Gustav Gilbert

The constitutional Antiquities of Sparta and Athens

Gustav Gilbert

The constitutional Antiquities of Sparta and Athens

ISBN/EAN: 9783743330313

Manufactured in Europe, USA, Canada, Australia, Japa

Cover: Foto ©ninafisch / pixelio.de

Manufactured and distributed by brebook publishing software (www.brebook.com)

Gustav Gilbert

The constitutional Antiquities of Sparta and Athens

THE
CONSTITUTIONAL ANTIQUITIES·

OF

SPARTA AND ATHENS

BY

Dr. GUSTAV GILBERT

Translated by

E. J. BROOKS, M.A. | T. NICKLIN, M.A.
Fellow of St. John's College | *Late Scholar of St. John's College*

With an Introductory Note by
J. E. SANDYS, Litt.D.
Public Orator in the University of Cambridge

London
SWAN SONNENSCHEIN & CO
NEW YORK: MACMILLAN & CO
1895

BUTLER & TANNER,
THE SELWOOD PRINTING WORKS,
FROME, AND LONDON.

INTRODUCTORY NOTE.

THERE are three different kinds of books which we may use in studying the Constitutional Antiquities of Greece. We may gather our information from articles in a Dictionary of Antiquities; or we may select the constitutional chapters in any comprehensive History of Greece; or, lastly, we may consult a Handbook specially devoted to this topic alone. Articles in a Dictionary are certainly useful for the study of minute details, but information derived from this source is apt to be disconnected and unsystematic. Again, the constitutional chapters in a History do not usually dwell on points of detail, while the total space which a historian can afford to assign to constitutional subjects is generally only a small part of the entire work. It may also be observed that the constitutional portions of Grote's *History of Greece*, originally published in 1846–1855, do not in any of the later editions take account of the important criticisms of Schömann, which appeared in 1854, and were translated into English in 1878, while, of course, they cannot include the results of more recent research in the same department of learning. As compared with a Dictionary, a good Handbook is at least as minute, while it is much more systematic; as compared with a History, it leaves much more room for full and comprehensive treatment. The popularity of the Handbook as a means of study may be exemplified by the fact that Potter's *Antiquities of Greece*, the early work of a future Archbishop of Canterbury, which was first published in 1697, passed through many editions and was long regarded as almost indispensable to the classical student.

At the present day, one of the very best Handbooks of Greek Constitutional Antiquities is that produced, in two volumes, by GUSTAV GILBERT, of Gotha, under the title:—*Handbuch der Griechischen Staatsalterthümer*, Leipzig (Teubner), 1881-5, the first volume containing the constitutions of Sparta and Athens. This important volume, the value of which has been widely recognised, has been considerably improved in the second edition, published in 1893. Not only has it been thoroughly revised by the light of recent research, but it has been further enriched by the results of the discovery and publication of Aristotle's *Constitution of Athens* (1891), the value of which is duly estimated in a special introductory chapter. Gilbert's own account of the constitutions of Sparta and Athens is divided into two parts, (1) a sketch of the historical development of the constitution; and (2) a detailed description of its component parts. It is interesting to notice that, in this division of the subject, he had unconsciously followed what we now know to have been the method adopted by Aristotle himself. In the notes, the ancient texts (including inscriptions) are generally quoted in full, while the references to the modern literature of the subject are usually limited to the best and the most accessible authorities, to the exclusion of inaccessible or obsolete works.

For the constitutional history of Athens and Sparta, Gilbert's first volume has become a recognised text-book in England, where the only drawback to its still wider usefulness is the fact that it is written in German. This drawback is now removed by the translation which is here offered to the public by two of my former pupils. The translation, so far as I have compared it with the original, appears to have been executed with skill and accuracy, and with a due regard to the differences between German and English idiom. The only part which has been minutely examined by myself is the introductory chapter on Aristotle's *Constitution of Athens*, where, besides revising the proof-sheets, I have added a few references to the more recent literature of the subject. I have also suggested a few *addenda* and *corrigenda* in other parts of the work. The volume, in its English dress, fully deserves to be warmly welcomed by every English student of Greek history, and to be extensively used in schools and colleges on either side of the Atlantic.

J. E. SANDYS.

CAMBRIDGE, *March*, 1895.

TRANSLATORS' PREFACE.

In preparing this translation we have not felt authorized to add anything, or to make any alterations in the original text, beyond correcting a very few trivial details including those noted in the author's preface. We have, however, supplied a few references to some of the more accessible English works and translations, and also to the general literature of the subject. For almost all of these last we are indebted to Dr. Sandys, to whom we would here express our best thanks for the kind interest he has taken in the work. We have also considered it advisable for the convenience of readers to make the Index fuller and more complete than that of the German edition. In a few quotations from the 'Αθηναίων Πολιτεία the text of Dr. Sandys' edition (1893) has been used instead of that of Prof. Blass. To help the reader to find references to the German editions the paging of the first edition is given on the left-hand side at the top of each page, and the paging of the second edition on the right. In the transliteration of Greek words the ordinary English spelling has been retained in words that have become familiar to the general English reader, for instance, Thucydides, Corinth. In more unusual words such as Kerykes, Skyros, *k* is written wherever *c* might lead to mispronunciation. For the *corrigenda* on p. xix we can only ask the reader's indulgence, and hope that the list is complete.

FROM THE AUTHOR'S PREFACE.

In this second edition of my Manual, as in the first, the Table of Contents and the Index are supplementary to one another; nothing has been admitted into the Index which could not be readily found in the Table. The edition which I have used of Aristotle's Ἀθηναίων Πολιτεία is that of Blass (1892). I was unable to make any use of Szánto's article on The Cleisthenian Trittyes in *Hermes*, 1892, p. 312 ff., or Milchhöfer's investigations of Cleisthenes' organization of the Demes in *Abhandl. der Berl. Akad.*, 1892. M. Fränkel's article in *N. Rh. Mus.*, 1892, 473 ff. (cf. p. 121[3]), with whose conclusions I cannot agree; J. E. Kirchner's on the Antigonis and Demetrias tribes in *N. Rh. Mus.*, 1892, 550 ff. (cf. p. 200[3]), Lolling's on More Psephisms of the time of the 13 tribes in Ἀρχ. δελτ., 1892, p. 42 (cf. p. 201[1]), and Dragumes' on the λέσχαι in *Mitth. d. dtsch. Inst. in Ath.* 17, 147 ff. (cf. p. 106[3]), all appeared too late for me to avail myself of them. Bruno Keil's work, however, on The Solonian Constitution in Aristotle's *Athenian Constitutional History*, 1892, was available for the revision of the Introduction. I must ask the reader's indulgence for any misprints which may have escaped my notice.

GUSTAV GILBERT.

Gotha, *November*, 1892.

TABLE OF CONTENTS.

INTRODUCTION. Aristotle's Ἀθηναίων Πολιτεία, xxi–1.

THE LACEDÆMONIAN STATE.

I. HISTORY.

Historical Development of the Lacedæmonian State with a Sketch of its Constitution under Roman Rule.

Λακωνική 3. Dorian immigration, Dual Kingship 4. Aigeidai 5. Synoikismos of Sparta 7. Conquest of Laconia 10. Land tenure 11. Nobles at Sparta 12. Distinction between landed estates of the Nobles and κλῆροι of the Commons 13. Lycurgus 15. Establishment of the Ephorate 16. Statute of Theopompos 17. Partheniai 18. Terpandros, Tyrtaios 19. Development of Ephorate 20. Attempts at Revolution, Loss of Messenia 22. Statute of Epitadeus 23. Agis IV. and Cleomenes III., End of Royalty, Rule of Despots 24. Sparta under Roman Rule, Classification of Citizens, πατρονόμοι 25. ἔφοροι, νομοφύλακες, γραμματοφύλαξ, βίδεοι, ἀγορανόμοι 26. πεδιανόμοι, ἐπιμεληταί, λοχαγός, ἱππάρχας, πρέσβυς, αἱ συναρχίαι, σύνδικοι, γερουσία 27. βουλή, Popular Assembly, Lycurgean Constitution, Eleutherolacones 28. Federal Officials, Constitutions of the individual towns 29.

II. ANTIQUITIES.

1. *Elements of the Population.*

A. *The Helots.*

Name, Place of Abode 30. Legal Status 31. Treatment 32. κρυπτεία 33. νεοδαμώδεις, μόθακες 34.

B. *Perioicoi.*

Place of Abode, Origin 35. Occupation, Legal Status 36.

C. *Spartiatai.*

Σπαρτιᾶται 37. Place of Abode, Numbers 38. Conditions necessary for citizenship, ὅμοιοι 39. ὑπομείονες, Political Classification 40.

2. *The Government.*

A. *The Kings.*

Royal Families, Succession 42. Prerogatives of Kings 43. Funeral obsequies 44. Religious functions 45. Judicial and Military functions 46. General position 47.

B. *The Council of Elders.*

Name, Number of Councillors 47. Mode of appointment 48. Powers 49.

C. *Apella.*

Name, One Apella 50. Place of Meeting, Powers 51.

D. *Ephors.*

A Board, How appointed, Official quarters 52. Entrance on office, Powers 53. Summoning and Presidency of Apella and Council of Elders 54. Foreign affairs 55. Police supervision 56. Supervision over Officials and Kings 57. Over Perioicoi and Helots, Xenelasia, Finance, Religious functions 58.

E. *Other Officials.*

In general, πρόξενοι, Πύθιοι, ἐμπέλωροι, ἁρμόσυνοι 59. παιδονόμος, ἀμπαιδες, ἁρμοσταί, ναύαρχος, ἐπιστολεύς, Military officers, ὁ ἐπὶ τῆς κρυπτείας τεταγμένος, ἱππαγρέται, ἀγαθοεργοί 60. Subordinate officials 61.

3. *Military Matters.*

Military Character of the State 61. Education 62. εἰσπνήλας and ἀίτας, Syssitia 65. Divisions of the Army 67. Liability to Service, ἱππεῖς 72. Equipment, Military Service of Helots, Skiritai 73. Light-armed Troops, Cavalry, Camp-followers, Engineers, Baggage 74. The King and his Staff 75. Army in the field 76. τρέσαντες, Fleet 77.

4. *Finance and Administration of Justice.*

The common metals as Standards of Value, Laconian Coinage 78. Gold and Silver in Laconia 79. Financial administration, Judicial administration, Court of Elders 80. Ephors, Kings 81.

5. *The Lacedæmonian League.*

Conquests of the Spartiatai 81. Sparta and Tegea, Establishment of Lacedæmonian Hegemony 82. Position of Sparta during Persian Wars 84. Sparta Hegemon of all Hellas 85. Liberation of Greeks of the Ægean, The Lacedæmonians Champions of the King's Peace 86. The Peloponnesian League 88. Rights and Duties of the presiding State and of the Allies 89.

THE ATHENIAN STATE.

I. HISTORY.

1. *The Athenian State from the earliest times till Solon.*

Physical features of Attica 95. Population 96. Political condition in earliest times 98. Independent communities on the site of Athens 99. Synoikismos of the city of Athens 100. Synoikismos of Attica 101. Nature of the Synoikismos 102. The Ionic Phylai 103. Attic Γένη 104. The old Attic system of Phylai and Phratries 105. Extension of the franchise 107. Conditions necessary for the franchise, oldest form of Constitution 109. Gradual diminution of the royal Power 110.

The higher annual magistrates 112. Κωλακρέται 113. Right to election and eligibility for office, Areopagus 114. Πολιτεία τῶν ἱππέων 115. Non-Eupatrid population 116. Ἐκτημόροι 117. Kylon 118. Draco 119. Πολιτεία τῶν ὁπλιτῶν 120. Council 121. Ecclesia, Areopagus 122. Jurisdiction of Ephetai and Prytaneis, ἐφέται 123. Πρυτάνεις, Draco's laws 125. Social conditions 126.

2. *From Solon to Eucleides.*

Social Conditions 126. Solon 127. Σεισάχθεια 128. Census-classes 130. Political Rights 131. Taxation 132. Naucrary-system 133. Basis of assessment-classes 134. Trade and industries 135. Magistrates, οἱ ἐννέα ἄρχοντες 126. Βουλή, Council of Areopagus 137. Ecclesia 138. Heliaia 139. Solon's Laws 140. Discontent, Damasias, Constitutional Changes 141. Local factions 142. The Peisistratidai 144. Their overthrow, Cleisthenes 145. Extension of the Franchise, New Phylai and Demes 146. Trittyes 147. New Phratry-system 148. The old Phylai, Conditions of citizenship 150. Classification on Decimal System 151. Ostracism 152. New arrangement of military officers, new mode of appointing the 9 Archons 153. Supremacy of the Areopagus, its overthrow 154. Nomophylakes 155. Athens as a Great Power 156. Admission of the Zeugitai to the Archonship, Deme-judges 157. New Franchise Law, The Peloponnesian War 158. Alterations under Eucleides 159.

3. *Constitutional History of Athens after B.C. 322, with Sketch of the Athenian Constitution under Roman Rule.*

Athens under Roman rule 162. Franchise, Magistrates 180. στρατηγοί 163. ἄρχοντες, ἀγορανόμοι 164. ἐπιμεληταί, σιτώνης, Financial officials, Council 165. Areopagus 167. Justice, Ecclesia 168.

II. ANTIQUITIES.

1. *Constituent Elements of the Population.*

A. *Slaves.*

Number and origin 170. Condition, Legal status 171. οἱ χωρὶς οἰκοῦντες. State slaves 173. Manumission 174. Freedmen 175.

B. *Metoicoi.*

Number and origin 176. προστάτης 177. Burdens imposed on Metoicoi, liability to military service 178. μετοίκιον, Market dues 179. Leiturgies, εἰσφορά 180. σκαφηφορία, Privileges 181. ἰσοτελεῖς, Tribunal 183.

C. *The Burgess body.*

Number 183. New citizens, Mode of creation 184. Political rights of new citizens 186. Plataeans, Old citizens, Descent 187. Marriage 188. Legal concubinage, Illegitimate children 190. Naming of children, Admission into Phratries 191. Enrolment in list of the Deme 197. Burgess rights, Their diminution, extension 199.

D. *Political Divisions of Burgess body, and Associations.*

Phylai 200. ἐπώνυμοι 201. Constitution of the Phylai 202. Demes 203. Constitution of the Demes 204. Trittyes 209. Phratries 210. Ionic Phylai, Γένη 211. Clan-associations, Private associations 212.

2. *Organs of Administration, and the Sovereign Power in the State.*

A. *Magistrates.*

(a) In general.

Classification of the magistrates 214, Their powers, Limitations to eligibility to office 215. Appointment, Time of appointment 216. Based on the Phylai, Candidature, Mode of appointment 217. Dokimasia 219. Entrance on office, and oath on taking office, 220. Emoluments 222. Collegiality, Epicheirotonia 223. εὔθυνα, Audit boards 224. Procedure at εὔθυνα 226. Assessors 228. Subordinate officials 229. Dignity of magistrates 230.

(b) The various Magistrates.

στρατηγοί 230. ταξίαρχοι, λοχαγοί, ἵππαρχοι 236. φύλαρχοι, δεκάδαρχοι, κωλακρέται, ἀποδέκται 237. πωληταί 239. πράκτορες, ἀντιγραφεύς 240. ταμίαι τῶν ἱερῶν χρημάτων τῆς Ἀθηναίας 241. ταμίαι τῶν ἄλλων θεῶν 242. Ἑλληνοταμίαι 243. ταμίας τοῦ δήμου 244. οἱ ἐπὶ τὸ θεωρικόν 245. ταμίας τῶν στρατιωτικῶν 247. ὁ ἐπὶ τῇ διοικήσει 248. Other treasurers, οἱ ἐννέα ἄρχοντες 250. ἄρχων 251. βασιλεύς 253. πολέμαρχος 254. θεσμοθέται 255. οἱ ἕνδεκα 256. ἀστυνόμοι 258. ἀγορανόμοι, μετρονόμοι 259. προμετρηταί, σιτοφύλακες, ἐπιμεληταὶ ἐμπορίου 260. ἐπιμεληταὶ τῶν νεωρίων, ὁ ἐπὶ τὰς κρήνας 261. ὁδοποιοί, οἱ ἱερῶν ἐπισκευασταί, ἱεροποιοί 262. ἀθλοθέται, βοῶναι, Extraordinary magistrates, ἐπιστάται τῶν δημοσίων ἔργων 263. ἀποστολεῖς, σιτῶναι, ζητηταί, ἐξετασταί 264. πορισταί 265.

B. *Council of 500, and Areopagus.*

Number and name, Method of appointment 265. Dokimasia, Oath on taking office 266. Honours and emoluments, ἐκφυλλοφορία and εὔθυνα 267. Council-officials 268. Prytaneis 271. πρόεδροι 274. Sittings of council 275. Business within competence of Council 277. Council as court of justice 281. Areopagus 282. Official functions 283.

C. *The Sovereign Power.*

Public assemblies, ordinary and extraordinary 285. Days of assembly, Convocation, place of meeting 287. Right of membership of Ecclesia and method of testing it 288. Pay, Maintenance of order in the Ecclesia 290. Order of business 291. Psephisms, how drawn up 297. γραφὴ παρανόμων 299. Legislation 301. προβολή 303. εἰσαγγελία 304. Full assemblies 307. ἄδεια 308. ὀστρακισμός 309. Business dealt with by Ecclesia 310.

3. *Military Matters.*

Military Oath and Freeman's Oath 310. Military training 311. Ephebia in later times 313. Hoplites 315. Conscriptions 316. Military lawsuits 318. Pay, Equipment, Tactical divisions of the hoplite forces 319. Light armed troops, Cavalry 320. Tactical divisions 323. The Knights as a corporate body, Hippotoxotai 324. Fleet, its strength 325. Equipment of an ἀπόστολος, Crews 326. Trierarchic crowns 327. Pay, Discipline 328.

4. Finance.

A. In general.

Coinage 328. Purchasing power of money 329. Interest on Capital 330. Economic condition of Athens 332. Main principles of fifth century finance 334. Finance of fourth century 338. Budget 339. Financial administration, checking and auditing of public accounts 341.

B. Expenditure.

Ordinary expenses, for religious purposes 342. Fees, μισθὸς δικαστικός 343. μισθὸς βουλευτικός 344. μισθὸς ἐκκλησιαστικός 345. Other fees, Largesses 346. Maintenance of orphans, Relief of ἀδύνατοι, Gifts as marks of honour 347. Expenses of setting up inscriptions, Maintenance of State slaves, Expenses for military purposes in time of peace, Maintenance and repair of public buildings 348. Extraordinary expenses, War expenses 349.

C. Revenue.

Ordinary direct revenues, τέλη, πεντηκοστή, ἐλλιμένιον 350. δεκάτη, ἐπώνιον 351. διαπύλιον, μετοίκιον, ξενικὸν τέλος, πορνικὸν τέλος 352. Tax-farmers, Rents, from mines 353. Land, buildings, Court-fees and fines 354. State-debtors 355. Remission of debts to the State, Classification of revenues 356. Tribute 357. Grand total of revenue, Ordinary indirect receipts 358. Choregia 359. Gymnasiarchia 360. ἑστίασις, ἀντίδοσις 361. Extraordinary direct receipts, ἐπιδόσεις 353. εἰσφορά 364. Assessment of Nausinicos 365. Symmories 368. Method of levying the Eisphora 369. Extraordinary indirect receipts, Trierarchia, Syntrierarchia 370. Trierarchic Symmories 371. Demosthenes' reform 373. Æschines' modification, Extent of the trierarchic duties 374. Cost of a trierarchy, Trierarchies put out on contract, returning the ship 375. Audit of trierarchs 376.

5. The Judicature.

Presiding Magistrates and Jury 376. εἰσαγωγεῖς, οἱ κατὰ δήμους δικασταί 377. ναυτοδίκαι, Judges 378. Permanent judges, Murder trials, Right of sanctuary 379. ἡ βουλὴ ἡ ἐξ Ἀρείου πάγου or ἐν Ἀρείῳ πάγῳ 380. τὸ δικαστήριον τὸ ἐπὶ Παλλαδίῳ 381. τὸ δικαστήριον τὸ ἐπὶ Δελφινίῳ 382. τὸ δικαστήριον τὸ ἐν Φρεαττοῖ, τὸ δικαστήριον τὸ ἐπὶ Πρυτανείῳ 383. Right to prosecute for homicide 384. Procedure in cases of homicide 385. Position of the slayer, Payment in compensation for homicide 387. Arbitrators 388. Diaitetai chosen by agreement, ἡλιαία 391. Heliasts' oath 392. Great court and little courts 393. Sections 394. New organization under Eucleides 395. System in Aristotle's time, Places where courts were held 396. Method of making up the court 397. Arrangements of the place where the court was held 402. Days of session,

Classes of lawsuits, Private suits, Public suits 404. Suits κατά τινος and πρός τινα, ἀγῶνες ἀτίμητοι and τιμητοί, διαδικασία, ἀπαγωγή, ἐφήγησις, ἔνδειξις 405. φάσις, ἀπογραφή, Regular procedure, Summons 406. Lodgement of suit, Court fees, Preliminary investigation, Special pleas 407. ἀντιγραφή, Evidence 408. Date of trial, The trial 409. The voting 410. Punishments, Execution of sentence 414. Restitutio in integrum, General criticism of the Athenian Judicature 415.

6. Athens as Mistress of a Confederation.

A. The First League.

Foundation and extension 416. Original object, Converted into an Athenian empire 417. Designation of the allies and their classification, Tribute 420. Tribute districts 421. Assessment 422. ἐπιφορά, Payment of tribute 424. εἰκοστή 425. Liability of allies to personal military service, Tithes paid to the gods 426. Constitutions of allied States 427. Supreme court of justice 429. Presiding officers at lawsuits of allies 431. Judicial procedure in δίκαι συμβόλαιαι 432.

B. The Second League.

Development 435. Object, Constitution of the League 439. Procedure in the conduct of Federal affairs 441. Competence of Federal Council, 442. Federal imposts, 443. Supreme tribunal 444.

C. The Athenian Cleruchies.

History 445. Various forms of Cleruchies 446. Object 447. Method of planting Cleruchies, Their religious cults 448. Relation of Cleruchs to Athens 449. Constitutions of Cleruchies 450. Jurisdiction in Cleruchies 452.

APPENDIX 454

INDEX 457

ADDENDA AND CORRIGENDA.

p. 108, l. 6. For "Phatries" read "Phratries."

p. 117, ll. 3, 8; note 1, ll. 5, 9, 13, 15, 18, 27, 31, read "ἐκτημόροι."

p. 117[1]. Ἐκτημόροι. In *Class. Rev.*, July, 1894, p. 296, Prof. H. Sidgwick maintains that the interpretation given in Liddell and Scott, "ἐκτημόριοι, those who paid one-sixth of the produce as rent," founded on Plutarch, *Sol.*, 13, and Hesychius, is confirmed by 'Αθ. Πολ., ch. 2, and also by Isocrates, *Areopag.*, § 32. This interpretation, which is also that of Dr. Sandys, is supported by Mr. E. S. Thompson, in *Class. Rev.*, Dec., 1894, p. 444.

p. 121[2], l. 9. For "ἢ" read "ἣ."

p. 133[2], l. 4. For "κᾱρ" read "κρῑ."

p. 136[2], l. 5. For "ἢ" read "ἣ."

pp. 136 and 141. Prof. H. Sidgwick, *Class. Rev.*, 1894, pp. 333-6, suggests that of the 8 non-eponymous Archons two were drawn by lot from the 10 nominated by each tribe, that the chief Archon was *chosen* from each tribe in rotation (cf. Arist. 13, 2) and the concurrence of the Areopagus was required for his election. One tribe being violently antagonistic to the Eupatrids, a deadlock occurred in the fourth year. Damasias continued in office, with the acquiescence of the Areopagus, to get over the third deadlock. But they did not approve his continuance in office for a third year, and after the compromise of the decemvirate simple election by the assembly was substituted for sortition.

p. 137[2], cf. p. 123. Gleue, *de Homicid. in Areop. Athen. Iudicio*, Göttingen, 1894, supposes that the Areopagus' jurisdiction was never interrupted; cf. Dem. 23, § 66. So Wayte, *Class. Rev.*, 1894, pp. 462-3.

p. 146[1] ult. For "Bernay's" read "Bernays."

pp. 147-8. Szánto, *Hermes*, 1892, p. 312, from inscriptions and Arist. 21, 4 makes it seem probable that the Paralian Trittyes lay along the coast, omitting Piræus; the Mesogaian from Parnes over the plain between Pentelicon and Hymettos; while the Metropolitan comprised Athens and the neighbourhood, *e.g.* Piræus and Lakiadai.

p. 149[1]. For Οἶκον read Οἶον Δεκελεικόν.

p. 164[2]. For "Swobeda" read "Swoboda."

p. 171[2]. For "*de Rep. Lac.*" read "*de Rep. Ath.*"

p. 175, l. 14. Omit "to."

p. 177[3]. For "did not pay the Demotikon" read "had no Deme-name."

p. 185[1]. For Θρασυβούλου read Θρασυβούλῳ.

p. 190, l. 10. For ";" read ","

p. 195. For Dekeleiai read Dekeleieis.

Addenda and Corrigenda.

p. 204⁴. For "ceremony" read "payment."

p. 207⁵. For "τὴν δήμαρχον" read "τὴν δημάρχου."

p. 209, top. For "II. 198–9" read "II. 231–2."

p. 293⁴. For a further refutation of Hartel's hypothesis, see Arnold Hug, *Studien aus d. Klass. Altert.*, i. 104–132.

For p. 308 (307⁴) *sub fin.* Müller's *Handb.* 3, 196 read 5, 3, 196.

p. 314¹. For the earliest ephebic inscr. (B.C. 334–3), see *Bull. Corr. Hell* xiii 253.

p. 348¹. Add "W. Larfeld, *Griech. Epigraphik*, p. 436 ff."

INTRODUCTION.

ARISTOTLE'S 'ΑΘΗΝΑΙΩΝ ΠΟΛΙΤΕΙΑ.

BETWEEN the appearance of the first and second editions of this volume came the discovery of the MS. of the 'Αθηναίων Πολιτεία, first published by Kenyon. As I have constantly quoted that treatise in this edition, it is my duty to review the controversy which has arisen as to its authorship and value, and to give in connected form my opinions on these points.[1]

With regard to the authorship, I hold that the work is an integral part of the Aristotelian collection of 158 Greek Πολιτεῖαι. Nissen thinks that it was written by Aristotle and his pupils for the use of practical statesmen, to provide the imperial government of Alexander with materials for deciding constitutional questions in the various Hellenic States. But on the evidence at our disposal this cannot be positively affirmed, nor does it appear intrinsically probable.[2] Numerous passages in ancient writers, which profess to be drawn from the 'Αθηναίων Πολιτεία that passed under the name of Aristotle, agree, some word for word, others in substance, with the statements of the newly discovered MS. Consequently, whoever denies the Aristotelian origin of the 'Αθηναίων Πολιτεία, will at least have to admit that the anonymous author had made a very extensive use of Aristotle, had indeed for the most part copied him word for word. The work was composed after the year

---

[1] That Aristotle was the author is denied by F. Cauer, *Hat Arist. die Schrift v. Staate der Ath. geschrieben?* 1891; and Rühl in *N. Rhein. Mus.*, 1891, 426 ff. and the 18th suppl. vol. of *Jahrb. f. cl. Phil.*, 1892, p. 675 ff.

[2] See Nissen's essay on Aristotle's political works in *N. Rhein. Mus.*, 1892, p. 161 ff. He has been answered by Bruno Keil, *die Solon. Verf. in Aristoteles Verfassungsgesch. Athens*, p. 127 ff.

329/8, for Kephisophon, the Archon of that year, is mentioned by name; and before the year 322, for Eucleides' constitution is still in force, and therefore the revision of the constitution in B.C. 322 had not yet taken place: what is more, the Athenians are still in possession of Samos, which they lost in 322.¹ It is clearly improbable that, at a time when Aristotle was still living, some unknown writer should have felt called upon to give a fresh description of the Athenian constitution, availing himself largely of the Aristotelian 'Αθηναίων Πολιτεία, but replacing several parts of Aristotle's constitutional history by a new account, which, in the judgment of those who doubt the Aristotelian origin of the work, is of little value. Still less probable is it that, while the chronological indications just referred to belonged to the original Aristotelian 'Αθηναίων Πολιτεία, the author of our treatise, writing long after Aristotle, thoughtlessly adopted these statements, although in several important points of constitutional history he departed from his authority and proceeded quite independently to give his own version.² The slavish dependence shown in the one case must, I think, to every sober judgment exclude the probability of an unfettered independence in the other. For my own part, these arguments convince me that we possess in the newly discovered MS. the genuine Aristotelian 'Αθηναίων Πολιτεία. In my opinion the only debatable question is whether the immediate author of the MS. was Aristotle himself, or one of his pupils—for in compiling his extensive work on the Greek Πολιτεῖαι, Aristotle no doubt availed himself of the assis-

---

¹ For the agreement of Aristotle's Fragments with our MS., cf. Kenyon, Introd., xiv ff., [and Sandys, 'Αθ. Πολ., Testimonia, and p. 256]. Kephisophon mentioned 54, 7. Eucleides' constitution still in force, 41, 1. On the revision of the constitution B.C. 322, see Diod. 18, 18; Plut., *Phok.*, 28. Samos still an Athenian possession: 62, 2; lost 322 B.C., Diod. 18, 18; Diog. L., 10, 1. The attempt to fix the composition of the 'Αθ. Πολ. precisely between October 324 and July 323 (as in Nissen 197/8) seems to me a failure. See also Bruno Keil, 148 ff. Neither can I bring myself to insist on the year 325/4 as the *terminus ante quem*. Even if Athens possessed seven penteremes by that year (C.I.A., 809 *d*, 90), Arist. 46, 1 might easily pass them over, as they formed only an insignificant fraction of the Athenian fleet compared with the 360 triremes and 50 tetreremes.

² The whole of the analytical part of the 'Αθ. Πολ. is based on the assumption of 10 tribes. Is it probable that the reviser who preserved so independent an attitude in regard to the constitutional history would altogether have ignored the increase of the tribes to 12, which took place in 306/5, if he had been writing after that date?

tance of his pupils.¹ The distinction, however, is of no great importance, for this reason: Aristotle being responsible for the undertaking, would certainly not have passed his pupil's account of the Ἀθηναίων Πολιτεία (if it was the work of a pupil) unless he approved of it. But unless Aristotle confined himself to a mere supervision of the whole—which we have no reason to assume—it is highly probable that he himself wrote the description of the Athenian constitution, the type of all democratic constitutions. In explanation of some trifling inconsistencies which may be found in the work, it is sufficient to assume that Aristotle died before he could complete his revision—an assumption which recommends itself by the evidence we possess for the date of the book. Probably no one would have hesitated to accept the Ἀθηναίων Πολιτεία as an authentic work of Aristotle's, if the second half alone had been preserved to us: what has raised suspicion is contained in the historical part of the MS. While it is not likely to be disputed that Aristotle used the political institutions of his own day as material for the analytical section,² the question of the sources of the historical part is not so simple, and requires therefore some consideration.

The historical part of the Ἀθηναίων Πολιτεία consists of narrative, of investigations and reflexions on political history, and of antiquarian discussions; and, to state my opinion at once, it was derived not only from literary sources of a historical and political character, but also from original documents. I shall begin my examination of Aristotle's sources with the period from Peisistratos to Cleisthenes, for here it is easiest to attain tangible results. It is demonstrable that Aristotle used Herodotus; he quotes him by

---

¹ At all events Theophrastus was in ancient times considered to have helped Aristotle in the preparation of the Πολιτεῖαι: Polyb. 12, 11, 5; 23, 8. [Susemihl, *Quaest. Arist.*, ii 13, 1893; "ex mea sententia satis otiosum quaerere, utrum hic liber ex ipsius magistri calamo profectus sit an in eius schola sub eius tutela extiterit."]

² For the assumption that Arist. did not put the last touches to the Ἀθ. Πολ., cf. Bruno Keil, 50 ff., 196. 230, 2. 231, 1. The δίκαι ἐμπορικαί were manifestly not ἔμμηνοι according to Arist. cf. 52, 2. 3 with 59, 5. In 342 B.C. they were ἔμμηνοι: (Dem.) 7, 12; in 397 they were not: Lys. 17, 5. 8. Bruno Keil, 232 *note*, thinks that for the passages cited above Arist. followed some authority earlier than 342 B.C. This seems scarcely probable: I should be much more inclined to believe that the δίκαι ἐμπορικαί had between 342 and 329/8 again ceased to be ἔμμηνοι.

name, he agrees with him word for word in several passages—in the account of Peisistratos as well as of Cleisthenes.[1]

But in spite of this it cannot be said that Herodotus was Aristotle's chief authority. We find repeatedly that, where Herodotus gives a detailed narrative, Aristotle's account is exceedingly brief and concise; at other times Aristotle gives in detail what we do not find in Herodotus, or at least do not find treated with the same completeness. So also with Thucydides; Aristotle shows an unmistakable acquaintance with his account of the despotism of the Peisistratidai, though there is nothing to prove that he actually copies Thucydides. It is true that the

---

[1] Hdt. quoted: 14, 4. Cf.

14, 3/4   with   Hdt. 1, 60.

οὔπω δὲ τῆς ἀρχῆς ἐρριζωμένης ὁμοφρονήσαντες οἱ περὶ τὸν Μεγακλέα καὶ τὸν Λυκοῦργον ἐξέβαλον αὐτὸν ἕκτῳ ἔτει μετὰ τὴν πρώτην κατάστασιν ἐφ' Ἡγησίου ἄρχοντος. ἔτει δὲ δωδεκάτῳ μετὰ ταῦτα περιελαυνόμενος ὁ Μεγακλῆς τῇ στάσει πάλιν ἐπικηρυκευσάμενος πρὸς τὸν Πεισίστρατον ἐφ' ᾧ τε τὴν θυγατέρα αὐτοῦ λήψεται, κατήγαγεν αὐτὸν ἀρχαίως καὶ λίαν ἁπλῶς.

καὶ τὴν τυραννίδα οὔ κω κάρτα ἐρριζωμένην ἔχων ἀπέβαλε, οἱ δὲ ἐξελάσαντες Πεισίστρατον αὖτις ἐκ νέης ἐπ' ἀλλήλοισι ἐστασίασαν. περιελαυνόμενος δὲ τῇ στάσι ὁ Μεγακλέης ἐπεκηρυκεύετο Πεισιστράτῳ, εἰ βούλοιτό οἱ τὴν θυγατέρα ἔχειν γυναῖκα ἐπὶ τῇ τυραννίδι. ἐνδεξαμένου δὲ τὸν λόγον καὶ ὁμολογήσαντος ἐπὶ τούτοισι Πεισιστράτου μηχανῶνται δὴ ἐπὶ τῇ κατόδῳ πρῆγμα εὐηθέστατον, ὡς ἐγὼ εὑρίσκω, μακρῷ.

20, 2   with   Hdt. 5, 70.

ἐπικαλεσάμενος τὸν Κλεομένην ὄντα ἑαυτῷ ξένον.

ἐπικαλέεται Κλεομένεα τὸν Λακεδαιμόνιον, γενόμενον ἑαυτῷ ξεῖνον.

20, 3: ἠγηλάτει (for which Blass writes ἀγηλατεῖ) τῶν Ἀθηναίων ἑπτακοσίας οἰκίας· ταῦτα δὲ διαπραξάμενος τὴν μὲν βουλὴν ἐπειρᾶτο καταλύειν, Ἰσαγόραν δὲ καὶ τριακοσίους τῶν φίλων μετ' αὐτοῦ κυρίους καθιστάναι τῆς πόλεως. τῆς δὲ βουλῆς ἀντιστάσης καὶ συναθροισθέντος τοῦ πλήθους οἱ μὲν περὶ Κλεομένην καὶ Ἰσαγόραν κατέφυγον εἰς τὴν ἀκρόπολιν, ὁ δὲ δῆμος δύο μὲν ἡμέρας προσκαθεζόμενος ἐπολιόρκει, τῇ δὲ τρίτῃ Κλεομένην μὲν καὶ τοὺς μετ' αὐτοῦ πάντας ἀφεῖσαν ὑποσπόνδους, Κλεισθένην δὲ καὶ τοὺς ἄλλους φυγάδας μετεπέμψατο.

5, 72: ἀπικόμενος δὲ ἀγηλατέει ἑπτακόσια ἐπίστια Ἀθηναίων, τά οἱ ὑπέθετο ὁ Ἰσαγόρης. ταῦτα δὲ ποιήσας δεύτερα τὴν βουλὴν καταλύειν ἐπειρᾶτο, τριηκοσίοισι δὲ τοῖσι Ἰσαγόρεω στασιώτῃσι τὰς ἀρχὰς ἐνεχείριζε. ἀντισταθείσης δὲ τῆς βουλῆς καὶ οὐ βουλομένης πείθεσθαι ὅ τε Κλεομένης καὶ ὁ Ἰσαγόρης καὶ οἱ στασιῶται αὐτοῦ καταλαμβάνουσι τὴν ἀκρόπολιν. Ἀθηναίων δὲ οἱ λοιποὶ τὰ αὐτὰ φρονήσαντες ἐπολιόρκεον αὐτοὺς ἡμέρας δύο. τῇ δὲ τρίτῃ ὑπόσπονδοι ἐξέρχονται ἐκ τῆς χώρης ὅσοι ἦσαν αὐτῶν Λακεδαιμόνιοι.

5, 73: Ἀθηναῖοι δὲ μετὰ ταῦτα Κλεισθένεα καὶ τὰ ἑπτακόσια ἐπίστια τὰ διωχθέντα ὑπὸ Κλεομένεος μεταπεμψάμενο. . . .

error, once current in Athens, that Hipparchos was actually tyrant, refuted in such detail by Thucydides, is not found in Aristotle: but then it had already been tacitly corrected by Herodotus.[1] The Aristotelian account of the murder of Hipparchos certainly coincides in some points with Thucydides'; but it also contains many deviations from it. Indeed Aristotle, in dealing with this event, actually enters on a polemic against Thucydides, though without mentioning him by name.[2] Aristotle's account of the sons of Peisistratos differs from that of Thucydides.[3]

From what has been said above as to the relation of Aristotle to Herodotus and Thucydides, it is obvious that he must have used other sources besides these two. Indeed, we have positive evidence that there were yet other authors from whom Aristotle drew material for this treatise.[4] Now the writings which would recommend themselves first and foremost as suitable for his pur-

---

[1] 18, 1 says: πρεσβύτερος δὲ ὢν ὁ Ἱππίας καὶ τῇ φύσει πολιτικὸς καὶ ἔμφρων ἐπεστάτει τῆς ἀρχῆς. Thuc. 6, 55 had explained ὅτι πρεσβύτατος ὢν Ἱππίας ἦρξεν, while οἱ πολλοί regarded Hipparchos as the actual tyrant, perhaps on the strength of the Scolion in *Athen.*, 15, 695 A.B. But Hdt. 5, 55 already has the true account.

[2] Cf. 18, 3   with   Thuc. 6, 57.

—ἰδόντες τινὰ τῶν κοινωνούντων τῆς πράξεως φιλανθρώπως ἐντυγχάνοντα τῷ Ἱππίᾳ, καὶ νομίσαντες μηνύειν—

Καὶ ὡς εἶδόν τινα τῶν ξυνωμοτῶν σφίσι διαλεγόμενον οἰκείως τῷ Ἱππίᾳ (ἦν δὲ πᾶσιν εὐπρόσοδος ὁ Ἱππίας) ἔδεισαν καὶ ἐνόμισαν μεμηνῦσθαί τε καὶ ὅσον οὐκ ἤδη ξυλληφθήσεσθαι.

Thucydides is contradicted on the following points:—According to 18, 3 Hippias was on the Acropolis when Hipparchos was assassinated; according to Thuc. 6, 57 in the Kerameicos. Aristogeiton and Harmodios undertook the murder, according to 18, 2 μετεχόντων πολλῶν, according to Thuc. 6, 56 ἦσαν δὲ οὐ πολλοὶ οἱ ξυνομωμοκότες ἀσφαλείας ἕνεκα. Again, ὁ λεγόμενος λόγος, ὡς ὁ Ἱππίας ἀποστήσας ἀπὸ τῶν ὅπλων τοὺς πομπεύοντας ἐφώρασεν τοὺς τὰ ἐγχειρίδια ἔχοντας, against which 18, 4 argues, is found in Thuc. 6, 58. Thuc., *ibid.*, says μετὰ γὰρ ἀσπίδος καὶ δόρατος εἰώθεσαν τὰς πομπὰς ποιεῖν (see also chap. 56); in 18, 4 we are told, οὐ γὰρ ἔπεμπόν πω μεθ' ὅπλων ἀλλ' ὕστερον τοῦτο κατεσκεύασεν ὁ δῆμος. According to 15, 4 (see also Polyain. 1, 21, 2) Peisistratos, after his last return, took all arms from the Athenians. Cf. also Hude in *Jahrb. f. cl. Phil.*, 1892, p. 173 ff.

[3] Cf. 17, 3. 4 with Thuc. 6, 55. According to Plut. also (*Cato*, 24) Timonassa, Iophon, and Thessalos were children of Peisistratos' Argive wife. Hdt. 5, 94 calls Hegesistratos, whom Peisistratos installed as ruler in Sigeion νόθον, γεγονότα ἐξ Ἀργείης γυναικός.

[4] In 14, 2 a statement is introduced with λέγεται: 14, 4 ἔνιοι are mentioned in opposition to Herodotus; 16, 6 has φασί; 17, 2 ληροῦσιν (οἱ) φάσκοντες: 17, 4 φασὶν οἱ μέν—οἱ δέ: 18, 5 οἱ δημοτικοί φασι and ἔνιοι.

pose, must have been the Atthides. Not to mention the Atthis of Hellanicos, those of Cleidemos and Androtion too had undoubtedly made their appearance by the time of the composition of the Aristotelian Ἀθηναίων Πολιτεία. In the passage where Aristotle speaks of Peisistratos' first return, he contrasts Herodotus' statements on the antecedents of Phye (the woman who, arrayed as Athena, brought back Peisistratos) with the accounts given by others—amongst them doubtless Cleidemos, as may be seen by comparing one of his extant fragments.[1] This proves that Aristotle made use of the Atthides. There are other statements of his which point in the same direction.

Herodotus says that the exiled Alcmeonidai, who were very wealthy, rebuilt the Delphian Temple with great magnificence. But Philochorus relates that the Alcmeonidai contracted for the building of the Temple, used the proceeds to raise an army, attacked the Peisistratids, and, after conquering them, rebuilt the Temple with great splendour. Aristotle's account, though somewhat obscure, is to the effect that the Alcmeonidai, after utter failure in their struggle against the Peisistratids, contracted to rebuild the Temple, and thus gained the means for the Lacedæmonian expedition for their support. We must take this to mean that the Alcmeonidai, as Philochorus said, used the building fund to collect troops, and that the Lacedæmonians made their expedition

---

[1] On the date of Androtion's *Atthis*, see Keil 190 ff. He supposes that Aristotle made extensive use of it. [Cf. Wilamowitz, *Aristoteles u. Athen*, i 123ⁿ, 277, 287 f., 305.] Cleidemos was ὁπόσοι τὰ Ἀθηναίων ἐπιχώρια ἔγραψαν ὁ ἀρχαιότατος (Paus. 10, 15, 5).

Cf. 14, 4   with   Cleidem. *ap.* Athen. 13, 609 C.

προδιασπείρας γὰρ λόγον, ὡς τῆς Ἀθηνᾶς καταγούσης Πεισίστρατον, καὶ γυναῖκα μεγάλην καὶ καλὴν ἐξευρών, ὡς μὲν Ἡρόδοτός φησιν (1, 60) ἐκ τοῦ δήμου τῶν Παιανιέων, ὡς δ᾽ ἔνιοι λέγουσιν ἐκ τοῦ Κολλυτοῦ στεφανόπωλιν Θρᾶτταν, ᾗ ὄνομα Φύη, τὴν θεὸν ἀπομιμησάμενος τῷ κόσμῳ, [συνεισή]γαγεν μετ᾽ αὐτοῦ, καὶ ὁ μὲν Πεισίστρατος ἐφ᾽ ἅρματος εἰσήλαυνε, παραιβατούσης τῆς γυναικός, οἱ δ᾽ ἐν τῷ ἄστει προσκυνοῦντες ἐδέχοντο θαυμάζοντες.

καὶ τὴν κατάγουσαν δὲ Πεισίστρατον ἐπὶ τὴν τυραννίδα ὡς Ἀθηνᾶς σώτειρας εἶδος ἔχουσαν καλήν φησι γεγονέναι, ἥτις καὶ τῇ θεῷ εἴκαστο τὴν μορφήν. στεφανόπωλις δὲ ἦν. καὶ αὐτὴν ἐξέδωκε πρὸς γάμου κοινωνίαν ὁ Πεισίστρατος Ἱππάρχῳ τῷ υἱῷ, ὡς Κλείδημος ἱστορεῖ ἐν ὀγδόῳ Νόστων. ἐξέδωκε δὲ καὶ Ἱππάρχῳ τῷ υἱεῖ τὴν παραιβατήσασαν αὐτῷ γυναῖκα Φύην τὴν Σωκράτους θυγατέρα καὶ Χάρμου τοῦ πολεμαρχήσαντος θυγατέρα ἔλαβεν Ἱππίᾳ περικαλλεστάτην οὖσαν τῷ μετ᾽ αὐτὸν τυραννεύσαντι.

According to Thuc. 6, 55 Hippias' wife was Myrrhine, the daughter of Callias.

against the Peisistratidai in order to assist the Alcmeonidai. Now it is a natural supposition that this new version was the one generally accepted in the Atthides, and that Aristotle derived his statements from Cleidemos and Androtion, whilst in Herodotus' day the prevalent opinion at Athens was that the Alcmeonidai established themselves at Delphi, won over the Pythia by bribery, and by that means induced the Lacedæmonians to enter on the expedition against the Peisistratidai.[1]

It is known that the Atthidographers grouped the events which they recorded according to the years of the Archons. Aristotle repeatedly marks the date by the Archon in that part of his work which we are now considering: and this seems to come from the Atthides.[2]

Cleidemos had evidently discussed very minutely the family relations of the Peisistratidai; it is probable that Aristotle's statements about the sons of Peisistratos, differing as they do from those of Thucydides, were taken from Cleidemos.[3] I am also inclined to ascribe the agreement of some passages in Aristotle with Plutarch's Life of Solon to a common Atthidographic source, which Plutarch perhaps consulted at second hand in the work of Hermippos.[4] Although I would not go so far as Niese, who con-

---

[1] Hdt. 5, 62–63. Philochor., *fr.* 70 in Müller, *fr. h. gr.*, 1, 390, states: λέγεται, ὅτι τὸν Πυθικὸν ναὸν ἐμπρησθέντα, ὥς φασιν, ὑπὸ τῶν Πεισιστρατιδῶν οἱ 'Αλκμαιωνίδαι φυγαδευθέντες ὑπ' αὐτῶν ὑπέσχοντο ἀνοικοδομῆσαι καὶ δεξάμενοι χρήματα καὶ συναγαγόντες δύναμιν ἐπέθεντο τοῖς Πεισιστρατίδαις καὶ νικήσαντες μετ' εὐχαριστηρίων πλειόνων ἀνῳκοδόμησαν τῷ θεῷ τὸ τέμενος ὡς Φιλόχορος ἱστορεῖ, to be compared with 19, 4: ἀποτυγχάνοντες οὖν (*sc.* οἱ 'Αλκμεωνίδαι) ἐν ἅπασι τοῖς ἄλλοις ἐμισθώσαντο τὸν ἐν Δελφοῖς νεὼν οἰκοδομεῖν, ὅθεν εὐπόρησαν χρημάτων πρὸς τὴν τῶν Λακώνων βοήθειαν. Cf. Isocr. 15, 232.

[2] Hellanicos had already in his *Atthis* grouped events according to Archons. See *Schol.* Arist., *Frogs*, 706 : τοὺς συνναυμαχήσαντας δούλους Ἑλλάνικός φησιν ἐλευθερωθῆναι καὶ ἐγγραφέντας ὡς Πλαταιεῖς συμπολιτεύεσθαι αὐτοῖς, διεξιὼν τὰ ἐπὶ 'Αντιγένους τοῦ πρὸ Καλλίου, whilst in Müller,*fr. h. gr.*, 1 p. 56,*fr.* 80, the last words are omitted. In Philochoros we observe this frequently; see *fr.* 90. 97. 98. 99. 107. 108. 111. 116. 117. 119. 132. 135. 144. Dating by Archons in Arist. 14, 1. 4. 17, 1 ; 21, 2. [Cf. Newman quoted by Sandys, 'Αθ. πολ., p. lvi ; and Wilamowitz, *Ar. u. Athen*, i 276].

[3] Cf. 17, 3. 4 ; 18, 1 with Cleidemos as quoted page xxvi, note 1.

[4] Plutarch is more detailed than Aristotle, and consequently can scarcely be following him.

Compare 14, 2 with Plut., *Sol.*, 30.

λέγεται δὲ Σόλωνα Πεισιστράτου τὴν φυλακὴν αἰτοῦντος ἀντιλέξαι καὶ εἰπεῖν, ὅτι τῶν μὲν εἴη σοφώτερος, τῶν δ' ἀνδρειό-

—ἀπῆλθεν εἰπών, ὅτι τῶν μὲν ἐστι σοφώτερος, τῶν δὲ ἀνδρειότερος· σοφώτερος μὲν τῶν μὴ συνιέντων τὸ πραττόμενον,

siders the historical part of the Ἀθηναίων πολιτεία a history of the changes in the Athenian constitution drawn by Aristotle from the literature accessible in his day, probably from an Atthis, yet I believe that the Atthid literature was one of Aristotle's main sources. Thus we must attribute to the influence of the Atthidographers not only the departures from Herodotus and Thucydides but also any novel views in the part of the Ἀθηναίων πολιτεία under consideration.

As to the value of these divergencies, Thucydides' account of the family relations of the Peisistratidai—resting as it does on the evidence of inscriptions—undoubtedly deserves to be preferred to that of Aristotle. The statement, too, that Thessalos, not Hipparchos, insulted Harmodios, is deserving of little credence, and is, I should suppose, taken from a source other than that from which what precedes and follows was derived.[1] On the other hand, Aristotle's assertion that the citizens under the Peisistratidai conducted the πομπή at the Panathenaia unarmed, seems more credible, and closely connected with it is the disarming of the citizens, after the last return of Peisistratos, mentioned by

[τερο]ς᾿ ὅσοι μὲν γὰρ ἀγνοοῦσι Πεισίστρατον ἐπιτιθέμενον τύραν[νίδι], σοφώτεροι εἶναι τούτων, ὅσοι δ᾿ εἰδότες κατασιωπῶσιν, ἀνδρειότερος. ἐπεὶ δὲ λέγων [οὐκ ἔπει]θεν, ἐξαράμενος τὰ ὅπλα πρὸ τῶν θυρῶν, αὐτὸς μὲν ἔφη βεβοηθηκέναι τῇ πατρίδι, καθ᾿ ὅσον ἦν δυνατός (ἤδη γὰρ σφόδρα πρεσβύτης ἦν), ἀξιοῦν δὲ καὶ τοὺς ἄλλους ταὐτὸ τοῦτο ποιεῖν.

ἀνδρειότερος δὲ τῶν συνιέντων μὲν ἐναντιοῦσθαι δὲ τῇ τυραννίδι φοβουμένων. And then after a new meeting of the people, at which Solon had spoken: οὐδενὸς δὲ προσέχοντος αὐτῷ διὰ τὸν φόβον ἀπῆλθεν εἰς τὴν οἰκίαν τὴν ἑαυτοῦ καὶ λαβὼν τὰ ὅπλα καὶ πρὸ τῶν θυρῶν θέμενος εἰς τὸν στενωπὸν "ἐμοὶ μὲν" εἶπεν "ὡς δυνατὸν ἦν βεβοήθηται τῇ πατρίδι καὶ τοῖς νόμοις."

16, 8.

ἔν τε γὰρ τοῖς ἄλλοι[ς προῃρεῖτο] πάντα διοικεῖν κατὰ τοὺς νόμους, οὐδεμίαν ἑαυτῷ πλεονεξίαν διδούς, [καί ποτ]ε προσκληθεὶς φόνου δίκην εἰς Ἄρειον πάγον αὐτὸς μὲν ἀπήντησεν ὡς ἀπολογησόμενος, ὁ δὲ προσκαλεσάμενος φοβηθεὶς ἔλιπεν.

Cf. Bruno Keil, 186 ff.

Plut., Sol., 31.

καὶ γὰρ ἐφύλαττε τοὺς πλείστους νόμους τοῦ Σόλωνος ἐμμένων πρῶτος αὐτὸς καὶ τοὺς φίλους ἀναγκάζων· ὅς γε καὶ φόνου προσκληθεὶς εἰς Ἄρειον πάγον ἤδη τυραννῶν ἀπήντησε κοσμίως ἀπολογησόμενος, ὁ δὲ κατήγορος οὐχ ὑπήκουσεν.

[Schulthess, in Bursian's *Jahrb.* 1894, lxxxi 158, regards it as very doubtful whether Hermippos was the intermediate authority between Ar. and Plutarch.]

[1] See Niese in *hist. Zeitschrift*, 1892, pp. 54/5. In 18, 1 Hipparchos is called ἐρωτικός, and it might be supposed that ἐρασθεὶς γὰρ κ.τ.λ. 18, 2 would refer to him. But Thessalos' name intervenes, although he is not mentioned again afterwards. [Wilamowitz, *Ar. u. Athen*, i 110.]

Aristotle.[1] Aristotle's chronological statements about the reign of the Peisistratidai—derived beyond a doubt from his Atthidographic source—cannot be correct as they stand. I do not believe that the dates of the two periods of exile and three periods of Peisistratos' rule rest on arbitrary calculation, as Köhler assumes; I consider them, so far as they are accurately preserved, to represent the approximate estimates of the Atthis here followed.[2] Again, the date given for Cleisthenes' reforms—the year of the Archon Isagoras—may be explained by supposing that the Atthis used by Aristotle described the legislative labours of Cleisthenes under this date, although his constitution was not actually adopted till Isagoras had left Athens. It is hardly probable that Aristotle engaged in chronological research on his own account.[3]

I should also refer to an Atthidographic source the account of the constitutional development of Athens, and the notices of various individuals which are found in chapters 22 to 28. This view is supported by two circumstances: we have the dating by Archons in these chapters; we have a close agreement between a passage in Aristotle and a fragment of Androtion.[4] In this sec-

---

[1] Contrast 18, 4 with Thuc. 6, 56. 88. Arist. is supported by the Scolion in honour of Harmodios and Aristogeiton, beginning ἐν μύρτου κλαδὶ τὸ ξίφος φορήσω, and the explanation in Suid. ἐν μύρτου κλαδί. The disarming of the citizens 15, 4 is mentioned also in Polyain. 1, 21, 2.

[2] The names of Archons in 14, 1. 4; 17, 1 point to an Atthidographic source. That Peisistratos' exile cannot have begun so late as ἔτει μάλιστα ἑβδόμῳ μετὰ τὴν κάθοδον (15. 1), and that the figures given are therefore incorrect, is clear from the words that follow οὐ γὰρ πολὺν χρόνον διακατέσχεν. See also Bauer, liter. u. hist. Forsch. z. Arist., 'Αθ. Πολ., p. 51 [and die Chronologie des Peisistratos u. seiner Söhne, in Analecta Graeciensia, 1893, pp. 79-98]. This consideration also demolishes the arbitrary dates of Köhler, Sitzungsber. d. Berl. Ak., 1892, pp. 339/40. Cf. Bruno Keil 51/2, [and Bury, Class. Rev., 1895, 106].

[3] Cf. Köhler 341/2. A justification of this dating may be found in the circumstance that Hdt. 5, 69 makes Cleisthenes propose an alteration of the constitution before his banishment, and 20, 1 is in harmony with this. That it is not improbable is shown by the consideration that in all probability Isagoras invoked the aid of Cleomenes, because he could not by himself make head against Cleisthenes. After his return Cleisthenes introduced the new constitution definitively. [Cf. Sandys, 'Αθ. πολ., p. 78a.]

[4] For the dating by Archons cf. 22, 2. 3. 5. 7. 8; 23, 5; 25, 2; 26, 2. 3. 4; 27, 2. For the conformity between Aristotle and Androtion compare

22, 3. 4 with Andr‍ot. ap. Harp. Ἵππαρχος.

θαρροῦντος ἤδη τοῦ δήμου, τότε πρῶτον ἐχρήσαντο τῷ νόμῳ τῷ περὶ τὸν ὀστρακισμόν, ὃς ἐτέθη διὰ τὴν ὑποψίαν τῶν ἐν

περὶ δὲ τοῦ (Ἱππάρχου τοῦ Χάρμου) Ἀνδροτίων ἐν τῇ δευτέρᾳ φησίν, ὅτι συγγενὴς μὲν ἦν Πεισιστράτου τοῦ

tion of the book we find a whole series of statements containing entirely novel information on various points of constitutional history. Among these, what has caused the greatest stir is Aristotle's account of the predominant position of the Areopagus after the battle of Salamis and until the year 462/1. Yet, taken strictly, this tells us no more than we knew already; it is merely somewhat more distinctly put. According to Solon's constitution (and in this respect Cleisthenes probably made no alteration) the Areopagus had the supervision of the laws and the control of the administration. Just as the Areopagus intervened directly in the administration during the siege of Athens at the close of the Peloponnesian war, so in all probability it intervened in the critical year 480. What failed to affect the course of events in 404 B.C. was attended with conspicuous success in the war against Persia. It is in this circumstance, I think, that we find the natural explanation of the fact that the Areopagus, as the war proceeded, converted its general right of supervision of the administration into a direct control, thus usurping functions of the Boule, the Ecclesia, and the Dicasteries.[1] After this supremacy of the Areopagites had been accepted for seventeen years, though not without protest, Ephialtes in 462/1 deprived them of

ταῖς δυνάμεσιν, ὅτι Πεισίστρατος δημαγωγὸς καὶ στρατηγὸς ὢν τύραννος κατέστη. καὶ πρῶτος ὠστρακίσθη τῶν ἐκείνου συγγενῶν Ἵππαρχος Χάρμου Κολλυτεύς, δι᾿ ὃν καὶ μάλιστα τὸν νόμον ἔθηκεν ὁ Κλεισθένης ἐξελάσαι βουλόμενος αὐτόν.

τυράννου καὶ πρῶτος ἐξωστρακίσθη, τοῦ περὶ τὸν ὀστρακισμὸν νόμου τότε πρῶτον τεθέντος διὰ τὴν ὑποψίαν τῶν περὶ Πεισίστρατον, ὅτι δημαγωγὸς ὢν καὶ στρατηγὸς ἐτυράννησεν.

[1] Cf. e.g. what Niese 64/5 and Köhler 343/4 have said on the credibility of the Aristotelian account of the supremacy of the Areopagus. It was already known to us from Arist., Pol., 8(5), 4, p. 201, 5 Bekker: οἷον ἡ ἐν Ἀρείῳ πάγῳ βουλὴ εὐδοκιμήσασα ἐν τοῖς Μηδικοῖς ἔδοξε συντονωτέραν ποιῆσαι τὴν πολιτείαν, and Cic., de off., 1, 22, 75: et Themistocles quidem nihil dixerit, in quo ipse Areopagum adiuverit, at ille vere a se adiutum Themistoclem; est enim bellum gestum consilio senatus eius, qui a Solone erat constitutus. The discrepancy between 23, 1 and Cleidem. ap. Plut., Them., 10, seems to be of no consequence, for Themistocles, as an ex-Archon, would be a member of the Areopagus. On the powers of supervision possessed by the Areopagus under Solon's constitution see 8, 4; for the intervention of that body at the end of the Peloponnesian war cf. Lys. 12, 69. That the Areopagus had usurped powers belonging to the Council, the popular assembly, and the law courts, follows from 25, 2: καὶ τὰ μὲν τοῖς πεντακοσίοις, τὰ δὲ τῷ δήμῳ καὶ τοῖς δικαστηρίοις ἀπέδωκεν. We need not be surprised that Hdt. tells us nothing of this predominant position of the Areopagus; for what do we learn from him about the internal history of Athens at this time?

the powers which they had arrogated to themselves, thus excluding them from all direct intervention in the administration; and subsequently Pericles and Archestratos took from them even the powers which constitutionally belonged to them.[1] This appears a very natural course for the development of the constitution to have taken, and for that reason I have no hesitation in accepting it as true.

For his full accounts of the Oligarchies of the Four Hundred and of the Thirty (chap. 29–40), Aristotle has mainly drawn on documentary evidence—for the Four Hundred, the psephism of Pythodoros, which directed the 30 συγγραφεῖς to be appointed, the proposals of these συγγραφεῖς, and the draft, in the form of psephisms, of the final and of the provisional constitution; for the Thirty, the treaty of peace between their adherents and the returned Democrats.[2] As regards the few historical notes about the Four Hundred, which are given in Aristotle side by side with what is derived from these documentary authorities, they may without doubt be traced to the Atthides, though there are some points of agreement with Thucydides. In proof of this, we might point to the exact chronological statements in Aristotle's account of the Four Hundred.[3] The events during the oligarchy of the

---

[1] The extended power of supervision, allowing a direct interference in the administration, is in 25, 2 called τὰ ἐπίθετα, δι' ὧν ἦν ἡ τῆς πολιτείας φυλακή. Arist. also styles this supremacy of the Areopagus, 25, 4, δύναμις, and 26, 1, ἐπιμέλεια. I would direct attention to the fact that Oncken, *Athen u. Hellas*, 236 ff., years ago demonstrated that the change introduced by Ephialtes was merely the restriction of the powers of the Areopagus within their original limits. He referred (p. 254) the passage in Æschylus' Eumenides (l. 693 sq.)—published in 458 B.C.—to the enlargement of the legal rights of the Areopagus. Of Pericles we read, 27, 1: καὶ γὰρ τῶν Ἀρεοπαγιτῶν ἔνια παρείλετο. Of the Thirty 35, 2 says: καὶ τούς τ' Ἐφιάλτου καὶ Ἀρχεστράτου νόμους τοὺς περὶ τῶν Ἀρεοπαγιτῶν καθεῖλον ἐξ Ἀρείου πάγο[υ].

[2] Pythodoros' psephism: Arist. 29, 2. 3; the proposals of the συγγραφεῖς 29, 4. 5; the draft of the ultimate constitution, 30; of the provisional, 31; brought in as a psephism, 32, 1. The treaty between the adherents of the Thirty and the Democrats, 39.

[3] Points of agreement with Thuc. Cf.

33, 1	with	Thuc. 8, 96.
πλείω γὰρ ἐκ τῆς Εὐβοίας ἢ τῆς Ἀττικῆς ἐτύγχανον ὠφελούμενοι.		ἐν ᾗ ναῦς τε καὶ τὸ μέγιστον Εὔβοιαν ἀπολωλέκεσαν, ἐξ ἧς πλείω ἢ τῆς Ἀττικῆς ὠφελοῦντο.
33, 1	with	Thuc. 8, 97.
κατέλυσαν τοὺς τετρακοσίους καὶ τὰ		ἐν ᾗπερ (ἐκκλησίᾳ) καὶ τοὺς τετρα-

Thirty Aristotle relates with far greater minuteness than those during the government of the Four Hundred. Yet he has not used Xenophon for his account of the Thirty. His version is much shorter and much more condensed than Xenophon's, and yet in some particulars more exact. The two narratives repeatedly disagree. Whether the words of Theramenes quoted by Aristotle are a reminiscence of Xenophon, or whether the expression is historical, and so may have been taken by Aristotle from some other authority, cannot be determined. Aristotle's authority for this part of the work too was, I am convinced, an Atthis, and of this the chronological statements seem again to be evidence. But any employment of Ephoros is very doubtful.¹

πράγματα παρέδωκαν τοῖς πεντακισχιλίοις τοῖς ἐκ τῶν ὅπλων, ψηφισάμενοι
μηδεμίαν ἀρχὴν εἶναι μισθοφόρον.

κοσίους καταπαύσαντες τοῖς πεντακισχιλίοις ἐψηφίσαντο τὰ πράγματα παρα-
δοῦναι· εἶναι δὲ αὐτῶν ὁπόσοι καὶ ὅπλα
παρέχονται· καὶ μισθὸν μηδένα φέρειν
μηδεμιᾷ ἀρχῇ.

Harp. συγγραφεῖς states, on the authority of Androtion and Philochoros, that 30 συγγραφεῖς were appointed. Thuc. 8, 67 says ten. As Harp. does not cite the psephism of Pythodoros (see 29, 2), but the Atthidographers, it is probable that the latter did not quote the actual words of the original document. For the chronological statements cf. 32, 1. 2; 33, 1.

¹ 37, 1 e.g. is more precise than Xen., *Hell.*, 2, 3, 51, and makes the proceedings against Theramenes much more intelligible. According to 37, 2 the Spartan garrison was called in after Theramenes' death, according to Xen. 2, 3, 13/4 before it. 37, 1 makes Phyle taken by Thrasybulos before the death of Theramenes, Xen. 2, 4, 2 after it.

For the words of Theramenes cf.—

   36, 2   with   Xen. 2, 3, 19.

Θηραμένης δὲ πάλιν ἐπιτιμᾷ καὶ
τούτοις, πρῶτον μὲν ὅτι βουλόμενοι
μεταδοῦναι τοῖς ἐπιεικέσι τρισχιλίοις
μόνοις μεταδιδόασι, ὡς ἐν τούτῳ τῷ
πλήθει τῆς ἀρετῆς ὡρισμένης, ἔπειθ᾽ ὅτι
δύο τὰ ἐναντιώτατα ποιοῦσιν, βίαιόν τε
τὴν ἀρχὴν καὶ τῶν ἀρχομένων ἥττω
παρασκευάζοντες.

ὁ δ᾽ αὖ Θηραμένης καὶ πρὸς ταῦτα
ἔλεγεν, ὅτι ἄτοπον δοκοίη ἑαυτῷ γε
εἶναι τὸ πρῶτον μὲν βουλομένους τοὺς
βελτίστους τῶν πολιτῶν κοινωνοὺς
ποιήσασθαι τρισχιλίους, ὥσπερ τὸν
ἀριθμὸν τοῦτον ἔχοντά τινα ἀνάγκην
καλοὺς καὶ ἀγαθοὺς εἶναι, καὶ οὔτ᾽ ἔξω
τούτων σπουδαίους οὔτ᾽ ἐντὸς τούτων
πονηροὺς οἱόν τε εἴη γενέσθαι· ἔπειτα δ᾽,
ἔφη, ὁρῶ ἔγωγε δύο ἡμᾶς τὰ ἐναντιώτατα
πράττοντας, βιαίαν τε τὴν ἀρχὴν καὶ
ἥττονα τῶν ἀρχομένων κατασκευαζο-
μένους.

Dates in 34, 1. 2; 35, 1; 40, 4; 41, 1. Cf. also 34, 3: ἔγραψε δὲ τὸ ψήφισμα Δρακοντίδης Ἀφιδναῖος with Philochor., *fr.* 135, in Müller 1, 406: τὰ δὲ χρήματ᾽ ἐψηφίσαντο πάντ᾽ εἶναι στρατιωτικά, Δημοσθένους γράψαντος. Bauer, *liter. und*

I turn now to that part of the Ἀθηναίων πολιτεία (chaps. 5–13) where Aristotle speaks of Solon and his legislation, and the circumstance of that age. To all appearance chapter 13, which deals with the time from Solon's leaving Athens to the beginning of Peisistratos' tyrannis, comes from an atthidographic source; for here, as elsewhere, we find exact dating such as we have before referred to. The account of the three στάσεις is essentially the same as Herodotus'. The close of the chapter is an inference of Aristotle's from the circumstance that the Atthis which he used mentioned a general Diapsephisis after the banishment of the Peisistratidai.[1] In chapter 12 Aristotle quotes the sources from which he derived his account of the political and social conditions before and immediately after the legislation of Solon. These are the poems of Solon himself, to which he repeatedly refers.[2] Besides these, he also cites other authors, evidently his atthidographic sources, but these have no value in his eyes except in so far as they agree with the primary authority, Solon's poems.[3]

To turn from the chapters on political matters, we have yet to consider the question, what were Aristotle's authorities for his antiquarian information as to the Solonian legislation.[4] And it will be well to extend this so as to include within the scope of our inquiry the source of his antiquarian statements as to the Draconian (chap 4) and Cleisthenian (chap. 21) constitutions. That antiquarian information was given in Aristotle's atthidographic sources cannot be doubted; that he used it appears—so

---

hist. Forsch. z. Arist. Ἀθ. πολ., p. 151 ff., tries to prove that Arist. has used Ephoros, but his arguments are hardly convincing. [Cf. Wilamowitz *Ar. u. Athen.*, i 305.]

[1] 13, 1. 2 gives the exact dates and the duration of the tyrannis. § 4 agrees with Hdt. i. 59; cf. also Plut., *Sol.*, 13, 29. § 5 is a combination of Aristotle's.

[2] 12 begins: ταῦτα δ' ὅτι τοῦτον ⟨τὸν⟩ τρόπον ἔσχεν οἵ τ' ἄλλοι συμφωνοῦσι πάντες καὶ αὐτὸς ἐν τῇ ποιήσει μέμνηται περὶ αὐτῶν ἐν τοῖσδε, and the quotations from Solon's poems follow. Chap. 5, where again Solon is repeatedly quoted, is a reconstruction from the Solonian poems. So probably is chap. 11, as the opening words of chap. 12 indicate. In 6, 4, again, another point is deduced from Solon's poems.

[3] Cf. the expressions ὡς ἔκ τε τῶν ἄλλων ὁμολογεῖται καὶ [αὐτὸς] ἐν τοῖσδε τοῖς ποιήμασιν μαρτυρεῖ (5, 3), καὶ ἐν τοῖς ποιήμασιν αὐτὸς πολλαχοῦ μέμνηται καὶ οἱ ἄλλοι συνομολογοῦσι πάντες (6, 4), ταῦτα δ' ὅτι τοῦτον ⟨τὸν⟩ τρόπον ἔσχεν οἵ τ' ἄλλοι συμφωνοῦσι πάντες καὶ αὐτὸς ἐν τῇ ποιήσει μέμνηται περὶ αὐτῶν ἐν τοῖσδε (12, 1).

[4] The discussions of political matters are contained in chap. 6, 2. 3 and 9; the antiquarian information in chap. 6, 1; 7; 8; 10.

far as the evidence before us warrants an opinion—very doubtful.[1] Besides these Atthides, it was open to Aristotle to use documentary evidence for the antiquarian information which he gives —above all to use the laws of Draco, Solon, and Cleisthenes. Did he consult these documents? Some writers maintain that he did not. Nissen is of opinion that Aristotle, in dealing with the earliest times, confined himself to literary sources, without attempting any specially profound research: that, for instance, he borrowed the description of the Draconian constitution from Critias or some similar pamphleteer.[2] According to Niese, Aristotle's description of the older Athenian constitution—Draco's as well as Solon's —is hypothetical, and is based mainly on the belief that Solon and Draco founded the Athenian democracy. But it is to be noticed that Solon's constitution was in point of fact a democracy, however limited, as indeed Solon himself says in one of his laws.[3]

---

[1] Cf. the different explanations of the σεισάχθεια (Plut., *Sol.*, 15) and in 6, 1; 12, 4, where Ar. contradicts Androtion 10, 1 though without mentioning him by name, remarking that the αὔξησις τοῦ νομίσματος took place after the σεισάχθεια. According to Androtion the ἀποδέκται were installed by Cleisthenes in place of the κωλακρέται, of whom Androt. had given an account elsewhere. See Androt., *fr.* 3=Harp. ἀποδέκται, and *fr.* 4=*Schol.* Arist., *Birds*, 1540. Arist. 7, 8 testifies to the existence of the κωλακρέται under Solon, but says nothing about the creation of the ἀποδέκται by Cleisthenes. Cleidemos, *fr.* 8=Phot. ναυκραρία declares that Cleisthenes established 50 naucraries simultaneously with the new 10 tribes. Aristotle knows nothing of this.

[2] See Nissen, p. 201. A similar opinion to Nissen's is held by Herzog, *zur Literatur. üb. d. Staat. der Athener*, Tübingen, 1892, p. 26 sqq., who holds that chap. 4 was taken from a pamphlet belonging to the partisan literature that emanated before 411 B.C. from the oligarchs as a preliminary to the events of that year, and presenting the constitution that the writer desired to establish, in the form of an ideal but fictitious Draconian institution. But the very existence of such a party literature before the year 411 is altogether a matter of doubt. [Nissen was anticipated in his conjecture by Mr. J. W. Headlam, *Class. Review*, 1891, p. 166; and Theod. Reinach, *la constitution de Dracon et la constitution de l'an 411* in *Rev. des ét. gr.*, iv (1891) 82–5, and *Aristot. ou Critias*, *ib.* 143–158.]

[3] Cf. Niese in the *hist. Zeitschrift*, 1892, 58 ff. Arist. 8, 4 gives as one of the functions of the Solonian Areopagus: καὶ τοὺς ἐπὶ καταλύσει τοῦ δήμου συνισταμένους ἔκρινεν, Σόλωνος θέντ[ος] νόμον . . . περὶ αὐτῶν. To this law doubtless the clause belonged which according to Andok., *de Myst.*, 95, was posted up ἐν τῇ στήλῃ ἔμπροσθεν τοῦ βουλευτηρίου:—ὃς ἂν ἄρξῃ ἐν τῇ πόλει τῆς δημοκρατίας καταλυθείσης, νηποινεὶ τεθνάναι καὶ τὸν ἀποκτείναντα ὅσιον εἶναι καὶ τὰ χρήματα ἔχειν τοῦ ἀποθανόντος. On this Andok. remarks: ἄλλο τι οὖν, ὦ Ἐπίχαρες, ἢ νῦν ὁ ἀποκτείνας σε καθαρὸς τὰς χεῖρας ἔσται, κατά γε τὸν Σόλωνος νόμον;

Niese is of opinion that the Solonian constitution was never reduced to writing, the only record actaully dating from Solon's time being his legal code, which contained also what had been retained of Draco's laws. And this code, he believes, contained only clauses dealing with family-rights, inheritances, legal processes and penalties, and police arrangements. But even if we must admit that there was no written Solonian constitution, at least in any systematic form such as we find in modern States, still Niese's idea of the contents of Solon's laws is much too limited. Without dwelling on the fact that we have the contents of the Solonian tables described as οἱ περὶ τῶν ἱερῶν νόμοι, οἱ πολιτικοὶ νόμοι, and οἱ περὶ τῶν ἰδιωτικῶν νόμοι, I think that a code of laws, which, in its regulations as to religion, prescribed the nature and the ritual of the sacrifices to be offered, cannot in the sphere of politics have remained silent upon constitutional arrangements.[1]

Niese himself admits that the laws presupposed a definite constitution, for which they may serve as evidence in so far as they enable us to draw inferences from them. Further, we have explicit testimony that the Solonian laws dealt with the powers of the ναύκραροι. This being so, it is scarcely probable that in the laws no mention was made of the system of Trittyes and Naucrariai as such, or at any rate that it was impossible to obtain from these incidental clauses on the ναύκραροι an accurate idea of their organization.[2] Even if we suppose that in the Solonian laws the powers of the Areopagus were not systematically defined, it was certainly possible from various clauses of the laws to form a true estimate of the functions of the Areopagus, as Aristotle did. The introduction of an appeal from the decisions of the Archons to a popular court, which Aristotle ascribes to Solon, could surely have been inferred by Aristotle from the Solonian code,

hence, on his own testimony, Solon's constitution is proved to be a democracy.

[1] On the contents of the Solonian tables see *Schol.* on Plat., *Pol.*, p. 298*d*. though there κύρβεις and ἄξονες are erroneously distinguished. Suid. κύρβεις Art. 1. In Lys. 80, 17 we read: θαυμάζω δέ, εἰ μὴ ἐνθυμεῖται, ὅταν ἐμὲ φάσκῃ ἀσεβεῖν λέγοντα, ὡς χρὴ θύειν τὰς θυσίας τὰς ἐκ τῶν κύρβεων καὶ τῶν στηλῶν κατὰ τὰς συγγραφάς, ὅτι καὶ τῆς πόλεως κατηγορεῖ. See also § 18.

[2] 8, 3: διὸ καὶ ἐν τοῖς νόμοις τοῖς Σόλωνος οἷς οὐκέτι χρῶνται πολλαχ[οῦ γέ]γραπται "τοὺς ναυκράρους εἰσπράττειν" καὶ "ἀναλίσκειν ἐκ τοῦ ναυκραρικοῦ ἀργυρ[ίου]." Cf. Phot. ναυκραρία: καὶ ἐν τοῖς νόμοις λέγει [for the MS. δὲ], "ἐάν τις ναυκραρίας ἀμφισβητῇ" καὶ "τοὺς ναυκράρους τοὺς κατὰ ναυκραρίαν."

since we are ourselves fortunately able to prove it by the documentary evidence of an extant law of Solon's. I cannot understand, therefore, how Niese can call the hypothesis that Solon founded the popular courts an entire anachronism.[1] We have evidence to show that there were laws of Solon prohibiting δανείζειν ἐπὶ τοῖς σώμασι, legalizing interest, and fixing a legal maximum for private landed property. Could not Aristotle have sketched from these and similar provisions, combined with Solon's poems, a true picture of the social condition of Athens before Solon's time? Must not laws, similar to the Solonian Epitimia-law in the 13th axon, have thrown a flood of light upon the character of the pre-Solonian constitution?[2]

These few instances are drawn from the scanty materials at our disposal. But, in spite of their small number, they serve to show that, if he wished, Aristotle might easily develop from the provisions of the codes of Draco, Solon, and Cleisthenes that general account of their constitutions which we find in the Ἀθηναίων πολιτεία. The only question therefore that remains is whether Aristotle was disposed to do so. According to Nissen and Niese he was not; in their opinion there is scarcely a trace of any study of original documents in the historical part of the work. And yet, when Aristotle began to write this treatise, he had written, as Nissen himself believes, five books περὶ Σόλωνος ἀξόνων, and was engaged with Theophrastos—as has been shewn by Usener, with whom Nissen agrees—on the composition of the συναγωγὴ τῶν νόμων, a compilation of the laws obtaining in the various States, and a description of the various authorities entrusted with their execution.[3] Thus we are asked to believe that

---

[1] For the Solonian Areopagus see 8, 4; on the popular dicastery 7, 2; 9, 2. Niese's view 65, 2. Lys. 10, 16 cites the Solonian law:—δεδέσθαι δ' ἐν τῇ ποδοκάκκῃ ἡμέρας πέντε τὸν πόδα, ἐὰν προστιμήσῃ ἡ ἡλιαία, whose authenticity is placed beyond doubt by the archaic expression ποδοκάκκη. See also the laws that follow.

[2] Prohibition of δανείζειν ἐπὶ τοῖς σώμασιν, 6, 1; 9, 1. Interest allowed Lys. 10, 18 τὸ ἀργύριον στάσιμον εἶναι, ἐφ' ὁπόσῳ ἂν βούληται ὁ δανείζων, with the explanation given by Lysias, ibid. On landed property see Arist., Pol., 2, 7 = p. 37, 26 ff. Bekker: οἷον καὶ Σόλων ἐνομοθέτησεν καὶ παρ' ἄλλοις ἐστὶ νόμος, ὃς κελεύει κτᾶσθαι γῆν, ὁπόσην ἂν βούληταί τις. Solon's epitimia law, cf. Plut., Sol., 19.

[3] Περὶ τῶν Σόλωνος ἀξόνων ε' is mentioned in a later catalogue of Aristotelian works (see Westermann, Biogr., 404) as a work of Aristotle's. Nissen 167/8 accepts it as authentic. On Aristotle's share in the συναγωγὴ τῶν νόμων, which went under the name of Theophrastos, see Usener in Preuss.

Aristotle, though in possession of documentary evidence, and though having unquestionably an accurate knowledge of that evidence, preferred to make no use of it in composing his Ἀθηναίων πολιτεία, but confined himself to the literary authorities then in existence. We are asked to believe that, on many questions lying on the border-land between constitutional law and jurisprudence, he voluntarily ran the risk of contradicting in this account of the Athenian constitution, drawn from literary sources, what had been stated in the συναγωγὴ τῶν νόμων, which was founded on documentary evidence, and this although the latter work went by his name, and certainly was partly edited by him. I maintain that the author need be no Aristotle to make such an assumption untenable. And indeed it is refuted by the Ἀθηναίων πολιτεία itself; the author refers repeatedly to the laws of Solon, which, after what has just been said, he can scarcely be supposed to have borrowed from his literary authority.

The peculiar character of the Aristotelian sketch of the Draconian, the Solonian and the Cleisthenian constitutions—where we miss many things that ought not to be absent from a systematic account, and find much that is of little intrinsic importance—may, I believe, be satisfactorily explained by supposing that the source on which Aristotle drew, was not a systematic work on the Athenian constitution, but a compilation of laws from which Aristotle gleaned for himself the character of the institutions of Athens.[1] To this another consideration must be added.

Jahrb. 53 p. 22; Nissen 183 ff. agrees. This joint authorship follows from the quotation by Arist. himself in *Pol.* 8 (5) 9 = p. 214, 21 ff. Bekker: ἁπλῶς δὲ ὅσα ἐν τοῖς νόμοις ὡς συμφέροντα λέγομεν ταῖς πολιτείαις, ἅπαντα ταῦτα σώζει τὰς πολιτείας; and from Philodem., *Rhet.* (Vol. Hercul. v. fol. 147) 11 ff.: πῶς [δ᾽] οὐχὶ θαυμ[ασ]μὸ[ν] ἐνέφ[υσ]ε μέγαν τῆς δ[υ]νάμεω[ς; ἐ]ξέστη λιπὼν δ[ὲ] τῆς οἰκείας πραγματείας καὶ διὰ ταῦτ᾽ ἐφωρᾶτο τούς τε νόμους συνάγων ἅμα τῷ μαθητεῖ καὶ τὰς τοσαύτας πολιτείας καὶ τὰ περὶ τῶν [τό]πων [δ]ικαιώματα καὶ τὰ πρὸς τοὺς καιροὺς καὶ πᾶν ὅσον τῆς τοιαύτη[ς ἐστι πραγματείας]. Aristotle had previously acted as a legislator for his native city Stageira (Diog. L. 5, 1, 6; Plut., *adv. Colot.*, 32, 9, p. 1377 Didot) which was rebuilt at his request (Plut., *Alex.*, 7; *vit. Arist.* in Westermann, *Biogr.*, p. 400, 58 ff.). He must then have made himself acquainted with the laws of Athens. Cf. Isocr. 15, 83: ἀλλὰ τοῖς μὲν τοὺς νόμους τιθέναι προαιρουμένοις προὔργου γέγονε τὸ πλῆθος τῶν κειμένων, οὐδὲν γὰρ αὐτοὺς δεῖ ζητεῖν ἑτέρους, ἀλλὰ τοὺς παρὰ τοῖς ἄλλοις εὐδοκιμοῦντας πειραθῆναι συναγαγεῖν.

[1] Reference to Solonian laws, 8, 3. 4. 5; 16, 10. Mention of Cleisthenian laws, 22, 1. In Plut., *Sol.*, 31, we read: ὡς δὲ Θεόφραστος ἱστόρηκε, καὶ τὸν τῆς ἀργίας νόμον οὐ Σόλων ἔθηκεν, ἀλλὰ Πεισίστρατος, ᾧ τήν τε χώραν ἐνεργοτέραν καὶ

The συναγωγὴ τῶν νόμων and the συναγωγὴ τῶν πολιτειῶν undoubtedly supplemented each other; accordingly, much that we now miss in the 'Αθηναίων πολιτεία must have been found in the 'Αθηναίων νόμοι. Aristotle therefore made his deductions from the provisions of the Solonian laws, and inferred from them the political institutions of Athens under the Solonian constitution, and the same observation will hold of the laws of Draco and Cleisthenes. It is therefore not impossible that one or two of his conclusions rested on insecure premisses, and would to-day appear rash inferences if we had the means of testing them. But in the absence of such means, conjectures of our own are certainly less trustworthy than Aristotle's conclusions, founded, as they are, on evidence such as this. In one case only has the philosopher permitted us a glimpse of the methods by which he arrived at his conclusions, and this bears out what has been said above. Aristotle informs us that Solon directed the magistrates to be taken from the three highest census-classes, ἑκάστοις ἀνὰ λόγον τῷ μεγέθει τοῦ τιμήματος ἀποδιδοὺς [τὴν ἀρ]χήν. This, as Aristotle himself remarks, is an inference from the clause in Solon's laws, that the treasurers of the goddess should be chosen from the Pentacosiomedimnoi, probably taken in connexion with the fact that in the year 457 the archonship was thrown open to the Zeugitai.[1] If all Aristotle's conclusions are as well founded—and this they seem to be, since he gives his data for this particular conclusion as being in his judgment not

---

τὴν πόλιν ἠρεμαιοτέραν ἐποίησεν. 16, 2. 3 is apparently an inference from this law. Arist., *Pol.*, 6 (4), 1, p. 146, 17 ff. Bekker, says: πρὸς γὰρ τὰς πολιτείας τοὺς νόμους δεῖ τίθεσθαι καὶ τίθενται πάντες, ἀλλ' οὐ τὰς πολιτείας πρὸς τοὺς νόμους. πολιτεία μὲν γάρ ἐστι τάξις ταῖς πόλεσιν ἡ περὶ τὰς ἀρχάς, τίνα τρόπον νενέμηνται καὶ τί τὸ κύριον τῆς πολιτείας καὶ τί τὸ τέλος ἑκάστης τῆς κοινωνίας ἐστίν· νόμοι δὲ κεχωρισμένοι τῶν δηλούντων τὴν πολιτείαν, καθ' οὓς δεῖ τοὺς ἄρχοντας ἄρχειν καὶ φυλάττειν τοὺς παραβαίνοντας αὐτούς. In 'Αθ. πολ. 9,1 and 10,1 this distinction is not made. Of these three institutions of Solon 9, 1 says: δοκεῖ δὲ τῆς Σόλωνος πολιτείας τρία ταῦτ' εἶναι τὰ δημοτικώτατα; 10, 1: ἐν[μὲν οὖν τ]οῖς νόμοις ταῦτα δοκεῖ θεῖναι δημοτικά; for Aristotle deduced the πολιτεία from the clauses of the Solonian νόμοι. In them Arist. could find no statement as to the standards for assessment in the Solonian census. This is the reason why he gives in 7, 4 his own estimate for the census of the ἱππεῖς as against that of other authors who were of a different opinion.

[1] Arist. 7, 8. 8, 1: σημεῖον δ' ὅτι κληρωτὰς ἐποίησεν ἐκ τῶν τιμημάτων ὁ περὶ τῶν ταμιῶν νόμος, ᾧ χρώμενοι [διατελο]ῦσιν ἔτι καὶ νῦν· κελεύει γὰρ κληροῦν τοὺς ταμίας ἐκ πεντακοσιομεδίμνω[ν], compared with 47, 1: πρῶτον μὲν γὰρ οἱ ταμίαι τῆς 'Αθηνᾶς εἰσὶ μὲν δέκα, κ[ληροῦται] δ' ε:ς ἐκ τῆς φυλῆς, ἐκ πεντακοσιομεδίμνων κατὰ τὸν Σόλωνος νόμ[ον· ἔτι γὰρ ὁ ν]όμος κύριός ἐστιν. For the change in b.c. 457 cf. 26, 2.

absolutely certain—we may safely accept his representation of the Draconian, Solonian, and Cleisthenian constitution as on the whole correct. From the point of view of modern research we often feel inclined to blame Aristotle for not putting us in a position to examine the methods by which he has arrived at his results by stating the data on which they were founded; this, however, is not a fault peculiar to Aristotle; all ancient authors are open to the same criticism. As regards the value, then, of the Ἀθηναίων πολιτεία for determining the character of the Draconian, Solonian, and Cleisthenian constitutions, my position is this: I regard its statements as valuable information, founded on documentary evidence, which we are not justified in rejecting in favour of conjectures of our own. If we approach Aristotle's statements with unprejudiced minds, we shall find that they can be perfectly well reconciled with the other evidence we possess. This cannot be said, however, of his representation of the pre-Draconian constitution. There can be no doubt that this is a reconstruction of Aristotle's from the statements in the Atthides, combined with his own interpretations of historical facts.[1] Still, I have thought it necessary to follow Aristotle even in his account of this, the earliest period of Athenian history, because he represents at all events the oldest tradition accessible to us, and because he and his authorities could still avail themselves of historical evidence which in its original form is lost to us.

I now turn to consider the discussions of questions of political history, which occur in a number of places in the historical part of the work. Among the conditions of peace imposed by Lysander upon the conquered Athenians, was one which bound them to govern their city henceforth according to the πάτριος πολιτεία. This immediately gave rise to a controversy between the various political parties; the democrats struggled to preserve the existing democracy, evidently on the pretext that this was the constitution inherited from their ancestors; aristocrats who were members of the *hetairiai*, and the exiles that returned on the conclusion of peace, demanded an oligarchy, evidently on the same plea as the democrats; while those who did not belong to a *hetairia* endeavoured to restore the real πάτριος πολιτεία. The leader of the last party was Theramenes. Lysander himself took the part of

---

[1] Arist. has employed a number of literary sources for chap. 3; he distinguishes his authorities into οἱ πλείους and ἔνιοι. For some statements he mentions historical facts as σημεῖα.

the oligarchs, and the oligarchy of the Thirty was established. But even the Thirty, to whom Theramenes also belonged, professed at first to be advocates of the πάτριος πολιτεία. They rescinded the laws of Ephialtes and Archestratos, which limited the powers of the Areopagus, and in order to deprive the dicasteries of their powers of passing sentence, they abrogated the ambiguous provisions in the laws of Solon. All this was done under pretence of restoring the constitution inherited from their ancestors, and making it unassailable.[1]

Thus the πάτριος πολιτεία signified the constitution established by Solon's legislation, that is, those forms of government which were expressed or implied in the laws of Draco and Solon. Whether the institutions of Cleisthenes also belonged to the πάτριος πολιτεία seems to have been a matter of dispute among its supporters.[2] Aristotle, himself an advocate of the πάτριος πολιτεία, plainly denies that they were, and approves of the Cleisthenian democracy only in its restricted form, as it existed when the Areopagus possessed extended powers. The constitution, which was in force for a short time after the overthrow of the Four Hundred, and which it was originally intended to adopt under the Four Hundred themselves, corresponded with Aristotle's constitutional ideal. He thus found himself in accord with Theramenes, and this explains the esteem which the philosopher shows for that politician.[3]

---

[1] Cf. 34, 3; similarly, though not in such detail, Diod. 14, 3; Arist. 35, 2.

[2] The psephism of Pythodoros in B.C. 411 must have directed the 30 συγγραφεῖς to examine the laws of Draco and Solon with a view to revising the constitution. This follows from Cleitophon's amendment, 29, 3: προσαναζητῆσαι δὲ τοὺς αἱρεθέντας ἔγραφεν καὶ τοὺς πατρίους νόμους, οὓς Κλεισθένης ἔθηκεν, ὅτε καθίστη τὴν δημοκρατίαν, ὅπως ⟨ἂν⟩ ἀκούσαντες καὶ τούτων βουλεύσωνται τὸ ἄριστον. Cleitophon, who in 404 was still a supporter of the πάτριος πολιτεία (34, 3), included in it therefore the laws of Cleisthenes. In the draft of the provisional constitution for the year 411, which enacted βουλεύειν μὲν τετρακοσίους κατὰ τὰ πάτρια (31, 1), τὰ πάτρια meant the Solonian constitution.

[3] In 29, 3 he remarks upon Cleitophon's amendment mentioned in the preceding note: ὡς οὐ δημοτικὴν ἀλλὰ παραπλησίαν οὖσαν τὴν Κλεισθένους πολιτείαν τῇ Σόλωνος. In 20, 1 he says τούτων δὲ γενομένων (i.e. through the institutions of Cleisthenes) δημοτικωτέρα πολὺ τῆς Σόλωνος ἐγένετο ἡ πολιτεία. Cf. 41, 2. Of the time of the supremacy of the Areopagus he says, 23, 2: καὶ ἐπολιτεύθησαν Ἀθηναῖοι καλῶς καὶ κατὰ τούτους τοὺς καιρούς, with which Isocr. 7, 15, 17 is to be compared. The last words of Arist. compare that period with the time after the overthrow of the Four Hundred, of which he says, 33, 2: δοκοῦσι δὲ καλῶς πολιτευθῆναι κατὰ τούτους τοὺς καιρούς. The same opinion in Thuc. 8, 97. The basis of the constitution of that date is described by Arist. 33, 1 in the

But the πάτριος πολιτεία of Theramenes was very far from satisfying the oligarchs of the *hetairiai* and the returned exiles. They had formed very different ideas of the constitution of their ancestors, which it was their endeavour to restore. Beyond question they regarded even Solon's constitution as a corruption of the πάτριος πολιτεία, and it seems as though Critias gave literary expression to this idea. Whether this was done, as Dümmler supposes, in order to furnish the Thirty with a programme, or rather, as appears to me more probable, to win Lysander over to the views of the oligarchs, is better left undecided. Neither can we determine whether this work appeared in the form of an 'Αθηναίων πολιτεία or of a pamphlet. Traces of it are to all appearance still discernible in the Aristotelian 'Αθηναίων πολιτεία. Critias accused Themistocles and Cleon of directing the policy of their country with a view to their own pecuniary advantage: and this may be the best place to mention Aristotle's statement that the same accusation had been brought by some against Solon. So too the accusation, referred to but contradicted by Aristotle, that Solon intentionally made his laws obscure and ambiguous in order that the Dicasteries might have more left to their discretion, seems to come from the Thirty, who struck out of Solon's laws those pro-

words: καὶ τὰ πράγματα παρέδωκαν τοῖς πεντακισχιλίοις τοῖς ἐκ τῶν ὅπλων, ψηφισάμενοι μηδεμίαν ἀρχὴν εἶναι μισθοφόρον. This agreed with the constitution drafted by the 30 συγγραφεῖς (29, 5), and with that of Draco (4, 2), to which the draft-constitution presents some other special points of resemblance. Cf. 30, 6 with 4, 3, and 31, 3 with 4, 3. Description of the best πολιτεία in Arist., *Pol.*, 6 (4) 11=p. 162, 19 ff. Bekker: δῆλον ἄρα ὅτι καὶ ἡ κοινωνία ἡ πολιτικὴ ἀρίστη ἡ διὰ τῶν μέσων καὶ τὰς τοιαύτας ἐνδέχεται εὖ πολιτεύεσθαι πόλεις, ἐν αἷς δὴ πολὺ τὸ μέσον καὶ κρεῖττον μάλιστα μὲν ἀμφοῖν (the ἄποροι and εὔποροι), εἰ δὲ μή, θατέρου μέρους· προστιθέμενον γὰρ ποιεῖ ῥοπὴν καὶ κωλύει γίνεσθαι τὰς ἐναντίας ὑπερβολάς (p. 164, 6 ff.). Its external form is defined by Arist., *Pol.*, 2, 6=p. 35, 19 ff., thus: ἡ δὲ σύνταξις ὅλη βούλεται μὲν εἶναι μήτε δημοκρατία μήτε ὀλιγαρχία, μέση δὲ τούτων, ἣν καλοῦσι πολιτείαν· ἐκ γὰρ τῶν ὁπλιτευόντων ἐστίν. The extreme form of democracy, in which αὐτὸς συνιὼν ὁ δῆμος χρηματίζει περὶ πάντων, usually occurs ὅταν εὐπορία τις ᾖ μισθοῦ τοῖς ἐκκλησιάζουσιν· σχολάζοντες γὰρ συλλέγονταί τε πολλάκις καὶ ἅπαντα αὐτοὶ κρίνουσιν. See Arist., *Pol.*, 6 (4), 15=p. 174, 16 ff. Cf. Arist., *Pol.*, 7 (6), 2=p. 180, 7 ff. On the Aristotelian μεσότης and the judgments Aristotle pronounced, in accordance with that principle, on men and institutions, see Bruno Keil 204 ff. This was also Theramenes' constitutional ideal (Xen. 2, 3, 48) for whom Arist. accordingly shows a special sympathy; cf. 28, 5, where he mentions Nikias, Thucydides, and Theramenes as ἄνδρας οὐ μόνον καλοὺς κἀγαθοὺς ἀλλὰ καὶ πολιτικοὺς καὶ τῇ πόλει πάσῃ πατρικῶς χρωμένους. See also 32, 2; 33, 2; 34, 3; 36. According to Isocr. 7, 16/7 Solon and Cleisthenes were the founders of the πάτριος πολιτεία.

visions which were likely to give rise to controversy. Hence Dümmler's idea, that Critias may be taken to be one of the critics referred to, appears highly probable.[1]

According to the oligarchs, therefore, even the Solonian constitution was a corruption of the πάτριος πολιτεία; Solon brought about the σεισάχθεια in order to enrich himself; the prohibition of δανείζειν ἐπὶ τοῖς σώμασι removed one of the most important supports of the rule of the aristocracy over the *Demos*; the right of appeal to the Ecclesia against irregularities on the part of officials weakened the magistrates' power; and the institution of popular law-courts made the *Demos* master of the administration.[2] On the other hand, to the eyes of the oligarchical party, the character of the rule of the Peisistratidai was not so black as the democrats painted it. Isagoras, Cleisthenes' opponent and the head of the oligarchs, was a friend of the Tyrants; and ostracism was introduced by Cleisthenes as a weapon against those members of powerful aristocratic families who were friends of the Tyrants.[3] Traces of the sympathy of the oligarchs for the Tyrants are to be seen in the traditional history. The traditional accounts agree in saying that Peisistratos administered the State in a moderate spirit. Compared with the government of his sons, his reign seemed like the golden age of Cronos.[4] But the oligarchic version went farther than this. Whilst the popular tradition affirmed that Aristogeiton and Harmodios re-established the Athenian

---

[1] Cf. Dümmler's arguments in *Herm.*, 1892, p. 260 ff., where he has collected everything which seems to show any trace of Critias' work. Critias' judgment of Themistocles and Cleon in Ælian, *Var. Hist.*, 10, 17. On the reproach against Solon of improperly enriching himself, see Arist. 6; Plut., *Sol.*, 15; on the intentional obscurity of his laws, Arist. 9, 2, compared with 35, 2. [On Critias, cf. Wilamowitz, *Ar. u. Athen.*, i 174.]

[2] On Solon's enriching himself by the σεισάχθεια see 6, 2; Plut., *Sol.*, 15. For the three δημοτικώτατα of Solon's mentioned in the text, cf. Arist. 9 and p. 138.

[3] On the opinion held by the Demos as to the Tyrants, see Thuc. 6, 53: on Isagoras, Arist. 20, 1; on the object of ostracism, 22, 3-6.

[4] The opinion about Peisistratos, Hdt. 1, 59; Thuc. 6, 54; Arist. 16, 2. 16, 7 says of him: διὸ καὶ πολλάκις ἐθ[ρυ]λλ[εῖ]το, ὡς ἡ Πεισιστράτου τυραννὶς ὁ ἐπὶ Κρόν[ου] βίος εἴη· συνέβη γὰρ ὕστερον δια[δεξαμένων] τῶν υἱέων πολλῷ γενέσθαι τραχυτέραν τὴν ἀρχήν. The contrast is here so pointed that Niese p. 48, 1 must be mistaken in assuming that Arist. borrowed this expression from Plat., *Hipparch.*, 229. For there the entire time of the Peisistratids, with the exception of the years after Hipparchos' murder, is compared to the age of Cronos. The words by which the saying is introduced in Plat., *Hipparch.*, καὶ πάντων ἂν τῶν παλαιῶν ἤκουσας refer, I believe, to a written tradition.

democracy by killing Hipparchos, in the oligarchic account the latter figured as an innocent victim, and his death was therefore held to justify Hippias' subsequent despotism. According to the version adopted by Aristotle, it was not Hipparchos, the patron of poetry and of poets, who insulted Harmodios, but his younger brother, the violent Thessalos, who was not one of the ruling members of the family at all. Another form of the tale was to the effect that Aristogeiton and Harmodios murdered Hipparchos,[1] because a handsome and noble youth, of whom Harmodios had been enamoured, had deserted him for Hipparchos.

But the democratic tradition also found expression in a literary form. Whether this appeared in reply to the work of Critias above mentioned, seems very questionable; and not less questionable is the attempt to father this literary embodiment of the democratic tradition on some particular author, as Dümmler endeavours to do. We know however that Euphranor, after the battle of Mantinea, painted the walls of the Stoa of Zeus Eleutherios in the agora at Athens, and on the one wall represented Theseus, Democracy, and the Athenian *Demos*,—while the subscription declared Theseus to be the founder of the Athenian democracy. Hence, by that date, this must have been the belief officially accepted at Athens, and this undoubtedly implies that it already had a literary foundation.[2] To all appearances, however, this belief, that Theseus was the founder of the Athenian de-

---

[1] For the popular tradition cf. the *scolion* in honour of Aristogeiton and Harmodios in Athen. 15, 695A. Thessalos insulted Harmodios according to 18, 2: cf. Hude in *Jahrb. f. cl. Phil.*, 1892, p. 171 ff. The other version appears in Plat., *Hipparch.*, 229, which, in contrast to what οἱ πολλοί believed, was accepted ὑπὸ τῶν χαριεστέρων ἀνθρώπων. Οἱ χαρίεντες, a euphemistic expression for the oligarchs, Arist., *Pol.*, 2, 7 = p. 39, 25 Bekker; Plut., *Phok.*, 29, *Dion* 28. οἱ χαριέστατοι, Diod. 11, 86, 87. Hipparchos the friend of poetry and poets, 18, 1, and Plat., *Hipparch.*, 228. According to Niese 48, Arist. borrowed this statement from Plat., *Hipparch.* But there Hipparchos is again τῶν Πεισιστράτου παίδων πρεσβύτατος.

[2] See Dümmler 276 ff. On the pictures of Euphranor in the Stoa of Zeus Eleutherios, see Paus., 1, 3, 3–4. Since Euphranor also depicted an episode in the battle of Mantinea, the painting must have been executed after that battle, though probably not very long after. Paus. 1, 3, 3 says: ἐπὶ δὲ τῷ τοίχῳ τῷ πέραν Θησεύς ἐστι γεγραμμένος καὶ Δημοκρατία τε καὶ Δῆμος · δηλοῖ δὲ ἡ γραφὴ Θησέα εἶναι τὸν καταστήσαντα Ἀθηναίοις ἐξ ἴσου πολιτεύεσθαι. κεχώρηκε δὲ φήμη καὶ ἄλλως ἐς τοὺς πολλούς, ὡς Θησεὺς παραδοίη τὰ πράγματα τῷ δήμῳ καὶ ὡς ἐξ ἐκείνου δημοκρατούμενοι, πρὶν ἢ Πεισίστρατος ἐτυράννησεν ἐπαναστάς. In 41, 2 ἡ ἐπὶ Θησέως γενομένη τάξις is, in opposition to this belief, characterized as μικρὸν παρεγκλίνουσα τῆς βασιλικῆς.

mocracy, first began to find general acceptance at Athens in the fourth century; the original opinion was evidently that which connected the institution of the democracy with the names of Solon and Cleisthenes.[1] The δημοτικοί quoted by Aristotle must also have maintained these views.[2]

It is the merit of Aristotle to have pointed out that the Athenian constitution had a history of its own, and had developed by progressive modifications from a monarchy into the advanced democracy of his own day. No one would maintain that he described this development with any special enthusiasm for the statesmen who had effected it, but he described it *sine ira et studio*. Nothing could be more unjust than Nissen's harsh verdict upon the Aristotle of the Ἀθηναίων πολιτεία. "In this work," he writes, "it is not an earnest inquirer in pursuit of truth who speaks, but a courtier exulting over fallen greatness with frivolous jests, calling the statesmen of Athens scamps and her generals bunglers." Aristotle saw with his own eyes how impotent and degenerate the democracy had become in his day, and his con-

---

[1] Isocrates in the *Helena* (10, 32 sqq.) still describes the political labours of Theseus in somewhat general terms and arrives § 36 at the cautious conclusion: τοσούτου δ' ἐδέησεν ἀκόντων τι ποιεῖν τῶν πολιτῶν, ὥσθ' ὁ μὲν τὸν δῆμον καθίστη κύριον τῆς πολιτείας, οἱ δὲ μόνον αὐτὸν ἄρχειν ἠξίουν ἡγούμενοι πιστοτέραν καὶ κοινοτέραν εἶναι τὴν ἐκείνου μοναρχίαν τῆς αὑτῶν δημοκρατίας. Even in the Panathenaic speech (12, 129) Isocr. uses a limiting ὡς λέγεται: καὶ ταῦτ' ἔπραξεν, οὐκ ἐπειδὴ πρεσβύτερος γενόμενος ἀπολελαυκὼς ἦν τῶν ἀγαθῶν τῶν παρόντων, ἀλλ' ἀκμάζων τὴν μὲν πόλιν, ὡς λέγεται, διοικεῖν τῷ πλήθει παρέδωκεν, αὐτὸς δ' ὑπὲρ ταύτης τε καὶ τῶν ἄλλων Ἑλλήνων διετέλει κινδυνεύων. In 12, 149 he appeals to tradition both oral and written on the point; may we suppose this to mean Androtion's *Atthis*? See Bruno Keil 91. (Dem.) 59, 75 says: ἐπειδὴ δὲ Θησεὺς συνῴκισεν αὐτοὺς καὶ δημοκρατίαν ἐποίησε. Theophr., *Char.*, 26, mentions as one of the characteristics of the oligarch: [καὶ] τὸν Θησέα πρῶτον φῆσαι τῶν κακῶν τῇ πόλει γεγονέναι αἴτιον· τοῦτον γὰρ ἐκ δώδεκα πόλεων εἰς μίαν καταγαγόντα [τὰ πλήθη ἀφεῖναι τὴν κατα]λυθεῖσαν βασιλείαν· καὶ δίκαια αὐτὸν παθεῖν· πρῶτον γὰρ αὐτὸν ἀπολέσθαι ὑπ' αὐτῶν. Solon introduced the democracy, and Cleisthenes restored it after the banishment of the Tyrants: Isocr. 7, 16. Greater emphasis on Cleisthenes than on Solon: 15, 232. Cleisthenes alone named: 15, 306. Similarly in the early speech περὶ τοῦ ζεύγους, 16, 26/7. According to Bruno Keil 78 ff., Arist. 8, 2 is a polemic against Isocr.

[2] They defended Solon against the reproach of having improperly enriched himself by the σεισάχθεια, Arist. 6, and they evidently thought it very much to Aristogeiton's credit that he represented the friends of the Tyrants as his accomplices and so injured the Tyrants even in his death, 18, 5: cf. Polyain. 1, 22. Bruno Keil 49 ff. supposes that Arist. found the statements of the δημοτικοί and of the oligarchs recorded already in the Atthis which he used.

stitutional history gives us a picture of the process by which this had come about, and of the politicians who were responsible for it. No doubt he fails to do adequate justice to the historical importance of the great Athenian statesmen of the fifth century; but in judging Aristotle we must consider the point of view from which he regards these men, and what influence they had upon the development of the Athenian constitution. Aristotle's ideal constitution, as has been already pointed out, was a State where the government was vested in those citizens who could equip and maintain themselves as hoplites in time of war at their own expense, and where the magistrates received no remuneration. This ideal corresponded with Draco's constitution, and with the constitutional scheme drawn up in the year 411, and this is the reason why the principles of that scheme are described by Aristotle' from his authorities in such detail. But even Solon's constitution meets with no disapproval from Aristotle, who gives hearty recognition to the work of the great political reformer. On the other hand Cleisthenes' constitution appeared to Aristotle far more democratic than that of Solon, and the progressive development towards complete democracy was in his opinion beneficially interrupted by the supremacy of the Areopagus during the seventeen years from 480–462. During that time Athens, he says,[1] was well governed, and in the conflicts of those years the Athenians gained experience in war, won great glory among the Hellenes, and secured in spite of the Lacedæmonians the empire of the sea. The leading men at that time were Themistocles and Aristeides—the latter of greater importance in constitutional history than the former. For it was Aristeides who organized the Athenian confederacy, and, when Athens had gained greater self-confidence from her victories, and the tribute of the allies had begun to swell her revenues, Aristeides was the statesman on whose advice the confederacy was changed into an empire. The change at once affected the course of internal development to a remarkable degree. To maintain the Athenian dominion over the allies was impossible, unless large numbers of men were drafted into the immediate service of the State: and this again could only be done, if the State paid them for their services. For this reason Aristeides introduced the system of payment for services rendered by citizens to the State, and this was the means of enticing the

[1] Arist. 23, 1 and 2.

poorer populace from the country into the city.[1] The supremacy of the Areopagus lasted for 17 years, though the foundations of the constitution were shaken by the attacks of the Demos, already becoming conscious of its strength, and beginning to demand an extension of its privileges. In 462/1 B.C. on the motion of Ephialtes, who was then προστάτης τοῦ δήμου, the Areopagus was stripped of the powers that it had usurped up to that time. Then followed a period, during which the aggression of ardent demagogues more and more disorganized the constitution, and the State was no longer administered in accordance with the laws. But, when Pericles came forward as the leader of the people, the constitution became more democratic still. The Areopagus was deprived of yet further functions. Pericles made the fleet the decisive factor in foreign politics, and thereby raised the self-esteem of the ὄχλος ναυτικός, who usurped the whole government of the State, that is, governed the city by resolutions of the Ecclesia. And the people began to have an even greater voice in the administration, when the whole Athenian population in consequence of the Peloponnesian war was confined within the walls of

---

[1] On Aristotle's ideal constitution see p. xl Nissen's judgment, 196. For Aristotle's opinion of Solon cf. Bruno Keil 203 ff., 225. The πολιτεία of Cleisthenes even was δημοτικωτέρα πολὺ τῆς Σόλωνος: Arist. 22, 1; see also 29, 3. Hence immediately afterwards we find the δῆμος, led by Xanthippos, opposed to the γνώριμοι, whose leader was Miltiades, 28, 2. In 485/4 B.C. Xanthippos was ostracized, 22, 6. In 483/2 B.C. Aristeides, probably as Themistocles' rival, 22, 7. In 481/0 all ostracized were recalled, 22, 8. Then followed the ascendency of the Areopagus, 23. Aristeides and Themistocles do not appear at this time as leaders of opposing parties, but both as προστάται τοῦ δήμου, 23, 3 and 28, 2. Both had an equal share in rebuilding the Athenian walls, 23, 4. The walls extended, Thuc. 1, 93. In this way room was made for the country population, which subsequently flocked to town. The historical results of this period, in which the Areopagus was supreme, are given by Arist. and Isocr. in almost the same words, perhaps from an *Atthis* used by both.

Arist. 23, 2:

συνέβη γὰρ αὐτοῖς περὶ τὸν χρόνον τοῦτον τά τε εἰς τὸν πόλεμον ἀσκῆσαι καὶ παρὰ τοῖς Ἕλλησιν εὐδοκιμῆσαι καὶ τὴν τῆς θαλάττης ἡγεμονίαν λαβεῖν, παρὰ ἀκόντων τῶν Λακεδαιμονίων.

Isocr. 7, 17:

οἱ μὲν γὰρ ἐκείνῃ χρώμενοι, πολλὰ καὶ καλὰ διαπραξάμενοι καὶ παρὰ πᾶσιν ἀνθρώποις εὐδοκιμήσαντες, παρ' ἑκόντων τῶν Ἑλλήνων τὴν ἡγεμονίαν ἔλαβον.

Aristeides organized the Confederacy, Arist. 23, 4–5. He advised the transformation of the Confederacy into an ἀρχή, and the introduction of pay. In consequence of this the poorer people migrated from the country to Athens, 24, 1–2.

Athens, freed from all anxiety for their daily bread by the receipt of military pay, and at liberty to devote themselves entirely to politics. After the death of Pericles the democracy degenerated still further, for the leadership of the people now fell into the hands of demagogues, who belonged themselves to the lower orders and so were held in contempt by the better classes. Such demagogues were Cleon, who contributed more than any other man to the demoralizing of the masses, and Cleophon, who introduced the Diobelia—both during the Peloponnesian war. Then followed a succession of demagogues, whose only ambition was to bring themselves into prominence by flattering the people as circumstances required. The rule of the Four Hundred and of the Thirty succeeded only for a short time in checking the progress of democracy. After the return of the democrats under Thrasybulos, the democracy was re-established, and subsequently developed itself more and more fully until the days of Aristotle. The *demos* in course of time made itself master of everything, decided everything by its *psephismata* and by the verdicts of its Dicasteries, and received, in return for its trouble, the Ecclesiasts' and Heliasts' fees.[1]

Such is the account which Aristotle gives of the development of the Athenian constitution up to its restoration after the return of Thrasybulos and the democrats in B.C. 403. It is an account manifesting neither love for those who influenced and determined this evolution, nor hatred against them. In chapter 28 Aristotle again enumerates these men and compares their merits, and comes to the conclusion that, leaving out of account the earlier statesmen, Nikias, Thoukydides, and Theramenes were the best of the political leaders of Athens, evidently because their political convictions were similar to his own.[1] Nor does Aristotle take up an attitude of hostility to the Athenian *Demos*. He praises its good qualities, its natural clemency, its hatred of those who had prompted the people to unworthy acts, and frankly acknowledges the historical justification of the democracy of his own day, in the fact that the Athenian *Demos* had successfully struggled unaided against the 30 tyrants, and had effected its own restoration to Athens.[2]

---

[1] On the development after Aristeides see 25–41; Bruno Keil 206 ff. For the reason that Arist. breaks off his historical sketch about 400 B.C. see Bruno Keil 231 ff.

[2] For Aristotle's favourable estimate of Theramenes (cf. also 32, 2; 34, 3) cf. p. xl³. In his judgment of Nikias, Aristotle was probably determined

xlviii   *Introduction.*

The fatal democratizing influence which, in Aristotle's opinion, was exercised by the introduction of the system of State-payments, and by its subsequent extension to an ever-increasing number of recipients, has induced Aristotle to devote special attention to this subject in his history of the development of the Athenian constitution. In his account of Aristeides' first introduction of pay —founded doubtless on some good contemporary evidence—he gives a list of those persons who received pay at Athens in the prime of the First Athenian Confederacy;[1] and he describes in

by Thuc. 7, 86. The same opinion of Theramenes was held by Theopompos, whom I agree with Fricke, *Untersuch. üb. d. Quellen d. Plut. im Nik. u. Alkib.*, p. 10 ff., in considering to be the source of Diod. 14, 3–5. The opposition of Athenian statesmen to one another, such as we find in Arist. 28, was also a peculiarity in Theopompos, who employed the verb ἀντιπολιτεύεσθαι of the opponents in these political duels; the word is not found however in this sense in Arist. See Theop., *fr.* 98, in Müller, *fr. h. gr.*, i 294. What Arist. 28, 3, says of Cleon occurs again almost word for word in Theop., *fr.* 99.

Arist.:   Theop.:

ὃς δοκεῖ μάλιστα διαφθεῖραι τὸν δῆμον   ὃς πρῶτος δημηγορῶν ἀνέκραγεν ἐπὶ
ταῖς ὁρμαῖς καὶ πρῶτος ἐπὶ τοῦ βήματος   βήματος καὶ ἐλοιδορήσατο κ. τ. ἀ.
ἀνέκραγε καὶ ἐλοιδορήσατο καὶ περιζω-
σάμενος ἐδημηγόρησε, τῶν ἄλλων ἐν
κόσμῳ λεγόντων.

So too the account of Kimon's liberality in Theop., *fr.* 94, (cf. also Plut., *Kim.*, 10; *Per.*, 9; Corn. Nep., 4) reads like an amplification and exaggeration of Arist. 27, 3 [*vid.* Sandys, *ad loc.*].

[2] Cf. 22, 4; 28, 3; 41, 1.

[1] See 24, 3. In the beginning, of course, there were not 20,000 recipients. The Dicast's fee, *e g.*, was introduced by Pericles, 27, 3. Köhler, in *Sitzungsber. d. Berl. Ak.*, 1892, 342/3, finds fault with the computation of the amount of these fees in Arist. 24, 3 as an instance of the "method" of the author of the πολιτεία. I would remark upon this: ἀπὸ τῶν φόρων καὶ τῶν τελῶν indicates the two chief sources of public revenue, while ἀπὸ τῶν συμμάχων refers to the fact that the allies had themselves to pay the Athenian garrisons and the ἀρχαὶ ὑπερόριοι. That this is correct for the ἐπίσκοποι is shewn by Arist., *Birds*, 1021 sq., and for the φρουραὶ by Zenob. 6, 32. With regard to the 700 ἀρχαὶ ἔνδημοι I would note that according to Arist. 6 (4), 15, p. 172, 22 sq., there are ἀρχαὶ πολιτικαὶ (including the military officials), οἰκονομικαὶ and ὑπηρετικαί. Hence among the 700 ἀρχαὶ ἔνδημοι we must place the civil and military officials and subalterns. Now, the knights, numbering 1,000 men, had 112 officers and subalterns, 2 Hipparchs, 10 Phylarchs, 100 Decadarchs. To these must be added the military officers and subalterns of the 2,500 Hoplites in regular service, of the 1,600 Toxotai of the 200 Hippotoxotai, of the 500 φρουροὶ νεωρίων: when to these we add all the civil magistrates with their ὑπηρέται, I think that there will be but few short of the 700 ἀρχαὶ ἔνδημοι. Of the ἀρχαὶ ὑπερόριοι we have less in-

several passages in his constitutional history the consequences which followed the introduction of the various kinds of fees. The introduction by Pericles of Dicasts' fees made the poorer people more eager than the rich to apply for allotment as jurors, and in consequence bribery of the juries became easier on account of the poverty of the mojority of the Dicasts. When the population of Attica during the Peloponnesian war crowded into Athens, and the *Demos* was freed from all anxiety for its living by the receipt of military pay, it usurped the control of the State. But at the close of the war, when that pay ceased, the attendance at the *Ecclesia* became so meagre that the Ecclesiast's fee, which at first there was no intention of paying, became necessary. The consequence was that from that time the *Demos* alone decided everything, both in the *Ecclesia* and in the law-courts, and even matters up to that time decided by the *Boule* were now brought under popular control.[1]

Aristotle's political conviction that the best πολιτεία consists ἐκ τῶν ὁπλιτευόντων explains why he traces the cause of the growth of the democracy, after the Areopagus was shorn of its power, to the fact that in the wars of that period thousands of citizens—the flower of the well-to-do classes, and indeed of the whole nation (for the *Thetes* did not serve as hoplites)—fell in the various campaigns, in consequence of the incapacity of *Strategoi*, elected simply because of their family connexions.[2]

---

formation. We have no knowledge how many ἐπίσκοποι were sent to the allied States. The 2,000 regular φρουροί in the confederate cities would have more than 200 officers, if they were organized in the same way as the corps of knights. Then in the navy, the sailors proper, called ὑπηρεσία, must be counted as subalterns. For the πεντηκόνταρχοι the title itself is sufficient evidence. Thus for the 20 νῆες φρουρίδες and 20 transport ships, there would be over 200 ὑπηρέται (see page 327). Hence the authority followed by Aristotle (who in this place gives us much valuable information, apart from the question of pay) was perhaps not quite so worthless as Köhler thinks. At most the error in Aristotle's calculation is that the military officers and subalterns are perhaps already counted among the troops.

[1] The introduction of the Dicasts' fee is attributed by Arist. 27, 3–4 to Pericles, who proposed it from personal motives. The authorities for the consequences of this step are cited as τινες, but Arist. evidently agrees with them. He apparently regards (27, 5) τὸ δεκάζειν also as a consequence of the δικαστήρια having become χείρω through the introduction of pay. For the further consequences of State-pay cf. 27, 2; 41, 2–3.

[2] The cause of the development of democracy after 462 B.C., 26, 1. In the words ἀλλ' αὐτῶν προεστάναι Κίμωνα τὸν Μιλτιάδου, νεώτερον ὄντα καὶ πρὸς

Introduction.

This is not the place to discuss the chronological details of the book, and their bearing on the general history of Athens. But, in forming an opinion about them, we must not forget that in all probability they are taken from an earlier *Atthis*, and therefore represent the oldest systematized chronological tradition which we possess.[1]

τὴν πόλιν ὀψὲ προσελθόντα, νεώτερος means " too inexperienced," *sc.* in προεστάναι (cf. Plat., *Phileb.*, 13, καὶ φανούμεθά γε νεώτεροι τοῦ δέοντος), and καὶ is the "explanatory καί"="for he had not devoted himself to home politics till late in life" (cf. Arist., *Plut.*, 29, κακῶς ἔπραττον καὶ πένης ἦν=I did not fare well, that is, I was poor). The passage αἰεὶ συνέβαινεν τῶν ἐξιόντων ἀνὰ δισχιλίους ἢ τρισχιλίους ἀπόλλυσθαι is probably a great exaggeration of Aristotle's or of his authority. If we accept the Aristotelian chronology, we may instance as Athenian disasters the defeats at Drabescos (Bauer 114 ff.) and at Tanagra (Bauer 121), the destruction of the Athenian army in Egypt (Bauer 119 ff.), and the defeat at Coroneia (Bauer 127). Niese, p. 68, remarks: "This is the way in which Arist. speaks of such generals as Kimon, Myronides, Pericles, Nikias, under whose command the Athenian citizen-army was superior to all other Greeks except the Spartans, whilst her navy gained the undisputed empire of the sea." According to our authorities the commanders at Drabescos were Sophanes and Leagros (Hdt. 9, 75; Paus. 1, 29, 4); the general at Tanagra is not expressly named, but from Plut., *Per.*, 10, Pericles seems to have been present; in Egypt Charitimides was in command (Ctes. 29, 32/3, p. 52 Didot); for the defeat at Coroneia Tolmides is made responsible by Pericles in Plut., *Per.*, 18. Arist. expresses the same opinion in the *Politics* too, 8 (5), 3, p. 197, 29 ff., where he shews that μεταβολαὶ τῶν πολιτειῶν occur when part of the population is increased παρὰ τὸ ἀνάλογον, οἷον τὸ τῶν ἀπόρων πλῆθος ἐν ταῖς δημοκρατίαις καὶ πολιτείαις. συμβαίνει δ' ἐνίοτε τοῦτο καὶ διὰ τύχας, οἷον—καὶ ἐν Ἀθήναις ἀτυχούντων πεζῇ οἱ γνώριμοι ἐλάττους ἐγένοντο διὰ τὸ ἐκ καταλόγου στρατεύεσθαι ὑπὸ τὸν Λακωνικὸν πόλεμον.

[1] For the chronological results obtainable from Aristotle, I would refer to Bauer, without however expressing unqualified approval of his views.

THE SPARTAN CONSTITUTION.

THE SPARTAN CONSTITUTION.

I.

HISTORICAL.

The Historical Development of the Constitution of the Lacedæmonians, with a Sketch of the Constitution under Roman Government.

THE district of the Peloponnesus called Λακωνική, together with Kynuria and the islands near the coast, covers an area of 2130 square miles. It is divided into three geographical sections. Λακωνική.

The eastern and western of these divisions are the districts of Parnon and Taygetos, each shaped like a peninsula. The latter is quite mountainous, and completely filled by the spurs which project from the main mountain chain. The former, in which the lower heights of Parnon extend more in the shape of isolated groups, contains some patches of level but barren plain.

The third division is the valley of the Eurotas, shut in between Parnon in the E. and Taygetos in the W. It contains an area of about 425 square miles. This valley, formed by the course of the main river of the country, contains two large plains. The more northerly of these commences near the confluence of the Oinos and the Eurotas, and is bounded on the S. by a ridge connecting Parnon and Taygetos, and attaining an elevation of about 1,500 feet. This is the plain of Sparta, and is 13 miles long by 5 miles broad.

Southwards from the above-mentioned ridge there extends as far as the mouth of the Eurotas, in the Laconian Gulf, the second extensive plain of the country, superior to the first in the fertility of its arable land and in the luxuriance of its meadows. Its south-eastern parts, however, were filled with marshes even in ancient times, as is shown by the name of the town there situated (Helos), though perhaps not to the same extent as now.¹

From this short description it may be seen that the plain of Sparta is the real centre of the country. Here an armed band of Dorian immigrants established themselves. In all probability they penetrated into the plain from the N., following in their march the course of the Eurotas. Then starting from the Spartan plain as their basis, they subdued the several towns of Laconia in wars which lasted for a century. For the internal history of these Dorians of Sparta before they began to extend their sway over the rest of the country, we have no satisfactory direct evidence.

Dorian Immigration.

We are therefore compelled to supplement our scanty records by inferences from the political institutions of historical times and by topographical considerations. The uncertainty of such conjectures obviously precludes any accurate knowledge of the most ancient form of the Spartan constitution.²

The existence of the dual kingship at Sparta in historical times is not explained satisfactorily by the legends of its origin in the birth of twin claimants to the throne. Several different theories have accordingly been propounded by various authorities to explain this peculiar institution. Among these the most plausible is that which regards the double kingdom as having arisen from an alliance between two royal houses, which represented two distinct communities.³

The Two Kings.

---

[1] For the geography of Laconia cf. Bursian, *Geogr. v. Griechenl.*, 2, 112 sqq. Kiepert, *Lehrb. d. alten. Geogr.*, § 237 sqq. Laconia, Kynuria and the adjacent islands contain altogether 5516·2 square kilometres; 55·16 sq. kilometres = 21·3 square miles. Cf. Beloch, *Bevölker. d. griech. röm. Welt*, p. 114.

[2] All our information about the condition of Laconia in the earliest times is obtained from late authors. In my opinion such statements are quite unworthy of credence, and cannot be used as materials for an account of the internal history of the Spartan constitution. They are collected and employed for this purpose by K. Fr. Hermann, *de statu Lacedæmoniorum ante Lycurgum* in the *Antiquitates Lacon.*, § 3 sqq.

[3] For the legend of the Spartan kings see Hdt. 6, 51 sqq. Different explanations of the dual kingship are given by Lachmann, *spart. Staatsverf.*, 134 sqq. Duncker, *Gesch. d. Alterth.*, 5⁵, 252 sqq. Curtius, *Greek Hist.* 1⁴, 166–7. [Ward's Eng. tr., vol. i. p. 186.] The explanation adopted in the text is essentially the same as the theory advocated and discussed in detail by C. Wachsmuth, in the *Jahrb. f. cl. Phil.*, 1868, p. 1 sqq. Cf. also the author's *Stud. z. altspart. Gesch.*, 57 sqq.

This theory is based chiefly on the topography of the town of Sparta.[1]

For we are able to point out within the area of the historical town, and close to the Acropolis, a quarter which bore the name 'Ἀγιάδαι, and included within its bounds the burial place of the Agiadai. It is therefore assumed with great probability that we must recognise in this district the ancestral home of the Agiads and of the community over which they ruled.

From this it is easy to conclude, further, that the original home of the Eurypontids and their subjects is to be found on the summit of New Sparta, where their dwelling place and their tombs may be pointed out.[2]

Whether these communities, ruled by the Agiadai and Eurypontidai respectively, were both of Dorian origin, or whether, as some have supposed, the Agiadai and their subjects were of Achæan stock, is better left undecided.[3]

To the two separate communities above mentioned I believe we must add yet a third, which united with the other two to form the town of Sparta.[4] The main argument for the existence of a third separate community previous to the συνοικισμὸς of Sparta is the testimony of Herodotus, that the Aigeidai still formed in his day a large Phyle in Sparta. Traditions more or less untrustworthy describe the Aigeidai as a Cadmean race, who either migrated from Thebes into the Peloponnesus along with the Dorians, or else were invited to Sparta

Aigeidai.

---

[1] No importance can be assigned to the traditions cited by Wachsmuth as proofs, from Polyain., 1, 10, and the chronographers.

[2] Hesych.: 'Ἀγιάδαι· τόπος ἐν Λακεδαίμονι καὶ οἱ βασιλεῖς δὲ οὕτω καλοῦνται ἀπὸ Ἀγιδος. The certain conjecture of Heringa, Paus. 3, 14, 2, ἐν 'Ἀγιαδῶν, enables us to locate this district, in accordance with the context in Pausanias, in the neighbourhood of the Acropolis hill. In this district were also the tombs of the Agiadai: Paus. 3, 14, 2. The cemetery of the Eurypontidai was on the highest part of New Sparta, Paus. 3, 12, 8. A comparison of Paus. 3, 16, 6 with Hdt. 6, 69 enables us to fix the dwelling place of the Eurypontidai in the same locality.

[3] Wachsmuth, loc. cit., has inferred from the saying of Kleomenes in Hdt. 5, 72: ἀλλ' οὐ Δωριεύς εἰμι, ἀλλ' Ἀχαιός, that the Agiadai were Achæans, since the mythical relationship of the Heraclidæ to the earlier Achæan rulers of Mykenæ was invented at a later period, in order to give an appearance of legitimacy to the Dorian conquest of Peloponnesus. It is, however, equally probable that this fiction was already recognised in the time of Herodotus, and that Kleomenes made himself out to be an Achæan on the strength of it.

[4] Cf. the author's *Stud. z. altspart. Gesch.*, 64 sq.

from Thebes at a later date by the Dorians, to help them in war against Amyklai.[1] According to tradition this clan obtained a very prominent position in Sparta. In the officially recognised legend of the Spartan kings we find Theras, the Spartan eponymous ancestor of the clan, mentioned as holding the position of a king in his capacity of guardian to his sister's child, the son of Aristodemos. From what has been said above as to the reasons assigned for the dual kingship in the official legend, it follows that this account of Theras can make no pretension to strict historical accuracy. Moreover it is obvious that the position assigned to Theras as guardian and prince regent, cannot be explained as an anachronistic anticipation of historical times, for in historical times a king who had not attained his majority was always represented in the Government by his nearest male relative (of proper age). We must therefore in all probability recognise in this regency of Theras the faint tradition of a once independent kingdom of the Aigeidai, which was adopted in the official legend at a time when this independent kingdom no longer existed, in order to give expression to the remembrance of the ancient power and dignity of the clan. That a dynasty of Aigid kings did once exist in Sparta, is proved to us by an inscription from Thera from the tomb of a priest of Apollo Karneios, a priesthood hereditary in the family of the Aigeidai, as we may with certainty infer. In that epitaph the dead priest claims to be descended from Spartan kings.[2]

---

[1] Hdt. 4, 149: Οἰολύκου δὲ γίνεται Αἰγεύς, ἀπ᾽ οὗ Αἰγεῖδαι καλεῦνται, φυλὴ μεγάλη ἐν Σπάρτῃ. According to Ephorus, *ap. Schol. Pind. Pyth.* 5, 101= Müller, *Fr. Hist. Gr.*, 1, 285, 11; 286, 13, the Aigeidai came into Peloponnesus from Thebes along with the Heraclidae; according to Aristot., *ap. Schol. Pind. Isthm.*, 6 (7), 18=Müller, *Fr. Hist. Gr.*, 2, 127, 75, they were summoned by the Heraclidae to assist them in war against Amyklai. What view Pindar himself took on the subject, *Isthm.*, 6, (7), 12 sqq., is quite uncertain. He says of the heroine Thebe: ἡ Δωρίδ᾽ ἀποικίαν οὕνεκεν ὀρθῷ—ἔστασας ἐπὶ σφυρῷ—Λακεδαιμονίων, ἕλον δ᾽ Ἀμύκλας—Αἰγεῖδαι σέθεν ἔκγονοι, μαντεύμασι Πυθίοις. I still believe I have proved that Pindar was not an Aigid in my *Stud. z. altspart. Geschicht.*, 65 sqq. I am pleased to find this view supported by Studniczka, whose *Cyrene*, Introd., p. 78 sqq., has brought the various points in question to a practically definite decision. For the arguments against the Cadmean origin of the Aigeidai cf. Studniczka, *ibid.*, 45 sqq., especially 85 sqq.

[2] For the position of Theras in Sparta cf. Hdt. 4, 147. In a tomb inscription from Thera, Admetus, son of Theokleidas and ἱερεὺς Ἀπόλλωνος Καρνηίου διὰ γένους, says of himself: οὐ μόνον (η)ὐχούμην Λακεδαιμο(νο)ς ἐκ βασιλήων, (ξ)υνὰ

Lastly, we find in our records still further traces of the importance and prominence of the Aigeidai at Sparta. The Aigid Timomachos assisted the Spartans in war against Amyklai and received high honour from them in return: the Aigid Euryleon was associated with the kings Theopompos and Polydoros, in the command of the Spartan army in the first Messenian war.[1]

Such being the nature of our records, I believe we may correctly assume that in the earliest period the Aigeidai exercised royal power in Sparta over their own community, which was originally autonomous and independent.

The Spartan State arose from the coalition of the separate communities of the Agiadai, the Eurypontidai, and   συνοικισμὸς the Aigeidai, and I believe we still possess in a so-   of Sparta. called Rhetra of Lycurgus the agreement upon which this coalition was based.[2]

δὲ Θετταλίης ἐκ προγόνων γενόμην; Boeckh. *kl. Schr.*, 6, 23=Kaibel, *Epigr. Gr.*, 192. The Aigeidai are the supporters of the cult of Apollo Karneios. Cf. Pind. *Pyth.*, 5, 68 sqq. Kallimach., *Hymn. in Apoll.*, 71 sqq. See also Luebbert, *Diatriba*, Bonn, 1883, 15 sqq. Hence Boeckh, *ibid.*, p. 3 sqq., 63, rightly concludes that Admetus was an Aigid because the priesthood of Apollo Karneios belonged to the Aigeidai. Gezler in the *N. Rh. Mus.*, 28, 13, identifies the Aigeidai and the Prokleidai, and believes that Eurypon drove the Aigeidai from the throne and won supremacy for his own clan. Luebbert in his *Diatriba*, 20-1, agrees. As proof of this is cited the fact that the names Prokles (I. G. A., 451), Soos (Boeckh, *kl. Schr.*, 6, p. 59), Prokleidas and Aristodamos (C. I. G., 2188) occur in Theraic inscriptions; the two last in the will of Epikteta, who was certainly of Aigid race, the two first in simple name inscriptions, without any certain reference to the Aigeidai. All four however are quite common names which occur frequently in the most widely separated districts of Greece.

[1] Concerning Timomachos the ally of the Spartans against Amyklai, we are told in Aristot., *loc. cit.*: μεγάλων δὲ παρ' αὐτοῖς ἠξιώθη τιμῶν καὶ τοῖς Ὑακινθίοις δὲ ὁ χάλκεος αὐτῷ θώραξ προτίθεται, τοῦτον δὲ Θηβαῖοι ὅπλον ἐκάλουν. Even supposing Studniczka, *Kyrene*, 86, is correct in considering Timomachos an old name of equestrian Apollo in Amyklai, still the metamorphosis of Apollo into an Aigid could only be possible if the Aigeidai possessed very considerable importance in Sparta. For Euryleon, cf. Paus., 4, 7, 8.

[2] This so-called Rhetra of Lycurgus, as preserved in Plut. *Lyc.*, 6, runs as follows, after the necessary emendations have been made: Διὸς Σελλανίου (for συλλανίου) καὶ Ἀθηνᾶς Σελλανίας (for συλλανίας) ἱερὸν ἱδρυσάμενον, φυλὰς φυλάξαντα καὶ ὠβὰς ὠβάξαντα, τριάκοντα γερουσίαν σὺν ἀρχαγέταις καταστήσαντα, ὥρας ἐξ ὥρας ἀπελλάζειν μεταξὺ Βαβύκας τε καὶ Κνακιῶνος, οὕτως εἰσφέρειν τε καὶ ἀφίστασθαι δάμῳ δὲ κυρίαν ἦμεν καὶ κράτος. On the original form of the Rhetra cf. the author's *Stud.*, 125 sqq. According to Ed. Meyer in the *N. Rh. Mus.*, 42, 81 sqq. this Rhetra was simply a formal statement of the

According to this authority, the coalition was first brought about by the establishment of a common worship of Zeus Sellanios and Athene Sellania; the religious centre of the whole state for the purposes of this cult being fixed in all probability at the place called Hellenion. Zeus Sellanios was the patron deity of the Agiads and Eurypontids, Athene Sellania was the goddess of the Aigeidai. The common worship of these two deities in historical Sparta, so far as it affected the political life of the State, finds its explanation in the nature of the συνοικισμός.[1]

system in force in the Spartan constitution, a system which, at least in the form described by Aristotle, was about fifty years old at most. I cannot agree with him. Meyer considers this Rhetra to possess the same degree of authority as the three other shorter Rhetrai, which are handed down to us as Lycurgean (Plut., *Lyc.*, 13; *Ages.*, 26, *de Esu Carn.*, 2, 2, 6, p. 1220, Didot); and argues accordingly that the long one cannot be recognised as genuine if the smaller ones are rejected: but he overlooks the fact that these three shorter Rhetrai are characterised as αἱ καλούμεναι τρεῖς ῥῆτραι, and therefore the long one is expressly distinguished from the others as belonging to a different class. I can find equally little justification for doubting the authenticity of the verses quoted from Tyrtæus in Plut. *Lyc.*, 6, which occur again in Diod., 7, 14, with a different beginning and with four additional lines at the end. Cf. Meyer, *ibid.*, 41, 571 sqq. That these verses cannot be regarded as in the same category with the Oracles recorded by Diodorus, is proved at once by their distichal form. Meyer declares (572): "I reflected that when lines which appeared in Ephorus (who was demonstrably Diodorus' authority in this passage) as anonymous, were assigned to some definite poet by name in later writers, we could easily tell what conclusion to adopt." But in the first place we do not know in the least whether they were anonymous in Ephorus or not, for the fact that they so appear in the short excerpts of Diodorus is certainly no proof at all that they were anonymous in Ephorus also. And secondly, even if that were so, the definite statement of Aristotle, whom Meyer himself (572, 1) seems to regard as the writer on whose authority the verses are assigned in Plut., *Lyc.* to Tyrtæus, leaves us no reason for suspicion. Plutarch's ποῦ instead of ἐν τῇ Εὐνομίᾳ καλουμένῃ proves nothing; compare the vague and general citation of the Solonian lines in Arist. 'Αθ. Πολ. 12, "ἐν τῇ ποιήσει." I therefore consider Meyer's doubts of the authenticity and antiquity of the Rheta unjustified. According to v. Wilamowitz in the *homer. Untersuch.*, 280 sqq., the Rhetra is the agreement between the kings and the nobles, by virtue of which the practical sovereignty was transferred from the king to the δᾶμος, i.e. the assembly of citizens of mature years, i.e. the caste of peers. According to Busson, *Lykurgos und die grosse Rhetra*, 16 sqq., Innsbruck, 1887, the Rhetra marked the change from government by the clan system to government by the popular assembly.

[1] Cf. *Stud.*, 128 sqq., 141 sqq. Ἑλλήνιον in Sparta: Paus. 3, 12, 6. Curtius, *Pelop.*, 2, 231. That Zeus was the clan deity of the Agiads and

The entire population of the community formed by this coalition was divided into the local Phylai and Obai, which we find still existing in historical times.[1]

At the head of the State stood a governing body of thirty members, consisting of the chieftains of the several separate communities, (who were called ἀρχαγέται because they were the founders of the New State,) assisted by a council of Gerontes or elders.[2]

The treaty of agreement further specifies that the people shall be convened in a regular Apella, or public assembly, at the time of full moon between Babyka and Knakion, *i.e.* in all probability within that portion of the plain of Sparta which is bounded on the N. by the Oinos, on the S. by the Tiasa. The area thus specified included the whole of the outskirts of the scattered villages which formed the town of Sparta. The concentration of these villages into a city surrounded by a fortified wall was contrary to Spartan ideas.[3]

Eurypontids I conclude from the fact that the Spartan kings, besides their general functions as high priests (Xen., *Hell.*, 3, 3, 4), were also priests in particular of Zeus Uranios and Lakedaimon, Hdt. 6, 56. Cf. Zeus Herkeios in the house of Demaratos: Hdt. 6, 67–8. Cf also the author's *Stud.*, 48 sqq., 62 sqq. Athene is the patron deity of Cadmus: Paus. 9, 12, 2: Theras is a Καδμεῖος by descent (Hdt. 4, 147); and the ἱερὸν he founded when he departed for Therus in accordance with this fact: Paus. 3, 15, 6, cf. *Stud.*, 70 sqq. Zeus and Athene together are the recognised state deities. Zeus Agoraios and Athene Agoraia: Paus. 3, 11, 9. Zeus Amboulios and Athene Amboulia: Paus. 3, 13, 6. Zeus Xenios and Athene Xenia: Paus. 3, 11, 11. Zeus Kosmetas is the guardian god of the Spartan Acropolis, and this honour is shared with him by Athene Poliouchos: Paus. 3, 17, 2; the ὑπερβατήρια for Zeus and Athene, cf. Xen., *de Rep. Lac.*, 13, 2; Polyain. 1, 10.

[1] Cf. *Studies*, 129 sqq., 142 sqq. The second passage must be modified by the corrections mentioned above, and by some others which are given later on.

[2] Cf. *Stud.*, 130 sqq., 149 sqq. In the time of Demetrios of Skepsis (cf. *Athen.*, 4, 141 E) there existed in Sparta 27 φρατρίαι, which still resumed some significance at the festival of the Karneia, which was a μίμημα στρατιωτικῆς ἀγωγῆς. If these Phratriai were of ancient standing—and there are no sufficient reasons to the contrary—then the 27 Gerontes who remained after subtracting the 3 ἀρχαγέται may have corresponded originally with the number of the Phratriai. But in later times the Gerontes can scarcely have been elected according to Phratries.

[3] Cf. *Stud.*, 131 sqq., 155 sqq. Sparta was κατὰ κώμας οἰκισθεῖσα: Thuc. 1, 10. ὁ μεταξὺ Βαβύκας τε καὶ Κνακιῶνος τόπος is a periphrasis for Sparta: Plut., *Pelop.* 17.

The government council above mentioned was required to bring its proposals before this Apella, which had the right of accepting or rejecting them. The decision of the Apella was final.[1]

After the three separate communities had become united in one single State in the manner described above, the power of this Conquest of State began to extend itself by degrees over the adLaconia. jacent territory. One natural and therefore credible extension of Spartan territory dates, according to our records, from the reign of Kings Archelaos and Charilaos, though the traditional accounts of the events and circumstances of that period give occasion for the most serious doubts.[2]

By these two kings and their immediate successors Aigytis in the N. was subdued, and the territory of the towns Amyklai, Pharis, Geronthrai and Helos was acquired.[3]

Although the towns thus subdued were now made communities enjoying the rights of Perioicoi (with the exception of Helos, whose inhabitants, according to the traditional account, were degraded to serfdom), yet I believe the Spartans did not hesitate to transfer to Sparta and adopt as members of their own State the Dorian families who had obtained admission into those towns when the Dorians first came into Laconia, and had been settled there ever since; just as in Attica also, when the συνοικισμὸς took place, the Eupatridai of the various hitherto independent communities were transferred to Athens and admitted to citizenship there.[4]

The greater part of the territory belonging to the conquered communities was taken from them and divided as the spoils of Tenure of victory among the burgesses of the victorious State. Land. Such a proceeding was in keeping with the character of

---

[1] Cf. *Stud.*, 134 sqq., 156 sqq.
[2] I think I have proved in *Stud.*, 72 sqq., that the traditional account of the earliest period of Spartan history previous to these kings, and also the statement of Ephorus, *ap. Strab.* 364–5 about the earliest condition of Laconia are both worthless. The accounts of the earliest warlike undertakings of the Spartans, which I have rejected as valueless, are referred by Gelzer in *N. Rh. Mus.*, 32, 259 sqq., to the migratory period of the Lacedæmonian Dorians.
[3] *Stud.*, 158 sqq.
[4] So I understand Aristot., *Pol.*, 2, 9=p. 47, 9 sqq. Bekker : λέγουσι δ' ὡς ἐπὶ μὲν τῶν προτέρων βασιλέων μετεδίδοσαν τῆς πολιτείας, ὥστ' οὐ γίνεσθαι τότε ὀλιγανθρωπίαν πολεμούντων πολὺν χρόνον. Cf. also Strab. 366. Hdt. 9, 33, 35 is true of later times only.

Sparta as a conquering State; and the peculiar ideas held by the Spartans about the employment of a subjugated district are sufficient proof that such was the case, apart from the various isolated statements of our authorities.[1]

The division and allotment of the territory conquered by Sparta naturally took place under the authority of the State itself, and just as naturally the State as a general rule divided the territory acquired on each occasion into parcels of equal value as far as possible. The result of this procedure must have been the formation of a large number of landed estates equal in size to one another; and this phenomenon was the cause in my opinion which induced some historians among the ancients to believe that a general distribution of land once took place in the Spartan community, and supplied a precedent for the land distribution proposed by Agis IV.[2]

---

[1] The Spartan notions on this subject may be inferred from the so-called Apophthegma of Polydorus, ap. Plut., Apophth. Lac. Polyd., 2, p. 285 Didot: ἐξάγοντος δὲ αὐτοῦ τὸ στράτευμα ἐπὶ Μεσσήνην ἤρετό τις, εἰ τοῖς ἀδελφοῖς μάχεσθαι μέλλει, οὔκ, ἔφη, ἀλλ' ἐπὶ τὴν ἀκλήρωτον τῆς χώρας βαδίζω. Cf. also the two lines of the Oracle given to the Spartans according to Hdt. 1, 66: δώσω τοι Τεγέην ποσσίκροτον ὀρχήσασθαι—καὶ καλὸν πεδίον σχοίνῳ διαμετρήσασθαι. Accounts of the division of the Messenian territory in Paus. 4, 24, 4. Strabo, 333, says of the Arcadians in their relations with the Dorians: καθάπερ συνέβη τοῖς τε Ἀρκάσι καὶ τοῖς Ἠλείοις, τοῖς μὲν ὀρεινοῖς τελέως οὖσι καὶ οὐκ ἐμπεπτωκόσιν εἰς τὸν κλῆρον.

[2] For the so-called Lycurgean land distribution see the author's Stud., 160 sqq., and the later authorities there quoted. The first to question the traditional account was Grote (vol. 2, p. 893 ff.), whose view is adopted with some modifications by H. Peter in the N. Rh. M., 22, 68 ff. Cf. also Oncken, Aristot., Pol., 2, 351 ff. The oldest witness for the equality of all Spartiatai in regard to the amount of their landed property is Ephorus, who is specially intended in the polemic of Polybius, 6, 45. It is said of him, Xenophon, Kallisthenes and Plato: τῆς μὲν δὲ Λακεδαιμονίων πολιτείας ἴδιον εἶναί φασι πρῶτον μὲν τὰ περὶ τὰς ἐγγείους κτήσεις, ὧν οὐδενὶ μέτεστι πλεῖον, ἀλλὰ πάντας τοὺς πολίτας ἴσον ἔχειν δεῖ τῆς πολιτικῆς χώρας. Cf. Just. 3, 3. The correct explanation of the passage of Polyb. has been given by Wachsmuth in the Gött. gel. Anz., 1870, p. 1814 sqq. and I agree with Wachsmuth, in spite of the eloquent arguments of Oncken, 2, 351 sqq., on the other side. That at the same time I do not believe in any general division of land or equality of property, is plain enough from what has been said in the text. For the equality in size of the estates cultivated by the Helots cf. Plut., Lyc., 8. Three further evidences of a distribution of land are given by Plut., Lyc. 8; cf. Schoemann, Op. Ac.1,139 sqq.—all three however may be later than the reforms of Agis and Cleomenes, just as Polybius also, 6, 48, was influenced by them. The numbers given in Plut., Lyc. 8 may have been taken from the scheme of distribution proposed by Agis IV., who after the ruin of

On the other hand the description given above of the development of the system of property in land within the Spartan State readily explains the fact that other ancient authors assert with especial emphasis that no redistribution of landed property ever took place at Sparta. If the so-called Lycurgean land distribution were a historical fact, these assertions would be difficult to explain; but on the theory that the system of landownership at Sparta was developed as explained above, they are perfectly intelligible, because any fresh distribution of land must have involved the complete subversal of all previous rights of landed property.[1]

The establishment of the historical fact of a gradual and progressive distribution of the land subjugated by the Spartan State **The Nobles at Sparta.** into equal allotments, by no means necessitates the assumption that the landed possessions of all Spartiatai were of equal value. It would be contrary to all historical anology to deny the existence in Sparta of a nobility, *i.e.*, according to Greek ideas, families distinguished from the common people by ability and by inherited wealth. Moreover, the existence of such a class of nobles is proved by the fact that the distinction at Sparta between rich and poor, eminent and ordinary, is attested by Herodotus and the ancient historians.[2]

Messene proposed to establish there 4,500 Spartan κλῆροι. Cf. Plut. *Ag.*, 8. Cf. also Plat., *Laws*, 3,684 : τοῖς δὲ δὴ Δωριεῦσι καὶ τοῦθ' οὕτως ὑπῆρχε καλῶς καὶ ἀνεμεσήτως, γῆν τε ἀναμφισβητήτως διανέμεσθαι, καὶ χρέα μεγάλα καὶ παλαιὰ οὐκ ἦν. Duncker also in the *Monatsber. d. Berl. Akad.*, 1882, p. 138 sqq.=*Abhandl. aus d. greich. Gesch.*, 1 ff., adopts the theory of a land distribution gradually effected with each successive increase of territory in the form of equal allotments.

[1] Plat., *Laws*, 5,736 : τόδε δὲ μὴ λανθανέτω γιγνόμενον ἡμᾶς εὐτύχημα, ὅτι καθάπερ εἴπομεν τὴν τῶν Ἡρακλειδῶν ἀποικίαν εὐτυχεῖν, ὡς γῆς καὶ χρεῶν ἀποκοπῆς καὶ νομῆς πέρι δεινὴν καὶ ἐπικίνδυνον ἔριν ἐξέφυγεν. Isokr. 12, 259 maintains that in the Spartan State no one can show οὐδὲ πολιτείας μεταβολὴν οὐδὲ χρεῶν ἀποκοπὰς οὐδὲ γῆς ἀναδασμὸν οὐδ' ἄλλ' οὐδὲν τῶν ἀνηκέστων κακῶν.

[2] Ed. Meyer in the *N. Rh. Mus.*, 41,586, 2, contends that it is wrong to assume the existence of a nobility of birth within the ranks of the Dorian Spartiatai. The "καλοὶ κἀγαθοί," from among whom the Gerontes were elected, according to Arist. 2, 9=p. 48, 6, do not imply an aristocracy of birth, if we believe Meyer's note, but "the best," *i.e.* those who have distinguished themselves and are competent to manage public affairs. Now Aristotle defines the Greek εὐγένεια as inherited wealth and ability. Cf. 6 (4), 3=159, 28 : ἡ γὰρ εὐγένειά ἐστιν ἀρχαῖος πλοῦτος καὶ ἀρετή. In this sense we can speak of a hereditary aristocracy among the Spartiatai. οἱ καλοὶ κἀγαθοί mean in the ordinary use of the term, as Aristotle testifies, οἱ

However, since the Spartiatai were forbidden to carry on any trade or industry, differences of fortune at Sparta could only depend upon the different size of the landed estates belonging to different individual Spartiatai. Just as the kings possessed estates in the territory of the conquered towns of the Perioikoi, so we may also suppose that the class next in rank to the kings, the nobles, represented in the governing body by the Gerontes, like their analogues the Patricii at Rome, took possession of large tracts of conquered territory; while the ordinary burgesses had each to be content with a fixed and definite quantum of land assigned to him by order of the State.[1]

Difference between the Landed Estates of the Nobility and the κλῆροι of the Commons.

εὔποροι. Cf. 6 (4), 8=159, 2: ὅθεν καὶ καλοὺς κἀγαθοὺς καὶ γνωρίμους τούτους (sc. τοὺς εὐπόρους) προσαγορεύουσιν. ἐπεὶ οὖν ἡ ἀριστοκρατία βούλεται τὴν ὑπεροχὴν ἀπονέμειν τοῖς ἀρίστοις τῶν πολιτῶν καὶ τὰς ὀλιγαρχίας εἶναί φασιν ἐκ τῶν καλῶν κἀγαθῶν μᾶλλον. 159, 24: σχεδὸν γὰρ παρὰ τοῖς πλείστοις οἱ εὔποροι⟨τὴν⟩ τῶν καλῶν κἀγαθῶν δοκοῦσι κατέχειν χώραν. We cannot suppose that Aristotle used καλοὶ κἀγαθοί in a different sense in 2, 9=48, 6. οἱ δὲ καλοὶ κἀγαθοὶ διὰ τὴν γερουσίαν, ἆθλον γὰρ ἡ ἀρχὴ αὕτη τῆς ἀρετῆς ἐστιν means that the Gerontes were chosen from among those of the well-to-do class who were distinguished for personal merit. According to Plut., *Lyc.* 17 the παιδονόμος was elected from among the καλοὶ κἀγαθοί; in Xen., *de Rep. Lac.*, 2, 2, we have the additional explanation ἐξ ὧνπερ αἱ μέγισται ἀρχαὶ καθίστανται; therefore this expression points to a definite class of eminent families. On καλοὶ κἀγαθοί= noble, cf. Welcker on Theogn., p. xx. sqq. Hdt. 7, 134, exactly corresponds with the Aristotelian definition of εὐγένεια. Σπερθίης τε ὁ Ἀνηρίστου καὶ Βοῦλις ὁ Νικόλεω ἄνδρες Σπαρτιῆται φύσι τε γεγονότες εὖ καὶ χρήμασι ἀνήκοντες ἐς τὰ πρῶτα. Cf. 6, 61. Thuc. 1, 6 distinguishes between οἱ πολλοί at Sparta and οἱ τὰ μείζω κεκτημένοι. The Spartiatai taken prisoners at Sphacteria belonged to the πρῶτοι ἄνδρες. Thuc. 5, 15; cf. 4, 108. Large pecuniary fines were inflicted on individual Spartiatai. Plut., *Pelop.*, 6, 13; *Ages.*, 34. Cf. also the extraordinary wealth of Lichas, who won a chariot race at Olympia in 420. Thuc. 5, 50; Xen., *Mem.*, 1, 2, 61; Plut., *Kim.*, 10. The ἱπποτροφία, which according to Hdt. 6, 125 was the sign of very great wealth, was pursued most zealously at the time of the Persian wars at Sparta: Paus. 6, 2, 1 sqq. Examples of this: Plut., *Ages.*, 20; *Apophth. Lac.*, p. 258, 49 Didot; Hdt. 6, 103. At the time of the battle of Leuctra οἱ πλουσιώτατοι accordingly supply horses for the cavalry: Xen. 6, 4, 11. Mention of πλούσιοι: Xen., *de Rep. Lac.*, 5, 3. Aristot. distinguishes πλούσιοι and πένητες: 6 (4), 9=p. 161, 6 sqq. The presence of wealth and wealthy men in Sparta in the earliest times can also be inferred from Alkaios (fr. 50): ὡς γὰρ δήποτ' 'Ἀριστόδαμόν φαισ' οὐκ ἀπάλαμνον ἐν Σπάρτᾳ λόγον—εἰπῆν· χρήματ ἀνήρ, πένιχρος δ' οὐδεὶς πέλετ' ἐσλὸς οὐδὲ τίμιος. See Grote, vol. 2, p. 393 sq., the author's *Stud.*, 151 ff. Duncker also, *op. cit.*, 149, 150=Abhandl. 7 ff. seems to contrast the families which possessed not more than the κλῆρος with other families more richly endowed. See also Bazin, *de Lycurgo*, 91 ff., Paris 1885.

[1] Spartiatai debarred from commerce and lucrative employment: Plut.,

Hence in discussing the landed estates of the Spartiatai, we must draw a distinction between the estates of the nobles and the properties which were granted to the nobles by the State as ordinary burgess allotments. And as a matter of fact we find this distinction clearly set forth in a trustworthy piece of evidence which treats of the alienation of landed property at Sparta. According to this authority it was, as a general rule, considered disgraceful at Sparta to sell land, but to sell the allotments assigned by the State was absolutely forbidden.[1]

Those lands whose sale was disgraceful but not absolutely forbidden, in contrast to the κλῆροι, whose sale was unconditionally prohibited, can have been nothing but freehold landed estates. On the other hand, the Kleroi are shown, by the legal regulations which were in force concerning them, to have been of the nature of state endowments. In the first place the law of Epitadeus allowed the occupiers of Kleroi to give away the Kleros in their lifetime even if they had descendants living, and also to make dispositions by will of the Kleroi before their death: therefore before this statute the Kleros must have lapsed in theory back to the State in case of failure of natural heirs. Early Greek religion dreaded the extinction of any family, and prevented it if possible; adoption was the usual remedy; yet in this case also the State maintained its right of property over the Kleros which was passing into strange hands by adoption, by insisting that the adoption must take place in presence of kings. For the same reason it was the kings again who decided in cases where the right to marry an heiress was disputed between several claimants.[2]

Lyc., 4; Ages., 26. Apophth. Lac., p. 260, 72; 296, 41. Ælian. Miscell., 6, 6. The Spartan kings possessed estates in the various towns of the Perioikoi. See Xen., de Rep. Lac., 15, 3. Plat., Alcib., 123.

[1] This evidence is found in a statement of the so-called Herakleides 2, 76. Müller, Fr. Hist. Gr., 2, 211. In my Stud., 162 ff. (cf. also Oncken d. Staatslehre d. Aristot., 2, 350, and in general 343 ff.) I have tried to make it probable that Herakleides obtains his information from Aristotle. His words are: πωλεῖν δὲ γῆν Λακεδαιμονίοις αἰσχρὸν νενόμισται, τῆς δὲ ἀρχαίας μοίρας οὐδὲ ἔξεστιν. With this should be compared Plut. Instit. Lacon., 22: ἔνιοι δ' ἔφασαν ὅτι καὶ τῶν ξένων ὃς ἂν ὑπομείνῃ ταύτην τὴν ἄσκησιν τῆς πολιτείας κατὰ τὸ βούλευμα τοῦ Λυκούργου μετεῖχε τῆς ἀρχῆθεν διατεταγμένης μοίρας, πωλεῖν δὲ οὐκ ἐξῆν. It is clear from the context that ἡ ἀρχαία μοῖρα and ἡ ἀρχῆθεν διατεταγμένη μοῖρα mean a Kleros granted by the State. Cf. Stud. 170 ff.

[2] In Lokroi also the sale of landed estates was allowed only on certain specified conditions. Aristot., Pol., 2, 7 = p. 37, 28 ff. Bekker. The statute of Epitadeus decreed: ἐξεῖναι τὸν οἶκον αὐτοῦ καὶ τὸν κλῆρον ᾧ τις ἐθέλοι καὶ ζῶντα

The development of the Spartan constitution as described up to this point, together with the constitutional ordinances contained in the so-called Rhetra of Lycurgus, as well as the arrangement of the land system, were all regarded by the traditional learning of later antiquity—of course from a standpoint of judgment and criticism quite different from the one adopted here—as a portion of the legislative activity of Lycurgus. In this historical sketch of the development of the Spartan constitution no mention has been made of any special legislation of Lycurgus. In the first place it is not certain that there ever existed such a person as Lycurgus; but apart from that, it is certain that the political institutions hitherto described cannot be ascribed to Lycurgus; and besides, the institutions generally ascribed to him are more social than political in character, and as such can find no place in this short abstract.[1]

In the reign of king Theopompos an extension and also an alteration of the Spartan constitution took place. The former is

---

δοῦναι καὶ καταλιπεῖν διατιθέμενον. See Plut. *Ag.*, 5. To the same subject also refer the words of Aristot., *Pol.*, 2, 9=p. 46, 26 ff.: ὠνεῖσθαι μὲν γὰρ ἢ πωλεῖν τὴν ὑπάρχουσαν ἐποίησεν οὐ καλόν, ὀρθῶς ποιήσας, διδόναι δὲ καὶ καταλείπειν ἐξουσίαν ἔδωκε τοῖς βουλομένοις. Previous to the decree of Epitadeus the Spartan land system was not free from the fault which Aristotle criticises. Cf. *Stud.* 172 ff. The reluctance to allow a family to die out reveals itself in the fact that at Sparta those men were employed but sparingly in war, who as yet had no children to leave behind them. See Hdt. 7, 205. For adoptions and disputed claims to heiresses see Hdt. 6, 57.

[1] Gelzer in the *N. Rh. Mus.*, 28, 1 ff., and I myself in *Stud.*, 80 ff., have almost simultaneously undertaken an examination of the traditions relating to Lycurgus. Though we differ in our explanations of the Lycurgus legend, yet we have both arrived at the common conclusion that the historical existence of a personal Lycurgus is to be denied. The same opinion was held at an earlier date by Zoëga (*Abhandlungen ed.* Welcker, p. 316), and Uschold (*üb. d. Entsteh. d. Verf. d. Spart.*, Amberg, 1843). For the elaboration and adornment of the traditional history of Lycurgus in the times of Agis IV. and Cleomenes III. see Oncken, *d. Staatslehre d. Aristot.*, 1, 219 ff. Ranke also *allgem. Weltgesch.*, 1, 178 (180), 1, relegates Lycurgus to the realm of myth. Von Wilamowitz in the *hom. Untersuch.*, 267 ff., especially 288 ff., regards Lycurgus as a hero who was styled Zeus Lykaios. "The hero's name supplied the peg whereon the legend of the legislator was hung." Ed. Meyer, *op. cit.*, 42, 97, agrees with von Wilamowitz, while Bazin, *de Lycurgo*, 1 ff., Paris, 1885, and Busson, *Lykurgos und die grosse Rhetra*, 3 ff., Innsbruck, 1887, attempt to rehabilitate the historical personality of Lycurgus. Winicker in the *Graudenz Programm*, 1884, regards Lycurgus as the originator of the συνοικισμὸς effected by means of the Rhetra found in Plut., *Lyc.* 6.

important only in its later development, but the latter had an immediate influence on the character of the constitution.
For it was by Theopompos that Ephors were first
instituted.[1]

Institution of the Ephorate.

The theories held by modern writers as to the original functions of these magistrates are widely divergent.[2]

The reason for their institution which is most probable, because it is given by tradition apparently trustworthy, is that the kings

---

[1] The authorities for the institution of Ephors by king Theopompos are Plato, *Laws*, 3, 692, who however does not mention that king by name, and also Aristot., *Pol.*, 8 (5), 11, p. 228, 25 sqq.: καὶ πάλιν Θεοπόμπου μετριάσαντος τοῖς τε ἄλλοις καὶ τὴν τῶν ἐφόρων ἀρχὴν ἐπικαταστήσαντος. Cf. Plut., *Lyc.*, 7; Cic., *de Rep.*, 2, 33; *de Leg.*, 3, 7. Hdt. 1, 65, and Xen., *de Rep. Lac.*, 8, 3, refer the institution conjecturally to Lycurgus. Cf. Pseudo-Plat. *Epist.*, 8, p. 354. Diog. Laert., 1, 31. Müller, *Dor.*, 2, 107 ff. (115), believes in the existence of Ephors before the time of king Theopompos—in fact regards them as an old Dorian institution (so also Spakler, *de Ephor. ap. Laced.*, 1842, 20 ff., and Gabriel, *de Magistratib. Lac.*, p. 38 sqq.. Berlin, 1845; Schaefer, *de Ephoris Lac.*, Greifswald, 1863, p. 7; Stein, *das spartan. Ephorat*, p. 14; Frick, *de Ephoris Spartanis. Diss.*, Goett., 1872, p. 8; Ed. Meyer, *N. Rh. Mus.*, 41, 583; Gachon, *de Ephoris Spart.*, 16 ff.). It appears that the Alexandrians had before them a list of the Ephors beginning with the year 755-4. See Ed. Meyer, *N. Rh. Mus.*, 42, 101. But it is questionable whether this list was authentic, or, as is more probable, the earlier names were the invention of later systematisers. The year 755-4 is given by the chronologists, but we cannot for that reason regard it as a historical datum. See Eusebius, *Chron.* ed. Schoene, 2, 80, 81. That the tradition that Theopompos instituted the Ephorate may very well be correct, has been well shown by Dum in his *Entst. u. Entwickel. d. spart. Ephorats*, Innsbruck, 1878, p. 81 ff.

[2] Müller, *Dor.*, 2, 111 (119), considers the supervision of traffic in the market to have been the original duty of the Ephors. Schaefer, p. 7, argues that the Ephors were originally the representatives of the kings in the five Lacedaemonian communities assumed by Ephorus, *ap.* Strab. 364-5, after the original kings of those communities were deposed. This view is supported by Oncken, *d. Staatslehre d. Aristot.*, 1, 276 ff. Stein, p. 14, believes that even before the time of Theopompos the Ephors stood at the head of the several κῶμαι of Sparta, with judicial functions, and as supervisors of the police; that Theopompos extended these functions over the Perioikoi; then after the Messenian wars the Ephors also decided disputes between the old burgesses and the Perioikoi who had been admitted to citizenship. Frick, 17 ff., thinks the Ephors were, after the time of Theopompos, the representatives of the Demos formed by the Minyan element of the community. According to Ed. Meyer, *ibid.*, 41, 583, 2, the political powers of the Ephors were developed out of their civil judicial functions. According to Gachon, *De Ephoris Spart.*, 55 ff., the Ephors were in possession of civil judicial functions before the time of Theopompos, and at the time of the Messenian wars when the power of the Oligarchy increased, they began to act as executive officers of the Gerousia.

were overburdened with business, so that as their own energies were entirely taken up by war, they entrusted certain of their friends with the civil jurisdiction, and very likely with the superintendence of police as well.[1]

Kings Theopompos and Polydoros introduced a change in the Spartan constitution by adding to the fundamental ordinances of the State, which were discussed above, the following rule:—that whenever the people made a wrong decision the Gerontes and the kings should be empowered to set it aside.[2] *The Statute of Theopompos.*

Through the addition of this ordinance the Gerontes and the kings obtained the right of refusing to carry out any decision of the Apella which they regarded as unadvisable. Up to this time the decision of the Apella had been final. Since therefore the Gerousia (as may be inferred, even for this early age, from the constitutional law of later times)[3] was composed of members of the Spartan aristocracy, this new regulation placed the entire

---

[1] With regard to the origin of the Ephorate, I have followed in my *Stud.*, 181 ff., the account given by Plut., *Kleom.*, 10, which in all probability is derived from Phylarchos. So also has Duncker, *Gesch. d. Alterth.*, 5⁵, 425–6. Dum, p. 39 ff., has shown that this account was the tradition generally accepted at Sparta, which is also attested by Plut., *Apophth. Anaxil.*, p. 265 Didot. I also agree with Dum now, that the original official function of the Ephors was κρίνειν, *i.e.* civil jurisdiction, which in later times too formed part of their official duties. See Aristot., *Pol.*, 3, 1 = p. 60, 15: οἷον ἐν Λακεδαίμονι τὰς τῶν συμβολαίων δικάζει τῶν ἐφόρων ἄλλος ἄλλας. Dum infers from the arrangements in force in later times that the Ephors possessed certain functions of police superintendence in the earliest stage of their development. The evidence of Phylarchos, however, does not exactly correspond with the dates given by the chronologists for the institution of the Ephorate. Plato, *Leg.*, 3, 692; Aristot., *Pol.*, 8 (5), 11 = p. 223, 24 ff.; cf. Plut., *Lyc.*, 7; Cic., *de Rep.*, 2, 33, 58; *de Leg.*, 3, 7, 16, Valerius Max., 4, 1, Ext. 8, all represent the establishment of the Ephorate as a weakening of the power of the kings, but this view is obviously an inference from the position of the Ephors in the state in later times.

[2] The part added to the so-called Lycurgean Rhetra by Theopompos and Polydoros reads as follows in Plut., *Lyc.*, 6: αἰ δὲ σκολιὰν ὁ δᾶμος ἕλοιτο, τοὺς πρεσβυγενέας καὶ ἀρχαγέτας ἀποστατῆρας ἦμεν. See the author's *Stud.*, 137 ff., 179 ff. That Theopompos and Polydoros were the originators of this innovation was proved to the satisfaction of Aristotle, who is the authority of Plut., *Lyc.*, 6, by the verses of Tyrtæus quoted by Plut., *ad loc.*, verses whose authenticity I consider it wrong to doubt. *Vid.* p. 8, 1.

[3] According to Aristot., *Pol.*, 2, 9 = p. 48, 6, cf. 6 (4), 9 = p. 161, 15, none but the καλοὶ κἀγαθοί were represented in the Gerousia, and there is no ground for supposing that it was otherwise in earlier times. See p. 13, 1.

control of the State in the hands of the kings and of the aristocrats.

We are told that the conspiracy of the Partheniai took place at Sparta not long after the end of the first Messenian war. The accounts we possess of this event are in such a condition that no clear comprehension of the conspiracy can be obtained from them.[1]

Partheniai.

The accomplices in this plot were, according to tradition, first, the Ἐπεύνακτοι, who seem to have been Helots assigned as husbands to Spartan widows to prevent their families from dying out; and secondly the Παρθενίαι, or sons of maidens, that is to say, not born in legitimate wedlock, though we are informed by a credible witness that their fathers were Spartiatai possessed of full burgess rights.[2]

To what extent these sexual relations were results of the first Messenian war, cannot be stated with certainty. On the other hand, it may be considered an established fact that the outbreak of the conspiracy was anticipated by a timely discovery, and that the conspirators were sent away as colonists and settled at Tarentum.[3]

---

[1] We possess two accounts of the Partheniai in the extracts in Strabo 278, 279, one taken from Antiochos, the other from Ephoros. The former contains without doubt the foundation legend of Tarentum; the version of Ephoros differs in many points. Dionys., Hal., 19, 1 (17, 1) and Justin 3, 4 are to all appearances based on Ephoros; while the short account found in Diod. 8, 21 seems to be derived from Antiochos, since the oracle recounted by Antiochos is found in Diodoros. According to Diodoros the Ἐπεύνακτοι also took part in the conspiracy, while Theopompos, *ap.* Athen., 6, 271 c, D. tells us that they afterwards became burgesses. Herakleid. *Fr.* 26 in Müller, *Fr. Hist. Gr.*, 2,220, seems to have possessed an independent version of the occurrence.

[2] The Ἐπεύνακτοι accomplices in the conspiracy, according to Diod. 8, 21. The explanation of the name Ἐπεύνακτοι is given by Theop., *loc. cit.*, with which should be compared the other regulations in force among the Spartans concerning sexual intercourse. See Xen., *de Rep. Lac.*, 1, 7 sqq., Plut., *Lyc.* 15. Ὁ παρθένιος is the child of a woman who is not married, and who is therefore still considered a παρθένος. See Hom., *Il.*, 16, 180. Hesych.: παρθένιοι:—καὶ οἱ ἐξ ἀνεκδότου λάθρα γεννώμενοι παῖδες ἀπὸ τοῦ δοκεῖν ἔτι παρθένους εἶναι τὰς γεννησαμένας αὐτούς. See also Suid., παρθένιοι. Arist., *Pol.*, 8 (5), 7=p. 207, 21 sqq., says of the Partheniai: ἐκ τῶν ὁμοίων γὰρ ἦσαν, which should be translated, "they were sons of the recognised ὅμοιοι," and not as Hermann does, *Antiqu. Lacon.*, 127, who holds that the words can only mean simply "they belonged to the ὅμοιοι."

[3] According to Justin, 3, 4, and Paus., 10, 10, 6, the leader of the colonists, Phalanthos was not a παρθενίας but a Σπαρτιάτης. Studniczka, *Kyrene*, 175 ff.,

There are some faint but unmistakable indications that the Aigeidai took part in this conspiracy. We may therefore venture to conjecture again that the influential position of the Aigeidai, which is attested for the time of the first Messenian war, was overthrown when this conspiracy was suppressed.[1]

The activity which Terpandros is said to have shown as a mediator at Sparta must on this supposition have benefited chiefly the new institution of the dual kingdom.[2] **Terpandros.**

Soon after the departure of the Παρθενίαι civil strife again arose in Sparta. This trouble was caused by the second Messenian war, which deprived those burgesses who had allotments in Messenia of the use of their land. Their agitation for a redistribution of landed property was appeased by the influence of Tyrtaios; but by what method we do not know.[3] **Tyrtaios.**

argues that Phalanthos was not a historical personality, but in his criticism of the history of the Partheniai, I think he carries his scepticism too far.

[1] For the Aigeid Euryleon in the first Messenian war, see Paus. 4, 7, 8. According to Antiochos, *ap.* Strab., 278, the plot was to have been carried out at the Hyakinthia, the festival of the Karneian Apollo, with which the Aigeids seem to have been especially connected. Compare what Aristot., *fr.* 75 in Müller, *Fr. Hist. Gr.*, 2,127, relates about the Aigeid Timomachos: καὶ τοῖς Ὑακινθίοις δὲ ὁ χάλκεος αὐτῷ θώραξ προτίθεται. The cult of Apollo Karneios found at Tarentum also: *Poll.*, 8, 30, 2, confirmed by the Tarentine coins in the *Annali dell' inst.*, 2,337. Just as Theras before setting out for Thera consecrated a ἱερὸν of Athene, so the colonists of Tarentum set up an ἄγαλμα to the same goddess: Paus., 3, 12, 5.

[2] Hermann, *Antiqu. Lacon.*, p. 69 ff., has shown that Terpandros was contemporary with the end of the first Messenian war. Hellanikos, *ap.* Athen., 14,635 E., says that Terpandros was the first victor at the Karneia; this is confirmed by Hellanikos's list of Karneian victors. C. Frick, however, in the *Jahrb. f. cl. Phil.*, 1872, p. 664–5, disputes the authenticity of that list. According to Sosibios, *ibid.*, and Africanus, in his list of Olympionicai, the Karneia were first instituted Ol. 26=676 B.C. The evidence for the activity of Terpandros at Sparta is Plut. *de Mus.* 42: Τέρπανδρον δ' ἄν τις παραλάβοι τὸν τὴν γενομένην ποτὲ παρὰ Λακεδαιμονίοις στάσιν καταλύσαντα. Cf. Diod., 8, 28, from Tzetz., *Hist.*, 1, 16. Apostol., 11, 27. Zenob., 5, 2.

[3] Aristot., 8 (5), 7=p. 207, 23 sqq., gives as one of the causes of στάσεις: ἔτι ὅταν οἱ μὲν ἀπορῶσι λίαν, οἱ δ' εὐπορῶσιν. καὶ μάλιστα ἐν τοῖς πολέμοις τοῦτο γίγνεται. συνέβη δὲ καὶ τοῦτο ἐν Λακεδαίμονι ὑπὸ τὸν Μεσσηνιακὸν πόλεμον. δῆλον δὲ καὶ τοῦτο ἐκ τῆς Τυρταίου ποιήσεως τῆς καλουμένης Εὐνομίας. θλιβόμενοι γάρ τινες διὰ τὸν πόλεμον ἠξίουν ἀνάδαστον ποιεῖν τὴν χώραν. More precise information, as it is given in the text, in Paus., 4, 18, 2/3. Whether the institution of the Karneian festival in 676 was connected with the reestablishment of concord by Tyrtaios or not, cannot be determined with certainty. Cf. the preceding note.

The further development of the Spartan constitution coincides with the development of the Ephorate. According to tradition the Ephor Asteropos[1] extended the powers of this office considerably, but we are not informed in what the increase of power consisted.[2]

Development of the Ephorate.

The Ephors were at first appointed by the kings, but in later times they were elected by the assembly of burgesses. So long as they were nominated by the kings they could scarcely have been in a position to exercise any considerable influence. Therefore the most natural theory is that the epoch-making significance of the Ephorate of Asteropos consisted in the fact that the Ephorate was thrown open to popular election during his administration.[3] Some authorities attribute a further increase of the power of the Ephors to Cheilon, but for this there is no sufficient evidence.[4]

The further development of the powers of the Ephors may be supposed to have been effected in something like the following fashion.[5]

[1] Niese, in Sybel's *hist. Zeitschr.*, 1889, 62, 58 ff., endeavours to establish the theory, that in the period of the Tyrtæan poems the Spartan constitution gradually developed into a democracy, and that the institution of the Ephorate was the result of this democratizing. According to him, the Ephors were from the first in full possession of all the powers they can be proved to possess in later times. I cannot agree with him. For Asteropos cf. Plut., *Cleom.*, 10: καὶ τὸν πρῶτον ἐπισφοδρύναντα τὴν ἀρχὴν καὶ ἀνατεινάμενον Ἀστερωπὸν ἡλικίαις ὕστερον πολλαῖς ἔφορον γενέσθαι.

[2] According to Stein, *ibid.*, p. 20 sq., Asteropos's innovation consisted in obtaining for the Ephors the presidency of the popular assemblies and a share in the discussions of the Gerousia. According to Frick, *ibid.*, p. 21, the Ephors ceased in Asteropos's day to be representatives of the Minyan plebs.

[3] Aristot., *Pol.*, 2, 10 = p. 52, 8 sqq. and 2, 9 = p. 48, 8 is our evidence that the Ephors were elected in later times by the burgesses. Duncker, *Gesch. d. Alterth.*, 6⁵, 343, and Schaefer, *op. cit.*, 15, both believe that Asteropos threw open the Ephorate to popular election.

[4] Diog. Laert., 1, 3, 68, says of Cheilon: γέγονε δὲ ἔφορος κατὰ τὴν πεντηκοστὴν πέμπτην ὀλυμπιάδα· Παμφίλη δέ φησι κατὰ τὴν ἕκτην. καὶ πρῶτον ἔφορον γενέσθαι ἐπὶ Εὐθυδήμου, ὥς φησι Σωσικράτης. καὶ πρῶτος εἰσηγήσατο ἐφόρους τοῖς βασιλεῦσι παραζευγνύναι· Σάτυρος δὲ Λυκοῦργον. The theories of Urlichs, *N. Rh. Mus.*, 6, 217 sqq., Duncker, *Gesch. d. Alterth.*, 6⁵, 349 sqq., Schaefer, *op. cit.*, p. 14 ff., Stein, *op. cit.*, 21 ff., on the innovations of Cheilon are pure conjectures. Cf. Dum., *op. cit.*, 21 ff.

[5] The theory here adopted coincides in its main points with that given by Dum, in the book quoted above, *Ensteh. u. Entwickel. d. spartan. Ephorats*. I believe, however, that the intervention of the Ephors in the

It might easily happen that the two kings would not agree. The dangers to the State which might arise from such disputes were provided against so far as military matters were concerned in the year 510 B.C., by a law which ordained that the two kings should never command simultaneously in the field. In time of peace such a remedy was not available. But it was natural enough that if the kings were at variance even in times of peace, they could not be then regarded as the representatives of the entire community.[1]

During such quarrels between the kings the influence of the Gerontes must have become more and more important. Since, however, this government board of twenty-eight members could not very well act as an executive committee, those duties were undertaken by the Ephors, who were already the representatives of the kings in the administration of civil justice. Thus the Ephors assumed the practical executive power, whenever the kings were not agreed, just as if they were their regular representatives.[2]

The Ephors ruled originally as temporary substitutes for the kings; but their power gradually became permanent, because after the death of Cleomenes I. the quarrels of the two kings became chronic. The establishment of the Ephors' control was still further promoted by the frequent cases in which kings were condemned for various offences during the fifth century. These condemnations in themselves did considerable damage to the moral prestige of royalty; and their further result, that the young children of the condemned had to be placed under the charge of guardians, was not calculated to produce energetic kings.[3]

Under these circumstances all the rights which belonged to royalty were gradually transferred to the Ephors during the

government, in case of dispute between the two kings, was not based on any particular statute, but merely on custom.

[1] Always one king and one only in the field after 510: Hdt. 5, 75. The narrative of Herodotus shows that it was only when they agreed together, that the Spartan kings were treated as representatives of the Spartan State. See Dum, *ibid.*, 62 ff.

[2] See Dum, 98 ff. According to Hdt. 5, 40, the Ephors and the Gerousia took joint action together before the time of Cleomenes I.

[3] See Dum, 74 ff. Aristot., *Pol.*, 2, 9 = p. 49, 16, says of the Lacedæmonians: καὶ σωτηρίαν ἐνόμιζον τῇ πόλει εἶναι τὸ στασιάζειν τοὺς βασιλεῖς. This is quite correct from the point of view of the Ephors who were in Aristotle's days the *de facto* rulers.

course of the fifth century. In the fourth century their rule degenerated into an absolute despotism.[1]

The attempts which were made to alter the course of constitutional development were frustrated by the watchfulness of the Ephors. Pausanias endeavoured in vain to overthrow the power of the Ephors. Lysander attempted to set up an elective dual monarchy in place of the hereditary one. Kinadon tried to break through the monopoly of political power held by the full burgesses.[2]

Attempts to overthrow the Ephors.

Thus the political development of the constitution was determined by the development of the Ephorate. Meanwhile social relations were also changing. In the first place the decline in the numbers of the Spartiatai had already altered the distribution of property in the period between the Persian and the Peloponnesian wars. The subsequent loss of Messenia had a very serious effect; and so had, thirdly, the law of Epitadeus. On the first invasion of Laconia by Epaminondas

Loss of Messenia.

---

[1] In Plat., *Leg.*, 4, 712, we are already informed: τὸ γὰρ τῶν ἐφόρων θαυμαστὸν ὡς τυραννικὸν ἐν αὐτῇ γέγονε. Cf. Dum, 105 ff. For the luxurious excesses of the Ephors and the bribes they took, cf. Aristot., *Pol.*, 2, 9=p. 47, 21 sqq. Plut., *Cleom.*, 6.

[2] See Aristot., *Pol.*, 8 (5), 1 = p. 194, 30 ff: ὥσπερ ἐν Λακεδαίμονί φασι Λύσανδρόν τινες ἐπιχειρῆσαι καταλῦσαι τὴν βασιλείαν καὶ Παυσανίαν τὸν βασιλέα τὴν ἐφορείαν. Ed. Meyer, in *N. Rh. Mus.*, 41, 578, holds that the Pausanias here mentioned was the king who was driven into exile after the battle of Haliartos, 395 B.C. (see Xen., *Hell.*, 3, 5, 25). This is in accordance with Meyer's general theory of the proceedings and the political position of this Pausanias. In my opinion the Pausanias mentioned by Aristot., *loc. cit.*, is the victor of Platæa, who moreover may perfectly well have composed the λόγος (Strab. 366), which plays so important a part in Meyer, *ibid.*, 575. Aristot. 8 (5), 7 = p. 208, 1 ff., gives as one of the causes of revolutions in aristocratic governments: ἔτι ἐάν τις μέγας ᾖ καὶ δυνάμενος ἔτι μείζων εἶναι, ἵνα μοναρχῇ, ὥσπερ ἐν Λακεδαίμονι δοκεῖ Παυσανίας ὁ στρατηγήσας κατὰ τὸν Μηδικὸν πόλεμον καὶ ἐν Καρχηδόνι Ἄννων. Judging by the sense, the same Pausanias is referred to in Aristot. 4 (7), 14 = p. 121, 21 ff.: ὅπερ (*i.e.* διώκειν, ὅπως δύνηται τῆς οἰκείας πόλεως ἄρχειν) ἐγκαλοῦσιν οἱ Λάκωνες Παυσανίᾳ, τῷ βασιλεῖ, καίπερ ἔχοντι τηλικαύτην τιμήν. In this passage and the one quoted above he is styled βασιλεύς, though he was only guardian of the king, but this is of no moment, because as guardian he exercised practically all the functions of royalty. Cf. also Thuc. 1, 132: ἐπυνθάνοντο δὲ καὶ ἐς τοὺς Εἴλωτας πράσσειν τι αὐτόν, καὶ ἦν δὲ οὕτως· ἐλευθερώσιν τε γὰρ ὑπισχνεῖτο αὐτοῖς καὶ πολιτείαν, ἢν ξυνεπαναστῶσι καὶ τὸ πᾶν ξυγκατεργάσωνται. For Lysander cf. further Plut., *Lys.*, 30. *Agesil.*, 20. *Apophth. Lac.*, p. 282, 14 Didot. Diod. 14, 13. Bazin, *la République des Lacédémoniens de Xénophon*, 178 ff., Paris, 1885. For Kinadon, Xen. 3, 3, 4 ff. Aristot. 8 (5), 7 = p. 207, 26 ff. Polyain. 2, 14.

in 370, Messenia became an independent State, and though the Lacedæmonians refused to recognise its independence, they never succeeded in recovering their lost possession. Under the Roman empire the two States were still disputing about their boundaries.[1]

By the loss of Messenia many Spartiatai were deprived of their estates, and thereby ran great risk of losing their full rights of citizenship also. For these depended on the sufficiency of their income to supply the regular contributions to the Syssitia.

The law of Epitadeus enacted that every burgess should be allowed to transfer his house and kleros to any one he pleased, either by gift during his own lifetime, or by bequest at his death. From what was said above on the character of the kleroi, it follows that the peculiar significance of this statute of Epitadeus lay in the fact that it changed these kleroi from allotments lent to individuals by the State into freehold properties. As a natural corollary of this change the same law gave the testator the right of bestowing the hand of his heiress-daughter as he pleased; and if the testator died without making any such arrangement, it gave the right of marrying the heiress to the nearest male relative. Previous to this statute the kings used to decide who was entitled to marry an heiress. The disgrace which attended the sale of freehold property was now attached to the alienation of kleroi also, but this could very easily be avoided by using the form of a deed of gift. The natural result of the law of Epitadeus was that by gift, inheritance, and marriage of heiresses, and most of all by sales under those forms, all the land of the country came into the possession of a few rich men who gave themselves up to the grossest luxury. Meanwhile trades and handicrafts still remained forbidden to Spartiatai, so that the main body of the full burgesses gradually sank into extreme poverty, which in its turn caused them to lose their rights of citizenship, since they were too poor to keep up their contributions to the Syssitia, or to bear the expense of the luxurious and

Law of Epitadeus.

---

[1] Augustus gave Pharai and Thyria to the Spartans: Paus. 4, 30, 2; 31, 2. Tiberius restored these and also the land of Deúthalioi to the Messenians: Tac., *Ann.*, 4, 43, since in the time of Pausanias the boundary ran through the χοίριος νάπη, near Gerenia, a narrow ravine through which ran a mountain stream. Cf. Curtius, *Pelop.*, 2, 160 and 162. A boundary stone from the frontier as fixed by Tiberius, is given in Le Bas' *Voyage archéol. explic. des inscr.*, 2, 167b.

costly Spartan Agoge. When Agis IV. came to the throne there were still 700 Spartiatai; of these 100 were landowners, who monopolised all the land, while the rest, deprived of their political rights, lived in open hostility to the existing constitution, without any voice in determining its fate.[1]

Of the reforms projected by Agis IV. and Cleomenes III., some were never carried out, and the rest were soon reversed, except one institution of Cleomenes, the πατρόνομοι, who survived till later times.[2] With this exception, the battle at Sellasia in 221 brought back the old constitution.[3]

Agis IV. and Cleomenes III.

Sparta remained without kings for three years only; then Agesipolis, of the Agiad family, and Lycurgos, an ordinary Spartiate, were elected kings.

End of the Royal Power.

Lycurgos drove out Agesipolis, and thereupon the double kingship came to an end for ever.[4]

After Lycurgos's death there ensued the lawless despotism of Machanidas from 211 to 206, then that of Nabis till 192. All the genuine Spartiatai still left in Sparta were slain or banished by Nabis, and there arose a new body of citizens composed of runaway slaves and criminals of every land.[5]

Rule of the Tyrants.

The existence of this new State was of no long duration. In

[1] On the Law of Epitadeus and its results, see Plut., *Ag.*, 5; Aristot., *Pol.*, 2, 9, p. 46, 21 ff. Ed. Meyer, in *N. Rh. Mus.*, 41, 589, 1, regards the narrative of the law of Epitadeus as an ætiological anecdote. According to Hermann, *Ant. Lac.*, 155 ff. (whose view is shared by Crome, *de turbata vetere quæ a Lycurgo instituta erat Lacedæmoniorum æqualitate*, Düsseldorf Progr., 1849), the equality of property was already destroyed by the decrease in the number of burgesses between the Persian and the Peloponnesian wars: Freese, in the Stralsund Progr., 1844, thinks this resulted still earlier, from the character of the Spartan constitution, the regulations in force concerning landed property, and the gradual increase of avarice. Luxurious living reached its climax in the reign of kings Areus and Acrotatus 309-265. Cf. Phylarch., *ap. Athen.*, 4, 142 B. It was increased by the circumstance that even in the time of Aristotle (*Pol.*, 2, 9=p. 45, 11 ff.) two-fifths of the landed property was in the hands of women who were greatly addicted to extravagance.

[2] For the reforms and general political activity of these two kings, cf. Droysen, *Gesch. d. Hellenism.*, 3, 1, 420 (407) ff., 3, 2, 74 (520) ff. Paus., 2, 9, 1, says of Cleomenes: καὶ τὸ κράτος τῆς γερουσίας καταλύσας πατρονόμους τῷ λόγῳ κατέστησεν ἀντ' αὐτῶν. On the survival of these officials in later times, see p. 25.

[3] Cf. Polyb. 2, 70, 1; 9, 29, 8. Paus. 2, 9, 2. Soon after Cleomenes' time we find Ephors and Gerontes again at Sparta (cf. Polyb. 4, 22, 5; 4, 35, 5).

[4] Cf. Polyb. 4, 35, 5 ff. Liv. 34, 36. Polyb. 24, 11.

[5] Polyb. 13, 6–8; 16, 18. Hertzberg, *Gesch. Griechenl.*, 1, 49 (44) ff.

195, after the defeat of Nabis by T. Quinctius Flamininus, the Laconian coast towns were set free from Spartan dominion and incorporated in the Achæan league. In 192, after Nabis had been slain by a troop of Ætolians, Philopœmen at length succeeded in inducing Sparta itself to join the Achæan league, to which it continued to belong, though perpetually at variance with the allies, and sometimes for short intervals independent, until the definite regulation of the affairs of Greece by the Romans in 146.[1]

By the new regulations of the Romans Sparta was classed among the *civitates fœderatœ*, which were liable to no tribute except what was explicitly required from them in their treaty with Rome, and were also exempted from the jurisdiction of the provincial governor.[2] Sparta under Roman Rule.

The following short sketch of the Spartan constitution in these times is based on the still existing inscriptions, without taking account of certain minor variations which occurred at various periods.[3]

The division of the citizens into the local Phylai and Obai remained the same as before.[4] Classification of Citizens.

The most important State officials were the πατρονόμοι, instituted by Cleomenes III., six, or perhaps twelve in number, and eligible for re-election. The πρέσβυς of these πατρονόμοι was the eponymous magistrate of the State, and had a corps of Epheboi as a guard of honour.[5] πατρονόμοι.

---

[1] Nabis conquered by T. Quinctius Flamininus, see Hertzberg, *ibid.*, 1, 85 (81) ff. To this date must be referred Liv. 35, 13: Achæis omnium maritimorum Laconum tuendorum a T. Quinctio cura mandata erat. Sparta induced by Philopœmen to join the Achæan league: Liv. 35, 37. Plut., *Philop.*, 15. Paus. 8, 51, 1. Hertzberg 1, 116–7 (113). For the fate of Sparta up to the year 146, see Hertzberg 1, 146 ff., 161 ff., 167, 169–70, 245–6, 250.

[2] Strabo, 365, says concerning the position of Sparta under Roman rule: ἀναλαβόντες δὲ σφᾶς ἐτιμήθησαν διαφερόντως καὶ ἔμειναν ἐλεύθεροι, πλὴν τῶν φιλικῶν λειτουργιῶν ἄλλο συντελοῦντες οὐδέν; *id.*, 376, says of the Spartans, as opposed to the Argives (who εἰς τὴν τῶν Ῥωμαίων ἐξουσίαν ἦλθον) καὶ διετέλεσαν τὴν αὐτονομίαν φυλάττοντες. Cf. also 414: καὶ παρὰ τούτοις (*i.e.* τοῖς Ῥωμαίοις) δὲ τιμώμενοι διατελοῦσι διὰ τὴν τῆς πολιτείας ἀρετήν. See Marquardt, *röm. Staatsverwalt.* 1², 327, and on the *civitates fœderatœ* in general: 1², 73 ff.

[3] Boeckh, in the C. I. G., 1, p. 604 ff.

[4] Compare what is said below about these divisions, and also Boeckh in the C. I. G., 1,609. For the state of affairs in the 2nd or 1st century B.C., cf. the Inscriptions in the *Mitth. d. dtsch. arch. Inst. in Ath.*, 3, 164 ff. The πρέσβυς ὡβᾶς, *e.g.* C. I. G., 1274, the πρέσβυς of the various φυλαί, *e.g.* 1,377.

[5] The πατρονόμοι were magistrates; see C. I. G., 1356: οἱ συνάρχοντες τῆς πατρονομίας. That they could hold office more than once is proved by

The five ἔφοροι held only the second rank among the magistrates; nothing is known for certain about their functions in this period.[1]

ἔφοροι.

νομοφύλακες. γραμματοφύλαξ.

We must mention further the five νομοφύλακες, and the γραμματοφύλαξ, whose duties were connected with those of the former.

βίδεοι.

The βίδεοι or βίδυοι, probably six in number, were the supervisors of the competitive exercises of the Epheboi.[2] The control of the police in the city was in the hands of a college of ἀγορανόμοι, eight in number, while the corresponding duties in the country devolved upon the πεδιανόμοι.[3]

ἀγορανόμοι. πεδιανόμοι.

Further, there were in Sparta ἐπιμεληταί, who occur once col-

C. I. G., 1341. In Le Bas' *Voyage archéologique* in the explanation of inscr. 2, no. 168, six πατρονόμοι are enumerated, but then there are added to these six σύναρχοι, one γραμματεύς, three ὑπογραμματεῖς, and one ὑπηρέτας. As a rule those who are styled σύναρχοι in Spartan inscriptions exercise the same functions as the man after whom their name comes. The one first mentioned is the πρέσβυς of the collegium, but usually only one name comes before the σύναρχοι. The inscription is not satisfactorily explained yet. See Foucart on no. 168. That their πρέσβυς, who is repeatedly mentioned, was the eponymos, and not the πρέσβυς of the Ephors as Paus. 3, 11, 2 says, is proved by Boeckh, *ibid.*, 605-6, who also gives a list of them. The proof is supplied by inscriptions such as C. I. G., 1251: νομοφύλακες οἱ περὶ Γ(οργιππον Γοργίππου) οἱ ἐπὶ πατρονόμων. Cf. 1241, 1258, 1259, 1268. Even in the lists of Ephors the name marking the year of their office is the name of the πρέσβυς πατρονόμων. See 1237, 1240-1245, 1249. For their honorary body-guard of Epheboi, see Boeckh. 612.

[1] Ephors five in number: C. I. G., I. 1237-8, and 1,240. A list of names of Ephors recorded Boeckh, *ibid.*, 608. They dined together: 1237. Paus., 3, 11, 2, mentions their ἀρχεῖον in the market place. What he says concerning their official functions: ἔφοροι δὲ τά τε ἄλλα διοικοῦσι τὰ σπουδῆς μάλιστα ἄξια καὶ παρέχονται τὸν ἐπώνυμον, is certainly wrong so far as the second clause is concerned. Religious societies too, and political subdivisions of the State, *e.g.* the ὠβὰ τῶν Ἀμυκλαιέων, have officials called Ephors in imitation of the State Ephors.

[2] Five νομοφύλακες: C. I. G., 1242-4-8-9; 1252, 1304. On the inscriptions which seem to give six, cf. Boeckh, *ibid.*, 608-9, and Foucart on Le Bas, 168g. One of them is styled γραμματοφύλαξ: 1239, 1240, 1242, 1247, 1251, 1304. But this last also occurs as a separate official, 1243. See Foucart, *ibid.* They also dined at State expense. Their ἀρχεῖον in the Agora: Paus. 3, 11, 2. The βίδεοι: 1254, 1270, 1271, or βίδυοι: 1241, 1242, 1255 (Paus. 3, 11, 2, calls them βιδιαῖοι); according to Paus., five in no.; acc. to C. I. G., 1271, 1364a, six; they had, acc. to Paus., the office τοὺς ἐπὶ τῷ πλατανιστᾷ καλουμένῳ καὶ ἄλλους τῶν ἐφήβων ἀγῶνας τιθέναι. Their ἀρχεῖον also in the Agora.

[3] In an inscr. in Le Bas, 168b., an ἀγορανόμος and seven σύναρχοι are recorded. ἀγορανόμος αἰώνιος, which occurs in C. I. G., 1363-4, 1375, 1379; Le Bas

lectively as a collegium of eight persons, but also as individual officials with separate special titles, as ἐπιμελητὴς πόλεως, ἐπιμεληταί. ἐπιμελητὴς Ἀμυκλῶν, ἐπι. Κορωνείας.[1]

We also find a λοχαγὸς and a ἱππάρχας, whose titles λοχαγὸς and explain themselves, and also ταμίαι.[2] ἱππάρχας.

At the head of the several colleges of magistrates πρέσβυς. stood a πρέσβυς as annual president.[3]

The whole body of magistrates probably formed a collective corporation, entitled αἱ συναρχίαι; to this body belonged αἱ συναρχίαι. the preliminary consideration of measures to be proposed in the public assembly.[4]

The σύνδικοι are to be regarded as judicial functionaries; of these we find mentioned in inscriptions a σύνδικος θεοῦ Λυκούργου, a σ. ἐπὶ τὴν μεγάλην συνδικίαν, one ἐπὶ τὰ ἔθη, another ἐπὶ σύνδικοι. τοὺς νόμους.[5]

We possess a complete list of members of the gerousia dating from the time of Hadrian. In it are mentioned a πρέσβυς, twenty-two γέροντες, a γραμματεύς, and a μάγειρος. The members γερουσία. were no longer elected for life, but for one year only. They were eligible for re-election.[6]

---

162 j, 178, 179, is only an honorary title. Cf. Foucart on 179. πεδιανόμοι are mentioned in Le Bas 168 c; on their duties, cf. W. Vischer, kl. Schr., 2, 32 ff.

[1] An ἐπιμελητάς and five σύναρχοι are mentioned in Le Bas 168 f. Four ἐπ. in Bulletin de Corresp. Hell., 1, 380, no. 4. ἐπ. πόλεως: C.I.G., 1241. ἐπ. Ἀμυκλῶν: 1338. ἐπ. Κορωνείας: 1243, 1255, 1258. The subordination of Corone to Sparta in that period has not yet been explained. See Hertzberg, Gesch. Griechenl., 2, 33.

[2] Λοχαγός: C.I.G., 1255, 1289. Ἱππάρχας is identified by Foucart on Le Bas 168 f., with the ἱππαγρέτης, but with little probability. 1241, 1248, 1345. Honorary title ἱππάρχας αἰώνιος, 1841. Hesych.: ἵππαρχος· ὁ τῶν νέων ἐπιμελητὴς παρὰ Λάκωσιν. ταμίαι: Le Bas 194 a.

[3] See, e.g., C.I.G., 1237, 1364 a. Le Bas 168 a, 168 b, 168 f. In C.I.G., 1299, πρέσβυς is translated by the Latin "princeps." See Boeckh 610.

[4] Foucart on Le Bas, 194 a, assumes that after the time of Cleomenes III. the Gerontes had either entirely lost the right of the προβούλευμα, or at any rate been compelled to share it with the magistrates. He bases this theory on the opening words of 194 a: πόθοδον ποιησαμένου Δαμῶνος τοῦ Θεοκρίτου Ἀμβρακιώτα περὶ προξενίας καὶ ἐπελθόντος ἐπί τε τὰς συναρχίας καὶ τὸν δᾶμον κ.τ.λ. For these and other συναρχίαι, cf. W. Vischer, kl. Schr., 2, 23 ff.

[5] The σύνδικοι were judges acc. to Boeckh, p. 610. σύνδικος θεοῦ Λυκούργου τὸ β': 1256. σύνδικος ἐπὶ τὴν μεγάλην συνδικίαν: 1242. σύνδικος ἐπὶ τὰ ἔθη: 1242. (συ)νδικῶν ἐπὶ τοὺς νόμους: 1241. σύνδικος καὶ δαμοσιομάστης: 1364 b. On the religious officials and their subordinates, see Boeckh, ibid., 610–11.

[6] The complete list of members of the gerousia is supplied by an inscription in Le Bas 173 a. According as we include the γραμματεύς or μάγειρος or

By the side of the gerousia there was in all probability yet
βουλή. another βουλή, which drew up decrees of its own, and seems to have had a share in the election of the magistrates.[1]

Public Assembly. The public assemblies were held in the Skias.[2]

The institutions of Lycurgus were nominally in force still, and Institutions there existed an interpreter whose special duty was to of Lycurgus. expound them.

So far as concerns the education of the young there are abundant proofs that the Lycurgean system still survived, though there may have been some changes in detail.[3]

The coast towns of Laconia remained independent of Sparta Eleuthero- after 146, and formed a community of their own, which lacones. was at first entitled κοινὸν τῶν Λακεδαιμονίων.

not we obtain a total of 23, 24, or 25 members. Foucart, *ad loc.*, includes the γραμματεὺς only, and so gives 24 members. The lists in C. I. G., 1260, 1262, are incomplete. The πρέσβυς of the gerontes in Le Bas, *ibid.*, and also in C. I. G., *e.g.*, 1261. βουλευτήριον τῆς γερουσίας in the Agora: Paus. 3, 11, 2.

[1] The member of the βουλή is called βουλευτής: C. I. G., 1375. ψήφισμα βουλῆς: 1345. An inscription styles a person who had held several offices αἱρεθέντα ὑπό τε τῆς λαμπροτάτης βουλῆς καὶ τοῦ ἱερωτάτου δήμου. See 1341. Mention of γραμματεὺς βουλᾶς: 1241, 1246, 1259, 1345. In 1253 his office is called an ἀρχή. Boeckh, C. I. G., 1, p. 610, considers the βουλή as distinct from the gerousia, while Foucart on Le Bas 173 a, regards the two as identical, or, if there was any distinction, considers the βουλή as composed of the γερουσία and the συναρχίαι.

[2] See Paus. 3, 12, 10: ἑτέρα δὲ ἐκ τῆς ἀγορᾶς ἐστιν ἔξοδος, καθ᾽ ἣν πεποίηται σφισι καλουμένη Σκιάς, ἔνθα καὶ νῦν ἐκκλησιάζουσι.

[3] As the Lycurgean constitution was abolished by Philopœmen in 188— see Liv., 38, 34—it must have been re-established in 146. Cic., *pro Flacco*, 26, 63, says of the Lacedæmonians: "Qui soli toto orbe terrarum septingentos iam annos amplius unis moribus et nunquam mutatis legibus vivunt." When Nero was making his tour in Achaia, 66–7 A.D., he did not visit Sparta, διὰ τοὺς Λυκούργου νόμους ὡς ἐναντίους τῇ προαιρέσει αὐτοῦ ὄντας (Dio. Cass. 63, 14). The title βουαγοί, which was retained even by adults, proves that the early system of education was still kept up. Cf. *e.g.*, νομοφύλαξ and βουαγός, 1240-1, 1251-2; Le Bas 168 g; ἔφορος and βουαγός, 1241, 1245; σπονδοφόρος and βουαγός, 1252; πρέσβυς ὡβᾶς and βουαγός, 1274; more rarely by itself, 1350, 1426, 1453, 1459; Le Bas 162 c. Further evidence is supplied by the title of honour, βωμονίκης, C. I. G., 1364 b; Le Bas 175 b; Bull., *de Cor. Hell.*, 1, 385, 14; Cic., *Tusc. Disp.*, 2, 14, 34. Cf. Müller, *Dor.*, 2, 306 (132). (σφ)αιρεῖς are mentioned, Le Bas 164; C. I. G., 1386, 1432; Bull., *de Cor. Hell.*, 1, 379, 2. Cf. also for the training of the young in this period Foucart on Le Bas, 162 j, p. 143. There was an ἐξηγητὴς τῶν Λυκουργείων, 1,364 b. We also find notice of ἐπιμέλεια τῆς τοῦ Λυκούργου, 1341. A person obtains a testimonial τῆς ἐν τοῖς πα(τ)ρίοις Λυκουργείοις ἔθεσιν εὐψυχίας καὶ πειθαρχίας χάριν, 1350. See Hertzberg, *Gesch. Griechenl.*, 2, 65–6.

It was reorganised perhaps by Augustus,[1] and the name changed, perhaps at the same time, to κοινὸν τῶν Ἐλευθερολακώνων.[2]

At the same time in all probability the number of allied towns was fixed at twenty-four, among which, however, only eighteen remained autonomous in the time of Pausanias.[3]

The highest official of the league was a στραταγός, who was also the ἐπώνυμος. By his side stood a ταμίας.[4] **Officers of the League.**

The constitutions of the several allied towns differed little from each other, and were modelled on the pattern of Sparta. For instance, we find at Kainepolis ἔφοροι, an ἐπιμελητής, a ταμίας, an ἀγορανόμος, and a βουλή;[5] in Oitylos, Geronthrai, Kotyrta, and Epidauros ἔφοροι;[6] at Gytheion ἔφοροι, ἀγορανόμοι, a ταμίας, οἱ τῆς πόλεως σύνεδροι, a βουλή, μεγάλαι ἀπέλλαι.[7] There is not sufficient material extant for more detailed information. **Constitution of the Individual Towns.**

---

[1] Strabo 366: συνέβη δὲ καὶ τοὺς Ἐλευθερολάκωνας λαβεῖν τινα τάξιν πολιτείας, ἐπειδὴ Ῥωμαίοις προσέθεντο πρῶτοι οἱ περίοικοι τυραννουμένης τῆς Σπάρτης, οἵ τε ἄλλοι καὶ οἱ Εἵλωτες. According to this passage Strabo obviously supposes that the Eleutherolacones enjoyed uninterrupted independence; on the other hand, Paus., 3, 21, 6, says that they were first set free from Sparta by Augustus. If so, we must suppose that in 146 they were again made subject to Sparta, which is not likely. Probably Augustus regulated the constitution of the league of Eleutherolacones, which was already in existence before his day. See Foucart on Le Bas, p. 111.

[2] The name κοινὸν τῶν Λακεδαιμονίων occurs in C. I. G., 1335; Le Bas 228 a, b, 255 d ; and on a coin of Kyparissia in the *Bullett. dell' Instit. Arch.*, 1861, p. 111. According to Foucart on Le Bas, p. 111, these documents and coins are older than the Imperial age. κοινὸν τῶν Ἐλευθερολακώνων: C. I. G., 1389; Le Bas 243 c, 244, 256. τὸ συνέδριον τὸ Ἐλευθερολακώνων: Paus. 3, 26, 8.

[3] Paus., 3, 21, 7, enumerates eighteen of the original twenty-four towns of the Eleutherolacones; the rest belonged to Sparta in his time.

[4] Στρατηγὸς τοῦ κοινοῦ τῶν Ἐλευθερολακώνων: *Mitth. d. dtsch. Arch. Inst. in Ath.*, 1, p. 156; Le Bas 243 c., 244, 256. The same official is meant in 228 a, b, 1. 36, 243 a, 1. 8, 243, 1. 33, 242 a, 1. 52. See Foucart on p. 111. The treasurer mentioned in Le Bas 255 d is without doubt the ταμίας of the league.

[5] Ἔφοροι: C. I. G., 1321, 1322=Le Bas 261, 262, and three in number, 261. ἐπιμελητής: C. I. G., 1322=Le Bas 262. ταμίας, *ibid.* ἀγορανόμος: C. I. G., 1393. βουλή: Le Bas 256 a, 257, 258=C. I. G., 1394.

[6] Ἔφοροι at Oitylos: C. I. G., 1323. In Geronthrai: C. I. G., 1334. Le Bas 228 a, b. In Kotyrta: Bull. 9, 242-3. In Epidauros: Ἐφ. ἀρχ., 1884, p. 85-6.

[7] ἔφοροι: Le Bas 242 a, 243, 243 e, five in number 245. *Anc. Inscr.*, 143. ἀγορανόμοι: 241 b, 244. ταμίας: 245. οἱ τῆς πόλεως σύνεδροι: 243 a. βουλή: 244. μεγάλαι ἀπέλλαι: 242 a, 243.

II.

ANTIQUITIES.

1. ELEMENTS OF THE POPULATION.

THE population of Laconia consisted of native serfs and vassals, ruled over by a race of warriors. Bought slaves only existed in isolated cases. Foreigners were as a rule forbidden to settle in the land.¹

A. *The Helots.*

The indigenous serfs of the Lacedæmonian State bore the name
Name. Εἵλωτες, which old historians, following an extremely doubtful etymology, declare almost unanimously to be derived from the town Helos.

To these so-called Helots belonged first of all that portion of the pre-Dorian population of Laconia, which was settled on what was
Place of Abode. afterwards the πολιτικὴ χώρα of the Spartiatai, *i.e.* particularly in the Eurotas valley; and secondly, after the definite subjugation of Messenia, the population of that land also, with the exception of a few coast towns.²

---

¹ *E.g.*, Alcman must have been a slave purchased by Agasidas, if the statement of Heracleid. Pont. *ap.* Müller, *Fr. Hist. Gr.*, 2, 210, 2, 2, is correct. On the exclusion of foreigners from Sparta, cf. Nikol. Damasc. *ap.* Müller, *Fr. Hist.*, 3, 458, 114, 5: ξένοις δ' ἐμβιοῦν οὐκ ἔξεστιν ἐν Σπάρτῃ.

² On the Helots, see Müller, *Dor.*, 2, 28 (29) ff. Kopstadt, *de rer. Lacon. constitution. Lycurg. origine et indole*, pp. 44 sqq. Hellanicos *ap.* Harp., εἱλωτεύειν, Ephoros *ap. Strab.*, 365, and Theopompos *ap. Athen.*, 6, 272 A, derive the name from the town Helos. So also in Apostol., 6, 59=Schol. on *Plat. Alkib.*, 1, 342. Modern authorities generally prefer the derivation from the root Ἑλ, so that Εἵλωτες is made to mean " captives," in support of which may be cited Et. M., εἵλωτες παρὰ Λακεδαιμονίοις εἰ νόθοι οἱ ἐξ αἰχμαλώτων δοῦλοι γινόμενοι. See Müller, *Dor.*, 2, 28 (29); *Proleg.*, 429. Another derivation from ἕλος, which according to Suid.=δίυλον δάσος, according to Et. Gud.=ὑγρὸς καὶ δασὺς τόπος, which makes Εἵλωτες mean the inhabitants of the marshes of the Eurotas. See Lachmann, *d. spart. Staatsverf.*, 113 ff. Kopstadt, whose view Müller adopts, gives on p. 45 ff. a criticism of the various etymologies. The forms

The number of the Helots must have been very considerable, though we cannot estimate it with precision.[1] Their position in the constitution was intermediate between that of the freemen and the slaves. Their position as subjects of the Spartiatæ, like that of the Penestæ, in Thessaly, depended upon certain recognised principles. The essential idea was that the Helots were vassals of the State, and therefore could neither be emancipated by their masters nor be sold off the land. The greater number of them were settled on their masters' estates, which they cultivated.[2]

Legal Status.

This they did on their own account, subject to an annual rent amounting for an estate of the ordinary size to 82 medimnoi of barley, and a corresponding quantity of oil and wine. The master was forbidden to raise this rent at pleasure.[3] Under these circumstances it was possible for the Helots to acquire property of their own.[4] But apart from this special tie of dependency, which united the several Helots to the possessors of the estates which

Εἴλωτες and Εἱλῶται are both found. Theop. *ap.*Athen.,6, 265 B.C. regards the Helots as Achæans; Müller, 2, 29 (31), thinks they are aborigines enslaved even earlier, whom the Dorians took over into their own service. So Kopstadt 47 ff. The Messenians Helots: Theop. *ap.* Athen., 6, 272 A. Thuc., i. 101.

[1] That the number was very great, follows from Thuc. viii. 40: οἱ γὰρ οἰκέται τοῖς Χίοις πολλοὶ ὄντες καὶ μιᾷ γε πόλει πλὴν Λακεδαιμονίων πλεῖστοι γενόμενοι. Büchsenschütz, *Besitz u. Erwerb.*, 138 sqq., shows how uncertain are the numbers given, for example, by Clinton, *Fast. Hellen.*, 421 (Krüger), who estimates them at 170,500, and by Müller, *Dor.*, ii. 41 (45) 224,000.

[2] For the Thessalian Penestæ see Archemach. *ap.*Athen., vi. 264A. Of the Helots, Ephor. *ap. Strabo*, 365, says: τοὺς δὲ Ἑλείους—καὶ κριθῆναι δούλους ἐπὶ τακτοῖς τισιν, ὥστε τὸν ἔχοντα μήτ᾽ ἐλευθεροῦν ἐξεῖναι μήτε πωλεῖν ἔξω τῶν ὅρων τούτους·—τρόπον γάρ τινα δημοσίους δούλους εἶχον οἱ Λακεδαιμόνιοι τούτους, κατοικίας τινὰς αὐτοῖς ἀποδείξαντες καὶ λειτουργίας ἰδίας. Paus., iii. 20, 6, calls the Helots δοῦλοι τοῦ κοινοῦ. Cf. too Livy xxxiv. 27: hi (*i.e.* the Ilotæ) sunt iam inde antiquitus castellani agreste genus. Poll., iii. 83, says: μεταξὺ δὲ ἐλευθέρων καὶ δούλων οἱ Λακεδαιμονίων εἵλωτες.

[3] See Plut., *Lyc.*, 8: ὁ δὲ κλῆρος ἦν ἑκάστου τοσοῦτος, ὥστε ἀποφορὰν φέρειν ἀνδρὶ μὲν ἑβδομήκοντα κριθῶν μεδίμνους, γυναικὶ δὲ δώδεκα, καὶ τῶν ὑγρῶν καρπῶν ἀναλόγως τὸ πλῆθος. *Inst. Lac.* 41: οἱ δὲ εἵλωτες αὐτοῖς εἰργάζοντο τὴν γῆν (ἀποφέροντες) ἀποφορὰν τὴν ἄνωθεν ἱσταμένην. Ἐπάρατον δ᾽ ἦν πλείονός τινα μισθῶσαι, ἵνα ἐκεῖνοι μὲν κερδαίνοντες ἡδέως ὑπηρετῶσιν· οὗτοι δὲ μὴ πλέον ἐπιζητῶσιν. Myron. *ap. Ath.*, xiv. 657D: καὶ παραδόντες αὐτοῖς (τοῖς εἵλωσι) τὴν χώραν ἔταξαν μοῖραν ἣν αὐτοῖς ἀνοίσουσιν ἀεί. Müller's calculation (*Dor.*, ii. 30 [32] ff.) of what would still remain for the Helots themselves after this payment is quite untrustworthy.

[4] Under Cleomenes III. as many as 6,000 Helots possessed at least 5 minæ apiece. Plut., *Cleom.*, 23.

they managed—on the landlord's death they were obliged to observe the usual ceremonies of mourning—any other Spartan who chose, and similarly the State as a whole, could demand the services of the Helots.[1] The latter event took place especially in time of war. Generally the State then employed them as light-armed troops and rowers in the fleet, but during the Peloponnesian war they were repeatedly used as hoplites[2] also.

We may be sure that the Spartan treatment of the Helots was cruel, although later writers perhaps misunderstood some of the facts which they interpreted in this way.[3] The Spartans regarded the Helots as their natural enemies, and treated them accordingly. The Helots saw in the Spartans the men who had suppressed their freedom and nationality, and repaid their hostility with secret hatred and on convenient opportunity with open insurrection.[4]

Treatment of the Helots.

In consequence the Spartans kept a careful watch over the Helots, and showed no hesitation to employ the most cruel measures against them, if they could thus prevent the possibility of their rising. For example, during the Peloponnesian war 2,000 Helots, who had been emancipated for their services in the war,

---

[1] On the funeral ceremonies of the Helots at their master's death see Ælian, *Var. Hist.*, vi. 1. Tyrt. *ap.* Paus., iv. 14, 5. For the employment of Helots belonging to others, Xen., *de Rep. Lac.*, vi. 3: ἡ περὶ τὸ δεῖπνον καὶ ὄψον διακονία, the business of the Helots: Plut., *Comp. of Numa and Lyc.*, 2.

[2] See Hdt. ix. 28 on the battle of Platæa: τούτων δὲ τοὺς πεντακισχιλίους ἐόντας Σπαρτιήτας ἐφύλασσον φιλοὶ τῶν εἱλωτέων πεντακισχίλιοι καὶ τρισμύριοι, περὶ ἄνδρα ἕκαστον ἑπτὰ τεταγμένοι. For the employment of the Helots in the fleet see Xen., *Hell.*, vii. 1, 12; as hoplites, Thuc. iv. 80; vii. 19.

[3] For the position of the Helots in general cf. Theoph. *ap.* Ath., vi. 272 A: τὸ δὲ τῶν εἱλώτων ἔθνος παντάπασιν ὠμῶς διοικεῖται καὶ πικρῶς. Details are given by Myron. *ap.* Ath., xiv. 657 D, where their costume also is described. His account is criticised by Müller, *Dor.*, ii. 35 sqq., [Eng. tr. 2, 37]. On the social injury to the Lacedæmonian State caused by the existence of the Helot class see Oncken, *d. Staatslehre d. Aristot.*, 1, 256 ff.

[4] Spartan mistrust of the Helots: Thuc. iv. 80; v. 14. In the treaty between Athens and Sparta in 421 are the words: ἢν δ' ἡ δουλεία ἐπανιστῆται, ἐπικουρεῖν 'Αθηναίους Λακεδαιμονίοις παντὶ σθένει κατὰ τὸ δυνατόν. See Thuc. v. 23. Precautions of the Spartans against the Helots in camp, Xen., *de Rep. Lac.*, xii. 4. Helot participation in Pausanias' conspiracy, Thuc. i. 132: in Kinadon's Xen. iii. 3, 6. Cf. generally Arist., *Pol.*, ii. 9 = p. 44, 27 sqq., Bekker, and the sentiment shared by all classes in the Lacedæmonian State who were not possessed of full citizen rights: οὐδένα δύνασθαι κρύπτειν τὸ μὴ οὐχ ἡδέως ἂν καὶ ὠμῶν ἐσθίειν αὐτῶν, i.e. τῶν Σπαρτιατῶν. Xen., *Hell.*, iii. 3, 6.

were suddenly put out of the way without leaving any trace, as the narrative of the event significantly expresses it.[1]

Remembering this Spartan act of barbarity, which is perfectly well attested, I feel no hesitation in believing the account of the κρυπτεία, as it was called, for which the original authority was Aristotle. The object of this κρυπτεία was on the one hand to harden the Spartan youths and practise them in actual military service, on the other to keep guard over the Helots, and immediately put down any possible movements they might make for freedom or national existence. Every year the Ephors on entering office inaugurated this κρυπτεία by proclaiming open war against the Helots, in order that no bloodguiltiness might ensue from any murders of Helots which might take place during their tenure of office.[2] Then the Spartan youths of a certain age were sent forth over the country, armed with swords and provided with an adequate supply of food.

During the day they generally kept themselves concealed, in order to observe in secret the proceedings of the Helots. If they believed they had anywhere detected any treasonable plot, they took steps against the Helots involved, and killed them out of hand. It is probable in itself that in such circumstances the suspected were at once regarded as guilty; and whoever considers the treacherous manner in which the Spartans, according to Thucydides, discovered who were the most conceited Helots, in order to kill them afterwards, will not discredit the assertion, resting upon

---

[1] Thuc., iv. 80: ἀεὶ γὰρ τὰ πολλὰ Λακεδαιμονίοις πρὸς τοὺς Εἴλωτας τῆς φυλακῆς περὶ μάλιστα καθεστήκει, where also a case is mentioned of the Spartans having 2,000 hoplites killed. See too Diod., xii. 76.

[2] Plut., Lyc., 28: Ἀριστοτέλης δὲ μάλιστά φησι καὶ τοὺς ἐφόρους, ὅταν εἰς τὴν ἀρχὴν καταστῶσι πρῶτον, τοῖς εἵλωσι καταγγέλλειν πόλεμον, ὅπως εὐαγὲς ᾖ τὸ ἀνελεῖν. Plato, Laws, i. 633, thus describes the κρυπτεία: ἔτι δὲ καὶ κρυπτεία τις ὀνομάζεται θαυμαστῶς πολύπονος πρὸς τὰς καρτερήσεις, χειμώνων τε ἀνυποδησίαι καὶ ἀστρωσίαι καὶ ἄνευ θεραπόντων αὐτοῖς ἑαυτῶν διακονήσεις νύκτωρ τε πλανωμένων διὰ πάσης τῆς χώρας καὶ μεθ' ἡμέραν. Cf. the Schol. on the passage. Müller, Dor., ii. 37 ff., Eng. tr. 2, 41, in his idealized picture of the Lacedæmonian constitution, gives a new interpretation of the passages cited in harmony with Plat., Leg., vi. 763. Hermann, § 47, regards the κρυπτεία as originally designed as a military exercise, and afterwards debased to a system of organized assassination. Schömann, Gk. Antiq., i. 206, regards it as a sort of police duty, but rejects the evidence contained in the following note. Kopstadt, ib., p. 52 ff., upholds this evidence, but refers it to the time subsequent to the 3rd Messenian war.

Aristotle's authority, that in the κρυπτεία the young men killed the strongest and most valiant Helots.[1]

Emancipations of Helots, which could only be granted by the State itself, were not unusual, and were given as rewards for military service and for other services to the State.[2] These emancipated Helots, whose numbers at the end of the fifth century B.C. must have been by no means insignificant, were called νεοδαμώδεις. We are not in a position to say wherein their rights consisted; but among their duties was the obligation to military service, to which they were in an especial degree liable.[3]

νεοδαμώδεις.

Another class of freedmen was formed by those Helots who were brought up as children with their masters' children, and shared in the Spartan ἀγωγή. These freedmen, who perhaps not unfrequently were born of Spartan fathers and Helot mothers, were called μόθακες or μόθωνες. Some of them were actually made Spartan citizens; generally, of course, the

μόθακες.

---

[1] In this way I believe we may interpret the words of Plutarch, *Lyc.*, 28, whose authority is Aristotle: ἦν δὲ τοιαύτη· τῶν νέων οἱ ἄρχοντες διὰ χρόνου τοὺς μάλιστα νοῦν ἔχειν δοκοῦντας εἰς τὴν χώραν ἄλλως ἐξέπεμπον, ἔχοντας ἐγχειρίδια καὶ τροφὴν ἀναγκαίαν, ἄλλο δὲ οὐδέν· οἱ δὲ μεθ' ἡμέραν μὲν εἰς ἀσυνδήλους διασπειρόμενοι τόπους ἀπέκρυπτον ἑαυτοὺς καὶ ἀνεπαύοντο, νύκτωρ δὲ κατιόντες εἰς τὰς ὁδοὺς τῶν εἱλώτων τὸν ἁλισκόμενον ἀπέσφαττον. πολλάκις δὲ καὶ τοὺς ἀγροὺς ἐπιπορευόμενοι τοὺς ῥωμαλεωτάτους καὶ κρατίστους αὐτῶν ἀνῄρουν. Cf. *Heraclid. Pont.*, II. 4, in Müller, *fr. hist. gr.*, ii. 210. Plut., *Cleom.*, 28, speaks of τὸν ἐπὶ τῆς κρυπτείας τεταγμένον. On the treacherous way in which the Helots were treated in the Peloponnesian war, see Thuc. iv. 80.

[2] Cf. Thuc. iv. 80. Xen., *Hell.*, vi. 5, 28. Thuc. iv. 26.

[3] On the νεοδαμώδεις cf. Schömann, *op. ac.*, i. 130 ff. The definition of the νεοδαμώδεις (Thuc. vii. 58, δύναται δὲ τὸ νεοδαμῶδες ἐλεύθερον ἤδη εἶναι) as Dindorf and v. Herwerden saw, was probably not written by Thuc., since the Scholiast, *ad loc.*, to judge by the explanation which he gives, νεοδαμώδης ὁ ἐλεύθερος παρὰ τοῖς Λακεδαιμονίοις, did not find the explanation in Thuc. According to Hesych., δαμώσεις are δημόται ἢ οἱ ἐντελεῖς παρὰ Λάκωσι. Poll. iii. 83, says: τοὺς μέντοι εἰς ἐλευθερίαν τῶν εἱλώτων ἀφιεμένους οἱ Λακεδαιμόνιοι νεοδαμώδεις καλοῦσι. Cf. Hesych., *ad verb.* The νεοδαμώδεις must be distinguished from the Βρασίδειοι, *i.e.*, from the Helots who had fought under Brasidas in his Thracian expedition, and of whom Thuc., v. 34, writes: οἱ Λακεδαιμόνιοι ἐψηφίσαντο τοὺς μὲν μετὰ Βρασίδου Εἵλωτας μαχεσαμένους ἐλευθέρους εἶναι καὶ οἰκεῖν ὅπου ἂν βούλωνται. Cf. Thuc. v. 34, 67. The νεοδαμώδεις employed in war as hoplites: Thuc. vii. 19; viii. 5. Xen. i. 3, 15; iii. 1, 4; 4, 20; v. 2, 24. How considerable their numbers were, can be judged from the fact that Agesilaus led 2,000 of them to Asia. Xen. iii. 4, 2. Plut., *Ages.*, 6.

citizenship was not conferred at once along with freedom.¹ What is told us of yet other classes of freedmen is too doubtful to deserve discussion.²

B. The Perioicoi.

The second class in the Lacedæmonian population consisted of the subjects of the Spartans, who were called Περίοικοι. The rights of Perioicoi were possessed by all the inland towns of the Eurotas valley, and the district adjoining Arcadia on the North, including Skiritis, and lastly the maritime towns from the frontiers of Argolis to Messenia. The inhabitants of these towns were of various origin: in the North, Arcadian; in Messenia, at any rate in part, Dorian; in Kynuria, Ionian; in the remaining inland districts, Achæan. That the number of these towns was considerable may be inferred from the fact that Laconia is called the land of a hundred cities, even if these words are hardly to be taken literally.³ The towns of the

Abode.

Origin.

---

[1] On the μόθακες cf. Schömann, op. ac., i. 127 ff. See Phylarchus ap. Ath., vi. 271 E: εἰσὶ δ' οἱ μόθακες σύντροφοι τῶν Λακεδαιμονίων. ἕκαστος γὰρ τῶν πολιτικῶν παίδων, ὡς ἂν καὶ τὰ ἴδια ἐκποιῶσιν, οἱ μὲν ἕνα οἱ δὲ δύο τινὲς δὲ πλείους ποιοῦνται συντρόφους αὐτῶν. εἰσὶν οὖν οἱ μόθακες ἐλεύθεροι μὲν οὐ μὴν Λακεδαιμόνιοι γε, μετέχουσι δὲ τῆς παιδείας πάσης. τούτων ἕνα φασὶ γενέσθαι καὶ Λύσανδρον τὸν καταναυμαχήσαντα τοὺς Ἀθηναίους πολίτην γενόμενον δι' ἀνδραγαθίαν. Harpocrat.: μόθων—μόθωνας δὲ καλοῦσι Λάκωνες τοὺς παρατρεφομένους τοῖς ἐλευθέροις παῖδας. Similarly Schol. on Arist., Plut., 279. Hesych.: μόθωνας. See also μόθακες. οἱ ἅμα τρεφόμενοι τοῖς υἱοῖς δοῦλοι παῖδες. Etym. Mag.: μόθων, μόθωνος· οὕτω καλοῦσι Λακεδαιμόνιοι τὸν οἰκογενῆ δοῦλον ὃν οἱ Ἀθηναῖοι οἰκότριβά φασι. Acc. to Ælian, Var. Hist., 12, 43, besides Lysandros, Kallikratides also and Gylippos were μόθακες; his explanation of the term is the same as Phylarchos's, but he adds: ὁ δὲ συγχωρήσας τοῦτο Λυκοῦργος τοῖς ἐμμείνασι τῇ τῶν παίδων ἀγωγῇ πολιτείας Λακωνικῆς μεταλαγχάνει. That all the μόθακες were not citizens, as Hermann, Ant. Lac., 132 ff., assumes, is rightly inferred by Schömann, ibid., from Xen., Hell., 5, 3, 8, where by the νόθοι τῶν Σπαρτιατῶν we must understand μόθακες to be meant. Cantarelli, in the Rivista di Filologia, 18, 465 ff., draws a distinction between μόθακες and μόθωνες, viz., that the latter are slaves, the former freemen children of Perioican families. I cannot agree with this. See also von Schoeffer in the Berl. phil. Wochenschr., 1891, 1013 ff.

[2] Cf. the ἐπεύνακτοι of Theopomp. ap. Ath., 6, 271 C, and the enumeration given by Myron ap. Ath., 6, 271 F.

[3] On the Perioicoi cf. Müller, Dor., ii. 16 sqq., Eng. tr., 2, 17; Kopstadt, de rer. Laconicar. constitutionis Lycurgeæ origine et indole, p. 81 ff. In Xen., iii. 5, 7, they are called αἱ περιοικίδες πόλεις. So Ages., ii. 24. According to Thuc. iii. 16, ἡ περιοικίς is the coast land, including the Messenian coast towns, for, according to Paus. iii., 3, 4, the Messenians were Helots, πλὴν οἱ τὰ ἐν τῇ

Perioicoi were in the main seats of trade and industry, and were **Occupation.** the centres of the Laconian manufactures of iron and other commodities much prized in Greek commerce. It is not to be disputed that the Perioicoi also engaged in agriculture, although the tale that Lycurgus assigned 30,000 allotments of land to them is certainly a fiction.[1] Gold and silver, of course, were current in these towns owing to the trade there, and the Perioicoi were also in possession of bought slaves.

Constitutionally the Perioicoi were the subjects of the Spartans. There were gradations of rank among the Perioicoi themselves. **Rights.** Although the towns in all probability retained their own communal administration, yet the Spartans interfered when they chose. Every year Sparta sent the κυθηροδίκης as governor to Cythera; and it has been surmised with some plausibility, on the strength of a passage which gives the number of the Harmosts as fixed at twenty, that these Harmosts acted as Spartan governors in the towns of the Perioicoi.[2] It may possibly be argued from the position of honour held by the Sciritæ on the left wing of the Lacedæmonian line, that there was some diversity in the constitutional position of the several towns, but on this question no certain conclusion can be arrived at.

θαλάσσῃ πολίσματα ἔχοντες, who were Perioicoi, as Thuc. i. 101 says expressly as regards Thyria and Aithaia. Xen. v. 2, 24 distinguishes the Sciritai from the Perioicoi, but perhaps only on account of their honourable position in the Lacedæmonian army. Hdt. vii. 234 speaks of πόλιες πολλαί of the Lacedæmonians. Strabo 362 says: τὸ δὲ παλαιὸν ἑκατόμπολιν φασιν αὐτὴν (i.e. τὴν Λακωνικήν) καλεῖσθαι καὶ τὰ ἑκατόμβαια διὰ τοῦτο θύεσθαι παρ' αὐτοῖς κατ' ἔτος, while he names about 30 towns in his own time. Under Augustus there were 24 towns of the Eleutherolacones: Paus. iii. 21, 6 ff. The expression ἑκατόμπολις Λακωνική is to be compared with Κρήτη ἑκατόμπολις, Hom., Il., ii. 649, which, according to Od., xix. 174, contained only 90 towns. A list of these towns, so far as they are known, is given by Clinton, Fast. Hell., ed. Krüger, 410g.

[1] See Müller, Dor., ii. 21 (24) ff. 30,000 allotments to the Perioicoi by Lycurgus: Plut., Lyc., 8; cf. also Isocr. xii. 179.

[2] The καλοὶ κἀγαθοὶ τῶν περιοίκων, Xen. v. 3, 9. χαριέστατοι τῶν περιοίκων, Plut., Cleom., 11. Only λογάδες of the Perioicoi were hoplites, Her. ix. 11, 29. This diversity of rank within the Perioican communities, assumed by Lachmann, d. spart. Staatsverf., 182, is wrongly denied by Kopstadt, ib. 39. On the political dependence of the Perioicoi cf. the picture, of course overdrawn, of Isocr. xii. 177 ff. His remark, ἔξεστι τοῖς ἐφόροις ἀκρίτους ἀποκτείναι τοσούτους, ὁπόσους ἂν βουληθῶσιν is scarcely to be doubted. The existence of permanent Spartan Harmosts in the Perioican towns has been conjectured from the Schol. on Pind., Ol, vi. 154: ἦσαν δὲ ἁρμοσταὶ Λακεδαιμονίων

One general obligation of all Perioicoi towards the Lacedæmonian state was military service.[1] So early as the battle of Platæa there fought 5,000 hoplites drawn from the Perioicoi, along with 5,000 from the Spartans, and later, as the number of the latter grew smaller continually, the Perioicoi furnished a far larger contingent than they. Moreover they were employed by the Spartans as commanders of divisions, especially in the fleet.[2] The Perioican towns seem further to have been subject to a fixed tribute to the Spartans, as also to the King's tax as it was called, from the royal domains within their boundaries.[3] The relation of the Spartans towards their Perioican subjects was perhaps originally a friendly one; but as time went on the Spartan rule became more and more oppressive.[4]

C. The Spartans.

Over against the Helot serfs and the subject Perioicoi stood the ruling citizen body. Its members, to distinguish themselves

εἴκοσι. The conjecture as to their original character was first made by Schömann, *Ant. iur. publ. Gr.*, p. 113, 5, with whom Haase, in his edition of *Xen. de rep. Lac.*, p. 286, and Arn. Schäfer, *de ephor. Laced.*, p. 12, agree. This was confirmed by an inscription found on Cythera, and dating from somewhere after 370, in which Μένανδρος ἁρμοστήρ is mentioned. See *Mitth. d. dtsch. arch. Inst. in Ath.*, v. 231, 239. The ἄρχων and φρουρά in Thyria in Thuc. iv. 57 was plainly not permanent. For Cythera cf. Thuc. iv. 53: καὶ Κυθηροδίκης ἀρχὴ ἐκ τῆς Σπάρτης διέβαινεν αὐτόσε κατ᾽ ἔτος, ὁπλιτῶν τε φρουρὰν διέπεμπον ἀεὶ καὶ πολλὴν ἐπιμέλειαν ἐποιοῦντο. Hesych.: Κυθηρο(δίκης). ἀρχή τις τὰ ξενικὰ διοικοῦσα.

[1] On the position of honour of the Skiritai, see Thuc. v. 67. Regard for the Amyclæans, Xen. iv. 5, 11.

[2] See Isocr. xii. 180. On the numbers at Platæa cf. Hdt. ix. 28. In the battle of Leuctra of the 1,000 Lacedæmonians who fell 600 were Perioicoi, Xen. vi. 4, 15. Δεινιάδης περίοικος, commander of a fleet, Thuc. viii. 22 cf. also viii. 6.

[3] Strabo, 365, Ἄγιν δὲ τὸν Εὐρυσθένους ἀφελέσθαι τὴν ἰσοτιμίαν καὶ συντελεῖν προστάξαι τῇ Σπάρτῃ. The Messenians when first conquered had to contribute to Sparta according to Tyrt. *ap.* Paus., iv. 14, 5, ἥμισυ παντὸς ὅσον καρπὸν ἄρουρα φέρει. The royal domains in the territories of the Perioicoi, Xen., *de Rep. Lac.*, xv. 3. Cf. Plat., *Alc.*, 123, ἔτι δὲ καὶ ὁ βασιλικὸς φόρος οὐκ ὀλίγος γίγνεται, ὃν τελοῦσιν οἱ Λακεδαιμόνιοι τοῖς βασιλεῦσι.

[4] Cf. Demaratus' opinion of the Perioicoi, Hdt. vii. 234. In the third Messenian War only the two Messenian Perioican towns Aithaia and Thyria revolted from Sparta, Thuc. i. 101. In Xen. iii. 3, 6, it is said with reference to the Perioicoi also as well as the Helots, ὅπου γὰρ ἐν τούτοις τις λόγος γένοιτο περὶ Σπαρτιατῶν, οὐδένα δύνασθαι κρύπτειν τὸ μὴ οὐχ ἡδέως ἂν καὶ ὠμῶν ἐσθίειν αὐτῶν. On the behaviour of the Perioicoi during the Theban invasions of Laconia, cf. Xen. vi. 5, 25, 32, vii. 2, 2; Plut., *Ages.*, 32.

from the rest of the population of Laconia, called themselves Σπαρ-τιᾶται, after the town Sparta, which they inhabited, while the official title of the State as such when opposed to other States was οἱ Λακεδαιμόνιοι.[1] The land immediately belonging to Sparta was identical with the districts peopled by the Helots, as before mentioned, and accordingly embraced the inland region between Parnon and Taygetos, bounded on the North by the stream of Pellene, and by Sellasia, and reaching on the South as far as Cape Malea (excluding however the Perioican towns lying within those boundaries); finally after the conquest of Messenia the greater part of that country.[2] In historical times the number of the Spartans was constantly diminishing. While we are informed of the existence of 8,000 Spartans as late as the Persian wars, their number in B.C. 371 barely exceeded 1,500. Aristotle reckons the number of Spartans in his own day at not quite 1,000, and at the accession of Agis IV. (244/3) there remained only 700.[3] It was natural that in view of this continual diminution of the Spartan population, the care of the State was in a very special degree directed to check it as far as possible. It is to

Σπαρτιᾶται.

Dwelling.

Numbers.

---

[1] That οἱ Λακεδαιμόνιοι denotes the Lacedæmonian State as such is shown by the documents in Thuc. v. 18, 23. While Herodotus still calls the Lacedæmonian State οἱ Λακεδαιμόνιοι and οἱ Σπαρτιᾶται, in Thuc. (with the exception of the episode, i. 128-134), and in Xen. also the Spartans as a political whole are regularly οἱ Λακεδαιμόνιοι, the individual as a member of the Spartan State opposed to the Perioicoi ὁ Σπαρτιάτης, in opposition to the citizens of other States ὁ Λακεδαιμόνιος. Οἱ Λακεδαιμόνιοι are the Spartans, and Perioicoi. Cf. Thuc. iv. 8, iv. 53; Xen. vi. 4, 15, vii. 4, 27.

[2] The boundaries of the χώρα πολιτική given in the text are those specified in the ῥήτρα of Agis, who in all probability wished to re-establish the earlier condition of affairs. See Plut., *Ag.*, 8; Müller, *Dor.*, ii. 43 (46).

[3] I disregard the statement in Isocr. xii. 255, according to which at the immigration into Laconia there were only 2,000 Spartans, that of Arist., *Pol.*, ii. 9, p. 47, 11, who gives 10,000 Spartans for the time of the first kings, and that in Plut., *Lyc.*, 8, about the 9,000 Spartan κλῆροι. 8,000 Spartans in the time of the Persian wars, Hdt. vii. 234. At the battle of Leuctra the 4 Spartan Morai engaged in the battle contained 700 Spartans of all ages up to 55. This gives for the whole 6 Morai, 1,050 Spartans between the ages of 20 and 55. See Xen. vi. 1, 1; vi. 4, 15 and 17. Accordingly, I have assumed 1,500 as the entire number of adult Spartans. Cf. Xen., *Ages.*, ii. 24, καὶ αὐτῶν Σπαρτιατῶν οὐ μειόνων ἀπολωλότων ἐν τῇ ἐν Λεύκτροις μάχῃ ἢ λειπομένων. Not 1,000 in Aristotle's day: Arist., *Pol.*, ii. 9, p. 47, 5. 700 at Agis IV.'s accession: Plut., *Ag.*, 5. Many Spartans perished in the earthquake B.C. 465: Diod. xi. 63, xv. 66, Plut., *Cim.*, 16.

this design that we must attribute the special privileges which in Aristotle's day were guaranteed to the father of three or more sons. We can discern it also in the fact that the man who either did not marry at all, or married too late, or made a bad choice of a wife, was punished.¹

The full rights of a citizen depended at Sparta not only on birth but on other conditions. Thus, apart from the question of birth, only those could be full citizens who had gone through the Spartan training, and only those remained full citizens who participated in the Syssitia and made the regular contributions to them.² Those who by satisfying these two requirements were in possession of the full rights of citizens, were all equally privileged and therefore were called ὅμοιοι.³ Those who did not fulfil the two re-

Conditions of citizenship.

ὅμοιοι.

---

¹ See Arist., *Pol.*, ii. 9, p. 47, 18 Bekker: ἔστι γὰρ αὐτοῖς νόμος τὸν μὲν γεννήσαντα τρεῖς υἱοὺς ἄφρουρον εἶναι, τὸν δὲ τέτταρας ἀτελῆ πάντων. Cf. Ælian, *Var. Hist.*, vi. 6. Δίκη ἀγαμίου, ὀψιγαμίου, κακογαμίου, Plut., *Lys.*, 30, *de amor. prol.*, 2; Poll. iii. 48, viii. 40. ἀτιμία of the unmarried, Plut., *Lyc.*, 15, *Apophth. Lac.*, p. 280, 14 Didot. In this connexion should be noticed also the customs which obtained concerning the begetting of offspring. See Xen., *de Rep. Lac.*, i. 7 ff., Plut., *Lyc.*, 15.

² See Plut., *Instit. Lacon.*, 21, τῶν πολιτῶν ὃς ἂν μὴ ὑπομείνῃ τὴν τῶν παίδων ἀγωγήν, οὐ μετεῖχε τῶν τῆς πόλεως δικαίων. See Xen., *de Rep. Lac.*, x. 7. The statement in Plut., *Inst. Lacon.*, 22, ἔνιοι δ' ἔφασαν ὅτι καὶ τῶν ξένων ὃς ἂν ὑπομείνῃ ταύτην τὴν ἄσκησιν τῆς πολιτείας κατὰ τὸ βούλημα τοῦ Λυκούργου μετεῖχε τῆς ἀρχῆθεν διατεταγμένης μοίρας· πωλεῖν δ' οὐκ ἐξῆν, I refer to the old days, when, according to Arist., *Pol.*, ii. 9, p. 47, 9 Bekker, λέγουσι δ' ὡς ἐπὶ μὲν τῶν προτέρων βασιλέων μετεδίδοσαν τῆς πολιτείας, strangers received the citizenship. L. Weber, *Quæst. Lacon. capita duo*, pp. 21/2, Gött., 1887, takes another view, but without convincing me. The ξένοι τῶν τροφίμων καλουμένων in Xen., *Hell.*, v. 3, 9, are plainly not Spartan citizens. Plutarch's statement in the pretended letter of Herakleitos in Boissonade, *Eunap.*, p. 425, is senselessly exaggerated. For the obligation of a citizen to share in the Syssitia, see Arist., *Pol.*, ii. 9, p. 49, 25 Bekker: μετέχειν μὲν γὰρ (τῶν συσσιτίων) οὐ ῥᾴδιον τοῖς λίαν πένησιν, ὅρος δὲ τῆς πολιτείας οὗτός ἐστιν αὐτοῖς ὁ πάτριος, τὸν μὴ δυνάμενον τοῦτο τὸ τέλος φέρειν μὴ μετέχειν αὐτῆς.

³ The ὅμοιοι, who, according to Arist., *Pol.*, viii. (v.) 7, p. 207, 22, already existed at the time of the first Messenian War (what Hermann, *Antiqu. Lac.*, p. 127, says on the meaning of ὅμοιοι in that place is mere arbitrary assertion), are mentioned in five places, while in a sixth, Dem. xx. 107, it is doubtful whether the word is used in a definite technical sense. See Schömann, *op. ac.*, i. 112 ff. Of the 5 other passages Xen., *Hell.*, iii. 3, 5, *de Rep. Lac.*, xiii. 1 and 7, tell us nothing as to the *special* meaning of ὅμοιοι. On the other hand, Xen., *de Rep. Lac.*, x. 7 (see too *Anab.*, iv. 6, 14) shows that their position depended on their education. Accordingly, Hermann, *Antiq. Lac.*, p. 148 (cf. his entire account 111 ff.), defined the ὅμοιοι as

quirements above mentioned lost the political, though probably
ὑπομείονες. they retained the civil, rights of citizenship. The
ὑπομείονες mentioned by only one authority in all
probability denoted this class of citizens.[1] This division of the
citizens is distinct from the division into nobles and δημόται, the
first of whom only were permitted to become members of the
Council of the Elders.[2]

The political classification of the citizens was twofold. First,
Political we must suppose that the three Dorian tribes, as they
Classification. were called, Ὑλλεῖς, Δυμᾶνες, and Πάμφυλοι, had existed at least in the earlier days of Sparta, although we can find
no precise statement to that effect.[3] The second division of the

in the text. At the same time he identifies them with Aristotle's καλοὶ
κἀγαθοί, but this supposition is refuted by Xen., *Hell.*, iii. 3, 5, according to
whom the ὅμοιοι are identical with the Σπαρτιᾶται, among whom Aristotle's
δῆμος was undoubtedly included. See Schömann, *op. cit.*, p. 138 ff. Kopstadt,
de rer. Laconicar. constitution. Lycurg. origine et indole, 87 ff., regards the
ὅμοιοι as the full citizens, who alone belonged to the hereditary tribes of
the Hylleis Dymanes and Pamphyloi, while the new citizens, the ὑπομείονες, were placed in the local Phylai. Lachmann, *d. Spart. Staatsverf.*
222 ff. explains the ὅμοιοι as Spartan nobles.

[1] The assertion of Teles *ap.* Stob. Flor., xl. 8, τὸν δὲ μὴ ἐμμείναντα (τῇ
ἀγωγῇ), κἂν ἐξ αὐτοῦ τοῦ βασιλέως, εἰς τοὺς εἵλωτας ἀποστέλλουσι καὶ τῆς πολιτείας
ὁ τοιοῦτος οὐ μετέχει is of course exaggerated to contrast effectively with the
context. That the Spartans with incomplete rights were styled ὑπομείονες
is a conjecture made as early as Cragius, *de Rep. Lac.*, i. 10, on the strength
of Xen., *Hell.*, iii. 3, 6, where they are distinguished from the Helots,
Neodamodes, and Perioicoi. Herm., *loc. cit.*, regards the ὑπομείονες as the
same as Aristotle's δῆμος (see also Kopstadt, *op. cit.*, 83). Schömann, p. 138 ff.,
thinks they were citizens with fewer rights, Dorians, who had originally been settlers in Perioican States. Rieger, *de ordinum homœorum et
hypomeionum qui apud Lacedæmonios fuerunt origine*, Giessen, 1858, 11 ff.,
believes them to be μόθακες and their descendants.

[2] On the difference in rights between the καλοὶ κἀγαθοί and the δῆμος see
Arist., *Pol.*, ii. 9, p. 48, 5 ff. From among the nobles were taken, so it seems, not
only the Gerontes, but also certain functionaries, *e.g.* the Paidonomos. Cf.
Plut. *Lyc.*, 17 with Xen., *de Rep. Lac.*, ii. 2. According to Schömann, op.
cit. p. 138 ff., the distinction between them was not *de iure* but merely *de
facto*. On the existence of nobles and inferiors see 12 ff.

[3] My present view, which is in opposition to that expressed in my *Stud.
z. alt. spart. Gesch.*, p. 142 ff., is an inference from the inscription found in
Thera : Ὑλλέων Νύμφαι. See *Mitth. d. dtsch. arch. inst. in Ath.*, ii. 78. As the
Ὑλλεῖς are found in the Spartan colony of Thera, we must suppose them to
have existed in the mother State too. On the existence of 3 Dorian Phylai
in other Dorian States see Müller, *Dor.*, ii. 70 (76) ff. A list of the older conjectures about the Spartan Phylai is given by Kopstadt, *de rer. Laconicar.
Constitution. Lycurg. origine et indole*, p. 65 ff.

citizens, which dates from the time of the composition of the so-called Lycurgean ῥήτρα, was a local division. The entire body of Spartan citizens was distributed among a certain number of local Phylai,—how many, we do not know. Among these we may reckon with tolerable certainty the Πιτανᾶται, Μεσοᾶται, Λιμναεῖς, and Κυνοουρεῖς, so called from Πιτάνη, Μεσόα, Λίμναι or Λιμναῖον, and Κυνόουρα, districts of Sparta. A fifth local Phyle in all likelihood is Δύμη.[1]

These Phylai, which lasted down into the Christian era, were divided again into several sub-divisions. This can be proved for the Christian period, in which we hear of the Κροτανοὶ as a subdivision of the Πιτανᾶται.[2] It would be natural to identify these sub-divisions of the Phylai with the Obai already spoken of in the Lycurgean ῥήτρα, and mentioned also in later inscriptions, were it not that in an inscription dating from the first or second century B.C. we find an ὠβὰ τῶν Ἀμυκλαιέων, which tempts us to suppose that in the Obai we must recognise a local division of the country not of the town Sparta. The statement of nearly the same date as the above-mentioned inscription, made by Demetrius of Skepsis to the effect that there were in Sparta 27 Phratries and probably 9 Phylai (if its authority can be used for the earlier days of Sparta —and against this no argument of weight can be adduced), not

---

[1] The Lycurgean ῥήτρα ap. Plut., Lyc., 6, φυλὰς φυλάξαντα καὶ ὠβὰς ὠβάξαντα undoubtedly refers to a local classification. See also K. Fr. Hermann, Ant. Lac., p. 46, n. 144. A collection of the earlier hypotheses about these Phylai may be found in Kopstadt, op. cit., 74 ff. While the other Phylai are only mentioned in late writers and inscriptions, Hdt. iii. 55 knows of the deme Πιτάνη. Its existence at the time of the founding of Tarentum, where Polybius, viii. 35, tells us many names indicated the connection with Sparta, is shown by Tarentine coins with the superscription Πιτανατᾶν περιπόλων. See Millingen, Anc. Coins, I. 1, 19, p. 13. By analogy we may suppose the rest of the Phylai to be equally old. Paus. iii. 16, 9 names the four Phylai together. Πιτάνη, C. I. G., 1425, 1426. Hesych., sub verb. Schol. Thuc. i. 20. Μεσόα, C. I. G., 1338. Steph. ad verb. Λίμναι (Strab. 363) or Λιμναῖον (Paus. iii. 16, 7). Λιμναέων φυλὴ, C. I. G., 1377, cf. 1241, 1243. Κυνόσουρα or Κυνοσουρίς in Hesych. Schol. Callimach. hymn. in Dian., 94; in Inscrr. φυλὴ Κυνοουρέων, C. I. G., 1347, 1272, 1386. Δύμη, according to Hesych., ἐν Σπάρτῃ φυλὴ καὶ τόπος. See Böckh in C. I. G., I. p. 609. Bergk in Phil., xii. p. 579, no. 23, assumes as a fifth κώμη of Sparta Θόρναξ, after Strabo 364, where he wishes to read: Μεσσόαν δ' οὐ τῆς χώρας εἶναι μέρος, ἀλλὰ τῆς Σπάρτης καθάπερ καὶ τὸ Λιμναῖον καὶ τὸν Θόρνακα.

[2] See Paus., iii. 14, 2, καὶ πλησίον ὀνομαζομένη λέσχη Κροτανῶν· εἰσὶ δ' οἱ Κροτανοὶ Πιτανατῶν 'μοῖρα. Λέσχαι are mentioned in Plut., Lyc., 16, 25, as meeting places of the φυλέται.

only supplies direct evidence as to the political classification of the citizens, but also gives us the Phratries as a sub-division of the Phyle in place of the doubtful Obai. However we must refrain from giving a definite opinion as to the nature of the ὠβά until the possible discovery of new inscriptions provides decisive information.[1]

2. THE GOVERNMENT.

A. The Kings.[2]

Royalty was represented at Sparta by a dual kingship, which was hereditary in the two families of the Agiads and Eurypontids.

Royal Families. Of these two families the former had the precedence in rank, but we cannot point to any distinction between the constitutional rights of the two.[3]

The right to the throne passed to the eldest son of the reigning prince, or, if he had had sons before his own accession and another

Succession. or several other sons were born afterwards, to the eldest born while his father was on the throne. But it was requisite that the heir should be born of a Spartan mother,

---

[1] In the Lycurgean ῥήτρα we read ὠβὰς ὠβάξαντα. Plut., *Lyc.*, 6. As to the etymological meaning of ὠβά see Curtius, *Grundz. d. griech. Etym.*,[2] p. 517. Curtius derives ὠβά from the root ΟϜ=ΑϜ(ἰαύω, I sleep), corresponding to the derivation of κώμη from κεῖσθαι. Hesych. ὠβαί (ὦβοι) τόποι μεγαλομερεῖς. ὡς τὰς κώμας. ὠγὴ κώμη. οὐαὶ φυλαί, Κύπριοι. We learn of the ὠβὰ τῶν Ἀμυκλαιέων from a newly discovered inscription. See *Mitth. d. dtsch. arch. Inst. in Ath.*, iii. 165. Whether there was a connexion between φυλή and ὠβά, cannot be decided with certainty from C. I. G., 1272, 1273, 1274. The existence of 27 φρατρίαι follows from Demetrius of Skepsis' description of the Carneia *ap.* Athen., iv. 141 E, F.

[2] For the Spartan kings, see Müller, *Dor.*, 2, 93 (100) ff.; Kopstadt, *de rer. Laconicar. constit. Lyc. origine et indole*, 94 ff.; Gabriel, *de magistratib. Lacedæmoniorum*, Berlin, 1845, p. 1 ff. Auerbach, *de Lacedæmoniorum regibus*, Berlin, 1863.

[3] The mythical ancestors of the two royal houses at Sparta were for the Agiads, Eurystheus or Eurysthenes, for the Eurypontids Procles. Both families traced their descent from Heracles through these ancestors. The official legend may be seen in Hdt. 6, 52, cf. 4, 147. Ἡρακλέης Γενάρχα in a late inscr., C. I. G., 1446. Other Spartiatai besides the two οἰκίαι βασιλικαί belonged to the γένος of the Heracleidæ. See Plut., *Lys.*, 2, 24, Diod. 11, 50. Attempts to explain why, in spite of the names of their ancestors, the royal families were called Agiads and Eurypontids, will be found in Ephor. *ap.* Strab., 366; Plut., *Lys.*, 2; *Apophth. Plistarch.*, i. p. 285 Didot. Paus. 3, 7, 1. See the author's *Stud. z. altspart. Gesch.*, p. 23 ff. The Eurypontids are styled οἰκίη ὑποδεεστέρη by Hdt. 6, 51, with the addition: κατὰ πρεσβυγένειαν δέ κως τετίμηται μᾶλλον ἡ (οἰκίη) Εὐρυσθένεος.

and since he had priestly functions to perform, that he should be free from serious bodily defects.¹ If there were no sons, or if the sons were disqualified for the reasons mentioned, then the next male agnate of the king succeeded; if the heir was a minor, the next male agnate of full age undertook his guardianship as πρόδικος, and during that time carried on the government.² If the legitimacy of the heir were challenged from any quarter, or if claims to the crown were made by several parties, the decision rested with the whole body of Spartiatai.³ The heir presumptive was exempt from the Spartan Agoge.⁴ The official title of the Spartan kings appears to have been ἀρχαγέται or βαγοί.⁵

Royalty at Sparta was richer in honours than in rights. Its possessors were regarded as heroes, and to lay hands on them was a serious offence.⁶ As to the honours and emoluments of the kings, they were in the first place supplied

Perogatives of the Kings.

---

¹ The definite statement of the rules of succession is given by Hdt. 7, 3: ἐπεί γε καὶ ἐν Σπάρτῃ ἔφη ὁ Δημάρητος ὑποτιθέμενος οὕτω νομίζεσθαι ἦν οἱ μὲν προγεγονότες ἔωσι πρὶν ἢ τὸν πατέρα σφέων βασιλεῦσαι, ὁ δὲ βασιλεύοντι ὀψίγενος ἐπιγένηται, τοῦ ἐπιγενομένου τὴν ἔκδεξιν τῆς βασιληίης γίνεσθαι, which is not contradicted by Hdt. 5, 42; 6, 52. Heidtmann in the *Jahrb. f. cl. Philol.*, 1883, pp. 255/6 doubts—I think, unreasonably—the genuineness of Hdt. 7, 3. That the mother of the heir presumptive must be a Spartan, I infer from Plut., *Ag.*, 11. The χρησμολόγος Diopeithes pronounced that it was not right for a lame man to be king in Sparta; still in spite of that Agesilaos became king. Plut., *Ages.*, 3; Xen., *Hell.*, 3, 3, 3.

² See Corn. Nep., *Ages.*, I. sin is (qui regnans decessisset) virilem sexum non reliquisset, tum deligebatur, qui proximus esset propinquitate. Cf. Xen. 3, 3, 2. The guardian of the infant king was called πρόδικος: Plut., *Lyc.*, 3; Xen., *Hell.*, 4, 2, 9. The regent was also called βασιλεύς. Cf. Hdt. 9, 76 with 10. Examples of regencies in Hdt., *loc. cit.*; Thuc. 1, 132; 1, 107; Diod. 11, 79; Thuc. 3, 26; Xen. 4, 2, 9. Cf. Gabriel, *de magistrat. Lacedæmonior.*, p. 29 ff.

³ For the first case cf. the example of Demaratos Hdt. 6, 65/6, and of Leotychidas, Xen. 3, 3, 1 ff.; for the second that of Kleonymos and Areus, Paus. 3, 6, 2, who makes the Gerousia the deciding tribunal.

⁴ This may be inferred from Plut., *Ages.*, 1.

⁵ The title ἀρχαγέται is given by the so-called Lycurgean Rhetra in Plut., *Lyc.*, 6; the title βαγὸς by the gloss of Hesych., which however is not altogether above suspicion: βαγὸς—καὶ βασιλεὺς καὶ στρατηγός. Λάκωνες. Βαγὸς according to Boeckh in C. I. G., I. p. 83, and Ross, *alte lokr. Inschr.*, p. 20, is to be derived from ἄγω with the Digamma.

⁶ See Xen., *de rep. Lac.*, 15, 9: αἱ δὲ τελευτήσαντι τιμαὶ βασιλεῖ δέδονται, τῇδε βούλονται δηλοῦν οἱ Λυκούργου νόμοι, ὅτι οὐχ ὡς ἀνθρώπους ἀλλ' ὡς ἥρωας τοὺς Λακεδαιμονίων βασιλεῖς προτετιμήκασιν. Plut., *Ages.*, 19, 9: οὐ θεμιτὸν οὐδὲ νενομισμένον βασιλέως σώματι τὰς χεῖρας προσφέρειν; cf. 21. This perhaps was the reason why condemned kings were, as a rule, allowed to go into exile.

with food at the State expense; if they attended the Syssitia they received a double portion; if they stayed at home, a specified quantity of bread and wine was sent to them.[1] Further, the kings possessed very considerable domains, within the district belonging to the Perioicoi; and the Perioicoi had to pay what was called the king's tax to the occupants of the throne for the cultivation and use of these lands.[2] Moreover the kings received as a share of honour a third of the booty, the hides, and in the field the back also of the beasts sacrificed, and out of every litter of pigs a porker. Whoever prepared a public sacrifice, had first to invite the kings, who on these occasions too received a double portion. At the public games the kings had places of honour, and everybody except the ephors had to rise from his seat before them.[3]

But the dignity of the kings showed itself most of all in the manner of their burial. When a king died, horsemen announced
Funeral of the Kings. his death through all Laconia, and in Sparta itself women went about beating brazen cymbals. Instantly, in every Spartan house two free persons, a man and a woman, had to put on mourning. From all Laconia came Perioicoi and Helots in great numbers to Sparta, to wail when the corpse was carried out, praising the dead king as the best that had ever ruled. If the king had died in the field, and his body had not been brought home to Sparta, an image of him was carried out on a beautiful ornamented bier, and, as though it were the body itself, was laid in the tomb of the Agiadai or the Eurypontides, according to the family of the dead man. The national mourning continued for ten days after the burial, and during that time the market was

[1] Cf. Xen., *Hell.*, 5, 3, 20: συσκηνοῦσι μὲν γὰρ δὴ βασιλεῖς ἐν τῷ αὐτῷ, ὅταν οἴκοι ὦσιν, paraphrased in Plut.,*Ages.*,20: συσσιτοῦσι γὰρ οἱ βασιλεῖς εἰς τὸ αὐτὸ φοιτῶντες φιδίτιον ὅταν ἐπιδημῶσιν. That they might also dine at home is plain from Hdt. 6, 57. For their διμοιρία and σύσκηνοι see Xen., *de rep. Lac.*, 15, 4; *Ages.*, 5; Hdt. 6, 57.

[2] See Xen., *de rep. Lac.*, 15, 3: καὶ γῆν δὲ ἐν πολλαῖς τῶν περιοίκων πόλεων ἀπέδειξεν ἐξαίρετον τοσαύτην, ὥστε μήτε δεῖσθαι τῶν μετρίων μήτε πλούτῳ ὑπερφέρειν. According to Plut., *Alcib.*, 1, 123, the Spartan kings are the wealthiest of the Hellenes: ἔκ τε γὰρ τῶν τοιούτων μέγισται λήψεις καὶ πλεῖσταί εἰσι τοῖς βασιλεῦσιν, ἔτι δὲ καὶ ὁ βασιλικὸς φόρος οὐκ ὀλίγος γίγνεται, ὃν τελοῦσιν οἱ Λακεδαιμόνιοι τοῖς βασιλεῦσι. Agis IV., before his attempt at reform, possssessed, besides a considerable landed estate, 600 talents in specie, Plut., *Ag.*, 9. The tribute of the Perioicoi was probably paid in money. See Auerbach, *op. cit.*, p. 52.

[3] For these various honours and emoluments of the kings, cf. Phylarch. ap. Polyb., 2, 62; Hdt. 6, 56-7; Xen., *de rep. Lac.*, 15, 3-6.

closed and public business ceased.¹ Only after this ten days' mourning did the king's successor enter on his reign with special festivities and sacrifices. He forgave at his accession all debts which were owing from individual Spartans to the king or the State.²

Originally, of course, the Lacedæmonian kings exercised the same functions as the Homeric, *i.e.* they were high-priests, supreme judges, and generals-in-chief; but in course of time their rights in all these directions were diminished. **Religious Functions.** As high priests the kings offered the sacrifices for the State, among which must be included the specially mentioned offerings to Apollo on the first and seventh days of each month. In the field the priestly powers of the kings were called into requisition no less than their generalship. Before the expedition set out, the king who was leading the army sacrificed to Zeus Agetor, at the frontier to Zeus and Athene; and similarly, during the campaign generally, the king had full power to offer all sacrifices, for which the State supplied him victims. Among the king's priestly functions must also be included the custom by which each of them selected two men, called Πύθιοι, to act as intermediaries in their dealings with Delphi, and take charge of the oracles received. In all probability the special priesthoods of Zeus Lacedaimon and Uranios were filled by the kings, for those two divinities were their family gods.³

---

¹ Cf. the description in Hdt. 6, 58; Paus. 4, 14, 4; Herakleid. Pont. *ap.* Müller, *fr. hist. gr.*, 2, p. 210, 5, differs from Hdt.: ὅταν δὲ τελευτήσῃ βασιλεύς, τρεῖς ἡμέρας οὐδὲν πωλεῖται καὶ ἀχύροις ἡ ἀγορὰ καταπάσσεται. The body of a king who died abroad was generally brought back to Sparta. Cf. Plut., *Ages.*, 40; Xen., *Hell.*, 5, 3, 19. The τάφοι of the Agiadai in Pitane, Paus. 3, 14, 2; those of the Eurypontides at the end of Aphetais, Paus 3, 12, 8. With the splendour of the king's funeral is to be compared the simplicity of ordinary burials. See Plut., *Lyc.*, 27.

² See Hdt. 6, 59: ἐπεὰν ἀποθανόντος τοῦ βασιλέος ἄλλος ἐνίστηται βασιλεύς, οὗτος ὁ ἐσιὼν ἐλευθεροῖ ὅστις τι Σπαρτιητέων τῷ βασιλέϊ ἢ τῷ δημοσίῳ ὤφειλε. Plut., *Ag.*, 13, mentions bonds, called κλάρια. The accession took place according to Xen., *Hell.*, 3, 3, 1, ἐπεὶ ὡσιώθησαν αἱ ἡμέραι. Thuc. 5, 16 must be explained by the fact that χοροί and θυσίαι were usual at the accession of the kings.

³ See Xen., *Hell.*, 3, 3, 4: θύοντος αὐτοῦ ('Αγησιλάου) τῶν τεταγμένων τινὰ θυσιῶν ὑπὲρ τῆς πόλεως. Sacrifice on the νουμηνία and the ἑβδόμῃ: Hdt. 6, 57. On the sacrifices in time of war, see Xen., *de rep. Lac.*, 13, 2 ff., 8, 11; Hdt. 6, 56. For the Πύθιοι, Hdt. 6, 57. Suid. *sub verb.* Plut., *Pelop.*, 21; Xen., *de rep. Lac.*, 15, 5. For their special priesthood of Ζεὺς Λακεδαίμων and Οὐράνιος, cf. Hdt. 6, 56 and the author's *Stud.*, p. 62 ff. Arist., *Pol.*, 3, 14 = p. 84, 20, says of the Spartan kings, ἔτι δὲ τὰ πρὸς τοὺς θεοὺς ἀποδέδοται τοῖς βασιλεῦσιν.

The independent judicial powers of the kings were of but little importance after the greater part of the civil jurisdiction had been **Judicial Functions.** transferred to the Ephors. The criminal jurisdiction, too, except in the very earliest times, was exercised by the Council of Elders. However, the kings undertook the decision of διαδικασίαι for the hands of heiresses, and in general all cases involving family rights; adoptions too took place before them. Further, they decided all cases which related to the public streets, and their delimitation from private property, which might often be a matter of dispute.[1]

But it was in their character of commanders-in-chief that the Lacedæmonian kings retained the greatest power and most privi- **Functions as Generals.** leges. They discharged this office in common until 510, when a law was made that only one king at a time might henceforth lead the army to war. According to Aristotle the Lacedæmonian kingship was an autocratic generalship with an unlimited term of office. Even in Herodotus' time the kings had nominally the right to begin war against any they chose, and whoever interfered with them in this was guilty of a grave offence. They were, however, liable to be called to account for their military undertakings when they were ended; and they therefore generally secured themselves by previously obtaining the consent of the Ephors and the Apella. Thus it was quite in accordance with the actual position of the kings, when in the 4th century they were only left the right of leading the army whither the State itself despatched it.[2] In the field the kings had un-

---

[1] See Hdt. 6, 57 : δικάζειν δὲ μούνους τοὺς βασιλέας τοσάδε μοῦνα· πατρούχου τε παρθένου πέρι, ἐς τὸν ἱκνέεται ἔχειν, ἢν μή περ ὁ πατὴρ αὐτήν ἐγγυήσῃ, καὶ ὁδῶν δημοσιέων πέρι· καὶ ἤν τις θετὸν παῖδα ποιέεσθαι ἐθέλῃ, βασιλέων ἐναντίον ποιέεσθαι. I give καὶ ὁδῶν δημοσιέων πέρι in accordance with Stein's explanation, ad loc.

[2] After 510 only one king with an army. Hdt. 5, 75; Xen., Hell., 5, 3, 10; Arist., Pol., 3, 14 = p. 84, 21, says: αὕτη μὲν οὖν ἡ βασιλεία οἷον στρατηγία τις αὐτοκράτωρ καὶ ἀΐδιός ἐστιν. Isocr. 3, 24; Hdt. 6, 56: καὶ πόλεμόν γε ἐκφέρειν ἐπ' ἥν ἂν βούλωνται χώρην, τούτου δὲ μηδένα εἶναι Σπαρτιητέων διακωλυτήν, εἰ δὲ μή, αὐτὸν ἐν τῷ ἀγεΐ ἐνέχεσθαι. Cleomenes I. still began all his wars at his own pleasure, and even in the time of Xenophon the kings seem still to have had the right to begin war and undertake expeditions on their own authority. Xen., Hell., 5, 1, 34; 2, 2, 7; 4, 7, 1; cf. too Thuc. 8, 5. But Xen., de rep. Lac., 15, 2, only attributes to the kings the right στρατιάν, ὅποι ἂν ἡ πόλις ἐκπέμπῃ, ἡγεῖσθαι. Dum, Entsteh. u. Entwickel. d. spart. Ephorats, p. 58 ff., 141 ff. Punishment of the kings for military expeditions badly carried out: Thuc. 5, 63. Xen., Hell., 3, 5, 25; Plut., Lys., 30. For the king's rights in time of war, see Dum, op. cit., p. 151 ff.

restricted power of life and death; all operations and movements depended upon their decision. The two Ephors, who accompanied the king on a campaign, had no voice officially in any matter.[1] The king's military powers were, however, seriously curtailed, by the independent commands occasionally given to ordinary Spartans, and by the creation of the Nauarchia.[2]

At the time of the matured ephorate the kings' influence on the government and administration of the State was not great, although it varied of course with the personal consideration in which the wearer of the crown for the time being was held. It is true the kings had a seat and a voice in the Council of the Elders, and might exercise a certain influence within that body; but they had lost their commanding position at the head of affairs, when the Ephors became the State executive.[3] *Their Position generally.*

B. The Council of Elders.[4]

The Lacedæmonian Council of Elders is called γερουσία in the so-called Lycurgean Rhetra in the form in which we have it handed down to us. Its members are described as πρεσβυγενεῖς in King Theopompos' law on the competence of the Apella. In later times its name seems to have been γεροντία or γερωχία.[5] In historical times *Name. Number.*

---

[1] Arist., *Pol.*, 3, 14 = p. 84, 9 says of the Spartan king: ὅταν ἐξέλθῃ τὴν χώραν, ἡγεμών ἐστι τῶν πρὸς τὸν πόλεμον '—κτεῖναι γὰρ οὐ κύριος, εἰ μὴ καθάπερ ἐπὶ τῶν ἀρχαίων ἐν ταῖς πολεμικαῖς ἐξόδοις ἐν χειρὸς νόμῳ. Cf. Thuc. 5, 66. Xen., *de rep. Lac.* 13, 10. For the two Ephors in the camp, Xen., *op. cit.*, 13, 5. *Hell.*, 2, 4, 36. The 10 σύμβουλοι, who were given Agis in 418, were plainly only a transitory institution. Thuc. 5, 63. The 30 σύμβουλοι, who from the 4th century onwards accompanied the kings on their more distant expeditions, formed their staff, without diminishing the military autocracy of the kings. Plut., *Ages.*, 6, 36. *Lys.*, 23. Xen., *Ages.*, 1, 7; *Hell.*, 3, 4, 2. 20; 5, 3, 8. Diod., 14, 79.

[2] Arist., *Pol.*, 2, 9 = pp. 49, 30, says, ἐπὶ γὰρ τοῖς βασιλεῦσιν οὖσι στρατηγοῖς ἀϊδίοις ἡ ναυαρχία σχεδὸν ἑτέρα βασιλεία καθέστηκεν. Agesilaos alone once had the command of the fleet as well. Plut., *Ages.*, 10.

[3] Hdt., 6, 57. Stein, *ad loc.*, has rightly observed that Hdt. does not state that each king had two votes in the Gerousia, as Thuc. 1, 20 supposed.

[4] For the Lacedæmonian Gerontia see Müller, *Dor.*, 2, 87 ff., Eng. tr. 94. Kopstadt, *de rer. Laconicar. constitut. Lycurg. origine et indole*, 107 ff. Gabriel, *de magistratib. Lacedæmonior.*, p. 31 ff.

[5] Both documents in Plut., *Lyc.*, 6. The form γεροντία is to be found in Xen., *de rep. Lac.*, 10, 1, 3, but γερωχία is the term used where the office of γέρων is actually meant, as may be inferred from Aristoph., *Lys.*, 980. Cf. Ahrens, *de dial. Dor.*, 62/3.

it consisted of 28 members, to whom were added the kings and later the Ephors.[1]

Election to the Council of the Elders was in Aristotle's time open to the nobles, and the nobles only; and as a similar distinction between nobles and commons is discernible even in the earliest times, we must infer a restriction of the right of elegibility to the former class even in those days.[2] Even among the nobles, however, only those were entitled to become candidates for the office of Geron, who had passed their 60th year. This plainly had reference to the fact that in this year the obligation to military service came to an end.[3] The Gerontes were elected by the people in a peculiar manner. The people assembled in the Apella, and the candidates for the office went through the assembly in an order previously determined by lot. He at whose passing the people raised the loudest cry, was held to be elected. The loudness of the cry was judged by men shut up in a house near the Apella, from which they could hear the cry, but could not see the place of assembly. The successful candidate, followed by a crowd of young people and women, who sang praises of his merits and good fortune, proceeded to the temples of the gods. In the houses of his friends feasts were prepared, to which he was invited. At their conclusion he went to the Syssition, where, on this occasion, he received two portions. He gave one to that one among the women

Mode of Appointment.

---

[1] See p. 9. For the number of the Gerontes, Hdt. 6, 57; Plato, *Laws*, 3, 691. The significance of the number 28 was already unknown in ancient times, as appears from the explanations given by Plut., *Lyc.*, 5.

[2] In Aristotle's days the Gerontes were chosen from the καλοὶ κἀγαθοί, the δῆμος possessing only the right of electing to this ἀρχή. Arist., *Pol.*, 2, 9 = p. 48, 6; 6 (4), 9 = p. 161, 14 ff. Hence the ἀρχή of the Gerontes is described as an ὀλιγαρχία: Arist., 2, 6 = p. 85, 30. Polyb., 6, 10, speaks of the Gerontes as κατ' ἐκλογὴν ἀριστίνδην κεκριμένοι. We have seen, p. 12 ff., that Nobles and Commons already existed in the earliest times. Arist. 8 (5), 6 = p. 206, 1 ff., calls the election of the Gerontes at Elis, δυναστευτικὴν καὶ ὁμοίαν τῇ τῶν ἐν Λακεδαίμονι γερόντων, where Sauppe, *Epist. crit.*, 148, inserts an οὐχ before ὁμοίαν. According to Arist., *Pol.*, 6 (4), 5 = p. 155, 11 ff., δυναστεία is that form of oligarchy in which the son succeeds the father, and persons, not laws, rule.

[3] Plut., *Lyc.*, 26; Arist., *Pol.*, 2, 9 = p. 49, 1 ff., finds fault because canvassing took place for vacancies in the Gerontia, a post which, according to him, was an ἆθλον τῆς ἀρετῆς, p. 48, 7, and ought to have been gained by the most worthy, whether he came forward as a candidate or not.

of his kindred who waited before the door of the Syssition, whom he wished especially to honour.[1]

The office of the Gerontes was held for life and irresponsible.[2] The Council of Elders, like the Athenian Council of 500, had twofold functions. It deliberated on questions which were to be transmitted to the Apella for decision; and at the same time it was an administrative body. As to the former of its two functions, the powers of the Council underwent changes in course of time. According to the so-called Lycurgean Rhetra, the Apella had the final decision on the measures introduced by the Council of Elders; according to king Theopompos' law, the latter was not bound by the decrees of the Apella, an arrangement which appears to have remained in force even in the 3rd century.[3] In the second place, the Council of Elders with the kings and Ephors formed the supreme executive magistracy.[4] The judicial powers of the Gerontes are treated in another place.

Functions.

C. *The Apella.*[5]

The assembly of the Spartans, which, according to the so-called

---

[1] The mode of election, characterized by Arist., *Pol.*, 2, 9=p. 49, 1, as παιδαριώδης, is described Plut., *Lyc.*, 26. It is the natural consequence of the voting of the Apella βοῇ καὶ οὐ ψήφῳ mentioned by Thuc., 1, 87.

[2] The γεροντία for life and irresponsible; Arist., *Pol.*, 2, 9=p. 48, 18 ff.; Plut., *Lyc.*, 26; Polyb. 6, 45, 5.

[3] The so-called Lycurgean Rhetra ordered οὕτως εἰσφέρειν τε καὶ ἀφίστασθαι· δάμῳ δὲ κυρίαν ἦμεν καὶ κράτος. Theopompos' law runs: αἰ δὲ σκολιὰν ὁ δᾶμος ἕλοιτο, τοὺς πρεσβυγενέας καὶ ἀρχαγέτας ἀποστατῆρας ἦμεν. See Plut., *Lyc.*, 6 and the explanation of these directions in my *Stud.*, p. 131, ff. If Plut., *Ag.*, 8–11, gives an accurate account of the proceedings in connexion with Agis's Land-distribution law, Theopompos' law was still in force then. Agis had his bill introduced by the Ephor Lysander εἰς τοὺς γέροντας (8), τῶν γερόντων εἰς ταὐτὸ ταῖς γνώμαις οὐ συμφερομένων. Lysander brought the law before the Apella, who manifestly were in its favour (9, 10). Nevertheless the Gerontes afterwards rejected it by one vote (11).

[4] Isocr. 12, 154, τὴν τῶν γερόντων αἵρεσιν τῶν ἐπιστατούντων ἅπασι τοῖς πράγμασι. Dem. 20, 107, ἐπειδάν τις εἰς τὴν καλουμένην γερουσίαν ἐγκριθῇ παρασχὼν αὑτὸν οἷον χρή, δεσπότης ἐστὶ τῶν πολλῶν. Polyb. 6, 45, 5, οἱ δὲ προσαγορευόμενοι γέροντες διὰ βίου, δι' ὧν καὶ μεθ' ὧν πάντα χειρίζεται τὰ κατὰ τὴν πολιτείαν. Dionys. Hal., 2, 14, ἡ γερουσία πᾶν εἶχε τῶν κοινῶν τὸ κράτος. Cf. Plut., *Lyc.*, 26. Æsch., *in Tim.*, 180. Lex. Seguer. 227, 29. Oncken, *d. Staatslehre d. Aristot.*, 1, 286, thinks that in the 4th century the Gerousia had been forced into a state of absolute insignificance.

[5] For the Lacedæmonian Apella, cf. Müller, *Dor.*, 2, 82 (87) ff.

Lycurgean Rhetra, was to be held regularly every month between Babyka and Knakion, *i.e.* within the scattered, isolated quarters of the town Sparta, bore apparently the official name ἀπέλλα.[1] It does not seem permissible to suppose, as some have done on the strength of a single and thoroughly untrustworthy quotation, that there was a second smaller Assembly existing side by side with this Apella. Every Spartan who had passed his 30th year might attend the Apella.[2]

Name.

One Apella only.

---

[1] The so-called Lycurgean Rhetra in Plut., *Lyc.*, 6, says: ὥρας ἐξ ὥρας ἀπελλάζειν μεταξὺ Βαβύκας τε καὶ Κνακιῶνος. The explanation of these words in my *Stud.*, p. 131 ff. Hesych. in his glosses: ἀπελλάζειν· ἐκκλησιάζειν, Λάκωνες. ἀπέλλαι· σηκοί, ἐκκλησίαι, ἀρχαιρεσίαι, introduces the same term, ἀπέλλα, which appears in the Rhetra. Cf. also the Μεγάλαι ἀπέλλαι in the inscriptions of Gytheion of a later time. Le Bas, *Voyage archéol. Explic. des Inscr.*, 2,242a, 243. We can see clearly from passages like Hdt. 1,125; 5, 29, 79, that when that writer, 7, 134, uses ἁλίη he does not intend to give us the proper title of the Spartan Assembly. Similarly the expressions repeatedly employed by Xen., ἐκκλησία, *Hell.*, 5, 2, 11; οἱ ἔκκλητοι, *Hell.*, 2, 4, 38; 5, 2, 33; 6, 3, 3, are not technical terms. Xen. certainly understands by οἱ ἔκκλητοι the same assembly as he denotes by ἐκκλησία; this appears from a comparison of *Hell.*, 6, 3, 3, with 5, 2, 11 and from 5, 2, 32, 33. Vid. Schömann, *op. ac.*, 1, 88 ff.

[2] The importance of the 30th year of age; οἱ μέν γε νεώτεροι τριάκοντα ἐτῶν τὸ παράπαν οὐ κατέβαινον εἰς ἀγοράν. See Plut., *Lyc.*, 25. The hypothesis of a second lesser Assembly is based upon Xen., *Hell.*, 3, 3, 8, ἀκούσαντες ταῦτα οἱ ἔφοροι ἐσκεμμένα τε λέγειν ἡγήσαντο αὐτὸν καὶ ἐξεπλάγησαν καὶ οὐδὲ τὴν μικρὰν καλουμένην ἐκκλησίαν ξυλλέξαντες, ἀλλὰ ξυλλεγόμενοι τῶν γερόντων ἄλλος ἄλλοθι (but gathering, one here, one there, some of the Gerontes about them) ἐβουλεύσαντο πέμψαι τὸν Κινάδωνα κ.τ.λ. The expression ἡ μικρὰ καλουμένη ἐκκλησία is quite indefinite. Ἐκκλησία is not a Spartan expression, and accordingly ἡ μικρὰ καλουμένη ἐκκλησία is only used by Xenophon to denote an assembly similar to the ἐκκλησία, but which was by no means a μικρὰ ἐκκλησία as is shown by the insertion of καλουμένη. The context shows that there is an opposition between the ordinary assembly of the small Ecclesia and the meeting of individual Ephors with individual Gerontes, one in one place, another in another. This leads us to conclude that the μικρὰ καλουμένη ἐκκλησία denotes that assembly which consisted of the 28 Gerontes, the 2 kings, and the 5 Ephors. Paus. 3, 5, 2. This was seen, it appears, by Lachmann, *d. spart. Staatsverf.*, 216, though of course I do not agree with the rest of his conclusions, p. 194 ff. There is no reason for supposing that the other magistrates sat in this assembly, as Tittman, *Darst. d. griech. Staatsverf.*, 99 ff., does. Schömann, *op. ac.*, 1, 92/3, regards as members of the μικρὰ καλουμένη ἐκκλησία the ὅμοιοι who happened to be in the town or seemed to the magistrates especially deserving of confidence. He has then to include in the great Ecclesia the ὑπομείονες, a hypothesis which appears to me entirely improbable. König, τὰ τέλη et οἱ ἐν τέλει *verbis quinam intel-*

During the proceedings in the Apella the members remained seated, as in the assemblies of other Greek States. The place of meeting was originally perhaps the market itself. In the 2nd century, A.D., the Skias, a building near the market place, was employed for this purpose.[1] The Apella was originally presided over by the kings, in historical times by the Ephors.[2]

Place of Meeting.

The so-called Lycurgean Rhetra recognised the right of the Apella to pronounce a final decision. This was withdrawn by King Theopompos' law, according to which the Council of Elders and the Kings were not to be bound any longer by the resolutions of the Apella.[3] After the introduction of this rule ordinary citizens in all probability lost also the right of raising opposition in the Apella to proposals introduced by the Gerontes. At any rate this right no longer existed in historical times, when manifestly none but the Kings, Ephors, Gerontes, and perhaps the other magistrates, were entitled to speak in the Apella; ordinary members could do nothing but applaud or the reverse.[4] Subject to these restrictions the Apella voted on ques-

Competence.

---

legendi sint, p. 4 ff., D. i. Jena, 1886, attacks my view of the passage, but he has not convinced me of the erroneousness of my interpretation. Neither has Thumser in Hermann, 169, 6.

[1] Paus. 3, 12, 10: ἑτέρα δὲ ἐκ τῆς ἀγορᾶς ἐστιν ἔξοδος, καθ' ἣν πεποίηταί σφισι καλουμένη Σκιάς, ἔνθα καὶ νῦν ἔτι ἐκκλησιάζουσι. That the Spartan Apella sat, appears from Thuc., 1, 87. See W. Vischer, *k. Schr.*, 1, 404 ff.

[2] Thuc., 1, 87.

[3] Plut., *Lyc.*, 6, gives the regulation in the Lycurgean Rhetra which concerns us here as follows: οὕτως εἰσφέρειν τε καὶ ἀφίστασθαι· δάμῳ δὲ κυρίαν ἦμεν καὶ κράτος. Theopompos' law: αἰ δὲ σκολιὰν ὁ δᾶμος ἕλοιτο, τοὺς πρεσβυγενέας καὶ ἀρχαγέτας ἀποστατῆρας ἦμεν. Cf. the interpretation of these regulations in the author's *Stud.*, 134 ff.

[4] We see that the members of the Apella did not possess the right of speaking from Arist., *Pol.*, 2, 11 = p. 54, 4 ff.: ἃ δ' ἂν εἰσφέρωσιν οὗτοι (οἱ βασιλεῖς μετὰ τῶν γερόντων at Carthage) οὐ διακοῦσαι μόνον ἀποδιδόασι τῷ δήμῳ τὰ δόξαντα τοῖς ἄρχουσιν, ἀλλὰ κύριοι κρίνειν εἰσὶ καὶ τῷ βουλομένῳ τοῖς εἰσφερομένοις ἀντειπεῖν ἔξεστιν, ὅπερ ἐν ταῖς ἑτέραις πολιτείαις (Crete and Lacedæmon) οὐκ ἔστιν. Cf. too Plut., *Lyc.*, 6. In the assembly too described by Thuc. 1, 67 ff., only the king Archidamos and the Ephor Sthenelaidas are introduced by name as speakers. And in the words in chap. 79, μεταστησάμενοι πάντας ἐβουλεύοντο κατὰ σφᾶς αὐτοὺς περὶ τῶν παρόντων. καὶ τῶν μὲν πλειόνων ἐπὶ τὸ αὐτὸ αἱ γνῶμαι ἔφερον there is nothing to prevent us from supposing those entitled to speak to be meant. The anecdote in Æsch., *in Tim.*, 180/1, Plut., *Praec. reip. ger.*, 4, 17, Didot, p. 978, is not equivalent to direct testimony. The manner of voting, κρίνουσι γὰρ βοῇ καὶ οὐ ψήφῳ. Thuc. 1, 87.

tions of peace and war, campaigns, treaties, and in general on all questions of foreign policy.[1] Further, the Apella appointed the generals, to whom definite commands were to be given; chose the Gerontes, the Ephors and probably various other magistrates; decided any disputed claims to the crown; decreed emancipations of Helots; and perhaps voted on proposed laws.[2]

D. *The Ephors.*

The board of Ephors consisted of five members, and had a permanent president who was the eponymous magistrate of the State. A majority of votes decided its policy.[3] After the Ephors ceased to be nominated by the kings, their appointment was made

Mode of Appointment. by election; every legitimate Spartan, who was of the proper age, was eligible. As to the method of election, which Aristotle characterizes as childish, nothing can

Official Residence. be affirmed with certainty.[4] The Ephors had an official residence in the market place, where they took

---

[1] The Apella decrees war and campaigns: Thuc., 1, 67–87. Xen., *Hell.*, 5, 2, 11. 20; 4, 6, 3; 6, 4, 3. Plut., *Ages.*, 6; peace, Xen., *Hell.*, 2, 2, 20; 6, 3, 8. 18; treaties, Hdt., 7, 149; Thuc., 5, 77; questions of foreign policy, Xen., *Hell.*, 2, 4, 38; 5, 2, 32 ff.

[2] The Apella appointed the generals, Xen., *Hell.*, 4, 2, 9; 6, 5, 10; chose the Gerontes, Plut., *Lyc.*, 26, the Ephors, and in general the magistrates, Just., 3, 3; decided claims to the throne, Hdt., 6, 65/6, Xen., *Hell.*, 3. 3, 1 ff.; freed Helots, Thuc., 5, 34; voted on proposed laws, Plut., *Ag.*, 9, 10.

[3] Five Ephors, Xen. *Ages.*, 1, 36: εἰ ἐν τῷ ἐφορείῳ ἔτυχεν ἑστηκὼς μόνος παρὰ τοὺς πέντε. Cic., *de Rep.*, 2, 33, 58. Arist., *Pol.*, 2, 10 = p. 51, 15 Bekker. Cf. the inscription found at Delos: ἐβασίλευον Ἆγις Παυσανίας· ἔφοροι ἦσαν Θυιωνίδας Ἀριστογενίδας Ἀρχίστας Σολόγας Φεδίλας. I. G. A., 91. One presided, Plut., *Lys.*, 30: Λακρατίδαν δὲ ἄνδρα φρόνιμον καὶ τότε προεστῶτα τῶν ἐφόρων. The president was, at the same time, ἐπώνυμος, Thuc., 5, 19. Cf. the inscription found at Tainaron, *Bullet. de corresp. Hell.*, 1879, p. 97. Decisions by a majority of votes: Xen., *Hell.*, 2, 3, 34, εἰ δὲ ἐκείνῃ (ἐν Λακεδαίμονι) ἐπιχειρήσειέ τις τῶν ἐφόρων ἀντὶ τοῦ τοῖς πλείοσι πείθεσθαι ψέγειν τε τὴν ἀρχὴν καὶ ἐναντιοῦσθαι τοῖς πραττομένοις, οὐκ ἂν οἴεσθε αὐτὸν καὶ ὑπ' αὐτῶν τῶν ἐφόρων καὶ ὑπὸ τῆς ἄλλης ἁπάσης πόλεως τῆς μεγίστης τιμωρίας ἀξιωθῆναι. Cf. 2, 4, 29. I cannot say what is to be deduced from the remark in Tim., *Lex. Plat.*, p. 128, ἔφοροι πέντε μείζους καὶ πέντε ἐλάττους. The notes of the Lexicographers on the Ephors are unimportant. See Suid., ἔφοροι, 2 Art. Phot. ἔφοροι. Et. M., ἔφοροι = Lex. Seguer. 257, 28, where the number of the Ephors is given as nine.

[4] Arist., *Pol.*, 2, 10 = p. 52, 8, describes the appointment of the Ephors as a αἵρεσις ἐκ πάντων, and says of their office, 2, 9 = 48, 8, καθίσταται ἐξ ἁπάντων. Other expressions used by Arist. are τὸ ἐκ τοῦ δήμου εἶναι τοὺς ἐφόρους, 2, 6 = 35, 82. γίνονται δ' ἐκ τοῦ δήμου πάντες, 2, 9 = 47, 23. That anyone and everyone might be elected appears from the expressions: γίνονται οἱ τυχόντες, 2, 10 = 52 6. οἱ ἐκ τῶν τυχόντων εἰσί, 2, 11 = 53, 21. ὄντες οἱ τυχόντες, 2, 9 = 48, 12.

their meals together.[1] They were responsible to their successors; and commenced their official duties about the autumn equinox with the remarkable order to the citizens to "cut their moustaches and obey the laws."[2]

Entrance on Office.

The official functions of the Ephors extended in course of time, as has already been shown in the his-

Functions.

Schömann *ad* Plut., *Ag.* and *Cleom.*, p. 119 (see too Stein., *d. Spartan. Ephoral.*, 17) has justly remarked that when Plato, *Laws*, 3, p. 692, speaks of τὴν τῶν ἐφόρων δύναμιν ἐγγὺς τῆς κληρωτῆς δυνάμεως, he merely means, as the whole context of the passage shows, that the election proceeded without any kind of regard to wealth or birth, just as was the case in lot-magistracies. Arist., 2, 9=48, 11, calls the mode of election for the Ephors childish, as he does that for the Gerontes, 2, 9=49, 1. As in the latter passage, he condemns the practice of the Gerontes canvassing for that office, but says nothing of the sort in the case of the Ephorate, it has been supposed that no canvassing took place for the Ephorate, and accordingly very various conjectures as to the mode of election have been made. I do not regard this as a necessary inference; for Aristot. might censure canvassing for an office for life, and irresponsible, which was according to him an ἆθλον τῆς ἀρετῆς, without necessarily expressing a similar condemnation in the case of the Ephorate, which lasted for a year, and was responsible. From Arist., *Pol.*, 6 (4) 9=p. 161, 14 ff., ἔτι τῷ δύο τὰς μεγίστας ἀρχὰς τὴν μὲν αἱρεῖσθαι τὸν δῆμον, τῆς δὲ μετέχειν· τοὺς μὲν γὰρ γέροντας αἱροῦνται, τῆς δ' ἐφορείας μετέχουσιν we can at most only conclude that the Demos did not itself elect the Ephors. We can say nothing for certain as to the mode of election. See also Schömann on Plut., *Ag.* and *Cleom.*, p. 116 ff. Schenkl, in the *Rivista di Filologia*, 2, 1874, p. 373 ff., regards it as identical with that for the Gerontes. Gachon, *de ephoris Spartanis*, 78 ff., Monspelii, 1888, supposes that the Gerousia chose from among the whole people those for whom the omens were favourable. Their names were then laid before the people, who chose from among them.

[1] Mention of the ἐφορεῖον, Xen., *Ages.*, 1, 36; in the *Agora*, Paus. 3, 11, 11. The ἐφορεῖον mentioned by Paus. 3, 11, 2 is a later building. Cf. Plut., *Lys.*, 20; *Ag.* 16. The συσσίτιον τῶν ἐφόρων mentioned in Plut., *Cleom.*, 8, was plainly in the ἐφορεῖον. Cf. also the position of the temple of Fear described in chap. 8, 9.

[2] The responsibility of the Ephors appears from Arist., *Rhet.*, 3, 18=p. 146, 32, καὶ ὡς ὁ Λάκων εὐθυνόμενος τῆς ἐφορίας. Plut., *Ag.*, 12, apparently deals with a similar case. That they gave in their accounts before their successors may be inferred from Arist., *Pol.*, 2, 9=48, 29, δόξειε δ' ἂν ἡ τῶν ἐφόρων ἀρχὴ πάσας εὐθύνειν τὰς ἀρχάς. Cf. Plut., *Ag.*, 12. The Ephors' decree with which they began their year of office according to Arist. *ap.* Plut., *Cleom.*, 9, κείρεσθαι τὸν μύστακα καὶ προσέχειν τοῖς νόμοις. See Plut., *de sera num. vind.*, 4. That the Ephors entered on their office about the Autumn equinox appears from the fact that those Ephors who were in office in the Attic month Elaphebolion, were Ephors no longer, τοῦ ἐπιγιγνομένου χειμῶνος. Cf. Thuc 5, 19 with 36.

torical section.[1] They are here brought together without regard to their historical development. In the first place the Ephors had **They Summon and Manage the Apella and Council of the Elders.** the right to summon the Apella, and to preside over its meetings. They possessed similar rights in regard to the Council of Elders.[2] The Ephors and the Council of Elders together represented the supreme governing power, the latter chiefly the deliberative, the former the executive side.[3] Before the Ephors as presidents of the Council of Elders accusations for criminal offences were made; these they either disposed of themselves or decided in conjunction

---

[1] Spakler, *de ephor. ap. Laced.*, 1842, p. 55 ff., has collected many incidents illustrating the Ephor's functions.

[2] The Ephors' right to summon the Apella, Xen., *Hell.*, 2, 2, 20; Plut., *Ag.*, 9; to manage it, Thuc. 1, 87. Cf. Xen., *Hell.*, 5, 2, 11. They deliberated with the Gerontes, Hdt. 5, 40. From Xen., *Hell.*, 3, 3, 8, we may conclude that they summoned the Gerousia; and from the circumstance that even in Herodotus' time the kings did not preside over its meeting, that the Ephors did so. Hdt. 6, 57 says of the kings merely, παρίζειν βουλεύουσι τοῖς γέρουσι. On the Ephors' right of initiating legislation, see Plut., *Ag.*, 5, 8.

[3] Plut., *Ages.*, 4, tells us of Agesilaos' age, τῶν ἐφόρων ἦν τότε καὶ τῶν γερόντων τὸ μέγιστον ἐν τῇ πολιτείᾳ κράτος. The expression τὰ τέλη used by ancient writers denotes in my judgment quite universally the highest authority in the Lacedæmonian State. Naturally the Ephors in their character of an executive magistracy were generally regarded by outsiders as the wielders of this authority; but the two expressions οἱ ἔφοροι and τὰ τέλη are not absolutely identical. This is shown clearly by Xen., *Anab.*, 2, 6, 2–4. The Ephors sent out Clearchos and recalled him, but he was condemned to death ὑπὸ τῶν ἐν Σπάρτῃ τελῶν, *i.e.* by the supreme authority, undoubtedly in this case the Gerousia under the Ephors' presidency. Xen., *Hell.*, 3, 2, 23, means, by τὰ τέλη, the same authority which immediately before he describes as οἱ ἔφοροι καὶ ἡ ἐκκλησία. In Xen., *Hell.*, 6, 4, 2/3 we must suppose similar representatives of the State's authority. When Plut., *Lyc.*, 14, the Ephors sent to Lysander introduced the terms of peace for Athens with the words, τάδε τὰ τέλη τῶν Λακεδαιμονίων ἔγνω, they meant, "The State of the Lacedæmonians considered the following terms just." I remark this in refutation of Trieber in the *Verh. d. 28 Philologenvers.*, 1872, p. 39 ff.; and König, τὰ τέλη et οἱ ἐν τέλει *verbis quinam intellegendi sint.*, D. i. Jena, 1886, both of whom identify τὰ τέλη with the Ephors. The more concrete οἱ ἐν τέλει, which Trieber regards as a council of war, serves, according to König, p. 52 ff., to designate the Ephors, Gerontes, and the other higher magistrates, including the kings. It perhaps denotes the magistrates as representatives of the State. Fleischhandel, *d. spartan. Verf. b. Xenoph.*, p. 39 ff., 129 ff., 1888, argues that Xenophon's expressions οἱ οἶκοι, οἱ οἶκοι ἄρχοντες, τὰ οἴκοι τέλη, τὰ τέλη, ἔφοροι καὶ οἱ ἔκκλητοι, ἔφοροι καὶ ἐκκλησία, κοινὸν τῶν Λακεδαιμονίων, πόλις are of a general character, and indicate the State. Spakler, *de ephor. ap. Laced.*, 1842, p. 77 ff., regards τὰ τέλη and οἱ ἐν τέλει ὄντες as those who were entitled to vote in the assembly.

with the Gerontes. Similarly the execution of the punishments was entrusted to them.[1] The political misdemeanours of the kings, whom the Ephors could throw into prison until a judicial decision had been pronounced, were judged before the same court and in the same way.[2]

As executive magistrates the Ephors carried out the decrees of the Council of Elders and of the Apella,—especially those which concerned foreign affairs. In our authorities very many measures within the sphere of foreign politics are represented as proceeding from the Ephors; but we obviously cannot suppose that these are all instances of independent decision on their part. All important resolutions were adopted by the Apella after previous deliberation in the Council of Elders; but since our authorities in most cases had no occasion to describe the full procedure, which a command issuing from the Ephors had passed through, what was perhaps merely the determination of the Apella, executed by the Ephors, often appears in our authorities as a direct command of the Ephors.[3] It is necessary in order to form an opinion of the powers and position of the Ephors, to bear this in mind when considering what is told us of the inter-

Foreign Affairs.

---

[1] Arist., *Pol.*, 3, 1=p. 60, 16, οἱ δὲ γέροντες τὰς φονικὰς (δικάζουσι). Xen., *Hell.*, 5, 4, 24, says, οἱ δ' ἔφοροι ἀνεκάλεσάν τε τὸν Σφοδρίαν καὶ ὑπῆγον θανάτου. This indictment took place before the Gerousia: for attempts were made εὐμενῆ εἰς τὴν κρίσιν παρασχεῖν Agesilaos in Sphodrias' interest. Xen., *ibid.*, § 26. Cf. *ibid.*, § 24. Plut., *Ages.*, 24, 25. In Plut., *apophth. Lac.*, p. 272 Didot, in a dictum of Thectamenes we have καταγνόντων αὐτοῦ θάνατον τῶν ἐφόρων; but evidently the Ephors are only mentioned there because they presided over the Gerousia and, as executive magistrates, carried out the sentence. Cf. Plut., *Ag.*, 19.

[2] Paus. 3, 5, 2, βασιλεῖ δὲ τῷ Λακεδαιμονίων δικαστήριον ἐκάθιζον οἵ τε ὀνομαζόμενοι γέροντες ὀκτὼ καὶ εἴκοσιν ὄντες ἀριθμόν, καὶ ἡ τῶν ἐφόρων ἀρχή, σὺν δὲ αὐτοῖς καὶ ὁ τῆς οἰκίας βασιλεὺς τῆς ἑτέρας. See also Plut., *Ag.*, 19. Hdt. 6, 82, tells us in regard to Cleomenes I., νοστήσαντα δέ μιν ὑπῆγον οἱ ἐχθροὶ ὑπὸ τοὺς ἐφόρους; but the real judicial proceedings, as appears from the end of the chapter, did not take place before the Ephors alone. Trial of Leotychidas, Hdt. 6, 85, 72; of Pleistoanax, Thuc. 2, 21, Plut., *Per.*, 22; of Agis I., Thuc. 5, 63; of Pausanias, Xen., *Hell.*, 3, 5, 25, Paus., *ibid.*; of Leonidas II., Plut., *Ag.*, 11; of Agis III., Plut., *Ag.*, 19. Thuc. 1, 131, says of Pausanias, καὶ ἐς μὲν τὴν εἱρκτὴν ἐσπίπτει τὸ πρῶτον ὑπὸ τῶν ἐφόρων (ἔξεστι δὲ τοῖς ἐφόροις τὸν βασιλέα δρᾶσαι τοῦτο).

[3] The Apella decrees war, Thuc. 1, 87. Xen., *Hell.*, 5, 2, 11. 20. 4, 6, 3, where we have ἔδοξε τοῖς τ' ἐφόροις καὶ τῇ ἐκκλησίᾳ, ἀναγκαῖον εἶναι στρατεύεσθαι. It decrees peace, Xen., *Hell.*, 2, 2, 20; 6, 3, 3. 18. Treaties, Hdt. 7, 149; Thuc. 5, 77. Cf. Dum, *Entsteh. u. Entwickel. d. spart. Ephorats.*, p. 149.

ference of the Ephors in foreign affairs. The Ephors either refused admittance to foreign ambassadors at the frontier, or allowed them to enter and carried on the negotiations with them. It rested with them to say whether they should have an interview with the Apella or not.[1] When war was to be undertaken the Ephors issued the order for mobilising the troops, stating the years that would have to serve, and gave the command to depart to the generals appointed by the Apella.[2] The Ephors, as presidents of the Council of Elders and of the Apella, were in direct communion with the generals, gave them instructions, and recalled them. In later days two Ephors regularly accompanied the kings on their expeditions.[3] The Ephors also interfered arbitrarily in the government of the allied cities.[4]

The police duties probably entrusted to the Ephors at their first institution, developed in course of time into a universal power of supervision over the whole State, with which was naturally connected the power of inflicting punish-

Police Supervision.

---

[1] Ambassadors refused admission by them at the frontier, Xen., *Hell.*, 2, 2, 13. Negotiations between the Ephors and foreign ambassadors, Hdt. 3, 46; 6, 106; 9, 7–9. Thuc. 1, 90. Xen. 3, 1, 1; 5, 2, 11. Polyb. 4, 34, 5. Plut., *Cim.*, 6. *Them.*, 19. Diod. 11, 40. Ambassadors made their proposals before the Ephors and the Apella: Xen. 2, 4, 38; 5, 2, 11. Polyb., 4, 34, 6, says of such an ambassador, τῷ δὲ Μαχάτᾳ συνεχώρησαν (sc. οἱ ἔφοροι) δώσειν τὴν ἐκκλησίαν.

[2] Xen., *de rep. Lac.*, 11, 2, πρῶτον μὲν τοίνυν οἱ ἔφοροι προκηρύττουσι τὰ ἔτη εἰς ἃ δεῖ στρατεύεσθαι. The technical expression for this is φρουρὰν φαίνειν. *Hell.*, 6, 4, 17. Xen. uses this repeatedly, *e.g.* 3, 2, 5; 3, 5, 6; 4, 2, 9; 5, 3, 18; 6, 5, 10. The Ephors despatched the generals and armies on special services. Hdt. 9, 10. Thuc. 8, 12. Xen., *Hell.*, 2, 4, 29; 5, 1, 33; 5, 4, 14; *Anab.*, 2, 6, 2. General's appointment regularly made by the Apella: cf. what Xen., *Hell.*, 4, 2, 9; 6, 5, 10, says of the general's appointment as contrasted with the φρουρὰ φαίνειν of the Ephors. Cf. Dum., *op. cit.*, 148. 151/2. 156.

[3] The Ephors gave the generals instructions: Thuc. 8, 11; Xen., *Hell.*, 3, 1, 1. 7; 3, 2, 6. 12; Diod. 14, 20; recalled them: Thuc. 1, 131, Plut., *Lys.*, 19, *Ages.*, 15; *Apophth. Lac.*, p. 257 Didot, 39, 41. First entry of the Ephors' official residence by the generals after their return, Plut., *Lys.*, 20. All instructions of importance were of course given by the Ephors only after they were authorized to do so by the Gerousia or Apella. Cf. *e.g.* Xen., 6, 4, 3, with Plut., *Ages.*, 28; and Xen. 5, 2, 32 ff. For the form in which orders were given to generals at a distance, *i.e.* for the σκυτάλη, as it was called, see Plut., *Lys.*, 19. Gell., *N.A.*, 17, 9. Schol. *ad* Arist., *Birds*, 1283. Auson., *epist.*, 23, 23. Two Ephors accompanied the kings in war: Xen., *Hell.*, 2, 4, 36. ὥσπερ γὰρ νομίζεται ξὺν βασιλεῖ δύο τῶν ἐφόρων ξυστρατεύεσθαι. Cf. *de rep. Lac.*, 13, 5. Hdt. 9, 76.

[4] Xen. 3, 4, 2. 5, 2, 9.

ment. The Ephors superintended the education of the young. Every ten days the Epheboi had to appear before the Ephors naked to be examined; their clothing and their quarters were subject to the Ephors' inspection. Moreover they supervised the relations of the older youths towards their protégés. In case of any particularly serious offence on the part of the boys or young men the Paidonomos brought the culprit before the Ephors for judgment. The Ephors annually appointed the three Hippagretai from among the young men, the Hippagretai again selecting the Hippeis.[1] Even when the young men had been enrolled among the adults, their outward behaviour remained under the control of the Ephors, who could punish any Spartan for any act which in their opinion was unseemly.[2]

This power of supervision and punishment possessed by the Ephors extended even to the other magistrates. They could suspend them from their offices, put them in prison, and impeach them on capital charges. Lastly the magistrates at the conclusion of their year of office had to render account of it before the Ephors.[3] The kings were in a similar position of dependence towards the Ephors, who exercised supervision over the minutest details even of their social conduct.[4] The kings were bound to appear before the Ephors at the third summons. The Ephors, unlike the other Spartans, did not rise from their seats in the king's presence. Every month

Supervision over the Magistrates and Kings.

---

[1] The summons issued by the Ephors on entering office, προσέχειν τοῖς νόμοις, is a particular manifestation of their general supervision of the laws. Plut., *Clem.*, 9. Examination and control of the Epheboi, Agatharchides *ap.* Ath., 12,550 C. Aelian, *Var. Hist.*, 14, 7. 3, 10. Punishment of the disobedient, Xen., *de rep. Lac.*, 4, 6. Selection of the ἱππαγρέται, Xen., *ibid.*, 4, 3. Dum., *op. cit.*, p. 120, concludes from Xen., *Hell.*, 6, 4, 16, that they also presided at the games. Cf. Plut., *Ages.*, 29.

[2] Xen., *de rep. Lac.*, 8, 4, ἔφοροι οὖν ἱκανοὶ μέν εἰσι ζημιοῦν ὃν ἂν βούλωνται, κύριοι δ' ἐκπράττειν παραχρῆμα. Examples in Dum., *ibid.*, 120 ff.

[3] Xen., *de rep. Lac.*, 8, 4, κύριοι δὲ καὶ ἄρχοντας μεταξὺ (καὶ) καταπαῦσαι καὶ εἷρξαί γε καὶ περὶ τῆς ψυχῆς εἰς ἀγῶνα καταστῆσαι. Arist., *Pol.*, 2, 9=p. 48, 29, δόξειε δὲ ἂν ἡ τῶν ἐφόρων ἀρχὴ πάσας εὐθύνειν τὰς ἀρχάς. Sphodrias impeached by the Ephors, Xen., *Hell.*, 5, 4, 24.

[4] The Ephors obliged King Anaxandridas to marry another wife, that the royal family should not die out, Hdt. 5, 40; they watched over the confinement of this king's wife, that no supposititious child should be foisted upon them, Hdt. 5, 41; they punished Agesilaos ὅτι τοὺς κοινοὺς πολίτας ἰδίους κτᾶται, Plut., *Ages.*, 5. The Ephors' supervision of the queens: Plat., *Alcib.*, 1, 121.

the kings took an oath before the Ephors to govern according to the laws of the State, when the Ephors answered by promising in that case to preserve the royal power undisturbed.[1] Every nine years, finally, the Ephors observed the heavens on a clear moonless night, and if they happened to see a shooting star, it was taken as a sign that the kings had been guilty of a religious offence. The Ephors then suspended them from their office, until an oracle favourable for the kings came from Delphi or Olympia.[2]

Superintendance of the Perioicoi and Helots. Again, the Ephors' supervision extended to the Perioicoi and Helots. They had the power of putting the former to death without trial; the κρυπτεία was under their direction.[3] Any evil foreign influences which became serious at Sparta were removed by the Ephors, sometimes by the Xenelasia, sometimes by some other direct mode of interposition.[4] The financial administration and the State treasury were under their special management and superintendence. Hence they received the war-booty, and managed the taxation.[5]

Xenelasia.

Control of the Finances.

Religious Functions. Lastly, the Ephors had certain religious duties. At any rate in later times they offered a public sacrifice

---

[1] Plut., *Cleom.*, 10, says that the king had to obey the Ephor's third summons. Xen., *de rep. Lac.*, 15, 6, tells us, καὶ ἕδρας δὲ πάντες ὑπανίστανται βασιλεῖ πλὴν οὐκ ἔφοροι ἀπὸ τῶν ἐφορικῶν δίφρων. The personal honour which, according to Plut., *Ages.*, 4, that king showed to the Ephors is made a duty of all kings in Plut., *praec. reip. ger.*, 21. The oaths of the kings and Ephors, Xen., *ibid.*, 15, 7: καὶ ὅρκους δὲ ἀλλήλοις κατὰ μῆνα ποιοῦνται ἔφοροι μὲν ὑπὲρ τῆς πόλεως, βασιλεὺς δ' ὑπὲρ ἑαυτοῦ. ὁ δὲ ὅρκος ἐστὶ τῷ μὲν βασιλεῖ κατὰ τοὺς τῆς πόλεως κειμένους νόμους βασιλεύσειν, τῇ δὲ πόλει ἐμπεδορκοῦντος ἐκείνου ἀστυφέλικτον τὴν βασιλείαν παρέξειν. Nicol. Dam. 114 *ap.* Müller., *fr. hist. gr.*, 3, 459, narrows down this reciprocal oath to a single oath of the king at his accession. Polyb. 24, 8b describes the relation of the kings towards the Ephors as that of children to their parents.

[2] Plut., *Ag.*, 11, δι' ἐτῶν ἐννέα λαβόντες οἱ ἔφοροι νύκτα καθαρὰν καὶ ἀσέληνον σιωπῇ καθέζονται πρὸς οὐρανὸν ἀποβλέποντες. ἐὰν οὖν ἐκ μέρους τινὸς εἰς ἕτερον μέρος ἀστὴρ διάξῃ, κρίνουσι τοὺς βασιλεῖς ὡς περὶ τὸ θεῖον ἐξαμαρτάνοντας καὶ καταπαύουσι τῆς ἀρχῆς, μέχρι ἂν ἐκ Δελφῶν ἢ Ὀλυμπίας χρησμὸς ἔλθῃ τοῖς ἡλωκόσι τῶν βασιλέων βοηθῶν.

[3] Isocr. 12, 181, whose declaration I do not hold myself at liberty to doubt. Cf. Xen., *Hell.*, 3, 3, 8. For the κρυπτεία see Aristot. *ap.* Plut., *Lyc.*, 28.

[4] Cf. Hdt. 3, 148. Plut., *Ag.*, 10; *Instit. Lac.*, 17.

[5] Receipt of the booty gained in war: Plut., *Lys.*, 16. Diod., 13, 106. Control of the taxes: Plut., *Ages.*, 16. *Vid.* Schömann, *z. St.*, p. 149/50.

to Athene Chalkioikos and regulated the calendar. It is possible that it was part of their religious functions to obtain the dream-oracles from the temple of Pasiphaa in Thalamai.[1] I deal with the judicial functions of the Ephors in another place.

E. Inferior Magistrates.

The remaining magistrates of the Lacedæmonian State were either elected in the Apella or appointed by the kings and Ephors. They were responsible to the Ephors, and could by them be suspended from their office, thrown into prison, and accused on charges involving life and limb.[2] All magistrates fell into two classes, civil and military. The civil magistrates included in the first place the πρόξενοι, appointed by the kings, and the four Πύθιοι, who likewise were appointed by the kings, each naming two. The former had to look after the strangers, who came on certain occasions to Sparta; the latter were the kings' intermediaries in the intercourse with Delphi. They dined with the kings.[3] The ἐμπέλωροι, for whom in Roman times we find ἀγορανόμοι, had the supervision of the market trade; the ἁρμόσυνοι supervised the women's behaviour.[4] At the head of the general education of the young

In General.

πρόξενοι.
Πύθιοι.

ἐμπέλωροι.
ἁρμόσυνοι.

---

[1] Polyb. 4, 35. Plut., *Ag.*, 16. For the dream oracle in the Temple of Pasiphaa, see Plut., *Ag.*, 9; *Cleom.*, 7. Cic., *de Divin.*, 1, 43, 96.

[2] Just. 3, 3, says, among other things of Lycurgus, "Populo sublegendi senatum vel creandi quos vellet magistratus potestatem permisit. The lot not in use at Sparta; Isocr. 12, 153/4. Arist., *Pol.*, 6 (4) 9=p. 161, 17 Bekker. The πρόξενοι and Πύθιοι were chosen by the kings, Hdt. 6, 57; the ἱππαγρέται by the Ephors, Xen., *de rep. Lac.*, 4, 3. Nothing further can be settled. Account given before the Ephors, Arist., *Pol.*, 2, 9=p. 48, 29. Their rights in relation to other magistrates, Xen., *op. cit.*, 8, 4.

[3] Hdt. 6, 67. Suid. Πύθιοι. For the duties of πρόξενοι in general, see Suid., προξένους ἐκάλουν τοὺς τεταγμένους εἰς τὸ ὑποδέχεσθαι τοὺς ξένους τοὺς ἐξ ἄλλων πόλεων ἥκοντας=Schol. Arist., *Birds*, 1021. Cf. Hesych., *sub verb*. Monceaux, *les proxénies grecques*, 6 ff., Paris, 1886, regards these πρόξενοι not as magistrates, but persons selected by the kings to receive strangers from a city which had no πρόξενος at Sparta. Hdt.'s turn of expression, however, makes me still think them magistrates. This naturally does not exclude the possibility that individual States had their own πρόξενοι in Sparta, and Sparta had hers in other States, as Monceaux, *op. cit.*, 146 ff., demonstrates.

[4] The single thing we know of the ἐμπέλωροι is the short gloss of Hesych., ἐμπέλωρος· ἀγορανόμος· Λάκωνες. For the later ἀγορανόμοι, see p. 26. Of the ἁρμόσυνοι we are similarly informed by Hesych. only ἁρμόσυνοι· ἀρχή τις ἐν Λακεδαίμονι ἐπὶ τῆς εὐκοσμίας τῶν γυναικῶν. I can make nothing of Hesych., γεροάκται· οἱ δήμαρχοι παρὰ Λάκωσιν and ἐμπασέντας· ἀρχεῖόν τι ἐν Λακεδαίμονι.

παιδονόμος. was the παιδονόμος; the ἄμπαιδες were perhaps his subordinates.[1] We must also mention the Κυθηροδίκης,
ἁρμοσταί. who was sent from Sparta to Cythera, and 20 ἁρμοσταί, with whom we have already dealt more fully.[2]

Military Officers. Of the military magistrates far the most important was the ναύαρχος, who, during his one year of office,
ναύαρχος. was in command of the Lacedæmonian fleet. The office of ναύαρχος, which might only be filled by the same person once, was styled by Aristotle a second kingship, and existed demoustrably in the time of the Persian wars.[3] The ναύαρχος'
ἐπιστολεύς. deputy in his office was the ἐπιστολεύς.[4] We must also mention, as military officers, the πολέμαρχοι with their συμφορεῖς, the λοχαγοί, πεντηκοντῆρες, ἐνωμοτάρχαι, ἱππαρμοσταί, the ἄρχων τῶν σκευοφόρων. The κρεωδαίτης, Ἑλλανοδίκαι, ταμίαι, and λαφυροπῶλαι acted indeed in war, but held no command.[5] All these will be dealt with in the section on the war department. Of commanders of separate divisions in the army we find ὁ ἐπὶ τῆς κρυπτείας τεταγμένος, who undoubtedly commanded the young
ἱππαγρέται. men of the age which was employed for the κρυπτεία,
ἀγαθοεργοί. and the three ἱππαγρέται, who commanded the select corps of the 300 ἱππεῖς. The five ἀγαθοεργοί, finally, were employed

---

[1] For the παιδονόμος vid. Xen., de rep. Lac., 2, 2; 4, 6. Plut., Lyc., 12, Hesych., παιδονόμος· ἀρχή τις παρὰ Λάκωσιν. The ἄμπαιδες again are only known to us from a gloss of Hesych., ἄμπαιδες· οἱ τῶν παίδων ἐπιμελούμενοι παρὰ Λάκωσιν. Perhaps this place was subsequently taken by the βίδεοι or βίδυοι. See for them, p. 26.

[2] For the Κυθηροδίκης, vid. Thuc., 4, 53. Our information about the 20 ἁρμοσταί is given by the Schol. ad Pind., Ol., 6, 154: ἦσαν δὲ ἁρμοσταὶ Λακεδαιμονίων εἴκοσι. Cf. p. 36. For the harmosts in the States of the league see below.

[3] On the Nauarchia in Sparta, see Beloch in the N. Rh. Mus., 34, 117 ff. Fleischhandel, d. spart. Verf. bei Xenophon, 57 ff., collects the passages in Xenophon. Arist., Pol., 2, 9 = p. 49, 30: ἐπὶ γὰρ τοῖς βασιλεῦσιν οὖσι στρατηγοῖς ἀϊδίοις ἡ ναυαρχία σχεδὸν ἑτέρα βασιλεία καθέστηκεν. Eurybiades is called ναύαρχος by Hdt. 8, 42. See also Diod. 11, 12. Beloch., ibid., 119 ff., shows that the Nauarchia lasted a year. οὐ γὰρ νόμος αὐτοῖς δὶς τὸν αὐτὸν ναυαρχεῖν. Xen., Hell., 2, 1, 7. Cf. Plut., Lyc., 7; Diod. 13, 100.

[4] That the ἐπιστολεύς was the vice-admiral appears from Poll. 1, 96; Xen., Hell., 2, 1, 7; Plut., Lys., 7. Cf. Xen. 1, 1, 23; 4, 8, 11; 5, 1, 5 and 6. Once we find, instead of ἐπιστολεύς the title ἐπιστολιαφόρος, Xen., 6, 2, 25. The ἐπιβάτης, mentioned, e.g., Thuc. 8, 61, Xen., Hell., 1, 3, 17, was a naval officer, but indubitably inferior in rank to the ἐπιστολεύς.

[5] For the military officers, see Gabriel, de magistratib. Lacedæmonior., p. 15 ff.

on courier-service. The five eldest of the young men just passing from the ἱππεῖς were appointed to this office.[1]

In conclusion, we must mention the subordinate officers: the heralds, flute-players, and cooks, whose occupations were hereditary.[2] **Subalterns.**

3. THE WAR DEPARTMENT.[3]

The onesided favour shown to military merit in the Lacedæmonian State was noticed even by the ancients, and Sparta's government was for this reason compared to that of a military camp.[4] The prohibition in force at Sparta against leaving the country without permission, and the threat of death for emigrating to a foreign land, show that this view of their State was familiar to the Spartans themselves.[5] This military character was impressed upon the Spartans' mode of life with irresistible strictness. The State institutions, which were expressions of this, merely fixed in formal law customs long prevalent. It must have been only after protracted wars that the Spartans subdued their country, beginning with the in- **Martial Character of the State.**

---

[1] ὁ ἐπὶ τῆς κρυπτείας τεταγμένος; Plut., Cleom., 28. Ἱππαγρέται; Xen., de rep. Lac., 4, 3. ἀγαθοεργοί; Hdt. 1, 67: οἱ δὲ ἀγαθοεργοί εἰσι τῶν ἀστῶν, ἐξιόντες ἐκ τῶν ἱππέων αἰεὶ οἱ πρεσβύτατοι, πέντε ἔτεος ἑκάστου, τοὺς δεῖ τοῦτον τὸν ἐνιαυτόν, τὸν ἂν ἐξίωσι ἐκ τῶν ἱππέων, Σπαρτιητέων τῷ κοινῷ διαπεμπομένους μὴ ἐλινύειν ἄλλους ἄλλῃ. See Suid. sub verb., Lex. Seguer. 209, 4; 333, 30.

[2] Hdt. 7, 134; 6, 60. Μάττων and Κεράων, the heroes of τῶν ἐν τοῖς φιδιτίοις ποιούντων τε τὰς μάζας καὶ κεραννύντων τὸν οἶνον διακόνων. Ath. 4, 173 F; 2, 39 c; 12, 550 D.

[3] Since the first edition this subject has been treated by Stehfen, de Spartanorum re militari. D. i. Greifswald, 1881; A. Bauer, in the Handb. d. cl. Alterth.-W., 4, 241 ff.; H. Droysen, Heerwesen und Kriegführ. der Griechen, 65–74 in Hermann.

[4] Cf. Isocr. 6, 81: ἐκεῖνο δ᾽ οὖν πᾶσι φανερόν, ὅτι τῶν Ἑλλήνων διενηνόχαμεν οὐ τῷ μεγέθει τῆς πόλεως οὐδὲ τῷ πλήθει τῶν ἀνθρώπων, ἀλλ᾽ ὅτι τὴν πολιτείαν ὁμοίαν κατεστησάμεθα στρατοπέδῳ καλῶς διοικουμένῳ καὶ πειθαρχεῖν ἐθέλοντι τοῖς ἄρχουσιν. Arist., Pol., 2, 9 = p. 50, 2, says: πρὸς γὰρ μέρος ἀρετῆς ἡ πᾶσα σύνταξις τῶν νόμων ἐστίν, τὴν πολεμικήν. See further Trieber, Forsch. z. spart. Verfassungsgesch., p. 1 ff.

[5] Τὸ μηδένα τῶν μαχίμων ἄνευ τῆς τῶν ἀρχόντων γνώμης ἀποδημεῖν given by Isocr., 11, 18 is extended to all Spartans by Arist. ap. Harp.: καὶ γὰρ τὸ μηδένα. See also Plut., instit. Lac., 19; Ag., 11: τὸν δὲ ἀπελθόντα τῆς Σπάρτης ἐπὶ μετοικισμῷ πρὸς ἑτέρους ἀποθνήσκειν κελεύει. Trieber, quæst. Lac., p. 57 ff., has collected all the passages bearing on this point.

terior of Laconia; and when this subjugation was completed, the very character of the State thus founded compelled its masters to be always on the watch against their subjects and slaves, who obeyed only unwillingly and under compulsion. The town, Sparta, was the permanent camp and base from which the conquerors held the conquered land in check. What they lacked in numbers, had to be made up by the highest development of warlike ability. But this could only be attained by giving up all other interests, and it was only by making this sacrifice that Spartans became the military artists of Greece, whose invincibility was, until the battle of Leuctra, an axiom of Greek popular faith.[1]

The constant discipline and practice required for the maintenance of this military excellence, was only possible for men, whose energies were not claimed by anything else. The allotment of fixed κλῆροι to the ordinary citizens (and even they were set free, thanks to the labours of the Helots, from the necessity of cultivating their lots) relieved them from any anxiety for their daily bread, so that they reserved their powers entire for the interests of the State.[2] But if the State thus secured to its citizens the possibility of consecrating themselves wholly to their military calling, it at the same time required this possibility to be used to the full, and therefore made the possession of citizen rights depend upon participation in the Spartan Agoge, and on regular contribution to the Syssitia.[3]

To pass on to the consideration of details. The reference to the Spartan boy's future military calling manifested itself immediately at his birth. It was not the father, as was usual elsewhere, who decided whether the new-born child was to be brought up or not. Instead of this the decision rested with the elders of the Phyle, who, after inspecting the child, if they found him strong and well formed, ordered him to be brought up; if not, they had him exposed in the Ἀποθέται, a gorge of Taygetus.[4] Those boys who had been pronounced fit to live were then

Education.

---

[1] Oncken, *d. Staatslehre d. Aristot.*, 1, 243 ff. The Spartans as τεχνῖται καὶ σοφισταὶ τῶν πολεμικῶν, Plut., *Pelop.*, 23, Xen., *de rep. Lac.*, 13, 5. Cf. Plut., *Ages.*, 26. Trieber, *quæst. Lac.*, p. 70/1.

[2] Cf. p. 33.

[3] Cf. p. 42.

[4] Plut., *Lyc.*, 16. When Plut. says of the elders of the Phyle, κλῆρον αὐτῷ (*i.e.*, the boy who was to be brought up) τῶν ἐνακισχιλίων προσνείμαντες, he can hardly be right in this general statement.

brought up in their several homes under the superintendence of the women till their seventh year. When they reached that age, the State took over their education, which was directed by the παιδονόμος.[1] Every boy was entered in one of the various βοῦαι, and inside this again in one of the ἶλαι, which were subdivisions of the βοῦαι.[2] Over each βοῦα was a βουαγός, over each ἴλα an ἴλαρχος; they were taken from the young men of more than twenty years of age.[3] The whole of the members of the βοῦαι were divided into three classes, the παῖδες from seven to eighteen years old, the μελλίρανες from eighteen to twenty, the ἴρανες from twenty to thirty. Of the latter again, the younger were called πρωτίρανες, the elder σφαιρεῖς.[4]

The entire mode of life of these boys and youths was directed to hardening their bodies. Beginning with their twelfth year, the boys were close cropped, made to go barefoot, and play habitually naked. From their twelfth year they went without underclothing, and slept together in their ἶλαι and βοῦαι, on beds of reeds gathered by their own hands from the banks of the Eurotas.[5] Every year the young men who had reached a certain age gave

---

[1] Xen., de rep. Lac., 2, 2; Plut., Lyc., 17.

[2] Plut., Lyc., 16, where the divisions are called ἀγέλαι and ἶλαι. See also Plut., Ages., 2; Inst. Lac., 6, p. 293. That ἀγέλη=βοῦα is shown by Hesych.: βοῦα· ἀγέλη παίδων. (Λάκωνες.) βουαγός· ἀγελάρχης, ὁ τῆς ἀγέλης ἄρχων παῖς Λάκωνες.

[3] From Plut., Lyc., 17: καὶ κατ' ἀγέλας αὐτοὶ προΐσταντο τῶν λεγομένων εἰρένων ἀεὶ τὸν σωφρονέστατον καὶ μαχιμώτατον, it would appear that the youths and boys themselves chose the βουαγός. But see Lyc., 16. For the head of the ἶλαι, see Xen., de rep. Lac., 2, 11: ἔθηκε τῆς ἴλης ἑκάστης τὸν τορώτατον τῶν εἰρένων ἄρχειν. Cf. Grasberger, Erzieh. u. Unterr., Th. 3. For the training of the Epheboi, cf. 57 ff.

[4] The ages can be determined, it appears to me, from Plut., Lyc., 17: εἴρενας δὲ καλοῦσι τοὺς ἔτος ἤδη δεύτερον ἐκ παίδων γεγονότας, μελλείρενας δὲ τῶν παίδων πρεσβυτάτους. οὗτος οὖν ὁ εἴρην εἴκοσι ἔτη γεγονὼς ἄρχει κ. τ. λ. On the correct forms of the names, vid. Kuhn's Zeitschr., 8, 53; Phil., 10, 431; Curtius, Stud., 4, 1, 116. Phot.: καταπρωτείρας· πρωτείραι (πρωτίρανες, as Mor. Schmidt writes κατὰ πρωτίρανας in Hesych.) οἱ περὶ εἴκοσι ἔτη παρὰ Λάκωσι. Paus. 3, 14, 6: οἱ δέ (sc. οἱ σφαιρεῖς) εἰσιν οἱ ἐκ τῶν ἐφήβων εἰς ἄνδρας ἀρχόμενοι συντελεῖν. Mention of σφαιρεῖς in inscriptions; C.I.G., 1386, 1432; Le Bas 164; Bullet. de corr. Hell., 1, 879, 2. For other designations of age, see Müller, Dor., 2, 296 (809–10).

[5] Plut., Lyc., 16; Inst. Lac., 5, 6, p. 298; Xen., de rep. Lac., 2, 3, 4. Photius on συνέφηβος says: Σπαρτιᾶται δὲ σιδεύνας (sc. τοὺς ἐφήβους καλοῦσι)· διέκρινον δὲ αὐτοὺς ἄρα τῇ ἥβῃ, τουτέστιν περὶ πεντεκαίδεκα καὶ ἐκκαίδεκα ἔτη γεγονότας τῶν νεωτέρων παίδων καὶ καθ' ἑαυτοὺς ἤσκουν ἀνδροῦσθαι.

public proof of their power of enduring bodily pain. This διαμαστίγωσις, as it was called, originally perhaps had had a religious significance; it took place at the altar of Artemis Orthia or Orthosia. The youths who took part in this competition were flogged till the blood came, and he came off conqueror—βωμονίκης —who bore the flogging longest and most stoically. It happened not seldom that they would hold out until they sank to the earth dead.[1] To train the youths in cunning and craftiness, they were allowed to steal provisions to eke out the very scanty supplies furnished to them. If they succeeded in this without being detected, they went unpunished; otherwise hunger and a flogging awaited them.[2] The particular exercises which the young Spartans practised all had the object of fitting them to become skilful warriors. Hence they zealously practised all the gymnastic exercises which aim at general bodily development.[3] Of particular warlike games, which they played side against side, we hear of the fight at the Platanistas, and the ball-match in the theatre.[4] Before the development of the body that of the mind had completely to give way. The Spartan boys were, from their earliest years, practised in the art of brief speaking, but in nothing else.[5]

---

[1] Lucian, *Anach.*, 38; Plut., *Lyc.*, 18; *Instit. Lac.*, 40, p. 296. Plut., *Lyc.*, 18, calls the competitors ἔφηβοι; *Instit. Lac.*, 40, παῖδες. Hygin., *fabul.*, 261: "ubi (sc. in Laconia) sacrificii consuetudo adolescentum verberibus servabatur, qui vocabantur βωμονῖκαι, quia aris superpositi contendebant, qui plura posset verbera sustinere." Trieber, *quæst. Lac.*, p. 25 ff., gives an accurate collection of all passages bearing upon this.

[2] Plut., *Lyc.*, 17, 18; *Instit. Lac.*, 12, 13, p. 293; *Apophth. Lac.*, p. 288, 32; Xen., *de rep. Lac.*, 2, 5 ff.; Isocr. 12, 211/2.

[3] For the various exercises, *vid.* Haase on Xen., *de rep. Lac.*, p. 219, 108.

[4] Description of the μάχη, at the Πλατανιστᾶς, Paus. 3, 14, 8 ff.; Lucian, *Anachars.*, 38; Cic., *Tusc. disp.*, 5, 27, 77. Of the ball-match, Lucian, *ibid.*, says: μέμνησο, ἤν ποτε καὶ ἐς Λακεδαίμονα ἔλθῃς, μὴ καταγελάσαι μηδὲ ἐκείνων μηδὲ οἴεσθαι μάτην πονεῖν αὐτούς, ὁπόταν ἢ σφαίρας πέρι ἐν τῷ θεάτρῳ συμπεσόντες παίωσιν ἀλλήλους κ.τ.λ. Particular form of the game—Demetr., *de elocut.*, § 122: ἔφορος ἐν Λακεδαίμονι τὸν περιέργως καὶ οὐκ ἐπιχωρίως σφαιρίσαντα ἐμαστίγωσεν. Schol. *ad* Plat., *Laws*, 1, 633: ἐνίοτε δὲ καὶ σφαῖραν ἢ ἄλλο τι ἐρρίπτουν, ὥστε τὸν πρῶτον ἁρπάσαντα νικᾶν.

[5] Plut., *Lyc.*, 18, 19. We cannot determine for certain how far the Spartan boys learnt the elements of reading and writing. Plut., *Lyc.*, 16, says: γράμματα μὲν οὖν ἕνεκα τῆς χρείας ἐμάνθανον, while Isocr., 12, 209, denies even this. Perhaps we may assume as certain that many Spartans learnt to read and write, but only by private instruction. On Laconism in speaking see Plat., *Protag.*, 342.

Although those ἴρανες, who were the heads of the βοῦαι and ἶλαι, were entrusted with the general instruction and supervision of the youths and boys belonging to their particular divi- εἰσπνήλας sions, it was customary for a friendship which lasted and ἀίτας. beyond the years of the Agoge to be formed between each youth of a greater age and a boy, the object being the education of the younger. The youth was called, with reference to this relation, εἰσπνήλας, because he was filled with love for his protégé; the boy ἀίτας, because he was to listen to the teaching and instruction of the εἰσπνήλας. This relation was regarded as that of lover and love, but its degradation to sensuality was visited with heavy punishment.[1]

The public Syssitia at Sparta had also, without doubt, a military object, and in their inner significance may be regarded as associations of mess-comrades in a camp. Indeed, their military character is attested by the designation of the members of such a Syssition as σύσκηνοι; by the Polemarchs' supervision of them; and by the explicit testimony of ancient writers.[2] At Sparta the Syssitia bore properly the name ἀνδρεῖα, Syssitia.

---

[1] On the duties of the ἴρανες, who were the heads of the divisions, see Plut., *Lyc.*, 17, 18. That the lovers were young men, is attested by Plut., *Lyc.*, 17: ἤδη δὲ τοῖς τηλικούτοις ἐρασταὶ τῶν εὐδοκίμων νέων συνανεστρέφοντο. They were responsible for the boy's conduct, *Lyc.*, 18; Aelian, *Var. Hist.*, 3, 10. Sensuality punished by lifelong Atimia, Aelian, *ibid.*, 3, 12; Plut., *Instit. Lac.*, 7. For the meaning of εἰσπνήλας and ἀίτας see Schömann ad Plut., *Cleom.*, 181 ff., and the authorities quoted *Ant. iur. publ. Gr.*, 137, no. 5. Εἰσπνήλας is to be regarded as the lover, ἀίτας as the love. *Vid. Et. M.*: ἀίτας· ὁ ἐρώμενος· παρὰ τὸ ἀείν, ὅ ἐστι πνέειν· ὁ εἰσπνέων τὸν ἔρωτα τῷ ἐραστῇ. φασὶ γὰρ γίνεσθαι τὸν ἔρωτα ἐκ τοῦ εἰσπνεῖσθαι ἐκ τῆς μορφῆς· τοῦ ἐρωμένου. ὅθεν καὶ εἰσπνήλας καλοῦσι τοὺς ἐραστὰς παρὰ Λάκωσιν. Accordingly, εἰσπνεῖν is used of the object of affection, εἰσπνεῖσθαι of the lover, as appears from Xen., *Symp.*, 4, 15: διὰ γὰρ τὸ ἐμπνεῖν τι ἡμᾶς τοὺς καλοὺς τοῖς ἐρωτικοῖς, and Plut., *Cleom.*, 3, where, in explaining ἐραστοῦ γεγονότος, he adds, τοῦτο δὲ ἐμπνεῖσθαι Λακεδαιμόνιοι καλοῦσιν. ὁ εἰσπνήλας, as the lover, must consequently have a passive sense, he who is breathed upon by love through the beloved. A passive meaning for εἰσπνήλας is assumed also by the explanation which makes εἰσπνήλας ὁ ἐρώμενος, which proceeds from the supposition that εἰσπνεῖν = ἐρᾶν. See Aelian, *Var. Hist.*, 3, 12; Et. M., εἰσπνήλης. Ἀίτας, according to Aristoph., in the Lex. Seguer., 348, 2, ὁ ἐρώμενος, is to be derived from ἀίω, not as the Et. M. gives, from ἀέω, ἄημι.

[2] On the Syssitia's military character, *vid.* Oncken, *d. Staatslehre des Aristot.*, 2, 325 ff. The members of a φιδίτιον were called σύσκηνοι, Xen., *de rep. Lac.*, 7, 4; 9, 4; 15, 5. Xen., 15, 4, calls the feeding together σκηνεῖν; the State guaranteed the kings a δημοσία σκηνή. Cf. Trieber, *op. cit.*, p.

and later φιδίτια.[1] In all probability all Spartans of more than twenty years old (with the exception of those ἴρανες who were the heads of βοῦαι or ἶλαι) were entitled and bound to be participants in the Phiditia.[2] Originally the kings seem to have been exempt from the duty of taking their meals in their Phidition; but later the Ephors compelled them to do so. Only those might absent themselves who were offering a family sacrifice or were away hunting. The Phiditia ceased only when a State sacrifice was being offered, with which general feasts were regularly connected.[3] The number of members of a Phidition was about fifteen; in order to secure complete harmony within the Phidition,[4] new members were admitted only by unanimous consent. The expenses of the king's table were met by the State; all other

---

21/2. The Polemarchs superintendence is attested by Plut., *Lyc.*, 12. In Plat., *Laws.*, 1, 633 the Athenian interrogates the Spartan, who replies in the affirmative: τὰ συσσίτια φαμὲν καὶ τὰ γυμνάσια πρὸς τὸν πόλεμον ἐξηυρῆσθαι τῷ νομοθέτῃ; Of the Cretan Syssitia, Plat., *ibid.*, 1, 625, says: ἐπεὶ καὶ τα συσσίτια κινδυνεύει ξυναγαγεῖν ὁρῶν, ὡς πάντες, ὁπόταν στρατεύωνται, τόθ' ὑπ' αὐτοῦ τοῦ πράγματος ἀναγκάζονται φυλακῆς αὐτῶν ἕνεκα ξυσσιτεῖν τοῦτον τὸν χρόνον. Cf. Dionys. Hal. 2, 23; Lex. Seguer. 303, 21. See Bielschowsky, *de Spartanorum syssitiis*, p. 32 ff.

[1] On the Syssitia cf. Müller, *Dor.*, 2, 198 (210) ff.; 269 (283), and Bielschowsky, *de Spartanorum syssitiis*, Breslau, 1869. For the oldest name, see the fragment of Alcman, quoted by Ephoros *ap.* Strab., 482: φοίναις δὲ καὶ ἐν θιάσοισιν—ἀνδρείων παρὰ δαιτυμόνεσσι πρέπει παιᾶνα κατάρχειν with which agrees Arist., *Pol.*, 2, 10 = p. 51, 11: καὶ τό γε ἀρχαῖον ἐκάλουν (sc. τὰ συσσίτια) οἱ Λάκωνες οὐ φιδίτια ἀλλ' ἀνδρεῖα, καθάπερ οἱ Κρῆτες. That φιδίτια—in the MSS. often changed into φειδίτια—is the right form, is shown by the line of Antiphanes, quoted in Ath. 4, 143 A., and by Plut., *Lyc.*, 12. For the etymology of the word φιδίτιον, see Plut., *Lyc.*, 12. Schömann, *Griech. Alterth.*, 1, 286, takes it to mean a "sitting"; Bielschowsky, p. 12, supposes the original full title was ἀνδρεῖα φιδίτια, meaning cenæ virorum, and derives it from ἔδειν.

[2] That the Spartan youths, after completing their twentieth year, took part in the Phiditia has been inferred from Plut., *Lyc.*, 15. See Bielschowsky, 14/15. Of course we cannot be absolutely certain. The ἴρανες who supervised divisions fed with their charges, Plut., *Lyc.*, 17, 18.

[3] According to Hdt., 6, 57, the kings might or might not attend the Phidition; this was not so later. Plut., *Lyc.*, 12; *Apophth. Lac.*, p. 278, 6; cf. Bielschowsky, p. 17; Plut., *Lyc.*, 12: ἐξῆν γὰρ οἴκοι δειπνεῖν ὁπότε θύσας τις ἢ κυνηγῶν ὀψίσειε, τοὺς δὲ ἄλλους ἔδει παρεῖναι. Hesych.: ἀφέδιτος (Cobet, ἀφίδιτος)· ἡμέρα παρὰ Λάκωσιν, ἐν ᾗ θύουσιν.

[4] Plut., *Lyc.*, 12: συνήρχοντο δὲ ἀνὰ πεντεκαίδεκα καὶ βραχεῖ τούτων ἐλάττους ἢ πλείους, where the mode of voting at the admission of a new member is also touched upon. See Bielschowsky, pp. 15/6.

Spartans had to contribute for the Phiditia every month a medimnos of barley-flour, 8 choes of wine, 5 minæ of cheese, $2\frac{1}{2}$ minæ of figs, and 10 Æginetan obols. Perhaps the money thus collected was spent in the purchase of the pigs for the meals.[1] The regular dish was the βαφὰ or αἱματία, *i.e.* pork cooked in blood, and seasoned with salt and vinegar. Of this, each had a certain quantity; but he might take as much as he liked of the bread and wine. The dessert consisted of cheese, olives, and figs.[2] Besides this regular fare members of the Phidition contributed not unfrequently extra delicacies, portions of sacrifices, game killed in the chase, and wheaten bread. When luxury invaded even Sparta, the extra dishes, then called ἔπαικλα, became the most important, while the αἱματία was only retained for form's sake.[3] All these Phiditia took place in a species of encampment or collection of tents, most probably in the Hyacinthian street.[4]

In the tactical organization of the Lacedæmonian army, various changes were introduced as time went on.[5] We find the establishment of ἐνωμοτίαι, τριακάδες, and συσσίτια

Organization of the Army.

---

[1] On the king's table, *vid.* Xen., *de rep. Lac.*, 15, 4, and Plut., *Lyc.*, 12, who gives the Laconian measures, while Dicaiarchos *ap.* Ath., 4, 141 c. has converted them into Attic measures. Cf. Hultsch, *griech. u. röm. Metrol.*,[2] 500; Bielschowsky, p. 23 ff.

[2] Plut., *Lyc.*, 12 calls the Spartan national dish ὁ μέλας ζωμός. The proper Spartan name is gathered from Poll. 6, 57: ὁ δὲ μέλας καλούμενος ζωμός, Λακωνικὸν μὲν ὡς ἐπὶ πολὺ τὸ ἔδεσμα, ἔστι δ' ἡ καλουμένη αἱματία. Hesych. says, βαφὰ ζωμός. Λάκωνες. The ingredients of the αἱματία are blood, as appears from the name, ὕειον κρέας ἐφθόν (Dicaiarch. *ap.* Ath. 4, 141 B), vinegar and salt, as may be inferred from Plut., *de sanit. præc.*, 12: καὶ καθάπερ οἱ Λάκωνες ὄξος καὶ ἅλας δόντες τῷ μαγείρῳ τὰ λοιπὰ κελεύουσι ἐν τῷ ἱερείῳ ζητεῖν. For the other ingredients see Dicaiarch. *ap.* Ath. 4, 141 A, B.

[3] The extras mentioned in the text are attested by Xen., *de rep. Lac.*, 5, 3; Plut., *Lyc.*, 12. It may be questioned whether such an extra was called ἔπαικλον in the earlier times. Cf. what Ath. 4, 138 B ff. has collected περὶ τῶν Λακωνικῶν συμποσίων. On the desuetude of the Syssitia in Sparta see Bielschowsky, p. 27 ff.

[4] Paus. 7, 1, 8, καὶ ἦν καὶ ἐς ἐμὲ ἔτι αὐτῷ τάφος ἔνθα τὰ δεῖπνα Λακεδαιμονίοις ἐστὶ τὰ φιδίτια καλούμενα. Their tent form is to be inferred from the fact that Xen. calls the members of a Phidition σύσκηνοι. *Vid.* p. 65. That the Phiditia were held in the Hyacinthian street, is the plausible deduction of Bielschowsky.pp. 22/3 from a comparison of Polemon's statement *ap.* Ath. 2, 39 C with that of Demetrios of Skepsis *ap.* Ath. 4, 173 F.

[5] The account of Beloch, *Bevölker. d. griech. röm. Welt*, 131 ff., does little to advance our knowledge of the historical development of the Lacedæmonian army.

attributed to Lycurgus. Whether these expressions really indicated divisions of the army, and, if so, how these divisions were subordinated one to another, or whether there was any such subordination at all, cannot be determined with certainty.[1]

On the other hand we may take it as a certain fact that in the earliest times—we know that it was so still in the Persian wars—the Spartans and Perioicoi had separate military organizations.[2] The army of the Spartans then consisted most probably of λόχοι.[3] Each of these bore a special name, either taken from a quarter of the town or given for some other reason.[4] The leaders of the λόχοι

---

[1] Hdt. 1, 65, μετὰ δὲ τὰ ἐς πόλεμον ἔχοντα ἐνωμοτίας καὶ τριηκάδας καὶ συσσίτια —ἔστησε Λυκοῦργος. Συσσίτια has either been taken to be the greater divisions in view of Plut., *Ag.*, 8 (so *e.g.*, Müller, *Dor.*, 2, 233 (Engl. Tr., 2, 253) Rüstow u. Koechly, *Gesch. d. griech. Kriegsw.*, 38; Stein, *d. Kriegsw. d. Spart. Konitz*, 1868, p. 6, or it has been identified with the companies for dining—of 15 men regularly—(see Plut., *Lyc.*, 12) and so Bielschowsky, *op. cit.*, p. 32 ff., who emends p. 28 ff., Plut., *Ag.*, 8. We must bear in mind that συσσίτια is certainly no Spartan expression, that in Sparta they were rather called in the earliest days ἀνδρεῖα, later φιδίτια (see p. 66). It is impossible to determine Herodotus' meaning. I would take συσσίτια in its general sense as associations of mess-companions; it is manifestly used so in Polyain. 2, 3, 11—see also Aelian, *Var. Hist.*, 2, 1, 15; 2, 3, 11—where, however, of course it does not denote any official subdivision. Cf. Stehfen, *de Spartanorum re militari*, 23 ff.; Trieber, *ibid.*, p. 15 ff., who explains Hdt.'s συσσίτια as different from the φιδίτια, takes it as meaning simply a military subdivision of the ἐνωμοτία, and strikes out τριηκάδας as a gloss.

[2] Tyrtæus' poems presume a Spartan citizen-army. Cf. especially fr. 11, 15, 16, in Bergk. I think we may argue the like for the Persian wars from Hdt. 9, 10. 11. 29.

[3] Hesych., in a gloss that is evidently incomplete, says: λόχοι . . . Λακεδαιμονίων φησὶν Ἀριστοφάνης (*Lysistr.*, 454) τέτταρας. πέντε γάρ εἰσιν, ὥς ςησι Ἀριστοτέλης. This has been filled up from Phot., λόχοι Λακεδαιμονίων τέτταρες, ὡς Ἀριστοφάνης, Θουκυδίδης δὲ πέντε, Ἀριστοτέλης δὲ ἐπτά. Only we must begin from Hesych. and suppose Aristotle really gave 5 lochoi, and alter Photius accordingly. For Thuc. 5, 68 in reality counts 7 Spartan lochoi, and therefore plainly his number has been interchanged with Aristotle's in Phot. See Rose, *Aristot. pseudep.*, p. 492, no. 154. I regard it as quite unallowable to explain the 5 Thucydidean lochoi in Phot. by the 5 Argive lochoi in Thuc. 5, 72, as *e.g.* Trieber, *ibid.*, p. 11, does.

[4] The Schol. on Arist., *Lysistr.*, 454, where 4 lochoi are mentioned, says, ἀργότερον τὸ Λακώνων ἔοικεν ἐξειργάσθαι ὁ ποιητής. λόχοι γὰρ οὐκ εἰσὶ τέτταρες ἐν Λακεδαιμονίᾳ, ἀλλὰ πέντε Ἔδωλος, Σίνις, Ἄριμας, Πλοάς, Μεσσοάγης. ὁ δὲ Θουκυδίδης ἐπτά φησι χωρὶς τῶν Σκιριτῶν. The Schol. on Thuc. 4, 8 calls the 5 λόχοι Αἰδώλιος, Σίνις, Σαρίνας, Πλοάς, Μεσσοάγης. Hesych. says under Ἐδωλός· λόχος Λακεδαιμονίων οὕτως ἐκαλεῖτο. Μεσοάγης undoubtedly is derived from the κώμη Mesoa, and the λόχος Πιτανάτης recorded Hdt. 9, 53 (cf. Herodian, 4, 8) presents nothing suspicious, especially as Hdt. was connected with the

were the λοχαγοί, in addition to whom there were already πολέμαρχοι who perhaps were employed on independent commands.[1]

We first hear of a change in the Lacedæmonian army organization in 425. The Spartan and Perioican hoplites were then amalgamated. This was probably due to the heavy losses which the Spartans had suffered in the great earthquake of 465. Spartans and Perioicoi were now incorporated in the same lochoi.[2] In consequence the number of lochoi was increased. In B.C. 418 the λόχοι were the largest divisions in the Lacedæmonian army: every λόχος contained 4 πεντηκοστύες, each πεντηκοστύς 4 ἐνωμοτίαι.[3] The

Pitanatan Archias. *Vid.* Hdt. 8, 55. We must then substitute Πιτανάτης for one of the lochoi names above given, the forms being plainly corrupt. If we follow Thuc. 1, 20 (see also Hesych. Πιτανάτης), who denies categorically the existence of the λόχος Πιτανάτης (*vid.* too Bauer in the *Phil.*, 50, 422 ff.), there still remains the hypothesis that Hdt. called the lochos, which he describes as that of the Pitanatai, λόχος Πιτανάτης because it was composed of them, though its official name perhaps was not taken from the κώμη Pitane. It is not open to us to substitute the names of the Spartan κῶμαι throughout for the lochoi names we find recorded, as Rüstow and Koechly do *ibid.*, p. 87, 7. Trieber, *op. cit.*, pp. 11/2 considers our authorities as so worthless that he passes them over with a few words. Stehfen, who *op. cit.* 6/7 regards Aristotle as the ultimate authority for the number 5 of the lochoi in the lexicographers, supposes (p. 8, 1), that this assertion was erroneously attributed to Aristotle, who was perhaps speaking of the 5 κῶμαι at Sparta. Harp. μόρα serves to refute the idea that Arist. attested the number 5. Whoever assumes, as Stehfen does, that in course of time changes were introduced in the tactical organization of the Spartan army, cannot possibly offer any objection to the various declarations of Arist. which refer to different periods. I still regard the views I propounded in my first edition as the most probable.

[1] Hdt. 9, 53, says, Ἀμομφάρετος λοχηγέων τοῦ Πιτανητέων λόχου. He is counted among the πρῶτοι, and evidently has a voice in the council of war, Hdt. 9, 55. Ταξίαρχοι in Hdt. 9, 53 is, judging by the context, not an official title. Cf. on this title Trieber, *ibid.*, p. 12 ff. Εὐαίνετος ὁ Καρήνου ἐκ τῶν πολεμάρχων ἀραιρημένος is mentioned, Hdt. 7, 173, as leading the Lacedæmonians at Tempe.

[2] The hoplites to garrison Sphacteria were drawn by lot ἀπὸ πάντων τῶν λόχων, Thuc., 4, 8, and consisted of Spartans and Perioicoi, Thuc. 4, 38.

[3] The number of the λόχοι, which in the first edition I estimated at 7, following Thuc. 5, 68, is better left undetermined. The hypothesis of Stehfen, *op. cit.*, 19 that there were 12 lochoi, is not proved. The account of the battle at Mantinea, Thuc. 5, 67-73, involves many difficulties. The following objections to Stehfen's views, p. 18 ff., suggest themselves: Thuc. 5, 64 says of the expedition of the Lacedæmonians ἐνταῦθα δὴ βοήθεια τῶν Λακεδαιμονίων γίγνεται αὐτῶν τε καὶ τῶν Εἱλώτων πανδημεὶ ὀξεῖα καὶ οἵα οὔπω πρότερον; undoubtedly he understands among the Helots the νεοδαμώδεις and Βρασίδειοι mentioned 5, 67, just as, Thuc. 7, 19, Helots and Neodamodeis are

λόχος was commanded by the λοχαγός, the πεντηκοστὺς by the πεντηκοντήρ, the ἐνωμοτία by the ἐνωμοτάρχης. The πολέμαρχοι were in immediate attendance on the king, transmitted his orders, and in difficult operations took command of separate lochoi.[1]

In the course of the Peloponnesian war yet another alteration was introduced in the tactical arrangement of the Lacedæmonian army. We first hear of it for the year 404.[2] From this time the Lacedæmonian army contained 6 μόραι, each μόρα 2 λόχοι, each mentioned together. If 5, 68 τὸ Λακεδαιμονίων τότε παραγενόμενον πλῆθος is counted by itself ἄνευ Σκιριτῶν, that is merely because the Neodamodeis and Brasideioi were not incorporated in the lochoi. According to the calculation in Thuc. 5, 68, the number of Lacedæmonians in the 7 lochoi on the left wing was about 3600 men. To these must probably be added the two lochoi mentioned Thuc. 5, 71: with Stehfen 18/9 I suppose from the context of chap. 71 that they were "on the right" (see Thuc. 5, 67). Thus about 4600 Lacedæmonians, Spartans and Perioicoi took part in the engagement. If to these be added τὸ ἕκτον μέρος, ἐν ᾧ τὸ πρεσβύτερόν τε καὶ τὸ νεώτερον ἦν (5, 64) that is, the men of the oldest and youngest years from the various lochoi, who were sent to the rear, we get as the sum total of the Lacedæmonians about 5400 men, a number not too small, when the obvious fact is borne in mind that only the well-to-do served as hoplites. In 394 at Corinth there fought 6000 men (Xen., *Hell.*, 4, 2, 16), although not all Lacedæmonians who were liable to serve were there; we must therefore notice that by that date another military reform had been introduced, vhose tendency undoubtedly was to increase the number of Perioicoi bound to serve. Thuc. 5, 68 gives us the tactical arrangement of the army. There we read: λόχοι μὲν γὰρ ἐμάχοντο ἑπτὰ ἄνευ Σκιριτῶν, ὄντων ἑξακοσίων, ἐν δὲ ἑκάστῳ λόχῳ πεντηκοστύες ἦσαν τέσσαρες καὶ ἐν τῇ πεντηκοστύι ἐνωμοτίαι τέσσαρες.

[1] As to the command in the army Thuc. 5, 66 tells us βασιλέως γὰρ ἄγοντος ὑπ' ἐκείνου πάντα ἄρχεται, καὶ τοῖς μὲν πολεμάρχοις αὐτὸς φράζει τὸ δέον, οἱ δὲ τοῖς λοχαγοῖς, ἐκεῖνοι δὲ τοῖς πεντηκοντῆρσιν, αὖθις δὲ οὗτοι τοῖς ἐνωμοτάρχαις, καὶ οὗτοι τῇ ἐνωμοτίᾳ. The two Polemarchs who in the battle of Mantinea led two lochoi (Thuc. 5, 71), were undoubtedly despatched by Agis, to execute the manœuvres which he designed.

[2] The Lacedæmonian Morai are first mentioned Xen., *Hell.*, 2, 4, 31. That the place of the λόχος was taken by the μόρα seems to be shown by Hesych., μόρα μέρη τινά. καὶ μέρη τοῦ στρατοῦ ἢ τάγμα. παρὰ γὰρ Λακεδαιμονίοις οἱ πατρίλοχοι (πρὶν λόχοι) μόρα αὖθις ὀνομασθέντες. Trieber, *ibid.*, p. 4 ff., tries to show that the Morai were an institution existing at Sparta from the very first. But in Hdt. 9, 60 μοῖρα certainly stands in merely the general signification of part, and we can draw no conclusion as to the existence of the morai from the fact that Hdt. and Thuc. mention Polemarchs, for in Thuc. 5, 71 the Polemarchs manifestly lead the lochoi. There is nothing strange in the simultaneous existence of lochagoi, for the Polemarchs regularly were in attendance on the king and conveyed his commands. *Vid.* Thuc. 5, 66.

λόχος 4 πεντηκοστύες, each πεντηκοστὺς 2 ἐνωμοτίαι. The μόρα was commanded by the πολέμαρχος, the λόχος by the λοχαγός, the πεντηκοστὺς by the πεντηκοντήρ, the ἐνωμοτία by the ἐνωμοτάρχης.[1] In this arrangement also, Spartans and Perioicoi were enrolled in the same Morai.[2]

We can say nothing definitely as to the principle observed in marshalling the individual soldiers within the Morai. We can only note that among the Spartans fathers, brothers, and sons did not belong to the same mora, and that the Amyclaioi were spread over the whole army.[3]

---

[1] The new organization of the Lacedæmonian army is attested by Xen., *de rep. Lac.*, 11, 4. But I suppose with E. Müller in the *Jahrb. f. cl. Phil.*, vol. 75, p. 99, on the strength of Xen., *Hell.*, 7, 4, 20, and 7, 5, 10 (where it is true the variant δέκα is found), that each μόρα contained only two λόχοι. The 4 λόχοι in Xen., *de rep. Lac.*, 11, 4, the number moreover in the expedition mentioned by Stob., *Flor.*, 44, 36, has arisen by changing δύο into δ'. So Schömann, *griech. Alterth.*, 1, 296, 1. Cf. Harp., μόρων, where we find φησὶ (sc. Ἀριστοτέλης) δὲ ὡς εἰσὶ μόραι ἐξ ὠνομασμέναι καὶ διῄρηνται εἰς τὰς μόρας Λακεδαιμόνιοι πάντες. See Müller, *fr. hist. gr.*, 2, 129, 83. 6 μόραι are the result too of a comparison of Xen., *Hell.*, 6, 1, 1, with 6, 4, 17. The circumstance that no lochoi are mentioned in the first six books of the *Hellenica*, that 4, 8, 15 ἥμισυ μόρας is used, which corresponds to one λόχος, that in 3, 5, 22; 4, 5, 7, where we should expect an express mention of the lochagoi, they are not named, while in the seventh book (cf. 7, 1, 30; 7, 4, 20; 7, 5, 10) λόχοι not μόραι meet us, has led Stehfen, 10 ff., to suppose that the Spartan army, when the Perioicoi formed the greater part of it, was divided into morai; when the Spartans alone marched out, into lochoi. I fully appreciate the importance of this extraordinary phenomenon in Xen. But since as a matter of fact Perioicoi were included even in the lochoi (cf. 7, 4, 20 with 27), I hold it wiser until we get further light on the subject to abide by the statement in Xen., *de rep. Lac.*, 11, 4, and to seek for other explanations of these peculiarities in the *Hell.* Xen., *de rep. Lac.*, 12, 6 mentions a πρῶτος πολέμαρχος, who, 'according to a conjecture of Gabriel, *de magistratib. Lacedæmonior.*, p. 17/8 is perhaps identical with the πρεσβύτατος τῶν περὶ δαμοσίαν of Xen., *ibid.*, 13, 7.

[2] Xen., *Hell.*, 4, 5, 11; 6, 1, 1, compared with 6, 4, 15. The expression μόραι πολιτικαὶ in Xen., *de rep. Lac.*, 11, 4, does not make against this. According to Xen., *Hell.*, 7, 4, 20, Archidamos marched out μετὰ τῶν πολιτῶν and left in Cromnos a garrison of three lochoi; among them, however, were both Spartans and Perioicoi. Xen. 7, 4, 27. Cf. Trieber in the *Jahrb. f. cl. Phil.*, 1871, p. 443 ff., who demonstrates that the πολιτικὸν στράτευμα indicates the Spartans and Perioicoi in opposition to the allies. However perhaps we ought to read in Xen., *de rep. Lac.*, 11, 4, ὁπλιτικῶν for πολιτικῶν; this reading is in Stob., *Flor.*, 44, 36.

[3] Xen., *Hell.*, 4, 5, 10, πολὺ πένθος ἦν κατὰ τὸ Λακωνικὸν στράτευμα, πλὴν ὅσων ἐτέθνασαν ἐν χώρᾳ ἢ υἱοὶ ἢ πατέρες ἢ ἀδελφοί· οὗτοι δ' ὥσπερ νικηφόροι λαμπροὶ καὶ ἀγαλλόμενοι τῷ οἰκείῳ πάθει περιῄεσαν. Sons, fathers, and brothers, then, of

Every Spartan, and also perhaps every Perioicos enrolled among the hoplites, was ἔμφρουρος, *i.e.* liable to military service. The liability continued for 40 years, from the 20th year of life to the 60th. An exception was made, perhaps only in later days, in the case of any Spartan who had 3 sons: he was not bound to serve in war.[1] It goes without saying that not all those who were liable to military service took part in every campaign; the Ephors specified certain ages for the levy, according to the force which it was necessary to raise. For dangerous expeditions it was usual to select only such men as left issue behind them in case of their death.[2] The varying number of the years levied for the several expeditions is the cause of the very diversified accounts given by the ancients of the strength of the morai.[3]

Liability to Service.

The 300 ἱππεῖς formed a *corps d'élite* among the hoplites,[4] and were selected annually from among the young men in the following manner. The Ephors chose three men in the prime of life, and then these three, called ἱππαγρέται, each selected at his own discretion 100 of the most valiant of the youths for service as ἱππεῖς, this being considered an especial honour.[5] The 300 ἱππεῖς obtained by this method formed in time of war the body

ἱππεῖς.

those who belonged to the annihilated mora were to be found in another mora of the army. As to the Amyclaioi, Xen., *Hell.*, 4, 5, 11, says καὶ τότε δὴ τοὺς ἐκ πάσης τῆς στρατιᾶς Ἀμυκλαίους κατέλιπεν Ἀγησίλαος ἐν Λεχαίῳ.

[1] Xen., *Hell.*, 5, 4, 13, tells us that those ὑπὲρ τεσσαράκοντα ἀφ' ἥβης were no longer bound to serve abroad. See Plut., *Ages.*, 24. The man liable was called ἔμφρουρος, Xen., *de rep. Lac.*, 5, 7. Exemptions for those who had three sons, Aristot., *Pol.*, 2, 9 = p. 47, 18; Aelian, *Var. Hist.*, 6, 6. αἱ ἐπ' ἀρχαῖς were also temporarily exempt, Xen., *Hell.*, 6, 4, 17.

[2] Xen., *de rep. Lac.*, 11, 2, πρῶτον μὲν τοίνυν οἱ ἔφοροι προκηρύττουσι τὰ ἔτη, εἰς ἃ δεῖ στρατεύεσθαι καὶ ἱππεῦσι καὶ ὁπλίταις, ἔπειτα δὲ καὶ τοῖς χειροτέχναις. Cf. Xen., *Hell.*, 6, 4, 17. On the various ages in the morai see Xen., *Hell.*, 2, 4, 32; 3, 4, 23; 4, 5, 14. 16; 4, 6, 10. See Stein, *op. cit.*, p. 18. Sparing employment in war of those who left no offspring behind them, Hdt. 7, 205.

[3] Xen. gives 576 as the number of men in a mora, 6, 4, 12; 600, 4, 5, 12; 1000, 4, 2, 16. The μόρα was according to Ephor. (*vid.* Diod. 15, 32) 500 men strong; according to Callisthenes, 700; according to others, 900; Plut., *Pelop.*, 17. Lex. Seguer. 279, 13, gives 800. The number 25 for the ἐνωμοτία in Suid. and Et. M. gives a strength of 400 for the μόρα. Cf. also Phot. μοῖρα.

[4] See Stein, *ibid.*, pp. 13, 14. That the ἱππεῖς, in spite of their name, were hoplites is shown by Strabo 481-2. Cf. Hesych.: ἱππαγρέτας· ἀρχὴ ἐπὶ τῶν ἐπιλέκτων ὁπλιτῶν. In Thuc. 5, 72, they are called οἱ τριακόσιοι ἱππῆς καλούμενοι. We find them mentioned as early as Hdt. 7, 205; 8, 124.

[5] For the method of selection, cf. Xen., *de Rep. Lac.*, 4, 1-4. Membership of the 300 was ἐν τῇ πόλει πρωτεύουσα τιμή: *Apophth. Lac. Pædareti*, 3, p. 284. Plut., *Lyc.*, 25.

guard of the king, and in time of peace were employed in services of particular importance.[1]

The equipment of the Spartan hoplites consisted of a red cloak, a cuirass, a helmet, a brass shield with a Λ as cognisance, a long thrusting spear and a short sword.[2] *Equipment.*

Before the Peloponnesian war the Helots were only employed as camp followers, or at most light armed troops; in that war it became customary to use select Helots even as hoplites. *Employment of Helots in War.*

After rendering such services to the State, they as a rule obtained their freedom, and after that were promoted to regular service in the army as νεοδαμώδεις. Besides this the Helots also served as shield bearers, each hoplite having one in attendance.[3]

Midway between the hoplites and the light-armed troops stood the Skiritai, or inhabitants of the territory called Skiritis, who formed a special division of the Lacedæmonian army. In time of war the Skiritai were employed on particularly perilous undertakings; they formed the vanguard; they began and ended the battle, and held the post of honour on the left wing.[4] *Skiritai.*

---

[1] The ἱππεῖς as royal body guard, Thuc. 5, 72. Dion. Hal. 2, 13. According to Hdt. 6, 56, the king's body guard consisted of only 100 ἄνδρες λογάδες. The guard of honour which escorted Themistocles to the frontier numbered 300: Hdt., 8, 124. The Ephors employed individuals from their ranks for police duties: Xen., *Hell.*, 3, 3, 9. See Trieber in the *Jahrb. f. cl. Phil.*, 1871, p. 443 ff.

[2] See Stein, *ibid.*, 4–5. For the φοινικίς, cf. Xen., *de Rep. Lac.*, 11, 3. Plut., *Inst. Lac.*, 24. Aristoph., *Ach.*, 320, and Schol. on *Pax.*, 1173. θώραξ and κράνος: Tyrt., *fr.* 12, 26; Plut., *Apophth. Lac. Demarati*, 2, p. 269. Great χαλκῇ ἀσπίς with the Λ as token: Tyrt., *fr.*, 11, 23–4; Xen., *loc. cit.*; Theop., *fr.* 325, *ap.* Müller, *fr. hist. gr.*, 1, 330. Long δόρατα: Hdt. 7, 224, 211. Short sword: Plut., *Apophth. Lac. Agid. Min.*, 1, p. 264, and *Antalk.*, 8, p. 266; Xen., *Anab.*, 4, 7, 16. H. Droysen, *Heerwesen u. Kriegführ. d. Griechen*, 24, believes we must say that the Spartans did not use the cuirass; but he is certainly wrong, as Tyrt., *fr.* 12, 26 shows. Tyrt., *fr.* 11 enumerates the weapons which could be seen in the phalanx; the cuirass was covered by the shield.

[3] Cf. Hdt. 9, 28. Thuc. 4, 80; 5, 34. Xen., *Hell.*, 6, 5, 28. νεοδαμώδεις employed in war: Thuc. 7, 19; 8, 5. Xen., *Hell.*, 1, 3, 15; 3, 1, 4; 3, 4, 20; 5, 2, 24; 3, 4, 2. Plut., *Ages.*, 6. On ὑπασπισταί, cf. Xen., *Hell.*, 4, 5, 14; 4, 8, 39.

[4] See Stein, 14. The Skiritai were infantry: Xen., *Hell.*, 5, 4, 53. Select division of 600 Skiritai: Thuc., 5, 68. Cf. Suid.: Σκιωρεῖται λόχος ἀνδρῶν χ' Ἀρκαδικός, ὁ ἀρχόμενός τε ἐν τοῖς πολέμοις καὶ τελευταῖος ἀναχωρῶν. Cf. Et. M.,

The Lacedæmonian army had no regular light armed troops of its own. When they are mentioned as present in armies commanded by Spartan generals they are either allies or mercenaries.[1]

Light armed Troops.

Neither can the institution of a cavalry force be said to date from before 424 B.C. In that year the Lacedæmonians, for the first time apparently, equipped 400 horsemen, whose number was increased to 600 in the year 394. This force was divided into six μόραι, each belonging to one of the six μόραι of infantry. Each μόρα was subdivided into two οὐλαμοί, and was commanded by a ἱππαρμοστής. The Lacedæmonian cavalry was of poor quality, for the horses (which were maintained at the expense of the richest of the citizens) were not selected for service until a levy was actually decided upon, and the men who were mounted upon them were those who were considered unfit for service as hoplites.[2]

Cavalry.

When an army took the field it was accompanied by a corps of handicraftsmen or engineers, taken from the Perioicoi, and a train of Helot attendants. These were under the orders of the ἄρχων τῶν σκευοφόρων.[3]

The kings were generals of the Lacedæmonian army by right of birth, and it was only on minor expeditions that their place was

---

Lex. Seguer. 305, 22. Skiritai in the vanguard: Xen., *de Rep. Lac.*, 13, 6.: in the most dangerous expeditions: Xen., *Kyrop.*, 4, 2, 1: on the left wing: Thuc. 5, 67. Cf. Diod., 15, 32.

[1] See Stein, 15 ff. Yet in Tyrt., *fr.* 11, 35 sqq., we find mentioned γυμνῆτες, who hurl stones and javelins.

[2] See Stein, p. 16. Equipment of 400 horsemen, 424 B.C. παρὰ εἰωθός: Thuc. 4, 55, cf. 5, 67. 394 B.C., 600 horsemen. Xen., *Hell.*, 4, 2, 16. Acc. to Xen., *de Rep. Lac.*, 11, 4, there were at that date six μόραι of cavalry, of which each contained 100 horsemen. By this arrangement the μόρα was divided into two οὐλαμοί, each being, according to Plut., *Lyc.*, 23, fifty men strong. The commander of a μόρα was entitled ἱππαρμοστής: Xen., *Hell.*, 4, 4, 10; 4, 5, 12, and was under the orders of the πολέμαρχος. See Xen., *Hell.*, 4, 5, 11 and 12. According to this, we must suppose there were six ἱππαρμοσταί. On the value and equipment of this corps, cf. Xen., *Hell.*, 6, 4, 10 and 11: τοῖς δὲ Λακεδαιμονίοις κατ' ἐκεῖνον τὸν χρόνον πονηρότατον ἦν τὸ ἱππικόν. ἔτρεφον μὲν γὰρ τοὺς ἵππους οἱ πλουσιώτατοι· ἐπεὶ δὲ φρουρὰ φανθείη, τότε ἧκεν ὁ συντεταγμένος· λαβὼν δ' ἂν τὸν ἵππον καὶ ὅπλα ὁποῖα δοθείη αὐτῷ ἐκ τοῦ παραχρῆμα ἂν ἐστρατεύετο· τῶν δ' αὖ στρατιωτῶν οἱ τοῖς σώμασιν ἀδυνατώτατοι καὶ ἥκιστα φιλότιμοι ἐπὶ τῶν ἵππων ἦσαν.

[3] On the χειροτέχναι in the Spartan army, cf. Xen., *de Rep. Lac.*, 11, 2. The ἄρχων τῶν σκευοφόρων took charge of the construction of the camp: Xen., *Hell.*, 3, 4, 22. Cf. also Xen., *de Rep. Lac.*, 13, 4.

occasionally taken by ordinary Spartiatai, who were then styled ἁρμοσταί. The subordinate officers under the commander-in-chief were the πολέμαρχοι, assisted by συμφορεῖς τῶν πολεμάρχων. Other officers were the λοχαγοί, πεντηκοντῆρες, ἐνωμοτάρχαι, ἱππαρμοσταί. The duties of these officers can be inferred from their names and from what has been said above.[1] Among these the six πολέμαρχοι belonged to the king's staff, the members of which were called οἱ περὶ δαμοσίαν, and were admitted to the king's mess table, so that he could consult with them at any time. Besides these, the king often summoned other officers to a council of war.[2] The king's staff also included 3 ὅμοιοι, who had to take charge of the commissariat. The κρεωδαίτης was probably one of these. Besides, there were also seers, doctors, and flute players.[3]

The King and his Staff.

Other functionaries employed on military expeditions without being themselves officers in the army were the ταμίαι, the λαφυροπῶλαι and the Ἑλλανοδίκαι.[4]

Fixed formalities were observed when the army set out to war.

---

[1] On the king as hereditary commander-in-chief, see page 46 ff. Ἁρμοστὴς as commander of Lacedæmonian army in war: Xen., *Hell.*, 2, 4, 28; 3, 1, 4; 4, 2, 5; 5, 2, 37; 5, 3, 20. When an ordinary Spartiates was in charge of an expedition, his probable successor seems to have always accompanied him, to provide for the possibility of his falling. Cf. Thuc. 4, 38. For the infantry officers, cf. Xen., *de Rep. Lac.*, 11, 4; 13, 4. For the ἱππαρμοσταί, Xen., *Hell.*, 4, 4, 10; 4, 5, 12. The πολέμαρχος commanded the μόρα of hoplites and the μόρα of cavalry both together: Xen., *Hell.*, 4, 5, 11. Cf. 4, 4, 7; 5, 4, 46 and 51. Also Fleischhandel 71 ff. οἱ συμφορεῖς τοῦ πολεμάρχου καλούμενοι: Xen., *Hell.*, 4, 4, 14.

[2] Cf. Xen., *de Rep. Lac.*, 13, 1: συσκηνοῦσι δὲ αὐτῷ (τῷ βασιλεῖ) οἱ πολέμαρχοι, ὅπως ἀεὶ συνόντες μᾶλλον καὶ κοινοβουλῶσιν, ἥν τι δέωνται. See Xen., *Hell.*, 6, 4, 14. In 3, 5, 22; 4, 5, 7, we find the πολέμαρχοι and πεντηκοντῆρες summoned to the council of war. The λοχαγοί are not mentioned. On the other hand, cf. those who were present at the θυσία of the king: Xen., *de Rep. Lac.*, 13, 4. If the king fell, the supreme command devolved upon the πολέμαρχοι: Xen., *Hell.*, 6, 4, 15 and 25.

[3] Cf. Xen., *de Rep. Lac.*, 13, 1: συσκηνοῦσι δὲ (τῷ βασιλεῖ) καὶ ἄλλοι τρεῖς ἄνδρες τῶν ὁμοίων. οὗτοι τούτοις ἐπιμελοῦνται πάντων τῶν ἐπιτηδείων, ὡς μηδεμία ἀσχολία ᾖ αὐτοῖς τῶν πολεμικῶν ἐπιμελεῖσθαι. I conjecture that the κρεωδαίτης also was one of these three ὅμοιοι. For him, or them, if there were more than one, cf. Plut., *quæst. symp.*, 2, 10, 2: Λακεδαιμόνιοι δὲ κρεωδαίτας εἶχον οὐ τοὺς τυχόντας ἀλλὰ τοὺς πρώτους ἄνδρας, ὥστε καὶ Λύσανδρον ὑπ' Ἀγησιλάου ἐν Ἀσίᾳ κρεωδαίτην ἀποδειχθῆναι. Cf. Plut., *Lys.*, 23. Poll. 6, 34. μάντεις καὶ ἰατροὶ καὶ αὐληταί: Xen., *ibid.*, 13, 7. On the tent companions of the king, cf. Gabriel, *de magistrat. Lac.*, 18 ff.

[4] Cf. Xen., *de Rep. Lac.*, 13, 11; *Hell.*, 4, 1, 26; *Ages.*, 1, 18.

First the king offered up sacrifice at home to Zeus Agetor before
he set out. If the sacrifice seemed propitious, the
army marched out, and the πυρφόρος carried with
the army fire from that sacrifice as far as the frontier, where the
usual ὑπερβατήρια were offered up to Zeus and Athene. From this
second sacrifice the πυρφόρος took fire to serve for all the other
sacrifices, which were performed by the king at all kinds of junctures throughout the whole campaign.[1] The camp constructed by
the Lacedæmonians in the field (the ἄρχων τῶν σκευοφόρων being
responsible for its erection), was circular in shape so far as the
nature of the ground permitted, and was, as a rule, surrounded
with a palisade of stakes.[2] The outposts were occupied by the
cavalry, and consisted of positions a certain distance away from
the camp, and affording a good outlook over the adjacent country.
Besides these, there was also a camp guard, whose main duty was
to keep watch over the Helots who were present. The Helots were
not allowed to lodge within the camp. No one was permitted to
move about in camp without his spear, or to go far away from it
when foraging. Bodily exercises were practised in camp as well
as at home, though the Spartiatai were not permitted to leave the
quarters of their mora, lest they should get too far away from their
weapons. In spite of all this, discipline was on the whole less
strict in camp than at home.[3] Before all military operations sacrifices were offered by the king or the highest officer in command.[4]
When the enemy were in sight, the king sacrificed once more, this
time a goat and to Artemis Agrotera.[5] Thereupon the army, with
wreaths on their heads, marched with leisurely steps against the
foe, accompanied with the music of the fifes, to which they sang

---

[1] Cf. Xen., de Rep. Lac., 13, 2-5. Hesych.: πυρσοφόρος. Nicol. Dam. ap. Müller, fr. hist. gr., 3, 458; 114, 14. Polyain. 1, 10. Trieber, quæst. Lac., p. 5 ff.

[2] Cf. Xen., de Rep. Lac., 12, 1. That the camp was surrounded with palisades may be concluded from the consideration that we cannot well think of a circular-shaped camp without them. Cf. Xen., Hell., 6, 2, 23. For the construction of a camp, cf. Xen., Hell., 3, 4, 22.

[3] Cf. Xen., de Rep. Lac., 12, 2 sqq.; Plut., Lyc., 22; Stein 31.

[4] See the collection of instances in Trieber, quæst. Lac., p. 7 ff. Trieber doubts the sacrifice to the Muses and Eros before battle which is attested by Plut., Lyc., 21; Apophth. Lac. Eudam., 10, p. 271; de cohib. ira, 10, and Athen. 13, 561 E.

[5] Cf. Xen., Hell., 4, 2, 20; Lyc., 22; Xen., de Rep. Lac., 13, 8; Trieber 13 ff.

their battle pæan.[1] If the enemy were defeated, the Lacedæmonians soon returned from pursuit, in order to sacrifice the thank-offering for victory to Ares. If the victory had been won in open fight, the sacrifice was a cock; if by a stratagem, an ox.[2]

"With the shield as victor or on the shield a corpse," as the well-known parting exhortation of the Spartan mother puts it— those were the instructions which the Lacedæmonian State gave its citizens. Those who did not obey this injunction but returned to Sparta defeated, were called τρέσαντες, and incurred a strict ἀτιμία. They lost all eligibility for office, and all power of bequest over their property, and were exposed to the deepest contempt. No one would eat with them, or practise gymnastic exercises with them. At choral festivals they must sit apart in seats especially appointed them: in the street they must give way to every one; they must rise from their seats before even their juniors. With beard half shorn and gay parti-coloured robes, they wandered about, treated everywhere with utter contempt, compelled even to submit to blows. If they had daughters, no one would marry them; if they themselves were unmarried, no one would give them their daughters to wife.[3]

τρέσαντες.

The Lacedæmonians had no fleet of any consequence; from the time of the Persian wars, however, and onwards, they possessed a few ships. At the sea-fight near Artemisium, ten of their ships took part; at Salamis, sixteen; in 413 B.C. they had twenty-five ships altogether. Their harbour for their war-ships was Gytheion.[4] We cannot tell for certain how the equipment of the fleet was managed, except that the trierarchs and crews were, as a rule, taken from among the Perioicoi.[5] The ναύαρχος and his deputy the ἐπιστολεύς have already been discussed above.[6]

Fleet.

---

[1] Cf. Plut., Lyc., 22; Instit. Lac., 16; de mus. 26. Xen., de Rep. Lac., 13, 8; Thuc., 5, 70; Polyain., 1, 10. For further passages, see in Auerbach, de Lacedæmoniorum reyib., 44–5.

[2] Cf. Plut., Lyc., 22; Apophth. Lac., p. 281, 30; Thuc. 5, 73; Inst. Lac., p. 295 ff.; Plut., Marcell., 22.

[3] Cf. Hdt. 7, 104. For the saying of the Spartan matron, cf. Apophth. Lac., 15, p. 299. On the τρέσαντες, cf. Hdt. 7, 231, and Thuc. 5, 34. Xen., de Rep. Lac., 9, 4 sqq. Plut., Ages., 30.

[4] Cf. Hdt. 8, 1, 43. Thuc. 8, 3. Γύθειον was the ἐπίνειον τῶν Λακεδαιμονίων, where were to be found the νεώρια τῶν Λ.: Diod. 11, 84. Paus. 1, 27 5. Thuc. 1, 108.

[5] Cf. Thuc. 4, 11. Xen., Hell., 5, 1, 11; 7, 1, 12.

[6] See page 60.

4. Finance and Justice.

The Common Metals as Measures of Value. Before the precious metals had become the usual standards of value in Greece, cattle and the ordinary metals were used as media of exchange. The latter were measured out by weight.

But at an early date the Greeks learnt from the people of Asia Minor and from the Phœnicians to make the pieces of metal of a convenient conventional shape, and stamp them with a device to guarantee the correctness of the weight. Bars and spits or obelisks were, according to an ancient tradition, the earliest forms in which these common metals circulated. Afterwards, when pieces of metal had become the customary measures of value, a flat shape was adopted, and from this the round coin was gradually developed.[1]

In Sparta the ancient custom of using a cheap metal, iron, as measure of value, was kept up till the end of the 4th century B.C.; **Laconian Coins.** for no silver coins were made there till after the time of Alexander the Great. Private persons were forbidden even to possess precious metals; nevertheless foreign silver coins were already in use among the Spartiatai at the time of the Persian wars. The most ancient form of native coin at Sparta also seems to have been bars weighing a mina each. At a later period the principal coin was struck in the shape of a sacrificial cake and called therefrom πέλανορ.[2] In value these

---

[1] See Hultsch, *griech. u. röm. Metrol.*,[2] 162 ff., 105–6. Plut., *Lys.*, 17: κινδυνεύει δὲ καὶ τὸ πάμπαν ἀρχαῖον οὕτως ἔχειν, ὀβελίσκοις χρωμένων νομίσμασι σιδηροῖς, ἐνίων δὲ χαλκοῖς. Cf. Et. M., δραχμή. Poll. 9, 77, tells that Pheidon, after causing coins to be made for the first time, consecrated the spits to Hera. Cf. Et. M.: ὀβελίσκος—πάντων δὲ πρῶτος Φείδων Ἀργεῖος νόμισμα ἔκοψεν ἐν Αἰγίνῃ καὶ διὰ τὸ νόμισμα ἀναλαβὼν τοὺς ὀβελίσκους ἀνέθηκε τῇ ἐν "Αργει "Ηρᾳ. See Mommsen, *Gesch. d. röm. Münzwesens*, 169.

[2] On the ancient establishment of iron coinage in the Peloponnesus, see Köhler in *Mitth. d. dtsch. Arch. Inst. in Athens*, 7, 1 ff., 377 ff. On the Laconian money Hultsch.,[2] 534 ff. Private persons forbidden to possess gold and silver: Xen., *de Rep. Lac.*, 7, 6. Cf. Stein in the *Jahrb. f. cl. Phil.*, 1864, 332 ff. Trieber, *quœst. Lac.*, p. 48 ff. Acc. to Poseidon. ap. Ath. 6, 233 F., private individuals deposited their cash in Arcadia. The document published by Kirchhoff in the *Ber. d. Berl. Ak.*, 1870, p. 51 ff., is a deed relating to such a deposit. Cf. Plut., *Lys.*, 17., Poll., 9, 79; 7, 105. Plut., *Lys.*, 17, seems to assume that at Sparta also money originally circulated in the form of obeliskoi. Hesych. says: πέλανορ τὸ τετράχαλκον. Λάκωνες. For the later Spartan silver coins, see Hultsch.[2] 536.

bars and cakes represented originally a silver obol or $\frac{1}{600}$ of the silver mina.

According to a later valuation, this Laconian πέλανορ was equivalent in weight to an Æginetan mina, and in value to four χαλκοῖ, or half an obol. This computation puts the ratio of value of iron to silver as 1 : 1200; and an Æginetan silver mina weighing 605 grams would therefore be worth 1200 Laconian iron minæ weighing altogether 726 kilograms.[1] This cheapness of iron forces us to the conclusion that so long as foreign coinage did not yet circulate in Laconia commerce was carried on mainly by barter, the iron coins being used merely to balance accounts.[2] In the towns of the Perioicoi their great export trade must always have required the use of the precious metals as a medium of exchange.[3]

As soon as the Spartan State began to take part in the general politics of Greece, and particularly during the Peloponnesian war, the possession of gold and silver became an absolute necessity. The attempt, made by the party of strict observance at the end of the Peloponnesian war, to prohibit the possession of precious metals even by the State, was obviously doomed to defeat, unless the Lacedæmonians deliberately intended to resign their hegemony. In the case of private persons, however, the prohibition was renewed at that period with threats of severe penalties; nevertheless it was frequently disregarded.[4]

Gold and Silver in Laconia.

Spartan finance was managed on a very simple system. It

---

[1] Cf. Plut., *Apophth. Lac. Lyc.*, 3, p. 278; οὐδὲ γὰρ νόμισμα παρ' αὐτοῖς εὔχρηστον εἴασε, μόνον δὲ τὸ σιδηροῦν εἰσηγήσατο, ὅ ἐστι μνᾶ ὁλκῇ Αἰγιναία, δυνάμει δὲ χαλκοῖ τέσσαρες. The weight of the Æginetan mina is given according to Hultsch.[2] 502. The Spartan leather money of which Nicol. Dam. *ap.* Müller, *fr. hist. gr.*, 3, 458, no. 114, 8, and Sen., *de benefic.*, 5, 14, speak, is a mere fable.

[2] According to the original ratio of silver to iron, 600 : 1, ten Æginetan minæ would represent 3,630 kilograms of Laconian iron coins; cf. Xen., *de Rep. Lac.*, 7, 5, Plut., *Lyc.*, 9. That barter prevailed in Laconia is attested by Polyb. 6, 49, and Just. 3, 2.

[3] See Müller, *Dor.*, 2, 21 (24) ff.

[4] Cf. Polyb. 6, 49. For the account of the discussions at the end of the Peloponnesian war, cf. Plut., *Lys.*, 17. Their result is described as follows: δημοσίᾳ μὲν ἔδοξεν εἰσάγεσθαι νόμισμα τοιοῦτον, ἂν δέ τις ἁλῷ κεκτημένος ἰδίᾳ, ζημίαν ὥρισαν θάνατον. Cf. Xen., *de Rep. Lac.*, 7, 6. On the observance of this law, see Müller, *Dor.* 2, 207 (220). Stein, 337, doubts whether such a law was passed.

cannot be supposed that the Spartiatai were liable to any taxation, but it is not unlikely that the Perioicoi paid tribute. The main revenues of the State consisted of booty won in war and subsidies paid at various times by foreign States, especially by the Persian king.[1] At the head of the financial administration stood the Ephors.[2]

Finance.

Justice. We possess no more definite information about the administration of justice than about finance. Criminal jurisdiction was exercised by the Council of Gerontes, and included murder cases and State trials.[3] The proceedings in capital cases extended over several days, and were subject to no *exceptio rei iudicatae*.[4] The Council of Gerontes could inflict money fines, atimia, banishment, or death.[5] Executions took place at night. Sometimes the prisoner was strangled in the Dechas, sometimes hurled down into a deep ravine called Kaiadas; into this, however, as a rule, only the corpses of the executed criminals were cast.[5]

Council of Gerontes.

---

[1] Cf. Plut., *Apophth. Lac. Anax.*, p. 265: πυνθανομένου τινός, διὰ τί χρήματα οὐ συνάγουσιν εἰς τὸ δημόσιον. In Thuc. 1, 80, Archidamos says: καὶ οὔτε ἐν κοινῷ (sc. χρήματα) ἔχομεν οὔτε ἑτοίμως ἐκ τῶν ἰδίων φέρομεν. Cf. Aristot., *Pol.*, 2, 9= p. 50, 10 sqq. Bekker. Acc. to Strabo 365, the Perioicoi, on their subjugation, undertook συντελεῖν τῇ Σπάρτῃ. See Trieber, *Quæst. Lac.*, p. 53 ff.

[2] The Ephors took possession of booty: Plut., *Lys.*, 16. Diod. 13, 106.

[3] On the Council of Elders as court of justice for δίκαι φονικαί cf. Aristot., *Pol.*, 3, 1=p. 60, 16. Acc. to Arist., *Pol.*, 2, 9=p. 48, 21, the Gerontes are κύριοι κρίσεων μεγάλων generally. That the Council of Elders was the court for State trials, follows from the case of Sphodrias, which was obviously pleaded before the Gerontes. Cf. Xen., *Hell.*, 5, 4, 24 sqq.; Plut., *Ages.*, 24, 25. For the kings brought to trial before the Council of Elders, cf. Paus., 3, 5, 2.

[4] Cf. *Apophth. Lac. Alexandr.*, 6, p. 265: ἐρωτῶντος δέ τινος αὐτόν, διὰ τί τὰς περὶ (τοῦ) θανάτου δίκας πλείοσιν ἡμέραις οἱ γέροντες κρίνουσιν, κἂν ἀποφύγῃ τις, ἔτι οὐδὲν ἧσσόν ἐστιν ὑπόδικος, Πολλαῖς μὲν, ἔφη, ἡμέραις κρίνουσιν, ὅτι περὶ θανάτου τοῖς διαμαρτάνουσιν οὐκ ἔστι μεταβουλεύσασθαι· νόμῳ δὲ ὑπόδικον δεήσει εἶναι, ὅτι κατὰ τοῦτον τὸν νόμον ἂν εἴη καὶ τὸ κρείττονα βουλεύσασθαι. The apprehension of miscarriages of justice here attested is mentioned also in Thuc., 1, 132.

[5] Acc. to Aristot., *Pol.*, 6 (4), 9=p. 161, 18, the Gerontes judge cases, punishable by death and banishment; acc. to Plut., *Lyc.*, 26, death, atimia, and severe punishments generally. Atimia, *e.g.*, for Paiderastai: Plut., *Inst. Lac.*, 7. An example of banishment: Thuc. 5, 72. A pecuniary fine was imposed, *e.g.*, on Phoibidas, who was certainly condemned by the Gerontes. Cf. Plut., *Pelop.*, 6. On the way in which death sentences were carried out, cf. Plut., *Ag.*, 19: τοῦτο δέ (*i.e.* ἡ καλουμένη Δέχας)

Lawsuits, arising out of contracts, were decided by the Ephors sitting as sole judges, except in cases where the dispute was settled by umpires chosen by mutual agreement.¹ The Ephors further exercised judicial functions in connexion with their duties as superintendents of police, and in this capacity could inflict punishments of very various kinds.² The kings had lost all their ancient civil jurisdiction, except in cases affecting family rights and the public roads.³

Ephors.

Kings.

5. THE LACEDÆMONIAN LEAGUE.⁴

After the Spartiatai had made themselves masters of the Eurotas valley, and of the communities on the adjacent coast, they by no means ended their career of conquest. In the second half of the 8th century they began the first Messenian war, which they carried on as a war of conquest.⁵

Conquests of the Spartiatai.

After a struggle of many years' duration, this war ended in the subjugation of Messenia. The inhabitants were reduced to a condition of oppression and serfdom under Spartan dominion, which was not rendered any less burdensome by their unfortunate rebellion, the so-called second Messenian war.⁶ Soon after the first

ἐστιν ἄκημα τῆς εἰρκτῆς, ἐν ᾧ θανατοῦσι τοὺς καταδίκους ἀποπνίγοντες. Hdt. 4, 146: κτείνουσι δὲ τοὺς ἂν κτείνωσι Λακεδαιμόνιοι νυκτός, μεθ' ἡμέρην δὲ οὐδένα. Thuc. 1, 134: καὶ αὐτὸν ἐμέλλησαν μὲν ἐς τὸν Καιάδαν οὗπερ τοὺς κακούργους ἐμβάλλειν. For a case of increased severity in the form of execution, cf. Xen., *Hell.*, 3, 3, 11.

¹ Cf. Aristot., *Pol.*, 3, 1 = p. 60, 15: οἶον ἐν Λακεδαίμονι τὰς τῶν συμβολαίων δικάζει τῶν ἐφόρων ἄλλος ἄλλας,—2, 9 = p. 48, 11: ἔτι δὲ καὶ κρίσεών εἰσι μεγάλων κύριοι, ὄντες οἱ τυχόντες, διόπερ οὐκ αὐτογνώμονας βέλτιον κρίνειν, ἀλλὰ κατὰ τὰ γράμματα καὶ τοὺς νόμους. Cf. Plut., *Apophth. Lac.*, 271. Eurycrad. Didot. On single arbitrators chosen by agreement between the litigants, cf. Plut., *Apophth. Lac. Archidam.*, 6, p. 267 Didot.

² Cf., *e.g.*, Athen. 4, 141 A.

³ Cf. Hdt. 6, 57.

⁴ An account of the historical development of the Lacedæmonian league down to the Peloponnesian war is given by Broicher, *de sociis Lacedæmoniorum*, Bonn, 1867, Diss. Inaug., and by Busolt, *d. Laked. u. ihre Bundesgen.*, vol. 1, 1878, down to the year 479.

⁵ The traditional accounts of the early history of Messenia and of the Messenian wars are quite untrustworthy. See Niese in *Hermes*, 26, 1 ff. The real cause of the war is without doubt given correctly in the Messenian account in Paus. 4, 4, 3: αἴτιον δὲ εἶναι τῆς χώρας τῆς Μεσσηνίας τὴν ἀρετήν.

⁶ On the serfdom of the Messenians, who obviously became Helots, except those who left the country, cf. Paus. 4, 14, 4 sqq.; 23, 1.

Messenian war the Spartiatai began war with the Argives for the district Thyreatis,[1] which lay on the frontier between the two States, and was not definitely secured by Sparta till the middle of the sixth century.[2]

Against their northern neighbours also, the Arcadians, the Spartans at first pursued the same aggressive policy.[3] But it was not till after repeated wars, and several defeats in the first decade of the sixth century, that they succeeded in defeating the people of Tegea about 550 B.C.[4] Even this victory was by no means decisive enough to afford the Spartans any good prospect of subduing the district of Tegea. On the contrary, they thereupon concluded peace with Tegea, and apparently abandoned all ideas of aggression in that direction. By the terms of this peace, the Tegeatai agreed to expel the Messenian fugitives from their territory, and to prosecute none of their own citizens for any dealings with the Spartans during the war.[5]

Sparta and Tegea.

The last proviso, which, according to Aristotle, was inserted by the Lacedæmonians in order to secure safety for the Lacedæmonian partisans in Tegea, clearly indicates the method by which the Spartans secured for themselves supremacy in the Peloponnesus. In the Greek States generally, the oligarchical factions agreed in their political theories

Foundation of the Lacedæmonian Hegemony.

---

[1] In Euseb. 2, 83, Schoene, there is recorded under Ol. 14: "bellum, quod in Thyrea inter Lacedæmonios et Argivos gestum est." Paus. 3, 7, 5: Θεοπόμπου δὲ ἔτι ἔχοντος τὴν ἀρχὴν ἐν Σπάρτῃ γίνεται καὶ ὁ περὶ τῆς Θυρεάτιδος καλουμένης χώρας Λακεδαιμονίοις ἀγὼν πρὸς Ἀργείους. I regard the traditions of earlier wars between the Spartans and Argives as unworthy of credence: see *Stud.*, p. 72 ff.

[2] According to the account in Hdt. 1, 82, the Thyreatis was first occupied and reduced by the Spartans immediately after the fight between the 300 Spartan and Argive λογάδες and the battle which followed. Cf. also Paus. 2, 38, 5.

[3] The aggressive tendency of Lacedæmonian policy in the 6th century (to be attributed likewise to the previous century) is correctly described by Busolt, *d. Laked. und ihre Bundesgen.*, 251 ff. Cf. also Hdt. 1, 66.

[4] Cf. Hdt. 1, 65 sqq. Busolt, *ibid.*, p. 257 ff.

[5] Cf. Plut., *Quæst. Gr.*, 5: Λακεδαιμόνιοι Τεγεάταις διαλλαγέντες ἐποιήσαντο συνθήκας καὶ στήλην ἐπ' Ἀλφειῷ κοινὴν ἀνέστησαν ἐν ᾗ μετὰ τῶν ἄλλων γέγραπται Μεσσηνίους ἐκβαλεῖν ἐκ τῆς χώρας καὶ μὴ ἐξεῖναι χρηστοὺς (cf. Hesych.: χρηστοί · οἱ καταδεδικασμένοι) ποιεῖν. ἐξηγούμενος οὖν ὁ Ἀριστοτέλης τοῦτό φησι δύνασθαι τὸ μὴ ἀποκτιννύναι βοηθείας χάριν τοῖς λακωνίζουσι τῶν Τεγεατῶν. Cf. also Plut., *Quæst. Rom.*, 52. The meaning of this proviso is without doubt what is given in the text. The Tegeatans had the post of honour in the Peloponnesian army on the left wing: Hdt. 9, 26. But it is not likely that this honour was secured them by the treaty.

with the principles of the Spartan constitution, and therefore supported Sparta, especially in wars against the Tyrannis, which rested on democratic sentiment. Again the oligarchs, who succeeded the despots in the possession of power, naturally found it to their interest to connect themselves closely with Sparta, in order to secure their own supremacy.[1] To this must be added, that in the 6th century, as a result of the aggressions of the Lydian kings against the Hellenic towns of Asia Minor, and of the immediately ensuing rise of the Persian power, a tendency towards centralization became apparent even among the Hellenes.[2] From all these considerations it will be understood how the influence of the Lacedæmonians, whose territory by itself already included two-fifths of the Peloponnesus, extended itself over the larger portion of the peninsula, without any definite record being handed down to us of the manner in which the several States became adherents of Sparta. In all Peloponnesus, only Argos and the Achæan towns stood aloof from the Lacedæmonian alliance.[3] The prominent and powerful position of the Lacedæmonians in Peloponnesus caused them to be regarded by foreigners about 550 B.C. as the leaders and representatives of the whole of Greece.[4] But as a matter of

---

[1] Overthrow of despots by the Lacedæmonians, according to Thuc., 1, 18: ἐπειδὴ δὲ οἵ τε Ἀθηναίων τύραννοι καὶ οἱ ἐκ τῆς ἄλλης Ἑλλάδος ἐπὶ πολὺ καὶ πρὶν τυραννευθείσης οἱ πλεῖστοι καὶ τελευταῖοι πλὴν τῶν ἐν Σικελίᾳ ὑπὸ Λακεδαιμονίων κατελύθησαν.—Muller, *Dor.*, 1, 172 (189). Interference with the constitutions of the separate States, Thuc. 1, 76: ὑμεῖς γοῦν, ὦ Λακεδαιμόνιοι, τὰς ἐν τῇ Πελοποννήσῳ πόλεις ἐπὶ τὸ ὑμῖν ὠφέλιμον καταστησάμενοι ἐξηγεῖσθε. 1, 19: οἱ μὲν Λακεδαιμόνιοι οὐχ ὑποτελεῖς ἔχοντες φόρου τοὺς ξυμμάχους ἡγοῦντο, κατ' ὀλιγαρχίαν δέ σφισιν αὐτοῖς μόνον ἐπιτηδείως ὅπως πολιτεύσωσι θεραπεύοντες—Aristot., *Pol.*, 6 (4), 11, p. 165, 18 ff. Bekker: ἔτι δὲ καὶ τῶν ἐν ἡγεμονίᾳ γενομένων τῆς Ἑλλάδος πρὸς τὴν παρ' αὑτοῖς ἑκάτεροι πολιτείαν ἀποβλέποντες οἱ μὲν δημοκρατίας ἐν ταῖς πόλεσι καθίστασαν, οἱ δ' ὀλιγαρχίας, οὐ πρὸς τὸ τῶν πόλεων συμφέρον σκοποῦντες, ἀλλὰ πρὸς τὸ σφέτερον αὐτῶν. That the Lacedæmonian hegemony was not developed in connexion with the Olympian festival and in alliance with Elis, as Curtius supposed *Gr. Hist.*,[4] 1, 218 (Ward's Eng. tr., 1, 234), is rightly shown by Busolt, *ibid.*, p. 57 ff., and *Forsch.*, 1 ff.

[2] On the tendency to centralization among the Greeks in the 6th century, see Busolt, *ib.*, p. 245 ff. ⅖ of the Peloponnese belonged to Sparta: Thuc. 1, 10. Of the time about 550 B.C., Hdt., 1, 68, already can say, ἤδη δέ σφι (τοῖς Λακεδαιμονίοις) καὶ ἡ πολλὴ τῆς Πελοποννήσου ἦν κατεστραμμένη, with which compare Busolt, *ib.*, p. 264 ff.

[3] On Argos, cf. Isocr. 12, 46, cf. 256; on Achaia, Paus. 7, 6 and 3, 4. Cf. also Thuc. 1, 9.

[4] Acc. to Hdt. 1, 69, Crœsus sends word to the Lacedæmonians: ὑμέας γὰρ πυνθάνομαι προεστάναι τῆς Ἑλλάδος. Compare Busolt, *ib.*, p. 269 ff.

fact their hegemony, after their attempt to extend it to include Athens also was defeated at the end of the 6th century, was confined to the limits of the Peloponnesus.[1]

It was the Persian War that first caused any considerable extension of the sphere of Spartan influence: for all the Greek States involved in that war, even Athens herself, acknowledged the hegemony of Sparta.[2] The constitutional forms in which this league expressed itself, corresponded with the objects which the league was intended to effect.

Position of Sparta during the Persian Wars.

The league included "the States well-disposed towards the Hellenes,"[3] which had bound themselves by mutual oaths to war against the Persians.[4]

The organising council of the league was the Synedrion of πρόβουλοι assembled at the Isthmus; they decided upon the measures adopted in preparation for the war. During the war itself, however, the generals of the several States concerned in each operation formed the regular council of war of the allies. The commander of the Lacedæmonians on each occasion was the generalissimo of the allies, whether on land or at sea.[5] In its capacity as federal council the council of war of the land-army

---

[1] Concerning the attempts of the Lacedæmonians to extend their Hegemony over Central Greece also, see Busolt, *ib.*, p. 284 ff.

[2] Thuc. 1, 18: καὶ μεγάλου κινδύνου ἐπικρεμασθέντος οἵ τε Λακεδαιμόνιοι τῶν ξυμπολεμησάντων Ἑλλήνων ἡγήσαντο δυνάμει προύχοντες.

[3] Acc. to Hdt. 7, 172: αἱ πόλεις αἱ τὰ ἀμείνω φρονέουσαι περὶ τὴν Ἑλλάδα. Cf. Hdt., 7, 145. For the States which belonged to this alliance, see Busolt, *ib.*, 387 ff. Compare also K. Ottfr. Müller, "History of the Hellenic Synedrion during the Persian Wars," in the *Prolegomena z. e. wissensch. Myth.*, p. 406 ff.

[4] In Hdt. 7, 148, they are called οἱ συνωμόται Ἑλλήνων ἐπὶ τῷ Πέρσῃ. Cf. also Hdt. 9, 106. On the other hand, we must regard as a pure invention the oath which the Hellenes are said to have sworn either at the Isthmus (cf. Hdt. 7, 132, Diod. 11, 3) or before the battle at Platæa (cf. Theop., *fr.* 167, *ap.* Müller, *fr. hist. gr.*, 2306, Diod. 11, 29, Lyk., *Leokr.*, 80–1) against those Hellenes who had submitted voluntarily to the Persians. See Wecklein, *üb. d. Tradit. d. Perserkr.*, 67 ff.

[5] The Synedrion at the Isthmus (cf. Diod. 11, 3) is denoted by the phrase πρόβουλοι τῆς Ἑλλάδος in Hdt. 7, 172. On its activity, cf. Busolt, *ib.*, p. 394 ff., who rightly shows, 407 ff., that the Synedrion of πρόβουλοι was an assembly for purposes of organisation. The general council of war at the Isthmus consisted of the Strategoi of the allied States; cf. Hdt. 7, 175, 177. See Busolt, p. 407, n. 125. That the πρόβουλοι did not assemble during the actual progress of hostilities is proved by Busolt, p. 408, n. 126. On the Synedrion of Strategoi as Federal assembly see Busolt, p. 410 ff. On the Hegemony of the Spartans by sea and land, cf. Hdt. 7, 161; 8, 2. Busolt, p. 410 ff.

after the battle of Platæa drew up a resolution that every year πρόβουλοι and θεωροὶ from all Hellas should assemble at Platæa. The latter undoubtedly were to come as religious representatives of the several States at the proposed annual sacrifices to the slain warriors, the former as their political envoys to deliberate on the affairs of the league. It was further decided to establish there a quadrennial festival called the Eleutheria, and the Platæans were to be considered sacred and inviolable on condition that they kept up the proper sacrifices to the Gods at the festival. For the war against the Persians it was determined to set on foot a standing army of 10,000 hoplites, 1,000 cavalry, and a fleet of 100 sail.[1] The alliance thus decreed, which is described by Thucydides as αἱ παλαιαὶ Παυσανίου μετὰ τὸν Μῆδον σπονδαί, existed, it is true, in form up to the third Messenian war, when the Athenians and their allies abandoned the alliance because of their dismissal by the Spartans from Messenia; but it never had any practical importance. For when the Greeks of the Ægean, in consequence of the presumption of Pausanias, elected the Athenians to be their leaders, the Lacedæmonians acquiesced in this decision, retired from the war against Persia, and again confined themselves to their former hegemony of the Peloponnesus.[2]

The attempts made in the interval between the Persian and Peloponnesian wars, first by Tegea and Argos, and again by all Arcadia except Mantinea,[3] to break down the Spartan supremacy, both failed. Sparta, therefore, was able to begin the Peloponnesian war as president of the Pelo- *Sparta Hegemon of all Hellas.*

---

[1] Cf. Plut., *Arist.*, 21: ἐκ τούτου γενομένης ἐκκλησίας κοινῆς τῶν Ἑλλήνων ἔγραψεν Ἀριστείδης ψήφισμα συνιέναι μέν εἰς Πλαταιὰς καθ' ἕκαστον ἐνιαυτὸν ἀπὸ τῆς Ἑλλάδος προβούλους καὶ θεωρούς, ἄγεσθαι δὲ πενταετηρικὸν ἀγῶνα τῶν Ἐλευθερίων. εἶναι δὲ σύνταξιν Ἑλληνικὴν μυρίας μὲν ἀσπίδας, χιλίους δὲ ἵππους, ναῦς δὲ ἑκατὸν ἐπὶ τὸν πρὸς βαρβάρους πόλεμον, Πλαταιεῖς δὲ ἀσύλους καὶ ἱεροὺς ἀφεῖσθαι τῷ θεῷ θύοντας ὑπὲρ Ἑλλάδος, cf. 19. The correctness of Plutarch's account is confirmed in certain points by Thuc. 2, 71, 72, 74; 3, 58, 68, but I do not therefore insist on the accuracy of Plutarch's account in points for which this confirmation is wanting. See Busolt, *ib.*, p. 463 ff. Broicher, *ib.*, p. 64 ff., doubts the accuracy of the account of Plutarch quoted above.

[2] αἱ παλαιαὶ Παυσανίου μετὰ τὸν Μῆδον σπονδαί is mentioned by Thuc. 3, 68. Thuc. 1, 102, says of the Athenians after their dismissal from Messenia: ἀφέντες τὴν γενομένην ἐπὶ τῷ Μήδῳ ξυμμαχίαν πρὸς αὐτούς (i.e. πρὸς τοὺς Λακεδαιμονίους). On the transference of the naval hegemony of the Greeks to Athens, cf. Thuc. 1, 95, Aristot., 'Αθ. π. 23, Diod. 11, 44, Plut., *Arist.*, 23, and *Kim.*, 6.

[3] For these wars we possess only the short account in Hdt. 9, 35. Paus. 3, 11, 7, 8, is based on Hdt.

ponnesian alliance; and the successful result of that war soon obtained for Sparta the supremacy over all Hellas.[1] In towns outside the Peloponnesus the Lacedæmonians exercised this supremacy by appointing Harmosts or governors of the garrisons maintained there in the Spartan interest, and also by establishing native oligarchical governments mostly in the form of Decarchies, or councils of ten.[2]

The haughtiness and tyranny which the Lacedæmonians displayed towards the various cities, soon produced in the latter a desire to get rid of the Spartan supremacy. Accordingly, when Conon with the Persian fleet defeated the Lacedæmonians off Cnidos in 394, the Greeks of the Ægean everywhere expelled the Lacedæmonian garrisons and Harmosts, and set themselves free.[3]

Liberation of the Greeks of the Ægean.

However, in 387 the Persian King decreed terms of peace to the Hellenes, and entrusted the Lacedæmonians with the duty of carrying out the provisions of his decree. This gave them many opportunities of interfering in the concerns of the other Greek States. On the other hand, the proviso that all Hellenic States were to be autonomous, had no effect on the relations of Sparta to its allied

The Lacedæmonians as Guardians of the Great King's Peace.

---

[1] The Spartans, about 400 B.C., πάσης τῆς Ἑλλάδος προστάται: Xen., *Hell.*, 3, 1, 3. In § 5 he says: πᾶσαι γὰρ τότε αἱ πόλεις ἐπείθοντο ὅτι Λακεδαιμόνιος ἀνὴρ ἐπιτάττοι. In *Anab.*, 6, 4, 13, Xen. says to the 10,000: καὶ γὰρ ἐν τῇ γῇ ἄρχουσι Λακεδαιμόνιοι καὶ ἐν τῇ θαλάττῃ τὸν νῦν χρόνον. Cf. 7, 1, 28. In Diod. 14, 10, we find: κατὰ δὲ τὴν Ἑλλάδα Λακεδαιμόνιοι καταλελυκότες τὸν Πελοποννησιακὸν πόλεμον ὁμολογουμένην ἔσχον τὴν ἡγεμονίαν καὶ κατὰ γῆν καὶ κατὰ θάλατταν.

[2] Cf. Diod., 14, 10: καταστήσαντες δὲ ναύαρχον Λύσανδρον τούτῳ προσέταξαν ἐπιπορεύεσθαι τὰς πόλεις ἐν ἑκάστῃ τοὺς παρ' αὑτοῖς καλουμένους ἁρμοστὰς ἐγκαθιστάντα· ταῖς γὰρ δημοκρατίαις προσκόπτοντες οἱ Λακεδαιμόνιοι δι' ὀλιγαρχίας ἐβούλοντο τὰς πόλεις διοικεῖσθαι. On the δεκαρχίαι or δεκαδαρχίαι, cf. Isocr. 5, 95; Paus. 9, 6, 4; Plut., *Lys.*, 5, 13, 14; Diod. 14, 13; Xen., *Hell.*, 3, 4, 2; 6, 3, 8. For the ἁρμοσταί, cf. Dem. 18, 96: Λακεδαιμονίων γῆς καὶ θαλάττης ἀρχόντων καὶ τὰ κύκλῳ τῆς Ἀττικῆς κατεχόντων ἁρμοσταῖς καὶ φρουραῖς, Εὔβοιαν, Τάναγραν καὶ Βοιωτίαν ἅπασαν, Μέγαρα, Αἴγιναν, Κλεωνάς, τὰς ἄλλας νήσους. Cf. Xen., *Anab.*, 6, 4, 13; Isocr. 14, 13; Xen., *Hell.*, 1, 1, 32; 1, 2, 18; 1, 3, 5; 1, 3, 15; 2, 3, 14; 4, 8, 3. 5. 39. See also Fleischhandel, *ib.*, 65 ff. Harp., ἁρμοσταί. Lex. Seguer. 206, 16; 211, 7; 445, 29. Even Helots are said to have been employed by the Lacedæmonians as Harmosts. Cf. Xen., *Hell.*, 3, 5, 12. See also Gabriel, *de magistratib. Lac.*, p. 92 ff.

[3] Cf. Diod. 14, 84: τοιαύτη τῆς μεταστάσεως σπουδή τις εἰς τὰς πόλεις ἐνέπεσεν, ὧν αἱ μὲν ἐκβαλοῦσαι τὰς φρουρὰς τῶν Λακεδαιμονίων τὴν ἐλευθερίαν διεφύλαττον, αἱ δὲ τοῖς περὶ Κόνωνα προσετίθεντο. καὶ Λακεδαιμόνιοι μὲν ἀπὸ τούτου τοῦ χρόνου τὴν κατὰ θάλατταν ἀρχὴν ἀπέβαλον.

towns in the Peloponnesus, for these were already at least nominally autonomous.¹ On the contrary, the Spartans used their position as guardians of the great King's peace, to reduce again under their influence Corinth which had cut itself adrift from the Peloponnesian league in 394: nor did they hesitate to modify the constitutions of various States such as Mantinea and Phlius in their own interests, in direct contravention of the terms of the peace.² And the Spartans did not confine their intermeddling to the Peloponnesian States. Their expedition against Olynthus, when that town was compelled by force to join the Spartan alliance, and also their occupation of the Kadmeia in 382 were open violations of the King's peace.³

The reaction was not long delayed. In 379 Thebes was liberated, and in 378 and the following years, the Athenians established their second league, which the Lacedæmonians, after repeated reverses, were compelled to recognise **Overthrow of the Lacedæ-** in 374 and at the general Peace Congress of 371.⁴ **monian Hegemony.** The hegemony of the Lacedæmonians by land was recognised at that conference, but received its death blow a few days after at the battle of Leuctra. Even the Peloponnesian allies then abandoned Sparta one after another, and the last remnant of them concluded a separate peace for themselves with Thebes in 366. Sparta herself was thus compelled to abandon her supremacy, which she never succeeded in regaining even in more favourable circumstances, after the battle of Mantinea, though she made repeated attempts.⁵

It was only the relations between the Lacedæmonians and their

---

¹ Cf. Xen., *Hell.*, 5, 1, 36: προστάται γὰρ γενόμενοι τῆς ὑπὸ βασιλέως καταπεμφθείσης εἰρήνης καὶ τὴν αὐτονομίαν ταῖς πόλεσι πράττοντες.—For the terms of the king's peace of 387 B.C., cf. Xen., *Hell.*, 5, 1, 31; Diod. 14, 110.

² Corinth, cf. Xen., *Hell.*, 5, 1, 36; Mantinea, Xen., *Hell.*, 5, 2, 1 sqq.; Phlius, Xen., *Hell.*, 5, 3, 10-17 and 21-25; Diod. 15, 19.

³ On Olynthus and the seizure of the Kadmeia, cf. Xen., *Hell.*, 5, 2, 11-5, 3, 9; 5, 3, 18-20 and 26. Also Diod. 15, 19-23.

⁴ Cf. Diod. 15, 38. Xen., *Hell.*, 6, 3, 18/19.

⁵ Cf. Isocr. 5, 47: οὗτοι (οἱ Λακεδαιμόνιοι) γὰρ ἄρχοντες τῶν Ἑλλήνων οὐ πολὺς χρόνος ἐξ οὗ καὶ κατὰ γῆν καὶ κατὰ θάλατταν εἰς τοσαύτην μεταβολὴν ἦλθον, ἐπειδὴ τὴν μάχην ἡττήθησαν τὴν ἐν Λεύκτροις, ὥστ' ἀπεστερήθησαν μὲν τῆς ἐν τοῖς Ἕλλησι δυναστείας. Cf. Xen., *Hell.*, 7, 2, 2. Separate peace made with Thebes by the remaining Peloponnesian allies of Sparta. Xen., *Hell.*, 7, 4, 9. In 362 those who were then allied with Sparta carried ὅπως ἐν τῇ ἑαυτῶν ἕκαστοι ἡγήσοιντο. Xen., *Hell.*, 7, 5, 3. On the later foreign affairs of Sparta in general, cf. Isocr. 5, 49.

Peloponnesian allies that were subject to any definite international regulations; in the case of the States outside the Peloponnesus, so long as the Spartan supremacy lasted, the rulers simply dictated and were obeyed. Even in regard to the Peloponnesian league, we are not in a position to state whether its constitution was based on a treaty of alliance, or simply upon ancient custom. But some of the federal obligations binding on all members of the alliance and dating from very ancient times are definitely known.

The Peloponnesian League.

According to these, all cities of the Peloponnese, great and small, were autonomous, and were bound to defend the Peloponnese from attack. They were also bound to assist any individual member of the league that might be attacked. If disputes arose between members of the alliance, they were bound to make an agreement together; if, however, they came to open hostilities, they were required to choose a third impartial State as arbitrator.[1] In spite of this, individual members of the league sometimes waged open war against each other; and we must therefore conclude that this was not explicitly forbidden by the constitution of the league.[2]

We know too little about the rights and obligations of the chief town of the league and of the other individual members to be able to give a systematic account of the confederation. Whenever

---

[1] The regulations given in the text are taken from the treaty between Sparta and Argos, as recorded in Thuc. 5, 77, 79: τὰς δὲ πόλιας τὰς ἐν Πελοποννάσῳ, καὶ μικρὰς καὶ μεγάλας, αὐτονόμως εἶμεν πάσας κατὰ πάτρια. αἰ δέκα τῶν ἐκτὸς Πελοποννάσω τις ἐπὶ τὰν Πελοπόννασον γᾶν ἴῃ ἐπὶ κακῷ, ἀλεξέμεναι ἀμοθεὶ βουλευσαμένως, ὅπᾳ κα δικαιότατα δοκῇ τοῖς Πελοποννασίοις in 77; cf. also 79, 1. The Argives invaded the territory of Epidauros, Ἐπιδαύριοι δὲ τοὺς ξυμμάχους ἐπεκαλοῦντο, ὧν τινες οἱ μὲν τὸν μῆνα (τὸν Καρνεῖον) προὐφασίσαντο, οἱ δὲ καὶ ἐς μεθορίαν τῆς Ἐπιδαυρίας ἐλθόντες ἡσύχαζον. Cf. Thuc. 5, 54: and 79 αἰ δέ τινι τᾶν πολίων ᾖ ἀμφίλογα, ἢ τᾶν ἐντὸς ἢ τᾶν ἐκτὸς Πελοποννάσω, αἴτε περὶ ὅρων αἴτε περὶ ἄλλου τινός, διακριθῆμεν. αἰ δέ τις τῶν ξυμμάχων πόλις πόλει ἐρίζοι, ἐς πόλιν ἐλθεῖν, ἄν τινα ἴσαν ἀμφοῖν ταῖς πολίεσσι δοκείοι. Example of such an arbitration in Thuc. 5, 81.

[2] In a war between Cleitor and Orchomenos, Agesilaos, being in need of the mercenary troops of the Cleitorians for his expedition against Thebes, ordered the Orchomenians, ἕως στρατεία εἴη, παύσασθαι τοῦ πολέμου. εἰ δέ τις πόλις στρατιᾶς οὔσης ἔξω ἐπὶ πόλιν στρατεύσοι, ἐπὶ ταύτην ἔφη πρῶτον ἰέναι κατὰ τὸ δόγμα τῶν συμμάχων, Xen., *Hell.*, 5, 4, 36 and 37. According to this, feuds between members of the league were forbidden by decree of the council of the league, but only during military expeditions of the league outside Peloponnesus.

on any occasion it was necessary to ascertain the opinion of the allies, Sparta, as president, summoned a federal council, consisting of envoys from the various States.[1] This assembly, as a regular rule, gave its vote previous to any warlike enterprises or declarations of war by the league, also before the conclusion of a peace or armistice.[2] Discussions on such questions took place apparently in the presence of the envoys of the allies before the Spartan Apella. When the Apella had come to a decision on the matter in question, the voting taking place probably after the envoys had left the assembly, the envoys in their turn voted on the question in their federal council, in which the representatives of Sparta voted in accordance with the decision of the Apella.[3] In such voting all members of the league were on an equality; all States, great or small, had one vote, and one only. The decision of the majority was binding upon all, provided that "the gods or the heroes offered no impediment."[4] The indefinite nature of this last formula made it possible for the several members of the league to avoid obeying a decision of the federal council. Yet the great influence which Sparta exerted over the league made such non-compliance very rare, while, on the other hand, the same formula secured the Lacedæmonians from being outvoted by the smaller States.

Rights and Obligations of the Leading State and of the Members of the League.

The decisions of the allies were naturally carried out by the head of the league, Sparta. Accordingly, the chief command of the allies in a war upon which they resolved belonged to Sparta. Sparta made the arrangements for furnishing troops, siege materials and ships. When an expedition was decided upon, Sparta sent into the allied towns ξεναγοί, who assumed the com-

---

[1] Cf. Thuc. 1, 87 and 119; 5, 17 and 36.

[2] Instances are Thuc. 1, 87; Xen., *Hell.*, 5, 2, 20; Thuc. 4, 118; 5, 17 and 18.

[3] The evidence on this point is not complete enough for us to be able to describe the course of procedure with certainty. Cf. Xen., *Hell.*, 5, 2, 11, 20 sqq.; 6, 3, 3, 18. Thuc. 1, 67 sqq., where, however, the whole council of the league was not assembled. In this case the allies who were present retired before the Apella debated and voted. Cf. 79. Thuc. 1, 119 sqq.

[4] Cf. Thuc. 1, 125: οἱ δὲ Λακεδαιμόνιοι ἐπειδὴ ἀφ' ἁπάντων ἤκουσαν γνώμην, ψῆφον ἐπήγαγον τοῖς ξυμμάχοις ἅπασιν ὅσοι παρῆσαν ἑξῆς καὶ μείζονι καὶ ἐλάσσονι πόλει καὶ τὸ πλῆθος ἐψηφίσαντο πολεμεῖν. In Thuc., 1, 141, the members of the league are said to be πάντες ἰσόψηφοι. Thuc., 5, 80: εἰρημένον κύριον εἶναι, ὅτι ἂν τὸ πλῆθος τῶν ξυμμάχων ψηφίσηται, ἢν μήτι θεῶν ἢ ἡρώων κώλυμα ᾖ.

mand over the troops of the allies and brought them to the Lacedæmonian generals.[1] But if the allies were not summoned by the Lacedæmonians to give their vote on a war, then they were not bound to obey the orders issued by Sparta for the purposes of that war.[2]

The military burdens of the several States were assessed, as might be expected, according to their size. The contingent which every State was expected to furnish to an expedition outside the limits of its own territory amounted to two-thirds of its entire population capable of bearing arms; but the State in whose territory the allied army was operating was bound to bring its whole force into the field.[3] When the employment of mercenaries became prevalent in Greece, it often happened that particular States avoided the burden of supplying troops by the payment of a fixed sum for every man required.[4]

The costs of the war were defrayed by the allied States in proportion to the size of each, but no permanent or regular tribute was exacted from them.[5]

---

[1] Cf. Thuc. 2, 10; 5, 17; 7, 18; 3, 16. Xen., *Hell.*, 5, 2, 37. On the ξεναγοί, cf. Thuc. 2, 75; Xen., *Hell.*, 3, 5, 7; 5, 1, 33; 2, 7; 7, 2, 3. Yet beside these the contingents of the allies seem also to have had their own στρατηγοί. Cf. Thuc. 2, 10. By decree of the league the Lacedæmonians were specially empowered to inflict punishment on those who were negligent in the fulfilment of their military duties. Cf. the decree of the league in Xen., *Hell.*, 5, 2, 22: εἰ δέ τις τῶν πόλεων ἐκλίποι τὴν στρατίαν, ἐξεῖναι τοῖς Λακεδαιμονίοις ἐπιζημιοῦν στατῆρι κατὰ τὸν ἄνδρα τῆς ἡμέρας.

[2] Compare the refusal of the allies to serve in the expedition of Cleomenes against Athens in Hdt. 5, 74 and 75. At the same time the influence of Sparta was not unfrequently strong enough to induce the allies to take part in a war concerning which their vote had not been taken. Cf. Thuc. 5, 54.

[3] In an ἔκδημος ἔξοδος the allies had to send two-thirds of their fighting men. Thuc., 2, 10; 3, 15. Compare the resolution of the federal council in Xen., *Hell.*, 5, 2, 20: πέμπειν τὸ εἰς τοὺς μυρίους ξύνταγμα ἑκάστην πόλιν. Cf. § 37. That the State, in whose territory the allied army was operating sent all its available forces, is attested by Thuc. 5, 57: Φλιάσιοι δὲ πανστρατιᾷ, ὅτι ἐν τῇ ἐκείνων ἦν τὸ στράτευμα.

[4] Cf. Xen., *Hell.*, 5, 2, 21: λόγοι δὲ ἐγένοντο (in the federal council) ἀργύριον τε ἀντ' ἀνδρῶν ἐξεῖναι διδόναι τῇ βουλομένῃ τῶν πόλεων, τριώβολον Αἰγιναῖον κατ' ἄνδρα, ἱππέας τε εἴ τις παρέχοι, (ἀντὶ) τεττάρων ὁπλιτῶν τὸν μισθὸν τῷ ἱππεῖ δίδοσθαι. Cf. also Diod. 15, 31: ἦν δὲ αὐτοῖς ὁ μὲν ὁπλίτης πρὸς δύο ψιλοὺς τεταγμένος, ὁ δ' ἱππεὺς πρὸς τέτταρας ὁπλίτας ἰσαζόμενος.

[5] Cf. Plut., *Apophth. Lac. Archid.*, 7, p. 268 Didot: τῶν δὲ συμμάχων ἐν τῷ Πελοποννησιακῷ πολέμῳ ἐπιζητούντων, πόσα χρήματα ἀρκέσει, καὶ ἀξιούντων ὁρίσαι

τὸν φόρον, ὁ πόλεμος, ἔφη, οὐ τεταγμένα ζητεῖ. That is the ἀργύριον ῥητὸν of Thuc. 2, 7. The apportionment of the war expenses according to the size of the allied towns follows from Diod. 14, 17, where the Lacedæmonians require from the Eleans τὰς δαπάνας τοῦ πρὸς Ἀθηναίους πολέμου κατὰ τὸ ἐπιβάλλον αὐτοῖς μέρος. No regular tribute; cf. Thuc. 1, 19: καὶ οἱ μὲν Λακεδαιμόνιοι οὐχ ὑποτελεῖς ἔχοντες φόρου τοὺς ξυμμάχους ἡγοῦντο—C. I. G. 1511= Dittenberger, *Syll.*, 34, contains a fragment of a list of war taxes paid by the allies to the Lacedæmonians.

ATHENS.

ATHENS.

I.

HISTORICAL.

1. The Athenian State from its Beginning down to Solon.

THE territory[1] in which the Athenian State arose, contained an area of about 1000 square miles. The peninsular shape of the country, and the numerous bays and openings into the land, produced a coast line of extraordinary length compared with its area. It was nearly 100 miles long. The bays supplied natural harbours in plenty; and between them and the mountains were enclosed coast plains, most of them suitable for cultivation. Of these plains, however, only two extended far into the interior of the country, namely, the plain of Eleusis and the plain of Athens, separated from each other by the rocky ridge of Aigaleos. The pieces of level land were but few in number, on account of the many mountain chains which stretch through Attica, and their calcareous soil was light and rather arid and stony. Many broad stretches of land, called φελλεῖς, where the rock was covered only by a thin layer of earth, were available for

<small>Natural Features of the Country.</small>

---

[1] For the description given in the text compare Bursian, *Geogr. v. Griechenl.* 1, p. 251 ff. Curtius in the *Ber. d. Berl Ak.*, 1877, p. 425 ff. C. Wachsmuth, *d. St. Ath.*, 1, 93 ff.; Kiepert, *Lehrb. d. alten Geogr.*, § 248 ff. According to Kiepert's computation, "as exact as the topographical material at present existing permits," Attica with its small adjacent islands, is about 1000 square miles in area. See Fränkel in Boeckh, *Staatsh. d. Ath.*,³ 2, 9, no. 67. In Beloch, *Bevölker. d. griech.-röm. Welt*, 55 ff., 1886, the area of Attica, including Oropos, Eleutherai, and the islands on the coast, is given as 2647 or 2658 square kilometres. 2650 sq. kilometres=1023 sq. miles.

nothing except pasturage for sheep and goats.[1] A further disadvantage, in addition to the unsatisfactory soil, was the complete absence of any adequate natural water supply. The climate, however, which prevailed in Attica was so mild and genial, that the inhabitants, by dint of very diligent cultivation, succeeded, in spite of these disadvantages, in growing crops of excellent quality, if scanty in quantity. Attica produced, for instance, capital barley, but not enough for the needs of its population.[2] The olive, the fig tree, and the vine were extensively cultivated; gardens were common and well kept. The considerable extent of the φελλεῖς favoured cattle breeding, which, however, was mostly confined to sheep and goats. The minerals found in Attica were silver ore, marble, and potters' clay.

Within the boundaries of this land there dwelt in historical times a population of Ionic race, who claimed for themselves the honour of being the aboriginal inhabitants.[3] But as in most cases where we find such pretensions advanced by any race, so in Attica, we cannot admit this claim to autochthony in the sense in which it was made by the historical Athenians. We must, on the contrary, assume that there were repeated immigrations of foreigners into the land. To this foreign element belonged in the first place, according to a perfectly credible tradition, a not inconsiderable number of noble families, who came to Attica from various districts of Hellas. Further, we must reckon among the immigrants in all probability those clans also which are personified in the legends under the names of Xuthus and Ion, and which dwelt originally on the east coast of the country.[4] But we are able to point to the presence of

Population.

---

[1] Thuc. 1, 2, calls the soil of Attica λεπτόγεων. For the φελλεῖς see Sauppe, *epist. crit.*, p. 59 ff. The Scholium on Aristoph., *Ach.*, 272, says, φελλεῖς δὲ ἔλεγον οἱ Ἀττικοὶ τοὺς πετρώδεις τόπους, οἵτινες κάτωθεν μέν εἰσι πετρώδεις, ἐπιπολῆς δὲ ὀλίγην ἔχουσι γῆν. The φελλεῖς especially devoted to goat pasturing: Schol. on Aristoph., *Clouds*, 71. Harp., φελλέα. Alkiphr., 3, 21.

[2] Cf. Xen., *de Vect.*, 1, 5: ἔστι δὲ καὶ γῆ, ἣ σπειρομένη μὲν οὐ φέρει καρπόν, ὀρυττομένη δὲ πολλαπλασίους τρέφει ἢ εἰ σῖτον ἔφερε. For the barley, cf. Theophr., περὶ φυτῶν ἱστορίας 8, 8, 2: Ἀθήνησι γοῦν αἱ κριθαὶ τὰ πλεῖστα ποιοῦσιν ἄλφιτα, κριθοφόρος γὰρ ἀρίστη.

[3] On the autochthony of the Athenians, cf. Hdt. 7, 161; Thuc. 1, 2; 2, 86. Eurip., *fr.* 862, 5. Dem. 19, 361. Isocr. 12, 124. Plat., *Menex.*, 288 C. Strab. 383.

[4] Cf. Thuc. 1, 2. Ephor. *ap.* Suid. Περιθοίδαι develops this into a law: νόμος δ' ἦν Ἀθήνησι ξένους εἰσδέχεσθαι τοὺς βουλομένους τῶν Ἑλλήνων. Aristeid.,

even non-Greek elements in the population of Attica. As such must be mentioned, in the first place, the Phœnicians, who came from Salamis to Attica, and established settlements of their own in Phaleron and Melite.¹ Further traces of the same nation meet us at Marathon and Athmonon.² The cult of Herakles, a deity of Phœnician origin, was especially characteristic of the Athenians.³ An immigration of Carians and Leleges is attested by the sepulchral relics which have been found, and by a number of names of localities in Attica.⁴ Still further, various cults and

Panath., 1, 173–8 Dind., who according to the not improbable theory of Maas in the *Gött. gel. Anz.*, 1889, p. 802, and 813, gets his information from Ephoros, develops the same idea still further. According to Aristeid., *op. cit.*, 177, the immigrants were οἱ περὶ Θήβας ἀτυχήσαντες καὶ πάσης τῆς Βοιωτίας συνεκπεσόντες and Θετταλῶν οἱ ταύτῃ τραπόμενοι καὶ Ταναγραίων οἱ μεταστάντες Δωριέων Πελοποννήσου κρατησάντων ὑπὸ τῶν ἐξάντων ἀναστάντες. In addition came immigrants ἀπ' ἀμφοτέρων τῶν αἰγιαλῶν τοῦ θ' ἑσπερίου καὶ τοῦ ἑῴου. On the immigration of the Περιθοῖδαι from Thessaly, see Maas, *ibid.*, 812–3; on the immigrants from Bœotia, *id.*, 813 ff.; on the Gephyraioi from Tanagra, Toepffer, *att. Geneal.*, 296 ff.; connexion between the Phytalidai and Troezen: Toepffer, *ib.*, 252 ff.; between Theseus and Troezen: 7 Suppl. vol. of the *Jahrb. f. cl. Phil.*, 233–4. Aristeid., *ibid.*, says of the immigrants from Thessaly and Bœotia: οὗτοι δ' ἦσαν Ἴωνες (so the Schol. for Ἰωνία) πάντες. Xuthos and Ion on the East coast of Attica. Xuthos in the Tetrapolis: Strab. 383. Ἰωνίδαι in Thorikos: Schol. Plat., *Apol.*, 23: Λύκων μέντοι πατὴρ ἦν Αὐτολύκου Ἰωνίδης (Meier, *de gent.*, 4, for Ἴων) γένος, δήμων Θορίκιος. The locality of the demos Ἰωνίδαι is uncertain. Τάφος Ἴωνος in Potamoi: Paus. 1, 31, 3; 7, 1, 5. See also Toepffer, *ibid.*, 267 ff. The Kephalidai also belong to this section. Kephalos on the mother's side grandson of Xuthos (Apollod. 1, 9, 4) in Thorikos: Apollod. 3, 15, 1. See Toepffer, 255 ff.

¹ For Salamis as the entrance to Attica for the Phœnicians, see Curtius, *erläut. Text d. 7 Karten*, p. 9 ff. *Stadtgesch. v. Athen.*, p. 23. Wachsmuth, *d St. Ath.*, 1, 442 ff. Phœnicians in Phaleron: Wachsmuth, 1, 439 ff.; in Melite, 1, 404 ff.

² On the Phœnicians in Marathon, see Wachsmuth, 1, 407; and in Athmonon, 1, 413.

³ Cf. Diod. 4, 39: Ἀθηναῖοι πρῶτοι τῶν ἄλλων ὡς θεὸν ἐτίμησαν θυσίαις τὸν Ἡρακλέα. Cult of Herakles as bond of union of the τετράκωμοι: Poll. 4, 105. Steph., Ἐχελίδαι; of the Μεσόγειοι: C. I. A., II. 602–3; in Melite: Wachsmuth, 1, 406 ff.; in Hephaistiadai: Diog. Laert., 3, 41; in Plotheia: C. I. A., II. 570; in Marathon: Paus. 1, 15, 3; 32, 4.

⁴ For Carians in Attica, cf. Philoch. *ap.* Strab., 397. On the ethnography of the Carians and Leleges, see Wachsmuth, 1, 445, 4. For the sepulchral remains at Spata, see Milchhöfer in the *Mitth. d. dtsch. Arch. Inst. in Ath.*, 2, 271 ff., and Köhler, 3, 1 ff. According to Köhler, the contents of the graves of Spata and Menidi have their nearest local analogues in the islands of the Ægean Sea, where a population of Carians and Leleges once dwelt. On the round tomb of Menidi, see the Publication *des*

places of worship show traces of having been founded by Leleges.¹ But it can no longer be considered probable that there ever existed a Thracian community at Eleusis.²

According to Thucydides' description of the condition of his country in the earliest ages, the inhabitants of Greece dwelt in those times in unfortified villages, situated some distance from the coast, through fear of the piracy that everywhere prevailed. It was not until the Greeks began to grow familiar with seafaring life that towns grew up on the coast. As prosperity increased, these were able to build town walls to protect themselves against attack from sea. Then the larger towns gradually reduced their smaller neighbours to subjection.³ In Attica therefore, as elsewhere, the population dwelt originally in small towns, some fortified, some not, but each independent of the rest in its political life. It is certain that many of the demes we meet with in historical times dated their first beginnings from the most remote antiquity.⁴

Condition of the country in the Earliest Period.

New forms of political life were developed in Attica by circumstances similar to those in operation in the rest of Greece. Certain large towns obtained sway over the smaller ones.⁵ In

---

deutschen Arch. Inst. in Ath., 1880, and *Mitth.*, 12, 139 ff. Acc. to Köhler, p. 9, the names of the Attic mountains ending in *ettos* agree in their suffix with many names of places in Caria. See Kiepert, *Lehrb. d. a. Geogr.*, 73, 3. By what route the Leleges reached Attica is uncertain acc. to Wachsmuth, 1, 444 ff.

¹ Lelegian character of the Artemis of Brauron and Munychia: Deimling, *die Leleger*, 179 ff.; of the Dioscuri and Helena, 153–4, of Nemesis at Rhamnus, 154; of the Amazons, 188 ff.; Wachsmuth, 1, 421 ff. On the encampment of the Amazons at Melite, see Wachsmuth, 1, 415 ff.

² See the convincing argument of Toepffer, *ibid.*, 26 ff. Wachsmuth, *ibid.*, 1, 401 ff., adopts the theory of a Thracian community at Eleusis.

³ Cf. Thuc. 1, 5, 7, 10. On the newer towns, Thuc. 1, 7, 8. Subjugation of the smaller πόλεις by the larger: Thuc. 1, 8.

⁴ Cf. Thuc. 2, 14, 15. I have shown in the 7 Suppl. vol. of the *Jahrb. f. cl. Phil.*, 202 ff., that the ἐν τοῖς ἀγροῖς διαιτᾶσθαι of 2, 14 is identical with the κατὰ πόλεις οἰκεῖσθαι of 2, 15. For the existence of demes before the time of Cleisthenes, see my remarks, *ibid.*, 206 ff. The recollection of their earlier autonomy was kept up in the traditions of the demes, cf. Paus. 1, 31, 5: γέγραπται δ' ἤδη μοι τῶν ἐν τοῖς δήμοις φάναι πολλοὺς ὡς καὶ πρὸ τῆς ἀρχῆς ἐβασιλεύοντο τῆς Κέκροπος. Cf. Paus. 1, 14, 7; 31, 5; 38, 1. Traditions of the demes distinguished from those of the town of Athens: Paus. 1, 14, 7: λέγουσι δὲ ἀνὰ τοὺς δήμους καὶ ἄλλα οὐδὲν ὁμοίως καὶ οἱ τὴν πόλιν ἔχοντες.

⁵ *E.g.* Βραυρὼν and Ἀφίδνα. As dependencies of Βραυρὼν may be reckoned Φιλαΐδαι, Ἁλαὶ Ἀραφηνίδες and Ἀραφήν. See Bursian, *Geogr.*, 1, 348 ff. To Ἀφίδνα belonged Τιτακίδαι (Hdt. 9, 73) and Περρίδαι (Hesych., *sub verb.*).

other neighbourhoods, towns more equal in size to one another joined together in religious leagues, each with some shrine worshipped by all the members as its centre.[1] The endeavour to describe this state of affairs as a symmetrical system, led to accounts such as that given by Philochoros, who tells us that before the time of Theseus, the inhabitants of Attica were united by Cecrops into a dodekapolis, or league of 12 cities. The number 12 seems to have been chosen on the analogy of the 12 Ionic cities of the Aigialeia and of Asia Minor, and the 12 pre-Cleisthenic phratries.[2]

The unification of the country first commenced in the plain which is shut in by the mountains Hymettos, Brilessos, Parnes and Aigaleos, and stretches from their feet to the sea. On the high ridge which extends into the plain, and round its flanks, arose one after the other three communities of three different nationalities. **Independent Communities on the Site of Athens itself.** The oldest was of aboriginal stock, and had established itself on the summit of the hill which was afterwards called the Acropolis, and on its S.E. side. They seem to have been specially identified with the worship of Zeus, Ge, Athene, Hephæstus, and the Chthonian deities.[3] On the Agra, a hill E. of the Akropolis, settlers of a different race had fixed their abode. The main bulk of these were Ionians: the deities they chiefly worshipped were Apollo Delphinius and Pythius and

---

[1] As examples of such religious leagues, which were kept up in historical times, may be mentioned Τρίκωμοι: Steph., Εὐπυρίδαι. *Mitth. d. dtsch. arch. Inst. in Ath.*, 12, 87, 27. Τετράκωμοι: Poll. 4, 105. Τετράπολις: Strab. 383. Steph., *sub verb.*, C.I.A., II. 601. Dedicatory inscr. in C.I.A., II. 1324. Ἐπακρεῖς: C.I.A., II. 570, Steph., Σημαχίδαι, Μεσόγειοι: C.I.A., II. 602-3. On the league for the worship of Athene Pallenis, see the author's *Altatt. Komenverf.*, *ib.*, pp. 212-3. On the positions of the demes that belonged to this league, see Bursian, 1,344 ff. Brückner in *Mitth. d. dtsch. arch. Inst. in Ath.*, 16, 200 ff. Milchhöfer in the *Berl. Phil. Wochenschr.*, 1892, p. 2 ff., 34 ff.

[2] Cf. Philoch. *ap.* Strab., 397, where eleven towns are mentioned: Kekropia, Tetrapolis, Epakria, Dekeleia, Eleusis, Aphidna, Thorikos, Brauron, Kytheros, Sphettos, Kephisia. Cf. *Parian Marble*, 84; Steph., Ἀθῆναι, Ἐπακρία. Theophr., *Char.*, 26. Haase in *Ath. Stammverf.* in the *Abh. d. hist. phil. Ges.*, Breslau, 1, 67 ff.; and Philippi, *Beitr. z. e. Gesch. d. att. Bürgerr.*, 257 ff., endeavour to explain Et. M., ἐπακρία χώρα, and Suid., ἐπακρία χώρα, as belonging to the genuine Philochorean tradition; but I still consider their attempt unsuccessful. See Author's *Komenverf.*, *ib.*, pp. 203-4.

[3] See Wachsmuth, *d. St. Athen.*, 1,387 ff.

Poseidon Helikonios. Clear indications point to the E. coast of Attica as the quarter whence the cult of Apollo was brought to the Agra hill.[1] Lastly, on a group of hills to the W. of the Acropolis was a settlement of Phœnician and Carian-Lelegian elements. To the Phœnicians we can trace the name of the district Melite, which is the Greek form of the Phœnician Melitáh, *i.e.* asylum or place of refuge; Hèrakles and Aphrodite Urania, who were worshipped there, are both deities of Phœnician origin; the Heptachalcon, *i.e.* building of seven metals, is to be explained as connected with the Chaldæan system of the seven planets. Carian-Lelegian settlers are indicated by the tombs of the Amazons, the Amazoneion and the place Chrysa.[2]

We possess no direct testimony about the unification of these independent settlements into the town of Athens; but the legend of Theseus' wars with the Amazons enables us to conclude that it was not effected without war; and since Theseus, the victor in those wars, is the representative of the Ionian community on the Agra, we may infer that

Synoikismos of the Town of Athens.

---

[1] Compare Wachsmuth, *ib.*, 1, 392 ff. The Cult of Apollo Delphinios was common to all Ionians: Strab. 179. Connexion of this Apollo with Aigeus: Poll. 8, 119, who dwelt in the Delphinion: Plut., *Thes.*, 12; and with Theseus: Plut. *Thes.*, 14, 18. The Pythion as an ancient shrine (Thuc. 2, 15) of Apollo Pythios, who after the time of Ion was the θεὸς πατρῷος of the Athenians: Arist. *ap.* Harp., Ἀπόλλων πατρῷος. At the Delphinion Theseus, who generally is represented as ἔπηλυς καὶ ξένος (Plut., *Thes.*, 13, 32), displayed the first proof of his strength on Athenian soil: Paus. 1, 19, 1. Theseus is connected with Poseidon also (cf. Plut., *Thes.*, 25, 36), who was his father according to Troizenian legend: Plut., *Thes.*, 6. Aigeus can scarcely be distinguished from Ποσειδῶν Αἰγαῖος (Pherekyd., *fr.* 115, in Müller, *fr. hist. gr.*, 1, 99). Compare Toepffer, *ib.*, 254. Acc. to Artemidor., *Oneirokrit.*, 2, 12, the billows were called αἶγες, and the epithet Ἑλικώνιος given to Poseidon on the Agra is also probably derived from the curling motion of the sea waves. See Wachsmuth, *ib.*, 1, 396, 2. That Poseidon Helikonios is an Ionic god, is shown by the fact that he was worshipped by the Ionians of Asia Minor also. Cf. Hdt. 1, 148. The theory that the Ionic worship of Apollo was introduced into the town from the E. coast of the land, agrees well with the tradition that the Kephalidai were admitted into Athens, and to the citizenship, and kept up their gentile sacra on the mountain ridge between the immediate territory of Athens and the borders of Eleusis. Cf. Paus. 1, 37, 6–7; Toepffer, *ib.*, 260 ff. A settlement from Thera on the Athenian town territory, which Wachsmuth tries to prove, *ib.* 1, 399 ff., I regard as improbable, as may be inferred from what is said above.

[2] See Wachsmuth, *ib.*, 1, 404.ff.

this community was the one which compelled the others to combine with it, though the Acropolis hill was adopted as the political centre of the new State because of its position and strength.[1]

The Panathenaic festival was held in honour and remembrance of this synoikismos of the town 'Ἀθῆναι, whose very name by its plural form points to the origin of the town in a group of independent settlements. The festival celebrating the synoikismos of the town was extended and developed into a national festival of the country, but not until the whole land was politically united with Athens.[2]

This political unification, and the classification of the entire community thus formed into Phylai are connected by tradition with the names of Theseus and Ion. Both of these men were immigrants and foreigners, and it was legendary genealogies that first made out any relationship by descent between them and the native Erechtheidai. It is, therefore, a very plausible conjecture that the newly arrived Ionic element of the population first brought about the amalgamation of all the communities who dwelt on the site which afterwards became the town of Athens; and then by the help of this consolidated State forced the other communities of the land into political

Synoikismos of the Country.

---

[1] See Wachsmuth, *ib.*, 1, 459 ff.

[2] The institution of the Panathenaia is ascribed to Erichthonios by Hellanikos and Androtion *ap.* Harp.=Παναθήναια. Phot. Suid., 2 Art.; and by Philochoros *ap.* Harp., Κανηφόροι, and by the Schol. on. Aristoph., *Wasps*, 544. On the *Parian Marble*, 17, 18 (Müller, *fr. hist. gr.*, 1, p. 544), it is said of the year 1506 B.C.: ἀφ' οὗ 'Εριχθόνιος Παναθηναίοις τοῖς πρώτοις γενομένοις ἅρμα ἔζευξε καὶ τὸν ἀγῶνα ἐδείκνυε καὶ 'Αθηναίους (ὢν)ό(μασε.) Apollod. 3, 15, 7, is to be explained by Diod. 4, 60. Plut., *Thes.* 24, based on the authority of Philochoros (see *Philolog.*, 1873, p. 60 ff.), attributes the institution of the Panathenaia to Theseus, in the words: καὶ Παναθήναια θυσίαν ἐποίησε κοινήν, *i.e.*, he converted the Panathenaia into a festival common to all Attica. The same thing is meant by Paus., when he says, 8, 2, 1, that after the unification of the country by Theseus the festival was called Panathenaia, having been previously called Athenaia. But Istros *ap.* Harp., Παναθήναια attributes the change of the name to Erichthonios. Suid., Παναθήναια, 1 Art., and Apost., 14, 6, speak of two establishments of the Panathenaia, first by Erichthonios, then by Theseus. Thuc. 2, 15 is equally ignorant of any re-modelling of the Panathenaia at the synoikismos. Wachsmuth's hypothesis, *ib.*, 1, 453 ff., on the synoikismos of the town of Athens, and the significance of the Panathenaia, has no sufficient justification in our authorities. On the significance of the plural form in names of towns, see Göttling, *Rhein. Mus.*, 1841, p. 162.

union.[1] According to Thucydides, this union meant the centralisation of the whole government in the metropolis Athens, by the abolition of the various governments of the hitherto autonomous States.[2]

The Eupatrid families which up to that time had governed the various independent communities, were now compelled to reside in Athens, where they obtained a share in the central government of the whole country.[3] The festival of the Συνοίκια or Μετοίκια, celebrated on the 16th of Hekatombaion, kept

Form of the Synoikismos.

---

[1] Ion, founder of the oldest form of government in Attica: Aristot., 'Αθ. πολ., 41, 2: πρώτη μὲν γὰρ ἐγένετο [κα]τάστασις τῶν ἐξ ἀρχῆς, Ἴωνος καὶ τῶν μετ' αὐτοῦ συνοικησάντων. Cf. also Arist. ap. Harp., Ἀπόλλων πατρῷος. Rose, Arist. pseudep., 406–7. Ion helped Erechtheus against the Eumolpidai: Philoch. ap. Harp., Βοηδρόμια. Cf. Suidas, sub verb. Et. M., Βοηδρομιών. Ion does not occur in the list of Attic kings. Hdt. 8, 44 calls him στρατάρχης of the Athenians, Aristotle, ib., 3, 2, Polemarch. So Schol. on Aristoph., Birds, 1527. Acc. to Strab. 383, the Athenians granted him the πολιτεία in return for his help. Euripides represents him, in contrast to Xuthos, as an autochthonous Athenian, son of Apollo and Kreusa, since none but an autochthon could rule over Athens. Cf. Ion, 589 sq., 1058 sq., 1069 sq. Cf. also the words of Kreusa, 1463 sq. Acc. to Hdt. 1, 143, the Athenians even in his day still disdained to be called Ionians. Acc. to Thuc. 2, 15, Theseus was the synoikist of Attica; for his opponent the Erechtheid Menestheus, cf. Plut., Thes., 32, 35, and 24, 25.

[2] Cf. Thuc. 2, 15: ἐπειδὴ δὲ Θησεὺς ἐβασίλευσε, γενόμενος μετὰ τοῦ ξυνετοῦ καὶ δυνατὸς τά τε ἄλλα διεκόσμησε τὴν χώραν καὶ καταλύσας τῶν ἄλλων πόλεων τά τε βουλευτήρια καὶ τὰς ἀρχὰς ἐς τὴν νῦν πόλιν οὖσαν ἓν βουλευτήριον ἀποδείξας καὶ πρυτανεῖον, ξυνῴκισε πάντας καὶ νεμομένους τὰ αὐτῶν ἑκάστους ἅπερ καὶ πρὸ τοῦ ἠνάγκασε μιᾷ πόλει ταύτῃ χρῆσθαι, ἣ ἁπάντων ἤδη ξυντελούντων ἐς αὐτὴν μεγάλη γενομένη παρεδόθη ὑπὸ Θησέως τοῖς ἔπειτα. Cf. Plut., Thes., 24, 32. That the synoikismos of Theseus did not involve a concentration of the whole population of Attica in Athens itself, is recognised by Kuhn, ub. d. Entsteh. d. Städte d. Alten, p. 160 ff., though few good authorities state the fact. Cf. Diod. 4, 61. Paus. 1, 22, 3; 26, 6. Apost. 14, 6. Cic., de Leg., 2, 2, 5. Valer. Max. 5, 3, 3. On the Synoikismos of Theseus see the author's Komenverf., p. 239 ff. In 3, 2, again Thuc. uses ξυνοικίζειν in its constitutional meaning, not literally.

[3] The settlement of the Attic Eupatridai in Athens is attested by Plut., Thes., 32 (Philoch.), where we are told of Theseus: εἰς ἓν ἄστυ συνείρξαντα πάντας (i.e. τοὺς εὐπατρίδας). Cf. also the description given in Plato, Critias, 110 c, which must be considered historical because it takes into account the three ἔθνη which then existed: ᾤκει δὲ τότ' ἐν τῇδε τῇ χώρᾳ, τὰ μὲν ἄλλα ἔθνη τῶν πολιτῶν περὶ τὰς δημιουργίας ὄντα καὶ τὴν ἐκ τῆς γῆς τροφήν, τὸ δὲ μάχιμον ὑπ' ἀνδρῶν θείων κατ' ἀρχὰς ἀφορισθὲν ᾤκει χωρὶς κ. τ. ἀ. τὸ μάχιμον, being contrasted with the Demiourgoi and Georgoi, can mean nothing but the Eupatridai, and their separate dwelling-place in opposition to the χώρα must be the

up the remembrance of this unification of the country.¹ The synoikismos and the many new settlers it brought to Athens naturally increased the size of the town, which now spread itself over the district N. of the Acropolis.²

The Synoikismos was accompanied by a distribution of the population into four Phylai. In the ordinary traditional accounts this classification is attributed to Ion, and the occurrence of the same Phylai in the Ionic colonies is a further proof that these Phylai were of Ionic origin. The names of the four Phylai, Αἰγικορεῖς, Ἀργαδεῖς, Ὅπλητες, and Γελέοντες, signify in literal meaning most probably "Goat-herds," "Agriculturists," "Warriors," and "the splendid" or "brilliant men," and, to all appearance, are an echo of some primeval caste-classification.³

The Ionic Phylai.

ἄστυ. Cf. also Et. M. Εὐπατρίδαι (Lex. Seguer. 257, 7 sqq.): ἐκαλοῦντο εὐπατρίδαι οἱ αὐτὸ τὸ ἄστυ οἰκοῦντες καὶ μετέχοντες βασιλικοῦ γένους, τὴν τῶν ἱερῶν ἐπιμέλειαν ποιοῦντες, γεωργοὶ δὲ οἱ τῆς ἄλλης χώρας οἰκήτορες, ἐπιγεώμοροι δὲ τὸ τεχνικὸν ἔθνος.

¹ Thuc. 2, 15, after the words quoted above, continues thus:—καὶ ξυνοίκια ἐξ ἐκείνου Ἀθηναῖοι ἔτι καὶ νῦν τῇ θεῷ ἑορτὴν δημοτελῆ ποιοῦσι. Cf. Charax ap. Steph., Ἀθῆναι. Schol. on Arist., Pax, 1019. Plut., Thes., 24: ἔθυσε δὲ καὶ Μετοίκια τῇ ἕκτῃ ἐπὶ δέκα τοῦ Ἑκατομβαιῶνος, ἣν ἔτι νῦν θύουσι. The festival could be called Μετοίκια in reference to the settlement of the Eupatridai in Athens. Μετοικεῖν = to change one's residence, to remove to a place. Paus. 2, 30, 9 ; 6, 22, 7. Kausel, however, de Thesei synœcismo, 13 sq., Marburg, 1882, shows that Μετοίκια can be also used as equivalent to Συνοίκια.

² Increase of the population of Athens by general immigration as well, Plut., Thes., 25: ἔτι δὲ μᾶλλον αὐξῆσαι τὴν πόλιν βουλόμενος ἐκάλει πάντας ἐπὶ τοῖς ἴσοις καὶ τὸ δεῦρ᾽ ἴτε πάντες λεῴ κήρυγμα Θησέως γενέσθαι φασὶ πανδημίαν τινὰ καθιστάντος. Thuc. 2, 15 is the authority for an extention of the area of the town of Athens in consequence of the Synoikismos of Theseus. The words of Thuc. are not self-contradictory, as has been supposed by some ; Wachsmuth, ib., 454 ff., is wrong in supposing that they refer to the Synoikismos of the town itself. Kausel, ib., 9 ff., also disagrees with Wachsmuth.

³ I regard the account of the pre-Ionic Phylai in Poll. 8, 109, as completely worthless. See Schömann, de comit., 347. Meier, de Gent. Att., p. 3. Ilgen, de Trib. Att., 6 ff. Arist., 41, 2, says: τότε (i.e. after Ion had established the πρώτη κατάστασις τῶν ἐξ ἀρχῆς) γὰρ πρῶτον εἰς τὰς τέτταρας συνενεμήθησαν φυλὰς καὶ τοὺς φυλοβασιλεῖς κατέστησαν. In other traditional accounts the four Ionic Phylai are either derived from the sons of Ion (as in Hdt. 5, 66; Eur., Ion., 1575 sqq. ; Plut., Sol., 23 ; Poll. 8, 109), or at any rate are recognised as instituted by Ion. Cf. Strab., 383. Steph., Αἰγικόρεως. Hdt. 5, 69, shows that these Phylai occurred among the Ionians generally. There is evidence of the existence in Teos of Γελέοντες : C. I. G., 378–9 ; in Kyzikos of Γελέοντες: 3664–5, Ἀργαδεῖς : 3664–5, Αἰγικορεῖς : 3657, 3663–4–5, and Ὅπλητες : 3665. Mitth. d. dtsch. arch. Inst. in Ath., 6, 44. Ἀργαδεῖς and Αἰγικορεῖς at Tomoi : Perrot, Mel. d'arch., 446 ff. Anc. Inscr., II. 178.

It is, therefore, a very plausible theory that the four Phylai were a system imported into Attica from abroad, and, if we follow the traditional account, from the Ionians. The symmetrical form of the clan organisation based on these four Phylai, and the conventional explanation of the expressions φυλή, φρατρία, and γένος, indicate that the whole system was not a historical growth, but artificial, which agrees admirably with the theory that the Phylai were a classification introduced into Attica from abroad.[1]

The investigation of these classifications based on kinship or family connection is one of the most difficult subjects in ancient history. Since the Ἀθηναίων πολιτεία of Aristotle, as we possess it, begins with the period after Kylon's enterprise, we have nothing better to consult than the statements of later grammarians and lexicographers; but they too seem to have obtained all the essential points of their information from Aristotle. The utmost result therefore which we can obtain, is to establish beyond doubt what were the views held on the subject by Aristotle and the authorities he followed. But, when that is done, we have made but little progress towards the discovery of the actual truth; for even Aristotle and his sources offer

Clan Divisions of Attica.

Γελεῦντες and Αἰγικορεῖς, at Perinthos: *Mitth.* 6, 49. An Ἀργαδίς at Delos: *Bull.*, 10, 478. A χιλιαστὺς Ἀργαδεῖς at Ephesus: Dittenberger, *Syll.*, 134, 10; 815, 5. Αἰγικορεῖς is to be explained as analogous to βουκόλος, with the common change of Λ into P. See Curtius, *Grundz. d. griech. Et.*, 2. Aufl., p. 412. Ἀργαδῆς is most probably a nomen agentis from ἐργάζομαι. See Curtius, p. 165, and 570. Philippi, *Beitr.*, p. 273 also considers them yeomen. Ὁπλῆτες =ὁπλῖται. Γελέοντες=the brilliant men. See Bergk in the *Jahrb. f. cl. Phil.*, vol. 65, 401. Hugo Weber, *etymol. Unters.*, 40 ff. Ζεὺς Γελέων in *Inscr.*: C. I. A., III. 2. Other explanations of the terms Αἰγικορεῖς and Ἀργαδεῖς are given by Maas in the *Gött. gel. Anz.* 1889, pp. 806–808, but I cannot agree with him. Schömann, *de comit. Athen.*, 357 ff., considers that the Γελέοντες were the priestly class; Haase, *d. ath. Stammverf.* p. 77, says they were the royal families. See also Preller in the *arch. Zt.*, 1854 p. 287. On Plato's views see Susemihl, *genet. Entwickel. d. plat. Phil.*, 2, 480. Even the ancient writers consider the names of the four Phylai to be connected with γένη τοῦ βίου. Cf. Plut., *Sol.*, 23; Strab. 383; Plat., *Tim.* 24.

[1] Philippi's conclusion, *Beitr.*, p. 290 ff., that the Phylai could not have been introduced into Attica from abroad, is based on premises which cannot be proved. The ancients were as ignorant of the original significance of the names as we are, as is proved by their connecting them with the sons of Ion, and by the attempts at explanation in Strabo, 383, and Plut., *Sol.*, 23. Koutorga, *la tribu*, p. 65 ff., supposes that Attica was once conquered by Ionians, who brought in along with them their own tribal divisions.

us, for the most part at any rate, nothing but the combinations and conjectures which seemed to them satisfactory. The statements of the orators concerning the earliest periods are of little weight, because they lived at a time when the constitution had already undergone many profound changes. With this warning as to the hypothetical nature of the following description, I now give a short survey of the old Attic clan divisions.

Aristotle seems to have discussed the old Attic Phylai and Phratries, while treating of the institution of the four so-called Ionic Phylai, with which he too connected the name of Ion: nor did he return to this theme until he came to describe the constitutional changes introduced by Cleisthenes.[1]

System of the old Attic Phylai and Phratries.

In the first place, it is now generally believed that even the pre-Cleisthenian Phylai were local in character [2]—were, in fact, topographical subdivisions of the country.[3] But the Phylai also served

---

[1] In his review of the various changes of constitution in cap. 41 Aristotle says: πρώτη μὲν γὰρ ἐγένετο [κα]τάστασις τῶν ἐξ ἀρχῆς, Ἴωνος καὶ τῶν μετ' αὐτοῦ συνοικησάντων· τότε γὰρ πρῶτον εἰς τὰς τέτταρας συνενεμήθησαν φυλὰς καὶ τοὺς φυλοβασιλέας κατέστησαν. The statements we find attributed to Aristotle on the subject of the old Attic Phylai and Phratries, belong without doubt to the section of the Αθ. Π. in which Aristot. treated of the institutions of Ion.

[2] Aristot., Αθ. π., 21, 3, gives as the reason which led Cleisthenes to make ten tribes: διὰ τοῦτο δὲ οὐκ εἰς δώδεκα φυλὰς συνέταξεν, [ὅπως α]ὐτῷ μὴ συμβαίνῃ μερίζειν κατὰ τὰς προϋπαρχούσας τριττῦς, ἦσαν γὰρ ἐκ δ' φυλῶν δώδεκα τριττύες, ὥστ' οὐ [συν]έπιπτεν (I consider it incorrect to supply ἂν to fill the lacuna, because I regard the statement as relating to the time before Cleisthenes) ἀναμίσγεσθαι τὸ πλῆθος. From this it follows that the twelve Solonian Trittyes were local districts. Therefore the Phyle made up of three Trittyes must have had a local character.

[3] Aristotle, 8, 3, expressly states that the Trittyes were a new creation of Solon's. Against his evidence little pretension to credibility can be made by the traditional information given by the lexicographers, which regards the expressions φρατρία, τριττύς, and ἔθνος as identical (Poll. 8, 111), or at any rate φρατρία and τριττύς (Harp., Suid., Moer., γεννῆται. Steph., φρατρία. Schol. Plat., Axioch., p. 465 Bekker. Lex. Patm. in *Bulletin* 1, 152=Aristot., ed. Kaibel et v. Wilamowitz, p. 88). Harp. (=Suid. Phot.) is without doubt correct: τριττύς ἐστι τὸ τρίτον μέρος τῆς φυλῆς. αὕτη γὰρ διῄρηται εἰς τρία μέρη, τριττῦς καὶ ἔθνη καὶ φρατρίας, ὥς φησιν Ἀριστοτέλης ἐν τῇ Ἀθηναίων πολιτείᾳ. But at the same time we must not suppose that the τριττύς was already in existence in the earliest times. [Sandys on Arist. 8, 3, ἐκ δὲ [τῆς] φυ[λῆς ἐκ]άστης ἦσαν νενεμημέναι τριττύες μὲν τρεῖς, ναυκραρίαι δὲ δώδεκα καθ' ἑκάστην takes the plupf. to show the existence of these divisions before Solon; and "every four of these districts (sc. the naucrariai) formed a group called a τριττύς, or third part of a tribe."]

as divisions of the burgess body; and as such included only those members of the population who were counted as citizens.[1] The further sub-divisions of the burgesses are represented in the traditional account given by the lexicographers as connected with the Phratries on the following system:—each Phyle contained three Phratries, each Phratry thirty γένη, each γένος thirty men.[2] This classification assumes for the system of Phratries and Phylai, connected by Aristotle with the name of Ion, a total population of 10,800 burgesses, a number which is scarcely consistent with the actual circumstances of that age. It seems probable, therefore, that the lowest step of the subdivision given by the lexicographers, *i.e.* the thirty men assigned to each γένος, did not form part of Aristotle's account of this early classification.[3]

Originally none but the Eupatrids were counted as members of the Phatries and γένη. When the Ionian conquerors had become

[1] That the account given in *Lex. Patm., ibid.*, with which *Schol.* Plat., *Axioch.*, p. 465 Bekker, agrees (cf. also Moer., γεννῆται), is not taken word for word from Aristotle, follows from the fact that Aristotle cannot have identified τριττὺs and φρατρία as their account does; besides, Aristotle calls the second ἔθνος not γεωργοί but ἄγροικοι. Cf. Arist. 18, 2. Therefore the statement that the whole πλῆθος of the Eupatrids (who are omitted in the *Lex. Patm.* as well as in the Schol.), the Georgoi, and the Demiurgoi all belonged to the Phratries and γένη, cannot be accepted as Aristotelian as it stands. I believe the genuine Aristotelian version to be that given by Harp., γεννῆται (=Suid., 2 Art.), in the words: διῃρημένων γοῦν ἁπάντων τῶν πολιτῶν κατὰ μέρη, though Harp. too in his article on τριττὺs makes the mistake of identifying τριττὺs and φρατρία.

[2] Poll. 8, 111, makes the ἔθνος the second subdivision. Other authorities as a rule make the Phratry the next subdivision after the φυλή, and then continue either down to 30 men in each γένος (Poll. 3, 52; *Schol. Plat., Axioch.*, 465; *Lex. Patm., ib.*), or else only to the 30 γένη in each φρατρία (Harp., γεννῆται; Suid., Art. 2).

[3] In *Lex. Patm., ib.*, and Suid., γεννῆται, Art. 1, the numbers given in this system are represented as connected with the year—the 4 Phylai with the 4 seasons, the 12 Phratries with the 12 months, the 360 γένη with the 360 days. According to the passage first quoted this idea is derived from Aristotle, which is not impossible. But this will not account for the 30 ἄνδρες in each γένος. As to the 360 γένη there is no reason to doubt their continued existence. Proklus refers to it on Hesiod, *Works and Days*, 492: καὶ γὰρ ἐν ʼΑθήναις ἦσαν τοιοῦτοι τόποι καὶ ὠνομάζοντο λέσχαι, ἐξήκοντα καὶ τριακόσιοι, καὶ ἐδρᾶτό τινα θέσμια παρ' αὐτούς, ἵνα οἱ λόγοι γίγνονται σὺν τοῖς συνιοῦσιν ἐπωφελεῖς. There has recently been discovered between the Areopagus and the Pnyx a small quadrangular building of porous stone, and near it two boundary stones *in situ* inscribed ὅρος λέσχης, also an altar *in situ*. See *Berl. phil. Wochenschr.*, 1892, p. 323.

masters of Attica, they formed, in conjunction with the most prominent native families, a new community classified into γένη or families. Even the autochthonous families, who already had the cult of Zeus Herkeios as family god established among them, now adopted the Apollo Patroos of the Ionic conquerors, whose worship superseded for the most part the cults hitherto kept up by the several clans.[1]

Whether these families or gentes were at their first institution really families, *i.e.* associations based ·on natural family relationship, or whether they were from the first artificial classifications made on the analogy of natural families, cannot be decided with certainty.[2]

New members were admitted into the Phratries, if not in earlier times, at any rate by the time of Draco, when all were admitted to citizenship who were able to equip themselves as hoplites. Hence, ever after the time of Draco at any rate, if not before, the burgess body, and therefore the Phratries also, contained non-Eupatrid members.[3] Whether

Extension of the Franchise.

---

[1] For Ζεὺς ἕρκειος, cf. Harp., ἕρκειος Ζεύς, ᾧ βωμὸς ἐντὸς ἕρκους ἐν τῇ αὐλῇ ἵδρυται. τὸν γὰρ περίβολον ἕρκος ἔλεγον. Paul. Festi, p. 101 M: Herceus Jupiter intra conseptum domus cuiusque colebatur, quem etiam deum penetralem appellabant. Ἀπόλλων πατρῷος is the special family god of Ion. Ἀπόλλων is called among the Ionians πατρῷος διὰ τὴν τοῦ Ἴωνος γένεσιν : Plat., *Euthyd.*, 302. Cf. Harp., *sub verb.* τὸν δὲ Ἀπόλλωνα κοινῶς πατρῷον τιμῶσιν Ἀθηναῖοι ἀπὸ Ἴωνος· τούτου γὰρ οἰκήσαντος Ἀττικήν, ὡς Ἀριστοτέλης φησί, τοὺς Ἀθηναίους Ἴωνας κληθῆναι καὶ Ἀπόλλω πατρῷον αὐτοῖς ὀνομασθῆναι. The θεοὶ πατρῷοι of the various γένη were originally the deities from whom each γένος traced its descent: *e.g.*, Hermes was ὁ πατρῷος to Andocides (cf. *Lys.*, 6, 11); the clan of Κήρυκες professed to be descended from Hermes and Aglauros (Paus. 1, 38, 3). See Toepffer, *att. Geneal.*, 80 ff. Whether Ζεὺς φράτριος (Plat., *Euthyd.*, 302; Dem. 43, 14; Kratinos *ap.* Athen., 11, 460 F), and Ἀθηνᾶ φρατρία (Plat., *ibid.*) were the patron deities of the Phratries even in the earliest times, I consider questionable. Probably they derived their origin from the reforms of Cleisthenes, which will be discussed below.

[2] The definition of γεννῆται given in the lexicographical tradition regards the γένη as artificial divisions. Cf. Harp., γεννῆται—οὐχ οἱ συγγενεῖς μέντοι ἁπλῶς καὶ οἱ ἐξ αἵματος γεννῆταί τε καὶ ἐκ τοῦ αὐτοῦ γένους ἐκαλοῦντο, ἀλλ᾽ οἱ ἐξ ἀρχῆς εἰς τὰ καλούμενα γένη κατανεμηθέντες. Suid., γεννῆται οὐχ οἱ ἐκ γένους καὶ ἀφ᾽ αἵματος προσήκοντες, ἀλλ᾽ οἱ ἐκ τῶν γενῶν τῶν συννενεμημένων εἰς τὰς φρατρίας. Cf. also Poll. 8, 111; Et. M., 226 γενῆται. Lex. Seguer. 227, 9 ff.; Rose, *Arist. Pseudep.*, 408, 5.

[3] Concerning Draco we are told in Arist., 4, 2: ἀπεδέδοτο μὲν ἡ πολιτεία τοῖς ὅπλα παρεχομένοις. [The tense implies that the franchise had already been given. (Sandys)]. That in the time of Draco others besides the Eupatrids were included in the Phratries, may be inferred from the ordinance of

these new burgesses were also admitted into the γένη must be left undecided; because Draco's ordinance concerning homicide makes no mention of the γένη, but regards the Phratry not the γένος as the next unit above the circle of immediate legal kinsmen or ἀγχιστεῖς.¹ Nor can we determine for certain whether the Phatries obtained additional members by the reforms of Solon or not. For civil dissensions broke out immediately after Solon's legislation; and therefore the enrolment of the Thetes into the burgess divisions of Phylai and Phratries was very possibly postponed for some considerable time.²

Draco quoted in Dem. 43, 57–8, a statute whose authenticity is established by C.I.A., 1, 61 (Dittenb. 45, Hicks 59). In it the following directions are given for the choice of the ten φράτερες: τούτους δ' οἱ πεντήκοντα καὶ εἷς ἀριστίνδην αἱρείσθων (for the MS. reading τούτοις see Philippi, d. Areop. u. d. Eph., 138). Here ἀριστίνδην can, in my opinion, mean nothing except "from among the Eupatrids" (see also Lachmann, *spart. Verf.*, 248; Zelle, *Beitr. z. ältern Verf. Ath.*, 20), and therefore cannot be equivalent to κατ' ἀρετήν, as is supposed by C. Schaefer in the *Pforta Progr.*, 1888, p. 27, and Ed. Meyer in the *N. Rh. Mus.*, 41, 586. ἀρετή cannot be seen from external signs, therefore the Ephetai would have been obliged to trust their own personal opinion. But they would have had to do that in any case without any such directions. Previous to Draco's legislation the Archons were appointed ἀριστίνδην καὶ πλουτίνδην, which without any doubt meant from among the rich Eupatrids. Cf. Arist. 3, 6.

¹ The Draconian statute concerning the prosecution of homicides runs as follows in Dem. 43, 57, and in the fragments of the same law from inscriptions in Dittenberger, *Syll.*, 45: προειπεῖν τῷ κτείναντι ἐν ἀγορᾷ ἐντὸς ἀνεψιότητος καὶ ἀνεψιῶν (so Philippi, *Areop. u. d. Eph.*, 72, for the MS. ἀνεψιοῦ), συνδιώκειν δὲ καὶ ἀνεψιοὺς καὶ ἀνεψιῶν παῖδας καὶ γαμβροὺς καὶ πενθεροὺς καὶ φράτερας. On the meaning of the words, see Philippi, *ibid.*, 71 ff. Had every citizen at that period still belonged to a γένος, the words καὶ γεννήτας would have been required before καὶ φράτερας.

² The political rights which Solon conceded to those who belonged to the Thetic census are described by Aristot. 7, 8: τοῖς δὲ τὸ θητικὸν τελοῦσιν ἐκκλησίας καὶ δικαστηρίων μετέδωκε μόνον—7, 4: τοὺς δ' ἄλλους θητικόν, οὐδεμιᾶς μετέχοντας ἀρχῆς. Nothing is told us about their enrolment into the Phylai and Phratries. In any case Cleisthenes found a considerable number of people who did not possess burgess rights. Cf. Arist. 21, 2: πρῶτον μὲν οὖν ⟨συ⟩νένειμε πάντας εἰς δέκα φυλὰς ἀντὶ τῶν τεττάρων, ἀναμεῖξαι βουλόμενος, ὅπως μετάσχωσι πλείους τῆς πολιτείας. Here ἀναμεῖξαι βουλόμενος gives the motive of the institution of the ten Phylai, each having its Trittyes scattered in various parts of the country; ὅπως μετάσ. πλ. τ. π. is the reason for including all the inhabitants in these new Phylai. From this it may be inferred that the four old Phylai did not include them all. I do not, however, think we are justified in taking these words in combination with the passage in the *Politics*, 3, 2=61, 11, πολλοὺς γὰρ ἐφυλέτευσε (Κλεισθένης) ξένους καὶ δούλους μετοίκους so as to make πάντας mean only strangers and metoikoi.

It appears that only those who were born of Athenian citizens both on the father's side and on the mother's were admitted into the classes discussed above.[1] **Restriction of Burgess Rights.**

The oldest form of political government in the Athenian State was, as in Greece generally, monarchical. At the head of the State stood a king who, after the unification of Attica, ruled over the whole country. He was assisted by a permanent council of φυλοβασιλεῖς, or Eupatrids, selected as representatives of the various phylai.[2] **Oldest form of Constitution.**

---

[1] Arist., *Pol.*, 3, 2=p. 60, 27 sqq. Bekker, says in general terms: ὁρίζονται δὴ πρὸς τὴν χρῆσιν πολίτην τὸν ἐξ ἀμφοτέρων πολιτῶν καὶ μὴ θατέρου μόνον, οἷον πατρὸς ἢ μητρός. This agrees fairly well with the information we possess about the Athenian franchise. According to a provision of the Draconian constitution candidates for the office of Strategos or Hipparchos were required to have παῖδας ἐκ γαμετῆς γυναικὸς γνησίους ὑπὲρ δέκα ἔτη γεγονότας (Arist. 4, 2). Deinarchos *contr. Dem.*, 71, states this qualification as valid in his day in the words παιδοποιεῖσθαι κατὰ τοὺς νόμους. That γαμετὴ γυνή meant an Athenian wife as opposed to a ξένη, follows from Arist. 17, 3, where the γαμετὴ γυνή of Peisistratos is contrasted with the Ἀργεία. Ἦσαν δὲ κύριοι μὲν τῶν πραγμάτων διὰ τὰ ἀξιώματα καὶ διὰ τὰς ἡλικίας Ἵππαρχος καὶ Ἱππίας(Arist. 18, 1), the sons of the γαμετὴ γυνή, where διὰ τὰ ἀξιώματα means "on account of their pure citizen blood." Hdt. 5, 94, calls Thessalos, the son of the Ἀργεία γυνή, a νόθος. In the factions which followed Solon's legislation Peisistratos was supported, besides his other adherents, by οἱ τῷ γένει μὴ καθαροὶ διὰ τὸν φόβον· σημεῖον δ' ὅτι μετὰ τὴν [τῶν] τυράννων κατάλυσιν ἐποίησαν διαψηφισμόν, ὡς πολλῶν κοινωνούντων τῆς πολιτείας οὐ προσῆκον (Arist. 13, 5). The τῷ γένει μ. καθ. are without doubt those whose citizen descent was not quite unquestionable. In the Solonian legislation a distinction was made between the γνήσιος and the νόθος παῖς, the νόθος=ὧν ξένης γυναικός (cf. Aristoph., *Birds*, 1650–1666). The νόθος could not claim ἀγχιστεία: Aristoph., *Birds*, 1661 sq., cf. Dem., 43, 51. The father has freedom of testamentary disposition, ἐὰν μὴ παῖδες ὦσι γνήσιοι: Dem. 20, 102, cf. Is. 3, 68. These νόθοι are doubtless meant in the glosses of Hesych.: ἐξ τριακάδος· οἱ μὴ μεταλαμβάνοντες παῖδες ἢ ἀγχιστεῖς κλήρου τελευτήσαντός τινος Ἀθήνησιν ἐκαλοῦντο. ἀτριάκοστοι· οἱ μὴ μετέχοντες τριακάδος Ἀθηναῖοι. Poll. 8, 111 identifies τριακάς with γένος, but the literal meaning of the word is certainly no less appropriate to the Phratry or complex of thirty γένη.

[2] For the mythic kings of Attica, see Büchsenschütz, *d. Könige v. Athen.*, Berl. Progr., 1855. For the manner in which the oldest list of Attic kings was gradually enlarged and lengthened see Brandis, *de temp. Græc. antiquiss. rationib.*, 7 ff. The list, as it was finally drawn up, and the chronology fixed, is in Euseb., *Chron.* ed. Schoene, 1183 ff. The powers of the φυλοβασιλεῖς, were, without doubt, far more comprehensive originally than in later times, and they apparently underwent the same process of change as those of the βασιλεύς, ending by being nothing more than purely religious func-

But the kings of Attica do not appear to have remained long in possession of full monarchical power. Earlier tradition credits Theseus with a restriction of the powers of the king; later versions represent him as the founder of the democracy.[1] We cannot state with certainty the steps by which this gradual diminution of the kingly power was brought about. Aristotle, who represents for us the most ancient tradition, made out from the authorities at his disposal, supplemented by his own conjectural combinations, the following account of the development. The βασιλεία remained in existence, it is true, but was considerably weakened in course of time by restrictions of the functions of the kings and shortening of their tenure of office.[2] The first step in the process, according to Aristotle, was the creation of the πολέμαρχος. Since Ion is given as the first πολέμαρχος, we are tempted to conjecture that the tradition which Aristotle followed represented the creation of this new military office as connected with the immigration of the conquering Ionians, whose eponym Ion has found no place in the list of Attic kings. Just as the chieftain of the Ionic immigrants now appears by the side of the King of the Attic autochthons, so we now find side by side with the βασιλεύς a πολέμαρχος; and it is not inconceivable that this new military magistracy was first introduced when the Ionic families coalesced with the autochthons to form the new political community, and that it was originally a here-

<small>*Marginal notes:* Gradual Weakening of the Power of the King.</small>

---

tions. Poll. 8, 111 says: οἱ δὲ φυλοβασιλεῖς ἐξ εὐπατριδῶν τέσσαρες (so Wecklein, *Monatsber. d. bayr. Ak.*, 1873, p. 88 for MS. δὲ) ὄντες μάλιστα τῶν ἱερῶν ἐπεμελοῦντο συνεδρεύοντες ἐν τῷ βασιλείῳ τῷ παρὰ τὸ βουκολεῖον, which, acc. to Arist., 3, 5, was the official residence of the βασιλεύς. In the 4th cent. the φυλοβασιλεῖς still exercised jurisdiction, conjointly with the βασιλεύς, ἐπὶ Πρυτανείῳ. Cf. Arist. 57, 4: δικάζει δ' ὁ βασιλεὺς καὶ οἱ φυλοβασιλεῖς καὶ τὰς τῶν ἀψύχων καὶ τῶν ἄλλων ζῴων.—Cf. Poll. 8, 120.

[1] Arist. 41, 2: δευτέρα δέ, καὶ πρώτη μετὰ ταῦτα ἔχουσα πολιτείας τάξιν, ἡ ἐπὶ Θησέως γενομένη, μικρὸν παρεγκλίνουσα τῆς βασιλικῆς. By this is meant the form of constitution described by Aristotle in Ch. 3, as is shown by the words which follow: μετὰ δὲ ταῦτα ἡ ἐπὶ Δράκοντος κ.τ.λ. Cf. Plut., *Thes.*, 25. Theseus as founder of the democracy: Paus. 1, 3, 3.

[2] Aristot. consulted several sources of information. Cf. 3, 3: [οἱ] μὲν γὰρ πλείους ἐπὶ Μέδοντος, ἔνιοι δ' ἐπὶ Ἀκάστου φασὶ γενέσθαι [βασιλέ]ως. However, even his authorities do not seem to have possessed any direct traditional version. The condition of affairs in the earliest periods was inferred from later σημεῖα. Plato also, in *Menex.*, 238, assumes the continuity of the later βασιλεία with the earlier kings: βασιλεῖς μὲν γὰρ ἀεὶ ἡμῖν εἰσίν. οὗτοι δὲ τοτὲ μὲν ἐκ γένους, τοτὲ δὲ αἱρετοί.

ditary office in the possession of the leading Ionic families.¹ The institution of the ἄρχων took place according to the most usual tradition under King Medon, but nothing is said about the original functions of the office.² The βασιλεία, diminished in importance by these changes, seems to have still remained in the hands of Medon's family for a number of generations; while the office of πολέμαρχος, which was probably at first hereditary in the family of Ion, was afterwards thrown open to all Eupatrids, as was the office of ἄρχων from its very first institution.³ The power of the

---

¹ Arist. 3, 2: μέγισται δὲ καὶ πρῶται τῶν ἀρχῶν ἦσαν βασ[ιλεὺς καὶ] πολέμαρχος καὶ ἄρχων· τούτων δὲ πρώτη μὲν ἡ τοῦ βασιλέως· αὕτη γάρ ἐξ [ἀρχ]ῆ[ς ἦν] [δευ]τέρα δ' ἐπικατέστη [πολε]μαρχία, διὰ τὸ γενέσθαι τινὰς τῶν βασιλέων τὰ πολεμικὰ μαλα[κούς, ὅθεν καὶ] τὸν Ἴωνα μετεπέμψαντο χρείας καταλαβούσης. Hdt. 8, 44, says: Ἴωνος δὲ τοῦ Ξούθου στρατάρχεω γενομένου Ἀθηναίοισι ἐκλήθησαν ἀπὸ τούτου Ἴωνες. Cf. also Paus. 7, 1, 5.

² Arist. 3, 3: τελευταία δ' ἡ [τοῦ ἄρχοντος· οἱ] μὲν γὰρ πλείους ἐπὶ Μέδοντος, ἔνιοι δ' ἐπὶ Ἀκάστου φασὶ γενέσθαι [βασιλέ]ως. τ[ούτῳ] δ' ἐπιφέρουσιν, [ὅτι] οἱ ἐννέα ἄρχοντες ὀμνύουσι καθάπερ ἐπὶ Ἀκάστου τὰ ὅρκια ποι[ή]σειν, ὡς ἐπὶ το[ύτου τῆς] βασιλείας παραχωρησάντων τῶν Κοδ[ρι]δῶν ἀντὶ τῶν δοθεισῶν τῷ ἄρχοντι δωρεῶν. τοῦτο μὲν οὖν ὁποτέρως ποτ' ἔχει, μικρὸν ἂ[ν διαλλάτ]τοι τοῖς χρόνοις. ὅτι [δὲ] τελευταία τούτων ἐγένετο τῶν ἀρχῶν, [ση]μεῖον καὶ [τὸ] μη[δ]ὲν τῶν [π]ατρίων τὸν ἄρχοντα διοικεῖν, ὥσπερ ὁ βασιλεὺς καὶ ὁ πολέμαρχος, ἀλλ[ὰ μόνον τ]ὰ [ἐπί]θετα. διὸ καὶ νεωστὶ γέγονεν ἡ ἀρχὴ μεγάλη, τοῖς ἐπιθέτοις αὐξη[θεῖσα]. There is no inconsistency between this passage and Arist., *Pol.*, 8 (6)., 10=p. 217, 26 ff., where Kodros is said to have secured for himself the royal dignity by saving Athens in time of war from being reduced to subjection. It is obvious that this account has no connection with the story of the death of Kodros given in Lyk., *Leokr.*, 84 ff. Paus. 4, 5, 10, Vell. Pat. 1, 2, and Justin, 2, 7, also tell us of a diminution of the regal power after the death of Kodros, *i.e.* under Medon, though by a process different from that given by Aristotle.

³ The Eupatrid family of the Medontidai can be proved to have been still in existence at Athens in later times. See Toepffer, *att. Geneal.*, 228 ff., where the relation of Kodros to this family is also discussed. An inscr. of the 5th cent. found just in front of the steps up to the Acropolis reads: ὅρο[ς χώ]ρας Μεδ(ον)τ(ι)δῶν. See C. I. A., I. 497. The Medontidai may have become βασιλεῖς, occupying at Athens a position similar to that of the Androklid βασιλεῖς at Ephesos. Cf. Strab. 633. There occur, however, in the list of Medontid kings, as given by the chronographers, names which in later times belonged to other Eupatrid gentes, *e.g.* Megakles and Alkmaion, suggesting the Alkmaionidai, Ariphron the Buzygai, Agamestor the Philaidai. See Toepffer, *ib.*, 241-2. Acc. to the usual chronology, the Medontidai retained possession of the βασιλεία till 712, but the last four only for ten years each. Euseb., *Chron.*. 1, 189-190 compared with Paus. 4, 13, 7. Phot. παρ' ἵππον καὶ κόρην=Suid. *ad verb*. Suid. Ἱππομένης. That they kept the title of king, see Lugebil in the 5 Suppl. vol. of the *Jahrb. f. cl. Phil.*, 589 ff. Arist. 3, 1, says of this oldest constitutional period: τὰς μὲν ἀρχὰς

archon was now diminished by limiting his tenure of office, which was originally held for life, to ten years.¹

The same tendency continued, and the decennial archon was reduced to a merely annual magistrate. Whether this was simultaneously accompanied by the institution of the new functionaries, the six θεσμοθέται, or whether these came at a later date, cannot be determined. The original official duties of the Thesmothetai were, we are told, to write down the law, *i.e.* the customary law which had grown up in the course of time, and to secure the administration of justice.² The six Thesmothetai were, from the very first, a collegium or board of magistrates; on the other hand the βασιλεύς, the πολέμαρχος, and the ἄρχων remained separate magistrates till the reforms of Solon, and had each his separate official residence and his distinct sphere of activity. The βασιλεύς occupied the building afterwards called the βουκόλιον, the πολέμαρχος the πολεμαρχεῖον, afterwards called 'Επιλύκειον, the ἄρχων the πρυτανεῖον, and the θεσμοθέται had their θεσμοθετεῖον.³ The functions of the three chief magistrates

Marginal note: The Superior Annual Magistrates.

[καθί]στασαν ἀριστίνδην καὶ πλουτίνδην, *i.e.* from among the nobles, the Eupatrids, for εὐγένεια is ἀρχαῖος πλοῦτος καὶ ἀρετή (Arist., *Pol.*, 6 (4), 8=p. 159, 28 Bekker), and εὐγενεῖς are οἷς ὑπάρχει προγόνων ἀρετὴ καὶ πλοῦτος (*ib.*, 8 (5), 1=p. 194, 14). In Plut., *Thes.*, 25, it is said of Theseus: εὐπατρίδαις δὲ γινώσκειν τὰ θεῖα καὶ παρέχειν ἄρχοντας ἀποδοὺς καὶ νόμων διδασκάλους εἶναι καὶ ὁσίων καὶ ἱερῶν ἐξηγητάς. Cf. Et. M., 895, εὐπατρίδαι=Lex. Seguer. 257, 7. Dionys., *Ant. R.*, 2. 8.

¹ Arist. 3, 1: ἦρχον δὲ τὸ μὲν πρῶτον [διὰ βίου], μετὰ δὲ ταῦτα [δεκα]έτειαν. The context shows that he refers to the three magistrates, the βασιλεύς, the πολέμαρχος, and the ἄρχων. Paus. 4, 5, 10 says the power of the Medontidai was weakened by the προθεσμία ἐτῶν δέκα. The date of this limitation is given as 752: Dionys., *Ant. R.*, 1, 71. Euseb., *Chron.*, 1, 189-90.

² Arist. 3, 4: [θεσ]μοθέται δὲ πολλοῖς ὕστερον ἔτεσιν ᾑρέθησαν, ἤδη κατ' ἐνιαυτὸν αἱρ[ουμένων] τὰς ἀρχάς, ὅπως ἀναγράψαντες τὰ θέσμια φυλάττωσι πρὸς τὴν τῶν [παρανομού]ντων κρίσιν. διὸ καὶ μόνη τῶν ἀρχῶν οὐκ ἐγένετο πλεῖον [ἢ] ἐνιαύσιος. [οὗτοι] μὲν οὖν [χρόνῳ] τοσοῦτον προέχουσιν ἀλλήλων. With the official functions of the θεσμοθέται should be compared the *edictum perpetuum* of the Roman praetor. See Mommsen, *röm. Staatsr.*¹ 1, 151; 2, 201. This definition of the duties of the θεσμοθέται is, however, nothing more than an inference drawn by Aristotle or his authorities from the etymology of the name. 682 [(Duncker., *Hist. of Greece*, ii. 135 E. T.) or 683 (Sandys)] is the conventional date for the first institution of the nine annual archons. Synkell. 399, 21, says: μετὰ τούτους ἄρχοντες ἐνιαυσιαῖοι εὑρέθησαν ἐξ εὐπατριδῶν ἐννέα τε ἀρχόντων 'Αθήνησιν ἀρχὴ κατεστάθη. Cf. Euseb., *Chron.*, 2, 84-5.

³ Arist. 3, 5: ἦσαν δ' οὐχ ἅμα πάντες οἱ ἐννέα ἄρχοντες, ἀλλ' ὁ μὲν βασιλεὺς εἶχε τὸ νῦν καλούμενον βουκόλιον πλησίον τοῦ πρυτανείου· (σημεῖον δέ· ἔτι καὶ νῦν γὰρ τῆς τοῦ βασιλέως γυναικὸς ἡ σύμμειξις ἐνταῦθα γίγνεται τῷ Διονύσῳ καὶ ὁ γάμος), ὁ δὲ

remained after the curtailment of their period of office the same as before. In the case of the Thesmothetai, even if their official activity was practically limited to writing down the law and providing for the administration of justice, yet we may perhaps venture to conjecture that each of the three superior magistrates had two Thesmothetai to assist him in his judicial functions.[1]

The final decision in judicial affairs lay in the hands of the three first magistrates, who indeed at that date transacted the bulk of public business generally.[2]

That other officials were already in existence in very early times by the side of these chief magistrates, admits of no doubt; but we possess no record of their names or functions. Only the κωλακρέται can with any certainty be specified, and Κωλακρέται. they merely on account of the archaic form of their title. Their name means dividers or carvers of the limbs of animals offered in

---

ἄρχων τὸ πρυτανεῖον, ὁ δὲ πολέμαρχος τὸ ᾽Επιλύκειον (ὃ πρότερον μὲν ἐκαλεῖτο πολεμαρχεῖον, ἐπεὶ δὲ ᾽Επίλυκος ἀνῳκοδόμησε καὶ κατεσκεύασεν αὐτὸ πολεμα[ρχή]σας ᾽Επιλύκειον ἐκλήθη), θεσμοθέται δ᾽ εἶχον τὸ θεσμοθετεῖον. ἐπὶ δὲ Σόλωνος ἅπαντες εἰς τὸ θεσμοθετεῖον συνῆλθον. For the first and last clauses, cf. Diog. L., Sol., 58: καὶ πρῶτος τὴν συναγωγὴν τῶν ἐννέα ἀρχόντων ἐποίησεν εἰς τὸ συνδειπνεῖν (so Hermann Staatsalt. § 138, 13, for συνειπεῖν), ὡς ᾽Απολλόδωρός φησιν ἐν δευτέρῳ περὶ νομοθετῶν. That the βουκόλιον was the original official residence of the βασιλεύς, is obviously only an inference made by Aristotle or his authorities. In historical times he occupied what was known as στοὰ ἡ βασίλεια. Suid. ἄρχων and Lex. Seguer. 449, 17 sqq., both based, though with some errors, on Aristotle, describe the official quarters of the ἄρχων as παρὰ τοὺς ἐπωνύμους. But they mean the πρυτανεῖον, as is shown by the Schol. to Aristoph., Pax, 1183: τόπος παρὰ πρυτανεῖον, ἐν ᾧ ἐστήκασιν ἀνδριάντες, οὓς ἐπωνύμους καλοῦσιν. The objections of Wachsmuth, d. St. Athen., 2, 1, 353, 1, are disproved by Aristot. Cf. also Plut., Arist., 27, where the daughters of Aristeides are given in marriage ἐκ τοῦ πρυτανείου, which must have belonged to the archon. The name Epilukos is known as occurring among the gentes Philaidai and Kerukes: Toepffer, ibid., 278-9. Suidas and the Lex. Seguer., ibid., have turned the Aristotelian ἦσαν δ᾽ οὐχ ἅμα πάντες οἱ ἐννέα ἄρχοντες into πρὸ μὲν τῶν Σόλωνος νόμων οὐκ ἐξῆν αὐτοῖς ἅμα δικάζειν. The emendation and restoration of these words proposed by Lange, d. Eph. u. d. Areop., 71 sqq., has been made superfluous by the discovery of Aristotle's treatise.

[1] The conjecture in the text affords an explanation of their strange number six. When they obtained from Solon a more independent position and a wider sphere of activity, their original places may have been filled by the two πάρεδροι of the first three archons.

[2] Arist. 3, 5: κύριοι δ᾽ ἦσαν καὶ τὰς δίκας αὐτοτελεῖς [κρίν]ειν καὶ οὐχ ὥσπερ νῦν προανακρίνειν. So Suid. and Lex. Seguer., ibid. Thuc. 1, 126, says of the period of Kylon: τότε δὲ τὰ πολλὰ τῶν πολιτικῶν οἱ ἐννέα ἄρχοντες ἔπρασσον.

sacrifice, and we may infer that they were the assistants of the king at sacrifices and at banquets connected with sacrifices, and that when the age of "kings who fed on gifts" was gone by, they became the treasurers of the chief magistrates.[1]

None were eligible for election, at any rate to the higher offices, except the rich Eupatridai; the right of electing belonged to the council on the Areopagus, who selected for office according to their personal opinions those who seemed to them most suitable.[2]

Right of Election Active and Passive.

This council on the Areopagus, consisting of life-members, recruited every year by the archons who had just vacated office, represented the highest administrative authority of the State. Since this council, as has been remarked before, nominated the archons themselves, it therefore practically elected its own members by cooptation, though indirectly. It also had power to enforce the law, and had the control of the great bulk of important State affairs, since it possessed the right to in-

The Areopagus.

---

[1] The high antiquity of the κωλακρέται is attested also by the occurrence of the expression κωλακρετεῖν in Kyzikos (C. I. G., 8660), to which town it may have been introduced from Athens viâ Miletus. Κωλακρέτης is correctly explained by Lange, *d. Eph. u. d. Areop.*, 65 A, 115, as a compound of κῶλα, "limbs" (of animals slaughtered in sacrifice), and κείρω, "I cut." κῶλαι pretty frequently mean the customary portions given to the priests from the victims offered up. Cf. Suid. κωλακρέται. Inscr. from Byzantium in the *Monatsber. d. Berl. Ak.*, 1877, p. 476; C. I. G., 2656, 9 ff.; 2265, 13. With reference to their original duties should be compared what C. I. A., II. 602, says of the ἄρχων of the Μεσόγειοι: ἐπεμελήθη δὲ (καὶ τῆς . . .) las καὶ τῆς κρεανομίας καὶ τῆς ἐπικοσ(μήσεως τῆς τ)ραπέζης. For the δωροφάγοι βασιλῆες, cf. Hes., *Works and Days*, 37 sqq., 220 sqq., 263 sqq. The title ταμίαι (from τέμνω) also seems to be derived from the carving of the sacrificial victims. See Lange, *ib.*, 68 A, 116.

[2] Arist., 3, 1: τὰς μὲν ἀρχὰς [καθί]στασαν ἀριστίνδην καὶ πλουτίνδην and 3, 6: ἡ γὰρ αἵρεσις τῶν ἀρχόντων ἀριστίνδην καὶ πλουτίνδην ἦν, ἐξ ὧν οἱ 'Αρεοπαγῖται καθίσταντο. That by ἀριστίνδην καὶ πλουτίνδην must be understood rich Eupatridai admits of no doubt. Cf. also Plut., *Thes.*, 25. Dionys., *Ant. R.*, 2, 8. Et. M., 395, Εὐπατρίδαι. In Philoch., *fr.* 58 (Müller, *fr. h. gr.*, 1, 394) it is said of this period: οὐ παντὸς ἀνδρὸς ἦν εἰς τὴν ἐξ'Αρείου πάγου βουλὴν τελεῖν. ἀλλ' οἱ παρ' 'Αθηναίοις πρωτεύοντες ἔν τε γένει καὶ πλούτῳ (*i.e.* rich Eupatrids) καὶ βίῳ χρηστῷ, ὡς ἱστορεῖ Φιλόχορος διὰ τῆς τρίτης τῶν αὐτῶν 'Ατθίδων. The election of the magistrates by the council on the Areopagus is attested by Arist., 8, 2: [Σόλ]ων μὲν οὖν οὕτως ἐνομοθέτησεν περὶ τῶν ἐννέα ἀρχόντων. τὸ γὰρ ἀρχαῖον ἡ ἐν 'Αρ[είῳ πάγῳ βου]λὴ ἀνακαλεσαμένη καὶ κρίνασα καθ' αὐτὴν τὸν ἐπιτήδειον ἐφ' ἑκάστῃ τῶν ἀρχῶν ἐπ' [ἐνι]α[υτ]ὸν [διατάξα]σα ἀπέστελλεν. The words τὸ ἀρχαῖον can only refer to the time previous to Draco, because acc. to Arist., 4, 2, οἱ ὅπλα παρεχόμενοι elected the nine archons after that date.

flict fines and penalties at its own discretion on those who violated the constitution.[1]

The Eupatrid constitution thus sketched out was without doubt a πολιτεία τῶν ἱππέων, which, according to Aristotle's evidence, was the oldest form of constitution in the Greek communities after the overthrow of the monarchies. This view is made more probable still by the fact that a similar constitution existed contemporaneously among the closely related Ionic families in Chalkis and Eretria, and also by the fact that ἱππεῖς already existed in Attica before the time of Solon. I therefore identify the ἱππεῖς, who went to battle in chariots or on horseback, with the Eupatrids. Among the Eupatrids the πεντακοσιομέδιμνοι, or great Eupatrid landowners—for they too can be proved to have existed before Solon—held all the highest offices, and after the expiration of their period of office still kept control of the government as members of the Areopagus.[2]

margin: πολιτεία τῶν ἱππέων.

---

[1] Arist. 3, 6: ἡ δὲ τῶν Ἀρεοπαγιτῶν βουλὴ τὴν μὲν τάξιν εἶχε τοῦ διατηρεῖν τοὺς νόμους, διῴκει δὲ τὰ πλεῖστα καὶ τὰ μέγιστα τῶν ἐν τῇ πόλει, καὶ κολάζουσα καὶ ζημιοῦσα πάντας τοὺς ἀκοσμοῦντας κυρίως. ἡ γὰρ αἵρεσις τῶν ἀρχόντων ἀριστίνδην καὶ πλουτίνδην ἦν, ἐξ ὧν οἱ Ἀρεοπαγῖται καθίσταντο· διὸ καὶ μόνη τῶν ἀρχῶν αὕτη μεμένηκε διὰ βίου καὶ νῦν. The view expressed by Schömann, *Antiqu.*, 172 A, 5, *op. ac.*, 1, 190 ff.; *Jahrb. f. cl. Phil.*, 1875, 153 ff., that the Areopagitic Boule is of prehistoric antiquity has been confirmed by Aristotle. The other conjectures on the subject of the Eupatrid State Council may be now regarded as exploded. I cannot agree with Peter Meyer's view in his *Aristot. Politik. u. d. Ἀθηναίων πολιτεία*, 1891, p. 32, that in the passage quoted above the words διῴκει δὲ κ.τ.λ. indicate an unconstitutional abuse of its influence on the part of the Areopagus; because in that case the preceding words also cannot mean that the Areopagus possessed any constitutional or legal right of supervising the laws. The clause ἡ γὰρ κ.τ.λ. gives the reason why the Areopagus was entitled to this commanding position in the Eupatrid State, *i.e.* because it was composed ἀριστίνδην καὶ πλουτίνδην; it was for the same reason too that the Areopagitai held their seats for life.

[2] Arist., *Pol.*, 6 (4), 13=p. 168, 21 ff: καὶ ἡ πρώτη δὲ πολιτεία ἐν τοῖς Ἕλλησιν ἐγένετο μετὰ τὰς βασιλείας ἐκ τῶν πολεμούντων, ἡ μὲν ἐξ ἀρχῆς ἐκ τῶν ἱππέων (τὴν γὰρ ἰσχὺν καὶ τὴν ὑπεροχὴν ἐν τοῖς ἱππεῦσιν εἶχεν· ἄνευ μὲν γὰρ συντάξεως ἀχρηστον τὸ ὁπλιτικόν, αἱ δὲ περὶ τῶν τοιούτων ἐμπειρίαι καὶ τάξεις ἐν τοῖς ἀρχαίοις οὐχ ὑπῆρχον, ὥστ' ἐν τοῖς ἱππεῦσιν εἶναι τὴν ἰσχύν). Concerning the Ἱπποβοτῶν πολιτεία in Chalkis, Arist. *ap.* Strab., 447, says: προέστησαν γὰρ αὐτῆς ἀπὸ τιμημάτων ἄνδρες ἀριστοκρατικῶς ἄρχοντες, *i.e.* the rulers of the State were those of the Hippobotai who, like the πεντακοσιομέδιμνοι at Athens, possessed property amounting to a certain fixed assessment. So in Eretria there was an ὀλιγαρχία τῶν ἱππέων: Arist., 6 (4), 3=p. 148, 16 ff., 8 (5), 6=p. 206, 20. Peisistratos on his last return to Athens found supporters from among τῶν ἱππέων τῶν ἐχόντων ἐν Ἐρετρίᾳ τὴν πολιτείαν: Arist., 15, 2. A stele in the sanctuary of the

The rest of the people were almost exclusively country farmers and agricultural labourers; for the artisan class, if any such existed at that early date, formed but an insignificant fraction of the population.[1]

The non-Eupatrid Population.

The agricultural population was, it appears, of two classes, peasant proprietors and labourers. The first class, whose numbers formed certainly only a minority of the agricultural population, comprised the so-called Zeugitai, who each possessed at least enough land to require a yoke of two oxen for its cultivation.[2]

Amarynthian Artemis specified τρισχιλίοις μὲν ὁπλίταις ἑξακοσίοις δ' ἱππεῦσιν ἑξήκοντα ἅρμασι ποιεῖν τὴν πομπήν: Strab. 448. That there were ἱππεῖς and πεντακοσιομέδιμνοι before Solon is proved by the Draconian ordinance in Arist. 4, 3. It is not very likely that Draco was the author of the classification. [Arist., 3, 1 implies the existence of some such classification, Sandys.] The authorities who acc. to Arist., 7, 4, used to define the ἱππεῖς as τοὺς ἱπποτροφεῖν δυναμένους very probably had these pre-Solonian ἱππεῖς in view. That only the wealthiest landowners were eligible for the highest offices is attested by Arist. 3, 6: ἡ γὰρ αἵρεσις τῶν ἀρχόντων ἀριστίνδην καὶ πλουτίνδην ἦν.

[1] Plut., *Thes.*, 25, attributes to Theseus the institution of the three ἔθνη of Εὐπατρίδαι, Γεωμόροι and Δημιουργοί. Cf. Poll. 8, 111. Hesych., ἀγροιῶται. In the Et. M., 395, Εὐπατρίδαι=Lex. Seguer. 257, 7 sqq., the Δημιουργοί are called Ἐπιγεώμοροι. Plato, *Critias*, 110, says: ᾤκει δὲ δὴ τότ' ἐν τῇδε τῇ χώρᾳ τὰ μὲν ἄλλα ἔθνη τῶν πολιτῶν περὶ τὰς δημιουργίας ὄντα καὶ τὴν ἐκ τῆς γῆς τροφήν, τὸ δὲ μάχιμον (i.e. the Eupatrids) ὑπ'·ἀνδρῶν θείων κατ' ἀρχὰς ἀφορισθὲν ᾤκει χωρίς. Dionys., *Ant. R.*, 2, 8, tells us what was certainly true for this early period: ἐκεῖνοι (i.e. οἱ Ἀθηναῖοι) μὲν γὰρ εἰς δύο μέρη νείμαντες τὸ πλῆθος εὐπατρίδας μὲν ἐκάλουν τοὺς ἐκ τῶν ἐπιφανῶν οἴκων καὶ χρήμασι δυνατούς, οἷς ἡ τῆς πόλεως ἀνέκειτο προστασία, ἀγροίκους δὲ τοὺς ἄλλους πολίτας, οἳ τῶν κοινῶν οὐδενὸς ἦσαν κύριοι· σὺν χρόνῳ δὲ καὶ οὗτοι προσελήφθησαν ἐπὶ τὰς ἀρχάς. Aristot., 2, distinguishes between rich and poor, the latter of whom form the rustic population. Arist., 2, 2, says of the time before Draco: ἡ δὲ πᾶσα γῆ δι' ὀλίγων ἦν, and the same of the time succeeding Draco: καὶ ἡ χώρα δι' ὀλίγων ἦν: 4, 5.

[2] The class of Zeugitai can be shown to have been in existence at the time of Draco. I identify them with the peasant proprietors. They in particular were the owners from whose estates Solon prides himself on having removed the mortgage stones. Cf. Arist., 12, 4. Cf. also Busolt in the *Phil.*, 1891, 50, 399. To their ranks belonged the people to whom, acc. to Ælian, *Var. Hist.*, 9, 25, Peisistratos said, when he observed them loafing idly in the market place: εἰ μέν σοι τέθνηκε ζεῦγος, παρ' ἐμοῦ λαβὼν ἄπιθι καὶ ἐργάζου· εἰ δὲ ἀπορεῖς σπερμάτων, παρ' ἐμοῦ σοι γενέσθω. Cf. also Arist. 16, 6. Their later descendants are the Georgoi of Aristophanes, who, when confined to the city in the Peloponnesian war, longed for peace and for their ζευγάριον οἰκεῖον βοοῖν. See the author's *Beitr. z. innern Gesch. Athens*, 97 ff. That the oldest ζεῦγος was a yoke of oxen, I infer from the fact that in Attica it was forbidden to sacrifice the ox from the plough. Ælian, *V. H.*, 5, 14. In later times we hear of ζεύγη of oxen, mules, and horses: Poll. 10, 53. Et. M. 409, ζεῦγος. Phot., *sub verb*. Lex. Seguer. 260, 29.

The field labourers called πελάται, i.e. euphemistically "neighbours" of the Eupatrid landlords who employed them, also bore the special name ἑκτήμοροι. That is to say, the oldest form of labour contract that we find in Attica, in those Ἑκτήμοροι. early times when no foreign slave element existed there, is the métayer system of co-operation still common in various countries for the association of Capital with Labour for the purpose of obtaining produce from the soil. The ἑκτήμοροι however found themselves in a situation unusual in such systems and perfectly desperate. They had to hand over to the landlords ⅚ of the produce of the patch of ground which they with their wives and children cultivated. The last sixth of the produce they kept as a reward for their labour.[1] This in itself unfavourable relation of the

[1] On the meaning of πελάται see Poll. iii. 82. πελάται δὲ καὶ θῆτες ἐλευθέρων ἐστὶν ὀνόματα διὰ πενίαν ἐπ' ἀργυρίῳ δουλεύοντες. Cf. Hesych., sub verb. Phot., Plat., Euthyphr., 4, ἐπεὶ ὅ γε ἀποθανὼν πελάτης τις ἦν ἐμός, καὶ ὡς ἐγεωργοῦμεν ἐν τῇ Νάξῳ, ἐθήτευεν ἐκεῖ παρ' ἡμῖν. For the explanation of their name cf. Phot. That the πελάται and ἑκτήμοροι in Attica were the same people, appears from Arist. 2, 2, and is expressly asserted by Poll. iv. 165. ἑκτημόριοι δὲ οἱ πελάται παρὰ τοῖς 'Αττικοῖς. See also Phot., sub verb. Arist. 2, 2 says καὶ δὴ καὶ ἐδούλευον (it was not at first a real slavery) οἱ πένητες τοῖς πλουσίοις καὶ αὐτοὶ [καὶ τ]ὰ τέκνα καὶ αἱ γυναῖκες, καὶ ἐκαλοῦντο πελάται καὶ ἑκτήμοροι· [κατὰ] ταύτην γὰρ τὴν μίσθωσιν [ἡ]ργάζοντο τῶν πλουσίων τοὺς ἀγρούς. I allow what Rühl contends (*N. Rh. Mus.*, 1891, p. 449; 18. Suppl. vol. of the *Jahrb. f. cl. Phil.*, p. 683 ff.) that the last words may easily be misunderstood, and this fact explains why, according to Phot., πελάται, and Hesych., ἑκτήμοροι, the ἑκτήμοροι kept ⅙ of the produce, while according to Plut., Sol., 13, Hesych., ἐπίμορτος, they had to give that to the landlord. The desperate case of the ἑκτήμοροι is only explicable if they had to hand over ⅚ of the produce. Had they kept ⅚, they would have been better off than the métayer tenants nowadays. The hypothesis that the ἑκτήμοροι kept ⅙, is further confirmed by the notice in Eustath. on *Odys.*, xix. 28, ἡ μορτὴ τὸ ἕκτον φασὶ μέρος τῶν καρπῶν, ἢ ἐδίδοτο τοῖς ἑκτημορίοις, ὡς ἐν ἀνωνύμῳ κεῖται λεξικῷ ῥητορικῷ. To judge by Poll., vii. 151, this explanation is derived from a law of Solon. Aristotle's words I take with Gomperz, *d. Schrift v. Staatswesen d. Ath. u. ihr. neuester Beurtheiler*, p. 11, to mean "they were called sixthers; for that was the agreement under which they cultivated the lands of the rich." The words τὰς μισθώσεις ἀποδιδόναι, which immediately follow, mean "pay the rent." Gomperz, *op. cit.*, should not have given up (p. 45 sqq.) his original view (p. 11 ff.), that the ἑκτήμοροι kept ⅙ of the produce. Πελάται is the Greek expression for the Roman Clients. See *e.g.* Plut., *Rom.*, 13. On the métayer system still in use in France, cf. *Schriften d. Vereins für Socialpolitik*, 27, 17; in Italy, *op. cit.*, 29, 124 sqq.; in America, Gilman-Katscher, *die Theilung des Geschäftsgewinns*, p. 9 ff. [Beloch *Griech. Gesch.*, p. 218, holds that the ἑκτήμοροι were harvest field labourers, who were paid one sheaf for every six they reaped.]

tenant to his landlord in regard to the division of the produce between them was made still more cruel by the fact that according to the customs of that day the former was liable to the latter in his own person for the fulfilment of the terms of their agreement, that is to say, the tenant, if he did not fulfil the agreement, became the slave of the landlord, and as such could be sold into slavery.[1] Even for the still independent Zeugitai the rights of creditors as they were then understood might prove fatal; for a loan was made only on the security of the debtor's person, not upon his land, so that to all appearance the debtor who did not fulfil the obligations which he had incurred fell, himself and his land, into the power of his creditor, who then probably as a rule left him as a ἑκτήμορος on his farm.[2]

Cylon. It is only natural that great dissatisfaction should have prevailed among those who did not belong to the class of the Eupatridai, in consequence of this unfavourable position of the tenant-farmer, a position the unpleasantness of which was accentuated by the complete absence of political rights. On this universal dissatisfaction of the lower classes it is possible that Cylon, the son-in-law of the tyrant Theagenes of Megara, reckoned, following the usual policy of tyrannoi, when he made his attempt to make himself master of the Acropolis and so seize the tyranny. The attempt failed however. Cylon and his brother escaped, but his followers were compelled to surrender by the Archon Megakles, and most of them were put to death.[3]

---

[1] Arist. 2, 2, after the words quoted in the previous note, continues: καὶ [εἰ μὴ] τὰς μισθώσεις [ἀπ]οδιδοῖεν, ἀγώγιμοι καὶ αὐτοὶ καὶ οἱ παῖδες ἐγίγνοντο. On the consequences of this state of affairs, cf. Solon ap. Arist. 12, 4, v. 8 ff.

[2] After his sketch of the position of the ἑκτήμοροι Arist. 2, 2 adds the general observation: καὶ ο[ἱ] δα[νεισ]μ[οὶ π]ᾶσιν ἐπὶ τοῖς σώμασιν ἦσαν μέχρι Σόλωνος· οὗτος δὲ πρῶτος ἐγέν[ετο τοῦ δήμο]υ προστάτης, where the last words seem to mean that Solon released the people from this miserable lot. Cf. also Arist. 4, 5, ἐπὶ δὲ τοῖς σώ[μα]σιν ἦσαν οἱ δα[νεισ]μ[οί, καθάπερ εἴρηται, καὶ ἡ χώρα δι' ὀλίγων ἦν.

[3] Arist. 2, 2, χαλεπώτατον μὲν οὖν καὶ πικρότατον ἦν τοῖς πολλοῖς τῶν κατὰ τὴν πολιτείαν τ[ὸ δουλ]εύειν· οὐ μὴν ἀλλὰ καὶ τοῖς ἄλλοις ἐδυσχέραινον· οὐδενὸς γάρ, ὡς εἰπεῖν, ἐτύγχανον μετέχοντες. On Cylon's attempt cf. Hdt. v. 7; Thuc. i. 126; Plut., Sol., 12. From Arist. 1 we see that this attempt belongs to the time before Draco, as Busolt, griech. Gesch., i. 504 ff., had already supposed. For determining Cylon's date we have the fact that he made his attempt in an Olympic year, after himself winning at Olympia in 640 (see African.). Vid. Thuc., ibid.

Draco.

The dissatisfaction prevalent among the agricultural population was met by Draco by his reforms of the constitution in so far as he admitted to a share in political rights the indepen- *Draco.* dent yeomen possessing a yoke of oxen, the class of the so-called Zeugitai. Draco was perhaps induced to make this extension of the franchise by the circumstance that, after the introduction of the hoplite system, those who served as hoplites—as the Zeugitai undoubtedly did—could not well be excluded from the citizenship.[1]

[1] Arist. 4, 1: μετὰ δὲ ταῦτα χρόνου τινὸς οὐ πολλοῦ διελθόντος ἐπ' Ἀρισταίχμου ἄρχοντος Δράκων τοὺς Θεσμοὺς ἔθηκεν. I do not consider as successful Peter Meyer's attempt, Arist., *Polit. u. d. Ἀθηναίων πολιτεία*, p. 81 ff., to prove the institutions described in Arist. 4 to be identical with what we find in Arist. 3, so that Draco would have only drawn up his code of laws to suit an already existent constitution, and thus there would be no contradiction with Arist., *Pol.*, ii. 12 = p. 58, 6. Δράκοντος δὲ νόμοι μέν εἰσι, πολιτείᾳ δ' ὑπαρχούσῃ τοὺς νόμους ἔθηκεν. The first words in Arist. 4 show clearly in my judgment that Arist. made a new organization of the State begin with Draco. This is shown also by c. 41, 2. For it is impossible to question that ἡ ἐπὶ Θησέως γενομένη (sc. μεταβολή), μικρὸν παρεγκλίνουσα τῆς βασιλικῆς is that described in c. 3, when we read the representation given there of the gradual weakening of the crown. I can therefore only see in Arist. 4 a further reason for doubting the genuineness of Arist., *Pol.*, ii. 12. The attempt to support it in Meyer, *ibid.*, 16 ff., seems to me to fail. See also Niemeyer in the *Jahrb. f. cl. Phil.*, 1891, p. 408. According to Paus. ix. 86, 8, Draco made his laws ἐπὶ τῆς ἀρχῆς, which in all probability means when he was archon. On the chronology of Draco's legislation we can say nothing for certain, since the Archon Aristaichmos is unknown to us. Cf. in general Fischer, *griech. Zeittafeln*, 103 ff. What we know of this legislation apart from the new information in Aristotle is collected by K. Fr. Hermann, *de Dracone legumlat. att. Ind. schol.*, Gött., 1849/50. Cf. for Draco's extension of the franchise, Arist., *Pol.*, 6 (4), 13 = p. 168, 21 ff.: καὶ ἡ πρώτη δὲ πολιτεία ἐν τοῖς Ἕλλησιν ἐγένετο μετὰ τὰς βασιλείας ἐκ τῶν πολεμούντων, ἡ μὲν ἐξ ἀρχῆς τῶν ἱππέων (τὴν γὰρ ἰσχὺν καὶ τὴν ὑπεροχὴν ἐν τοῖς ἱππεῦσιν ὁ πόλεμος εἶχεν· ἄνευ γὰρ συντάξεως ἄχρηστον τὸ ὁπλιτικόν, αἱ δὲ περὶ τῶν τοιούτων ἐμπειρίαι καὶ τάξεις ἐν τοῖς ἀρχαίοις οὐχ ὑπῆρχον, ὥστ' ἐν τοῖς ἱππεῦσιν εἶναι τὴν ἰσχύν), αὐξανομένων δὲ τῶν πόλεων καὶ τῶν ἐν τοῖς ὅπλοις ἰσχυσάντων μᾶλλον πλείους μετεῖχον τῆς πολιτείας. Cf. also Arist. 7 (6), 7 = p. 188, 10 ff. That the Zeugitai in reality did belong to the πολιτεία after Draco is plain from Arist. 4, 3. We should compare Arist., *Pol.*, 6 (4), 4 = p. 152, 6 Bekker: καὶ γὰρ ὁπλιτεύειν καὶ γεωργεῖν συμβαίνει τοῖς αὐτοῖς πολλάκις. We see from the passage just quoted from Aristotle's *Politics* that the πολιτεία τῶν ὅπλα παρεχομένων was a regular stage in the early historical development of the Greek States. The πολιτεία τῶν ὅπλα παρεχομένων, established, according to Arist. 4, 2, by Draco, very well harmonises with the character of the age, and it appears to me more likely that the πεντακισχίλιοι οἱ ἐκ τῶν ὅπλων, who were provided for in the constitution of the 400 (Arist. 29, 5; 32, 3), but first came into actual existence after their

In any case, in consequence of his reforms, all those who were πολιτεία able to arm themselves at their own cost as hoplites τῶν ὁπλιτῶν obtained a share in political rights.[1]

Meanwhile, these political rights were divided into various grades. The βασιλεύς, the πολέμαρχος, the ἄρχων, the θεομοθέται, and the ταμίαι, were still to be chosen from the class of the πεντακοσιομέδιμνοι, *i.e.* the Eupatrid landowners; the other elective magistracies were filled from the number of those who could arm themselves, *i.e.* besides the πεντακοσιομέδιμνοι from the classes of the Eupatrid ἱππεῖς and the yeomen Zeugitai. Still, to hold the office of a Strategos and Hipparchos, the possession was necessary of an estate worth at least 100 minæ, and free from mortgage, and of children over 10 years of age, born in lawful wedlock.[2]

For the Strategoi and the Hipparchs the peculiar rule was made, that the Prytaneis, in all probability those of the Council, must, until those officers had given in their accounts, guarantee that they possessed the requisite amount of property, while to secure the Prytaneis four sureties were produced by the Strategoi and Hipparchs, with the same rating as they themselves had to have. This peculiar regulation may perhaps be explained conjecturally as follows:—The State did not make a regular assess-

---

overthrow (Arist. 88, 1) were copied from the πάτριοι νόμοι (Arist. 29, 3) than the converse, that a pamphleteer fabricated the Draconian constitution in imitation of that of the 400, as Nissen (*N. Rh. Mus.*, 1892, p. 201) has conjectured. [But cf. Dr. Sandys, *Ath. Pol.*, 4, 2 note].

[1] Arist. 4, 2: ἀπεδέδοτο μὲν ἡ πολιτεία τοῖς ὅπλα παρεχομένοις.

[2] Arist. 4, 2: ᾑροῦντο δὲ τοὺς μὲν ἐννέα ἄρχοντας καὶ τοὺς ταμίας οὐσίαν κεκτημένους οὐκ ἐλάττω δέκα μνῶν ἐλευθέραν, τὰς δ' ἄλλας ἀρχὰς ⟨τὰς⟩ ἐλάττους ἐκ τῶν ὅπλα παρεχομένων, στρατηγοὺς δὲ καὶ ἱππάρχους οὐσίαν ἀποφαίνοντας οὐκ ἔλαττον ἢ ἑκατὸν μνῶν ἐλευθέραν καὶ παῖδας ἐκ γαμετῆς γυναικὸς γνησίους ὑπὲρ δέκα ἔτη γεγονότας. That the reading δέκα μνῶν is wrong, goes without saying. The ἐννέα ἄρχοντες, as they were afterwards called, were the highest magistrates in the State, and they must therefore have possessed a larger property than the Strategoi and the Hipparchs, who undoubtedly even then were inferior to the Polemarch. Whether we ought to write διακοσίων or τριακοσίων or something else, we cannot say. In any case the property qualification specified in this passage corresponded to that of the Pentakosiomedimnoi. We cannot determine how large an estate, free of mortgage, represented a yearly income of 500 Æginetan medimnoi. The magistracies mentioned in the above quoted words of Arist. are the elective magistracies, as Gomperz, *op. cit.*, 31 ff., assumes—and I agree with him—and as indeed the ᾑροῦντο shows. Why no magistracies appointed by the lot can remain over and above the elective officers here indicated, as Rühl, *N. Rh. Mus.*, 1891, 445/6, maintains, is not obvious.

ment: the families of the Pentakosiomedimnoi, who alone had a share in the government before Draco, were known; and the lowest class again was limited by the power to arm oneself as a hoplite from one's own resources; but the citizens between these extreme classes were not officially classified, so that the possession of an estate worth 100 minæ, and free from mortgage, required as a qualification for the Strategia and Hipparchia, could not be actually demonstrated. Accordingly the Prytaneis, who perhaps presided over the meeting for election, undertook to answer for the fulfilment of this requirement if four sureties, whose estates were likewise estimated at 100 minæ, were produced, to be responsible to the Prytaneis, until the Strategoi and Hipparchoi had given in their accounts, for the existence of the amount of property required of those magistrates.[1]

The lot-magistracies, and the Council, whose members were likewise chosen by lot, were open to all citizens of at least 30 years of age. But no one might be drawn a second time for the Council or a lot office, until all the other citizens had participated in the administration of these magistracies.[2]

A new institution of Draco's was the Council just mentioned, consisting of 401 members. This council, which was not always sitting, was apparently represented by a standing committee of πρυτάνεις, as to whose organization no further information has come down to us.[3]

Council.

---

[1] Arist. 4, 2: τούτους δ' ἔδει διε[γγυ]ᾶ[σθαι] τοὺς πρυτάνεις καὶ τοὺς στρατηγοὺς καὶ τοὺς ἱππάρχους τοὺς ἔνους μέχρι εὐθυνῶν, ἐγγ[υη]τὰς δ' ἐκ τοῦ αὐτοῦ τέλους δεχομένους (not [παρα]σχομένους), οὕπερ οἱ στρατηγοὶ καὶ ἵππαρχοι. The subject in the accusative and inf. clause is τοὺς πρυτάνεις, the object τούτους, which refers to the previously mentioned Strategoi and Hipparchoi, and is again taken up by καὶ τοὺς στρατηγοὺς καὶ τοὺς ἱππάρχους. This is borne out by the relative clause at the end, and δεχομένους is therefore to be retained.

[2] Arist. 4, 3: βουλεύειν δὲ τετρακοσίους καὶ ἕνα τοὺς λαχόντας ἐκ τῆς πολιτείας. κληροῦσθαι δὲ καὶ ταύτην καὶ τὰς ἄλλας ἀρχὰς τοὺς ὑπὲρ τριάκοντ' ἔτη γεγονότας, καὶ δὶς τὸν αὐτὸν μὴ ἄρχειν πρὸ τοῦ πάντας ἐ[ξ]ελθεῖν (or perhaps comparing Arist., Pol., p. 169, 32; 175, 11 διελθεῖν)· τότε δὲ πάλιν ἐξ ὑπαρχῆς κληροῦν. For the last requirement, cf. Arist., Pol., 6 (4) 14 = p. 169, 29 ff.: καὶ ἐν ἄλλαις δὲ πολιτείαις βουλεύονται αἱ συναρχίαι συνιοῦσαι, εἰς δὲ τὰς ἀρχὰς βαδίζουσι πάντες κατὰ μέρος ἐκ τῶν φυλῶν καὶ τῶν μορίων τῶν ἐλαχίστων παντελῶς, ἕως ἂν διέλθῃ διὰ πάντων. Ib. id. 6 (4) 15 = p. 175, 8 ff., where he discusses the various ways of appointing magistrates: ἢ γὰρ πάντες ἐκ πάντων αἱρέσει, ἢ πάντες ἐκ πάντων κλήρῳ, καὶ ἢ ἐξ ἁπάντων ἢ ὡς ἀνὰ μέρος, οἷον κατὰ φυλὰς καὶ δήμους καὶ φρατρίας, ἕως ἂν διέλθῃ διὰ πάντων τῶν πολιτῶν, ἢ ἀεὶ ἐξ ἁπάντων, καὶ τὰ μὲν οὕτω, τὰ δὲ ἐκείνως.

[3] Arist. 4, 3. βουλεύειν δὲ τετρακοσίους καὶ ἕνα τοὺς λαχόντας ἐκ τῆς πολιτείας. Rühl (Suppl. vol. of the Jahrb., 18, 687/8) thinks Plutarch cannot have read in

Besides the Council there was also an Ecclesia, composed undoubtedly of all citizens. Any member of the Council who missed a sitting of the Council or an assembly of the Ecclesia, had to pay if a πεντακοσιομέδιμνος a fine of 3 drachmae, if a ἱππεὺς 2, if a ζευγίτης 1 drachma.[1]

Ecclesia.

The great powers which the Council of the Areopagus possessed in the government before Draco, were considerably curtailed by him. For whereas the Areopagus before Draco, and again subsequently to Solon's reforms, exercised judicial functions, and could inflict corporal punishment and fines;

Areopagus.

Aristotle of the establishment of a βουλή by Draco, because he ascribes to Solon the establishment of a second βουλή (Plut., *Sol.*, 19. Comp. of *Sol. and Public.* 2). But Plutarch did not write an Athenian Constitutional History, but a biography of Solon. He only recorded what Solon did, and therefore could very well write as he has. For the Prytaneis cf. the passage of Arist., quoted and explained, p. 121, 1. Πρυτάνεις in the Greek States either form a committee of the council (see Part 2, 316 ff.) or are single magistrates (Part 2, 326). Since at Athens we only hear of them in the former character, I do not hesitate to regard them here too as a committee of the council. In Thuc. ii. 15 we read that before Theseus the several Attic πόλεις had their separate πρυτανεῖά τε καὶ ἄρχοντας. Theseus made them all into one, καταλύσας τῶν ἄλλων πόλεων τά τε βουλευτήρια καὶ τὰς ἀρχὰς εἰς τὴν νῦν πόλιν οὖσαν, ἓν βουλευτήριον ἀποδείξας καὶ πρυτανεῖον. Here πρυτανεῖον once corresponds to the βουλευτήριον, then to the ἀρχαί. The πρυτανεῖον was at Athens the official residence of the ἀρχων: Arist. 3, 5, but also a councilroom of the πρυτάνεις, Plut., *Sol.*, 19. The πρυτάνεις τῶν ναυκράρων in Hdt. 5, 71, have nothing to do with Draco's πρυτάνεις, for they are an invention of Herodotus.

[1] Arist. 4, 3: εἰ δέ τις τῶν βουλευτῶν, ὅταν ἕδρα βουλῆς ἢ ἐκκλησίας ᾖ, ἐκλείποι [τὴν]σύνοδον, ἀπέτινον ὁ μὲν πεντακοσιομέδιμνος τρεῖς δραχμάς, ὁ δὲ ἱππεὺς δύο, ὁ ζευγίτης δὲ μίαν. Cauer (*Hat Arist. d. Schrift vom Staate d. Ath. geschrieben?* p. 70) takes offence at these fines, since Draco, according to Pollux 9, 61, καὶ μὴν κἂν τοῖς Δράκοντος νόμοις ἔστιν ἀποτίνειν εἰκοσάβοιον still employed cattle as the measure of value. Rühl (Suppl. vol. 689) rightly rejects this, for according to Poll., *ibid.*, the Didrachmon was then called βοῦς, and so εἰκοσάβοιον is only an antiquated expression for 40 Drachmæ. Nevertheless, Rühl thinks this passage untrustworthy. Of course we must not regard it as evidence for believing that Solon found his 4 property classes already existent. How the expressions are to be understood has been shown in the course of the text. Busolt (*Phil.*, 1891, 399) thinks that in Draco's laws compensation in cattle and fines subsisted side by side. Fines graduated according to the person's property, for absence from the Assembly and the Council-meetings were an ὀλιγαρχικὸν σόφισμα τῆς νομοθεσίας. Cf. Arist. 6 (4) 13=p. 167, 14 ff. περὶ ἐκκλησίαν μὲν τὸ ἐξεῖναι ἐκκλησιάζειν πᾶσι, ζημίαν δ' ἐπικεῖσθαι τοῖς εὐπόροις, ἐὰν μὴ ἐκκλησιάζωσιν, ἢ μόνοις ἢ μείζω πολλῷ—καὶ περὶ τὰ δικαστήρια τοῖς μὲν εὐπόροις εἶναι ζημίαν, ἂν μὴ δικάζωσι, τοῖς δ' ἀπόροις ἄδειαν, ἢ τοῖς μὲν μεγάλην τοῖς δὲ μικράν, ὥσπερ ἐν τοῖς Χαρώνδου νόμοις.

so long as Draco's constitution lasted, that council was merely the guardian of the laws, and superintended the magistrates to ensure their administering their office in accordance with the laws. Whoever believed that he had suffered injustice at the hands of a magistrate might bring an Eisangelia before the Council of the Areopagus.[1] Draco transferred the judicial powers which the Areopagus had previously possessed to two new bodies which he created, the Ephetai and the Prytaneis.[2] In the first place, as to cases of homicide, which undoubtedly were tried by the Areopagus before the time of Draco, he transferred these to a board of fifty-one Eupatrids over 50 years of age.[3] These fifty-one judges

Jurisdiction of the Ephetai and Prytaneis.

'Εφέται.

---

[1] Arist. 4, 4, ἡ δὲ βουλὴ ἡ ἐξ' Ἀρείου πάγου φύλαξ ἦν τῶν νόμων καὶ διετήρει τὰς ἀρχὰς ὅπως κατὰ τοὺς νόμους ἄρχωσιν. ἐξῆν δὲ τῷ ἀδικουμένῳ πρὸ[ς τὴν τῶν] 'Ἀρεοπαγιτῶν βουλὴν εἰσαγγέλλειν, ἀποφαίνοντι παρ' ὃν ἀδικεῖται νόμον. On the other hand, of the βουλὴ τῶν 'Ἀρεοπαγιτῶν in the times before Draco we read: καὶ κολάζουσα καὶ ζημιοῦσα πάντας τοὺς ἀκοσμοῦντας κυρίως. Arist. 3, 6: for the times after Solon: καὶ τοὺς ἁμαρτάνοντας ηὔθυνεν κυρία οὖσα [καὶ ζη]μι[οῦν] καὶ κολάζειν. Arist. 8, 4.

[2] That Ephetai and Prytaneis sat before Solon, follows from the Solonian law of Epitimia in Plut., *Sol.*, 19: ἀτίμων ὅσοι ἄτιμοι ἦσαν, πρὶν ἢ Σόλωνα ἄρξαι, ἐπιτίμους εἶναι πλὴν ὅσοι ἐξ' Ἀρείου πάγου ἢ ὅσοι ἐκ τῶν ἐφετῶν ἢ ἐκ πρυτανείου καταδικασθέντες ὑπὸ τῶν βασιλέων ἐπὶ φόνῳ ἢ σφαγαῖσι ἢ ἐπὶ τυραννίδι ἔφευγον, ὅτε ὁ θεσμὸς ἐφάνη ὅδε. Like Philippi (*N. Rh. Mus.*, 29, 7/8, vid. too Areop. u. Eph., 238), I suppose that καταδικασθέντες ὑπὸ τῶν βασιλέων relates to all three courts, and that by βασιλεῖς we must understand the successive βασιλεῖς (see also Lange, *d. Eph. u. d. Areop.*, 41 ff.; *Leipz. Stud.*, 2, 116 ff. Hauvette-Besnault, *de Archonte Rege*, 2 ff.). I agree with Lange that as the double ὅσοι and double ἐπὶ show, a bipartition of the courts and of the offences is indicated. Adopting these hypotheses, I interpret the law to mean by the ὅσοι ἐξ' Ἀρείου πάγου those condemned by the Areopagus before the introduction of Draco's reforms, by the ὅσοι ἐκ τῶν ἐφετῶν ἢ ἐκ πρυτανείου those condemned, after Draco's reforms, by the Ephetai and the Prytaneis. Further, φόνος and σφαγαί go together, meaning premeditated murder and assassinations in political party fights (Lange, *op. cit.*, 46); in opposition to this stands τυραννίς—an attempt to gain the Tyrannis. Before Draco perhaps the Areopagus tried all three crimes; afterwards perhaps the Ephetai took φόνος and σφαγαί, the Prytaneis τυραννίς.

[3] Cf. Poll. 8, 125: ἐφέται τὸν μὲν ἀριθμὸν εἰς καὶ πεντήκοντα, Δράκων δ' αὐτοὺς κατέστησεν ἀριστίνδην αἱρεθέντας· ἐδίκαζον δὲ τοῖς ἐφ' αἵματι διωκομένοις ἐν τοῖς πέντε δικαστηρίοις. Σόλων δὲ αὐτοῖς προσκατέστησε τὴν ἐξ' Ἀρείου πάγου βουλήν. This statement of Poll. was first called in question by Philippi in the *Jahrb. f. cl. Phil.*, 1872, 578 ff., especially 604. See too *d. Areop. u. d. Eph.* 189 ff. He was followed by Lange, *d. Eph. u. d. Areop.*, 3 ff., Wecklein in the *Sitzungsber. d. bayr. Ak.*, 1873, 5/6, Wachsmuth, *d. St. Athen.*, 1, 479, 1, and by the author in his first edition. Schömann opposed this view in the *Jahrb.*

in murder cases bore the name ἐφέται, by which probably they were designated as being those who by their decision determined what was to be done with the accused.[1]

Whether Draco himself introduced, or merely codified in accordance with customs already existing, the system by which murder cases were tried at Athens, and which even measured by the standard of to-day is tolerably complete, can as little be decided with certainty as can the question whether he was the founder of the 5 different courts, at which in later times the trial was held

---

f. cl. Phil., 1875, 158 ff. Poll.'s account was supposed to have had its origin in the false reading of Draco's law in Dem. 43, 57, τούτοις (for τούτους) δ' οἱ πεντήκοντα καὶ εἷς ἀριστίνδην αἱρείσθων. This supposition was possible but not necessary. Now that our knowledge has been enlarged by Aristotle, I cannot agree with it, but see in the passage in Poll. a satisfactory testimony agreeing well with the process of constitutional development at Athens, for the institution of the Ephetai by Draco. The number of the Ephetai, 51 : C. I. A., I. 61 ; Dem. 43, 57 ; Poll. 8, 125 ; over 50 years old : Suid. Phot. Et. M. ἐφέται, Lex. Seguer. 188, 30 ff. The number 51 is perhaps best explained with Schömann, *op. ac.*, 1, 196, as composed of 3 ἐξηγηταί of sacred law—see (Dem.) 47, 68 sq.—and 12 Ephetai from each Phyle. Against this Lange, *d. Eph. u. d. Areop.*, 20 ff. The Ephetai as ἀριστίνδην αἱρεθέντες (Poll. 8, 125) must have been Eupatrids. See the ἀριστίνδην καὶ πλουτίνδην in Arist. 3, 1. 6. That in the Aristotelian ᾿Αθηναίων πολιτεία there is nothing said of the institution of the Ephetai by Draco, may be due to the fact that in the συναγωγὴ τῶν νόμων written as a companion to the collection of Constitutions the organs of the administration of justice were likewise treated. See Nissen in the *N. Rh. Mus.*, 1892, 184 ff.

[1] On the etymology of ἐφέται cf. Lange, *de ephetarum Atheniensium nomine*. Leipzig, 1874 ; *d. Eph. u. d. Areop.*, 13/4. Lange explained οἱ ἐφέται as οἱ ἐπὶ τοῖς ἔταις ὄντες, i.e. as the presidents of the citizens optimo iure, and regarded them as the old Council. This explanation the author accepted in the first edition (see too Philippi, *d. Areop. u. d. Eph.*, 213 ; Oesterberg, *de ephetarum Atheniensium origine*, 70/1. Upsala, 1885). Now, however, that another βουλή is attested by Aristotle for the period before Solon, we cannot acquiesce in Lange's theory. I now regard as most satisfactory the explanation of Schömann, *op. ac.*, 1, 196, who explains the Ephetai as those who by their verdict determined (ἐφίεσθαι) what was to be done with the accused. The possibility of this view is admitted also by Lange, *op. cit.*, 7, though he regards it as improbable, since this would be applicable to all judges. See too Philippi, *op. cit.*, 213. The other etymologies are disproved by Lange, *op. cit.*, 3 ff. Since Lange, Forchhammer, *Phil.*, 34, 465 ff., has proposed to derive the word from the root ἑ, ἧμαι, making οἱ ἐφέται, "those who sit in judgment upon something," and Joh. and Theod. Baunack in the *Stud. auf. d. Geb. d. griech. u. ar. Sprachen* I., 1, suggest the Sanskrit sabha=a judicial assembly, corresponding to which a Greek word, ὁ ἔφος, might have been formed.

according to the nature of the case.¹ The other judicial powers which before Draco had been exercised by the Areopagus, with the exception of the cases of homicide just discussed, were apparently transferred by Draco to the Prytaneis, the standing committee of the newly established Council. Πρυτάνεις. The βασιλεύς, who still acted as chief magistrate, kept the presidency even in those new courts of the Ephetai and the Prytaneis, just as he had beyond a doubt presided before Draco in the Areopagus.²

Besides the constitutional reforms just described, the codification of the unwritten laws then obtaining is attributed to Draco. Of this code, whose regulations a later age regarded as excessively severe, we know practically nothing except the laws concerning homicide which Solon adopted with slight alterations.³ The social problem was unaffected by

¹ The θεσμοὶ φονικοί of Draco contained, so far as we are acquainted with them, no provisions about the places where the various kinds of homicide were to be tried. See C. I. A., I. 61., Philippi, *d. Areop. u. d. Eph.*, 333 ff. On the contrary, all Draco's blood-laws were called φονικοὶ οἱ ἐξ Ἀρείου πάγου: Dem. 23, 22, cf. *Lys.*, 6, 15. Moreover, the law about the δίκαιος φόνος is cited, *Lys.*, 1, 30, ἐκ τῆς στήλης τῆς ἐξ Ἀρείου πάγου.

² As has been already remarked, p. 123, 2, the author refers the ἐκ πρυτανείου of the Solonian law on Epitimia in Plut., *Sol.*, 19, to the πρυτάνεις mentioned in Arist. 4, 2. Plut., too, in his explanation of ἐκ πρυτανείου, uses the word πρυτάνεις. The crime which they had to judge, according to the law just mentioned, was undoubtedly τυραννίς. For the punishment decreed for an attempt to gain the Tyrannis, cf. Arist., 16, 10.; θέσμια τάδε Ἀθηναί[οις] καὶ πάτρια· ἐάν τινες τυραννεῖν ἐπανιστῶνται ἢ τὴν τυραννίδα τις συγκαθιστῇ, ἄτιμον εἶναι καὶ αὐτὸν καὶ γένος. There is nothing strange in this judicial power of the Prytaneis; the Council of the 500 too after Cleisthenes possessed jurisdiction over certain offences, and could inflict fines, imprisonment and death. See Aristot. 45, 1; C. I. A., I. 57. The βασιλεύς is indicated as president of the Ephetai and Prytaneis in the Solonian Epitimia-law (p. 123, 2), and in C. I. A., I. 61. Curtius, on the contrary, *Monatsber. d. Berl. Ak.*, 1873, 290, understands by the βασιλεῖς there mentioned the 9 archons, or the three first of them; Schoell, *Herm.*, 6, 21, and Wachsmuth, *d. St. Ath.*, 1, 468 ff. the φυλοβασιλεῖς; Schömann in *Jahrb. f. cl. Phil.*, 1876, 16, the Archons and the φυλοβασιλεῖς.

³ Arist., *Pol.*, 2, 12=p. 58, 7, Bekker—a passage, however, which is hardly genuine—pronounces on Draco's laws: ἴδιον δ' ἐν τοῖς νόμοις οὐδέν ἐστιν ὅτι καὶ μνείας ἄξιον πλὴν ἡ χαλεπότης διὰ τὸ τῆς ζημίας μέγεθος. A dictum of Demades, ὅτι δι' αἵματος, οὐ διὰ μέλανος τοὺς νόμους ὁ Δράκων ἔγραψεν, Plut., *Sol.*, 17. The Athenians, says Arist., 7, 1, after Solon τοῖς Δράκοντος θεσμοῖς ἐπαύσαντο χρώμενοι πλὴν τῶν φονικῶν. Solon introduced the Areopagus again as the court for φόνος ἑκούσιος; but he retained Draco's laws on that subject, and began his πρῶτος ἄξων with Draco's regulation about φόνος ἀκούσιος. That the

Draco's legislation. The ἑκτήμοροι continued to be personally liable
Social for the fulfilment of their obligations. The increasing
Position. indebtedness of the still independent Zeugitai threatened to reduce them also sooner or later to slavery.[1]

2. From Solon to Euclides.

Draco's revision of the constitution was not such as to produce internal harmony among the various classes of the community. Not only did it fail to remove the existing social distress,
Social. but by codifying the laws relating to debt, it actually sanctioned that state of affairs for the future. The mortgaging of the small peasant properties proceeded unchecked. Whoever could not meet his financial obligations, fell in the end into slavery, and was either sold out of the country, or led a slave's life in Attica.[2] Furious internal struggles of the people against the aristocrats and

definition of φόνος ἑκούσιος preceded this in Draco's laws, may be inferred from the καί at the beginning of the πρῶτος ἄξων. See C. I. A., I. 61.

[1] Arist. 4, 5, concludes his account of Draco's legislation with the words: ἐπὶ δὲ τοῖς σώ[μα]σιν ἦσαν οἱ δαν[εισ]μοί, καθάπερ εἴρηται, καὶ ἡ χώρα δι' ὀλίγων ἦν.

[2] Even for the time after Draco, Arist., 4, 5, says: ἐπὶ δὲ τοῖς σώ[μα]σιν ἦσαν οἱ δαν[εισ]μοί, καθάπερ εἴρηται, καὶ ἡ χώρα δι' ὀλίγων ἦν. The δανείζειν ἐπὶ τοῖς σώμασιν (Arist. 6, 1; see too Plut., *Sol.*, 13) lasted down to Solon, *i.e.* Attic law before Solon knew no credit on real security, but only a personal-credit. Even in case of the ὅροι on the plots of ground the debtor was personally liable, and therefore could not free himself of the debt by cession of the property mortgaged. Solon describes the position of affairs before his legislation as follows: ταῦτα μὲν ἐν δήμῳ στρέφεται κακά· τῶν δὲ πενιχρῶν —ἱκνοῦνται πολλοὶ γαῖαν ἐς ἀλλοδαπήν—πραθέντες δεσμοῖσί τ' ἀεικελίοισι δεθέντες, —καὶ κακὰ δουλοσύνης στυγνὰ φέρουσι βίᾳ (Sol. fr., 4, 23 ff.=Dem. 19, 255). Further, in Aristot., 12, 4:

συμμαρτυροίη ταῦτ' ἂν ἐν δίκῃ χρόνου
μήτηρ μεγίστη δαιμόνων ['Ολυ]μπίων
ἄριστα, Γῆ μέλαινα, τῆς ἐγώ ποτε
ὅρους ἀνεῖλον πολλαχῇ πεπηγότα[ς]
[πρόσθ]εν δὲ δουλεύουσα, νῦν ἐλευθέρα.
πολλοὺς δ' Ἀθήνας, πατρίδ' εἰς θεόκτιτον,
[ἀνή]γαγον πραθέντας, ἄλλον ἐκδίκως,
ἄλλον δικαίως, τοὺς δ' ἀναγκαίης ὕπο
χρειοῦς φυγόντας γλῶσσαν οὐκέτ' Ἀττικὴν
ἱέντας, ὡς ἂν πολλαχῇ πλαν[ωμένους],
τοὺς δ' ἐνθάδ' αὐτοῦ δουλίην ἀεικέα
ἔχοντας, ἤθη δεσποτῶν τρομευμέν[ους],
ἐλευθέρους ἔθηκα.

Solon.

the well to do threatened the existence of the State with the most serious dangers, and it was high time that Pallas Athene, who, according to Solon's expression, held her protecting hand over Athens, should send a saviour, if it really was the will of Zeus and of the blessed gods that the State should not perish. This saviour appeared in the person of Solon. Born of a Eupatrid family, but by the amount of his property and his station in life belonging to the middle classes, he appeared to both parties a suitable mediator, when in a political elegy he depicted the miserable circumstances of his native city, attributed them to greed and arrogance, and concluded by calling on all to lay aside their civil feuds.[1] If Solon had joined either party now, he would have found it an easy task to secure the Tyrannis. He disdained to do so, and contented himself with becoming the lawgiver of his country and the mediator in her social disputes. The result was that during his lifetime he found but scant recognition for his institutions, but after his death was famed for centuries as the founder of the Athenian constitution.[2] By a compromise between the contending parties, Solon was chosen to be peacemaker, and charged with the reform of the constitution, a duty which he carried out in his official capacity as archon in 594 B.C.[3]

---

[1] Arist. 5, 1: τοιαύτης δὲ τῆς τάξεως οὔσης ἐν τῇ πολιτείᾳ καὶ τῶν πολλῶν δουλευόντων τοῖς ὀλίγοις, ἀντέστη τοῖς γνωρίμοις ὁ δῆμος. For Solon's origin and social position see Arist. 5, 3: ἦν δ᾽ ὁ Σόλων τῇ μὲν [φύ]σει καὶ τῇ δόξῃ τῶν πρώτων, τῇ δ᾽ οὐσίᾳ, καὶ τοῖς πράγμασι τῶν μέσων κ. τ. ἀ. According to Plut., Sol., 1, Solon was a descendant of Codrus. Cf. too Toepffer, att. Geneal., 284, 1. On the contents of the elegy, which indicated Solon as suitable for a mediator, see Arist. 5, 2, 3. From it too probably comes Sol., fr. 4=Dem. 19, 25, where the verses quoted in the text are also to be found.

[2] See Sol., fr. 32, 33, in Plut., Sol., 14. That his reforms failed to satisfy most citizens, is shown by his verses in Arist. 12, and fr. 87=Aristid. 2, 537. See also Arist. 11. Arist., 6, 3, says he was so moderate, and so thoughtful of the general good [ὥ]στ᾽ ἐξὸν αὐτῷ τοὺς [ἑτ]έ[ρο]υς ὑποποιησάμενον τυραννεῖν τῆς πόλεως, ἀμφοτέροις ἀπεχ[θ]έσθαι καὶ περὶ πλείονος ποιήσασθαι τὸ καλὸν καὶ τὴν τῆς πόλεως σωτηρίαν ἢ τὴν αὑτοῦ πλεονεξίαν. Cf. too Arist. 11, 2: . . . [ἀμ]φοτέροις ἠναντιώθη καὶ ἐξὸν αὐτῷ μεθ᾽ ὁποτέρων ἠβούλετο συστά[ντι] τυραννεῖν εἵλετο πρὸς ἀμφοτέρους ἀπεχθέσθαι, σώσας τὴν πατρίδα καὶ τὰ βέ[λτι]στα νομοθετήσας.

[3] Arist., 5, 2, ἰσχυρᾶς δὲ τῆς στάσεως οὔσης καὶ πολὺν χρόνον ἀντικαθημένων ἀλλήλοις εἵλοντο κοινῇ διαλλακτὴν καὶ ἄρχοντα Σόλωνα καὶ τὴν [πολι]τείαν ἐπέτρεψαν αὐτῷ κ. τ. ἀ. Solon was archon, according to Sosikrates, Ol., 46, 3=594/3: Diog. L. 1, 2, 15. Cf. Cyril, adv. Jul., 1, p. 12 e, Aubert., Clem. Strom. 1, 14. According to the Armen. Euseb., Solon's legislation, Ol., 47, 3=590, according to Jerome, Ol., 47, 1=592. Solon succeeded Philombrotos, Plut.,

While the people hoped his mediation would secure a general redistribution of property, the aristocrats expected at most an insignificant alteration of the existing state of affairs.

Σεισάχθεια.

Solon however, like a true mediator, did not completely accede to the wishes of either party; but by far-reaching changes in the laws of property he ended the social distress without attacking the social foundations of the State. The measure which effected this object was the σεισάχθεια, as it was called—the shaking off of burdens.[1] Even in ancient times opinions were divided as to the meaning of this σεισάχθεια. The general view, which Aristotle and Philochoros represent, regarded the σεισάχθεια as a cancelling of debts.[2] Androtion, on the other hand, supposed that Solon's measure merely meant the relief of debtors by a reduction of the rate of interest and depreciation of the coinage. According to the new standard

---

Sol., 14. Stettiner, *ad Solon. ætatem quæst. crit.*, 47 ff., Königsberg, 1885, conjectures that Solon was αἰσυμνήτης for 20 years. Holzapfel, *Beitr. z. griech. Gesch.*, 1 ff., 1888 (cf. too Fr. Cauer, *Parteien u. Politiker in Megara u. Athen.*, 56 ff., 1890), wishes to throw Solon's legislation forward to the year 584. Certainty is perhaps impossible; the year 594, however, seems to be the best attested. See Bauer, *Lit. u. hist. Forsch. zu Aristot.* 'Αθηναίων πολιτεία, p. 44 ff. That Solon exercises his legislative powers as archon, is proved by the form of the Solonian law in Dem. 44, 67/8.

[1] Arist. 11, 2: ὁ μὲν γὰρ δῆμος ᾤετο πάντ' ἀνάδαστα ποιήσειν αὐτόν, οἱ δὲ γνώριμοι πάλιν [(εἰς)] τὴν αὐτὴν τάξιν ἀποδώσειν ἢ [μικρὸν] παραλλάξ[ειν.] For the σεισάχθεια see Arist. 6, 1: καὶ χρεῶν ἀποκοπὰς ἐποίησε καὶ τῶν ἰδίων καὶ τῶν δημοσίων, ἃς σεισάχθειαν καλοῦσιν, ὡς ἀποσεισάμενοι τὸ βάρος. Arist. 10, 1: ἐν [μὲν οὖν τ]οῖς νόμοις ταῦτα δοκεῖ θεῖναι δημοτικά, πρὸ δὲ τῆς νομοθεσίας ποιήσα[ς τὴν τῶν χρ]εῶ[ν ἀπο]κοπὴν καὶ μετὰ ταῦτα τὴν τε τῶν μέτρων καὶ σταθμῶν καὶ τὴν τοῦ νομίσματος ἐπαύξησιν. According to Plut., *Sol.*, 14, Solon carried the σεισάχθεια as archon and then was appointed διορθωτὴς καὶ νομοθέτης τῆς πολιτείας, Plut., *Sol.*, 16. This is not probable; by the σεισάχθεια he undeceived both parties, and therefore would hardly have been chosen to legislate afterwards.

[2] Cf. Plut. *Sol.*, 15: οἱ δὲ πλεῖστοι πάντων ὁμοῦ φασι τῶν συμβολαίων ἀναίρεσιν (τὴν τῶν χρεῶν ἀποκοπὴν) γενέσθαι τὴν σεισάχθειαν καὶ τούτοις συνᾴδει μᾶλλον τὰ ποιήματα. Arist. 6, 1: κύριος δὲ γενόμενος τῶν πραγμά[τω]ν Σόλων—καὶ χρεῶν ἀποκοπὰς ἐποίησε καὶ τῶν ἰδίων καὶ τῶν δημοσίων, ἃς σεισάχθειαν καλοῦσιν, ὡς ἀποσεισάμενοι τὸ βάρος. Cf. the whole chapter. Philoch.'s version is in Phot. Suid. σεισάχθεια. Apostol. 15, 39: σεισάχθεια χρεωκοπία δημοσίων καὶ ἰδιωτικῶν, ἣν εἰσηγήσατο Σόλων. εἴρηται δὲ παρ' ὅσον ἔθος ἦν Ἀθήνησι τοὺς ὀφείλοντας τῶν πενήτων σώματι ἐργάζεσθαι τοῖς χρήσταις, ἀποδόντας δὲ οἱονεὶ τὸ ἄχθος ἀποσείσασθαι· ὡς Φιλοχόρῳ δὲ δοκεῖ, ἀποψηφισθῆναι τὸ ἄχθος. The σεισάχθεια was regarded as a cancelling of debts by Herakleid., 1, 5 (Müller, *fr. hist. gr.*, 1, 208). Dionys., 5, 65. Dion., *Chrysost.*, 31, 69. Diog. L. 1, 2, 1.

100 new drachmas were worth only 73 of the old standard; and the change must have acted in favour of the debtors because the capital received in the old heavy coinage was repaid in the new light money.[1] Of these two views—both already current in ancient times—the first is the better attested, since Aristotle and Philochoros adopt it. Moreover the consequences which, according to Solon's own declaration, attended the Seisachtheia, the removal of the mortgage pillars from the estates, and the emancipation of the enslaved debtors, are of such a character that they could not have been effected by a partial cancelling of debts to the extent of 27 %. And the reduction of the rate of interest which Androtion considered a part of the Seisachtheia is expressly contradicted by a law of Solon's, which has been preserved for us, and which leaves the rate of interest entirely at the pleasure of the lender.[2] Accordingly in my view of the Seisachtheia I follow Aristotle and Philochoros, and regard it as a complete cancelling of debts. The financial injury to the rich involved in the measure was justified in Solon's eyes not only by reasons of statesmanship, but also by his ideas of morality, for, according to his own testimony, their riches had been gained by unrighteous means.[3] The emancipation of the enslaved debtors was a consequence of the provisions for cancelling of debts, and of course was accompanied by compensation to the creditor in whose possession they were. But we cannot say how the debtors already sold as slaves abroad were brought back to Athens by Solon.[4] To guard against the recurrence of similar circumstances

---

[1] See Androtion ap. Plut. Sol., 15: καίτοι τινὲς ἔγραψαν, ὧν ἐστὶν 'Ανδροτίων, οὐκ ἀποκοπῇ χρεῶν, ἀλλὰ τόκων μετριότητι κουφισθέντας ἀγαπῆσαι τοὺς πένητας καὶ σεισάχθειαν ὀνομάσαι τὸ φιλανθρώπευμα τοῦτο καὶ τὴν ἅμα τούτῳ γενομένην τῶν τε μέτρων ἐπαύξησιν καὶ τοῦ νομίσματος τιμὴν κ. τ. ά. Arist., 10, 1, distinguishes the two in express terms: πρὸ δὲ τῆς νομοθεσίας ποιῆσα[ς τὴν τῶν χρ]εω[ν ἀπο]κοπὴν καὶ μετὰ ταῦτα τήν τε τῶν μέτρων καὶ σταθμῶν καὶ τὴν τοῦ νομίσματος αὔξησιν. Hultsch., griech. u. rom. Metrol.,[2] 200 ff. Curtius, Gk. Hist., 1[5], 816 ff. (Ward's Eng. tr. 1, 829 ff.) formerly followed Androtion. Schömann, griech. Alterth., 1[3], 347; Grote, vol. 2, p. 476, take the right view.

[2] Solon's own description of the results of his legislation in Arist. 12, better than in Aristid. 2, 536=fr. 36. Cf. in regard to the limitation of interest the law of Solon ap. Lys. 10, 18: τὸ ἀργύριον στάσιμον εἶναι, ἐφ' ὁπόσῳ ἂν βούληται ὁ δανείζων with the explanation τὸ στάσιμον τοῦτό ἐστιν, ὦ βέλτιστε, οὐ ζυγῷ ἱστάναι, ἀλλὰ τόκον πράττεσθαι, ὁπόσον ἂν βούληται.

[3] Cf. Sol., fr. 4, 11=Dem. 19, 255. Arist., 5, 3, says of Solon: καὶ ὅλως αἰεὶ τὴν αἰτίαν τῆς στάσεως ἀνάπτει τοῖς πλουσίοις.

[4] That they were so brought back, he tells us himself, fr. 36, 6 ff., Arist.

in the future, Solon forbade ἐπὶ τοῖς σώμασι δανείζειν, and ensured the existence of small holdings by fixing a maximum, which no individual citizen's estate was to exceed.[1]

After Solon had removed the immediate distress, he laid the foundations of the new constitution. Even before Draco there had been four grades in society, with the names πεντακοσιομέδιμνοι, *i.e.* the Eupatrid large landowners, ἱππεῖς, *i.e.* Eupatrid knights, ζευγῖται, peasants masters of a team of oxen, and the θῆτες, *i.e.* the dependent manual labourers. These names Solon employed to indicate the four classes which he instituted for purposes of taxation. For each class except the last he fixed a certain minimum of property. The πεντακοσιομέδιμνοι had to be in receipt of 500 measures of dry or fluid produce from land of their own, *i.e.* either 500 medimnoi of corn, or 500 metretai of oil or wine—the amount to be measured by the new measure which was nearly 50 % less than the old. The ἱππεῖς had to have a revenue of 300 measures, the ζευγῖται 200; while all those whose yearly income from land of their own did not reach the minimum of the ζευγῖται were included in the class of the θῆτες.[2]

Classes.

12. Hugo Landwehr in the 5. Suppl. vol. of the *Phil.*, 135/6 supposes Solon made the return of many to their country possible by granting freedom to any who escaped from their masters abroad and came to Attica. In that case Solon chose a very strong expression when he said: πολλοὺς δ' 'Αθήνας, πατρίδ' εἰς θεόκτιτον,—[ἀνή]γαγον πραθέντας, ἄλλον ἐκδίκως,—ἄλλον δικαίως.

[1] See Arist. 6, 1: κύριος δὲ γενόμενος τῶν πραγμά[τω]ν Σόλων τόν τε δῆμον ἠλευθέρωσε καὶ ἐν τῷ παρόντι καὶ εἰς τὸ μέλλον κωλύσας δ[ανε]ίζειν ἐπὶ τοῖς σώμασιν. According to Plut., *Sol.*, 15 the prohibition ἐπὶ τοῖς σώμασι μηδένα δανείζειν belongs to the σεισάχθεια. For the holdings see Arist., *Pol.*, 2, 7 = p. 37, 26 ff. Bekker: οἷον καὶ Σόλων ἐνομοθέτησεν καὶ παρ' ἄλλοις ἐστὶ νόμος, ὃς κωλύει κτᾶσθαι γῆν, ὁπόσην ἂν βούληταί τις.

[2] On the earlier existence of the four grades mentioned in the text, see p. 114 ff., 122. Previously they were not classes for the purpose of taxation, with the exception of the πεντακοσιομέδιμνοι. On this point I agree with Gomperz, *d. Schrift vom Staatswesen d. Ath. u. ihr neuester Beurtheiler*, 1891, p. 40 ff., who is only mistaken in making πεντακοσιομέδιμνος too an indefinite expression like our millionaire. The πεντακοσιομέδιμνοι are the people who carried on the government in the pre-Draconian constitution, and they must have had a minimum-census, just as did the governing class among the Hippobotai. But the πεντακοσιομέδιμνος of Solon is socially a different person from the πεντακοσιομέδιμνος before Draco (see too Busolt, *Phil.*, 1891, p. 396). For the proportion of the Solonian system of measures to the Æginetan is: An Æginetan medimnos = 72·74 litres, a Solonian = 52·53, an Æginetan metretes = 54·56 litres, a Solonian = 39·39. See Hultsch, *griech. u. röm. Metrol.*,[2] 499 ff., 505. By the assumption in the text the titles of the classes, so extraordinary if taken as classes for taxation, become clear

The extent of the political rights possessed by each burgess depended upon the assessment class to which he belonged. The 9 ἄρχοντες, the ταμίαι, the πωληταί, the ἕνδεκα and the κωλακρέται were all chosen from among the first three classes, but not all of them from all three classes without distinction; the ἄρχοντες were elected from among the πεντακοσιομέδιμνοι and the ἱππεῖς, the ταμίαι from the πεντακοσιομέδιμνοι, the rest from all three classes. Only the members of the first three classes were liable to military service. The Thetes were exempt from service, at any rate from serving as hoplites; they were not eligible for any public office; they merely possessed the right of attending the ἐκκλησία and serving as jurymen.[1]

Political Rights.

(see Gomperz, *ibid.*); and at the same time the passage in Aristotle, 7, 3: καθάπερ διῄρητο καὶ πρότερον, becomes intelligible. Busolt., *ibid.*, justly notices that the Pentacosiomedimnoi after Solon should have been called properly Pentacosiometroi. The retention of the old name shows how Solon clung to what already existed. In Arist. 7, 3 we read concerning these taxation-classes: ⟨τὰ⟩τιμήματα διεῖλεν εἰς τέτταρα τέλη, καθάπερ διῄρητο καὶ πρότερον, εἰς πεντακοσιομ[έδιμ]ν[ον καὶ ἱππέα] καὶ ζευγίτην καὶ θῆτα. 7, 4: ἔδει δὲ τελεῖν πεντακοσιομέδιμνον μὲν ὃς ἂν ἐκ τῆς οἰκείας ποιῇ πεντακόσια μέτρα τὰ συνάμφω ξηρὰ καὶ ὑγρά, ἱππάδα δὲ τοὺς τριακόσια ποιοῦντας, ὡς δ' ἔνιοί φασι τοὺς ἱπποτροφεῖν δυναμένους. After Aristotle had refuted the latter view, he proceeds: ζευγίσιον δὲ τελεῖν τοὺς διακόσια τὰ συνάμφω ποιοῦντας, τοὺς δ' ἄλλους θητικὸν κ.τ.λ. Cf. Plut., *Sol.*, 18. Harp.: πεντακοσιομέδιμνοι. ἱππάς. θῆτες καὶ θητικόν. Poll. 8, 129, 130. Phot.: πεντακοσιομέδιμνοι. ἱππάς. ζευγήσιον. θητεὺς καὶ θητικόν. Hesych.: ἐκ τιμημάτων. ἱππάς. ζευγίσιον. θητικόν. Suid.: πεντακοσιομέδιμνον. ἱππεῖς. ἱππάς. θῆτες καὶ θητικόν. Et. M., 410: ζευγίσιον. θητικόν. Lex S:guer. 261, 20; 264, 19; 267, 18; 298, 20, all of which are drawn from Arist. Boeckh's view (*St. d. Ath.*, 1, 647, Lamb's Eng. tr. of Boeckh's *Publ. Ec. of Ath.*, p. 641) was that the minimum assessment of the Zeugitai was 150 μέτρα. He inferred this from a law preserved in Dem. 43, 54. But this view is now no longer tenable on account of Aristotle's testimony.

[1] Arist. 7, 3: καὶ τὰς [[με[γίστ]ας]] ἀρχὰς ἀπένειμεν ἄρχειν ἐκ πεντακοσιομεδίμνων καὶ ἱππέων καὶ ζευγιτῶν, τοὺς ἐννέα ἄρχοντας καὶ τοὺς ταμίας καὶ τοὺς πωλητὰς καὶ τοὺς ἕνδεκα καὶ τοὺς κωλακρέτας, ἑκάστοις ἀνὰ λόγον τῷ μεγέθει τοῦ τιμήματος ἀποδιδοὺς [τὴν ἀρ]χήν. τοῖς δὲ τὸ θητικὸν τελοῦσιν ἐκκλησίας καὶ δικαστηρίων μετέδωκε μόνον. 7, 4: τοὺς δ' ἄλλους θητικόν, οὐδεμιᾶς μετέχοντας ἀρχῆς. Cf. Arist., *Pol.*, 2, 12 = p. 56, 32 sqq. Bekker: τὰς δ' ἀρχὰς ἐκ τῶν γνωρίμων καὶ τῶν εὐπόρων κατέστησε πάσας, ἐκ τῶν πεντακοσιομεδίμνων καὶ ζευγιτῶν καὶ τρίτου τέλους τῆς καλουμένης ἱππάδος· τὸ δὲ τέταρτον θητικόν, οἷς οὐδεμιᾶς ἀρχῆς μετῆν. Poll. 8, 130. Harp. θῆτες—ὅτι δὲ οὐκ ἐστρατεύοντο, εἴρηκε καὶ Ἀριστοφάνης ἐν Δαιταλεῦσιν. In general cf. Sol., *fr.* 18. Arist. 26, 2: οἱ δὲ (viz. οἱ ἐννέα ἄρχοντες) πρὸ τούτου (*i.e.* before 457/6) πάντες ἐξ ἱππέων καὶ πεντακοσιομεδίμνων ἦσαν, οἱ ⟨δὲ⟩ ζευγῖται τὰς ἐγκυκλίους ἦρχον, εἰ μή τι παρεωρᾶτο τῶν ἐν τοῖς νόμοις. When Plut., *Arist.*, 1, says that Demetrios of Phaleron cited as proof of the easy circumstances of Aristides τὴν ἐπώνυμον ἀρχήν, ἣν ἦρξε τῷ κυάμῳ λαχὼν ἐκ τῶν γενῶν τῶν τὰ μέγιστα τιμήματα κεκτημένων, οὓς πεντακοσιομεδίμνους προσηγόρευον, the last ex-

Solon seems to have arranged the incidence of taxation on the same principle on which he distributed political rights. If Boeckh's ingenious combination is correct, he graduated the financial burdens of the burgesses on a system of extraordinary originality for such early times, according to the census-class to which each burgess belonged. Regarding the 500, 300 and 200 measures as the net income, computed from the amount of rent the estate brought in, then, since Solon regarded the medimnos as equivalent to a drachma, it follows, if we assume a ratio of income to property of $8\frac{1}{3}$ % (which is the ratio supported by evidence from later periods), that the minimum value of landed property for the πεντακοσιομέδιμνοι was one talent, for ἱππεῖς 3,600 drachmas, for the Zeugitai 2,400 drachmas. Now to secure an equitable distribution of taxation for state purposes among the classes two methods were available: the different classes might have been taxed at different rates per cent. upon their entire property; or, the assessed capital might be made to vary from the actual capital in different ratios in the different classes, while the taxes were levied at the same rate per cent. of assessed capital in all. Solon adopted the latter course. The πεντακοσιομέδιμνοι were assessed at the entire value of their landed estates, the ἱππεῖς at 3,000 drachmas, the ζευγῖται at 1,000. These numbers represent the minimum assessment on a member of each class, and also show the ratio at which the assessed capital stood to the real capital for each member of the class.[1]

planatory words may be Plutarch's own. In the Draconian constitution the ἄρχοντες and ταμίαι had the same assessment (Arist. 4, 2); according to the Solonian the latter had to be Pentacosiomedimnoi (Arist. 8, 1).

[1] For the system of Boeckh's given in the text see *Publ. Econ.*, 1, 643 (495) ff. It is based on Poll. 8, 130. The $8\frac{1}{3}$ % assumed by Boeckh as the ratio of rent to value of landed property is supported by the 12 minae as rent for an ἀγρὸς worth 150 minæ in Is. 11, 12. For the worth of a medimnos in Solon's time=one drachma, cf. Plut., *Sol.*, 23. The objections of Bake, *Schol. hypomnem.*, 4, 123 ff., have been answered by Thumser, *de Civium Atheniensium munerib.*, 29 ff. Beloch has criticised Boeckh's combination in Herm. 20, 245/6. A graduated taxation so complicated as that Boeckh assumes cannot be admitted for the period when financial science was still in its infancy; even the Pisistratidai still levied $\frac{1}{20}$ of the produce of the soil in kind. At any rate it must always be recognised that Boeckh's scheme is merely a hypothesis. On the other hand, the statements in Pollux show that there was a graduated system of some kind or other. Therefore the only doubt remaining is whether such a scheme can date as early as Solon himself. If this is considered probable, then it must be assumed that Pisistratos reverted to what was undoubtedly the original system of taxes

Solon's Taxation.

The employment of the census-classes for purposes of finance was effected by means of the system of Naucraries instituted by Solon. Starting with the four Ionic Phylai, he divided each Phyle into 3 τριττύες, each τριττύς into 4 ναυκραρίαι; the whole country was thus mapped out into 48 local divisions or Naucraries.[1] At the head of each Naucrary stood a ναύκραρος or "ship-furnisher," who derived his name from his duty, the equipment of a ship of war: when the ship was completely furnished he also acted as its captain or commander.[2] This etymology is corroborated by the fact that according to our

System of Naucraries.

---

paid in kind. Cf. Thuc. 6, 54; Arist. 16, 4; Zenob. 4, 76. On the other hand, the statements of Arist. 8, 3 on Solon's arrangement of the Naucraries show that the Naucraries levied an εἰσφορὰ in coin. The comparison of the Naucrary with the Symmory in Phot. seems to point to the same conclusion.

[1] Arist. 8, 3: φυλαὶ δ' ἦσαν δ' καθάπερ πρότερον καὶ φυλοβασιλεῖς τέτταρες. ἐκ δὲ [τῆς φυλῆς ἑκ]άστης ἦσαν νενεμημέναι τριττύες μὲν τρεῖς, ναυκραρίαι δὲ δώδεκα καθ' ἑκάστην, [ἐπὶ δὲ τῶν] ναυκραριῶν ἀρχὴ καθεστηκυῖα ναύκραροι, τεταγμένη πρὸς τε τὰς εἰσφορὰς καὶ τὰς δαπ[άνας] τὰς γιγνομένας· διὸ καὶ ἐν τοῖς νόμοις τοῖς Σόλωνος οἷς οὐκέτι χρῶνται πολλαχ[οῦ γέ]γραπται "τοὺς ναυκράρους εἰσπράττειν" καὶ "ἀναλίσκειν ἐκ τοῦ ναυκραρικοῦ ἀργυρ[ίου]." Cf. also Phot. ναυκραρία· τὸ πρότερον οὕτως ἐκάλουν ναυκραρία καὶ ναύκραρος· ναυκραρία μὲν ὁποῖόν τι ἡ συμμορία καὶ ὁ δῆμος, ναύκραρος δὲ ὁποῖόν τι ὁ δήμαρχος, Σόλωνος οὕτως ὀνομάσαντος, ὡς καὶ Ἀριστοτέλης φησί. καὶ ἐν τοῖς νόμοις λέγει (for the MSS. δὲ), "ἐάν τις ναυκραρίας ἀμφισβητῇ" καὶ "τοὺς ναυκράρους τοὺς κατὰ ναυκραρίαν"· ὕστερον δὲ ἀπὸ Κλεισθένους δῆμοι εἰσιν καὶ δήμαρχοι ἐκλήθησαν· ἐκ τῆς Ἀριστοτέλους πολιτείας ὃν τρόπον διέταξε τὴν πόλιν ὁ Σόλων· φυλαὶ δὲ ἦσαν τέσσαρες καθάπερ πρότερον καὶ φυλοβασιλεῖς τέσσαρες· ἐκ δὲ τῆς φυλῆς ἦσαν νενεμημέναι τριττύες μὲν τρεῖς, ναυκραρίαι δὲ δώδεκα καθ' ἑκάστην. See Rose, *Aristot. Pseudep.*, 410, 7. That the explicit testimony of Aristotle outweighs the casual notice of Hdt. 5, 71 admits of no further question, now that we have Aristotle himself (see also Stein, *ad loc.* For Hdt.'s knowledge of Athenian institutions, see 5, 69). The Schol. on Arist., *Clouds*, 37: οἱ πρότερον ναύκραροι εἴτε ὑπὸ Σόλωνος κατασταθέντες εἴτε καὶ πρότερον, who immediately before quoted from Aristotle, has obviously in view the evidence of both Aristot. and Hdt. in his annotation. I have fully discussed my view of the date of the institution of the Naucraries in the *Jahrb. f. cl. Phil.*, 1875, p. 9 ff., where the views of other writers are also stated. Schömann has raised objections in the *Jahrb. f. cl. Phil.*, 1875, p. 452 ff. [See Sandys' *Ath. Pol.*, 8, 13.]

[2] On the etymology of ναύκραρος cf. G. Meyer in Curtius' *Stud.*, 7, 175 ff., who rightly rejects the explanation of ναύκραροι as "householders" given by Wecklein in the *Sitzungsber. d. K. Bayr. Ak.* 1878, p. 42. In Meyer's view Ναύκραρος is compounded of ναῦς and the root κᾱρ, with metathesis κρᾱ, which appears in the verb κραίνω "fulfil." With this meaning should be compared Lex. Seguer. 283, 20: ναύκραροι· οἱ τὰς ναῦς παρασκευάζοντες καὶ τριηραρχοῦντες καὶ τῷ πολεμάρχῳ ὑποτεταγμένοι. We are expressly told that there was only one Naucraros in each Naucrary. Cf. Poll. 8, 108. Hesych. ναύκλαροι.

authorities each Naucrary had to furnish a ship and two horsemen.[1] The Naucraroi levied all the contributions from the members of their Naucrary, and disbursed all the sums necessary for that purpose.[2] To judge from a fragment of a Solonian law, a citizen's claims to the office of Naucraros depended upon the amount of his wealth. This supposition at any rate will explain how disputes could arise who among many candidates was entitled to the office of Naucraros.[3]

It is characteristic of the Solonian census classes, and at the same time in perfect accord with the political ideas of that age, *Census Classes based on Landed Estate.* that no kind of wealth except landed property was taken into account in the assessment of the classes, and therefore in the distribution of political rights also. "The agricultural Demos is the best," says Aristotle, and with justice: the landowner is most closely involved in the destiny of his country; and according to the testimony of Socrates agricultural life produces for the State the best and most patriotic citizens. Attica, however, from the nature of its soil and the configuration of the country, is but little suited for extensive agriculture; and it therefore speaks well for Solon's insight into the circumstances of the case that he made not merely the produce of agriculture, but also the revenues from tree cultivation the basis of his class system. It was obviously with a view to encourage the cultivation of the olive, that Solon, while he attempted to keep up the somewhat scanty returns from the soil by a general prohibition of exportation, made an exception in the case of olive oil, which could not all be consumed in Attica, if olive cultivation was developed to any great extent.[4]

---

[1] Cf. Poll. 8, 108: ναυκραρία δ' ἦν τέως φυλῆς δωδέκατον μέρος καὶ ναύκραροι ἦσαν δώδεκα, τέτταρες κατὰ τριττὺν ἑκάστην. τὰς δὲ εἰσφορὰς τὰς κατὰ δήμους διεχειροτόνουν οὗτοι καὶ τὰ ἐξ αὐτῶν ἀναλώματα. ναυκραρία δ' ἑκάστη δύο ἱππέας παρεῖχε καὶ ναῦν μίαν, ἀφ' ἧς ἴσως ὠνόμαστο.

[2] Cf. Arist., loc. cit., Hesych. ναύκλαροι—τινὲς δὲ ἀφ' ἑκάστης φυλῆς δώδεκα, οἵτινες ἀφ' ἑκάστης χώρας τὰς εἰσφορὰς ἐξέλεγον. That the amount to be levied by the Naucrary was computed according to the assessment of the individual members, is natural in itself, and is attested also by the comparison of the Naucrary to a Symmory. Cf. Phot., ναυκραρία—ναυκραρία μὲν ὁποῖόν τι ἡ συμμορία.

[3] The Solonian fragment reads as follows in Phot. ναυκραρία—ἐάν τις ναυκραρίας (i.e. the office of ναύκραρος) ἀμφισβητῇ. For such ἀμφισβήτησις for priesthoods, cf. Poll. 8, 90. Phot. ἡγεμονία δικαστηρίου.

[4] Arist. 7 (6), 4 = p. 182, 3 sqq. Bekker: βέλτιστος γὰρ δῆμος ὁ γεωργικός ἐστιν, ὥστε καὶ ποιεῖν ἐνδέχεται δημοκρατίαν, ὅπου ζῇ τὸ πλῆθος ἀπὸ γεωργίας ἢ νομῆς. In

This partiality in favour of the agricultural population did not prevent Solon's devising careful and energetic measures in the interest of the traders and handicraftsmen, who already existed in Attica in his day. The alteration of the system of weights and of coinage was intended to make the trade of Athens independent of Ægina, and open a new region as a market for its produce. Solon made special enactments to encourage Attic industry and handicrafts, and facilitate the settlement of foreign craftsmen at Athens. Further, those who belonged to this class were not absolutely excluded from political rights. Anyone who invested his earnings in landed property to the requisite amount, became thereby a member of the privileged classes; and that land should not be difficult to procure, was secured by the Solonian law, which prohibited the acquisition of landed property above a fixed maximum amount. Similarly the law which can be proved to have been in force in the 5th and 4th centuries prohibiting ἔγκτησις γῆς by Metoicoi, was also intended to facilitate the acquisition of land by Athenian burgesses.[1]

Trade and Manufactures.

case the enemy invade the land, the γεωργοί are eager ἀρήγειν τῇ χώρᾳ, the τεχνῖται on the other hand are willing to sacrifice the country and defend the town only: Xen., Oecon., 6, 5–7. διὰ ταῦτα δὲ καὶ εὐδοξοτάτη (so also § 10), εἶναι πρὸς τῶν πόλεων αὕτη ἡ βιοτεία (i.e. ἡ γεωργία), ὅτι καὶ πολίτας ἀρίστους καὶ εὐνουστάτους παρέχεσθαι δοκεῖ τῷ κοινῷ. After treating of agriculture, Xen., Oecon., 19, discusses ἡ τῶν δένδρων φυτεία, so far as concerns the vine, the fig, and the olive tree. Prohibition of export τῶν γιγνομένων with exception of oil: Plut., Sol., 24. State protection of the olive tree: Boeckh. 1, 60 (41) ff. Arist. 60, 2. Attica as original home of olive culture: Hdt. 5, 82. Later Pisistratos is said to have paid special attention to its encouragement: Dio Chrysost. 25, p. 181.

[1] In Diod. 9, 18 the division of the πολιτεία into Eupatridai, Georgoi and Demiourgoi is attributed to Solon, while Plut., Thes. 25 assigns it to Theseus. For this classification cf. also Poll. 8, 111. Hesych. ἀγροιῶται. Et. M. 395. εὐπατρίδαι=Lex. Seguer. 257, 7. Sol., fr. 13, 43 sqq., speaks of the classes of merchants, countrymen, and artisans. In the introduction of the new coinage Solon adopted the Euboeo-Corinthian system, with the object of obtaining Sicily and Chalkidike as markets for Athenian trade. See Köhler in the Mitth. d. dtsch. arch. Inst. in Ath., 10, 151 ff. Imhoof in the Ber. d. Berl. Ak., 1881, 656 ff. Droysen, ib., 1882, 1202. Special decrees of Solon's for the encouragement of Industry and Manufactures:—A son need not maintain his father, if his father had taught him no trade: Plut., Sol., 22. Solon granted citizenship to foreigners, πανεστίοις Ἀθήναζε μετοικιζυμένοις ἐπὶ τέχνῃ: Sol., 24. Concerning the political rights of δημιουργοί in general, Arist., Pol., 3, 4=p. 65, 6, says: διὸ παρ' ἐνίοις οὐ μετεῖχον οἱ δημιουργοὶ τὸ παλαιὸν ἀρχῶν, πρὶν δῆμον γενέσθαι τὸν ἔσχατον. Solon himself practised a trade: Arist. 11, 1. For the possibility of rising out of the class of Thetes to a

Athens.

For the appointment of magistrates (of whom we have attested as existing in Solon's time οἱ ἐννέα ἄρχοντες, οἱ ταμίαι, οἱ πωληταί, οἱ ἕνδεκα and οἱ κωλακρέται) Solon introduced a combination of election and allotment. The 9 Archons, whose method of appointment cannot have been essentially different from that of the rest, were selected in the following way: each of the 4 Phylai elected from its own numbers 10 citizens belonging to the two first census classes; then from among these 40 the 9 archons were taken by lot.[1]

Magistrates.

These 9 Archons became by Solon's legislation a Collegium or board of colleagues; at this date they must have first obtained the official title οἱ ἐννέα ἄρχοντες. This board met in the Thesmotheteion. The president was not the βασιλεύς, but the official already known before the time of Solon as ἄρχων: his position must have given him the preponderant influence on the board. The official powers of these 9 Archons were diminished by Solon to the extent that he permitted litigants to appeal to the public assembly against their legal decisions.[2]

οἱ ἐννέα ἄρχοντες.

---

higher class, see the example of Anthemion in Arist. 7, 4. Poll. 8, 131. Maximum limit of landed property: Arist., *Pol.*, 2, 7 = p. 37, 26 sqq.

[1] On the magistrates who existed in Solon's time, cf. Arist. 7, 3. On the method of appointing magistrates, cf. Arist. 8, 1: τὰς δ' ἀρχὰς ἐποίησε κληρωτὰς ἐκ προκρίτων, οὓς [ἑκάσ]τη προκρίνειε τῶν φυλῶν. προύκρινε δ' εἰς τοὺς ἐννέα ἄρχοντας ἑκάστη δέκα καὶ ⟨ἐκ⟩ τού[των ἐκλ]ήρουν· ὅθεν ἔτι διαμένει ταῖς φυλαῖς τὸ δέκα κληροῦν ἑκάστην, εἶτ' ἐκ τούτων κυαμεύειν. σημεῖον δ' ὅτι κληρωτὰς ἐποίησεν ἐκ τῶν τιμημάτων ὁ περὶ τῶν ταμιῶν νόμος, ᾧ χρώμενοι [διατελο]ῦσιν ἔτι καὶ νῦν· κελεύει γὰρ κληροῦν τοὺς ταμίας ἐκ πεντακοσιομεδίμνω[ν. Σόλ]ων μὲν οὖν οὕτως ἐνομοθέτησεν περὶ τῶν ἐννέα ἀρχόντων. From ὅθεν ἔτι δ. τ. φ. τ. δ. κλ. ἐκ. we must understand that this method of appointment was abolished for a long period and not reintroduced till the time of Eucleides. The method of appointment mentioned in Arist. 55, 62 must be this one. But in 487 one slightly different was substituted, which in turn must have been abolished afterwards. Cf. Arist. 22, 5, where the words οἱ δὲ πρότεροι πάντες ἦσαν αἱρετοί are explained by the fact that the Solonian system remained in force only a very short time because of the civil wars which followed and the domination of the Pisistratidai. That the method described in Arist. 8, 1 is not inconsistent with Arist., *Pol.*, 3, 11 = p. 76, 9 sqq., 77, 12 sqq., is correctly shown by Meyer, *Aristot. Pol. u. d. 'Αθηναίων πολιτεία*, p. 44 ff., and Niemeyer in *Jahrb. f. cl. Phil.*, 1891, p. 408.

[2] Cf. Arist. 3, 5: ἐπὶ δὲ Σόλωνος ἅπαντες εἰς τὸ θεσμοθετεῖον συνῆλθον. In Diog. L., *Sol.*, 58, it is said of Solon: καὶ πρῶτος τὴν συναγωγὴν τῶν ἐννέα ἀρχόντων ἐποίησεν εἰς τὸ συνδειπνεῖν (adopting the cj. of Hermann, *Staatsalt.*, § 138, 13 for συνειπεῖν) ὡς Ἀπολλόδωρός φησιν ἐν δευτέρῳ περὶ νομοθετῶν. Acc. to Arist. 9, 1 ἡ εἰς τὸ δικ[αστήριον] ἔφ[εσις] dates from Solon. The expression used by Aristotle, ἔφεσις, seems to necessitate the conclusion that the

Solon retained the βουλή as established by Draco, except that its 400 members were now to be chosen 100 from each Phyle, by the same method perhaps by which the 9 Archons were appointed; *i.e.* the requisite number were chosen by βουλή. lot from among a larger number of candidates elected by vote by each separate tribe. This council formed an advising body whose duty was to consider beforehand and prepare all business intended for the consideration of the Ecclesia, and to lay before the Ecclesia appropriate proposals.[1]

The council of the Areopagus, into which just as before the Archons were to enter after the expiration of their term of office, obtained again from Solon most of the powers taken from it by Draco. It retained the power which it had previously held of supervising the law and the constitution, and in addition was invested with increased judicial powers, which made it again competent to inflict fines and even death. More especially cases of homicide and attempted homicide, of arson, and of attempts to overthrow the constitution, were placed under its jurisdiction.[2]

The Council of the Areopagus.

Archons pronounced sentence, and that thereupon the litigant could appeal against the sentence if he chose, or else declare his acquiescence. The influential position of the Archon is shown by the description given us of the faction-wars which followed Solon's reforms. Cf. Arist. 13, 2: ᾧ καὶ δῆλον ὅτι μεγίστην εἶχεν δύναμιν ὁ ἄρχων· φαίνονται γὰρ αἰεὶ στασιάζοντες περὶ ταύτης τῆς ἀρχῆς. From this period certainly dates the κήρυγμα made when he entered on his office: Arist. 56, 2. That ὁ ἄρχων is here used collectively, as Gomperz, *ib.*, 31 supposes, is not very probable. The official meant is without doubt the ἄρχων ἐπώνυμος who was raised by Solon to the position of president of the board.

[1] Arist. 8, 4: [βουλ]ὴν δ' ἐποίησε τετρακοσίους, ἑκατὸν ἐξ ἑκάστης φυλῆς. That Solon's βουλή was no new creation, is shown by Arist. 4, 3. Plut., *Sol.*, 19, in the words: δευτέραν προσκατένειμε βουλὴν ἀπὸ φυλῆς ἑκάστης τεττάρων οὐσῶν ἑκατὸν ἄνδρας ἐπιλεξάμενος, οὓς προβουλεύειν ἔταξε τοῦ δήμου καὶ μηδὲν ἐᾶν ἀπροβούλευτον εἰς ἐκκλησίαν εἰσφέρεσθαι seems to be describing a new institution of Solon's; but we must remember that Plut. was writing a biography of Solon not a constitutional history of Athens, and therefore took no account of anything Draco had done. The method of appointment given in the text is attested first by the analogy of the appointment of Archons (Arist. 8, 1), and again by the method by which the 400 were nominated in 411, which was κατὰ τὰ πάτρια. Cf. Arist. 31, 1: βουλεύειν μὲν τετρακοσίους κατὰ τὰ πάτρια, τετταράκοντα ἐξ ἑκάστης ⟨τῆς⟩ φυλῆς, ἐκ προκρίτων οὓς ἂν ἕλωνται οἱ φυλέται τῶν ὑπὲρ τριάκοντα ἔτη γεγονότων.

[2] Arist. 8, 4: τὴν δὲ τῶν Ἀρεοπαγιτῶν ἔταξεν ἐ[πὶ τὸ] νομοφυλακεῖν, ὥσπερ ὑπῆρχεν καὶ πρότερον ἐπίσκοπος οὖσα τῆς πολιτείας, [καὶ] τά τε ἄλλα τὰ πλεῖστα καὶ τὰ μέγιστα τῶν πολιτ⟨ικ⟩ῶν διετήρει καὶ τοὺς ἁμαρτάνοντας ηὔθυνεν κυρία οὖσα [καὶ

The Ecclesia had been in existence since the time of Draco at any rate. The right of taking part in its proceedings was granted by Solon even to Thetes. Aristotle in the *Politics* attributes to Solon among other legislators the honour of having given to the multitude the right of electing the magistrates and of calling them to account; drawing a distinction between the rights so described and the right of actually holding office in person. This however does not say that the business of the Ecclesia was confined to these two functions. On the contrary it seems a more natural inference from the method of election of magistrates instituted by Solon, and described above, that the active power of election was exercised by the multitude not in the Ecclesia at all, but rather in the tribal assemblies of the Phylai; on the other hand the right to call magistrates to account before the Ecclesia belonged certainly to every citizen who thought himself aggrieved. Therefore the passage just quoted from Aristotle's *Politics* does not in any way prevent us from concluding that other matters came before the Ecclesia for decision.[1]

Ecclesia.

ζη]μι[οῦν] καὶ κολάζειν καὶ τὰς ἐκτίσεις ἀνέφερεν εἰς πόλιν, οὐκ ἐπιγράφουσα τὴν πρόφασι[ν τοῦ πράττ]εσθαι, καὶ τοὺς ἐπὶ καταλύσει τοῦ δήμου συνισταμένους ἔκρινεν Σόλωνος θέντ[ος] νόμον εἰσα[γγ]ελ[ίας] περὶ αὐτῶν. Plut., *Sol.*, 19, says simply: τὴν δ' ἄνω βουλὴν ἐπίσκοπον πάντων καὶ φύλακα τῶν νόμων ἐκάθισεν. Acc. to Poll. 8, 125 Solon added the court of the Ephetai to the Areopagus as a court of justice to deal with cases of homicide. On the competence of the Areopagus in this department, cf. the law quoted in Dem. 23, 22. Arist. 57, 3. Poll. 8, 117. On the composition of the Areopagus, cf. Plut., *Sol.*, 19: συστησάμενος δὲ τὴν ἐν Ἀρείῳ πάγῳ βουλὴν ἐκ τῶν κατ' ἐνιαυτὸν ἀρχόντων. Cf. Plut., *Per.*, 9.

[1] Arist. 7, 3: τοῖς δὲ τὸ θητικὸν τελοῦσιν ἐκκλησίας καὶ δικαστηρίων μετέδωκε μόνον. Apart from the passage in the doubtful 12th chap. of Bk. 2 of the *Politics* = p. 56, 29 sqq.,'ἐπεὶ Σόλων γε ἔοικε τὴν ἀναγκαιοτάτην ἀποδιδόναι τῷ δήμῳ δύναμιν, τὸ τὰς ἀρχὰς αἱρεῖσθαι καὶ εὐθύνειν· μηδὲ γὰρ τούτου κύριος ὢν ὁ δῆμος δοῦλος ἂν εἴη καὶ πολέμιος. τὰς δ' ἀρχὰς ἐκ τῶν γνωρίμων καὶ τῶν εὐπόρων κατέστησε πάσας κ.τ.λ., the passage of the *Politics* to which Arist. 7, 2 corresponds is 3, 11 = p. 76, 9 sqq.: διόπερ καὶ Σόλων καὶ τῶν ἄλλων τινὲς νομοθετῶν τάττουσιν (sc. τὸ πλῆθος) ἐπί τε τὰς ἀρχαιρεσίας καὶ τὰς εὐθύνας τῶν ἀρχόντων, ἄρχειν δὲ κατὰ μόνας οὐκ ἐῶσιν. That these εὔθυναι τῶν ἀρχόντων were nothing more than the auditing of accounts of magistrates at the end of their year of office as was customary in later times, I do not consider at all probable. I am more disposed to connect these εὔθυναι with the regulation which Aristot. 9, 1 counts among the three δημοτικώτατα of Solon's, τὸ ἐξεῖναι τῷ βουλομένῳ τιμωρ[εῖν]· ὑπὲρ τῶν ἀδικουμένων. Cf. also Plut., *Sol.*, 18. Draco granted to a burgess aggrieved by a magistrate—the context clearly shows that such is meant, and not one ill-treated by a private citizen—the right to prosecute the magistrate by

Another concession of Solon's to the Thetes was the right of taking part in the administration of Justice. For Solon instituted a great popular tribunal consisting of a fixed number of jurymen chosen by lot from among all burgesses 'Ηλιαία. over 30 years of age who offered their services. This great popular tribunal was called 'Ηλιαία, and was probably divided into a number of sections even as early as the time of Solon.[1] With regard to the judicial powers of this Heliaia we must remember, that up to the time of Solon the sentences pronounced by the Archons were final in all processes, after Solon's reforms appeal to the Heliaia was permitted. We must however hold that this right of appeal was limited to certain specified cases, because in the 4th century

Eisangelia before the Areopagus. Cf. Arist. 4, 4. Solon made a distinct advance in the direction of democracy by substituting the Ecclesia for the Areopagus. On the other hand, the right to prosecute a private individual for injustice is not a specially democratic institution,—not to mention that it must have been long in existence at Athens before this time. Therefore Solon's measure was the precursor of the later Epicheirotonia of magistrates. What other matters were subject to the decision of the Areopagus, we do not know. Schömann, *Verf.*, 53 ff., and Wachsmuth 1, 497 attribute legislative powers to the Ecclesia. Solon's own words in Arist. 12, 1: δήμῳ μὲν γὰρ ἔδωκα τόσον γέρας ὅσσον ἀπαρ[κε]ῖ,—τιμῆς οὔτ' ἀφελὼν οὔτ' ἐπορεξάμενος show that he had no very great veneration for the rights of the Demos or Ecclesia either.

[1] Arist. 7, 3: τοῖς δὲ τὸ θητικὸν τελοῦσιν ἐκκλησίας καὶ δικαστηρίων μετέδωκε μόνον. That the 'Ηλιαία was established by Solon follows from the wording of a Solonian law preserved in Lys. 10, 16, the authenticity of which there is no reason to doubt: δεδέσθαι δ' ἐν τῇ ποδοκάκκῃ ἡμέρας πέντε τὸν πόδα, ἐὰν προστιμήσῃ ἡ ἡλιαία. That the jurymen were chosen by lot from among citizens who volunteered their services, I infer from the fact that this was obviously the method practised at the time when payment for the jurymen was introduced by Pericles. Cf. Arist. 27, 5: ἀφ' ὧν (through the introduction of μισθοφορὰ) αἰτιῶνταί τινες χεῖρω γενέσθαι (sc. τὰ δικαστήρια), κληρουμένων ἐπιμελῶς ἀεὶ μᾶλλον τῶν τυχόντων ἢ τῶν ἐπιεικῶν ἀνθρώπων. The ἡλιαία appears as a great board of dicasts in C.I.A., IV. 27a. (Dittenb. 10. Hicks 28). Cf. Antiph., *de Chor.*, 21. Demad. περὶ δωδεκαετίας, *fr.* 52 in Hermes 13, 494. For the position of the ἡλιαία building cf. Eustath. on *Od.*, 1430, 22: ἦν . . . ἀγορὰ Κερκώπων πλησίον ἡλιαίας. Wachsmuth 1, 496; 2, 1, 359. That there was a distinction between the Heliaia and the Demos is clearly shown by Plut., when in his *Comp. of Solon and Poplicola*, 2, he says of the latter: καὶ γὰρ ἀρχόντων καταστάσεως κυρίους ἐποίησε τοὺς πολλοὺς καὶ τοῖς φεύγουσι δίκην ἐπικαλεῖσθαι τὸν δῆμον, ὥσπερ ὁ Σόλων τοὺς δικαστάς, ἔδωκεν. It is uncertain whether Solon at once divided the Heliaia into sections. Aristot. in the passage quoted above speaks of δικαστήρια, but in c. 9, 2 of δικαστήριον. The Solonian statute quoted above designates the Heliaia as a court of justice.

the magistrates still possessed the power to inflict fines up to a maximum amount specified by law, and this appears to be a survival of an original power of delivering final judicial sentences.[1] Moreover the right of participating in the administration of justice granted to the Thetes by Solon was at that date more important theoretically than in actual practice; for so long as the jurymen were unpaid, it was only in exceptional cases that Thetes were willing or able to devote their time to the tedious business of jurisdiction.

While Solon retained the Draconian laws concerning homicide, with the modifications explained above, he abolished all the rest of Draco's statutes, and secured complete Epitimia to all who had been condemned under them, with but few exceptions. The Draconian laws were replaced by the code of statutes drawn up by Solon, and this code remained the standard of Athenian legal obligations for all departments of public and private life. The Solonian laws were written out on square-based pyramidal pillars, which were called ἄξονες because they were mounted so as to admit of being turned round, and κύρβεις, because of their shape. These were placed in the στοὰ βασίλειος. The 9 Archons had to take an oath at their entry upon office that they would observe the laws, and would dedicate a golden statue at Delphi if they transgressed.[2]

Solon's Laws.

---

[1] Arist. 9, 1: τρίτον δὲ, ⟨ᾧ⟩ μάλιστά φασιν ἰσχυκέναι τὸ πλῆθος, ἡ εἰς τὸ δικ[αστήριον] ἔφ[εσις]. κύριος γὰρ ὢν ὁ δῆμος τῆς ψήφου κύριος γίγνεται τῆς πολιτείας κ.τ.λ. Plut., *Sol.*, 18: ὃ (τὸ δικάζειν) κατ' ἀρχὰς μὲν οὐδέν, ὕστερον δὲ παμμέγεθες ἐφάνη· τὰ γὰρ πλεῖστα τῶν διαφόρων ἐνέπιπτεν εἰς τοὺς δικαστάς. καὶ γὰρ ὅσα ταῖς ἀρχαῖς ἔταξε κρίνειν, ὁμοίως καὶ περὶ ἐκείνων εἰς τὸ δικαστήριον ἐφέσεις ἔδωκε τοῖς βουλομένοις κ.τ.ἀ. Cf. also Aristot., *Pol.*, 2, 12 = p. 56, 8 sqq. Bekker, on the judicial institutions of Solon. The right of appeal to the Heliaia is attested also by Plut., *Comp. of Sol. and Popl.*, 2: καὶ τοῖς φεύγουσι δίκην ἐπικαλεῖσθαι τὸν δῆμον, ὥσπερ ὁ Σόλων τοὺς δικαστάς, ἔδωκε. Arist. 8, 5 says of the powers of the magistrates under the earliest form of constitution: κύριοι δ' ἦσαν καὶ τὰς δίκας αὐτοτελεῖς [κρίν]ειν καὶ οὐχ ὥσπερ νῦν προανακρίνειν. Suid. ἀρχων = Lex. Seguer. 449, 24 connects this limitation of power to ἀνακρίνειν with the legislation of Solon, obviously basing the statement on the words of Aristotle 3, 5.

[2] The Solonian law of Epitimia, Plut., *Sol.*, 19. Solon describes his own work as lawgiver in the words: θεσμοὺς δ' ὁμοίως τῷ κακῷ τε κἀγαθῷ,— εὐθεῖαν εἰς ἕκαστον ἁρμόσας δίκην,—ἔγραψα. Cf. Arist., 12, 4. Arist., 7, 1, says: πολιτείαν δὲ κατέστησε καὶ νόμους ἔθηκεν ἄλλους, τοῖς δὲ Δράκοντος θεσμοῖς ἐπαύσαντο χρώμενοι πλὴν τῶν φονικῶν. ἀναγράψαντες δὲ τοὺς νόμους εἰς τοὺς κύρβεις ἔστησαν ἐν τῇ στοᾷ τῇ βασιλείῳ καὶ ὤμοσαν χρήσεσθαι πάντες. I now consider it wrong

The auspices under which Solon had brought about his reforms seemed to promise but little permanency for his new constitution. The poor were disappointed because there had been no general redistribution of wealth; the rich were discontented because they considered themselves unjustly robbed of their political rights and of their social position. Solon came to the conclusion that the discontented elements would most readily acquiesce in the new *régime* if he himself left the country, and so deprived them of all prospect of any peaceable alteration in the existing state of affairs. He therefore, in perfect self-denial, started upon a long course of travels, which kept him for ten years far away from his fatherland.[1] *Discontent at Athens.*

Solon's hopes, however, were doomed to disappointment. The struggle which broke out a few years after his departure was carried on, it appears, among the Eupatrid Hetairiai or factions, and its object was the possession of the office of first Archon. Solon's reforms had made this the most influential post in the State, and the Eupatrid Hetairiai were therefore eager to secure it for their own leaders, so as to get the control of the State into their own hands. As a result of these dissensions, the office of senior Archon was vacant altogether in the fifth year after Solon's departure, and again in the tenth. After this Damasias became senior Archon, and kept *Damasias. Constitutional Changes.*

---

to distinguish ἄξονες from κύρβεις as made of different materials, as Wachsmuth does in his *St. Ath.*, 1, 585, 1. Both were made of wood. Harp, ἄξονι, Plut., *Sol.*, 25 and Cratinus *ap.* Plut., *Sol.*, ib. The wood decayed in course of time, and for that reason the laws were copied out again at a later date, and preserved in the archives. Cf. C.I.A., 1, 61. [Hicks, 59. Cf. Dem. in Macart., 1069.] The λείψανα of the wooden originals were put in the Prytaneion: Harp. ἄξονι; Plut., *Sol.*, 25; Paus., 1, 18, 3. In 409 B.C. the originals had already disappeared from the στοὰ βασίλειος, otherwise there would have been no need for the resolution recorded in C.I.A., 1, 61. The statement of Anaximenes *ap.* Harp., ὁ κάτωθεν νόμος, that Ephialtes removed the ἄξονες and κύρβεις from the Acropolis to the Bouleuterion and the Agora, is, according to Köhler in Herm. 6, 98, 2, based on a false interpretation of Dem. 23, 28. Wachsmuth, *ib.*, however, disputes this. The question scarcely admits of a certain solution. C.I.A., 1, 61, shows that they were no longer there in 409 B.C. For the Archons' oath cf. Arist., 7, 1: οἱ δ' ἐννέα ἄρχοντες ὀμνύντες πρὸς τῷ λίθῳ κατεφάτιζον ἀναθήσειν ἀνδριάντα χρυσοῦν, ἐάν τινα παραβῶσιν τῶν νόμων· ὅθεν ἔτι καὶ νῦν οὕτως ὀμνύουσι. Cf. Plut., *Sol.*, 25. For the significance of this oath see below.

[1] The Athenians not satisfied with Solon's institutions: cf. Arist., 11, 12; Solon's travels, Arist., 11, 1.

possession of office for more than two years, until he was deposed by force. Thereupon an attempt was made to modify the constitution so as to render such an intolerable state of affairs impossible. In place of the board of nine Archons, in which the first or senior Archon had the preponderating influence, it was resolved to appoint ten Archons theoretically equal in power, five from among the Eupatrids, three from the agricultural class, 2 from the artisans. The measure was a compromise made by the Eupatrids with the well-to-do farmers and artisans, in order to obtain the help of the latter in overthrowing Damasias. We do not know that this board of ten maintained its existence for any length of time; but it was at any rate a departure from Solon's constitution.[1] After this time the relation of the several classes to the Solonian constitution still continued to be the decisive factor in the grouping of political factions, which assumed more and more a local character. First came the party formed by those rich Eupatrids who were discontented with the new régime. These owned land in the fruitful plain of Athens, and were therefore called πεδιακοί. Their leader at that moment was Lycurgos, and their political object was the establishment of an oligarchy.[2]

Local Factions.

---

[1] The text is based on Arist. 13, 1: Σόλωνος δ' ἀποδημήσαντος ἔτι τῆς πόλεως τεταραγμένης, ἐπὶ μὲν ἔτη τέτταρα διῆγον ἐν ἡσυχίᾳ· τῷ δὲ πέμπτῳ μετὰ τὴν Σόλωνος ἀρχὴν οὐ κατέστησαν ἄρχοντα διὰ τὴν στάσιν, καὶ πάλιν ἔτει πέμπτῳ ⟨διὰ⟩ τὴν αὐτὴν αἰτίαν ἀναρχίαν ἐποίησαν. μετὰ δὲ ταῦτα διὰ τῶν αὐτῶν χρόνων Δ[α]υα[σίας α]ἱρεθεὶς ἄρχων ἔτη δύο καὶ δύο μῆνας ἦρξεν, ἕως ἐξηλάθη βίᾳ τῆς ἀρχῆς. εἶτ' ἔδοξεν αὐτοῖς διὰ τὸ στασιάζειν ἄρχοντας ἑλέσθαι δέκα, πέντε μὲν εὐπατριδῶν, τρεῖς δ' ἀ[γρ]οίκων, δύο δὲ δημιουργῶν, καὶ οὗτοι τὸν μετὰ Δαμασίαν ἦρξαν ἐνιαυτόν. ᾧ καὶ δῆλον ὅτι μεγίστην εἶχε δύναμιν ὁ ἄρχων· φαίνονται γὰρ ἀεὶ στασιάζοντες περὶ ταύτης τῆς ἀρχῆς. The theory of Landwehr, in the 5th Suppl. vol. of *Phil.*, 105 ff., and Diels, in the *Abh. d. Berl. Ak.*, 1885, 10 ff., that by Damasias is meant the second Archon of that name known to us, has now been confirmed by Aristotle. Diels, *ib.*, 11, had fixed his year of office at 586/5, or, at any rate, between 590 and 580, which agrees with Aristotle. That the new arrangement only lasted one year, as Busolt supposed in his *griech. Gesch.*, 1, 544, does not necessarily follow from the text of Aristotle. See also Diels, *ib.*, 19. Nor does Aristotle give any justification for the theory that Damasias obtained support as tyrannos from the non-Eupatrid classes, as Diels, *ib.*, 13 ff., and Holzapfel, *Beitr. z. griech. Gesch.*, 14 ff., 1888, suppose. Arist., 13, 3, gives τὴν πρὸς ἀλλήλους φιλονικίαν as a sign of the long-continued νοσεῖν τὰ πρὸς ἑαυτούς. I take this as referring to Eupatrid Hetairiai, such as we meet with in the history of Cleisthenes (cf. Arist., 20, 1); they were analogous to the ξυνωμοσίαι ἐπ' ἀρχαῖς of the period of the Peloponnesian war: Thuc., 8, 54.

[2] Arist. 13, 3 proceeds as follows: ὅλως δὲ διετέλουν νοσοῦντες τὰ πρὸς ἑαυτούς, οἱ μὲν ἀρχὴν καὶ πρόφασιν ἔχοντες τὴν τῶν χρεῶν ἀποκοπὴν (συνεβεβήκει

The faction of the Alcmeonidai found its chief supporters among the παράλιοι, the inhabitants of those coast plains which were most suitable for cultivation; for in those districts Solon's reforms had created a free population of peasants or small landowners. The leader of the Alcmeonidai and of the παράλιοι was Megacles; their political programme was the maintenance of the Solonian constitution.[1] Lastly came a third faction, led by Peisistratos, who from the first had the tyrannis in view as the goal of his efforts. With him were leagued all sections of the community who hoped to profit by a subversion of the existing constitution, all who had been reduced to poverty and distress by Solon's remission of debts, and all those who were apprehensive of losing the political rights to which their birth gave them but a questionable title. Further, since Peisistratos seemed to be more democratic and friendly to the common people than the other leading men, he was supported by the Diacria also, *i.e.* by the mountain districts of North Attica, and by the hilly coast country to the south as far as Brauron; for these parts were too mountainous to afford room for a middle class of farmers. Such inhabitants as there were managed with difficulty to eke out a penurious existence. Ever since the time of Solon's legislation these people had indulged in hopes of a general redistribution of property, and Peisistratos contrived to encourage these restless expectations well enough to be able to calculate on their support.[2]

γὰρ αὐτοῖς γεγονέναι πένησιν), οἱ δὲ τῇ πολιτείᾳ δυσχεραίνοντες διὰ τὸ μεγάλην γεγονέναι μεταβολήν, ἔνιοι δὲ διὰ [τὴν] πρὸς ἀλλήλους φιλονικίαν· ἦσαν [δὲ] αἱ στάσεις τρεῖς· μία μὲν τῶν παραλίων, ὧν προειστήκει Μεγακλῆς ὁ Ἀλκμέωνος, οἵπερ ἐδόκουν μάλιστα διώκειν τὴν μέσην πολιτείαν. ἄλλη δὲ τῶν πεδια[κῶν], οἱ τὴν ὀλιγαρχίαν ἐζήτουν· ἡγεῖτο δ' αὐτῶν Λυκοῦργος. Οἱ τῇ πολιτείᾳ δυσχεραίνοντες διὰ τὸ μ. γ. μεταβολήν formed without doubt the nucleus of the πεδιακοί, who, acc. to Arist., *Pol.*, 8 (5), 5=p. 203, 21 ff., are identical with the πλούσιοι. Arist., 13, 5, says of the party divisions: εἶχον δ' ἕκαστοι τὰς ἐπωνυμίας ἀπὸ τῶν τόπων, ἐν οἷς ἐγεώργουν; cf. also Plut., *Sol.*, 13 and 29 (where, acc. to Diels' (*ib.*, 19 ff.) more probable theory, 13 is a dittography of 29), and Hdt. 1, 59.

[1] Arist., 13, 4: μία μὲν τῶν παραλίων, ὧν προειστήκει Μεγακλῆς ὁ Ἀλκμέωνος, οἵπερ ἐδόκουν μάλιστα διώκειν τὴν μέσην πολιτείαν. The μέση πολιτεία is the constitution of Solon, who, according to Arist. 5, 3, belonged τῇ οὐσίᾳ καὶ τοῖς πράγμασι τῶν μέσων. Thuc. 2, 55 includes in the πάραλος or παραλία γῆ the coast districts facing the Peloponnesus, as well as those towards Euboia and Andros.

[2] Arist. 13, 4: τρίτη δ' ἡ τῶν διακρίων, ἐφ' ᾗ τεταγμένος ἦν Πεισίστρατος, δημοτικώτατος εἶναι δοκῶν. προσεκεκόσμηντο δὲ τούτοις οἵ τε ἀφῃρημένοι τὰ χρέα διὰ τὴν ἀπορίαν (these are the same of whom it is said, 13, 3: οἱ μὲν ἀρχὴν καὶ πρόφασιν ἔχοντες τὴν τῶν χρεῶν ἀποκοπήν, συνεβεβήκει γὰρ αὐτοῖς γεγονέναι πένησιν)

With the help of these classes Peisistratos established himself as Tyrannos in 561. He was twice driven out of Attica by his combined opponents, and twice recovered the supremacy, which, after his death, about 528/7 B.C., his sons maintained until 511/10.[1] The rule of the Peisistratidai, which was a domination of a family rather than a personal autocracy, is described as gentle and law-abiding in the main, with the exception of the last years of Hippias. They observed the established laws, taking care only that one of their family always had a place among the chief magistrates of the State. We are told that Peisistratos, accused of murder, pleaded in his own defence before the Areopagus. He took special care of the interests of the agricultural population, so that they might possess satisfactory means of obtaining a livelihood, and therefore remain contented with the existing *régime* and abstain from interfering in politics. Again, in order that the country population might not be obliged to come up to Athens to settle their legal disputes, Peisistratos instituted κατὰ δήμους δικασταί, who made circuits through the country, and settled the less important cases on the spot. The taxes levied by the Peisistratidai consisted of a fixed percentage on the produce of the harvest.[2]

The Peisistratidai

καὶ οἱ τῷ γένει μὴ καθαροὶ διὰ τὸν φόβον· σημεῖον δ', ὅτι μετὰ τὴν [τῶν] τυράννων κατάλυσιν ἐποίησαν διαψηφισμόν, ὡς πολλῶν κοινωνούντων τῆς πολιτείας οὐ προσῆκον. Hdt., 1, 59, says of Peisistratos: καταφρονήσας (with designs upon) τὴν τυραννίδα ἤγειρε τρίτην στάσιν, συλλέξας δὲ στασιώτας καὶ τῷ λόγῳ τῶν ὑπερακρίων προστὰς μηχανᾶται τοιάδε κ.τ.λ. Plut., *Sol.*, 29, says of the Diacrioi: ἐν οἷς ἦν ὁ θητικὸς ὄχλος καὶ μάλιστα τοῖς πλουσίοις ἀχθόμενος. The extent of the Diacria is given in Hesych. Διακριεῖς as ἡ ἀπὸ Πάρνηθος ἕως Βραυρῶνος, sc. χώρα.

[1] For the tyrannis of the Peisistratidai cf. Hdt. 1, 59; Plut., *Sol.*, 80; Arist., *Pol.*, 8 (5), 5 = p. 208, 18 sqq.; Arist., 'Ἀθ. π., 14–19. On the chronological inconsistency between the two passages of Arist., which however can supply no argument against the authenticity of the 'Ἀθ. π., see Peter Meyer, *Arist. Pol. and the* 'Ἀθ. π., pp. 48/9; Gomperz, *d. Schrift v. Staatswesen d. Ath. u. ihr neuester Beurtheiler*, 1891, p. 21 ff. For the chronology of the Peisistratidai cf. Toepffer, *quæstiones Peisistrateæ*, 115 ff., 1886; Bauer, *Lit. u. hist. Forsch. z. Arist.* 'Ἀθ. π., 50 ff. The statements in the text seem fairly certain.

[2] The rule of the Peisistratidai, Arist. 16; Thuc. 6, 54; Hdt. 1, 59; Plut., *Sol.*, 31. Always one of them ἐν ταῖς ἀρχαῖς: Thuc. 6, 54. That at that date the magistracies had again been made elective follows from the words οἱ δὲ πρότεροι πάντες ἦσαν αἱρετοί, in Arist. 22, 5, defined more accurately by the preceding words, μετὰ τὴν τυραννίδα. Government according to the laws: Thuc., *ib.*; Arist. 16, 8. Peisistratos before the Areopagus: Arist. 16, 8, 9; Aristot., *Pol.*, 8 (5), 12 = p. 229, 32. Patronising of the agricul-

All the leading families of Athens who had not become adherents of the Peisistratidai had been driven into exile. The attempt they made under the leadership of the Alcmeonidai to expel the Peisistratidai was frustrated by their defeat at Leipsydrion. But soon afterwards the Alcmeonidai won over to their side the priests of Delphi, who induced the Lacedæmonians to undertake the task of deposing the despots. The first expedition of the Lacedæmonians was unsuccessful, but a second, led by Cleomenes I., and aided by the Athenian exiles, effected its object in 511.¹ *Overthrow of the Peisistratidai.*

Immediately after the expulsion of the Peisistratidai a fierce struggle for supremacy broke out between the returned exiles, led by the Alcmeonid Cleisthenes, and the old adherents of the Peisistratidai, led by Isagoras. Cleisthenes was overpowered, and thereupon put himself at the head of the democracy. *Cleisthenes.*

This reform of the constitution introduced in Isagoras' archonship in 508 was generally accepted, after Isagoras' attempted reaction with Lacedæmonian help had failed in consequence of the opposition of the Athenian people, and Cleisthenes, who had left Athens,

---

tural population: Arist. 16, 2 sqq. Cauer, in his treatise, *Hat Arist. die Schrift v. Staate d. Ath. geschrieben?* pp. 64/5, has given Peisistratos credit, which he scarcely deserved, for services in this direction. Οἱ κατὰ δήμους δικασταί: Arist., 16, 5. An εἰκοστὴ τῶν γιγνομένων is attested by Thuc. 6, 54; a δεκάτη ἀπὸ τῶν γιγνομένων by Arist. 16, 4; a δεκάτη τῶν γεωργουμένων by Zenob. 4, 76.

¹ Arist. 16, 9: ἐβούλοντο γὰρ καὶ τῶν γνωρίμων καὶ τῶν [δημο]τικῶν οἱ πολλοί· τοὺς μὲν γὰρ ταῖς ὁμιλίαις, τοὺς δὲ ταῖς εἰς τὰ ἴδια βοηθείαις προσ[ή]γετο καὶ πρὸς ἀμφοτέρους ἐπεφύκει καλῶς. Miltiades also was opposed to Peisistratos, and for that reason retired to the Chersonnesus. Cf. Hdt. 6, 35. Οἱ φυγάδες, ὧν οἱ Ἀλκμεωνίδαι προεϊστήκεσαν Arist. 19, 3 calls them, and the Scolion styles those who fell at Leipsydrion εὐπατρίδας. Exiles at Leipsydrion: Arist. 19, 3; Hdt. 5, 62; the Scolion in Arist. 19, 3, and Athen. 15, 695 E. Behaviour of the Delphian priesthood: Hdt. 5, 63; Arist. 19, 4. According to Arist. 19, 4, with which Philoch., *fr.* 70 (Müller, *fr. hist. gr.*, 1, 395), agrees, the Alcmeonidai undertook the repair of the Delphian temple. By this means they obtained possession of large resources, which they employed in expelling the Peisistratidai, then built the temple afterwards. According to Hdt. 5, 62, they won the favour of the Delphian priests by repairing the temple, and the priests thereupon supported their interests. This temple-building cannot be the same as that which, according to Hdt. 2, 180, took place during the rule of Amasis. According to Paus. 10, 5, 13, the temple of Delphi was burnt down in 548. For the expulsion of the Peisistratidai cf. Hdt. 5, 63 sqq.; Thuc. 6, 59; Arist. 19.

had returned with the other exiles.¹ Our knowledge of these reforms of Cleisthenes is very defective. We know that the or-
Extension of the Franchise. ganization of the Athenian citizen-body, as we find it in the 5th and 4th centuries, was his work. Cleisthenes made the constitution more democratic; he admitted to citizenship all free inhabitants of Attica, not only those Athenians who until then had not been in possession of full citizenship, but also the strangers domiciled in Athens, and those slaves, who by emancipation had attained the standing of Metoicoi.²

With this extension of the franchise Cleisthenes combined a new political arrangement of the citizens. The object of this was to break
New Phylai and Demes. up the connexion of old-established local interests, by which the old local Phylai had been governed, and to bring the political antagonisms which in earlier days were bound

---

¹ Isagoras is described by Arist. 20, 1 as φίλος τῶν τυράννων, and the same sentiments must have been entertained by the Hetairiai to whom Cleisthenes, according to Arist., succumbed. The contest between Isagoras and Cleisthenes was at first a mere contest περὶ δυνάμιος, Hdt. 5, 66. It was only when Cleisthenes was beaten, when, that is, Isagoras had been elected Archon, that he won the Demos to his side, ἀποδιδοὺς τῷ πλήθει τὴν πολιτείαν, Arist. 20, 1. The reform of the constitution was carried out ἐπὶ Ἰσαγόρου ἄρχοντος (Arist. 21, 1), i.e. 508. Marm. Par. 46, Dionys. Hal. 1, 74; 5, 1. On the events described in the text, cf. Hdt. 5, 66, 69 ff.; Thuc. 1, 126; Arist. 20.

² Arist. 20, 1 describes the result of Cleisthenes' reforms by the words, ἀποδιδοὺς τῷ πλήθει τὴν π. The same expression is used Arist. 4, 2 in describing the constitution of Draco, ἀπεδέδοτο μὲν ἡ πολιτεία τοῖς ὅπλα παρεχομένοις. It is true Solon had (Arist. 7, 3) given a share ἐκκλησίας καὶ δικαστηρίων τοῖς τὸ θητικὸν τελοῦσιν, but in the disturbances which followed Solon's legislation and under the rule of the Pisistratids the Thetes hardly had any rights at all. It is not probable that they were included in the four old Phylai. Arist. 21, 2 says πρῶτον μὲν οὖν συνένειμε πάντας εἰς δέκα φυλὰς ἀντὶ τῶν τεττάρων, ἀναμεῖξαι βουλόμενος, ὅπως μετάσχωσι πλείους τῆς πολιτείας : the ἀναμεῖξαι βουλόμενος gives the reason for the establishment of the ten Phylai in place of the previous four, but the final clause describes the object which Cleisthenes had in view when he included πάντας in the Phylai. Not all then can have been enrolled in the Phylai before this. It seems scarcely probable that this inclusion ought to be limited to strangers and freed slaves, on the strength of Arist., *Pol.*, 3, 2, p. 61, 9 ff. οἷον Ἀθήνησιν ἐποίησε Κλεισθένης μετὰ τὴν τῶν τυράννων ἐκβολήν· πολλοὺς γὰρ ἐφυλέτευσε ξένους καὶ δούλους μετοίκους. Such a limited extension of the franchise could hardly be called ἀποδιδόναι τῷ πλήθει τὴν πολιτείαν. Peter Meyer, *des Arist. Polit. u. d. Ἀθ. πολ.*, p. 50, makes the final clause depend on ἀναμεῖξαι βουλόμενος. But how this intermingling was to make more people take a real share in the government is incomprehensible, for the relations of dependence, where they did exist, remained in the new Phylai as much as in the old. On the paraphrase of the passage in Aristotle's *Politics* given in the text, see Bernay's *d. herakleit. Briefe*, 155.

up with the triple division of the country to a peaceable settlement in each of the ten new Phylai. So far from following the example of Solon in artificially creating 48 Naucraries, Cleisthenes in this purely political arrangement of the land and the citizens proceeded on the basis of the local townships or villages which had arisen in the course of natural historical development. To these he gave official names, and made them into independent unities under the style of δῆμοι, each with a δήμαρχος at its head.[1] The Demes thus formed were grouped by Cleisthenes into thirty local and contiguous τριττύες. The number of demes assigned to one τριττύς varied with their size. Ten Trittyes were formed from the districts of the plain of Athens, 10 from those of the coast, 10 from those of the Mesogaia, which beyond a doubt is identical with the Diacria. From each of these three divisions, each of 10 Trittyes, he assigned by lot one Trittys to each φυλή, the largest unit in this system of organization. Thus each Phyle formed was made up of three Trittyes, one in each

Τριττύες.

---

[1] For the object of the new arrangement see Arist. 21, 2: πρῶτον μὲν οὖν συνένειμε πάντας εἰς δέκα φυλὰς ἀντὶ τῶν τεττάρων, ἀναμεῖξαι βουλόμενος, ὅπως μετάσχωσι πλείους τῆς πολιτείας.—διὰ τοῦτο δὲ οὐκ εἰς δώδεκα φυλὰς συνέταξεν, [ὅπως α]ὐτῷ -μὴ συμβαίνῃ μερίζειν κατὰ τὰς προϋπαρχούσας τριττῦς· ἦσαν γὰρ ἐκ δ' φυλῶν δώδεκα τριττύες ὥστ' οὐ [συνέ]πιπτεν ἀναμίσγεσθαι τὸ πλῆθος. On the institution of the demes see Arist. 21, 5: κατέστησε δὲ καὶ δημάρχους τὴν αὐτὴν ἔχοντας ἐπιμέλειαν τοῖς πρότερον ναυκράροις· καὶ γὰρ τοὺς δήμους ἀντὶ τῶν ναυκραριῶν ἐποίησεν. προσηγόρευσε δὲ τῶν δήμων τοὺς μὲν ἀπὸ τῶν τόπων, τοὺς δὲ ἀπὸ τῶν κτισάντων· οὐ γὰρ ἅπαντες ὑπῆρχον ἐν τοῖς τόποις. The pre-Cleisthenic existence of the Attic Demes appears from what Plat., *Hipparch.*, 228/9, says as to Hipparchos' erection of Hermai as finger-posts. Cf. Wachsmuth, *d. St. Athen*, 1, 498, 3. Moreover the villages and hamlets without doubt had names before Cleisthenes; he only gave them official recognition. On the origin of these names cf. Et. M. 327, 33 ff. That Cleisthenes originally established 100 Demes (though Strab. 396 gives 174 as the number of the Attic Demes, and the Demes we know outnumber 100) appears to be nevertheless the meaning of Hdt. 5, 69: τὰς φυλὰς μετωνόμασε καὶ ἐποίησε πλεῦνας ἐξ ἐλασσόνων· δέκα δὲ δὴ φυλάρχους ἀντὶ τεσσέρων ἐποίησε, δέκα δὲ καὶ τοὺς δήμους κατένειμε εἰς τὰς φυλάς. This is confirmed, it has been believed, by Herodian π. μ. λέξ., pp. 17, 8, Ἀραφὴν εἷς τῶν ἑκατὸν ἡρώων. Wachsmuth, *d. St. Athen*, 2, 1, 248, 1. Sauppe, *de dem. urb.,* 5; Landwehr in the 5th Suppl. vol. of the *Phil.*, 161 ff., attacks this. Perhaps the 100 ἥρωες are to be explained from Arist. 21, 6: ταῖς δὲ φυλαῖς ἐποίησεν ἐπωνύμους ἐκ τῶν προκριθέντων ἑκατὸν ἀρχηγετῶν, οὓς ἀνεῖλεν ἡ Πυθία δέκα. Cf. Poll. 8, 110. The notice of Cleidemos ap. Phot., ναυκραρία: ὁ Κλείδημος ἐν τῇ τρίτῃ φησίν, ὅτι Κλεισθένους δέκα φυλὰς ποιήσαντος ἀντὶ τῶν τεττάρων συνέβη καὶ εἰς πεντήκοντα μέρη διαταγῆναι· αὐτοὺς δὲ ἐκάλουν ναυκραρίας perhaps is due to a confusion with the 30 τριττύες.

district.¹ By constituting the Demes independent communities and subdivisions of the State, he bound together the members of the several demes, making them feel personally united; henceforth every citizen was officially designated as member of some particular Deme, and all official distinction between old and new burgesses disappeared.²

Another reform of Cleisthenes was the supplementing and extension of the old arrangement of the Phratries. This was rendered necessary by the creation of so many new citizens.³ Cleisthenes formed from the new citizens a certain number of θίασοι or religious societies; in so doing perhaps he recognised as θίασοι some private associations of this kind already in existence. These θίασοι had the same importance for the new citizens as τὰ καλούμενα γένη for the old.⁴ While the old citizens remained in the Phratries, to which they had previously belonged, the θίασοι of the new citizens were, it appears, arranged within the old Phratries already existing, or in other cases new Phratries were formed by a union of a certain number of θίασοι. In doing this Cleisthenes naturally proceeded in such a manner

New Arrangement of the Phratries.

---

¹ Arist. 21, 4 : διένειμε δὲ καὶ τὴν χώραν κατὰ δήμους τριάκοντα μέρη, δέκα μὲν τῶν περὶ τὸ ἄστυ, δέκα δὲ τῆς παραλίας, δέκα δὲ τῆς μεσογείου, καὶ ταύτας ἐπονομάσας τριττῦς, ἐκλήρωσεν τρεῖς εἰς τὴν φυλὴν ἑκάστην, ὅπως ἑκάστη μετέχῃ πάντων τῶν τόπων.

² Arist. 21, 4 : καὶ δημότας ἐποίησεν ἀλλήλων τοὺς οἰκοῦντας ἐν ἑκάστῳ τῶν δήμων, ἵνα μὴ πατρόθεν προσαγορεύοντες ἐξελέγχωσιν τοὺς νεοπολίτας, ἀλλὰ τῶν δήμων ἀναγορεύωσιν· ὅθεν καὶ καλοῦσιν Ἀθηναῖοι σφᾶς αὐτοὺς τῶν δήμων. In Aristotle's times the Athenians called themselves πατρόθεν and by the Deme to which they belonged. The πατρόθεν in this place, if it is not struck out, must therefore have a different sense from that it usually bears. I understand by it that the Athenians till Cleisthenes' time called themselves by their family names, e.g. Κλεισθένης ὁ Ἀλκμεωνίδης.

³ Arist., Pol., 7(6)4 = p. 184, 30 ff. : ἔτι δὲ καὶ τὰ τοιαῦτα κατασκευάσματα χρήσιμα πρὸς τὴν δημοκρατίαν τὴν τοιαύτην, οἷς Κλεισθένης τε Ἀθήνησιν ἐχρήσατο βουλόμενος αὐξῆσαι τὴν δημοκρατίαν καὶ περὶ Κυρήνην οἱ τὸν δῆμον καθιστάντες· φυλαί τε γὰρ ἕτεραι ποιητέαι πλείους καὶ φρατρίαι καὶ τὰ τῶν ἰδίων ἱερῶν συνακτέον εἰς ὀλίγα καὶ κοινά. This is not contradicted by Arist. 21, 6 : τὰ δὲ γένη καὶ τὰς φρατρίας καὶ τὰς ἱερωσύνας εἴασεν ἔχειν ἑκάστους κατὰ τὰ πάτρια. This has been rightly emphasized by Peter Meyer, de Aristot. Polit. u. die Ἀθ. πολ., p. 51 ff., and Niemeyer in the Jahrb. f. cl. Phil., 1891, p. 409.

⁴ The actual evidence that the Phratria was divided into a number of θίασοι, is supplied for the age after Eucleides by the decree of the Phratria Demotionidai, most easily accessible, in a complete form, in Sauppe, de phratriis Att., II. p. 3 ff., Ind. schol. Goett., 1890/1, the first half in C.I.A., II. 811b, the second in Berl. phil. Wochenschr., 1889, 225 ff.

that as far as possible all members of any one particular Deme, so far as they did not already belong to an old Phratria, were attached to the same Phratria, so that the majority of the members of a Deme or of several demes were united in one and the same Phratria.[1] The members of the θίασοι, who were also called ὀργεῶνες, had citizen rights now just as much as the members of the γένη, and the Phrateres were bound henceforth to receive the former no less than the latter into the Phratria.[2]

---

[1] The θίασος to which Aeschines' family belonged was, it appears, incorporated into an old Phratria. I infer this from his words *de falsa leg.*, 147; εἶναι δ' ἐκ φρατρίας τὸ γένος, ἧ τῶν αὐτῶν βωμῶν 'Ετεοβουτάδαις μετέχει. The Phratria Demotionidai, in whose decree only θίασοι are spoken of, was a new Phratria, or one in which τὰ καλούμενα γένη had died out. R. Schoell in the *Sitzungsber. d. bayr. Ak.*, 1889, 2, p. 22, says of Cleisthenes' new arrangement of the Phratries: "It is not the family or γένος, but the deme which is the basis of the Phratria." This is so far right that Cleisthenes as far as possible assigned whole Demes to the Phratries. Thus in all likelihood Myrrhinus was the centre of the Phratria Dyaleis, for the φράτριον was there. Cf. C.I.A., II. 600. Similarly Dekelea was the centre of the Phratria Demotionidai. See the last note. But other Demes also belonged to this Phratria, for otherwise the direction l. 115 ff., ὅπως δ' ἂν εἰδῶσι οἱ φράτερες τοὺς μέλλοντας εἰσάγεσθαι, ἀπογράφεσθαι τῷ πρώτῳ ἔτει ἢ ᾧ ἂν τὸ κουρεῖον ἄγει τὸ ὄνομα πατρόθεν καὶ τοῦ δήμου κ.τ.ἀ., would be as far as the last words are concerned superfluous. Moreover the Phratriarch is from Οἶκον Δεκελεικόν, l. 11/12. With Schoell, *ibid.*, 21, I take the οἶκος of the Dekeleans to be the whole of those who belonged to the deme Dekelea, to which as chief deme fell the leading position in the Phratria. Hence the Phratria-notices were made ὅπου ἂν Δεκελειῆς προσφοιτῶσιν ἐν ἄστει, l. 60 ff., 120 ff. Cf. Lys. 23, 3.

[2] This is definitely stated by an old fragment of a law preserved by Philochoros, *fr.* 94, in Müller, *fr. hist. gr.*, 1, 399 (=Suid. Phot., ὀργεῶνες), belonging to the 4th book of the Atthis (cf. *fr.* 94 with *fr.* 91 = Harp. γεννῆται), a book which covered the period from 456–403 B.C. This fragment, belonging perhaps to the legal enactments drawn up at the revision of the laws in 403, is derived in all probability from a law of Cleisthenes, Schoell, *ibid.*, 16 ff. It runs τοὺς δὲ φράτορας ἐπάναγκες δέχεσθαι καὶ τοὺς ὀργεῶνας καὶ τοὺς ὁμογάλακτας, οὓς γεννήτας καλοῦμεν. The explanatory relative clause is, without doubt, an addition of Philochoros. The meaning of the words is clear. Cf. Schoell, *ibid.*, p. 17. Ὀργεῶνες appear as early as Solon's laws (see Seleucos *ap.* Phot., ὀργεῶνες. I now agree with Schoell, *ibid.*, 15, 1, that he refers to the law preserved in Dig. 44, 22, 4), but without reference to the organization of the citizen-body. The ὀργεῶνες mentioned Is. 2, 14. 16, before whom an adopted son was brought, I now regard as the members of a subdivision of the Phratria. Isolated lexicographers identify ὀργεῶνες and γεννῆται (Et. M. 226, 13 ff., Lex. Seguer. 227, 9 ff.): they probably arrive at this from the general meaning of the ὀργεῶνες as a religious association (Harp. Suid., ὀργεῶνες), because after the reconstitution of the Phratria γεννῆται and ὀργεῶνες attend to similar religious ceremonies.

The cult of Ζεὺς Ἑρκεῖος and Ἀπόλλων Πατρῷος, hitherto the possession of the γένη alone, was now undertaken also by the new citizens, and henceforth counted as a proof and condition of Athenian citizenship. In earlier days perhaps this cult had been observed in the individual families only: now Zeus Herkeios and Apollo Patroos became guardian-gods of the Phratries, in which character the former meets us in the cults of the Phratria side by side with Ἀθηνᾶ Φρατρία as Ζεὺς Φράτριος.[1]

The Old Phylai. It seems to be abundantly proved that Cleisthenes left the 4 old Phylai standing in some form or other.[2]

In harmony with the tendency to increase the citizen-body, which Cleisthenes followed in his enfranchisement of the strangers and Conditions of emancipated slaves, the rule was now established, that Citizenship. citizen descent on one side of the family was sufficient to secure Athenian citizenship. This appears to be demonstrated by the isolated examples of which we hear.[3] We do not know what

[1] In Plat., *Euthydem.*, 302, Socrates says: ἔστι γάρ ἐμοίγε καὶ βωμοὶ καὶ ἱερὰ οἰκεῖα καὶ πατρῷα καὶ τἄλλα ὅσαπερ τοῖς ἄλλοις Ἀθηναίοις τῶν τοιούτων. As appears from what follows, he means the cult of Ζεὺς Ἑρκεῖος and Φράτριος, Ἀπόλλων Πατρῷος and Ἀθηνᾶ Φρατρία. Harp. ἑρκεῖος Ζεύς says, ὅτι δὲ τούτοις μετῆν τῆς πολιτείας, οἷς εἴη Ζεὺς ἑρκεῖος, δεδήλωκεν καὶ Ὑπερίδης ἐν τῷ ὑπὲρ δημοποιήτου, εἰ γνήσιος, καὶ Δημήτριος ἐν τοῖς περὶ τῆς Ἀθήνησι νομοθεσίας. At the Archon's dokimasia the candidate was asked, εἰ ἔστιν αὐτῷ Ἀπόλλων πατρῷος καὶ Ζεὺς ἑρκεῖος καὶ ποῦ ταῦτα τὰ ἱερά ἐστιν. Arist. 55, 3. The last clause shows clearly, that it is not here a question of a private worship of the gods named. The question means, To what Phratria do you belong? Cf. the question in Dinarchus (Harp., ἑρκεῖος Ζεύς), εἰ φράτορες αὐτῷ καὶ βωμοὶ Διὸς ἑρκείου καὶ Ἀπόλλωνος πατρῴου εἰσίν. Both gods became exclusively Phratria-divinities. Schoell., *ibid.*, 23 ff. This explains the inscription in C.I.A., II. 1652, (ἱ)ερὸ(ν Ἀπόλ)λων(ος πατρ)ωίου φ(ρατρία)ς (Θ)ερρικ(ιαδ)ῶν. Cf. the recent discovery given in Sauppe, *de phratriis Att.*, II. 11: (ὅ)ρος τεμένους Ἀπόλλωνος πατρῴου Ἐλασιδῶν, where however it is a question whether Elasidai represents a Phratria or a γένος. Apollo Patroos is perhaps meant also in C.I.A., II. 1653, (ἱ)ερὸν (Ἀ)πόλλωνος ἑβδομείου φρατρίας Ἀχνιαδῶν. The Ἀπόλλωνος πατρῴου καὶ Διὸς ἑρκείου γεννῆται mentioned Dem. 57, 66 are the members of an old family. Ζεὺς Φράτριος and Ἀθηνᾶ Φρατρία, Plat., *Euthyd.*, 302. Dem. 43, 14. Cratin. *ap.* Ath. 11, 460 F. Schol. *ad* Arist. Ach. 146. Suid. ἀπατούρια. C.I.A., II. 841 b. *Berl. phil. Wochenschr.*, 1889, 225/6 = Sauppe, *de phratiis Att.*, II. 3 ff.; *Ind. schol. Goett.*, 1890/1.

[2] Ζεὺς Γελέων in an inscription so late as the time before the introduction of the Hadrianis, C.I.A., III. 2. The continuance of the old Phylai as corporations seems to be shown by the continuance of the φυλοβασιλεῖς, Poll. 8, 111.; Arist. 57, 4, and by the payments still made in the 4th century for sacrifices ἐκ τῶν φυλοβασιλικῶν. C.I.A., II. 844.

[3] Themistocles, although a νόθος on the mother's side (Plut., *Them.*, 1; Ath. 13, 576 C) was nevertheless Archon. (Thuc. 1, 93; Arist. 25, 3).

else Cleisthenes did to make his constitution more democratic than that of Solon.[1] His arrangements for the organization of the government were based on the number 10 of the new Phylai. He raised the number of the members of the council of 400 to 500, taking 50 from each tribe. The number 10 was also adopted for the boards of magistrates either introduced by Cleisthenes or subsequent to him. *Classification on Decimal System.* We are not in a position to say what magistrates were established by Cleisthenes, and what only later. We only know that the Apodectai were his creation.[2]

Lastly the institution of ostracism, which lasted till 418, is due to Cleisthenes.[3] It was specially directed against the followers

---

Schenkl, in the *Wiener Stud.*, 1888, 23, has doubted this without reason. See also Wachsmuth in the *Wiener Stud.*, 1885, 159/160: Schenkl's reply, *ibid.*, 337 ff., is not at all conclusive. Cimon too was a νόθος, Hdt. 1, 39; Plut., *Cim.*, 4. The νόθοι received their public gymnastic training in the Kynosarges, Plut., *Themist.*, 1; Lex. S:guer. 274, 21 ff. That fact, it is true, put them to a certain extent on a lower level than the general citizens. With the tendency of Cleisthenes' institutions agrees very well the remark in Arist., *Pol.*, 7 (6) 4 = p. 184, 16 ff. πρὸς δὲ τὸ καθιστάναι ταύτην τὴν δημοκρατίαν καὶ τὸν δῆμον ποιεῖν ἰσχυρὸν εἰώθασιν οἱ προεστῶτες τῷ προσλαμβάνειν ὡς πλείστους καὶ ποιεῖν πολίτας μὴ μόνον τοὺς γνησίους, ἀλλὰ καὶ τοὺς νόθους καὶ τοὺς ἐξ ὁποτερουοῦν πολίτου.

[1] Arist. 22, 1 says: τούτων δὲ γενομένων δημοτικωτέρα πολὺ τῆς Σόλωνος ἐγένετο ἡ πολιτεία· καὶ γὰρ συνέβη τοὺς μὲν Σόλωνος νόμους ἀφανίσαι τὴν τυραννίδα διὰ τὸ μὴ χρῆσθαι, νόμους δ' ἄλλους θεῖναι τὸν Κλεισθένην στοχαζόμενον τοῦ πλήθους, ἐν οἷς ἐτέθη καὶ ὁ περὶ τοῦ ὀστρακισμοῦ νόμος. Cf. 41. πέμπτη δ' ἡ μετὰ ⟨τὴν⟩ τῶν τυράννων κατάλυσιν ἡ Κλεισθένους δημοτικωτέρα τῆς Σόλωνος. On the other hand in Cleitophon's supplementary proposal during the discussions which preceded the establishment of the 400, we find, Arist. 29, 3: Κλειτοφῶν δὲ τὰ μὲν ἄλλα καθάπερ Πυθόδωρος εἶπεν, προσαναζητῆσαι δὲ τοὺς αἱρεθέντας ἔγραψεν καὶ τοὺς πατρίους νόμους, οὓς Κλεισθένης ἔθηκεν, ὅτε καθίστη τὴν δημοκρατίαν, ὅπως ⟨ἂν⟩ ἀκούσαντες καὶ τούτων βουλεύσωνται τὸ ἄριστον, ὡς οὐ δημοτικὴν ἀλλὰ παραπλησίαν οὖσαν τὴν Κλεισθένους πολιτείαν τῇ Σόλωνος.

[2] Arist. 21, 3 ἔπειτα τὴν βουλὴν πεντακοσίους ἀντὶ τετρακοσίων κατέστησεν, πεντήκοντα ἐξ ἑκάστης φυλῆς· τότε δ' ἦσαν ἑκατόν. Harp., ἀποδέκται—ὅτι δὲ ἀντὶ τῶν κωλακρετῶν οἱ ἀποδέκται ὑπὸ Κλεισθένους ἀπεδείχθησαν, Ἀνδροτίων β'. On the "Constructive plan of the political reform carried out by Cleisthenes," see Wachsmuth, *d. St. Ath.*, 1, 506 ff.

[3] Arist. 22, 1, καινοὺς ἄλλους θεῖναι τὸν Κλεισθένη στοχαζόμενον τοῦ πλήθους, ν οἷς ἐτέθη καὶ ὁ περὶ τοῦ ὀστρακισμοῦ νόμος. Philoch. in the Lex. Cantabr., p. 675 = Müller, *fr. hist. gr.*, 1, 396, 79b: μετὰ τοῦτον (Ὑπέρβολον) δὲ κατελύθη τὸ ἔθος ἀρξάμενον νομοθετήσαντος Κλεισθένους, ὅτε τοὺς τυράννους κατέλυσεν, ὅπως συνεκβάλῃ καὶ τοὺς φίλους αὐτῶν. Cf. Heracl., *fr.* I. 7 = *fr. hist. gr.*, II., 209. Ælian, *Var. Hist.*, 13, 24; Diod. 11, 55. Lugebil in the 4th Suppl. vol. of the *Jahrb. f. cl. Phil.* p. 163 ff., makes the ostracism introduced after 496; its abrogation 418, according to Philoch., *ibid.*, cf. Schol. ad Arist., *Eq.*, 855. See my *Beitr.*,

and friends of the Pisistratids, and was not employed till afterwards against other prominent political personages also. Cleisthenes wished by its help to prevent men who from their wealth, their many friends, or personal importance, attained a leading position in the State, from ever again proving fatal to the continuance of the constitution, as they had done in the past. In ostracism he gave the assembly of the people the power of banishing men of this character from the State for a period of 10 years without any definite accusation. A vote for this purpose was taken once in each year.[1] It was only in later times that ostracism began to be misused for party ends. Of this improper application of ostracism the description holds good which has mistakenly been regarded as true of its original character: that it was a contest between two parties for the preponderating influence in the State, and was decided by the temporary banishment of the leader of one party.[2]

Ostracism.

---

etc., 231, 237. Lugebil, p. 174, assumes the year of Eucleides for its abrogation. So Seeliger in the *Jahrb. f. cl. Phil.*, 1877, p. 742, 10, and Zurborg, *ibid.*, p. 836.

[1] Arist. 22, 3, τότε (488) πρῶτον ἐχρήσαντο τῷ νόμῳ τῷ περὶ τὸν ὀστρακισμόν, ὃς ἐτέθη διὰ τὴν ὑποψίαν τῶν ἐν ταῖς δυνάμεσιν, ὅτι Πεισίστρατος δημαγωγὸς καὶ στρατηγὸς ὢν τύραννος κατέστη· καὶ πρῶτος ὠστρακίσθη τῶν ἐκείνου συγγενῶν Ἵππαρχος Χάρμου Κολυττεύς, δι' ὃν καὶ μάλιστα τὸν νόμον ἔθηκεν ὁ Κλεισθένης, ἐξελάσαι βουλόμενος αὐτόν. οἱ γὰρ Ἀθηναῖοι τοὺς τῶν τυράννων φίλους, ὅσοι μὴ συνεξημάρτανον ἐν ταῖς ταραχαῖς, εἴων οἰκεῖν τὴν πόλιν, χρώμενοι τῇ εἰωθυίᾳ τοῦ δήμου πρᾳότητι· ὧν ἡγεμὼν καὶ προστάτης ἦν Ἵππαρχος.—22, 5, καὶ ὠστρακίσθη Μεγακλῆς Ἱπποκράτους Ἀλωπεκῆθεν. ἐπὶ μὲν οὖν ἔτη τρία τοὺς τῶν τυράννων φίλους ὠστράκιζον, ὧν χάριν ὁ νόμος ἐτέθη, μετὰ δὲ ταῦτα τῷ τετάρτῳ ἔτει καὶ τῶν ἄλλων εἴ τις δοκοίη μείζων εἶναι μεθίσταντο. 22, 8, καὶ τὸ λοιπὸν (after 481) ὥρισαν τοῖς ὀστρακιζομένοις ἐκτὸς (so we should read for the MS. ἐντὸς) Γεραιστοῦ (south coast of Euboea) καὶ Σκυλλαίου (east coast of Argolis) κατοικεῖν, ἢ ἀτίμους εἶναι καθάπαξ. Cf. on the importance of ostracism Aristotle's comments, *Pol.*, 3, 13 = p. 82, 13 ff., διὸ καὶ τίθενται τὸν ὀστρακισμὸν αἱ δημοκρατούμεναι πόλεις διὰ τὴν τοιαύτην αἰτίαν· αὗται γὰρ δὴ δοκοῦσι διώκειν τὴν ἰσότητα μάλιστα πάντων, ὥστε τοὺς δοκοῦντας ὑπερέχειν δυνάμει διὰ πλοῦτον ἢ πολυφιλίαν ἤ τινα ἄλλην πολιτικὴν ἰσχὺν ὠστράκιζον καὶ μεθίστασαν ἐκ τῆς πόλεως χρόνους ὡρισμένους. The ostracism directed against Pisistratus' followers, according to Androt. *ap.* Harp., Ἵππαρχος—τοῦ περὶ τὸν ὀστρακισμὸν νόμου τότε πρῶτον τεθέντος διὰ τὴν ὑποψίαν τῶν περὶ Πεισίστρατον. Cf. Heracl., *ibid.*; Diod. 11, 87. Hipparchos, son of Charmos, a relation of Pisistratus, is mentioned also by other authors as the first to suffer ostracism. Androt., *ibid.*, Cleitodemos *ap.* Ath., 13, 609 D. Plut., *Nic.*, 11. Valeton in *Mnemosyne*, 1887, p. 129 ff., thinks the principal demagogues were all suspected of aiming at tyrannis, and therefore Cleisthenes gave the people the power to banish any of them it chose. The banishment was a means of deterring those who remained behind.

[2] Arist., *Pol.*, 3, 13 = p. 83, 26, οὐ γὰρ ἔβλεπον πρὸς τὸ τῆς πολιτείας τῆς οἰκείας

Cleisthenes. [GILBERT II. 169-170.

In the year 501 the Athenian constitution was further developed by a new arrangement of the military officials. From this year onwards 10 Strategoi were elected each year, one from each Phyle; they commanded the men of their Phyle, while the Polemarch retained the command-in-chief of the whole army.[1]

New Arrangement of the Military Magistrates.

In the year 487 a new mode of appointing the 9 Archons was introduced. The peculiar mode of selection by lot established by Solon had been replaced again by election under the rule of the Pisistratids. In 487 a return was made to the lot; 500 candidates were nominated by the Demes perhaps in numbers proportional to their size; from these 500 the 9 Archons and their secretary were drawn by lot, one from each tribe. We cannot definitely determine whether the lot was also introduced for other magistrates in some form or other.[2]

New mode of appointing the 9 Archons.

συμφέρον, ἀλλὰ στασιαστικῶς ἐχρῶντο τοῖς ὀστρακισμοῖς. A list of the conflicting parties and party leaders from Cleisthenes to the end of the Peloponnesian War is given by Arist. 28. The whole of Aristotle's account, *Pol.*, 3, 13, seems to me to testify expressly to the change in the meaning of ostracism given in the text. It explains too the universal tradition of antiquity that by the ostracism those were attacked who towered above their fellow-citizens. Lugebil, p. 154 ff., explains this tradition as arising from the debates preceding ostracism, in which each side reproached the other with aiming at tyrannis. This seems very improbable. His explanation of the character and historical significance of ostracism is correct for the time of its improper use in the 5th century. He starts from a remark of Roscher, *über Leben, Werk, und Zeitalter d. Thukyd.*, p. 381 ff.

[1] Arist. 22, 2, ἔπειτα τοὺς στρατηγοὺς ᾑροῦντο κατὰ φυλάς, ἐξ ἑκάστης ⟨τῆς⟩ φυλῆς ἕνα, τῆς δ' ἁπάσης στρατιᾶς ἡγεμὼν ἦν ὁ πολέμαρχος. The time is defined by the words that follow: ἔτει δὲ μετὰ ταῦτα δωδεκάτῳ νικήσαντες τὴν ἐν Μαραθῶνι μάχην ἐπὶ Φαινίππου ἄρχοντος. So at Marathon the Polemarch was commander-in-chief, Hdt. 6, 109 ff. See Lugebil in the 5th Suppl. vol. of the *Jahrb. f. cl. Phil.*, 585 ff.

[2] Arist. 22, 5, εὐθὺς δὲ τῷ ὑστέρον ἔτει ἐπὶ Τελεσίνου ἄρχοντος ἐκυάμευσαν τοὺς ἐννέα ἄρχοντας κατὰ φυλὰς ἐκ τῶν προκριθέντων ὑπὸ τῶν δημοτῶν πεντακοσίων τότε μετὰ τὴν τυραννίδα πρῶτον· οἱ δὲ πρότεροι πάντες ἦσαν αἱρετοί. For the Solonian mode of selection by lot see p. 186. The drawing of the 9 Archons by tribes would proceed as in later times (Arist. 55, 5)—their secretary made up the necessary number 10. The candidates were nominated from the two highest classes, Arist. 26, 2. The statement in Hdt. 6, 109 that Callimachos, Polemarch in 490, and that of Demetrios of Phaleron on Plut., *Arist.*, 1, that Aristides, Archon 489, were chosen by lot, are thus cleared up. Idomeneus *ap.* Plut., *ibid.*, maintained that Aristides was elected. Cf. Lugebil, *ibid.*, 585 and 659 ff. Plut., *Arist.*, 22 (Aristides) γράφει ψήφισμα κοινὴν εἶναι τὴν πολιτείαν καὶ τοὺς ἄρχοντας ἐξ Ἀθηναίων πάντων αἱρεῖσθαι cannot

The gradual development of the constitution in a democratic direction received a check from the circumstance that in the dangers of the second Persian War the council of the Areopagus alone showed itself equal to the situation.

Rule of the Areopagus.

The consequence was that the supreme power in the State was transferrred *de facto*, but without any special resolution to that effect, to the Areopagus. The foundation and establishing of the first Athenian League was carried out under the Areopagus' guidance.[1]

The Athenian Demos, whose self-reliance was considerably raised by the happy issue of the Persian war, submitted to the usurped powers of the Areopagus by no means without resistance. Still that body for 17 years practically maintained its position. It was in the year 462 that this usurpation of the Council of the Areopagus was brought to a close by a resolution of the people; and apparently other limitations of their powers followed in the next years.[2] It would be a hopeless

Its overthrow.

be correct as it stands. The lot as a democratic institution was adopted pretty extensively in ancient times. Hdt. 3, 80. Plat., *Laws*, 6, 757. Arist. in various passages collected by Lugebil, *ibid.*, 571 A, 53. Grote, vol. 3, p. 361, also regards it as a democratic measure. Perrot, *le droit public d'Athènes*, 56, 1.

[1] Arist. 41, 2 makes his sixth μεταβολὴ τῆς πολιτείας ἡ μετὰ τὰ Μηδικά, τῆς ἐξ Ἀρείου πάγου βουλῆς ἐπιστατούσης. Cf. Arist. 23, 1. τότε μὲν οὖν μέχρι τούτου προῆλθεν ἡ πόλις ἅμα τῇ δημοκρατίᾳ κατὰ μικρὸν αὐξανομένη· μετὰ δὲ τὰ Μηδικὰ πάλιν ἴσχυσεν ἡ ἐν Ἀρείῳ πάγῳ βουλὴ καὶ διῴκει τὴν πόλιν, οὐδενὶ δόγματι λαβοῦσα τὴν ἡγεμονίαν, ἀλλὰ διὰ τὸ γενέσθαι τῆς περὶ Σαλαμῖνα ναυμαχίας αἰτία. τῶν γὰρ στρατηγῶν ἐξαπορησάντων τοῖς πράγμασι καὶ κηρυξάντων σῴζειν ἕκαστον ἑαυτόν, πορίσασα δραχμὰς ἑκάστῳ ὀκτὼ διέδωκε καὶ ἐνεβίβασεν εἰς τὰς ναῦς. διὰ ταύτην δὴ τὴν αἰτίαν παρεχώρουν αὐτῆς τῷ ἀξιώματι, καὶ ἐπολιτεύθησαν Ἀθηναῖοι καλῶς καὶ κατὰ τούτους τοὺς καιρούς. συνέβη γὰρ αὐτοῖς περὶ τὸν χρόνον τοῦτον τά τε εἰς πόλεμον ἀσκῆσαι καὶ παρὰ τοῖς Ἕλλησιν εὐδοκιμῆσαι καὶ τὴν τῆς θαλάττης ἡγεμονίαν λαβεῖν, ἀκόντων τῶν Λακεδαιμονίων. See also Arist., *Pol.*, 8 (5) 4=p. 201, 5. Plut., *Them.*, 10. Cic., *de Off.*, 1, 22, 75. On the establishment of the first Athenian League, see Arist. 23, 2.

[2] Arist. 25, 1 says, ἔτη δὲ ἑπτακαίδεκα μάλιστα μετὰ τὰ Μηδικὰ διέμεινεν ἡ πολιτεία προεστώτων τῶν Ἀρεοπαγιτῶν καίπερ ὑποφερομένη κατὰ μικρόν. With this Arist., *Pol.*, 8 (5) 4=p. 201, 5 ff., very well agrees: οἷον ἡ ἐν Ἀρείῳ πάγῳ βουλὴ εὐδοκιμήσασα ἐν τοῖς Μηδικοῖς ἔδοξε συντονωτέραν ποιῆσαι τὴν πολιτείαν, καὶ πάλιν ὁ ναυτικὸς ὄχλος γενόμενος αἴτιος τῆς περὶ Σαλαμῖνα νίκης καὶ διὰ ταύτης τῆς ἡγεμονίας διὰ τὴν κατὰ θάλατταν δύναμιν τὴν δημοκρατίαν ἰσχυροτέραν ἐποίησεν. See Peter Meyer, *des Arist. Pol. u. d. Ἀθ. πολ.*, 55 ff. Arist. 41, 2 describes the curtailment of the Areopagus' powers in these words: ἑβδόμη δὲ ἡ μετὰ ταύτην (sc. μεταβολή), ἣν Ἀριστείδης μὲν ὑπέδειξεν, Ἐφιάλτης δὲ ἐπετέλεσεν καταλύσας τὴν Ἀρεοπαγῖτιν βουλήν. ἐν ᾗ πλεῖστα συνέβη τὴν πόλιν διὰ τοὺς δημαγωγοὺς ἁμαρτάνειν διὰ τὴν τῆς θαλάττης ἀρχήν. What Aristides, though indirectly,

task to try to determine precisely how the official powers of the Areopagus were constituted in the 17 years of its rule. The Areopagus had simply usurped its supremacy during these years, so that of course there can be no question of a constitutional limitation of it. The Areopagus appropriated all the powers it could. Ephialtes, according to Aristotle's testimony, restored the powers that he took from the Areopagus to the Council of 500, the Ecclesia, and the Heliast courts; therefore those powers must have been administrative and judicial. In general we may suppose that from the laws of Ephialtes, Archestratos, and Pericles dates the restriction of the Areopagus in its judicial powers to murder-cases, the γραφὴ πυρκαϊᾶς, and the γραφὴ ἀσεβείας, and in its administrative activity to those functions which it still exercised at Athens in the 2nd half of the 5th and the 4th century.[1]

The supposition that the new office of the νομοφύλακες was established to discharge certain isolated duties taken from the Areopagus by Ephialtes, is not adequately proved nor does such an institution appear to be in harmony with the tendency of contemporary constitutional development.[2]

Νομοφύλακες.

contributed to the restriction of the Areopagus' powers, is shown by Arist. 24, 3, κατέστησαν δὲ καὶ τοῖς πολλοῖς εὐπορίαν τροφῆς, ὥσπερ Ἀριστείδης εἰσηγήσατο. Ephialtes' activity in this direction, Arist. 25, 2: καὶ πρῶτον μὲν ἀνεῖλεν πολλοὺς τῶν Ἀρεοπαγιτῶν, ἀγῶνας ἐπιφέρων περὶ τῶν διῳκημένων· ἔπειτα τῆς βουλῆς ἐπὶ Κόνωνος ἄρχοντος ἅπαντα περιείλετο τὰ ἐπίθετα, δι' ὧν ἦν ἡ τῆς πολιτείας φυλακή, καὶ τὰ μὲν τοῖς πεντακοσίοις, τὰ δὲ τῷ δήμῳ καὶ τοῖς δικαστηρίοις ἀπέδωκεν. I refrain for the present from expressing an opinion on Themistocles' share in this, contradicting as it does all we had known hitherto, but cf. Bauer, *Lit. u. hist. Forsch. z. Arist. 'Aθ. πολ.*, p. 67 ff. Quite general accounts are given by Arist., *Pol.*, 2, 12=p. 56, 20. Plut., *præs. ger. reip.*, 10, 15; Diod. 11, 77; Paus. 1, 29, 15. Plut., *Cim.*, 15, tells us, οἱ πολλοὶ ἀφείλοντο τῆς ἐξ Ἀρείου πάγου βουλῆς τὰς κρίσεις πλὴν ὀλίγων ἁπάσας καὶ τῶν δικαστηρίων κυρίους ποιήσαντες εἰς ἄκρατον δημοκρατίαν ἐνέβαλον τὴν πόλιν, and Cimon seeks πάλιν ἄνω τὰς δίκας ἀνακαλεῖσθαι. According to Plut., *Per.*, 9, Pericles contrived ὥστε τὴν μὲν (βουλὴν) ἀφαιρεθῆναι τὰς πλείστας κρίσεις δι' Ἐφιάλτου. Arist. 35, 2 mentions τοὺς τ' Ἐφιάλτου καὶ Ἀρχεστράτου νόμους τοὺς περὶ τῶν Ἀρεοπαγιτῶν. Of Pericles, Arist. 27, 1 says, καὶ γὰρ τῶν Ἀρεοπαγιτῶν ἔνια περιείλετο. The limitations of the Areopagus' power carried by Archestratos and Pericles belong perhaps to the time after Ephialtes.

[1] The δίκαι φονικαί always remained in the hands of the Areopagus. Philippi, *d. Areop. u. d. Eph.*, 264 ff., γραφὴ πυρκαϊᾶς, 161/2, γραφὴ ἀσεβείας, 156/7. On the Areopagus' administrative activity in later times, cf. Philippi, *ibid.*, 307 ff.

[2] Strenge, *quæst. Philochoreæ*, Gött., 1868, p. 5 ff., following Boeckh in his *Kl. Schr.*, 5, 424 ff., has in my judgment (see also Wachsmuth; *d. St. Ath.*, 1, 584, 2), demonstrated that the νομοφύλακες are not earlier than the age of

In the period of the Areopagus' supremacy, and the age following thereupon falls the time of Athens' development into a great power. This was accompanied by a marvellous change and development in political life. To fulfil all those duties which their position at the head of the league laid upon the Athenians, it was necessary for all the people to take their share in the political business of the State. It was simply impossible to escape this necessity unless they were willing to resign their leading position within the league. This is shown by one characteristic circumstance. The way for this development was prepared by Aristides, under the aristocratic guidance of the Areopagus; and one is inclined to attribute conservative tendencies to this statesman rather than democratic. After the powers of the Areopagus were curtailed, this expansion proceeded with an accelerated rapidity. The inhabitants of Attica migrated more and more to Athens, where they found employment and maintenance in military and political duties. More than 20,000 men found employment and support in the service of the State, either as soldiers, jurymen, bouleutai, or magistrates. The State, as indeed under the existing conditions it was forced to do, made heavy demands upon the services of its citizens: and it could do so only by the employment of an extensive system of salaries. It is in this period of the foundation and expansion of the Athenian League that the μισθὸς στρατιωτικός, βουλευτικός, and ˙δικαστικὸς must have been introduced. We are told indeed that the last was brought in by Pericles. At the same time there must have been a great increase in the number of magistrates. In general the Athenian State acquired in the brilliant period of the Pentecontaeteia those forms of constitution and government which were peculiarly characteristic of the political life of Athens in the 5th century. But we are not in a position to adduce details in consequence of the silence of our authorities.[1]

Demetrios of Phaleron. Philippi, *d. Areop. u. d. Eph.*, 185 ff., believes we must maintain their institution by Ephialtes, but he can tell us nothing as to their duties. Starker, *de nomophylacib. Atheniensium*, p. 89 ff., Diss. inaug., Breslau, 1880, supposes we may transfer to the νομοφύλακες instituted by Ephialtes all the functions which are recorded by the lexicographers under their name. I do not consider he has succeeded in his attempt to prove (p. 22 ff.) the credibility of the statement in the Lex. Cantabr., νομοφύλακες: ἑπτὰ δὲ ἦσαν καὶ κατέστησαν, ὡς Φιλόχορος, ὅτε Ἐφιάλτης μόνα κατέλιπε τῇ ἐξ Ἀρείου πάγου βουλῇ τὰ ὑπὲρ τοῦ σώματος.

[1] On the changes for which the way was prepared under the govern-

We read that from and after 457 the candidates nominated by the Demes for selection by lot for the 9 archonships were drawn from the Zeugitai as well as the other classes: up to this time the Zeugitai were eligible only for the inferior offices.[1] In the year 453 an institution first introduced by Pisistratus, and after the expulsion of the Pisistratids perhaps abolished, was re-established. This was the 30 Deme-judges, who journeyed about Attica and gave final sentence in cases where the amount in dispute did not exceed 10 drachmæ. Under the government of the Pisistratids this institution had had a political character; it was now reintroduced merely to relieve the Heliast courts from the business of deciding unimportant cases.[2]

Admission of the Zeugitai to the Archonship.

Deme-judges.

The easiness of the conditions upon which Cleisthenes had made the attainment of the Athenian franchise to depend, had greatly increased the numbers of the citizens, especially through the great

---

ment of the Areopagus see Arist. 24. We do not possess definite information as to the introduction of the μισθὸς στρατιωτικὸς and βουλευτικός. Arist., *Pol.*, 2, 12 = p. 56, 20 ff., connects Pericles' introduction of the μισθὸς δικαστικὸς with the limitation of the Areopagus' power: καὶ τὴν μὲν Ἀρείῳ πάγῳ βουλὴν Ἐφιάλτης ἐκόλουσε καὶ Περικλῆς, τὰ δὲ δικαστήρια μισθοφόρα κατέστησε Περικλῆς. Arist. 27, 3 says: ἐποίησε δὲ καὶ μισθοφόρα τὰ δικαστήρια Περικλῆς πρῶτος, ἀντιδημαγωγῶν πρὸς τὴν Κίμωνος εὐπορίαν. 27, 4, ἐπεὶ τοῖς ἰδίοις ἡττᾶτο (sc. Περικλῆς), διδόναι τοῖς πολλοῖς τὰ αὑτῶν, κατεσκεύασε μισθοφορὰν τοῖς δικαστηρίοις, ἀφ' ὧν αἰτιῶνταί τινες χεῖρω γενέσθαι, κληρουμένων ἐπιμελῶς ἀεὶ μᾶλλον τῶν τυχόντων, ἢ τῶν ἐπιεικῶν ἀνθρώπων. According to Arist. 24, 3, the ἀρχαὶ ἔνδημοι required 700 men yearly, besides the ἀρχαὶ ὑπερόριοι. There were 6000 δικασταί, Arist. 24, 3. Arist. 26, 1 says of the time after the overthrow of the Areopagus, μετὰ δὲ ταῦτα συνέβαινεν ἀνίεσθαι μᾶλλον τὴν πολιτείαν διὰ τοὺς προθύμως δημαγωγοῦντας. 26, 2, τὰ μὲν οὖν ἄλλα πάντα διῴκουν οὐχ ὁμοίως καὶ πρότερον τοῖς νόμοις προσέχοντες.

[1] Arist., 26, 2: τὴν δὲ τῶν ἐννέα ἀρχόντων αἵρεσιν οὐκ ἐκίνουν, ἀλλ' [ἢ] ἕκτῳ ἔτει μετὰ τὸν Ἐφιάλτου θάνατον ἔγνωσαν καὶ ἐκ ζευγιτῶν προκρίνεσθαι τοὺς κληρωσομένους τῶν ἐννέα ἀρχόντων, καὶ πρῶτος ἦρξεν ἐξ αὐτῶν Μνησιθείδης. οἱ δὲ πρὸ τούτου πάντες ἐξ ἱππέων καὶ πεντακοσιομεδίμνων ἦσαν, οἱ ⟨δὲ⟩ ζευγῖται τὰς ἐγκυκλίους ἦρχον, εἰ μή τι παρεωρᾶτο τῶν ἐν τοῖς νόμοις. Plut., *Arist.*, 22, can hardly be right, as the words stand, when he says of Aristides, γράφει ψήφισμα κοινὴν εἶναι τὴν πολιτείαν καὶ τοὺς ἄρχοντας ἐξ Ἀθηναίων πάντων αἱρεῖσθαι. Cf. Arist. 7, 4, διὸ καὶ νῦν ἐπειδὰν ἔρηται τὸν μέλλοντα κληροῦσθαί τιν' ἀρχήν, ποῖον τέλος τελεῖ, οὐδ' ἂν εἷς εἴποι θητικόν. But in the 4th century at all events the Thetes do not appear to have been excluded by law from the archonship, although perhaps on account of the expenses incident thereto they refrained from standing for it. See Lys. 24, 13, (Dem.) 59, 72.

[2] Arist., 26, 3: ἔτει δὲ πέμπτῳ μετὰ ταῦτα ἐπὶ Λυσικράτους ἄρχοντος οἱ τριάκοντα δικασταὶ κατέστησαν πάλιν, οἱ καλούμενοι κατὰ δήμους. On their functions see Arist. 53. On the object of Pisistratus' introduction of them, Arist. 16, 5.

attraction which Athenian citizenship must have had for the members of the Confederacy of which Athens was the
mistress. In the year 451, therefore, on the motion of
Pericles, it was resolved that from that time forth no one should
be an Athenian citizen who was not of citizen parentage on both
sides.[1]

New Franchise Law.

The foundation and development of the Athenian Confederacy
had prepared the way for a larger and larger participation by the
entire people in political life. This was rendered complete by the Peloponnesian War, when the whole
population of Attica was shut up for years in Athens,
and gained a yet more absolute control over the government and
direction of the State.[2]

The Peloponnesian War.

The oligarchic interregna of the 400, and of the 30, which the
Peloponnesian War brought in its train, were of too short duration to deserve a place in this brief review of the development of
the Athenian constitution.[3]

The last alteration which the Athenian constitution underwent
during the period of independence dates from the year of

---

[1] Arist. 26, 4: καὶ τρίτῳ μετ' αὐτὸν ἐπὶ 'Αντιδότου διὰ τὸ πλῆθος τῶν πολιτῶν Περικλέους εἰπόντος ἔγνωσαν μὴ μετέχειν τῆς πόλεως, ὃς ἂν μὴ ἐξ ἀμφοῖν ἀστοῖν ᾖ γεγονώς. Cf. Plut., *Per.*, 37; Ælian, *Var. Hist.*, 6, 10; 13, 24. Suid. δημοποίητος. This settles the discussions of Duncker in the *Ber. der Berl. Ak.* 1883, 935 ff. = *Abh. z. griech. Gesch.*, 124 ff., and of Zimmermann, *de nothorum Athenis condicione*, p. 32 ff., Berlin, 1886. In 445/4 on occasion of a distribution of corn from Amyrtaios (Duncker, *ibid.*, 132 ff.) there was a great ξενηλασία of about 5000 persons at Athens (Plut., *Per.*, 37, Philoch., *fr.* 90 in Müller, *fr. hist. gr.*, 1, 398/9). The doubts which H. Schenkl in the *Wiener Stud.*, 2, 170 ff., and 1883, pp. 4/5, 25 ff., has raised upon this point, I regard as unjustified. Cf. Wachsmuth in the *Wiener Stud.*, 1885, 159/60; he has been answered by Schenkl, *ibid.*, 337 ff. The means of deciding in such cases seems to me to have more probably been the διαψήφισις than the γραφὴ ξενίας, for which Philippi, *Beitr.*, 34 ff., and Duncker, *ibid.*, 944 ff., have pronounced. Cf. Lipsius on Meier and Schömann, *de att. Proc.*,[2] 439, N. 704.

[2] Arist. 27, 2: ἐν ᾧ (τῷ πρὸς Πελοποννησίους πολέμῳ) κατακλησθεὶς ὁ δῆμος ἐν τῷ ἄστει καὶ συνεθισθεὶς ἐν ταῖς στρατείαις μισθοφορεῖν, τὰ μὲν ἑκών, τὰ δὲ ἄκων προῃρεῖτο τὴν πολιτείαν διοικεῖν αὐτός.

[3] Arist. 41, 2 reckons the establishment of the 400 as the eighth change in the constitution, as the ninth the restoration of the democracy, and as the tenth the rule of the 30. Arist. 29-40 describes the history and constitution of the 400 and the 30 at great length. What was previously known on the subject from other sources has been collected, as far as the rule of the 400 is concerned, in my *Beitr. z. innern Gesch. Athens*, 300 ff., for that of the 30 by Scheibe, *die oligarch. Umwälzung zu Ath. am Ende des pelop. Krieges.*

Eucleides' archonship. This new constitution, showing a strong democratic tendency, continued essentially unchanged until the destruction of Athenian political independence, although, it is true, some reforms were introduced in the course of the 4th century. The antiquarian section will have to deal with the details of this constitution.[1]

Alterations under Eucleides.

3. INTERNAL HISTORY OF ATHENS AFTER 322, AND SURVEY OF THE ATHENIAN CONSTITUTION UNDER ROMAN RULE.

The Athenians took part in the Lamian War, and this in 322 led to the destruction of their independence. They were compelled to receive a Macedonian garrison in the harbour-fortress of Munychia, and all Athenians who did not possess a fortune of at least 2,000 drachmas—there were 12,000 of them—were deprived of burgess-rights.[2] After Antipater's death Polysperchon restored the democratic government at Athens as elsewhere, 319 B.C.[3] Its duration however was but short. Nicanor kept possession of Munychia and the Piræus in the interest of Cassandros, and the Athenians thereby found themselves compelled in 318 to make peace with the latter by agreeing that Cassandros should remain in possession of Munychia, and that the franchise should be restricted to those who were assessed as possessing at least 1,000 drachmas. Finally, in compliance again with a demand of Cassandros, Demetrios of Phaleron was made administrator of the State [4]

---

[1] Arist. 41, 2: ἐνδεκάτη δ' ἡ μετὰ τὴν ἀπὸ Φυλῆς καὶ ἐκ Πειραιέως κάθοδον, ἀφ' ἧς διαγεγένηται μέχρι τῆς νῦν ἀεὶ προσεπιλαμβάνουσα τῷ πλήθει τὴν ἐξουσίαν. ἁπάντων γὰρ αὐτὸς αὑτὸν πεποίηκεν ὁ δῆμος κύριον καὶ πάντα διοικεῖται ψηφίσμασιν καὶ δικαστηρίοις, ἐν οἷς ὁ δῆμός ἐστιν ὁ κρατῶν. καὶ γὰρ αἱ τῆς βουλῆς κρίσεις εἰς τὸν δῆμον ἐληλύθασιν. καὶ τοῦτο δοκοῦσι ποιεῖν ὀρθῶς· εὐδιαφθορώτεροι γὰρ ⟨οἱ⟩ ὀλίγοι τῶν πολλῶν εἰσιν καὶ κέρδει καὶ χάρισιν. According to Cauer, *Hat Arist. d. Schrift v. Staate d. Ath. geschrieben ?* p. 47 ff., this passage in some marvellous manner furnishes the main proof of the spuriousness of the Ἀθηναίων πολιτεία. A satisfactory refutation of this view has been given by Peter Meyer, *des Arist. Polit. u. d. Ἀθ. πολ.*, 59 ff., Niemeyer in the *Jahrb. f. cl. Phil.*, 1891, 410 ff., and Crusius in *Phil.*, 1891, 174 ff.

[2] Cf. Diod. 18, 18. Plut., *Phok.*, 28. Schwarz, *die Demokratie von Athen*, 582 ff. Spangenberg, *de Atheniensium publicis institutis aetate Macedonum commutatis*, 2 ff., Halle, 1884.

[3] Decree of general freedom in Hellas, cf. Diod. 18, 56. For the re-establishment of the democracy in Athens cf. Plut., *Phok.*, 32. Droysen, *Gesch. d. Hell.*, 2, 1, 214 (197) ff. Schwarz, *ib.*, 587 ff.

[4] Cf. Diod. 18, 74. The 1,000 drachmas mean probably not the entire

What powers he had in that capacity cannot be determined with certainty; he held at the same time various special offices. He seems to have left the democracy unimpaired, at any rate so far as outward form went; and the prosperity and population of the country increased under his rule.[1] A new institution of his was the office of the νομοφύλακες, whose chief duties were to see that the magistrates observed the laws, and to prevent the vote of the Ecclesia being taken if an illegal or harmful decree was about to be passed.[2] Another was the office of the γυναικονόμοι, who exercised a sort of censorship of morals.[3]

In 307 Demetrios, the son of Antigonos, expelled Demetrios of

property, but merely the τίμημα. See Bergk in the *Jahrb. f. cl. Phil.*, vol. 65, 398. In Diod. Demetrios is styled ἐπιμελητὴς τῆς πόλεως. But in the honorary decree of the Demos Aixonai to Demetrios Köhler reads καὶ σ(ῖτον εἰσήγαγεν τοῖς Ἀ)θηναίοις καὶ τεῖ χώ(ρᾳ καὶ ἐπιστάτης or προστάτης αἱρ)εθείς, since the gap is not large enough to admit of ἐπιμελητής. Ἐπιστάτης is supported by Strabo 398 and Diod. 20, 45; προστάτης by Polyb. 12, 13, 9. Cf. C.I.A., II. 584, and Köhler's remarks there. Vischer, *kl. Schriften*, 2, 87 ff., conjectures that the official title of Demetrios was στρατηγός. Demetrios was condemned to death along with Phokion, but was absent at the time. Cf. Plut., *Phok.*, 35. See Droysen, *ib.*, 226/7 (205) and 233 ff.

[1] Demetrios was Archon 309/8: Athen. 12, 542ε. Diog. L. 5, 5, 8=77. Diod. 20, 27. He was also four times στρατηγός: Dittenberger, *Syll.*, 121. Strab. 398 concludes from Demetrios's commentaries on his own government, that οὐ μόνον οὐ κατέλυσε τὴν δημοκρατίαν, ἀλλὰ καὶ ἐπηνώρθωσε. Plut., *Demetr.*, 10, calls the rule of Demetrios λόγῳ μὲν ὀλιγαρχική, ἔργῳ δὲ μοναρχικὴ κατάστασις. The revenues increased by Demetrios: Diog. L. 5, 5, 2=75. Acc. to Duris of Samos *ap.* Ath. 12, 542c he had control of 1,200 talents per annum. Cf. also Polyb. 12, 13. Acc. to Ctesicles *ap.* Ath. 6, 272B, the population in the archonship of Demetrios amounted to 21,000 citizens, 10,000 metoikoi, and 400,000 slaves. On the last number see, however, Beloch, *Bevölker. d. griech.-rom. Welt.*, 87 ff. For the literature on Demetrios see in Wachsmuth 1, 610. Compare Droysen, *ib.*, 2, 2, 106 (408) ff.; Schwarz, *ib.*, 542 ff.; Spangenberg, *ib.*, 8 ff.

[2] Cf. Suid., νομοφύλακες. Phot. Lex. Seguer. 191, 20; 283, 16; Poll. 8, 94; Harp. Lex. Cantabr. 674. See also Starker, *de nomophylacib. Atheniens.*, p. 9 ff., Breslau, 1880. That they were first instituted by Demetrios has been proved by Strenge, *quaest. Philoch.*, p. 5 ff., Goett. 1868, who follows Boeckh., *Kl. Schr.*, 5, 424 ff. See Spangenberg, *ib.*, 18 ff.

[3] Cf. Philoch. *ap.* Ath. 6, 245c: οἱ γυναικονόμοι μετὰ τῶν Ἀρεοπαγιτῶν ἐσκόπουν τὰς ἐν ταῖς οἰκίαις συνόδους ἔν τε τοῖς γάμοις κἂν ταῖς ἄλλαις θυσίαις. Cf. Poll. 8, 112. Hesych., πλάτανος. The mention of the γυναικονόμοι in the comic poets Timocles and Menandros *ap.* Ath. 6, 245B sq., marks them as a new institution rightly attributed by Boeckh, *Kl. Schr.*, 5, 421 ff., to Demetrios. See Spangenberg, *ib.*, 11 ff. Stojentin, *de Poll. Att. Ant.*, 50 ff., maintains that the γυναικονόμοι were already in existence before Demetrios's time, and Wachsmuth 2, 1, 390, 2 agrees with him.

Phaleron, drove out the Macedonian garrison from Munychia, and gave back to the Athenians their freedom and their old constitution.[1] Soon afterwards Lachares set up in Athens a new Tyrannis, which, after one year's duration, was overthrown by Demetrios Poliorketes again, B.C. 295. This time Poliorketes restored the democracy once more, it is true, but retained in his own power Munychia, the Piræus, and the fortified Museion hill.[2] The Athenians dislodged the garrison of the Museion in 287, but Munychia and the Piræus remained in the possession of Demetrios and of his son Antigonos after him.[3]

In the Chremonidean war the Athenians, after regaining possession of the harbour fortifications Munychia and Piræus, attempted once more to maintain their independence. But in spite of their vigorous resistance Antigonos compelled them to capitulate in 263, and insisted on their submitting to permanent Macedonian garrisons in Salamis, Sunion, Munychia, and also on the Museion. In 256 Antigonos withdrew the last, and restored Athens to nominal freedom;[4] but the other fortresses remained in the hands of the Macedonians, until the death of Demetrios the successor of Antigonos in 229. At that date Aratus effected an agreement by which Diogenes, the Macedonian Phrourarch, evacuated Attic territory on payment of 150 talents. Thus the Athenians recovered their freedom, and henceforth held themselves aloof from all Hellenic affairs, seeking to obtain the support of Rome.[5]

Upon the settlement of the affairs of Greece by the Romans after the sack of Corinth, Athens became one of the *civitates*

---

[1] Cf. Plut., *Demetr.*, 10; Diod. 20, 45; Droysen, 2, 2, 114 (412) ff.

[2] See Droysen 2, 2 (538) ff., 272 (559) ff. Plut., *Demetr.*, 34. C.I.A., II. 300. Paus. 1, 25, 5. Acc. to Droysen the occupation of the Museion took place a few years later than that of the Piræus and Munychia; acc. to Wachsmuth 1, 617, 1 they were all three occupied at the same time.

[3] Droysen 2, 2, 299 (585) ff.

[4] Paus. 3, 6, 6; 2, 8, 6. Jerome and the Armenian version of Eusebius remark on the year of Abraham 1761=256 B.C. "Antigonus Atheniensibus reddidit libertatem." See Euseb., ed. Schoene, pp. 120, 121. For the Chremonidean war see Wachsmuth 1, 626 ff. Droysen 3, 1, 225 ff.

[5] Wachsmuth, 680 ff.; Droysen, 3, 2, 55 (487) ff. A Roman embassy was sent to Athens immediately after the defeat of the queen of Illyria in 228. The Athenians granted to the Romans the right of admittance to the Mysteries, and also the Athenian franchise. Cf. Polyb. 2, 12. Zonar. 8, 19.

fœderatæ.[1] Such States were recognised by Rome as independent, except that they were not allowed to adopt an independent foreign policy; they possessed full power to coin money and full rights of exilium. In internal affairs they were exempt from any interference by Roman officials, and possessed full jurisdiction not only over their own citizens, but also over Roman citizens residing in their territory, at any rate in civil cases. They paid no taxes and were subject to no burdens of any kind, except those expressly stipulated in the fœdus.[2] In spite, however, of the fact that Athenian independence was maintained and respected, there is no reason to suppose that Athens escaped all interference with her constitution; for it was the usual practice of the Romans when they arranged the affairs of new provinces to alter the constitutions of the allied cities in the direction of timocracy. At Athens this alteration seems to have consisted chiefly in the restriction of the powers of the Ecclesia and the law courts.[3] The following is a short summary of the main facts known to us concerning the Athenian constitution under Roman supremacy. No account is taken of minor points of difference between one period and another.

Athens under Roman rule.

---

[1] On Athens under Roman sway see Ahrens, *de Athenarum statu politico et literario inde ab Achaici foederis interitu usque ad Antoninorum tempora.* Goett., 1829. Neubauer, *Atheniensium reipublicae quaenam Romanorum temporibus fuerit condicio.* Halle, 1882. On Athens as *civitas fœderata* cf. Strabo 898. Tac., *Ann.*, 2, 53: hinc ventum Athenas foederique sociae et vetustae urbis datum, ut uno lictore uteretur. In Plin., *N. H.*, 4, 7, 24, Athens is called a *libera civitas*. Cf. Plin., *Ep.*, 8, 24. Dio Chrysost. 31, 343 M., 622 R. Aristides 14, 224. For the subsequent fate of Athens under the Roman empire see Wachsmuth 1, 650 ff.

[2] See Marquardt, *röm. Staatsverwalt.*, 1², 78 ff. On the Athenian right of exilium cf. Cic., *Tusc.*, 5, 37, 108. Also C. I. A., III. 44, of the time of Septimius Severus (οἱ ὑπὸ τοῦ δήμ)ου (?) φυγὴν κατεγνωσμέν(οι).

[3] That the Romans had already effected changes in the Athenian constitution can be seen from Appian, *Mithr.*, 39, where it is said of Sulla after his capture of Athens: καὶ νόμους ἔθηκεν ἅπασιν ἀγχοῦ τῶν πρόσθεν αὐτοῖς ὑπὸ Ῥωμαίων ὁρισθέντων. The nature of these regulations can be inferred from the words of Aristion just before the defection of Athens from the Romans in 86, as recorded by Poseidonios *ap.* Athen. 5, 213 D, though they are undoubtedly exaggerated: καὶ μὴ περιίδωμεν—τὸ θέατρον ἀνεκκλησίαστον, ἄφωνα δὲ τὰ δικαστήρια καὶ τὴν θεῶν χρησμοῖς καθωσιωμένην πύκν' ἀφῃρημένην τοῦ δήμου. Ahrens 24 ff., Hertzberg, *Gesch. Griechenl. unter der Herrsch. der Römer*, 1, p. 308 (288) ff, and Wachsmuth 1, 650/1 all suppose that a constitutional change of that kind took place about 146 B.C. For the political restrictions of Athens under the empire see Neubauer 10 ff.

The purity of the burgess body was so little valued at Athens in this period that the franchise was offered for sale, until Augustus prohibited the practice.[1] Under the Roman supremacy as before the magistrates seem to have been appointed some by election some by lot.[2]

Burgess-rights.

Magistrates.

The collegium of Strategoi of equal power remained in existence apparently till the year of the battle of Pharsalia, 48 B.C. At that date the στρατηγὸς ἐπὶ τὰ ὅπλα, otherwise called στ. ἐπὶ τοὺς ὁπλίτας or simply στρατηγός, acquired the preeminent position in the State in which he afterwards appears. It is doubtful whether he was assisted by other Strategoi or not.[3] Immediately upon the first occurrence of the title, the στρατηγὸς ἐπὶ τοὺς ὁπλίτας appears as eponymous magistrate by the side of the

στρατηγοί.

---

[1] Cf. Nicol. Dam. in Müller, *fr. hist. gr.*, 3, 355, 6: κατεγέλα δὲ καὶ τῶν καθ' αὑτὸν σοφιστῶν, οἳ μεγάλοις τιμήμασιν ἐωνοῦντο Ἀθηναῖοι ἢ Ῥόδιοι καλεῖσθαι. Dio Cass. 54, 7: καὶ προσέτι (ὁ Αὔγουστος) καὶ ἀπηγόρευσέ σφισι μηδένα πολίτην ἀργυρίου ποιεῖσθαι. See Hertzberg 1, 434.

[2] See Sauppe, *de creatione archontum att.*, p. 27 ff., whose view is adopted by Dittenberger on C.I.A., III. 87, though it is generally supposed that appointment by lot was entirely abolished. Appointment by lot is attested in the case of a γραμματεύς: C.I.A., III. 87, and in a fragment, no. 81, we find (κλήρ)ῳ λαχών. No. 1 shews that the στρατηγὸς ἐπὶ τὰ ὅπλα was elected; the inscription on the chair of the ἐξηγητὴς ἐξ Εὐπατριδῶν in the theatre, no. 267, shows that his office too was elective. Another fragment, no. 96, has (χει)ροτονητοί. The ἐπιμελητὴς ἐπὶ τὸν λιμένα was elected: C.I.A., II. 475. Philostrat., *Vit. Apollon. Tyan.*, 8, 16, says of the Athenians: τυράννοις λοιπὸν χαρίζονται τὸ κεχειροτονημένους αὐτῶν ἄρχειν.

[3] In the time before Augustus, acc. to the inscrr., οἱ στρατηγοί shared the superintendence of the Epheboi between them (C.I.A., II. 470, 471), and were responsible for the proclamation of the victor's wreaths (II. 469, 470, 471, 478/9, 480. *Mitth. d. dtsch. arch. Inst.*, 5,329); 3 (στρα)τηγοὶ οἱ ἐπὶ τὸν Πειραιᾶ acc. to Köhler in the year 95/4; C.I.A., II. 1207. Cf. also 1206. In the years 102-94, B.C., στρατηγὸς ἐπὶ τὸ ναυτικόν, στρατηγὸς ἐπὶ τὴν παρασκευὴν τὴν ἐν ἄστει, 985. The στρατηγὸς ἐπὶ τοὺς ὁπλίτας is first mentioned in C.I.A., II. 481, drawn up bet. 52–42 B.C. Köhler in his note on the inscr. conjectures that this innovation dates from Caesar and the battle of Pharsalia. This στρατηγός, called sometimes ἐπὶ τὰ ὅπλα, sometimes ἐπὶ τοὺς ὁπλίτας, sometimes simply ὁ στρατηγός (so on his theatre-seat στρατηγοῦ, C.I.A., III. 248, cf. 10, 38, 651), occurs throughout the whole imperial age. In C.I.A., II., 481, in which the στρατηγὸς ἐπὶ τοὺς ὁπλίτας first appears, we still find mention of στρατηγοί in line 52. But we cannot from this infer, as Neubauer 43 ff., and Hauvette-Besnault, *les stratèges Athéniens*, 175, Paris, 1885, do, that other Strategoi still existed, for these στρατηγοί do not belong to the same year as the στρατηγὸς ἐπὶ τοὺς ὁπλίτας Mnaseas, but to the year before. But in a list of Prytaneis, dating from 90-100 A.D., a στρατηγὸς still occurs by the side of the στ. ἐπὶ τὰ ὅπλα. Cf. C.I.A., III. 1020.

Archon, and so repeatedly throughout the principate.[1] According to Hadrian's decree concerning the exportation of oil the Strategos possessed the power of convening the Boule and the Ecclesia.[2] According to our literary authorities he stood at the head of the Athenian State, took charge of the corn trade and corn supply, and supervised the training of the Epheboi.[3]

The collegium of the 9 Archons, who were all together styled θεσμοθέται, continued in existence. The ἄρχων, who as eponymous magistrate is often at this date called ἄρχων ἐπώνυμος, was, together with the Strategos, the most important official in the State. The βασιλεύς, the πολέμαρχος, and the six θεσμοθέται, though of less importance than the ἄρχων, nevertheless were high officials, and, like the others mentioned, possessed seats of honour in the theatre.[4] Other magistrates of the times of independence who still remained in existence were the ἀγορανόμοι, whose number was now diminished to two, and also the ἀστυνόμοι.[5] As in Sparta, so also at Athens, we meet

ἄρχοντες.

ἀγορανόμοι.

---

[1] C.I.A., II. 481, and for examples from imperial times III. 63, 65, 68, 158, 457, 616.

[2] C.I.A., III. 38. Compare Swobeda in *N. Rh. Mus.*, 1890, 809/10.

[3] Cf. Philostrat., *Vit. Soph.*, 1, 23, 1. προὔστη δὲ καὶ τοῦ Ἀθηναίων δήμου στρατηγήσας αὐτοῖς τὴν ἐπὶ τῶν ὅπλων· ἡ δὲ ἀρχὴ αὕτη πάλαι κατέλεγέ τε καὶ ἐξῆγε ἐς τὰ πολέμια, νυνὶ δὲ τροφῶν ἐπιμελεῖται καὶ σίτου ἀγορᾶς. Cf. 2, 16; 2, 20, 1. Plut., *Quaest. Symp.*, 9, 1, 1: Ἀμμώνιος Ἀθήνησι στρατηγῶν ἀπόδειξιν ἔλαβε τῷ Διογενίῳ τῶν γράμματα καὶ γεωμετρίαν καὶ τὰ ῥητορικὰ καὶ μουσικὴν μανθανόντων ἐφήβων. On the Strategoi, cf. Ahrens, 42 ff.

[4] See Neubauer, 36 ff. For the lists of the 9 Archons, who are called οἱ συνάρχοντες in C.I.A., III. 710, and θεσμοθέται in 716, see C.I.A., III. 1005 ff. Along with them we find mentioned in these lists· the κῆρυξ τῆς ἐξ Ἀρείου πάγου βουλῆς, the κῆρυξ ἄρχοντος, an αὐλητής, and a λειτουργός. See 1005, 1007/8, 1013. The dating of the years acc. to the first Archon, who is not unfrequently called ἐπώνυμος (81, 130, 623, 655/6, 659, 662, 676, 1006) continues through the whole imperial age. Seat of honour at the theatre: 254. Dio Cass. 69, 16 calls his office ἡ μεγίστη ἀρχή. The same office is meant also, I believe, in Philost., *Vit. Soph.*, 2, 20, 1: ἔν τε λειτουργίαις, ἃς μεγίστας Ἀθηναῖοι νομίζουσι, τήν τε ἐπώνυμον καὶ τὴν ἐπὶ τῶν ὅπλων ἐπετράπη, where λειτουργία seems to mean the same as ἀρχή, though as a rule it meant nothing more than the ὑπηρεσία of the δημόσιοι. Cf. C.I.A., II. 404, 476, line 53. Cf. also the λειτουργὸς mentioned above and the λειτουργὸς ἐπὶ τὴν Σκιάδα, C.I.A., III. 1020. Special mention of the βασιλεύς: III. 95, 680, 717. His chair at the theatre: 255; mention of the πολέμαρχος: 91, his theatre-chair 256; mention of the θεσμοθέται: 690, their chairs, 257–60.

[5] ἀγορανόμοι mentioned, C.I.A., III. 160, 682, 725. An ἀγορανόμος dedicates (τὸν) ζυγὸν καὶ τὰ μέτρα: 98. 461 shows that there were only two of them: ἀγορανομούντων αὐτοῦ τε Διονυσίου Μαραθωνίου καὶ Κοΐντου Ναιβίου Ῥούφου

with various ἐπιμεληταί.[1] Under Augustus a σιτωνικὸν ταμιεῖον was established, under the control of a σιτώνης and of ταμίαι τῶν σιτωνικῶν. Hadrian's decree concerning oil exportation established ἐλεῶναι also.[2]   **σιτώνης.**

The ταμίας τῶν στρατιωτικῶν, who appears to have been the supreme official of general Athenian finance in the last century B.C., still occurs under the principate of Domitian.[3] Under Hadrian the state ταμιεῖον seems to have been placed under the control of ἀργυροταμίαι; and there was also a συνήγορος τοῦ ταμιείου, whose duty was to represent the interests of the State in lawsuits concerning fiscal matters.[4] In the 2nd century B.C. there occurs a ταμίας τῶν πρυτανείων. An inscription of the last century B.C. mentions οἱ ἄρχοντες ἐπὶ τὴν δημοσίαν τράπεζαν.[5]   **Financial Officials.**

The Boule also continued in existence under the Roman rule, though with repeated changes in the number of its members. After the Phylai were increased in number to 12, 600 was the usual number of Bouleutai, but in 126/7 A.D. the old number 500 was restored. Whether this last change coincided in date with the creation of the new tribe Hadrianis, or whether it came later, must be left undecided. In an inscription dating before 267 A.D., we find a council of 750 members, while at the end of the 4th century A.D. the number of Bouleutai   **Boule.**

Μελιτέως. The existence of ἀστυνόμοι as state officials may be inferred from their occurrence among the governors of the Epheboi. Cf. C.I.A., 1114, 1147, 1199. See Neubauer, 45/6.

[1] Ἐπιμελητὴς τοῦ ἐν Πειραιεῖ λιμένος, also ἐπιμελητὴς Πειραιέως, ἐπιμελητὴς τοῦ λιμένος, or ἐπὶ τὸν λιμένα: C.I.A., II. 985, 475/6. See Wachsmuth 2, 1, 819. III. 458. ἐπιμελητὴς τῆς πόλεως: III. 68, 556, 721. ἐπιμελητὴς τῆς κατὰ τὴν πόλιν ἀγορᾶς: Neubauer 45. ἐπιμελητὴς πρυτανείου: III. 90. ἐπιμελητὴς τοῦ Λυκείου: III. 89.

[2] On the date of the institution of the σιτωνικὸν ταμιεῖον see Dittenberger on C.I.A., III. 645, where a σιτώνης is mentioned, as also in no. 708, about 200 A.D. ταμίαι τῶν σιτωνικῶν: III. 646. Ἐλεῶναι, οἵτινες ἀεὶ προνοοῦσιν τῆ(ς δημοσίας χρεία)ς: III. 38.

[3] C.I.A., III. 654. On his occurrence in inscriptions before the Christian era see the collection of instances in Hartel, Stud. ü. att. Staater. u. Urkundenw., 135/6.

[4] Ἀργυροταμίαι, C.I.A., III. 88/9. The title ἀπὸ συνη(γ)οριῶν ταμ(ιε)ίου, III. 712a and Dittenberger's note.

[5] ταμιεύων ἐπὶ τὰ πρυτανεῖα, C.I.A., II. 1201/2, 1358. οἱ ἄρχοντες ἐπὶ τὴν δημοσίαν τράπεζαν, C.I.A., II. 476, lines 4, 28. On δημοσία τράπεζα, cf. Boeckh 2, 856 ff., Wachsmuth in N. Rh. M., 24, 471.

has diminished to 300.¹ An extension of the official powers of the council, coinciding with a restriction of the rights of the popular assembly, can be assigned with considerable probability to the year 48 B.C.; but our authorities tell us just as little about the powers of the Boule as they do concerning the difference between its powers and those of the Areopagus. In the inscriptions the Boule repeatedly grants its consent to private persons to put up dedicatory offerings: in Hadrian's decree on oil exportation the Boule was empowered to decide cases arising out of the transgression of that decree, up to a specified maximum amount.² Among officials of the Boule we find in the Prytany-lists a γραμματεὺς βουλῆς καὶ δήμου, a γραμματεὺς κατὰ πρυτανείαν, also styled περὶ τὸ βῆμα, an ἀντιγραφεύς, a κῆρυξ βουλῆς καὶ δήμου, and a ὑπογραμματεύς; all these belonged to the ἀΐσιτοι. The ταμίας τῆς βουλῆς was not counted among the ἀΐσιτοι. Further, the πρυτάνεις, whose ἐπιστάτης held office throughout the entire Prytany, had their own clerk, the γραμματεὺς βουλευτῶν, their ταμίας τῆς φυλῆς, and their ἐπώνυμος, whose full title seems to have been ἱερεὺς ἐπωνύμου. The meetings of the Council, and also of the Ecclesia, were presided over, as in earlier times, by the πρόεδροι.³

---

¹ See Ahrens 29 ff.; Neubauer 26 ff. Institution of the 13th tribe Hadrianis: Paus. 1, 5, 5. On the manner of its formation, see Dittenberger in *Herm.*, 9, 386 ff. The βουλὴ τῶν πεντακοσίων, repeatedly mentioned in the inscriptions of the imperial age, was introduced at the same time as the Hadrianis, acc. to Hirschfeld, *Herm.*, 7, 55, with whom Dittenberger, *ib.*, 221, agrees, though on different grounds. According to Neubauer, 27 ff., the Hadrianis came later. The question is best left undecided. C.I.A., III. 716, which Dittenberger, in *Commentat. Mommsen*, 246, puts not later than 267 B.C., gives a βουλή of 750 members; III. 635, 719, gives one of 300.

² On the increase of the powers of the Council see Köhler on C.I.A., II. 481. Dedications by private persons, κατὰ τὰ δόξαντα τῇ βουλῇ, C.I.A., III. 809, 77a. κατὰ τὸ ἐπερώτημα τῆς βουλῆς, 697, 780b. Ψηφισαμένης τῆς βουλῆς, 822a. The Boule as court of justice, III. 38.

³ The lists of the ἀΐσιτοι, among whom were counted also a number of religious functionaries, and also a λειτουργός, i.e. a ὑπηρέτης, the ἐπὶ Σκιάδος, see C.I.A., III. 1019 ff. III. 1020 gives the accurate term, (λι)τουργὸς ἐπὶ τὴν Σκι(άδα). See Neubauer, 32 ff., ταμίας τῆς βουλῆς, III. 646, 650, 1297. That the ἐπιστάτης πρυτανέων remained unchanged through the entire Prytany, follows from the fact that the lists of Prytanies obviously know only one ἐπιστάτης. See 1025/6, 1047, 1053, 1055, 1058. γραμματεὺς βουλευτῶν, 1030, 1032–37–40–57. In 1042 he seems to be counted among the ἀΐσιτοι. ταμίας τῆς φυλῆς, i.e., τῶν πρυτανέων, 648, 1019, 1023, 1057. ἐπώνυμος, 1030, 1032, 1037, 1040, 1047, 1049, 1053, 1054–58, 1062, 1065, 1075. ἱερεὺς ἐπων(ύμου), 1051. Mention of πρόεδροι, 2, 10.

Another governing body was ἡ ἐξ Ἀρείου πάγου βουλή, which at that date was certainly not recruited in the same way as in old days. In earlier times the State was represented by Council and public assembly; now it was represented by the Areopagus, the Council, and the public assembly. These three together drew up decrees and dedicated votive offerings. Written communications to the State from foreign powers were addressed to all three. Cases, however, occur where a dedication is made by the Areopagus and Demos only, or decrees are drawn up by the Boule and Demos.[1] As to the special competence of the Areopagus, we can only give isolated details. The Areopagus made votive offerings on its own account and granted its permission for dedications, a right which, however, belonged to the Boule also, as we have seen.[2] It also granted permission for repair of houses, and supervised education.[3] The Areopagus exercised judicial as well as administrative functions.[4] In the first place it was still the tribunal for cases of homicide.[5] Our other information as to its judicial activity is limited to two cases. In a decree, dating before the Christian

---

[1] Cic., *de Deor. Nat.*, 2, 29, 74 : si quis dicat Atheniensium rempublicam consilio regi, desit illud Areopagi.—Plut., *Per.*, 9, describes the Solonian method of appointing Areopagites as an institution of the bygone past. Decree of the Areopagus, Boule, and Demos, C.I.A., III. 10. Dedications by all three, III. 454, 457/8, 461/2, 464, 556, 578, 604, 618, 642/3/4, 706. Letters addressed to the three, III. 31, 40/1. Dedications by Areopagus and Demos, III. 452/3, 558, 566. Decree of Boule and Demos, III. 2. On the Areopagus at this date see Ahrens., 34 ff.; Philippi, *d. Areop. u. d. Eph.*, 309 ff.; Neubauer, 14 ff.

[2] Dedications by the Areopagus, C.I.A., III. 546, 567. The permission of the Areopagus for the dedication of votive offerings is stated in the inscriptions in various formulae. κατὰ τὰ δόξαντα τῇ ἐξ Ἀρείου πάγου βουλῇ or the like : III. 703, 687, 714, 675a, 775a, 830a. Ψηφισαμένης τῆς ἐξ Ἀρείου πάγου βουλῆς, III. 751; κατὰ τὸ ἐπερώτημα τῆς ἐξ Ἀρείου πάγου βουλῆς, III. 732, 965 a, b, c. καθ' ὑπομνηματισμὸν τῆς ἐξ Ἀρείου πάγου βουλῆς or similar phrase, III. 843, 806, 938, 772b, 832a. The dedicator had to ask the consent of the Areopagus : see III. 704, 710, 735, 746, 774a. Occasionally the Areopagus and Boule give their joint sanction, III. 639, 707, or the Areopagus, Boule, and Demos, III. 716.

[3] Repair of houses : Cic., *ad Fam.*, 13, 1 ; *ad Att.*, 5, 11. The Areopagus gave permission to the Peripatetic Cratippus to teach in Athens : Plut., *Cic.*, 24.

[4] Lucian, *Bis Accusat.*, 4, 12, 14; *Vitar. Auct.*, 7, represents the Areopagus as the centre of the Athenian judicial system generally.

[5] This follows from Paus. 1. 28, 5, though I agree with Philippi, p. 314/5, that no special weight should be assigned to the anecdotes in Ælian, *Var. Hist.*, 5, 18, Quint. 5, 9, 13, and Gell. 12, 7.

era, and treating of the introduction and use of new standards of weight and measure, the Areopagus is empowered to punish the transgressor of the regulations, κατὰ τοὺς ἐπὶ τῶν κακούργων κειμένους νόμους. The other case is from the beginning of the first century A.D.: the Areopagus condemned a man for forgery, but the particular details are not recorded.[1] The office of κῆρυξ τῆς ἐξ 'Αρείου πάγου βουλῆς was held in high honour; we may regard him as the chairman of the Areopagus.[2]

No certain information can be given concerning the administration of justice apart from the cases which belonged to the Areopagus. Hadrian's decree on oil exportation provides that the transgressor of its provisions shall be condemned by the Boule if the amount in question does not exceed 50 amphorai, if it be greater by the Ecclesia. In the latter case appeal was permitted to the emperor or to the governor of the province, and the people were to appoint σύνδικοι to represent the interests of the State if appeal were made.[3] Yet there seem still to have been other permanent courts of justice besides the Areopagus. For there are mentioned in the inscriptions four annual ἐπιμεληταὶ δικαστηρίων with two γραμματεῖς, who must have been presidents of such courts.[4]

Justice.

The Demos was of little importance after 48 B.C. It is true that the Athenian populace still assembled in the theatre to draw up decrees, still elected Strategoi in the Pnyx, and, indeed, had a certain judicial competence under

Ecclesia.

---

[1] C.I.A., II. 476, line 59/60. Tac., *Ann.*, 2, 55, where it is said of Cn. Piso: offensus urbi propria quoque ira, quia Theophilum quendam Areo iudicio falsi damnatum precibus suis non concederent.

[2] See Köhler on C.I.A., II. 481. He and the στρατηγὸς together arranged for the proclamation of the victors' wreaths. Not to mention religious officials, he is mentioned along with the ἄρχων ἐπώνυμος and the στρατηγός: III. 10. 721, and with the στρατηγὸς and βασιλεύς: 680. The theatre-seat inscribed κήρυκος, III. 250, belonged without doubt to him. In C.I.A., III. 57, he gives presents to the Areopagus. He is introduced into the list of Archons: III. 1005, 1007, 1008, 1013. If the κῆρυξ mentioned III. 38, 39, is the κῆρυξ of the Areopagus, he apparently had a share in the financial administration. Perhaps Plut. refers to him in *An seni sit ger. resp.* 20: οὐδὲ γὰρ ἐν ἀρχαῖς τὸν τηλικοῦτον ὥρα φέρεσθαι, πλὴν ὅσαι γε μέγεθος κέκτηνται καὶ ἀξίωμα καθάπερ ἣν σὺ νῦν 'Αθήνῃσι μεταχειρίζῃ τῆς ἐξ 'Αρείου πάγου βουλῆς ἐπιστασίαν.

[3] C.I.A., III. 38.

[4] Cic., *pro Balbo*, 12, 30, draws a distinction bet. iudices and Areopagitæ. For ἐπιμεληταὶ δικαστηρίων see C.I.A., III. 1017, 1018.

Hadrian; but they no longer possessed the influence which they enjoyed in the period of fully developed democracy.[1]

[1] For the date of the restriction of the Demos see Köhler on C.I.A., II. 481. Ecclesia in the theatre in the Psephisma in Joseph., *Ant. Jud.*, 14, 8, 5. The Demos-decrees of this period are mostly honorary decrees: C.I.A., II. 490; III. 1, 2, 3. Decree concerning the disputes of the Lemnian Cleruchs, II. 488. Decree on the Epheboi sharing in the Eleusinian festival, 5, 6. Decree for a festival to celebrate the appointment of Getas as joint emperor, 209 A.D., 10. Election of στρατηγὸς at the Pnyx: Hesych. Πνύξ. The Ecclesia as court of justice, C. I. A., III. 38. See also Neubauer 21 ff.

II.

ANTIQUITIES.

1. THE ELEMENTS OF THE POPULATION.

A. *The Slaves.*[1]

THE number of the slave population in Attica cannot be stated with precision, but can scarcely have ever amounted to much **Number and** more than 100,000.[2] These were naturally divided **Origin.** in very various proportions among the different householders. For quite apart from the difference in wealth between the various slave-owners, a difference which determined the number of slaves in each household, the number of a citizen's slaves at any moment depended also on the question whether the slaves were kept simply for household service, or whether the owner had invested part of his fortune in purchasing and keeping slaves for the prosecution of manufacture or mining, or to get a profit from their strength and skill by letting out their services on hire to others.[3] There were but few slaves born from slave-parents in Attica; the demand for fresh slaves was supplied mainly by importation from barbarian lands; we are told that the chief supply came from Lydia, Phrygia, Paphlagonia, Syria, and the countries of the Black Sea. In private households the slaves

---

[1] On the slaves in general see Büchsenschütz, *Besitz. u. Erwerb. im griech. Alterth.*, 104 ff.

[2] Acc. to Ctesikles *ap.* Ath. 6, 272B, there were 400,000 slaves in Attica when Demetrios of Phaleron was ruler. The impossibility of the truth of this statement is proved by Beloch, *die Bevölker. d. griech.-röm. Welt*, 87 ff. 1886. Acc. to Thuc. 7, 27, 20,000 slaves even were a very considerable number.

[3] Cf. Dem. 27, 9. Lys. 12, 19. Slaves hired out to employers in the mines: Xen., *de Vect.*, 4, 14, 15. Lex. Seguer. 212, 12: Ἀνακεῖον Διοσκούρων ἱερόν, οὗ νῦν οἱ μισθοφοροῦντες δοῦλοι ἑστᾶσιν refers to slaves hired for particular jobs. On the servants of Κολωνὸς ἀγοραῖος cf. Harp., Κολωνίτις.

were called either by their national name, or by a proper name suggesting their origin, *e.g.* a Phrygian would be called Midas.¹

The life of the slaves in Attica was a comparatively comfortable one. Their behaviour is described as impudent and shameless, and we are told that freedom of speech was enjoyed at Athens even by aliens and slaves. They were not distinguished from the ordinary citizen either in dress or by close-cropped hair. In their owner's household they were treated as members of the family. When a newly bought slave entered into the house the master or mistress scattered figs, dates, nuts, and other dainties over him, declaring, symbolically, that his life in the house would be a pleasant one.² Condition of the slaves.

The slave was permitted to enter the public sanctuaries, and to be present at religious festivals, but was not allowed to visit the Ecclesia or the Palæstra. He could only appear as a witness before a judicial tribunal in cases of homicide, in all other cases his evidence, to be valid, had to be given under torture.³ On the other hand, the law protected the slave against ill-treatment by strangers by allowing the owner of the injured slave a γραφὴ ὕβρεως against the injurer;⁴ and also against his owner by establishing considerable restrictions on the right of the owner to inflict punishment. Thus the owner Legal position of the slaves.

---

¹ Strab. 304. Compare Büchsenschütz 117 ff. No slave was allowed to have the name Harmodios or Aristogeiton: Gell. 9, 2, 10.

² General condition of slaves in Attica: (Xen.) *de Rep. Lac.*, 1, 10 sqq. Dem. 9, 8. Their clothing and method of wearing the hair: Xen., *ib.*, 1, 10; Arist., *Birds*, 911. For the symbolic act of reception of the slave into the house cf. καταχύσματα. Lex. Seguer. 269, 9: καταχύσματα ἰσχάδες καὶ φοίνικες καὶ κάρυα ἄλλα τοιαῦτα ἐδώδιμα κατέχεον αἱ κύριαι τῶν οἴκων κατά τι ἔθος ἐπὶ τὰς κεφαλὰς τῶν ἄρτι ἐωνημένων δούλων παραδηλοῦσαι, ὅτι ἐπὶ γλυκέα καὶ ἡδέα πράγματα εἰσεληλύθασιν. Cf. Suid. Art. 1.=Phot. Art. 2. Schol. on Arist., *Plut.*, 768.

³ Cf. (Dem.) 59, 85; Plut., *Phok.*, 34. Æsch. c. *Tim.*, 138. Antiph., *de cæde Herod.*, 48: εἴπερ γὰρ καὶ μαρτυρεῖν ἔξεστι δούλῳ κατὰ τοῦ ἐλευθέρου τὸν φόνον. This competence of the slave to give evidence in homicide cases is disputed by Guggenheim, *d. Bedeut. d. Folter. im att. Proc.*, 7 ff., Zurich, 1882; he believes that the μαρτυρεῖν used with reference to slaves is used by the Attic orators for μηνύειν also. His arguments are answered correctly by Lipsius in Meier,² 875, no. 806. On the legal competence of slaves in general see Meier,² 749 ff.

⁴ Cf. Hyper. ap. Ath. 6, 266 F: ἔθεσαν οὐ μόνον ὑπὲρ τῶν ἐλευθέρων, ἀλλὰ καὶ ἐάν τις εἰς δούλου σῶμα ὑβρίσῃ, γραφὰς εἶναι κατὰ τοῦ ὑβρίσαντος. See Lipsius in Meier,² 399 ff. The owner is the legal representative of his slave as a general rule. Cf. Dem. 53, 20. Antiph., *de cæd. Her.*, 48.

possessed no power of life and death over his slave; the slave's life could not be forfeited except by judicial sentence; the slave could further obtain protection against any inhuman treatment by his master, by taking asylum in a temple. The temples used for this purpose at Athens were the temple of Theseus and the shrine of the Σεμναί.[1] In them the slave not merely obtained protection against immediate ill-treatment, but could also, under certain circumstances, either as a right or as a customary piece of humanity, get his owner compelled to sell him.[2]

The slaves, known as οἱ χωρὶς οἰκοῦντες, occupied a peculiar posi-

---

[1] The death penalty cannot be inflicted on a slave except by decision of a legal tribunal: Ant., de caed. H., 48. For the temples of refuge cf. Schol. on Arist., Eq., 1312: εἰς τὸ Θησεῖον· ἐνταῦθα οἱ καταφεύγοντες τῶν οἰκετῶν ἀσυλίαν εἶχον. ἐπὶ τῶν σεμνῶν· εἰς τὸ τῶν Ἐρινύων ἱερόν. καὶ ἐνταῦθα δὲ οἱ οἰκέται ἔφευγον. Similarly Suid. Θησεῖον. The Θησεῖον alone is mentioned as the asylum by Phot., Hesych., Et. M., Lex. Seguer. 264, 21. Cf. also Plut., Thes., 36. Diod. 4, 62. Teles ap. Stob. Flor. 567 speaks in quite general terms: ὥσπερ οἰκέτης πρὸς κύριον ἐφ' ἱερὸν καθίσας δικαιολογεῖται· τί μοι μάχῃ; μή τι σοὶ κέκλοφα; οὐ πᾶν τὸ προσταττόμενον ὑπὸ σοῦ ποιῶ; οὐ τὴν ἀποφορὰν εὐτάκτως σοι φέρω;

[2] The technical term is πρᾶσιν αἰτεῖν. Cf. Poll. 7, 13: ὃ δὲ οἱ νῦν φασὶ τοὺς οἰκέτας πρᾶσιν αἰτεῖν, ἔστιν εὑρεῖν ἐν ταῖς Ἀριστοφάνους Ὥραις:

ἐμοὶ
κράτιστόν ἐστιν εἰς τὸ Θησεῖον δραμεῖν,
ἐκεῖ δ', ἕως ἂν πρᾶσιν εὕρωμεν, μένειν.
ἄντικρυς δὲ ἐν ταῖς Εὐπόλιδος πόλεσι
κακὰ τοιάδε
πάσχουσα μηδὲ πρᾶσιν αἰτῶ.

Who had to decide whether the πρᾶσις should be granted to the slave, we are not told. In the Et. M. Θησεῖον it is said: Θησεῖον τέμενός ἐστι τῷ Θησεῖ, ὃ τοῖς οἰκέταις ἄσυλον ἦν· ἐλέγοντο δὲ δίκαι ἐνταῦθα, with which however should be compared Meier,[2] 179/80. In the Mystery-inscrr. of Andania, Dittenberger 388, 80 sqq., it is said: ὁ δὲ ἱερεὺς ἐπικρινέτω περὶ τῶν δραπετικῶν, ὅσοι κα ἦνται ἐκ τᾶς ἁμετέρας πόλεος καὶ ὅσους κα κατακρίνει, παραδότω τοῖς κυρίοις· ἂν δὲ μὴ παραδιδῷ ἐξ(έσ)τω τῷ κυρίῳ ἀποτρέχειν ἔχοντι. In the accounts of the ἐπιστάται Ἐλευσινόθεν, dating from 329/8 B.C., we find C.I.A., II. 834b, Col. I. 65: κόφινοι παρ' Ἀμεινίου ἐκ τοῦ Θησείου. 68: ἧλοι ταῖς θυραῖς ἐκ τοῦ Θησείου: Col. II. 30/1: ἥλων στ(α)τῆρες τρεῖς, ὁ στατὴρ ⊢⊢⊢, τρεῖς παρὰ Φίλωνος ἐκ τοῦ Θησέου. 55/6: ἀμφιδέαι ταῖς θυροκυκλίσιν τέτταρες παρὰ Φίλωνος ἐκ τοῦ Θησέου. Köhler remarks on 834b, Col. I.: servos, qui a dominis male habiti ad heroes confugerant, interdum in area templi constitisse et tabernas collocasse non est veridissimile, probably in order to purchase their liberty with their earnings.

tion.[1] They were those slaves who lived by themselves, and on their own resources, and simply had to pay their masters a fixed sum annually. Such slaves were able to amass a respectable fortune in course of time, and these are obviously the slaves referred to, when complaints are made of the luxurious and sumptuous life of slaves at Athens.[2] Sometimes, also, several slaves worked together in a workshop or factory under a foreman or overseer, himself also a slave, paid their master the stipulated amount, and then shared between themselves any surplus profits.[3] *οἱ χωρὶς οἰκοῦντες.*

The State employed slaves in various public services. For instance, the Athenian police force was composed entirely of slaves. They were called bowmen because armed with bows, Scythians from the country whence they were obtained, or Speusinii from the name of the founder of the force. *State slaves.*

These Skythai, who were encamped in tents in earlier days in the market-place, but afterwards on the Areopagus, were employed to keep order in the public assembly, in the courts of justice, in the open spaces of the city, and when public works or functions were proceeding.[4] The magistrates employed them in

---

[1] Cf. Lex. Seguer. 316, 11: χωρὶς οἰκοῦντες· οἱ ἀπελεύθεροι, ἐπεὶ χωρὶς οἰκοῦσι τῶν ἀπελευθερωσάντων ἢ δοῦλοι χωρὶς οἰκοῦντες τῶν δεσποτῶν.

[2] (Xen.) *de Rep. Ath.*, 1, 10 ff. Teles *ap.* Stob. Flor. 95, 21: οἰκέται οἱ τυχόντες αὐτοὺς τρέφουσι καὶ μισθὸν τελοῦσι τοῖς κυρίοις. These are the ἀνδράποδα μισθοφοροῦντα, Is. 8, 35. ἀποφορά, mentioned also by Teles *ap.* Stob. Flor. 5, 67. Theophr., *Char.*, 30. The slave mentioned by Andok., *de Myst.*, 38, as bringing in an ἀποφορά, was not an independent workman, but a slave let on hire to an employer. See Boeckh, *kl. Schr.*, 5, 46 sqq.

[3] Æsch., c. Tim., 97: χωρὶς δὲ οἰκέτας δημιουργοὺς τῆς σκυτοτομικῆς τέχνης ἐννέα ἢ δέκα, ὧν ἕκαστος τούτῳ δυ' ὀβολοὺς ἀποφορὰν ἔφερε τῆς ἡμέρας, ὁ δ' ἡγεμὼν τοῦ ἐργαστηρίου τριώβολον.

[4] For these see Boeckh 1, 290 (206) sqq; Poll. 8, 131/2: οἱ μέντοι πρὸ τῶν δικαστηρίων καὶ τῶν ἄλλων συνόδων δημοσίου ὑπηρέται, οἷς ἐπέτατον ἀνείργειν τοὺς ἀκοσμοῦντας καὶ τοὺς ἃ μὴ δεῖ λέγοντας ἐξαίρειν καὶ Σκύθαι ἐκαλοῦντο καὶ τοξόται καὶ Σπευσίνιοι ἀπὸ τοῦ πρώτου συντάξαντος τὴν περὶ αὐτοὺς ὑπηρεσίαν. Schol. Aristoph. *Ach.*, 54: εἰσὶ δὲ οἱ τοξόται δημόσιοι ὑπηρέται, φύλακες τοῦ ἄστεος, τὸν ἀριθμὸν χίλιοι, οἵτινες πρότερον μὲν ᾤκουν τὴν ἀγοράν μέσην σκηνοποιησάμενοι, ὕστερον δὲ μετέβησαν εἰς Ἄρειον πάγον κ.τ.ἀ. = Suid. τοξόται. Cf. Phot. τοξόται. Acc. to Lex. Seguer. 234, 15 sqq. they were told off πρὸς ὑπηρεσίαν τῶν δικαστηρίων καὶ τῶν κοινῶν τόπων καὶ ἔργων. In an inscr. about 440 B.C. there are specified as sentinels on the acropolis: φύλακας δὲ (εἶ)ναι τρεῖς μὲν τοξό(τ)ας ἐκ τῆς φυλῆς τῆς (π)ρυτανευούσης: Bull. 14, 77 = 'Αρχ. δελτ. 1889, 254 = C.I.A., IV. 3, 26a. I consider these τοξόται as τοξόται ἀστικοί, not as Wernicke in Herm. 26, 51, Skythai. Classification of the former by Phylai is attested *e.g.* by C.I.A.,

personal services connected with their spheres of office.[1] The formation of this corps of bowmen dates from the time of Pericles' expedition to the Pontos, on which occasion, probably, the first 300 were bought. The number was afterwards increased to 1,200.[2] Whether the executioners, torturers, and similar officers were taken from among these Skythai or not, must remain undecided. At all events, the duties of these people also were performed by slaves.[3] It was customary, too, to employ slaves skilled in writing and reckoning as clerks and accountants in the financial departments, because slaves could be put to the torture if necessary.[4] The State possessed no slave for mere manual labour except those employed in the mint.[5] Slaves were employed as oarsmen in the fleet only in exceptional cases, *e.g.* in the sea fight at Arginusæ.[6]

A slave could obtain his freedom by decree of the people, or by the voluntary permission of his master, or by purchasing his freedom himself. The State granted emancipation to the slaves by decree of the people, apart from wholesale grants of freedom for service in war, to those slaves who had given information of offences against the State. In this case the

Emancipation.

I. 79, but for the latter it is not at all probable. Nor can I identify the Skythai with the ἱπποτοξόται. Foucart in the Bull., *ib.*, supposes that a few words have been lost after τοξό(τ)ας.

[1] The Prytaneis have archers in attendance upon them (Arist., *Ach.*, 54; *Thesm.*, 940, 1002 sqq.); so have the Proboùloi who represented them (Arist., *Lysistr.*, 441 sqq.). Such attendants must have been specially numerous in the case of police officials such as the Astynomoi and Agoranomoi.

[2] So we find in Andok., *Pax*, 5 and 7. Æsch., *de Fals. Leg.*, 173/4. See Boeckh, 1, 292 (208). Scheibe in Phil. 3, 542 ff. makes the words ἑτέρους τοσούτους found in both passages, refer to the 300 first bought, and accordingly makes 600 the maximum number ever reached, but he is refuted by Funkhaenel in the *Zeitschr. f. A.-W.*, 1856, p. 41 ff. The number 1000 given by the Schol. Arist., *Ach.*, 54 = Suid. τοξόται, is of no weight against these statements of the orators. Duncker was the first to make the plausible conjecture that Pericles bought the first 300 Skythai on his expedition to Pontos, which he puts in 444 B.C. Duncker, *Abhandl. z. griech. Gesch.*, (158), 147.

[3] Poll. 8, 71; Harp. Et. M., δημόκοινος. Lex. Seguer. 236, 8. Büchsenschütz, *ib.*, 164, 5.

[4] For authorities see the section on financial administration.

[5] Andok. in the Schol. on Arist., *Vesp.*, 1007, περὶ Ὑπερβόλου λέγειν αἰσχύνομαι· οὗ ὁ μὲν πατὴρ ἐστιγμένος ἔτι καὶ νῦν ἐν τῷ ἀργυροκοπείῳ δουλεύει τῷ δημοσίῳ.

[6] See the author's *Beitr. z. innern Gesch. Ath.*, p. 367. The χωρὶς οἰκοῦντες in Dem. 4, 36 mean, without doubt, freedmen. So they are explained in Harp.=Phot. Suid., τοὺς χωρὶς οἰκοῦντας. See Büchsenschütz in *N. Rh. Jhrb. f. cl. Phil.*, Bd. 95, 20 ff.

State paid compensation to the owner for the value of the slave, if the slave belonged to a private person.[1] In the same way, if a slave rendered signal service to his master, he might be emancipated by the voluntary act of his owner.

We have no definite information about the forms by which a slave could purchase his own freedom, and it must therefore be left undecided whether the owner was bound to set his slave free whenever the latter paid the amount for which he was purchased, or an amount previously agreed upon, or whether in this case also the emancipation depended upon the will and pleasure of the owner.[2] Nor do we know upon what formalities the legal validity of the emancipation depended. We hear of emancipations taking place before a court of justice, and also in the theatre.[3]

The freedman[4] obtained, roughly speaking, to the same rights, and became subject to the same obligations, as the Metoicoi. He was bound to render certain services to his former master even after his emancipation, but what these were we do not know, except that he was obliged to choose his emancipator as προστάτης. If he neglected to do this, his former master was entitled to proceed against him by a δίκη ἀποστασίου, in which case an adverse verdict made the freedman once more the slave of his emancipator; if, on the other hand, the freedman won his case, he was released from all obligations towards his former owner.[5]

The Freedmen.

---

[1] Lys. 7, 16, εὖ γὰρ ἂν εἰδείην, ὅτι ἐπ' ἐκείνοις (sc. τοῖς δούλοις) ἦν καὶ ἐμὲ τιμωρήσασθαι καὶ αὐτοῖς μηνύσασιν ἐλευθέροις γενέσθαι. Plat., *Leg.*, 1, 914, δοῦλος δ' ἐὰν ᾖ, μηνύσας μὲν ἐλεύθερος ὑπὸ τῆς πόλεως ὀρθῶς γίγνοιτ' ἂν ἀποδιδούσης τῷ δεσπότῃ τὴν τιμήν. On the slave's right to μήνυσις see Guggenheim, *die Bedeut. d. Folter. im att. Proc.*, 5 ff.

[2] Dio Chrysost. 15, 453 R, 241 M, gives no definite information to decide this question. A case of purchase of freedom in (Dem.) 59, 29–30.

[3] Is. ὑπὲρ Εὐμάθους, *fr.* 15, 3, εἰδὼς ἀφειμένον ἐν τῷ δικαστηρίῳ ὑπὸ Ἐπιγένους. Emancipation in the theatre, Æsch., *in Ctes.*, 41.

[4] The freedman was styled ἀπελεύθερος or ἐξελεύθερος. Cf. Harp. in Dindorf's Oxford ed., praef. VII., ἀπελεύθερος· ὁ δοῦλος ὤν, εἶτα ἀπολυθεὶς τῆς δουλείας, ὡς καὶ παρ' Αἰσχίνῃ. ἐξελεύθερος δὲ ὁ διά τινα αἰτίαν δοῦλος γεγονώς, εἶτα ἀπολυθείς. ἔστι δ' ὅτε καὶ οὐ διαφέρουσιν.

[5] Harp., ἀποστασίου δίκη τίς ἐστι κατὰ τῶν ἀπελευθερωθέντων δεδομένη τοῖς ἀπελευθερώσασιν, ἐὰν ἀφιστῶνταί τε ἀπ' αὐτῶν ἢ ἕτερον ἐπιγράφωνται προστάτην καὶ ἃ κελεύουσιν οἱ νόμοι μὴ ποιῶσιν. καὶ τοὺς μὲν ἁλόντας δεῖ δούλους εἶναι, τοὺς δὲ νικήσαντας τελέως ἤδη ἐλευθέρους. So Suid. Art. 1. Et. M. Lex. Seguer. 201, 5 sqq., 434, 24 sqq. Another form of the ἀποστασίου δίκη was directed against a slave who gave himself out to be a free man, and thus deserted his master's service. Suid., Art. 2. Lex. Seguer. 434, 30 sqq., 184, 25. Platner, *Proc.*, 239.

It seems to have become customary towards the end of the 4th century—no earlier instance has been found—for the freedman acquitted in a δίκη ἀποστασίου to dedicate to Athena a silver bowl called φιάλη ἐξελευθερική of 100 drachmas in weight, as a thank-offering for his liberation.[1]

If a freedman died childless, his property reverted to his emancipator.[2]

B. The Metoicoi.

The second non-citizen element of the Attic population consisted of the resident aliens.[3] Over and above the fluctuating alien population which must be supposed to have existed in Athens as in every large commercial town, there were also aliens who had definitely settled there either permanently or for long periods of time. At Athens all aliens who remained in residence longer than a legally specified time were obliged to get themselves enrolled as μέτοικοι.[4] The State en-

μέτοικοι. Their Number and Origin.

---

[1] In an inventory of the treasurers of Athena, C.I.A., II. 720, we have mention of silver hydriai made ἐκ τῶν φιαλῶν τῶν ἐξελευθερικῶν. Köhler in *Mitth. d. arch. Inst. in Ath.*, 8, 172 ff., compares with this the fragmentary inscriptions which record dedications of cups—C.I.A., II. 768–775, 776 b. 'Εφ. ἀρχ., 1889, p. 60. *Ber. d. Berl. Ak.*, 1887, 1070, 1199; 1888, 251. 'Αρχ. δελτ., 1888, 174; 1890, 58 ff.—in formulæ such as (M)άνης Φαληρε(ί) οἰκῶν, γεωργὸς (ἀπ)οφυγὼν Νικίαν 'Ολύνθιον, φιάλη (σταθμ)όν H (768), and infers that slaves when emancipated were accustomed to dedicate such cups to Athena. In the apparently analogous inscription, C.I.A., II. 776, the word (ἀπ)οστασίου still legible indicates that these offerings are to be attributed to those set free by acquittal in δίκη ἀποστασίου, and this is corroborated by the meaning of ἀποφυγεῖν. See also Köhler on C.I.A., II. 768; H. Schenkl in *d. Zeitschr. f. österr. Gymn.*, 1881, 167 ff.; *Wiener Stud.*, 2, 213 ff. Lipsius in Meier and Schömann, *att. Proc.*,[2] 621, No. 373. Wachsmuth, 2, 1, 151, 2, thinks they refer to emancipations by purchase taking place in courts of justice under the form of a δίκη ἀποστασίου. But this is not at all probable, because the defendant in a δίκη ἀποστασίου must be already a freedman. [Cf. Buck, in *Amer. J. of Archæol.*, 1888, p. 149 ff.]

[2] Is. 4, 9.

[3] De Bruyn de Neve Moll, *de peregrinorum ap. Athen. conditione*, Ludg. Bat., 1839. H. Schenkl, *de metoecis att.* in *Wien. Stud.*, 1880, 161 ff. V. Thumser, *Untersuch. u. d. att. Metoeken*, in *Wien. Stud.*, 1885, 45 ff. v. Wilamowitz-Moellendorf in *Hermes*, 22, 107 ff., 211 ff., 1887, whose views are not made at all more tenable by the air of certainty with which they are put forward. Cf. Thalheim in the *Berl. phil. Wochenschrift*, 1888, 1344/5.

[4] Arist. Byc. in Boissonade Herodian. Epimer., p. 287=Nauck, *fragm. Arist.* 38, p. 198: μέτοικός ἐστιν, ὁπόταν τις ἀπὸ ξένης ἐλθὼν ἐνοικῇ τῇ πόλει,

couraged their settlement because they contributed not a little to the prosperity of Attic industries, and supplied valuable recruits for the navy.[1] In the census taken during the government of Demetrios of Phaleron the number of Metoicoi was given as 10,000, *i.e.* that was the number of those who paid the Metoikion; therefore we must assume at least an equal number for the Metoicoi at Athens in the 5th and 4th centuries. At Athens there were Greeks, Lydians, Phrygians, Syrians and barbarians from all parts.[2] In Athenian parlance the Metoicoi, as distinguished from the burgesses, were spoken of not as Demesmen but as dwellers in the Demes.[3]

Every Metoicos was bound to choose for himself a burgess as προστάτης to represent his interests. The respectability of the Metoicos was generally estimated by the dignity of his προστάτης; the Metoicoi therefore were careful to choose men of special eminence as prostatai, and they in their turn obtained honour from being patrons of as many Metoicoi as possible. Metoicoi that had no προστάτης were liable to a γραφὴ ἀπροστασίου, involving confiscation of their property if decided against them. To what extent this representation by a προστάτης was necessary for all the Metoicos' affairs cannot be accurately

---

τέλος τελῶν εἰς ἀποτεταγμένας τινὰς χρείας τῆς πόλεως· ἕως μὲν οὖν ποσῶν ἡμερῶν παρεπίδημος καλεῖται καὶ ἀτελής ἐστιν, ἐὰν δὲ ὑπερβῇ τὸν ὡρισμένον χρόνον, μέτοικος ἤδη γίγνεται καὶ ὑποτελής. Cf. Harp. μετοίκιον. In C.I.A., II. 86, the Sidonians are excused the necessity of enrolling themselves as Metoicoi after the legal interval: ὁπόσοι δ' ἂν Σιδωνίων οἰκοῦντες ἐς Σιδῶνι καὶ πολιτευόμενοι ἐπιδημῶσιν κατ' ἐμπορίαν Ἀθήνησι, μὴ ἐξεῖναι αὐτοὺς μετοίκιον πράττεσθαι μηδὲ χορηγὸν μηδένα καταστῆσαι μηδ' εἰσφορὰν μηδεμίαν ἐπιγράφειν. See Schenkl, *ib.*, 189. The μέτοικοι not enrolled were called ἀδιάτακτοι, Poll. 3, 37.

[1] (Xen.), *de rep. Ath.*, 1, 12. Cf. the measures proposed in Xen., *de Vect.*, 2, to attract Metoicoi to Athens in still greater numbers.

[2] Ctesicl. *ap.* Athen. 6, 272 B gives 10,000 Metoicoi. Beloch, *Bevölker. d. griech.-röm. Welt*, 58/9, 73. For their nationality cf. Xen., *de Vect.*, 2, 3.

[3] *e.g.* C.I.A., 1, 324: Τεῦκρος ἐν Κυδαθηναίῳ οἰκῶν, cf. C.I.A., II. 768–776. v. Wilamowitz-Moellendorf., *ib.*, 107 ff., gives a collection of the evidence on this point. In 213 ff. he argues from the formula οἰκῶν ἐν τῷ δεῖνι δήμῳ that the Metoicoi were members of Deme, Phyle, and State, and accordingly credits them with quasi-burgess rights, and refuses to admit that the Metoicos stood in client-relationship to any individual Athenian This arbitrary conclusion cannot be accepted. The Metoicos did not pay the Demotikon; he is merely styled "resident in such and such a Deme." We have no more right to assume from that a quasi-burgess right of the Metoicos than we have to assume that an Englishman, said to be resident in Göttingen, must therefore be a German citizen.

determined, but it can be shown that the Metoicoi sometimes conducted their own cases in court themselves.[1]

The Metoicoi were under restrictions as to their rights of ownership, being prohibited from acquiring landed property in Attic territory;[2] further, they were subject to various liabilities towards the Athenian State. They were liable to military service, the wealthier among them as hoplites, the rest as oarsmen in the fleet. But they were not employed as cavalry even if they possessed the census of the ἱππεῖς.[3]

Burdens of the Metoicoi.

Military Service.

---

[1] The Metoicos judged of by his προστάτης: Isocr. 8, 53. Harp., προστάτης· οἱ τῶν μετοίκων Ἀθήνησι προεστηκότες προστάται ἐκαλοῦντο · ἀναγκαῖον γὰρ ἦν ἕκαστον τῶν μετοίκων πολίτην τινὰ Ἀθηναίων νέμειν προστάτην. So Suid., Phot., προστάτης. Acc. to Suid. νέμειν προστάτην, ἀπροστασίου, and Lex. Seguer. 435, 1 sq., 298, 2 sq., the μέτοικος μετὰ προστάτου pays the μετοίκιον. Harp., ἀπροστασίου εἶδος δίκης κατὰ τῶν προστάτην μὴ νεμόντων μετοίκων· ᾑρεῖτο γὰρ ἕκαστος ἑαυτῷ τῶν πολιτῶν τινὰ προστησόμενον περὶ πάντων τῶν ἰδίων καὶ τῶν κοινῶν. So Et. M., Suid., ἀπροστασίου. Lex. Seguer. 201, 12 ff. Results of the δίκη ἀπροστασίου: Phot., πωληταί, 1 Art. = Suid., πωληταί, Art. 2. For these trials cf. Meier and Schömann, *att. Proc.*,[2] 388 ff. Choosing a προστάτης was called τὸν δεῖνα προστάτην ἐπιγράψασθαι (Aristoph., *Pax*, 684) or νέμειν (Suid., νέμειν προστάτην. Harp., προστάτης. Lex. Seguer. 298, 2 ff.). Independent appearance in court of justice is attested by Demosthenes' 56th speech, where the speaker is a μέτοικος. See Meier and Schömann, *att. Proc.*,[2] 753/4. Cf. Herondas Mimiamb. 2, where the πορνοβοσκός, who pleads in person before a Coan court of justice, is obviously a Metoicos, cf. v. 15, 40, 92 sqq. In my opinion the evidence—especially Isocr. 8, 53—is quite clear enough to justify us in adhering, in spite of v. Wilamowitz-Moellendorf, *ib.*, 223 ff., to the old view that even in the 4th century every Metoicos was obliged to have a Prostates. In a decree of the people init. 4th century, the Athenians grant a person who undoubtedly was a Metoicos, besides other privileges, (πρόσοδον) εἶναι αὐτῷ πρὸς τὸν πολέμαρχον (καθάπερ) το(ῖ)ς ἄλλοις προξένοις: it appears from this that the πρόσοδος πρ. τὸν π. was only allowed to the πρόξενοι, while the ordinary Metoicoi had to obtain formal introduction by their patron. C.I.A., II. 42.

[2] Xen., *de Vect.*, 2, 6, and the decrees by which ἔγκτησις γῆς καὶ οἰκίας was granted to individual Metoicoi, *e.g.* C.I.A., II. 41, 42, 70, 186. For this reason mortgages on houses or land were of no value to Metoicoi. Cf. Dem. 36, 6.

[3] Hoplites: Thuc. 2, 13. 31; 4, 90. Xen., *de Vect.*, 2, 2. In earlier times they were only employed, as a rule, for the defence of Attic territory; in Demosthenes' day for service abroad as well. In this I agree with Thumser, *ib.*, 62 ff., against Schenkl, *ib.*, 196 ff. At any rate they seem from Thuc. 2, 13 to have been employed in cases where οἱ πρεσβύτατοι καὶ οἱ νεώτατοι were also used. Acc. to (Xen.), *de Rep. Ath.*, 1, 12, the Athenians needed the services of the Metoicoi διὰ τὸ ναυτικόν. Cf. Harp., μετοίκιον. Dem. 4, 36. The Metoicoi not ἱππεῖς: Xen., *de Vect.*, 2, 5.

Further, the Metoicoi paid an annual tax called μετοίκιον. This amounted to 12 drachmas for a man, 6 for a widow. The latter, however, ceased to pay as soon as any son of hers attained his majority and became liable on his own account for the ordinary 12 drachmas.[1] It need scarcely be said that the freedmen also paid the Metoikion, because by emancipation they obtained the status of Metoicoi. We also hear that they were liable to an extra tax of 3 obols, but the point cannot be certainly determined.[2] Those Metoicoi who failed to pay the metoikion were brought before the Poletai, and if convicted were sold into slavery.[3]

Besides this tax, paid as the price of state protection, every alien, and therefore without doubt every Metoicos, as soon as he began to trade in the market, was required to pay a fee for the privilege of using the market place. The exact amount is not specified.[4]

Market dues.

Further burdens imposed by the State on the Metoicoi were

---

[1] Isaeus ap. Harp., μετοίκιον = Phot., sub verb.: 'Ισαῖος δ' ἐν τῷ κατ' 'Ελπαγόρου καὶ Δημοφάνους ὑποσημαίνει, ὅτι ὁ μὲν ἀνὴρ δώδεκα δραχμὰς ἐτέλει μετοίκιον, ἡ δὲ γυνὴ ἕξ, καὶ ὅτι τοῦ υἱοῦ τελοῦντος ἡ μήτηρ οὐκ ἐτέλει· μὴ τελοῦντος δ' ἐκείνου αὐτὴ τελεῖ. Cf. Lex. Seguer. 281, 19 sqq. Hesych. under μετοίκιον gives incorrectly 10 drachmas per man, under μέτοικοι he gives the correct amount. The Schol. on Plat., Legg., 8,850, gives both versions. In C. I. A., IV. 27a, line 52 ff., occurs the formula τοὺς δὲ ξένους τοὺς ἐν Χαλκίδι ὅσοι οἰκοῦντες μὴ τελοῦσι 'Αθήναζε: Schenkl, *Wiener Stud.*, 2, 195, proposes simply to omit the words ὅσοι οἰκ. μὴ as written by mistake; Kirchhoff would emend to οἰκοῦντας ὅσοι μὲν; Welsing, *de inquilinorum et peregr. ap. Ath. iudiciis*, Münster, 1887, 31, 5, conjectures ὅσοι μετοικοῦντες. The words refer to those Metoicoi who, though settled at Chalkis, continued to pay the Metoikion at Athens. See v. Wilamowitz in *Herm.* 27, 249, 1. Welsing, *loc. cit.* The elaborate conclusions deduced from this by v. Wilamowitz in the *Phil. Untersuch.*, 1, 36 ff., do not admit of proof. See also Welsing, *loc. cit.*, 30/1.

[2] Harp., μετοίκιον—ὅτι δὲ καὶ οἱ δοῦλοι ἀφεθέντες ὑπὸ τῶν δεσποτῶν ἐτέλουν τὸ μετοίκιον, ἄλλοι τε τῶν κωμικῶν δεδηλώκασι καὶ 'Αριστομένης. Μένανδρος δ' ἐν 'Ανατιθεμένῃ καὶ ἐν Διδύμαις πρὸς ταῖς δώδεκα δραχμαῖς καὶ τριώβολόν φησι τούτους τελεῖν, ἴσως τῷ τελώνῃ. The last clause was added by Harp. or the author he followed, and occurs again but without the ἴσως in Hesych. μετοίκιον. Poll. 3, 55 says the τριώβολον was paid to the γραμματεύς. Boeckh 1, 447 (330) ff. infers from this τριώβολον, combined with the passage in Xen., *de Vect.*, 4, 25, that there was a tax on slaves of 3 obols a head, which freedmen after their emancipation had still to pay. See also Thumser, *de civ. Athen. munerib.*, 1 ff., 1880.

[3] Harp., μετοίκιον—οἱ μέντοι μὴ τιθέντες τὸ μετοίκιον μέτοικοι ἀπήγοντο πρὸς τοὺς πωλητὰς καὶ εἰ ἑάλωσαν ἐπιπράσκοντο, ὥς φησι Δημοσθένης ἐν τῷ κατ' 'Αριστογείτονος =(Dem.) 25, 57; cf. Poll. 8, 99.

[4] Dem. 57, 31. 34. Boeckh 1, 449 (332). Schaefer, Dem. 1¹, 124.

λειτουργίαι. those described as λειτουργίαι τῶν μετοίκων, which included the Choregia, Gymnasiarchia and Hestiasis.[1]

For the purposes of the εἰσφορά the Metoicoi were classified, when the symmories were introduced, into μετοικικαὶ συμμορίαι, each headed by a ταμίας. They were assessed for the εἰσφορά by officials called ἐπιγραφεῖς. Of these the individuals whose names are recorded were certainly Metoicoi, and it is probable enough that all of them were of that class.[2]

εἰσφορά.

---

[1] Dem. 20, 18. 20 draws a distinction between αἱ τῶν μετοίκων λειτουργίαι and αἱ πολιτικαί. I now agree with Thumser, op. cit., 57 ff., that Dem. 20, 18–22 proves that the leiturgies of the Metoicoi included the Choregia Gymnasiarchia and Hestiasis. In C.I.A., II. 86, which is a document dating between Ol. 101–104 (B.C. 376–361) and releasing the Sidonians from all pecuniary contributions to the State, we find the words: μὴ ἐξεῖναι αὐτοὺς μετοίκιον πράττεσθαι μηδὲ χορηγὸν μηδένα καταστῆσαι μηδ' εἰσφορὰν μηδεμίαν ἐπιγράφειν: but this does not prove that the Metoicoi were not liable to other leiturgies also, because the word χορηγίαι was often used as a general term for all leiturgies. See Thumser, de civ. Ath. munerib., 58, and ib. 59/60. Choregia by Metoicoi at the Lenaia mentioned by Schol. to Arist., Plut., 953. Acc. to Dem. 20, 20 Metoicoi had not yet been made liable to the trierarchy in 355 B.C. Schenkl, ib., 190, asserts, in opposition to Boeckh, Seeurk., 170, that no Metoicos was ever made trierarch; but Thumser, ib., 60, 55, quotes C.I.A., II. 414, where a Byzantine is granted ἔγκτησις and a vote of thanks to him is recorded ἐπαινέσαι—καὶ τοὺς μετ' αὐτοῦ τριηράρ(χ)ους. Nevertheless it is possible that the person honoured in this decree may have undertaken the trierarchy voluntarily. See Fränkel on Boeckh, 2, p. 124, no. 840. The question is best left open.

[2] Poll. 8, 144: καὶ τὸ παρ' Ὑπερίδῃ μετοικικῆς συμμορίας ταμίας. Isocr. 17 is spoken by a Metoicos who was himself ἐπιγραφεύς (cf. § 41). v. Wilamowitz regards the εἰσφορά here mentioned as an εἰσφορά of the ξένοι παρεπιδημοῦντες, not of the μέτοικοι; but the speaker of Isocr. 17 paid the tribute along with Pasion (§ 41) who must have been a Metoicos at that time. That the speaker could evade the payment by leaving Athens is natural enough even for a metoicos. Cf. C.I.A., II. 413 (B.C. 200–197), where it is said of a Metoicos: καὶ τάς τε εἰσφορὰς ἀπ(ὰσ)ας ὅσας ἐψήφισται ὁ δῆμος ε(ἰ)σενεγκεῖν τοὺς μετοίκους (ε)ὐτάκτως εἰσενήνοχεν. And the εἰσφοραί mentioned in C. I. A., II. 270 are war taxes in spite of Schenkl, ib., 188, and Thumser, ib., 56. Nicandros and Polyzelos are honoured in that inscr. for contributing not only for the building of dockyards and arsenals according to the εἰσφορά levied each year from 347/6–328/2 to the amount of 10 tal., but also for the equipment of the fleet in the Lamian war. According to my view it had been resolved to defray the expenses of building the docks and arsenals by exacting an εἰσφορά of 10 tal. per ann. from the Metoicoi until the works were completed. Therefore the εἰσφορά was a tax to meet war expenses in this case too. See also Pauske, de magistratib. att. qui saec. a Chr. n. IV. pecunias publicas curabant, 27 ff., Leipz. 1890. v. Wilamowitz, ib., 218, 4, supposes that here again an εἰσφορά of the ξένοι παρεπιδημοῦντες is

The property of Metoicoi must have been assessed for the purposes of war-taxes at a higher rate than that of burgesses, because it was often granted as a privilege to Metoicoi εἰσφορὰς μετὰ Ἀθηναίων εἰσφέρειν.[1]

The functions which the Metoicoi had to discharge at the religious festivals, especially in the Panathenaic processions, formed another burden which fell upon them exclusively. In these processions the males had to march σκαφηφορία. clad in purple, and crowned with chaplets of oak, and carry brazen and silver vessels full of sacrificial cakes; their women had to carry pitchers of water and sunshades. They took part in other state festivals also, *e.g.* in the Hephaistia and Prometheia, where they received a specified portion of the flesh offered in sacrifice; and probably also in the festivals of the Deme in which they happened to reside.[2]

Individual Metoicoi were granted special privileges by decree of the people. Among these were the titles πρόξενος and εὐεργέτης granted by decrees of the people, sometimes separately, sometimes both together. They are to be regarded as Privileges.

meant just as in C.I.A., II. 86, although the εἰσφορὰ is mentioned here in connexion with the μετοίκιον.

[1] C.I.A., II. 121, lines 28 and 176. For the expression τὸ ἕκτον μέρος εἰσφέρειν μετὰ τῶν μετοίκων in Dem. 22, 61, see Boeckh 1, 696/7; his view however is only conjectural. The same may be said of Thumser, *de civ. Atheniens. munerib.*, pp. 47/8.

[2] Harp. σκαφηφορία = Phot.: Δημήτριος γοῦν ἐν γ' νομοθεσίας φησίν, ὅτι προσέταττεν ὁ νόμος τοῖς μετοίκοις ἐν ταῖς πομπαῖς αὐτοὺς μὲν σκάφας φέρειν, τὰς δὲ θυγατέρας αὐτῶν ὑδρεῖα καὶ σκιάδια. Cf. Poll. 3, 55. The σκαφηφόριαι were called μετοίκων λειτουργίαι: Phot., σκαφηφορεῖν. Lex. Seguer. 280, 1 sq. The σκάφαι full of offerings: Phot. σκάφας σκαφηφορεῖν. Lex. Seguer. 304, 27 sq. Purple chiton and oak chaplet: Phot. σκάφας. Lex. Seguer. 214, 6 sq., 242, 3 sq. Special mention of Panathenaia: Hesych. σκάφαι. Lex. Seguer. 242, 3 sq. Cf. Ælian, *Var. Hist.*, 6, 1: τὰς γοῦν παρθένους τῶν μετοίκων σκιαδηφορεῖν ἐν ταῖς πομπαῖς ἠνάγκαζον ταῖς ἑαυτῶν κόραις, τὰς δὲ γυναῖκας ταῖς γυναιξί, τοὺς δὲ ἄνδρας σκαφηφορεῖν. Cf. Zenob. 5, 95. Full collection of passages in Michaelis, *Parthenon*, 330, no. 191 ff. Cf. also Schenkl, *ib.*, 204 ff., with the corrections of Thumser, *ib.*, 60 ff. Wilamowitz, 220, argues with some plausibility that the sunshades were carried to honour Athena, and that Ælian is mistaken in supposing them to have been for the convenience of the Athenian ladies. An inscr. in the Ἐφ. ἀρχ., 1883, pp. 167/8, line 16 = *Ber. d. bayr. Ak.*, 1887, p. 5, referring apparently to the sacrifices at the Hephaistia and Prometheia, runs thus: δοῦναι δὲ (κ)αὶ τοῖς μετοίκοις τρεῖς βοῦς τούτων τ(ῶν βοῶν καὶ οἱ) ἱεροποιοὶ (νε)μόντω(ν αὐ)τοῖς ὠμὰ τὰ κρέα. C.I.A., I. Suppl. 2, as restored by v. Wilamowitz 254 ff., justifies us in concluding that the Metoicoi took part in the festivals of the Deme at Scambonidai.

mere honorary titles; but the πρόξενος seems to have been entitled to πρόσοδος πρὸς τὸν πολέμαρχον, *i.e.* could appear in his court without introduction by a προστάτης, which was required in the case of other ͵Metoicoi.[1] Other rights granted by special favour, sometimes separately, sometimes in combination, were (1) the ἀτέλεια, which probably referred to the leiturgies, and the μετοίκιον, (2) ἔγκτησις γῆς καὶ οἰκίας, sometimes subject to a maximum limitation, (3) πρόσοδος πρὸς τὴν βουλὴν καὶ τὸν δῆμον, (4) τὰς εἰσφορὰς εἰσφέρειν μετὰ Ἀθηναίων, (5) στρατεύεσθαι τὰς στρατιὰς μετὰ Ἀθηναίων.[2]

[1] Schubert, *de Proxenia Att.*, Leipzig, 1881. Monceaux, *les Proxenies grecques*, 91 ff., Paris, 1886. Acc. to Dem. 20, 60, aliens who had done good service to Athens received προξενίαν, εὐεργεσίαν, ἀτέλειαν ἁπάντων. But the ἀτέλεια was not included in the προξενία. Dem. 20, 133: οὐ γάρ ἐστιν οὔθ᾽ οὗτος οὔτ᾽ ἄλλος οὐδεὶς πρόξενος ὢν ἀτελής, ὅτῳ μὴ διαρρήδην ἀτέλειαν ἔδωκεν ὁ δῆμος. This is the reason why the ἀτέλεια is expressly mentioned, when granted, together with προξενία. C.I.A., II. 91. Nor was ἔγκτησις γῆς καὶ οἰκίας included in the προξενία: cf. C.I.A., II. 41, where προξενία is mentioned in the probouleuma of the βουλή, the ἔγκτησις γῆς καὶ οἰκίας added by an additional clause in the Ecclesia. See also C.I.A., II. 70, 186. Schubert also, 10 ff., regards the προξενία as a mere title of honour, but infers from C.I.A., II. 42: καὶ (πρόσοδον) εἶναι αὐτῷ πρὸς τὸν πολέμαρχον (καθάπερ) το(ῖ)ς ἄλλοις προξένοις (see also II. 131) that the πρόξενοι required no introduction by their προστάτης to the πολέμαρχος. In C.I.A., IV. 3, 551 it is decreed: (καὶ ἀτ)έλειαν εἶναι α(ὐτῷ) καὶ δίκας, ἐάν (τις) ἀδικῇ αὐτὸν Ἀ(θήν)ησιν πρὸς τὸν (πολέ)μαρχον ἄνευ π(ρυταν)είων. The εὐεργεσία also is a mere title: Schubert 25 ff. Monceaux 98, 6 infers from C.I.A., II. 208, in my opinion incorrectly, that in certain periods all πρόξενοι possessed the ἔγκτησις γῆς καὶ οἰκίας. Dittmar, in the *Leipz. Stud.*, 13, 142 ff., seeks to prove that the ἐγκτ. γῆς καὶ οἰκίας was by law included in the προξενία and εὐεργεσία in the years 325–315, and so he explains the words κατὰ τὸν νόμον. Monceaux 102 infers that the πρόξενοι paid neither μετοίκιον nor market dues, but he must be wrong, for the ἀτέλεια was not included in the προξενία.

[2] ἀτέλεια in general: C.I.A., II. 42, 91. ἀτέλεια τοῦ μετοικίου: II. 27. ἔγκτησις γῆς καὶ οἰκίας: II. 41, 70, 186, limited to the value of from 3,000 drachmæ up to 1 talent for houses, and from 1 up to 2 talents for land. See the inscrr. on the point collected by A. Wilhelm in *Herm.*, 24, 1889, 331 ff. The clause κατὰ τὸν νόμον sometimes found added to ἔγκτησις γῆς καὶ οἰκίας probably refers to the Solonian law. Arist., *Pol.*, 2, 7=p. 87, 26 sqq.: οἷον καὶ Σόλων ἐνομοθέτησεν καὶ παρ᾽ ἄλλοις ἐστὶ νόμος, ὃς κωλύει κτᾶσθαι γῆν, ὁπόσην ἂν βούληταί τις. For the meaning of ἐγκτήματα cf. Lex. Seguer. 251, 1 ff.; 260, 4 ff. πρόσοδος πρὸς τὴν βουλὴν καὶ τὸν δῆμον: II. 41, 91. τὰς εἰσφορὰς εἰσφέρειν μετὰ Ἀθηναίων: C.I.A., II. 121. στρατεύεσθαι τὰς στρατιὰς καὶ τὰς εἰσφορὰς εἰσφέρειν μετὰ Ἀθηναίων: C.I.A., II. 176. *Mitth. d. dtsch. arch. Inst. in Ath.*, 8, 218. Δελτίον ἀρχ., 1889, p. 91, l. 53 ff. τὰς εἰσφορὰς εἰσφέρειν καὶ τὰ τέλη τελεῖν καθάπερ Ἀθηναῖοι καὶ τὰς στρατείας στρατεύεσθαι μετὰ Ἀθηναίων: Δελτ. ἀρχ., 1888, p. 224.

The ἰσοτελεῖs were a special class of Metoicoi, so called because they were liable to the same burdens as fell upon the burgesses, and to no others.[1] But ἰσοτέλεια does not seem to have necessarily included the ἔγκτησις γῆς καὶ οἰκίας; at any rate the latter privilege is found granted in decrees by express provision along with the ἰσοτέλεια.[2]

Ἰσοτελεῖς.

The tribunal for all Metoicoi, including the privileged classes, was the court of the πολέμαρχος.[3]

Tribunal.

C. *The Athenian Burgess-body.*

In the census taken under the administration of Demetrios Phalereus the number of Athenian burgesses amounted to 21,000.[4] Writers of the 5th century B.C. state the number as 30,000.[5] Modern computations, which in the absence

Number.

---

[1] Lys. and Theophr. *ap.* Harp., ἰσοτελής=Phot. Lex. Seguer. 267, 1; ἰσοτελεῖς μέτοικοι τὰ μὲν ξενικὰ τέλη μὴ τελοῦντες, τὰ δὲ ἴσα τοῖς ἀστοῖς τελοῦντες: cf. Phot., ἰσοτελεῖς. This explains C.I.A., II. 54: εἶναι δὲ καὶ τοί(ς) μ(ετ)ὰ Ἀστυκράτους ἐκπεπτωκόσι (ἰ)σοτέλειαν καθάπερ Ἀθηναίοις. On ἰσοτέλεια see Schubert 49 ff. and Thumser 65 ff; for the meaning of τέλος Thumser, *de civ. Athen. munerib.*, 108 ff. In epitaph inscriptions the ἰσοτελεῖς are expressly described as such, *e.g.* C. I. A., III. 2723 sqq.

[2] C.I.A., II. 176, 413. If Lysias, an ἰσοτελής, possessed houses (Lys. 12, 18), that was because the decree which granted him ἰσοτέλεια contained also a clause granting him ἔγκτησις οἰκίας, as was usually the case. Boeckh 1, 197 c, takes a different view, but the inscrr. in my opinion refute him. Xen., *de Vect.*, 4, 12, does not prove that ἰσοτελεῖς could hold property in mines. The meaning of the passage is that the State had granted ἰσοτέλεια to those who had consented to work in the mines. See Schubert 53; Thumser 66.

[3] Arist. 58, 2; Poll. 8, 91; Harp. πολέμαρχος. See Schenkl, 213 ff., and Welsing, *de inquilinor. et peregrinor. ap. Ath. judiciis*, 1 ff., Münster, 1887, where there is also a discussion of some exceptions and changes, which probably occurred after the Peloponnesian war. The Polemarch, however, referred the private suits of the Metoicoi to the judges in the Demes, and these brought them before the Diaitetai. See Arist., *loc. cit.*: δίκαι δὲ λαγχάνονται πρὸς αὐτὸν (*i.e.* τὸν πολέμαρχον) ἴδιαι μέν, αἵ τε τοῖς μετοίκοις καὶ τοῖς ἰσοτελέσι καὶ τοῖς προξένοις γιγνόμεναι. καὶ δεῖ τοῦτον λαβόντα καὶ διανείμαντα δέκα μέρη, τὸ λαχὸν ἑκάστῃ τῇ φυλῇ μέρος προσθεῖναι, τοὺς δὲ τὴν φυλὴν δικάζοντας (these are, acc. to Arist. 53, οἱ τετταράκοντα) τοῖς διαιτηταῖς ἀποδοῦναι. Poll. 8, 91 is confused.

[4] For the population of Attica see Beloch, *die Bevölker. d. griech.-röm. Welt.*, 57 ff. 21,000 citizens under Demetrios of Phaleron: Ctesicles *ap.* Ath. 6, 272B. This is corroborated by the other data of that period in Plut., *Phok.*, 28. (Dem.) 25, 21. Philochor., *fr.* 12 (Müller, *fr. hist. gr.*, 1, 386.) The last obviously computes the population in the age of Kecrops from the facts of his own time.

[5] Hdt. 5, 97; Aristoph., *Eccl.*, 1132. The δύο μυριάδες τῶν δημοτικῶν in

of satisfactory statistics can never be more than approximations to the truth, give for the beginning of the Peloponnesian war a total of between 40,000 and 47,000 citizens, corresponding to a free population of between 120,000 and 140,000 souls.[1] To these must be added about 10,000 Athenian citizens dwelling in the cleruchies, a number which may be considered fairly accurate for the 4th century also.[2]

The Athenian citizens were of two classes, old citizens and new. The latter, who were called ποιητοὶ or δημοποίητοι πολῖται, **New Burgesses.** obtained their burgess-rights by decree of the people.[3] Such grants of citizenship to non-burgesses could lawfully be made only in cases where the recipients had done good **Mode of Creation.** service to the Athenian State, and in the examples of these decrees that we possess this is regularly stated as the motive of the grant.[4] After the Ecclesia had passed the vote bestowing the franchise, the grant had yet to be confirmed in a second assembly in which not less than 6,000 citizens voted. Even after this any Athenian citizen who chose was entitled to oppose the decree by a γραφὴ παρανόμων, in which he had to prove that the person favoured with the grant of citizenship was unworthy of the honour and his admission to citizenship illegal.[5]

Aristoph., *Vesp.*, 709, include only the poorer citizens. (Plat.), *Axioch.*, 369A, says 30,000 citizens were present at the trial of the generals after Arginusai, and obviously means to include the whole body of citizens.

[1] See the calculation in Beloch, 60 ff., and for the statements of Philoch., *fr.* 90 (Müller 1, 398) and Plut., *Per.*, 37, about the number to whom corn was distributed in 445/4 B.C., see Beloch, 75 ff.

[2] Beloch, 81 ff.

[3] Harp. δημοποίητος. Poll. 3, 56. Distinction between γένει πολῖται and ποιητοὶ πολῖται: Dem. 45, 78.

[4] (Dem.) 59, 89. Szánto, *Untersuch. ü. d. att. Bürgerr.*, p. 26 ff.

[5] (Dem.) 59, 89–91, delivered in 340 B.C. See Schaefer, *Dem. u. seine Zeit*, 3¹, 2, 183. The earliest inscr. in which the second assembly is undoubtedly mentioned is C.I.A., II. 54, 363/2 B.C., and it was probably mentioned in II. 51, 369/8 B.C.; this however does not prove that the two assemblies were not necessary even earlier than that date. The context of the passage in (Dem.) shows clearly that the trial in the law court did not take place unless a γραφὴ παρανόμων was brought against the grant of franchise. The special regulation adopted when the Platæans were admitted to citizenship, namely, that they should be required to prove in courts of justice that they were Platæans and democrats, is clearly an exceptional measure due to the large number who were admitted on that occasion. Cf. (Dem.) 59, 105/6, and Pseudoplut., *vit. Lys.*, 8. Fränkel, 34 ff., argues that every grant of the franchise was necessarily accompanied by a dokimasia before a law-court.

The formal statements in the extant decrees are consistent with this course of procedure. Up to the middle of the 4th century the newly admitted citizens seem to have been at liberty to select for themselves the Phyle, Deme, and Phratry in which they desired to be enrolled. After that period it seems that the freedom of choice was limited to certain specified subdivisions of the burgess-body.[1]

At the end of the 4th century B.C. it seems to have become a regular rule that newly admitted citizens should be subjected to a dokimasia held before a court of 501 jurors, the Thesmothetai acting as εἰσαγωγεῖς.[2]

Till lately conflicting views were held concerning the political

---

Hartel, too, in his *Stud. üb. att. Staatsr. u. Urkundenw.*, 271, supposes that a judicial test of fitness was necessary from the very first, and thinks that the term γραφὴ παρανόμων cannot be taken here in its strict technical sense. His view is with good reason opposed by Szánto, *Untersuch. üb. d. att. Bürgerr.*, p. 7 ff., who however is led to other untenable results by adopting Hartel's hypothesis about the double reading of the decrees in the Ecclesia. Buermann, in *Jahrb. f. cl. Phil.* Suppl. vol., 10, 361, and Meier, *Intell.-Bl. z. Allg. Lit.-Zeit.*, 1884, p. 254, rightly date the introduction of the dokimasia for this purpose in the time of Demetrios of Phaleron.

[1] The oldest formula of franchise-grants in the inscriptions runs thus: εἶναι δὲ Θρασυ(βούλου φυλῆς τε εἶναι καὶ δήμου κ)αὶ φρατρίας ὧ(ν ἂν βούληται): C.I.A., I. 59. About 370 B.C. the formula appears expanded as follows: εἶναι τὸν δεῖνα Ἀθηναῖον αὐτὸν καὶ ἐκγόνους αὐτοῦ καὶ εἶναι αὐτῷ γράψασθαι φυλῆς καὶ δήμου καὶ φρατρίας ἧς ἂν βούληται. τοὺς δὲ πρυτάνεις δοῦναι περὶ αὐτοῦ τὴν ψῆφον τῷ δήμῳ εἰς τὴν πρώτην ἐκκλησίαν. Cf. C.I.A., II. 51, 54, 108. Soon after the middle of the 4th century the addition ὧν οἱ νόμοι λέγουσι sometimes appears immediately after ἧς ἂν βούληται (see C.I.A., II. 115 b), but it was soon supplanted by the clause κατὰ τὸν νόμον, which obviously means the same thing, as Buermann admits without reservation in the 10th Suppl. vol. of the *Jahrb. f. cl. Phil.*, 648 ff. Dittmar's explanation of κατὰ τὸν νόμον in the *Leipz. Stud.*, 13, 140 ff., 153 ff., will scarcely convince anybody. See also Schmitthenner, *de coronar. ap. Ath. honorib.*, 81 ff., Berlin, 1891. A collection of inscriptions on the subject will be found in Hartel 272.

[2] The formula given in the last note remained in use till about 320 B.C., with only a few formal changes in its second clause, but at that date or thereabouts an additional clause appears (cf. C.I.A., II. 228, 229) to the following effect: τοὺς δὲ θεσμοθέτας εἰσαγαγεῖν αὐτῷ τὴν δοκιμασίαν τῆς δωρεᾶς (or τῆς πολιτείας) εἰς τὸ δικαστήριον, ὅταν πρῶτον οἷόν τ' ᾖ. Cf. C.I.A., II. 309. Inscriptions of still later date, soon after the end of the Chremonidean war (Buermann, *ibid.*), show the following wording: δεδόσθαι δὲ αὐτῷ καὶ πολιτείαν δοκιμασθέντι ἐν τῷ δικαστηρίῳ κατὰ τὸν νόμον, τοὺς δὲ θεσμοθέτας, ὅταν πρῶτον πληρῶσιν δικαστήριον εἰς ἕνα καὶ πεντακοσίους δικαστάς, εἰσαγαγεῖν αὐτῷ τὴν δοκιμασίαν κατὰ τὸν νόμον καὶ εἶναι αὐτῷ δοκιμασθέντι γράψασθαι φυλῆς καὶ δήμου καὶ φρατρίας ἧς ἂν βούληται. Cf. C.I.A., II. 895. Collection of inscriptions, Hartel, 272/3.

status of the new citizens at Athens, especially with regard to their relation to the Phratries :[1] but we have now at our disposal numerous inscriptions of the 5th, 4th, and 3rd centuries supplying ample evidence that the new citizens were admitted into a Phyle, Deme, and Phratry on the strength of the decree which granted them the franchise.[2] The limitations of the rights of the new citizens, as compared with the old burgesses, were but unimportant. They could not hold the office of any of the 9 Archons, nor a priesthood; but any sons of theirs born after their reception into the burgess-body, and in legal wedlock with an Athenian freewoman, were eligible for both. If, on the other hand, the sons were born before the admission of their father to citizenship, they were admitted as a rule to citizenship at the same time as their father, but then stood under the same restrictions as their father, and the full rights of old burgesses could only be obtained by their sons again in the next generation born from legal wedlock with a free Athenian wife.[3]

Political Rights of New Citizens.

[1] The various theories are stated in Philippi, *Beitr. z. e. Gesch. d. att. Bürgerrechtes*, 107 ff. He then held that a new citizen could obtain entrance into a Phratry for himself only by adoption, for his son by an Athenian free woman by admission of such son into the Phratry of his maternal grandfather. This view he has now abandoned; *Jahrb. f. cl. Phil.*, 1879, p. 418. Yet Hruza, *Beitr. z. Gesch. d. griech. u. röm. Familienrechtes*, 136/7, 1892, still considers it doubtful whether the new citizens were at all periods permitted or compelled to belong to a Phratry.

[2] *e.g.* C.I.A., I. 59 of 410/9 B.C.; II. 54, 363/2 B.C.; II. 121, B.C. 338, 7; II. 300, n.c. 295. Buermann in *Jahrb. f. cl. Phil.*, 9th Suppl. vol., p. 597 ff., had demonstrated clearly that other arguments also independently of epigraphical evidence prove that new citizens were enrolled at once in the Phratries.

[3] (Dem.) 59, 92. 106. Arist., 55, 3, gives the question put at the δοκιμασία of the 9 Archons as follows: τίς σοι πατὴρ καὶ πόθεν τῶν δήμων καὶ τίς πατρὸς πατήρ, καὶ τίς μήτηρ καὶ τίς μητρὸς πατὴρ καὶ πόθεν τῶν δήμων; cf. Lex. Cantabr., p. 670, 14. Inquiry was made concerning the maternal grandfather and his Deme, because in the official name of an Athenian citizen lady the Deme-name was given after the name of her father or husband. The name of the paternal grandfather was asked, because in cases where burgess rights had been granted to an alien and to his living descendants, those descendants had, it is true, a citizen for their father, and so far the form of question given in (Dem.) was sufficient, but they were not citizens by inheritance from their father, but because citizenship had been specially conferred on themselves. See also Philippi 117, 99. The version in Poll. 8, 85: εἰ Ἀθηναῖοί εἰσιν ἑκατέρωθεν ἐκ τριγονίας probably arose from a misunderstanding of the full form of question as given above. Philippi, 109/10, and before him Meier, *de bonis damnat.*, 285, refer the statements of (Dem.) and Poll. to different periods.

The theory that the Platæans formed a peculiar class of Athenian citizens, and that the slaves who were liberated because of their services at the battle of Arginusai became Platæans, must be modified. The fact is that those freedmen received a number of allotments of land in the territory of Skione which had been in the possession of the Platæans since 422/1 B.C., and their names were entered in the list of Cleruchs next after those of the Platæans.[1] *The Platæans.*

The new citizen owed his admission to the franchise simply to his good services to the State; the old burgess, on the other hand, was entitled to citizenship by hereditary descent. To define this, the Athenians re-enacted in the archonship of Eucleides the decree of Pericles of 451 B.C., which provided that only those who were descended from Athenian citizens both on the father's side and on the mother's should be entitled to the rights of citizens. For those however who were born before the archonship of Eucleides a concession was made; for them citizen descent on one side was declared sufficient.[2] From this concession we may infer that the Periclean law had become obsolete in consequence of the great losses which had thinned the ranks of the burgess body in the course of the Peloponnesian war: this seems to be corroborated by the restoration by Alcibiades of the synteleia of half-blood citizens in the Kynosarges.[3] The half-blood Athenians were under disadvantages *Old Burgesses. Descent.*

---

[1] The correct explanation of Hellan. *ap.* Schol. to Aristoph., *Frogs*, 694, is that given by Kirchhoff in the *Abh. d. Berl. Ak.*, 1878, pp. 9/10. Skione in hands of the Platæans from 422/1, Thuc. 5, 32. Diod. 12, 76. Isocr. 4, 109. For the relations between Athens and Platæa see Szánto in the *Wiener Stud.*, 6, 159 ff. The discussion by Heinr. Wiegand, *die Platœer in Athen*. in the *Ratzeburg Progr.*, 1888, is of little importance.

[2] Arist. 42, 1 says of the form of constitution after Eucleides: μετέχουσιν μὲν τῆς πολιτείας οἱ ἐξ ἀμφοτέρων γεγονότες ἀστῶν. For Pericles' law cf. Arist. 26, 4. To the decree in the archonship of Eucleides belong the statements of Carystios *ap.* Ath. 13, 577 C : 'Ἀριστοφῶν δὲ ὁ ῥήτωρ ὁ τὸν νόμον εἰσενεγκὼν ἐπ' Εὐκλείδου ἄρχοντος, ὃς ἂν μὴ ἐξ ἀστῆς γένηται νόθον εἶναι and of Eumelos *ap.* Schol. to Æsch. 1, 89 : Εὔμηλος ὁ περιπατητικὸς ἐν τῷ γ´ περὶ τῆς ἀρχαίας κωμῳδίας φησὶ Νικομένη τινὰ ψήφισμα θέσθαι μηδένα τῶν μετ' Εὐκλείδην ἄρχοντα μετέχειν τῆς πόλεως, ἂν μὴ ἄμφω τοὺς γονέας ἀστοὺς ἐπιδείξηται, τοὺς δὲ πρὸ Εὐκλείδου ἀνεξετάστους ἀφεῖσθαι. To this decree Dem. 57, 30. Is. 8, 43 refer.

[3] For the Gymnasium Kynosarges cf. Plut., *Them.*, 1, Lex. Seguer. 274, 21 sqq.: Κυνόσαργες γυμνάσιόν τι Ἀθήνησι καλούμενον, εἰς ὃ ἐνεγράφοντο καὶ οἱ νόθοι ἐκ τοῦ ἑτέρου μέρους ἀστοί. The comparison in Dem. 23, 213 shows that those who were of Athenian blood on the mother's side only were also admitted to the training given in the Kynosarges. Cf. Buermann in the

after 403 B.C. in civil matters also; for the law of Solon, nominally still valid but practically obsolete, which deprived all νόθοι of the rights of kinship in all matters sacred or profane, was also reenacted in that year.[1] In the course of the 4th century these enactments about the franchise were made still more severe by the absolute prohibition of mixed marriages both between citizens and alien women, and also between aliens and Athenian women; if the law was broken, the alien offenders were to be sold into slavery. These rigorous laws, however, do not seem to have been strictly carried out; at any rate they failed to exclude the half-bloods from citizen-rights in practice. The foisting of their names into the burgess-rolls remained a busy and successful trade, as is clearly proved by the διαψήφισις or revision of lists carried out in 346/5 B.C., when many such intruders were ejected from the burgess-body.[2]

But, for admission into the Phratries and thereby into the Athenian burgess-body, pure citizen descent was not sufficient; it was also necessary that the applicant for

Marriage.

7th Suppl. vol. of the *Jahrb. f. class. Phil.*, 633/4. Schenkl however in the *Wiener Stud.*, 1883, 17 A, 22, denies it. Reorganisation of the synteleia of νόθοι by Alcibiades: Polemon *ap.* Ath. 6, 234 E. Schenkel 18/9 without good reason identifies this Alcibiades with Cleisthenes' colleague of that name. Dem. 23, 213 shews that in the 4th century the synteleia of νόθοι no longer existed. An unprejudiced interpretation of Aristoph., *Birds*, 1649-1670 will show that the νόθοι were not *ipso facto* citizens in the eye of the law in the period of the Peloponnesian War. Isocr. 8, 88, on the other hand, shews that as a matter of fact they were surreptitiously enrolled in the burgess lists, for he tells us that in the Peloponnesian war the Phratries and Demes were filled τῶν οὐδὲν τῇ πόλει προσηκόντων.

[1] Is. 6, 47: τοὐναντίον τοίνυν συμβέβηκεν ἢ ὡς ὁ νόμος γέγραπται· ἐκεῖ μὲν γάρ ἐστι νόθῳ μηδὲ νόθῃ εἶναι ἀγχιστείαν μήθ' ἱερῶν μήθ' ὁσίων ἀπ' Εὐκλείδου ἄρχοντος. So Dem. 43, 51. That the law on ἀγχιστεία of νόθοι was enacted by Solon is attested by Aristoph., *Birds*, 1660 sqq.

[2] (Dem.) 59, 17: τοῦ μὲν νόμου τοίνυν ἀκηκόατε, ὦ ἄνδρες δικασταί, ὃς οὐκ ἐᾷ τὴν ξένην τῷ ἀστῷ συνοικεῖν οὐδὲ τὴν ἀστὴν τῷ ξένῳ οὐδὲ παιδοποιεῖσθαι, τέχνῃ οὐδὲ μηχανῇ οὐδεμιᾷ· ἐὰν δέ τις παρὰ ταῦτα ποιῇ, γραφὴν πεποίηκε κατ' αὐτῶν εἶναι πρὸς τοὺς θεσμοθέτας, κατὰ τε τοῦ ξένου καὶ τῆς ξένης, κἂν ἁλῷ, πεπρᾶσθαι κελεύει. For the διαψήφισις of the year 346/5, cf. Harp. *s.v.*, Hypoth. to Is. 12 and to Dem. 57. It was proposed by Demophilus, Æsch. c. *Tim.* 86, Schol. 1, 77 Dind. On this occasion many were ejected from the citizen-body, Dem. 57, 2, but were readmitted after the battle of Chæronea, Suid. ἀπεψηφισμένοι. In the Attic tomb-inscrr. we find mention of Athenian citizens' wives who came from Amphissa, C.I.A., II. 2786; Tolophon, 3395; Locris, 3142; Andros, 2788; Elis, 2894; Heracleia, 2916, 2962, 2964; Thebes, 3006; Laconia, 3127; Miletus, 3215, 3218; Sikyon, 3333.

admission should be the offspring of a legal marriage. Now apart from the above-mentioned conditions of citizenship for the parents, marriages were valid in the eyes of the law at Athens, if the betrothal was formally effected either by ἐγγύησις, *i.e.*, the formal giving away of the bride by her κύριος to the bridegroom, which regularly took place in presence of witnesses, or else, in cases of heiresses (ἐπίκληροι) by means of the ἐπιδικασία, in which the ἀγχιστεύς, who was by law entitled to marry the heiress, declared before the ἄρχων (or if he was a Metic before the πολέμαρχος) that the heiress was his wife. In the latter case the consent of the magistrate was a mere formality, unless the right of the ἐπιδικαζόμενος were called in question and the case brought before the law courts.[1] The formal betrothal thus described was followed by the γάμος or marriage ceremony. On the meaning of the phrase εἰσφέρειν γαμηλίαν ὑπὲρ τῆς γυναικὸς τοῖς φράτορσιν nothing certain can be said; the most probable view is that the γαμηλία was a payment or contribution which the bridegroom was expected to make to his Phratry, but was not considered a legal obligation upon him, nor as an indispensable requirement for a regular and formal marriage contract.[2] At marriage the wife as a rule brought her husband a dowry, but this was not legally essential for a valid marriage.[3]

Lawful concubinage has been set forth as a second form of

---

[1] On the formalities of betrothal see Hruza, *Beitr. z. Gesch. d. griech. u. röm. Familienrechtes*, I. 1892. The distinction between ἐγγύησις and ἐπιδικασία appears as early as Is. 6, 14. On the κύριος, Meier.,[2] 505; Van den Es, *de iure familiarum ap. Ath.*, 6 ff.; Hruza 54 ff. On the ἐπίδικος ἐπίκληρος, Is. 3, 64/5; Poll. 3, 33. On ἐγγύησις, Hruza 18 ff.; for ἐπιδικασία, id. ib., 90, ff. At the introduction of the child into the Phratry the father had to swear: ἦ μὴν ἐξ ἀστῆς καὶ ἐγγυητῆς γυναικὸς εἰσάγειν, Is. 8, 19; we must therefore suppose that in the case of ἐπιδικασθεῖσαι the ἐγγύησις was regarded as effected by the law concerning ἐπίδικοι. Acc. to the Phratry decree of the Demotionidai the witnesses had simply to give evidence: μαρτυρῶ ὃν εἰσάγει ἑαυτῷ υἱὸν εἶναι τοῦτον γνήσιον ἐγ γαμετῆς; Ind. Schol. Goett., 1890/1, p. 4, l. 108 ff. Cf. Hruza 111/2. The son not ἐγ γαμετῆς is νόθος. Cf. Poll. 3, 21: καὶ γνήσιος μὲν ὁ ἐκ γυναικὸς ἀστῆς καὶ γαμετῆς (ὁ δὲ αὐτὸς καὶ ἰθαγενής), νόθος δὲ ὁ ἐκ ξένης ἢ παλλακίδος. The class of νόθοι born of citizen παλλακίδες was certainly only a small one at Athens.

[2] On the meaning of γάμος, which as a rule followed immediately after the ἐγγύησις, see Hruza 125 ff., 45 ff. Εἰσφέρειν γαμηλίαν ὑπὲρ τῆς γυναικὸς τοῖς φράτορσιν, Is. 3, 76. 79; 8, 18. 20; Dem. 57, 43. 69. The explanations in the Lexicographers are contradictory. Hruza 133, 2. For the meaning of γαμηλία see Hruza 133 ff., who, 144, 17, infers from Is. 3, 79, perhaps rightly, that the γαμηλία was not compulsory.

[3] Meier 513 ff. Schömann on Is., p. 233.

legally valid union between man and woman at Athens. After fresh consideration of the question I can no longer give this theory the complete approval that I once expressed.[1] The Demosthenic speeches against Boiotos and the speech of Isaios on the estate of Philoctemon, which were considered the strongest evidence for the existence of lawful concubinage, seem to admit of a satisfactory explanation in the circumstances described in them without having recourse to this theory.[2] The other evidence adduced is not sufficiently strong to prove the case;[3] if the support of Demosthenes and Isaios is withdrawn, especially as there is also a piece of direct evidence against the existence of the usage and all its assumed legal consequences.[4]

Lawful concubinage.

Children not born in lawful wedlock were νόθοι even if their father and mother were both Athenians. They could not properly be enrolled in a Phratry because the father could not take the necessary oath that the child was born of a free Athenian woman betrothed to him by ἐγγύησις. These νόθοι

Illegitimate children.

---

[1] The theory of the existence of lawful concubinage was set forth with arguments in its support by Buermann in the 9th Suppl. vol. of the *Jahrb. f. cl. Phil.*, 569 ff. Philippi, *ib.*, 1879, p. 418 ff., agrees in general, but considers that in the general looseness of Athenian legal forms this legal concubinage has not been sufficiently described by our authorities. In the first edition the author assented to Buermann's view. For arguments against it, see Zimmermann, *de nothorum Athenis condicione*, p. 10 ff., Berlin 1886; and Hruza 25 ff.

[2] For the circumstances of Dem. 39, 40 and Is. 6, cf. the appendix at the end of this book.

[3] For Is. 3 it is sufficient to refer to Zimmermann 19 ff. and Hruza 30 ff. The old Draconian law in Dem. 23, 58, which mentions παλλακή, ἣν ἂν ἐπ' ἐλευθέροις παισὶν ἔχῃ most probably means the class of mistresses described by Is. 3, 39. ἐλεύθερος is not, as Buermann 573 thinks, the same as γνήσιος. Cf. Zimmermann, *ib.*, p. 24.

[4] (Dem.) 59, 118, quoted by Zimmermann 25–6: θαυμάζω δ' ἔγωγε τί ποτε καὶ ἐροῦσι πρὸς ὑμᾶς ἐν τῇ ἀπολογίᾳ, πότερον ὡς ἀστή ἐστι Νέαιρα αὕτη, καὶ κατὰ τοὺς νόμους συνοικεῖ αὐτῷ; ἀλλὰ μεμαρτύρηται ἑταίρα οὖσα καὶ δούλη Νικαρέτης γεγενημένη. ἀλλ' οὐ γυναῖκα εἶναι αὐτοῦ, ἀλλὰ παλλακὴν ἔχειν ἔνδον; ἀλλ' οἱ παῖδες ταύτης ὄντες καὶ εἰσηγμένοι εἰς τοὺς φράτερας ὑπὸ Στεφάνου καὶ ἡ θυγάτηρ ἀνδρὶ Ἀθηναίῳ ἐκδοθεῖσα περιφανῶς αὐτὴν ἀποφαίνουσι γυναῖκα ἔχοντα. From this it follows that the children of a παλλακή could not be enrolled in the Phratry. Cf. also § 122: τὸ γὰρ συνοικεῖν τοῦτ' ἔστιν, ὃς ἂν παιδοποιῆται καὶ εἰσάγῃ εἴς τε τοὺς φράτερας καὶ δημότας τοὺς υἱεῖς καὶ τὰς θυγατέρας ἐκδιδῷ ὡς αὑτοῦ οὔσας τοῖς ἀνδράσι. τὰς μὲν γὰρ ἑταίρας ἡδονῆς ἕνεκ' ἔχομεν, τὰς δὲ παλλακὰς τῆς καθ' ἡμέραν θεραπείας τοῦ σώματος, τὰς δὲ γυναῖκας τοῦ παιδοποιεῖσθαι γνησίως καὶ τῶν ἔνδον φύλακα πιστὴν ἔχειν. Schaefer's article in the *Phil. Anz.*, 1887, p. 403 ff., does nothing to invalidate this. Cf. also Thalheim, *Berl. phil. Wochenschr.*, 1888, p. 1345 ff.

however belonged probably to the Phyle of their mother, and were accordingly admitted when of proper age into the mother's Deme also. They therefore became Athenian citizens by this reception, but could not claim the full family rights which depended upon membership of a Phratry; none of their father's property could be bequeathed to them except the so-called νοθεῖα, which was not allowed to exceed a specified sum.[1]

I here give a short account of the formalities with which the young Athenian was admitted into the burgess-body. The child received its name as a rule on the 10th day after birth.[2] The parents had free choice in selecting what name they pleased, and could also alter a name once given if they chose. Nevertheless it was the custom that the eldest son should be called after his paternal grandfather, while for the other children they usually selected names from among their relations on the father's or mother's side.[3] The naming was a private festival, but the admission into the Phratry secured to the child its full family rights. For the ceremonies of this admission only the general rules, apparently, were fixed by the State; the special arrangements were left to the discretion of the individual Phratries.[4] Even as to the age of the children admitted there seem to have been no universally applicable rules;

Naming of Children.

Admission into the Phratry.

[1] Oath at introduction to Phratry, Is. 7, 16. Dem. 57, 54. But any one not enrolled in a Phratry is νόθος: Is. 3, 75. I now believe that the νόθοι ex cive Attica were *ipso facto* citizens. See Caillemer in the *Annuaire de l'association pour l'encouragement des études grecques en France*, 1878, p. 184 ff. Boiotos already belonged to the Phyle Hippothontis before Mantias acknowledged him. Cf. Dem. 39, 25, 28. See Lipsius in Meier 533, 143. Acc. to Arist., *Rhet.*, 2, 23, περὶ τῶν τέκνων αἱ γυναῖκες πανταχοῦ διορίζουσι τἀληθές; therefore the declaration of the Athenian mother that the child was the son of a citizen father would be sufficient to secure the franchise of the child until he was admitted into a Deme. For admission to the Deme the only requirement made with regard to the candidate for admission was εἰ ἐλεύθερός ἐστι καὶ γέγονε κατὰ τοὺς νόμους, where the κατὰ τοὺς νόμους merely refers to the clause immediately preceding: μετέχουσιν μὲν τῆς πολιτείας οἱ ἐξ ἀμφοτέρων γεγονότες ἀστῶν. See Arist. 42, 1. The maximum νοθεῖα, acc. to Harp., was 1000 dr.; acc. to Schol. on Aristoph., *Birds*, 1626, 5 minæ.

[2] The δεκάτη the regular day for naming children. Aristoph., *Birds*, 922/3. 494 with the Schol.; Dem. 39, 20. 22; 40, 28. Cf. also Lex. Seguer. 237, 26 sqq. On the ἑβδόμη see Harp. ἑβδομευομένου.

[3] On the right of selecting or altering names: Dem. 39, 39. On the choice of names: Dem. 39, 27; 43, 74. An adoptive son names his own son after his adoptive father, ἵνα μὴ ἀνώνυμος ὁ οἶκος αὐτοῦ γένηται (Is. 2, 36).

[4] That these ceremonies varied in the different Phratries is shewn by the

which indeed was reasonable enough, for the possibility of enrolling children of tender years on a fixed day in the year undoubtedly depended very much on accidental circumstances. It is however probable that the admission took place in one of the first years of the child's life.[1] The festal occasion for this was supplied by the Apaturia, a festival celebrated by the members of each phratry; the third day of the festival, the so-called κουρεῶτις, was set apart for the enrolment of the children.[2] This was accompanied by an

fact that the orators considered it necessary to give special descriptions of the formalities in special Phratries. Thus Is. 7, 16 says of the Phratry of Apollodoros: ἔστι δ' αὐτοῖς νόμος ὁ αὐτός, ἐάν τέ τινα φύσει γεγονότα εἰσάγῃ τις ἐάν τε ποιητόν. Cf. especially the decrees of the Phratry Demotionidai, C.I.A., II. 841 b, with the continuation in the 'Εφ. ἀρχ. 1888. 3, 1 ff.=Berl. phil. Wochenschrift, 1889, pp. 225/6. The entire inscr. is now to be found in Sauppe, de Phratriis Att., II. 3 ff., in the Ind. Schol. Goett., 1890/91. The discussions on the Inscr. which appeared before the second part of it came to light, Szánto in the N. Rh. Mus., 1885, 40, 506 ff., myself in the Jahrb. f. cl. Phil., 1887, 23 ff., and C. Schaefer, Pforta Progr., 1888, have now been superseded by the appearance of the actual text. The entire inscr. is discussed by R. Schoell in the Sitzungsber. d. bayr. Ak., 1889, 2, 1 ff., and Sauppe, loc. cit. It contains 3 distinct decrees, and mentions in line 14 in Sauppe's copy (which I am quoting) τὸν νόμον τὸν Δημοτιωνιδῶν, to which also line 70 τοὺς δὲ μάρτυρας τρεῖς οὓς εἴρηται probably refers.

[1] Et. M., 118, 54 ff. ('Απατούρια): ἐν ταύτῃ τῇ ἑορτῇ τοὺς γεννωμένους ἐν τῷ ἐνιαυτῷ ἐκείνῳ παῖδας τότε ἐνέγραφον. Schol. Plat. Tim., 21: ἐν ταύτῃ (τῇ κουρεώτιδι) γὰρ τοὺς κόρους ἐνέγραφον εἰς τοὺς φράτερας, τριετεῖς ἢ τετραετεῖς ὄντας. The speaker of Is. 8 says § 19 he was enrolled, ἐπειδὴ ἐγενόμεθα; Callias in Andoc., Myst., 127, τὸν παῖδα ἤδη μέγαν ὄντα εἰσάγει εἰς Κήρυκας; in Dem. 48, 11, the enrolment takes place, ἐπειδὴ οὑτοσὶ ὁ παῖς ἐγένετο καὶ ἐδόκει καιρὸς εἶναι. In the Demotionidai inscr. the first decree l. 45 sqq. says: ἐπι(ψ)ηφίζειν δὲ τὸν φρατρίαρχον περὶ ὧν ἂ(ν) διαδικάζειν δέῃ κατὰ τὸν ἐνιαυτὸν ἕκαστον; in the second decree the persons to be enrolled are repeatedly called simply παῖδες (ll. 69, 79, 104); in the third and latest decree line 115 sqq. it is decreed: ὅπως δ' ἂν εἰδῶσι οἱ φράτερες τοὺς μέλλοντας εἰσάγεσθαι, ἀπογράφεσθαι τῷ πρώτῳ (meaning προτέρῳ) ἔτει ἢ ᾧ ἂν τὸ κούρειον ἄγῃ τὸ ὄνομα πατρόθεν καὶ τοῦ δήμου καὶ τῆς μητρὸς πατρόθεν καὶ τοῦ δήμου πρὸς τὸν φρατρίαρχον, τὸν δὲ φρατρίαρχον ἀπογραψαμένων ἀναγράψαντα ἐκτιθέναι, ὅπου ἂν Δεκελειῆς προσφοιτῶσι, ἐκτιθέναι δὲ καὶ τὸν ἱερέα ἀναγράψαντα ἐν σανιδίῳ λευκῷ ἐν τῷ ἱερῷ τῆς Λητοῦς.

[2] For the Apaturia see Meier, de gent. Att., 11 ff. Mommsen, Heort., 302 ff. Xen., Hell., 1, 7, 8: μετὰ δὲ ταῦτα ἐγίγνετο ἀπατούρια, ἐν οἷς οἵ τε πατέρες καὶ οἱ συγγενεῖς σύνεισι σφίσιν αὐτοῖς. 'Απατούρια=ὁμοπατόρια: Meier, ib., 11. Absurd etymology in the Et. M. 118, 54 ff. ('Απατούρια). For the κουρεῶτις cf. Schol. on Aristoph., Ach., 146: τὴν δὲ τρίτην κουρεῶτιν ἀπὸ τοῦ τοὺς κούρους καὶ τὰς κόρας ἐγγράφειν εἰς τοὺς φρατρίας. So also Suid. 'Απατούρια. In Hesych. the word is obviously taken as derived from κείρειν. So also Mommsen, ib., 310. In the first decree of the Demotionidai inscr. we read l. 26 sqq.: τὴν δὲ διαδικασίαν τὸ λοιπὸν εἶναι τῷ ὑστέρῳ ἔτει ἢ ᾧ τὸ κούρειον θύσῃ τῇ κουρεώτιδι 'Απατουρίων, cf. l. 60 sqq.

offering to Zeus Phratrios called κούρειον for the boys, while the sacrifice customary at enrolments of girls was probably called μεῖον.[1] The introducer of the new member had to give a sheep or a goat, a certain quantity of cake and wine, and a fixed sum in money for the expenses of the sacrifice, of which the members of his Phratry all received a share.[2] The sacrifice was accompanied by a vote taken on the question of admitting the boy into the Phratry. For this admission into the Phratry, which thenceforth served as proof of the boy's συγγένεια, and so of his right of inheritance, the following formalities are laid down in the second decree of the Phratry Demotionidai. The act of admission consisted of two parts, ἀνάκρισις and διαδικασία. In the former the introducer had to bring 3 witnesses, who were required to affirm upon oath that the boy introduced was his legitimate son by a lawfully married wife; in other Phratries, however, the father himself had to take this oath.[3] In the Diadicasia which followed

---

[1] Κούρειον the offering customary at the introduction of boys, Is. 6, 22. Demotionidai-inscr. l. 28 and 117. Lex. Seguer. 273, 1 ff.; κούρειον—ἰδίως δὲ καὶ τὸ διδόμενον ὑπὸ τῶν πατέρων τοῖς φράτορσιν, ὅταν εἰσφέρωσι τοὺς παῖδας εἰς φρατρίας. τὸ οὖν θυόμενον τότε ἱερεῖον κούρειον ἐκαλεῖτο. That the μεῖον and κούρειον were distinct from one another, follows from the Demotionidai-inscr., l. 5, 59/60, though the Et. M., 533, 30 sq., makes them identical. Nothing definite is known about the μεῖον. Cf. Harp. μεῖον καὶ μειαγωγός. Poll. 3, 52. Schol. to Aristoph., *Frogs*, 798. Both sacrifices were offered at the Apaturia: Demotionidai-inscr., l. 58 sq. The inscr. shows that μεῖον meant the smaller offering, as Mommsen, *ib.*, 308, conjectured. I now conjecturally identify the μεῖον with the sacrifice offered at the enrolment of girls (cf. Is. 3, 73. 75. 76. 79). Sauppe 9/10 and others regard μεῖον as the offering made at the first introduction of girls and boys, κούρειον as the offering made at a second introduction of the child supposed by them to have taken place from a passage in Poll. 8, 107. But since that passage contains an error on the subject of the γαμηλία as well, I cannot attach such importance to it as to infer from it the fact of a second, and indeed the decisive, introduction. The case of Callias in Andoc., *de Myst.*, 127, introducing a boy ἤδη μέγαν ὄντα, is obviously something unusual. See also Philippi, *Beitr.*, 101/2.

[2] For the animals sacrificed cf. Poll. 3, 52: καὶ δῦς φράτηρ καὶ φράτριος αἴξ ἡ θυομένη τοῖς φράτορσιν. The wine offering was called οἰνιστήρια. The other gifts are known from the Demotionidai-inscr., where in line 4 sqq. we have specified as ἱερώσυνα for the priest of Zeus Phratrios; ἀπὸ τοῦ μείου κωλῆν πλευρόνος, ἀργυρίου 111 (30b); ἀπὸ τοῦ κουρείου κωλῆν πλευρόνος, ἐλατῆρα χοινικιαῖον οἴνου ἡμίχουν, ἀργυρίου ⊢ (1 Dr.). For the μερίδες received by the φράτερες cf. Dem. 43, 82; Harp. μεῖον.

[3] Suid. φράτορες—τὸ δὲ γράφεσθαι εἰς τοὺς φράτορας σύμβολον εἶχον τῆς συγγένειας. In the 2nd decree of the Demotionidai-inscr., l. 67 sq., we read: Νικόδημος εἶπε τὰ μὲν ἄλλα κατὰ τὰ πρότερα ψηφίσματα, ἃ κεῖται περὶ τῆς εἰσαγωγῆς

the Phratriarch first caused the Thiasotai of the applicant to vote by ballot for or against the enrolment of the child in the presence of all the Phrateres. If the Thiasotai voted for admission, but the general body of Phrateres voted against it in the general vote which next took place, then a money fine was inflicted on all the Thiasotai who could not prove that they had opposed the admission.[1] If, on the other hand, the Thiasotai refused the admission, and on appeal to the general body of Phrateres their decision was reversed, then the child in question was enrolled in the Phratry-list. If however the general vote was given against the appellant, he was required to pay a fine of 100 drachmas. If no appeal was made against rejection by the Thiasotai, their decision was held valid and sufficient. In all votes of the whole body the Thiasotai of the member immediately interested were forbidden to give a vote.[2] In the first decree of the Phratry Demotionidai the formalities of admission differ somewhat from those in the second. It is certainly an almost inevitable inference that here also the first vote on the question of reception of the

τῶν παίδων καὶ τῆς διαδικασίας, τοὺς δὲ μάρτυρας τρεῖς οὓς εἴρηται ἐπὶ τῇ ἀνακρίσει παρέχεσθαι ἐκ τῶν ἑαυτοῦ θιασιωτῶν μαρτυροῦντας τὰ ὑπερωτώμε(να) καὶ ἐπομνύντας τὸν Δία τὸν φράτριον· μαρτυρεῖν δὲ τοὺς μάρτυρας καὶ ἐπομνύναι ἐχομένους τοῦ βωμοῦ· ἐὰν δὲ μὴ ὦσι ἐν τῷ θιάσῳ τούτῳ τοσοῦτοι τὸν ἀριθμόν, ἐκ τῶν ἄλλων φρατέρων παρεχέσθω. The ὅρκος μαρτύρων ἐπὶ τῇ εἰσαγωγῇ τῶν παίδων, line 107 sqq., reads thus: μαρτυρῶ ὃν εἰσάγει ἑαυτῷ ὑὸν εἶναι τοῦτον γνήσιον ἐγγαμετῆς· ἀληθῆ ταῦτα νὴ τὸν Δία τὸν Φράτριον· εὐορκοῦ(ν)τι μέν μοι πολλὰ καὶ ἀγαθὰ εἶναι· εἰ δ' ἐπιορκοίην, τἀναντία. In other Phratries, where the father himself had to take the oath, the νόμιμος ὅρκος was: ἢ μὴν ἐξ ἀστῆς καὶ ἐγγυητῆς γυναικὸς εἰσάγειν. Cf. Is. 8, 19; 7, 16. Dem. 57, 54. Andoc., de Myst., 127. In (Dem.) 59, 59/60 the γένος of the Brytidai voted without this oath being taken, the applicant not being required to take it till he came before the Diaitetes.

[1] The inscr. quoted continues, line 77 sq.: ὅταν δὲ ᾖ ἡ διαδικασία, ὁ φρατρίαρχος μὴ πρότερον διδότω τὴ(ν) ψῆφον περὶ τῶν παίδων τοῖς ἅπασι φράτερσι, πρὶν ἂν οἱ αὐτοῦ τοῦ εἰσαγομένου θιασῶται κρύβδην ἀπὸ τοῦ βωμοῦ φέροντες τὴν ψῆφον διαψηφίσωνται· καὶ τὰς ψήφους τὰς τούτων ἐναντίον τῶν ἁπάντων φρατέρων παρόντων ἐν τῇ ἀγορᾷ ὁ φρατρίαρχος διαριθμησάτω καὶ ἀναγορευέτω, ὁπότερ' ἂν ψηφίσωνται· ἐὰν δέ, ψηφισαμένων τῶν θιασωτῶν εἶναι αὐτοῖς φράτερα, οἱ ἄλλοι φράτερες ἀποψηφίσωνται, ὀφειλόντων ἑκατὸν δραχμὰς ἱερὰς τῷ Διὶ τῷ Φρατρίῳ οἱ θιασῶται, πλὴν ὅσοι ἂν τῶν θιασωτῶν κατήγοροι ἢ ἐναντιούμενοι φαίνωνται ἐν τῇ διαδικασίᾳ.

[2] Ibid., line 93 sqq.: ἐὰν δὲ ἀποψηφίσωνται οἱ θιασῶται, ὁ δὲ εἰσάγων ἐφῇ εἰς τοὺς ἅπαντας, τοῖς δὲ ἅπασι δόξῃ εἶναι φράτερ, ἐγγραφέσθω εἰς τὰ κοινὰ γραμματεῖα· ἐὰν δὲ ἀποψηφίσωνται οἱ ἅπαντες, ὀφειλέτω ἑκατὸν δραχμὰς ἱερὰς τῷ Διὶ τῷ Φρατρίῳ. ἐὰν δέ, ἀποψηφισαμένων τῶν θιασωτῶν, μὴ ἐφῇ εἰς τοὺς ἅπαντας, κυρία ἔστω ἡ ἀποψήφισις ἡ τῶν θιασωτῶν· οἱ δὲ θιασῶται μετὰ τῶν ἄλλων φρατέρων μὴ φερόντων τὴν ψῆφον περὶ τῶν παίδων τῶν ἐκ τοῦ θιάσου τοῦ ἑαυτῶν.

children was given by the separate θίασοι, and that from their adverse decision the applicant could appeal to the general body of the Phratry. In that case the Dekeleiai, *i.e.* the family or clan of the Dekeleiai, who formed the main body of the Phratry, had to choose from among themselves 5 men over 30 years of age to represent before the Phratry as συνήγοροι the interests of the θίασος in opposition to the appellant.[1] If the appellant was refused by the entire Phratry also, he had to pay a fine of 1,000 drachmas to Zeus Phratrios.[2] The literary evidence agrees in essential points with this epigraphical account of the procedure at enrolments in the Phratry. It seems however that in certain old families, which formed sub-divisions of the Phratries by the side of the purely religious θίασοι, the vote of the Gennetai was sufficient in itself for the enrolment into the Phratry also, mainly of course because the members of such a family on account of their immediate or more remote right of inheritance had a greater interest in the child's membership of the family in question, than the members of a θίασος who were not connected by a similar family descent.[3] In some circumstances it seems to have been

[1] *Ibid.* 26 sqq.: τὴν δὲ διαδικασίαν τὸ λοιπὸν εἶναι τῷ ὑστέρῳ ἔτει ἢ ᾧ ἂν τὸ κούρειον θύσῃ τῇ κουρεώτιδι Ἀπατουρίων, φέρειν δὲ τὴν ψῆφον ἀπὸ τοῦ βωμοῦ· ἐὰν δέ τις βούληται ἐφεῖναι ἐς Δημοτιωνίδας ὧν ἂν ἀποψηφίσωνται, ἐξεῖναι αὐτῷ· ἑλέσθαι δὲ ἐπ' αὐτοῖς συνηγόρους τὸν Δεκελειῶν οἶκον πέντε ἄνδρας ὑπὲρ τριάκοντα ἔτη γεγονότας, τούτους δὲ ἐξορκωσάτω ὁ φρατρίαρχος· καὶ ὁ ἱερεὺς συνηγορήσειν τὰ δικαιότατα καὶ οὐκ ἐάσειν οὐδένα μὴ ὄντα φράτερα φρατρίζειν. These words lay down the procedure for the future, as τὸ λοιπὸν—(cf. also line 44/5: ταῦτα δὲ εἶναι ἀπὸ Φορμίωνος ἄρχοντος)—plainly shows; they have nothing to do with the procedure described in line 15 sqq., which took place αὐτίκα μάλα, though Schoell *op. cit.*, 8/9, supposes they have. Even in Schoell's explanation of the passage the strange fact remains that one and the same corporation gives the verdict both in the first instance and at the appeal. Ὁ νόμος ὁ Δημοτιωνιδῶν (line 14), which is apparently referred to in line 70 also, must have contained more precise details about the method of examination and admission, so as to explain the allusion in the words quoted above. I regard the separate θίασοι as the bodies which voted in the first instance here also. For the Δεκελειῶν οἶκος see Schoell, in the *Sitzungsber. d. bayr. Ak.*, 1889, p. 21, and above, p. 149, 1.

[2] The same inscr., 88 sqq.: ὅτου δ' ἂν τῶν ἐφέντων ἀποψηφίσωνται Δημοτιωνίδαι, ὀφειλέτω χιλίας δραχμὰς ἱερὰς τῷ Διὶ τῷ Φρατρίῳ. This fine is reduced to 100 drachmas in the second decree, 89/90.

[3] The statements in Is. 7, 15–17; 8, 19; Dem. 43, 14, 82; 57, 54, agree in all essentials with the Demotionidai-inscr. As regards exceptions in the case of certain old families, in Andoc., *de Myst.*, 127, for instance the Κήρυκες admit the son of Callias in spite of the opposition of Callides, and that obviously settled the question. In (Dem.) 59, 59 sqq. Phrastor introduced

possible for a private individual to offer opposition to the enrolment. The objector did this by the symbolic act of removing the sacrifice from the altar, and he was bound to make good his case by bringing a lawsuit before a court of justice, probably by a γραφὴ ξενίας or ὑποβολῆς.[1]

After admission to the Phratry had been granted, the name of the new member was entered in the κοινὸν γραμματεῖον of the φράτερες, also called φρατερικὸν γραμματεῖον.[2] Introductions into the Phratry at any other time except the Apaturia were generally speaking quite unusual, but they must have been sometimes allowable, at any rate in the case of adoptions, where it might be extremely important to the adoptor to obtain the full legal rights of a son for the person adopted as soon as

his son εἰς τοὺς φράτερας καὶ εἰς τοὺς Βρυτίδας, ὧν καὶ αὐτός ἐστιν ὁ Φράστωρ γεννήτης. But there is no question about any vote of the Phrateres. Phrastor appealed, when the Brytidai refused the enrolment, but not to the Phratry; he brought the case before a Diaitetes, and as he failed to take the customary oath before the Diaitetes the case was apparently decided against him. Perhaps however Phrastor did not venture to appeal to the Phrateres, and therefore the decision of the Gennetai remained valid on the same principle as in the Demotionidai-inscr., l. 99 sqq.: ἐὰν δέ, ἀποψηφισαμένων τῶν θιασωτῶν, μὴ ἐφῇ εἰς τοὺς ἅπαντας, κυρία ἔστω ἡ ἀποψήφισις ἡ τῶν θιασωτῶν. Again in an inscr. acknowledged to be genuine by Dittenberger, *Syll. inscr. gr.*, 98, 5, and Herm. 20, 5, 1, οἱ γεννῆται οἱ καλοῦνται Βρυτίδαι formed an old family of the same kind. Appeal to a judicial decision occurs also in the speech of Deinarchos πρὸς Κήρυκας (for κατὰ Κηρύκων acc. to Meier[2] 760, 38a), in which there is a question περί τινος ἀποψηφισθέντος obviously by the family of the Κήρυκες. See Meier, *de bon. damnat.*, 90, 299.

[1] Is. 6, 22: ἐπειδὴ οὔθ' ὁ υἱὸς αὐτῷ Φιλοκτήμων συνεχώρει οὔθ' οἱ φράτορες εἰσεδέξαντο, ἀλλ' ἀπηνέχθη τὸ κούρειον: here therefore the ἀπενεγκεῖν τὸ κούρειον seems to have been the result of the unfavourable decision of the Phrateres. On the other hand acc. to Dem. 43, 14. 82, it was possible for an individual to prevent an admission into the Phratry by himself removing the sacrifice from the altar; this proceeding involved κινδυνεύειν (14) or ὑπεύθυνον αὑτὸν ποιεῖν (82), *i.e.* a lawsuit on the subject before the dicasteria. In Is. 3, 37 a man is prosecuted by a Phrater for ξενίας, but apparently when he was already of mature age. The only mention of the γραφὴ ὑποβολῆς is in Lex. Seguer. 311, 33: ὑποβολῆς γραφή τί ἐστιν; εἶδος ἐγκλήματος. εἴ τις ἐγκαλοίη τινί, ὡς ὑποβολιμαῖος εἴη, ἐγράφετο ὑποβολῆς καὶ ἁλόντα αὐτὸν ἔδει πεπρᾶσθαι. See Meier[2] 441/2.

[2] Κοινὸν γραμματεῖον: Is. 7, 16. 17; Harp. Phot. Suid. *sub v.*; Demotionidai-inscr. 96/7; φρατερικὸν γραμματεῖον: Dem. 44, 41. In the Demot.-inscr. l. 20/1 mention is made of τὸ γραμματεῖον τὸ ἐν Δημοτιωνιδῶν καὶ τὸ ἀντίγραφον; the ἀντίγραφον probably belonged to the Δεκελειῶν οἶκος. This proceeding is termed εἰσάγειν εἰς τοὺς φράτερας: Is. 6, 21; 8, 19; Dem. 39, 4; 43, 13; 57, 54; ἐγγράφειν εἰς τοὺς φρ.: Dem. 39, 4; Is. 7, 17.

possible.[1] After enrolment in the Phratry-list the child remained under the care of its family and relatives; the State did not interfere in its education at all.

The individual Athenian first entered into legal relations with the State when he was admitted into his Deme. This took place upon the completion of his 17th year.[2] In two recorded cases of adoption the time of year when this enrolment took place is given as the Archairesia, meaning the Archairesia of the Demes; for ordinary enrolments no specified date is given, though they probably took place at the same date in all the Demes.[3] The method of procedure was as follows.

Enrolment in the Deme-list.

After the Demotai had taken an oath that they would decide uprightly, they examined the youth and voted on the question whether he was of the age required by law, and whether his pedigree satisfied the conditions legally necessary for burgess rights. If the Demotai refused to accept him and appeal was made to the

---

[1] In Is. 7. 15 the enrolment of an adopted son takes place at the Thargelia. For adoption see Meier ² 539 ff.

[2] Arist. 42, 1: ἐγγράφονται δ' εἰς τοὺς δημότας ὀκτωκαίδεκα ἔτη γεγονότες—cf. also the Schol. on Æsch. *in Ctes.*, 122: πολλάκις ἔγνωμεν, ὅτι ἀπὸ ὀκτωκαίδεκα ἐτῶν ἐνεγράφοντο εἰς τὸ ληξιαρχικὸν οἱ Ἀθηναῖοι, a note based on Aristotle (cf. Schol. on Arist., *Wasps*, 578). That ὀκτωκ. ἔτ. γεγ. means the year after completion of the 17th year of life, is proved by the case of Demosthenes, who was 7 years old when his father died (Dem. 27, 4), was a few days more than ten years under guardianship (Dem. 27, 6 and Schaefer Dem. 3¹, 2, 43 ff.), and then came of age, *i.e.* was enrolled in the ληξιαρχικὸν γραμματεῖον. For the time one attained one's majority in Attic law cf. Schaefer 3¹, 2, 19 ff.; and for a refutation of the theory that enrolment in the ληξ. γραμμ. did not take place till the 20th year, *id. ib.* 87/8.

[3] Passages on enrolments of adopted sons, Dem. 44, 39 and Is. 7, 27/8. Lipsius in *Jahrb. f. cl. Phil.*, 1878, 299 ff., makes a distinction between the enrolment of adopted sons and the ordinary enrolment. That the regular Dokimasia of the Epheboi took place at the beginning of the Athenian official year, is an inference drawn by Lipsius, p. 302, from Lys. 21, 1, which would find some confirmation in the fact that in the 2nd cent. B.C. the Epheboi-year began on the 1st of Boedromion. But Ad. Schmidt, *Handb. d. Griech. Chronol.*, 313 ff., seems to be justified in holding that the Dokimasia at the beginning of the Attic official year attested by Lysias was an exceptional occurrence of the year 411 B.C. caused by the exceptional circumstances produced by the domination of the 400. Philippi, *N. Rh. Mus.*, 34, 610/1, puts the Archairesia at the beginning of the year, and supposes that both natural and adopted sons were admitted at the same time on that date. I still consider the Archairesiai mentioned by Is. and Dem. to have been the Archairesiai of the Demes.

law courts, the Demotai elected from amongst themselves 5 prosecutors. If the verdict of the dicastery was against the appellant, he was sold into slavery for the benefit of the state treasury; if in his favour, they were compelled to enrol him in their Deme. After this there was yet another examination by the Boule, who inflicted a fine on the Demotai, if the new Demesman had not attained the requisite age.¹ The list in which his name was entered, is sometimes called by the same title as the Phratry-list κοινὸν γραμματεῖον,² but is generally termed ληξιαρχικὸν γραμματεῖον, *i.e.* the list of those who possessed the right of inheriting (λῆξις) their κλῆρος and their οὐσία.³

Upon entrance into the Deme the Athenian acquired his complete citizen-name, which consisted of his own name, the name of his father in the genitive case, and his Deme-name,⁴ and became a political personality. From this time the State presumed that the young Athenian was acquainted with its laws, and was com-

¹ Arist. 42, 1: ἐγγράφονται δ' εἰς τοὺς δημότας ὀκτωκαίδεκα ἔτη γεγονότες. ὅταν δ' ἐγγράφωνται, διαψηφίζονται περὶ αὑτῶν ὀμόσαντες οἱ δημόται, πρῶτον μὲν εἰ δοκοῦσι γεγονέναι τὴν ἡλικίαν τὴν ἐκ τοῦ νόμου, κἂν μὴ δόξωσι, ἀπέρχονται πάλιν εἰς παῖδας, δεύτερον δ' εἰ ἐλεύθερός ἐστι καὶ γέγονε κατὰ τοὺς νόμους. ἔπειτ' ἂν μὲν ἀποψηφίσωνται μὴ εἶναι ἐλεύθερον, ὁ μὲν ἐφίησιν εἰς τὸ δικαστήριον, οἱ δὲ δημόται κατηγόρους αἱροῦνται πέντε [ἂν]δρας ἐξ αὑτῶν, κἂν μὲν μὴ δόξῃ δικαίως ἐγγράφεσθαι, πωλεῖ τοῦτον ἡ πόλις· ἐὰν δὲ νικήσῃ, τοῖς [δ]ημόταις ἐπάναγκες ἐγγράφειν. μετὰ δὲ ταῦτα δοκιμάζει τοὺς ἐγγραφέντας ἡ βουλή, κἄν τις δόξῃ νεώτερος ὀκτωκαίδεκ' ἐτῶν εἶναι, ζημιοῖ [το]ὺς δημότας τοὺς ἐγγράψαντας. Cf. Is. 7, 28; Dem. 57, 61. The expressions for reception among the Demotai are ἐγγραφῆναι εἰς τὸ ληξιαρχικὸν γραμματεῖον, εἰς τοὺς δημότας, also briefly ἐγγραφῆναι or δοκιμασθῆναι and the like.

² Dem. 57, 60; Lex. Seguer. 272, 27 sqq.

³ Is. 7, 27; Dem. 44, 35; Harp. ληξιαρχικὸν γραμματεῖον· Αἰσχίνης ἐν τῷ κατὰ Τιμάρχου (§ 18), εἰς ὃ ἐνεγράφοντο οἱ τελεωθέντες τῶν παίδων, οἷς ἐξῆν ἤδη τὰ πατρῷα οἰκονομεῖν, παρ' ὃ καὶ τοὔνομα γεγονέναι, διὰ τὸ τῶν λήξεων ἄρχειν· λήξεις δ' εἰσὶν αἵ τε κλῆροι καὶ αἱ οὐσίαι, ὡς καὶ Δείναρχος ἐν τῇ ά καθ' Ἡγελόχου συνηγορίᾳ ὑπὲρ ἐπικλήρου. For the ληξιαρχ. γραμμ., see L. Lange, *Leipz. Stud.*, 1, 194 ff.

⁴ Dem. 39, 9: καὶ τίς ἤκουσε πώποτε ἢ κατὰ ποῖον νόμον προσπαραγράφοιτ' ἂν τοῦτο τὸ παράγραμμα ἢ ἄλλο τι πλὴν ὁ πατὴρ καὶ ὁ δῆμος; so *e.g.* Δημοσθένης Δημοσθένους Παιανιεύς. A decree of the Boule of 343/2 B.C. directs that on an ἄγαλμα of Athena shall be inscribed (τοὺς βουλ)ευτὰς πατρόθεν καὶ τοῦ δήμ(ου): C.I.A., II. 114 B. In the case of the Phratry Demotionidai a list was to be drawn up every year of the children to be admitted, and it was to contain τὸ ὄνομα πατρόθεν καὶ τοῦ δήμου καὶ τῆς μητρὸς πατρόθεν καὶ τοῦ δήμου, Sauppe in *Ind. Schol. Goett.*, 1890/1, p. 4, l. 115 ff. In names of Athenian freewomen the Deme-name was put after the name of the father or husband with or without the addition of θυγάτηρ or γυνή; the tomb-inscrr. supply numerous examples. What was the custom in case of *νόθοι ex cive Attica* admitted into the Deme, is uncertain.

petent to distinguish right from wrong, and therefore dealt with him henceforth directly in person.[1] If the newly enrolled Demesman was the son of an ἐπίκληρος, or was an orphan, he received by admission to the Deme the right of disposal over his property.[2]

The πίναξ ἐκκλησιαστικός, in which Athenians had to be enrolled at the beginning of their 20th year, was simply a copy of the ληξιαρχικὸν γραμματεῖον prepared for the ληξίαρχοι to help them in their supervision of the meetings of the Ecclesia. The right of attending the Ecclesia legally belonged to the Athenian as soon as he was declared of age; but during the period of military training which followed his enrolment in the Deme he was seldom able to exercise this right in practice.[3] Leaving out of consideration the particular rights which he could not claim till later in life,[4] the youth enrolled in the ληξιαρχικὸν γραμματεῖον thereby entered into full possession of all the political rights included in the term ἐπιτιμία. The corresponding negative expression was ἀτιμία, which might be either partial or total. Total ἀτιμία meant deprivation of all political rights; partial ἀτιμία, called ἀτιμία κατὰ προστάξεις, meant loss of some rights while the rest were retained.[5] As full political rights could be diminished by Atimia, so additional rights could be granted by special grants of honour. The commonest of these rights were ἀτέλεια, i.e. exemption from λειτουργίαι; προεδρία, i.e. right to a seat of honour at festival assemblies; σίτησις ἐν Πρυτανείῳ, or the right

Burgess-rights.

Diminution of Burgess-rights.

Increase of rights.

---

[1] Æsch. *in Tim.* 18.

[2] Harp., ληξιαρχικὸν γραμματεῖον. Poll. 8, 104. For the sons of ἐπίκληροι cf. Is. *ap.* Suid., τέως; Is. 8, 31; 10, 12; for orphans, Æsch. *in Tim.* 103. Orphans were however exempted from Leiturgies during the first year after coming of age: Lys. 32, 94.

[3] So Schaefer 36 rightly holds, in opposition to Boeckh., *kl. Schr.*, 4, 154. See also Dittenberger, *de ephebis Att.*, p. 10. It is proved by Xen., *Mem.*, 3, 6, 1. Dem. 44, 35 mentions the πίναξ ἐκκλησιαστικός.

[4] 30 years was the minimum age for Bouleutai (Xen., *Mem.*, 1, 2, 35) and Heliasts (Arist. 63, 3; Poll. 8, 122), 50 for Ephetai (Poll. ἐφέται Art. 2; Suid., *id.*; Lex. Seguer. 188, 30), 60 for Diaitetai (Arist. 53, 4; Poll. 8, 126). For Athenian usage in this matter cf. the author's *Beitr.*, 25.

[5] The *locus classicus* for the various kinds of ἀτιμία is Andoc., *de Myst.*, 73 sqq. Atimia with confiscation of property is not a special form of Atimia but the combination of two forms of punishment, as Lipsius in Bursian's *Jahresber.*, 15, 343, rightly infers from Dem. 20, 155 sqq. On Atimia cf. Meier, *de bonis damnat.*, 101 ff. and van Lelyveld, *de infamia iure Attico comment.*, Amsterdam, 1885.

to dine in the Prytaneion either on one occasion or for life; and, lastly, distinguished men were often publicly presented with a crown or chaplet.[1]

D. *Political Divisions of the Burgess Body and other Associations.*

The entire free population of Athens was divided by Cleisthenes into 10 Phylai or tribes: the following is the list of their names in their official order: Ἐρεχθηίς, Αἰγηίς, Πανδιονίς, Λεοντίς, Ἀκαμαντίς, Οἰνηίς, Κεκροπίς, Ἱπποθωντίς, Αἰαντίς, and Ἀντιοχίς.[2] To these 10 old tribes were added in 306/5 B.C. the Ἀντιγονίς, named after Antigonos I., and the Δημητρίας, named after Demetrios Poliorketes, and in the official order the Antigonis was assigned the first place, the Demetrias the second.[3] To these 12 the Πτολεμαίς was afterwards added, so that for

[1] For these public honours see Westermann, *de publ. Atheniens. honorib. ac praemiis*, 1830. For Ateleia the exhaustive investigation by Thumser, *de civ. Atheniens. munerib.*, p. 108 ff. σίτησις ἐν Πρυτανείῳ was generally granted to victorious Strategoi (Æsch., *de Fals. Leg.*, 80), and returning ambassadors (*id. ib.*, 46, 53). For this right see Westermann p. 45 ff., and R. Schoell in *Herm.*, 6, 14 ff., who has discussed the subject in a note upon a fragmentary decree of the people (C.I.A., I. 8) which contains an enumeration of all those who could claim the right of dining during their whole life in the Prytaneion. For crowns and public announcement of grants of crowns see Köhler in *Mitth. d. dtsch. archäol. Inst. in Ath.*, 3, 131 ff.; Schmitthenner, *de coronarum apud Athenienses honoribus*, Berlin, 1891.

[2] All the 10 Phylai occur in official order in C.I.A., II. 172, and in the list of Diaitetai in C.I.A., II. 943, also in Ἐφ. ἀρχ., 1883, pp. 123/4, l. 50 sqq. (Dem.) 60, 27–31, also gives them in official order with the names of their eponymi. For these last cf. Paus. 1, 5, 2 sqq. Incomplete lists of the Phylai, but in official order so far as they go, in C.I.A., I. 443, 446, 447. See also A. Mommsen in *Phil. N. F.*, 1, 450 ff., 1888, where he seeks to prove (465) that the official order was influenced partly by the relation of their eponymi to the customary ceremonies of the tenth of the year which fell under their presidency, partly by the rank of the eponymi. To me the whole argument and its results seem of very doubtful validity.

[3] For the creation of the Antigonis and the Demetrias cf. Plut., *Demetr.*, 10; Droysen, *Gesch. d. Diad.*, 2, 119/20 (416). The Phyle Demetrias is attested in inscrr. for the year 306/5: C.I.A., II. 246. On the other hand the circumstance that the 5th Prytany falls in the 6th month Poeseideon in C.I.A., II. 238, dating from 307/6, while after the institution of the twelve tribes the Prytany in any ordinary year nearly always coincides with the corresponding month, serves to prove that in 307/6 B.C. there were still only 10 tribes. See Köhler in Herm. 5, 349 ff. C.I.A., II. 335, shows the official place of the Antigonis and the Demetrias in the lists. See Dittenberger in *Herm.* 9, 399, and J. E. Kirchner, *N. Rhein. Mus.*, 1892.

some time there were 13 tribes. In 200 B.C., when the 'Ατταλίς was created in honour of king Attalus I., the Antigonis and Demetrias were abolished, and the number of the tribes again became 12.[1]

In the official order of the tribes the Ptolemais took the 5th, the Attalis the 12th place.[2]

The ἐπώνυμοι of the Phylai were called in unofficial language ἀρχηγέται; statues representing them were erected on the slope leading up to the Acropolis and Areopagus; they had also special shrines in which heroic honours were paid to them.[3] They also possessed property consecrated to them, chiefly parcels of land, which were let out on lease.[4]

ἐπώνυμοι.

At the head of each tribe stood several ἐπιμεληταὶ τῆς φυλῆς,

---

[1] From the inscr. published in the 'Εφ. ἀρχ., 1887, p. 177, it appears that under the archonship of Diocles there were 13 tribes and a council of 650 members. Since this inscr. can only have been made in the period between the creation of the Antigonis and Demetrias and that of the Attalis, it is a very plausible inference that the Antigonis Demetrias and Ptolemais existed side by side for some time, and that the two first were abolished when the Attalis was created. See Philios 179 ff. For the list of Proedroi in 'Αθην. 6, p. 271, no. 4, the explanation I suggested in Phil. 39, 873 ff., will not hold good, and some other must be found. See Spangenberg, *de Athen. publicis institutis aetate Maced. commutatis*, p. 34/5, Halle, 1884; Beloch, in the *Jahrb. f. cl. Phil.*, 1884, 481 ff.; Philios 182, 3. Acc. to Paus. 1, 8, 6; 1, 6, 8; 1, 5, 5 the Ptolemais was founded in honour of Ptolemy Philadelphos (285–247); acc. to Beloch, who argues from the datum that the Ptolemais and the Demos Berenikidai (cf. Steph. *sub v.*) were founded simultaneously, it was in honour of Ptolemy Euergetes (247–221). Foundation of Attalis in honour of Attalos I., Polyb. 16, 25; Liv. 31, 15; Paus. 1, 5, 5; 1, 8, 1.

[2] For the position of the Ptolemais and Attalis in the official order of the tribes cf. C.I.A., II. 465, 471.

[3] Paus. 1, 5, 1. Wachsmuth 1, 165; 2, 1, 243 ff. Ἐπώνυμοι is their usual name (cf. *e.g.* Suid. *s.v.*) they are called ἀρχηγέται by Aristoph. *ap.* Lex. Seguer. 449, 14. Among special shrines of the Eponymoi, who naturally all had their Heroa, I may mention the Ἱπποθώντιον on the road to Eleusis: Paus. 1, 88, 4; C.I.A., II. 567b; the ἱερὸν τοῦ Πανδίονος: C.I.A., II. 553, 556, 559, 554b, whose priest is mentioned C.I.A., II. 1179, 554b; the ἱερὸν τοῦ Κέκροπος: C.I.A., I. 322, col. 1, l. 9, 58, 62, 83; 324a, col. 2, l. 24; III. 1276. 'Αρχ. δελτίον, 1889, p. 11 = Bull. 13, 257; the Αἰγεῖον: Harp., *s.v.* Lex. Seguer. 354, 8; Paus. 1, 22, 5. A ἱερεὺς of Erechtheus: Bull. 12, 331. Ἀττάλου ἐπωνύμου: C.I.A., II. 1670, III. 300; a ἱερεὺς τοῦ ἐπωνύμου: II. 393, 431, cf. II. 1664.

[4] Cf. Dem. 24, 8. (Dem.) 58, 14. The presidents of the Erechtheis are to have supervision over the lands leased: C.I.A., II. 564; see also 565. In Samos has been found a ὅρος τεμένους ἐπωνύμων Ἀθήνηθ(ε)ν: C. Curtius, *Inschr. u. Stud. z. Gesch. v. Samos.*, p. 9, Lübeck, 1877.

who were chosen annually by the Phyle, probably by election,[1] and were bound to give in accounts of their year of office at its expiration.[2] The ἐπιμεληταὶ τῆς φυλῆς had in their hands the administrative business of the tribe, and had to see that the decrees passed by the tribe were carried out. Among the particular tasks incumbent upon them are mentioned holding the tribal-assemblies, supervising the property of the Phyle, recording and publishing tribal decrees, receipt of rents, and, if necessary, distraint against the tenants, and payment of moneys voted by the Phyle. In their financial business they were assisted by a ταμίας.[3] The members of the various tribes assembled on fixed dates in Athens in tribal assemblies called ἀγοραί, where they voted in secret on matters concerning their particular tribe.[4] These tribal ἀγοραί elected their own officials, and also a special class of state-officials who, as e.g. the extraordinary τειχοποιοί, ταφροποιοί, and τριηροποιοί, were responsible for the performance of that portion (i.e. a tenth part) of any public work that was imposed on their tribe.[5]

Further, the Choregoi Gymnasiarchoi and Hestiatores were also elected at these ἀγοραί.[6] Of the tribal decrees that have been

[1] C.I.A., II. 564: οἱ ἐπιμεληταὶ οἱ ἀεὶ καθιστάμενοι κατ' ἐνιαυτόν. 3 ἐπιμεληταί: C.I.A., II. 1209.

[2] C.I.A., 567b: ἀναγράψαι δὲ τόδε τὸ ψήφισμα τοὺς ἐπιμελητὰς τῆς φυλῆς ἐν στήλαις λιθίναις καὶ στῆσαι τὴν μὲν ἐν τῷ Ἀσκληπιείῳ, τὴν δὲ τῷ Ἱπποθωντίῳ ὅτι δ' ἀνάλωμα γένηται, λογίσασθαι τῇ φυλῇ. The εὔθυνη is proved by (Dem.) 58, 14–18. There it says of the Phyletai, § 15: ὥστ' ἐκείνους κλοπὴν αὐτοῦ καταγνῶναι, but perhaps without legal effect, for that would certainly require a verdict of a dicastery.

[3] Holding tribal assemblies: C.I.A., II. 564. Supervision of property of tribe: II. 564. Recording tribal decrees: II. 554, 557. Receipt of rents and distraint on tenants: II. 565. Making payments: II. 558, 559. Mention of a ταμίας: II. 565, 1209.

[4] C.I.A., II. 555: τῇ κυρίᾳ ἀγορᾷ κρύβδην ψηφισαμένων τῶ(ν φυλετῶν) ἐν ἀκροπόλει. Decree of the Pandionis, ἐν τῇ ἀγορᾷ(ι) τῇ μετὰ Πάνδια: II. 554b. Mommsen, Heort., 389, places the Pandia sacrifice on the 14th of Elaphebolion just after the State Dionysia, from which we may conclude that the κύριαι ἀγοραὶ were held at the convenient time of state festivals, when most members of the tribe were present in Athens. C.I.A., II. 564 says of the ἐπιμεληταί: ἐάν τινος δέηται (sc. Ἀριστομάχη) ἐμφανίζοντας τεῖ φυλεῖ ὅταν ἀγορὰν ποιῶσιν.

[5] Æsch. in Ctes. 27, 30. As a rule the Boule appointed from among its own members a committee of 10 τριηροποιοί. Cf. Arist. 46, 1: ποιεῖται (ἡ βουλὴ) δὲ τὰς τριήρεις δέκα ἄνδρας ἐξ α[ὑτῶν] ἑλομένη τριηροποιούς. (But Sandys following Kenyon reads ἁ[πάντων].)

[6] Dem. 39, 7; 21, 13. Antiph., de Choreut., 11; cf. also 13.

preserved, most are decrees of honour, sometimes in favour of Choregoi, praising them for excellent performance of their Choregiai, granting them crowns or even Ateleia either temporarily or for life; sometimes other private individuals are honoured in the same way for various reasons.[1] There are, however, some Phyle decrees which have reference to the administration of the property of the Phyle.[2]

Each Phyle was composed of a number of Demes. Whether these were originally 10 in each Phyle can neither be affirmed nor denied with certainty. In later times at any rate the total number of Demes had risen considerably above 100, for we have literary evidence that there were 174 of them, and the Demes known to us by name outnumber even this.[3] It goes without saying that the Demes varied considerably in size. Acharnai, for instance, and the metropolitan Demes certainly had a very large number of inhabitants, while on the other hand at a Diapsephesis in Halimus only 73 demotai were present, and at Myrrhinus the quorum at a meeting of the Deme was 30 members.[4]

Demes.

---

[1] Decrees of honour to Choregoi: C.I.A., II. 553, 554; to a σωφρονιστής: Bull. 12, 149. Decrees granting Ateleia one for several years, the other for life, in return for leiturgies: II. 557, 554b. Other decrees of honour: II. 555, 558, 559, 562, 567. Cf. also Æsch. *in Ctes.* 41.

[2] Tribe decree concerning supervision of tribe property: C.I.A., II. 564; for letting the same: II. 565.

[3] For the administration of the Attic Demes cf. Otto Muller, *de demis Att.*, Göttingen, 1880. B. Haussoullier, *la vie municipale en Attique*, Paris, Thorin, 1884. 100 Demes the original number: Hdt. 5, 69. Herodian, π. μ. λέξ., p. 17, 8: 'Αραφὴν εἶς τῶν ἑκατὸν ἡρώων. Cf. Sauppe, *de dem. urb.*, p. 5. But see p. 147, 1 and Strab. 396: 'Ελευσῖνά τε εἰπὼν ἕνα τῶν ἑκατὸν ἑβδομήκοντα δήμων πρὸς δὲ καὶ τεττάρων, ὥς φασιν, οὐδένα τῶν ἄλλων ὠνόμακεν. Köhler's suggestion in *Mitth. d. dtsch. arch. Inst.*, 10, 108 ff., that the increase in the number of Demes took place by a single act of the sovereign people at the time of the second founding of the fleet by Themistocles and the institution of the Trittyes, now loses its main support through the discovery of the fact that Cleisthenes had already created the Trittyes before. Cf. Arist. 21, 4.

[4] Acharnai the largest Deme: Thuc. 2, 19, 20. See Herbst in *Phil.*, 46, 571 ff. Piræus was divided into a number of τριακάδες: C.I.A., II. 589. For Halimus cf. Dem. 57, 9, 10, for Myrrhinus C.I.A., II. 578. I do not think it probable that the 30 demotai at Myrrhinus had to be unanimous for their resolution to be valid, as Szánto, *Untersuch. üb. d. att. Burgerr.*, 33 ff., thinks. To judge by the Prytany lists there must have been in Attica Demes which kept aloof from public affairs, and were not represented in the Boule. See Köhler, in *Mitth. d. dtsch. arch. Inst. in Ath.*, 4, 105/6.

As in the case of the Phylai, so the Demes also had their especial Eponymoi worshipped in the Deme as heroes.[1]

Constitution of the Demes. The Attic demes were communities with communal constitutions, but without separate political rights; the Deme of Eleusis was the only one which still retained from the period of its old autonomy the right of coinage.[2] The entire citizen population of the individual Demes was divided into δημόται, members domiciled within the Deme concerned, and the so-called ἐγκεκτημένοι, who merely resided in the Deme concerned but had their proper domicile in another Deme. In return for the privilege of residing in a Deme not their own the ἐγκεκτημένοι paid a fixed contribution called ἐγκτητικόν, from which they might indeed be released by decree of the Deme, but even in that case their status in the Deme remained that of strangers.[3]

The ἐγκτητικόν, together with the financial contributions of the Demotai and the revenues from the communal property of the Deme (which consisted mostly of landed estates, let out to tenants), formed the funds of the Deme treasury out of which the communal expenses of the Deme were met.[4]

For the communal government of the Deme no universally valid scheme can be made out.[5] All Demes had a δήμαρχος or president,

---

[1] Sauppe, *de demis urb.*, p. 6 ff., gives a collection of all the known deme-eponymi. Cf. C.I.A., II. 1191, found at Rhamnus, which mentions a ἱερεὺς ἥρωος ἀρχηγέτου.

[2] For Eleusis see Köhler in *Mitth. d. dtsch. arch. Inst. in Ath.*, 4, 261 ff.

[3] Dem. 50, 8 distinguishes δημόται and ἐγκεκτημένοι. C.I.A., II. 589 = decree of Piræus in honour of Callidamas from Cholleidai: τελεῖν δὲ αὐτὸν τὰ αὐτὰ τέλη ἐν τῷ δήμῳ ἅπερ ἂν καὶ Πειραιεῖς καὶ μὴ ἐκλέγειν παρ' αὐτοῦ τὸν δήμαρχον τὸ ἐγκτητικόν. But that Callidamas was still not counted a Demotes follows from the words: καὶ συνεστιᾶσθαι Καλλιδάμαντα μετὰ Πειραιέων ἐν ἅπασι τοῖς ἱεροῖς πλὴν εἴ που αὐτοῖς Πειραιεῦσιν νόμιμόν ἐστιν εἰσιέναι, ἄλλῳ δὲ μή. Cf. II. 582.

[4] μισθώσεις τεμενῶν part of the receipts of the Deme treasury, Dem. 57, 63. We possess leases of communal property granted by Aixone and Piræus. C.I.A., II. 1055, 1059. Cf. also II. 570. Communal pasture land at Aixone whose ἐννόμιον was let by lease: *Mitth. d. dtsch. arch. Inst. in Ath.*, 4, 201. At Piræus the theatre too was the property of the Deme. See II. 573. In II. 588 occurs a peculiar ceremony in some deme of unknown name, ἐπαρχή, ἣν ἐπάρχονται οἱ δημόται ἀπὸ τῆς ἀρχῆς ἕκαστος ἧς ἂν λάχει. On the financial payments of the Demotai for purposes of the Deme see Thumser, *de civ. Atheniens. munerib.*, p. 102 ff. For the difficult inscr. C.I.A., II. 570, see Szánto *Untersuch. ab. d. att. Bürgerr.*, 37 ff.

[5] For the Deme officials see O. Müller 49 ff., and for the Demarchoi, Haussoulier, 94 ff.

appointed apparently by lot and annually.[1] Just like the state officials, the δήμαρχος had the right ἐπιβολὴν ἐπιβάλλειν within his sphere of duty.[2] Since the Deme was a subdivision of the State, the Demarch exercised both state functions and communal ones. To the former class belonged the duty of collecting debts due to the State, and, if necessary, distraining for them; collecting the tithes or percentage of the crops of the demotai due to the Eleusinian deities; drawing up the list of demotai liable to be recruited for manning the fleet; and lastly keeping the survey book or cadastral register of his Deme.[3] In his capacity as communal official, the Demarch kept the ληξιαρχικὸν γραμματεῖον, convoked and presided over meetings of the Deme, and saw that the decrees of the Deme were carried out.[4] He further was responsible for public order in his Deme; had to offer certain sacrifices at certain festivals; and was at the head of the entire finance management of the Deme, in which last duty he was assisted by one or two ταμίαι, who were likewise appointed by lot in all probability.[5] Besides the Demarch there were in some Demes

---

[1] Lex. Seguer. 237, 8: δήμαρχος· ὁ τοῦ δήμου ἄρχων. ἕκαστος δὲ τῶν κατὰ τὴν χώραν δήμων ἄρχοντα εἶχε τὸν προϊστάμενον αὐτοῦ. Müller, 49/50, rightly infers from C.I.A., II. 570: τοὺς μὲν ἄρχοντας τοῦ ἀργυρίου ἀ(ξιό)χρεως κυαμεύειν ὅσου ἑκάστῃ ἡ ἀ(ρχὴ ἄ)ρχει that the Demarch was appointed by lot, for he too had charge of funds. Cf. also Dem. 57, 25.

[2] C.I.A., II. 573b. Decree of the Deme Piræus: ἐάν τίς τι τούτων παρὰ ταῦτα ποιεῖ (enters the Thesmophorion without permission of the priestess), ἐπιβολὴν ἐπ(ι)βαλόντα τὸν δήμαρχον κ.τ.ά.

[3] C.I.A., I. 79: ἐκπραττόντων δὲ οἱ δήμαρ(χοι). Cf. the καταδίκη of Archeptolemos and Antiphon in Plut., Antiph., 27; Didot, p. 1016. Harp., Suid., Hesych., s. verb. Lex Seguer. 199, 4; 237, 8; 242, 16. Schol. on Aristoph., Clouds, 37. Dittenberger, Syll., 13. Out of every 100 medimnoi of barley one ἑκτεύς, every 100 medimnoi of wheat one ἡμιεκτέον had to be given τοῖν θεοῖν. ἐκλέγειν δὲ [τοὺς δ]ημάρχους κατὰ τοὺς δήμους καὶ παραδιδόναι τοῖς ἱεροποιοῖς τοῖς Ἐλευσινόθεν Ἐλευσινάδε. Drawing up the κατάλογοι: Dem. 50, 6. For the land-register kept by the Demarch, cf. Harp., δήμαρχος, and compare with that passage, C.I.A., II. 1055, 1059. The distribution of the Theoricon was likewise a duty of the Demarchs. Cf. Dem. 44, 37; and C.I.A., II. 163.

[4] Keeping the ληξιαρχικὸν γραμματεῖον: Dem. 57, 60. Harp. δήμαρχος. Convoking and presiding over the assembly of the Demes: Harp., ib.; C.I.A., II., 578. Recording and publishing decrees of Deme: C.I.A., II., 573, 575, 579, 581, 585. Ἐφ. ἀρχ., 1888, 23. The Demarch conducted into the theatre those honoured with Proedria: C.I.A., II. 589. Mitth. d. dtsch. Arch. Inst. in Ath., 4, 196. Ἐφ. ἀρχ., 1888, 23.

[5] Acc. to the law quoted in Dem. 43, 57/8 the Demarch had to see to the burial of those who died in the Deme. Cf. also C.I.A., II. 573b, 841, where

other ordinary or extraordinary officials of very varied character, mostly religious functionaries.[1] In the case of Piræus for instance we hear of ὁρισταί.[2] In a decree of honour from Aixone mention is made of 4 officials selected by lot ἱεροποιοὶ εἰς τὸ τῆς Ἥβης ἱερόν, 2 σωφρονισταί and a κῆρυξ, who were all employed in the παννυχὶς of Hebe; further a ἱερεὺς τῶν Ἡρακλειδῶν, a ἱέρεια τῆς Ἥβης καὶ τῆς Ἀλκμήνης, and an ἄρχων also in the service of those deities.[3] Again, for Halimus we have evidence of a priest of Heracles appointed by lot from among the most prominent Demotai.[4] A decree of Athmonon is passed in honour of 6 μεράρχαι, who obviously were officials responsible for the sacrifices at the Amarysia.[5] The 3 ἐπιτιμηταί or valuers at Piræus who are mentioned in connexion with the letting of the theatre to the lessees must be regarded as a special committee for the purpose, and so also must the 3 Demotai of Aixone who assisted the Demarch and the treasurers at the sale of the olive trees on a parcel of land let on lease.[6]

Like the State magistrates, the officials of the Deme had to undergo a dokimasia before entering upon office, to take an oath of good conduct in their office, and also to render their accounts

---

it is decreed that if any Demotes took wood, faggots, leaves, etc., from the ἱερὸν of Apollo Erithaseos, ἂν δὲ ἐλεύθερος ᾖ, θοάσει αὐτὸν ὁ ἱερεύ(s) μετὰ τοῦ δημάρχου πεντήκοντα δραχμαῖς καὶ παραδώσει τοὔνομα αὐτοῦ τῷ βασιλεῖ καὶ τῇ βουλῇ κατὰ τὸ ψήφισμα τῆς βου(λ)ῆς καὶ τοῦ δήμου τῶν Ἀθηναίων. Sacrifices offered by the Demarch: II. 578, 570. Ἐφ. ἀρχ., 1887, p. 93. He collects the μισθώσεις τεμενῶν that are due: Dem. 57, 63, and also the ἐγκτητικόν: C.I.A., II. 589. Demarch and Tamiai directed by Deme decree to make payments out of funds of Deme: C.I.A., II. 579, 585. C.I.A., II. 570, shows 2 Tamai, but at Eleusis there seems to have been only one: II. 574; in Ἐφ. ἀρχ. 1884, 73/4 payment is made by the Demarch at Eleusis. C.I.A., II. 570, shews that the ταμίαι at Plotheia were chosen by lot. That there was an ἀντιγραφεὺς in all Demes, cannot be inferred with certainty from the solitary example of Myrrhinus in C.I.A., II. 575.

[1] See Haussoullier, 136 ff. for the priestly officials, 151 ff. on the sanctuaries and cults, 162 ff. on the festivals of the various Demes.

[2] C.I.A., II. 573b: ἀναγράψαι δὲ τόδε τὸ ψήφισμα τοὺς ὁριστὰς μετὰ τοῦ δημάρχου καὶ στῆσαι πρὸς τῇ ἀναβάσει τοῦ θεσμοφορίου. This psephism gives regulations for the use of the θεσμοφόριον at Piræus. For ὁρισταί, cf. Lex. Seguer. 287, 18. Hypereid. pro Euxenipp., 18 ff. Boeckh in C.I.Gr., III. 705.

[3] C.I.A., II. 581.

[4] Dem. 57, 46. 62.

[5] C.I.A., II. 580: ἐπειδὴ οἱ μεράρχαι οἱ ἐπ' Ἀντικλείους ἄρχοντος καλῶς καὶ φιλοτίμως τῶν θυσιῶν ἐπεμελήθησαν καὶ τῶν κοινῶν κ.τ.ἀ. Köhler rightly regards them as treasurers of some kind.

[6] C.I.A., II. 573, 1055.

for scrutiny after laying down office.¹ This scrutiny took place before the εὔθυνος.² In the Deme Myrrhinus the audit tribunal consisted of an εὔθυνος, who acted as judge and assessed the damages for any offence proved against the ex-official, next a λογιστής, who checked the accounts, lastly 10 elective συνήγοροι, who gave their verdict by ballot after being sworn in by the Demarch, who also presided over the tribunal.

From this verdict appeal could be made to the assembly of the Deme, which gave the final decision under oath. In case of condemnation by the assembly of the Deme the fine previously imposed was increased fifty per cent.³ In all affairs of the Deme the final decision rested with the Deme-assembly or ἀγορά.⁴ That body decided both judicial and administrative matters. Judicial decisions took place at the εὔθυνα of the Deme-officials under certain circumstances, as we have seen. Again, in a decree of the Deme Piraeus mention is made of a court of justice, from which the Demarch obtains confirmation of an ἐπιβολή imposed by him, he himself acting as εἰσαγωγεύς; this court is to be identified with the Deme-assembly.⁵ In Aixone the Deme-assembly acted as a court of arbitration in cases brought by the Demarch, who, as representative of the Deme-interests, was assisted by σύνδικοι, against those who had covenanted to pay ἐννόμιον, but had for

---

¹ Dokimasia of Deme-officers: Dem. 57, 25/6. 46. 47. A fragment of a Deme-official's oath on entering on office is contained in a decree of Scambonidai of the 5th century: καὶ τὰ κοιν(ὰ) τὰ Σκαμβωνιδῶν σωῶ καὶ ἀποδώσω παρὰ τὸν εὔθυνον τὸ καθῆκον. Kirchhoff conjectures that the officials who took this oath were the ἱεροποιοί. Cf. also C.I.A., I. 2. Oath of the εὔθυνος and λογιστής at Myrrhinus: II. 578. We have proof that εὔθυνα was required from the δήμαρχος (C.I.A., II. 578), the ἱεροποιοί (II. 581), and the ταμίαι (II. 571).

² C.I.A., I. 2 and II. 571 make the scrutiny take place before the εὔθυνος and in the second inscr. he is assisted by πάρεδροι.

³ The system of εὔθυνα described above as in force in the Deme Myrrhinus, is recorded in C.I.A., II. 578. I believe the context there justifies my identification of the συνήγοροι mentioned in line 14 with the 10 elective officers mentioned in ll. 17 and 24. That the audit officials here concerned were merely Deme-officials is correctly maintained by Köhler, ad loc., in opposition to R. Schoell, de Synegoris att., p. 29 ff.

⁴ On the Deme meetings cf. Müller 83 ff.; Haussoullier 11 ff. Ἀγορά means (1) the market-places of the various Demes: C.I.A., I. 2; II. 571, 573, (2) the assembly of the Demotai: II. 585., Dem. 44, 36; Lex. Seguer. 827: ἀγορὰ συνέδριον φυλετῶν καὶ δημοτῶν οἱονεὶ σύλλογος.

⁵ C.I.A., II. 578, 573b: ἐάν τίς τι τούτων παρὰ ταῦτα ποιεῖ, ἐπιβολὴν ἐπ(ι)βαλόντα τὴν δήμαρχον εἰσάγει(ν) εἰς τὸ δικαστήριον χρώμενον τοῖς νόμοις οἳ κεῖνται περὶ τούτων.

some reason or other omitted to do so.¹ The Deme-assembly acted as a judicial tribunal in the διαψήφισις also. This last process was instituted, sometimes by decree of the whole people in all Demes alike, in order to detect those who had illegally obtained enrolment as citizens; sometimes in single Demes, by decree of the Deme, *e.g.* if the ληξιαρχικὸν γραμματεῖον had been lost.² In this case also the Demotai were first sworn in to give their verdict impartially. Then the names of the individual Demotai were called over, and each name was voted upon by ballot, by means of pebbles placed in a balloting urn.³ If any one were ejected from the Deme by this vote and he acquiesced in the verdict, he simply lost his burgess-rights. If however he appealed to a heliastic court, as he was legally entitled to do, and the court confirmed the decision of the Deme, the appellant was sold into slavery.⁴ Lastly, the Deme-assembly exercised judicial functions at the above described enrolment of young Athenians in the ληξιαρχικὸν γραμματεῖον, which was always preceded by a ballot to decide whether the enrolment should be allowed or not.

It was a common characteristic of all judicial decisions of the

¹ Cf. the decree of the Deme Aixone, published and explained by Lolling in *Mitth. d. dtsch. arch. Inst. in Ath.*, 4, 199 ff. Σύνδικοι are mentioned again in another inscr. from Aixone, *ib.*, 196. Cf. also Haussoullier 87 ff.

² The general διαψήφισις in the archonship of Callias 346/5 is the only one about which we possess detailed information. Cf. Philoch. and Androt. *ap.* Harp, *s.v.* Schol. to Æsch. *in Tim.* 77, Dionys. *Dein.* 11. διαψήφισις in an individual Deme is attested by Dem. 57, 26. 60. Cf. Blass, *att. Beredsamk.*, 2, 534 ff.; 3, 428. The Potamioi were notorious, ὡς ῥᾳδίως δεχόμενοι τοὺς παρεγγράπτους. Cf. Harp., Ποταμός. For Halimus cf. Harp., Ἀγασικλῆς.

³ The oath of the Demotai was: ψηφιεῖσθαι γνώμῃ τῇ δικαιοτάτῃ καὶ οὔτε χάριτος ἕνεκ' οὔτ' ἔχθρας. Cf. Dem. 57, 63. For the special procedure at διαψήφισις cf. Dem. 57, 8–14. Acc. to Poll. 8, 18 φύλλα were used as ψῆφοι at the ballot. Suid., *s.v.*, also says that the voting took place κρύβδην. Cf. also Harp., Suid., Hesych., *s.v.*, Lex. Seguer. 439, 32.

⁴ Dionys., *Hypoth.*, to Is. 12: ἐξέτασιν γενέσθαι τῶν πολιτῶν κατὰ δήμους, τὸν δὲ ἀποψηφισθέντα ὑπὸ τῶν δημοτῶν τῆς πολιτείας μὴ μετέχειν· τοῖς δὲ ἀδίκως ἀποψηφισθεῖσιν ἔφεσιν εἰς τὸ δικαστήριον εἶναι, προσκαλεσαμένοις τοὺς δημότας, καὶ ἐὰν τὸ δεύτερον ἐξελεγχθῶσι, πεπρᾶσθαι αὐτοὺς καὶ τὰ χρήματα εἶναι δημόσια to which may be added from Lex. Seguer. 440, 3: εἰ δὲ ἐκράτει, ἀνελαμβάνετο εἰς τὴν πολιτείαν. The matter could also be brought before a Diaitetes after the διαψήφισις, and before it came before the heliastic court. Cf. Is. 12, 11. The case is brought against the Demarch and Demotai. Cf. Is. 12, 11. But nevertheless the representative of the Demos has the first word, and is therefore accuser. Cf. Dem. 57, 1. 4. For judicial proceedings of this kind see Dem. 57, 60; Æsch. *in Tim.* 77, 78. 114.

Deme that the Demotai had to take an oath before voting.[1] Further, all the more important decisions affecting the administration of the Deme were passed by the Deme-assembly. The Deme-decrees we possess shew that this assembly decreed crowns, proedria, ateleia and exemption from ἐγκτητικόν; made rules for the auditing of the accounts of the officials; passed measures about the leasing of the estates of the Deme; voted out of the yearly revenues specified sums of money for specified purposes, and laid down general directions for the management and use of the communal property of the Deme.[2]

The τριττύες instituted by Cleisthenes were intermediate in size between the Phylai and the Demes. They were undoubtedly uniform in size or nearly so, and formed therefore a more convenient basis for the distribution of State taxation than the Demes which were so unequal to one another. Every Phyle was divided into 3 such τριττύες, which again were divided into a number of Demes, varying according to the size of the Demes. The Trittyes known to us are as follows: in the tribe Pandionis, Παιανιεῖς, Μυρρινούσιοι, and probably Κυδαθηναιεῖς; in Acamantis, Κεραμεῖς; in Oineis, Λακιάδαι, Θριάσιοι and perhaps Ἐπακριεῖς; in Hippothontis, Ἐλευσίνιοι and Πειραιεῖς.[3]

From these names which, with one exception, are identical with names of Demes, we may infer that the τριττύς was named as a rule after the largest of the Demes composing it. The system

Trittyes.

---

[1] So at the audits: C.I.A., II. 578, 1..20 sqq.; if the Deme-assembly acted as court of appeal: *Mitth. d. dtsch. arch. Inst. in Ath.*, 4, 201, 205; at the διαψήφισις: Dem. 57, 9. 26; Æsch. *in Tim.* 78; at enrolments in the ληξιαρχικὸν γραμματεῖον: Dem. 57, 61; Is. 7, 28; Arist. 42, 1.

[2] Honour-decrees: C.I.A., II. 573, 574, 575, 579, 580, 581, 582, 584, 585, 589. *Mitth.*, 4, 194/5, 196/7. Decrees about εὔθυνα: II. 571, 578. Decree as to leasing the theatre at Piræus: II. 573. Votes of money, ἀπὸ τῆς προσόδου τῶν δημοτῶν: II. 579; ἐκ τῆς διοικήσεως τῶν περιόντων χρημάτων τῶν ἐπὶ Θεοφράστου ἄρχοντος: II. 585. Decree giving general directions for finance: II. 570.

[3] For the institution of these Trittyes by Cleisthenes, cf. Arist. 21, 4. (Δ)εῦρε Πα(ι)ανιῶν τριττὺς τελ(ε)υτᾷ, ἄρχεται δὲ Μυρρινουσί(ων) τριτ(τύς): Dittenberger, *Syll.*, 301=C.I.A., IV. 2, 517a. Παιανιέων τριττύς and K—: C.I.A., II. 2, 871, where, acc. to Köhler, *Mitth. d. arch. Inst. in Ath.*, 7, 110, K(υδαθηναιέων τριττύς), should probably be read. (Κερ)αμέων τριττύς: C.I.A., I. 500; Λακιαδῶν τριττύς: I. 502; (δ)ε(ῦρ') Ἐπ(ακρ)έων τριττὺς τελευτᾷ, Θρασίων δὲ ἄρχεται τριττύς: Dittenberger 300=C.I.A., IV. 2, 517b; Ἐπακρέων τριττύς: II. 1053; (δεῦρ' Ἐλε)υσινίων (τρ)ιττὺς τελ(ε)υτᾷ Πειραιῶν δὲ τριττὺς ἄρχεται: Dittenberger 299=C.I.A., I. 517. Cf. also Hesych., Ῥωπῖτις from ῥωπῆτις.

See Gmil Szanto in *Hermes*, 1892, p. 312 sq.

of the Trittyes, with a τριττύαρχος at the head of each, was afterwards used mainly for military purposes.¹

Another kind of subdivision of the Athenian burgess body was the φρατρίαι or φατρίαι, reorganised by Cleisthenes. Of such

Phratries. Phratries we may now regard as attested by inscriptions, 'Αχνιάδαι and Δημοτιωνίδαι with certainty, by restoration Θερρικωνίδαι or Θερρικιάδαι, and with some probability Δυαλεῖς.² At the head of the Phratry stood, as a rule, a ἱερεὺς of the patron god of the Phratry, and also the φρατρίαρχος, who was elected by the Phrateres or members of the Phratry, and had custody of the κοινὸν γραμματεῖον, managed the business of the Phratry, and presided at its meetings. In the larger Phratries there may have been several φρατρίαρχοι.³ Every Phratry had its own place of assembly, where its religious central point was situated, and could pass resolutions which were valid so far as the authority of the Phratry extended.⁴

¹ Acc. to Æsch. *in Ctes.* 80, the Trittyes elected officers, τὰ δημόσια χρήματα διαχειρίζειν. That they served military purposes seems to be shown by Plat., *Rep.*, 5, 475, where Socrates says to Glaucon: καὶ μὴν φιλοτίμους γε, ὡς ἐγῷμαι, καθορᾷς, ὅτι, ἂν μὴ στρατηγῆσαι δύνωνται, τριττυαρχοῦσι. In the proposition of Dem. 14, 23, each Trittys was to supply crews for 10 ships. Kirchhoff makes C.I.A., I. 517 refer to this. C. Schaefer, in *Mitth. dtsch. arch. Inst. in Ath.*, 5, 85 ff., seems to make too much of the military importance of the Trittys. In late inscrr. (first instance 299/8 B.C.), the τριττύαρχοι in conjunction with the ἐξεταστής supply money for erecting inscr.-stelai: C.I.A., II. 297, 298, and statues: II. 300.

² For the Phratries, cf. 148 ff. 'Αχνιάδαι: C.I.A., II. 1653; *Mitth.*, 12, 287; Δημοτιωνίδαι: C.I.A., II. 841b; *Ind. Schol. Goett.* 1890/1. p. 3; Θερρικωνίδαι, *Mitth.*, 2, 186, or Θερρικιάδαι: II. 1652; Δυαλεῖς: II. 600. Ζακυάδαι (II. 1062) and 'Ελασίδαι (*Ind. Schol. Goett.* 90/1, p. 11) may just as probably be families. It does not necessarily follow from Æsch., *Fals. Leg.*, 147, that the Phratry to which the Eteobutadai belonged was called by their name. Sauppe, *de phratriis Att.*, 10 ff., Gött., 1886, counts the Κήρυκες and the Τιτακίδαι and Θυργωνίδαι among the Phratries, on the authority of Et. M. 760, 38 sqq. C. Schaefer in the *Pforta Progr.*, 1888, p. 30 ff., regards 'Αχνιάδαι, Δημοτιωνίδαι and Θερρικωνίδαι as complexes of several Phratries.

³ A ἱερεὺς of Ζεὺς Φράτριος: *Ind. Schol. Goett.* 90/1, p. 3; φρατρίαρχος: C.I.A., II. 599. 841b, *Ind. Schol. Goett., ib.* For the functions of the φρατρίαρχος see especially the inscrr. last quoted. Two φράτριαρχοι in the κοινὸν Δυαλέων: II. 600. Dem. 57, 23 shows that the φρατρίαρχος was elected; II. 841b, that the κοινὸν γραμματεῖον was in his keeping.

⁴ Phratry-decrees, C.I.A., II. 598, 599, 600, 841b; *Ind. Schol. Goett.* 1890/1, p. 3 ff.; C.I.A., II. 599 was set up (ἔμπροσθεν τ)οῦ φρατρ(ίου), 841b, πρόσθεν τοῦ βωμοῦ Δεκελειᾶσιν. Cf. Steph. Byz., φρατρία· λέγεται καὶ φράτριον τόπος, ἐν ᾧ οἱ τῆς αὐτῆς φρατρίας συνάγονται. Cf. also Poll. 3, 52. A meeting of the Phrateres is called ἀγορά in *Ind. Schol. Goett.*, p. 4, l. 85.

Phratries, etc.

There seems sufficient evidence to prove that the Ionic tribes continued to exist, nominally at any rate, even after the reforms of Cleisthenes.[1] **Ionic Phylai.**

It is natural enough in itself, and also attested by express evidence, that the old families or clans continued in existence after the time of Cleisthenes, though without retaining any political importance.[2] As a rule each genos was headed by an ἄρχων τοῦ γένους, and other officers also are mentioned.[3]   **Γένη.**

These old families still kept their lists of members after Cleisthenes, as they had done before, and in those lists the new-born children were entered.[4] It was in itself allowable for the newly instituted θίασοι to keep lists of members and to enrol the names of new-born children in these lists at the Apaturia. But since the θίασοι had no family traditions, and the lists would have only private importance, it is not very probable that such lists were kept by them at all. The cult of Zeus Herkeios and

---

[1] In an inscr. composed before the establishment of the Hadrianis, C.I.A., III. 2, mention is made of a Ζεὺς Γελέων, who, however, acc. to Benfey in the *Gött. Nachr.*, 1877, p. 1 ff., may simply be Zeus the god of lightning, from γελεῖν, which, acc. to Hesych. = λάμπειν, a word used of lightning. In the *Bulletin*, 1879, 3, p. 69 = C.I.A., II. 844, in an Attic inscr. of the 4th cent. payments for sacrifices are made ἐκ τῶν φυλοβασιλικῶν, which again speaks for the continued existence of the Ionic tribes. See also Droysen in Herm. 14, 587. Philippi, *Beitr.*, p. 168, 172, also agrees that they still survived. Arist. 57, 4 shows that there were still φυλοβασιλεῖς in Aristotle's day.

[2] Arist. 21, 6. The latest treatise on Attic families is Toepffer, *att. Genealogie*, 1889. For such families becoming extinct, Isocr. 8, 88.

[3] For the internal constitution of the γένη see Dittenberger in Herm. 20, 7 ff. Toepffer, *att. Geneal.*, p. 20 ff. One ἄρχων of the Eumolpides and Kerykes: 'Εφ. ἀρχ., 1883, p. 83, and so also perhaps in C.I.A., II. 605, where Toepffer reasonably considers ἄρχοντα a stonecutter's blunder for ἄρχοντας. Ἄρχων of the Amynandridai: C.I.A., III. 1276; of the Bacchiadai: II. 1325, III. 97; of the Salaminioi: *Mitth.*, 4, 265. For the method of appointment of the ἄρχων we have two pieces of information: 'Εφ. ἀρχ. 1883, p. 83: τοὺς ἄρχοντας τοὺς ἀεὶ καθισταμένους ἐξ ἑκατέρου τοῦ γένους. Ἀθήν. VI. 274: (τ)ὸν ἀεὶ λαν(χ)άνοντα ἀρχ(οντα τοῦ γέν)ους. These are not sufficient for definite conclusions. A ταμίας of the Amynandridai: III. 1276; of the Eumolpidai: III. 5. Ἀρχιερεὺς καὶ γενε(άρχης) of the Kerykes: III. 1278; ἱερομνήμονες in the family of the Salaminioi: *Mitth.*, 4, 265. Decrees of families occur in C.I.A., II. 596, 597, 605. 'Εφ. ἀρχ., 1883, 83.

[4] Enrolment of a child among the γεννῆται is attested by Is. 7, 15–17, 43; in the case of the Brytidai by (Dem.) 59, 59–61; the Kerykes, Andoc., *de Myst.*, 125 sqq. See also Philippi, *Beitr.*, etc., p. 168 ff.

Apollo Patroos was common to all the families, as also to the θίασοι.[1]

Religious Unions of Communes. There still survived from ancient times a number of federations of communities for religious purposes, of which I will here mention only the three attested by inscriptions: the Ἐπακριεῖς, the Μεσόγειοι and the Τετραπόλεις. There was an ἄρχων at the head of the Μεσόγειοι and the Τετραπόλεις.[2] Beside these associations instituted by the State and either still possessing constitutional importance or retaining recollections and survivals of it from former times, there was at **Private Associations.** Athens, as a result of the unlimited freedom of association permitted there, a considerable number of private societies. In a law attributed to Solon we read of θιασῶται and ὀργεῶνες, dining-clubs and burial-clubs, shipping, trading, and privateer companies, whose agreements or bye-laws were binding on all their members provided they were not contrary to the laws of the State.[3] Among these associations the θιασῶται and ὀργεῶνες occur most frequently, and next to these, what are not mentioned in the so-called Sólonian law, the ἐρανισταί.[4] However we are not in a position to draw a clear distinction between these various associations. Even the ἔρανοι, which originally simply provided banquets at the expense of all the members, obtained later, judging by the inscriptions, a

---

[1] The Ἀπόλλωνος πατρῴου καὶ Διὸς ἑρκείου γεννῆται mentioned in Dem. 57, 67, are an old family. See Philippi, *Beitr.*, 169. But the Dokimasia of the Archons shows that the θίασοι also worship both those deities, cf. Arist. 55, 3; Poll. 8, 85, cf. Harp. ἑρκεῖος Ζεύς; Suid., Phot., *s. verb.*; Harp., Ἀπόλλων πατρῷος; Plat., *Euthyd.*, 302.

[2] See page 99. The Ἐπακριεῖς are attested by a decree of the Deme Plotheia: C.I.A., II. 570. We possess several decrees of the Μεσόγειοι: II. 602, 603. The latter gives as religious functionaries τὸν ἱερέα τοῦ Ἡρακλ(έ)ους καὶ τὸν τοῦ Διόμου καὶ τοὺς μνήμονας καὶ τὸν πυρφόρον καὶ τὸν κοραγωγὸν καὶ τὸν κήρυκα καὶ τὸν πάτριον. Decree of the Tetrapolis, in a fragmentary state: II. 601. Cf. also the dedicatory inscr. C.I.A., II. 1324: τετραπόλεες τῷ Διονύσῳ ἀνέθεσαν, Λυσανίας Καλλίου Τρικορύσιος ἦρχεν. Ἱεροποιοί· Φανόδωρος Μαραθώνιος, Μελάνωπος Τρικορύσιος, Φ(α)νοκλῆς Οἰναῖος, Ἀντικράτης Προβαλίσιος.

[3] Gaius, Bk. 3, Dig. 47, 22 quotes as a Solonian law: ἐὰν δὲ δῆμος ἢ φράτορες ἢ ἱερῶν ὀργεῶνες (for ὀργίων) ἢ ναῦται ἢ σύσσιτοι ἢ ὁμόταφοι ἢ θιασῶται ἢ ἐπὶ λείαν (for λίαν) οἰχόμενοι ἢ εἰς ἐμπορίαν ὁτιοῦν (for ὅτι ἂν τούτων) διαθῶνται πρὸς ἀλλήλους, κύριον εἶναι, ἐὰν μὴ ἀπαγορεύσῃ δημόσια γράμματα. Conjectures on this passage are given by Meier in *Ind. schol. Halle*, 1848/9; Lobeck, *Aglaoph.*, 305; Petersen, *d. geh. Gottesdienst bei den Griechen*, p. 42.

[4] For treatises on the religious associations see Lüders, *die Dionysischen Künstler*, p. 1 ff. 1873; Foucart, *des associations religieuses chez les Grecs*, 1873; C. Schäfer in the *Jahrb. f. cl. Phil.*, 1880, p. 417 ff.

religious character.[1] So far as our knowledge goes these three classes of clubs were societies of a religious type for practising the cult of some deity or other; and in later times, when the native faith began to decay, they were often devoted to foreign deities; nevertheless it is still possible enough that they at the same time pursued other objects not connected with religion.[2] They held meetings at regular fixed dates; sometimes had a priest, sometimes a priestess; in some cases again had ἐπιμεληταί, ἱεροποιοί, a γραμματεύς, and a ταμίας, subject to εὔθυνα.[3]

The expenses of the sacrifices or other religious duties were defrayed from the temple property of the deity concerned and from the contributions of the members.[4] Admission into such a society was accompanied by the taking of an oath, but was probably open to any person on payment of a specified entrance fee.[5] These

---

[1] Ath. 8, 362 E: καλεῖται δὲ ὁ αὐτὸς καὶ ἔρανος καὶ θίασος καὶ οἱ συνιόντες ἐρανισταί καὶ συνθιασῶται. So too the ὀργεῶνες cannot be distinguished from the θιασῶται and ἐρανισταί. Phot. says: ὀργεῶνες οἱ τοῖς ἰδίᾳ ἀφιδρυμένοις θεοῖς ὀργιάζοντες; Harp. ὀργεῶνες: οἱ ἐπὶ τιμῇ θεῶν ἢ ἡρώων συνιόντες which almost exactly coincides with his explanation of θιασιῶται: θίασος τὸ ἀθροιζόμενον πλῆθος ἐπὶ τελετῇ καὶ τιμῇ θεοῦ. For the ἔρανοι in their original meaning see Meier.[2] 687. For the close connexion between all three forms of association cf. Lüders, p. 2 ff.

[2] Cults forming the nucleus of such religious societies are *e.g.* that of Zeus of Labranda: C.I.A., II. 613, that of Μήτηρ τῶν θεῶν: II. 614, of Ζεὺς Σωτήρ, Ἡρακλῆς and the Σωτῆρες: II. 616, Σδράπις: II. 617, Βένδις: II. 620, Ἀφροδίτη Συρία: II. 627, Ἀθηνᾶ Ὀργάνη: II. 1329, Ζεὺς φίλιος: II. 1330.

[3] Decrees of ὀργεῶνες: C.I.A., II. 610, 618, 619, 621, 622, 623, 624, 627. *Mitth.* 9, 288. Decrees of ἐρανισταί: II. 615, 616, 617, 630, cf. 1330; of θιασῶται: II. 611, 613, 614, 620, cf. 1329, 1331. Their meetings were called ἀγοραί. In II. 610 an ἀγορά of the ὀργεῶνος is to take place τῇ δευτέρᾳ ἱσταμένου τοῦ μηνὸς ἑκάστου. In other cases we often find in decrees of ὀργεῶνες the phrase, Μουνυχιῶνος ἀγορᾷ κυρίᾳ: II. 610, 619, 621, 622, 623, 624; ἀγορὰ κυρία τῶν θιασωτῶν: II. 611. The officers mentioned in the text occur in inscrr., sometimes all together, sometimes separately. See also C.I.A., II. 1326, 1332, 1333, 1334, 1337. In the case of ἐρανισταί we find mentioned besides these a προερανίστρια: II. 617, and an ἀρχερανιστής: II. 630. εὔθυνα of religious functionaries: II. 611, 617. On the organisation of these societies cf. Foucart, p. 5 ff.

[4] C.I.A., II. 610, line 17: διδόναι δὲ (τοῖς ἱ)εροποιοῖς εἰς τὴν θυσίαν ⊢⊢ δραχμὰς ἕκαστον τῶν ὀργεώνων κ.τ.ἑ. Payment of the contribution is a necessary condition of membership: II. 630. The Εἰκαδεῖς have κοινά, ἀφ' ὧν τὰ ἱερὰ τοῖς θεοῖς θύουσιν κ.τ.ἑ.: II. 609.

[5] On admission and the oath at admission see C.I.A., II. 610 l. 20 sqq. An oath mentioned: II. 609, 616. The enrolment of new members on the list was accompanied by a dokimasia. II. 610 l. 22: τ(οὺς δὲ γεγραμμ)ένους εἰς τὴν στήλην δο(κιμάζ)ειν τοὺς ὀργεῶνας. l. 1 ff. ὁπόσοι ἐν τῇ(ι στήλ)η(ι ἐ)γ(γεγρα)μμένοι

societies styled themselves sometimes by the general terms ὀργεῶνες θιασῶται or ἐρανισταί, sometimes they had also special names.¹

Other private guilds were the dining and burial-societies, σύσσιτοι and ὁμόταφοι. About the former we know nothing; the latter were burial-societies, some confined to separate families, others not.² Mention must also be made of shipping, trade, and privateer associations, the first two of which were probably often owners' societies and trade companies, while the privateer associations would only be formed in time of war. We have evidence from inscriptions of a guild of the πλυνῆς and a κοινὸν τῶν ἐργαζομένων.³

2. THE MINISTERS OF THE GOVERNMENT AND THE SOVEREIGN POWER OF THE STATE.

A. *The Magistrates.*

(a) *General.*

The Athenian magistrates⁴ (ἄρχοντες, ἀρχαί) fall into two main divisions, which can again be subdivided into particular classes.

Classification of the Magistrates. The two main divisions are the ordinary and extraordinary officials. Of these the former, who were regularly chosen annually, and who transacted business distinctly prescribed by the constitution, were either elected or chosen by lot. The extraordinary officials, who were chosen in cases of necessity, and who undertook any duty imposed upon them by the voice of the people, were of 3 classes, (1) overseers of the public works, (2) those entrusted with the completion of some

εἰσὶν ἢ το(ὺς τ)ούτων ἐκγόνους would seem to show that sons were *eo ipso* members of the Orgeones to which their father had belonged. In an inscr. from Cnidos also quoted in Lüders, p. 163, no. 38, sons are admitted to the θίασος.

¹ *E.g.* Εἰκαδεῖς: C.I.A., II. 609. Σαραπιασταί: II. 617. Ἡροϊσταί: II. 630. Διονυσιασταί: *Mitth.* 9, 288.

² σύσσιτοι are mentioned by Is. 4, 18. Dem. 43, 79 mentions a μνῆμα Βουσελιδῶν. In Dem. 57, 67 those act as witnesses οἷς ἤρια ταὐτά. Cf. Arist. 55, 3.

³ For the ship and trade associations reference may be made to Harp.: κοινωνικῶν·—τῶν ἑκούσιον κοινωνίαν συνθεμένων ἐμπορίας ἤ τινος ἄλλου, ὧν ἕκαστος οὐκ εἶχε τὸ ὅλον τίμημα τῆς κοινῆς οὐσίας. Cf. C.I.A., II. 1339. For the privateer associations see the passages in Schoemann's *Antiqu.*, 367, 8. οἱ πλυνῆς: C.I.A., II. 1327. κοινὸν τῶν ἐργαζ(ομένων): II. 1332.

⁴ In general cf. K. Fr. Hermann, *de iure et auctoritate magistratuum apud Athenienses.*

state business for a period exceeding 30 days, (3) those who, elected by the tribes, had to perform a task to be carried out partly at state expense.[1]

Aristotle classifies the most important powers of magistrates under three heads, deliberative, judicial, and executive.[2] All these powers the Athenian magistrates possessed, and had accordingly the ἡγεμονία δικαστηρίου for lawsuits in their several departments, and the power of inflicting money fines up to a specified maximum amount on any one who did not carry out their official commands.[3] To hold the same office for several consecutive years was only permitted in the case of military offices; in the non-military offices not even a two years' tenure was permissible. Similarly, for the same person to hold several offices at once was unusual.[4]

_{Their Powers.}

[1] The above classification is indicated by Æschin. *in Ctes.* 13-15, 28-30. On this passage see Philippi in the *N. Rh. Mus.*, 34, 611. In one way this is confirmed by C.I.A., I. 315, in which the ἐπιστάται over the building of the Propylaia designate themselves as ἀρχή.

[2] See Arist., *Pol.*, 172, 26 ff., Bekker: μάλιστα δ' ὡς ἁπλῶς εἰπεῖν ἀρχὰς λεκτέον ταύτας, ὅσαις ἀποδέδοται βουλεύσασθαί τε περί τινων καὶ κρῖναι καὶ ἐπιτάξαι καὶ μάλιστα τοῦτο· τὸ γὰρ ἐπιτάττειν ἀρχικώτατόν ἐστιν. Hermann, *ibid.*, 33, 36, translates the three infinitives by *deliberare, decernere*, and *imperare* or *edicere*.

[3] In Æschin. *in Ctes.* 27 Demosthenes is called a τειχοποιός: καὶ ἐπιβολὰς ἐπέβαλλε, καθάπερ οἱ ἄλλοι ἄρχοντες, καὶ δικαστηρίων ἡγεμονίας ἐλάμβανε. Description of the ἡγεμονία δικαστηρίου in the Lex. Seguer. 262, 21: ἄρχοντες ἦσαν εἰσαγωγεῖς δικῶν τινων εἰς τὰ δικαστήρια, προανακρίνοντες τὰς δίκας καὶ προσκαθεζόμενοι τοῖς δικαστηρίοις, καὶ εἶχον τὴν τῶν δικαστηρίων ἡγεμονίαν, probably all who were in office for more than 30 days: Æschin. *in Ctes.* 14. Power of the Archon ἐπιβολὴν ἐπιβάλλειν: Arist. 56, 7; of the Strategoi: Arist. 61, 2. Further examples of the officials' power, ἐπιβολὴν ἐπιβάλλειν, in Siegfried, *de multa quae ἐπιβολή dicitur. Diss. inaug.*, Berlin, 1876, p. 2 ff. But he seems to me to extend the power of ἐπιβολή to too many persons. The ἐπιβολή as the official's punishment for disobedience to his commands or for smaller offences: Siegfried 18 ff. The maximum ἐπιβολή which the magistrates could inflict probably varied according to the dignity of the magistrate; for the Boule it amounted to 500 drachmæ. The maximum ἐπιβολή of the ἱεροποιοί of the Hephaisteia amounted to 50 drachmæ. *Sitzungsber. d. bayr. Akad.*, 1887, p. 18. It was the same in the case of those who damaged the trees in the holy precinct of Apollo Erithaseos, and was imposed by the priest together with the Demarchs: C.I.A., II. 841.

[4] See Arist. 62, 3: ἄρχειν δὲ τὰς μὲν κατὰ πόλεμον ἀρχὰς ἔ[ξεσ]τι πλεονάκις, τῶν δ' ἄλλων οὐδεμίαν πλὴν βουλεῦσαι δίς. Prolongation of the strategia in the case of Pericles, Plut., *Per.*, 16; in the case of Phokion, Plut., *Phok.*, 8, 19. Prolongation of the hipparchia: Hyper., *pro Lycophr.* XIV. 2 ff. In general see Dem., *prooem.* 55, 1461: δεινότατοι γάρ ἐστ' ἀφελέσθαι μὲν ὅσ' ὑμῖν ὑπάρχει

Appointment. The appointment of the magistrates proceeded either by lot or by election. Election, apart from the above-mentioned tribal elections, was reserved as it seems for the military officials, the ταμίας τῶν στρατιωτικῶν, and those ἐπὶ τὸ θεωρικόν, ἐπὶ τὰς κρήνας and ἐπὶ τῇ διοικήσει; the remaining magistrates were elected by lot.[1]

When Appointed. The time of the official elections is attested by an inscription of the 3rd century as the end of the month Munychion, whereas, at least in Aristotle's time, the military officials seem to have been elected in the month Anthesterion. These early dates confirm the supposition that between election and entering upon office a sufficiently long interval had to elapse, to allow time for the customary dokimasia and any lawsuits arising from it.[2] To the same date we must for the same reasons assign the choosing of the officials by lot, for they were all chosen together.[3]

καὶ νόμους περὶ τούτων θεῖναι, ἄν τις ἀστυνομήσῃ δὶς ἢ τὰ τοιαῦτα, στρατηγεῖν δ' ἀεὶ τοὺς αὐτοὺς ἐάν. The same man can only once be elected σύνδικος: Dem. 20, 152; cf. also Lys. 30, 29. It is not a cumulation of offices in the hands of one person when the functions of one office are added to those of another, as in Æsch. *in Ctes.* 25, or in a decree of the people in the year 320, Dittenberger 337: ἐπειδὴ δὲ καὶ ἡ τῶν ἀστυνόμων ἐπιμέλεια προστέτακται τοῖς ἀγορανόμοις.

[1] See Æschin. *in Ctes.* 13. Arist. 43, 1: τὰς δ' ἀρχὰς τὰς περὶ τὴν ἐγκύκλιον διοίκησιν ἀπάσας ποιοῦσι κληρωτὰς πλὴν ταμίου στρατιωτικῶν καὶ τῶν ἐπὶ τὸ θεωρικὸν καὶ τοῦ τῶν κρηνῶν ἐπιμελητοῦ.—χειροτονοῦσι δὲ καὶ τὰς πρὸς τὸν πόλεμον ἀπάσας. For the election of the magistrate ἐπὶ τῇ διοικήσει vid. Pseudoplut., *vit. Lyc.*, 3.

[2] The 22 Munychion as the time of the ἀρχαιρεσίαι in the year of the Archon Symmachos in the time of the 12 tribes: C.I.A., II. 416. Arist. 44, 4 tells us: ποιοῦσι (i.e. οἱ πρόεδροι) δὲ καὶ ἀρχαιρεσίας στρατηγῶν καὶ ἱππάρχων καὶ τῶν ἄλλων τῶν πρὸς τὸν πόλεμον ἀρχῶν ἐν τῇ ἐκκλησίᾳ, καθ' ὅτι ἂν τῷ δήμῳ δοκῇ· ποιοῦσι δ' οἱ μετὰ τὴν ς (ἕκτην) πρυτανεύοντες, ἐφ' ὧν ἂν εὐσημία γένηται. δεῖ δὲ προβούλευμα γενέσθαι καὶ περὶ τούτων. The question has been discussed in my *Beitr.*, etc., 5 ff., with reference to the election of the Strategoi, and to this I have nothing important to add. For the Strategoi-elections in spring or early summer see Wilamowitz, *aus Kydathen*, 58; Paulus, *Maulbronn Progr.*, 1883, 1 seq.; Beloch, *att. Polit. seit Perikles*, 265 seq.; Belser in the *Korresp. Bl. für d. Gel. u. Realschulen*, 1886, 4 ff., Tübingen; Hauvette Besnault, *les stratèges Athéniens*, 37 ff., Paris, 1885. The theory of Ad. Schmidt, in the *Handb. d. griech. Chronol.*, 301 ff., that the elections up to the year 306, according to the hypothesis to Dem. 22, 590, were held during the last days of the year, and only after 306 in the last days of the month Munychion, is now exploded by Aristotle.

[3] C.I.A., I. 32: ταμίας δὲ ἀποκυαμεύει(ν γ)όντων τῶν χρημάτων ὅτανπερ τὰς ἄλλας ἀρχάς, καθάπερ τοὺς τῶν ἱ(ερῶ)ν τῶν τῆς Ἀθηναίας.

[GILBERT I. 207–8.] *Appointment of Magistrates.* [GILBERT II. 241.

The nomination of magistrates was either so conducted that for every official college of ten, one member was chosen from each tribe, or else so that the members of the college were all chosen from among all the Athenians,[1] each tribe getting roughly its fair share of representation. *Regard paid to their Tribes.*

For both elective magistracies and those filled by lot, canvassing took place; in the former case this consisted in a regular Ambitus, while in the latter case a simple application for office sufficed.[2] *Canvassing.*

The elective offices were filled at the elections (ἀρχαιρεσίαι) held under the supervision of the πρόεδροι by cheirotonia (show of hands).[3] The method of nominating the officials by lot underwent some change in process of time. The arrangement made in 487 that the 9 Archons should be appointed by lot, one for each tribe, out of 500 candidates elected by the Demes, was changed in course of time; each tribe in a body nominated 10 candidates, and out of these hundred applicants the 9 Archons with their secretary were appointed by lot, one from each tribe. The rest of the officials chosen by lot were originally nominated either in the former or the latter way, so that the nominators were either the Demes or the tribes. Afterwards as bribery occurred among the Demes in these nominations, they all, with the sole exception of the βουλευταὶ and φρουροί, were placed in the hands of the tribes. From those thus nominated, the 9 Archons then nominated the officials by a lottery held in the Theseion, and if any failed to pass the dokimasia, others were subsequently nominated in a *How Appointed.*

---

[1] Compare the remarks on the several offices. The Hellenotamiai, about whose method of nomination we know nothing for certain, seem, C.I.A., I. 259, 260, to have been nominated with regard for the tribes, while I. 188 the Acamantis and the Aiantis are twice represented in the college. Even in the case of the 9 Archons, the tribes were taken into consideration. This supposition of Sauppe, *de creat. archont. att.* Goett., 1864, is now confirmed by Arist. 55, 1: [νῦν] δὲ κληροῦσιν θεσμοθέτας μὲν ἐξ καὶ γραμματέα τούτοις, ἔτι δ' ἄρχοντα καὶ βασιλέα καὶ πολέμαρχον κατὰ μέρος ἐξ ἑκάστης ⟨τῆς⟩ φυλῆς.

[2] For the Ambitus see my *Beitr.*, etc., p. 14 ff. The application for offices filled by lot appears in Isocr. 15, 150; Lys. 6, 4; 31, 33; Harp. ἐπιλαχών, and against this Suid. ληξιαρχικὸν and Phot., Art. 2, are valueless. It is suggestive too that Poll. 8, 55 obviously does not know of any ἐξωμοσία of offices, though according to the method of drawing by lot given by Suid., Phot., it must certainly have been permissible.

[3] See Arist. 44, 4; Æschin. *in Ctes.* 13.

similar manner to fill their place.¹ The lottery itself must be imagined to have proceeded thus. In one urn were tablets with the names of the candidates, in another a corresponding number of beans, of which one was white, the rest black. Out of the two urns were drawn at the same time a tablet with a name inscribed on it, and a bean, and that candidate with whose name the white bean was drawn was nominated.² Corrupt practices at elections are reported not only in the case of the offices filled by sortition, but also of those filled by election: but nothing can be definitely said as to the methods adopted.³

Each official appointed either by vote or by lot had to pass a Dokimasia before entering on office.⁴ In the case of the 9

¹ For the method of nominating the 9 Archons introduced in 487 see Arist. 22, 5. Comp. p. 158. In place of this they reverted to the method introduced by Solon, about which Arist. 8, 1 says: προύκρινεν δ' εἰς τοὺς ἐννέα ἄρχοντας ἑκάστη (namely φύλη) δέκα καὶ ⟨ἐκ⟩ τού[των ἐκλ]ήρουν· ὅθεν ἔτι διαμένει ταῖς φυλαῖς τὸ δέκα κληροῦν ἑκάστην, εἶτ' ἐκ τούτων κυαμεύειν. For the intervention of the tribes at the nomination of the 9 Archons see the preceding note. With regard to the other officials elected by lot cf. Arist. 62, 1: αἱ δὲ κληρωταὶ ἀ[ρχ]αὶ πρότερον μὲν ἦσαν αἱ μὲν μετ' ἐννέα ἀρχόντων [ἐκ] τῆς φυλῆς ὅλης κληρούμεναι, αἱ δ' ἐν Θησείῳ κληρούμεναι διῃροῦντο εἰς τοὺς δήμ[ο]υς· ἐπειδὴ δ' ἐπώλουν οἱ δῆμοι, καὶ ταύτας ἐκ τῆς φυλῆς ὅλης κληροῦσι πλὴν βουλευτῶν καὶ φρουρῶν. τούτους δ' εἰς τοὺς δημότας ἀποδιδόασι. In the time of Æschines, the 9 Archons selected by lot all those officials in the Theseion: Æschin. *in Ctes.* 18. For Æschines evidently takes the θεσμοθέται for the 9 Archons, on the analogy of the election by lot of the dicasts by the 9 Archons (cf. Arist. 59, 7; 63, 1). That for every official elected by lot, a substitute had to be also elected by lot at the same time, as Harp. ἐπιλαχών thinks, is probably only true of the Bouleutai. A bye-election by lot was held when magistrates had failed to pass the dokimasia or had died. See Lex. Seguer. 256, 3, (Dem.) 58, 29 and especially Lys. 26, 6. Köhler wishes the phrase ἐπὶ Νικίου ἄρχοντος ὑστέ(ρου) C.I.A., II. 299, to be taken as evidence for an ἐπιλαχών of the ἄρχων, on the strength of a fragment of a decree of the people in the *Mitth. d. dtsch. arch.-Inst.*, 5, 326 (ἐπὶ Νικίου ἄρ)χοντος ὑ(στέ)ρου, and (ἐπὶ—ι)οδώρου ἄρχοντος δεύτε(ρου), II. 299b. But cf. Droysen, *Gesch. d. Hell.*, 2, 2, 388 (646) ff. and Unger in the Phil. 38, 445.

² The ἄρχοντας ἀπὸ κυάμου καθιστάναι (Xen., *Mem.*, 1, 2, 9) is, in the Lex. Cantabr. 671, explained as follows: κυαμεύονται· κληροῦνται. ἐχρῶντο γὰρ κυάμοις οἱ Ἀττικοὶ ἐν ταῖς κληρώσεσι τῶν ἀρχῶν μέλασι καὶ λευκοῖς. Καὶ ὁ τὸν λευκὸν ἀναρπάσας ἦρχεν, cf. Hesych. κυαμοτρώξ. Phot. Κυαμίτης. Dem. 39, 10. 12.

³ For the elective offices see Isocr. 8, 50, for the others Aeschin. *in Tim.* 107, *in Ctes.* 62. A form of corruption in voting was τὸ δυοῖν πινακίοιν τὸν ἕνα πληροῦσθαι in Dem. 39, 12, where the πινάκιον signifies the tablet with the name of the candidate. For the γραφὴ δεκασμοῦ see Meier and Schömann, *att. Proc.*,² 444/5.

⁴ The following have treated of the Dokimasia of magistrates: Fränkel, *d. att. Geschwornenger.*, 28 ff. Herm. 13, 561 ff., Thalheim in the Herm. 13,

Archons this inquiry was a double one, first before the council, then in a law court; the other officials were examined in the law court only.[1] The dokimasia of the 9 Archons, which does not seem to have differed materially from that which the others had to pass, was conducted in the following way: the applicant had to prove by witnesses his citizen descent for three generations back, and to show that he followed the cult of Apollo Patroos and of Zeus Herkeios, that he had a family tomb, that he respected his parents as he should, that he belonged to a class so assessed as to entitle him to hold this office, and that he had fulfilled his military duties.[2]

After the witnesses had given evidence on these points, it was asked whether any of those present had any complaint to make against the candidate. If a complainant appeared, a legal trial was undertaken, and only after consequent prosecution and de-

---

866 ff., *Jahrb. f. cl. Phil.*, 1879, 601 ff., C. Schäfer in the *Jahrb. f. cl. Phil.*, 1878, 821 ff. What was then still a matter of dispute has now been set at rest by Arist., who confirms Schäfer's theory. That all officials had to pass the Dokimasia, Arist. 55, 2 affirms: π[άντες γὰρ καὶ] οἱ κληρωτοὶ καὶ οἱ χειροτονητοὶ δοκιμασθέντες ἄρχουσιν. Cf. Æschin. *in Ctes.* 14, 15; Poll. 8, 44.

[1] See Arist. 55, 2: δοκιμάζονται δ' οὗτοι (οἱ ἐννέα ἄρχοντες) πρῶτον μὲν ἐν τῇ (βουλῇ) τοῖς φ' πλὴν τοῦ γραμματέως, οὗτος δ' ἐν δικαστηρίῳ μόνον ὥσπερ οἱ ἄλλοι ἄρχον[τες], (π[άντες γὰρ καὶ] οἱ κληρωτοὶ καὶ οἱ χειροτονητοὶ δοκιμασθέντες ἄρχουσιν), οἱ δ' ἐννέ' ἄρχοντε[ς ἔ]ν τε τῇ βουλῇ καὶ πάλιν ἐν δικαστηρίῳ. καὶ πρότερον μὲν οὐκ ἦρχεν ὄντ[ιν' ἀ]ποδοκιμάσειεν ἡ βουλή, νῦν δ' ἔφεσίς ἐστιν εἰς τὸ δικαστήριον καὶ τοῦτο κύριόν ἐστι τῆς δοκιμασίας. Cf. also Arist. 45, 3: δοκιμάζει δὲ (ἡ βουλὴ) καὶ τοὺς βουλευτὰς τοὺς τὸν ὕστερον ἐνιαυτὸν βουλεύσοντας καὶ τοὺς ἐννέα ἄρχοντας. καὶ πρότερον μὲν ἦν ἀποδοκιμάσαι κυρία, νῦν δὲ ⟨καὶ⟩ τούτοις ἔφεσίς ἐστιν εἰς τὸ δικαστήριον. τούτων μὲν οὖν ἄκυρός ἐστιν ἡ βουλή. That this double dokimasia was held in every case, is also clear from Dem. 20, 90: τοὺς μὲν θεσμοθέτας τοὺς ἐπὶ τοὺς νόμους κληρουμένους δὶς δοκιμασθέντας ἄρχειν ἔν τε τῇ βουλῇ καὶ παρ' ὑμῖν ἐν τῷ δικαστηρίῳ. In Lys. 26, 12 the Dokimasia of the council περὶ τῶν ἄλλων ἀρχῶν can only refer to the bouleutai. See Lipsius in Meier and Schömann, *att. Proc.*,[2] 244, 10. Dokimasia of the Taxiarchs in court: Dem. 40, 34, of the Strategoi: Lys. 15, 2, of the ἐπιμεληταὶ τοῦ ἐμπορίου: Dein. *in Aristog.* 10.

[2] Arist. 55, 3: ἐπερωτῶσιν δ', ὅταν δοκιμάζωσιν, πρῶτον μὲν "τίς σοι πατὴρ καὶ πόθεν τῶν δήμων καὶ τίς πατρὸς πατὴρ καὶ τίς μήτηρ καὶ τίς μητρὸς πατὴρ καὶ πόθεν τῶν δήμων· μετὰ δὲ ταῦτα εἰ ἔστιν αὐτῷ Ἀπόλλων πατρῷος καὶ Ζεὺς ἑρκεῖος καὶ ποῦ ταῦτα τὰ ἱερά ἐστιν, εἶτα ἠρία εἰ ἔστιν καὶ ποῦ ταῦτα, ἔπειτα γονέας εἰ εὖ ποιεῖ [καὶ] τὰ τέλη τελεῖ (cf. Arist. 7, 4: διὸ καὶ νῦν ἐπειδὰν ἔρηται τὸν μέλλοντα κληροῦσθαί τιν' ἀρχήν, ποῖον τέλος τελεῖ, οὐδ' ἂν εἰς εἴποι θητικόν) καὶ τὰς στρατείας εἰ ἐστράτευται. ταῦτα δ' ἀνερωτήσας "κάλει, φησίν, τούτων τοὺς μάρτυρας." Cf. also Lex. Cantabr. 670; Poll. 8, 85; Dem. 57, 66. 67. 70; (Dem.) 59, 92. That the anacrisis of the other officials did not materially differ from that of the 9 Archons is evident from Deinarch. *in Aristog.* 17; Xen., *Mem.*, 2, 2, 13.

fence did the epicheirotonia in the Council, the final verdict in the law court, take place. If there was no complainant, the voting immediately began. In the judicial Dokimasia, before a law-court, the Thesmothetai presided over the proceedings.[1] For special officials the judicial inquiry required proof of special qualities, e.g. the treasurers of Athene and probably those of the other gods had to prove that they belonged to the first assessed class, the 9 Archons to show that their bodies were faultless, the Basileus that he was married to a woman who had never married before, the Strategoi that they lived in lawful wedlock and that they possessed property within the boundaries of Attica.[2] At the same time the Dokimasia did not limit itself to the points here enumerated; the whole life of the nominee was subjected to examination, and he could be refused office on various other grounds.[3] Rejection at the Dokimasia implied, it seems, a partial atimia, which involved the loss of the right of appearing as a speaker before the people.[4]

The Athenian year of office corresponded to the civil year, and for this reason the officials usually took office on the first of Hecatombaion. The treasurers of Athene, however, and those of the other gods succeeded to office at the Panathenaia, holding it till the following Panathenaia,

Entrance on Office: the Oath.

[1] Arist. 55, 3: ἐπειδὰν δὲ παράσχηται τοὺς μάρτυρας, ἐπερωτᾷ, "τούτου βούλεταί τις κατηγορεῖν;" κἂν μὲν ᾖ τις κατήγορος, δοὺς κατηγορίαν καὶ ἀπολογίαν, οὕτω δίδωσιν ἐν μὲν τῇ βουλῇ τὴν ἐπιχειροτονίαν, ἐν δὲ τῷ δικαστηρίῳ τὴν ψῆφον· ἐὰν δὲ μηδεὶς βούληται κατηγορεῖν, εὐθὺς δίδωσι τὴν ψῆφον· καὶ πρότερον μὲν εἷς ἐνέβαλλε τὴν ψῆφον, νῦν δ' ἀνάγκη πάντας ἐστὶ διαψηφίζεσθαι περὶ αὐτῶν, ἵνα, ἄν τις πονηρὸς ὢν ἀπαλλάξῃ τοὺς κατηγόρους, ἐπὶ τοῖς δικασταῖς γένηται τοῦτον ἀποδοκιμάσαι. The Thesmothetai as εἰσαγωγεῖς in the Dokimasia before a court of law: Lys. 15, 2. Poll. 8, 88.

[2] The authorities for this are Arist. 47, 1; Poll. 8, 97; Lys. 24, 13. Et. M. ἀφελής. (Dem.) 59, 75. Dein. in Dem. 71. The Thetes do not seem to have been excluded by law from the archonship, at any rate in the 4th century, although the expense connected with it perhaps deterred them from standing for the office. See Lys. 24, 13. (Dem.) 59, 72. Beyond this Arist. 7, 4. says nothing: διὸ καὶ νῦν ἐπειδὰν ἔρηται τὸν μέλλοντα κληροῦσθαί τιν' ἀρχήν, ποῖον τέλος τελεῖ, οὐδ' ἂν εἷς εἴποι θητικόν.

[3] See Lys. 16, 9: ἐν δὲ ταῖς δοκιμασίαις δίκαιον εἶναι παντὸς τοῦ βίου λόγον διδόναι. The nominated official can be refused office for ἑταιρεῖν (Æschin. in Tim. 19), for his previous political conduct (Lys. 13, 10. 26).

[4] This Atimia is recognised by K. Fr. Hermann, de iure et auctorit. magistratuum ap. Atheniens., p. 27, from (Dem.) 25, 30, according to which it was forbidden, among other things, to speak before the people, τοῖς ἀποδεδοκιμασμένοις ἄρχειν λαχοῦσιν.

in the 5th and perhaps also in the 4th century, as did also the Hellenotamiai in the 5th, and in the 4th the ταμίας τῶν στρατιωτικῶν, οἱ ἐπὶ τὸ θεωρικόν, and ὁ ἐπὶ τὰς κρήνας.[1] Just before the taking of office, came the oath of office which all Athenian officials had to swear.[2] This oath (which was probably different for the different offices, but in every case, as it seems, contained the obligation not to accept bribes), was taken just before entering on office, first at the stone of witness in the Agora and then again on the Acropolis.[3] I conjecture that on the first of Hekatombaion,

[1] That the year of office of the Strategoi was the same as that of the Archons, a thing often doubted,—see my *Beitr.*, etc., 13/4—can be proved true of the 3rd century by inscriptions. See C.I.A., II. 331. I cannot place such reliance on C.I.A., I. 273, as authority for the taking of office of the Strategoi in Hecatombaion as do Loeschcke, *de aliquot titulis Att.*, 25 ff. and Arnold, *de Atheniens. prætorib.*, II. p. 3 ff. Bautzen, 1876, since I cannot convince myself of the existence of a permanent chairman of the board of Strategoi. The year of office too of the Taxiarchs is identical with that of the Archons in 339: C.I.A., II. 562. Those who hold that the taking of office by the Strategoi took place on 1 Hecatombaion are the same as those who fix the election in spring or summer. See p. 216, 2. So also Hauvette-Besnault, *ibid.*, 29 ff. Entering on office of the ταμίαι τῆς θεοῦ at the Panathenaia on the 28th Hecatombaion : C.I.A., 179. Boeckh, *kl. Schr.*, 6, 78 seq. C.I.A., I. 189 *a*, *b*, goes from Metageitnion to Hecatombaion (the 20th Hecatombaion is mentioned). See Kirchhoff in the C.I.A., I. p. 88. I. 188 is not against it, as the expenses of the first prytany may have come after the 28th Hecatombaion. Neither is I. 180, where according to Müller-Strübing in the *N. Rhein. Mus.*, 33, 87 ff., the first payment of the treasurers is made on the 32nd day of the first prytany. After the time of Eucleides the treasurers' years of office, as Boeckh, *ibid.*, 85, concludes from C.I.G., 150, 151=C.I.A., II. 652, 667, were the same as those of the Archons. Panske, *de magistratib. att. qui saec. a Chr. n. IV. pecunias publ. curabant*, 20 ff., 1890, Leipzig, takes the Panathenaia as the term of office in the 4th century also. Arist. 43, 1 is not conclusive against this, as he there only speaks of elective offices. The entering on office of the ταμίαι τῶν ἄλλων θεῶν took place at the same time. See C.I.A., I. 32. The Hellenotamiai also, according to Boeckh's conjecture in the *St. d. Athen.*, 1, 244. For the other officials mentioned in the text see Arist. 43, 1.

[2] See Lyc., *Leokr.*, 79.

[3] For the oath of the 9 Archons see Arist. 55, 5: δοκιμασθέν⟨τες⟩ δὲ τοῦτον τὸν τρόπον βαδίζουσι πρὸς τὸν λίθον ἐφ' οὗ τὰ τόμι' ἐστίν, ἐφ' οὗ καὶ οἱ διαιτηταὶ ὀμόσαντες ἀποφαίνονται τὰς διαίτας καὶ οἱ μάρτυρες ἐξόμνυνται τὰς μαρτυρίας, ἀναβάντες δὲ ἐπὶ τοῦτον ὀμνύουσιν δικαίως ἄρξειν καὶ κατὰ τοὺς νόμους καὶ δῶρα μὴ λήψεσθαι τῆς ἀρχῆς ἕνεκα, κἄν τι λάβωσιν, ἀνδριάντα ἀναθήσειν χρυσοῦν. ἐντεῦθεν δ' ὀμόσαντες εἰς ἀκρόπολιν βαδίζουσιν καὶ πάλιν ἐκεῖ ταὐτὰ ὀμνύουσι, καὶ μετὰ ταῦτα εἰς τὴν ἀρχὴν εἰσέρχονται. See also 7, 1. Compare also for the oath Plut., *Sol.*, 25. Plat., *Phædr.*, 235. Herakl. I. 11=Müller, *fr. hist. gr.*, 2, 209. This

the officials, after they had taken the oath of office at the stone of witness, went in procession to the Acropolis, while a table was carried in front, on which lay myrtle twigs. After they had there renewed the oath before the statue of Athene Polias, they were crowned with these myrtle twigs, and were thus symbolically inducted into office.[1] Then followed the inaugural sacrifice, with which the officials entered on office.[2] The different officials had as a rule their special places of business, in which they held their sittings, and also, in most cases, dined together.[3] Some of the offices were remunerated, others were not, but nothing more can be said upon the point.[4]

passage as to willingness to dedicate at Delphi, in case of corruption, a χρυσῆν εἰκόνα ἰσομέτρητον (Plat.)—Arist. has ἀνδριάντα χρυσοῦν ἀναθήσειν— Bergk in the *N. Rhein. Mus.*, 13, 448 seq., has acutely explained in this way:—The magistrate convicted of bribery was to dedicate at Delphi a golden image equal in weight to the weight in silver of the money received, the ratio of gold to silver being as 10 : 1 (Boeckh, *St. d. Ath.*, 1, 42, *metr. Unters.*, 130): an ancient formula for the usual tenfold punishment of bribery. See Dein. *in Dem.* 60, *in Aristog.* 17. The oath of the Strategoi included the special obligation τοὺς ἀστρατεύτους καταλέξειν: Lys. 9, 15. The obligation of not allowing themselves to be bribed, seems to follow in their case from Dein. *in Philokl.* 2. For the addition to the oath of the Strategoi in the Peloponnesian war, see Plut., *Per.*, 30. For the stone of witness see Wachsmuth, *d. St. Athen.*, 2, 1, 351/2.

[1] The account given in the text rests on Arist. 55, 5; Poll. 8, 86, and on the statement in Dein. *in Philokl.* 2, that the oath of the Strategoi was given μεταξὺ τοῦ ἕδους καὶ τραπέζης, where ἕδος, according to Bergk, *ibid.*, 456, is the statue of Athene Polias (see Lex. Seguer. 246, 3: ἕδος αὐτὸ τὸ ἄγαλμα) while I associate the τράπεζα with the note in Poll. 10, 69, that in Aristophanes' *Georgoi*, occurs the term τραπεζοφόρος before ἐπὶ τοῦ τὴν τράπεζαν φέροντος, ᾗ ἐπῆσαν τοῖς ἄρχουσι αἱ μυρρίναι. For the symbolic meaning of the myrtle-wreath for the officials see Lys. 26, 8. Phot. μύρρινος μυρρινῶν. Hesych. μυρρινῶν. The apocheirotonia of an official is the taking away of his wreath. See Dem. 26, 5. (Dem.) 58, 27.

[2] See Lex. Seguer. 245, 20: εἰσιτήρια θυσίας ὄνομα, ὅταν βουλεύειν ἢ ὅταν ἄρχειν τις χειροτονηθῇ. With this I compare (Dem.) 59, 72, where it says of Stephanos's dealings with the ἄρχων βασιλεύς Theogenes: συμπαραγενόμενος αὐτῷ δοκιμαζομένῳ καὶ συνευπορήσας ἀναλωμάτων, ὅτε εἰσῄει εἰς τὴν ἀρχήν.

[3] See Dem. 19, 190.

[4] (Xen.) *de rep. Ath.*, 1, 3, says: for offices like the Strategia or Hipparchia, the Demos does not trouble itself, ὁπόσαι δ' εἰσὶν ἀρχαὶ μισθοφορίας ἕνεκα καὶ ὠφελείας εἰς τὸν οἶκον, ταύτας ζητεῖ ὁ δῆμος ἄρχειν. Yet in my *Beiträgen*, etc., p. 81, I have held that we are bound to suppose that the Strategoi must have received pay in time of war. Isocr. 12, 145: ἔδει γὰρ τοὺς ἄρχειν αἱρεθέντας τῶν τε κτημάτων τῶν ἰδίων ἀμελεῖν καὶ τῶν λημμάτων τῶν εἰθισμένων δίδοσθαι ταῖς ἀρχαῖς ἀπέχεσθαι μηδὲν ἧττον ἢ τῶν ἱερῶν, ἃ τίς ἂν ἐν τοῖς νῦν καθεστῶσιν ὑπομείνειεν; is probably thinking more of indirect gain. See also 15,

Particular magistrates had also special honorary privileges.[1]

As the officials, whose deliberations seem usually to have been public, regularly formed committees of ten members, one of them had to preside. This position was either filled (as for example in the committee of the Archons by the first Archon), by the same man throughout the year, or by the several committee men in turn.[2] Every official had to hand in to the Council every Prytany a report concerning his official proceedings, especially regarding the money he administered and expended. A commission of auditors, consisting of 10 λογισταί, whom the council elected by lot from among its own members, audited this account; and the council probably decided on their report, whether the account should be accepted as correct or not. If the decision of the council was unfavourable, it was open to the official in question to appeal to the Heliaia. Even private citizens could bring in an eisangelia against any official before the Council, against whose decision in this case too the accused was allowed to appeal to the Heliaia. Besides, every official was subject every Prytany to the epicheirotonia in the κυρία ἐκκλησία, that is, the

Boards of Magistrates: Presidents.

ἐπιχειροτονία.

---

145. The σωφρονισταί received daily a drachma εἰς τροφήν. Arist. 42, 3. Lex. Seguer. 301, 7. Phot., *sub verb.*, says the 9 Archons each received 4 obols daily, εἰς σίτησιν, with which they had also to support a herald and a flute-player, the ἄρχων εἰς Σαλαμῖνα, 1 drachma, the Ἀμφικτύονες εἰς Δῆλον, 1 drachma. The ἀρχαί for Samos, Skyros, Lemnos, and Imbros were also paid: Arist. 62, 2. Under the 400 all ἀρχαί had to be ἄμισθοι, with the exception of the 9 Archons and the Prytanes: Arist. 29, 5. In the best days of the Athenian confederacy Arist. 24, 3 counts 700 members of the ἀρχαί ἔνδημοι as receiving pay. The officials gained indirect advantages, by allowing themselves to be bribed. Vid. *e.g.* for the Prytanes: Lys. 6, 29. Arist., *Thesm.*, 936/7. Müller-Strübing, *Aristoph.*, 347 seq.

[1] Thus, for instance, the Prytanes, the 9 Archons, the ταμίαι τῆς θεοῦ, the ἱεροποιοί, the Strategoi and the Taxiarchs received pieces of the sacrifice at the Panathenaia as a mark of honour: C.I.A., II. 163: ἀθλοθέται δ' ἐν πρυτανείῳ δειπνοῦσι τὸν Ἑκ[ατο]μβειῶνα μῆνα, ὅ[τ]αν ᾖ τὰ Παναθήναια, ἀρξάμενοι ἀπὸ τῆς τετράδος ἱσταμένου: Arist. 62, 2.

[2] See Poll. 8, 99: πρυτανεύει ἐξ αὐτῶν (τῶν πωλητῶν) εἷς, ὃς τὰ πωλούμενα βεβαιοῖ. The ταμίαι τῆς θεοῦ had an annual president. This is proved by inscriptions marking a whole year by the formula: ἐπὶ τῆς τοῦ δεῖνος ἀρχῆς καὶ ξυναρχόντων. See *e.g.* C.I.A., I. 273. That the Hellenotamiai had an annual president has been generally inferred from C.I.A., I. 237, 238, 242, etc., but 188, 189 throw some doubt on the point. For the Strategoi see my *Beitr.*, etc., p. 38. The publicity of the deliberations I gather from (Dem.) 25, 23, for the cases mentioned there are obviously exceptional.

question was put to the assembly, whether the officials seemed to them to be doing their duty well. Charges could then be brought against any official. If the ecclesia considered them serious, then the official in question was suspended, and the charge brought against him was brought before the Heliaia for final decision.[1] Further, every official,[2] at the end of his term of office, was bound to give an account of his trust, and was answerable in his person and property for any faults or negligences during his term of office. He was not permitted to leave the country before giving an account of his office, neither could he in the interval be adopted into another family, nor dispose of his fortune as he wished; so that he could not in any way defraud the State of its public money:[3] and it was not allowable, before his examination, to decree to any official a crown of honour for the way in which he had conducted his office.[4]

About the constitution of those bodies, before which the audits took place, our information varies according as it refers to the time before or after Eucleides.[5] For the time

Boards of Auditors.

---

[1] Lys. 30, 5: ἀλλ' οἱ μὲν ἄλλοι τῆς αὐτῶν ἀρχῆς κατὰ πρυτανείαν λόγον ἀναφέρουσι. From this Fischer in the *Progr. d. Kneiphöfischen Stadtgymn.* in Königsberg, 1886, 10 seq., rightly concludes that all officials had to render an account in each Prytany. Arist. 48, 3, says: [κ]ληροῦσι δὲ καὶ λογιστὰς ἐξ αὐτῶν οἱ βουλευταὶ δέκα τοὺς λογιουμένους ταῖς ἀρχαῖς κατὰ τὴν πρυτανείαν ἑκάστην. With this I compare Arist. 45, 2: κρίνει δὲ τὰς ἀρχὰς ἡ᾽ βουλὴ τὰς πλείστας, μάλισθ' ὅσαι χρήματα διαχειρίζουσιν· οὐ κυρία δ' ἡ κρίσις, ἀλλ' ἐφέσιμος εἰς τὸ δικαστήριον. ἔξεστι δὲ καὶ τοῖς ἰδιώταις εἰσαγγέλλειν ἣν ἂν βούλωνται τῶν ἀρχῶν, μὴ χρῆσθαι τοῖς νόμοις· ἔφεσις δὲ καὶ τούτοις ἐστὶν εἰς τὸ δικαστήριον, ἐὰν αὐτῶν ἡ βουλὴ καταγνῷ. To the regular daily routine of the κυρία ἐκκλησία, belonged τὰς ἀρχὰς ἐπιχειροτονεῖν, εἰ δοκοῦσι καλῶς ἄρχειν : Arist. 48, 4. Arist. 61, 2 describes the epicheirotonia more fully with regard to the Strategoi: ἐπιχειροτονία δ' αὐτῶν ἐστι κατὰ τὴν πρυτανείαν ἑκάστην, εἰ δοκοῦσι καλῶς ἄρχειν. κἄν τινα ἀποχειροτονήσωσιν, κρίνουσιν ἐν τῷ δικαστηρίῳ κἂν μὲν ἁλῷ, τιμῶσιν, ὅτι χρὴ παθεῖν ἢ ἀποτεῖσαι, ἂν δ' ἀποφύγῃ, [π]άλ[ιν] ἄρχει. That the epicheirotonia took place under the presidency of the 9 Archons, as has been concluded from Poll. 8, 87, is hardly likely, since the passage from Poll., a quotation from Arist. 61, has probably only reached its present place through a blunder. Examples of such an epicheirotonia in (Dem.) 26, 5. 58, 27/8.

[2] von Wilamowitz-Moellendorff tries in the *phil. Untersuch.*, Heft 1, p. 59 sqq., to prove that no real account was given by the Strategoi, at least not in the 5th century. I hold this view to be wrong.

[3] The regulations for the rendering of these accounts in Aeschin. *in Ctes.* 17–22; cf also Lex. Seguer. 247, 10.

[4] See Æschin. *in Ctes.* 9–12; C.I.A., II. 114, 329.

[5] The question is interesting on account of the well-known controversy between Gottfr. Hermann on Prof. Boeckh's *Behandl. d. griech. Inschr.*, p.

previous to Eucleides, the existence of a body of 30 λογισταί is proved by epigraphical evidence; they are also called simply οἱ τριάκοντα; they drew up all money accounts required by the State, and audited the officials' accounts of their tenure of office. Besides these λογισταί we can prove from inscriptions the existence at the same time of εὔθυνοι, with their πάρεδροι.[1] For the time subsequent to Eucleides the inscriptions mention as officials who took part at the auditing of accounts, λογισταί and εὔθυνοι, with their πάρεδροι and συνήγοροι.[2] With this Aristotle is in agreement, who speaks of 10 λογισταί, 10 συνήγοροι and 10 εὔθυνοι, each with their 2 πάρεδροι, all of them being chosen by lot.[3] Whether the 30 λογισταί of the time before Eucleides were after his time reduced to ten, or whether the 30 represented the three committees of ten members each, cannot be determined with certainty.[4]

73 sqq., 220 sqq., and Boeckh in the *Rhein. Mus.*, Bd. 1, now in the *Kl. Schr.*, 7, 280 sqq. Boeckh's somewhat modified view now in the *Staatsh. d. Ath.*, 1, 263 sqq. (*Pub. Econ.*, Bk. 2, ch. 8). Recently the question has been treated by R. Schoell, *de Synegoris Atticis*, Jena, 1876. See in general for such a body, Aristot., *Pol.*, 7, (6), 8, p. 192, 7 sqq. Bekker: ἐπεὶ δὲ ἔνιαι τῶν ἀρχῶν, εἰ καὶ μὴ πᾶσαι, διαχειρίζουσι πολλὰ τῶν κοινῶν, ἀναγκαῖον ἑτέραν εἶναι τὴν ληψομένην καὶ προσευθυνοῦσαν, αὐτὴν μηθὲν διαχειρίζουσαν ἔτερον· καλοῦσι δὲ τούτους οἱ μὲν εὐθύνους οἱ δὲ λογιστὰς οἱ δὲ ἐξεταστὰς οἱ δὲ συνηγόρους.
[1] Accounts of the moneys due to the gods, drawn up by the Logistai: C.I.A., I. 32. Calculation of the capital borrowed from the gods, together with the interest, C.I.A., I. 273. The so-called tribute-lists in the C.I.A., I. 226 sqq. (lists of the ἀπαρχή, due to the goddess from the tribute=μνᾶ ἀπὸ ταλάντου), were drawn up by the Hellenotamiai and then undoubtedly audited by the logistai. Cf. Christ., *de publicis populi Atheniensis rationibus*, p. 28, D. i. Greifswald 1879, οἱ λογισταὶ οἱ τριάκοντα: C.I.A., I. 32, οἱ τριάκοντα: I. 226, 228. Receiving of the report by them, I. 32: καὶ τὸ λοιπὸν ἀναγραφόντων οἱ αἰεὶ ταμίαι ἐς στήλην καὶ λόγον διδόντων τῶν τε ὄντων χρημάτων καὶ τῶν προσιόντων τοῖς θεοῖς καὶ ἐάν τι ἀ(π)αναλίσκηται κατὰ τὸν ἐνιαυτὸν πρὸς τοὺς λογιστὰς καὶ εὐθύνας διδόντων καὶ ἐκ Παναθηναίων ἐς Παναθήναια τὸλλόγον διδόντων. Εὔθυνος and his πάρεδροι: I. 34, in the Demos Scambonidai: I. 2. See also the Psephism of Patrocleides in Andoc., *de Myst.*, 78.
[2] C.I.A., II. 444, 446, for the λογισταί, Boeckh, *Seeurk.*, 14b, p. 466=C.I.A., II. 809b, 1 sqq., and the Deme-decree, C.I.A., II. 571, for the εὔθυνοι and their πάρεδροι; for all three classes the Deme-decree C.I.A., II. 578.
[3] See Arist. 54, 1. 2: κληροῦσι δὲ καὶ τάσδε τὰς ἀρχάς·—καὶ λογιστὰς δέκα καὶ συνηγόρους τούτοις δέκα, πρὸς οὓς ἅπαντας ἀνάγκη τοὺς τὰς ἀρχὰς ἄ[ρξαντ]ας λόγον ἀπενεγκεῖν. Arist. 48, 4: κληροῦσι δὲ καὶ εὐθύνους, ἕνα τῆς φυ[λῆς] ἑκάστης καὶ παρέδρους β' ἑκάστῳ τῶν εὐθύνων—cf. Rose., *Aristot. pseudep.*, p. 444/5, no. 61. 62. 63.
[4] Boeckh, *Staatsh. d. Ath.* 1, 266 (*Publ. Econ.*, Bk. 2, ch. 8), accepts the former, Schoell, *de Synegoris Att.*, p. 38 sqq. the latter hypothesis.

G.A.

The method of giving account was as follows. Each official on leaving office had to hand in to the Logistai a report of the State Procedure at money which he had received and expended, or a εὔθυνα. declaration to the effect that he had neither received nor expended public funds. The correctness of the several accounts was then tested by the Logistai who probably divided the work; this was done by comparing the items of the report with the official documents in the archives.[1] If the result of this scrutiny was that the official had, during his tenure of office, been guilty of forgery, receipt of bribes, or of the offence called ἀδίκιον, then, after the 10 συνήγοροι, at a preliminary investigation, had satisfied themselves of the justice of the charges brought by the Logistai, the matter was brought before a court of the Heliaia, consisting of 501 members, in the form of a γραφὴ κλοπῆς δημοσίων

[1] Arist. 54, 2 continues the passage quoted on page 225 note 3 thus: οὗτοι γάρ εἰσι μόνοι τοῖς ὑπευθύνοις λογιζόμενοι καὶ τὰς εὐθύνας εἰς τὸ δικαστήριον εἰσάγοντες. Cf. Harp. λογισταὶ καὶ λογιστήρια· ἀρχή τις παρ' Ἀθηναίοις οὕτω καλουμένη· εἰσὶ δὲ τὸν ἀριθμὸν δέκα, οἳ τὰς εὐθύνας τῶν διῳκημένων ἐκλογίζονται ἐν ἡμέραις τριάκοντα, ὅταν τὰς ἀρχὰς ἀποθῶνται οἱ ἄρχοντες. Lex. Cantabr. 672 says under λογισταὶ καὶ συνήγοροι· 'Αριστοτέλης ἐν τῇ 'Αθηναίων πολιτείᾳ οὕτω λέγει· λογιστὰς δὲ αἱροῦνται δέκα, παρ' οἷς διαλογίζονται πᾶσαι αἱ ἀρχαὶ τά τε λήμματα καὶ τὰς γεγενημένας δαπάνας. καὶ ἄλλους δέκα συνηγόρους οἵτινες συνανακρίνουσι τούτοις· καὶ οἱ τὰς εὐθύνας διδόντες παρὰ τούτοις ἀνακρίνονται (for the MSS. ἀνακρίνοντες) πρῶτον, εἶτα ἐφίενται εἰς δικαστήριον εἰς ἕνα καὶ πεντακοσίους. But these remarks are not quoted directly from Aristotle. The technical expression for the giving of account is λόγον διδόναι πρὸς τοὺς λογιστὰς καὶ εὐθύνας διδόναι (C.I.A., I. 32) or, ἀποφέρειν λόγους εἰς τὸ μητρῷον καὶ πρὸς τοὺς λογιστὰς καὶ τὰς εὐθύνας διδόναι (C.I.A., II. 444. 446) or, τούς τε λόγους ἐνφέρειν πρὸς τοὺς λογιστὰς καὶ εἰ(ς) μητρῷον καὶ τὰς εὐθύνας διδόναι ἐν τῷ δικαστηρίῳ κατὰ τοὺς νόμους: 'Εφ. ἀρχ., 1887, p. 177, l. 26 sqq. See Schoell, *ibid.*, 27, 1. In the formula in Æschin. *in Ctes.* 15: καὶ λόγον καὶ εὐθύνας ἐγγράφειν πρὸς τὸν γραμματέα καὶ τοὺς λογιστάς, the clerk of the council, not the ἀντιγραφεύς, as Schömann, *op. ac.*, 1, 293 seq., thinks, is meant as the president of the archives, the expression πρὸς τὸν γραμματέα being equivalent to the εἰς τὸ μητρῷον. The clerk of the council handed over to the Logistai the official statistics from the metroon, where they were kept (Harp., ἀποδέκται). In the metroon or in the adjacent bouleuterion were most probably the separate λογιστήρια (Harp., λογισταί—λογιστήρια δ' ἐστὶ τὰ τῶν λογιστῶν ἀρχεῖα) and here the reports were received. Pseudoplut., *vit. Lyc.*, 26, p. 1027, Didot. He who had had no money in his control, gave the declaration in writing: οὔτ' ἔλαβον οὐδὲν τῶν τῆς πόλεως οὔτ' ἀνήλωσα: Aeschin. *in Ctes.* 22. Fischer, *quaestionum de praetorib. att. Saec. V. et IV. a. Chr. n. specimen*, p. 26 sqq., D. i. Königsberg, 1881, doubts the special εὔθυνα of Strategoi assumed from Poll. 8, 88 (οἱ θεσμοθέται εἰσάγουσι) καὶ στρατηγοῖς εὐθύνας. See also Hauvette-Besnault, *les Stratèges Athéniens.*, p. 56 sqq. This statement of Poll. is now proved to be correct by Arist. 59, 2. Ambassadors also had to render account, Dem. 19, 211; Harp. εὐθῦναι.

χρημάτων.[1] If the result of the scrutiny undertaken by the logistai gave no cause for raising any accusation against the official, his account of office, after being passed by the συνήγοροι, was sent to the court of the Heliaia with the recommendation that the official in question should receive his discharge.[2] But even after this discharge had been granted, three days were set apart, during which it was open to any private citizen to bring an accusation against the official with regard to any of his acts during office. This was done before the εὔθυνοι; every εὔθυνος with his two πάρεδροι received any accusations before the statue of the Eponymos of his tribe. With his πάρεδροι he also tested the soundness of these charges, and if he acknowledged their validity, he handed them over, if they were of a private nature, to those Deme judges who conducted the litigation of the tribe in question, but if they were of a public

---

[1] Arist. 54, 2 says of the Logistai: οὗτοι γάρ εἰσι μόνοι τοῖς ὑπευθύνοις λογιζόμενοι καὶ τὰς εὐθύνας εἰς τὸ δικαστήριον εἰσάγοντες. κἂν μέν τινα κλέπτοντ' ἐξελέγξωσι, κλοπὴν οἱ δικασταὶ καταγιγνώσκουσι καὶ τὸ ⟨κατα⟩γνωσθὲν ἀποτίνεται δεκαπλοῦν· ἐὰν δέ τινα δῶρα λαβόντα ἀποδείξωσιν καὶ καταγνῶσιν οἱ δικασταί, δώρων τιμῶσιν, ἀποτίνεται δὲ καὶ τοῦτο δεκαπλοῦν· ἂν δ' ἀδικεῖν καταγνῶσιν, ἀδικίου τιμῶσιν, ἀποτίνεται δὲ τοῦθ' ἁπλοῦν, ἐὰν [πρὸ τῆς] θ' πρυτανείας ἐκτείσῃτις, εἰ δὲ μή, διπλοῦται τὸ ⟨δὲ⟩ δεκαπλοῦν οὐ διπλοῦται. For the charges here mentioned see Meier and Schömann, *att. Proc.*,[2] 454/5. 444. 426 sqq. These are the charges which were to have been brought against Pericles, according to the psephisma of Hagnon, Plut., *Per.*, 32 It seems according to this that the rendering of account was not then usual in the form in which it existed in the fourth century. For the work of the συνήγοροι cf. Lex. Cantabr. 672 under λογισταὶ καὶ συνήγοροι: καὶ ἄλλους δέκα συνηγόρους, οἵτινες συνανακρίνουσι τούτοις καὶ οἱ τὰς εὐθύνας διδόντες παρὰ τούτοις ἀνακρίνονται (for the MSS. ἀνακρίνοντες) πρῶτον, εἶτα ἐφίενται εἰς δικαστήριον εἰς ἕνα καὶ πεντακοσίους. Cf. Schoell., *ibid.*, 24 sqq. More accurate knowledge of the functions of the λογισταί and συνήγοροι is gained by analogy from the functions of the audit officials of the Deme Myrrhinus, who received accounts (see Köhler on C.I.A., II. 578 against Schoell., *ibid.*, 29 sqq.) in the C.I.A., II. 578: ὀμνύναι (δ)ὲ τὸν ὅρκον καὶ τὸν λογιστὴ(ν) λογιεῖσθαι ἃ ἄν μοι δοκεῖ ἀ(νηλ)ωκέναι (καὶ) τ(οὐ)s σ(υν)ηγό(ρ)ους συν(η)γορήσειν τῷ δήμῳ τ(ὰ) (δ)ίκαια καὶ (ψηφι)εῖσθαι, ἃ ἄν μοι δοκεῖ δικαιότατα εἶναι.

[2] For the proceedings in court see C.I.A., II. 469: καὶ περὶ πάντων τῶν (κατὰ τὴν ἀ)ρχὴ(ν) (ἔδωκεν τὰς εὐθύνα)s ἐν τῷ δ(ικασ)τηρίῳ κατὰ τὸν νόμον. 470 l. 42. Ἐφ ἀρχ., 1887, p. 177, l. 29/30: καὶ τὰς εὐθύνας δεδώκασιν ἐν τῷ δικαστηρίῳ κατὰ τοὺς νόμους. Even in the court, the herald of the logistai seems to have asked: τίς βούλεται κατηγορεῖν; private citizens could then still call in question the correctness of the report. See Æschin. *in Ctes.* 23; Dem. 18, 117; Lex. Seguer. 245, 6. That all reports were under the cognizance of the dicasteries is emphasized by Schoell, *ibid.*, 13 sqq. The official perhaps received his discharge by having his account sealed. See Boeckh, *St. d. Ath.*, 1, 272 c.=Publ. Ec. Bk. 2, ch. 8.

nature, to the Thesmothetai to bring them before a court of the Heliaia.[1] Against any official, who did not hand in his account of office within an interval of 30 days, the ἀλογίου δίκη was admissible.[2]

Various officials had πάρεδροι, i.e. assessors. Some magistrates, for instance the three senior Archons, chose their own assessors; for others, e.g. the εὔθυνοι, they were appointed by lot.

Assessors. The πάρεδροι of the Archons, and probably those of the other officials, had to pass a dokimasia, and were bound to render an account on leaving office. We know for certain that this was so in the case of the assessors of the first three Archons, of the εὔθυνοι and of the Hellenotamiai.[3]

---

[1] See Arist. 48, 4: κληροῦσι δὲ καὶ εὐθύνους, ἕνα τῆς φυ[λῆς] ἑκάστης, καὶ παρέδρους β' ἑκάστῳ τῶν εὐθύνων, οἷς ἀναγκαῖόν ἐστι ταῖς [εὐθύν]αις κατὰ τὸν ἐπώνυμον τὸν τῆς φυλῆς ἑκάστο[ι]ς καθῆσθαι, κἂν τις βούλ[ηταί] τινι τῶν τὰς εὐθύνας ἐν τῷ δικαστηρίῳ δεδωκότων, ἐντὸς γ' ἡ[μερῶν ἀφ'] ἧς ἔδωκε τὰς εὐθύνας, εὔθυναν ἄν τ' ἰδίαν ἄν τε δ[ημοσίαν ἐ]μβαλέσθαι, γράψας εἰς πινάκιον λελευκωμένον τοὔνομα τὸ [αὐτοῦ] καὶ τὸ τοῦ φεύγοντος, καὶ τὸ ἀδίκημ' ὅτι ἂν ἐγκαλῇ καὶ τίμημα [ἐπιγραψά]μενος ὅτι ἂν αὐτῷ δοκῇ, δίδωσιν τῷ εὐθύνῳ· ὁ δὲ λαβὼν τοῦτο καὶ ἀ[ναγνούς], ἐὰν [μὲν] καταγνῷ, παραδίδωσιν τὰ μὲν ἴδια τοῖς δικασταῖς τοῖς κατὰ δ[ήμους, τοῖς] τὴν φυλὴν ταύτην εἰσάγουσιν, τὰ δὲ δημόσια τοῖς θεσμοθέτα[ις, ἐπι]γράφει. οἱ δὲ θεσμοθέται, ἐὰν παραλάβωσιν, πάλιν εἰσάγουσιν [τὴν] εὔθυναν εἰς τὸ δικαστήριον, καὶ ὅτι ἂν γνῶσιν οἱ δικαστ[αί, τοῦτο κύ]ριόν ἐστιν. To the procedure described in the preceding words I refer the direction in the Psephisma of Patrocleides: καὶ ὅσων εὔθυναί τινές εἰσι κατεγνωσμέναι ἐν τοῖς λογιστηρίοις ὑπὸ τῶν εὐθύνων καὶ (for ἢ) τῶν παρέδρων καὶ (for ἢ) μήπω εἰσηγμέναι εἰς τὸ δικαστήριον γραφαί τινές εἰσι περὶ τῶν εὐθυνῶν. See Andok., de Myst., 78. The εὔθυνος of Myrrhinus (see Schoell, 30, 1) in the C.I.A., II. 578 has to swear: (κα)ὶ ἐάν (μοι δ)οκεῖ ἀδικεῖν, κα(τευθ)υν(ῶ) α(ὑτ)οῦ (καὶ τιμήσ)ω, οὗ (ἄ)ν μ(ο)ι (δ)ο(κ)εῖ ἄξιον εἶναι τὸ ἀδί(κ)η(μ)α. According to the schol. on Plat., p. 459, Bekker, the εὔθυνοι collected the money due to the State from the officials: ἐκπράσσει δὲ ὁ εὔθυνος, ὅσα ἐπὶ τῆς ἀρχῆς, ᾗ προστέτακται, ὠφλόν τινες εἰς τὸ δημόσιον. See also the confused note in Poll. 8, 100. The direction in the decree of the people in Boeckh, Seeurk., 14b, p. 466 = C.I.A., 809 b, 1 sqq.: ἐὰν δέ τις μὴ ποήσει, οἷς ἕκαστα προστέτακται, ἢ ἄρχων ἢ ἰδιώτης, κατὰ τόδε τὸ ψήφισμα, ὀφειλέτω ὁ μὴ ποήσας μυρίας δραχμὰς ἱερὰς τῇ Ἀθηνᾷ, καὶ ὁ εὔθυνος καὶ οἱ πάρεδροι ἐπανάγκες αὐτῶν καταγιγνωσκόντων ἢ αὐτοὶ ὀφειλόντων is certainly a case of an extraordinary commission. Such private accusations are meant in Lys. 10, 16; 20, 10.

[2] See Lex. Cantabr. 664: ἀλογίου δίκη· ὅταν τινὲς λαβόντες χρήματα εἰς ἀναλώματα δημόσια μὴ ὦσιν τοὺς λόγους ἀπενηνοχότες (see Schoell. 27, 1) τοῖς δικασταῖς. Poll. 8, 54; Suid., Hesych., Et. M. sub verb. The giving of account within 30 days after leaving office: Harp. λογισταί. For the length of time during which liability to εὔθυνα continued see Poll. 8, 45.

[3] The first three Archons elected their πάρεδροι themselves: Arist. 56, 1; the εὔθυνοι, on the other hand, each received two who were elected by lot for them: Arist. 48, 4. The method of the nomination of the πάρεδροι for the Hellenotamiai, of whom each had one πάρεδρος (see C.I.A., I. 183. 188, 6 pryt.)

Subordinate Officials.

The magistrates had secretaries, under-secretaries, heralds and servants to assist them in their official duties. Whether the secretaries, who can be shown to have assisted certain **subordinate officials**, were chosen by them or were assigned to them, cannot be definitely asserted.[1] If the secretaryship in any particular department was specially arduous, an under-secretary was appointed to assist.[2] Both secretaries and under-secretaries were paid.[3] The profession of secretary was held in disrepute at Athens. It was natural that in course of time they should win for themselves more importance in their particular departments than the magistrates themselves, and on that account should have great influence with them. In order to limit this secretarial influence as much as possible, no one was allowed to serve as under-secretary to the same office twice.[4] The heralds were held in the same estimation; their services were required by the magistrates

is unknown. The Archons had also the right of dismissing their πάρεδροι at pleasure. See (Dem.) 59, 72. 83.

[1] I note a γραμματεὺς τῶν Ἑλληνοταμιῶν (C.I.A., I. 226 sqq., 260, 315), τῶν ταμιῶν (I. 117 sq., 179 sq., 318), by whose names the boards are distinguished and dated, a γραμματεὺς τῶν ἕνδεκα (Boeckh, Seeurk., p. 535. Poll. 8, 102: see Stojentin, de Jul. Poll. auctor., p. 30), τῶν ἐπιστατῶν (I. 284 sqq.), τῶν εἰσαγωγέων (I. 37), τῶν στρατηγῶν (II. 122), τῶν ἐπιμελητῶν τῶν νεωρίων (Seeurk., p. 165. C.I.A., II. 811 c, 165), τῶν σιτωνῶν (II. 335), τῶν ταμιῶν, τῶν σιτωνικῶν, τῶν ἐπὶ τῇ διοικήσει: Ἐφ. ἀρχ. 1887, p. 187; τῶν ἐμπορίου ἐπιμελητῶν (Dem.) 58, 8. C.I.A., II. 61. mentions besides the clerk of the council τοὺς ἄλλους γραμμα(τέ)as τοὺς ἐπὶ τοῖ(s δ)ημοσίοις γράμμασιν. The secretary of the 9 Archons was appointed by lot at the same time as the Archons themselves: Arist. 55, 1. In C.I.A., II. 861 a board of 5 officials have a γραμματεὺς κληρωτός, a γραμματεὺς αἱρετὸς and a ὑπογραμματεύς. A freedman as γραμματεύς: II. 772, 5.

[2] A ὑπογραμματεὺς τῶν θεσμοθετῶν is mentioned by Antiph., de Chor., 85, a ὑπογραμματεὺς τῶν ποριστῶν, τῶν πωλητῶν, τῶν πρακτόρων in Antiph., ibid., 49, and a ὑπογραμματεὺς τῶν ταμιῶν τῆς θεοῦ in C.I.A., II. 730. See also C.I.A., II. 1177, 1198.

[3] The epistatai of the public works compute as μισθὸς ὑπογραμματεῖ Πυργίωνι Ὀτ(ρ)ινεῖ ΔΔΔ : C.I.A., I. 324.

[4] Compare the expressions of Demosthenes about Æschines, as ὄλεθρο γραμματεύς (18, 127), πανοῦργος οὗτος καὶ θεοῖς ἐχθρὸς καὶ γραμματεύς (19, 95). According to Aristophanes, Frogs, 1183, sqq., Euripides causes every evil in Athens by his tragedies: κᾆτ' ἐκ τούτων ἡμῶν ὑπογραμματέων ἀνεμεστώθη. Dio Chrysost., 7, 258 R, says of the most ancient times of Athens: οὔκουν οὐδὲ ἐκείνοις ἀσύμφορος ἡ τοιαύτη δίαιτα ἐγένετο οὐδὲ ἀγεννεῖς ἤνεγκε φύσεις πολιτῶν, ἀλλὰ τῷ παντὶ βελτίους καὶ σωφρονεστέρους τῶν ἐν ἄστει τρεφομένων ὕστερον ἐκκλησιαστῶν καὶ δικαστῶν καὶ γραμματέων, ἀστῶν ἅμα καὶ βαναύσων. Dem. 19, 200 refers to the bribing of the secretaries. For the limitation of the service of the ὑπογραμματεῖς see Lys. 30, 29.

for public announcements.[1] Both slaves and freemen were employed as subordinate attendants on the officials.[2]

Respect paid to magistrates. The democratic sentiment of the Athenians precluded any special deference to the magistrates, although they were protected by law against personal injury or slander.[3]

C. The Individual Offices.

στρατηγοί. At the head of the Athenian officials, both in powers and political importance, were the war officials, and among these again the στρατηγοί, who had their official quarters in the στρατηγεῖον situated in the market-place.[4]

The ten Athenian Strategoi were without doubt elected one from each tribe, so long as each of them commanded his own tribe; at a later date, when the taxiarchs had become the commanding officers of the separate tribes, the strategoi were all elected from the entire burgess body without regard to the tribes.[5]

---

[1] For the guild of the heralds, who had to pass a dokimasia for their εὐφωνία (Dem. 19, 338), see (Xen.) *de rep. Ath.*, 1, 18. Archipp. *ap.* Ath., 7. 322 A. Antiphan. *ap.* Stob. Flor., 74, 9. Poll. 6, 128 counts the heralds among the βίοι, ἐφ' οἷς ἄν τις ὀνειδισθείη. See Eurip., *Troad.* 424 sqq. The herald of the poletai received the comic (see Poll. 7, 8) nickname πρατίας. See Hesych., Phot., *s. v.* Α κῆρυξ κληρωτός: C.I.A., II. 1198. Dedicatory inscription of a herald: C.I.A., IV. 3, 482. Ὁ κῆρυξ τοῦ δήμου of the year 332/1. Ἐφ. ἀρχ., 1891, p. 82.

[2] Æschines had been a ὑπηρέτης: Dem. 18, 261. Such a ὑπηρέτης I take the δοκιμαστής, who was under the supervisors of the docks, to have been; he acted as judge in purely technical matters. See *Seeurk.* II. 56, p. 288= C.I.A., II. 791, 1. 56. *Mitth. d. dsch. arch. Inst. in Ath.*, 5, p. 44. App. IV. c. 77 sqq.=C.I.A., II. 794 c. 77 sqq. For the services of such ὑπηρέται see Dem., 25, 23; 50, 31. 46. 51. (Dem.) 47, 35. Poll. 8, 131 calls the Σκύθαι ὑπηρέται. Generally the slaves employed by the State are called δημόσιοι. See Lex. Seguer. 234, 15. For these δημόσιοι see C.I.A., II. 61. *Seeurk.*, XVI. b, 135, p. 536=C.I.A., II. 811 c, 128: (ὁ) δημόσιος ὁ ἐν (τοῖς νεωρίοις).

[3] Xen., *Mem.*, 3, 5, 16: πότε δὲ οὕτω πείσονται τοῖς ἄρχουσιν, οἳ καὶ ἀγάλλονται ἐπὶ τῷ καταφρονεῖν τῶν ἀρχόντων; Atimia was the penalty for slander or personal injury of an official: Dem. 21, 32/3; according to Lys. 9, 6. 9. 10, perhaps only if perpetrated during the execution of his official duties.

[4] For the details I refer to my *Beitr.*, etc., 2 sqq.; Hauvette-Besnault, *Les stratèges Athéniens.*, Paris, Thorin, 1885; Heinr. Swoboda in the *N. Rh. Mus.*, 1890, 288 sqq. Cf. *e.g.* Lys. 26, 20: τοιγάρτοι ἀντὶ τούτων αὐτοὺς ὁ δῆμος ταῖς μεγίσταις τιμαῖς τετίμηκεν ἱππαρχεῖν καὶ στρατηγεῖν καὶ πρεσβεύειν ὑπὲρ αὐτῶν αἱρούμενοι. For the στρατηγεῖον see Wachsmuth, *d. St. Athen.*, 2, 1, 356/7.

[5] Arist. 61, 1: χειροτονοῦσι δὲ καὶ τὰς πρὸς τὸν πόλεμον ἀρχὰς ἁπάσας, στρατηγοὺς δέκα, πρότερον μὲν ἀφ' ⟨ἑκάστης τῆς⟩ φυλῆς ἕνα, νῦν δ' ἐξ ἁπάντων. Poll. 8, 87 is a quotation from Aristotle. Cf. Æschin. *in Ctes.* 13. This

At first, apparently, the ten Strategoi acted together as a collegiate board, with general powers of control over military matters; in the second half of the fourth century we have evidence that special duties were assigned to individual strategoi. For instance, in the second half of the fourth century there was a στρατηγὸς ἐπὶ τοὺς ὁπλίτας, who had the chief command in foreign campaigns; another, ἐπὶ τὴν χώραν, who attended to the protection of the country and took the command against hostile incursions; a third, ἐπὶ τὴν Μουνιχίαν; and another ἐπὶ τὴν Ἀκτήν, whose duty it was to see to the defence of the ports; another again, ἐπὶ τὰς συμμορίας, who nominated the Trierarchs, received the challenges to antidosis which occurred in the Trierarchia, and prepared those cases for judicial decision. The five remaining Strategoi had no special powers, but were employed as necessity arose.[1]

election of the strategoi ἐξ ἁπάντων is authenticated by a series of cases in which in the same year two strategoi belong to the same tribe. These cases have now been most completely collected in Beloch, *d. att. Politik seit Perikles*, 276/7. The construction indeed which Beloch, 274 sqq., has put upon this fact has been proved by Aristot. to be false. When the change in the method of election mentioned by Arist. was introduced we cannot say with precision, certainly before 441. Cf. the list of the strategoi of the year 441/440 in the Atthis of Androtion in Müller, *fr. h. gr.*, 4, p. 645, and to these 8 names we must add Γλαυκέτης Ἀξηνιεὺς and Κλειτοφῶν Θοραιεύς. See von Wilamowitz, *de Rhesi scholiis*, p. 13. Theories in Fischer, *quaest. de praetorib. att. saec. V. et IV. a. Chr. n. specimen*, 13 sqq., D. i. Königsberg, 1881. Belser, in the *Korresp.-Bl. f. d. Gel. u. Realschulen*, 1886, Tübingen, p. 13 sqq. The election by tribes which Droysen in *Herm.* 9, 1 sqq. inferred from Xen., *Mem.*, 3, 4, 1, can hardly be maintained in face of Aristot. Formerly I agreed with him in my *Beitr.*, 16 sqq.; and so did Paulus in the *Progr. v. Maulbronn*, 1883, 34 sq.; Belser, *ibid.*, and Hauvette-Besnault, 19 sqq. An adequate explanation of the passage in Xenophon has not yet been found.

[1] Arist. 61, 1: καὶ τούτους διατάττουσι τῇ χειροτονίᾳ, ἕνα μὲν ἐπὶ τοὺς ὁπλίτας, ὃς ἡγεῖται τῶν ὁπλιτῶν, ἂν ἐξίωσι, ἕνα δ' ἐπὶ τὴν χώραν, ὃς φυλάττει, κἂν πόλεμος ἐν τῇ χώρᾳ γίγνηται, πολεμεῖ οὗτος· δύο δ' ἐπὶ τὸν Πειραιέα, τὸν μὲν εἰς τὴν Μουνιχίαν, τὸν δὲ εἰς τὴν Ἀκτήν, οἳ τῆς. φ[υ]λακῆς ἐπιμελοῦνται [καὶ] τῶν ἐν Πειραιεῖ· ἕνα δ' ἐπὶ τὰς συμμορίας, ὃς τούς τε τριηράρχους καταλέγει καὶ τὰς ἀντιδόσεις αὐτοῖς ποιεῖ καὶ τὰς διαδικασίας αὐτοῖς εἰσάγει· τοὺς δὲ ἄλλους πρὸς τὰ παρόντα πράγματα ἐκπέμπουσιν. Ὁ στρατηγὸς ὁ ἐπὶ τοὺς ὁπλίτας has been supplied on an inscription for the year 293/2 with great probability: *C.I.A.*, II. 302; soon after 272: II. 331; often in later inscriptions. In II. 331 we read, χειροτονηθεὶς δὲ ὑπὸ τοῦ δήμου ἐπὶ τὰ ὅπλα στρατηγὸς τὸν ἐνιαυτὸν τὸν ἐπὶ Κίμωνος ἄρχοντος διετέλεσεν ἀγωνιζόμενος ὑπὲρ τῆς κοινῆς σωτηρίας καὶ περιστάντων τῇ πόλει καιρῶν δυσκόλων διεφύλαξεν τὴν εἰρήνην τῇ χώρᾳ ἀποφαινόμενος αἰεὶ τὰ κράτιστα καὶ τὸν σῖτον ἐκ τῆς χώρας καὶ τοὺς ἄλλους καρποὺς αἴτιος ἐγένετο εἰσκομισθῆναι συμβουλεύσας τῷ δήμῳ συντελέσαι . . . καὶ τὴν πόλιν ἐλευθέραν καὶ δημοκρατου-

After Aristotle's time we meet with further special powers of single Strategoi. At the end of the fourth and at the beginning of the third century we have mention in inscriptions of a στρατηγὸς ἐπὶ τὸ ναυτικόν, another ἐπὶ τὴν χώραν τὴν ἐπ' Ἐλευσῖνος, a third ἐπὶ τὴν χώραν τὴν παραλίαν, another ἐπὶ τὴν παρασκευήν, and yet another ἐπὶ τοὺς ξένους.[1]

There was not as a rule a Strategos-in-chief as permanent head of the board of Strategoi, at least in the fifth and fourth centuries. But in time of need the chief place in the college was probably given temporarily to one of the Strategoi by a decree of the people, though ordinarily all the members of the college had

μένην αὐτόνομον παρέδωκεν καὶ τοὺς νόμους κυρίους τοῖς μεθ' ἑαυτόν. Literary evidence for the existence of this special power I can find neither in Lys. 32, 5, nor in Xen., *Hell.*, 4, 15, 13. But this Strategos seems to be meant in Dem. 4, 26. Ὁ στρατηγὸς ὁ ἐπὶ τὴν φυλακὴν τῆς χώρας in the year 352 : Bull. 13, 434 (see 443), l. 18 sqq.; ὁ στρατηγὸς ὁ ἐπὶ τὴν χώραν not long after 296/5: C.I.A., II. 331, cf. Plut., *Phok.*, 32. Ὁ στρατηγὸς ὁ ἐπὶ τὴν Μουνιχίαν καὶ τὰ νεώρια in the year 325/4: Dein. *in Philokl.* 1. See Schaefer, *Dem. u. s. Zeit*, 3¹, 279. I think that this Strategos is also meant in Boeckh, *Seeurkunden*, XVI. *b*, 196, p. 536=C.I.A., II. 811 *b*, 188. C.I.A., II. 1206 about 100 B.C. mentions one στρατηγήσας ἐπὶ τὸν Πειρα(ιᾶ). Ὁ ἐπὶ τὴν Ἀκτὴν probably had charge of the large harbours of the Piræus and Zea. See Wachsmuth in the *N. Rh. Mus.*, 46, 2, 3. Ὁ στρατηγὸς ὁ ἐπὶ τὰς συμμορίας in the year 325/4 : *Seeurk.*, XIV. 214, p. 465=C.I.A., II. 809, col. a. 210, certainly not appointed before the institution of the trierarchic symmories (357/6). In a statement of accounts of the dockyard supervisors probably in the year 334/3, οἱ στρατηγοί still superintend the arrangements for the Symmoriai: Köhler in the *Mitth. d. dtsch. Inst. in. Ath.*, 4, 79, sq. App. A. 72 sq.=C.I.A., II. 804, col. a. 63 sqq.

[1] Ὁ στρατηγὸς ὁ ἐπὶ τὸ ναυτικὸν of the year 315/4 in the C.I.A., II. 331, seems to me to have a new special function, which occurs again about 100 : C.I.A., II. 985. In the time of Demetrios of Phaleron an Aristophanes is honoured χειροτονηθεὶς στρατηγὸς ἐπ' Ἐλευσῖνος τὸ δεύτερον : 'Εφ. ἀρχ., 1884, pp. 137/8, l. 14, cf. also 19. He had command over the troops in Eleusis, Panakton, Phyle: *ibid.*, pp. 135/6, l. 20 sq. More correctly he is called χειροτονηθεὶς στρατηγὸς ἐπὶ τὴν χώραν τὴν ἐπ' Ἐλευσῖνος : 'Εφ. ἀρχ., 1887, p. 3 sqq., 1890, 85/6. Ὁ στρατηγὸς ὁ ἐπὶ τὴν χώραν τὴν παραλίαν after 287/6. C.I.A., II. 1194, 1195. Ὁ στρατηγὸς ὁ ἐπὶ τὴν παρασκευήν in the year 296/5. C.I.A., II. 331. Mentioned on committee for superintending the melting of the images offered to the ἥρως ἰατρός: II. 403, 404. See also II. 836, 839, 858. Ἀρχ. δελτ. 1891, p. 127. In II. 985 he is called στρατηγὸς ἐπὶ τὴν παρασκευὴν τὴν ἐν ἄστει. Ὁ στρατηγὸς ὁ ἐπὶ τοὺς ξένους soon after 296/5: II. 331. Of this one it is said : τὴν πᾶσαν ἐποιήσατο σπουδήν, ὅπως ἂν οἱ στρατιῶται ὡς ἄριστα κατ(ε)σκευασμένοι παρέχωνται τὰς χρείας τῷ δήμῳ. If the restoration στρατ-(ηγῶν τῶν ἐπὶ τὴν τοῦ πολέμου παρασκ)ευὴν κεχει(ροτονημένων) in the C.I.A., II. 733 is right, this seems to have been a temporary commission for the Strategoi in question.

equal rights and the presidency seems to have been taken in turn by them.[1] Usually, the Ecclesia appointed from among the Strategoi those who were to undertake the different military enterprises; sometimes all the Strategoi taking part in the same expedition had equal right to take the supreme command, sometimes one of them was entrusted with it.[2] At times the Ecclesia waived some of its proper rights in favour of one or several Strategoi, to facilitate the conduct of military enterprises.[3]

The high political position of the Strategoi is shown by the fact that they had the right of submitting motions to the Council, and of calling together the Ecclesia, which they were probably in the

[1] Beloch tries to prove the existence of a permanent chief Strategos at Athens, *ibid.*, 274 sqq. I cannot agree with him. Paulus, 22 sqq., Hauvette-Besnault, 50 sqq., Belser, 22. sqq., are of my opinion. Although Herodotus may not have represented correctly the arrangements at the battle of Marathon, yet, if in his day a permanent chief Strategos had existed at Athens, he would not have written, 6, 110: μετὰ δὲ οἱ στρατηγοί, τῶν ἡ γνώμη ἔφερε συμβάλλειν, ὡς ἑκάστου αὐτῶν ἐγίνετο πρυτανηίη τῆς ἡμέρας, Μιλτιάδῃ παρεδίδοσαν, ὁ δὲ δεκόμενος οὔτι κω συμβολὴν ἐποιέετο, πρίν γε δὴ αὐτοῦ πρυτανηίη ἐγένετο. This changing presidency is noticed also by Diod. 13, 97: τῶν δ' Ἀθηναίων ὁ στρατηγὸς Θράσυλλος, ὃς ἦν ἐπὶ τῆς ἡγεμονίας ἐκείνην τὴν ἡμέραν, εἶδε κατὰ τὴν νύκτα τοιαύτην ὄψιν. Cf. also 13, 106. Pericles took up a leading position within the college of the Strategoi in the Samian war and at the beginning of the Peloponnesian war, expressed in Thuc. 1, 116, and 2, 13 by στρατηγὸς δέκατος αὐτός. See my *Beitr.* 41 sqq. Hauvette-Besnault, 76 sqq. Fellner *z. Gesch. d. att. Finanzverw.*, 91 sqq., does not consider my explanation of these words right, nor does Paulus, 31 sq.; but Beloch, 285 sq., agrees with me. Cf. Thuc. 2, 65, Diod. 12, 42 and the similar expression with reference to Alcibiades in Thuc. 8, 82. Alcibiades in 408 στρατηγὸς αὐτοκράτωρ: Plut., *Alcib.*, 33. Diod. 13, 69. Xen., *Hell.*, 1, 4, 10. 20.

[2] Appointment of a Strategos from the college for a particular mission: C.I.A., II. 62. In Thuc. 4, 28 Nicias in the Ecclesia ἐξίστατο τῆς ἐπὶ Πύλῳ ἀρχῆς in favour of Cleon, though he had himself been commissioned with it before. This he could do, as the people agreed to it. See Hauvette-Besnault, 80/1. Nicias, Alcibiades, and Lamachos had equal power in the command of the Sicilian expedition: Thuc. 6, 8. A subordination of the Strategoi taking part in an expedition to one of themselves as chief Strategos is to be inferred where Thucydides only gives the name of one Strategos with the addition of an ordinal number and the pronoun αὐτός. Cf. for instance, Thuc. 1, 61: καὶ Καλλίαν τοῦ Καλλιάδου πέμπτον αὐτὸν στρατηγόν, with 1, 62: Καλλίας ὁ τῶν Ἀθηναίων στρατηγὸς καὶ οἱ ξυνάρχοντες, whereas Diod. 12, 37 speaks only of one strategos Callias. Cf. Thuc. 3, 3 with Diod. 12, 55. Further examples in Thuc, 2, 79; 3, 19; 4, 42.

[3] Thus, for instance, in the Sicilian Expedition. Thuc. 6, 8. 26; Diod. 13, 2.

habit of doing by means of the Prytanes.¹ The Strategoi had the chief command of all the troops of the Athenian State, and the jurisdiction over military offences. I shall speak of these in the chapter on military affairs. But it was the duty of the Strategoi not only to conduct war, but also to find funds for the purpose. Accordingly the trierarchs were nominated every year by the Strategoi; any refusals of the Trierarchia were brought by the Strategoi before the court of the Heliaia for decision.² It is also clear that the Strategoi took part in the assessment for the εἰσφορά, which may be called a special war-tax, and for the προεισφορά also; they also acted as εἰσαγωγεῖς for the antidosis of the Trierarchia.³ To the official duties of the Strategoi belonged also the defence of Athens against foreign and domestic foes, in which I include the preservation of the ports, city walls and fortresses,⁴ and in a

---

[1] The right of the Strategoi of submitting motions to the Council, appears from the Probouleuma in the *Sitzungsber. d. Berl. Ak.* 1888, p. 244, no. 20: ἔδοξεν τῇ βουλῇ καὶ τῷ δήμῳ· Ἀκαμαντὶς ἐπρυτάνευε· Ἀρχικλῆς ἐγραμμάτευε· γνώμη στρατηγῶν κ. τ. ά. Cf. Swoboda in the *N. Rh. Mus.* 1890, 299 sqq. They introduce foreigners to the Council: Ἀρχ. δελτ. 1891, p. 46. For the right of calling together the Ecclesia, see the record of the armistice of Laches in Thuc. 4, 118: ἐκκλησίαν δὲ ποιήσαντας τοὺς στρατηγοὺς καὶ τοὺς πρυτάνεις πρῶτον περὶ τῆς εἰρήνης βουλεύσασθαι Ἀθηναίους, and C.I.A., I. 40, where it is said of the Prytanes: συν(ε)χῶς δὲ ποιεῖν τ(ὰς ἐκκλησία)ς ἕως ἂν δι(απρ)αχθῇ, ἄλλο δὲ προχρηματ(ίσαι τούτῳ)ν μηδέν, ἐαμμήτι οἱ στρατηγοὶ δέωντα(ι). Cf. also Swoboda, 305 sq.

[2] Evidence at the time of the Symmoriai, Dem. 39, 8: τίνα δ' οἱ στρατηγοὶ τρόπον ἐγγράψουσιν, ἂν εἰς συμμορίαν ἐγγράφωσιν ἢ ἂν τριήραρχον καθιστῶσιν. 35, 48: οὐκοῦν ὑπόλοιπόν ἐστιν οἱ στρατηγοί. ἀλλὰ τοὺς τριηράρχους καθιστᾶσιν. Appendix A. 72 ff., *Mitth. d. dtsch. arch. Inst. in Ath.*, 4, p. 80; cf. Ælian., *Var. Hist.*, 2, 10. At the end of the fourth century these duties were undertaken by the στρατηγὸς ἐπὶ τὰς συμμορίας, of whom it is said in Arist. 61, 1: ὃς τούς τε τριηράρχους καταλέγει καὶ τὰς ἀντιδόσεις αὐτοῖς ποιεῖ καὶ τὰς διαδικασίας αὐτοῖς εἰσάγει. Suid. ἡγεμονία δικαστηρίου—τῷ στρατηγῷ περὶ τριηραρχίας καὶ ἀντιδόσεως (sc. ἐφεῖτο δίκας εἰσάγειν). In the same way the Strategoi nominated even in the fifth century the annual 400 Trierarchs: (Xen.) *de rep. Ath.*, 3, 4; Thuc. 2, 24. Cf. also the decree of the people in the year 405 in the Ἀρχ. δελτίον 1889, pp. 25/6.

[3] See the passages quoted in the foregoing notes. For the duties of the Strategoi in the antidosis see (Dem.) 42, 5. Meier u. Schömann *att. Proc.*² 736/7.

[4] Ἐπιδόσεις εἰς τὴν σωτηρίαν τῆς πόλεως καὶ τὴν φυλακὴν τῆς χώρας to be announced and written out before the Strategoi: C.I.A., II. 334. For the φυλακὴ τῆς χώρας, probably effected by bodies of armed patrols in the interior of the country and by vessels of war lying off the coast, see Thuc. 2. 24; Xen., *Mem.*, 3, 6, 10/11. Boeckh, *Seeurk.*, p. 467. This φυλακὴ also extended to Euboea. C.I.A., IV. 27a in 445 B.C.: περὶ δὲ φυλακῆς Εὐβοίας τοὺς στρατηγοὺς ἐπιμελεῖσθαι ὡς ἂν δύνωνται ἄριστα, ὅπως ἂν ἔχῃ ὡς βέλτιστα Ἀθηναίοις.

still wider sense the security of the corn supply necessary for Athens,[1] the prevention and punishment of treason, and the protection of the democratic constitution.[2]

The Strategoi had charge of foreign affairs, and were the representatives of the State in relation to foreign countries. As such they made treaties with foreign states or recommended their acceptance to the Council, swore to the treaties in combination with various other corporate bodies, looked after the States and persons taken under Athenian protection by decree of the people, and foreigners who received special honorary rights at Athens.[3] The Strategoi exercised religious functions[4] at certain sacrifices The special powers of the later στρατηγὸς ἐπὶ τὴν χώραν and ἐπὶ τὴν χώραν τὴν παραλίαν probably included this φυλακή.

[1] For this παραπομπὴ τοῦ σίτου by the Strategoi see Dem. 50, 17. 20. 58. Boeckh, Seeurk., XIII. a. 39, p. 423=C.I.A., II. 808a. 37 sqq.: (τετρήρεις τ)άσδε ἔδομεν (κατὰ ψήφισ)μα δήμου, ὃ Πο(λύευκτος Κ)υδαντίδης εἶπε, (μετὰ στρατ)ηγοῦ Θρασυβού(λου Κολλυτέω)ς ἐπὶ τὴν (παραπομπὴ)ν τ(οῦ) σίτου.

[2] Cf. the proceedings of the Strategoi against the traitors Antiphon and his accomplices in Pseudoplut., Vit. Antiph., 28. In C.I.A., II. 331 a Strategos for the hoplites is commended, because he had concerned himself ὑπὲρ τῆς κοινῆς σωτηρίας—καὶ τὴν πόλιν ἐλευθέραν καὶ δημοκρατουμένην αὐτόνομον παρέδωκεν καὶ τοὺς νόμους κυρίους τοῖς μεθ' ἑαυτόν.

[3] Report of the Strategoi upon foreign affairs, Isocr. 7, 81: καὶ περὶ μὲν τοῦ μίσους τῶν Ἑλλήνων αὐτῶν ἀκηκόατε τῶν στρατηγῶν. A proxenia-decree is agreed upon as result of the γνώμη στρατηγῶν: Bull. 12, 143=Sitzungsber. d. Berl. Ak., 1888, p. 244, 20. Conclusion and recommendation of treaties, C.I.A., IV. 61a, II. 609. Mitth. d. arch. Inst. in Ath., 2, 142. They swear to keep them: Mitth., 2, 144, in conjunction with the Trierarchs and hoplites: IV. 61a, with the Council: IV. 71, II. 64 and Mitth., 2, 211, with the Hipparchs: Bull. 12, 139, with the Taxiarchs: II. 12, Mitth., 2, 139, with the Hipparchs, Phylarchs, and Taxiarchs according to the probable restoration: II. 90, 112, with the Council, Hipparchs and Hippeis. Mitth., 2, 201, with Council and the Hippeis: Mitth., 2, 212. Protection given to Euagoras: I. 64; to Neapolis in Thrace: IV. 51; Arybbas of Epirus: II. 115, the Pelagonian Menelaos: II. 55. They see to the ratification of treaties by oath of the Athenians: ὅπως δ' ἂν (δ)μόσωσιν ἅπαντες, ἐπιμελόσθων οἱ στρατηγοί.—ὅπως δ' ἂν τάχιστα γίγνηται (the taking of the oath), ἐπιμελόσθων οἱ στρατηγοί: IV. 27a and receive the oath from the foreign States: στρατηγοὶ ἐχ(σ)ορκ: I. 84, see Bull. 12, 139. Care for the πρόξενοι and εὐεργέται: II. 40. 69. 121. 124. 209. 225.

[4] For the religious functions of the Strategoi see Hauvette-Besnault, 148 sqq. C.I.A., IV. 27a says: ὅπως ἂν τάχιστα τυθῇ (i.e. τὰ ἱερὰ τὰ ἐκ τῶν χρησμῶν ὑπὲρ Εὐβοίας), οἱ στρατηγοὶ ἐπιμελόσθων καὶ τὸ ἀργύριον ἐς ταῦτα παρεχόντων. The treasurers of the goddess and οἱ ᾑρημένοι ἐπὶ τὰς νίκας καὶ τὰ πομπεῖα in the years 334 sqq. received from the Strategoi hide-money (δερματικόν) ἐκ τῆς θυσίας τῷ Ἑρμῇ τῷ Ἡγεμονίῳ, ἐκ τῆς θυσίας τῇ Εἰρήνῃ, ἐκ τῆς θυσίας τῷ Ἄμμωνι, ἐγ Διονυσίων τῶν ἐν ἄστει, ἐκ τῆς θυσίας τῇ Δημοκρατίᾳ, ἐγ Διονυσίων τῶν ἐν Πειραιεῖ, ἐκ τῆς θυσίας τῇ Ἀγαθῇ Τύχῃ. But even in these accounts the hide-money

and at Pompai. In conclusion I will remark that the Strategoi bore the State seal.¹

ταξίαρχοι. Subordinate to the Strategoi were the Taxiarchs, the commanders of the Athenian hoplites, whose office was probably instituted after the Strategoi had become the highest executive officials of the State. There were in Athens ten Taxiarchs, who were elected one from each tribe, and each commanded the hoplites of his own tribe.² The Taxiarchs formed the council of war, together with the Strategoi, and supported the latter in their administrative business.³

λοχαγοί. Next in position to the Taxiarchs in command of the army of hoplites were the λοχαγοί, of whom as little definite can be said as of other subordinate officers.⁴ They were nominated by the Taxiarchs.⁵

After the Strategia, the Hipparchia was the most distinguished military office in the State.⁶ There were two ἵππαρχοι. ἵππαρχοι, who were chosen from among all the Athenians and each commanded the cavalry of five tribes.⁷ At the head of

---

from the before-mentioned sacrifices is not received regularly from the Strategoi, but sometimes from other persons. See C.I.A., II. 741; Boeckh, *St. d. Ath.*, 2, 120 sqq.=Bk. 3, ch. 7. For the Strategoi at the Panathenaia see Dem. 4, 26; Thuc. 6, 56; Mommsen, *Heort.*, 178.

¹ C.I.A., II. 443: (τοὺς δὲ) στρατηγοὺς διαπέμ(ψαι ἀντίγραφον— —σφραγισαμένους τῇ δημοσί)α(ι σ)φραγῖδι.

² Von Wilamowitz-Möllendorff, in *phil. Untersuch.*, Heft. 1, p. 57 sqq., seems to prove that the Taxiarchs were not instituted until between 490 and 480. Belser, 13 sqq., places the introduction of the Taxiarchs soon after 479, when the Polemarch lost the conduct of military affairs, and the Strategoi were no longer leaders of the tribes. For the Taxiarchs cf. Arist. 61, 3: χειροτονοῦσι δὲ καὶ ταξιάρχους δέκα, ἕνα τῆς φυλῆς ἑκάστης· οὗτος δ' ἡγεῖται τῶν φυλετῶν καὶ λοχαγοὺς καθίστησιν. See also Dem. 4, 26; Poll. 8, 87; Lex Seguer. 306, 12 sqq. The Taxiarch the commander of one tribe: Dem. 39, 17; Æschin., *de Fals. Leg.*, 169. The Taxiarch from the tribe which he commanded: Thuc. 8, 92; C.I.A., II. 444. 446. 1214. In Bull. 8, 327, in a decree of honour of the third century: οἱ ταξίαρχοι οἱ ἐπὶ Φιλοκράτου ἄρχοντ(ος) (ἀ)ρ(ξαντες) appear as a college.

³ See Thuc. 7, 60; and 4, 4. Thus the Taxiarch could represent the Strategos in military cases: Dem. 39, 17.

⁴ Mention of Lochagoi in Isocr. 15, 117; Is. 9, 14.

⁵ See Arist. 61, 3.

⁶ See Lys. 26, 20; Xen., *Symp.*, 1, 4; Hipparch. 1, 23. Cf. Martin, *les cavaliers Athéniens*, p. 874 sqq.; Paris, 1886.

⁷ Arist. 61, 4: χειροτονοῦσι δὲ καὶ ἱππάρχους δύο ἐξ ἁπάντων· οὗτοι δ' ἡγοῦνται τῶν ἱππέων, διελόμ[ενοι] τὰς φυλὰς ε' ἑκάτερος· κύριοι δὲ τῶν αὐτῶν εἰσιν ὧνπερ οἱ στρατηγοὶ κατὰ τῶν ὁπλι[τῶν]. Part of this information from Arist. in Poll.

each tribe was a φύλαρχος, who in every instance belonged to the tribe which he commanded.¹ φύλαρχοι.

The next cavalry officers were the δεκάδαρχοι, who were appointed by the Hipparchs.² δεκάδαρχοι.

Of the finance ministers, the κωλακρέται, from the antiquity of their office, are entitled to be mentioned first. Although from the time of Cleisthenes their place had been taken by the ἀποδέκται, as far as their chief duties were concerned, κωλακρέται. yet even in the fifth and fourth century they still managed the public dinners in the Prytaneion, and the payment of the jurymen. We possess no evidence of their number.³ The office of the ἀποδέκται was instituted by Cleisthenes, and existed to our knowledge to the end of the fourth century.⁴ The ἀποδέκται, ten in number, appointed by lot, one for each tribe, were the general treasurers of the State. Tribute, war-taxes, tolls and ἀποδέκται.

8, 87. 94; Harp., Suid., Phot. Ἵππαρχοι. See also Dem. 4, 26; Xen., *Hipparch.*, 3, 11; C.I.A., II. 445. In a dedicatory inscription of the ἱππεῖς, soon after 450, three ἵππαρχοι are mentioned: C.I.A., IV. 3. 418h=p. 184. Dedicatory inscription of a ἱππαρχήσας: C.I.A., IV. 3. 422¹⁷=p. 186.

¹ For the Phylarchoi cf. Martin, 894. Arist. 61, 5 says: χειροτονοῦσι δὲ καὶ φυλάρχους ⟨ί⟩, ἕνα τῆς φυλῆς, τὸν ἡγ[ησό]μενον ⟨τῶν ἱππέων⟩, ὥσπερ οἱ ταξίαρχοι τῶν ὁπλιτῶν. Arist. repeated in Poll. 8, 94; Harp., Suid., φύλαρχος, Lex. Seguer. 312, 32. Cf. also Dem. 4, 26, C.I.A., II. 968, 969, 1678. The Phylarchs belong to the tribes which they command, C.I.A., II. 444, 445.

² See Xen., *Hipparch.*, 2, 2.

³ For the change made by Cleisthenes see Androt. *ap.* Harp., ἀποδέκται. The fullest information about their functions in the Schol. to Aristoph., *Birds*, 1541, referring to the time after Cleisthenes: Ἀριστοφάνης ὁ γραμματικὸς τούτους ταμίας εἶναί φησι τοῦ δικαστικοῦ μισθοῦ (cf. Hesych., κωλακρέται; Arist., *Vesp.*, 695, 724; *Birds*, 1541) and further below: ταμίαι δὲ ἦσαν καὶ προεστῶτες τῆς δημοσίας σιτήσεως. See Boeckh, 1, 239/40=Bk. 2, ch. 6. They make payments to ἱεροποιοί: Ἐφ. ἀρχ., 1883, pp. 167/8, l. 14, pay the ἐπιστάται in Eleusis; C.I.A., IV. 3, 288a, give money for publishing the people's decrees; C.I.A., I. 20, 45; IV. 27; Ἀθήν. 8, 405 sqq.; *Ind. Schol. Goett.* 1880/1, p. 4; Ἐφ. ἀρχ., 1884, 161/2, l. 28. The ἐπιστάται of the public works receive (πα)ρὰ κωλακρετῶν: C.I.A., I. 285. See Fellner, *z. Gesch. d. att. Finanzverw.*, 24/5. There is no inscriptional evidence as yet for the κωλακρέται in the fourth century.

⁴ For the ἀποδέκται cf. Panske, *de magistratib. Att. qui saec. a Chr. n. IV. pecunias publicas curabant.*, p. 46 sqq. Leipzig 1890; Fellner, *z. Gesch. d. att. Finanzverw.*, 20 sqq.; Boeckh, 1, 214 sqq.=Bk. 2, ch. 4. See Harp. ἀποδέκται —ὅτι δὲ ἀντὶ τῶν κωλακρετῶν οἱ ἀποδέκται ὑπὸ Κλεισθένους ἀπεδείχθησαν, Ἀνδροτίων β'. Christ *de publicis populi Atheniensis rationib.*, p. 15 sqq., 26 sqq. Greifswald, 1879, thought that the ἀποδέκται dated only from the fourth century, but apart from the evidence of Androtion, this is contradicted by C.I.A., IV. 53a, where we meet with the ἀποδέκται for the year 418/7. They are

debts to the State were paid in to them, and for this purpose the δημόσιος of the Council handed over to them a list of debtors when the appointed times for payment came. After they had crossed out the payments that had been made and put a mark against the name of the debtors in arrear, they gave back the list to the δημόσιος. They could settle claims made by or against the customs-collectors when it was a matter of 10 drachmæ or less; in case of larger amounts the dispute was brought by them as a δίκη ἔμμηνος, to be decided by a court of the Heliaia.[1] After the apodectai had received the payments, and had on the same day distributed the money among the several boards of officials in the proportion directed by the laws, they submitted this allotment and their accounts for the approval of the Council on the following day. They do not seem to have had a special Exchequer.[2]

mentioned for the last time in inscriptions for the year 323/2: C.I.A., II. 811, Col. c. 78 sqq. Spangenberg, de Atheniens. publ. institutis œtate Macedonum commutatis, p. 43, supposes that they were abolished by Demetrios of Phaleron.

[1] See Arist. 48, 1: [εἰσὶ] δ' ἀποδέκται δέκα, κεκληρωμένοι κατὰ φυλάς· οὗτοι δὲ παραλαβόντες τὰ [γρα]μματεῖα (for these see chap. 47) ἀπαλείφουσι τὰ καταβαλλόμενα χρήματα, ἐναντίον τ[ῆς βουλῆς] ἐν τῷ βουλευτηρίῳ καὶ πάλιν ἀποδιδόασιν τὰ γραμματεῖα [τῷ δη]μοσίῳ· κἄν τις ἐλλίπῃ καταβολήν, ἐνταῦθ' ἐγγέγραπται, καὶ διπλ[οῦν] [ἀ]νάγκη τὸ [ἐλλ]ειφθὲν καταβάλλειν ἢ δεδέσθαι καὶ ταῦτα εἰσπρά[ττειν ἡ βο]υλὴ καὶ δῆσαι [κυρ]ί[α κατὰ τοὺς νόμους ἐστίν. Harp., ἀποδέκται. Suid., Et. M., 124, 41 sqq. Lex. Seguer. 198, 1 sqq., 427, 13 sqq., which all draw from Arist. Poll., 8, 97: ἀποδέκται δὲ ἦσαν δέκα, οἳ τοὺς φόρους καὶ τὰς εἰσφορὰς καὶ τὰ τέλη ὑπεδέχοντο καὶ τὰ περὶ τούτων ἀμφισβητούμενα ἐδίκαζον. εἰ δέ τι μεῖζον εἴη, εἰσῆγον εἰς δικαστήριον. Arist. 52, 3: οἱ δ' ἀποδέκται τοῖς τελώναις καὶ κατὰ τῶν τελωνῶν τὰ μὲν μέχρι δέκα δραχμῶν ὄντες κύρι[οι], τὰ δ' ἄλλ' εἰς τὸ δικαστήριον εἰσάγοντες ἔμμηνα. Arist. 47, 5: εἰσφέρεται (by the Poletai) μὲν οὖν εἰς τὴν βουλὴν τὰ γραμματε[ῖα τὰ] τὰς καταβολὰς ἀναγεγραμμένα, τηρεῖ δ' ὁ δημόσιος· ὅταν δ' ᾖ χρ[ημάτων κατα]βολή, παραδίδωσι τοῖς ἀποδέκταις αὐτὰ ταῦτα καθελ[ὼν] ἀπ[ὸ τῶν] ἐπιστυλίων, ὧν ἐν ταύτῃ τῇ ἡμέρᾳ δεῖ τὰ χρήματα καταβληθ[ῆναι καὶ ἀπ]αλειφθῆναι· τὰ δ' ἄλλα ἀπόκειται χωρίς, ἵνα μὴ προεξαλ[ειφθῇ]. The payments of the accounts made out by the ἐπιμεληταὶ τῶν νεωρίων were handed by them to the Apodectai (C.I.A., II. 807, Col. b, 15 sqq., 28 sqq., 33) or else the debtors paid direct to the Apodectai (II. 809 c, 70 sqq., 126 sqq., 200 sqq.). The collectors for the τέμενος of Codros, Neleus and Basile in 418 make payment to the Apodectai, who then give the money to the " treasurers of the other gods ": C.I.A., IV. 53a.

[2] Arist. 48, 2 goes on to say: τῇ μὲν οὖν προτεραίᾳ δέχονται τὰ χρ[ήματα] καὶ μερίζουσι ταῖς ἀρχαῖς, τῇ δ' ὑστεραίᾳ τόν τε μερισμὸν εἰσ[φέρο[υσι γράψαντες ἐν σανίδι καὶ καταλέγουσιν ἐν τῷ βουλευτηρίῳ καὶ προ[τιθ]έασιν ἐν τῇ βουλῇ, εἴ τίς τινα οἶδεν ἀδικοῦντα περὶ τὸν μερισ[μὸν ἢ ἄρ]χοντα ἢ ἰδιώτην, καὶ γνώμας ἐπιψηφίζουσιν, ἐάν τις τι δοκῇ ἀδ[ικεῖν]. Cf. Arist., Pol., 7 (6) 8 = p. 190, 12 sqq. Bekker: ἄλλη δ' ἀρχή, πρὸς ἣν αἱ πρόσοδοι τῶν κοινῶν ἀναφέρονται, παρ' ὧν φυλαττόντων

Finance Ministers.

The πωληταί, who already existed in Solon's time, became later ten in number, appointed by lot one from each tribe. They farmed out the tolls, mines and the other state undertakings, sold property confiscated by the State, and gave out contracts for the carrying out of state works.[1] They also sold the property of those who owed money to the State, and had not paid it within the specified time, and of those whose payments of the εἰσφορά were in arrear, as also the goods and persons of those condemned in a γραφὴ ξενίας, and of those metics who were condemned by a γραφὴ ἀπροστασίου, or had not paid their μετοίκιον.[2]

μερίζονται πρὸς ἑκάστην διοίκησιν· καλοῦσι δ' ἀποδέκτας τούτους καὶ ταμίας. Cf. C.I.A., II. 38: με(ρ)ίσαι δὲ (τ)ὸ ἀργύριον τὸ εἰρημένον (a reward) τοὺς ἀποδέκτας ἐκ τῶν καταβαλλομένων χρημά(τ)ων, ἐπειδὰν τὰ ἐκ τῶν νόμων μερ(ίσωσι). The Apodectai are commissioned to expend money for crowns: Dittenberger, *Syll.*, 101. C.I.A., II. 809a, 200 sqq., for the travelling expenses of the architheoroi to the Nemean games: II. 181, for a pension: II. 115, b, for the erection of a στήλη: 'Αρχ. δελτίον, 1889, p. 204, to the ἐπιστάται Ἐλευσινόθεν: C.I.A., 834b, and in complete form, Ἐφ. ἀρχ., 1883, p. 109 sqq., A. 39 sqq., B. 3, a. 39, β. 29, 34. The payments were reckoned by the Prytany: Panske, 57.

[1] Existence of the πωληταί already in Solon's time: Arist. 7, 3. He says 47, 2: ἐπειθ' οἱ πωληταὶ ι' μέν εἰσι, κληροῦται δ' εἷς ἐκ τῆς φ[υλῆς. μ]ισθοῦσι δὲ τὰ μισθώματα πάντα καὶ τὰ μέταλλα πωλοῦσι καὶ τὰ τέλη [μετὰ] τοῦ ταμίου τῶν στρατιωτικῶν καὶ τῶν ἐπὶ τὸ θεωρικὸν ᾑρημένων ἐναντ[ίον τῆς βουλῆς] κατακυροῦσιν, ὅτῳ ἂν ἡ βουλὴ χειροτονήσῃ, καὶ τὰ πραθέντα μέταλλα [τά τ'] ἐργάσιμα τὰ εἰς τρία ἔτη πεπραμένα καὶ τὰ συγκεχωρημένα, τὰ ε[ἰ]s [ἔτη] πέπραμένα. καὶ τὰς οὐσίας τῶν ἐξ Ἀρείου πάγου φευγόντων καὶ τῶν [ἄλλοθεν ἐ]ν[αντίον τῆς β]ουλῆς πωλοῦσιν, κατακυροῦσι δ' οἱ θ' ἄρχοντες. Harp. draws from Aristotle—πωληταὶ καὶ πωλητήριον. οἱ μὲν πωληταὶ ἀρχή τίς ἐστιν Ἀθήνησι, δέκα τὸν ἀριθμὸν ἄνδρες, εἷς ἐκ τῆς φυλῆς ἑκάστης· διοικοῦσι δὲ τὰ πιπρασκόμενα ὑπὸ τῆς πόλεως πάντα, τέλη καὶ μέταλλα καὶ μισθώσεις καὶ τὰ δημευόμενα.—πωλητήριον δὲ καλεῖται ὁ τόπος, ἔνθα συνεδρεύουσιν οἱ πωληταί. From the same source Suid. πωληταί. Phot. πωληταὶ καὶ πωλητήριον. Lex Seguer. 291, 17 sqq., where there is added: καὶ φροντίζουσιν, ὅπως ἡ τιμὴ τῶν πιπρασκομένων ἀποδοθῇ τῇ πόλει. For the situation of the πωλητήριον, see Wachsmuth, *d. St. Athen.*, 2, 1, 357/8. The Poletai give contracts for stelai for inscriptions: C.I.A., I. 61; II. 1, 2; IV. 27. Ἀθήν. 8, 405 sqq.= *Ind. schol. Goett.*, 1880/1, p. 4, the building of the Athenian walls between 334-326; II. 167, any public work: Ἀρχ. δελτίον, 1889, p. 255 = Bull. 14, 178, the enclosing of the ἱερὸν of Codros, Neleus and Basile: C.I.A., IV. 53a, μέταλλα: Ἐφ. ἀρχ., 1890, 222. C.I.A., I. 274-281 contains accounts of the Poletai for property confiscated and sold by the State. Cf. *Seeurk.*, XVI. b. 184 sqq., p. 542, with Boeckh's note= C.I.A., II. 811, Col. c. 195. C.I.A., II. 780-783. 782b contain descriptions made by the Poletai of the positions of mines; II. 777. 779. lists of property sold.

[2] Suid. πωλητής—καὶ πωληταί· οὗτοι τῶν ὀφειλόντων τῷ δημοσίῳ κατὰ προθεσμίαν καὶ μὴ ἀποδιδόντων ἐπίπρασκον τὰς οὐσίας. ὑπέκειντο δὲ τοῖς πωληταῖς καὶ ὅσοι τὸ διαγραφὲν ἀργύριον ἐν πολέμῳ μὴ εἰσέφερον· ἔτι καὶ οἱ ξενίας ἁλόντες καὶ ὁ μέτοικος

Of the goods thus sold and leased, the Poletai drew up lists, clearly stating the times of payment stipulated on by themselves and the purchasers or leaseholders, and these they handed in to the Council. There they were kept by the δημόσιος of the Council until the appointed day of payment, and then were given to the Apodectai for them to get in the money.[1]

To collect the fines imposed by the courts was the duty of the πράκτορες, who, for this purpose, received from the Hegemones of the courts a list of those who had been sentenced in court to pay fines, and the fines to which they had been sentenced.[2] That there were 10 Praktores, and that they were appointed by lot, one for each tribe, may be accepted as certain.[3]

πράκτορες.

The control of the money, which was paid in by the Apodectai to the Council-house, was the duty of the ἀντιγραφεὺς τῆς διοικήσεως, the controller of the treasury. He had also in every Prytany to draw up an account for the people, of the money which had been received during the preceding

ἀντιγαφεύς.

ὁ προστάτην οὐκ ἔχων καὶ ὁ ἀπροστασίου γραφείς. τούτων γὰρ τὰς οὐσίας πωλοῦντες παρακατέβαλλον εἰς τὸ δημόσιον. So Phot. πωληταί. Cf. Poll. 8, 99, where it says towards the end: ἀπήγοντο δὲ πρὸς τούτους καὶ οἱ μετοίκιον μὴ τιθέντες. See Harp. μετοίκιον. (Dem.) 25, 57. Boeckh, *Publ. Econ.*, 209/10=Bk. 2, ch. 3.

[1] Arist. 47, 2, says further: καὶ τὰ τέλη τὰ εἰς ἐνιαυ[τὸν] πεπραμένα, ἀναγράψαντες εἰς λελευκωμένα γραμματεῖα τόν τε πριάμενον καὶ [ὅσου] ἂν πρίηται, τῇ βουλῇ παραδιδόασιν. ἀναγράφουσιν δὲ χωρὶς μὲν οὓς δεῖ κατὰ ⟨τὴν⟩ πρυ[τ]ανείαν ἑκάστην καταβάλλειν, εἰς δέκα γραμματεῖα, χωρὶς δὲ οὓς τ[ρὶς τοῦ] ἐνιαυτοῦ, γραμματεῖον κατὰ τὴν καταβολὴν ἑκάστην ποιήσαντες, χωρὶς δὲ οὓς [ἐπὶ] τῆς ἐνάτης πρυτανείας. ἀναγράφουσι δὲ καὶ τὰ χωρία καὶ τὰς οἰκίας τ[ὰ ἀπο]γρ[αφ]έντα καὶ πραθέντα ἐν τῷ δικαστηρίῳ (cf. C.I.A., II. 884)· καὶ γὰρ ταῦθ' οὗτοι πωλ[οῦσιν. ἔστι] δὲ τῶν μὲν οἰκιῶν ἐν ε' ἔτεσιν ἀνάγκη τὴν τιμὴν ἀποδοῦναι, τῶν δὲ χωρίων ἐν δέκα· καταβάλλουσιν δὲ ταῦτα ἐπὶ τῆς ἐνάτης πρυτανείας. ε[ἰσφέ]ρει δὲ καὶ ὁ βασιλεὺς τὰς μισθώσεις τῶν τεμενῶν (C.I.A., IV. 58a), ἀναγράψας ἐν γραμματε[ίοις λελευ]κωμένοις. ἔστι δὲ καὶ τούτων ἡ μὲν μίσθωσις εἰς ἔτη δέκα, καταβάλλεται δ' ἐπὶ τῆς [θ'] πρυτανείας· διὸ καὶ πλεῖστα χρήματα ἐπὶ ταύτης συλλέγεται τῆς πρυτανείας. εἰσφέρεται μὲν οὖν εἰς τὴν βουλὴν τὰ γραμματ[εῖα τὰ] τὰς καταβολὰς ἀναγεγραμμένα, τηρεῖ δ' ὁ δημόσιος· ὅταν δ' ᾖ χρ[ημάτων κατα]βολή, παραδίδωσι τοῖς ἀποδέκταις αὐτὰ καθελ[ὼν] ἀπ[ὸ τῶν] ἐπιστυλίων, ὧν ἐν ταύτῃ τῇ ἡμέρᾳ δεῖ τὰ χρήματα καταβληθ[ῆναι καὶ ἀ]παλειφθῆναι· τὰ δ' ἄλλα ἀπόκειται χωρίς, ἵνα μὴ προεξαλ[ειφθῇ].

[2] See (Dem.) 58, 48: οὐδ' ἐστὶ δίκαιον τούτους ὑπολαμβάνειν ὀφείλειν, ὧν οὐδεὶς παρέδωκε τοῖς πράκτορσι τὰ ὀνόματα. See the law in Dem. 43, 71: ὅτου δ' ἂν καταγνωσθῇ, ἐγγραφόντων οἱ ἄρχοντες, πρὸς οὓς ἂν ᾖ ἡ δίκη, τοῖς πράκτορσιν, ὃ τῷ δημοσίῳ γίγνεται· ὃ δὲ τῇ θεῷ γίγνεται, τοῖς ταμίαις τῶν τῆς θεοῦ, and in Æschin. in Tim., 35. Andoc. 1, 77. C.I.A., I. 47, fr. e., 1. 3, 4 (τῷ δ)ημοσίῳ ὀφειλ—and οἱ πράκ(τορες) occur in close connexion with one another.

[3] See Lex. Seguer. 190, 26: κληρωταὶ ἀρχαὶ πρακτόρων, ἐκλογέων καὶ ἀντιγραφή.

Prytany. It is probable that the ἀντιγραφεὺς τῆς διοικήσεως was elected by the Council from among its members.[1]

Of the Finance-officials, who managed separate treasuries, mention must first be made of the ταμίαι τῶν ἱερῶν χρημάτων τῆς Ἀθηναίας, who can be proved to have existed as early as the time of Solon.[2] These treasurers of Athene were ten in number, and were appointed by lot, one from each tribe from among the Pentacosiomedimnoi, and

ταμίαι τῶν ἱερῶν χρημάτων τῆς Ἀθηναίας.

---

[1] In the lexicographers Harp., Suid., Lex. Seguer. 410, 3 sqq. the official business of the ἀντιγραφεὺς is thus described: ἀντιγραφεὺς ὁ καθιστάμενος ἐπὶ τῶν καταβαλλόντων τινὰ τῇ πόλει χρήματα, ὥστε ἀντιγράφεσθαι ταῦτα, wherewith cf. Æsch. in Ctes. 25 : πρῶτον μὲν τοίνυν, ὦ Ἀθηναῖοι, ἀντιγραφεὺς ἦν χειροτονητὸς τῇ πόλει, ὃς καθ' ἑκάστην πρυτανείαν ἀπελογίζετο τὰς προσόδους τῷ δήμῳ. The conclusion in Harp., διττοὶ δὲ ἦσαν ἀντιγραφεῖς, ὁ μὲν τῆς διοικήσεως, ὥς φησι Φιλόχορος, ὁ δὲ τῆς βουλῆς, ὡς Ἀριστοτέλης ἐν Ἀθηναίων πολιτείᾳ is a blunder, for Aristotle says nothing about the ἀντιγραφεὺς at all. The secretary of the Prytany had, according to Arist. 54, 3, the ἀντιγραφή in the Council (see also C.I.A., II. 61). Out of this the lexicographical tradition makes a special ἀντιγραφεὺς τῆς βουλῆς, and says of him what Arist. tells of the secretary of the Prytany; see Poll. 8. 98. Thus there was only one ἀντιγραφεὺς τῆς διοικήσεως, of whom we read in an inscription of the third century in the Ἀρχ. δελτίον, 1889, p. 58 (if it be correctly restored, but this is not certain): ἐπιμεληθῆναι δὲ (τῆς ποιήσεως τὸν ἀντιγραφέα τὸ)ν τῆς διοικήσε(ως). This ἀντιγραφεὺς was χειροτονητὸς (Æschin. in Ctes. 25) and that by the Council, if Riedenauer (Verh. d. philos. Ges. in Würzburg, 77 sq.), has, as I think likely, rightly identified him with the official of the Council whose duties are described (C.I.A., II. 114 B) in the following terms: ἐπεμελήθη τῆς διοικήσεως ὑπὸ τῆς βουλῆς ἐφ' ἣν ᾑρέθη καὶ τῆς ἄλλη(ς εὐκοσμί)ας τῆς βουλῆς μετὰ τῶν πρυτάνεων τῶν ἀεὶ πρυτανευόντων. See also II. 114 c. That the official here described cannot, according to the words of the inscription, have been a bouleutes, I cannot concede to C. Schaefer, de Scribis Senatus populique Athen., p. 38, 2, Greifswald, 1878. Mention is also made of an ἀντιγραφεὺς in a fragmentary list of Prytanes in the beginning of the fourth century: Mitth. d. Arch. Inst. in Ath., 4, 98=C.I.A., II. 865, and in a prescript, II. 408. Dem. 22, 38 mentions an ἀντιγραφεὺς, who with other members acts as leader of the Council. We also meet with one among the ἄσιτοι in the time of the empire. See Hille in the Leipz. Stud., 1, 232. Boeckh, St. de Ath., 1. 261 sqq.(= Publ. Econ., Bk. 2, ch. 8) supposes there were 2 ἀντιγραφεῖς, and with him Hille 232 sq. agrees. Schömann, griech. Alt., 1, 401, 5, leaves the question undecided. Droege, de Lycurgo Ath. pecuniar. publicar. administratore, p. 34, Bonn, 1880, supposes there was only one ἀντιγραφεύς.

[2] Their complete title was ταμίαι τῶν ἱερῶν χρημάτων τῆς Ἀθηναίας (C.I.A., I. 117 sqq. 188), shortened to ταμίαι τῆς θεοῦ (I. 324; II. 17. 61. 667. 730. 733), into ταμίαι (I. 273. 299), to ταμίαι τῶν τῆς θεοῦ (C.I.A. 809a, line 215. 612. 677. 698). Existent in Solon's time: Arist. 7, 3. 8, 1: σημεῖον δ', ὅτι κληρωτὰς ἐποίησεν ἐκ τῶν τιμημάτων, ὁ περὶ τῶν ταμιῶν νόμος, ᾧ χρώμενοι [διατελο]ῦσιν ἔτι καὶ νῦν· κελεύει γὰρ κληροῦν τοὺς ταμίας ἐκ πεντακοσιομεδίμνω[ν]. In one inscription, older than 550, οἱ ταμίαι dedicate to Athene τάδε χαλκία. Five names are

had a Prytanis for the year at their head.[1] They had the custody of the treasury of Athene,[2] and in general, the Acropolis and everything on it seems to have been under their immediate control.[3]

In the year 453/4 the treasures of the other gods also were placed in the Opisthodomos of the Parthenon, and for the control over these a new treasury-board was established, ταμίαι τῶν ἄλλων θεῶν. nominated in the same way and under the same conditions as the treasurers of Athene. They had the doors of the Opisthodomos under lock and seal, and were officially styled ταμίαι τῶν ἄλλων θεῶν.[4] Of the number of these treasurers we

mentioned: the end of the inscription is mutilated. C.I.A., IV. 3. 373²³⁶, p. 199.

[1] Their appointment by lot is testified by C.I.A., I. 32. From I. 299 we see there was one from each tribe: in that inscr. there is a list of the Tamiai in the official order of the tribes, and complete with the exception of the name of the tenth, which is lost. See also I. 140; II. 648. 652. 653. In Arist. 47. 1 we find: πρῶτον μὲν γὰρ οἱ ταμίαι τῆς Ἀθηνᾶς εἰσι μὲν δέκα, κ[ληροῦται] δ' εἶς ἐκ τῆς φυλῆς, ἐκ πεντακοσιομεδίμνων κατὰ τὸν Σόλωνος νόμ[ον (ἔτι γὰρ ὁ ν]όμος κύριός ἐστιν), ἄρχει δ' ὁ λαχών, κἂν πάνυ πένης ᾖ. Cf. Poll. 8, 97; Suid., ταμίαι, Art. 1.=Lex. Seguer. 306, 7 sqq. For the annual Prytanis see such phrases as ἐπὶ τῆς τοῦ δεῖνος ἀρχῆς καὶ ξυναρχόντων: C.I.A., I. 273, or τάδε οἱ ταμίαι τῶν ἱερῶν χρημάτων τῆς Ἀθηναίας, οἷς ὁ δεῖνα ἐγραμμάτευε, ὁ δεῖνα καὶ ξυνάρχοντες παρέδοσαν: C.I.A., I. 117 sqq., 188.

[2] See Arist. 47, 1: παραλαμβάνου[σι] δὲ τό τε ἄγαλμα τῆς Ἀθηνᾶς καὶ τὰς Νίκας καὶ τὸν ἄλλον κόσμον καὶ τὰ χρ[ήματ]α ἐναντίον τῆς βουλῆς. Following Arist., Harp., ταμίαι, Phot., Suid., Art. 2. In Suid. Art. 1. and in the Lex. Seguer. 306, 7 sqq., we read: οἱ τὰ ἐν τῷ ἱερῷ τῆς Ἀθηνᾶς ἐν ἀκροπόλει χρήματα ἱερά τε καὶ δημόσια καὶ αὐτὸ τὸ ἄγαλμα τῆς θεοῦ καὶ τὸν κόσμον φυλάττουσι. Cf. C.I.A., I. 32 = Dittenberger, Syll., 14 B, 23: τα(μιενέσθω τὰ μὲν τῆς Ἀθη)ναίας χρήματα (ἐν τῷ) ἐπὶ δεχσιὰ τοῦ ὀπισ(θοδόμου). See the list of treasures in Michaelis, der Parthenon, 288 sqq.; C.I.A., I. 117 sqq.; II. 642 sqq. For the fourth century see Fellner, z. Gesch. d. att. Finanzverwalt., p. 33 sq.

[3] They are therefore present at the valuation of the Chalcotheke: C.I.A., II. 61; they are authorised to destroy a Stele: Mitth. d. dtsch. Arch. Inst., 2, p. 291. They preserve on the Acropolis the oil obtained from the holy μορίαι, and at the Panathenaia they mete it out to the Athlothetai for the victors: Arist. 60, 3.

[4] The institution of treasurers of the other gods is spoken of C.I.A., I. 32 =Dittenberger, Syll., 14. Beloch, in the N. Rh. Mus., 43, 113 sq., 1888, places C.I.A., I. 32 between the end of 419/8 and the spring of 416, and takes the new arrangement decreed in the inscription to be the increasing of the treasurers of the other gods to ten, while they had before been only five. I cannot agree with him. See also Panske, de magistratib. ath. qui sœc. a. Chr. n. IV. pecunias publicas curabant, p. 13, 5, Leipz., 1890. Fragments of accounts rendered by these treasurers: C.I.A., I. 194-225; II. 672. 682c. Enumeration of the several gods: I. 273. Their official title, ταμίαι τῶν ἄλλων θεῶν : I. 194; II. 682c.

have no information, but as their constitution is based on that of the college of the treasurers of Athene, we may conclude that it was ten.[1] At the beginning of the fourth century (we have evidence from the time of the Archon Eucleides) the treasuries of Athene and of the other gods were united, and the control was vested in a college of ten members. Yet there is evidence again so soon as B.C. 385/4 of ταμίαι τῆς θεοῦ, by the side of whom there again existed, at least for a time, the ταμίαι τῶν ἄλλων θεῶν.[2]

The most important treasury office of the fifth century, next to the treasurers of Athene, was that of the Ἑλληνοταμίαι. Established as they were when the Athenian league was founded, they had their seat of office at first at Delos.[3] When the treasury of the league was transferred to Athens, they migrated thither, and in 454 probably became Athenian officials. There were at that time ten Ἑλληνοταμίαι,[4] of whom each had a

---

[1] See C.I.A., I. 32: ταμίας δὲ ἀποκυαμεύει(ν) (το)ύτων τῶν χρημάτων, ὅταμπερ τὰς ἄλλας ἀρχάς, καθάπερ τοὺς τῶν ἱ(ερῶ)ν τῶν τῆς Ἀθηναίας. Kirchhoff, who, in the *Abh. d. Berl. Ak.*, 1864, 5 sq., concluded that there were five treasurers from among all the Athenians, conjectures C.I.A., I., p. 92, on no. 194/5, and on 818 that there was a college consisting of ten persons. See also Dittenberger, *Syll.*, 14, 7; Panske 13, 5.

[2] We possess statements of accounts of οἱ ταμίαι τῶν ἱερῶν χρημάτων τῆς Ἀθηναίας καὶ τῶν ἄλλων θεῶν, ten in number: C.I.A., II. 642 sqq. In the year of Eucleides both colleges of treasurers were united: 'Εφ. ἀρχ., 1885, p. 129; Lehner, *d. att. Schatzverzeichnisse d. 4. Jahr.*, p. 12 sqq., Strassburg, 1890, assigns the change to the year 406/5. We have evidence of ταμίαι τῆς θεοῦ again for the year 385: C.I.A., II. 667. In 376/5 there were again two different boards of treasurers, as is evident from a comparison of C.I.A., II. 671 with 672, both of which belong to the same year. Ταμίαι τῶν ἄλλων θεῶν even in 363: II. 682c. Last mention of these 343, if II. 702 has been rightly restored. Lists of the different boards of treasurers of the fourth century in Panske 36 sqq. Lehner 119/20 considers that the two colleges were united again by Lycurgus 338. From the fact that in a statement of accounts, most probably of the year 321/20, the treasurers of Athene call themselves simply οἱ ταμίαι, Köhler, on C.I.A., II. 719, concludes that at that time there were no longer any treasurers of the other gods. Yet at later dates they are styled sometimes simply ταμίαι: II. 721. 722. 726. 728. 736; sometimes ταμίαι τῆς θεοῦ: II. 730. 733. 737=p. 508. 739. The Eleusinian goddesses had in 329 their own treasurers: II. 834, *b*. See also Kirchhoff on C.I.A., IV. 3, 225B, p. 167. Michaelis, *Parthenon*, 29, also thinks that the renewed separation of the two colleges of treasurers did not last long. The treasurers of the goddess are authenticated to the end of the fourth century, *e.g.* in the year 300: C.I.A., II. 612.

[3] See Thuc. 1, 96. For the Hellenotamiai cf. Boeckh, 1, 241 ff.=Bk. 2, ch. 7.

[4] The Hellenotamiai, ten in number, and one from each tribe: C.I.A., I. 259. 260. Of the eleven Hellenotamiai in the C.I.A., I. 188, I take

πάρεδρος.[1] The Hellenotamiai received the tribute of the allies, which was paid at the Dionysia, and kept accounts of it.[2] They kept a special treasury for the tribute-money, out of which they had annually to pay $\frac{1}{60}$ of the incoming revenue as ἀπαρχή to the treasury of Athene.[3] The payments out of the treasury of Athene for military purposes and for festivals passed mostly through their hands.[4]

The ταμίας τοῦ δήμου, whose existence can be proved to the end of the 4th century, had in that century the control of the money out of which the expenses of erection and

Phrasitelides of Icaria, mentioned in the first Prytany, to be the Πάρεδρος. It says there inaccurately: Ἐ(λλη)νοταμίαις παρεδόθη Καλλιμάχῳ Ἀγνουσίῳ, Φρασιτελίδῃ Ἰκαριεῖ, while by analogy of the sixth Prytany it ought to be: Ἑλληνοταμίᾳ Καλλιμάχῳ Ἀγνουσίῳ καὶ παρέδρῳ Φρασιτελίδῃ Ἰκαριεῖ. In C.I.A., I. 188 there are three Hellenotamiai from the Acamantis and two from the Aiantis, while the Aigeis, Leontis, Hippothontis are not represented. Of the mode of their appointment nothing definite can be said.

[1] Ἑλληνοταμίαις καὶ παρέδροις: C.I.A., I. 180–183. Ἑλληνοταμίᾳ καὶ παρέδρῳ: I. 183. 188. 6th Pryt.

[2] Thuc. I. 96: καὶ Ἑλληνοταμίαι τότε πρῶτον Ἀθηναίοις κατέστη ἀρχή, οἳ ἐδέχοντο τὸν φόρον. Hesych. Ἑλληνοταμίαι οἱ τοῦ κομιζομένου φόρου παρὰ Ἀθηναίοις ταμίαι. Harp., Suid., s.v. Poll. 8, 114, assigns them a wider sphere of duties, but with little probability. The payment of the tribute at the Dionysia is testified by Eupolis in the Schol. on Aristoph. Ach. 504. See also the Schol. on 378. They keep accounts of the tribute. C.I.A., I. 38. fr. c. d.: ἀναγ(ραφόντων δὲ οἱ Ἑλλ)ηνοτ(αμ)ίαι ἐσσανίδι τὰς—σας τοῦ φ(όρ)ου καὶ τῶν ἀπαγόντ(ων τὰ ὀνόματα. κα)ὶ τιθέναι (ἐ)κάστοτε πρόσθε—.

[3] That they had a separate treasury is evident from C.I.A., I. 32= Dittenberger, Syll., 14, where τὰ χρήματα τὰ παρὰ τοῖς Ἑλληνοταμίαις ὄντα νῦν are mentioned. Payment of the ἀπαρχή is ordered in the same decree of the people, B. 18 sqq.: (ἐκ δὲ τῶν φόρω)ν κατατιθέναι κ(ατὰ τὸ)ν ἐνιαυτὸν τὰ ἑκά(στοτε γενόμενα παρὰ το)ῖς ταμίασι τῶν (τῆς Ἀθ)ηναίας τοὺς Ἑλληνο(ταμίας). From the year 454 $\frac{1}{60}$ of the annual tribute is set apart as ἀπαρχή for Athens. The accounts of this ἀπαρχή form the so-called tribute lists: C.I.A., I. 226–272. I now concur in the theory of Christ, de publicis populi Atheniensis rationib., 28 sqq., Greifswald, 1879, that the ἀρχή mentioned in the so-called tribute-lists is not that of the Logistai but that of the Hellenotamiai. Cf. Bannier, de titulis aliquot att. rationes pecuniarum Minervae exhibentibus, p. 6 sqq., Berlin, 1891.

[4] The Hellenotamiai received money for the Strategoi from the treasurers of Athene: C.I.A., I. 180. 181. 188; for the payment of the troops: I. 188. 188; for the athlothetai of the Panathenaia: I. 183; for the diobelia: I. 188. 189. They give money for posting up the resolutions of the people: C.I.A., I. 59. 61. And yet the treasurers of Athene make payments direct to certain persons and authorities without the mediation of the Hellenotamiai: C.I.A., I. 188. 189. For the duties of the Hellenotamiai see Fellner, z. Gesch. d. att. Finanzverwalt., p. 13 sqq.

restoration of the records of decrees of the people were defrayed.[1] Out of the same treasury the ταμίας τοῦ δήμου paid the travelling expenses of ambassadors and money for the making of wreaths.[2] Lastly we must speak of three other finance offices, whose institution seems to have stood in a certain chronological relation to one another.

The first finance office to be mentioned here is that of οἱ ἐπὶ τὸ θεωρικόν, which, as it seems, was instituted under the influence of Eubulos between 354 and 339. After the introduction of the theoricon by Cleophon, it was customary to refund the entrance money for the theatre to its frequenters and to grant the people on festive occasions a general bounty. These bounties were at a later time renewed and increased by Agyrrhios. Then Eubulos during his period of ascendency laid down the principle that all surplus funds of the exchequer should be divided among the people. The attempt, which was made in the year 348 or 350, by Apollodoros, to restrain this waste, was frustrated by Eubulos.[3] For the control of this new fund, into which under the administration of Eubulos all the balances of the exchequer flowed, a new finance office was necessary, the holders of which were elected to hold office from one Panathenaia to the following Panathenaia,

οἱ ἐπὶ τὸ θεωρικόν.

---

[1] The ταμίας τοῦ δήμου pays ἐκ τῶν (εἰς τὰ) κατὰ ψηφίσματα ἀναλισκομένων τῷ δήμῳ, or, as it is also put, ἐκ τῶν κατὰ ψηφίσματα μεριζομένων τῷ δήμῳ (C.I.A., II. 115. Ἐφ. ἀρχ. 1891, 89). C.I.A., II. 47 before 376, 50=372, cf. 54. 69. 114. 119. 120. 147. 150. 167. 171. 176. 186. 210. 228. 235. 252. 272–277. 286. 293–296. In the year 332: Ἐφ. ἀρχ., 1891, p. 86 ; 329 : Ἐφ. ἀρχ., 1891, p. 89. From the year 299/8 to 295/4 the ἐξεταστὴς and the τριττύαρχοι pay : C.I.A., II. 297. 298. 300. The ταμίας τοῦ δήμου pays ἐκ τῶν κοινῶν χρημάτων : II. 243, without further intimation of the fund from which payment is made : II. 52c (in the year 368). 65. 90. For this cf. Fellner, 43 sqq. According to Köhler, in d. Mitth. d. dtsch. arch. Inst. in Ath., 4, 325, the office of the ταμίας τοῦ δήμου certainly did not exist in 295, and was probably abolished some years earlier.

[2] The ταμίας τοῦ δήμου pays from the same fund ἐφόδια to ambassadors : II. 64. 89. Bull. 13, 436, l. 58 sq., sees to the making of a wreath : II. 254.

[3] For the financial measures of Eubulos see Schaefer, Dem. u. s. Zeit., 1¹, 174. The proposal of Apollodoros and the certainly very questionable law of Eubulos : 1¹, 184/5. For the history of the θεωρικὸν see Harp. θεωρικά=Suid. θεωρικά, Art. 1 and 2., Suid. θεωρικόν. Et. M. θεωρικόν. Boeckh, 1, 306=Bk. 2, ch. 13.. The doubtful remark in Plut., Per., 9, that Pericles had bribed the people θεωρικοῖς, cannot be upheld in the face of Arist. 28, 3 : τοῦ δὲ δήμου Κλεοφῶν ὁ λυροποιὸς, ὃς καὶ τὴν διωβελίαν ἐπόρισε πρῶτος. καὶ χρόνον μέν τινα διεδίδοτο, μετὰ δὲ ταῦτα κατέλυσε Καλλικράτης Παιανιεύς, πρῶτος ὑποσχόμενος ἐπιθήσειν πρὸς τοῖν δυοῖν ὀβολοῖν ἄλλον ὀβολόν.

and were entitled οἱ ἐπὶ τὸ θεωρικόν.[1] The position of these finance-ministers was so important that for a time they exercised the functions of the Apodectai and of the ἀντιγραφεύς and in fact controlled the whole State finance.[2] Even after the year 339, this office retained its authority, though indeed with considerable limitations.[3]

The financial system of Eubulos was abolished in the year 339.

---

[1] That there were several, and, as Boeckh, 1, 249, sq.=Bk. 2, ch. 7, supposes, perhaps 10 ἐπὶ τὸ θεωρικόν, is evident now from Arist. 43, 1; 47, 2, and in this sense Æschin. *in Ctes.* 25, is also now to be understood. Suid. θεωρικά art. 1 and 2, θεωρικόν. Et. M. θεωρικόν speak of one only. Harp., θεωρικόν, quotes Æschin. and speaks of ἀρχή τις ἐπὶ τοῦ θεωρικοῦ. Lex. Seguer. 264, 7, θεωρικὴ ἀρχή=οἱ ἄρχοντες τῶν θεωρικῶν χρημάτων; several also in Poll. 8, 99. Aristotle and Æschines, *loc. cit.*, testify to the election. That this office was newly introduced under Eubulos, I consider very probable. In the fifth century the Hellenotamiai paid the theoricon—C.I.A., I. 188. 189 A.B.; later undoubtedly those Tamiai had charge of the surplus funds. That a theoricon treasury or οἱ ἐπὶ τὸ θεωρικόν existed is not to be supposed, since it was never the duty of the latter to actually distribute the theoricon. Lucian, *Tim.* 49; Benndorf, in *d. Ztschr. f. d. östr. Gymn.*, 1875, 22/3. Fellner., z. *Gesch. d. att. Finanzverwaltung*, p. 33 sq., is of opinion that there were 10 presidents of the theoricon and that they were probably instituted in the year 396/5. The official ἐπὶ τὸ θεωρικὸν in the C.I.A., II. 114, now that the plurality of these finance ministers is established, can only have been a council official with unknown functions.

[2] Æschin. *in Ctes.* 25 : διὰ δὲ τὴν πρὸς Εὔβουλον γενομένην πίστιν ὑμῖν οἱ ἐπὶ τὸ θεωρικὸν κεχειροτονημένοι ἦρχον μέν, πρὶν ἢ τὸν Ἡγήμονος νόμον γενέσθαι, τὴν τοῦ ἀντιγραφέως ἀρχήν, ἦρχον δὲ τὴν τῶν ἀποδεκτῶν καὶ νεώριον καὶ σκευοθήκην ᾠκοδόμουν, ἦσαν δὲ καὶ ὁδοποιοὶ καὶ σχεδὸν τὴν ὅλην διοίκησιν εἶχον τῆς πόλεως. For the termination of the supremacy of οἱ ἐπὶ τὸ θεωρικόν 339/8 see Schaefer, 1¹, 188/189. The beginning I place after the peace of Philocrates, because there is inscriptional evidence for Apodectai for 347/6 (see the decree of honour for the sons of Leucon: Dittenberger, *Syll.*, 101), and because the building of the σκευοθήκη mentioned by Æschines was then begun. See Schaefer, 2¹, 288. But perhaps the above-named officials existed throughout the period of the ascendency of οἱ ἐπὶ τὸ θεωρικὸν as their subordinates. For the financial measures of Eubulos see Plut., *praec. ger. reip.*, xv. 23, p. 992 Didot. Aphobetos, the brother of Æschines, was one τῶν ἐπὶ τὸ θεωρικόν. For after the words of Æschines *in Ctes.* 25, on the theoricon board—καὶ σχεδὸν τὴν ὅλην διοίκησιν εἶχον τῆς πόλεως—I do not hesitate to refer the remark of Æschines about Aphobetos, *de Fals. Leg.*, 149 : καλῶς δὲ καὶ δικαίως τῶν ὑμετέρων προσόδων ἐπιμεληθείς, ὅτε αὐτὸν ἐπὶ τὴν κοινὴν διοίκησιν εἵλεσθε to this office.

[3] Demosthenes was ὁ ἐπὶ τὸ θεωρικόν after the battle of Chaeronea : Æschin. *in Ctes.* 24; Dem. 18, 113. See Schaefer 1¹, 189. To this office Plut., *praec. ger. reip.*, xxv. 1. p. 999, must have reference, if any weight is to be attached to such testimony. This is rightly recognised by Fickelscherer, *de theoricis Athen. pecuniis*, 34 sqq., Leipz. 1877. See Boeckh, 1, 229; 2, 117. In Arist. too 43, 1; 47, 2 οἱ ἐπὶ τὸ θεωρικόν are mentioned even after 329.

At the instance of Demosthenes, it was decided that all State funds should be employed for military purposes. Connected with this radical change of the finance administration, it seems, was the institution of a new finance official, the ταμίας, τῶν στρατιωτικῶν.[1] This ταμίας τῶν στρατιωτικῶν, whose year of office ran from the Panathenaia to the following Panathenaia, was appointed by election, and had apparently the control of the whole financial administration. He was present in the Council along with the ἐπὶ τὸ θεωρικόν officials when the Poletai made leases; in 329, in co-operation with the Apodectai and the τραπεζίτης, he advanced money to the Epistatai and treasurers of the Eleusinian goddesses; in conjunction with the Council he saw to the completion of the Nike statues, and procured the prizes for the Panathenaia; in 334 (the most probable date) he paid to the treasurers of Athene and to the commission appointed for the purpose, money for the restoration of the Nike statues and the articles used in processions, saw to the making of a golden wreath for Amphiaraos and gave the money for it. These examples of the activity of the ταμίας τῶν στρατιωτικῶν hardly suit the special official duties of a treasurer of war, but necessarily follow from his conjectured position at the head of the Athenian finance administration.[2]

---

[1] Philochor., *fr.* 135, in Müller, *fr. h. gr.*, 1, 406, says: Λυσιμαχίδης Ἀχαρνεύς. ἐπὶ τούτου τὰ μὲν ἔργα τὰ περὶ τοὺς νεωσοίκους καὶ τὴν σκευοθήκην ἀνεβάλοντο διὰ τὸν πόλεμον πρὸς Φίλιππον· τὰ δὲ χρήματ' ἐψηφίσαντο πάντ' εἶναι στρατιωτικά, Δημοσθένους γράψαντος. The ταμίας τῶν στρατιωτικῶν is first mentioned in literature in connexion with the year 338 B.C.: Pseudoplut., *vit. Lyc.*, 27. p. 1027 Didot; in inscriptions probably for the year 334: C.I.A., II. 739, certainly for the year 332/1: Ἐφ. ἀρχ. 1891, p. 82. Boeckh, 1. 246 (Bk. II. ch. 7), assigns the institution of this office to the year of Eucleides; Fränkel, in the *Phil.-hist. Aufs. für E. Curtius*, p. 43, sqq. 1884, to the year 347. That in this year the ταμίας τῶν στρατιωτικῶν did not yet exist, I conclude from the fact that in 347 the Apodectai still paid ἐκ τῶν στρατιωτικῶν χρημάτων: Dittenberger, *Syll.*, 101. See Schaefer in the *N. Rh. Mus.*, 33. p. 431.

[2] Arist. 43, 1: τὰς δ' ἀρχὰς τὰς περὶ τὴν ἐγκύκλιον διοίκησιν ἁπάσας ποιοῦσι κληρωτὰς πλὴν ταμίου στρατιωτικῶν καὶ τῶν ἐπὶ τὸ θεωρικὸν καὶ τοῦ τῶν κρηνῶν ἐπιμελητοῦ. ταύτας δὲ χειροτονοῦσιν, καὶ οἱ χειροτονηθέντες ἄρχουσιν ἐκ Παναθηναίων εἰς Παναθήναια. 47, 2: [μ]ισθοῦσι δὲ τὰ μισθώματα πάντα καὶ τὰ μέταλλα πωλοῦσι, καὶ τὰ τέλη [μετὰ] τοῦ ταμίου τῶν στρατιωτικῶν καὶ τῶν ἐπὶ τὸ θεωρικὸν ᾑρημένων ἐναντ[ίον τῆς βουλῆς] κατακυροῦσιν.—The participation of the ἐπὶ τὸ θεωρικὸν officials was probably a survival from their former position of importance. In the report of the ἐπιστάται Ἐλευσινόθεν for the year 329 in C.I.A., II. 834b, col. i. l. 89, we find: καὶ τὸ προδανεισθὲν εἰς τὸ διατείχισμα τὸ Ἐλευσῖνι παρὰ ταμίου (σ)τρατιωτικῶν καὶ παρ' ἀποδεκτῶν καὶ παρὰ τοῦ τραπεζίτου; Arist. 49, 3: καὶ τῆς ποιήσεως τῶν Νικῶν καὶ τῶν ἄθλων τῶν εἰς τὰ Παναθήναια συνεπιμελεῖται

In the third century it was the duty of the ταμίας τῶν στρατιωτικῶν to assign and distribute the State moneys, a work which he either did alone or with the aid of ὁ ἐπὶ τῇ διοικήσει.[1]

ὁ ἐπὶ τῇ διοικήσει. To the end of the fourth century belongs also the institution of the official ἐπὶ τῇ διοικήσει, whose office seems to have taken the place of that of the Apodectai, either under the rule of Demetrios of Phaleron or after his deposition.[2] Lycurgus accordingly cannot have held the office of ἐπὶ τῇ διοικήσει; so that all the details which have been taken from the financial policy of Lycurgus to characterize the functions of this office are irrelevant.[3] We are therefore really reduced to the evidence of

(sc. ἡ βουλὴ) μετὰ τοῦ ταμίου τῶν στρατιωτικῶν. Payment for the making of νῖκαι and πομπεῖα: C.I.A., II. 739. A golden wreath for Amphiaraos and payment for the same: 'Εφ. ἀρχ., 1891, pp. 81/2.

[1] In 306/5 the treasurers of Athene make payments to the ταμίας τῶν στρατιωτικῶν to meet the freight charges for ship-building timber: C.I.A., II. 737 l. 28 sq., p. 508. In 305/4 the ταμίας and 5 Areopagites make payments to the treasurers of the goddess: ibid. l. 32 sqq. The expression usual before of the Apodectai—μερίσαι—is used of the ταμίας paying for the erection of inscription stelai: C.I.A., II. 335. 370. 375. 380. 396. 411. 420. 423. 467. l. 57. Bull. 15, p. 346. 356. See the list in Hartel, Stud. üb. att. Staatsrecht. u. Urkundenw., 135. C.I.A., II. 368, he pays ἐκ τῶν εἰς τὰ κατὰ ψηφίσματα ἀναλισκομένων τῷ δήμῳ, a fund which was formerly controlled by the ταμίας τοῦ δήμου. The ταμίας τῶν στρατιωτικῶν is also (C.I.A., II. 334) meant where, in the time of the Chremonidean war, we read ll. 9 sqq.: (ὅπως ἂν χρημάτων π)ορισθέντων ἔχει ὁ ταμίας μερίζειν τὰ (δεόμενα, ἵνα κ)ατὰ τὸν κατάλοιπον χρόνον τοῦ ἐνιαυτοῦ συνκ(ομισθῶσιν οἱ ἐκ γῆς? κ)αρποὶ μετ' ἀσφαλείας. So Bull. 15, 349. 350/1, where mention is made of the ταμίας only. The ταμίας supplies funds in conjunction with ὁ ἐπὶ τῇ διοικήσει: C.I.A., II. 327. 'Αρχ. δελτ. 1891, pp. 45/6. Bull. 15. p. 355.

[2] That the office of the ἐπὶ τῇ διοικήσει did not yet exist between 329 and 322, is proved by the silence of Aristotle. For even if it be supposed that chapter 60 was followed by the account of the offices mentioned in chap. 43, 1, yet mention of the ἐπὶ τῇ διοικήσει, if he had at that time existed, must have been made in chap. 43, 1. See also B. Keil, in the Berl. phil. Wochenschr. 1891, pp. 614/5. There is no notice of the Apodectai after the time of Demetrios of Phaleron; last mention 325 B.C.: C.I.A., II. 809. c. 70 sqq. e, 147 sqq. Spangenberg, de Atheniens. publ. institutis aetate Macedonum commutatis, p. 43, thinks that they were abolished by that Demetrios. The first ἐπὶ τῇ διοικήσει mentioned in inscriptions is Habron, the son of Lycurgus: C.I.A., II. 167. That this inscription is later than 307 (see Wachsmuth, d. St. Ath., 1, 616), and does not belong to the time of Lycurgus, is further proved by the fact that Habron was ταμίας τῶν στρατιωτικῶν in 306/5: C.I.A., II. 737, 31, p. 510.

[3] Boeckh, 1, 222 (Bk. 2, ch. 6) ff., has taken his representation of the office of ὁ ἐπὶ τῇ διοικήσει from what is said in Pseudoplut. of Lycurgus. The decree of Stratocles, which calls Lycurgus ταμίας τῆς κοινῆς προσόδου, is certainly

inscriptions for the description of the official duties of the ἐπὶ τῇ διοικήσει; and from these little can be learnt. Yet we know that there was only one ἐπὶ τῇ διοικήσει each year till the end of the year 295/4, while from 286/5 for some time several ἐπὶ τῇ διοικήσει are mentioned. Previous to the Chremonidean war, however, they were again replaced by one. At the end of the third century we again meet with several ἐπὶ τῇ διοικήσει, who are once more reduced to one in the second century.[1] The ἐπὶ τῇ διοικήσει, who was ap-

spurious, in its present form at any rate. See Droege, *de Lycurgo Atheniensi*, p. 23 sqq., Bonn, 1880; Fränkel, in Boeckh., *St. d. Ath.*, 2. p. 44. No. 270. Whether Lycurgus held a definite constitutional office at all, is according to this doubtful. In Diod. 16, 88 it is said of Lycurgus: δώδεκα ἔτη τὰς προσόδους τῆς πόλεως διοικήσας, i.e. probably by his personal authority. In Hyper, *fr.* 121, ed. Blass, he is described as ταχθεὶς ἐπὶ τῇ διοικήσει τῶν χρημάτων. The fragmentary inscription in C.I.A., II. 162, decrees probably at the instance of Lycurgus (a. *b*, 15) the establishment of the commission, which C.I.A., II. 739-741 specifies. A τετραετία (162 c, 17) seems to be fixed as its term of duration. This commission, to which without doubt Lycurgus belonged (see the decree of Stratocles in *Pseudoplut.*, 1038) was in office from 334 to 331. See II. 741. So far as the buildings of Lycurgus are concerned, the naval arsenal had just come into use in 330: Boeckh, *Seeurk.*, 70; work was still being done on the Theatre and the Stadion just before the Panathenaia of the year 330: C.I.A., II. 176; the building of the sanctuary of Pluto in Eleusis and of the Eleusinion was still proceeding in 329, with the co-operation of Lycurgus: C.I.A., II. 834 *b*. In 329/8 Lycurgus belonged to the 10 χειροτονηθέντες ὑπὸ τοῦ δήμου ἐπὶ τὴν ἐπιμέλειαν τοῦ ἀγῶνος καὶ τῶν ἄλλων τῶν περὶ τὴν ἑορτὴν τοῦ 'Αμφιαράου: 'Εφ. ἀρχ. 1891, p. 89. According to Köhler in *Herm.*, 1., 321, special offices were created for Lycurgus; according to Fellner, *zur Gesch. d. ath. Finanzverw.*, 58 sqq., he held a commissioner's office for re-organizing the treasury on the Acropolis and for the supply of materials of war. Droege 41 makes him exercise the last-named function as στρατηγὸς ἐπὶ τὴν παρασκευήν, whereas, according to Arist. 61, 1, this official did not at that time exist. These remarks disprove also what Pseudoplut., *vit. Lyc.*, 3, p. 1025, Didot, in a rather unintelligible context says of the time-limitation of the unknown office of Lycurgus. If Lycurgus during his politico-financial ascendancy ever temporarily held a definite office, it probably was that of the ταμίας τῶν στρατιωτικῶν, which his brother-in-law Callias held in 338, probably as the first treasurer of war. See Pseudoplut., *vit. Lyc.*, 27. Fellner, 51 sqq., puts the year of the institution of the ἐπὶ τῇ διοικήσει at 378, von Wilamowitz at 354 at the earliest. Cf. Droege, 29 sqq. Philippi, in the *N. Rh. Mus.*, 34, 612. 1, considered Eubulos to have been the first ἐπὶ τῇ διοικήσει.

[1] Habron, son of Lycurgus, ὁ ἐπὶ τῇ διοικήσει after 307: C.I.A., II. 167: ὁ ἐπὶ τῇ διοικήσει still in the year 295/4: II. 300. οἱ ἐπὶ τῇ διοικήσει in the year 286/5: II. 311. 312. In the year 284/3: 'Εφ. ἀρχ., 1890, 71 sqq. Again ὁ ἐπὶ τῇ διοικήσει not long before the Chremonidean war: II. 331. Οἱ ἐπὶ τῇ διοικήσει at the end of the third century: Bull. 15. p. 355. ὁ ἐπὶ τῇ διοικήσει again in the second century; C.I.A., II. 453.

pointed by election and held his office without doubt for a year, had the supervision of the revenue and expenditure of the State. Thus with the Poletai he contracted for the public works, directed the making of wreaths of honour and statues, and provided the money for the posting of the decrees of the people.[1]

The number of the Athenian treasurers is by no means exhausted by the preceding enumeration. On the contrary, every official, through whose hands large sums of money passed during his year of office, had his treasurer. Only it cannot always be decided whether it was a private treasurer or one appointed by the State.[2]

Other Treasurers.

Next to the finance ministers come the administrative and judicial officials, among whom the Archons must first be mentioned.

οἱ ἐννέα ἄρχοντες. The nine ἄρχοντες, who were also collectively styled θεσμοθέται, were appointed by lot and formed a college at whose head was the first ἄρχων.[3] After they had laid down their office and had passed the regular scrutiny they became ordinary members in the Council of the Areopagus.[4] Although for most

---

[1] Poll. 8, 113: ὁ δὲ ἐπὶ τῆς διοικήσεως αἱρετὸς ἦν ἐπὶ τῶν προσιόντων καὶ ἀναλισκομένων. Contracts for public works in conjunction with the Poletai: C.I.A., II. 167. The ἐπὶ τῇ διοικήσει directed by decree of the people to see to the making of wreaths of honour and statues: II. 251. 311. 312; has to μερίσαι the money for posting up psephisms: II. 300. 311. 316. 325. 326. 328. 331. 393. Occasionally the ταμίας τῶν στρατιωτικῶν assists the ἐπὶ τῇ διοικήσει in this: C.I.A., II. 327. 'Αρχ. δελτ., 1891, pp. 45/6. Bull. 15. pp. 355. Collection of the inscriptions bearing on this subject in Hartel, *Stud. üb. att. Staatsr. u. Urkundenw.*, 135.

[2] Thus e.g. ταμίαι τῶν τειχοποιῶν are mentioned: in Æsch. *in Ctes.* 27, ταμίας τῶν ἀδυνάτων: Aristot. 49, 4, ταμίας κρεμαστῶν: C.I.A., II. 809 B. 212 sqq., ταμίας εἰς τὰ νεώρια: II. 803 D, 4, 13, ταμίας τριηροποιϊκῶν: II. 803 C. 128 sqq.= ὁ τῶν τριηροποιῶν ταμίας: Dem. 22, 17. The ταμίαι τῶν ἱερῶν τριήρων: Arist. 61, 7. Harp. ταμίας. Ἀμμωνίς. Lex. Cantabr. 675. 28. Phot., Πάραλοι· ταμίαι. Rose, *Arist. pseudep.*, 443, 59. For the position of these ταμίαι, see Köhler in the *Mitth. d. arch. Inst. in Ath.* 8, 168 sqq. The ταμίας of the trierarch Philippos was probably a private one (Dem.) 49, 14. 15, as also that of the strategos Timotheos: (Dem.) 49, 6. I infer the private character of this ταμίας from Dem. 8, 47, since according to this passage the strategos was responsible for the financial administration of his office. But see (Dem.) 49, 9. 10. Eupol. *ap.* Harp., ταμίαι. Compare in general Boeckh, *Economy of Athens*, 1, 234 (=Bk. 2, ch. 6) ff.

[3] οἱ ἐννέα ἄρχοντες=οἱ θεσμοθέται: Dem. 57, 66, compared with 70. Plut., *Sol.*, 25. Poll. 8, 85. Lex. Seguer. 311, 10. Boeckh, C.I.G., I. p. 440. The first Archon president: Hesych., ἄρχων πρύτανις Ἀθήνησιν ἐπώνυμος τῶν ἀρχόντων. Archon lists: C.I.A., II. 859. 862. 863.

[4] Poll. 8, 118. (Dem.) 26, 5. Lipsius, in the *Leipz. Stud.*, 4, 151 sqq.

matters separate duties were assigned to individual Archons, yet certain functions were discharged by the whole college collectively, *e.g.* the drawing of the jurymen by lot for the several suits, and perhaps the appointment by lot of the magistrates.[1]

The ἄρχων was at a later date called also ἄρχων ἐπώνυμος because various annual lists of names were distinguished by being designated after his name. He had his official residence in the Prytaneion.[2] Probably we should regard as a survival from early times the custom by which the Archon, immediately on accession to office, made proclamation by herald that whatever any man then possessed, the Archon would allow him possession until the end of his archonship.[3] The ἄρχων was the

ἄρχων.

refuses to believe there was a formal dokimasia of the Archons by the Areopagus before their admission to that body; and conjectures on the authority of Lys. 7, 22 ; 26, 11, that the Archons even during their term of office had seats and votes in the Areopagus. I do not doubt that the Archons took part in those sittings of the Areopagus at which matters connected with their office were discussed. The theory of a dokimasia before their admission at the end of their year of office is supported by Arist. 60, 3.

[1] The remarks of Poll. 8, 86/7 on the business devolving on the 9 Archons collectively are not over trustworthy in themselves. Aristotle does not confirm the statement that they pronounced the death sentence in the case of those who had illegally returned to Athens. Dem. 23, 31 has the vague expression θεσμοθέται. Their election of the military officials is contradicted, Arist. 44, 4. Their appointment of the jurymen is confirmed, Arist. 63, 1. Although their sortition of the athlothetai is given in Poll. simply through his misunderstanding Arist. 60, 1, yet the sortition of the magistrates may be set down as a collective function of the 9 Archons on the analogy of the jurymen, though Æschin. *in Ctes.* 13 vaguely says: ἀρχὰς δὲ φήσουσιν ἐκείνας εἶναι, ἃς οἱ θεσμοθέται ἀποκληροῦσιν ἐν τῷ Θησείῳ. The epichirotonia of the officials by the Archons is likewise questionable: for the passage in Poll.—an extract from Arist. 61—must surely have reached its present place by some mistake.

[2] His official title in the Macedonian age even is ἄρχων simply : Kirchhoff *in Herm.* 2, 161 sqq. He was called ἐπώνυμος not because he was ἐπώνυμος τοῦ ἐνιαυτοῦ, but because as the result of his official position he stood at the head of various official lists of names, *e.g.* ἐπώνυμος τῶν ἡλικιῶν, τῶν λήξεων : L. Lange, in the *Leipz. Stud.*, 1, 159 sqq. His official residence in the Prytaneion: Arist. 3, 5. This only refers, of course, to the time before Solon. Lex. Seguer. 449, 22, and Suid. ἄρχων, both based upon Arist., give παρὰ τοὺς ἐπωνύμους for the place. But it is a question whether this is not due to an inference of the grammarian who has confused the Tholos, the seat of the Prytanes, near to the ἐπώνυμοι, with the Prytaneion. See Judeich, in the *N. Rh. Mus.*, 1892, p. 59. 2.

[3] Arist. 56, 2: καὶ ὁ μὲν ἄρχων εὐθὺς εἰσελθὼν πρῶτον μὲν κηρύττει, ὅσα τις εἶχεν, πρὶν αὐτὸν εἰσελθεῖν εἰς τὴν ἀρχήν, ταῦτ' ἔχειν καὶ κρατεῖν μέχρι ἀρχῆς τέλους.

eponymous official of the State. His official duties comprised the supervision of family matters, protection of parents against their children, protection of widows, the chief wardship of orphans and heiresses and the providing of guardians for them; he received notices of divorce, and made provision for the continuance of individual families.[1] He had jurisdiction in all suits in which family rights of citizens came into question.[2] His religious duties consisted in conducting the great Dionysia, for which he appointed the Choregoi and arranged any consequent antidoseis; conducting the Thargelia; arranging for the Pompe in honour of Asclepios and Zeus Soter, and for the Theoroi to be sent to Delos or elsewhere.[3] In the conduct of the Dionysia the ἄρχων was assisted by 10 elected ἐπιμεληταὶ τῆς πομπῆς τῷ Διονύσῳ.[4] In his ordinary official duties he was assisted by two πάρεδροι nominated by himself.[5]

[1] Arist. 56, 6. 7; Dem. 35, 48; and the law in Dem. 43, 75; Poll. 8, 89. Care of the ἐπίκληροι: Dem. 37, 45/6 of the ὀρφανοί: Lex. Seguer. 201, 25 sqq. The providing of guardians: Poll. 8, 89. ἀπόλειψις: Plut., *Alcib.*, 8. Andok. *in Alcib.*, 14. Care that the families did not die out: Is. 7, 30.

[2] Meier und Schömann, *att Proc.*,[2] 55 sqq. List of suits within the Archon's jurisdiction in Arist. 56, 6. 7. Poll. 8, 89. Lex. Seguer. 310, 1 sqq.; 199, 9 sqq. Suid., Phot., ἡγεμονία δικαστηρίου. Harp. under the same word and under εἰς ἐμφανῶν κατάστασιν. Lex. Cantabr. εἰς δατητῶν αἵρεσιν.

[3] Arist. 56, 3 sqq.: ἔπειτα χορηγοὺς τραγῳδοῖς καθίστησι τρεῖς ἐξ ἁπάντων Ἀθηναίων τοὺς πλουσιωτάτους· πρότερον δὲ καὶ κωμῳδοῖς καθίστη πέντε, νῦν δὲ τούτους αἱ φυλαὶ φέρουσιν. ἔπειτα παραλαβὼν τοὺς χορηγοὺς τοὺς ἐνηνεγμένους ὑπὸ τῶν φυλῶν εἰς Διονύσια ἀνδράσιν καὶ παισὶν καὶ κωμῳδοῖς καὶ εἰς Θαργήλια ἀνδράσιν καὶ παισὶν (εἰσὶ δ' οἱ μὲν εἰς Διονύσια κατὰ φυλάς, εἰς Θαργήλια [δὲ] δυεῖν φυλαῖν εἷς· παρέχει δ' ἐν μ[έρει] ἑκατέρα τῶν φυλῶν), τούτοις τὰς ἀντιδόσεις ποιεῖ καὶ τὰς σκήψεις εἰσ[άγει] κ.τ.ἀ. καθίστησι δὲ καὶ εἰς Δῆλον χορηγοὺς καὶ ἀρχιθέω[ρον τ]ῷ τριακοντορίῳ τῷ τοὺς ἠθέους ἄγοντι. πομπῶν δ' ἐπιμελεῖτ[αι τῆς τε] τῷ Ἀσκληπιῷ γινομένης, ὅταν οἰκουρῶσι μύσται, καὶ τῆς Διονυσίων τῶν μ[εγά]λων μετὰ τῶν ἐπιμελητῶν, οὓς πρότερον μὲν ὁ δῆμος ἐχειροτόνει δέκα ὄντας κ[αὶ τὰ] εἰς τὴν πομπὴν ἀναλώματα παρ' αὐτῶ[ν ἀ]νήλ[ισκ]ον, νῦν δ' ἕνα τῆς φυλῆ[ς ἑκ]άστης κληροῖ καὶ δίδωσιν εἰς τὴν κατασκευὴν ἑκατὸν μνᾶς. ἐπιμελ[εῖτα]ι δὲ καὶ τῆς εἰς Θαργήλια καὶ τῆς τῷ Διὶ τῷ Σωτῆρι. διοικεῖ δὲ καὶ τὸν ἀγῶνα τῶ[ν Διον]υσίων οὗτος καὶ τῶν Θαργηλίων. ἑορτῶν μὲν οὖν ἐπιμελ[εῖ]ται τούτων. Lex. Cantabr. 670: ἐπώνυμος ἄρχων—ἔχειν δὲ ἐπιμέλειαν χορηγοὺς καταστῆσαι εἰς Διονύσια καὶ Θαργήλια· ἐπιμελεῖται δὲ καὶ τῶν εἰς Δῆλον καὶ τῶν ἀλλαχόσε πεμπομένων Ἀθήνηθεν χορῶν. See Poll. 8, 89. Compare the psephism in the Ἀθήν. 7, p. 480, no. 3.

[4] For the ἐπιμεληταὶ see Arist. 56, 4 in the preceding note. Cf. Dem. 21, 15; 4, 35. Ten ἐπιμεληταὶ τῆς πομπῆς τῷ Διονύσῳ are mentioned by name in a psephism of the year of the Archon Nikias: Dittenberger, *Syll.*, 382. See Mommsen, *Heort.*, 397.

[5] Arist. 56, 1; Poll. 8, 92; Is. 6, 32: ἐναντίον τοῦ ἄρχοντος καὶ τῶν παρέδρων. Cf. Æschin. *in Tim.* 158. (Dem.) 58, 32. The two πάρεδροι of the ἄρχων are

The second ἄρχων, who was called βασιλεύς, had his official quarters in the στοὰ βασίλειος by the market.[1] The βασιλεύς, who retained the name and religious functions of the early kings, superintended the holy places and the religious rites and ordinances. It was his special office to preside over and conduct the Mysteries, the Lenaia, and the torch-races, for which he probably nominated the gymnasiarchs.[2] He had jurisdiction in matters of public worship and religion, and also in murder cases, on account of the religious significance attached to blood-guiltiness.[3] His wife, the βασίλισσα or βασίλιννα, represented the

βασιλεύς.

mentioned by name in a psephism of the year of the Archon. Nikias: Dittenberger, *Syll.*, 882.

[1] Wachsmuth, *d. St. Athen.*, 2, 1, 344 sqq. ἡ στοὰ ἡ βασίλεια: C.I.A., I. 61. Paus. 1, 3, 1: πρώτη δέ ἐστιν ἐν δεξιᾷ καλουμένη στοὰ βασίλειος, ἔνθα καθίζει βασιλεὺς ἐνιαυσίαν ἀρχων καλουμένην βασιλείαν. ἡ τοῦ βασιλέως στοὰ the official quarters of the βασιλεύς: Plat. Euthyphr. *ad init.*, Theæt. *ad fin.* For earlier times see Arist. 3, 5.

[2] For the βασιλεὺς cf. Hauvette-Besnault, *de archonte rege*, Paris, 1884. See the passage in a psephism passed about 446, in Dittenberger 13 = C.I.A., IV. 27, *b*: τὸν δὲ βασ(ι)λέα ὁρίσαι τὰ ἱερὰ τὰ ἐν τ(ῷ)ι Πελαργικῶι καὶ τὸ λοιπὸν μὴ ἐν ἱδρύεσθαι βωμοὺς ἐν τῷι Πελαργικῶι ἄνευ τῆς βουλῆς καὶ τοῦ δήμου, μηδὲ τοὺς λίθους τέμνειν ἐκ τοῦ Πελαργικοῦ, μηδὲ γῆν ἐχσάγειν μηδὲ λίθους. ἐὰν δέ τις παραβαίνηι τούτων τι, ἀποτινέτω πεντακοσίας δραχμάς· ἐσαγγελλέτω δὲ (ὁ) βασιλεὺς ἐς τὴν βουλήν. Those on whom an ἐπιβολή was imposed for taking wood, brush-wood, or leaves from the sacred precinct of Apollo Erithaseos, were to be accused before the βασιλεὺς and the βουλή: C.I.A., II. 841. The βασιλεὺς contracts for the enclosing of the τέμενος τοῦ Κόδρου καὶ τοῦ Νηλέως καὶ τῆς Βασίλης: Ἐφ. ἀρχ., 1884, pp. 161/2 = C.I.A., IV. 53a. Cf. Ἐφ. ἀρχ., 1888, 113/4 = Bull. 13, 434. Ath. 6, 234F, 235A. Arist. 57, 1: [ὁ] δὲ βασιλεὺς πρῶτον μὲν μυστηρίων ἐπιμελεῖ[ται μετὰ τῶν ἐπιμελητῶν, οὓς] ὁ δῆμ[ος χ]ειροτονεῖ, δύο μὲν ἐξ Ἀθηναίων ἁπάντων, ἕνα δ' ἐξ [Εὐμολπιδῶν, ἕνα] δ' ἐκ Κηρ[ύκω]ν. ἔπειτα Διονυσίων τῶν ἐπὶ Ληναίῳ· ταῦτα δ' ἐστὶ [πομπὴ καὶ ἀγών. τὴν] μὲν οὖν πομπὴν κοινῇ πέμπουσιν ὅ τε βασιλεὺς καὶ οἱ ἐπιμεληταί, τὸν δὲ ἀγῶνα διατίθησιν ὁ βασιλεύς. τίθησι δὲ καὶ τοὺς τῶν λαμπάδων ἀγῶνας ἅπαντας· ὡς δ' ἔπος εἰπεῖν καὶ τὰς πατρίους θυσίας διοικεῖ οὗτος πάσας. Poll. 8, 90: ὁ δὲ βασιλεὺς μυστηρίων προέστηκε μετὰ τῶν ἐπιμελητῶν καὶ Ληναίων καὶ ἀγώνων τῶν ἐπὶ λαμπάδι καὶ τὰ περὶ τὰς πατρίους θυσίας διοικεῖ. Schol. to Aristoph., *Ach.*, 1224. For the βασιλεὺς at the Mysteries see also (Lys.) 6, 4/5. The βασιλεὺς and the πάρεδροι and the ἐπιστάται Ἐλευσινόθεν and the ἐπιμεληταὶ τῶν μυστηρίων contract for the μισθώματα for the Mysteries: Ἐφ. ἀρχ., 1883, pp. 121/2, l. 30, pp. 123/4, l. 31. The fourteen γεραραὶ nominated by the βασιλεύς: Poll. 8, 108; Et. M., 227, 36. Law-suits of the γυμνασίαρχοι before the βασιλεύς: Dem. 35, 48. Cf. Suid. ἐπιώψατο.

[3] For the cases within the jurisdiction of the βασιλεὺς see Arist. 57, 2 sqq. Poll. 8, 90. Lex. Seguer. 219, 14 sq.; 310, 6. Harp. ἡγεμονία δικαστηρίου. Phot. Art. 2. Suid. under the same word. Meier und Schoemann, *att. Proc.*,[2] 61 sqq.

consort of the god[1] in the symbolical marriage of Dionysus at the Anthesteria. In conducting the Mysteries the βασιλεύς was assisted by the four ἐπιμεληταὶ τῶν μυστηρίων, of whom the people annually elected two from among all the Athenians, a third from the Eumolpidai and the fourth from the Kerykes.[2] In his other official duties he was assisted, like the first ἄρχων, by two πάρεδροι nominated by himself.[3]

The third ἄρχων, styled πολέμαρχος, whose official quarters were in the Epilykeion,[4] in the course of the fifth century lost the control of military affairs, which was originally his.[5]

πολέμαρχος. The only survival of this ancient power of his consisted in this, that he offered the sacrifice made to Artemis Agrotera and Enyalios, and the ἐπιτάφια. He also offered the sacrifices in honour of Harmodius and Aristogeiton.[6] The πολέμαρχος had jurisdiction in those cases which had to do with the political position of the Metoicoi and freedmen in the State and with questions of family rights among them, and further in most private suits in which the defendant was a foreigner.[7]

---

[1] See Arist. 3, 5; Poll. 8, 90. 108; (Dem.) 59, 72 sqq. Mommsen, *Heort.*, 856 sqq.

[2] See Toepffer, *att. Geneal.*, 78 sqq. Harp. ἐπιμελητὴς τῶν μυστηρίων.— Ἀριστοτέλης ἐν Ἀθηναίων πολιτείᾳ φησὶν οὕτως· ὁ δὲ βασιλεὺς πρῶτον μὲν τῶν μυστηρίων ἐπιμελεῖται μετὰ τῶν ἐπιμελητῶν, οὓς ὁ δῆμος ἐχειροτόνει, δύο μὲν ἐξ Ἀθηναίων ἁπάντων, ἕνα δ' ἐξ Εὐμολπιδῶν, ἕνα δ' ἐκ Κηρύκων=Arist. 57, 1. See Poll. 8, 90; Dem. 21, 171; Lex. Seguer. 279, 20; 219, 15. Decrees of honour for the ἐπιμεληταὶ τῶν μυστηρίων: C.I.A., II. 315. 376. Ἐφ. ἀρχ., 1887, pp. 172, 177. For the participation of the γένος of the Κήρυκες in the conduct of the Mysteries see C.I.A., II. 597.

[3] Arist. 56. 1; Poll. 8, 92; (Dem.) 59, 72. 81. C.I.A., II. 597. Ἐφ. ἀρχ., 1883, 121/2, 123/4.

[4] Arist. 3, 5: ὁ δὲ πολέμαρχος τὸ Ἐπιλύκειον· ὃ πρότερον μὲν ἐκαλεῖτο πολεμαρχεῖον, ἐπεὶ δὲ Ἐπίλυκος ἀνῳκοδόμησε καὶ κατεσκεύασεν αὐτὸ πολεμα[ρχή]σας, Ἐπιλύκειον ἐκλήθη. From this Suid. ἀρχων. Lex. Seguer. 449, 21. But Hesych. also has ἐπὶ Λύκ(ε)ιον (for which Ἐπιλύκειον is to be read). ἀρχεῖον τοῦ πολεμάρχου Ἀθήνησιν.

[5] Arist. 22, 2 says of the year 511: τῆς δὲ ἁπάσης στρατιᾶς ἡγεμὼν ἦν ὁ πολέμαρχος. Cf. Hdt. 6, 109. 111. Lex. Seguer. 288, 20.

[6] Arist. 58, 1: ὁ δὲ πολέμαρχος θύει μὲν θυσίας τήν τε τῇ Ἀρτέμιδι τῇ ἀγροτέρᾳ καὶ τῷ Ἐνυαλίῳ, διατίθησι δ' ἀγῶνα τὸν ἐπιτάφιον [καὶ] τοῖς τετελευτηκόσιν ἐν τῷ πολέμῳ καὶ Ἁρμοδίῳ καὶ Ἀριστογείτονι ἐναγίσματα ποιεῖ. From this Poll. 8, 91. Cf. Lex. Seguer. 290, 27. The sacrifice to Artemis in commemoration of the victory at Marathon on the sixth of Boedromion: Xen., *An.*, 3, 2, 12. Boeckh, *Mondcycl.*, 64 sqq.

[7] Arist. 58, 2: δίκαι δὲ λαγχάνονται πρὸς αὐτὸν ἴδιαι μὲν αἵ τε τοῖς μετοίκοις καὶ τοῖς ἰσοτελέσι καὶ τοῖς προξένοις γιγνόμεναι.—αὐτὸς δ' εἰσάγει δίκας τάς τε τοῦ

The πολέμαρχος, too, was assisted in his official duties by two πάρεδροι.[1]

The remaining six members of the College of Archons, who had the general title of θεσμοθέται, had their official residence in the θεσμοθετεῖον, and supervised the laws.[2] These they had annually to revise, and, when necessary, recommend the repeal of old laws and the promulgation of new. International agreements for the administration of justice (σύμβολα) had to be ratified by the court of the Heliaia under their presidency, and they prepared and drew up the resulting δίκαι ἀπὸ συμβόλων.[3] As regards specially important judicial business, the Thesmothetai directed and introduced the following classes of lawsuits:—the Endeixis in certain cases; the Eisangelia and Probole; the Dokimasia of the officials, and the Euthyne of the Strategoi; the public charges which were made by any private person when the officials' accounts were audited; penal sentences of the Council which had to receive judicial confirmation; appeals against the rejection of a candidate by the Demotai; the Nomothesia; and the γραφαὶ παρανόμων.[4] But, besides this, the Thesmothetai con-

θεσμοθέται

ἀ[προσ]τασίου καὶ ἀπροστασίου καὶ κλήρων καὶ ἐπικλήρων τοῖς μετοίκοις, καὶ τἆλλ ὅσα τοῖς πολίταις ὁ ἄρχων, ταῦτα τοῖς μετοίκοις ὁ πολέμαρχος. Cf. Poll. 8, 91. Harp. πολέμαρχος. (Dem.) 46, 22. Suid. Phot. πολέμαρχος. Harp. ἡγεμονία δικαστηρίου = Phot. sub verb. Art. 1, Suid. Art 2. Meier und Schömann, att. Proc.,[2] 64 sqq. In a decree of honour for a πρόξενος we find: καὶ (πρόσοδον) εἶναι αὐτῷ πρὸς τὸν πολέμαρχον (καθάπερ) το(ῖ)ς ἄλλοις προξένοις: C.I.A., II. 42. The δίκαι συμβολαίων between Athens and Phaselis before the Polemarch: C.I.A., II. 11.

[1] Arist. 56, 1. Poll. 8, 92. Harp. πάρεδρος.

[2] Their official quarters: Arist. 3, 5. In Suid. ἄρχων, and Lex. Seguer. 449, 22, we find παρὰ τὸ θεσμοθέσιον. Wachsmuth, d. St. Athen., 2, 1, 353 sqq. Harp. θεσμοθέται· Δημοσθένης ἐν τῷ κατ' Ἀνδροτίωνος. ἀρχή τίς ἐστιν Ἀθήνησιν ἡ τῶν θεσμοθετῶν ἐξ τὸν ἀριθμὸν ὄντων, εἰσὶ δὲ ἐκ τῶν καλουμένων ἐννέα ἀρχόντων. καλοῦνται δὲ οὕτως, ὅτι τῶν νόμων τὴν ἐπιμέλειαν εἶχον· θεσμοὶ δὲ ἐκαλοῦντο οἱ νόμοι, ὡς προείπομεν. ὅτι δὲ τοὺς νόμους οὗτοι διώρθουν κατ' ἐνιαυτὸν ἕκαστον, εἴρηκεν Αἰσχίνης τε ἐν τῷ κατὰ Κτησιφῶντος καὶ Θεόφραστος ἐν τρίτῃ Νόμων. Cf. Phot., sub verb. Lex. Seguer. 264, 15 sqq.

[3] For the revision of the laws see the section on the Nomothesia. For the conclusion of σύμβολα with foreign states see Arist. 59, 6 : καὶ τὰ σύμβολα τὰ πρὸς τὰς πόλεις οὗτοι κυροῦσι καὶ τὰς δίκας τὰς ἀπὸ συμβόλων εἰσάγουσι. Poll. 8, 88. (Dem.) 7, 9. Fränkel, d. att. Geschworenenger. 40 sqq.

[4] Arist. 59, 2: ἔτι δὲ τὰς εἰσαγγελίας εἰσαγγέλλουσιν εἰς τὸν δῆμον καὶ τὰς καταχειροτονίας καὶ τὰς προβολὰς ἁπάσας εἰσάγουσιν οὗ[τοι] καὶ γραφὰς παρανόμων καὶ νόμον μὴ ἐπιτήδειον θεῖναι καὶ προεδρικὴν καὶ ἐπιστατικὴν καὶ στρατηγοῖς εὐθύνας. 4: εἰσάγουσιν δὲ καὶ τὰς δοκιμασίας ταῖς ἀρχαῖς ἁπάσαις καὶ τοὺς ἀπεψη-

ducted all public and private suits which did not fall within some other official's special sphere of administration or jurisdiction.[1] The Thesmothetai decided the times for taking the various cases, and allotted the courts to the several magistrates.[2]

The college of the ἕνδεκα, who certainly existed as far back as Solon's time, consisted of ten ordinary members, appointed by lot one from each tribe, and their clerk.[3] The ἕνδεκα formed the executive board of the Athenian State and consequently had the superintendence of the prisons and saw that the death-sentences pronounced by the jurors were carried out.[4] They kept a list of State debtors, probably in order that, when an

marginal note: οἱ ἕνδεκα.

φισμένους ὑπὸ τῶν δημοτῶν καὶ τὰς καταγνώσεις τὰς ἐκ τῆς βουλῆς. 45, 1: καὶ νόμον ἔθετο, ἄν τινος ἀδικεῖν ἡ βουλὴ καταγνῷ ἢ ζημιώσῃ, τὰς καταγνώσεις καὶ τὰς ἐπιζημιώσεις εἰσάγειν τοὺς θεσμοθέτας εἰς τὸ δικαστήριον, καὶ ὅτι ἂν οἱ δικασταὶ ψηφίσωνται, τοῦτο κύριον εἶναι. 48, 5: If private persons brought charges at the scrutiny of accounts, the εὔθυνος τὰ δημόσια τοῖς θεσμοθέτα[ις ἐπι]γράφει. οἱ δὲ θεσμοθέται, ἐὰν παραλάβωσιν, πάλιν εἰσάγουσιν [τὴν] εὔθυναν εἰς τὸ δικαστήριον, καὶ ὅτι ἂν γνῶσιν οἱ δικαστ[αί, τοῦτο κύριόν] ἐστι. 52, 1: εἰσάγουσι δὲ τῶν ἐνδείξεών τινας καὶ οἱ θεσμοθέται. See also Poll. 8, 87. 88. Schol. to Æschin. I. 16, ed. Dindorf: οἱ θεσμοθέται ἄλλα μὲν ποιοῦσι κοινῇ, ἰδίᾳ δὲ πότε δεῖ δικάζειν τὰ δικαστήρια καὶ τὰς εἰσαγγελίας εἰσάγειν εἰς τὸν δῆμον καὶ τὰς χειροτονίας καὶ τὰς προβολὰς εἰσάγουσι καὶ τὰς τῶν παρανόμων γραφὰς καὶ ἕτερα.

[1] For the cases which the Thesmothetai directed see Arist. 59; Poll. ibid.; Harp., Suid., Phot., ἡγεμονία δικαστηρίου. Lex. Seguer. 310, 12 sqq. Harp. δωροξενία, παράστασις. Meier und Schömann, att. Proc.,[2] 72 sqq.

[2] Arist. 59, 1: οἱ δὲ θεσμοθέται πρῶτον μὲν τοῦ προγράψαι τὰ δικαστήριά εἰσι κύριοι, τίσιν ἡμέραις δεῖ δικάζειν, ἔ[π]ε[ιτα] τοῦ δοῦναι ταῖς ἀρχαῖς· καθότι γὰρ ἂν οὗτοι δῶσιν, κατὰ τοῦτο χρῶνται. 59, 5: καὶ ἐπικληροῦσι ταῖς ἀρχαῖς οὗτοι τὰ δικαστήρια τὰ ἴδια καὶ τὰ δημόσια I consider to be a non-Aristotelian gloss. See also Poll. ibid., Schol. to Æschin. ibid. For the ἐπικληροῦν τὰ δικαστήρια see the section on the judicature.

[3] The ἕνδεκα in Solon's time: Arist. 7, 3; Poll. 8, 102: οἱ ἕνδεκα εἷς ἀφ' ἑκάστης φυλῆς ἐγίνετο καὶ γραμματεὺς αὐτοῖς συνηριθμεῖτο. In the Lex. Seguer. 250, 4, it says: κληρωτοὶ ἄρχοντες ἦσαν, ἕνδεκα τὸν ἀριθμόν. C.I.A., II. 811c, 130 sq., 144 sqq. mentions τὸγ γραμματέα τῶν ἕνδεκα. This expression is not utterly inconsistent with the explanation of Poll. For papers on the ἕνδεκα I may mention Fr. W. Ullrich in the appendix to the treatise *Vier platonische Gespräche, Menon, Kriton, der erste und zweite Alkibiades*, Berlin, 1821; Crome, *de undecemviris Atheniensium*, Düsseldorf Progr., 1828, in which, p. 2, n. 1, the literature at that time available for the subject is given; Wachsmuth., d. St. Athen., 2, 1, 383 sq.

[4] Arist. 52, 1: καθιστᾶσι δὲ καὶ τοὺς ἕνδεκα κληρωτούς, ἐπιμελησομένους τῶν ἐν τῷ δεσμωτηρίῳ. From this Poll. 8, 102. For the prison compare Wachsmuth, ibid. See Lex. Seguer. 250, 4 sqq. Et. M. ἕνδεκα. Carrying out of the death sentence through their ὑπηρέται: Xen., Hell., 2, 3, 54; Plat., Phæd., 116 B; Lys. 22, 2. These ὑπηρέται were called παραστάται: Lex. Seguer. 296, 32; Phot. s.v.

ἔνδειξις was brought against a State debtor who had suffered atimia for having exercised rights to which he was not entitled, they might at once know whether he could be punished with imprisonment as a man caught in the act.[1] Sometimes the ἕνδεκα were employed to get in State-debts, so that, in case of inability to pay, they might carry off the debtor to prison.[2] To their jurisdiction belonged the judicial procedure of ἀπογραφή, by which property which had come into private hands could be reclaimed for the State; and ἀπαγωγή, which was directed against a certain class of wrong-doers for whom arrest in the very act seems to have been the recognised procedure. In this class we find mentioned house-breakers, thieves, kidnappers, footpads and murderers. Finally in certain cases, the ἔνδειξις came into their court.[3] Of the ten ἀστυνόμοι appointed by lot, five managed the police in

---

[1] C.I.A., II. 811 c, 130 sqq., 144 sqq.: καὶ τὸγ γράμματέα τῶν ἕνδεκα ἀπαλεῖψαι ἀπὸ τοῦ ὠφλημένου Σωπόλιδι ἀργυρίου, ὅτι ἂν ἀποφάνῃ αὐτῷ ὁ ταμίας παρειληφ(ώς), κ.τ.λ. Ἔνδειξις against ἄτιμοι before the ἕνδεκα: Lex. Seguer. 250, 10 sqq., probably against the state-debtors who had lost their citizen rights (Boeckh, 1, 512=2, 111), against whom the ἔνδειξις was usual: (Dem.) 58, 14.

[2] They were the executive authority when payment of state-debts was enforced, so as to be ready to throw the debtor into prison: Dem. 22, 49. 52. 53.

[3] Arist. 52, 1: καθιστᾶσι δὲ καὶ τοὺς ἕνδεκα κληρωτούς, ἐπιμελησομένους τῶν ἐν τῷ δεσμωτηρίῳ καὶ τοὺς ἀπαγομένους κλέπτας καὶ τοὺς ἀνδραποδιστὰς καὶ τοὺς λωποδύτας (see Lys. 10, 10), ἂν μὲν [ὁμολογ]ῶσι, θανάτῳ ζημιώσοντας, ἂν δὲ ἀμφισβητῶσιν, εἰσάξοντας εἰς τὸ δικαστήριον, κἂν μὲν ἀποφύγωσιν, ἀφήσοντας, εἰ δὲ μή, τότε θανατώσοντας καὶ τὰ ἀπογραφόμενα χωρία καὶ οἰκίας εἰσάξοντας εἰς τὸ δικαστήριον καὶ τὰ δόξαντα δ[ημ]όσια εἶναι παραδώσοντας τοῖς πωληταῖς καὶ τὰς ἐνδείξεις εἰσάξοντας· καὶ γὰρ ταύτας εἰσάγουσιν οἱ ἕνδεκα. Cf. Poll. 8, 102; Lex. Seguer. 310, 14; Phot. ἡγεμονία δικαστηρίου. ἕνδεκα; Suid. ἕνδεκα. Lex. Seguer. 250, 4 sqq., also adds the φονεῖς, that is, originally those who were caught ἐπ' αὐτοφώρῳ. See Philippi, d. Areop. u. d. Ephelen., p. 102 sqq. Sorof, in the Jahrb. f. cl. Phil., 1883, 105 sqq., 1885, 10 sqq., thinks that the ἀπαγωγή was at first only used against those who committed murder with robbery, after 403 against murderers ἐπ' αὐτοφώρῳ; according to Meuss, de ἀπαγωγῆς actione ap. Athen., 27 sqq., D. i. Breslau, 1884, only when the murderer was a foreigner. Dem. 35, 48 mentions τοιχωρύχους καὶ κλέπτας καὶ τοὺς ἄλλους κακούργους τοὺς ἐπὶ θανάτῳ, Isocr. 15, 237, τοὺς κακουργοῦντας in general. In later times the list of offences for which the ἀπαγωγὴ was admissible seems to have been enlarged; Meuss, 22 sqq., denies this. See Meier und Schömann² 86/7, 274/5. Sorof, ibid., 1885, 14 sqq.: in general cf. Meier und Schömann² 81 sqq. Cf. the law in Dem. 24, 146: τὸν δ' ἐνδειχθέντα ἢ ἀπαχθέντα δησάντων οἱ ἕνδεκα ἐν τῷ ξύλῳ. For ἔνδειξις and ἀπαγωγὴ cf. Meier und Schömann² 270 sqq. Et. M. under ἕνδεκα agrees with Arist.: εἰσῆγον δὲ καὶ τὰ ἀπογραφόμενα χωρία, οἰκίας· καὶ τὰ δημόσια εἶναι δόξαντα παρεδίδουν τοῖς πωληταῖς. εἰσῆγον δὲ ἐνίας ἐνδείξεις. For the ἀπογραφή see Meier und Schömann² 302 sqq.

the city, five in the Piræus. As to their police duties, special mention is made of the surveillance of the flute girls and harp players, and the punishment of those who wore indecent dress.[1] They had moreover street police duties and saw that the streets were kept clean; the scavengers were under their management: they inspected buildings; saw that the streets were not encroached on, that the balconies of the houses did not project too far into the streets, that the rain from the roofs did not run into the streets, and that the doors of houses did not open outwards toward the street.[2] They seem also to have had a kind of police duty at festivals, for at religious Pompai they saw that the streets and the holy precincts of the gods to which these Pompai proceeded, presented an appearance worthy of the occasion.[3] They

ἀστυνόμοι.

---

[1] Haederli, *d. hell. Astynomen und Agoranomen* in the 15. Suppl. vol. of the *Jahrb. f. cl. Phil.*, 69 sqq.; Wachsmuth, *d. St. Athen.*, 2, 1, 267 sqq.; Meier und Schömann² 105 sqq. Arist. 50, 2: κληροῦνται δὲ (see also Dem. 24, 112) καὶ ἀστυνόμοι δέκα· τούτων δὲ ε' μὲν ἄρχουσιν ἐν Πειραιεῖ, πέντε δ' ἐν ἄστει, καὶ τάς τε αὐλητρίδας καὶ τὰς ψαλτρίας καὶ τὰς κιθαριστρίας οὗτοι σκοποῦσιν, ὅπως μὴ πλείονος ἢ δυεῖν δραχμαῖν μισθωθήσονται, κἂν πλείους τὴν αὐτὴν σπουδάσωσι λαβεῖν, οὗτοι διακληροῦσι καὶ τῷ λαχόντι μισθοῦσιν. From this Harp. s.v., Lex. Seguer. 455, 24 sqq., Suid. ἀστυνόμος. In Diog. Laërt. 6, 5, 90 it says of Crates: ὑπὸ τῶν Ἀθήνησιν ἀστυνόμων ἐπιτιμηθείς, ὅτι σινδόνα ἠμφίεστο.

[2] Arist. 50, 2: καὶ ὅπως τῶν κοπρολόγων μηδεὶς ἐντὸς ί σταδίων τοῦ τείχους καταβαλεῖ κόπρον ἐπιμελοῦνται (see Harp. βολεῶνες)· καὶ τὰς ὁδοὺς κωλύουσι κατοικοδομεῖν καὶ δρυφάκτους ὑπὲρ τῶν ὁδῶν ὑπερτείνειν (see Heracl., *fr.* 1, 10 in Müller, *fr. h. gr.*, 2, 209) καὶ ὀχετοὺς μετεώρους εἰς τὴν ὁδὸν ἔκρουν ἔχοντας ποιεῖν καὶ τὰς θυρίδας [windows with shutters opening outwards on to the streets, Sandys *ad loc.*] εἰς τὴν ὁδὸν ἀνοίγειν· καὶ τοὺς ἐν ταῖς ὁδοῖς ἀπογιγνομένους ἀναιροῦσιν, ἔχοντες δημοσίους ὑπηρέτας. Cf. Arist., *Pol.*, 7 (6), 8=189, 31, sqq. Bekker: ἑτέρα δὲ ἐπιμέλεια ταύτης ἐχομένη καὶ σύνεγγυς ἡ τῶν περὶ τὸ ἄστυ δημοσίων καὶ ἰδίων, ὅπως εὐκοσμία ᾖ, καὶ τῶν πιπτόντων οἰκοδομημάτων καὶ ὁδῶν σωτηρία καὶ διόρθωσις καὶ τῶν ὁρίων τῶν πρὸς ἀλλήλους, ὅπως ἀνεγκλήτως ἔχωσιν, καὶ ὅσα τούτοις ἄλλα τῆς ἐπιμελείας ὁμοιότροπα. καλοῦσι δ' ἀστυνομίαν οἱ πλεῖστοι τὴν τοιαύτην ἀρχήν.

[3] That they had a kind of police duty at festivals is evident from a psephism of the year 320, in Dittenberger., *Syll.*, 337: ἐπειδὴ δὲ καὶ ἡ τῶν ἀστυνόμων ἐπιμέλεια προστέτακται τοῖς ἀγορανόμοις, ἐπιμεληθῆναι τοὺς ἀγορανόμους τῶν ὁδῶν τῶν πλατειῶν, ᾗ ἡ πομπὴ πορεύεται τῷ Διὶ τῷ Σωτῆρι καὶ τῷ Διον(ύ)σῳ, ὅπως ἂν ὁμαλισθῶσιν καὶ κατασκευασθῶσιν ὡς βέλτιστα· τὰ δὲ ἀναλώματα εἶναι εἰς ταῦτα ἐκ τοῦ ἀργυρίου, οὗ οἱ ἀγορανόμοι διαχειρίζουσιν· ἐπαναγκαζόντων δὲ καὶ τοὺς τὸν χοῦν καταβεβληκότας εἰς τὰς ὁδοὺς πάντας ἀναι(ρ)εῖν τρόπῳ ὅτῳ ἂν ἐπίστωνται. Moreover an Athenian psephism of the year 284/3 ὅπως ἂν οἱ ἀστυνόμοι οἱ ἀεὶ λαγχ(ά)νοντες ἐπιμέλειαν ποιῶντα(ι) τοῦ ἱεροῦ τῆς Ἀφροδίτης τῆς Πανδήμου κατὰ τὰ πάτρια decrees: τοὺς ἀστυνόμους ποιῆσαι λαχόντας, ὅταν ᾖ ἡ πομπὴ τῇ Ἀφροδίτῃ τῇ Πανδ(ή)μῳ, παρασκευάζειν εἰς κάθαρσι(ν τ)οῦ ἱεροῦ περιστερὰν καὶ περιαλε(ῖψαι) τοὺς βωμοὺς καὶ πιττῶσαι τὰ(ς) ὀροφὰς) καὶ λοῦσαι τὰ ἕδη, παρασκευά(σαι δὲ κα)ὶ πορφύραν ὁλκὴν ⊢⊢ (⊢)—: Bull. 13, 163.

had jurisdiction in disputes concerning matters that fell within the sphere of their official duties. The ten ἀγορανόμοι appointed by lot, of whom, as with the ἀστυνόμοι, 5 officiated in the city and 5 in the Piræus, were controllers of the market.[1] They collected the dues which foreigners had to pay for their market stalls,[2] and saw that order was kept in the market and that punishment was inflicted for any fraud practised there.[3] But in maintaining order they probably could not inflict corporal punishment except in the case of foreigners or slaves.[4] Further, it was the duty of the ἀγορανόμοι to supervise the Hetairai, for whom they assessed the amount of tax each had to pay.[5] The duty of keeping the places of traffic in the market clean, which Plato assigned to his Agoranomoi, actually belonged to the Athenian officials, as inscriptions demonstrate.[6] Not only the Agoranomoi but also the μετρονόμοι took care

ἀγορανόμοι.

μετρονόμοι.

---

[1] Cf. Haederli, ib. Arist. 51, 1: κληροῦνται δὲ καὶ ἀγορανόμοι, πέντε μὲν εἰς Πειραιέα, ε' δ' εἰς ἄστυ. τούτοις δὲ ὑπὸ τῶν νόμων προστέτακται τῶν ὠνίων ἐπιμελεῖσθαι πάντων, ὅπως καθαρὰ καὶ ἀκίβδηλα πωλῆται. See also Harp., ἀγορανόμοι οἱ τὰ κατὰ τὴν ἀγορὰν ὤνια διοικοῦντες ἄρχοντες· (Lex. Seguer. 199, 24; 330, 13. Et. M. s.v., Lys. 22, 16: ἀγορανόμοι ἐπὶ τοῖς ὠνίοις φύλακες) Δημοσθένης ἐν τῷ κατὰ Τιμοκράτους (Dem. 24, 112). Ἀριστοτέλης δ' ἐν Ἀθηναίων πολιτείᾳ κληροῦσθαί φησι πέντε μὲν εἰς Πειραιᾶ, πέντε δὲ εἰς ἄστυ. Cf. Aristoph., Acharn., 968. Summons before the Agoranomoi for damage done to goods: Aristoph., Wasps, 1406 sqq. Cf. Meier und Schömann[2] 100 sqq. Büchsenschütz, Besitz und Erwerb., 536. They also had their ἀγορανόμιον in the Piræus: Dittenberger Syll., 337. A dedicatory inscription of the ἀγορανόμοι in the C.I.A., II. 1208 b.

[2] See Schol. to Aristoph., Acharn., 896: ἔθος ἦν τὸ παλαιὸν ὡς καὶ μέχρι τοῦ νῦν τοὺς ἐν τῇ ἀγορᾷ πιπράσκοντας (but this is to be limited to strangers: Dem. 57, 31/2) τέλος διδόναι τοῖς λογισταῖς with which Schol. to line 723 is to be compared: ἀγορανόμους δέ, οὓς νῦν λογιστὰς καλοῦμεν. Stamps inscribed ἀγορανόμων, probably serving as receipts for the market duty when paid, are given by Benndorf, in the Zeitschr. f. d. östr. Gymn., 1875, p. 595.

[3] See Theophr. ap. Harp., κατὰ τὴν ἀγορὰν ἀψευδεῖν (=Phot. s.v.) Θεόφραστος γοῦν ἐν τοῖς περὶ νόμων φησὶ δυοῖν τούτων ἐπιμελεῖσθαι δεῖν τοὺς ἀγορανόμους τῆς τε ἐν τῇ ἀγορᾷ εὐκοσμίας καὶ τοῦ ἀψευδεῖν μὴ μόνον τοὺς πιπράσκοντας, ἀλλὰ καὶ τοὺς ὠνουμένους. See also Xen., Symp., 2, 20.

[4] For the power of corporal punishment, see Poll. 10, 177. Schol. to Aristoph., Acharn., 724.

[5] See Suid., διάγραμμα, and Meier und Schömann, att. Proc.,[2] 103, no. 188.

[6] See Plato, Laws, 6, 764. Aristot., Pol., 7. (6), 8, p. 189, 24 sqq. Bekker. Psephism of the year 320 in Dittenberger 337: ὅπως ἂν ἡ ἀγορὰ ἡ ἐν Πειραιεῖ (κα)τασκευασθεῖ καὶ ὁμαλισθεῖ ὡς κάλλιστα καὶ τὰ ἐν τῷ ἀγορανομίῳ ἐπισκευασθεῖ ὧν ἂν προσδεῖται ἅπαντα, ἀγαθῇ τύχῃ δεδόχθαι τῷ δήμῳ, τοὺς ἀγορανόμους τοὺς ἐν Πειραιεῖ ἐπιμεληθῆναι ἁπάντων τούτων· τὸ δ' ἀνάλωμα εἶναι εἰς ταῦτα ἐκ τοῦ ἀργυρίου, οὗ οἱ ἀγορανόμοι διαχειρίζουσιν.

that the sellers used correct weights. The Metronomoi were ten in number, and were appointed by lot, five for the city and five for the Piræus.[1] I consider the προμετρηταί their attendants,

προμετρηταί. who kept the official standards for re-measuring commodities, and seem to have received a certain fee out of what they re-measured.[2]

The corn and bread trade was under the direction of a board consisting originally of ten members appointed by lot, called οἱ σιτοφύλακες, of whom five acted in the city and five in

σιτοφύλακες. the Piræus; but towards the end of the fourth century this business was superintended by 20 officials in the city and 15 in the Piræus.[3] These σιτοφύλακες kept statistics of the quantity of corn imported, probably to control the corn merchants; and they had to see that the grain was sold legally, and the flour and bread according to the right weight and price.[4]

The 10 ἐπιμεληταὶ ἐμπορίου, appointed by lot, superintended the

ἐπιμεληταὶ Athenian mercantile ports. They had to see that the
ἐμπορίου. merchants conveyed to Athens two-thirds of the grain

---

[1] Arist. 51, 2: κληροῦνται δὲ καὶ μετρονόμοι, πέντε μὲν εἰς ἄστυ, ἐ δὲ εἰς Πειραιέα· καὶ οὗτοι τῶν μέτρων καὶ τῶν σταθμῶν ἐπιμελοῦνται πάντων, ὅπως οἱ πωλοῦντες χρήσονται δικαίοις. By this the conflicting statements concerning the number of members of this college of officials are disposed of. Cf. Harp., Suid., Phot., Lex. Seguer. 278, 25 sqq. By the ἄρχοντες mentioned in C.I.A., II. 476, the μετρονόμοι are to be understood. In the last century before Christ there were statute weights and measures in the Skias, in the Piræus and at Eleusis: C.I.A., II. 476.

[2] In the Lex. Seguer. 290, 34 sqq. the προμετρηταί are called ἄρχοντές τινες ἐναύσιοι οἱ τῷ δικαίῳ μέτρῳ διαμετροῦντες τὰ ὄσπρια καὶ τοὺς πυροὺς ἐν τῇ ἀγορᾷ. After Harp. προμετρητὴς (=Phot. προμετρητὰς) I can only consider them a kind of ὑπηρέται. In the statement of accounts of the ἐπιστάται Ἐλευσινόθεν of the year 329 we find the item προμετρητεῖ μισθὸς ἀπὸ τῶν ἑκατὸν (probably μεδίμνων) ⊢IC: Ἐφ. ἀρχ., 1883, pp. 125/6 β. 78. ἀπὸ τούτου προμετρητεῖ ⊢⊢ : pp. 125/6 γ. 3.

[3] Lys. 22, 16. Arist. 51, 3: ἦσαν δὲ καὶ ⟨δέκα⟩ σιτοφύλακες κληρωτοί, πέντε μὲν εἰς Πειραιέα, πέντε δ᾽ εἰς ἄστυ, νῦν δ᾽ εἴκοσι μὲν εἰς ἄστυ, πεντεκαίδεκα δ᾽ εἰς Πειραιέα. But here also the numbers vary with the lexicographers. See Harp., Suid., Phot. Five σιτοφύλακες in Lys. 22, 8 acc. to the emendation of Bergk, Rel. com. Gr., p. 18.

[4] They kept statistics of the imported grain: Dem. 20, 32. Cf. Lys. 22. For their official duties see Arist. 51, 3: οὗτοι δὲ ἐπιμελοῦνται πρῶτον μὲν ὅπως ὁ ἐν ἀγορᾷ σῖτος ἀργὸς ὤνιος ἔσται δικαίως, ἔπειθ᾽ ὅπως οἵ τε μυλωθροὶ πρὸς τὰς τιμὰς τῶν κριθῶν τὰ ἄλφιτα πωλήσουσιν καὶ οἱ ἀρτοπῶλαι πρὸς τὰς τιμὰς τῶν πυρῶν τοὺς ἄρτους καὶ τὸν σταθμὸν ἄγοντας, ὅσον ἂν οὗτοι τάξωσιν· ὁ γὰρ νόμος τούτους κελεύει τάττειν. Cf. Lex. Seguer. 300, 19 sqq., Harp., Suid., Phot.

that passed through the Athenian ports.¹ Besides this, all we know of their official business is that they were the authorities before whom were brought cases of φάσις against citizens or Metics who lent money on ships which had not taken cargo for the harbour of Athens.²

Just as the Athenian mercantile port had its inspectors, so also had the war harbour, which was guarded by five hundred sentinels chosen from the Demes. These inspectors were styled ἐπιμεληταί οἱ τῶν νεωρίων ἐπιμεληταί. It may be accepted as certain τῶν νεωρίων. that they too were ten in number, and appointed by lot, one from each tribe.³ According to our authorities, chiefly inscriptions, they had the superintendence of the docks and arsenals. They gave out ships and equipment to the Trierarchs and had them examined by an expert after the Trierarchs had returned them. They kept account of those who owed money to the docks, collected the debts, and presided over those courts which had to give judgment in naval matters.⁴

Probably on account of the scarcity of water from which Attica suffered, the office of superintendent of the wells seems to have been one of great importance. This can be gathered ὁ ἐπὶ τὰς from the fact that he was elected, and acted alone, κρήνας.

---

¹ Arist. 51, 4: ἐμπορίου δ' ἐπιμελητὰς δέκα κληροῦσιν (cf. Dein. in Arist. 10) τούτοις δὲ προστέτακται τῶν τ' ἐμπορίων ἐπιμελεῖσθαι καὶ τοῦ σίτου τοῦ καταπλέοντος εἰς τὸ ἀστικὸν ἐμπόριον τὰ δύο μέρη τοὺς ἐμπόρους ἀναγκάζειν εἰς τὸ ἄστυ κομίζειν. From this source: Harp. ἐπιμελητὴς ἐμπορίου. Suid. ἐπιμεληταί and ἐπιμελητὰς ἐμπορίου. Et. M. ἐπιμεληταί. Lex. Seguer. 255, 22 sqq. A late inscription (C.I.A., II. 475) mentions an elective ἐπιμελητὴς ἐπὶ τὸν λιμένα.

² Dem. 35, 51; (Dem.) 58, 8/9. We possess no accurate, detailed information about the ἐπιμεληταί ἐμπορίου. Baumstark, de curatoribus emporii et nautodicis ap. Athen., 1827, discusses all the possible theories.

³ Φρουροὶ νεωρίων πεντακόσιοι are mentioned in Arist. 24, 3, and with these the φρουροί of 62, 1 are identical. In an Athenian psephism of the year 405/4 οἱ νεωροί (cf. Hesych. νεωρός· νεωριοφύλαξ) are mentioned as a board ('Αρχ. δελτίον, 1889, pp. 25/6, 1. 80. Cf. C.I.A., IV. 3, 78a), who in the fifth century seem to have had the superintendence of the Athenian warharbour. In the fourth century they are called οἱ τῶν νεωρίων ἐπιμεληταί: Seeurk., XVI. b. 121, p. 585. 107, p. 584=C.I.A., II. 811 b, 105 sqq.· οἱ τῶν νεωρίων ἄρχοντες: XVI. b, 139, p. 586=II. 811b, 140. οἱ ἐν τοῖς νεωρίοις ἄρχοντες: X. c. 125, p. 878=II. 808c, 121. They made out the statements of accounts given in Boeckh, Seeurk.=C.I.A., II. 789-812. Particulars in Boeckh 49 sqq. For their number, ten, see Köhler, Mitth. d. dtsch. arch. Inst. in Ath., 4, pp. 84/5.

⁴ All this is obtained from inscriptions; Boeckh 55 sqq. For evidence from literature cf. Dem. 22, 63. (Dem.) 47, 22. Lex. Seguer. 282, 6 sqq. The expert is called ὁ δοκιμαστής, II. 56, p. 288=II. 794c, 88.

without a colleague. ὁ ἐπὶ τὰς κρήνας held office from one Panathenaia to the next, and was responsible for the repair of wells, conduits and the subterranean water pipes.[1]

The repairing of the public roads was entrusted to the ὁδοποιοί, who were appointed by lot, annually, and were five in number.[2]

ὁδοποιοί.

Οἱ ἱερῶν ἐπισκευασταί, ten in number, and appointed by lot, received 30 minæ annually from the Apodectai, and had to provide for any necessary repairs of the sanctuaries of Attica.[3]

οἱ ἱερῶν ἐπισκευασταί.

In conclusion we must mention some officials with religious functions. Among these must be first named the two colleges of the ἱεροποιοί. The first of these colleges consisted of ten ἱεροποιοί οἱ ἐπὶ τὰ ἐκθύματα, who were appointed by lot and had to prepare sacrifices decreed by oracle, and, when necessary, to assist the seers at sacrificial auspices.[4] Besides these there were ten ἱεροποιοὶ οἱ κατ' ἐνιαυτόν, appointed by lot, who had to offer certain sacrifices and to manage all penteterid festivals, with the exception of the great Panathenaia.[5]

ἱεροποιοί.

[1] For this official cf. Arist. 43, 1, where he is called ὁ τῶν κρηνῶν ἐπιμελητής. In a psephism of B.C. 333 it is said of a certain Pytheas: αἱρεθεὶς ἐπὶ τὰς κρήνας τῶν τε ἄλλων τῶν ἐν τῇ ἀρχῇ ἐπιμελεῖται καλῶς καὶ φιλοτίμως καὶ νῦν τήν τε πρὸς τῷ τοῦ Ἄμμωνος ἱερῷ κρήνην καινὴν ἐξῳκοδόμηκεν καὶ τὴν ἐν Ἀμφιαράου κρήνην κατεσκεύακεν καὶ τῆς τοῦ ὕδατος ἀγωγῆς καὶ τῶν ὑπονόμων ἐπιμεμέληται. Pytheas is honoured with a golden crown, ἀρετῆς ἕνεκα καὶ δικαιοσύνης τῆς περὶ τὴν ἐπιμέλειαν τῶν κρηνῶν, ὅπως ἂν καὶ οἱ ἄλλοι οἱ (ἀ)εὶ χειροτονούμενοι ἐπὶ τὰς κρήνας φιλοτιμῶνται ἕκαστοι εἰς τὸν δῆμον: Ἐφ. ἀρχ., 1889, pp. 15/6. According to Plut., Them., 31, Themistocles as ἐπιστάτης ὑδάτων punished τοὺς ὑφαιρουμένους τὸ ὕδωρ καὶ παροχετεύοντας. Cf. Poll. 8, 113. Phot., κρηνοφύλαξ. For the condition of the water supply of Attica, see Plut., Sol., 23.

[2] Arist. 54, 1: κληροῦσι δὲ καὶ τάσδε τὰς ἀρχάς· ὁδοποιοὺς πέντε, οἷς προστέτακται δημοσίους ἐργάτας ἔχουσι τὰς ὁδοὺς ἐπισκευάζειν. The ὁδοποιοί are mentioned again in Æschin. in Ctes. 25.

[3] Arist. 50, 1: κληροῦνται δὲ καὶ ἱερῶν ἐπισκευασταί, δέκα ἄνδρες, οἳ λαμβάνοντες τριάκοντα μνᾶς παρὰ τῶν ἀποδεκτῶν ἐπισκευάζουσιν τὰ μάλιστα δεόμενα τῶν ἱερῶν.

[4] Arist. 54, 6: κληροῖ δὲ καὶ ἱεροποιοὺς δέκα, τοὺς ἐπὶ τὰ ἐκθύματα καλουμένους, [οἳ] τά τε μ[αν]τευτὰ ἱερὰ θύουσιν, κἄν τι καλλιερῆσαι δέῃ καλλιεροῦσι μετὰ τῶν μάντε[ων]: Et. M., p. 468, ἱεροποιοί, Phot. s.v., Lex. Seguer. 265, 22 sqq., have confused the functions of these and of the ἱεροποιοί next to be treated of [Sandys, p. 197].

[5] Arist. 54, 7: κληροῖ δὲ καὶ ἑτέρους δέκα, τοὺς κατ' ἐνιαυτὸν καλουμένους (C.I.A., I. 188, 5 sqq. Ἐφ. ἀρχ., 1883, p. 121 sqq. β. 8, 38), οἳ θυσίας τέ τινας θύουσι [καὶ τ]ὰς [πεντε]τηρίδας ἁπάσας διοικοῦσιν πλὴν Παναθηναίων. ε[ἰσὶ δὲ] πεντετηρίδες, μία μ[ὲν ἡ εἰ]ς Δῆλον (ἔστι δὲ καὶ ἑπτετηρὶς ἐνταῦθα), δευτέρα δὲ Βραυρώνια, τρίτη [δὲ Ἡράκλει]α (for which Schoell, Sitzungsber. d. bayr. Ak., 1887, 1, 13/4 plau-

The management of the penteterid part of the great Panathenaia was the duty of ten Athlothetai, appointed by lot, one from each tribe, and holding office for four years. They had to make preparations for the great Panathenaia, to ἀθλοθέται. arrange the Pompe, and manage the gymnastic, equestrian, and musical contests.¹

The office of the βοῶναι was given to distinguished citizens as a mark of honour. They were elected to buy oxen for the sacrifices.² βοῶναι.

Besides the ordinary officials enumerated above, there were extraordinary officials who were appointed by special Extraordinary officials. psephism, at special times and under special conditions.

In the first place, mention must be made of the ἐπιστάται τῶν δημοσίων ἔργων, who were elected in varying number, ἐπιστάται probably from among all Athenians, to superintend τῶν δημοσίων the state buildings. The technical supervision was ἔργων. entrusted to an expert.³ But it was a common practice to divide

sibly conjectures Ἡφαίστια), τετάρτη δὲ Ἐλ[ευσίνια, πέμπτη] δὲ Πα[ν]αθηναια, καὶ τούτων οὐδεμία ἐν τῷ αὐτῷ ἐν[ιαυτῷ] γίγνε[ται]. Cf. Poll. 8, 107. The connexion of these ἱεροποιοί with the Panathenaia, proved by inscriptions—C.I.A., II. 163—must be compared with the statement of Aristotle that at the great Panathenaia they performed what was annually performed, while all that was peculiar to the quinquennial festival belonged to the office of the Athlothetai. Mommsen, *Heort.*, 118. This explains C.I.A., I. 188. 5 sqq., II. 741. The διοίκησις described in C.I.A., II. 163 refers to the annual Panathenaia. The theory of Schoell, 11 sqq., is now disproved by the authentic text of Aristotle. Ἱεροποιοί for Artemis Brauronia are mentioned in C.I.A., II. 729, for the Hephaistia in the inscr. in Schoell, p. 24: τὴν δὲ λ(αμπάδα ποιεῖν τῇ πεν)ετηρίδι (καὶ τοῖς Ἡφ)αιστίοις ποιούντω(ν δ)ὲ οἱ ἱερο(ποιοὶ ὡς ἄριστα). They are expressly designated ἱεροποιοὶ κατ' ἐνιαυτὸν in the Eleusinian accounts in the Ἐφ. ἀρχ., 1883, 121 sqq., β. 35 sqq. An inscription referring to the Eleusinian penteteris in Ἐφ. ἀρχ. 1883, 121 ff. β 46 ff. These permanent ἱεροποιοί were different from the committees of ἱεροποιοί nominated for special occasions. For these cf. Schoell 1 sqq.

¹ Arist. 60, 1: κληροῦσι δὲ καὶ ἀθλοθέτας δέκα ἄνδρας, ἕνα τῆς φυλῆς ἑκάστης. οὗτοι δὲ δοκιμασθέντες ἄρχουσι τέτταρα ἔτη καὶ διοικοῦσι τήν τε πομπὴν τῶν Παναθηναίων καὶ τὸν ἀγῶνα τῆς μουσικῆς καὶ τὸν γυμνικὸν ἀγῶνα καὶ τὴν ἱπποδρομίαν καὶ τὸν πέπλον ποιοῦνται καὶ τοὺς ἀμφορεῖς ποιοῦνται μετὰ τῆς βουλῆς καὶ τὸ ἔλαιον τοῖς ἀθληταῖς ἀποδιδόασι. Cf. the rest of the chapter. Poll. 8, 93. 88. C.I.A., I. 188. 5 sqq.

² Suid. βοώνης. οὗτος παρὰ τῆς πόλεως ᾑρεῖτο (Dem. 21, 171), ἵνα βοῦς αὐτῇ πρίηται, πρὸς τὰς θυσίας. ἦν δὲ λαμπρὸν τὸ βοώνην γενέσθαι (cf. Harp. *s.v.*), ἐπειδὴ στρατηγοὺς φασι βοώνας μάλιστα χειροτονεῖσθαι. Lex. Seguer. 219, 22 sqq. That there were several βοῶναι is apparent from C.I.A., II. 163, 741.

³ Æschin. *in Ctes.* 14. 29. C.I.A., I. 289 sqq. Bull. 13. 174 sqq. The number of these ἐπιστάται, according to what evidence we have, varies

the expense of constructing public works among the tribes, who then appointed from their number a board of overseers to supervise their share of the work. The most important of these tribe-commissions were the τειχοποιοί, ταφροποιοί, and τριηροποιοί.[1]

To the extraordinary officials belonged also the ten ἀποστολεῖς, ἀποστολεῖς. who were elected from among all the Athenians, in case of need, to see to the despatch of the fleet required.[2] The ἀποστολεῖς in addition had the right of punishing dilatory Trierarchs, and supported the inspectors of the dockyards in settling any questions arising from the despatch of the fleet.[3]

In times of famine at Athens corn was bought partly at the State's expense, partly from voluntary contributions, and was then distributed to the poor from the public granaries, probably σιτῶναι. at less than cost price. The purchase of this corn was entrusted sometimes to one, sometimes to several elected σιτῶναι.[4]

We meet too with other committees: ζητηταί, with judicial and ζητηταί. financial duties;[5] ἐξετασταί, who had to count the troops enrolled by the State, so that the Strategoi ἐξετασταί. could not defraud the State with respect to the

between 2, 3 and 5: *e.g.* three ἐπιστάται τοῦ νεῶ for the building of the Erectheion with an ἀρχιτέκτων and a γραμματεὺς, 409 B.C.: C.I.A., I. 322. ἀγάλματος (of Athene Parthenos) ἐπιστάται with a γραμματεύς: C.I.A., I. 298. Bull. 13. 172, where also seven ταμίαι are mentioned.

[1] Æschin. *in Ctes.* 14. 27. 30. Αἰγεῖδος τειχοπ(οιοί) in B.C. 394/3: C.I.A., II. 830. τειχοποιο(ί) Πανδιονίδ(ος) B.C. 855/4: II. 833. Sometimes, too, the council appointed council-commissions for this purpose. Arist. 46, 1: ποιεῖται δὲ τὰς τριήρεις δέκα ἄνδρας ἐξ α[ὑτῶν] ἑλομένη τριηροποιούς. [Sandys, p. 169.]

[2] Seeurk. xiv. b. 20 sqq., p. 466=C.I.A., II. 809b, 20 sqq.: ἑλέσθαι δὲ καὶ ἀποστολέας τὸν δῆμον δέκα ἄνδρας ἐξ Ἀθηναίων ἁπάντων, τοὺς δὲ αἱρεθέντας ἐπιμελεῖσθαι τοῦ ἀποστόλο(υ) καθάπερ τῇ βουλῇ προστέτακται. Cf. Harp. ἀποστολῆς = Suid., Lex. Seguer. 203, 22 sqq. = 435, 29 sqq.

[3] The Trierarchs put in prison by the ἀποστολεῖς: Dem. 18, 107; cf. Dem. 51, 4. The ἀποστολεῖς and the inspectors of the dockyards bring διαδικασίαι about the σκεύη into court: (Dem.) 47, 26. 33.

[4] Boeckh 1, 123 (Bk. i. c. 15) sqq. Demosthenes was, apparently, σιτώνης without a colleague: Dem. 18, 248. C.I.A., II. 335, a decree of honour to the σιτῶναι and their γραμματεύς, mentions ten σιτῶναι. They were elected according to C.I.A., II. 353. Under the Archon Menecles a single ταμίας τῶν σιτωνικῶν is mentioned, though at an earlier date there were several. Ἐφ. ἀρχ., 1887, p. 187.

[5] Elected ζητηταί after the mutilation of the Hermæ: Andoc., *de Myst.* 36. 40. 65. Financial ζητηταί, to discover what private persons possessed state property: Lys. 21, 16; Dem. 24, 11. See Harp. ζητητής. Phot. ζητητής and ζητηταί. Poll. 8, 115. Lex. Seguer. 261, 4 sqq. The μαστῆρες, I do not consider Attic. Harp., Phot., *s.v.*

amount of money due for soldiers' pay;[1] and πορισταί, whose duty it was to procure for the State the money necessary to meet a deficiency.[2]   πορισταί.

B. *The Council of the 500 and the Council of the Areopagus.*

After the constitutional changes of Cleisthenes, the Athenian Council consisted of 500 members, a number which was raised to 600 on the introduction of an eleventh and twelfth Number and tribe. The full title of this Council was ἡ βουλὴ οἱ Name. πεντακόσιοι, and later ἡ βουλὴ οἱ ἑξακόσιοι, but this was regularly shortened into ἡ βουλή.[3] Every Athenian citizen, who had reached his thirtieth year, and was possessed of full citizen- Mode of ship, was eligible for the βουλεία, i.e. for the post appointment. of councillor; but it could not be held more than twice by the same person.[4] The councillors were appointed by lot, 50 from each tribe, and probably in this way:—each Deme nominated a certain number of candidates proportionate to the size of the Deme, and from these were appointed by lot—probably with due regard to the size of the individual Demes—first the councillors, and then those who were to replace them in case of eventuali-

---

[1] Their duty is so described in Lex. Seguer. 252. 6 sqq., which is in harmony with Æschin. *in Tim.* 113, and *de fals. leg.* 177.

[2] *Beitr.*, 387 sqq. Beloch in *N. Rhein. Mus.*, 39, 249 sqq. I have not spoken here of the offices temporarily instituted during times of rapid constitutional change. For these I refer the reader to *Beitr.*, where the πρόβουλοι are treated, p. 289 sqq.; the καταλογεῖς, 314 sqq.; the ἀναγραφεῖς τῶν νόμων, p. 326 sqq., the συγγραφεῖς, p. 341 sqq. See also R. Schoell in *Commentat. phil. in honor. Mommseni*, p. 458 sqq. Foucart in Bull. 4, 248 sqq. For the σύνδικοι and συλλογεῖς, who were in office for several years after the downfall of the Thirty, see Schoell, *Quaest. fisc. iuris att. ex Lysiae orationib. illustratae*, 1873, and Meier [2], 123 sqq.

[3] The Dissertation of C. van Osenbruggen, Haag, 1834, which is now to a large extent out of date, and Heydemann, *de senatu Atheniensium* in *Dissertat. philol. Argentoratens. Sel.* 4, p. 151 sqq., deal specially with the Athenian Council of 500. ἡ βουλὴ οἱ πεντακόσιοι: Lyc., *Leocr.*, 37. Æschin. *in Ctes.* 20. ἡ βουλὴ οἱ ἑξακόσιοι: C.I.A., II. 476. Probably after the institution of the Ptolemaïs tribe there were for a short time 13 tribes. At any rate there is evidence of a council of 650 members. ἡ βουλὴ οἱ ἑξακόσιοι καὶ πεντήκοντα: 'Εφ. ἀρχ., 1887, p. 177, l. 25/6.

[4] For the definition of βουλεία see Harp. *s.v.* The βουλεία could only be held twice by the same person. Arist. 62. 3: ἄρχειν δὲ τὰς μὲν κατὰ πόλεμον ἀρχὰς ἔ[ξεσ]τι πλεονάκις, τῶν δ' ἄλλων οὐδεμίαν πλὴν βουλεῦσαι δίς. [Headlam, *On the lot*, p. 50.] The age of thirty: Xen., *Mem.*, 1, 2, 35.

ties.[1] After nomination the Bouleutai had to pass a Dokimasia before the old Council; in this examination the candidate's whole life, public and private, was subject to criticism, and any Athenian who chose could bring charges against him. In early times this Dokimasia was final; but afterwards the rejected candidate was at liberty to appeal from the decision of the Council to a court of the Heliaia.[2]

Dokimasia.

Before their entrance on office (which, it seems, took place in the middle of Skirophorion, and was attended with festal εἰσιτήρια), the Bouleutai took an oath of office, by which they bound themselves to administer their office according to the laws, to keep the statutes of Solon, to give the people the best advice, to reject the unworthy at the Dokimasia of the next

Oath of Office.

---

[1] Arist. 43, 2: βουλὴ κληροῦται φ´, ν´ ἀπὸ ⟨τῆς⟩ φυλῆς ἑκάστης. The method of nomination is described in Arist. 62, 1, and with this p. 153 should be compared. It was not obligatory to nominate candidates for the βουλεία, and consequently insignificant Demes took no part, and held themselves aloof from politics, as the lists of the Prytanies shew: Köhler, in *Mitth. d. dtsch. arch. Inst. in Ath.*, 4, 105/6. We find from inscrr. that the number of Bouleutai supplied by the same Deme was practically identical in various different years; from this we may infer that in the nomination of the Bouleutai the size of the individual Demes was taken into account. Cf. Beloch, *d. Bevölker. der griech-röm. Welt*, 102 sqq. Lists of the Prytanies in C.I.A., II. 864–874. That men gave notice of their candidature is proved by Lys. 31, 33, where it says of a candidate for the βουλεία: ὥσπερ νῦν προθύμως κληρωσόμενος ἦλθε. Difference between λαχόντες and ἐπιλαχόντες: Æschin. *in Ctes.* 62. That for each councillor there was a substitute allotted to take his place if necessary is to be inferred from the Platonic Hyperbolos in Meineke 2, 670: εὐτυχεῖς ὦ δέσποτα.—B. τί δ' ἔστιν; A. βουλεύειν ὀλίγου 'λαχες πάνυ.—ἀτὰρ οὐ λαχὼν ὅμως ἔλαχες, ἢν νοῦν ἔχῃς.—B. πῶς ἦν ἔχω νοῦν; A. ὅτι πονηρῷ καὶ ξένῳ—ἐπέλαχες ἀνδρί, μηδέπω γὰρ ἐλευθέρῳ . . . B. ἀπερρ'· ἐγὼ δ' ὑμῖν τὸ πρᾶγμα δὴ φράσω—Ὑπερβόλῳ βουλῆς γὰρ, ἄνδρες, ἐπέλαχον. Cf. *Beiträge*, etc., 81; Harp. ἐπιλαχών, where however what is correct in the case of the Bouleutai is wrongly made to apply to the magistrates as well: ἐπιλαχών—ἐκληροῦντο οἱ βουλεύειν ἢ ἄρχειν ἐφιέμενοι, ἔπειτα ἑκάστῳ τῶν λαχόντων ἕτερος ἐπελάγχανεν, ἵν', ἐὰν ὁ πρῶτος λαχὼν ἀποδοκιμασθῇ ἢ τελευτήσῃ, ἀντ' ἐκείνου γένηται βουλευτὴς ὁ ἐπιλαχὼν αὐτῷ. For the selection by lot with beans in the case of councillors see Thuc. 8, 69: τοῖς ἀπὸ τοῦ κυάμου βουλευταῖς. [Headlam 41–56. 86. 188].

[2] Dem. 21, 111; (Dem.) 59, 3. The Dokimasia takes place before the old council: Lys. 31, 1. Arist. 45, 3: δοκιμάζει δὲ (sc. ἡ βουλὴ) καὶ τοὺς βουλευτὰς τοὺς τὸν ὕστερον ἐνιαυτὸν βουλεύσοντας καὶ τοὺς ἐννέα ἄρχοντας. καὶ πρότερον μὲν ἦν ἀποδοκιμάσαι κυρία, νῦν δὲ ⟨καὶ⟩ τούτοις ἔφεσίς ἐστιν εἰς τὸ δικαστήριον. For the nature of this Dokimasia see Lys. 16, 9: ἐν δὲ ταῖς δοκιμασίαις δίκαιον εἶναι παντὸς τοῦ βίου λόγον διδόναι. Lys. 31 is a speech for the prosecution, Lys. 16 a speech for the defence in such a Dokimasia.

Council, and only under certain specified conditions to consent to imprison an Athenian.[1] The Bouleutai wore wreaths as their emblem of office; their privileges were freedom from military service during their year of office, and a seat of honour in the theatre; they received as salary one drachma per day, at the end of the fourth century five obols.[2] It was customary for the people to vote crowns of honour to the Council at the end of its year of office, if its administration had been satisfactory.[3]

Honours and Emoluments.

The Council as a whole had a certain disciplinary power over its members: for instance, it could provisionally expel a member by ἐκφυλλοφορία, which was either confirmed or reversed by a subsequent formal and judicial trial before the Council.[4] At the end of its year of office the Council

ἐκφυλλοφορία and Account of Office.

---

[1] Their entrance on office in the middle of the month Skirophorion seems to follow from Arist. 32, 1. Εἰσιτήρια at the Council's accession to office, Thuc. 8, 70; Dem. 19, 190; 21, 114. The βουλευτικὸς ὅρκος dated from soon after Cleisthenes' time. Arist. 22, 2: πρῶτον μὲν οὖν ἔτει πέμπτῳ μετὰ ταύτην τὴν κατάστασιν ἐφ' Ἑρμοκρέοντος ἄρχοντος τῇ βουλῇ τοῖς πεντακοσίοις τὸν ὅρκον ἐποίησαν, ὃν ἔτι καὶ νῦν ὀμνύουσιν. Particulars of the βουλευτικὸς ὅρκος: κατὰ τοὺς νόμους βουλεύσειν: Xen., Mem., 1. 1. 18, τοὺς Σόλωνος νόμους ἐμπεδώσειν: Plut., Sol., 25, τὰ βέλτιστα βουλεύσειν τῷ δήμῳ τῶν Ἀθηναίων: (Dem.) 59, 4. Lys. 31, 1, ἀποφαίνειν, εἴ τίς τινα οἶδε τῶν λαχόντων ἀνεπιτήδειον ὄντα βουλεύειν: Lys. 31, 2. Cf. 26, 8. The clause relating to imprisonment of Athenian citizens is given in Dem. 24, 144. For an addition of the year 410/9 in Philoch. in the Schol. Aristoph. Plut. 972, see Beitr., 348 sqq.; and for another in the year of Eucleides, Andoc., de Myst., 91. See Taylor, Lect. Lys., p. 325. Hofmann, de iuris iurandi ap. Athenienses formulis, p. 38 sqq., Darmstadt, 1886.

[2] For the wreath: Lyc., Leocr., 122. Exemption from military service Lyc., Leocr., 37. Seat of honour in the theatre=βουλευτικὸς τόπος: Aristoph., Birds, 794, with the Schol. Hesych. βουλευτικόν. Suid., βουλευτικός. Poll. 4. 122. The βουλευτικὸς μισθὸς of one drachma: Hesych. βουλῆς λαχεῖν. Thuc. 8, 69. In Aristotle's time five obols: Arist. 62, 2. Köhler understands the καθέσιμον τῆς βουλῆς mentioned in C.I.A., II. 444. 445. 446, as payment to the Council, which the Agonothetes of the Theseia pays ἐκ τῶν ἰδίων.

[3] See the second Hypothesis to Dem. 22, p. 590: νόμος δὲ ἦν τὴν βουλὴν τὴν δόξασαν τῷ δήμῳ καλῶς βεβουλευκέναι στεφανοῦσθαι. But the council could not expect this honour, if it had built no triremes: Dem. 22, 12. 36. Arist. 46, 1: ἂν δὲ μὴ παραδῶσιν ἐξειργασμένα ταῦτα (everything connected with shipbuilding for the navy) τῇ νέᾳ βουλῇ, τὴν δωρεὰν οὐκ ἔστιν αὐτοῖς λαβεῖν. ἐπὶ γὰρ τῆς ὑστέρων βουλῆς λαμβάνουσιν.

[4] Harp. ἐκφυλλοφορῆσαι· εἰ ἐδόκει τις τῶν βουλευτῶν ἀδικεῖν, διεψηφίζετο ἡ βουλὴ περὶ αὐτοῦ, εἰ χρὴ αὐτὸν μηκέτι βουλεύειν· ἀντὶ δὲ ψήφων φύλλοις ἐχρῶντο, δι' ὧν ἕκαστος ἐπεσημαίνετο τὴν αὐτοῦ γνώμην. Δείναρχος ἐν τῷ κατὰ Πολυεύκτου ἐκφυλλοφορηθέντος. Cf. Lex. Seguer. 248, 7 sqq. For the final decision see Æschin. in Tim. 129: μετὰ ταῦτα ὡς ἐπανῆλθεν ἡ βουλὴ εἰς τὸ βουλευτήριον,

had to render account; every single member was responsible for his official acts.[1]

Officials of the Council. The Council had a number of officials and servants, of whom the secretaries occupy the first place.[2] The first and original clerk of the Council was at first elected and changed with the Prytany; his full title was accordingly ὁ κατὰ πρυτανείαν γραμματεὺς τῆς βουλῆς, a title usually shortened however to ὁ γραμματεὺς τῆς βουλῆς. He had to see to the drafting, writing, and setting up of inscriptions, superintended the archives, and kept copies of documents.[3] About the middle

ἐξεφυλλοφόρησε μὲν αὐτόν, ἐν δὲ τῇ ψήφῳ κατεδέξατο, on which a Schol. says: διὰ φύλλων γὰρ οἱ βουλευταὶ ἐψηφίζοντο ἐν τῇ πρώτῃ δοκιμασίᾳ, ἐν δὲ τῇ δευτέρᾳ ψήφοις. δεύτερον γὰρ ἐβουλεύοντο περὶ τοῦ αὐτοῦ. Et. M. ἐκφυλλοφορῆσαι—μετὰ δὲ τὸ ἁλῶναι κακουργοῦντα Ξενότιμον τὸν ὑπηρέτην ἐν τοῖς κυάμοις, οὕτως ἡ τῶν φύλλων ἐπενοήθη. ἐξῆν μέντοι ἐν τῷ δικαστηρίῳ καταδέχεσθαι τοὺς ἐκφυλλοφορηθέντας, ὡς καὶ Δημοσθένης φησὶν ἐν τῷ κατὰ Νεαίρας, where, however, nothing is said about it. If the statement of Et. M. is correct, we must understand by δικαστήριον the council acting as a court of justice. Deinarchos' speech κατὰ Πολυεύκτου ἐκφυλλοφορηθέντος was delivered before the Council. The δικαστήριον mentioned in Æschin. in Tim. 129, 130, is the Dicastery which would have tried the case if Timarchos had been accused of κλοπὴ δημοσίων χρημάτων.

[1] Æschin. in Ctes. 20: πάλιν τὴν βουλὴν τοὺς πεντακοσίους ὑπεύθυνον πεποίηκεν ὁ νομοθέτης. According to Dem. 22, 38/9 every single Bouleutes is accountable. C.I.A., II. 114, the Bouleutes Phanodemos is to be crowned ἐπειδὰν τὰς εὐθύνας δῷ.

[2] The following have written on the clerks of the Council:—C. Schaefer, de scribis senatus populique Atheniensium, Greifswald, 1878. Hille, de scribis Atheniensium in Leipziger Stud., vol. 1. Kornitzer, de scribis publicis Atheniensium in the Progr. von Hernals, 1882/3. Hartel, Stud. üb. att. Staatsrecht und Urkundenwesen, 119 sqq., and the author in the Phil. 89, 131 sqq. To what extent I have altered my views on account of the evidence of Arist. 54, 3 sqq., will appear from what is said in the text.

[3] In Aristotle's time there were three secretaries to the Council. The first he describes, 54, 3, in the following terms: κληροῦσι δὲ καὶ γραμματέα τὸν κατὰ πρυτανείαν καλούμενον, ὃς τῶν γραμμάτων ⟨τ'⟩ ἐστὶ κύριος καὶ τὰ ψηφίσματα τὰ γιγνόμενα φυλάττει καὶ τἆλλα πάντα ἀντιγράφεται καὶ παρακάθηται τῇ βουλῇ. πρότερον μὲν οὖν οὗτος ἦν χειροτονητὸς καὶ τοὺς ἐνδοξοτάτους καὶ πιστοτάτους [ἐχειρ]οτόνουν· καὶ γὰρ ἐν ταῖς στήλαις πρὸς ταῖς συμμαχίαις (e.g. C.I.A., II. 17), καὶ προξενίαις (e.g. I. 45), καὶ πολιτείαις (e.g. I. 59) οὗτος ἀναγράφεται· νῦν δὲ γέγονε κληρωτός. Harp. γραμματεύς only notices this secretary, while Poll. 8, 98 gives a complete extract from Aristotle. In C.I.A., I. 61 the ἀναγραφῆς τῶν νόμων are to receive Draco's laws as to murder, παρὰ (τ)οῦ (κατὰ πρυτανείαν γραμμα)τέως τῆς βουλῆς. I consider this reading of Köhler's (Herm., 2, 27) undoubtedly correct, not Schaefer's attempt, 13 sqq., παρὰ (τ)οῦ (βασιλέως μετὰ τοῦ γραμμα)τέως τῆς βουλῆς, especially as there is evidence of the scribe changing with the Prytany before Eucleides. See C.I.A., I. 188, 58, IV. 51,

of the sixties in the fourth century the character of this clerk of the Council changes: he seems after this to have been appointed by lot for the whole year. His title was the same as before, except that the abbreviation γραμματεὺς κατὰ πρυτανείαν, which meets us for the first time B.C. 358/7 or 354/3, became more and more frequent, alternating with γραμματεὺς τῆς βουλῆς, until the latter died out.[1] The fact that, after this change in the character of the secretary to the Council, the abbreviation of his title γραμματεὺς κατὰ πρυτανείαν becomes more common, is most easily explained, if we suppose that when this change was made the second secretaryship spoken of by Aristotle had been established.

This second secretary was appointed by lot, and had to fulfil the same duties with respect to the laws as the first secretary had to perform with respect to the decrees of the Council and people. There are no traces of this second secretary in the inscriptions, but he was without doubt styled γραμματεὺς τῆς βουλῆς; so that it was probably in order to distinguish him from the first secretary

---

I. 59, and the formula for designating the year, ἐπὶ τῆς βουλῆς, ᾗ ὁ δεῖνα πρῶτος ἐγραμμάτευεν: I. 33, 176, 188, 273, 301. If besides this scribe, who changed with the Prytanies, there had been an annual one, it would have been more natural to use his name to designate the year. The writing and setting up of the psephisms was regularly intrusted to the secretary to the Council. For his official functions as keeper of the archives cf. Ath. 9, 407 c; C.I.A., IV. 51, *fr. f. gr.* 28 sqq., 61 a, 26 sqq., II. 17, 63 sqq., 49, 12 sqq. Ἀρχ. δελτίον, 1889, p. 26, 25 sqq. Dittenberger, *Syll.* 101, 60 sqq. ἀντιγράφεσθαι and ἀντίγραφα ποιήσασθαι: II. 61.

[1] As the secretary mentioned in the prefaces to decrees is found in the later inscriptions of the fourth century in different Prytanies in the same year, Boeckh, *epigr. chron. Stud.*, 38 sqq., concluded that from some time in the fourth century onwards this scribe held office for a year. The earliest instance, so far as I can discover, is in B.C. 363/2, when Nicostratos of Pallene was secretary to the Acamantis, Oineis, and Aiantis tribes. See C.I.A., II. 54. 55, Ἀθήν., 5, 516. Now as we know that in B.C. 368/7 there were different secretaries for the first and sixth Prytanies (C.I.A., II. 52 b, 52 c) we may conjecture that the extension of the secretary's term of office took place somewhere between the years 368/7 and 363/2. Schaefer, p. 29; Hartel 120; Hille 209/10. With this extension of the term of office the change in the method of nomination attested by Aristotle was probably connected. The phrase in the prefaces to decrees ἐπὶ τῆς—πρυτανείας, ᾗ ὁ δεῖνα ἐγραμμάτευεν, still found after the secretary became annual, was retained as a traditional formula. Hartel 29. The title γραμματεὺς κατὰ πρυτανείαν first in C.I.A., II. 61. For the occurrence of the title γραμματεὺς κατὰ πρυτανείαν and γραμματεὺς τῆς βουλῆς in the same inscription see *Phil.*, 39, 136/7. In B.C. 322/1, for the last time so far as I am aware, γραμματεὺς τῆς βουλῆς: C.I.A., II. 186.

that the abbreviation γραμματεὺς κατὰ πρυτανείαν came more and more into use for the first secretary, instead of the abbreviation usual up to that time, γραμματεὺς τῆς βουλῆς.[1]

Finally, a third secretary was elected by the people to produce in the assembly of the people and in the Council papers which had to be read aloud. He seems to have existed even in the fifth century. I should identify him with the γραμματεὺς τῆς βουλῆς καὶ τοῦ δήμου, sometimes mentioned in inscriptions.[2]

The office of secretary for the laws probably remained in existence for only a short time; on the other hand, the γραμματεὺς τῆς βουλῆς καὶ τοῦ δήμου (who after B.C. 307/6 is as a rule called simply γραμματεὺς τοῦ δήμου) was entrusted with additional duties, temporarily at any rate; for during the first few years after 307 B.C. we find him in the inscriptions commissioned alternately with the γραμματεὺς κατὰ πρυτανείαν to write and set up public inscriptions.[3]

---

[1] Arist. 54, 4, says: κληροῦσι δὲ καὶ ἐπὶ τοὺς νόμους ἕτερον (cf. Poll. 8, 98). ὃς παρακάθηται τῇ βουλῇ καὶ ἀντιγράφεται καὶ οὗτος πάντας. In the fifth century ὁ κατὰ πρυτανείαν γραμματεὺς τῆς βουλῆς still had charge of the original copies of the laws. C.I.A., I. 61. That this new secretary is not met with in psephisms is quite natural. If the document in Dem. 24, 42 is genuine and subsequent to the introduction of this second secretary, the γραμματεὺς τῆς βουλῆς mentioned in it must be the ἐπὶ τοὺς νόμους of Aristotle.

[2] Arist. 54. 5: χειροτονεῖ δὲ καὶ ὁ δῆμος γραμματέα τὸν ἀναγνωσόμενον αὐτῷ καὶ τῇ βουλῇ καὶ οὗτος οὐδενός ἐστι κύριος ἀλλ' ἢ τοῦ ἀναγνῶναι. In Thuc. 7. 10, ὁ γραμματεὺς ὁ τῆς πόλεως reads documents in the assembly of the people. According to the arrangement introduced by Lycurgos at the representation of plays of Æschylus, Sophocles, and Euripides, ὁ τῆς πόλεως γραμματεὺς was to follow the play in a copy belonging to the State, to see that no changes were introduced: Pseudoplut., vit. Lyc., 11. p. 1026, Didot. This evidently unofficial designation corresponds to ὁ γραμματεὺς τῆς βουλῆς καὶ τοῦ δήμου. He was probably mentioned in the lists of the Prytanes (C.I.A., II. 865, 867, 869, 870. Bull. 13. 348), because the honours were decreed to the Prytanes by the people and Council. See Köhler on II. 865. In C.I.A., II. 114A, which the γραμματεὺς κατὰ πρυτανείαν is to draw up, the words καὶ ἀνα(γνῶ)ναι τόδε τὸ ψήφισμα τὸγγραμματέα τῷ δήμῳ must be taken as referring to this third secretary. Probably both Æschines and Aphobetos held this office; τὸ τελευταῖον ὑφ' ὑμῶν γραμματεῖς χειροτονηθέντες δύ' ἔτη ἐτράφησαν ἐν τῇ θόλῳ: Dem. 19. 249. Cf. 19, 70, where ὑπογραμματεύων καὶ ὑπηρετῶν is probably a depreciatory phrase for γραμματεύων.

[3] The abbreviation γραμματεὺς τοῦ δήμου is usual after 307/6 (Pseudoplut., vit. X or. decr. iii. 8, p. 1038, Didot). The full title γραμματεὺς τῆς βουλῆς καὶ τοῦ δήμου only occurs in isolated cases. C.I.A., II. 309, 393, 431, 488. Soon after the beginning of the third century the γραμματεὺς τοῦ δήμου disappears from the inscriptions; and they are again set up by the γραμματεὺς κατὰ πρυτανείαν alone. Köhler on C.I.A., II. 415. Mitth. d. dtsch. arch. Inst. in Ath., 1, 262. But both secretaries lasted down to Roman times; the

Temporary assistance in publishing the psephisms was given to the secretary of the Council by ὁ ἐπὶ τὰ ψηφίσματα, of whom there is evidence for B.C. 343/2, and by the ἀναγραφεύς, attested for the years 321–318:[1] his regular assistant was the ὑπογραμματεύς.[2] The Council elected from among its members two treasurers, who had control over the money which had to be paid for the publication of the decrees of the Council and for certain sacrifices.[3] Lastly must be mentioned the herald of the Council, who was a paid official.[4]

As the whole Council could not always be together, the administration was arranged for in the following way:—to transact current business and to prepare proposals for the Council, the 50 councillors of each tribe formed a permanent committee for the tenth part of a year. They were called πρυτάνεις, and the order of the tribes for this purpose was settled each year by lot.[5] This tenth of the year was called a πρυτανεία, and in the ordinary year consisted of 35 or 36 days, in

Prytanies.

γραμματεὺς κατὰ πρυτανείαν, also called περὶ βῆμα,—the identity of these two can be deduced from C.I.A., III. 10 (see Hille 220/1),—and the γραμματεὺς βουλῆς καὶ δήμου, also probably called simply γραμματεὺς βουλῆς (C.I.A., III. 1038, 1045), are δίσιτοι : C.I.A., III. 1029 sqq.

[1] For the former see C.I.A., II. 114, for the latter II. 227. 228. 229. Ἀθήν. 6. 133. Bull. 12, 147. Schaefer 31 sqq. C.I.A., II. 190: ἐπειδὴ ὁ ἀναγραφεὺς Καλλικρατίδης καλῶς καὶ δικαίως ἐπιμεμέληται τῆς ἀναγραφῆς τῶγγραμμάτων.

[2] For the ὑπογραμματεὺς τῆς βουλῆς see C.I.A., II. 329. 393. 431. 441. Hille 230 sqq.

[3] Two βουλῆς ταμίαι B.C. 343/2: C.I.A., II. 114. They controlled τὰ κατὰ ψηφίσματα ἀναλισκόμενα τῇ βουλῇ : II. 114 B, 61. From the end of the fourth century there seems to have been only one ταμίας (Fellner, z. Gesch. d. att. Finanzverwalt., p. 50), perhaps also in the fifth century, as the ταμίας mentioned in a psephism of the year 405/4 is probably the treasurer of the Council. Ἀρχ. δελτίον, 1889, pp. 26. 39. C.I.A., II. 329, at the beginning of the third century, says: Ν(ι)κο(κ)ράτης βουλεύειν λαχών—καὶ ταμίας αἱρεθεὶς ὑπὸ τῆς βουλῆς εἴς τε τὰ(ς) θυσίας τοῖς—σιν μεμέρικεν τοῖς ἱεροποιοῖς. Cf. II. 375. Ἀθήν., 6. 270. He was responsible to the Council: καὶ ὑπὲρ ἁπάντων (ὧν ὠ)ικ(ο)νόμηκεν ἀπολελόγισται τεῖ βουλεῖ ὀρθῶς καὶ δικαίως.

[4] C.I.A., II. 73. 329. Later he is called κῆρυξ τῆς βουλῆς καὶ τοῦ δήμου: C.I.A., II. 393. 394. 431.

[5] Harp. πρυτάνεις· τὸ δέκατον μέρος τῆς βουλῆς τῶν πεντακοσίων πεντήκοντα ἄνδρες ἀπὸ μιᾶς φυλῆς, οἱ διοικοῦντες ἅπαντα τὰ ὑπὸ τῆς βουλῆς πραττόμενα πρυτάνεις ἐκαλοῦντο. ἐπρυτάνευον δὲ ἐκ διαδοχῆς ἀλλήλαις αἱ δέκα κλήρῳ λαχοῦσαι· Αἰσχίνης ἐν τῷ κατὰ Κτησιφῶντος. So Suid., Phot. s.v., Lex. Seguer. 291. 4 sqq. Arist. 43, 2 says: πρυτανεύει δ᾽ ἐν μέρει τῶν φυλῶν ἑκάστη καθ᾽ ὅτι ἂν λάχωσιν, αἱ μὲν πρῶται τέτταρες ἓξ καὶ λ᾽ ἡμέρας ἑκάστη, αἱ δὲ ς᾽ αἱ ὕστεραι πέντε καὶ λ᾽ ἡμέρας ἑκάστη. κατὰ σελήνην γὰρ ἄγουσιν τὸν ἐνιαυτόν.

leap year of 38 or 39 days.[1] It was only after the number of the tribes was raised to twelve that a Prytany generally corresponded to a month.[2] The presidency in this committee of the Council was held by the ἐπιστάτης τῶν πρυτάνεων who was appointed by lot for one day and one night, and could only hold this office once during the Prytany. He kept the keys of the state-treasury and the archives, and the Athenian state-seal, and had to be continually present with a third of the Prytanes in their official chambers.[3] The Prytanes in office elected from their number a

---

[1] The Athenian year was a lunar year of 12 lunar months, six full months with 30 days each and six hollow with 29 days each, in all 354 days; in leap year a thirteenth month of 30 days was added. The months of the Athenian year, which began in the first half of our July, were Ἑκατομβαιών, Μεταγειτνιών, Βοηδρομιών, Πυανεψιών, Μαιμακτηριών, Ποσειδεών, Γαμηλιών, Ἀνθεστηριών, Ἐλαφηβολιών, Μουνυχιών, Θαργηλιών, Σκιροφοριών. The Athenian intercalary month Ποσειδεών Β or ὕστερος (C.I.A., II. 191) came after the sixth month. For Hecatombaion intercalated (an inference from Dittenberger, *Syll.*, 13 l. 54 = C.I.A., IV. 2. 27 b) see Ad. Schmidt in *Jahrb. f. cl. Phil.*, 1885, 681 sqq.; and for the Attic Calendar see his *Handb. d. griech. Chronol.*, 1888. The four days remaining after the division of the 354 or 384 days of the year by 10 were probably assigned by lot to 4 Prytanies. Schmidt, 235 sqq. Arist. 43, 2 says: πρυτανεύει δ' ἐν μέρει τῶν φυλῶν ἑκάστη, καθ' ὅτι ἂν λάχωσιν, αἱ μὲν πρῶται τέτταρες ἒξ καὶ λ' ἡμέρας ἑκάστη, αἱ δὲ ς' αἱ ὕστεραι πέντε καὶ λ' ἡμέρας ἑκάστη· κατὰ σελήνην γὰρ ἄγουσιν τὸν ἐνιαυτόν. For the last expression, if it is not to be considered a gloss which has crept into the text, cf. Gomperz, *d. Schrift vom Staatswesen d. Ath. und ihr neuester Beurtheiler*, 1891, pp. 39, 40. We cannot admit a further division of the Prytany into 5 divisions of 7 days each, during which time 10 Prytanes are said to have been πρόεδροι. K. Fr. Hermann, *epicrisis de proedris ap. Ath.*, Gött., 1843, and—a completion of his work—Prill, *de senatus Atheniens. epistatis et proedris*, p. 13 sqq. Münster, 1858.

[2] Until the introduction of the twelve tribes, we find the double dating in documents according to Prytanies and months; afterwards months and Prytanies for the most part coincide. Poll. 8, 115.

[3] Arist. 44, 1: ἔστι δ' ἐπιστάτης τῶν πρυτάνεων εἷς ὁ λαχών· οὗτος δ' ἐπιστατεῖ νύκτα καὶ ἡμέραν καὶ οὐκ ἔστιν οὔτε πλείω χρόνον οὔτε δὶς τὸν αὐτὸν γενέσθαι. τηρεῖ δ' οὗτος τάς τε κλεῖς τὰς τῶν ἱερῶν, ἐν οἷς τὰ χρήματ' ἐστὶν καὶ ⟨τὰ⟩ γράμματα τῇ πόλει, καὶ τὴν δημοσίαν σφραγῖδα καὶ μένειν ἀναγκαῖον ἐν τῇ θόλῳ τούτοις ἐστιν καὶ τριττὺν τῶν πρυτάνεων, ἣν ἂν οὗτος κελεύῃ. From Arist. comes Telephos *ap.* Eustath. on *Od.* 17, 455. 1827: γίνεται γάρ, φησιν, ἐπιστάτης Ἀθήνησιν ἐκ τῶν πρυτάνεων εἷς, ὃς ἐπιστατεῖ νύκτα καὶ ἡμέραν μίαν καὶ πλείω χρόνον οὐκ ἔξεστιν οὐδὲ δὶς τὸν αὐτὸν γενέσθαι τάς τε κλεῖς, ἐν οἷς τὰ χρήματά εἰσι, φυλάσσει καὶ τὰ γράμματα τῆς πόλεως καὶ τὴν δημοσίαν σφραγῖδα. Less complete are Suid. ἐπιστάτης, Art. 2. Et. M. ἐπιστάται. Poll. 8. 96. Cf. Harp. ἐπιστάτης. Suid., Art. 3. Lex. Seguer. 244, 31 sqq. Fellner, *z. Gesch. d. ath. Finanzverwalt.*, p. 14 sqq. On the custody of the State-seal see Ἐφ. ἀρχ., 1888, pp. 114/5 = Bull. 13. 435, l. 30 sqq: ὁ δὲ ἐπιστά(της) τῶ)μ πρυτάνεων κατασημη(νάσ)θ(ω τῇ τοῦ δήμου or probably

treasurer and a secretary to serve during the Prytany.¹ The Prytanes met in the Skias, where they dined together at the expense of the State.² They formed a political corporation, and, as such, had the right to bestow crowns of honour, while they themselves were at times crowned by the Council and people.³ To the Prytanes foreign ambassadors would first go; to them notices and announcements were sent in; the Toxotai, or police who kept public order, were under the direction of the Prytanes.⁴ It was their duty also to convene the Council, and that under ordinary circumstances by a written πρόγραμμα, in which notice was given of the order of the day's business, and to put the Council in posses-

more correctly τῇ δημοσίᾳ) σφραγῖδι. This δημοσία σφραγίς = δημόσιον σήμαντρον (Xen., de Vect., 4, 21); the device on the seal was probably the Athenian owl or Gorgon's head. Curtius in *Abh. d. Berl. Ak.*, 1874, p. 88.

¹ The ταμίας is first mentioned for B.C. 341/40; C.I.A., II. 872, γραμματεὺς and ταμίας perhaps about 350: II. 869. The secretary first occurs for certain at the beginning of the third century: II. 329. For this ταμίας cf. Fellner, z. *Gesch. d. att. Finanzverwalt.*, p. 48 sqq.; for the so-called γραμματεὺς τῶν βουλευτῶν, Hille in *Leipz. Stud.*, 1, 236 sqq., with whom however I cannot agree as to the date of the institution of this office. That the ταμίας was elected, is evident from C.I.A., II. 481: the secretary was probably elected likewise.

² Arist. 43, 3: οἱ δὲ πρυτανεύοντες αὐτῶν πρῶτον μὲν συσ[σι]τοῦσιν ἐν τῇ θόλῳ, λαμβάνοντες ἀργύριον παρὰ τῆς πόλεως—and Arist. 62, 2 and Ammonios *ap.* Harp. θόλος—ὁ δὲ τόπος, ὅπου ἐστιῶνται (Dem. 19, 190) οἱ πρυτάνεις, καλεῖται θόλος, ὑπ' ἐνίων δὲ σκιὰς διὰ τὸ οὕτως ᾠκοδομῆσθαι αὐτὸν στρογγύλον παρόμοιον θολίᾳ. Lex. Seguer. 264, 26. Phot. σκιάς. Poll. 8, 155. Paus. 1, 5, 1. In the inscriptions generally Σκιάς: C.I.A., III. 1048. 1051. 1064; II. 445. 476: θόλος: Ἐφ. ἀρχ., 1883, p. 103. For its shape see Hagemann, *de Græcorum Prytaneis.* p. 80 sqq. Breslau, 1881. Wachsmuth, 2, 1, 315 sqq. ὁ δημόσιος ὁ ἐν τῇ σκιάδι καθεσταμένος: C.I.A., II. 476. The Prytanes at times in the Skias throughout the night: Andoc., *de Myst.*, 45.

³ For instance, C.I.A., II. 190. For the crowning of the Prytanes Köhler in *Mitth. d. arch. Inst. in Ath.*, 4, 97 sqq., and the fragment of an inscription edited by Köhler in *Mitth.*, 10. 111/2: ἐπα(ινέσαι καὶ) ἀναγράψαι (δικαιο)σύνης ἕνεκα, ὅτι ἔκρινεν αὐτοὺς ἡ βουλὴ νικᾶν τὰς ἄλλας φυλὰς ὡς ἄριστα πρυτανεύσα(ν)τας τῇ πόλει at the beginning of the fourth century: it is evident from this that in early times only one tribe was thus honoured. Cf. C.I.A., II. 864. 866. 871. 872. 1188. For later times, when crowning was a regular honour, see Köhler in *Herm.*, 5. 331 sqq. To this age belongs also the list in Bull. 13, 346 sqq.

⁴ Arist. 43, 6: προσέρχονται δὲ καὶ οἱ κήρυκες καὶ οἱ πρέσβεις τοῖς πρυτάνεσιν πρῶτον, καὶ οἱ τὰς ἐπιστολὰς φέροντες τούτοις ἀποδιδόασι. Notices and announcements to the Prytanes: Aristoph., *Equit.*, 300; *Thesm.* 654. 764. Dem. 18, 169. Lys. 22, 1/2. ὁ πρύτανις (called in l. 854, τῶν πρυτάνεών τις) κὼ τοξότης appear when Mnesilochos intrudes at the Thesmophoria. The former has Mnesilochos put in the stocks: Arist., *Thesm.*, 923. 929 sqq.

sion of any information received.[1] They had the same rights in the case of the assembly of the people.[2] In the fifth century their ἐπιστάτης presided not only in the Council but also in the Ecclesia.[3] In the fourth century, however—we have evidence of it first in 378/7—the presidency in the Council and the Assembly πρόεδροι. passed over to the ἐπιστάτης τῶν προέδρων.[4] These πρόεδροι were nine in number, and were selected by lot before every sitting of the Council and every meeting of the people by the ἐπιστάτης τῶν πρυτάνεων, one from each of the nine tribes not

---

[1] Arist. 43, 3: ἔπειτα συνάγουσιν καὶ τὴν βουλὴν καὶ τὸν δῆμον, τὴν μὲν [[οὖν]] βουλὴν ὅσαι ἡμέραι, πλὴν ἐάν τις ἀφέσιμος ᾖ, τὸν δὲ δῆμον τετράκις τῆς πρυτανείας ἑκάστης. καὶ ὅσα δεῖ χρηματίζειν τὴν βουλήν, [[καὶ ὅτι]] ἐν ἑκάστῃ τῇ ἡμέρᾳ καὶ ὅπου καθίζειν, οὗτοι προγράφουσι. προγράφουσι δὲ καὶ τὰς ἐκκλησίας οὗτοι. Cf. Poll. 8, 95. Dem. 19, 185. (Dem.) 47, 42. C.I.A., II. 61: ἐπειδὰν δὲ ταῦτα παρασκ(ευα)σθεῖ, το(ὺς) πρυτάνε(ι)ς προγράψαι περὶ τούτων (ἐν βουλευ)τηρίῳ, ὅτ(α)ν οἷόν τε ᾖ. Compare the formula not seldom used of the Prytanes in the inscriptions, e.g. C.I.A., II. 417. 459, and elsewhere: ἐπεμελήθησαν δὲ καὶ τῆς συλλογῆς τῆς τε βουλῆς καὶ τοῦ δήμου καὶ τῶν ἄλλων ἁπάντων, ὧν αὐτοῖς προσέταττον οἱ νόμοι. In extraordinary circumstances the Boule is of course convened without the programma, e.g. in Dem. 18. 169. Presidency of the Prytanes in the Council: Aristoph., Equit., 674.

[2] Arist. in the previous note. Poll. 8. 95. Æschin., de Fals. Leg., 58, in Ctes., 39. They bring proposals before the Ecclesia: Dem. 18, 170. Cf. the section on the Ecclesia.

[3] For the sittings of the Council see the description in Aristoph., Equit., 624 sqq., especially 665. 674; for the Ecclesia Aristoph., Ach., 40 sqq., and, Plato, Gorg., 473 E.; Apol., 32 B. Xen., Mem., 1, 1, 18; 4, 4, 2. In the inscriptions of the fifth century the ἐπιστάτης belongs to the φυλὴ πρυτανεύουσα.

[4] Meier, de epistatis Atheniens., Halle, 1855, whose account can now be supplemented by more precise information from inscriptions. In C.I.A., II. 17, n.c. 378/7 during the Prytany of the Hippothontis tribe, the Epistates comes from Athmonon, i.e., the Kecropis tribe. Cf. in the same year II. 17b. In B.C. 404/3 the ἐπιστάτης is still from the φυλὴ πρυτανεύουσα: II. 1b. = 'Αρχ. δέλτ., 1889, p. 26. In the fifth century the formula for the president in the prefaces is ὁ δεῖνα ἐπεστάτει; afterwards we find this used to designate the ἐπιστάτης τῶν προέδρων, and τῶν προέδρων ἐπεψήφιζεν ὁ δεῖνα is also used at least from 378/7 to 347/6. C.I.A., II. 109. From that time forward the last formula is constant. The further addition καὶ οἱ συμπρόεδροι does not occur before 319/8: C.I.A., II. 187. Köhler on C.I.A., II. 193. 222. Sometimes there is an enumeration of the συμπρόεδροι by name: C.I.A., II. 230. 236. 244. 245. 336. 371. Hartel, Stud. üb. att. Staatsrecht u. Urkundenw., p. 15 sqq. Schaefer, de scribis senatus populique Athen., p. 25 sqq. Greifswald 1878. For the presidency of the πρόεδροι in the assembly of the people, see also Æschin., de Fals. Leg., 82–85, in Ctes. 39; in the Council, Æschin., in Tim. 104. C.I.A., II. 168. 179.

represented in the Prytany. From these nine again the ἐπιστάτης τῶν προέδρων was chosen by lot.[1]

The Council was usually convened by a πρόγραμμα of the Prytanes, or a summons of the herald; in critical times it probably sat permanently.[2] It assembled every day except festivals and unlucky days.[3] The sittings, called ἕδραι, were generally held in the βουλευτήριον, but under special circumstances in other places, e.g. in the Eleusinion, at the χῶμα, in the dock-yards, on the Acropolis, in later times in the Theseion as well, in the theatre, and in the Panathenaic Stadion.[4] They were as a rule public, and the audience were only

Meetings.

---

[1] Arist. 44, 2: καὶ ἐπειδὰν συναγάγωσιν οἱ πρυτάνεις τὴν βουλὴν ἢ τὸν δῆμον, οὗτος (ὁ ἐπιστάτης τῶν πρυτάνεων) κληροῖ προέδρους ἐννέα, ἕνα ἐκ τῆς φυλῆς ἑκάστης πλὴν τῆς πρυτανευούσης, καὶ πάλιν ἐκ τούτων ἐπιστάτην ἕνα καὶ παραδίδωσι τὸ πρόγραμμα αὐτοῖς· οἱ δὲ παραλαβόντες τῆς τ' εὐκοσμίας ἐπιμελοῦνται καὶ ὑπὲρ ὧν δεῖ χρηματίζειν προτιθέασιν καὶ τὰς χειροτονίας κρίνουσιν καὶ τὰ ἄλλα πάντα διοικοῦσιν καὶ τοῦ [[τ']] ἀφεῖναι κύριοί εἰσιν. καὶ ἐπιστατῆσαι μὲν οὐκ ἔξεστιν πλεῖον ἢ ἅπαξ ἐν τῷ ἐνιαυτῷ, προεδρεύειν δ' ἔξεστιν ἅπαξ ἐπὶ τῆς πρυτανείας ἑκάστης. From Arist., Suid. ἐπιστάτης, Art. 2, is taken. Cf. Telephos ap. Eustath. on Od. 17, 455. 1827. Vaguer and less correct is Harp. πρόεδροι=Phot., Art. 2, Lex. Seguer. 290, 8 sqq. Cf. Harp., ἐπιστάτης. Et. M., ἐπιστάται. Poll. 8, 96. This view is borne out by the enumeration of the πρόεδροι in the inscriptions: C.I.A., II. 386. 371, and especially 'Αθήν. 6, 271, No. 4. The opinion of Köhler in *Mitth. d. dtsch. arch. Inst.*, 5, 269 sqq., that at the end of the fourth century the functions and the title of the ἐπιστάτης τῶν πρυτάνεων passed over to the ἐπιστάτης τῶν προέδρων, is questioned by Dittenberger, *Syll.*, 130, 2, and Foucart in *Bull.* 13. 451—probably rightly. The first instance of votes of thanks to the πρόεδροι is in Hypereid., *in Philippid.* § 4, in *Jahrb. f. cl. Phil.*, 1892, pp. 101/2: τὸ δὲ ψήφισμα τὸ κρινόμενον ἔπαινος προέδρων. ὅτι δὲ προσήκει τοὺς προέδρους κατὰ τοὺς νόμους προεδρεύειν, οὗτοι δὲ παρὰ τοὺς νόμους προηδρεύκασιν, αὐτῶν τῶν νόμων ἠκούετε ἀναγιγνωσκομένων. According to Köhler in *Monatsber. d. Berl. Ak.*, 1891, 931 sqq., the date of the delivery of this speech was winter 336/5; according to Blass in *Jahrb. f. cl. Phil.*, 1892, p. 99, B.C. 337; Rühl, p. 47, says it was not delivered till shortly after the Lamian war, and then not by Hypereides.

[2] For the programma of the Prytanes see above. Summons by the herald: Andoc., *de Myst.*, 36. C.I.A., II. 439 says: βουλὴ ἐμ βουλευτηρίῳ σύγκλητος. For the σημεῖον then used, according to Andoc., see Schoemann, *de comit.*, 152/3, with whom Boeckh at last agreed (*Kl. Schr.*, 4. 117/8). The Council sitting permanently on the Acropolis: Andoc., *ib.*, 45.

[3] Daily sittings of the Council: Arist. 43, 3 (see page 274¹). Harp., κυρία ἐκκλησία, Poll. 8, 95 copy him. Festivals an exception: (Xen.) *de Rep. Ath.* 3, 2, e.g. the Apaturia; Athen. 4, 171 E, Thesmophoria; Arist., *Thesm.*, 79/8 the Kronia; Dem. 24, 26; and the ἀποφράδες ἡμέραι: Plut., *Alcib.*, 34.

[4] The sittings, called ἕδραι (C.I.A., I. 31. 40. 59) usually in the Bouleuterion: C.I.A., II. 179. 439. 475. 482—cf. Wachsmuth 2, 1, 320 sqq.—after the celebration of the Mysteries in the Eleusinion: Andoc., *de Myst.*, 111.

separated by a barrier from the members of the Council;[1] but secret meetings were sometimes held, from which the public were excluded.[2] Private citizens were probably not admitted to address the Council, unless introduced by the Prytanes or specially summoned before the Council.[3] A clause introduced into the Council-oath in B.C. 410/9 directed that the Bouleutai should sit together according to their tribes; before this they probably sat according to their political views. The φυλὴ πρυτανεύουσα and later the πρόεδροι of course occupied a special place.[4] About the order of business at the Council's meetings we are very insufficiently informed, but from the few statements which we possess, we may suppose that it resembled that of the Ecclesia.[5]

The Athenian Council in early times possessed very extended

C.I.A., II. 872. 481; at an ἀπόστολος ἐπὶ χώματι: Seeurk. XIV. b. 15 sqq., p. 466=C.I.A., II. 809b, 15—for the position of the χῶμα see Wachsmuth 2, 1, 95—ἐν τῷ νεωρίῳ in C.I.A., I. 40; sometimes on the Acropolis: Xen., Hell., 6, 4, 20. And., de Myst., 45; in the Theseion: C.I.A., II. 481; in the theatre and in the Panathenaic Stadion: C.I.A., II. 482. See Hartel, 62.

[1] Dem. 19, 17: τὸ γὰρ βουλευτήριον μεστὸν ἦν ἰδιωτῶν. δρύφακτα (Xen., Hell., 2, 8, 50. 55), or a κιγκλίς (Aristoph., Equit., 641) excluded the public; but yet those standing outside the barrier could hear the speeches of the Bouleutai. See the description in Aristoph., Equit., 624 sqq.

[2] Æschin. in Ctes. 125: εἰσελθὼν εἰς τὸ βουλευτήριον καὶ μεταστησάμενος τοὺς ἰδιώτας. On such occasions too they seem to have had a κιγκλίς, put perhaps at a further distance than usual from where the Bouleutai sat. (Dem.) 25, 28: τὸ τὴν βουλὴν τοὺς πεντακοσίους ἀπὸ τῆς ἀσθενοῦς τοιαυτησὶ κιγκλίδος τῶν ἀπορρήτων κυρίαν εἶναι καὶ μὴ τοὺς ἰδιώτας ἐπεισιέναι. Cf. Harp., ἀπεσχοινισμένος.

[3] Schol. to Aristoph., Pax, 905: τοῖς πρυτάνεσιν ἔθος ἦν προσαγαγεῖν τοὺς δεομένους εἰς τὴν βουλήν; so too in the case of magistrates, cf. Andoc., de Myst., 111. In C.I.A. 81 the Ecclesia grants this πρόσοδος to a private person. Cf. Swoboda in N. Rh. Mus., 1890, 296 sqq. Even then he was not allowed to propose a motion.

[4] Philoch. ap. Schol. to Aristoph., Plut., 972: φησὶ γὰρ Φιλόχορος ἐπὶ Γλαυκίππου καὶ ἡ βουλὴ κατὰ γράμμα τότε πρῶτον ἐκαθέζετο καὶ ὀμνύσιν ἀπ᾽ ἐκείνου καθεδεῖσθαι ἐν τῷ γράμματι, ᾧ ἂν λάχωσι and the explanation in my Beitr., etc., 348 sqq. Wachsmuth 2, 1, 823, 1 takes another view. Special seats for the Prytanes in Lys. 13. 37: οἱ μὲν γὰρ τριάκοντα ἐκάθηντο ἐπὶ τῶν βάθρων (sc. ἐν τῇ βουλῇ), οὗ νῦν οἱ πρυτάνεις καθέζονται. When this speech was delivered "about 398 or even later" (Blass, att. Beredsamk., 1, 557), the Prytanes still presided.

[5] Before the sitting began the Bouleutai prayed to Ζεὺς Βουλαῖος and Ἀθηνᾶ Βουλαία (Antiph., de Chor., 45), to whom the ἑστία, which was situated in the place of meeting, was probably dedicated (Andoc., de Myst., 44; Xen., Hell., 2, 3, 52). Wahcsmuth 2, 1, 820 sqq. Before beginning the herald recites the usual ἀρά: Dem. 19, 70; 23, 97. Order kept by the Toxotai in the fifth century: Aristoph., Equit., 665.

powers of punishment. Later it had a double position in the State. It was at once a committee of the Assembly **Competence** to prepare business for its consideration, and also the **of the Council** highest administrative and executive power in the State. In its first capacity it had to deliberate beforehand upon all matters which were to be brought before the Ecclesia, and to draw up resolutions in regard to them, which should serve as propositions for the Assembly to consider.[1]

In its second capacity the Council could pass binding resolutions in matters within its competence so long as they did not contravene the laws.[2] At the same time no complete distinction between these two functions can be made; the Council not only prepared bills for the Assembly to discuss, but also had to carry them out when passed. How they were to be carried out was sometimes definitely stated in the decree of the assembly, sometimes left undetermined. In the latter case the Council had full power to pass independent resolutions on the lines of the Ecclesia's decree; while at times full powers were explicitly granted to the Council to deal with certain specified matters.[3] As the supreme administrative

---

[1] Arist. 45, 1: ἡ δὲ βουλὴ πρότερον μὲν ἦν κυρία καὶ χρήμασιν ζημιῶσαι καὶ δῆσαι καὶ ἀποκτεῖναι. This right was subsequently withdrawn, as Arist. relates. To this curtailment of its powers perhaps C.I.A., I. 57 refers. Arist. 45, 4 continues: προβουλεύει δ' εἰς τὸν δῆμον καὶ οὐκ ἔξεστιν οὐδὲν ἀπροβούλευτον οὐδ' ὅτι ἂν μὴ προγράψωσιν οἱ πρυτάνεις ψηφίσασθαι τῷ δήμῳ. κατ' αὐτὰ γὰρ ταῦτα ἔνοχός ἐστιν ὁ νικήσας γραφῇ παρανόμων. Cf. Plut., *Sol.*, 19: μηδὲν ἐᾶν ἀπροβούλευτον εἰς ἐκκλησίαν εἰσφέρεσθαι. More on this topic will be found in the section on the Ecclesia.

[2] (Dem.) 47, 34 and the law in Dem. 23, 87: ψήφισμα δὲ μηδὲν μήτε βουλῆς μήτε δήμου νόμου κυριώτερον εἶναι. For ψήφισμα and ψηφίζεσθαι, said of the βουλή, see Kirchhoff, *Abh. d. Berl. Ak.*, 1865, p. 74. It cannot be definitely settled whether in Dem. 23, 92 (cf. Lex. Seguer. 289, 29) ψήφισμα stands for προβούλευμα, as Hartel (*demosth. Stud.* 2, 54, 1; *Stud. üb. att. Staatsr. u. Urkundenw.* 261) supposes, with whose further remarks however I do not agree; or whether the words ὁ νόμος δ' ἐπέτεια κελεύει τὰ τῆς βουλῆς εἶναι ψηφίσματα, refer to the independent decisions of the Council and to the Probouleumata. A γραφὴ παρανόμων was admissible against a ψήφισμα of the Council: (Dem.) 47. 34. A collection of the psephismata of the Council which remain to us is given by Hartel, pp. 60/1. They are decrees of honour, or the like, with few exceptions. (Nomination of a herald: C.I.A., II. 73, 1. Decisions on matters of religion: II. 404. 489b; on financial affairs: II. 74. Re-erection of an inscription-stele destroyed by the Thirty: II. 3. Permission to private citizens to erect statues of honour: II. 475, 487). See Heydemann, p. 157 sqq. Their prefaces are constructed like those of the decrees of the people.

[3] In a decree of the assembly about the equipment of an ἀπόστολος which

authority in the State the Council had the magistrates under its control, and to it they had to report. It gave them the necessary warrants, and could call them to account for their conduct.[1]

The competence of the Council accordingly extended to all affairs which came up for discussion before the Ecclesia.[2] Some of the most important matters that it dealt with may here be mentioned. The Council attended to the efficiency of the national forces, and consequently superintended the shipbuilding, repairs, and general supplies for the fleet and the dockyards, for the cavalry, and without doubt for the hoplites too.[3] It examined

the Council was to direct in accordance with the provisions of the psephisma, it says at the end: ἐὰν δέ του προσδέει τόδε τὸ ψήφισμα τῶν περὶ τὸν ἀπόστολον, τὴν βουλὴν κυρίαν εἶναι ψηφίζεσθαι μὴ λύουσαν μηθὲν τῶν ἐψηφισμένων τῷ δήμῳ: Seeurk., XIV. b, 32, p. 467=C.I.A., II. 809b, 82. For full powers given to the Council in special cases see C.I.A., I. 32: συναγωγῆς δὲ τῶλλογιστῶν ἡ βουλὴ αὐτοκράτωρ ἔστω. IV. 22a. fr. d. e., l. 18. II. 17. l. 34/5. 66b. The Council αὐτοκράτωρ in the enquiry as to the mutilation of the Hermæ (Andoc., de Myst., 15), in negotiations for peace (Dem. 19, 154).

[1] Examples in inscriptions of reports from officials, ambassadors, priests, etc., to the Council are collected by Swoboda in N. Rh. Mus., 1890, 289 sqq. Arist. says twice, 47, 1 and 49, 5, of the Council: συνδιοικεῖ δὲ καὶ ταῖς ἄλλαις ἀρχαῖς τὰ πλεῖστα. Cf. 45. 2: κρίνει δὲ τὰς ἀρχὰς ἡ βουλὴ τὰς πλείστας, μάλιστα ὅσαι χρήματα διαχειρίζουσιν· οὐ κυρία δ' ἡ κρίσις, ἀλλ' ἐφέσιμος εἰς τὸ δικαστήριον. ἔξεστι δὲ καὶ τοῖς ἰδιώταις εἰσαγγέλλειν ἣν ἂν βούλωνται τῶν ἀρχῶν μὴ χρῆσθαι τοῖς νόμοις· ἔφεσις δὲ καὶ τούτοις ἐστὶν εἰς τὸ δικαστήριον, ἐὰν αὐτῶν ἡ βουλὴ καταγνῷ. The Council sends for the Strategoi, and commissions them: Andoc., de Myst., 45; Dem. 18, 169, other ἀρχαί: C.I.A., II. 61, calls to account the Poristai, Poletai, Practores: Antiph., de Chor., 49.

[2] A general account of its work is given in (Xen.) de Rep. Ath., 3, 2: τὴν δὲ βουλὴν βουλεύεσθαι πολλὰ περὶ τοῦ πολέμου, πολλὰ δὲ περὶ πόρου χρημάτων, πολλὰ δὲ περὶ νόμων θεσίας, πολλὰ δὲ περὶ τῶν κατὰ πόλιν ἀεὶ γιγνομένων, πολλὰ δὲ καὶ τοῖς συμμάχοις καὶ φόρον δέξασθαι καὶ νεωρίων ἐπιμεληθῆναι καὶ ἱερῶν.

[3] The Council attends to the ἀπόστολος: Seeurk., XIV. b. 10 sqq., p. 466= C.I.A., II. 809b, 10 sqq., cf. Dem. 50, 6; has ships girded: XIII. b. 85, p. 433=808b, 82 sqq. XIV. b. 120, p. 472=809b, 122 sqq.; sells tackle: XIII. b. 154 sqq., p. 486=808b, 152 sqq. XIV. b. 190, p. 476=809b, 188 sqq.; doubles the number of triremes given to the trierarchs: XIII. c. 1 sqq., p. 488=808b, 1 sqq. XIV. d. 141 sqq., p. 495=809d, 138 sqq. XVI. b. 185 sqq., p. 544=811c, 183 sqq. (see Boeckh, Seeurk., 225); arranges other things of this kind: XI. c. 5 sqq., p. 413=807c, 1 sqq. XVI. b. 104 sqq., p. 534=811c, 104 sqq. Arist. 46, 1: ἐπιμελεῖται δὲ καὶ τῶν πεποιημένων τριήρων καὶ τῶν σκευῶν καὶ τῶν νεωσοίκων καὶ ποιεῖται καινὰς τριήρεις ἢ τετρήρεις, ὁποτέρας ἂν ὁ δῆμος χειροτονήσῃ, καὶ σκεύη ταύταις καὶ νεωσοίκους· χειροτονεῖ δ' ἀρχιτέκτονας ὁ δῆμος ἐπὶ τὰς ναῦς. ἂν δὲ μὴ παραδῶσιν ἐξειργασμένα ταῦτα τῇ νέᾳ βουλῇ, τὴν δωρεὰν οὐκ ἔστιν αὐτοῖς λαβεῖν. ἐπὶ γὰρ τῆς ὑστέρον βουλῆς λαμβάνουσιν. ποιεῖται δὲ τὰς τριήρεις, δέκα ἄνδρας ἐξ α[ὑτῶν] ἑλομένη τριηροποιούς. The Council filled up the number of the knights, and inspected them and their horses:

the claims for relief of those incapable of work, and attended to the repair of public buildings. It was the channel of communication between the Ecclesia and foreign States, swore to treaties, and saw to the security of the πρόξενοι and εὐεργέται.[1] It managed everything relating to the confederacy, and consequently made the estimates for the assessment of tribute.[2] It formed part of the legislature, and saw to the public sanctuaries, festivals, and religious ceremonies.[3] Lastly, its chief function was the conduct and control of the finances. The Council had to provide the necessary money for the Budget.[4] It farmed out the taxes to the tax-gatherers through the Poletai, the contract prices being paid to the Apodectai in the presence of the Council.[5] It collected

Arist. 49. Xen., *Oik.*, 9, 15. *Hipparch.* 3, 9–14. It exercised a general supervision over them: *Hipparch.* 1, 8, 13. Perhaps it reviewed the hoplites also, after they began to be drilled in military exercises; at any rate it certainly reviewed the epheboi in later times: C.I.A., II. 467, 468. Dittenberger, *de Epheb. Att.*, p. 27.

[1] For the examination of the infirm see Arist. 49. 4: δοκιμάζει δὲ καὶ τοὺς ἀδυνάτους ἡ βουλή· νόμος γάρ ἐστι, ὃς κελεύει τοὺς ἐντὸς τριῶν μνῶν κεκτημένους καὶ τὸ σῶμα πεπηρωμένους, ὥστε μὴ δύνασθαι μηδὲν ἔργον ἐργάζεσθαι, δοκιμάζειν μὲν τὴν βουλήν, διδόναι δὲ δημοσίᾳ τροφὴν δύο ὀβολοὺς ἑκάστῳ τῆς ἡμέρας. καὶ ταμίας ἐστὶν αὐτοῖς κληρωτός. For the inspection of public buildings see Arist. 46. 2: ἐξετάζει δὲ καὶ τὰ οἰκοδομήματα τὰ δημόσια πάντα.—For foreign affairs see Æschin., *F. L.*, 58: ταῖς δὲ ξενικαῖς πρεσβείαις ἡ βουλὴ τὰς εἰς τὸν δῆμον προσόδους προβουλεύει. C.I.A., II. 49. 51. 54. The first audience of ambassadors was given in the Council: Thuc. 5. 45. Plut., *Nik.*, 10. Aristoph., *Equit.*, 667 sqq. The Council communicated decrees of the Ecclesia to foreign states: Dittenberger, *Syll.*, 13, 23 sqq.=C.I.A., IV. 27 b. The Council swore to treaties and alliances: Thuc. 5. 47. C.I.A., I. 52. IV. 27a, 71. II. 64. *Mitth. d. dtsch. arch. Inst. in Ath.* 2, 201. 211. 212. Heydemann 182 sqq. gives an exact list of all those bodies which swore to peaces and treaties. The Council looked after εὐεργέται and πρόξενοι: C.I.A., I. 59, IV. 94, II. 40. 69. 121. 124. 151. 209. 289.

[2] C.I.A., I. 37, 266. Heydemann 176 sqq., with whom however I do not agree, as will presently be shown.

[3] See the section on Nomothesia. Supervision of the ἱερά: (Xen.), *de Rep. Ath.*, 3, 2. Heydemann 174 sqq., 195 sqq. The Council saw to the εὐκοσμία at the Dionysia: C.I.A., II. 114, to the Panathenæa: Arist. 49, 3. Members of the Council went as θεωροί to the Pythian games: Dem. 19, 128. Whoever disregards the regulations about the Pelargicon, ἀποτινέτω πεντακοσίας δραχμάς· εἰσαγγελλέτω δὲ (ὁ) βασιλεὺς ἐς τὴν βουλήν: Dittenberger, *Syll.* 13, 58 sqq.=C.I.A., IV. 27 b.

[4] Lys. 30, 20: εἰδὼς δέ, ὅτι ἡ βουλὴ ἡ βουλεύουσα, ὅταν μὲν ἔχῃ ἱκανὰ χρήματα εἰς διοίκησιν, οὐδὲν ἐξαμαρτάνει, ὅταν δὲ εἰς ἀπορίαν καταστῇ, ἀναγκάζεται εἰσαγγελίας δέχεσθαι καὶ δημεύειν τὰ τῶν πολιτῶν καὶ τῶν ῥητόρων τοῖς τὰ πονηρότατα λέγουσι πείθεσθαι. See Fellner, *z. Gesch. d. att. Finanzverwalt.*, p. 12.

[5] Lease of the πορνικὸν τέλος: Æschin. *in Tim.* 119, of the πεντηκοστή:

debts due to the State, and had power to imprison State debtors if they did not pay in time. Informations against those who had State-property in their possession were laid before it.[1] The Council also received all voluntary gifts to the State, and published lists of the προεισφέροντες.[2] In presence of the Council took place the cancelling of names in the debtors' lists by the Apodectai or Practores, and the transfer of the sacred monies by the various treasurers to their successors; the inventories of the sacred treasures were drawn up under the supervision of the Council.[3] Finally, the Council transacted any current business which was too unimportant to require to be brought before the Ecclesia.[4]

The execution of measures decreed either by the Council or by the people was probably carried out as a rule by special commissioners from amongst the Council, or by dividing the business between the various tribes of the Council, who again subdivided it among their members.[5]

Andoc., de Myst., 134. Cf. Arist. 47, 2 sqq. The Council, together with the ἱεροποιοί τοῖν Θεοῖν sells the tithe-corn which had been delivered to the Eleusinian deities: Dittenberger 13, 41 sqq.=C.I.A., IV. 27b. Payment of the τέλη: (Dem.) 59, 27. Arist. 48, 1. 2.

[1] Collection of debts due to the State: Dem. 24, 96 sqq. Lex. Seguer. 199, 4 sqq. In the naval inscriptions the formula for the payment of moneys due to the State is usually: τοῦτο κατεβλήθη ἀποδέκταις; once or twice: ὁ εἰς βουλευτήριον κατέβαλεν: e.g. Seeurk., X. d. 100, p. 384, 150, p. 385 =C.I.A., 803d, 89 sqq., which means the same as the first formula. Proceedings by the Council against defaulting state-debtors: Dem. 24, 144. Andoc., de Myst., 93. Μήνυσις against those who had State-monies in their private possession: Dem. 24, 11.

[2] ἐν τῇ βουλῇ γιγνομένων ἐπιδόσεων: Dem. 21, 161. Lists of προεισφέροντες: Dem. 50, 8.

[3] Payment of debts: Andoc., de Myst., 79. Arist. 47. Harp. ἀποδέκται. Lex. Seguer. 198, 1 sqq. Cf. C.I.A., I. 32. Transfer of sacred monies: Arist. 47, 1. Harp. ταμίαι. Poll. 8, 97. Lex. Seguer. 306, 7 sqq. Inventory ἐναντίον τῆς βουλῆς: C.I.A., I. 32.

[4] (Xen.), de rep. Ath., 3, 21: τὴν δὲ βουλὴν βουλεύεσθαι—περὶ τῶν κατὰ πόλιν ἀεὶ γιγνομένων.

[5] Seeurk., X. c. 166, p. 379=C.I.A., II. 803c, 162, gives under the heading Αἰγηΐδος B.C. 346/5 Μνησικλῆς Κολλυ(τεὺς) αἱρεθεὶς ἐκ τῆς βουλῆς as giving out tackle for the ships. For each of the remaining 9 tribes we must assume a αἱρεθεὶς ἐκ τῆς βουλῆς, all together forming the Harbour-Board. A ship-building committee in Arist. 46, 1: ποιεῖται δὲ (sc. ἡ βουλὴ) τὰς τριήρεις, δέκα ἄνδρας ἐξ α[ὐτῶν] ἑλομένη τριηροποιούς; a finance committee in Arist. 48, 3: [κ]ληροῦσι δὲ καὶ λογιστὰς ἐξ αὐτῶν οἱ βουλευταὶ δέκα τοὺς λογιουμένους τ[αῖς ἀρ]χαῖς κατὰ τὴν πρυτανείαν ἑκάστην. The 30 συλλογεῖς τοῦ δήμου (vid. inf.) were another committee of the Council. In 341/40 B.C. the 10 ἱεροποιοὶ οἱ τὰ

Lastly, there were cases in which the Council exercised judicial functions. Eisangeliai could be laid before the Council, and if the offence required not more than a fine of 500 drachmas, the maximum fine which the Council was permitted to inflict, then the case could be finally disposed of. Otherwise, the Eisangeliai were referred either to the Ecclesia or to a court of Heliasts. The proceedings in such an Eisangelia before the Council lasted two days. First the plaintiff and the defendant were granted a hearing, and then the Councillors voted by ballot whether the latter were guilty or not. If their decision was in the affirmative, they would vote on the second day whether the defendant was to be fined by the Council, or whether the case should go before a Heliastic court for trial. The Council could also deal with cases of Endeixis, Apagoge, and Phasis.[1]

The βουλή as a Court of Justice.

The high political importance of the Council at Athens made the βουλεία a coveted office; an orator who held a prominent place in the Council had a great influence over the government and administration of the State.[2]

μυστήρια ἱεροποιήσαντες 'Ελευσῖν(ι) were a committee of the Aigeis the φυλὴ πρυτανεύουσα, C.I.A., II. 872. On other occasions these festival committees were not limited to the members of the φυλὴ πρυτανεύουσα. In 'Εφ. ἀρχ., 1888, pp. 167/8, for the Hephaistia we have: (δια)κληρωσάτω δὲ καὶ ἡ β(ουλ)ὴ σφῶν αὐτῶν ἱεροπ(οι)οὺς δέκα ἄνδρ(ας, ἕνα ἐκ τῆς φυλ)ῆς ἑκάστη(ς). Cf. 'Αθήν., 6, 483. Ἱεροποιοὶ ἐγ βουλῆς for Eleusis, 'Εφ. ἀρχ., 1888, pp. 123/4, l. 67. 71; pp. 125/6, l. 1. 3. 76. Cf. R. Schoell in *Sitzungsber. d. bayr. Ak.*, 1887, p. 9 sqq. Committees for special objects appear also in C.I.A., IV. 27 a, II. 114 A.B., 404. *Mitth. d. dtsch. arch. Inst. in Ath.*, 2, 212. Lys. 13, 23/4. I should suppose a division of labour between the tribes for the collection of state-debts: Lex. Seguer. 199. 4 sqq., for drawing up the muster rolls before an ἀπόστολος: Dem. 50, 6, for drafting the lists of προεισφέροντες: Dem. 50, 8, for the conduct of the διαψήφισις: Dem. 57, 8. In this the Bouleutai were assisted by the Demarchs for their several Demes.

[1] For the Eisangelia before the Council see Poll. 8, 51. Isocr. 15, 314. The account in the text is drawn from (Dem.) 47, 42/3, which refers to an Eisangelia against a man, who by retention of tackle, etc., belonging to the State, delayed an ἀπόστολος. See also *Seeurk.* XV. b 151 sqq., p. 540=C.I.A., II. 811c, 153 sqq. The βασιλεὺς is to bring an Eisangelia against any one who infringes the laws regarding the Pelargicon: Dittenberger, *Syll.*, 13, 54 sqq.=C.I.A., IV. 27 b. Endeixis and Apagoge before the Council: Andoc., *de Myst.*, 91. Phasis: Isocr. 17, 42; 18, 6. Arist., *Equit.*, 300 sqq. That the Council had in earlier times a far more extended power of punishment is evident from Arist. 45, 1. Cf. C.I.A., I. 57. Arist. 46, 2 says: κἂν τις ἀδικεῖν αὐτῇ (sc. τῇ βουλῇ) δόξῃ, τῷ τε δήμῳ τοῦτον [ἀπ]οφαίνει καὶ καταγνόντος παραδίδωσι δικαστηρίῳ. Cf. Heydemann 167 sqq.

[2] Dem. 22, 36 sqq., distinguishes between λέγοντες and ἰδιῶται in the

After 462/1 B.C. the Council of the Areopagus (of whose judicial powers I shall speak in another place) had not so much control over the administration of the State as the Council of the 500.[1] The Council of the Areopagus consisted of the ex-archons, who entered it on the expiration of their year of office, after first passing their εὔθυνα.[2] But it appears that, before taking their seats, they had also to undergo Dokimasia before the Areopagus, which sometimes ended in the rejection of a candidate.[3] The Council of the Areopagus had also power to provisionally expel offending members; but to become final this expulsion required the confirmation of a Heliastic court, before which the Areopagus had to bring the case.[4] The Areopagus was also bound to pass a εὔθυνα before the Logistai, and as the Areopagites held office for life we must suppose this εὔθυνα to have been held either at the close of each year or on the completion of some particular task.[5] The meetings of the Council of the Areopagus were held on the Areopagus, or in the βασίλειος στοά, and seem to have been private.[6]

Council of the Areopagus.

Council. For such a speaker in the Council see C.I.A., II. 114. In general compare my *Beitr.*, etc., p. 80 sqq. Perrot, *le droit public d'Athènes*, p. 63 sqq. [Headlam, pp. 68 sq. 75 sq.].

[1] The title of the Areopagus runs ἡ βουλὴ ἡ ἐξ Ἀρείου πάγου: C.I.A., II. 252. Dem. 18, 133. Dem. *in Dem.* 50. Æsch. *in Tim.* 82. ἡ ἐξ Ἀρείου πάγου βουλή: Æsch. *in Ctes.* 252. ἡ βουλὴ ἡ ἐν Ἀρείῳ πάγῳ: Æsch. *in Tim.* 81. ἡ ἐν Ἀρείῳ πάγῳ βουλή: Lyc., *Leocr.*, 52.

[2] See page 250. Poll. 8, 118: οἱ δ' ἐννέα ἄρχοντες οἱ καθ' ἕκαστον ἐνιαυτὸν μετὰ τὸ δοῦναι τὰς εὐθύνας ἀεὶ τοῖς Ἀρεοπαγίταις προσετίθεντο. Cf. Xen., *Mem.*, 3, 5, 20. Plut., *Sol.*, 19. *Per.* 9. (Dem.) 26, 5. Arist. 60, 3.

[3] Athen. 13, 566 F: Ὑπερείδης δ' ἐν τῷ κατὰ Πατροκλέους, εἰ γνήσιος ὁ λόγος, τοὺς Ἀρεοπαγίτας φησὶν ἀριστήσαντά τινα ἐν καπηλείῳ κωλῦσαι ἀνιέναι εἰς Ἄρειον πάγον. Cf. Isocr. 7, 38.

[4] Dein. *in Dem.* 56: διόπερ τὸν παρ' αὐτῶν ἀποστερήσαντα τὸ ναῦλον τὸν πορθμέα ζημιώσασα (ἡ ἐξ Ἀρείου πάγου βουλή) πρὸς ὑμᾶς ἀπέφηνε· πάλιν τὸν τὴν πεντεδραχμίαν ἐπὶ τῷ τοῦ μὴ παρόντος ὀνόματι λαβεῖν ἀξιώσαντα καὶ τοῦτον ὑμῖν ἀπέφηνε καὶ τὸν τὴν μερίδα τὴν ἐξ Ἀρείου πάγου τολμήσαντα ἀποδόσθαι παρὰ τὰ νόμιμα τὸν αὐτὸν τρόπον ζημιώσασα ἐξέβαλε. The concluding words—τὸν αὐτὸν τρόπον ζημιώσασα ἐξέβαλε—seem to show that expulsion was the punishment inflicted by the Areopagus in the first two cases as well. Confirmation or cassation of this by the Heliasts: § 57. Cf. Æschin. *in Ctes.* 20 about the Areopagites: ἀλλ' οὐκ ἀγαπῶσιν, ἐάν τις παρ' αὐτοῖς μὴ ἀδικῇ, ἀλλ' ἐάν τις ἐξαμαρτάνῃ, κολάζουσιν.

[5] Æsch. *in Ctes.* 20: πρῶτον μὲν γὰρ τὴν βουλὴν τὴν ἐν Ἀρείῳ πάγῳ ἐγγράφειν πρὸς τοὺς λογιστὰς ὁ νόμος κελεύει λόγον καὶ εὐθύνας διδόναι καὶ τὸν ἐκεῖ σκυθρωπὸν καὶ τῶν μεγίστων κύριον ἄγει ὑπὸ τὴν ὑμετέραν ψῆφον.

[6] (Dein.) 25, 23: τὸ τὴν ἐξ Ἀρείου πάγου βουλήν, ὅταν ἐν τῇ βασιλείῳ στοᾷ

As to the official functions of the Areopagus, it appears that it exercised a certain supervision in matters of religion. Thus it looked after the sacred olive trees which belonged to Athene, checked their number every month, and appointed annually from among its own members inspectors called γνώμονες to see to them. Whoever uprooted a sacred olive tree was brought to account before the Areopagus. The Areopagus also saw that religious ritual was duly observed, and it appears that it had also some power of punishing offences against religion.[1] In the inscriptions of the third century we find committees of two Areopagites entrusted with extraordinary religious duties. On the other hand, it is very doubtful whether the Areopagus in the time of the orators heard γραφαὶ ἀσεβείας.[2] Even the supervision of the Areopagus over education and morals was probably very limited after the reforms of Ephialtes. Our authorities are silent on this point, and therefore we cannot speak with certainty.

Functions.

καθεζομένη περισχοινίσηται, κατὰ πολλὴν ἡσυχίαν ἐφ' ἑαυτῆς εἶναι καὶ ἅπαντας ἐκποδὼν ἀποχωρεῖν. See however Wachsmuth 2, 1, 346. A meeting on the Areopagus in (Dem.) 59, 79 sqq., which according to § 79, 80 was secret. Dem. 18, 134 speaks of a special method of voting, ἀπὸ τοῦ βωμοῦ φέρειν τὴν ψῆφον.

[1] For the supervision of the μορίαι by the Areopagus see Arist. 60, 2. 3, Lys. 7. Special committee of Areòpagites for this purpose: § 7. 25. Supervision of the ἱερὰ ὀργὰς and the other τεμένη: 'Εφ. ἀρχ., 1888, 113/4=Bull. 13, 434 l. 15 sqq. I infer from (Dem.) 59, 79 sqq. that the Areopagus watched over the ritual. Philippi, *d. Areop. u. d. Eph.*, 166/7, sees in the action of the Areopagus towards Theogenes there described, only steps which it had to take at the Dokimasia of a future member. This seems to me impossible. In my opinion the Dokimasia of the Archons is not at all in question, for Theogenes, according to § 83, is still in office. The possession by the Areopagus of a limited power of punishment in such matters is indicated in § 80: καὶ ἐζημίου τὸν Θεογένην ὅσα κυρία ἐστίν, ἐν ἀπορρήτῳ δὲ καὶ διὰ κοσμιότητος· οὐ γὰρ αὐτοκράτορές εἰσιν, ὡς ἂν βούλωνται 'Αθηναίων τινὰ κολάσαι. If the passage in the Psephisma of Tisamenos in Andoc., *de Myst.*, 84: ἐπειδὰν δὲ τεθῶσιν οἱ νόμοι, ἐπιμελείσθω ἡ βουλὴ ἡ ἐξ 'Αρείου πάγου τῶν νόμων, ὅπως ἂν αἱ ἀρχαὶ τοῖς κειμένοις νόμοις χρῶνται is genuine, it will explain the action of the Areopagus against Theogenes.

[2] Two members of the Areopagus on the committee for melting up images and erecting from the metal obtained an Anathema for the ἥρως ἰατρός: C.I.A., II. 403. Two members of the Areopagus and the στρατηγὸς ὁ ἐπὶ τὴν παρασκευὴν supervised τὴν καθαίρεσιν καὶ τὴν ἐπισκευὴν τῶν ἐν τῷ 'Ασκληπιείῳ: C.I.A., II. 839. For various cases of γραφαὶ ἀσεβείας see Meier[2] 366 sqq. Platner, *Proc. u. Klagen*, 2, 138 sqq. The Areopagus did not hear γραφαὶ ἀσεβείας in the time of the orators: Lipsius in Meier, pp. 373/4. Philippi 156/7 reduces the powers of the Areopagus in this respect to the lowest possible minimum.

The γραφὴ ἀργίας, which before the reforms of Ephialtes had to come before the Areopagus, was in later times tried by a Heliastic court.[1]

For the supposed control of markets and buildings by the Areopagus we have no reliable authority.[2] A committee of five members of the Areopagus had a share in the management of certain financial business. So much inscriptions of B.C. 305/4 tell us; but we know nothing more.[3]

If the legal competence of the Areopagus was very much restricted after Ephialtes' reforms, as we should judge from the silence of our authorities, yet even after that time it still maintained its moral influence.[4] This must be the reason why the Areopagus was not infrequently entrusted by the people with a commission of enquiry. The result of such an enquiry would be conveyed to the people in the form of an ἀπόφασις, to be either referred, after the nomination of public prosecutors, to a heliastic

---

[1] The description of Isocrates 7, 37 sqq. does not refer to the orator's own days, but to the past. The testimony of Pseudoplat., Axioch., 367 A: καὶ πᾶς ὁ τοῦ μειρακίσκου χρόνος ἐστὶν ὑπὸ σωφρονιστὰς καὶ τὴν ἐπὶ τοὺς νέους αἵρεσιν τῆς ἐξ Ἀρείου πάγου βουλῆς is of no practical value. Phanodem. and Philoch. ap. Athen., 4, 168 A : ὅτι δὲ τοὺς ἀσώτους καὶ τοὺς μὴ ἔκ τινος περιουσίας ζῶντας τὸ παλαιὸν ἀνεκαλοῦντο οἱ Ἀρεοπαγῖται καὶ ἐκόλαζον, ἱστόρησαν Φανόδημος καὶ Φιλόχορος ἄλλοι τε πλείους: but this probably refers to the time before Ephialtes. What Athen. adds from the biographies of Menedemos and Asclepiades, and what Diog. Laërt. 7, 5, 2 relates about the philosopher Cleanthes, cannot be taken as sufficient evidence. The νόμος περὶ τῆς ἀργίας still existed in Demosthenes' time. See Dem. 57, 32. According to Plut., Sol., 22, Solon ordained that the Areopagus should try these cases. At the time of the orators they came before a heliastic court. Meier[2] 364. For the Areopagus' supervision of morals and education cf. Philippi 162 sqq.

[2] Philippi, p. 158 sqq. On p. 160 sq. he infers from Æschin. in Tim. 80 sqq. that the Areopagus was competent to deal with questions of building regulations. I cannot consider this correct. According to § 81, the Areopagus, in the proceedings which Æschines is describing, was acting as a committee, and I cannot see why the Ecclesia should not have given such a commission to the Areopagus, whether the supervision of buildings was a regular function of the Areopagus or not. Nor do I look upon the jurisdiction of the Areopagus in the γραφὴ πυρκαϊᾶς as a consequence of its supervision of buildings. But on this I shall have more to say when I come to the murder trials.

[3] According to accounts of the treasurer τῆς θεοῦ of the year 305/4, five members of the Areopagus and the ταμίας τῶν στρατιωτικῶν made payments to him. See Mitth. d. dtsch. arch. Inst. in Ath., 5, 277. 281=C.I.A., II. 737, p. 508. Cf. C.I.A., II. 252, at the end of the year 305/4, and Plut., Them., 10.

[4] Æschines in Tim. 84.

court, or else dealt with by the Ecclesia directly.¹ But it appears that the Areopagus was also entitled to institute an enquiry merely on its own initiative, and to bring the result before the people in an ἀπόφασις for definitive sentence.²

Lastly, the Areopagus was sometimes specially entrusted by the people with independent jurisdiction over certain crimes.³

C. *The Sovereign Power in the State.*⁴

The sovereign power of the State was represented by the people of Athens, *i.e.* in theory the whole of the citizens who were in full possession of political rights—but in fact those Athenians who happened to be present in the Ecclesia. The people of Athens exercised these rights of sovereignty ordinarily at regular assemblies, of which a fixed number were held within fixed intervals of time; in special circumstances at extraordinary assemblies held whenever occasion required. In each Prytany there were, according to Aristotle, four ordinary assemblies of the people, of which one was specially called κυρία ἐκκλησία.⁵

---

¹ See for this form of ζήτησις and ἀπόφασις by the Areopagus, Dein. *in Dem.* 50 sqq. This proceeding in the Harpalos case: Dein. 8, 82 sqq., against Polyeuctos: Dein. 58. Other instances in Dein. 62/3. The Areopagus was commissioned by the people to institute an enquiry whether Æschines might be nominated as σύνδικος in the dispute about the Delian sanctuary. Dem. 18, 134. It inquires, at the instance of Timarchus, whether the neighbourhood of the Pnyx may be built on. Æsch. *in Tim.* 80 sqq. Cf. the § in Philippi 170 sqq.

² That the Areopagus on its own initiative might hold an enquiry and make a report, we see from Dein. *in Dem.* 51/2. In spite of Philippi 177 ff. I take the enquiry of the Areopagus about Antiphon in Dem. 18, 132/3 to be held on its own initiative. Dein. 63 appears to me to make more for than against this view, considering that, in the other cases there mentioned, we find more express indication of Demosthenes' activity.

³ The Areopagus took proceedings of this kind after the battle of Chaeronea against those who had betrayed their country in the battle. Lyc., *Leocr.*, 52. Æschin. *in Ctes.* 252. Cf. Philippi 179 sqq.

⁴ Cf. Schömann, *de comitiis Atheniensium*, 1819. Leop. Schmidt, *de Atheniensis reipublicæ indole democratica* in *Ind. lect.*, Marburg, 1865. Adam Reusch, *de dieb. contionum ordinar. ap. Athenienses* in *Diss. phil. Argentorat. sel.*, 3, 1 sqq. J. W. Headlam, *Election by lot at Athens*, Cambridge, 1891. The author in a close and convincing argument—though many of his details I cannot accept—shows that the Athenian Demos was the real sovereign on whom the entire government depended.

⁵ Arist. 43, 3 says expressly of the Prytanes: συνάγουσιν—τὸν δὲ δῆμον τετράκις τῆς πρυτανείας ἑκάστης, and then gives the agenda for these various meetings. From Arist. are drawn Harp. κυρία ἐκκλησία. Phot., Suid., Lex.

In this κυρία ἐκκλησία the Epicheirotonia of the officials took place, the Council reported on the state of the corn-market and the security of the country, Eisangeliai were brought before the people, and a list was read of all confiscations made since the preceding κυρία ἐκκλησία, and of all suits for the right of succession to inheritances or of marrying heiresses (the object being to bring any vacant estate to every one's notice). In addition to this the κυρία ἐκκλησία of the 6th Prytany had to vote whether ostracism was to take place during that year; and probably the κυρία ἐκκλησία in every Prytany had to discuss any προβολαί, which had been brought against Sycophantai or against any one who had not kept a promise made to the people. Another ordinary meeting was set apart for receiving petitions on private and public matters and deciding about them. The two remaining ordinary meetings were devoted to other business; questions of ritual, foreign politics, and State administration seem to have been discussed in a certain fixed order and within certain time-limits.[1] In case of extraordinary events demanding immediate attention, an extraordinary meeting was called, which was designated σύγκλητος

Cantabr., Poll. 8, 95/6. According to other evidence—Phot. κυρία ἐκκλησία; Schol. Arist., Ach., 19; Schol., Dem. 24, 20—there were each month three meetings of the people, all of which were called κυρίαι ἐκκλησίαι. See the complete list of passages quoted in Reusch 50 sqq. It is now certain from Arist. 43, 4 that in Aristotle's day there was only one κυρία ἐκκλησία. Considering the express statement of Aristotle, I cannot agree with Ad. Schmidt, Hdb. d. griech. Chronol., 356 sqq., who assumes three meetings in the month. In the inscriptions there is only one κυρία discoverable in each Prytany. See the list in Reusch 66/7, and especially Mitth., 8, 216/7. Earliest mention of the κυρία ἐκκλησία C.I.A., I. 25; Arist., Ach., 19. In Æschin., F. L., 72, the ordinary meetings of the people are called ἐκκλησίαι αἱ τεταγμέναι ἐκ τῶν νόμων.

[1] Arist. 43, 4: προγράφουσι δὲ καὶ τὰς ἐκκλησίας οὗτοι (οἱ πρυτάνεις) μίαν μὲν κυρίαν, ἐν ᾗ δεῖ τὰς ἀρχὰς ἐπιχειροτονεῖν εἰ δοκοῦσι καλῶς ἄρχειν καὶ περὶ σίτου καὶ περὶ φυλακῆς τῆς χώρας χρηματίζειν καὶ τὰς εἰσαγγελίας ἐν ταύτῃ τῇ ἡμέρᾳ τοὺς βουλομένους ποιεῖσθαι καὶ τὰς ἀπογραφὰς τῶν δημευομένων ἀναγιγνώσκειν καὶ τὰς λήξεις τῶν κλήρων καὶ τῶν ἐπικλήρων [ἀναγιγνώσκειν], ὅπως μηδένα λάθῃ μηδὲν ἔρημον γενόμενον. ἐπὶ δὲ τῆς ἕκτης πρυτανείας πρὸς τοῖς εἰρημένοις καὶ περὶ τῆς ὀστρακοφορίας ἐπιχειροτονίαν διδόασιν, εἰ δοκεῖ ποιεῖν ἢ μή, καὶ συκοφαντῶν προβολὰς τῶν Ἀθηναίων καὶ τῶν μετοίκων μέχρι τριῶν ἑκατέρων κ[ἄν τι]ς ὑποσχόμενός τι μὴ ποιήσῃ τῷ δήμῳ. ἑτέραν δὲ ταῖς ἱκετηρίαις, ἐν ᾗ θεὶς ὁ βουλόμενος ἱκετηρίαν [ὑπὲρ] ὧν ἂν βούληται καὶ ἰδίων καὶ δημοσίων διαλέξεται πρὸς τὸν δῆμον. αἱ δὲ δύο περὶ τῶν ἄλλων εἰσίν, ἐν αἷς κελεύουσιν οἱ νόμοι τρία μὲν ἱερῶν χρηματίζειν, τρία δὲ κήρυξιν καὶ πρεσβείαις, τρία δ' ὁσίων. For the meaning of περὶ σίτου see Xen., Mem., 3, 6, 13. The φυλακὴ τῆς χώρας is referred to in Xen. 3, 6, 10. C.I.A., II. 225. 334. 809b, 38. 811c, 155. Cf. Reusch 71 sqq.

or κατάκλητος ἐκκλησία.[1] But even the ordinary meetings, the κυρία ἐκκλησία and the other ἐκκλησίαι alike, with perhaps one or two exceptions, were not fixed for certain days of the Prytany or of the month. This was indeed impossible; for it was not customary to hold a meeting on festival days or unlucky days, and these did not always fall on the same day in the several Prytanies and months.[2] Hence it was customary for the Prytanes to give five days' notice of the ordinary meetings in a πρόγραμμα which contained also the agenda for the meeting.[3] The same procedure was no doubt followed in the case of the σύγκλητοι ἐκκλησίαι, except when unforeseen events necessitated the immediate calling of the meeting; in such a case this seems to have been done by a trumpeter.[4]

Days of meeting.

Notice.

The place where the Ecclesiai were held was different at different times. In the earliest times Apollodoros makes them meet near the Sanctuary of Aphrodite

Place of meeting.

---

[1] Harp. σύγκλητος ἐκκλησία—εἰ δέ τι ἐξαίφνης κατεπείξειεν, ὥστε γενέσθαι ἐκκλησίαν, αὕτη ἐκαλεῖτο σύγκλητος ἐκκλησία· Δημοσθένης ἐν τῷ κατ' Αἰσχίνου. See Poll. 8, 116. Et. M. Suid. s.v. Reusch 5. Æschin., F. L., 72 is speaking of such critical times, πλείους δὲ ἐκκλησίας συγκλήτους ἠναγκάζεσθε ἐκκλησιάζειν μετὰ φόβου καὶ θορύβου ἢ τὰς τεταγμένας ἐκ τῶν νόμων. See Stojentin, de Iul. Poll. auctor., p. 58.

[2] The inscriptions shew that meetings might be held on any day of the month, except a few days which have not yet been accounted for. See Reusch 54 sqq. The κυρία ἐκκλησία too, as we see from inscriptions, took place on quite different days on different occasions. See the list in Reusch 69 sqq. Reusch assumes, p. 57, the eleventh Hecatombaion as a fixed day for the first Ecclesia of the year, inferring this from Dem. 24, 20. 26, and the day after the Pandia for the ἐκκλησία ἐν Διονύσου from Dem. 21, 8. 9. During the ερομηνία there was no Ecclesia, nor during the Panathenaia: Dem. 24, 29, nor on the feast of Asclepios: Æschin. in Ctes. 67. For unlucky days, ἀποφράδες ἡμέραι, cf. Lucian, Pseudolog., 12: ἀποφρὰς ἡμέρα, ὅταν μήτε αἱ ἀρχαὶ χρηματίζωσι μήτε εἰσαγώγιμοι αἱ δίκαι ὦσι. Particular ἀποφράδες ἡμέραι in Plut., Alcib., 34. Hesych., Et. M. s.v.

[3] Arist. 43, 4: προγράφουσιν δὲ καὶ τὰς ἐκκλησίας οὗτοι (=οἱ πρυτάνεις). From this come Poll. 8, 95; Harp., κυρία ἐκκλησίαι; Lex. Seguer. 296, 8: πρόπεμπτα· τὸ πρὸ πέντε ἡμερῶν τῆς ἐκκλησίας προγράφειν, ὅτι ἔσται ἐκκλησία κ. τ. δ. Cf. Phot., πρόπεμπτα. Reusch 79 sqq. To this previous arrangement of the agenda by means of a programma several days beforehand, I would take the formula used in several inscrr. in regard to the πρόεδροι to refer: ὅταν αἱ ἡμέραι αἱ ἐκ τοῦ νόμου ἐξήκωσιν, χρηματίσαι περὶ κ. τ. δ. See C.I.A., II. 309. 318. 331. Cf. Jahrb. f. cl. Phil., 1879, p. 234, against Hartel, Stud. ub. att. Staatsr. u. Urkundenw., 170 sqq. Reusch 58 sqq. has come to the same conclusion as myself.

[4] See the ἐκκλησία σύγκλητος in Dem. 18, 169. Reusch 83/4.

Pandemos, *i.e.* to the south of the Acropolis, on the spot where at a later date stood the Odeion of Herodes Atticos.[1] In the 5th and 4th centuries the meetings were as a rule held on the Pnyx, but it is impossible to determine with any degree of certainty where this was.[2] Still it had become customary even in the fifth century to hold meetings on special occasions in the theatre, and by the time of Demosthenes this had became the rule for the first meeting after the festival of the city Dionysia.[3] Later still the theatre became the ordinary place of meeting, only exchanged for the Pnyx for the Archairesiai.[4] It was also customary even in the time of Demosthenes to hold Ecclesiai at the Piræus, perhaps in the theatre there, in certain cases when questions relating to shipping and navigation were to be considered.[5] In the last centuries B.C. it appears that the meetings were held alternately at Athens and the Piræus.[6] The only meetings which we can prove to have been held in the Agora are those for voting ostracism. But it is highly probable that besides this, citizenship and ἄδεια were voted in the Agora.[7]

Every adult Athenian was entitled to attend the Ecclesia, unless he had lost this right by some form of Atimia. To see

[1] Harp. πάνδημος Ἀφροδίτη. I consider the ἀρχαία ἀγορὰ there mentioned as ἐκκλησιαστικὸς τόπος. So does Wachsmuth 1, 484 sqq.

[2] Assemblies on the Pnyx during the Peloponnesian war: Thuc. 8, 97. Arist., *Equit.*, 750/1, *Ach.*, 20, *Wasps*, 31, *Eccl.*, 283. See Wachsmuth 1, 538. That the Pnyx was a usual place of meeting even in B.C. 338 is evident from Dem. 18, 169. For the situation of the Pnyx see Wachsmuth 1, 368 sqq. Ὅρος Πυκνός: C.I.A., I. 501. Later the Pnyx the place of meeting only for the Archairesiai: Poll. 8, 133. Hesych. Πνύξ.

[3] For the time of the Peloponnesian war see Thuc. 8, 94; for the assembly of the people after the Dionysia: Dem. 21, 9. Æschin., *F. L.*, 61.

[4] Poll. 8, 132/3. Hesych., Πνύξ. ἐκκλησία ἐν Διονύσου: C.I.A., II. 307 = 290/89, cf. 420. ἐκκλησία ἐν τῷ θεάτρῳ: II. 378. 381. 392. 403. 408. 435. 439. 454. 468. 471. See Wachsmuth 1, 647. Reusch, p. 4, gives a collection of inscriptions bearing on the subject.

[5] Ἐκκλησία ἐν Πειραιεῖ περὶ τῶν ἐν τοῖς νεωρίοις: Dem. 19, 60. Lys. 13, 32. 55.

[6] Citizen rights conferred by an ἐκκλησία ἐμ Πειραιεῖ: C.I.A., II. 401; such a meeting decrees crowns to the Prytanes: II. 417. In the decrees of honour for the Epheboi we have mentioned: ἐκκλησίαι ἐν ἄστει καὶ ἐμ Πειραιεῖ: II. 466 sqq. II. 459 says: (ἐκκλησία ἐν τῷ) θεάτρῳ ἡ μεταχθεῖ(σα) ἐκ Πειραιέως κατὰ τὸ ψήφι(σμα ὃ—εἶπ)εν. Reusch, p. 4, gives the inscriptions bearing on the subject.

[7] Philoch., *fr.*, 79b. Müller, *fr. hist. gr.*, 1, 396. Plut., *Arist.*, 7. Poll. 8, 20. Cf. E. Curtius, *att. Stud.*, 2, 40. The views of this scholar in the *Monatsb. d. Berl. Ak.*, 1878, p. 77 sqq., are for the most part doubtful hypotheses.

that none but those qualified were admitted to the meetings, there were 6 ληξίαρχοι, with 30 assistants, who apparently were 3 members from each tribe of the Council, and who were called συλλογεῖς τοῦ δήμου. It was their duty to ascertain the personality of all at the meetings, whom they did not know. With this object they held in their hand the ἐκκλησιαστικοὶ πίνακες of the separate Demes. It was they who gave out the tickets for the μισθὸς ἐκκλησιαστικός, and brought those to account who after receiving a ticket did not attend the meeting.[1] A further duty of the ληξίαρχοι is said to have been to have those Athenians who were in the Agora driven into the Ecclesia by the Toxotai.[2] The Toxotai are said to have used for this purpose a rope, steeped in red dye, with which they surrounded the market-place, and then by drawing it in drove those who were there assembled into the only open exit, which led to the Pnyx.[3]

The right of attendance, and exclusion of the unqualified.

[1] Poll. 8, 104: ληξίαρχοι ἐξ καθίσταντο τῶν πολιτῶν ἐγγεγραμμένων ἐν λευκώματι καὶ τριάκοντα ἀνδρῶν αὐτοῖς προσαιρεθέντων τοὺς μὴ ἐκκλησιάζοντας ἐζημίουν καὶ τοὺς ἐκκλησιάζοντας ἐξήταζον. In Phot. and Hesych., τριάκοντα, these thirty assistants are called δικασταί. See Stojentin, *de Iul. Poll. auctor.*, 32. C. Schaefer, in *Mitth. d. dtsch. arch. Inst.*, 5. 85 sqq., identifies the τριάκοντα with the 30 τριττύαρχοι, assuming that the people were arranged in the Pnyx, not only by tribes, but even by Trittyes. Köhler, in *Mitth. d. dtsch. arch. Inst. in Ath.*, 7, 102 sqq., seems to have arrived at the truth. The Prytanes of the tribe Aigeis, in the year 341/40, honour three of their own number, ἐπειδὴ καλῶς κ(αὶ δι)καίω(s) ἐπεμελήθησαν τῆς συλλογῆς τοῦ δήμου καὶ τῆς (δ)ιαδόσε(ω)s τῶν συμβόλων. See C.I.A., II. 872. Köhler assumes that each tribe of the Council nominated three members, forming a committee, presided over by the three members of the φυλὴ πρυτανεύουσα, for the time being. Köhler identifies these 30 men with the 30 assistants of the ληξίαρχοι. These are the συλλογεῖς τοῦ δήμου mentioned elsewhere, for the year 351/50: C.I.A., II. 1174, for 334/3: II. 741, for 324/3: II. 607. An ἐκκλησιαστικὸς πίναξ of the Deme Otryneis is mentioned in Dem. 44, 35.

[2] Poll. 8, 104 goes on to say: καὶ σχοινίον μιλτώσαντες διὰ τῶν τοξοτῶν συνήλαυνον τοὺς ἐκ τῆς ἀγορᾶς εἰς τὴν ἐκκλησίαν. Phot. σχοινίον μεμιλτωμένον· εἰ βραδύνοιεν ἐπὶ τὴν ἐκκλησίαν, οἱ τοξόται σχοινίον μιλτοῦντες συνήλαυνον καὶ τὰ πρατήρια διέκλειον. From the same source comes the *Schol.* to Arist., *Ach.*, 22 =Suid., σχοινίον and μεμιλτωμένον. Hesych., σχοινίον τὸ μεμιλτωμένον ἔρραινον ὑπὲρ τοῦ σοβῆσαι τὴν ἀγοράν, ὁπότε βραδύνοιεν ἐπὶ τὴν ἐκκλησίαν. Cf. *Schol.* to Aristoph., *Eccl.*, 378. Stojentin 102.

[3] The quotations in the preceding note, which speak of this, all refer to verses from the comic writers: Arist., *Ach.*, 21/2, *Eccl.*, 378/9, and Plat. *ap.* Schol. to *Ach.*, 22. Leop. Schmidt in *Ind. lect.*, Marburg, 1867/8, p. 9 sqq., supposes that the rope painted with red lead was used to shut out from the Pnyx those not entitled to be there. Wachsmuth 2, 1, 454 agrees with him. v. Wilamowitz-Moellendorff, in his *phil. Unters.*, Heft 1, p. 165, 77,

Athens.

After the introduction of the ἐκκλησιαστικὸς μισθός, which we may assume to have been soon after the Archonship of Eucleides, **Pay.** those present at the Ecclesiai received a regular fee, at first one, and later two and three obols. In the time of Aristotle this pay was raised to as much as 1½ drachmas for the κυρία ἐκκλησία and 1 drachma for the other meetings.[1] It appears, however, that in the beginning at any rate all members of the Ecclesia did not receive this pay, whether it was that those who arrived too late lost it, or whether only a certain amount was to be expended for each Ecclesia.[2] Those who went received on entering tickets, which at the close of the meeting were exchanged for money by the Thesmothetai.[3]

In the fifth century order was kept by the Toxotai; from **Maintenance** about 345 by a tribe of the Ecclesia appointed for the **of order.** purpose; yet later by the Epheboi.[4] The ordinary

advances the same opinion. It is difficult to find this in Arist., *Ach.*, 22, and if the Scholiast quotes Plato aright, it is he from whom the traditional account comes. Cf. Valeton in *Mnemosyne*, 1887, 27 sqq.

[1] That the μισθὸς ἐκκλησιαστικὸς stood first at 1 obol, but at the time of the representation of the Ecclesiazusai at 3 obols, is evident from Arist., *Eccl.*, 300 sqq. Arist. says in 41, 3, of the age after Eucleides: μισθοφόρον δὲ ἐκκλησίαν τὸ μὲν πρῶτον ἀπέγνωσαν ποιεῖν· οὐ συλλεγομένων δ᾽ εἰς τὴν ἐκκλησίαν, ἀλλὰ πολλὰ σοφιζομένων τῶν πρυτάνεων, ὅπως προσιστῆται τὸ πλῆθος πρὸς τὴν ἐπικύρωσιν τῆς χειροτονίας, πρῶτον μὲν Ἀγύρριος ὀβολὸν ἐπόρισεν, μετὰ δὲ τοῦτον Ἡρακλείδης ὁ Κλαζομένιος ὁ βασιλεὺς ἐπικαλούμενος διώβολον, πάλιν δ᾽ Ἀγύρριος τριώβολον. For Heracleides cf. Plat., *Ion.*, 541D, to which Immisch, in *Berl. phil. Wochenschr.*, 1891, pp. 707/8, has called attention. Cf. Köhler's remarks on him in *Herm.*, 1892, p. 68 sqq. Of Aristotle's own age we read, 62, 2: μισθοφοροῦσι δὲ πρῶτον [μὲν ὁ δῆμος] ταῖς μὲν ἄλλαις ἐκκλησίαις δραχμήν, τῇ δὲ κυρίᾳ ἐννέα ⟨ὀβολούς⟩.

[2] That not all present at the Ecclesia received pay is shewn by Arist., *Eccl.*, 185 sqq. That those who came too late did not get it may be concluded from lines 289 sqq. Line 380 seems to suggest a certain sum set aside for each Ecclesia. Cf. Wuerz, *de mercede Eccl. Atheniens.*, Berlin, 1878, 34 sqq. See also vol. 2, 310, 2.

[3] This assumption is, in view of Aristoph., *Eccl.*, 289 sqq., 297 sqq., the most probable, and is confirmed by the inscription cited on p. 289.[1] Cf. Benndorf in *Ztsch. f. d. östr. Gymn.*, 1875, p. 597 sqq., who, however, is opposed by Wuerz, p. 34, and rightly as regards payment in kind. It is true that so far it has not been possible to prove such a σύμβολον. Against Benndorf, who deals with this, pp. 601/2, see Fränkel in *Sallets numismat. Ztschr.*, 3, 384; Wuerz 36, 3.

[4] οἱ τοξόται: Arist., *Ach.*, 54 sqq.; *Eccl.*, 143. 258/9. Plat., *Prot.*, 319c, ἡ προεδρεύουσα (Foucart in the *annaire de l'association pour l'encouragement des études grecques*, 1876, p. 137 sqq., wishes to read προσεδρεύουσα on the strength of the inscription quoted below) φυλή, τὸ δέκατον μέρος τῆς πόλεως, *i.e.* accord-

Ecclesia began, it appears, early in the morning.[1] A σημεῖον, probably a flag, was hoisted in the immediate neighbourhood just before beginning.[2]

The meeting, at which the people sat without any distinction of tribes, began with a sacrifice of purification. Preceded by the περιστίαρχοι, the purificatory-victims called περίστια— slain sucking pigs—were carried round the assembled people.[3] Next probably the herald pronounced the curse against

Order of business.

ing to Schäfer, *Dem.*, 2¹, 291, of the Council: Æschin. *in Ctes.* 4. Cf. (Dem.) 25, 90. Æschin. *in Tim.* 33: καθ' ἑκάστην ἐκκλησίαν ἀποκληροῦν φυλὴν ἐπὶ τὸ βῆμα, ἥτις προεδρεύσει. Philippi in the *N. Rh. Mus.*, 34, 612, understands by this a tribe of the Ecclesia. See too Fränkel in *Sallets numismat. Ztschr.*, 3, 388. οἱ ἔφηβοι, according to the formula in the decrees of honour: παρήδρευσαν—or προσήδρευσαν, see, *e.g.*, C.I.A., II. 470—δὲ καὶ ταῖς ἐκκλησίαις ἁπάσαις ἐν ὅπλοις ταῖς τε ἐν ἄστει καὶ ἐμ Πειραιεῖ: C.I.A., II. 466 sqq.

[1] Arist., *Ach.*, 19/20. *Thesm.*, 375. *Eccl.*, 100 sqq., 289 sqq.
[2] Arist., *Thesm.*, 277/8 with the *Schol.*=Suid., σημεῖον. ὅτε ἔμελλε γίνεσθαι ἐκκλησία, σημεῖον ἐτίθετο.
[3] Istr. *ap.* Suid., περιστίαρχος· "Ιστρος δὲ ἐν τοῖς 'Αττικοῖς "περίστια, φησί, προσαγορεύεται τὰ καθάρσια καὶ οἱ τὰ ἱερὰ καθαίροντες περιστίαρχοι· ἔξωθεν γὰρ περιέρχονται χοιροφοροῦντες." The closing words are not certain. [See Müller, *fr. hist. gr.*, 1, 422, *fr.* 32. Cf. Harp.=Phot.=Suid., καθάρσιον. Poll. 8, 104. Lex. Seguer. 269, 16. Suid., περιστίαρχος, Art. 5=*Schol.* to Arist., *Eccl.*, 128: περιστίαρχος· ὁ τῶν καθαρσίων προηγούμενος ἐν ταῖς ἐκκλησίαις. περίστια γὰρ τὰ καθάρσια. Cf. Arist., *Ach.*, 43/4: πάριτ' εἰς τὸ πρόσθεν, Πάριθ' ὡς ἂν ἐντὸς ἦτε τοῦ καθάρματος. *Eccl.*, 128. Æschin. *in Tim.* 23, with the *Schol.* It does not seem to me very probable that the benches were sprinkled with the blood of the sucking pig (*Schol.* to Arist., *Ach.*, 44). To these opening ceremonies I formerly referred the words in some inscriptions which direct that certain persons are to be introduced into the Ecclesia, ἐν ἱεροῖς or πρῶτοι μετὰ τὰ ἱερά. C.I.A., II. 325. 373b. 605; I. 36; II. 52c. 164. But I am now doubtful whether these expressions are not to be regarded, as Hartel 173 sqq. thinks, as referring to the order of business, μετὰ τὰ ἱερά meaning "after religious questions have been discussed." Schubert, *de proxenia Attica*, 36 sqq., Leipzig, 1881, also understands by ἱερά *actiones de rebus sacris*. In two Samian decrees we find μετὰ τὰ ἱερὰ καὶ βασιλικά (C. Curtius in *Progr. von Lübeck*, 1877, pp. 29, 33). Similarly, in a decree from Ephesus in Wood, *Discoveries at Ephesus*, Inscr. from the temple of Diana, No. 11, p. 20, and in one from Bargylia in Lebas, *Asie Min.*, 87. Even if we follow Sauppe in Curtius, p. 30, and understand by τὰ βασιλικά messages or edicts of kings, we can still think of τὰ ἱερά as the religious opening ceremonies of the Ecclesia. But C.I.G. 3640 presents difficulty: μετὰ τὸγ χρηματισμὸν (τ)ὸμ περὶ τῶν ἱρων. That the people sat at an Ecclesia is proved for the fifth century by Arist., *Ach.*, 24/5, for the fourth by Arist., *Eccl.*, 103/4. Dem. 18, 169. Cf. W. Vischer, *Kl. Schr.*, 1, 402 sqq. Fränkel in *Sallets numismat. Ztschr.*, 3, 385 sqq., refutes the opinion advanced by Benndorf in *Zeitschr. f. d. östr. Gymn.*, 1875, p. 18 sqq., that the people sat together by tribes in the Assembly.

those who by their speeches tried to deceive the people and who had received bribes to do so.[1] After this probably followed a communication from the Prytanes that the sacrifice made to certain deities with reference to the meeting had proved favourable, and that therefore these deities would not interrupt the intended meeting. This custom however can only be proved to have existed in later times.[2] If, notwithstanding, an inauspicious omen did occur during the sitting, then the meeting was dissolved. Such interruptions, or διοσημίαι, were lightning, thunder, rain, a storm, an eclipse, an earthquake.[3] As to when such a διοσημία was to be considered as having occurred, this seems to have depended on the decision of the Exegetai.[4]

After the presidency of the Ecclesia was transferred from the πρυτάνεις to the πρόεδροι, the ἐπιστάτης of the πρυτάνεις, before the meeting could proceed to business, had first to choose the πρόεδροι by lot, and from among them again an ἐπιστάτης had to be drawn. He presided, using a herald to address the meeting.[5]

When these formalities had been gone through, actual business

---

[1] Dem. 19, 70. Æschin. *in Tim.* 23. Dein. *in Arist.* 14. For the nature of the curse see Dem. 23, 97; 18, 282. Dein. *in Demosth.* 47, *in Arist.* 16. A free parody of this ἀρὰ in Arist., *Thesm.*, 295 sqq., 331 sqq. See Schömann, *de comit.*, 92 sqq.

[2] The μικροφιλότιμος in Theophr., *Char.*, 21, wishes to appear wreathed before the Ecclesia and make the announcement: ὦ ἄνδρες 'Αθηναῖοι, ἐθύομεν οἱ πρυτάνεις τῇ μητρὶ τῶν θεῶν καὶ ὑμεῖς δέχεσθε τὰ ἀγαθά· τὰ γὰρ σφάγια καὶ τὰ ἱερὰ καλά. Cf. the formula found in later inscriptions, *e.g.* C.I.A., II. 417, 459: ὑπὲρ ὧν ἀπαγγέλλουσι οἱ πρυτάνεις τῆς—ίδος ὑπὲρ τῶν θυσιῶν ὧν ἔθυον τά τε πρὸ τῶν ἐκκλησιῶν τῷ Ἀπόλλωνι τῷ Προστατηρίῳ καὶ τῇ Ἀρτέμιδι τῇ Βουλαίᾳ καὶ τοῖς ἄλλοις θεοῖς οἷς πάτριον ἦν, ἀγαθῇ τύχῃ δεδόχθαι τῷ δήμῳ τὰ μὲν ἀγαθὰ δέχεσθαι τὰ γεγονότα ἐν τοῖς ἱεροῖς οἷς ἔθυον ἐφ' ὑγιείᾳ καὶ σωτηρίᾳ τῆς βουλῆς καὶ τοῦ δήμου καὶ τῶν συμμάχων. See Köhler in *Herm.*, 5, 333. Schoell. 6, 56. Perhaps C.I.A., II. 416, is to be explained as referring to this consultation of the gods by sacrifice preliminary to the Ecclesia: ἀρχαιρεσίαι κατὰ τὴν μαντ(είαν). For earlier times this custom is not proved as yet. In a psephism of B.C. 362/1 we find the declaration that the herald had vowed sacrifices to certain gods in case the resolution turned out well for the Athenians. II. 57b, p. 57.

[3] Arist., *Ach.*, 170/1; *Clouds*, 579 sqq.; Thuc. 5. 45. Suid. διοσημία.

[4] Poll. 8, 124: ἀνίστατο δὲ τὰ δικαστήρια, εἰ γένοιτο διοσημία· ἐξηγηταὶ δ' ἐκαλοῦντο οἱ τὰ περὶ τῶν διοσημιῶν καὶ τὰ τῶν ἄλλων ἱερῶν διδάσκοντες. What is said of the courts may be taken as applying also to popular assemblies. In Arist., *Ach.*, 170/1, the Ecclesia is dissolved in consequence of a private intimation of a διοσημία.

[5] Arist. 44, 2; Suid., ἐπιστάτης, Art. 2. For the Prytanes and Proedroi compare p. 271 sqq.

began with the reading by the herald of the προβούλευμα of the Council. Sometimes in extraordinary cases the Prytanes would make a verbal communication of their proposals to the Assembly.[1] It was illegal to bring anything before the Ecclesia without a προβούλευμα of the Council.[2] In this προβούλευμα the Boule either made definite proposals, which was generally the case, or it contented itself with formally bringing the matter before the Ecclesia. In the first case the Council proposed a definite resolution in the προβούλευμα; in the latter the Council left it to the Ecclesia to decide for itself, without laying before it any motion.[3]

The reading of the προβούλευμα was followed by the προχειροτονία as it was called. We gather from the definitions of the grammarians, which agree with what we are told of various instances in which it was employed, that this was a preliminary vote of the Ecclesia on the question whether the Council's proposal should be accepted as it stood or whether a debate should be opened on it.[4]

---

[1] The former custom may be gathered from the imitation in Arist., *Thesm.*, 371; the latter seems to follow from Dem. 18, 170.

[2] Arist. 45, 4: προβουλεύει δ' εἰς τὸν δῆμον καὶ οὐκ ἔξεστιν οὐδὲν ἀπροβούλευτον οὐδ' ὅτι ἂν μὴ προγράψωσιν οἱ πρυτάνεις ψηφίσασθαι τῷ δήμῳ· κατ' αὐτὰ γὰρ ταῦτα ἔνοχός ἐστιν ὁ νικήσας γραφῇ παρανόμων. Even for the Archairesiai a Probouleuma was necessary. Arist. 44, 4. Cf. Plut., *Sol.*, 19: μηδὲν ἐὰν ἀπροβούλευτον εἰς ἐκκλησίαν εἰσφέρεσθαι. For the definition of προβούλευμα see Harp.=Phot. προβούλευμα. Lex. Seguer. 289, 26 sqq.

[3] The first alternative is the commoner, as we see in numerous psephisms after the time of Eucleides. Thus we have, with slight variations: ἐψήφισται τῇ βουλῇ τοὺς προέδρους οἳ ἂν λάχωσιν προεδρεύειν εἰς τὴν πρώτην ἐκκλησίαν (προσαγαγεῖν τὸν δεῖνα καὶ) χρηματίσαι περὶ τούτων, γνώμην δὲ ξυμβάλλεσθαι τῆς βουλῆς εἰς τὸν δῆμον, ὅτι δοκεῖ τῇ βουλῇ; then follows the way in which the Council proposes to deal with the matter. On the gradual development of this formula see Hartel, *Stud. üb. att. Staatsr. u. Urkundenw.*, 166 sqq. The second alternative is seen in C.I.A., II. 168. The Council here resolves: τοὺς προέδρους οἳ ἂν λάχωσι προεδρεύειν εἰς τὴν πρώτην ἐκκλησίαν προσαγαγεῖν αὐτοὺς καὶ χρηματίσαι, γνώμην δὲ ξυμβάλλεσθαι τῆς βουλῆς εἰς τὸν δῆμον, ὅτι δοκεῖ τῇ βουλεῖ, ἀκούσαντα τὸν δῆμον τῶν Κιτιείων περὶ τῆς ἱδρύσεως τοῦ ἱεροῦ καὶ ἄλλου Ἀθηναίων τοῦ βουλομένου βουλεύσασθαι, ὅτι ἂν αὐτῷ δοκεῖ ἄριστον εἶναι. Cf. for Probouleumata of this kind the list in Hartel 226 sqq.

[4] Harp.=Phot., Suid., προχειροτονία. ἔοικεν Ἀθήνησι τοιουτό τι γίγνεσθαι· ὁπόταν τῆς βουλῆς προβουλευσάσης εἰσφέρηται εἰς τὸν δῆμον ἡ γνώμη, πρότερον γίγνεται χειροτονία ἐν τῇ ἐκκλησίᾳ, πότερον δοκεῖ περὶ τῶν προβουλευθέντων σκέψασθαι τὸν δῆμον ἢ ἀρκεῖ τὸ προβούλευμα. ταῦτα δ' ὑποσημαίνεται ἐν τῷ Λυσίου πρὸς τὴν Μιξιδήμου γραφήν. Arist. 43, 6, after an account of the order of business at the four ordinary assemblies, continues: χρηματίζουσιν ἐνίοτε καὶ ἄνευ προχειροτονίας. See Dem. 24, 11. Æschin. *in Tim.* 23. The hypothesis as to the meaning of προχειροτονία advanced by Hartel, *Demosth. Stud.* 2, p. 46 sqq., and in *Stud. üb. att. Staatsrecht u. Urkundenwesen*, 179 sqq., I think I

It was probably not usual to adopt the προβούλευμα without discussion except where minor details were in question; for we may assume as certain that the Probouleuma was voted upon section by section.¹

If it was resolved by the Procheirotonia to discuss a clause of the προβούλευμα, the herald put the question to the meeting, "Who wishes to speak?" According to a law of Solon, a senior member had precedence over his juniors, but that custom seems to have been soon abandoned.² Whoever obtained leave to speak put on a wreath before beginning to address the meeting.³ It was usual

have refuted in the *Jahrb. f. cl. Phil.*, 1879, p. 225 sqq. To Hartel's rejoinder in *Wiener Stud.*, 1. 269 sqq., I have replied in the *Jahrb. f. cl. Phil.*, 1880, p. 529 sqq. A detailed refutation from the inscriptions is given in the work of Miller, *de decretis att. quæstiones epigraphicæ*, Breslau, 1885. Höck, in the same *Jahrb.*, 801 sqq., agrees with me in the rejection of Hartel's hypothesis, but thinks that we may infer from Æschin. *in Tim.* 23 that the προχειροτονία meant preliminary questions περὶ ἱερῶν καὶ ὁσίων and on foreign affairs, which in urgent cases preceded the proper business of the Assembly. The opinion advanced by Bake, *Schol. hypomnem.*, 4. 279 sqq., on the προχειροτονία is also incorrect. Miller, in *phil. Abhandl. für M. Hertz*, p. 189 sqq., attempts a new explanation based on Dem. 24, 11. sqq., and Æschin. *in Tim.* 28; but he has misunderstood the former passage, which deals (§ 14) with a γραφὴ παρανόμων—compare § 15—and in the second is forced to change the position of καὶ μετὰ ταῦτ' in order to make them serve his purpose. What I have said about this passage, *ib.* 288 sqq. and 530 sqq., I still hold to be correct, and the statement in Harp. (particularly as the short notice in Arist. gives us no help) must be considered authoritative until an inscription proves it erroneous.

¹ For instance, the introduction of foreign ambassadors moved in a Probouleuma would usually be agreed to at once by προχειροτονία, whilst the policy recommended by the Council would be considered and voted upon after the introduction of the ambassadors. Cf. C.I.A., II. 49. 50. 54. 55.

² Æschin. *in Tim.* 23. In Arist., *Ach.*, 45 ; *Thesm.*, 379; *Ecc.*, 130; Dem. 18, 170, the formula is simply : τίς ἀγορεύειν βούλεται; according to the law of Solon: τίς ἀγορεύειν βούλεται τῶν ὑπὲρ πεντήκοντα ἔτη γεγονότων καὶ πάλιν ἐν μέρει τῶν ἄλλων Ἀθηναίων. See Æschin., *loc. cit.*, and *in Ctes.* 4, where also, § 1 sqq., the discontinuance of this custom is shown.

³ Arist., *Thesm.*, 380. *Eccl.*, 131. 148. 163. Τὸ δοκιμασίαν ἐπαγγέλλειν (Æschin. *in Tim.* 32) or ἐπαγγελίαν ἐπαγγέλλειν (81) against the speaker, when some member of the Ecclesia declared that the speaker had been guilty of a misdemeanour which was punishable with Atimia, did not force him to resume his seat. It was only afterwards and in a heliastic court that the justice of the accusation was determined. See Lipsius in Meier,² 248 sqq., where the difference between the ἔνδειξις and the ἐπαγγελία is also discussed. Certain cases in which this ἐπαγγελία was admissible are given by Æschin., *ibid.*, 27 sqq. Poll. 8, 45. The punishment was atimia : Poll., Dem. 19, 284.

perhaps for the man who had moved the προβούλευμα in the Council to defend it in the Ecclesia.[1] Any citizen present in the Ecclesia might propose amendments to the Probouleuma; if adopted, the amendments were appended to the Probouleuma when written out as a psephisma. He might also formulate his views in a new resolution based on the Probouleuma, and propose that for the acceptance of the Ecclesia.[2]

Similarly any member might oppose the Probouleuma and move its rejection, or move in place of it a different resolution; such a counter resolution could be adopted by the Ecclesia without contravening the law mentioned above, since a Probouleuma on the same subject, though to a different effect, had come before the Ecclesia.[3] This is manifest from the second form of προβούλευμα, where the Council called on the Ecclesia to formulate its own view; for in such cases the Council was considered to have given its advice though it had made no substantive proposition.

It was also permissible for a private citizen in the Ecclesia to take the initiative in the consideration of some matter by bringing in a motion asking the Council to pronounce an opinion upon it. The course adopted in such a case, supposing the Ecclesia declared itself for the motion, was to direct the Council to submit to the popular assembly a προβούλευμα on the subject.[4] The Council

---

[1] In the psephisms he is designated by ὁ δεῖνα εἶπεν.

[2] In the psephisms the formula for the first kind of amendments is ὁ δεινὰ εἶπεν· τὰ μὲν ἄλλα καθάπερ τῇ βουλῇ or καθάπερ ὁ δεῖνα, then follows the amendment. Cf. C.I.A., I. 38, II. 38, 186; 86, 331. A collection of inscrr. of this class in Hartel 221 sqq. See however Miller 42 sqq. An instance of a new resolution based on the Probouleuma is found in the inscr. in the *Mitth. d. dtsch. etc.*, 8, 211/2, compared with 213. See Köhler, 214/5.

[3] This follows from Xen., *Hell.*, 7, 1, 1-14 on which passage I agree with Schömann, *de comit.*, 98; Leop. Schmidt, *de auctorit. προβουλεύματος in rep. Ath.*, Ind. lect. Marburg, 1876/7, p. 6, as against Hartel in *commentat. phil. in honor. Mommseni*, 520/1.

[4] Köhler in *Herm.* 5, 13 sqq. Hartel 183 sqq., where the inscriptions relating to this point are collected. The formula in such a psephisma runs somewhat as follows: δεδόχθαι or ἐψηφίσθαι τῷ δήμῳ προβουλεύσασαν τὴν βουλὴν ἐξενεγκεῖν ἐς τὸν δῆμον περί, and then follows the matter on which the Ecclesia desired a Probouleuma. C.I.A., II. 76. 98. 126. 82b. In the case of Heracleides of Salamis—see *Mitth.*, 8, 211 sqq.—it was proposed in the Ecclesia by Telemachos of Acharnae: ἐψηφίσθαι τῷ δήμῳ, τὴν βουλὴν προβουλεύσασαν ἐξενεγκεῖν εἰς τὴν πρώτην ἐκκλησίαν περὶ Ἡρακλείδου, καθότι εὑρήσεται ἄν τι δύνηται ἀγαθὸν παρὰ τοῦ δήμου τοῦ Ἀθηναίων. Then Kephisodotos in the Boule moves the necessary Probouleuma, and on the basis of this Telemachos proposes in a subsequent Ecclesia the final psephism. A

then carried out this order either by sending to the Ecclesia a Probouleuma with definite proposals, or by simply submitting the matter to its consideration by a formal προβούλευμα, leaving the speakers in the Ecclesia to move what they chose. A second way for a private citizen to gain leave to propose resolutions was to petition the Council to allow him to speak in the Ecclesia on a certain subject; in other words, to give that subject a place in the agenda of the Ecclesia.[1]

All motions submitted to the Ecclesia, whether amendments to a προβούλευμα or independent proposals, were formulated by the mover in writing and handed to the president or to his secretary, or else proposed by word of mouth and afterwards put in writing with the assistance of the secretary.[2]

Administrative measures requiring popular sanction were frequently proposed in the first instance by those bodies of officials to whose department they belonged, and then were brought by the Council before the Ecclesia in the ordinary course of business.[3]

similar procedure must be assumed for the resolution in honour of Pytheas, 333 B.C., beginning ἔδοξεν τῷ δήμῳ, where we find : Χαιριωνίδης Λυσανίου Φλυεὺς εἶπεν· περὶ ὧν ὁ δῆμος προσέταξεν τῇ βουλῇ προβουλεύσασαν ἐξενεγκεῖν περὶ Πυθέου, καθότι τιμηθήσεται ὑπὸ τοῦ δήμου, τύχῃ ἀγαθῇ δεδόχθαι τῷ δήμῳ κ. τ. ἁ. : 'Εφ. ἀρχ., 1889, pp. 15/6.

[1] That ordinary private citizens had the right of bringing forward motions in the Ecclesia appears also in Xen., Mem., 3, 6. Glaucon is not yet 20 years of age, and therefore cannot think of obtaining the βουλεία : and when, in spite of this, he endeavours προστατεύειν τῆς πόλεως and makes speeches in the Ecclesia (§ 1) we can only suppose that he is making independent motions in the Ecclesia. The same follows from 3, 7, where Socrates advises Charmides to turn his political activities to the Ecclesia (see § 6), and also from the context in Plat., Protagor., 319D. The second way for a private citizen to obtain the opportunity of proposing a motion in the Ecclesia we learn from Isocr. 7, 1. 15. The technical expression seems to have been τὴν πρόσοδον ἀπογράφεσθαι.

[2] For the first alternative see Æschin., F.L., 68. 83, for the second Arist., Thesm., 432. I do not think it probable that there was in Athens in the fifth century a committee of συγγραφεῖς, annually elected, to draw up documents, whom the Council and people employed under certain circumstances to put resolutions in writing, as Sauppe assumes in the Ind. schol. Goett., 1880/1, p. 10, on the ground of some inscriptions, viz., C.I.A., I. 58, IV. 22a, in which Foucart in Bulletin de correspondance hellénique, 1880, p. 251, restores (τάδε οἱ χσυγγραφῆς χ)συνέγρα(ψαν), and 'Αθήν. 8, 405 sqq.=Ind. schol. Goett., 1880/1, p. 3.

[3] C.I.A., II. 430 : βουλὴ ἐμ βουλευτηρίῳ σύνκλητος στρατ(ηγῶν) παραγγειλάντων καὶ ἀπὸ βουλῆς ἐκκλησία (κυρία) ἐν τῷ θεάτρῳ—γνώμη στρατηγῶν : Bull. 12, 142, no. 8. γνώμη τῶν συγγραφέων : C.I.A., I. 58. τάδε οἱ ξυγγραφῆς ξυνέγραψαν : C.I.A., IV. 22a. 27b. γνώμη Κλεισόφου καὶ συνπρυτάνεων : 'Αρχ. δελτίον, 1889,

The Ecclesia.

If a motion were not of a purely political character, and technical questions had to be considered, the Ecclesia heard the opinion of experts, and, if the motion fell within the province of any board of magistrates, the latter were also called upon to give their opinion.[1]

If no one had any further wish to discuss the motion before the Ecclesia, the voting took place. The president might refuse to put the question, if he considered the motion under discussion illegal.[2] The presidents could, however, be made answerable for refusing to proceed with the voting, by an ἔνδειξις.[3] The voting regularly took place by χειροτονία, i.e., by show of hands. The president through the herald first asked those who were in favour of the motion to hold up their hands, and then those who were against it. A count probably only took place when the voting was close.[4] A second but more unusual form of voting was by ballot; this was employed in the full assemblies, i.e. at the Ostrakismos, in granting citizenship and ἄδεια, and occasionally in other extraordinary cases.[5] In this case two urns were placed, either for each tribe or for the whole Ecclesia, the one for the ayes, the other for the noes.[6] After the voting had taken place, the president announced the result and dismissed the meeting by means of the herald, if there was no other business.[7]

The psephism of the Ecclesia was deposited in the State archives in the Metroon; and besides this, in case further publicity seemed desirable, it was inscribed on a stele, placed usually on the Acropolis. In this case the psephism contained a special order that this should be done, as also that the cost of the erection of the stele should be charged to

Construction of Decrees.

---

p. 25. Proposal of a single Strategos: C.I.A., IV. 61a. 1. 26 sqq. Bull. 13. 154. Dittenberger, Syll., 79. C.I.A., II. 439. 481. Cf. Köhler in Herm., 2, 326. Swoboda, die griech. Volksbeschlüsse, 84.

[1] Plato, Protagor., 319 B. Æschin. in Tim. 81. See Hartel 242/3.

[2] See for the Prytanes: Plat., Gorg., 473 E. Apol., 32 B. Xen., Mem., 1, 1, 18; 4, 4, 2: for the Proedroi, Æschin., F.L., 84.

[3] This seems to follow from Plat., Apol., 32 B. Cf. the law in Dem. 24, 22.

[4] A meeting dismissed without a division taking place: τότε γὰρ ὀψὲ ἦν καὶ τὰς χεῖρας οὐκ ἂν καθεώρων: Xen., Hell., 1, 7, 7. The method of voting is given in Phot. = Suid., κατεχειροτόνησαν. Compare Dem. 24, 20.

[5] Plut., Arist., 7. (Dem.) 59, 89. 90. Dem. 24, 45/6.

[6] (Dem.) 59, 90, speaks in general terms of καδίσκοι. Two urns for each tribe according to Xen., Hell., 1, 7, 9.

[7] Æschin. in Ctes. 8. The herald says in Arist., Ach., 173: οἱ γὰρ πρυτάνεις λύουσι τὴν ἐκκλησίαν.

the State treasury.¹ The psephisms thus engraved and set up contain two parts, the preface and the decree proper. The form of the first underwent various changes in the course of time. The fullest formulæ of the time before Eucleides contain the names of the Archon and the Secretary to the Council, the formula of sanction (ἔδοξεν τῇ βουλῇ καὶ τῷ δήμῳ), the names of the φυλὴ πρυτανεύουσα, the president of the Ecclesia, and the mover; we do not, however, find all these particulars in all inscriptions. After Eucleides this old formula was gradually remodelled and brought more into accord with the style of the age, and new matter was added in order to state with greater precision the date of the decree and the class of decrees to which it belonged. These additions were introduced gradually, and consisted of the day of the Prytany and of the month on which the Ecclesia had taken place, the character of the meeting and the place of meeting, and sometimes, at a later period, the subject of the resolution.² The sanction-formula appears in the inscriptions after Eucleides in the two forms ἔδοξεν τῇ βουλῇ καὶ τῷ δήμῳ and ἔδοξεν τῷ δήμῳ. The first form is usually connected with the above-mentioned formula of the προβούλευμα, which made definite proposals, but also appears without it; in the second form this formula is sometimes found, but is more frequently absent. The resolutions which we find recorded by inscriptions are accordingly to be distinguished in this way:—not only the resolutions with the sanction-formula ἔδοξεν τῇ βουλῇ καὶ τῷ δήμῳ without the probouleuma-formula, but also those documents supplied with the sanction-formulæ ἔδοξεν τῇ βουλῇ καὶ τῷ δήμῳ and ἔδοξεν τῷ δήμῳ, both in connexion with the probouleuma-formula, are all alike based on probouleumata

---

¹ For the management of the archives see Boeckh, *Kl. Schr.*, 4, 293 sq. C. Curtius, *d. Metroon*, p. 15 sqq. Hartel, *Stud. üb. att. Staatsr. u. Urkundenw.*, 52 sqq. Wachsmuth, 2, 1, 327 sqq. According to Wilamowitz-Moellendorf in *Phil. Unters.*, vol. i. p. 205, the Metroon was not used for the archives before the second half of the fourth century, but this view is rightly rejected by Wachsmuth 2, 1, 326, 1. 343/4. Phot., μητρῷον· τὸ ἱερὸν τῆς μητρὸς τῶν θεῶν, ἐν ᾧ γράμματα δημόσια καὶ οἱ νόμοι. Dem. 19, 129: ἀλλ' ὑπὲρ μὲν τῆς ἐξωμοσίας ἐν τοῖς κοινοῖς τοῖς ὑμετέροις γράμμασιν ἐν τῷ μητρῴῳ ταῦτ' ἐστίν, ἐφ' οἷς ὁ δημόσιος τέτακται, καὶ ψήφισμα ἄντικρυς περὶ τούτου τοῦ ὀνόματος γέγραπται. Contents of the archives: Wachsmuth 334 seq. Not all decrees engraved and erected: Hartel., 149 sqq. Meaning of this erection of the decrees on the Acropolis: Hartel 156/7. For the assignment of money to pay for the stele, and on the scale of charges see Hartel 129 sqq.

² An exhaustive account of the matter of which these preface-formulæ consisted is given by Hartel p. 4 sqq.

with definite proposals; on the other hand, the decrees characterized simply by ἔδοξεν τῷ δήμῳ are framed after a merely formal opinion of the Council.[1]

The sovereignty of the Athenian people, which finds expression in the psephisms of the Ecclesia, was limited by law. This is plainly shown by the use made of the γραφὴ παρανόμων, γραφὴ which was considered a safeguard of the democratic παρανόμων. constitution, because by means of it unconstitutional resolutions could be impugned.[2] This γραφὴ παρανόμων, which any Athenian was at liberty to bring, was permissible against every resolution of the people and against every law not passed with the proper legal forms. Notice that such an indictment would be laid against a psephism was given by oath either before or after the vote was taken in the Ecclesia, and this oath called by the same name as the application for adjournment in an ordinary lawsuit, ὑπωμοσία, resulted in the suspension of the psephism until the matter had been decided in a heliastic court.[3] At the trial the plaintiff had to prove that the resolution in question was in contravention of some existing law.[4] To prove this, he wrote out the

---

[1] In Plat., Phædr., 258, we find: ἔδοξέ πού φησι τῇ βουλῇ ἢ τῷ δήμῳ ἢ ἀμφοτέροις. The differences in the sanction-formula of the Attic decrees were first pointed out by Hartel 59 sq. I have followed him in the text, with the alterations suggested by Miller, 14 sqq.

[2] See Dem. 24, 154. Thuc. 8, 67. Arist. 29, 4. Holm, griech. Gesch., 2, 234, points out, with good reason, that the responsibility of the mover was a check upon frivolous motions.

[3] Poll. 8, 56: ὑπωμοσία δέ ἐστιν, ὅταν τις ἢ ψήφισμα ἢ νόμον γραφέντα γράψηται ὡς ἀνεπιτήδειον· τοῦτο γὰρ ὑπομόσασθαι λέγουσι. καὶ οὐκ ἦν μετὰ τὴν ὑπωμοσίαν τὸ γραφέν, πρὶν κριθῆναι, κύριον. Poll. 8, 44. For the request for delay in ordinary suits see Harp., ὑπωμοσία. For this action see Schömann, de comit., 159 sqq., 272 sqq. Meier [2] 428 sqq. According to Hartel, Stud. üb. att. Staatsr. u. Urkundenw., 251 sqq., notice of the γραφὴ παρανόμων had to be made between the first and second readings which he supposes. But such a conclusion does not follow from the authorities quoted by Hartel. The words in (Dem.) 26, 8, rather indicate a definite decision of the Ecclesia, after which the γραφὴ παρανόμων was entered. I believe it unnecessary to assume with Madvig, Kl. Schr., 379, that in cases of administrative resolutions of the people, which were to be carried out as soon as possible, the suspensory power of the γραφὴ παρανόμων was limited by law, since we may be sure that in practice no one would dare to enter a γραφὴ in such a case. A γραφὴ παρανόμων before the voting of the Ecclesia: Xen. 1, 7, 12, after it: (Dem.) 59, 4. 5.

[4] Thus e.g. if a psephism had been passed without a Probouleuma: Arist. 45, 4. With reference to Dem. 23, 100. 101, we must admit with Madvig, ibid., 378 sqq., that the inexpediency of a proposed psephisma or law was in

proposed psephisma and the laws it contravened on a wooden tablet side by side, and submitted it to the Thesmothetai, who then had to bring the case before a heliastic Court. In the trial the plaintiff spoke first and was followed by the defendant. If the verdict went against the latter, the resolution, to which objection had been made, was definitively set aside; and then, as the γραφὴ παρανόμων was a γραφὴ τιμητὸς, a new trial ensued to fix the penalty. This was either a fine, or (but most probably only in extraordinary cases) a sentence of death.[1] The proposer of a resolution was responsible for it only for a year. After the expiration of that time, only the psephism or law could be attacked, not its proposer.[2] Whoever had been condemned three times on a γραφὴ παρανόμων incurred a partial atimia; he lost the right of proposing motions in the Ecclesia.[3]

As already mentioned, the psephisms had to keep within the existing laws; hence, as a natural consequence, the Ecclesia had its share in the proceedings preliminary to legislation, but not in legislation itself. The method of legislation in the 4th century itself no reason for its being proceeded against by a γραφὴ παρανόμων. The fact that in such speeches as we possess delivered in these cases, the injuriousness of the motion under discussion is not infrequently dwelt upon, is perfectly explicable if we consider that this would influence the judgment of the court. If in the Leptines the injuriousness of the law is insisted upon almost exclusively, we can explain the fact by the consideration that Phormio had already dealt with its illegality. See Lipsius in *Bursian's Jahresber.*, 1878, pp. 313/4. Poll. 8, 44 is explained by the stress laid by the orators on the inexpediency of the law in question in each case.

[1] For the form of procedure see Æschin. *in Ctes.* 197 sqq. The Thesmothetai as εἰσαγωγεῖς: Poll. 8, 87. Hypereid., *Euxenipp.*, xxi. 27. Dem. 20, 98/9, as the causa Leptinea is a γραφὴ παρανόμων. Schömann, *op. ac.*, 1, 237 sqq. Sentence of death: Dem. 24, 208. Fines: 10 talents, Dem. 21, 182. (Dem.) 58, 43. 15 talents, (Dem.) 59, 6. 100 talents: Æschin., *F.L.*, 14. Valeton in *Mnemosyne*, 1887, p. 44 sqq., is certainly right in emending ἑξακισχιλίοις into ἑνὶ καὶ χιλίοις in Andoc., *de Myst.*, 17, where it is said of the γραφὴ παρανόμων of the father of Andocides against Speusippos: καὶ ἠγωνίσατο ἐν ἑξακισχιλίοις Ἀθηναίων καὶ μετέλαβε δικαστῶν τοσούτων οὐδὲ διακοσίας ψήφους ὁ Σπεύσιππος. The μετέλαβε δικαστῶν τοσούτων οὐδὲ διακοσίας ψήφους corresponds to the formula τὸ πέμπτον μέρος τῶν ψήφων οὐ μεταλαμβάνει: Æschin., *F. L.*, 14, or more briefly τὸ μέρος τῶν ψήφων ὁ διώκων οὐκ ἔλαβεν: Dem. 18, 103.

[2] Dem. 20, 144: ἐξῆλθον οἱ χρόνοι καὶ νυνὶ περὶ αὐτοῦ τοῦ νόμου πᾶς ἐστιν ὁ λόγος, τούτῳ δ' οὐδείς ἐστι κίνδυνος. In the argument to Dem. 20, p. 453, it says: νόμος γὰρ ἦν τὸν γράψαντα νόμον ἢ ψήφισμα μετὰ ἐνιαυτὸν μὴ εἶναι ὑπεύθυνον.

[3] Diod. 18, 18: ἦν γὰρ τρὶς ἡλωκὼς παρανόμων καὶ διὰ τοῦτο γεγονὼς ἄτιμος καὶ κωλυόμενος ὑπὸ τῶν νόμων συμβουλεύειν. Athen, 10, 451 A.

was as follows.[1] On the eleventh of Hecatombaion in each year, at the meeting of the Ecclesia regularly held on that day, an Epicheirotonia of the laws took place, *i.e.*, after a debate, a vote on the several classes of laws was taken as to whether they were satisfactory as they stood, or whether this or that class of laws appeared to need improvement. If the Ecclesia pronounced in favour of the latter alternative, any private citizen was at liberty to put up a notice of amendments to the laws under revision, in front of the statues of the Eponymoi, that all might see. A copy of his amendments had to be given to the secretary to the Council, and he had to read them out in the next Ecclesia. At the fourth ordinary assembly in the Prytany a resolution was passed as to the choice of Nomothetai (who were selected from the heliasts), the number of Nomothetai to be nominated, the amount of their fees, and the duration of their powers. At the same time the meeting chose 5 συνήγοροι to defend the laws under revision before the Nomothetai.[2]

---

[1] The forms of Nomothesia have been repeatedly discussed: *e.g.*, by Schömann, *de Comit.*, 248 sqq., *op. ac.*, 1, 247 sqq., in criticism of the confused account of Bake in *Schol. hypomnem.*, 4, 1 sqq., who took up the question again, *ib.*, 5. 236 sqq. Westermann, *Abh. d. Sächs. Ges. d. W.*, 2. Schäfer, *Demosth.*, 1¹, 337. Köhler, *Urk. u. Unters. z. Gesch. d. del.-att. Bundes*, 65 sqq. Fränkel 24 sqq. Höffler, *de Nomothesia att.* Kieler Diss., 1877. Neubauer, *üb. d. Anwend. der* γραφὴ παρανόμων *bei d. Ath. z. Abschaff. v. Gesetzen*. Pr. v. Marburg (Steiermark) 1880. Lastly, R. Schoell in *Ber. d. bayr. Ak.*, 1886, p. 83 sqq., to whom belongs the credit of having proved the genuineness of the laws quoted in the Timocrates (Dem. 24, 20 sqq., 33) as against Westermann, *ibid.*, 7 sqq., 47 sqq. I have followed him in the main in this edition. But it seems that the method of legislation described in the text only dates from the fourth century. At least Pericles answers the question of Alcibiades in Xen., *Mem.*, 1, 2, 42 : τί ἐστι νόμος; with the words πάντες γὰρ οὗτοι νόμοι εἰσίν, οὓς τὸ πλῆθος συνελθὸν καὶ δοκιμάσαν ἔγραψε, φράζον ἅ τε δεῖ ποιεῖν καὶ ἃ μή, an answer which is not in accordance with the Nomothesia in vogue in the fourth century.

[2] See the law in Dem. 24, 20–23, which is confirmed by the statements of the orator, §§ 18. 25. 26. 47. 48. Cf. Dem. 20, 94. Cf. Schoell, *ib.*, 84 sqq. Τὴν τελευταίαν τῶν τριῶν ἐκκλησιῶν (§ 21), for which Dem. § 25 puts τὴν τρίτην ἐκκλησίαν, I consider with Schoell 101, and against Ad. Schmidt, *Handb. d. griech. Chronol.*, 359/60, as the third after the first, *i.e.*, the fourth ordinary meeting of the Prytany, as four ordinary meetings in every Prytany are spoken of by Arist. 43, 4 sqq. 1,000 Nomothetai in Poll. 8, 101, who, however, seems to have derived this statement, as Schoell 102 justly assumes, from the 1,001 Nomothetai in Dem. 24, 27 ; 500 in the psephism of Tisamenos in Andoc., *de Myst.*, 84. Schömann, *de Comit.*, 257, had already held that the number varied.

After the Nomothetai had been appointed from among the heliasts by the Prytanes of the Council, the πρόεδροι chosen by lot from the members of the Council for the conduct of the proceedings of the Nomothetai, and presided over by their ἐπιστάτης, brought before the Nomothetai the laws proposed for revision, the amendments proposed, and also probably an opinion of the Council's upon them. They first heard the arguments of the advocates, who had been nominated to defend the existing laws, and those of the proposers of amendments, and then took a vote as to whether the law was to be retained as it stood. If the decision was against this, a second vote was taken to decide whether the amendment was to be accepted as law. It depended on the decision of the Nomothetai whether the old law was confirmed or the proposed amendment substituted for it.[1] Against every law thus enacted a γραφὴ παρανόμων was admissible, in case the new law seemed to be prejudicial to the interests of the Athenian people or to contravene other legal enactments. This γραφὴ παρανόμων was likewise admissible if an attempt was made to pass a law without observing the method of legislation just described.[2]

Distinct from this procedure for the enactment of laws was the revision of existing laws which devolved upon the Thesmothetai. They had annually to examine the existing laws, to ascertain

[1] Compare Schoell 111 sqq. That the Prytanes of the Council appointed the Nomothetai is proved by the psephism in Dem. 24, 27, the genuineness of which is discussed by Schoell 119 sqq. The expression too in Æschin. *in Ctes.* 40: τῶν δὲ πρυτάνεων ἀποδόντων τοῖς νομοθέταις ἀνῄρητ' ἂν ὁ ἕτερος τῶν νόμων, which has reference to the revision of the laws by the Thesmothetai, seems to confirm this. For the participation of the Council compare the psephism just quoted, and (Xen.) *de rep. Ath.*, 3, 2; and for the extraordinary revision of the laws in B.C. 403, the psephism of Tisamenos in Andoc., *de Myst.*, 84. For the proceedings before the Nomothetai see the law in Dem. 24, 33, with which cf. Dem. 20, 89. 93; 24, 34. Οἱ πρόεδροι καὶ ὁ ἐπιστάτης τῶν νομοθετῶν in an inscription immediately after B.C. 350, C.I.A., II. 115 b., to which there has now been added a psephism of 335 B.C. in Ἐφ. ἀρχ., 1885, p. 131=Herm. 24, 136 sqq. In this psephism too πρόεδροι of the Nomothetai are mentioned. Schoell 115 sqq. adds as a third piece of evidence Æschin. *in Ctes.* 39, where, striking out the bracketed τῷ δήμῳ, he reads: τοὺς δὲ πρυτάνεις ποιεῖν ἐκκλησίαν ἐπιγράψαντας νομοθέτας, τὸν δὲ ἐπιστάτην τῶν προέδρων διαχειροτονίαν διδόναι (τῷ δήμῳ). That these πρόεδροι with their ἐπιστάτης are to be taken to be members of the Council, seems to me now, considering Schoell's arguments, the most probable view.

[2] Compare Schoell, 133 sqq. The law about the γραφὴ παρανόμων in Dem. 24, 33, with which should be compared the remarks of the orator, §§ 61. 68. 108. Poll. 8, 87. Γραφὴ παρανόμων in case of illegality in the method of legislation: Dem. 24, 18. 108.

whether there were laws contradicting one another or which had become obsolete, or whether there were several laws deciding the same point in different ways. If the Thesmothetai in the course of their revision found such anomalies, they posted up these laws on a board before the statues of the Eponymoi, and had a meeting of the Ecclesia summoned by the Prytanes to decide on the appointment of Nomothetai. The subsequent procedure was doubtless the same as that above described.[1]

The judicial functions of the Ecclesia were limited to two cases, the προβολή and the εἰσαγγελία. The προβολή was a criminal information brought before the Ecclesia.[2] This προβολή was, according to our authorities, admissible at the κυρία ἐκκλησία of each Prytany against Sycophantai, and those who had not kept their promises to the people, and also, probably, at all meetings, against those who were not well-disposed to the people or who had caused disturbance at the festivals in any way.[3]

προβολή.

---

[1] For the course followed in revising the laws cf. Æschin. *in Ctes.* 38–40. A concise account is contained in the words: κἄν τι τοιοῦτον εὑρίσκωσιν, ἀναγεγραφότας ἐν σανίσιν ἐκτιθέναι κελεύει πρόσθεν τῶν ἐπωνύμων, τοὺς δὲ πρυτάνεις ποιεῖν ἐκκλησίαν ἐπιγράψαντας νομοθέτας, τὸν δ' ἐπιστάτην τῶν προέδρων διαχειροτονίαν διδόναι τῷ δήμῳ καὶ τοὺς μὲν ἀναιρεῖν τῶν νόμων, τοὺς δὲ καταλείπειν, ὅπως ἂν εἷς ᾖ νόμος καὶ μὴ πλείους περὶ ἑκάστης πράξεως. It seems to me, therefore, immaterial whether we strike out τῷ δήμῳ after διδόναι, as Schoell proposes, and supply in thought after νομοθέτας: "after the Ecclesia has resolved upon the appointment of Nomothetai and that body has been constituted," or whether τὸν δ' ἐπιστάτην τῶν προέδρων διαχειροτονίαν διδόναι τῳ δήμῳ is understood as relating to the decision of the assembly about the appointment of the Nomothetai, and the proceedings before the latter are meant by the words καὶ τοὺς μὲν ἀναιρεῖν τῶν νόμων, τοὺς δὲ καταλείπειν. That the proceedings were the same as for legislation is evident from § 40.

[2] Harp. προβολάς=Suid. s.v.: ἡ προβολὴ τοὔνομα γέγονεν ἀπὸ τοῦ προβάλλεσθαί τινα ἀδικεῖν. In Lex. Seguer. 288, 18 it is thus defined: τὸ παράγειν εἰς τὴν ἐκκλησίαν τὸν βουλόμενον καὶ ἀποφαίνειν ὡς ἠδίκησεν, εἴ τις δοκοίη ἀδικεῖν.

[3] Poll. 8, 46: προβολὴ δὲ ἦν κλῆσις εἰς δίκην κατὰ τῶν κακῶνως πρὸς τὸν δῆμον διακειμένων. προβολαὶ δ' ἐγίνοντο τοῦ δήμου ψηφισαμένου καὶ τῶν εὐνουστάτων τῇ πόλει, ὡς Λυσίας ἐν τῷ κατὰ Θεοσδοτίου περὶ ἀμφοῖν λέγων. προβολαὶ δὲ ἦσαν καὶ αἱ τῆς συκοφαντίας γραφαί. Λυσίας ἐν τῷ πρὸς Ἱπποκράτην αἰκίας. ἐγίνοντο δὲ καὶ περὶ τῶν ἐξυβρισάντων ἢ ἀσεβησάντων περὶ τὰς ἑορτάς, ὡς ἡ κατὰ Μειδίου προβολή. Arist. 43, 5 gives among the agenda for the κυρία ἐκκλησία (for the προβολή can hardly have been limited to that in the sixth Prytany): καὶ συκοφαντῶν προβολὰς τῶν Ἀθηναίων καὶ τῶν μετοίκων μέχρι τριῶν ἑκατέρων κἄ[ν τι]ς ὑποσχόμενός τι μὴ ποιήσῃ τῷ δήμῳ. The προβολή was employed against offences at the Dionysia and at the Mysteries, and against Sycophantia also according to Lex. Seguer. 288, 20; this is also testified by Dem. 21, 9. 11. 175. Æschin. *F. L.*, 145. Isocr. 15, 314. A προβολή against officials is

The procedure at the προβολή was as follows. After the criminal information had been brought before the Ecclesia, the accused defended himself, and in this he was assisted by his friends. Thereupon the Ecclesia voted by show of hands on the guilt of the accused. If the vote went against him, it served as a moral judgment in favour of the accuser, who could either rest satisfied with this decision of the Ecclesia, which involved no legal consequences, or might enter a regular lawsuit against the offender. In the latter case the suit, in which the Thesmothetai acted as εἰσαγωγεῖς, came before a heliastic court, which, however, was not bound by the vote of the assembly.[1]

The second case in which the Ecclesia exercised judicial functions was in what was called εἰσαγγελία.[2] This was similarly limited to a special class of offences. It was originally only admissible against serious and flagrant offences, requiring immediate condemnation, but not provided for specifically by law.[3] It was not till later, perhaps at the revision of

εἰσαγγελία.

---

mentioned by Harp. καταχειροτονία: Lex. Seguer. 268, 27 sqq., which Schömann 229 sqq. limits to the regular Epicheirotonia of the officials; probably the term προβολή is in this case a vague expression of the grammarian's. See Lipsius in Meier[2] 337. A προβολὴ κατὰ τῶν δημόσια μέταλλα ὑπορυττόντων in Lex. Cantabr. 667, under προβολή, should doubtless be regarded as a φάσις. See Lipsius 340, no. 896.

[1] The procedure in a προβολή, as given in the text, follows from Dem. 21, 1/2. 7. 9. 206. Compare Schömann 227 sqq., and in *Philolog.*, 2, 593 sqq., against Bake, who holds that a judicial condemnation was pronounced by the Ecclesia, while the law-court had only to determine the fine—see *Schol. hypomnem.*, 1844, 31 sqq.—an opinion which K. Fr. Hermann accepted in his *quæstiones de probole apud Athen.*, Ind. Schol. Goett., 1847/8, p. 9 sqq. Compare Meier[2] 335 sqq. Since the dicasts had the power of acquittal in the suit against Meidias—see Dem. 21, 97. 199. 204. 216. 218. 222—they cannot have been bound by the verdict of the Ecclesia, which had condemned Meidias; the case before them was therefore *res integra*. See too Fränkel 87/88. The Thesmothetai as εἰσαγωγεῖς: Arist. 59, 2. Poll. 8, 87.

[2] For the εἰσαγγελία see Schömann 180 sqq. Hager, *quæst. Hyperid.*, Diss. Leipzig, 1870, p. 47 sqq. *Journal of Philol.*, 1872, p. 74. Bohm., *de εἰσαγγελίαις ad comitia Ath. delatis*, Diss. Halle, 1874. Fränkel 71 sqq. Lipsius in Meier[2] 312 sqq.

[3] See Hyper., *Euxenipp.*, xix. 6 sqq.: οὕτως ὑπὲρ μεγάλων ἀδικημάτων καὶ περιφανῶν αἱ εἰσαγγελίαι τότε ἦσαν. Harp. εἰσαγγελία=Suid. εἰσαγγελία, Art. 3: ἡ μὲν γοῦν ἐπὶ δημοσίοις ἀδικήμασι μεγίστοις καὶ ἀναβολὴν μὴ ἐπιδεχομένοις καὶ ἐφ' οἷς μήτε ἀρχὴ καθέστηκε μήτε νόμοι κεῖνται τοῖς ἄρχουσι, καθ' οὓς εἰσάξουσιν.—Cf. Poll. 8, 51. Suid. εἰσαγγελία, Art. 2=Lex. Seguer. 244, 18 sqq. Lex. Cantabr. 667, in which the expression, ἄγραφα ἀδικήματα, has been derived from the schools of rhetoric.

the laws under the Archon Eucleides, that the various cases in which the Eisangelia had hitherto been used were catalogued, and it was sanctioned for the future as the legal procedure for such cases, without, however, completely excluding its application in other cases. It was probably in the time of the orators that it became the custom to apply the Eisangelia in unimportant cases.[1] According to our authorities, Eisangelia was admissible against any one who made an attempt to overthrow the Athenian democracy, or joined in a conspiracy to overthrow it, or who established a Hetairia, or betrayed a city, a ship, soldiers or sailors, or who went to the enemy without being sent, or lived with them, or took the field with them, or who deceived the people by false promises, or, being an orator, allowed himself to be bribed to bring in a motion detrimental to the State. But Eisangelia was also permissible against those who had committed an offence at the dockyards, or had contravened the corn and harbour laws.[2]

The Eisangelia could be introduced either directly in the Ecclesia or before the Council.[3] The κύρια ἐκκλησία of each Prytany was appointed for Eisangeliai, but this probably did not ex-

---

[1] Hyper., *Euxenipp.*, xix. 10 sqq., says, when submitting instances of the use of Eisangelia in his time: νυνὶ δὲ τὸ γιγνόμενον ἐν τῇ πόλει πάνυ καταγέλαστόν ἐστιν, and then continues: ὧν οὐδεμ(ία) δήπου τῶν αἰτι(ῶ)ν τούτων οὐδὲν κοινωνεῖ τῷ εἰσαγγελτικῷ νόμῳ. See Fränkel 78. That the νόμος εἰσαγγελτικὸς dates only from a time subsequent to the restoration of the democracy is justly held by Bohm, p. 32, and Fränkel, p. 77.

[2] The εἰσαγγελτικὸς νόμος, in Hyper., *Euxenipp.*, xxii. 13 sqq., xxiii. 2 sqq., which must be completed from Theophrast. *ap.* Poll. 8, 52. Lex. Cantabr. 667. (Dem.) 49, 67. Boeckh, *Seeurk.*, xv. b, 151 sqq., p. 540=C.I.A., 811 c, 152 sqq.: εἶναι δὲ καὶ εἰσαγγελίαν αὐτῶν εἰς τὴν βουλήν, καθάπερ ἐάν τις ἀδικῇ περὶ τὰ ἐν τοῖς νεωρίοις. See also (Dem.) 47, 41. An Eisangelia against the corn merchants is inferred by Hager, pp. 64/5 from Lys. 22, and against those who contravened the harbour laws, p. 93 sqq., from Dem. 34, 50. See also Lipsius, *ibid.*, 319. The gradual growth of the several provisions of the εἰσαγγελτικὸς νόμος out of actual cases is particularly exemplified in the Eisangelia against Antiphon and his companions, who were arraigned περὶ προδοσίας (Pseudoplut., *vit. Antiph.*, 26), whereas later, evidently in consequence of this case, the Eisangelia was admissible, κατὰ τῶν πρὸς τοὺς πολεμίους ἄνευ τοῦ πεμφθῆναι ἀπελθόντων. I regard as an appendix to the law of Eisangelia the psephism in C.I.A., II. 65, which again was passed in view of an actual case. The Council is to bring in a Probouleuma as to how those, in view of whose offence the psephism is passed, are to be punished. As this decree could have no retrospective effect, their trial had to be conducted under another section of the εἰσαγγελτικὸς νόμος.

[3] Harp. εἰσαγγελία=Suid. εἰσαγγελία, Art. 3.

clude the right of introducing them at other meetings as well.[1] When an Eisangelia was submitted to the Ecclesia, the people, after hearing the plaintiff and defendant, decided first whether it was to be taken into consideration. If their decision was in the affirmative, the Eisangelia was referred to the Council, which was at the same time directed to submit to the Ecclesia a Probouleuma on the matter. Things took a similar course if the Eisangelia was brought before the Council; for that body could not decide such a matter itself, unless the penalty did not exceed the maximum fine within the competence of the Council, 500 drachmas. If it exceeded this sum, then the Eisangelia—provided that the Council did not at once refer it to a heliastic court—was taken to the Ecclesia, which decided whether it was to be accepted for trial or rejected at once, and in the former case the Council was then requested to draw up a Probouleuma on the subject.[2] This Probouleuma of the Council proposed either that the Eisangelia should be decided in the Ecclesia, or that it should be referred to a heliastic court.[3] If it were resolved that the Ecclesia should judge the Eisangelia, a special meeting was called, in which, after the accuser and accused had both been heard, the verdict was given by ballot.[4] But even in case of the Eisangelia being referred to a heliastic court, the Council or the Ecclesia, in the fifth century, determined beforehand by what penalty the defendant, if condemned, was to be punished; in the fourth century the

---

[1] Arist. 43, 4. Poll. 8, 95. Harp. κυρία ἐκκλησία.

[2] That the Council was empowered to refer the decision of an Eisangelia which had been submitted to it to a heliastic court, is seen from (Dem.) 47, 43. See also the Probouleuma of the Council in Pseudoplut., *vit. Antiph.*, 23 sqq. Cf. Heydemann, *de senatu Atheniensium*, Diss. philol. Argentorat. sel. 4, 167 sqq. For the proceedings in the Council see p. 281. Introduction of the Eisangelia before the Ecclesia, by the Council is attested by Suid. εἰσαγγελία, Art. 2=Lex. Seguer. 244, 18: εἰσαγγελία δὲ κυρίως ἡ περὶ καινῶν καὶ δημοσίων ἀδικημάτων εἰσαγομένη δίκη ὑπὸ τῶν πρυτάνεων. That in this first Ecclesia it was not permissible to determine, without a Probouleuma on the subject, how the Eisangelia was to be actually decided, follows from the *Hypothesis* to (Dem.) 25, p. 767, see Schömann 207. 109. The first part of C.I.A., II. 65 is a psephism ordering the Council to introduce a Probouleuma, with regard to the form of conducting an Eisangelia case.

[3] Fränkel, *ibid.*, 78/9. Evidently Arist., *Wasps*, 590/1, refers to the Eisangelia: ἔτι δ' ἡ βουλὴ χὠ δῆμος, ὅταν κρῖναι μέγα πρᾶγμ' ἀπορήσῃ,—ἐψήφισται τοὺς ἀδικοῦντας τοῖσι δικασταῖς παραδοῦναι. Examples of decisions by the Ecclesia in Dem. 19, 31; 24, 134. (Dem.) 49, 9. Lyc., *Leocr.*, 117.

[4] Xen., *Hell.*, 1, 7, 9.

provisions of the εἰσαγγελτικὸς νόμος were followed.[1] The heliastic court, which tried the Eisangelia, under the presidency of the Thesmothetai, consisted of 1,000 dicasts—after the government of Demetrios of Phaleron 1,500.[2] The accuser was in early times liable to no punishment, if the defendant were acquitted; but later on, to prevent abuse of the Eisangelia, he was punished by the usual fine of 1,000 drachmas, if he failed to obtain the fifth part of the votes.[3]

Ordinarily the resolutions of those Athenians who happened to be assembled in the Ecclesia were considered to express the will of the entire people. But there were cases where a quorum of at least 6,000 Athenians was necessary. These full meetings of at least 6,000 Athenians were held in the market, and the place was divided, according to the number of the tribes, into 10 compartments, in each of which—as the voting had to be secret—there were two urns for the reception of the voting pebbles. Such a full meeting of the people was necessary for passing certain ψηφίσματα ἐπ' ἀνδρί, i.e., for the granting of privileges as to which no resolution could legally be passed if there were not 6,000 voters present. Such ψηφίσματα ἐπ' ἀνδρί in Athenian constitutional law included grants of ἄδεια, grants of citizenship, and the ostrakismos.[4]

Full Assemblies.

---

[1] Pseudoplut., *vit. Antiph.*, 26: ὅτου δ' ἂν καταψηφίσηται τὸ δικαστήριον, περὶ αὐτοῦ ποιεῖν κατὰ τὸν νόμον, ὃς κεῖται περὶ τῶν προδόντων. Cf. Xen., *Hell.*, 1, 7, 20. 22.

[2] The Thesmothetai as εἰσαγωγεῖς: Arist. 59, 2. Pseudoplut., *vit. Antiph.*, 26. Poll. 8, 87/8 should be emended accordingly. For the number of Dicasts see Lex. Cantabr. 667, which makes Poll. 8, 53 clear. For the voting see Lyc., *Leocr.*, 146. 149.

[3] Poll. 8, 52. Lex. Cantabr. 677. When the speech of Hypereides for Lycophron was delivered, the plaintiff was still exempt from punishment, although the defendant was acquitted. See x. 5 sqq. From Dem. 18, 250 it is evident that the plaintiff was liable to punishment in B.C. 330. See Lipsius, *ibid.*, 329. Harp., εἰσαγγελία, it is true does not agree with this previous immunity of the plaintiff.

[4] Valeton in *Mnemosyne*, 1887, p. 7 sqq., distinguishes, on the strength of Dem. 23, 218, between νόμοι ἐπ' ἀνδρί and ψηφίσματα ἐπ' ἀνδρί: the latter (with the exception of those mentioned in the text) were admissible, if they did not contravene the laws; νόμοι ἐπ' ἀνδρί were altogether forbidden. The addition given in Andoc., *de Myst.*, 87, limiting this prohibition—ἐὰν μὴ ἑξακισχιλίοις δόξῃ κρύβδην ψηφιζομένοις—is not confirmed by Andoc., *ib.*, 89. Dem. 23, 86. 218; 24, 18. 59. 188. (Dem.) 46, 12. 6,000 voters necessary for conferring ἄδεια: Dem. 24, 46, for granting citizenship (Dem.) 59, 89—at the ostrakismos: Plut., *Arist.*, 7. Philoch., *fr.*, 79 b in Müller, *fr. hist. gr.*, 1,

Any one who intended to move the restitution of his rights to a citizen that was atimos, or the cancelling of a State debtor's liability or permission for him to make part payments, needed, we know, a grant of ἄδεια. A meeting of the assembly was regularly appointed in each Prytany for such business. Any one who wished to address the Ecclesia on such a matter deposited an olive branch on the altar in the Pnyx, or wherever else the Ecclesia was being held, and thus placed himself under divine protection, and in this way could state his case without fear of punishment. His motion in this Ecclesia would evidently be that he should receive permission to ask for a full assembly to vote on the question of ἄδεια for a motion he would subsequently propose. If this request was acceded to, the Council had to draw

ἄδεια.

---

396. That 6,000 Athenians were regarded in Athenian constitutional law as identical with the whole body of Athenians, as Fränkel, 14 sqq., tries to prove, appears to me now rather questionable, since this assumption has practically no support except in Dem. 24, 46. 48. See also Valeton, *ib.*, 40 sqq. That the Agora was the meeting-place for the Ostrakismos we are expressly told, and that it was the place of assembly for the granting of the citizenship we may infer from (Dem.) 59, 90, and for the ἄδεια by analogy. See Wachsmuth 2, 1, 313/14. For the method of voting compare (Dem.) 59, 90; Plut., *Arist.*, *ibid.*; Philoch., *ibid.*, with which Xen., *Hell.*, 1, 7, 9, is to be compared. That 6,000 votes in all, not 6,000 affirmative votes, were necessary for ostracism, and similarly for the other ψηφίσματα ἐπ' ἀνδρὶ mentioned in the text, was first demonstrated by Lugebil., *üb. d. Wesen u. hist. Bedeut. d. Ostr.*, 141 sqq. Valeton, *ibid.*, 32 sqq., tries to reestablish the opposite theory. He thinks that, assuming the correctness of Lugebil's views, the correct policy for the opponents of the motion would be to abstain from voting. But grants of ἄδεια and of citizenship were surely not matters of such importance that the citizens should reflect in the way that Valeton suggests, and for this reason absent themselves from the meeting, losing thereby in the fourth century their fee. In the case of ostracism, which was abrogated so early as 418, and which was originally directed against the Peisistratidai (Arist. 22, 3 sqq.), the law of Solon, that every one in the State must take one side or other in a stasis, was applicable. See Arist. 8, 5. Thuc. 8, 72 is by no means to be limited to the time of the Four Hundred: καίτοι οὐ πώποτε Ἀθηναίους διὰ τὰς στρατείας καὶ τὴν ὑπερόριον ἀσχολίαν ἐς οὐδὲν πρᾶγμα οὕτω μέγα ἐλθεῖν βουλεύσοντας, ἐν ᾧ πεντακισχιλίους ξυνελθεῖν. Six thousand ayes would presuppose an attendance incompatible with the statement of Thucydides. See also Goldstaub, *de ἀδείας notione et usu in iure publ. att.*, Breslau, 1890, 111 sqq. [Cf. Szanto, *Bürgerrecht*, p. 408, 1.; Lipsius, *Ber. der sächs. Gesellsch. d. Wissensch.* 1887, p. 4 ff.; Alb. Müller, *Bühnenaltert.*, 177 f. and 330 ff.; Öhmichen in Müller's *Handb.*, 3, 196 ff.; Buck in *American Journ. of Arch.*, V. 1, pp. 18 ff.; Reisch, *Griech. Weihgeschenke*, Wien, 1890, p. 63 ff.; Bodensterner, *Comment. Philol. Monach.* 1891, p. 38 ff.]

up a Probouleuma in accordance with the Assembly's resolution, and to introduce it at the full assembly which was called by the Prytanes. If this Assembly definitely granted the ἄδεια for the motion, the ψήφισμα ἐπ' ἀνδρὶ was complete. The acceptance or rejection of the motion, for the introduction of which the ἄδεια had been necessary was then voted in an ordinary Ecclesia.[1]

The second kind of ψήφισμα ἐπ' ἀνδρὶ, the granting of the citizenship, has already been discussed.[2]

The third and politically the most important ψήφισμα ἐπ' ἀνδρὶ was ostracism. It proceeded as follows:—[3] In the κυρία ἐκκλησία of the sixth, or in leap year the seventh, Prytany, a vote was taken whether ostracism should be adopted during the current year. ὀστρακισμός. If the decision was in the affirmative, the Ostracophoria proper took place in a full assembly in the Agora.[4] In a part specially marked off for the purpose, the vote was taken by tribes, the men of each several tribe placing an earthenware tablet, on which they had written the name of the man they wished ostracised, in the urn of their division. The nine Archons and the Council superintended the voting. When it was finished, the first count was to see whether 6,000 votes had been cast. If this had not been done, then the vote was null and void. If, however, 6,000 votes had been given, the man who had received most was proclaimed by the herald to be ostracised. He had then to leave the country within 10 days and remain in exile for 10 years, unless it were specially resolved to recall him earlier; but he retained possession of his property. No ostracised citizen was permitted

---

[1] Arist. 43, 6: ἑτέραν δὲ ταῖς ἱκετηρίαις, ἐν ᾗ θεὶς ὁ βουλόμενος ἱκετηρίαν [ὑπὲρ] ὧν ἂν βούληται καὶ ἰδίων καὶ δημοσίων διαλέξεται πρὸς τὸν δῆμον. Poll. 8, 96: ἡ δὲ δευτέρα ἐκκλησία ἀνεῖται τοῖς βουλομένοις, ἱκετηρίαν θεμένοις, λέγειν ἀδεῶς περί τε τῶν ἰδίων καὶ τῶν δημοσίων. The ἄδεια was, we know, necessary in the two cases mentioned in the text: Dem. 24, 46. 47. Goldstaub, ib., 10 sqq., makes it seem probable that it was also necessary for one who wished to move the recall of an ostracised citizen before the expiration of the legal term, or the recall of an exile, or a reprieve for a man condemned to death.

[2] Page 184 sqq.

[3] For the nature and historical importance of ostracism, see pp. 151/2 sqq.

[4] Arist. 43, 5: ἐπὶ δὲ τῆς ἕκτης πρυτανείας (i.e., ἐν τῇ κυρίᾳ) πρὸς τοῖς εἰρημένοις καὶ περὶ τῆς ὀστρακοφορίας ἐπιχειροτονίαν διδόασιν, εἰ δοκεῖ ποιεῖν ἢ μή. From this comes Lex. Cantabr. 672, 13 sqq. Philoch., fr., 79 b, says: προχειροτονεῖ μὲν ὁ δῆμος πρὸ τῆς ὀγδόης πρυτανείας, εἰ δοκεῖ τὸ ὄστρακον εἰσφέρειν. Ad. Schmidt, Handb. d. griech. Chronol., 259/60, explains these different marks of time by supposing that Philoch. takes into account leap year, in which the ostracophoria took place in the seventh Prytany.

during his exile to approach nearer to the borders of Attica than certain specified limits.¹

It is scarcely necessary to speak of the business dealt with by the Ecclesia. The Athenian Demos was the sovereign power in the State, and therefore everything that the Council or the magistrates could not or would not settle was brought before the Ecclesia. This body, it is true, was subject to the laws even in passing decrees, but still cases occurred not unfrequently, especially in the period of extreme democracy, in which the decrees of the Ecclesia were regarded as superior to the laws. During the 5th century it only happened once, and then in a meeting of the Ecclesia excited by passion, that the maxim—soon repented of by the Athenians—was asserted, that the Demos might do just as it chose: in the 4th century an orator formulated and stated the principle in the sentence: "The popular assembly has unlimited competence to carry out its own pleasure in all affairs of the State."²

Business of the Ecclesia.

3. MILITARY MATTERS.

When the young Athenian on the completion of his 17th year was declared to be of age by enrolment in the ληξιαρχικὸν γραμματεῖον, he went to the Temple of Aglauros and took his oaths of allegiance as a soldier and a citizen. He swore that he would not disgrace his arms nor desert his comrade in battle, but would fight for his country's

Military oath and Freeman's oath.

---

¹ We obtain our information about the procedure at ostracism from a comparison of Philoch., *ibid.* (whom the *Schol.* to Arist., *Equit.*, 855, has made use of without mentioning his name), Plut., *Arist.*, 7, Poll. 8, 19. 20, Et. M. 349. 15. Philoch. is represented as stating that the 10 years of exile was lowered to 5; but this arose from the excerptor of the fragment misunderstanding a comparison made by Philoch. between Ostracism and the πενταετὴς πεταλισμός of the Syracusans. Cf. Diod. 11, 87. Arist. 22, 8: καὶ τὸ λοιπὸν ὥρισαν τοῖς ὀστρακιζομένοις ἐκτὸς (so we should read for ἐντὸς) Γεραιστοῦ καὶ Σκυλλαίου κατοικεῖν ἢ ἀτίμους εἶναι καθάπαξ. Cf. Philoch., *ib.*, καρπούμενον τὰ ἑαυτοῦ μὴ ἐπιβαίνοντα ἐντὸς πέρα τοῦ Εὐβοίας ἀκρωτηρίου. A fragment of pottery with the inscr. scratched upon it: Μεγακλῆς (Ἱππο)κράτους Ἀλωπεκῆθε (cf. Arist. 22, 5): C.I.A., IV., 3, 569, p. 192; others with Ξάνθιππος Ἀρρίφρονος (Arist. 22, 6): IV., 3. 570. 571.

² Cf. Aristot., *Pol.*, p. 153, 32 sqq., Bekker. Arist. 41, 2 says of the Athenian constitution after Eucleides: ἁπάντων γὰρ αὐτὸς αὑτὸν πεποίηκεν ὁ δῆμος κύριον καὶ πάντα διοικεῖται ψηφίσμασιν καὶ δικαστηρίοις, ἐν οἷς ὁ δῆμός ἐστιν ὁ κρατῶν· καὶ γὰρ αἱ τῆς βουλῆς κρίσεις εἰς τὸν δῆμον ἐληλύθασιν; Xen., *Hell.*, 1, 7, 12; (Dem.) 59, 88. On the business that was entirely managed by the Ecclesia see Schömann, *de comit.*, 281 ff.

shrines and leave his fatherland not feebler than he found it, but greater and mightier; that he would obey the orders of his commanders; that he would keep the laws, not stand idly by if any one violated or disregarded them, but do his best to maintain them, and that he would honour the shrines of his native land.[1]

After taking this oath the Athenian youths, now called Epheboi, spent the next two years in a course of military training. In the first year they were instructed in the use of their weapons and served as guards at the various temples and in the Piræus. They were classified by Phylai, every Phyle being commanded by a σωφρονιστής, appointed in the following manner:—in each Phyle the fathers of the Epheboi of the current year nominated 3 men over forty years of age, and of these 3 one was elected by the entire burgess-body to act as σωφρονιστής of that Phyle. The Epheboi of each tribe dined together at the expense of the State and were under the supervision of their σωφρονιστής. The entire body of Epheboi were under the supervision of a κοσμητής, elected from the entire burgess-body. They received gymnastic training from instructors elected by the people; other teachers elected in the same way instructed them in hoplite-combat, archery, spear-throwing, and the use of artillery-engines. At the end of the first year the Epheboi were publicly inspected in the theatre, and every one who passed this test satisfactorily was presented by the State with a spear and shield. These two weapons together with a Petasos and a Chlamys formed their complete equipment.[2]

Military training.

---

[1] Cf. Lyc., *Leocr.*, 76; Dem. 19, 303. The form of oath is preserved in slightly different form in Stob., *Flor.*, 43, 48 and Poll. 8, 105. Cf. Dittenberger, *de ephebis att.*, p. 9; Dumont, *essai sur l'éphébie Attique*, 1, 9 ff; Hofmann, *de iuris iurandi ap. Athenienses formulis*, p. 28 ff., Darmstadt 1886. A clause not contained in these versions is mentioned by Plut., *Alcib.*, 15; Cic., *de Rep.*, 3, 9. Yet Cobet, *novæ lect.*, 223, is scarcely justified in doubting the general authenticity of this oath. See also Grasberger, *Erzieh. u. Unterr. im class. Alterth.*, 3, 29 ff.

[2] Arist. 42, 2: ἐπὰν δὲ δοκιμασθῶσιν οἱ ἔφηβοι, συλλεγέντες οἱ πατέρες αὐτῶν κατὰ φυλὰς ὀμόσαντες αἱροῦνται τρεῖς ἐκ τῶν φυλετῶν τῶν ὑπὲρ τετταράκοντα ἔτη γεγονότων, οὓς ἂν ἡγῶνται βελτίστους εἶναι καὶ ἐπιτηδειοτάτους ἐπιμελεῖσθαι τῶν ἐφήβων, ἐκ δὲ τούτων ὁ δῆμος ἕνα τῆς φυλῆς ἑκάστης χειροτονεῖ σωφρονιστὴν καὶ κοσμητὴν ἐκ τῶν ἄλλων Ἀθηναίων ἐπὶ πάντας, συλλαβόντες δ' οὗτοι τοὺς ἐφήβους, πρῶτον μὲν τὰ ἱερὰ περιῆλθον, εἶτ' εἰς Πειραιέα πορεύονται καὶ φρουροῦσιν οἱ μὲν τὴν Μουνυχίαν, οἱ δὲ τὴν Ἀκτήν. χειροτ[ονεῖ] δὲ καὶ παιδοτρίβας αὐτοῖς δύο καὶ διδασκάλους, [οἵ]τινες ὁπλομαχεῖν καὶ τοξεύειν καὶ ἀκοντίζειν καὶ καταπάλτην ἀφιέναι διδάσκουσιν. δίδωσι δὲ καὶ εἰς τρο[φὴ]ν τοῖς μὲν σωφρονισταῖς δραχμὴν α΄ ἑκάστῳ, τοῖς

In the second year the Epheboi were acquainted with garrison duty and field service as περίπολοι. During this time they formed the garrisons of the fortresses in Attica, patrolled the frontiers, and were exercised in marching, digging trenches, throwing up fortifications, and carrying out siege-works.[1] The supreme super-

δ' ἐφήβοις τέτταρας ὀβολοὺς ἑκάστῳ τὰ δὲ τῶν φυλετῶν τῶν αὑτοῦ λαμβάνων ὁ σωφρονιστὴς ἕκαστος ἀγοράζει τὰ ἐπιτήδεια πᾶσιν εἰς τὸ κοινόν (συσσιτοῦσι γὰρ κατὰ φυλὰς) καὶ τῶν ἄλλων ἐπιμελεῖται πάντων. καὶ τὸν μὲν πρῶτον ἐνιαυτὸν οὕτως διάγουσι, τὸν δ' ὕστερον ἐκκλησίας ἐν τῷ θεάτρῳ γενομένης ἀποδειξάμενοι τῷ δήμῳ τὰ περὶ τὰς τάξεις καὶ λαβόντες ἀσπίδα καὶ δόρυ παρὰ τῆς πόλεως περιπολοῦσι τὴν χώραν καὶ διατρίβουσιν ἐν τοῖς φυλακτηρίοις. φρουροῦσι δὲ τὰ δύο ἔτη, χλαμύδας ἔχοντες. This is the source of Harp., Suid., Phot., περίπολος. On the σωφρονισταί see further Lex. Seguer. 301, 7 ff.; Phot.; Et. M.; (Plat.) Axioch., 367. Mention is made of a σωφρονιστής of the Kecropis elected by the people in 334/3 B.C.: Ἀρχ. δελτ. 1889, pp. 11/12=Bull. 12, 257; another of the Pandionis 303 B.C.: Bull. 12, 148/9 = Ber. d. Berl. Ak., 1888, 247. After the beginning of the 3rd cent. the σωφρονισταί no longer occur: Köhler in Mitth. 4, 328. On the σωφρονισταί see also Girard, l'éducation athénienne, 43 ff., Paris, 1889. The presentation of the shield and spear, after they passed their review, is analogous to the κατάστασις of the knights, and not to be taken in connexion with the presentation of a πανοπλία to the sons of men who had fallen in war when they came of age (Æsch. in Ctes. 154; Isocr. 8, 82; Plat., Menex., 249), as Boeckh, Kl. Schr., 4, 152, and Schaefer, Dem. u. s. Zeit, 3, 2, 33/4, suppose. This latter presentation perhaps referred to in (Xen.) de rep. Ath., 3, 4, where we hear that the council ὀρφανοὺς δοκιμάσαι. See Dittenberger, p. 12; Heinrichs, d. Kriegsdienst bei d. Ath., p. 14., Progr. d. königstädt. Realsch. in Berlin 1864. πέτασος and χλαμύς worn by Epheboi: Philemon ap. Poll. 10, 164. See Grasberger, Erzieh. u. Unterr. im cl. Alterth., 3, 42 ff.

[1] Cf. Aristot. quoted in previous note; Poll. 8, 105: περίπολοι. ἔφηβοι περιῄεσαν τὴν χώραν φυλάττοντες, ὥσπερ ἤδη μελετῶντες τὰ στρατιωτικά; Plat., Leg., 6, 778: τὸ δ' ἡμέτερον ἔτι πρὸς τούτοις γέλωτ' ἂν δικαίως πάμπολυν ὄφλοι, τὸ κατ' ἐνιαυτὸν μὲν ἐκπέμπειν εἰς τὴν χώραν τοὺς νέους, τὰ μὲν σκάψοντας, τὰ δὲ ταφρεύσοντας, τὰ δὲ καὶ διά τινων οἰκοδομήσεων εἴρξοντας τοὺς πολεμίους, ὡς δὴ τῶν ὅρων τῆς χώρας οὐκ ἐάσοντας ἐπιβαίνειν. Æsch., Fals. Leg., 167, who says he was περίπολος τῆς χώρας for two years, means by that no doubt his entire two years' service as Ephebos. φρουροῦσι δὲ τὰ δύο ἔτη in Arist. is correct, for the Epheboi, even in their first year, φρουροῦσιν οἱ μὲν τὴν Μουνυχίαν, οἱ δὲ τὴν Ἀκτήν. Patrol service of the περίπολοι: Xen., de Vect., 4, 47; Aristoph., Birds, 1177. Garrison duty: Eupolis ap. Meineke, fr. com. gr., edit. min., p. 220, LVI. 2, 566: καὶ τοὺς περιπόλους ἀπιέν' εἰς τὰ φρούρια. Attic φρούρια Anaphlystos, Thoricos, Sunion, Rhamnus, Eleusis, Phyle, Aphidna: Xen., de Vect., 4, 43; Skyl., Peripl., 58. Psephism in Dem. 18, 68. See Boeckh, Publ. Econ., 1, 282-3 (Bk. II. c. 10). Whether Ἀθηναίων οἱ τεταγμένοι Ἐλευσῖνι, ἐν Πανάκτῳ, ἐπὶ Φυλῇ in the time of Demetrius of Phaleron were περίπολοι or not, is uncertain. Cf. C.I.A., II. 1217; Ἐφ. ἀρχ. 1884, 135 ff.; 1887, 3 ff., 187/8. We cannot regard as περίπολοι the στρατιῶται οἱ παρὰ τῇ πόλει στρατευόμενοι: Εφ. ἀρχ. 1884, pp. 135/6, l. 21, nor οἱ ὕπαιθροι: Ἐφ. ἀρχ. 1887, pp. 3/4, l. 2.

vision and military command over the Epheboi naturally belonged to the Strategoi, to whom the various other officers of the Epheboi were subordinated.[1] To prevent their military education being interrupted, the Epheboi were not allowed to bring a law-suit against any one during their two years of training, nor could any one bring one against them; exceptions were allowed in cases of inheritance, of disputed right to marry an Epicleros, or Diadicasia for a hereditary priesthood.[2]

For the period after the end of the 4th century numerous inscriptions give us detailed information about the system of the Ephebia, which however had assumed an entirely different character by that date. In the first place, the Ephebia now lasted only one year—from Boedromion to Boedromion—and secondly, the enrolment among the Epheboi no longer took place at a fixed age, nor was it now compulsory. The Ephebia of that date was an institution under State supervision and control for the education of the youth of the rich upper classes of Athenians. The Epheboi of that time occupied about the same social position as the knights of the 5th and 4th century.[3]

The Epheboi in later times.

[1] Dein. in Philocl. 15: καὶ ὁ μὲν δῆμος ἅπας οὔτ' ἀσφαλὲς οὔτε δίκαιον νομίζων εἶναι παρακαταθέσθαι τοὺς ἑαυτοῦ παῖδας ἀπεχειροτόνησεν αὐτὸν (i.e. τὸν Φιλοκλέα τὸν στρατηγόν, cf. § 1) ἀπὸ της τῶν ἐφήβων ἐπιμελείας. Dumont, sur l'éphébie Attique, pp. 169/70, erroneously supposes Philocles was κοσμητής. In the 2nd half of the 4th cent. the Eleusinioi pass a vote of thanks to the Strategos Derkylos, ἐπειδὴ Δέρκυλος ὁ στρατηγὸς φιλοτιμεῖται περὶ τὸν δῆμον τὸν Ἐλευσινίων τά τε ἄλλα καὶ ὅπως ἂν οἱ παῖδες παιδεύωνται οἱ ἐν τῷ δήμῳ: Dittenberger, Syll., 345. Æsch., Fals. Leg., 167, mentions ἄρχοντες τῶν ἐφήβων. The περιπόλαρχοι attested for the year 352 B.C. may have been commanders of the Athenian περίπολοι, but it is not certain (see Bull. 13, 434, 1. 15 ff. = Ἐφ. ἀρχ. 1888, pp. 31/2, 1. 15 ff.). They are mentioned again in C.I.A., II. 1219; Ἐφ. ἀρχ. 1888, 21 ff. Foucart in the Bull. 13, 265/6 regards them as commanders of mercenaries, and Girard 274 ff. agrees with him. The περίπολοι in Thuc. 8, 92 are certainly mercenaries (cf. 8, 69), and so too are those mentioned in 4, 67. Acc. to the inscr. of 334/3 B.C. in the Ἀρχ. δελτ. 1889, pp. 11/2 = Bull. 13, 257, the σωφρονιστής seems to have been in charge of the Epheboi in the year of Peripoly service as well: ἐπιμελοῦνται τῆς φυλακῆς Ἐλευσῖνος ὁ(ἱ) τῆς Κεκροπί(δ)ο(ς ἐφηβ)οι καὶ ὁ σωφρονιστὴς αὐτῶν.

[2] Arist. 42, 5: καὶ δίκην οὔτε διδόασιν οὔτε λαμβάνουσιν, ἵνα μὴ π[ρ]ὁ[φ]ασις ᾖ τ[ο]ῦ ἀπιέναι, πλὴν περὶ κλήρου καὶ ἐπικλήρου κἄν τινι κατὰ τὸ γένος ἱερωσύνη γένηται διε[ξ]ελθόντων δὲ τῶν δυεῖν ἐτῶν ἤδη μετὰ τῶν ἄλλων εἰσίν.

[3] That the Ephebia afterwards lasted only one year can be seen from the formula in honour-decrees: ἔφηβοι οἱ ἐπὶ τοῦ δεῖνος ἄρχοντος ἐφηβεύσαντες. This occurs as early as C.I.A., II. 816. The Ephebia year began with Boedromion, Dittenberger, de ephebis att., 21 ff; Dumont, 37 ff. That this

The κοσμητής was then at the head of the entire institution; the σωφρονισταί no longer existed. The κοσμητής was elected by the people annually; at the end of his year of office he had to undergo εὔθυνα. He had the right of appointing the instructors of the Epheboi.[1] Of these we find in inscriptions, just as we do in the 4th century, the παιδοτρίβης, the ὁπλομάχος, the ἀκοντιστής, the τοξότης, and the καταπελταφέτης, or, briefly, ἀφέτης. In addition a γραμματεύς and a ὑπηρέτης of the Epheboi are mentioned.[2] Though the Epheboi even at that date were under the command of the Strategoi, yet the original military character of the institution was almost entirely abandoned.[3] The only remembrance of it

shortening of the course was already introduced in 305/4 B.C. has been made probable by Köhler in *Mitth.* 4, p. 326; see also Girard, 290 ff. That entrance into the ranks of Epheboi was no longer restricted to any particular age, is inferred by Köhler, p. 333, from the fact that we repeatedly find in Epheboi-lists of the same year two or several Epheboi with the same father and from the same Deme, who therefore must be brothers. If entrance to the Ephebia was restricted to youths of some particular age, two brothers could not be Epheboi at the same time, except in the case of twins; and the occurrence of such Epheboi names is too frequent for that. See *Mitth.*, *ib.*, 329; C.I.A., II. 324. Nor is the explanation of Dumont, p. 41 ff., any more satisfactory, viz. that the similarity of patronymics and of Deme names is only an accidental coincidence in each case. The sudden decrease in the numbers of the Epheboi is what leads Köhler, pp. 332/3, to conclude that Ephebia was no longer compulsory. In 305/4 B.C. two Phylai produced at least 84 Epheboi, in 283 or 282 B.C. all the Phylai together had only 33. Cf. C.I.A., II. 316, and also C.I.A., II. 324. 388. It follows that it was still obligatory in 305/4 B.C. Boeckh on C.I.G., 272, and Dittenberger, pp. 16/7, both hold that the Ephebia of later times was optional.

[1] In 305 B.C. the κοσμητής and the σωφρονισταί still appear side by side: *Mitth.*, 4, 327. In 303 B.C. we still find σωφρονισταί: *Bull.* 12, 148/9=*Ber. d. Berl. Ak.*, 1888, 247, but they were probably abolished soon after. The election of the κοσμητής is attested by the repeatedly employed formula: χειροτονηθεὶς κοσμητὴς ἐπὶ τοὺς ἐφήβους εἰς τὸν ἐπὶ τοῦ δεῖνος ἄρχοντος ἐνιαυτόν: C.I.A., II. 465. 467. 469. 471. In l. 56 we are told that the Demos: καὶ καθίστησ(ιν ἐκ) τῶν ἄριστα βε(βι)ωκότων. He is a magistrate: ἦρξεν τὴν ἀρχὴν κατὰ τοὺς ν(όμο)υς καὶ τὰ ψηφίσματα: II. 467. εὔθυνα: II. 469, l. 60. 470, 41. 471, 88. διδάσκαλοι appointed by the κοσμήτης: C.I.A., II. 470, 21: ἐγένοντο δὲ καὶ κατήκο(οι το)ῦ τε κο(σ)μητοῦ καὶ τῶν κατασταθέντων ὑφ' ἑαυτοῦ διδασκάλων ποιούμενοι τὰς μελέτας ἐν τοῖς ὅπλοις. The κοσμητής is discussed by Dittenberger, p. 29 ff.; Dumont, p. 166 ff.

[2] See Köhler on C.I.A., II. 478. For the various masters and the exercises they superintended see Dittenberger, 34 ff., 54 ff.; Dumont, 177 ff.; Grasberger, 3, 462 ff.

[3] C.I.A., II. 471, l. 52 certainly still gives as the reason for a decree of the people: ἐπειδὴ διὰ παντὸς ὁ δῆμος τὴν πλείστην σπουδ(ὴν ποι)εῖται τῆς τῶν

was to be found in the facts that the Epheboi were frequently conducted to the various fortresses of Attica by the κοσμητής, and were practised in drawing ships ashore and launching them.[1] There still remains to be mentioned a political function of the Epheboi: they were quartered near the place of meeting of the Ecclesia and did police-duty at its assemblies.[2]

In the 5th and 4th century the young Athenians, when they entered the ranks of the Epheboi, were at the same time enrolled in the muster-roll of their tribe, which was kept most probably by the Taxiarch of the tribe for the time being. **Hoplites.** These muster-rolls or lists of the 10 tribes contained the names of all the citizens belonging to the 3 first Solonian census-classes and therefore liable to military service as Hoplites from 18 years of age to 60. Thus there were, in any given year, 42 sets of Hoplites liable to military service belonging to 42 different years, and the men of each year were arranged under the name of the Archon of the particular year in which they were originally enrolled and of his predecessor in office. These 42 Archons were accounted the ἐπώνυμοι of the 42 yearly sets of Hoplites, and every year the oldest of the 42, and the men enrolled under his name, fell out of the roll, their places being taken by the Archon of the current year, as ἐπώνυμος of the list of new Hoplites enrolled during the year.[3] The 42 yearly sets of Athenians liable to

ἐφήβων ἀγωγῆς καὶ εὐταξίας βουλόμενος το(ὺ)ς ἐκ τῶν πα(ί)δων μεταβαίνοντας εἰς τοὺς ἄνδρας ἀγαθοὺς γίνεσθαι τῆς πατρίδος διαδ(ό)χους καὶ προσέταξεν διὰ τῶν νόμω(ν) τ(ῆ)ς τε χώρας κα(ὶ) τῶν φρουρίων καὶ τῶν ὁρίων τῆς Ἀττικῆς ἐμπείρους γίνεσθαι ἔν τε τοῖς ὅπλοις τὴν εἰς πόλεμον ἀνήκουσαν ἄσκησι(ν) ποιεῖσθαι. The Epheboi have to obey the commands of the Strategoi: C.I.A., II. 469, l. 58. 470, 19. 38. 471, 62. 481, 51.

[1] C.I.A., II. 467, 22: ἐξῆλθον δὲ καὶ ἐπὶ τὰ φρούρια καὶ τὰ ὅρια τῆς Ἀττικῆς πλεονάκις ἐν ὅπλοις καθὼς ἐπέταττον αὐτοῖς τὰ ψηφίσματα τῆς τε βουλῆς καὶ τοῦ δήμου. Cf. line 65, where it is said that the κοσμητής conducted them. Cf. II. 470, 15; 471, 24. 65. Grasberger 3, 115 ff. On their exercises with ships cf. C.I.A., II. 467, 37. 470, 19. Grasberger 3, 136.

[2] C.I.A., II. 467, 35: παρήδρευσαν δὲ καὶ ταῖς ἐκκλησ(ίαις ἀπά)σαις ἐν ὅπλοις ταῖς τε ἐν ἄστει καὶ ἐμ Πειραιεῖ. Cf. 468, 21. 469, 20. In C.I.A., 470, 22, the verb προσεδρεύειν is used, in 471, 20. 76 ἐφεδρεύειν. Cf. Philostrat., *Life of Soph.*, 2, 1, 5. This is not the place to enter into a discussion of the Ephebia of the 3rd century, and trace its developments under the Roman empire, because in those periods the Epheboi had no longer any real political importance. For this I simply refer to the works of Dittenberger, Dumont and Grasberger, to which I have so often referred.

[3] Even Epheboi served as Hoplites. See Grasberger 3, 89. For these lists cf. Arist. 53, 4: εἰσὶ γὰρ ἐπώνυμοι δέκα μὲν οἱ τῶν φυλῶν, δύο δὲ καὶ

Hoplite-service were divided into two categories, one containing those under 20 and over 50 years of age, the other those between 20 and 50. The first were not as a rule employed except for the defence of Attica itself; the second alone were called upon to serve outside the country.[1]

For such expeditions sometimes the entire military force of the State was employed, including all liable to service abroad; in other cases, a levy took place on the basis of the muster-rolls.[2] Campaigns, for which levies were raised according to the muster-rolls, were again of two classes. The first,

Levies.

τετταράκοντα οἱ τῶν ἡλικιῶν. οἱ δ' ἔφηβοι ἐγγραφόμενοι πρότερον μὲν εἰς λελευκωμένα γραμματεῖα ἐνεγράφοντο καὶ ἐπεγράφοντο αὐτοῖς ὅ τ' ἀρχων, ἐφ' οὗ ἐνεγράφησαν, καὶ ὁ ἐπώνυμος ὁ τῷ πρότερον ἔ[τει] δεδιαιτηκώς, νῦν δ' εἰς στήλην χαλκῆν ἀναγράφονται καὶ ἵσταται ἡ στήλη πρὸ τοῦ βουλευτηρίου παρὰ τοὺς ἐπωνύμους. This passage is the source of Harp. στρατεία ἐν τοῖς ἐπωνύμοις. Cf. Harp. ἐπώνυμοι, Phot. Suid., Art. 1. On the Archons as ἐπώνυμοι of the muster-rolls see L. Lange, *Leipz. Stud.*, 1, 160 ff. Schwartz, *ad Atheniens. rem militarem studia Thucydidea.* Kiel inaug. diss. 1877, p. 5 ff., holds that the only list kept was the ληξιαρχικὸν γραμματεῖον, without any special muster-roll of Hoplites, but his view is refuted by Arist. quoted above. See Lange, *Leipz. Stud.*, 1, 164 ff. O. Mueller, *de demis att.*, 27ff. Goett., contends that the levies were not made according to the muster rolls. But in the passage he quotes in support of his view, Dem. 50, 6, the decree there preserved: καὶ τοὺς βουλευτὰς καὶ τοὺς δημάρχους καταλόγους ποιεῖσθαι τῶν δημοτῶν καὶ ἀποφέρειν ναύτας refers merely to the conscription for the fleet, as §§ 7 and 16 clearly show. And Thuc. 3, 87 supplies certain and clear testimony for the existence of muster-rolls of men liable to military service: τετρακοσίων γὰρ ὁπλιτῶν καὶ τετρακισχιλίων οὐκ ἐλάσσους ἀπέθανον ἐκ τῶν τάξεων καὶ τριακοσίων ἱππέων, τοῦ δὲ ἄλλου ὄχλου ἀνεξεύρετος ἀριθμός. See Müller-Strübing, *Aristophanes*, 642. That Thetes were not Hoplites is seen from Harp. θῆτες and from the passage of Thuc. just quoted. If they were employed as such during the Peloponnesian war (see Usener in the *Jahrb. f. cl. Phil.*, 1873, p. 162) that was an exceptional step. Their names were not put down in the lists even during that war. Cf. Thuc. 6, 43. Even Delbrück, *die Perserkriege und die Burgundenkriege*, 125 ff., 309 ff., has not convinced me of the contrary.

[1] Æsch., *Fals. Leg.*, 167, shows that the περίπολοι were not employed on expeditions abroad; and it may be fairly inferred from Lyc., *Leocr.*, 39/40, that the same was the rule for those ὑπὲρ πεντήκοντα ἔτη γεγονότας. Cf. also Plut., *Phok.*, 24. Thuc. 1, 105 calls the two classes οἵ τε πρεσβύτατοι καὶ οἱ νεώτατοι. Those over sixty years of age are οἱ ὑπὲρ τὸν κατάλογον: Poll. 2, 11. (Dem.) 13, 5. Beloch, *Bevölker. d. griech.-röm. Welt*, 66 ff., gives a conspectus of the records that have been preserved of the numbers of the Athenian Hoplites; with him compare Delbrück, 123 ff., 309 ff.

[2] The first kind of levy is described by Thuc. as πανστρατιᾷ or πανδημεί: 2, 31; 4, 90. 94, the second kind he calls ἐκ καταλόγου. In view of passages such as Thuc. 6, 43; 8, 24; Aristot., *Pol.*, 8 (5), 3, p. 198, 12 ff. Bekker, I

στρατεῖαι ἐν τοῖς ἐπωνύμοις, took place when certain years were specified by decree and the entire number of men belonging to those years were called upon to serve.[1] The others, στρατεῖαι ἐν τοῖς μέρεσι, were those for which only a certain number of men were taken out of each year specified in the psephism, just enough to make up a force of the strength resolved upon and decreed by the Ecclesia.[2] The method of conscription varied according to the kind of campaign that the Ecclesia decreed. For the στρατεῖαι ἐν τοῖς ἐπωνύμοις the Strategoi had merely to announce that the Hoplites of a certain age or belonging to certain years were to present themselves prepared for the campaign at a certain date.[3] For the στρατεῖαι ἐν τοῖς μέρεσι the Strategoi, or their representatives, the Taxiarchs, selected from the lists of the years specified by the Ecclesia the men they thought suitable, until the total number decreed by the Ecclesia was made up. The lists of men drawn for service were posted up for all to see near the statues of the Eponymoi.[4]

cannot agree with the view of Schwarz, 14 ff., that ἐκ καταλόγου has nothing to do with the muster-roll of the Hoplites, but means merely e delectu= publico delectu habito.

[1] Arist. 53, 7: χρῶνται δὲ τοῖς ἐπωνύμοις καὶ πρὸς τὰς στρατείας, καί, ὅταν ἡλικίαν ἐκπέμπωσι, προγράφουσιν, ἀπὸ τίνος ἄρχοντος καὶ ἐπωνύμ[ου] μέχρι τίνος (so we should read instead of τίνων cf. Harp. στρατεία ἐν τοῖς ἐπωνύμοις and Phot. s.v.) δεῖ στρατεύεσθαι. A decree of this kind is mentioned by Æsch., Fals. Leg., 133: τοὺς μέχρι τριάκοντα ἔτη γεγονότας ἐξιέναι.

[2] The description given in the text of the στρατεία ἐν τοῖς μέρεσι sc. τῶν ἐπωνύμων is discussed and proved in my Beitr., etc., 51 ff. The locus classicus for the kinds of στρατεῖαι is Æsch., de Fals. Leg., 168, where Æschines says of his own military service: πρώτην δ' ἐξελθὼν στρατείαν τὴν ἐν τοῖς μέρεσι καλουμένην, and again further on: καὶ τὰς ἄλλας τὰς ἐκ διαδοχῆς ἐξόδους τὰς ἐν τοῖς ἐπωνύμοις καὶ τοῖς μέρεσιν ἐξῆλθον. According to this passage the ἐκ διαδοχῆς ἔξοδοι include τὰς ἐν τοῖς ἐπωνύμοις καὶ τοῖς μέρεσιν ἐξόδους, and the ἐκ διαδοχῆς means nothing more than "the successive campaigns one after another." ἐκ διαδοχῆς may, it is true, under certain circumstances, e.g. in Dem. 4, 21, mean the relieving of one division of soldiers by another taking their place; but it certainly has not that meaning here. I cannot accept therefore the explanation of this passage given by Boeckh, kl. Schr. 4, 156, and Schwartz 20, or Rüstow and Köchly, Gesch. d. griech. Kriegsw. 96, nor that of Schömann, griech. Alterth. 1, 449, nor yet Hamaker's omission of καὶ τοῖς μέρεσι which is adopted by Lange, Leipz. Stud., 1, 160, 2.

[3] Aristot., ibid. Lysias 14, 6, discussing the question who had to serve in the army, indicates this method of conscription, by the question οὐχ οἵτινες ἂν τὴν ἡλικίαν ταύτην ἔχωσιν;

[4] Lys. 14, 6 in the context described in note [3] indicates this method of conscription by the question: οὐχ οὓς ἂν οἱ στρατηγοὶ καταλέξωσιν; The selection of men from the muster-rolls of the appointed years is what is

Appeals against conscription had to be brought before the Strategoi; those who took the law into their own hands and did not appear in their place when the army set out were prosecuted by γραφὴ ἀστρατείας, brought by the Strategoi or their representatives the Taxiarchs before a jury composed of comrades of the accused. The same method was followed in the γραφαὶ λειποταξίου and δειλίας, which were employed against those who abandoned a post assigned them by their commander, or were guilty of cowardly conduct. The punishment for these offences was a partial Atimia without confiscation of property; the condemned man was excluded from the market place and from the Ecclesia.[1] But in all these cases the trial was probably postponed until the army returned home from the campaign. The right of punishing or rewarding soldiers in the actual field belonged apparently to the Strategoi alone.[2]

<small>Lawsuits arising from military matters.</small>

referred to in the official oath of the Strategoi; τοὺς ἀστρατεύτους καταλέξειν: Lys. 9, 15. Posting the list by the statues of the Eponymoi: Aristoph., *Peace*, 1181 sqq., with the Schol. For details see my *Beiträge*, etc., 52 ff.

[1] Appeals before the Strategoi: Lys. 9, 4. Classes exempt from military service were the Bouleutai: Lyc., *Leocr.*, 37, the tax-farmers: (Dem.) 59, 27 and in all probability the magistrates. With regard to the Choreutai it is probable that they were regularly excused from service on appeal: Dem. 21, 15; 39, 16. Under certain circumstances ἔμποροι also were excused; cf. Arist., *Eccl.*, 1027; Boeckh, *Publ. Econ.*, 1, 122 (Bk. I. c. 15). A roll-call was taken before marching out, probably in the Lykeion (cf. Arist., *Peace*, 354, with Schol. Lex. Seguer. 277, 10 ff. Other places of rendezvous in the city Andoc., *de Myst.*, 45) according to the conscript lists, before the Taxiarchs (Poll. 8, 115), who took these lists with them on campaign also (Lys. 15, 5). γραφὴ ἀστρατείας against those who absented themselves without leave: Lys. 14, 7. These and the γραφὴ λειποταξίου and δειλίας formed the military lawsuits: Æsch. *in Ctes.* 175. Rosenberg in the *Phil.* 34, 1876, p. 65 ff., maintains that there was no such thing as γραφὴ δειλίας at all, but Thalheim in the *Jahrb. f. cl. Phil.*, 1877, p. 269 ff. affirms, in my opinion correctly, the existence of all three forms of military offences. The other names of military cases seem to be simply special titles of the three classes of cases mentioned above. Cf. Andoc., *de Myst.*, 74. Poll. 8, 40. The Strategoi presided at military cases: Lys. 14, 21; 15, 1. The Taxiarchs acted as their substitutes: Dem. 39, 17. The στρατιῶται as jurymen: Lys. 14, 15. For the punishments cf. Æsch. *in Ctes.* 175; Andoc., *de Myst.*, 74. Further details in my *Beitr.*, etc., 54 ff.

[2] The Strategos can order executions in the field: Lys. 13, 67, or put a man in chains: Dem. 50, 51. Cf. also Arist. 61, 2, where it is said of the Strategoi: κύριοι δέ εἰσιν, ὅταν ἡγῶνται, καὶ δῆσαι τὸν ἀτακτοῦντα καὶ ⟨ἐκ⟩[κη-]ρύξαι καὶ ἐπιβολὴν ἐ[πι]βάλλειν· οὐκ εἰώθασι δὲ ἐπιβάλλειν. The punishments for insubordination were light. Cf. Lys. 3, 45. Military rewards, *e.g.* wreath: Æsch., *de Fals. Leg.*, 169, and panoply: Plut., *Alcib.*, 7; Plut., *Symp.*, 220.

After the introduction of pay for the troops the conscript received pay during the time he was on campaign, and also a fixed sum for his maintenance; the two together amounted to a sum varying between a drachma and 4 obols a day.[1] **Pay.**

The Athenian hoplite was armed with a πανοπλία which consisted, as among the Greeks generally, of shield, helmet, breastplate, greaves, sword and thrusting-spear.[2] **Weapons.**

The Athenian hoplite force, being a citizen-militia, was classified according to the divisions of the burgess-body, and accordingly was divided into 10 Phylai, otherwise called τάξεις. The hoplite served in the same Phyle to which he belonged as a civilian.[3] Similarly the hoplites belonging to the class of Metoicoi beyond a doubt served in the ranks of the Phyle to which the Deme where they resided belonged.[4] Hence it naturally followed that the numerical strength of the military Phylai was only approximately uniform. For expeditions on which the entire fighting strength of the State was not employed, field battalions were formed of a strength determined according to the total strength of the levy decreed by the people; and these battalions were also called φυλαί.[5] The tactical **Tactical divisions of the hoplite forces.**

The δημόσιος τάφος for the slain (see the passages in Schaefer, *Dem.*, 3, 1¹, 31, 4) also had to be proposed by the Strategos: Aristoph., *Birds*, 395 sqq. Children of men slain in war were reared at the expense of the State: Thuc. 2, 46; Aristot., *Pol.*, 2, 8, p. 41, 10 sqq. Bekker.

[1] Boeckh, *Publ. Econ.*, 1, 377 ff. (Bk. II. c. 22). In the Peloponnesian war we hear of hoplites receiving daily a sum, including both the μισθός and the σιτηρέσιον, of a drachma for themselves and another for their servants, Thuc. 3, 17. Dem. 4, 28 puts down as daily σιτηρέσιον 2 obols, to which we must add another equal sum as μισθός. In the Peloponnesian war the hoplite as a rule took with him provisions for 3 days: Aristot., *Ach.*, 197; *Peace*, 312. In the archonship of Menecles (B.C. 282?) οἱ 'Αθηναῖοι οἱ τεταγμένοι 'Ελευσῖνι pass a vote in honour of a certain Dion, who, as γραμματεύς of the ταμίας τῶν σιτωνικῶν, πολλὴν σπουδὴν πεποίηται περὶ τὴν τοῦ σίτου δόσιν καὶ τῶν ἐκκλη(σ)ιαστικῶν τῶν διδομένων ἐπὶ τὸν σῖτον: 'Εφ. ἀρχ., 1887, p. 187.

[2] A πανοπλία was given to the orphan sons of men fallen in battle: Æsch. *in Ctes.* 154.

[3] 10 Phylai of the army: Xen., *Hell.*, 4, 2, 19; cf. Hdt. 6, 111. φυλὴ τῶν ὁπλιτῶν: Thuc. 6, 98. 101. φυλή=τάξις: Lys. 13, 82 compared with 79; 16, 16. Cf. Thuc. 3, 87. The hoplite served in the same Phyle to which he belonged as a burgess: Is. 2, 42; Plat., *Symp.*, 219/20. Plut., *Alcib.*, 7, may still be justified in spite of this theory.

[4] Xen., *de Vect.*, 2, 3. In C.I.A., II. 176, a certain Eudemus is granted the title εὐεργέτης: καὶ στρατεύεσθαι αὐτὸν τὰς στρατείας καὶ τὰς εἰσφορὰς εἰσφέρειν μετὰ 'Αθηναίων.

[5] See the φυλὴ τῶν ὁπλιτῶν in Thuc. 6, 98, 101.

subdivisions of the several Phylai are not known; it is however probable that to form these mobilised Phylai a number of Demes, more or fewer according to the size of the several Demes, were combined to form a Lochos, each Lochos being commanded by a Lochagos appointed probably by the Strategos.[1]

The military forces of the State included also light armed troops, who were recruited from among the Thetes, though this class was employed on other service also on occasion.[2] The only common characteristic of these troops was that none of them were armed with complete hoplite armour; Athens possessed no specially equipped light-armed troops. In the fifth century, however, we hear of a corps of bowmen, commanded by τόξαρχοι, and recruited from among the citizens.[3]

Light armed Troops.

The most distinguished portion of the Athenian militia was the cavalry or ἱππεῖς. In 490 B.C. the Athenians were still destitute of cavalry, but they gradually increased the number of their horsemen till in 431 B.C. it reached 1,000, and this total was maintained during the fourth century.[4] Every

Cavalry.

---

[1] Lochoi among the Athenians: Arist., *Ach.*, 1074; Xen., *Hell.*, 1, 2, 3. Lochagoi: Isocr. 15, 117; Xen., *Memor.*, 3, 4, 1; Is. 9, 14. The hoplites of Acharnai probably formed one or more Lochoi by themselves on account of their numerical strength (cf. Thuc. 2, 20). Is. 2, 42 shows that demotai served together.

[2] We find them taking part in expeditions undertaken, πανδημεί or πανστρατιᾷ. Cf. Thuc. 2, 81. 4, 90. 91.

[3] Thuc. 4, 94: ψιλοὶ δὲ ἐκ παρασκευῆς μὲν ὡπλισμένοι οὔτε τότε παρῆσαν οὔτε ἐγένοντο τῇ πόλει. This statement is not affected by the fact that *e.g.* in C.I.A., I. 54. 55 Athenian πελτασταί are mentioned. Pericles speaks of 1,600 bowmen at the beginning of the Peloponnesian war: Thuc. 2, 13, and Arist. 24, 3 supports this. Nikias obtained for the Sicilian expedition τὴν δὲ ἄλλην παρασκευὴν ὡς κατὰ λόγον καὶ τοξοτῶν τῶν αὐτόθεν καὶ ἐκ Κρήτης καὶ σφενδονητῶν: Thuc. 6, 25. Τοξόται οἱ ἀστικοί: C.I.A., I. 79. (κατὰ) φυλὰς τοχ(σόται δέ)κα: I. 54. Cf. also I. 55. 433. 446. οἱ τόξαρχοι: I. 79.

[4] The Athenian knights have been discussed by K. Fr. Hermann, *de equitibus att.*; Lejeune Dirichlet, under the same title, Königsberg, 1882: Martin, *les cavaliers Athéniens*, Paris, 1886, especially 121 ff. No cavalry yet in 490 B.C., Hdt. 6, 112. 1,000 in 431 B.C.: Thuc. 2, 13, and Arist. 24, 3, compared with Aristoph., *Eq.*, 225, and Philoch. *ap.* Hesych. ἱππῆς—Φιλόχορος δὲ ἐν τετάρτῳ (probably dealing with the period 456-404 B.C.) εἴρηκεν πότε κατεστάθησαν·χίλιοι. The same number in the fourth century, Xen., *Hipparch.* 9, 3. Dem. 14, 13.—Philoch., *ibid.*, continues: διάφορα γὰρ ἦν ἱππέων πλήθη κατὰ χρόνον Ἀθηναίοις. As regards the successive steps by which the number of the cavalry was increased, no great reliance can be placed on the *Schol.* to Arist., *Eq.*, 627, nor yet on Andoc., *de Pace*, 5, 7, or Æsch., *de Fals. Leg.*, 173. 174; see Wachsmuth 1, 558, 1. Hermann, p. 35 ff.

citizen who was physically competent, and possessed the property qualifying for cavalry service, was bound to enter the corps of knights. If he refused to do so at the request of the Hipparchoi, who were responsible for the recruiting of the corps, he could be compelled by judicial procedure. In Aristotle's time 10 καταλογεῖs, elected by the people, had the duty of enrolling every year all the men, of the age liable to service, who were under obligation to cavalry-service, and were competent for it. They handed over the list of these men to the Phylarchoi, and the Phylarchoi and Hipparchoi brought it before the Council. The muster-roll of the cavalry was then revised in the Council; first, the Council erased the names of all the men of former years, who stated on oath that they were no longer physically capable of serving as horsemen, then the list of new recruits was examined. Any who could show on oath that they were physically or financially incompetent were excused service; the rest were examined to see whether they were suitable or not, and, according to the result, were entered on the roll of knights or rejected.[1] The recruit

---

Martin, p. 121 ff. puts the date of the organisation of the corps of knights between 447 B.C., in which year, at the battle of Coroneia, there was still no Athenian cavalry, and 488 B.C., the date of the completion of the Parthenon, on the frieze of which building the knights are represented.

[1] ἱπποτροφία, Xen., Œc., 2, 6. Lyc., Leocr., 189, does not mean, as Hermann 28 ff. supposes, the maintenance of the cavalry horse, though the verb ἱπποτροφεῖν is used in that sense also (cf. Xen., Hipparch., 1, 11) but the keeping of race-horses. See Martin 295 ff. Though horse racing and horse breeding was a favourite form of sport among the upper classes—cf. e.g., Plat., Lysis, 205. Hdt. 6, 35. 125. Aristoph., Clouds—and we read in Plat., Lach., 182: καὶ ἅμα προσήκει μάλιστ' ἐλευθέρῳ τοῦτό τε τὸ γυμνάσιον καὶ ἱππική, yet the men liable to cavalry service probably had, as a rule, only one horse (Is. 11, 41. Dem. 42, 24). A horse could not be purchased in Attica for less than 3 minæ (cf. Is. 5, 43). A good charger would certainly be considerably dearer than that. In Aristoph., Clouds, 21 ff., a κοππατίας costs 12 minæ, and another in Lyc. 8, 10 just as much. See Thumser, de civ. Atheniens. munerib., p. 80 ff. For the men liable to cavalry service cf. Xen., Hipparch., 1, 9: τοὺς μὲν τοίνυν ἱππέας δῆλον ὅτι καθιστάναι δεῖ κατὰ τὸν νόμον τοὺς δυνατωτάτους καὶ χρήμασι (i.e., probably the two first Solonian census classes. Hermann 11 ff.) καὶ σώμασιν ἢ εἰσάγοντα εἰς δικαστήριον ἢ πείθοντα. See also Dirichlet 25/6. Cf. Xen., de re Equestri, 2, 1. Hermann 21 ff. Precepts for the Hipparchoi as to how they are to induce youths to enlist as volunteers in the cavalry: Xen., Hipparch., 1, 11/2, cf. Arist., Birds, 1442/3, where the Diitrephes mentioned was a Hipparch, cf. 798 sqq. I agree with Thalheim, Berl. phil. Wochenschr., 1887, 1815, that the system elaborated by Martin 319 ff. from Xen., Hipparch., 9, 5, is erroneous, for Xen. is there discussing simply a proposal or suggestion of his own. Arist.

newly entered by the Council on the roll received, for the expenses of his equipment, a sum of money called κατάστασις, which he had to refund to the State when he left the service.[1] The training of the horsemen belonged to the duties of the Hipparchoi. They had to instruct them in mounting and dismounting, hurling spears on horseback, charging, wheeling, leaping walls and ditches, and riding up and down steep slopes. Further, the Hipparchoi had to test the horses to see if they were suitable for the services required.[2] In general the Hipparchoi directed the entire military

49, 2 informs us about his own times: τοὺς δ' ἱππέας καταλέγουσιν οἱ καταλογεῖς, οὓς ἂν ὁ δῆμος χειροτονήσῃ δέκα ἄνδρας. οὓς δ' ἂν καταλέξωσι, παραδιδόασι τοῖς ἱππάρχοις καὶ φυλάρχοις, οὗτοι δὲ παραλαβόντες εἰσφέρουσι τὸν κατάλογον εἰς τὴν βουλὴν καὶ τὸν πίνακ' ἀνοίξαντες, ἐν ᾧ κατασεσημασμένα τὰ ὀνόματα τῶν ἱππέων ἐστί, τοὺς μὲν ἐξομνυμένους τῶν πρότερον ἐγγεγραμμένων μὴ δυνατοὺς εἶναι τοῖς σώμασιν ἱππεύειν ἐξαλείφουσι (cf. Xen., Hipparch., 1, 2) τοὺς δὲ κατειλεγμένους καλοῦσι, κἂν μέν τις ἐξομνύηται μὴ δύνασθαι τῷ σώματι ἱππεύειν ἢ τῇ οὐσίᾳ, τοῦτον ἀφιᾶσιν, τὸν δὲ μὴ ἐξομνύμενον διαχειροτονοῦσιν οἱ βουλευταί, πότερον ἐπιτήδειός ἐστιν ἱππεύειν ἢ οὔ· κἂν μὲν χειροτονήσωσιν, ἐγγράφουσιν εἰς τὸν πίνακα, εἰ δὲ μή, καὶ τοῦτον ἀφιᾶσιν. This muster-roll must be meant by the σανίδιον in Lys. 16, 6. 13, and by the σανίδες produced in 26, 10. Those who possessed the requisite property probably became liable to cavalry service as soon as they left the Peripoloi. Dexileos, who fell at Corinth while serving as a ἱππεύς in 394/3, was born in 414/3: C.I.A., II. 2084. Νέοι and πρεσβύτεροι in the corps: Xen., Hipparch., 1, 17; 2, 3. Νεανίσκοι: Thuc. 8, 92. Arist., Knights, 731. μειράκια: Arist. 1442.

[1] Xen., Hipparch., 1, 9, says that the Hipparchoi, καθιστάναι τοὺς ἱππέας, and so from the point of view of the Council the κατάστασις is the definitive enlistment of a knight after the Dokimasia described by Arist. Cf. Lex. Seguer. 270, 30: ἡ ὑπὸ τῆς βουλῆς τῶν ἱππέων δοκιμασία κατάστασις ἐλέγετο. The Dokimasia just mentioned is the one which occurs in Lys. 14, 8, which Sauppe in the Phil. 15, 69 ff. has rightly distinguished from the Dokimasia described by Xen., Hipparch., 1, 13 sqq., and so also has Dirichlet 27 ff. On the κατάστασις, in the sense of a sum of money, cf. Harp., Suid., Phot., Lys. 16, 6 sqq. Bake, schol. hypomnem., 5, 134 ff., tries to prove that the κατάστασις existed in the time of the 30 only, but he is refuted by Sauppe. I now agree with Martin 335 ff. who, on the authority of Harp. κατάστασις, holds that this had to be paid back to the State on leaving the cavalry service.

[2] The younger men learnt ἀπὸ δόρατος ἀναπηδᾶν ἐπὶ τοὺς ἵππους, the older men learnt to mount in the Persian style: Xen., Hipp., 1, 17, de re Equestri, 6, 12; 7, 1, 3. Cf. Mnesimach. ap. Ath. 9, 402 F: Στεῖχ' εἰς ἀγορὰν πρὸς τοὺς Ἑρμᾶς Οὗ προσφοιτῶσ' οἱ φύλαρχοι Τούς τε μαθητὰς τοὺς ὡραίους, Οὓς ἀναβαίνειν ἐπὶ τοὺς ἵππους Μελετᾷ Φείδων καὶ καταβαίνειν. Xen., Mem., 3, 3, 5. Practice in ἀκοντίζειν: Hipp., 1, 6, 21; in ἀνθιππασία: Hipp., 1, 20, in which each Hipparch commands 5 tribes: 3, 11. For the other employments of a πολεμιστήριος ἵππος: de re Eq., 3, 7: 8, 1 sqq.; 7, 13 sqq. Examination of the horses: Xen., Mem., 3, 3, 3/4. Phot. ἱππότροχος. The definitive rejection of a horse probably required a vote of the Council. This reviewing of the horses Körte

arrangements of the cavalry; nothing was fixed by the State except the classification into Phylai.[1] Every year, and probably early in the year, the cavalry were repeatedly reviewed by the Boule, to see whether the horses were good enough for the services required.[2] Horsemen not rejected at the revision of the muster-roll in the Boule, could not be called upon to serve as hoplites in the current year; on the other hand, no one was permitted to serve in the cavalry in any year without passing the Dokimasia for that year.[3]

The Athenian cavalry was divided into 10 Phylai, corresponding to the 10 Phylai of the burgess body. Out of these the necessary number of cavalry for each campaign was levied according to the muster-roll, probably by the Phylarchs.[4] Every horseman received, even in time of peace, an allowance to pay for the keep of his horse.[5]

Tactical Divisions.

believes to be the subject represented on a drinking cup of Orvieto, which he has published in the *Archäol. Zt.*, 1881, p. 117 ff. However, the two men called Bouleutai in Körte's explanation are probably the two Hipparchoi, and Körte's Hipparch a Phylarch.

[1] Cf. *Hipparch.*, 2, 1 sqq. Νόμοι of the Hipparch for the cavalry: Dem. 21, 173.

[2] The Boule reviewed the exercises of the cavalry in Acontismos at the Lykeion, in Anthippasia in the Hippodrome, in riding and wheeling on difficult ground in the Academy: Xen., *Hipp.*, 3, 1, 6 sq. Horses tested by the Boule: 1, 13 sq. Arist. 49, 1: δοκιμάζει δὲ καὶ τοὺς ἵππους ἡ βουλὴ κἂν μέν τις καλὸν ἵππον ἔχ]ων κακῶς δοκῇ τρέφειν, ζημιοῖ τῷ σίτῳ, τοῖς δὲ μὴ δυναμένοις [ἀκολ]ουθεῖν ἢ μὴ 'θέλουσιν μένειν ἀλλ' ἀνάγουσι, τροχὸν ἐπὶ τὴν γνάθ[ον ἐπιβάλλει, καὶ ὁ τ]οῦτο παθὼν ἀδόκιμός ἐστι. Cf. Hesych. τρυσίππιον. Ἵππου τροχός. This is the Dokimasia of horses and riders by the Council: Xen., *Œc.*, 9, 15. *Hipp.*, 3, 9. General supervision by the Council: *Hipp.*, 1, 8, 13. See Martin 326 ff.

[3] Knights duly enrolled could not be conscripted as hoplites: Lys. 15, 7. Those not duly enrolled were not allowed to serve in the cavalry: Lys. 15, 11; 14, 10; 16, 13. Any one who entered the cavalry illegally was liable to atimia and confiscation of property: Lys. 14, 8. 9.

[4] 10 φύλαι τῶν ἱππέων: Xen., *Hipp.*, 3, 11. Phot. Ἵππαρχοι. Each was commanded by a Phylarch: Harp. Suid. φύλαρχος. Lex. Seguer. 313, 32. In an inscr. of the first half of the 4th cent., belonging probably to a statue in honour of the commanding Phylarch, occur the words: ἡ φυλὴ ἡ τῶν ἱππέων. See *Mitth. d. dtsch. arch. Inst.*, 5, 319 = C.I.A., II. 1213. In Lys. 16, 13 Orthoboulos must be supposed to have been a Phylarch.

[5] Xen., *Hipp.*, 1, 23 speaks of μισθός for the cavalry, and in 1, 19 he computes the annual cost of the cavalry at about 40 talents, which would make the cost of each horseman 240 drachmas *per annum*, if the total number was 1000. The μισθός mentioned by Xen. is probably the σῖτος which each horseman received for his horse's keep (cf. Arist. 49, 1): for, according to the

The knights, or cavalry, formed a political corporation, and as such were entitled to decree crowns of honour: and the members **The Cavalry** of the corps occasionally swore to treaties with foreign **as a** States.[1] The Athenians regarded the knights as the **Corporation.** ornament of their State, and accordingly employed them in processions at festivals such as the Panathenaia and the feast of Zeus, to give the necessary éclat to the proceedings.[2]

Besides the 1,000 knights there were also, at any rate at the beginning of the Peloponnesian war, 200 ἱπποτοξόται, who were **Hippotoxotai.** employed as skirmishers.[3] We now have Aristotle's evidence that the combination of light infantry with cavalry, known as ἄμιπποι, was likewise employed at Athens.[4]

words spoken by the knights in Aristoph., *Knights*, 576/7, ἡμεῖς δ' ἀξιοῦμεν τῇ πόλει Προῖκα γενναίως ἀμύνειν καὶ θεοῖς ἐγχωρίοις, they seem to have received no pay for their own services, at any rate in Aristophanes' time. And accordingly the *Schol.* to Dem. 732 says: καὶ γὰρ καὶ οἱ ἱππεῖς μισθὸν ἐλάμβανον ἐν τῇ εἰρήνῃ ὑπὲρ τοῦ τρέφειν τοὺς ἵππους. Cf. Boeckh, *Publ. Ec.*, 1, 352 (Bk. II., c. 19). For the σῖτος of the ἱππεῖς cf. also C.I.A., II. 612, 300 B.C.: ἐπεμελήθησαν (i.e. οἱ ταμίαι) (μετὰ τ)ῶν ἱππάρχων, ὅπως ἂν οἱ (ἱππ)ε(ῖ)ς τόν τε σῖτον κομίσων(ται π)αρὰ τοῦ δήμου τὸν ὀφειλ(όμενον) αὐτοῖ(ς)—. In 410/9 B.C. the treasurers of Athene paid more than 16 Tal. in 4 Prytanies to the Hellenotamiai for σῖτος ἵπποις: C.I.A., I. 188.

[1] The ἱππεῖς presented crowns to the treasurers of the goddess: C.I.A., II. 612; to their Hipparch: Hyper., *Lycophr.*, XIII. 21 sqq.; dedicated a statue to the same officer: C.I.A., II. 962, cf. 1358; swore to treaties: C.I.A., II. 49. *Mitth. d. dtsch. arch. Inst. zu Ath.*, 2, 201. 212. See Martin 412 ff.

[2] In Aristoph., *Frogs*, 652, Dionysos explains his exclamation ἰοὺ ἰοὺ by ἱππέας ὁρῶ, on which the Schol. remarks ὡς θαυμάζων ἱππέων ἔφοδον. Festal processions were called, according to the *Schol.* on Arist., *Knights*, 627, θυσίαι ἱππάδες. The knights at the Panathenaic procession: Xen., *Hipp.*, 3, 2. Mommsen, *Heort.*, 176. Wachsmuth 1, 305. Michaelis, *der Parthenon*, 215 ff., 331; on the 19th of Munychion: Plut., *Phok.*, 37. Cf. also Dem. 4, 26; 21, 171. 174. Martin 145 ff.

[3] The number 200 is obtained by combining Thuc. 2, 13 and Arist. 24, 3 with Aristoph., *Eq.*, 225. The ἱπποτοξόται rode out before the Hipparchs: Xen., *Mem.*, 3, 3, 1. Cf. the πρόδρομοι in Xen., *Hipp.*, 1, 25. Since the πρόδρομοι also were mounted (cf. Arist. 49, 1: δοκιμάζει δὲ καὶ (sc. ἡ βουλή) τοὺς προ[δρόμους, ὅσοι ἂν α]ὐτῇ δοκῶσιν ἐπιτήδειοι προδρομεύειν εἶναι, κἄν τιν' ἀποχειροτονήσῃ, καταβέβηκεν οὗτος), I would identify them with the ἱπποτοξόται. Their number 200 shows at once that Wernicke, *Hermes*, 26, 67 ff., is wrong in supposing that they had anything to do with the police corps of Scythians. The context in Arist. 24, 3, where they are included in the 1,200 knights, shows clearly that they were citizens, as Thuc. 2, 13 indicates. Service in the ἱπποτοξόται was apparently thought less honourable: Lys. 15, 6.

[4] Arist. 49, 1: δοκιμάζει δὲ καὶ τοὺς ἀμίππους (sc. ἡ βουλή) κἄν τιν' ἀποχειροτονήσῃ, πέπαυται μισθοφορῶν οὗτος. Xen., *Hipp.*, 5, 13, recommends πεζοὶ

The main strength of Athens lay in its fleet. At the beginning of the Peloponnesian war the fleet consisted of 300 triremes fit for service at sea, and to this number we must probably add 100 select ships, which were not to be employed except in case of an attack upon the Piræus. All ships of war still possessed by Athens at the end of that war, except twelve, had to be surrendered to the Lacedæmonians. In 378 B.C. the Athenians had again collected a considerable fleet, which had grown to 349 triremes in 353 B.C., 392 triremes and 18 quadriremes in 330 B.C., 360 triremes, 50 quadriremes, and 7 quinqueremes in 325 B.C. The ships were kept in special docks in the war harbours.[1] In the most flourishing days of Athens, at any rate, the triremes which had become unfit for service were continually replaced by new ones. Any Boule which, during its year of office, failed to get the usual number of triremes prepared, lost all claim to receive crowns of honour at the end of its year.[2] The wood, canvas, and rigging was kept partly in the docks, partly in the naval arsenals.[3]

Fleet. Its Strength.

If the people decided upon an ἀπόστολος, then the trierarchs

ἄμιπποι for the Athenian cavalry; they must, therefore, have been introduced after his time. ἄμιπποι are heard of in Bœotia also. Cf. Thuc. 5, 57. Xen., Hell., 7, 5, 24. Diod. 15, 85.

[1] In 431 B.C. Pericles reckons 300 seaworthy ships: Thuc. 2, 13, while in Thuc. 2, 24 another 100 τριήρεις ἐξαίρετοι are also mentioned. Cf. also Andoc., de pace, 7, 9. Æsch., de Fals. Leg., 174/5. The fleet usually consisted of 300 ships: Xen., An., 7, 1, 27. Aristoph., Ach., 544/5. Every year 400 trierarchs were nominated in anticipation: (Xen.) de Rep. Ath., 3, 4; and, acc. to Strab. 395, the Athenian ναύσταθμον was built for 400 ships. At the peace of Lysander Athens retained 12 war-ships: Xen. 2, 2, 20. Andoc., de Pace, 12. Plut., Lys., 15. In 378 B.C. the Athenians manned 100 ships acc. to Polyb. 2, 62, 200 acc. to Diod. 15, 29. Condition of the fleet in 353 B.C.: C.I.A., II. 795, l. 138; in 330 B.C.: C.I.A., II. 807b, l. 79; in 325 B.C.: C.I.A., II. 809d, 62 sqq. Even in the middle of the 4th cent. we find again 100 τριήρεις ἐξαίρετοι: Wachsmuth 2, 1, 91/2. For the development of the Athenian fleet see Köhler in the Mitth. d. dtsch. arch. Inst. in Ath., 6, 28 ff. After the restoration of the docks by Lycurgus there were 372 ships altogether, 82 at Munychia, 196 at Zea, and 94 in the harbour of Kautharos: Seeurk., XIo., p. 414 and p. 67 ff. = C.I.A., II. 807c, 27 sqq. On the still existing remains of the Athenian sheds and arsenals see Wachsmuth 2, 1, 51 ff.

[2] Dem. 22, 12. 36. In the financial programme set forth in C.I.A., I. 32 we read: ἐπειδὰν δὲ ἀποδεδομένα ᾖ τοῖς θεοῖς (τὰ χρ)ήματα, ἐς τὸ νεώριον καὶ τὰ τείχη τοῖς περιοῦσι χρῆσθαι χρήμασ(ιν). For the way in which Themistocles built the first 100 triremes cf. Arist. 22, 7 and Polyain. 1, 30, 6.

[3] Boeckh, Seeurk., 68 ff.

(who in the 5th century were appointed at the beginning of each year in anticipation of any naval expedition that might be necessary, but in the 4th century were not appointed till immediately before the actual armament of the fleet), had to equip at their own expense the triremes assigned to them, together with a quantity of rigging and the like, by the Harbour-superintendents, or, at a later date, by allotment.[1] The Trierarchs had the triremes which were assigned to them moved from the ship-sheds to the harbour-dock or to the pier, where they were then equipped with oars, sails, and all other necessary tackle.[2]

Equipment of an ἀπόστολος.

After this was done the trireme was manned. Each ship when fully manned carried about 200 men, drawn from three different classes of men.[3] The first class were the ἐπιβάται or marines, who were hoplites, and were employed as fighting men in defence or attack. There were about 10 of these on each trireme.[4] The second, and far the most numerous class, consisted of the actual crew or oarsmen. They sat in three rows, one over the other: 62 θρανῖται, who worked the upper row of oars, 54 ζυγῖται at the middle row, and 54 θαλαμῖται in the lowest row.[5] These oarsmen, called ναῦται or ναυβάται, were recruited in

Crews and Men.

---

[1] For the arrangements in the 5th cent. cf. (Xen.), *de Rep. Ath.*, 8, 4; for the 4th cent. Dem. 4, 36. See, however, Boeckh, *Seeurk.*, 168. It was probably always usual for the Trierarchs to receive the tackle from the State, though not complete on every occasion: Boeckh, *Seeurk.*, 201 ff. I shall deal with the details of the trierarchy in the section on finance. For what follows cf. the remarks of Kirchhoff in the *Abh. d. Berl. Ak.*, 1865, p. 80 ff.; *Seeurk.* XIVa, 184 ff., p. 462=C.I.A., II. 809a, 180: ἐψηφίσθαι τῷ (δήμ)ῳ τοὺς μὲν τῶν νε(ωρί)ων ἐπιμελητὰς πα(ραδο)ῦναι τοῖς τριηρά(ρχοις τ)ὰς ναῦς καὶ τὰ σκεύη (κατὰ τὰ) δεδογμένα τῷ δή(μῳ).

[2] *Seeurk.*, XIVa, 189 ff., p. 462=C.I.A., II. 809a, 181, where Kirchhoff, *ib.*, p. 75, 25, completes the inscr. undoubtedly correctly: (το)ὺς δὲ τριηράρχους (τοὺς καθ)εστηκότας παρα(κομίζει)ν τὰς ναῦς ἐπὶ τὸ (χῶμα ἐ)ν τῷ Μουνυχιῶνι (μηνὶ π)ρὸ τῆς δεκάτης (ἱσταμέ)νου καὶ παρέχειν (παρεσ)κευασμένας εἰς (πλοῦν). Cf. Dem. 50, 6; 51, 4.

[3] Dem. 50, 29. 30.

[4] On the numbers and composition of the crews see Boeckh, *Publ. Econ.*, 1, 384 ff. (Bk. II. c. 22). For the ἐπιβάται, Harp. ἐπιβάτης—οὕτως ἐκάλουν τῶν ἐν ταῖς τριήρεσι στρατευομένων τοὺς μὴ κωπηλατοῦντας, ἀλλὰ μόνον πρὸς τὸ μάχεσθαι ἐπιτηδείους. Cf. Thuc. 7, 63. ἐπιβάται taken from the Thetes: Thuc. 6, 43. Hoplites from the hoplite-list compelled to serve as ἐπιβάται: Thuc. 8. 24. Each ship had 10 ἐπιβάται: Thuc. 2, 23; 2, 69 compared with 92, 102; 3, 91 with 95; 4, 76 with 101. Boeckh 1, 390 (Bk. II. c. 22); Schwartz, p. 32.

[5] Boeckh, *Seeurk.*, 114 ff. For the numbers of the Thranitai, Zygitai and

the 5th century, during the supremacy of the Athenians and their league, partly, indeed, from the poorer citizens, but chiefly from foreign mercenaries and Metoicoi. In the 4th century, besides the Metoicoi, the poorer citizens seem to have been taken into service as rowers in larger numbers.[1] The third class of men on board consisted of regular seamen, technically skilled in navigation, the κυβερνήτης, the πρῳρεύς or πρῳράτης, the κελευστής, probably three πεντηκόνταρχοι, and one or two ναυπηγοί.[2] The entire complement of men on board was under the command of the Trierarch, who had power to inflict punishment if necessary.[3]

When the ship was manned, and its oarsmen trained for their work by a few practices,[4] the Trierarch could announce to the Council, or to the ἀποστολεῖς, that his ship was ready for service at sea. In order to increase the keenness of the Trierarchs and so expedite the armament of the ἀπόστολος, it was the custom for a golden crown to be offered by decree of the people, as a prize for the Trierarch whose trireme was first ready to sail. Occasionally the Trierarchs of the first three ships ready received these wreaths of honour.[5]

Trierarchic Crowns.

The pay and maintenance money for the crews varies in the

Thalamitai, see Boeckh 118 ff., 54, not 58 Zygitai: Köhler in the *Mitth. d. dtsch. arch. Inst. in Ath.*, 6, 38.

[1] In the battle of Salamis the crews were still formed of citizens: Aristoph., *Eq.*, 785. Thuc. 1, 121: ὠνητὴ γὰρ Ἀθηναίων ἡ δύναμις (τῶν ναυβατῶν) μᾶλλον ἢ οἰκεία. ξένοι among the ναῦται: Thuc. 1, 143; 7, 63; Isocr. 8, 48. Cf. what Thuc. 8, 73 explicitly says of the crew of the Paralos. Metoicoi as oarsmen: (Xen.), *de Rep. Ath.*, 1, 12: διότι δεῖται ἡ πόλις μετοίκων—διὰ τὸ ναυτικόν. Zeugitai, Thetes and Metoicoi man the ships under special circumstances: Thuc. 3, 16; cf. 1, 143. The citizens were probably employed chiefly as Thranitai, for they received higher pay; cf. Thuc. 6, 31. Hence, ὁ θρανίτης λεώς in Aristoph., *Ach.*, 162; cf. however (Xen.), *de Rep. Ath.*, 1, 19/20. For the practice of the 4th century cf. Isocr. 8, 48; Dem. 50, 6, 7; 4, 36.

[2] Thuc. 1, 143: κυβερνήτας ἔχομεν πολίτας καὶ τὴν ἄλλην ὑπηρεσίαν πλείους καὶ ἀμείνους ἢ πᾶσα ἡ ἄλλη Ἑλλάς. The men mentioned by (Xen.), *de Rep. Ath.*, 1, 2, κυβερνῆται, κελευσταί, πεντηκόνταρχοι, πρῳρᾶται, ναυπηγοί form the ὑπηρεσία; cf. also Aristoph., *Eq.*, 541 sqq.; Xen., *Œc.*, 8, 14. For their number see Köhler, *Mitth. d. dtsch. arch. Inst. in Ath.*, 8, 177 ff.

[3] Dem. 50, 18. 19. 50; 51, 11.

[4] Dem. 51, 5/6.

[5] Dem. 51, 1. Poll. 1, 128. *Seeurk.*, XIV a, 195 ff., p. 463 = C.I.A., II. 809a, 190 sqq.: τὸν δὲ πρῶτον πα(ρακομί)σαντα στεφανωσά(τω ὁ δῆ)μος χρυσῷ στεφά(νῳ ἀ)πὸ πεντακοσίων δραχμῶν, (τὸν δὲ) δεύτερον ἀπὸ τριακοσίων (δραχμ)ῶν, τὸν δὲ τρίτον ἀ(πὸ—) καὶ ἀναγορευσά(τω ὁ κῆ)ρυξ τῆς βουλῆς Θαρ(γηλίων) τῷ ἀγῶνι τοὺς στε(φάνους). See Kirchhoff, *ib.*, p. 67 ff.

calculations of average pay given in our authorities, from various periods, between 3 obols and 1 drachma a day per man.[1]

Pay.

The discipline in the fleet was better than among the hoplites and cavalry, though complaints were made of the insubordination of the sailors also.[2]

4. FINANCE.

A. General.

Every financial administration must have for its basis a regular monetary system. The Athenian State possessed in the 5th and 4th centuries a silver currency, admired by Hellenes and barbarians for the purity of its metal, and therefore readily accepted.[3] The introduction of this coinage dated from the times of Solon. He had abolished the earlier coinage of Athens, which was identical with the Æginetan system, and introduced the Euboic; this did not involve, however, any alteration in the system of subdivision or in the names of the various smaller coins; but the Tetradrachm became the chief coin of the State, in place of the Didrachm customary until then.[4] The Athenian silver coins bore, in all probability from the days of Peisistratos, the head of Pallas as device on the obverse, and an owl on the reverse; and that, almost without exception, though in the extant examples

Coinage.

---

[1] The same distinction was made in the case of ships' crews between μισθός and σιτηρέσιον: Dem. 50, 10. A drachma, at the beginning of the Peloponnesian war and for the Sicilian expedition: Thuc. 3, 17; 6, 31: 3 obols: Thuc. 8, 45. Dem. 4, 28 reckons 20 minæ as monthly σιτηρέσιον for a ship, i.e., for a complement of 200 men an average daily σιτηρέσιον of 2 obols per man, to which must be added a daily μισθός of 2 obols; see Boeckh, *Publ. Econ.*, 1, 381 ff. (Bk. II. c. 22). The burgess crew of the Paralos also received 4 obols a day. Cf. Harp. Πάραλος.

[2] Xen., *Mem.*, 3, 5. 18. 19. Instance of insubordination of a hoplite, Lys. 3, 45. And according to Xen.'s manual for the Hipparch, that officer had to deal with the knights more by persuasion than by command. Complaints of ναυτικὴ ἀναρχία in Eurip., *Hec.*, 606 sqq.

[3] Cf. Aristoph., *Frogs*, 717 sqq. Xen., *de Vect.*, 3, 2. Uttering false coins was punished by death: Dem. 20, 167. The Attic coins were not alloyed: Hultsch, *Metrol.*[2], 232 ff.

[4] For the agreement of the pre-Solonian coinage with the Æginetan see Hultsch, *Metrol.*[2], 200 ff. The Solonian coinage was based on the light Babylonian gold talent, and the Attic talent is equal to the Eubœan: Hultsch[2] 203 ff., 507/8. Cf. also Köhler in the *Mitth.*, 10, 151 ff.

various periods of minting can be distinguished.[1] The coinage of gold, the ratio of whose value to silver at Athens varied between 14–10 : 1, and the coinage of copper, which was first coined to any great extent after Alexander the Great, were both very limited in the 4th century.[2] The Athenian system of silver coins, which were coined in varying amounts, was as follows: τάλαντον = 60 μναῖ, μνᾶ = 100 δραχμαί, δραχμή = 6 ὀβολοί or 12 ἡμιωβόλια. The normal weights of these coins and their approximate values in English money are as follows:—

> τάλαντον = 57·752 lbs. Avoirdupois = £230.
> μνᾶ = 6737·76 grains Troy = £4.
> δραχμή = 67·3776 grains = 9·2d.
> ὀβολός = 11·2 grains = 1·5d.[3]

Since the purchasing power of a coinage depends upon the ratio of its value to that of other commodities and on the interest paid for capital, it is necessary, in order to appreciate rightly the amounts of the separate heads of the Athenian budget, to collect here various data with regard to these ratios.

First, as concerns the ratio of value of money to other commodities, I will simply state some prices recorded for corn and cattle. In Solon's time a medimnos of corn cost—it is not stated whether it was wheat or barley—1 drachma, while for the same bulk of wheat in 390 B.C. 3 drachmas were given, and in a tariff for sacrifices in 380 B.C. as much as 6 drachmas. In 335 B.C. the medimnos of wheat cost 5 drachmas. In 330 B.C. the delivery of 3,000 medimnoi of wheat, at 5 drachmas the medimnos, is reckoned a special act of kindness, and in 329 B.C. a decree of the people fixed the price at which the offerings of corn, which were yearly made to the Eleusinian temple, should be sold, at 6 drachmas per medimnos for wheat, and 3 drachmas for a medimnos of barley.[4] In Solon's time an ox was ordinarily

Value of Money. Purchasing Power.

---

[1] Regular system of Attic coinage, of full weight, stamped with owl and head of Pallas, introduced by Peisistratos: Hultsch[2] 220 ff. For the various periods of coinage: 213 ff.

[2] For the gold coinage see Hultsch[2] 223 ff. Ratio of gold to silver as 14–10 : 1, Hultsch[2] 236 ff.; as 14 : 1, C.I.A., I., p. 160. On Attic copper coinage Hultsch[2] 227 ff. Foreign gold coins were tested by a δοκιμαστής: *Mitth.* 5, 277.

[3] On the weight and value of the coins in German money see Hultsch[2] 208 ff. 234/5. For the fractions or smaller coins see Poll. 9, 51 sqq.

[4] 1 drachma: Plut., *Sol.*, 23. 3: Aristoph., *Eccl.*, 547/8. 6: Inscr. con-

reckoned worth 5 drachmas, but it is to be noticed that the price for oxen for sacrifice was even then considerably higher; in 410 B.C. an ox for sacrifice is reckoned at about 51 drachmas, 347 B.C. about 77, in 329 B.C. at 400.[1] In Solon's time a sheep cost 1 drachma, in the 4th century the price apparently varied between 10 and 20 drachmas, in 329 B.C. a sheep or goat cost 30.[2] It is impossible to institute a comparison between the worth of money then and its present value on such unsatisfactory data.

On the other hand, it may be shown with certainty that the rate of interest on capital at Athens was considerably greater **Interest of** than it is with us. The usual rate of interest on bor-**Capital.** rowed capital was 12–18 per cent., on money lent on bottomry on an average 20 per cent.[3] Capital invested in land produced less interest, about 8–12 per cent.; in case of house property about 8 per cent.[4] For money laid out in slaves, who

---

taining a sacrifice-tariff in Boeckh, *kl. Schr.*, 4, 404 ff., 409. 5; Dem. 34, 39. In Socrates' time a medimnos of ἄλφιτα cost 2 drachmas, though we have no direct contemporary evidence for this: Plut., *de tranquill. animi*, 10. 6 drachmas for the medimnos of κριθή follows from (Dem.) 42, 20, cf. with 31. For the price in 380 and 329 B.C. see *Mitth. d. dtsch. arch. Inst. in Ath.*, 8, 213 and 'Εφ. ἀρχ., 1883, pp. 123/4, 1. 69 ff.

[1] Plut., *Sol.*, 23. In 410/9 B.C. 5,114 drachmas are reckoned for a ἑκατόμβη, which gives for each ox, supposing that the Hecatombe consisted of exactly 100 oxen, an average price of 51·14 drachmas: C.I.A., I. 188. In 374/3 B.C. 109 oxen for sacrifice cost 8419 dr., giving an average of $77\frac{23}{109}$: C.I.A., II. 814. In 329 B.C. 400 dr. are reckoned for one ox: 'Εφ. ἀρχ., 1883, pp. 125/6, β. 77.

[2] Plut., *Sol.*, 23. Lys. 32, 21 mentions as a high price for an ἄρνιον 16 dr. Acc. to (Dem.) 47, 52. 57, compared with 64, about 20 dr. might be reckoned as the approximate cost of a πρόβατον μαλακόν. Acc. to Menand. *ap.* Ath. 4, 146 E, a προβάτιον ἀγαπητόν cost 10 dr. Price of a sheep in the time of Lycurgus 12 dr., of a ram 17 dr.: C.I.A., II. 834c, l. 62. In 329 B.C. 30 dr. are reckoned as the price for a sheep and a goat: 'Εφ. ἀρχ., 1883, pp. 125/6 β 76.

[3] On the rate of interest see Boeckh, *Publ. Econ.*, 1, 181 ff. (Bk. I. c. 22), and for interest on bottomry Xen., *de Vect.*, 3, 9. Fränkel in Boeckh, *St. d. Ath.*[3], 2, p. 37, no. 224. According to the usual idiom the rate of interest was expressed either by the number of obols or drachmas payable per month per mina, *e.g.* ἐπ' ὀκτὼ ὀβολοῖς=16 per cent., or by the proportion of the capital paid as interest per annum, *e.g.* τόκοι ἐπόγδοοι=$12\frac{1}{2}$ per cent. See Boeckh 173.

[4] Land in Thria worth 150 minæ produced 12 minæ rent, *i.e.* 8 per cent. of the capital: Is. 11, 42. A χωρίον 5,000 dr. in value brought in a yearly rent of 600 dr., *i.e.* 12 per cent: Is., *ibid.* So also C.I.A., II. 600. The house rent of two houses in Melite and Eleusis, worth both together 3,500 dr., was 300 dr., *i.e.* $8\frac{4}{7}$ per cent of the capital: Is., *ibid.*

were hired out to labour in the mines, we may reckon according to some statements of Xenophon's a profit or interest of 30–38 per cent., but this high amount was caused by the rapid depreciation to which such capital was liable.[1]

The value of free labour was but moderate, on account of the vast numbers of the slaves. In the 5th century, when the Parthenon and other great buildings were erected, the regular daily wages of an artizan seem to have been 1 drachma; less skilled work was of course paid less. Towards the end of the 4th century 3 obols a day were reckoned as the cost of maintenance of a state slave; the usual day's wage amounted on the average to $1\frac{1}{2}$ drachmas, while more skilled artizans were paid as much as $2\frac{1}{2}$ drachmas per day.[2]

On the other hand, the cost of living was not great, because of the well-known abstemiousness of the Athenians; and actual poverty does not seem to have existed during the time of Athens' greatness, because there were so many possibilities of earning a subsistence either on the fleet, or as a workman, or as heliast; in its period of decadence poverty grew more and more universal.[3]

---

[1] The passage is Xen., *de Vect.*, 4, 23. 1,200 slaves, each of whom brings in 360 obols annually, can be increased in number by means of this income to 6,000 in 5 or 6 years. If it be assumed that with the income of every year fresh slaves were to be purchased, who would work along with the rest in the next year, then the calculation of the capital so laid out forms a problem of the following kind:—The amount of capital must be determined which produced 360 obols a year interest. The rate of interest is determined by the datum that 1,200 times that capital increases by compound interest in 5 or 6 years to 6,000 times the same amount. This gives as the rate of compound interest, if we assume 5 years, 37·97 per cent.; if 6 years, 30·76 per cent; so that a yearly return of 360 obols represents in the first case the interest on 948·01 obols, in the second case on 1,170·35 obols. The value of a mining slave was accordingly between 158 and 195 drachmæ, and Boeckh's statement in *Kl. Schr.*, 5, 46, must be modified accordingly.

[2] In the statement of accounts for the building of the Erechtheion, 408 B.C., the work is mostly contract or piecework. Still a πρίστης received daily 1 drachma, an amount which is set down for other workmen also. Cf. C.I.A., I. 325, 324. IV. 3, 321. Payment by the piece also occurs: IV. 3, 321. A day's pay of 4 obols for porters and 3 obols for πηλοφοροῦντες may probably be inferred from Poll. 7, 133 and *Eccl.*, 308 sqq. In the statement of accounts of the ἐπιστάται Ἐλευσινόθεν 329 B.C. in the 'Εφ. ἀρχ., 1883, p. 109 ff., we have 3 obols reckoned as τροφή for a δημόσιος: A 4/5, 42. B 5/6, a 40; as ordinary day's wages $1\frac{1}{2}$ dr.: A 28 ff., 32 ff., 45 ff., 60 ff., B 23 ff., $2\frac{1}{2}$ dr.: A 26 ff. 2 dr.: B 41 ff., a 33 ff.

[3] On the simplicity of Athenian meals cf. the description by Lynkeus

As regards the financial economy of Athens, it rested on a thoroughly unsound basis. Reduced to its own resources, the **Prosperity of the people.** State would have found its economical existence impossible as things were arranged; it was merely the political supremacy, which lucky circumstances and the energy of its citizens had created, that secured its financial solvency. The cause of this unfavourable economical condition lay in the fact that Attica consumed far more in value than it could produce, and as a result the exports were less in value than the imports, and therefore every year a considerable amount of precious metal went from the country abroad.[1] The importation of corn alone, to which special attention was devoted by the State, and which according to a computation made in ancient times amounted to 800,000 medimnoi per annum, represented a yearly value of at least 250 talents.[2] To this must be added the importation of materials for shipbuilding, including timber, iron, brass, flax and wax,[3] imports of salt fish, articles of luxury, slaves and raw material for the Attic industries.[4] While the imports were so

ap. Ath. 4, 181 F, where the Perinthian says of himself and a Rhodian, οὐδέτερος ἡμῶν ἥδεται τοῖς 'Αττικοῖς—δείπνοις. Cf. Alexis *ap.* Ath., 4, 137 E. The δεῖπνον of Philocleon is a φυστὴ μᾶζα of barley meal: Arist., *Wasps*, 610, and for his triobolon he purchases wood, pearl-barley and condiments: *Wasps*, 300 sqq. Cf. *Eccl.*, 306 sqq. Isocr. 7, 83 says: τότε μὲν οὐδεὶς ἦν τῶν πολιτῶν ἐνδεὴς τῶν ἀναγκαίων οὐδὲ προσαιτῶν τοὺς ἐντυγχάνοντας τὴν πόλιν κατῄσχυνε, νῦν δὲ πλείους εἰσὶν οἱ σπανίζοντες τῶν ἐχόντων.

[1] On Attic exports and imports see Büchsenschütz, *Besitz und Erwerb*, 439 ff. Drain of coin from the country abroad: Xen., *de Vect.*, 8, 2.

[2] Dem. 20, 32 calculates from the account books of the σιτοφύλακες a yearly corn importation of 800,000 medimnoi, which Boeckh, *Publ. Econ.*, 1, 111 (Bk. I., c. 15) considers less than the truth. The value of this would be more than 250 tal., if we take 2 drachmas as purchasing price for the medimnos, which can scarcely be too high considering the price of corn in Attica. Of all the corn brought into the Athenian market two-thirds had by law to be brought to Athens: Arist. 51, 4. Harp., ἐπιμελητὴς ἐμπορίου. It was forbidden σιτηγεῖν to any other place than Athens: Dem. 35, 50. To estimate how much corn must be imported in every year was one of the statesman's duties acc. to Xen., *Mem.*, 3, 6, 13. Cf. Boeckh, *Publ. Econ.*, 1, 115 ff. (Bk. I., c. 15).

[3] Timber for shipbuilding: Thuc. 4, 108, (Dem.) 17, 28. Other timber: Dem. 21, 167. C.I.A., II. 834b, col. 1, l. 66. 'Εφ. ἀρχ. 1883, p. 125 γ, l. 8, Other ship-building materials: (Xen.) *de Rep. Ath.*, 2, 11.

[4] Fish formed a staple article of food with the Athenians. The Athenian slaves were mostly bought slaves. Influx of commodities from every land to the Piræus: Thuc. 2, 38. (Xen.) *de Rep. Ath.* 2, 7. Isocr. 4, 42: Antiphan. *ap.* Ath. 1, 27 D, E. With regard to the importation of raw

[Gilbert I. 817–8.] *State of the Finances.* [Gilbert II. 372–3.

considerable the exports were limited to a few raw products such as oil, figs, honey, wool and marble, all of which combined represented no very considerable value,[1] and some products of Attic industry, among which earthenware was by far the most important.[2] If in spite of all these unfavourable circumstances Athenian finances, at any rate before the beginning of the Peloponnesian war, were in an excellent state, the cause of this is to be found first in the great influx of precious metal to Athens caused by the payments of tribute by the allies, secondly in the silver mines of the country, and lastly in the profits of the transport trade with all Hellas, of which the Piræus was the centre.[3] But after the Peloponnesian war had destroyed the first and third sources of their wealth, the tide of Athenian prosperity turned and ebbed irrevocably; and this was only partially checked by the foundation of the second Athenian league, while the financial administration of the 4th century became more careless and extravagant every year.[4]

material for Attic industries, considerable interest attaches to the commercial treaty between Athens and Keos about 350 B.C., providing that the red chalk of Keos should be exported to Attica exclusively (C.I.A., II. 546): this ruddle or red chalk was employed to colour the earthenware: Suid. Κωλιάδος κεραμῆς.

[1] The exportation of oil, attested as early as Solon (Plut., *Sol.*, 24) is said by the *Schol.* on Pind., *Nem.*, 10, 64, certainly without justification, to have been laid under restrictions: οὐκ ἔστι δὲ ἐξαγωγὴ ἐλαίου ἐξ Ἀθηνῶν εἰ μὴ τοῖς νικῶσι. At the Panathenaia more than 1,200 amphorai of oil were distributed to the victors: Mommsen, *Heort.*, 151, 141. 153. C.I.A., II. 965. 3 κοτύλαι of oil cost acc. to a sacrifice tariff of 380 B.C. 1½ obols (Boeckh, *kl. Schr.*, 4, 404 ff. 409); therefore a μετρητής would be 6 dr. On the exportation of figs see Boeckh, *Publ. Econ.*, 1, 61 ff. (Bk. I. c. 8). Attic honey was famous. Plut., *de tranquill. animi*, 10, reckons a κοτύλη of a specially fine quality as worth 5 drachmas, while on a sacrifice tariff the κοτύλη costs 3 obols. On the excellence of Attic wool cf. Plut., *de audiendo* 9. Ath. 12 540 D. Attic marble: Xen., *de Vect.*, 1, 4.

[2] A great number of τέχναι at Athens: (Xen.) *de Rep. Ath.*, 1, 21. Earthenware vases, sent as articles of commerce (Hdt. 5, 88) as far as Libya (Skyl., *Peripl.*, 111); not high priced; Boeckh, *Publ. Econ.*, 1, 151/2 (Bk. I. c. 19). Praise of Attic potter's art in Critias, *Eleg.*, 1, 12 sqq.

[3] On the Piræus as a commercial emporium see Boeckh, 1, 85 (Bk. I. c. 9). On the wealth of the silver mines at Laureion see Xen., *de Vect.*, 1, 5, and Æsch., *Pers.*, 233: ἀργύρου πηγή τις αὐτοῖς ἐστι, θησαυρὸς χθονός.

[4] Wealth of Athens before the Pelop. war: Thuc. 1, 80; after the war feeble revenues and general impoverishment: Lys. 21, 18; 12, 6; 19, 11. Isocrates' descriptions indicate great poverty: 8, 20 sqq. 46; 7, 83. The people subsist merely by μισθός obtained in one way or another: Isocr. 7, 82; 8, 130; 15, 152.

In early times it was apparently the custom to distribute among the people any surplus revenue of the State.¹ After the foundation of the first Athenian league, on account of the continued wars with the Persians, the Athenians first began to feel the necessity of a permanent war chest, from which to defray the expenses of the war. Such a fund was formed by the treasury of the allies at Delos, which was kept full by the tribute paid by the members of the league. Afterwards when the war with the Persians came to an end, and the allies gradually fell into the position of dependencies of Athens, the Delian treasury of the allies was removed to Athens about 454 B.C., and there, just as the constitutional position of Athens in the league had altered, the allied treasury too changed its character and became an Athenian State chest. The monies brought to Athens were consecrated to Athene Polias and thus amalgamated with the temple treasures, and after the completion of the Parthenon these were kept in the Opisthodomos of that temple under the custody of the treasurers of Athene.² The

Main Principles of 5th Century Finance.

---

¹ I infer this from the proposal to distribute the 100 tal. which came into the State treasury in payment for concessions on the discovery of the silver mines at Maroneia. Cf. Arist. 22, 7. That Athens had no State treasury at the time of the Persian wars is shown by Arist. 23, 1. Cf. Plut., *Them.*, 10.

² In this second edition I have been induced by the discussions of Beloch in the *N. Rh. Mus.*, 39, 49 ff., and of Holwerda in *Mnemosyne*, 1886, 103 ff., to return to the view of Boeckh, *Publ. Econ.*, 1, 575 ff. (Bk. III., c. 20) that the State treasury of the Athenians was identical with the treasury of Athene Polias. Kirchhoff, in the *Abh. d. Berl. Ak.*, 1876, 21 ff., inferred the existence of a separate State chest in addition to the temple treasury on the following grounds:—Acc. to Thuc. 2, 13, the amount of coined money in the Acropolis at the beginning of the Peloponnesian war was 6,000 tal., of which 1,000 tal., acc. to Thuc. 2, 24, was put by as a reserve fund. Cf. also Thuc. 8, 15. Philoch., *fr.*, 116. Now Kirchhoff argues that these 5,000 tal. must have been spent by the beginning of 428/7 B.C., because an εἰσφορά was decreed in that year. Cf. Thuc. 3, 19. But acc. to the accounts of the Logistai in C.I.A., I. 273 not more than about 4,750 tal. were taken from the temple treasures in the 7 years from 433/2–427/6 B.C.; that is, not so much as was taken from the balances in the Acropolis up to the beginning of 428/7. Therefore Kirchhoff infers there must have existed besides the sacred treasury yet another reserve, namely the State chest proper. On the other hand, Beloch and Holwerda maintain that the decree of an Eisphora in the beginning of 428/7 does not necessarily imply the complete exhaustion of the State chest. Holwerda 104/5 translates the words of Thuc. 3, 17: καὶ τὰ χρήματα τοῦτο μάλιστα ὑπανήλωσε μετὰ Ποτειδαίας and τὰ μὲν οὖν χρήματα οὕτως ὑπανηλώθη τὸ πρῶτον by: "atque pecunias haec res maxime

ordinary revenues of this sacred treasury consisted of the rents of the temple estates, the tithes of confiscated goods, and the ἀπαρχή of $\frac{1}{60}$ of the annual tribute.[1] Besides this, however, the sacred treasury had extraordinary receipts. For instance, every year, so it seems, it was decided by decree of the Ecclesia, how the surplus from the tribute and from the government administration, if there were a surplus, should be employed. If there were no special needs to meet, the surplus seems to have been consecrated to Athene and incorporated with the sacred treasures.[2]

cum Potidæa consumere cœpit," and "pecuniæ igitur hoc modo primum consumi cœptæ sunt." Further the calculations of Beloch, *ib.*, 52 ff., show that the disagreement supposed by Kirchhoff between the statements of Thuc. and the accounts of the logistai does not exist. Lastly, the computation of the ἐπέτεια of the temple treasury at 200 tal. per annum by Kirchhoff is acc. to Beloch 56 ff. much too high. Fränkel has declared himself against Beloch in the *phil. u. hist. Aufs. für E. Curtius* 1884, pp. 48/9, and on Boeckh, *Publ. Ec.*, 2³, 43, no. 268, to which Beloch has replied in the *N. Rh. Mus.*, 43, 114. Fränkel cites as an analogous case the fact that in Delos the ἱεροποιοί had the ἱερά and the δημοσία κιβωτὸς under their supervision and issued separate accounts for each. See *Bull.* 6, p. 6.

[1] The ἀπαρχή of the tribute paid to the goddess was μνᾶ ἀπὸ τοῦ ταλάντου: C.I.A., I. 226. 260. 315. The Hellenotamiai paid it to the goddess and their accounts were checked by the Logistai. Documents concerning these payments are extant, C.I.A., I. 226-272. To this regular payment of this ἀπαρχή to the sacred treasury I refer, as does Holwerda, *ibid.*, 113/4, the passage in the decree of the Ecclesia C.I.A., I. 32, which I here quote from Dittenberger, *Syll.*, 14: (ἐκ δὲ τῶν φόρω)ν κατατιθέναι κ(ατὰ τὸ)ν ἐνιαυτὸν τὰ ἑκά(στοτε γενόμενα παρὰ τ)οῖς ταμίασι τῶν (τῆς Ἀθ)ηναίας τοὺς Ἑλληνο(ταμίας). Holwerda rightly takes as the basis of his explanation the expression in C.I.A., I. 40: ὅσον τῇ θε(ῷ ἀπὸ τ)οῦ φόρου ἐγίγ(ν)ετο. Kirchhoff, *ib.*, 33, understands by it the surpluses from the tribute, which he says were paid as deposit to the temple treasury to be kept in the custody of the treasurers of Athene. With regard to the date of the decree just quoted I agree with Kirchhoff and assign it to 435/4 B.C. Beloch's date (*ib.* 43, 121/2) between the end of 419/8 B.C. and the spring of 416 is impossible; for the inscription makes provision for the institution of treasurers of the other gods, and other inscriptions prove that those treasurers existed as early as 429/8 B.C. Cf. C.I.A., I. 191. On the other hand the wording of the document prevents our supposing as Beloch does, *ib.*, 43, 118/9, that the new arrangement recommended in it was merely the increase of the number of those treasurers to 10.

[2] In the decree of the Ecclesia 435/4 B.C., it is enacted, that after the monies due to the gods have been paid, for which purpose are to be employed τά τε παρὰ τοῖς Ἑλληνοταμίαις ὄντα νῦν καὶ τἆλλα ἃ ἐστι τούτων τῶν χρημάτων καὶ τὰ ἐκ τῆς δεκάτης ἐπειδὰν πραθῇ—εἰς τὸ νεώριον καὶ τὰ τείχη τοῖς περιοῦσι χρῆσθαι χρήμασ(ιν . . .). See Dittenberger, *Syll.*, 14. I conjecture that as a rule the employment of the περιόντα χρήματα was determined by decree of the Ecclesia, as indeed was natural.

The employment of this money paid into the temple treasury was subject to certain formalities. Although a fixed annual amount could be spent without any special decree, on improvements in the festival appointments, and for other purposes that can no longer be ascertained; this fixed amount could not be exceeded—at any rate, not beyond a margin of 10,000 drachmas.[1] Money from the sacred treasury could not be used in greater amounts than this, except by decree of the Ecclesia; and any one who proposed such a decree had to have a special ἄδεια voted for him by a full meeting of the Ecclesia.[2] If this ἄδεια were granted, and a formal decree of the Ecclesia then passed concerning the employment of monies from the sacred treasury, the treasurers of the goddess thereupon paid out the sum decided upon by the decree to the persons specified by name in it. The advances from the sacred treasury made under these conditions were as a rule advances which the State undertook to repay with interest calculated up to the time of repayment.[3] It appears also that the treasurers of Athene took

---

[1] The Ecclesia-decree of 435/4 B.C. enacted, after certain provisions in the mutilated beginning of the decree as to the employment of a certain sum of money: (τοῖς δ)ὲ ἄλλοις χρήμασ(ιν παρ)ὰ τῆς Ἀθηναίας, το(ῖς τε νῦν οὖσιν ἐμ πόλει κα)ὶ ἅττ' ἂν τὸ λο(ιπὸν ἀν)αφέρηται, μὴ χρῆσ(θαι μηδὲ ἀπαναλίσκειν ἀ)π' αὐτῶν ἐς ἄλλο (τι, μηδὲ) ἐς ταῦτα ὑπὲρ μυ(ρίας δραχμὰς δοῦναι κελ)εύειν, ἐάν τι δέῃ. See Dittenberger 14 B, 11 ff.

[2] The Ecclesia decree of 435/4 B.C. in Dittenberger, *Syll.*, 14 B, 15 ff., enacts in regard to this: (ἐς ἄλλ)ο δὲ μηδὲν χρῆσθα(ι τοῖς χρήμασιν, ἐὰν μὴ τ)ὴν ἄδειαν φσηφ(ίσηται ὁ) δῆμος ἐάνπερ ἡ (ἐκκλησία ᾖ περὶ τῆς ἐσφο)ρᾶς. ἐὰν δέ τις (εἴπῃ ἢ)ἐπιφσηφίσῃ μὴ ἐ(φσεφισμένης του τῆς ἀδεί)ας, χρῆσθαι το(ῖς χρήμ)ασιν τοῖς τῆς Ἀθη(ναίας, ἐνεχέσθω τοῖς αὐ)τοῖς οἷσπερ ἐὰ(ν . . .) φέρειν εἴπῃ ἢ ἐπι(φσηφίσῃ).

[3] The items introduced in the accounts of the treasurers of Athene under the heading Ἀθηναῖοι ἀνήλωσαν with the name of the Archon of the year contain the sums which were taken from the sacred treasury in C.I.A., I. 180-183 with the explicit addition ψηφισαμένου τοῦ δήμου τὴν ἄδειαν. It is usually said of the treasurers παρέδομεν or παρέδοσαν. ἐδανείσαμεν occurs once in 183 instead, but I regard it as merely a more precise expression for παρέδομεν. On this point I cannot agree with Kirchhoff, *ib.*, 41 A, nor with Beloch 39, 58. That advances were made from the treasury of Athene and of the other gods is shown by the wording at the beginning of the decree of 435/4 B.C.: ἀποδοῦναι τοῖς θεοῖς (τ)ὰ χρήματα τὰ ὀφειλόμενα, ἐπειδὴ τῇ Ἀθηναίᾳ τὰ τρισχίλια τάλαντ(α) ἀνενήνεγκται ἐς πόλιν ἃ ἐφσέφιστο, νομίσματος ἡμεδαποῦ. See Dittenberger 14 A, 2 ff. In this 3,000 tal. were certainly included the 1,276 tal. for the Samian war, and the 128 tal. for some unknown purpose, which are mentioned in C.I.A., I. 177. Cf. also the calculation by the Logistai of the interest on the sum of about 5,500 tal. advanced in the 11 years 438-423 B.C., from the treasuries of Athene Polias, Nike and the other gods. C.I.A., I. 273. I do not regard the inscriptions C.I.A., I. 177-192 as records of debts as Kirchhoff does, but as accounts rendered by the treasurers of

temporary charge of those sums in any current year, concerning the employment of which no decree had yet been passed. From such monies the treasurers could make advances on the strength of a mere vote of the Ecclesia.[1] To all appearance the sacred treasury on the Acropolis never again during the 4th century became large enough for money to be advanced from it for war purposes.[2] The reason of this I believe to be that in the 4th

Athene. Kirchhoff's theory is opposed by the introductory words 'Ἀθηναῖοι ἀνήλωσαν, as Beloch 39, 58 observes. The treasurers of Athene without doubt received, at every payment they made, a receipt or acknowledgment from those officials to whom they advanced the money. Cf. the provisions for repayment of the moneys owing to the gods in the Ecclesia-decree of 435/4 B.C. Dittenberger 14 A, 10 ff.: ἀποδόντων (δὲ τ)ὰ χρήματα οἱ πρυτάνεις μετὰ τῆς βουλῆς καὶ ἐχσαλειφόντων, ἐπει(δὰν) ἀποδῶσι, ζητήσαντες τά τε πινάκια καὶ τὰ γραμματεῖα καὶ ἐάμ π(ου ἄλ)λοθι ᾖ γεγραμμένα. ἀποφαινόντων δὲ τὰ γεγραμμένα οἵ τε ἱερ(ῆς κ)αὶ οἱ ἱεροποιοὶ καὶ εἴ τις ἄλλος οἶδεν. When these advances were made, the treasuries had not yet been centralised on the Acropolis.

[1] These are the so-called ἐπέτεια out of which according to the preamble of C.I.A., I. 188 the treasurers of Athene in 410/9 B.C. had paid or advanced at least 180 tal. That all these monies were included in the regular yearly revenue of the temple of Athene, as Kirchhoff, ib., 49 ff., assumes, I agree with Beloch, ib, 39, 56 ff. in considering impossible. Beloch has already remarked, p. 59, that the payments are obviously made from different funds. All the same τὰ ἐκ Σάμου sc. χρήματα from which in I. 188 money is assigned to the amount of over 95 tal. have not yet been satisfactorily explained, though attempts have been made by Beloch, ib., 36 ff., 60/1. Holwerda, ib., 107/8, and Busolt in the *N. Rh. Mus.* 38, 309. In C.I.A., I. 184/5 also, 412/1 B.C., the treasurers make payments from various funds (ἐκ τῶν εἰς τὰς τρι)ήρεις (cf. Thuc. 2, 24; 8, 15. Philoch., *fr.*, 116), ἐκ τοῦ Παρθενῶνος ἀρ(γυρίου—χρυ)σίου οὗ οἱ ξύμμαχο(ι—)ΤΧΧΧΧ 'Αθηναίας Ν(ίκης. Part of the treasury therefore consisted of a fund into which the allies made payments. Out of the ἐπέτεια the treasurers made payments or assigned money ψηφισαμένου τοῦ δήμου, where Kirchhoff wishes to supply τὴν ἄδειαν. Goldstaub, *de ἀδείας notione et usu in iure publico*, 56, 4, Breslau, 1889, holds that the ἄδεια was not necessary for proposals concerning the employment of the ἐπέτεια.

[2] There is no explicit evidence that advances were made from the temple treasury in the 4th cent. What is meant by τὰ δέκα τάλαντα from which acc. to C.I.A., II. 17. 44. 84. 86, the treasurers of the goddess in 378 B.C. were to pay the expenses of setting up inscr.-stelai, is quite uncertain. Hartel, *Stud. üb. att. Staatsr. u. Urkundenwesen*, 131 ff.; Fellner, *z. Gesch. d. att. Finanzverwalt.*, 33 ff.; Fränkel in the *Aufs. f. Curtius*, 47; Panske, *de magistratib. att. qui saec. a. Chr. n. IV. pecunias publ. curabant*, 21 ff., Leipzig, 1890, all explain it as an advance from the temple treasury from which the treasurers, they say, paid money in case of need. I hold with Köhler in the *Herm.* 5, 12 that it was a fund to meet current expenses, deposited with the treasurers of the goddess.

G.A.

century the surpluses of the league's revenues remained in the federal treasury, and that the surpluses of the administration, if there ever were any, were used for the Theoricon, which had been already set on foot in the last years of the Peloponnesian war. Thus at the end of the war there was no money in hand which by consecration to Athene could be put in reserve in the temple treasury for future needs.[1]

The practice of appropriating the government surpluses for the Theoricon, was limited by law by the rule that these surpluses **Finance of the fourth century.** were to be used for military purposes at any rate in time of war.[2] But even this rule was neglected in practice while Eubulos was in power: the surpluses were then under all circumstances distributed in the form of Theorica. The proposal of Apollodoros to restore the Theoric fund to its original use, though adopted in 348 B.C. or 350 by the Ecclesia, was attacked in a γραφὴ παρανόμων and again rescinded.[3]

---

[1] The existence of a federal treasury in the 2nd Athenian league follows from C.I.A., II. 17. 44 sqq. For the history of the Theoricon in the 4th cent. see Fickelscherer, *de theoricis Atheniens. pecuniis*, 19 ff., Leipzig, 1877. Harp. θεωρικά· θεωρικὰ ἦν τινα ἐν κοινῷ χρήματα ἀπὸ τῶν τῆς πόλεως προσόδων συναγόμενα. ταῦτα δὲ πρότερον μὲν εἰς τὰς τοῦ πολέμου χρείας ἐφυλάττετο καὶ ἐκαλεῖτο στρατιωτικά, ὕστερον δὲ κατετίθετο εἴς τε τὰς δημοσίας κατασκευὰς καὶ διανομάς, ὧν πρῶτος ἤρξατο Ἀγύρριος ὁ δημαγωγός. So also Suid. θεωρικά, Art. 2. Arist., *Pol.*, 2, 7, p. 39, 27 sqq., and 7 (6), 5, p. 186, 17 sqq. Bekker discusses the gradual increase of the Theoric fund. The statement in Plut., *Per.*, 9, that Pericles introduced the Diobelia is contradicted by Arist. 28, 3, according to whom it was Cleophon who was responsible. Aristotle is corroborated by the fact that in 410 B.C., when Cleophon was the leading demagogue (see my *Beitr.*, 335 ff.), the treasurers of Athene for the first time made payments out of the ἐπέτεια for the Diobelia. Cf. C.I.A., I. 188. This supplied the demagogues with a means of agitation, as may be seen from what Xen., *Hell.*, 1, 7, 2, according to Dindorf's emendation, says about Archedemos. It goes without saying that even in the 4th cent. sums of money were temporarily deposited for safety in the custody of the treasurers of Athene. This explains C.I.A., II. 737, p. 508. But it cannot be stated for certain what part was taken by the treasurers of the goddess in C.I.A., II. 612.

[2] (Dem.) 59, 4 : κελευόντων μὲν τῶν νόμων, ὅταν πόλεμος ᾖ, τὰ περιόντα χρήματα τῆς διοικήσεως στρατιωτικὰ εἶναι.

[3] Æsch. *in Ctes.* 251. For the proposal of Apollodoros cf. (Dem.) 59, 4, 5. For its date Schaefer, *Dem. u. s. Zeit*, 2¹, 77, who puts it 350 B.C.; Blass, *att. Beredsamk.*,¹ 3, 1, 276, who with Weil gives 348 B.C. Justin. 6, 9 assumes as *terminus a quo* the surpluses were used as Theorica, the death of Epaminondas. Dem. 1, 19; 3, 10/11 allude to the motion of Apollodoros. For the law which Eubulos is said to have carried in consequence of Apollodoros's motion, cf. *Schol.* on Dem. 1, 1 : ἐπιχειρήσαντος Ἀπολλοδώρου τινὸς πάλιν

It was not till 339/8 B.C. that it was resolved on the motion of Demosthenes to employ all surpluses of the State revenues for war purposes.[1]

No regular budget, *i.e.* estimate of the annual revenues and expenditure, was ever drawn up at Athens, but in the course of time a series of observations had been made, quite enough to show how far the various receipts sufficed to meet the various items of expenditure. The practice thus arose of assigning certain definite sources of revenue to meet definite expenses to which they were pretty nearly equal in amount; *e.g.* expenses of administration were met by the customs, and those of the judicature were defrayed out of the court-fees of the litigants and the fines inflicted on the condemned.[2] All State revenues were paid in at fixed dates to the Apodectai before the Boule, and they paid them over into the chests of the various boards of magistrates after the Boule had given its consent to the scheme of distribution they proposed.[3] Of the sums thus distributed we find some mentioned in Inscriptions under specified heads, *e.g.* τὰ (εἰς τὰ) κατὰ ψηφίσματα ἀναλισκόμενα τῷ δήμῳ, τὰ κατὰ

Budget.

αὐτά (τὰ θεωρικά) ποιῆσαι στρατιωτικὰ βουλόμενος Εὔβουλος ὁ πολιτευόμενος, δημαγωγὸς ὤν, πλείονα εὔνοιαν ἐπισπάσασθαι τοῦ δήμου πρὸς ἑαυτόν, ἔγραψε νόμον τὸν κελεύοντα θανάτῳ ζημιοῦσθαι, εἴ τις ἐπιχειροίη μεταποιεῖν τὰ θεωρικὰ στρατιωτικά. Similarly Liban. in the *Hypothesis* to the *Olynthiac* speeches. The accuracy of this statement is called in question by Sauppe on *Ol.*, 1, § 19, Boehnecke, *Forsch. auf. d. Geb. d. att. Redner*, 1, 184, Hartel, *demosth. Stud.*, 1, 31 ff., etc., but Schaefer, *Dem. u. s. Zeit*, 1¹, 184/5, and Blass, *op. cit.*, 277, regard it as historically true.

[1] Cf. Philoch., *fr.* 135 = Müller, *fr. hist. gr.*, 1, 406. In the archonship of Lysimachides 339/8: τὰ δὲ χρήματ' ἐψηφίσαντο πάντ' εἶναι στρατιωτικά, Δημοσθένους γράψαντος.

[2] The τέλη for the διοίκησις: Dem. 24, 96 sqq.; the administration of justice paid for by the πρυτανεῖα: (Xen.), *de Rep. Ath.*, 1, 16; Poll. 8, 38; Phot. *sub verb.*; and by the fines: Aristoph., *Eq.*, 1358 sqq.; Lys. 27, 1. Cf. Arist. Byz. *ap.* Boissonade Herodian, *Epimer.*, p. 287 = *fr.* 38 Nauck: μέτοικος δέ ἐστιν, ὁπόταν τις ἀπὸ ξένης ἐλθὼν ἐνοικῇ τῇ πόλει, τέλος τελῶν εἰς ἀποτεταγμένας τινὰς χρείας τῆς πόλεως.

[3] Aristot., *Pol.*, 7 (6), 8, p. 190, 12 sqq.: ἄλλη δ' ἀρχή, πρὸς ἣν αἱ πρόσοδοι τῶν κοινῶν ἀναφέρονται, παρ' ὧν φυλαττόντων μερίζονται πρὸς ἑκάστην διοίκησιν· καλοῦσι δ' ἀποδέκτας τούτους καὶ ταμίας. Arist. 48, 2 says of the Apodectai: τῇ μὲν οὖν προτεραίᾳ δέχονται τὰ χρ[ήματα] καὶ μερίζουσι ταῖς ἀρχαῖς, τῇ δ' ὑστεραίᾳ τόν τε μερισμὸν εἰσ[φέρου]σι γράψαντες ἐν σανίδι καὶ καταλέγουσιν ἐν τῷ βουλευτηρίῳ καὶ προ[τιθ]έασιν ἐν τῇ βουλῇ, εἴ τίς τινα οἶδεν ἀδικοῦντα περὶ τὸν μερισ[μὸν ἢ ἀρ-]χοντα ἢ ἰδιώτην, καὶ γνώμας ἐπιψηφίζουσιν, ἐάν τίς τι δοκῇ ἀδ[ικεῖν]. Cf. also ch. 47, and the section on the Apodectai, p. 287 sqq.

ψηφίσματα ἀναλισκόμενα τῇ βουλῇ, τὰ δέκα τάλαντα.[1] The titles and amounts of these separate items were fixed by law.[2] Any increase temporary or permanent could only be effected by a decree passed on the motion of the Nomothetai.[3]

[1] See Hartel, *Stud. üb. att. Staatsrecht u. Urkundenwesen*, 130 ff. The expenses of publishing decrees of the Ecclesia were defrayed by the ταμίας τοῦ δήμου ἐκ τῶν (εἰς τὰ) κατὰ ψηφίσματα ἀναλισκομένων τῷ δήμῳ. So e.g. C.I.A., II. 47. 50. 54. 69. 114. 120. 176. 186. From the same fund the same ταμίας pays ἐφόδια to envoys: C.I.A., II. 64. 89. 251. 366, and pays for wreaths of honour: 'Αθήν. 6, p. 153. A slightly different title for this fund is ἐκ τῶν (εἰς τὰ) κατὰ ψηφίσματα τῷ δήμῳ μεριζομένων: 'Αθην. 6, p. 153. C.I.A., II. 115; ἐκ τῶν κοινῶν χρημάτων: C.I.A., II. 243. The ταμίαι τῆς βουλῆς pay ἐκ τῶν κατὰ ψηφίσματα ἀναλισκομένων τῇ βουλῇ: C.I.A., II. 61. The ταμίαι τῆς θεοῦ make payments ἐκ τῶν δέκα ταλάντων for posting up decrees of the Ecclesia: C.I.A., II. 17. 44. 84. 86. *Bull.* 12, 141/2. I cannot agree with Hartel, p. 132, and Fellner, *z. Gesch. d. att. Finanzverwalt.*, 35/6, in identifying this fund with τὰ δέκα τάλαντα of C.I.A., II. 270. I agree with Köhler, *Herm.*, 5, 12 and regard τὰ δέκα τάλαντα as a fund for current expenses deposited with the treasurers of the goddess. See also page 337[2]. τὰ στρατιωτικὰ too (from which the Apodectai of 347/6 B.C. make an advance in Dittenberger 101, and 349/8 money is taken εἰς τὴ(ν πα)ράληψιν τοῦ σίτου: C.I.A., II. 108) can at that date signify nothing more than a special fund, probably for current expenses of armament, not the surpluses of the administration.

[2] This is to be inferred from C.I.A., II. 38: με(ρ)ίσαι δὲ τὸ ἀργύριον (τ)ὸ εἰρημένον τοὺς ἀποδέκτας ἐκ τῶν καταβαλλομένων χρημά(τ)ων, ἐπειδὰν τὰ ἐκ τῶν νόμων μερ(ίσωσι), i.e. the Apodectai are to assign the sum specified out of the monies paid to them, after they have paid away the items directed by law (τὰ ἐκ τῶν νόμων). μερίσαι however does not mean "use up," as Hartel 134 and Fellner, *z. Gesch. d. att. Finanzverwalt.*, pp. 21/2, contend, but signifies the assignment of the monies to the various funds. See also Panske 51 ff.

[3] Cf. C.I.A., II. 115*b*, where the ταμίας τοῦ δήμου is directed by decree of the Ecclesia to pay a drachma per day to Peisitheides ἐκ τῶν κατὰ ψηφίσματα ἀναλισκομένων τῷ δήμῳ; in line 40 ff. occur these words: ἐν δὲ τοῖς νομοθέται(s) τ(οὺς πρόεδρ)ους οἳ ἂν προεδρεύωσιν (καὶ τὸν ἐ)π(ισ)τάτην προσνομοθετῆ(σαι τὸ ἀργύρ-)ιον τ(ο)ῦτο μερίζειν τ(οὺς ἀποδ)έκτας τῷ ταμίᾳ τοῦ δήμ(ου κατὰ τὸ)ν ἐνιαυτὸν ἕκαστον, ὁ δὲ τ(αμίας ἀπ)οδότω Πει(σι)θείδει κατὰ (τὴν πρυτ)α(νε)ίαν ἑκάστην. Fränkel, *d. att. Geschworenenger.*, p. 24, holds that a decree of the Nomothetai was necessary for any permanent burden on the State chest. Valeton in *Mnemos.*, 1887, 15 ff., says that such a decree was necessary for every temporary as well as permanent increase of any items which had been once legally fixed. The latter theory is supported by the fragmentary decree of 335 B.C. in the 'Εφ. ἀρχ., 1885, p. 131 ff.= *Herm.*, 24, 136 ff., where the ταμίας τοῦ δήμου pays for golden crowns ἐκ τῶν ε(ἰς τ)ὰ κατὰ ψηφ(ίσματα ἀναλισκομένων τῷ δήμ)ῳ. The Nomothetai are to be summoned, ὅπως δ' ἂν ὁ (ταμ)ίας ἀπολάβ(ῃ τὸ ἀργύριον———). Similarly the injunction in a decree of 329 B.C.: τὸ δὲ ἀργύριον τ(ὸ) εἰς τὴν θυσίαν (in honour of Amphiaraos) προδανεῖσαι τὸν ταμίαν τοῦ δήμου, ἐν δὲ τοῖς πρώτοις νομοθέταις προσνομοθετῆσαι τῷ ταμ(ί)ᾳ, δοῦναι δὲ καὶ τὰς τριάκοντα δ(ρ)αχμὰς τὸν ταμίαν τοῦ δήμου τοῖς (α)ἱρεθεῖσιν ἐπὶ τὸν ἀγῶνα, ἃς εἴρηται διδόναι ἐν τῷ νόμῳ τῷ αἱρεθέντι ἐπὶ τὴν εὐταξίαν: 'Εφ. ἀρχ., 1891, p. 89. Dem. 24, 26-28 also admits

The management of financial matters was properly in the hands of the Boule; but the Ecclesia was also kept informed of the condition of the finances by reports sent in every Prytany by the ἀντιγραφεὺς τῆς διοικήσεως concerning the receipts, and by the provisional εὔθυναι in each Prytany of the monies expended by the various officials.[1] *Disposers of the Finances.*

Finance was controlled on the one hand by the Boule, inasmuch as payments were made to the Apodectai before the Boule, and the names of State-debtors were erased in presence of the Boule; on the other hand all officials on leaving office had to render account to the Logistai.[2] It was further customary for the State to give each financial official a slave, who knew how to write, as an assistant; these slaves did the actual work of drawing up the accounts, and so exercised a control over the officials.[3] *Control of Finance.*

of explanation on this theory. See Schaefer, *Dem. u. s. Zeit*, 1¹, 334. As regards the νομοθέτας that occur in an Ecclesia decree of 320 B.C. in Dittenberger 337, Köhler would emend to ἀθλοθέτας, (see *Ber. d. bayr. Ak.*, 1886, p. 115, 1). In *Seeurk.* XIV.a, 200 ff., p. 464=C.I.A. II. 809a, 200 sqq. the Apodectai are instructed by decree of the Ecclesia to pay out money for the trierarchic crowns, but in this case most probably a fixed amount was appointed by law. C.I.A., II. 38, 181, is too fragmentary to admit of any certain inference. In Dittenberger 101, 40 ff., the Apodectai simply advance money ἐκ τῶν στρατιωτικῶν χρημάτων. We must also regard as a financial grant the decision of a δικαστήριον chosen by lot concerning the pattern of the πέπλος for the Panathenaia, cf. Arist. 49, 3: ἔκρινεν δέ ποτε καὶ τὰ παραδείγματα τὰ εἰς τὸν πέπλον ἡ βουλή, νῦν δὲ τὸ δικαστήριον τὸ λαχόν· ἐδόκουν γὰρ οὗτοι καταχαρίζεσθαι τὴν κρίσιν.

[1] On the Boule as supreme financial authority see pp. 279/80. Of the ἀντιγραφεύς, Aesch. *in Ctes.* 25 says: καθ' ἑκάστην πρυτανείαν ἀπελογίζετο τὰς προσόδους τῷ δήμῳ. Provisional rendering of accounts by the officials in each Prytany: Lys. 30, 4. 5.

[2] Control by the Boule, pp. 279/80; rendering of accounts before the Logistai, p. 216 ff.

[3] *Schol.* on Dem., 2, 19: δούλους εἶχον δημοσίους οἱ Ἀθηναῖοι ἀπὸ αἰχμαλώτων ποιήσαντες καὶ ἐδίδασκον τούτους γράμματα καὶ ἐξέπεμπον αὐτοὺς ἐν τοῖς πολέμοις μετὰ τῶν ταμιῶν καὶ στρατηγῶν, ἵνα ἀπογράφοιεν τὰ ἀναλισκόμενα. οὐκ ἀκαίρως δὲ τοῦτο ἐποίουν, ἀλλ' ἵνα διὰ τὸ δύνασθαι τούτους τύπτειν ὡς δούλους ἔχωσι μανθάνειν τὸ ἀληθές. Cf. Arist. 47, 48. Accordingly we find mention of δημόσιοι for the φυλακὴ τῶν χρημάτων in the case of the Strategoi: Dem. 8, 47, a δοῦλος as ἀντιγραφεύς for the receipt of εἰσφορά: Lex. Seguer. 197, 24 sqq. Dem. 22, 70. In C.I.A., II. 403, where it is resolved to appoint a commission for making a dedicatory offering out of the τύποι of the ἥρως ἰατρός which were to be melted up, we find the words: ἃ δὲ ἂν οἰκονομήσωσιν, λόγον καταβαλέσθαι αὐτούς· ἑλέσθαι(ι) δὲ καὶ δημόσιον τὸν ἀντιγραψόμενον, ὅπως ἂν τούτων γενομένων ἔχει καλῶς καὶ εὐσεβῶς τεῖ βουλεῖ καὶ τῷ(ι) δήμῳ τὰ πρὸς τοὺς θεούς. See also Köhler in *Mitth. d. dtsch. arch. Inst. in Ath.*, 5, 269.

B. The Expenditure.

The expenditure of the Athenian State was divided into ordinary and extraordinary expenses. To the ordinary expenses
Ordinary Expenditure. belonged first the expenditure for religious purposes, *i.e.* for the sacrifices and festivals.[1] The cost of the State religious ceremonies was defrayed by the State; the ex-
Religion. penses of the festivals and sacrifices of particular corporations were paid by those corporations themselves.[2] The Athenians had twice as many festivals as the other Greeks, and the State expenses they involved must have been very considerable, even allowing for the fact that the temple revenues were also available to defray them.[3] Besides the actual victims for sacrifice, which were supplied by the State, considerable expense was involved in the musical, gymnastic, and equestrian competitions connected with the various festivals, though this was partly met by Leiturgies.[4] Another item of expenditure connected with the festivals was the θεωρικόν, which was originally introduced by Cleophon and was afterwards distributed at all the more important festivals to enable the poorer citizens to celebrate them with a better meal than usual: finally during the period of Eubulos' influence all the surplus revenues of the

---

[1] εἰς τὴν ἱερὰν διοίκησιν = εἰς τὰς θυσίας: Dem. 24, 96/7. On these expenses see Boeckh, *Publ. Econ.*, 1, 293 ff. (Bk. II., c. 12) and Fränkel in Boeckh³ 2, p. 60; no. 378 ff.

[2] Lex. Seguer. 240, 28 sqq.: τὰ μὲν δημοτελῆ θύματα ἡ πόλις δίδωσιν, εἰς δὲ τὰ δημοτικὰ οἱ δημόται, εἰς δὲ τὰ ὀργεωνικὰ οἱ ὀργεῶνες, οἱ ἂν ὦσιν ἑκάστου τοῦ ἱεροῦ, εἰς δὲ τὰ τῶν γονέων τὰ γένη. Cf. Harp. δημοτελῆ καὶ δημοτικὰ ἱερά. Hesych. δημοτελῆ ἱερά.

[3] Cf. (Xen.) *de Rep. Ath.*, 2, 9: θύουσιν οὖν δημοσίᾳ μὲν ἡ πόλις ἱερεῖα πολλά. 3, 8: καὶ ἄγουσι μὲν (οἱ 'Αθηναῖοι) ἑορτὰς διπλασίους ἢ οἱ ἄλλοι. Contributions from the temple revenues: Harp. ἀπὸ μισθωμάτων. Δίδυμός φησιν ὁ γραμματικὸς ἀντὶ τοῦ ἐκ τῶν τεμενικῶν προσόδων. ἑκάστῳ γὰρ θεῷ πλέθρα γῆς ἀπένεμον, ἐξ ὧν μισθουμένων αἱ εἰς τὰς θυσίας ἐγίγνοντο δαπάναι. See Boeckh, *Publ. Econ.*, 1, 296a (Bk. II., c. 12).

[4] Occasionally 300 oxen for one sacrifice: Isocr. 7, 29. In C.I.A., I. 188, 5,114 drachmai are estimated as the cost of the hecatomb at the great Panathenaia. The δερματικόν, which formed an item in the State revenues, amounted in 7 months of the year 334/3 B.C. to 5,148¾ drachmai: C.I.A., II. 741. In 410/9 B.C. the Athlothetai received εἰς Παναθήναια τὰ μεγάλα 5 tal. 1,000 dr.: C.I.A., I. 188. Prizes for the contests in music (Mommsen, *Heort.*, 139, 140), gymnastics (Mommsen, p. 141, 150 ff.), and horse-racing (Mommsen, pp. 153, 160 ff.). Cf. Arist. 60, 3. See also the collection of instances in Michaelis, *der Parthenon*, 321 ff. Cf. Dem. 4, 35: εἰς ἃ (Παναθήναια καὶ Διονύσια) τοσαῦτ' ἀναλίσκετε χρήματα ὅσα οὐδ' εἰς ἕνα τῶν ἀποστόλων.

State were swallowed up by the Theoricon.[1] Lastly, expenditure was also required for the Theoriai sent to foreign festivals, especially to the national Greek games.[2] It is impossible to estimate the total amount spent for religious purposes.

Another most important item of ordinary annual expenditure was the pay given under various forms and titles.[3] The oldest form of this pay was the μισθὸς δικαστικός, introduced by Pericles.[4] Its original amount cannot be determined with certainty; the analogy of the Ecclesiasts' fee makes 1 obol appear probable; the evidence we have, which however comes mostly from later periods, is in favour

Pay.

μισθὸς δικαστικός.

---

[1] According to the explicit statement of Arist. 28, 3 the Diobelia was introduced by Cleophon; against this the general statement of Plut., *Per.*, 9, has no weight. Arist. is corroborated by the fact that the Diobelia appears in the accounts for the first time in 410 B.C.: C.I.A., I. 188. 2 obols for each of the three festival days of the Dionysia amount to one drachma. This explains Philoch. *ap.* Harp., θεωρικά. See Sauppe in the *Abh. d. Sächs. Ges. d. Wissensch.*, 1855, p. 20 ff. The Theoricon was afterwards distributed not only for the Dionysia and Panathenaia (cf. Dem. 44, 37), but also for all the great festivals. Harp. θεωρικά—ἄλλοτε μέντοι ἄλλως ὡρίσθη τὸ διδόμενον εἴς τε τὰς θέας καὶ εἰς τὰς θυσίας καὶ ἑορτάς. Cf. Phot. θεωρικόν Art. 1. Even at the Dionysia, in addition to the free tickets for the theatre (see Benndorf in the *Zeitschr. f. d. östr. Gymn.*, 1875, p. 23 ff.), money for the festival was also distributed. Cf. Philin. *ap.* Harp., θεωρικά, with Isocr. 8, 82. In 407/6 B.C. money is paid in the second Prytany εἰς τὴν διωβολίαν Ἀθηναίᾳ Νίκῃ: C.I.A., I. 189a. See Benndorf, *op. cit.*, 606/7. In 410/9 B.C. in the 3rd, 4th, 5th and 7th Prytanies a total amount of 15 tal. 4,787 dr. 3½ ob. was paid εἰς διωβελίαν: C.I.A., I. 188. Boeckh, *Publ. Econ.*, 2, 11, 12, 17, gives a scheme showing how this amount was divided between the several festivals. In the *N. Rh. Mus.*, 39, 239 ff., Beloch regards the διωβελία mentioned in the inscr. quoted above as a contribution towards the Dicasts' pay, which he believes to have been 2 obols at that date on the strength of Aristoph., *Frogs*, 140. But in verse 141: φεῦ· ὡς μέγα δύνασθον πανταχοῦ τὼ δύ' ὀβολώ certainly refers to the entrance money for the Theatre, and the εἰς τὴν διωβολίαν Ἀθηναίᾳ Νίκῃ in C.I.A., I. 189a certainly does not support Beloch's explanation of the Diobelia. On the Theoricon see Boeckh 1, 306 ff. (Bk. 2, ch. 13) and also Fickelscherer, *de theoricis Atheniensium pecuniis*, Leipzig, 1877.

[2] Cf. *e.g.* Androt. *ap.* Schol., Aristoph., *Aves*, 1541: τοῖς δὲ ἰοῦσι Πυθῶδε θεωροῖς τοὺς κωλακρέτας διδόναι ἐκ τῶν ναυκληρικῶν ἐφόδιον ἀργύρια καὶ εἰς ἄλλο ὅτι ἂν δέῃ ἀναλῶσαι.

[3] Dem. 24, 97 reckons as a special item of expenditure for the διοίκησις, τὰ εἰς τὰς ἐκκλησίας καὶ τὰς θυσίας καὶ τὴν βουλὴν καὶ τοὺς ἱππέας. Arist. 24, 3 estimates that in the period of prosperity of the first Athenian league there were in Athens 20,000 men receiving pay.

[4] Cf. Aristot., *Pol.*, 2, 12, p. 56, 22 Bekker: τὰ δὲ δικαστήρια μισθοφόρα κατέστησε Περικλῆς. Aristot. 27, 3: ἐποίησε δὲ καὶ μισθοφόρα τὰ δικαστήρια Περικλῆς πρῶτος, ἀντιδημαγωγῶν πρὸς τὴν Κίμωνος εὐπορίαν. Cf. Plut., *Per.*, 9.

of 2 obols as the original Dicast's fee.[1] In 425/4 B.C. Cleon increased the original fee to 3 obols, and it seems to have remained at that amount during the whole of the 4th century.[2] The total amount spent annually on Dicasts' fees cannot be estimated with exactness.[3]

Another class of fees paid by the State was the μισθὸς βουλευτικός, also introduced by Pericles in all probability.[4] It amounted to a drachma per day, afterwards 5 obols, and we must suppose that it was paid even on days when the Boule did not sit.[5] On this assumption the fees of the Bouleutai amounted to about 25–30 talents per annum.

μισθὸς βουλευτικός.

[1] The analogy of the μισθὸς ἐκκλησιαστικός is emphasized by Boeckh, *Publ. Econ.*, 1, 328 (Bk. II., c. 15), who on p. 328 ff. seeks to prove that 1 obol was the original fee. See also Pflug in the *Waldenburg Progr.*, 1876, p. 11 ff. I cannot agree with Boeckh, p. 329 (Bk. II., c. 15), that Aristoph., *Clouds*, 863, is evidence for this theory. Schol. on Aristoph., *Wasps*, 300: ἦν μὲν γὰρ ἄστατον τὸ τοῦ μισθοῦ. ποτὲ γὰρ διωβόλου ἦν, ἐγίνετο δὲ ἐπὶ Κλέωνος τριώβολον. Schol. on Aristoph., *Wasps*, 88: ἐδίδοτο δὲ αὐτοῖς χρόνον μέν τινα δύο ὀβολοί, ὕστερον δὲ Κλέων στρατηγήσας τριώβολον ἐποίησε ἀκμάζοντος τοῦ πολέμου τοῦ πρὸς Λακεδαιμονίους. Cf. Schol. on Aristoph., *Birds*, 1541. *Frogs*, 140. Fritzsche, *de mercede iudicum*, Rostock, 1839, supposes from this that 2 obols was the original fee.

[2] Increased to 3 obols by Cleon., Schol. on Aristoph., *Wasps*, 88, 300. The date is determined by the consideration that in the Acharnians there is no allusion to the increased fee, but in the Knights it is mentioned. See Müller-Strübing, *Aristoph.*, p. 149 ff. C. Wachsmuth in *N. Rh. Mus.*, 34, 161 ff., argued that there was a further increase to 4 obols, quoting Theopomp. *ap.* Poll. 9, 64, explained by Phot. τετρωβολίζων· τὸ δικαστικὸν τετρώβολον λαμβάνων. ἐγένετο γὰρ καὶ τοσοῦτόν ποτε. Kock in *N. Rh. Mus.*, 35, 488 ff., and Boeckh, *Publ. Econ.*, 1, 168 (Bk. I., c. 21), 378b (Bk. II., c. 22), considers the passage from Theopomp. to refer to the pay of the military troops. So Fränkel in Boeckh[3], 2, p. 67, no. 437. Lipsius in *Meier und Schömann att. Proc.*,[2] 1, 166, 89. In Aristot.'s time the Dicasts' fee was 3 obols: Arist. 62, 2. Zenob. 6, 29 (Suid., Phot., Diogenian. 8, 62) says in explanation of the phrase ὑπὲρ τὰ Καλλικράτους: Ἀριστοτέλης δέ φησιν ἐν τῇ Ἀθηναίων πολιτείᾳ Καλλικράτην τινὰ πρῶτον τῶν δικαστῶν τοὺς μισθοὺς εἰς ὑπερβολὴν αὐξῆσαι, ὅθεν καὶ τὴν παροιμίαν εἰρῆσθαι, but the statement is erroneous. Zenobius alludes to Arist. 28, 3, where Callicrates is said to have increased the Diobelia.

[3] Aristophanes' computation in the *Wasps*, 661 sqq., of 150 tal., putting the number of Heliasts at 6,000, and therefore making them sit 300 days in every year, is too high; though we have the evidence of Arist. 24, 3 that there were 6,000 Heliasts when the power of the first Athenian league was in its zenith.

[4] It was paid in the best period of the first Ath. league: Arist. 24, 3. And also in 412/1 B.C.: Thuc. 8, 69.

[5] Hesych.: βουλῆς λαχεῖν· τὸ λαχεῖν βουλευτὴν καὶ δραχμὴν τῆς ἡμέρας λαβεῖν. Arist. 62, 2: εἶθ' ἡ βουλὴ (sc. μισθοφορεῖ) πέντε ὀβολούς. τοῖς δὲ πρυτανεύουσιν εἰς σίτησιν [ὀβολός (so Blass fills up the lacuna) π]ροστίθεται [[δέκα προστίθενται]].

The introduction of the μισθὸς ἐκκλησιαστικός, which was originally 1 obol, is attributed to Agyrrhios, and took place soon after the archonship of Eucleides. It was soon raised to 2 obols, and shortly before the publication of Aristophanes' *Ecclesiazusæ* was further increased by Agyrrhios to 3 obols. In the course of the 4th century it was increased still further, so that in Aristotle's time the μισθὸς ἐκκλησιαστικὸς for the κυρία ἐκκλησία was 9 obols, and for other meetings of the Ecclesia 1 drachma.[1] It appears that a specified sum of money was assigned to defray the costs of each meeting of the Ecclesia, at any rate in the beginning of the 4th century. When the

That it was paid every day seems to be attested by Hesych. and also by Thuc. 8, 69: ἔφερον δὲ αὑτοῖς τοῦ ὑπολοίπου χρόνου παντὸς (sc. τὸν μισθὸν) αὑτοί καὶ ἐξιοῦσιν ἐδίδοσαν. The βουλεία was a stipendiary office, and the fee for it cannot be compared with the Ecclesiasts' fee.

[1] Arist. 41, 3: οὐ συλλεγομένων δ' εἰς τὴν ἐκκλησίαν (after the constitutional changes of Eucleides' archonship) ἀλλὰ πολλὰ σοφιζομένων τῶν πρυτάνεων, ὅπως προσιστῆται τὸ πλῆθος πρὸς τὴν ἐπικύρωσιν τῆς χειροτονίας, πρῶτον μὲν 'Αγύρριος ὀβολὸν ἐπόρισεν, μετὰ δὲ τοῦτον Ἡρακλείδης ὁ Κλαζομένιος ὁ βασιλεὺς ἐπικαλούμενος διώβολον, πάλιν δ' 'Αγύρριος τριώβολον. For Heracleides, Immisch in the *Berl. phil. Wochenschr.*, 1891, pp. 707/8, quotes Plat., *Ion.*, 541 D: Ἀπολλόδωρον οὐ γιγνώσκεις τὸν Κυζικηνόν; ποῖον τοῦτον; ὃν 'Αθηναῖοι πολλάκις ἑαυτῶν στρατηγὸν ᾕρηνται ξένον ὄντα· καὶ Φανοσθένη τὸν Ἄνδριον καὶ Ἡρακλείδην τὸν Κλαζομένιον, οὓς ἥδε ἡ πόλις ξένους ὄντας, ἐνδειξαμένους ὅτι ἄξιοι λόγου εἰσί, καὶ εἰς στρατηγίας καὶ εἰς τὰς ἄλλας ἀρχὰς ἄγει. Cf. also Athen. 11, 506 A. Ælian, *Var. Hist.*, 14, 5. Aristoph., *Eccl.*, 183 sqq., also attests that Agyrrhios was concerned in the introduction or increasing of the Ecclesiast's fee. Aristoph., *Eccl.*, 300 sqq., shows that it was raised to 3 obols shortly before the publication of the *Ecclesiazusæ*, which Goetz (*Acta phil. soc. Lips.*, ed. Ritschl 2, 335 ff.) assigns to 390 B.C., Velsen (*phil. Anz.*, 6, 392 ff.) 391 B.C. Aristot. 62, 2 says of his own day: μισθοφοροῦσι δὲ πρῶτον [μὲν ὁ δῆμος] ταῖς μὲν ἄλλαις ἐκκλησίαις δραχμήν, τῇ δὲ κυρίᾳ ἐννέα ⟨ὀβολούς⟩. It is however quite possible that the statement in the Append. Vat., no. 411, *parœmiogr.*, Goett. 1, 437: ὀβολὸν εὗρε Παρνύτης (so we should read with Boeckh, *Publ. Ec.*, 1, 320d (Bk. II., c. 14) acc. to Hesych. Παρνόπη)· Καλλίστρατος 'Αθήνησι πολιτευσάμενος, ἐπικαλούμενος δὲ Παρνύτης, μισθὸν ἔταξε τοῖς δικασταῖς καὶ τοῖς ἐκκλησιασταῖς· ὅθεν σκωπτόντων αὐτὸν τῶν κωμικῶν εἰς παροιμίαν ἦλθε τὸ γελοῖον refers to this increase of the μισθὸς ἐκκλησιαστικός. We must suppose that the statesman Callistratos of Aphidna is meant; being nephew of Agyrrhios, he followed his uncle's policy. If so, the increase took place probably between 387 and 362 B.C. Dem. 24, 135, says of him: καὶ ἐπ' ἐκείνῳ Καλλίστρατος δυνάμενος καὶ ἀδελφιδοῦς ὢν αὐτοῦ οὐκ ἐτίθει νόμους. In the *N. Rh. Mus.*, 46, 459/60, Rühl calls in question the accuracy of the information in Arist. It is not clear what is meant in the resolution of the Athenians at Eleusis in the archonship of Menecles (283 or 282 B.C.) in honour of the ταμίας τῶν σιτωνικῶν by the words: πολλὴν σπουδὴν πεποίηται περὶ τὴν τοῦ σίτου δόσιν καὶ τῶν ἐκκλη(σ)ιαστικῶν τῶν διδομένων ἐπὶ τὸν σῖτον ('Εφ. ἀρχ., 1887, p. 187).

tokens representing this specified sum were all distributed, the Ecclesiasts who arrived later received no pay.[1] In the case of the μισθὸς ἐκκλησιαστικὸς again, no satisfactory computation of the annual total cost can be made.

Other fees. Besides these three main classes of fees there still remain to be mentioned the fees of the magistrates, which were subject to the rule that no magistrate should receive two fees.[2]

Bounties. Another item of State expenditure was the bounties given to the whole people or to particular individuals. The only general largesses to the whole people to be mentioned, with the exception of the Theoricon discussed already in another connexion, are the distributions of corn. This was sometimes given to the people absolutely gratis, particularly on occasions when foreign princes made presents of corn to Athens; at other times corn was purchased by the State by means of a fund raised by voluntary private contributions, or at State expense, and then sold at a low price to individual citizens.[3] It was only in the latter cases that the State finances were affected.

[1] Aristoph., *Eccl.*, 380 sqq., 185 sqq. Wuerz, *de mercede eccl. Atheniens.*, Berlin, 1878, p. 35 ff. The citizens attending were first given σύμβολα. Cf. *Eccl.*, 298 sqq. For these σύμβολα see Benndorf, *Zeitschr. f. d. östr. Gymn.*, 1875, pp. 597/8, and Wuerz, p. 36, 3.

[2] The rule μὴ διχόθεν μισθοφορεῖν : Dem. 24, 123. That various magistrates received pay is stated by (Xen.), *de Rep. Ath.*, 1, 3 : ὁπόσαι δ' εἰσὶν ἀρχαὶ μισθοφορίας ἕνεκα καὶ ὠφελείας εἰς τὸν οἶκον, ταύτας ζητεῖ ὁ δῆμος ἄρχειν. According to Arist. 24, 3, when the first Athenian league was at its strongest, ἀρχαὶ ἔνδημοι μὲν εἰς ἑπτακοσίους ἄνδρας, ὑπερόριοι δ' εἰς ἑπτακοσίους received their τροφὴ ἀπὸ τῶν φόρων καὶ τῶν τελῶν καὶ τῶν συμμάχων. For the payment of magistrates see p. 222. Salary of ἐπίσκοπος : Aristoph., *Birds*, 1025. Fee of συνήγοροι one dr. : Arist., *Wasps*, 691 and Schol. *ad loc.* Salaries of subordinate officials : Dem. 19, 249. C.I.A., I. 324 : μισθὸς ὑπογραμματεῖ Πυργίωνι ʼΟτ(ρ)υνεῖ Δ Δ Δ. Envoys paid 2 dr. : Aristoph., *Ach.*, 66. The inscr. speak of ἐφόδια only : C.I.A., II. 64. 89. 251. 366. Cf. Lex. Seguer. 296, 12 : πορεῖον· τὸ διδόμενον τοῖς πρεσβευταῖς ὑπὲρ τοῦ πορευθῆναι εἰς τὴν πρεσβείαν ὥσπερ ἐφόδιον. So Et. M., *sub verb.* For these and other classes of salaries see Boeckh, *Publ. Econ.*, 1, 336 ff. (Bk. 2, ch. 16).

[3] Corn distributed gratis: Aristoph., *Wasps*, 715. Bounties of foreign princes Boeckh, *Publ. Econ.*, 1, 125 sq. (Bk. 1, ch. 15), and Fränkel's additions in Boeckh[3] 2, p. 25, no. 156 ff. C.I.A., II. 811. 812. 314. Poll. 8, 103 : καὶ ἐν ταῖς σιτοδοσίαις ἐγίνοντο σίτου ἐπιγραφεῖς, ὡς ʼΑντιφῶν. Sale at low price : Dem. 34, 37. Voluntary contributions, εἰς τὴν σιτωνίαν τὴν ὑπὲρ τοῦ δήμου: Dem. 34, 39. Fund for purchase of corn: Dem. 20, 33. Such a purchase of corn by the State is meant in the decree published in the *Mitth. d. dtsch. arch. Inst. zu Ath.*, 5, 321.

Among gratuities to individuals the first to be mentioned are those given for the orphans of citizens slain in war. These orphans, of whom there was a considerable number because of the numerous wars, were reared at State expense till they attained their majority, and were then presented with a πανοπλία.[1] Maintenance of orphans.

The State relief, probably given originally only to those citizens who had been invalided in war, was afterwards extended, on account of the increase of poverty at Athens, to those invalids or cripples who possessed less than 3 minæ.[2] This relief, given every Prytany by the Boule on proof that it was needed, seems to have amounted at first to an obol per day, and to have been afterwards increased to 2 obols.[3] Maintenance of ἀδύνατοι.

Among the bounties given to individuals must also be counted those presentations as marks of honour which were made by the State either directly in the form of cash, or indirectly in the form of permanent or temporary right of dining in the Prytaneion, presentation of a golden crown of honour, or the erection of statues.[4] Gifts as marks of honour.

---

[1] Aristot., *Pol.*, 2, 8, p. 41, 11 sqq. Bekker. Plat., *Menex.*, 249. Æsch. *in Ctes.* 154. Large number of orphans: Isocr. 8, 82.

[2] Plut., *Sol.*, 31, attributes to Peisistratos ὁ νόμος ὁ τοὺς πηρωθέντας ἐν πολέμῳ δημοσίᾳ τρέφεσθαι κελεύων. On the other hand, the speaker of Lys. 24 obviously was not invalided on military service, otherwise he would certainly have mentioned the fact in his speech.

[3] See Boeckh, *Publ. Econ.*, 1, 342 ff. (Bk. 2, ch. 17). Arist. 49, 4: δοκιμάζει δὲ καὶ τοὺς ἀδυνάτους ἡ βουλή· νόμος γάρ ἐστιν, ὃς κελεύει τοὺς ἐντὸς τριῶν μνῶν κεκτημένους καὶ τὸ σῶμα πεπηρωμένους, ὥστε μὴ δύνασθαι μηδὲν ἔργον ἐργάζεσθαι, δοκιμάζειν μὲν τὴν βουλήν, διδόναι δὲ δημοσίᾳ τροφὴν δύ' ὀβολοὺς ἑκάστῳ τῆς ἡμέρας· καὶ ταμίας ἐστὶν αὐτοῖς κληρωτός. Cf. also Harp. ἀδύνατοι· (Suid. Hesych. in a more concise form) Αἰσχίνης ἐν τῷ κατὰ Τιμάρχου. οἱ ἐντὸς τριῶν μνῶν κεκτημένοι τὸ σῶμα πεπηρωμένον (τὸ δὲ σῶμα πεπηρωμένοι, Lex. Seguer.). ἐλάμβανον δὲ οὗτοι δοκιμασθέντες ὑπὸ τῆς βουλῆς δύο ὀβολοὺς τῆς ἡμέρας ἑκάστης ἢ ὀβολόν, ὥς φησιν Ἀριστοτέλης ἐν Ἀθηναίων πολιτείᾳ, ὡς δὲ Φιλόχορός φησιν ἐννέα δραχμὰς κατὰ μῆνα. ἔστι δὲ καὶ λόγος τις ὡς Λυσίου περὶ τοῦ ἀδυνάτου, ἐν ᾧ ὡς ὀβολὸν λαμβάνοντος (Lys. 24, 13, 26) μέμνηται. According to the Lex. Seguer. 345, 15 sqq., Lys. puts the amount of relief at one obol (cf. 24, 13. 26), Aristot. at 2, Philochor. at 5. The numbers given in the text are what appear to me most probable. On Philochor.'s statements see Boeckh, *Publ. Econ.*, 1, 345 (Bk. 2, ch. 17). Distribution every Prytany: Æsch. *in Tim.* 104. Hullemann, *quæst. græcæ*, II., p. 1 ff., supposes that up to Aristotle's time 2 obols a day was given, then a monthly dole was introduced.

[4] Gifts of cash: Æsch. *in Ctes.* 187. Dem. 20, 115. Plut., *Arist.*, 27. The Prytanes dine in the Tholos: Harp. θόλος, and probably other officials too: Dem. 19, 190. For the dining in the Prytaneion see R. Schoell in

Another item of annual expenditure was the expense of inscribing decrees of the people on stone, and setting up such inscriptions; it varied from 10 to 60 drachmas for each inscription.[1]

Expenses of publishing inscription-documents.

There was also considerable outlay incurred for the maintenance and supply of the State slaves, especially the 1,200 Scythian bowmen.[2]

Maintenance of State slaves.

Even in time of peace provision had to be made for war, and money had to be spent for war purposes.[3] Among such expenses come the cost of maintenance of the cavalry, amounting to 40 tal. per annum; pay of the crew of the Paralos, and the other express ships[4] of the State; money for providing war materials, for the maintenance of the fleet, and the repairing of the walls and fortifications.[5]

Expenses for war-purposes in time of peace.

A specified sum had also to be devoted every year to keep in repair the other public buildings and the streets.[6]

Repairs of public buildings.

Herm., 6, 14 ff. Arist. 24, 3 mentions πρυτανεῖον in discussing those who were supported ἀπὸ τῶν κοινῶν. Presentation of golden crowns: Seeurk., XIVa., 195 ff., p. 463 = C.I.A., II. 809a, 190 sqq. Erection of statues: Dem. 20, 70. Æsch. *in Ctes.* 243. See Boeckh, *Publ. Econ.*, 1, 347 (Bk. 2, ch. 18) ff.

[1] See R. Schoene, *griech. Reliefs*, 18 ff., whose statements, however, are modified by Hartel, *Stud. üb. att. Staatsrecht u. Urkundenwesen*, 140 ff. See also Fränkel on Boeckh, *St. d. Ath.*,[3] 2, p. 34, n. 204.

[2] Boeckh, *Publ. Econ.*, 1, 290 (Bk. 2, ch. 19) ff.

[3] The monies used for this purpose were in my opinion τὰ στρατιωτικὰ χρήματα, from which in 347/6 B.C. the Apodectai made an advance: Dittenberger, *Syll.*, 101, and in 349/8 B.C. money was assigned εἰς τὴ(ν πα)ράληψιν τοῦ σίτου: C.I.A., II. 108.

[4] τὰ εἰς τοὺς ἱππέας (Dem. 24, 97) amounted acc. to Xen., *Hipparch.*, 1, 19, to nearly 40 tal. per ann. In 410/9 B.C. more than 16 tal. were paid by the treasurers of Athena to the Hellenotamiai for σῖτος ἵπποις in 4 Prytanies: C.I.A., I. 188. Cf. also II. 612. The crew of the Paralos, also free Athenians (Thuc. 8, 73), received 4 obols per day per man: Harp. Πάραλος = Suid. Πάραλος, Art. 2. Other sacred Triremes were the Salaminia (Thuc. 3, 33. 77; 6, 53), and at a later date the Ammonias, the Antigonis, Demetrias, Ptolemais. Philoch. *ap.* Lex. Cantabr. 676. On the sacred Triremes see Boeckh., *Publ. Econ.*, 1, 339 (Bk. 2, ch. 6, etc.) ff. Seeurk., 76 ff. Köhler, in *Mitth. d. dtsch. arch. Inst. in Ath*, 8, 168 ff. For other military and police expenses in the more prosperous days of the 1st Ath. league cf. Arist. 24, 3.

[5] For the provision of war material cf. Pseudoplut., *vit. Lyc.*, 3, 5. C I.A., I. 32: ἐπειδὰν δὲ ἀποδεδομένα ᾖ τοῖς θεοῖς (τὰ χρ)ήματα, ἐς τὸ νεώριον καὶ τὰ τείχη τοῖς περιοῦσι χρῆσθαι χρήμασ(ιν). Aristoph., *Daitaleis ap.* Suid. ἀναλίσκειν. εἰς τὰς τριήρεις δεῖν ἀναλοῦν ταῦτα καὶ τὰ τείχη,—εἰς οἷ' ἀνάλουν οἱ πρὸ τοῦ τὰ χρήματα. Cf. Arist. 46, 1.

[6] In an Ecclesia-decree of 320/19 B.C. the Agoranomoi are instructed to

Examples of extraordinary expenditure are the costs of new public buildings, which amounted to very considerable sums under the supremacy of Pericles, and again when Lycurgus was the financial administrator of the State.[1]   *Extraordinary expenditure.*

The heaviest extraordinary expenditure was, naturally, that caused by war. The pay of the troops and their maintenance, the equipment of the fleet, and the providing of war materials, swallowed up large sums of money proportionate to the strength of the forces mobilised on each occasion.[2]   *War expenses.*
To give an idea of the amount of these war expenses, it may be mentioned that the crew of one trireme cost 30–40 minæ per month; the expenses of the Samian war, which lasted 9 months, amounted to 1,000–1,200 talents; and the siege of Potidaia, for 2 years and a few months, cost 2,000–2,400 talents.[3]

C. *The Revenues.*

The revenues of the Athenian State can be classified into ordinary and extraordinary, and each of these categories can be again divided into direct and indirect receipts.

act for the Astynomoi and see to the repairing of the street followed by the Pompe to the temple of Zeus Soter and of Dionysos, and in their own official capacity they are to undertake the plastering of the marketplace and the repair of the Agoranomion in the Piræus. τὸ δ'ἀνάλωμα εἶναι εἰς ταῦτα ἐκ τοῦ ἀργυρίου, οὗ οἱ ἀγορανόμοι διαχειρίζουσιν: Dittenberger, *Syll.*, 337. Cf. Arist., 50, 1: κληροῦνται δὲ καὶ ἱερῶν ἐπισκευασταὶ δέκα ἄνδρες, οἱ λαμβάνοντες τριάκοντα μνᾶς παρὰ τῶν ἀποδεκτῶν ἐπισκευάζουσιν τὰ μάλιστα δεόμενα τῶν ἱερῶν.

[1] Boeckh., *Publ. Econ.*, 1, 281 (Bk. 2, ch. 10) ff. For the great building operations under the administration of Pericles see E. Curtius, *Stadtgeschichte von Athen*, 138 ff., and under Lycurgos, E. Curtius, *ib.*, 213 ff., C. Curtius in the *Phil.*, 24, 260 ff.

[2] On the pay and money for maintenance see Boeckh, *Publ. Econ.*, 1, 377 (Bk. 2, ch. 19) ff., on the cost of equipment and war materials, *id.*, 1, 397 ff.

[3] Tissaphernes paid the Spartans in the Peloponnesian war 36 minæ per ship (Thuc. 8, 29), though he need only have paid 30 minæ; Xen., *Hell.*, 1, 5, 5. Dem. 4, 28 puts down as monthly σιτηρέσιον for 1 trireme 20 minæ, to which an equal amount must be added for the μισθός. See Boeckh 1, 381/2 (Bk. 2, ch. 22). War expenses for the Samian war of 9 months (Thuc. 1, 117): Isocr. 15, 111. Nep., *Timoth.*, 1, C.I.A., I. 177, seem to show that 1,276 tal. were borrowed from the temple treasury for this war. The entire cost of the war was perhaps still more: Busolt, in *N. Rh. Mus.*, 38, 309. Cost of siege of Potidaia 2,000 tal.: Thuc. 2, 70; 2,400: Isocr. 15, 113.

Ordinary direct revenues. The main source of ordinary direct revenue was the τέλη, including customs, tolls, and taxes.

Among the customs the first to be mentioned is the πεντηκοστή, levied to the amount of 2 per cent. on the value of all articles of commerce brought into or taken out of Athenian harbours.[1] The duty was levied apparently when the ship was loaded or unloaded; and the annual sum paid by the tax-farmers for these dues is stated at 36 talents on the one occasion recorded, an amount which enables us to estimate the total value of the imports and exports at about 2,000 talents.[2] As to the levying of customs on imports and exports carried by land we have no definite information.

1) τέλη.
a) πεντηκοστή.

Nor can we tell for certain what was the amount of the dues called ἐλλιμένιον, or for what purpose they were paid; though Boeckh's conjecture, that they were levied as a charge for the use of the harbour, seems very plausible.[3]

b) ἐλλιμένιον.

---

[1] Lex. Seguer. 297, 22 sqq.: τῶν εἰσαγομένων εἰς τὸν Πειραιᾶ φορτίων καὶ ἀνδραπόδων ἐκ τῆς ἀλλοδαπῆς πεντηκοστὴν ἐτέλουν οἱ ἔμποροι. καὶ τοῦτο ἐκαλεῖτο πεντηκοστεύεσθαι. So Et. M. πεντηκοστευόμενον. Duty levied on imported corn: (Dem.) 58, 27, on ruddle from Keos: C.I.A., II. 546, on clothing and drinking vessels: Dem. 21, 133. The duties on exports are attested by Dem. 34, 7, and by the statement of accounts of the Delian Amphictyones in Boeckh 2, 95 = C.I.A., II. 814, where the πεντηκοστή is reckoned even on a sacrificial ox belonging to an Athenian Theoria sent to Delos. On the πεντηκοστή see Boeckh, *Publ. Econ.*, 1, 425 ff. Beloch, in the *N. Rh. Mus.*, 39, 47 ff., argues from (Xen.), *de Rep. Ath.*, 1, 17, that the duty on exports and imports during the Archidamian war was a ἑκατοστή, since (Xen.) does not mention the amount of revenue produced by the πεντηκοστή. Beloch supposes that it was increased to a πεντηκοστή during the progress of the war. Boeckh 1, 432 ff. identifies the ἑκατοστή in (Xen.) with the ἐλλιμένιον.

[2] The customs were levied on unloading: Dem. 35, 29, and therefore probably when the cargo was loaded also. Andoc., *de Myst.*, 133/4, mentions an annual contract sum of 36 tal., which represents an import and export of 1,800 tal., to which something must be added because of the cost of collection and the profits of the tax-farmers.

[3] Lex. Seguer. 251, 30: ἐλλιμενισταί· οἱ ἐν τοῖς λιμέσι τελῶναι. Aristoph., *Wasps*, 659, puts down λιμένας as one source of revenue. Poll. 8, 132 and Aristoph. *ap.* Poll. 9, 31 leave the matter vague. Eupol. *ap.* Poll. 9, 30: ἐλλιμένιον δοῦναι πρὶν εἰσβῆναί σε δεῖ seems to make the ἐλλιμένιον a toll on embarkation, which should be compared with the ἐπιβατικὸν mentioned in C.I.A., I. 35, l. 7; 34, l. 12. See Wachsmuth, *d. St. Ath.*, 2, 1, 153, 1 Boeckh, *Publ. Econ.*, 1, 431 ff.

The δεκάτη or toll of 10 per cent. can be proved to have been levied in certain periods on the cargoes of ships passing through the straits of Byzantium. Besides this there must have been another kind of δεκάτη, concerning the nature of which nothing definite is known.[1]   *c) δεκάτη.*

The ἐπώνιον was a tax on sales, paid to the State treasury by the purchaser at every sale. The amount varied: but since the ἐπώνιον seems at various times to have been 1 per cent., it may be plausibly identified with the ἑκατοστή, the exact nature of which is uncertain.[2]   *d) ἐπώνιον.*

[1] Lex. Seguer. 185, 21: δεκάτη καὶ εἰκοστή· οἱ Ἀθηναῖοι ἐκ τῶν νησιωτῶν ταῦτα ἐλάμβανον. Harp., δεκατευτάς. Poll. 9, 28/9. Xen., *Hell.*, 1, 1, 22 says of Alcibiades and the other Athenian Strategoi of 411 B.C.: ἐντεῦθεν δ' ἀφικόμενοι τῆς Καλχηδονίας εἰς Χρυσόπολιν ἐτείχισαν αὐτὴν καὶ δεκατευτήριον κατεσκεύασαν ἐν αὐτῇ καὶ τὴν δεκάτην ἐξέλεγον τῶν ἐκ τοῦ Πόντου πλοίων. The δεκάτη we are told was re-established by Thrasybulus about 390 B.C.: Xen., *Hell.*, 4, 8, 27. 31. Dem. 20, 60. Acc. to Polyb. 4, 44, 4 the establishment of the δεκάτη by Alcibiades was its first institution. The circumstances described in the decree concerning Methone, C.I.A., I. 40, and the Ἑλλησποντοφύλακες there mentioned can therefore have nothing to do with the δεκάτη. I now agree with Kirchhoff, *Sitzungsber. d. Berl. Ak.*, 1888, 1179 ff., that the inscr. refers to a temporary embargo on the corn trade. Duncker's hypothesis (*Abhandl. z. griech. Gesch.*, 160 ff.) that the δεκάτη was instituted on the occasion of Pericles' expedition to the Pontos must also be rejected for the same reason. Nothing certain can be stated as to the nature of the δεκάτη mentioned in a decree of 435/4 B.C., C.I.A., I. 32.

[2] Lex. Seguer. 255, 1: ἐπώνια μὲν τὰ ἐπὶ τῇ ὠνῇ προσκαταβαλλόμενα, ὥσπερ ἑκατοσταί τινες. Cf. Poll. 7, 15. Aristoph., *Wasps*, 658 mentions as a source of revenue τὰς πολλὰς ἑκατοστάς, because they were paid at the various sales. The ἑκατοστὴ ἡ ἐν Πειραιεῖ in (Xen.), *de Rep. Ath.*, 1, 17, can scarcely have been such a tax on sales. In the *Ber. der Berl. Ak.*, 1865, 541 ff., Köhler computes from data supplied by the lists of goods confiscated by the State and sold by the Poletai (cf. C.I.A., I. 274-281; IV. 3, 277c, p. 177) that the ἐπώνιον was 1·obol for a purchase amounting to 1-4 drachmæ, 3 ob. for one of 5-50 dr., 1 dr. for 50-100 dr. In a list of this kind dating from the first decade after Eucleides out of a sum of 410 dr. 9 dr., *i.e.* a πεντηκοστή, is put down as ἐπώνιον. See Köhler, *ib.*, p. 546 ff.=C.I.A., II. 777. On the other hand, in C.I.A., II. 784-788, a ἑκατοστή occurs in the case of sales of land, and Köhler on C.I.A., II. 784 argues from C.I.A., II. 721A, col. 1. 10-12, that this was paid into a temple-treasury. But this inference is not inevitable, for the inscription quoted does not admit of any definite conclusion. The πέμπτη in Harp. ἐπώνια (so also Suid., Et. M.) is merely a conjecture. See on the subject of the ἐπώνιον Thumser, *de civium Atheniens. munerib.*, Vienna, 1880, p. 8 ff.; he rightly rejects the theory of Büchsenschütz, *Besitz und Erwerb.*, 557, 4, who on the strength of Theophrast. *ap.* Stob. Flor. 44, 22 maintains that the ἑκατοστή was a species of judicial caution-money.

Similar in character to the ἐπώνιον was the toll levied either at the city gates or at the market place on commodities brought to Athens for sale. It varied in amount according to the nature of the commodity.[1]

e) διαπύλιον.

Among taxes levied on persons the μετοίκιον, or fee paid by the Metoicoi for State-protection, brought in the greatest revenue. It amounted to 12 drachmas per annum for each man, and 6 drachmas for a woman; women however ceased to pay when their sons attained their majority. Assuming that there were 10,000 Metoicoi, which was actually the case in 309 B.C., the μετοίκιον produced an annual revenue of 20 talents.[2]

f) μετοίκιον.

The payment of the tax for State protection did not suffice to secure the Metoicos the right of doing business in the market place; indeed he was forbidden to do so by a law of Solon's re-enacted by Aristophon. To obtain this privilege he had to pay special market dues.[3]

g) ξενικὸν τέλος.

Lastly, the πορνικὸν τέλος must be mentioned. Its amount in each case appears to have been assessed by the Agoranomoi.[4]

h) πορνικὸν τέλος.

The State did not collect these tolls and taxes directly by means of officers of its own, but sold them for a definite annual price to

---

[1] Boeckh., *Publ. Econ.*, 1, 438 ff. Hesych. διαπύλιον· τέλος τι παρ' Ἀθηναίοις οὕτως ἐκαλεῖτο. In the *Acharnians*, 896, Dicaiopolis demands from the Boeotian an eel as ἀγορᾶς τέλος, on which the Schol. remarks: ἔθος ἦν τὸ παλαιόν, ὡς καὶ μέχρι τοῦ νῦν, τοὺς ἐν τῇ ἀγορᾷ πιπράσκοντας τέλος διδόναι τοῖς λογισταῖς. Cf. *Schol.* to 723. That the impost varied for different commodities follows from the *Schol.* on Il. 21. 203: καὶ ἐν τῷ ἀγορανομικῷ δὲ νόμῳ Ἀθηναίων διέσταλται ἰχθύων καὶ ἐγχελύων τέλη and from the story about the peasant Leucon (for the real significance of this tale see Boeckh, *ib.*) who brought in skins filled with honey, and κριθὰς οὖν τοῖς φορμοῖς ἐμβαλών, ὡς ὑπὲρ κριθῶν ὀλίγον εἰσπραχθησόμενος τέλος, ἐκόμιζε: Zenob. 1, 74.

[2] Is. *ap.* Harp. μετοίκιον—Ἰσαῖος ὑποσημαίνει, ὅτι ὁ μὲν ἀνὴρ δώδεκα δραχμὰς ἐτέλει μετοίκιον, ἡ δὲ γυνὴ ἕξ, καὶ ὅτι τοῦ υἱοῦ τελοῦντος ἡ μήτηρ οὐκ ἐτέλει· μὴ τελοῦντος δ' ἐκείνου αὐτὴ τελεῖ. For details see p. 179. 10,000 Metoicoi in 309 B.C.: Ath. 6, 272 B.

[3] The Solonian law, Dem. 57, 31. 32. See Schaefer, *Dem.*, 1¹, 124. For the market dues cf. Dem. 57, 34: ἀλλ' εἰ μὲν ξένη ἦν, τὰ τέλη ἐξετάσαντας τὰ ἐν τῇ ἀγορᾷ (προσῆκε μαρτυρεῖν), εἰ ξενικὰ ἐτέλει καὶ ποδαπὴ ἦν ἐπιδεικνύντας. See Boeckh, *Publ. Econ.*, 1, 449.

[4] Aesch. *in Tim.* 119. The improbable statement of Suid. διάγραμμα τὸ μίσθωμα· διέγραφον γὰρ οἱ ἀγορανόμοι, ὅσον ἔδει λαμβάνειν τὴν ἑταίραν ἑκάστην is explained by Boeckh, *Publ. Econ.*, 1, 450, very plausibly, in the manner indicated in the text.

tax-farmers,¹ who were exempted from military service during the year for which they had bought the taxes.² Since the sums offered for the taxes were as a rule very heavy, it was generally companies or associations of tax-farmers who made the agreements with the State. Such companies had as their president a tax-farmer-in-chief, and included tax-farmers, guarantors and collectors, all of whom were interested to a greater or less extent in the profits of the bargain.³ The farmers of the πεντηκοστὴ kept accounts of the freights of all ships that entered or left the port, and had power to examine cargoes for customs purposes.⁴ Attempts at smuggling were punished by seizure of the wares that had not paid duty, and offenders could be brought before the dicasteries by the form of action called Phasis.⁵

<small>Tax-farmers.</small>

The second head of ordinary direct revenue consisted of the revenue obtained by letting out on lease the mines at Laureion and the lands and houses owned directly by the State.⁶

<small>2) Leases of state property.</small>

The most important item under this head was the proceeds of the silver mines at Laureion. The State sold to each lessee the right of exploiting a specified space in the mine district. The lessee took the space so assigned on hereditary lease, agreeing to pay $\frac{1}{24}$ of the annual profits as permanent rent to the State; the rights of the lessee could be transferred to a third party by purchase or inheritance.⁷

<small>a) The mines.</small>

---

¹ For the tax-farmers see Boeckh 1, 451 ff. The τελῶναι are described from their relation to the State, or to those who had to pay some impost, either as tax-farmers, e.g. πορνοτελῶναι, or as tax-collectors, e.g. πεντηκοστολόγοι. Cf. Poll. 9, 28 sqq. As regards the various kinds of tolls we find πεντηκοστολόγοι in Dem. 21, 133 ; 34, 7 ; ἐλλιμενισταί, in Lex. Seguer. 251, 30, εἰκοστολόγοι Aristoph., Frogs., 363, δεκατηλόγοι, Poll. 9, 29. Harp. δεκατευτάς, farmers of the διαπύλιον, Zenob. 1, 74, of the μετοίκιον, Harp. μετοίκιον ; πορνοτελῶναι, Æsch. in Tim. 119. Philonid. ap. Poll. 9, 29 ; 7, 202.

² Tax-farmers were in evil repute: Poll. 9, 32. Their exemption from military service : (Dem.) 59, 27.

³ For such a company of tax-farmers with an ἀρχώνης as their director cf. Andoc., de Myst., 133/4. For the 3 classes τελῶναι, ἐγγυηταί and ἐκλέγοντες (Dem.) 24, 144.

⁴ Dem. 34, 7 ; 21, 133.

⁵ Seizure of smuggled goods by tax-farmers: Zenob. 1, 74. Φάσις against smugglers: Poll. 8, 47.

⁶ Boeckh, kl. Schr., 5, 1 ff., Publ. Ec., 1, 413 ff.

⁷ Boeckh, kl. Schr., 5, 32 ff., J. H. Hansen, de metallis att. Comment. prior., Strassburg, 1885. The right of working new mines was purchased: Dem. 37, 37, cf. Arist. 47, 2, on which is based Harp. πωληταί. The 100 tal. which

Since it was the practice of the State to sell confiscated property, the amount of landed property owned directly by the State cannot have been very large. All such property was let on lease. The same course was pursued in the case of temple properties, whose rents were used to meet the expenses of religious ceremonies.[1]

b) Of land.

c) House-property. The receipts from rents of houses and buildings owned by the State, including the theatre, were likewise only moderate in amount.[2]

The third class of ordinary direct revenues consisted of the court fees and fines.[3] The court fees which were paid in almost all private or public legal cases, were either fixed at a certain proportion of the value of the object in dispute, or in other cases were a fixed sum of money paid for bringing the action.[4] The fine-monies consisted first of the fines, which the accuser had to pay, if he abandoned a public suit, or if he failed to obtain $\frac{1}{5}$ of the dicasts' votes, or in certain specified cases if he

3) Court fees and fines.

Themistocles used for building the fleet were the proceeds of the sale of mining rights in the newly discovered mines of Maroneia: Arist. 22, 7. Maroneia in Attica: Dem. 37, 4. Harp., *sub verb*. For the yearly payments, cf. Suid.: ἀγράφου μετάλλου δίκη· οἱ τὰ ἀργύρεια μέταλλα ἐργαζόμενοι ὅπου βούλοιντο καινοῦ ἔργου ἄρξασθαι φανερὸν ἐποιοῦντο τοῖς ἐπ' ἐκείνοις τεταγμένοις ὑπὸ τοῦ δήμου καὶ ἀπεγράφοντο τοῦ τελεῖν ἕνεκα τῷ δήμῳ εἰκοστὴν τετάρτην τοῦ καινοῦ μετάλλου. Cf. Harp. ἀπονομή. The right of sale and therefore of inheritance also follows from Æsch. *in Tim*. 101. C.I.A., II. 780–783 contain fragments of boundary marks of mining concessions.

[1] Aristoph., *Wasps*, 658 sqq., mentions among the sources of State revenue not only τέλη and μέταλλα but also μισθούς. Cf. Arist. 47, 2. 4. Andoc., *de Myst*., 92, mentions the sale of the proceeds of certain tithes belonging to the State. Athenian state-lands in the territory of Chalkis let on lease Ælian, *Var. Hist.*, 6, 1. Μισθώσεις of confiscated landed estates: C.I.A., IV. 3, 277a, p. 177. On the use made of the revenues from temple property cf. Harp. ἀπὸ μισθωμάτων.

[2] Leasing of houses belonging to the State, Xen., *de Vect.*, 4, 19.

[3] $\frac{1}{10}$ of the fine-monies belonged in certain cases to Athena, cf. the law in Dem. 43, 71. Andoc., *de Myst.*, 96; Xen., *Hell.*, 1, 7, 10; Pseudoplut., *vit. Antiph.*, 27, p. 1016 Didot. The State debtors were then debited with $\frac{9}{10}$ of the fine to the Practores, and $\frac{1}{10}$ to the treasurers of the goddess. Monies due to the State were recorded on a register kept in the temple of Athena on the Acropolis. Cf. (Dem.) 25, 70; 58, 48. Harp.=Suid. ψευδεγγραφή. Suid. ψευδέγγραφος δίκη. Boeckh, *P. Econ.*, 1, 509.

[4] For the first kind of court fees, the πρυτανεῖα, cf. Poll. 8, 38, for the second, the παράστασις Arist. 59, 3. Poll. 8, 39. Phot. παράστασις. Revenues ἀπὸ δικαστηρίων, Thuc. 6, 91. Arist., *Wasps*, 659, counts πρυτανεῖα among the public revenues.

merely lost the case: secondly, the fines inflicted on the accused in public suits if condemned; these in some cases were sums of an amount fixed by law, in other cases confiscation of property: lastly, the ἐπιβολαί inflicted by the Boule or by the magistrates.[1]

Any one who failed to pay at the appointed time money due to the State, whether rent or fines or otherwise, became a State debtor and incurred *ipso facto* the form of Atimia peculiar to such men.[2] At the same time the amount of the debt was doubled, and the State secured payment for itself by the sale of the debtor's property.[3] Further, when the time allowed for payment had elapsed, the State had power to put the debtor in prison till the debt was paid, a punishment not infrequently put in force as a deterrent against dilatoriness.[4]

State debtors.

---

[1] The fine inflicted on the accuser, if he failed to obtain ⅕ of the votes, amounted in public cases to 1000 dr.: Poll. 8, 53—the same amount if he allowed a public accusation to fall through—in private cases the Epobelia had to be paid to the defendant. Harp. ἐπωβελίαι. The State also received one class of παρακαταβολαί,—where the accuser had to pay ⅕ of the value of the object in dispute, if he laid claim to property confiscated by the State. Cf. Poll. 8, 39. Phot. παρακαταβολή, Art. 2. For the fines inflicted on condemned defendants see Boeckh, *P. Ec.*, 1, 488 ff., and on the confiscation of property 1, 516 ff. Arist., *Wasps*, 659 δημιόπρατα among the public revenues. On the ἐπιβολαί see Siegfried, *de multa quae ἐπιβολή dicitur*. Berlin, 1876, p. 69 ff.

[2] The money paid by the tax-farmers for the tolls was paid in to the State κατὰ πρυτανείαν: (Dem.) 59, 27. Cf. Arist. 47, 2 sqq., for the duties of the Poletai. They prepared lists of payments for each Prytany. The chief time for payments was the 9th Prytany. Houses purchased from the State had to be paid for within 5 years, lands within 10 years. Men punished by money fines became State debtors if the fine was not paid within a certain interval of grace allowed after the sentence was passed; as a rule probably the 9th Prytany was the limit: (Dem.) 59, 6/7, but in cases of ὕβρις, acc. to the law in Dem. 21, 47, Æsch. *in Tim.* 16, only 11 days' grace was allowed. Cf. (Dem.) 58, 49. The status of State-debtor involved Atimia, which, in case the father failed to pay, was inherited by his descendants: Dem. 22, 34. (Dem.) 25, 4; 58, 15; 59, 6. On State debtors see Boeckh, *Pub. Econ.*, 1, 506 ff.

[3] Cf. Arist. 48, 1: κἄν τις ἐλλίπῃ καταβολήν, ἐνταῦθ' ἐγγέγραπται (*i.e. ἐν τοῖς γραμματείοις*) καὶ διπλ[οῦν ἀ]νάγκη τὸ [ἐλλ]ειφθὲν καταβάλλειν ἢ δεδέσθαι καὶ ταῦτα εἰσπρά[ττειν ἢ βο]υλὴ καὶ δῆσαι [κυρ]ία κατὰ τοὺς νόμους ἐστίν. Doubling of fines overdue in the 9th Prytany, the usual time for payment: (Dem.) 59, 7, Harp. ἀδικίου; rents in arrear: Andoc., *de Myst.*, 73. The share due to the goddess increased tenfold: Dem. 24, 82.

[4] This was a provision of the τελωνικοὶ νόμοι which the Boule carried out against lessees, guarantors, and tax-farmers. Cf. Dem. 24, 144. That this provision applied to the other μισθούμενοι too, is shown by the exception

State debts could be remitted in two ways. The first method was by decree of the Ecclesia; but for this it was requisite that the proposer of the decree first obtained ἄδεια for making his proposition, by means of a ψήφισμα ἐπ' ἀνδρί. The same preliminary was necessary for a proposal to grant the debtor a period of grace within which to pay his debt.[1] Secondly, a debt might be remitted less formally by a legal fiction; the State accepted the performance of some slight service or other in lieu of the sum due.[2]

Remission of State debts.

The revenues of the State, as described up to this point, fell into two categories. The receipts from tolls, taxes, and rents were of fixed and known amounts, and could therefore supply a financial basis for the administration; the receipts from court fees and fines were naturally subject to fluctuations. Accordingly these revenues were divided into (1) regular payments, καταβολαί, including the returns from tolls and taxes let out to the tax-farmers, and from rents and leases, and (2) additional receipts, προσκαταβλήματα, consisting of the court fees and fine-monies.[3]

Classification of revenues.

made in the law of Timocrates in Dem. 24, 41. Finally Dem. 24, 96 shows that it could be extended to apply to all who had money belonging to the State in their hands. Cf. the passage from Arist. quoted in the last note.

[1] Cf. the laws quoted in Dem. 24, 45. 50, which are confirmed by § 46. Boeckh, *Publ. Ec.*, 1, 515/6; Goldstaub, *de ἀδείας notione et usu in iure publ. att.*, 32 ff. Breslau, 1889.

[2] See Boeckh in Meineke, *fr. com. gr.*, 2, 527/8 and *Publ. Econ.*, 1, 514/5. Acc. to Androt. *ap Schol.*, Aristoph., *Pax*, 347, Phormio owed the State 100 minæ, and was therefore Atimos, ὁ δὲ δῆμος βουλόμενος λῦσαι τὴν ἀτιμίαν ἀπεμίσθωσεν αὐτῷ ῥ' μνῶν τοῦ Διὸς θυσίαν; so I read with Müller-Strübing, *Aristoph.*, 689. Cf. also Plut., *Dem.*, 27, referring to a similar remission of debt: τῆς δὲ χρηματικῆς ζημίας αὐτῷ μενούσης (οὐ γὰρ ἐξῆν χάριτι λῦσαι καταδίκην) ἐσοφίσαντο πρὸς τὸν νόμον.

[3] So I explain Dem. 24, 96 sqq. The orator says there is a law in accordance with which the Boule are to employ against τοὺς ἔχοντας τά τε ἱερὰ καὶ τὰ ὅσια χρήματα, if they failed to pay, the laws laid down in the case of tax-farmers, *i.e.* put them in prison (cf. § 144): § 96. In the interest of Androtion and his associates, who had monies of this kind in their hands, and should have been dealt with κατὰ τοὺς νόμους τοὺς τελωνικούς (§ 101), Timocrates made a new law to the effect that, with the exception of tax-farmers and lessees, other debtors, if they gave sureties, should not be put in prison unless they failed to pay in the 9th Prytany. Cf. § 89 sqq. Now Dem. says in § 97, that through fear of the former law, *i.e.* of imprisonment, the προσκαταβλήματα are paid in, if τὰ ἐκ τῶν τελῶν χρήματα fall short of the government expenses. § 98 describes the serious results which must

Lastly, the most important revenues of the State during the existence of the first Athenian league were supplied by the tribute of the allies. This amounted originally to 460 talents. This total, for some time diminished in some of the items, but again brought up to the original sum by the assessment of 439/8 B.C., was then increased at the assessment of 425/4 B.C. to 1,200 talents, though as a matter of fact only 8–900 talents per annum were actually paid.[1] We have no precise information concerning the amount of the financial contributions of the mem-

Tribute.

follow the acceptance of Timocrates' law. In this § τὰ προσκαταβλήματα τοὺς μὴ τιθέντας corresponds to τοὺς ἔχοντας τά τε ἱερὰ καὶ τὰ ὅσια χρήματα of § 96, as is clear from the context of both §§. The meaning of § 98 is therefore as follows:—" If the ordinary receipts from the taxes are not sufficient for the needs of the administration, but leave a large deficit which cannot be met till the end of the year, *i.e.* till the 9th Prytany; and if, on the other hand, the Boule or Dicastery has not the power to imprison those who fail to pay the προσκαταβλήματα but by giving sureties they can delay payment till the 9th Prytany, the result must be chaos in the State." This seems to me to prove the correctness of the explanation of προσκαταβλήματα given in the text. ἱερά = the fine-monies in so far as they belonged to Athena. See p. 354[3]. Other theories, which I cannot accept, are given by Platner, *Proc.*, 1, 40; Telfy in the *Phil.*, 16, 365 ff.; Boeckh, *Publ. Ec.*, 1, 459 ff.; Schaefer, *Dem.*, 1[1], 342, 1. The statements in Suid. Phot. προσκαταβολὴ are of little weight against (Dem.) 59, 27.

[1] Ὁ πρῶτος φόρος, assessed by Aristeides acc. to Arist. 23, 5 in 478 B.C., amounted to 460 tal.: Thuc. 1, 96. Diod. 11, 47. Plut., *Arist.*, 24. Kirchhoff (*Herm.* 11, 27 ff.) argues that the tribute did not reach this amount till after the battle at the Eurymedon. Herbst in the *Phil.* 40, 318 ff., Beloch, *N. Rh. Mus.*, 43, 104 ff., Nöthe, *d. del. Bund*, p. 6, Magdeburg, 1889, reject this view. In Boeckh, *St. d. Ath.*[3], 2, 88, no. 626, Fränkel argues with considerable plausibility, from details given by Thuc., that at the time of the foundation of the league the States undertook to pay amounts considerably higher than were necessary at a later date, after the league had extended itself and the barbarian power had been decisively broken. The φόρος of the Athenian allies has been discussed by Köhler in the *Urk. u. Untersuch. z. Gesch. d. del.-att. Bundes*, but his results must be corrected in acc. with the exhaustive investigations of Busolt, in the *Phil.* 41, 652 ff. See also Guirand, *de la condition des alliés pendant la première confédération Athénienne*, 46 ff. Paris, 1888. The statement of Thuc. 2, 13, that circ. 431 B.C. ὡς ἐπὶ τὸ πολὺ 600 tal. per annum was received from the tribute is disproved by the tribute lists. Busolt, *ib.*, 703 suggests that the 600 tal. includes the war indemnity which the Samians had to pay (Thuc. 1, 117). The increase of tribute from 460 to 600 tal. in Plut., *Arist.*, 24, is a combination of Plutarch's own from Thuc. 1, 96 and 2, 13. Beloch, *N. Rh. Mus.*, 39, 34 ff., gives a different explanation of Thuc.'s 600 tal. C.I.A., I. 37, is a fragment of the assessment list of 425/4 B.C. [Hicks, no. 47]. The total of this assessment 1,200 tal. Andoc., *de pace*, 9. Æsch., *de Fals. Leg.*, 175.

bers of the second Athenian league, but they must have been considerably less than the tribute of the first league.¹

Though we cannot estimate the revenue from the various items, their amount being for the most part unknown to us, we nevertheless possess some information about the total. For example, at the beginning of the Peloponnesian war the entire revenues amounted to quite 1,000 tal., in 422 B.C., after the increase of the tribute, to almost 2,000.² Lycurgos, during his twelve years' tenure of power from 338-326 B.C., spent 18,900 tal., a total corresponding to an average annual revenue of 1,575 tal.; and even under the rule of Demetrius of Phaleron the revenues still amounted to 1,200 tal. per annum. These figures are not so much at variance with those of the 5th century as at first appears, for the value of money had fallen considerably in the interval.³ It need scarcely be said that in times of depression the annual revenues fell considerably below the amounts just given.⁴

Total amount of the entire State revenues.

Besides the direct revenues, the State received further sums indirectly, in the financial burdens imposed upon rich citizens. These public burdens, called λῃτουργίαι, were undertaken in turn by the well-to-do citizens in a fixed cycle.⁵ Besides the Trierarchia and the προεισφορά,

Ordinary indirect revenues.

---

¹ Schaefer, *Dem.*, 1¹, 26 ff.
² Boeckh., *Publ. Ec.*, 1, 566 ff. Xen., *Anab.*, 7, 1, 27, says with reference to the beginning of the Pelop. war: προσόδου οὔσης κατ' ἐνιαυτὸν ἀπό τε τῶν ἐνδήμων καὶ ἐκ τῆς ὑπερορίας οὐ μεῖον χιλίων ταλάντων : of this total 460 tal. were tribute; the other receipts therefore amounted to 540 tal. With regard to the statement of Aristoph., *Wasps*, 660, 422 B.C.: τούτων πλήρωμα τάλαντ' ἐγγὺς δισχίλια γίγνεται ἡμῖν, if we may venture to suppose that at that date the tribute amounted to 1,200 tal., that Aristoph. exaggerates, and lastly that the οὐ μεῖον in Xen. is put by litotes for "fully 1,000 or more," we may reconcile the statements of the two writers.
³ This estimate of the yearly revenues under Lycurgos is based on the decree concerning Lycurgos in Plut., p. 1,038, Didot: διανείμας ἐκ τῆς κοινῆς προσόδου μύρια καὶ ὀκτακισχίλια καὶ ἐνακόσια τάλαντα. In the *Vita Lyc.*, 25, p. 1,027, 1,200 tal. are given as the annual revenue. For Demetrios's administration cf. Duris *ap.* Ath. 12, 542c.
⁴ Cf. *e.g.* (Dem.) 10, 37.
⁵ For the etymology of λῃτουργία (this is the spelling in inscrr. till the 3rd cent. Cf. Lex. Seguer. 277, 29) cf. Ulpian on Dem. 494: λεῖτον (*i.e.* λήϊτον) ἐκάλουν οἱ παλαιοὶ τὸ δημόσιον, ὅθεν λειτουργεῖν τὸ εἰς τὸ δημόσιον ἐργάζεσθαι ἔλεγον. See Bremi's Wolf's ed. of *Lept.*, p. 48, 1. Curtius, *Grundz. d. griech. Etym.²*, p. 362, no. 585, puts under the same root λαός, λάϊτος, λήϊτος, λειτουργία. For the regular leiturgies—from which Atelia was granted

which must be discussed among the extraordinary revenues, the leiturgies included the Choregia, Gymnasiarchia, and ἑστίασις, or giving feasts to the tribesmen, for which last in most cases the Phyle concerned nominated the men who had to serve.[1]

The first of these leiturgies, the χορηγία, for which the Choregoi were as a rule appointed by the various tribes, was required for all those festivals which were accompanied by dramatic, lyric, or orchestic competitions; we know this was the case with the Panathenaia, Dionysia, Thargelia, Prometheia, and Hephaisteia. It was the duty of the Choregos to collect his chorus, pay them, supply their expenses during the time of training, and all the requisites for their performance at the festival. Further, the Choregos had to pay the χοροδιδάσκαλος who trained the chorus. The expenses involved in the Choregia varied considerably according to the character of the chorus to be provided; in the cases recorded they amounted to between 300 and 5,000 drachmæ. In the course of the Peloponnesian war so many families became impoverished that it often became necessary to allow two Phylai to take one Choregia between them, or two citizens of one Phyle to undertake one Choregia together. In Aristotle's time the Archon nominated the three richest of all the Athenians as Choregoi for the performance of the tragedies; for the comedies and for the cyclic choruses at the Dionysia each Phyle appointed one Choregos; for the cyclic choruses at the Thargelia one was appointed by every two tribes. In the time of Demetrius of Phaleron the Phylai no longer appointed the Choregoi

Choregia.

only in very few cases (cf. Dem. 20, 21)—there were about 60 persons required every year acc. to Dem. 20, 21. Boeckh, 1, 598, makes the number greater. A citizen who had in one year performed a leiturgy was free for the next: Dem. 20, 8, and no one need undertake more than one leiturgy at a time: Dem. 20, 19; 50, 9. Orphans were exempt for a year after they attained their majority: Lys. 32, 24. Cf. Arist. 56, 3, where it is said of the ἄρχων: καὶ τὰς σκήψεις εἰσ[άγει, ἐά]ν τις ἢ λελητουργη[κέ]ν[αι] φῇ π[ρ]ότερον ταύτην τὴν λῃτουργ[ίαν, ἢ ἀ]τελὴς εἶναι, λελῃτ[ουργηκὼς ἑ]τέραν λῃτουργίαν καὶ τῶν χρόνων αὐτῷ [τῆς ἀτελ]είας μὴ ἐξεληλυθό[των, ἢ τὰ] ἔτη μὴ γεγονέναι· δεῖ γὰρ τὸν ταῖς παι[σὶν χορη]γοῦντα ὑπὲρ τετταρά[κον]τα ἔτη γεγονέναι. See Boeckh, *Pub. Ec.*, 1, 593 ff.

[1] Dem. 20, 21: πόσοι δήποτ' εἰσὶν οἱ κατ' ἐνιαυτὸν τὰς ἐγκυκλίους λειτουργίας λειτουργοῦντες χορηγοὶ καὶ γυμνασίαρχοι καὶ ἑστιάτορες; acc. to Lex. Seguer. 250, 22, ἐγκύκλιοι meant αἱ κατ' ἐνιαυτὸν γινόμεναι. Dem. 39, 7: οἴσουσι νὴ Δία οἱ φυλέται τὸν αὐτὸν τρόπον ὅνπερ καὶ τοὺς ἄλλους. οὐκοῦν Μαντίθεον Μαντίου Θορίκιον οἴσουσιν, ἐὰν χορηγὸν ἢ γυμνασίαρχον ἢ ἑστιάτορα ἢ ἐάν τι τῶν ἄλλων φέρωσιν. For other leiturgies see Thumser, *de civ. Atheniens. munerib.*, p. 95 ff.

for the musical competitions; but the people entrusted the equipment of the choruses to an ἀγωνοθέτης, whose ἐπιμέλεια lasted for a year. This officer, nominated from among the richest of the citizens, had to defray at his own expense the entire cost of providing the choruses; in one case known to us this amounted to 7 tal. It is not known for certain whether this system was kept up in the two last centuries B.C. In the imperial age the old system of the Choregia was again in force.[1]

The γυμνασιαρχία, to which citizens were nominated doubtless by the Phylai, consisted in defraying the expenses of the competitors in the torch races,[2] which took place at the Panathenaia, Hephaisteia, Prometheia, and at the

Gymnasiarchia.

---

[1] On the Choregia see Boeckh, *Publ. Ec.*, 1, 600. Thumser, *de civ. Atheniens. mun.*, p. 83 ff., where the literature bearing on the subject can be found. Subsequent treatises are Brink, *inscr. Graecae ad choregiam pertinentes.* Halle, 1885. Reisch, *de musicis Graecorum certaminibus*, Vienna, 1885, p. 10 ff., 25 ff.; Lipsius, in the *Ber. d. sächs. Ges. d. W.*, 1885, 411 ff. Examples of the expenses involved are given in Lys. 21, 1-4: χορηγία τραγῳδοῖς 3,000 dr., ἀνδρικὸς χορός at the Thargelia 2,000 dr., εἰς πυρριχιστάς at the great Panathenaia 800 dr., χορηγία ἀνδράσιν εἰς Διονύσια 5,000 dr., κυκλικὸς χόρος at the lesser Panathenaia 300 dr., παιδικὸς χόρος 1,500 dr.; χορηγία κωμῳδοῖς 1,600 dr., χορηγία πυρριχισταῖς ἀγενείοις 700 dr. Acc. to Dem. 21, 156, the χορηγία αὐληταῖς ἀνδράσι cost more than τραγῳδοῖς. For the appointment of Choregoi by the Phylai cf. Dem. 20, 130. Lipsius, *ib.*, 411 ff., proved, mainly from C.I.A., II. 971, cf. also 553, that the Choregoi for tragedies and comedies competed in their own names, and therefore were not nominated by the Phylai; his view is now confirmed by Arist. 56, 3. Aristot. *ap. Schol.* Aristoph., *Ranae*, 404, attests for 412/1 B.C. ὅτι σύνδυο ἔδοξε χορηγεῖν τὰ Διονύσια τοῖς τραγῳδοῖς καὶ κωμῳδοῖς. Choregoi for two tribes at once: C.I.A., IV. 2, 387a. So too C.I.A., II. 1236 for 365/4 B.C., 1237 B.C. 364/3, 1240 B.C., 344/3. Cf. also 1251, 1255, 1261. For the system in force in Aristotle's time cf. Arist. 56. C.I.A., II. 553, shows that musical performances took place not only at the Panathenaia, Dionysia, and Thargelia, but also at the Prometheia and Hephaisteia. On the later alterations of the choregic system see Köhler, in the *Mitth. d. dtsch. arch. Inst. in Ath.*, 3, 229 ff., and Reisch 82 ff. Decrees in honour of Agonothetai: C.I.A., II. 302, 314, 317, 331, 379. For the cost of such an Agonothesia cf. C.I.A., II. 379: καὶ ἀγωνοθέτης ὑπακούσα(ς ἀνήλω)σεν ἑπτὰ τάλαντα καὶ πάλιν τὸν υἱὸν δοὺς (ἐπὶ ταύτην) τὴν ἐπιμέλειαν καὶ καλῶς τὴν ἀγωνοθεσί(αν ἐκτελέσας) προσανήλωσεν οὐκ ὀλίγα χρήματα.

[2] For the Gymnasiarchia see Boeckh, *Publ. Ec.*, 1, 609 ff. Thumser, *ib.*, p. 88 ff. The Phyle is the victor in the competitions: C.I.A., II. 1229 sqq. Xen., *de Vect.*, 4, 53, shows that the expenses of the γυμνασιαρχούμενοι were paid. Lex. Seguer. 228, 11 sqq.: γυμνασίαρχοι οἱ ἄρχοντες τῶν λαμπαδοδρομιῶν εἰς τὴν ἑορτὴν τοῦ Προμηθέως καὶ τοῦ Ἡφαίστου καὶ τοῦ Πανός, ὑφ' ὧν οἱ ἔφηβοι ἀλειφόμενοι κατὰ διαδοχὴν τρέχοντες ἧπτον τὸν βωμόν.

festivals of Pan and Bendis. The expenses of a Gymnasiarchia at the Prometheia are given as 1,200 drachmae.[1]

No definite information can be given concerning the ἑστίασις, or duty of giving a banquet to a tribe: this took place at State festivals, but it was a matter which belonged to the internal management of the Phyle itself.[2] *Feasting the tribe.*

If any one thought he was unfairly treated by being nominated for a leiturgy, for which some other citizen seemed better able to bear the expense, he was allowed, if he could prove his contention, to transfer his liability to the other. *ἀντίδοσις.*

The formal process by which this was effected was called ἀντίδοσις,[3] a term which literally signifies giving in exchange, a gift in exchange for what a person has received, and then further the reciprocal relation of a mutual exchange of gifts. This signification of an exchange of property was the original meaning of ἀντίδοσις in Athenian constitutional law, and it was only in a

---

[1] See Wecklein, *Herm.*, 7, 1873, p. 437 ff. Torch races at the Panathenaia: C.I.A., II. 1181, 1229. Lex. Seguer. 277, 22 sqq. Phot. λαμπάδος; at the festival of Hephaistos: C.I.A., II. 1340. Lex. Seguer. *ib.* and 228, 11 ff; of Prometheus: Phot. λαμπάς, Lex. Seguer. *ib.*; of Pan: Hdt. 6, 105. Phot. λάμπας. Lex. Seguer. *ib.*; Bendis: Plat., *de Rep.*, 1,327 sqq. Mommsen, *Heort.*, 425/6. Costs of the Gymnasiarchia: Lys. 21, 3.

[2] The ἑστίασις is counted among the ἐγκύκλιοι λειτουργίαι by Dem. 20, 21, cf. 21, 156. Boeckh 1, 616/7. Thumser, p. 90 ff. *Schol.* to Dem. 20, 21 in the *Bull.* 1, 147: ἑστιάτορες· οἱ τὰς φυλὰς ἐν τοῖς Διονυσίοις καὶ Παναθηναίοις τρέφοντες. Is. 3. 80: καὶ ἐν τῷ δήμῳ κεκτημένος τὸν τριτάλαντον οἶκον, εἰ ἦν γεγαμηκώς, ἠναγκάζετο ἂν ὑπὲρ τῆς γαμετῆς γυναικὸς καὶ θεσμοφόρια ἑστιᾶν τὰς γυναῖκας.

[3] Boeckh, *Publ. Ec.*, 1,749 ff., supposed that the ἀντίδοσις might be decided in any of the following ways: The person challenged undertook the leiturgy, or else a judicial trial took place to decide who should be required to perform the leiturgy. If the challenger lost the case and was ordered to serve, the question was settled. If the verdict was given against the person challenged, he could either undertake the leiturgy or exchange properties with the challenger, in which case the latter had to take the property of the other and perform the leiturgy with it. Dittenberger, in *Rudolstadt Progr.*, 1872, denied the possibility of an actual exchange of property; and his view is accepted by Blaschke, *de antidosi*, Berlin, 1876, and Max Fränkel, *Herm.*, 18, 442 ff., 1883, the latter directing his arguments especially against the view set forth by Thalheim, in the *Jahrb. f. cl. Phil.*, 1877, 613 ff., and here adopted in the text. Thalheim replied in *Herm.*, 19, 80 ff., 1884, and his main conclusions are accepted by Illing, *de antidosi*. Berlin, 1885. Fränkel again replied in Boeckh, *St. d. Ath.*[3], 2, 130, no. 883 ff. See also Lipsius in Meier[2] 737 ff. The Antidosis is attested in the case of the Choregia by Lys. 24, 9. Xen., *Œc.*, 7, 3; for the Trierarchia by Dem. 21, 78. Xen., *ibid.*; for the προεισφορά by (Dem.) 42, 5. [Cf. Lécrivain *Revue Hist.*, xiv. 276 ff.].

derived sense that the term served to denote the judicial process which became the usual substitute for the actual exchange.[1] This follows from the various ways in which the question of Antidosis could be settled.[2] The citizen who considered himself wrongly called upon to serve a leiturgy, challenged the man who, he considered, ought to perform the leiturgy rather than himself, to undertake the duty.[3] If the person challenged accepted the leiturgy, the dispute was settled. If he refused, the other could challenge him to Antidosis, *i.e.*, to exchange of properties. If this challenge was accepted—and there is evidence that this sometimes happened—an actual exchange of property took place, and the challenger then performed the leiturgy by means of the property he received in exchange for his own.[4] But, as a rule,

[1] Dittenberger, p. 12 *note*, supposes that the original form of Antidosis was an actual exchange of properties, but without judicial trial. I cannot endorse D.'s view, p. 8 ff., that in the times of Dem. and Lys. ἀντίδοσις and ἀντιδιδόναι never meant anything more than the compulsory exchange of the properties before the judicial trial. Nor is the view of Blaschke, p. 6 ff., more probable, that the object of ἀντιδιδόναι is always τὴν λειτουργίαν. When, on account of more complicated social and economical relations, the actual exchange of property had become unusual, ἀντιδιδόναι and ἀντίδοσις were used to denote the legal procedure of Antidosis generally, or its preliminaries; see Illing, *loc. cit.*, 16 ff., Lipsius in Meier², 743/4. Ἀντιδιδόναι is used both of the challenger and of the person challenged; cf. Dem. 28, 17.

[2] For the three possible solutions of a question of Antidosis see Thalheim, p. 613 ff., with whom I agree, though I do not follow him in regarding the πρόκλησις mentioned in (Dem.) 42, 19 as the first challenge to an Antidosis; see Fränkel, in *Herm.*, 18, 458 ff., Illing, *op. cit.*, 4 ff. The Lexicographers represent the Antidosis as an actual exchange of property, *e.g.* Lex. Seguer. 197, 3 sqq., Lex. Cantabr. 663.

[3] Hence the leiturgy itself is found put loosely as the object of the verb ἀντιδιδόναι; Dem. 21, 78: ἀντιδιδόντες τριηραρχίαν, Xen., *Œc.*, 7. 3: ὅταν γέ με εἰς ἀντίδοσιν καλῶνται τριηραρχίας ἢ χορηγίας.

[4] Those who hold that actual and complete exchange of properties was impossible base their theory on general considerations; see especially Fränkel, *Herm.*, 18, 442 ff. But Lys. 3, 20 gives evidence that at Athens property was sometimes obtained as a result of Antidosis; for in that passage I cannot consider δίκας ἰδίας ἐξ ἀντιδόσεως to be anything else than legal processes connected with claims obtained by the exchange of properties. The explanation of these words given by Fränkel, *ib.*, 461, is refuted by Illing 13/4. The other passages which seem to prove the possibility of an actual exchange are Dem. 20, 40; (Dem.) 42, 27; Lys. 24, 9; in these cases those who hold the opposite view have suggested various explanations, all more or less arbitrary. Dittenberger 11 regards the passage in (Dem.) 42, 27 as an unsolved problem, Blaschke 15 ff., and Fränkel 447 ff., attempt

the person challenged, if he did not consider himself justly called upon to perform the leiturgy, refused this challenge, and appealed to a judicial Diadicasia. In this case, the challenger had the property of the other marked and sealed, and the person challenged did the same to his opponent's, that neither party might fraudulently misrepresent the amount of his property. Both parties bound themselves by a judicial oath taken before the magistrate who presided over the Diadicasia to produce accurate inventories of their properties within three days. Armed with these inventories, whose correctness had to be attested once more by oath, or, if they were suspected to be false, by further proof, the litigants pleaded their case before a Heliastic court, which decided which of the two must perform the leiturgy.[1] I do not think it probable that the person challenged could still accept the exchange of property as at first offered, and so get rid of the obligation to serve the leiturgy, after being ordered to serve by the verdict of the Dicastery; but before the verdict, he could always accept either the leiturgy or the exchange.[2]

Besides the ordinary revenue the State had extraordinary receipts, which may again be divided into direct and indirect. *Extraordinary direct Revenues.*

To the direct receipts of this class belonged first the ἐπιδόσεις or voluntary contributions. These were given either for purposes of war and the defence of the country, or for religious purposes, sometimes in cash, sometimes in natural pro- *ἐπιδόσεις.*

to explain away the difficulties. Fränkel suggests that there may have been a private compromise practically equivalent to an exchange of properties; but in that case, as Thalheim rightly observes in *Herm.* 19, 83. 90, exchange of properties, even from Fränkel's own point of view, cannot have been so absolutely unknown at Athens. For the case where Demosthenes was challenged to Antidosis by Thrasylochos (Dem. 28, 17; 21, 77 sqq.) cf. Illing 24 ff.

[1] For the procedure at a judicial Antidosis cf. (Dem.) 42. The Strategoi were ἡγεμόνες of the judicial Antidosis in the case of the Proeisphora and Trierarchia: (Dem.) 42, 4; Arist. 61, 1. See the author's *Beitr.*, etc., 58 ff. The ἄρχων presided in the case of the Choregia at the Dionysia and Thargelia: Arist. 56, 3.

[2] I agree with Dittenberger, pp. 8/9, that exchange was no longer allowed after the verdict of the Dicastery. Demosthenes's case shows that it was possible to accept before the verdict was given. Remnants of lists of judicial decisions in such Diadicasiai concerning leiturgies from the first half of the 4th cent.: Köhler, *Mitth. d. dtsch. arch. Inst. in Ath.*, 7, 96 ff.= C.I.A., II. 945 (where Lipsius in Meier,[2] 742, no. 756, wishes to read διεδικάσαντο) 946, 947. Stschonkareff, in the *Mitth.*, 12, 181 ff.

ducts.[1] Voluntary contributions were invited by decree of the people, which sometimes specified the maximum and minimum amounts to be accepted. Announcements of Epidoseis were made either at once in the Ecclesia, or in the Boule and to the Strategoi.[2] Not unfrequently voluntary presents were made in special circumstances without such invitation.[3]

The εἰσφορά was devoted to war purposes, and admitted of no Ateleia, not even in the case of orphans, nor if it was required at the same time as the Trierarchia.[4] It was an extraordinary income-tax, and was imposed on each particular occasion by special decree of the Ecclesia.[5] It is uncertain on what system it was assessed in the 5th century. There is no doubt that the assessment was based on the 4 Solonian census classes, which can be shown from inscriptions to have been still in existence in 387/6 B.C.: but it must be supposed that as early as the Peloponnesian war, the first period in which war-taxes were frequently levied, these census classes were so far modified that movables as well as landed property were taken into account.[6] In all probability even before Nausinicos there were occasional

εἰσφορά

---

[1] Ἐπιδόσεις for war and defence of the country: Dem. 18, 171; Is. 5, 38; C.I.A., II. 334, 380. For religious purposes: C.I.A., II. 980, 981; Plut., *Phok.*, 9. For building a tower: II. 982. For repairs of the theatre: II. 984. ἐπίδοσις of a ship: Dem. 21, 163. ἐπιδόσεις for improvements in triremes: C.I.A., II. 804 Bb, 65 sqq. 807c. 51 sq. 808d, 105 sq. ἐπίδοσις of cheap corn: *Mitth. d. dtsch. arch. Inst. in Ath.*, 8, 211 ff.

[2] C.I.A., II. 334, where 200 dr. is given as maximum, 50 dr. minimum. Announcement of ἐπιδόσεις immediately in the Ecclesia: Dem. 21, 162; Plut., *Alcib.*, 10; Ath. 4, 168 F.

[3] Instances in Boeckh, *Publ. Ec.*, 1, 764/5.

[4] Dem. 20, 18; Xen., *Œc.*, 2, 6; Dem. 20, 28; Thumser, *de civ. Athen. munerib.*, p. 22 ff. For the orphans cf. Dem. 27, 7; 28, 4.

[5] The εἰσφορά was not a leiturgy: Thumser 25 ff. Cf. Is., *fr.*, 23. Whether ἄδεια was necessary for the proposer of an Eisphora, I can no longer venture to decide; the passage in point, C.I.A., I. 32, is too fragmentary—see Dittenberger, *Syll.*, 14 B. 15 ff. An instance in inscrr. of εἰσφοραί in the 5th cent.; C.I.A., I. 25, 55. See Thumser 19 ff.

[6] The Solonian census classes appear in inscrr. 444 B.C.: C.I.A., I. 31; in 387/6 B.C.: C.I.A., II. 14. They are also mentioned 428/7 B.C. by Thuc. 3, 16, cf. 6, 43, and 354/3 B.C. by Is. 7, 39 (Blass, *att. Bereds.*, 2, 517). Acc. to Thuc. 3, 19 the first Eisphora was in 428/7, *i.e.*, in the Peloponnesian war: see my *Beitr.*, etc., 128 ff. Aristoph., *Eq.*, 923 sqq. draws a distinction between the rich and the poorer citizens in connexion with the Eisphora. Acc. to Isocr. 17, 49 which was delivered before 392 B.C. (Blass, *att. Beredsamk.*, 2, 210) even property in slaves was assessed. Beloch, *Herm.*, 20, 245/6 holds that the transition from contributions in kind to payments in money

revisions of the assessment-lists, when the taxpayers were, if necessary, reclassified according to their wealth.[1] The citizens liable to the tax apparently made their own estimates of the amount of their property, which were then accepted or corrected by a committee of ἐπιγραφεῖς, probably a separate committee for each of the census classes.[2]

In 378/7 B.C. in the Archonship of Nausinicos a new system of assessment for the purposes of Eisphora was introduced, in connexion with the institution of Symmories for the same purpose. The entire amount of the property of the Athenians, as declared on this occasion, reached, according to Polybios, the sum of 5,750 talents; and the total assessment remained, according to the evidence we possess, at approximately the same amount up to the end of the 4th century.[3] Boeckh, arguing from the consideration that the total amount of the property of the Athenians at that date must be estimated at between 30 and 40

Assessment of Nausinicos.

---

was first effected in the 5th cent., and Poll. 8, 130 refers to the adjustment of the old census classes to the coinage system current in the 5th cent.

[1] Cf. the epigram of Anthemion in Arist. 7, 4; Poll. 8, 131, a man who was promoted from the Thetes to the class of Hippeis.

[2] The account given in the text is attested in the case of the Metoicoi by two passages in Isocr. 17, a speech delivered not later than 392 B.C., and therefore before the assessment under Nausinicos. See Blass, *att. Bereds.*, 2, 210. Isocr. 17, 49: τὸν αὐτὸν δὲ τοῦτον ἀπεγράψατο (Πασίων) μὲν ἐν τοῖς τιμήμασιν ὡς δοῦλον μετὰ τῶν οἰκετῶν τῶν ἄλλων—41: πρὸς δὲ τούτοις εἰσφορᾶς ἡμῖν προσταχθείσης καὶ ἑτέρων ἐπιγραφῶν γενομένων ἐγὼ πλεῖστον εἰσήνεγκα τῶν ξένων, αὐτὸς δὲ αἱρεθεὶς ἐμαυτῷ μὲν ἐπέγραψα τὴν μεγίστην εἰσφοράν, ὑπὲρ Πασίωνος δ' ἐδεόμην τῶν συνεπιγραφέων λέγων, ὅτι τοῖς ἐμοῖς χρήμασι τυγχάνει χρώμενος. Harp. too mentions ἐπιγραφεῖς, as a term found in Lysias; ἐπιγραφέας τοὺς καθεστηκότας ἐπὶ τῷ γράφειν, ὁπόσον ὀφείλουσιν εἰσφέρειν εἰς τὸ δημόσιον. Λυσίας ἐν τῷ περὶ τῆς εἰσφορᾶς. Cf. also Lex. Cantabr. 670. Lex. Seguer. 254, 5. Poll. 8, 103. The statement of the last writer ἐπιγραφεῖς τοὺς οὐκ εἰσφέροντας εἰσῆγον εἰς τὸ δικαστήριον seems to me improbable.

[3] Philoch. ap. Harp., συμμορία—διῃρέθησαν δὲ πρῶτον Ἀθηναῖοι κατὰ συμμορίας ἐπὶ Ναυσινίκου ἄρχοντος, ὥς φησι Φιλόχορος ἐν τῇ ἑ Ἀτθίδος. Whether the 100 Symmories in Cleidem. ap. Phot., ναυκραρία refer to these or to the Trierarchic Symmories, is uncertain. Polyb. 2, 62, 6/7 says: τίς γὰρ ὑπὲρ Ἀθηναίων οὐχ ἱστόρηκε, διότι καθ' οὓς καιροὺς μετὰ Θηβαίων εἰς τὸν πρὸς Λακεδαιμονίους ἐνέβαινον πόλεμον καὶ μυρίους μὲν ἐξέπεμπον στρατιώτας, ἑκατὸν δ' ἐπλήρουν τριήρεις, ὅτι τότε κρίναντες ἀπὸ τῆς ἀξίας ποιεῖσθαι τὰς εἰς τὸν πόλεμον εἰσφορὰς ἐτιμήσαντο τήν τε χώραν τὴν Ἀττικὴν ἅπασαν καὶ τὰς οἰκίας, ὁμοίως δὲ καὶ τὴν λοιπὴν οὐσίαν· ἀλλ' ὅμως τὸ σύμπαν τίμημα τῆς ἀξίας ἐνέλιπε τῶν ἑξακισχιλίων διακοσίοις καὶ πεντήκοντα ταλάντοις. Boeckh, *Publ. Ec.*, 1, 637, saw that this statement refers to the assessment of Nausinicos. Dem. 14, 9 estimates the τίμημα τὸ τῆς χώρας for 354/3 B.C. at 6,000 tal., and so too Philochor., *fr.*, 151 in Müller, *Fr. Hist. Gr.*, 1, 409, in his 10th book.

thousand talents, explains the 5,750 talents of Polybios as the amount not of the entire property of the people, but of their assessed capital: he regards the Eisphora of Nausinicos's system as a property tax so arranged, that though the tax was levied at an uniform rate per cent., the same for all classes, the wealthier citizens had to pay heavier amounts, the poorer classes less; *i.e.*, the assessed capital differed from the actual capital in proportions varying according to the census class, a larger proportion being assessed in the higher classes and smaller proportions in the lower. His theory is controverted by Rodbertus, who regards Polybios's 5,750 tal. as the total amount of the annual incomes of the citizens, and endeavours to prove that the Eisphora introduced in the Archonship of Nausinicos was a graduated income-tax arranged in 4 classes; the graduation, he supposes, began with the 2nd class, and in the 4th class the tax was 20 per cent. of the income.[1] The evidence, however, which Rodbertus quotes for his theory, cannot be regarded as conclusive; while Boeckh's theory can be reconciled with our authorities, if his hypothesis that the assessed capital differed from the actual capital be admitted.[2] But this hypothesis has been attacked more recently by Beloch, who in view of the fact that in assessments for taxes a large amount of property as a rule escapes assessment, recognises the 5,750 tal. of Polybios as being really the entire assessed total of the property of Athenian citizens in 378 B.C.[3] Beloch's computation of the Athenian property, obtained partly from recent discoveries, seems to rest on a sounder basis than Boeckh's; and it is further recommended by the fact that it explains the evidence of ancient authorities without recourse to strained interpretations.[4] On the

---

[1] Boeckh's calculation of the amount of Athenian property in *Publ. Ec.*, 1, 638 ff. Eisphora system of Nausinicos's Archonship: *Publ. Ec.*, 1, 667 ff. Rodbertus's views, to which Wachsmuth, *d. St. Athen.*, 1, 582, 1, gives complete assent, may be found in the *Jahrb. f. Nationalökonomie und Statistik herausg. v. Hildebrand*, 8, 453, 75, 1857.

[2] Rodbertus's view has been opposed by Lipsius, *Jahrb. f. cl. Phil.*, 1878, p. 289 ff., Thumser, *de civium Ath. munerib.*, 31 ff., and Fränkel, *Herm.*, 18, 314 ff.

[3] See Beloch in *Herm.* 20, 237 ff.

[4] Beloch estimates the property of the Attic people as follows: *Slaves*, estimated at 60–80,000 in number (cf. Beloch, *Bevölker. d. griech.-röm. Welt*, 84 ff.), and worth on an average $1\frac{1}{2}$ minæ=1,500–2,000 tal. *Movables*,—in the time of Polybios (2, 62, 4), when luxury was at its height and money depreciated in value, the ἔπιπλα χωρὶς σωμάτων of the entire Peloponnese did not reach a total value of 6,000 tal., therefore those of Athens in 378/7

other hand, we cannot accept Beloch's remarks on the institution of the Symmories, and on the manner of assessment of Demosthenes' property; two points used by Boeckh as the main supports of his hypothesis.[1] But the passages in question may perhaps be satisfactorily explained, from Beloch's point of view, if we conjecture that in the highest class, to which Demosthenes belonged, 5 minæ on 25 minæ, *i.e.*, 20 per cent. of the capital, was the maximum Eisphora which could be demanded, but that as an ordinary rule only a specified percentage of that maximum was exacted. In the lower classes the ratio of the maximum Eisphora to a man's total capital would be diminished progressively, being least in the lowest class.[2] The assessment during Nausinicos's would not be more than 1,000 tal. *Arable land*: the annual harvest may be estimated at 700,000 medimnoi, which at 2½ dr. per medimnos=in round numbers 300 tal., less 50 per cent. for cost of production=150 tal., representing at 8 per cent. (Is. 11, 42) a capitalised value of 2,000 tal. 700,000 medimnoi is a liberal estimate for the annual yield, for in 329/8 B.C., according to the accounts of the Eleusinian temple in the *Bull.* 8, 194 compared with Dittenberger, *Syll.*, 13, Attica produced only 366,000 medimnoi of barley and 39,600 med. of wheat, that is in round numbers a total of 400,000 med. *Vineyards, olive plantations, woods, pasture land*, and *buildings* 2,000 tal. Grand total about 7,000 tal.

[1] Beloch's statements in 247 ff. (see also *Herm.*, 22, 371 ff.) I consider erroneous. See Fränkel in Boeckh, *St. d. Ath.*³, 2, p. 121. But Beloch rightly observes in opposition to Fränkel, *Herm.*, 18, 814 ff., that in the lease in C.I.A., II. 1058: ἐὰν δέ(τις) εἰσφορὰ γίγνηται ἢ ἄλλο τι ἀπ(ότε)ισμα τρόπῳ ὁτ(ῳ)οῦν, εἰσφέρειν Εὐκράτην κατὰ τὸ τίμημα καθ' ἑπτὰ μνᾶς the τίμημα must represent, at any rate approximately, the entire value of the property. For if that was the case, the rent of 54 drachmas represents 7⅘ per cent. interest on the capital value, *i.e.* the usual rent; if, on the other hand, the τίμημα was only ⅕ of the value of the piece of property, the interest would be only 1½ per cent. or even less. Fränkel's rejoinder in Boeckh, *St. d. Ath.*³, 2, pp. 121/2 is answered by Beloch in *Herm.* 22, 376/7.

[2] Demosthenes the father left a property of about 14 tal., Dem. 27, 4. 11. 59. The guardians in their assessment returns stated the property of the young Demosthenes at 15 tal., πρὸς πεντεκαιδεκαταλάντους οἴκους: 28, 11, *i.e.*, in the first assessment-class: 27, 7. The total property was to the maximum Eisphora in the ratio of five to one: 27, 7; 28, 4; 29, 59. Dem. 27, 9: δῆλον μὲν τοίνυν καὶ ἐκ τούτων (*i.e.*, from the Symmory schedule in which the maximum Eisphora was set down as 3 tal.) ἐστὶ τὸ πλῆθος τῆς οὐσίας. πεντεκαίδεκα ταλάντων γὰρ τρία τάλαντα τίμημα· ταύτην ἠξίουν εἰσφέρειν τὴν εἰσφοράν means that for an estate worth 15 talents the Eisphora was assessed on 3 talents. "The guardians considered 3 talents to be the proper Eisphora for my estate." Though 14 tal. would increase to more than three times that sum in 10 yrs. (Dem. 27, 59), still a maximum Eisphora of ⅕ the entire estate for the first class seems a monstrous amount to our ideas; but it may

archonship seems to have been carried out as before: individuals liable to Eisphora, and also corporations holding property, sent in returns estimated by themselves; these returns were then accepted or corrected by a special assessment-committee.[1] I do not think it probable that re-assessments took place at fixed or regular intervals; it is more likely that revisions of the assessment were instituted only on extraordinary occasions by special decree of the Ecclesia. Yet there must have been some method by which a person who had suffered losses and consequently found himself assessed too high could get his assessment altered.[2]

The citizens liable to be taxed were classified into a number of Symmories, each headed by a ἡγεμών, who was the richest man in the Symmory, and each representing an approximately equal part of the entire wealth of the State. The 300 richest men formed the first assessment class.[3] It was the duty

Symmories.

seem credible when we remember the high rate of interest yielded by capital and the great sacrifices demanded from rich citizens in ancient Athens, especially if the tax actually levied never reached the theoretical maximum. Demosthenes in the 10 yrs. of his minority paid 18 minae as Eisphora: 27, 37. There were maximum and minimum limits in the case of ἐπιδόσεις also: C.I.A., II. 834. In *Herm.* 22, 218, 3 v. Wilamowitz calls attention to a similar system in force in Mecklenburg. Enquiries made on the spot have shown that in that State in the case of the Landessteuer, a tax assessed according to income and property, on many occasions not the full amount but only ⅔ or ⅓ of it is levied.

[1] Cf. Is. 7, 39: καὶ μὴν καὶ αὐτὸς Ἀπολλόδωρος οὐχ ὥσπερ Προνάπης ἀνεγράψατο μὲν τίμημα μικρόν—a passage which may very well refer to the assessment of Nausinicos. For the chronology of the speech see Schömann, p. 352 ff. For individuals making their own assessment returns cf. also Dem. 27, 7; 29, 59. Eisphora from property held by corporations: C.I.A., II. 600, 1055, 1058, 1059, and see also *Bull.* 15, 211. We are justified in supposing that there was an assessment-committee by the fact that there was such a committee before Nausinicos's year. To this committee I refer the εἰσφορὰν εἰσφέρειν in C.I.A., II. 86. Any one who tried to avoid being assessed probably had his property confiscated. Köhler regards the fragmentary list of names in C.I.A., II. 779, under the heading: (τ)άδ' ἐπράθη ἐδ(άφη) . . . ἀτίμητα ὄντα, as a list of such confiscations.

[2] Such a revision of assessments by decree of the Ecclesia is attested by Suid. ἀνασύνταξις· τὰ διαγεγραμμένα τιμήματα ταῖς συμμορίαις ὅταν δόξῃ τῷ δήμῳ χρῄζειν προσθήκης ἢ ἀφαιρέσεως καὶ ἕλωνται τοὺς τοῦτο πράξοντας, τοῦτο ἀνασύνταξιν καλοῦσιν. It must have been possible to obtain a modification of the assessment even without a general re-assessment, not only in the case of the 300 προεισφέροντες, (Dem.) 42, 5, but for the other persons assessed as well.

[3] I agree with Lipsius in the *Jahrb. f. cl. Phil.*, 1878, p. 294 ff., that the Symmories included all persons liable to the tax, not merely the 1,200 richest. The 1,200 formed the trierarchic Symmories. This view is con-

of the Strategoi to distribute the citizens liable to be taxed among the various Symmories.[1]

When an Eisphora had been ordered by decree of the Ecclesia, the sum specified in the decree was first apportioned out among the various Symmories. Each Symmory then drew up a list in which the payments to be demanded from the members of the Symmory were calculated according to the assessment of each.[2] According to these lists the Eisphora was collected from the citizens; and for some time after the archonship of Nausinicos this was done directly by the State.[3]

---

firmed by the fact that Philochor. discussed the institution of the Symmories in Nausinicos' year in book 5 (cf. Harp. συμμορία), but did not mention the 1,200 till Book 6 (cf. Harp. χίλιοι διακόσιοι); and also that there is no trace of the 1,200 previous to the time when the Symmory-system was applied to the Trierarchy. Direct evidence against the existence of the 1,200 before that time is supplied by Dem. 21, 155, who tells of the creation of the trierarchic Symmories in the words: ὅτε·πρῶτον μὲν διακοσίους καὶ χιλίους πεποιήκατε συντελεῖς ὑμεῖς. This hypothesis also gets rid of the strange peculiarity of the system as represented by Boeckh, *Publ. Econ.*, 1, 684 ff., viz. that all citizens liable paid the tax, but all were not members of the Symmories. Dem. 1, 20; 2, 31 shows that all had to pay. Demosthenes was ἡγεμὼν συμμορίας during the ten years of his minority: Dem. 28, 4; 21, 157. Harp. ἡγεμὼν συμμορίας. Acc. to Is. 6, 60 delivered 364/3 B.C. (Schömann, p. 822), οἱ τριακόσιοι must have formed the first assessment class long before that. It does not necessarily follow from Dem. 14, 16. 17. that there were 20 Symmories for the Eisphora, for that passage refers to the trierarchic Symmories.   [1] Dem. 39, 8.

[2] Each Symmory kept a list of the assessments of its members. Cf. Lex. Seguer. 236, 9: διάγραμμα τὸ συντίμημα τῆς οὐσίας διάγραμμα ἐκαλεῖτο, ἐν ᾧ ἐνεγέγραπτο, τί ἕκαστος ἔχει, and Suid. ἀνασύνταξις · τὰ διαγεγραμμένα τιμήματα ταῖς συμμορίαις. The list of the various sums which had to be paid towards a particular Eisphora by the various members of the Symmory, was drawn up in each Symmory by the διαγραφεύς on the basis of the assessment-lists and was called διάγραμμα. Cf. Harp. διάγραμμα. Ὑπερίδης ἐν τῷ πρὸς Ἐπικλέα. τὸ ταττόμενον ἐν ταῖς συμμορίαις, ὁπόσον ἕκαστον ἄνδρα εἰσφέρειν δεῖ. ἐτάττετο δὲ οὐ τὸ αὐτὸ πᾶσιν, ἀλλὰ πρὸς τὴν τίμησιν τῆς οὐσίας. περὶ τούτων σαφέστατα δεδήλωκεν Ὑπερίδης ἐν τῷ κατὰ Πολυεύκτου περὶ διαγράμματος. διαγραφεὺς μέντοι ἐστὶν ὁ καθιστάμενος ἐν ταῖς συμμορίαις ἐπὶ τῷ διακρῖναι, πόσον ἕκαστος ἀνὴρ εἰσενεγκεῖν ὀφείλει, ὡς ὁ αὐτὸς πάλιν φανερὸν ποιεῖ ἐν τῷ κατὰ Πολυεύκτου. Cf. Suid. διάγραμμα. διαγραφεύς. διαγράμματα. Lex. Seguer. 241, 3; 236, 13. The double meaning of διάγραμμα here assumed is not surprising. See Boeckh, *Seeurk.*, 204.

[3] Dem. 22, 54; 24, 166; Lys. 29, 9. When payments of Eisphora were made the accounts were kept by public slaves as ἀντιγραφεῖς. Lex. Seguer. 197, 24; Dem. 22, 70/1. Acc. to Suid. ἐκλογεῖς the Eisphora was paid to the ἐκλογεῖς. Any one who failed to pay had his property confiscated. Cf. Suid. πωλητής. Phot. πωληταί. The Symmories of the Metoicoi had ταμίαι. Poll. 8, 144.

Not long after 362/1 B.C. a modification was introduced; the 300 richest citizens were required to advance the entire amount of Eisphora decreed; they then had to recover the amounts owing from other citizens according to the lists.[1] This payment in advance by the rich citizens was called προεισφορά, and was so far regarded as a leiturgy, that Antidosis was applicable to it.[2]

The extraordinary indirect revenue of the State consisted in the τριηραρχία which private individuals had to perform. This term was still retained after Tetreremes and Penteremes were introduced. The Trierarchia could not be required again of the same person till two years had elapsed since he last served.[3] It admitted of very few cases of exemption. Originally one individual performed the duty by himself. In the course of the Peloponnesian war the wealth of individual citizens was much diminished, and two Trierarchs were allowed to join in equipping one vessel. The first instance of this is in 405/4 B.C. The duty might be performed for a whole year by one man acting for himself and his partner, or they might take it for six months each. Trierarchy and Syntrierarchy, according to the wealth of the persons called upon to serve, co-existed side by side after the conclusion of the Peloponnesian war, till the establishment of the trierarchic Symmories.[4]

Extraordinary indirect revenues.

Trierarchia.

Syntrierarchia.

---

[1] For the change in the method of levying see Lipsius, *ib.*, p. 297 ff. The earliest mention of the προεισφορά is in 362/1 B.C., when the Bouleutai were to draw up a list of citizens required to pay the προεισφορά for their demesmen: Dem. 50, 8. I conjecture that this method too was soon found awkward, and abandoned in favour of making the 300 richest citizens liable to pay the προεισφορά, as was the case in (Dem.) 42, 25. The προεισφέροντες recovered the sums due from the poorer members: Dem. 50, 9. The προεισφορά is still found mentioned in inscriptions in the 3rd cent.: C.I.A., II. 380.

[2] Cf. (Dem.) 42, 4. 5. The rules laid down for the other leiturgies—that none need serve two leiturgies at once, or the same leiturgy two years in succession—cannot have applied to the προεισφορά. This follows from the nature of the προεισφορά, in spite of Dem. 50, 9.

[3] Trierarchs of Triremes and Tetreremes: *Seeurk.*, XVIIa. 18 ff. p. 563 = C.I.A., II. 812a. 17 sq., of a τριακόντορος: XIVa. 95 ff. p. 455 = C.I.A., II. 809a, 91 sq. Trierarch of a Pentereme, Polyb. 16, 5, 1. See Boeckh, *Seeurk.*, 167. For the whole of the account which follows I may refer once for all to the exhaustive investigations of Boeckh, *Publ. Econ.*, 1, 699 ff., *Seeurk.*, 166 ff., though my account varies from his in many points. See also Thumser, *de civ. Ath. munerib.*, p. 58 ff.

[4] First instance of Syntrierarchia 405/4 B.C.: Isocr. 18, 59, 60. Lys. 32,

In 357/6 B.C. by the decree of Periandros the Symmory system already established for the purposes of the Eisphora was extended with some modifications to the Trierarchy also.[1] The 1,200 richest men in the Eisphora-Symmories were classified into 20 trierarchic Symmories of 60 members each.[2] In this case again the classification must naturally have been so arranged that each Symmory represented an approximately equal part of the total assessed wealth of the whole 1,200; and accordingly the 300 mentioned above must have been distributed equally among the 20 Symmories.[3] In these Symmories, as in those for Eisphora purposes, the richest members were ἡγεμόνες; there were also ἐπιμεληταί of the Symmories. With these ἐπιμεληταί I should identify "the twenty," as they were called, who undertook in conjunction with the Strategoi the apportionment of the trierarchic burdens among the members of the Symmories.[4] This theory of

The Trierarchic Symmories.

---

24 supplies no definite data. One Syntrierarch relieves the other at the end of 6 months: Dem. 50, 39. 68. For the existence of Trierarchy and Syntrierarchy side by side cf. Is. 5, 36, delivered about 390 B.C. (Schömann on Is. p. 290 ff.): ἀλλὰ μὴν τριηράρχων τοσούτων κατασταθέντων οὔτ' αὐτὸς ἐτριηράρχησεν οὔθ' ἑτέρῳ συμβέβληκεν ἐν τοιούτοις καιροῖς. See Boeckh, *Publ. Econ.*, 1, 708 ff. The two years' interval between two Trierarchies is attested by Is. 7, 38. Exemption of the 9 Archons: Dem. 20, 18. 27. 28. Other cases of exemption are given in Dem. 14, 16. See Boeckh, *Publ. Econ.*, 1, 702 ff. Thumser, p. 118 ff.

[1] Voluntary Trierarchs: Dem. 18, 99, 358/7 B.C. The first instance of Trierarchy on the Symmory-system is in 357/6 B.C.: (Dem.) 47, 44. ὁ δὲ νόμος ὁ τοῦ Περιάνδρου—καθ' ὃν αἱ συμμορίαι συνετάχθησαν: (Dem.) 47, 21. Boeckh, *Publ. Econ.*, 1, 720 ff. *Seeurk.*, 184/5.

[2] This is Lipsius' theory, which he has in my opinion convincingly substantiated in the *Jahrb. f. cl. Phil.*, 1878, p. 294 ff. The normal scheme of 20 Symmories of 60 members each is attested by Dem. 14, 17. For the total 1,200 cf. also Dem. 21, 155. Lex Seguer. 238, 31; 300, 23. Harp. χίλιοι διακόσιοι. The naval inscriptions show that the Symmories were not classified acc. to the Phylai: see Boeckh, *Seeurk.*, p. 186.

[3] For the τριακόσιοι, in the trierarchic Symmories cf. Dein. c. *Dem.* 42. I refer the words, quoted, without their context, from Hypereid. ap. Harp. συμμορία· εἰσὶ γὰρ ἐν τῇ συμμορίᾳ ἑκάστῃ πεντεκαίδεκα ἄνδρες, to the 15 members of the 300 who belonged to each Symmory. This explanation was first proposed by Parreidt, *disput. de instituto eo Athen., cuius ordinat. et correct. or. περὶ συμμοριῶν inscripta suadet Dem.*, Marburg, 1827, p. 36. Boeckh's objection, *Seeurk.*, p. 180, does not seem to me valid.

[4] Dem. 18, 102 ff., 312, shows that the Hegemones of the Symmories were the richest members. Dem. 18, 103 mentions also τοὺς δευτέρους καὶ τρίτους. (Dem.) 47, 21. 22. 24, mentions ἐπιμεληταὶ οἱ ἐν ταῖς συμμορίαις. In a statement of accounts of the supervisors of the dockyards, probably 334/3 B.C., we read: τούτῳ συντριήραρχον οἱ στρατηγοὶ καὶ εἴκοσιν κατέστησαν κατὰ μνᾶν τοῦ

the trierarchic Symmories, with its fixed numbers, cannot have been exactly carried out in practice, because among the 1,200 richest Athenians who formed these Symmories there was always a large number temporarily exempt from the Trierarchy. The consequence was that the full number of 1,200, appointed by law to perform the Trierarchy, was never actually available.[1]

On the earlier system the men-of-war were assigned to individual Trierarchs; when the Symmory-system was in force the vessels were assigned to the various Symmories.[2] The financial burden laid on the Symmories varied according to the number of ships to be equipped. The arrangement seems to have been that in each Symmory a certain number of members, varying in each case according to the wealth of each man and the number of ships, were formed into a Syntelia to undertake the equipment of each ship. Each Syntelia deputed one of its members as Trierarch to do the actual work of supervising the equipment; this deputy was relieved at the end of his term of office by another member of the same Syntelia.[3]

διαγράμμ(α)τος 'Ονήτορα 'Ον(ήτορος Μελι)τέα. See App. A, 72 ff. in the *Mitth. d. dtsch. arch. Inst. in Ath.*, 4, 80 = C.I.A., II. 804b, 63 sqq., where it seems to me more reasonable to identify the 20 with the ἐπιμεληταί, than with the ἡγεμόνες, as Köhler, p. 87, prefers to do.

[1] Acc. to the computation of Dem. 14, 16, 480 out of the 1,200 were exempt: these exemptions included the estates of Epicleroi and orphans, those sent out by the State as cleruchs, and the cases of undivided inheritances held in common by brothers or relatives who were none of them individually possessed of the trierarchic census (see Boeckh, *Publ. Econ.*, 1, 704/5. Schaefer, *Dem.*, 1¹, 421, 4. Lipsius, however, in Meier ² 602, 321 understands by κοινωνικά property held by corporations). In addition to these the ἀδύνατοι must have been exempt *ipso facto*, i.e. those who no longer possessed the trierarchic census, though they were still nominally members of the 1,200. See Boeckh, *ib.*, 703.

[2] See *Seeurk.*, vii., viii., p. 347 ff. = C.I.A., II. 800. 801, where this is expressed in the manner shown in the following example: vii. 30, p. 349 = C.I.A., II. 800b, 27 sqq. Περιστερά, ἐπισκε(υῆς) δεο(μένη) 'Ηγησίου ἔργον, Κηφισίου Τρικορυ(σίου) συμ(μορία). Boeckh, *Seeurk.*, p. 185, conjectures with great probability that the name governed by συμμορία indicates the Hegemon of the Symmory.

[3] Dem. 21, 155 calls the 1,200 συντελεῖς. Dem. 20, 23 advises εἰς συντέλειαν ἀγαγεῖν τὰς χορηγίας ὥσπερ τὰς τριηραρχίας. These συντελεῖς are explained in Et. M. συντελὴς—ὅτε οἱ τριηραρχοῦντες νεὼς μιᾶς ἅμα ἐπεμελοῦντο, συντελεῖς ἐλέγοντο. To such συντέλειαι must be referred the words of Hypereid. ap. Harp. συμμορία· ἕως μὲν οἱ πλουσιώτατοι παρακρουόμενοι τὴν πόλιν σύμπεντε καὶ σύνεξ τριηραρχοῦντες μέτρια ἀνήλισκον, ἡσυχίαν ἦγον οὗτοι. The *Seeurkunden* give instances of συντέλειαι of three members (IVh.=C.I.A., II. 793h. Vd. 15 ff.=795c. Xc.

Trierarchic Symmories.

Since it was the richest members in each Symmory who made all arrangements and allotted the services to be required of each individual, these rich men soon began to arrange the **The reform of burdens in such a way that they themselves escaped Demosthenes.** payment as far as possible.[1] To remove this abuse Demosthenes, when Director of the Admiralty, most probably in 340/39 B.C., set on foot a reform of the trierarchic leiturgies. He had already in 354 B.C. introduced a programme of reform to the consideration of the citizens in his speech on the Symmories; but the scheme he now carried out was based on a different idea to that proposed in the speech.[2] The law carried by Demosthenes in 340/39 B.C., while leaving the Symmories intact, secured that the trierarchic burdens imposed on every individual should be actually and prac-

---

=808c.) of 5, 6 and 7 (X*e. f.*=808 *e. f.*). The character of the Symmory-system does not prevent our inferring, that when a large fleet was to be equipped, if the duty was fairly apportioned out, two individuals or even one would sometimes have to undertake the entire trierarchy of a ship. Syntrierarchs during the period of the Symmories: Dem. 24, 11, (Dem.) 47, 78. *Seeurk.*, V*d.* p. 337 ff.=C.I.A., II. 795 *f.*, where in 795*d* in one instance a ship has only one Trierarch; we are not told how long he had to serve. So again 808*e*. The Trierarch hands over the equipments τῷ διαδόχῳ, ὃς ἂν ἔλθῃ ἐκ τῆς συμμορίας ἐπὶ τὴν ναῦν: (Dem.) 47, 29. Thumser, *de civ. Ath. munerib.*, p. 65 ff., explains the varying numbers of men in the Synteleiai, by supposing that the 1,200 were divided into various classes, and that for each class it was fixed how many partners should undertake a Trierarchy.

[1] The abuses which had arisen in the distribution of the burdens within the Symmories are described by Dem. 18, 102 sqq.; 21, 155. When Dem. 18, 104 speaks of Synteleiai of 16 persons each for one Trierarchy, he can only refer to a time when the State needed very few ships, and when therefore large Synteleiai could be formed in the Symmories for each ship: for it is certain that the number of men in each Synteleia must have varied according to the size of the fleet to be equipped. In all probability during the whole period of the Symmories a number of ships had definite individuals from among the Symmories assigned to them as Trierarchs, each Trierarch being the representative of a Synteleia; and this was done even in time of peace when the ships were lying in dock. See Boeckh, *Seeurk.*, p. 168. These Synteleiai may have consisted as a rule of 16 persons, and this is what Demosthenes contrasts with his own system, with rhetorical exaggeration.

[2] For the programme of reform in the Symmory-speech cf. Dem. 14, 16 sq. Boeckh, *P. Econ.*, 1, 727 ff.; Schaefer, *Dem.*, 1¹, 417 ff. I agree with Schömann, *de comit.*, 291, 20, and Schaefer, *ib.*, 424, that this programme was not carried out. For the date of the reform Dem. actually carried out see Boeckh, *Pub. Econ.*, 1, 741 ff. *Seeurk.* 189 ff. Schaefer, *Dem.*, 2¹, 494. That Dem. then held the extraordinary office of ἐπιστάτης τοῦ ναυτικοῦ is attested by Æsch. *in Ctes.* 222.

tically in proportion to his assessment: the equipment of two ships was fixed as the maximum leiturgy to be demanded from any one. Any one who did not possess sufficient wealth for a complete Trierarchy, had to give help to others in performing a Trierarchy in proportion to the wealth he did possess. Similarly in the case of those who had means more than sufficient for one Trierarchy but not enough for two; they were required to take one Trierarchy by themselves, and in addition to contribute their fair share towards a second Trierarchy. No one was required to perform more than two Trierarchies at the same time.[1]

Not long after Demosthenes passed his law, Æschines effected some alteration of its provisions, but we are not informed to what *Modification* extent the law was changed. At any rate the general *of Æschines.* principles of Demosthenes' reform seem to have been retained in subsequent times.[2]

As concerns the nature of the services performed by the Trierarchs, the State supplied the Trierarch with the ships, and as a Extent of the general rule with the apparatus belonging to it, and trierarchic with the pay and ration-money for the crew. The duties. Trierarch was then required to keep the ship and all its belongings in good condition and repair during the period of his Trierarchy. It need scarcely be said that any one could do more than this as a voluntary service if he chose.[3]

---

[1] Dem. 18, 102 sq. gives a general statement of the principle of his law. I reject as spurious the portion of a law inserted in Dem. 18, 106 (see Schaefer, *Dem.*, 2¹, 490, 3), mainly because according to § 104 the double Trierarchy seems to have been the highest burden imposed by the Demosthenic law. The fact that the 300 richest citizens were especially affected by this law explains expressions like νομοθετήσας περὶ τῶν τριακοσίων in Æsch. *in Ctes.* 222, and ἐπειδὴ δὲ ταῦτα κατιδὼν Δημοσθένης νόμους ἔθηκε τοὺς τριακοσίους τριηραρχεῖν καὶ βαρεῖαι γεγόνασιν αἱ τριηραρχίαι in Hypereid. *ap.* Harp. συμμορία. Cf. also Poll. 8, 100. Examples of Trierarchies and of partial contributions in Boeckh, *Seeurk.*, p. 191 ff. Cf. C.I.A., II. 804a, 72 sq., b 16 sq., 43 sq., Bb 1 sq., 808a, 37 sq., 809a, 1 sq. On Demosthenes' law see also Schaefer, *Dem.*, 2¹, 490 ff.

[2] Dem. 18, 312. Æsch. *in Ctes.* 222. Boeckh, *Pub. Econ.*, 1, 745a. Schaefer, *Dem.*, 2¹, 493, 4. For the continued validity of Demosthenes's main principles see Boeckh, *Seeurk.*, 191 ff., 209. A στρατηγὸς ὁ ἐπὶ τὰς συμμορίας is mentioned as late as 325/4 B.C.: *Seeurk.*, XIVa, 214/5, p. 465=C.I.A., II. 809a, 205 sq. It is uncertain whether the 100 symmories which Cleidem. *ap.* Phot. ναυκραρία mentions as existing in his day were the Eisphora-Symmories or the trierarchic.

[3] See Boeckh, *Pub. Econ.*, 1, 712 ff., 725 ff., *Seeurk.*, 194 ff. Thuc. 6, 31 says that for the Sicilian expedition the State supplied the pay and ναῦς κενάς.

The Trierarchy.

The expenses involved in serving as sole Trierarch for one year amounted to 40–60 minæ, and were called τριηράρχημα. The outlay caused by prolongation of the Trierarchy beyond its legal duration by the failure of the successor to appear at the right time, was called ἐπιτριηράρχημα, and could be recovered by the Trierarch from his successor.[1]

Cost of the Trierarchy.

Both before and after the introduction of the Symmory-system Trierarchs often had their duties performed for them for hire by contractors. Trierarchs who did this were under certain circumstances liable to be prosecuted by a γραφὴ λειποταξίου; but in practice this rule was seldom enforced.[2]

Trierarchies put out on Contract.

The Trierarchs were bound to return their ships to the State at the end of their time of service in proper condition, unless they could prove that the vessel had been rendered useless by the enemy or by storms. Any question whether this was the case or not, was decided in the form of a diadicasia between the State and the Trierarch before a Heliastic court. If the Council decided in favour of the Trierarch, he had, as a rule, merely to restore the beak of the disabled vessel; if the verdict went against him, he had either to build a new ship and hand it over to the State,—the old ship, with the exception of the beak, remaining in his hands,—or else to return the old ship to the State, and pay in addition 5,000 drachmas for the building of

Returning the ship.

But we may infer from Aristoph., *Eq.*, 911 sqq., that at that date it was already customary for the State to supply the general apparatus as well. See *Seeurk.*, 201 ff. For later times cf. Dem. 21, 155; (Dem.) 47, 20 ff. From the description in Dem. 50 of the voluntary trierarchic contributions of Apollodoros it may be seen that the Trierarch was not obliged to perform any services beyond what are given in the text; though in the 4th cent. it was not very unusual for the Trierarch to supply also the pay of the ὑπηρεσία: Isocr. 18, 60. Dem. 51, 6. See also Thumser, *de civ. Ath. mun.*, p. 59 ff.

[1] Dem. 50 shows that the Trierarchy lasted one year reckoned from the day of entry on duty. See Boeckh, *Seeurk.*, 172 ff. Cost of Trierarchy 40 minæ: Dem. 21, 8. 154. 48 minæ: Lys. 32, 24 sq. Trierarchy for 7 years, 6 tal., *i.e.* 51½ minæ, *per annum*: Lys. 21, 2. 1 tal.: Dem. 21, 155. See also Boeckh, 482 *note.* Harp. τριηράρχημα τὸ εἰς τὴν τριηραρχίαν ἀνάλωμα. Δημοσθένης ἐν τῷ περὶ τοῦ τριηραρχήματος. ἐπιτριηράρχημα δὲ τὸ ἀναλισκόμενον μετὰ τὸν τῆς τριηραρχίας χρόνον. For the ἐπιτριηράρχημα cf. also Dem. 50, 38 sq.

[2] The earliest instance of contracting out of the Trierarchia is 364/3 B.C., Dem. 21, 80. 154. For an instance after the institution of the Symmory-system cf. Dem. 21, 155. Dem. 51, 8 shows the possibility of the γραφὴ λειποταξίου.

a new one. If, notwithstanding the sentence of the court, the Trierarch did not build another vessel, and did not pay the 5,000 drachmas, his liability might be doubled by a court of law, and in exceptional cases even by a resolution of the Council.[1]

Responsibility of the Trierarchs. It is needless to say that the Trierarch had to pass an audit with respect to his Trierarchia; for the money for the wages and keep of the crew passed through his hands.[2]

5. THE JUDICATURE.

There is evidence to show that from very early times, in all those lawsuits which were decided by the vote of a jury, a sharp distinction was drawn at Athens between the conduct **Presiding Magistrates and Jury.** of the legal proceedings by the presiding magistrate and the finding of the verdict by the jury. It was in the Areopagus alone that the βασιλεύς took part in the voting, and then not until he had laid aside his character of magistrate, by taking off his wreath;[3] and only the δικασταὶ κατὰ δήμους, to be presently mentioned, at once presided in certain lawsuits and decided them. This direction of the legal proceedings by the president of the court—the ἡγεμονία δικαστηρίου, as it was termed —included receiving the accusation, holding the preliminary inquiry, presiding at the trial, and seeing to the execution of the

---

[1] Cf. the inscription in the *Mitth. d. dtsch. arch. Inst. in Ath.*, 4. 79 sqq., with Köhler's remarks; the theories of Boeckh, *Seeurk.*, 210 sqq., must be modified in several points accordingly. See also Lipsius in Meier [2] 467/8. In the recently discovered naval inscriptions in the *Mitth. d. dtsch. arch. Inst. in Ath.*, 5, p. 43 sqq., the Trierarchs, after the return of the ships, are directed by the presidents of the dockyards to repair them (App. III. *b*, 41 sqq.=C.I.A., II. 794 *b*, 40 sqq.); they seem occasionally, however, to have received some assistance from the State, 10 per cent. of the expenses being reimbursed to them (App. IV. *c*, 1 sqq., 77 sqq.=C.I.A., II. 794 *c*, 1 sqq., 89).

[2] Æschines *in Ctes.* 19. Dem. 50, 10. 50.

[3] The laws of Draco, C.I.A., I. 61, already distinguish between the δικάζειν of the βασιλεύς and the διαγνῶναι of the ἐφέται. [Cf. J. W. Headlam, *The Procedure of the Gortynian Inscription*, in the *Journal of Hellenic Studies*, xiii., p. 69]. For the exception in the case of Areopagus, see Arist. 57, 4 : εἰσάγει δ' ὁ βασιλεὺς καὶ δικάζουσιν . . . καὶ ὑπαίθριοι, καὶ ὁ βασιλεύς, ὅταν δικάζῃ, περιαιρεῖται τὸν στέφανον, and Poll. 8, 90: καὶ τὰς τοῦ φόνου δίκας εἰς Ἄρειον πάγον εἰσάγει (*sc.* ὁ βασιλεύς) καὶ τὸν στέφανον ἀποθέμενος σὺν αὐτοῖς δικάζει. In Æschyl., *Eum.*, 726 ff., Athena, the president of the court, votes herself; this is copied from the voting of the βασιλεύς. See Kirchhoff, *Ber. d. Berl. Ak.*, 1874, p. 105 ff. Schömann, *Jahrb. f. cl. Phil.*, 1876, p. 12 ff., attacked Kirchhoff's view, but without justification.

sentence.¹ This *hegemonia* was generally the duty of the magistrate, to whose province the subject of the charge belonged.² Only in certain cases was the presidency held by special magistrates, whose duties were strictly and entirely judicial. To this class of magistrate belonged the εἰσαγωγεῖς, the δικασταὶ κατὰ δήμους and the ναυτοδίκαι.

The five εἰσαγωγεῖς were appointed by lot, each representing two tribes; they presided at the ἔμμηνοι δίκαι, and seem to have had the *hegemonia* in cases arising out of the assessment of the allies for tribute.³   εἰσαγωγεῖς.

The judges of the Demes, οἱ κατὰ δήμους δικασταί, at first 30 in number, then, after the rule of the Thirty Tyrants, increased to 40, and so called οἱ τετταράκοντα, were certainly appointed by lot in the fourth century. In earlier times they were circuit-judges, travelling over the Demes and giving judgment there; in later times they apparently sat at Athens. Before their court were brought lawsuits about property, each case coming before the four judges belonging to the tribe of the defendant. Actions, involving sums not exceeding 10 drachmas, they decided themselves; actions involving greater amounts they brought before a Diaitetes, and, if the parties were not satisfied with his decision, before a Heliastic court.⁴   οἱ κατὰ δήμους δικασταί.

---

¹ Meier², p. 41 ff.
² Meier², p. 53 ff.
³ Arist. 52, 2: κληροῦσι δὲ καὶ εἰσαγωγέας ε´ ἄνδρας οἳ τὰς ἐμμήνους εἰσάγουσι δίκας, δυοῖν φυλαῖν ἕκαστος, and then the various δίκαι ἔμμηνοι, which they brought into court, are enumerated. Cf. Poll. 8, 93. 101; Lipsius, *Ber. d. Sächs.-Ges. d. Wiss.*, 1891, pp. 56/7. They are mentioned in the assessment lawsuits of the allies, C.I.A., I. 37. That they did not preside at all cases which were treated as ἔμμηνοι δίκαι, is evident from C.I.A., I. 38, where οἱ ἐπιμεληταί introduce, as ἐμμήνους δίκας, suits to recover tribute from defaulters. The Apodectai, too, presided over actions against tax-farmers, for sums above 10 drachmas, as ἐμμήνους δίκας: Arist. 52, 3.
⁴ Arist. 53, 1: κλήρουσι (cf. Dem. 24, 112) δὲ καὶ τετταράκοντα, τέτταρας ἐκ τῆς φυλῆς ἑκάστης, πρὸς οὓς τὰς ἄλλας δίκας λαγχάνουσιν, οἳ πρότερον μὲν ἦσαν τριάκοντα καὶ κατὰ δήμους περιιόντες ἐδίκαζον, μετὰ δὲ τὴν ἐπὶ τῶν τριάκοντα ὀλιγαρχίαν τετταράκοντα γεγόνασιν. καὶ τὰ μὲν μέχρι δέκα δραχμῶν αὐτοτελεῖς εἰσι [κρίνει]ν, τὰ δ´ ὑπὲρ τοῦτο τὸ τίμημα τοῖς διαιτηταῖς παραδιδόασιν. The Euthynoi and the Polemarch send on cases to them: Arist. 48, 5; 58, 2. If the parties are not satisfied with the decision of the Diaitetai, the latter hand over the case to the 4 of the τετταράκοντα, who belong to the same tribe as the accused, and they have then to bring the case before a Heliastic court. They are called in Arist. 58, 2, οἱ τὴν φυλὴν δικάζοντες, 58, 2, οἱ δ᾽ οἱ τὴν φυλὴν τοῦ φεύγοντος δικάζοντες. Cf. Lys. 23, Harp. ὅτι, passages from which Lipsius

The ναυτοδίκαι were in all probability instituted in the fifth century, when, during the first Athenian confederacy, many mercantile suits were brought to Athens for decision.[1]

ναυτοδίκαι. That the ναυτοδίκαι, before whose tribunal the δίκαι ἐμπορικαί and the γραφὴ ξενίας came, only presided in these cases, and did not give the verdict, I believe we may assume on the strength of an extant inscription.[2] As our authorities mention the ναυτοδίκαι for the last time in B.C. 397, and in the fourth century, the Thesmothetai presided at commercial suits and at γραφαὶ ξενίας, we may reasonably conclude that the office of the ναυτοδίκαι was abolished soon after the beginning of the fourth century.[3]

As regards the judges, we have to <u>distinguish</u> at Athens between permanent judges, arbitrators, and juries.

Judges. The permanent judges were the Council of the Areopagus, composed of ex-Archons, and the Ephetai. The latter,

in Meier[2] 90 had already deduced what Aristotle now proves. According to Dem. 37, 33, ἡ αἰκία καὶ τὰ τῶν βιαίων belonged to the jurisdiction of the τετταράκοντα. When Aristotle wrote, the δίκη αἰκίας belonged to the εἰσαγωγεῖς. See Arist. 52, 2, the source of Harp. κατὰ δήμους δικασταί; Poll. 8, 100; Suid. κατὰ δήμους δικασταί; Phot. τετταράκοντα; Lex. Seguer. 306, 15 sqq. The τετταράκοντα are mentioned in C.I.A., II. 849. Cf. Meier[2] 88 sqq., 643 sqq.

[1] Mention of the ναυτοδίκαι in Aristophanes (Harp. ναυτοδίκαι) in the Daitaleis, in Cratinos (Schol. to Aristoph., Aves, 766), and in C.I.A., I. 29, which, according to Kirchhoff, is not later than 444 B.C. The psephism from the collection of Crateros ap. Harp., in which they are mentioned, I agree with Philippi, Beitr. z. e. Gesch. d. att. Bürgerr., 40 sqq., in referring to the year 404/3.

[2] They are styled ἀρχή or ἄρχοντες in Harp., Poll. 8, 126, δικασταί in Hesych. ναυτοδίκαι. Schömann, Verf. Ath., 47/8, on the strength of Lys. 17, 5: νυνὶ δὲ λαχόντος ἐν τῷ Γαμηλιῶνι μηνὶ οἱ ναυτοδίκαι οὐκ ἐξεδίκασαν, takes them to be judges as well as presidents. That they were only presidents I conclude from C.I.A., I. 29, lines 4, 5, where ναυτοδίκαι and δικαστήριον are evidently distinguished. So Lipsius in Meier[2] 97. Cf. Lys. 17, 8, in which τοὺς ἄρξαντας evidently means the same as τοὺς ναυτοδίκας, though Baumstark, de curatorib. emporii et nautodicis, p. 71, 1827, understands the Thesmothetai by τοὺς ἄρξαντας. Their duties as judges in mercantile suits: Suid. ναυτοδίκαι ἄρχοντές εἰσι τοῖς ναυκλήροις δικάζοντες καὶ τοῖς περὶ τὸ ἐμπόριον ἐργαζομένοις. Cf. Lex. Seguer. 283, 3. Hesych., s.v. For the γραφὴ ξενίας before the ναυτοδίκαι see Harp., Poll., Hesych., ibid.

[3] Last mention of the ναυτοδίκαι, in Lys. 17, 5. 8, delivered in B.C. 397. See Blass, Gesch. d. att. Beredsamk., 1, 629. After this date γραφαὶ ξενίας and δίκαι ἐμπορικαί belong to the jurisdiction of the Thesmothetai: Meier[2] 77. 80. I do not attach much weight to the mention of ναυτοδίκαι in Lucian, Dialogi Meretricii, 2, 2. See Meier[2] 95 sqq.

however, were replaced about 400 B.C. by Heliasts in the court at the Palladion, and we may probably infer, by analogy, that the same change was made in the courts at the Delphinion and in Phreatto.[1]   **Permanent Judges.**

Before these permanent judges came all cases of manslaughter. At Athens this was a religious matter, dealt with according to Divine Law. And this was the reason that the three Exegetai or Interpreters of Divine Law were required to instruct those who desired to proceed against a murderer, but were ignorant of the law, as to the proper steps to take.[2] The procedure was indeed not of the simplest. In the heroic age, and at Sparta apparently even in historical times, the issue in a trial for bloodshed was, whether the accused was guilty or not guilty; at Athens a distinction was drawn, which we first hear of in the laws of Draco, between premeditated, unpremeditated, and justifiable homicide; and not only did the legal consequences vary accordingly, but also the place where the trial was held.[3]   **Cases of Homicide.**

Among the Greeks, when blood was shed, the relatives of the murdered man usually set themselves to wreak vengeance on the murderer. If he did not quit the country immediately after the deed, he could only secure himself by taking refuge in a sanctuary until he had made compensation to the relatives of his victim. From his sanctuary, protected by the right of asylum, he could enter into negotiations with them as to what compensation must be paid. When the State took into its   **Right of Sanctuary.**

---

[1] For the Archons see (Dem.) 26, 5; Poll. 8, 118; Plut., *Per.*, 9. The Ephetai are mentioned as still judging at the Palladion in B.C. 409/8: C.I.A., I. 61, while, according to Isocr. 18, 52. 54 (a speech which, as §§ 27 sqq. and 45 sqq. show, cannot have been delivered later than B.C. 397), 700 dicasts, *i.e.* Heliasts, sat at the Palladion, or, according to (Dem.) 59, 10, 500. For the 4th century, Poll. 8, 125, applies: κατὰ μικρὸν δὲ κατεγελάσθη [there is no necessity for Forchhammer's conjecture, κατηγελάσθη, in the *Kiel. Ind. lect.*, 1844, *de ephetis non ludibrio habitis*] τὸ τῶν ἐφετῶν δικαστήριον. Arist. 57, 4, after mentioning the courts on the Areopagus, at the Palladion and Delphinion, and in Phreatto says: δικάζουσι δ' οἱ λαχόντες τα[ῦτα δικασταὶ or ἡλιασταί] πλὴν τῶν ἐν Ἀρείῳ πάγῳ γιγνομένων. The addition, λαχόντες τα(ῦτα), points to Heliasts as the judges. For the Ephetai, see p. 123–4.

[2] For the interpreters of Divine Law I would refer the reader to Otf. Müller, *Eumen.*, 162 sqq., and Chr. Petersen in the 1st suppl. vol. of *Phil.*, p. 155 ff. That they gave the prosecutor advice in murder cases is clear from Plato, *Euthyphro*, 4; (Dem.) 47, 68 sqq. See Petersen, p. 174 sqq.

[3] On trials for homicide in heroic times cf. Philippi, *d. Areop. u. d. Eph.*, p. 4; for Sparta Xen., *An.*, 4, 8, 25.

own hands the regulation of vengeance for bloodshed it respected the right of sanctuary in so far that the three places of trial were connected with three sanctuaries.[1]

The most venerable tribunal at Athens for cases of bloodshed was ἡ βουλὴ ἡ ἐξ Ἀρείου πάγου or ἐν Ἀρείῳ πάγῳ, that is, the Council of, or on, the hill of the Ἀραί, the goddesses of curse and vengeance, who had their sanctuary at the foot of the hill.[2] The precincts of the sanctuary of these goddesses were still a place of refuge in the fifth century,[3] and the murderer who took refuge there—when private vengeance for bloodshed was still permitted—escaped the vengeance of man by surrendering himself to the vengeance of the goddesses. After the abolition of private vengeance, when the State took into its own hands the punishment of the murderer, it judged, so to say, as the representative of the goddesses of vengeance, keeping the court of homicide connected with the old sanctuary. Premeditated murder, premeditated wounding with intent to kill, arson, which was regarded as a crime against life and limb, and premeditated poisoning resulting in the death of the victim, were all within the jurisdiction of this court on the

(margin: ἡ βουλὴ ἡ ἐξ Ἀρείου πάγου or ἐν Ἀρείῳ πάγῳ.)

---

[1] Köhler in *Herm.*, 6, 102 sqq., has justly insisted that the origin of all the Athenian courts for trying homicide is the right of sanctuary.

[2] Wachsmuth, *d. St. Athen im Alterthum*, 1, 428, considers the Ἄρειος πάγος to be the hill of cursing or expiation, and very properly denies any connexion between the murder-court on the Areopagus and the Ares-cult. The other explanations of the name are brought together in Philippi, *ib.*, p. 8 sqq. But, I think, Wachsmuth cannot be right in connecting the origin of the name of the hill with Athena ἀρεία, the only goddess who had a shrine on the hill (Paus. 1, 28, 5); it is rather connected with the Σεμναί, whose name, Ἀραί, is found in Æsch., *Eumen.*, 417. For the shrine of the Σεμναί cf. Æsch., *Eumen.*, 804 sqq.; *Schol.* Eurip., *Orest.*, 1650: φασὶ δὲ, ὅτι καὶ ἱερὸν οὗτος (ὁ Ὀρέστης) ἐν Ἀρείῳ πάγῳ τῶν θεῶν (τῶν Εὐμενίδων) ἱδρύσατο; *Schol.*, Lucian III., p. 68 (Jacobitz): σεμνὰς θεὰς τὰς Ἐρινύας· τούτων γὰρ τὸ ἱερὸν πλησίον τοῦ Ἀρείου πάγου. A connexion between the court on the Areopagus and the Σεμναί is further shown in the oath taken before these goddesses (Dein. *in Dem.*, 47), and in the sacrifice offered in their sanctuary by those acquitted (Paus. 1, 28, 6). Otfr. Müller, *Eum.*, 154, had previously directed attention to this connexion. The derivation of the adjective ἄρειος, from ἀρά, is no difficulty. Ἀρεία is, without doubt, originally an adjectival derivative from ἀρά, accentuated like ἀδελφειός from ἀδελφός; and the differently accentuated ἄρειος was introduced as the adjectival form after ἀρεία had become a substantive.

[3] Cf. Arist., *Thesm.*, 224, with the *Schol.*: ἄσυλον γὰρ εἶχον οἱ καταλαμβάνοντες τὰ ἱερὰ τῶν Ἐρινύων.

Areopagus.[1] The penalties, which the court on the Areopagus imposed, were, in case of premeditated murder, death and confiscation of property; for premeditated wounding with intent to kill, exile and confiscation; for premeditated poisoning with intent to kill, probably either the penalty for murder or that for intentional wounding, according to the circumstances of the case.[2]

The second Athenian court for cases of bloodshed sat on the east side of the city, outside the walls, at the Palladion, the old sanctuary of Pallas.[3] This court at the Palladion judged unpremeditated manslaughter, the crime of instigating another to do bodily harm to a third person, whether with intent to kill or not, and the murder of a slave, a metic, or a foreigner.[4] The punishments inflicted by the court

τὸ δικαστήριον τὸ ἐπὶ Παλλαδίῳ.

---

[1] Cf. the law in Dem. 23, 22: δικάζειν δὲ τὴν βουλὴν τὴν ἐν Ἀρείῳ πάγῳ φόνου καὶ τραύματος ἐκ προνοίας καὶ πυρκαϊᾶς καὶ φαρμάκων, ἐάν τις ἀποκτείνῃ δούς. Arist. 57, 3: εἰσὶ [δὲ] φ[όνου] δίκαι καὶ τραύματος, ἂν μὲν ἐκ προνοίας ἀποκτείνῃ ἢ τρώ[σ]ῃ, ἐν Ἀρείῳ πάγῳ, καὶ φάρμακον ἐὰν ἀποκτείνῃ δούς, καὶ πυρκαᾶς· [ταῦ]τα γὰρ ἡ βουλὴ μόνα δικάζει. So Poll. 8, 117. Cf. Philippi, ib., 23 sqq. In the τραῦμα ἐκ προνοίας there must have been intent to murder, as is proved by Lys. 3, 41: ἔπειτα δὲ καὶ οὐδεμίαν ἡγούμην πρόνοιαν εἶναι (τραύματος), ὅστις μὴ ἀποκτεῖναι βουλόμενος ἔτρωσεν. For poisoning, see the law just cited and Philippi 51/2. I do not agree with the common view (see Heffter, ath. Gerichtsverf., 180. Meier [2] 387. 541. Philippi, d. Areop. u. d. Eph., 161), which regards the γραφὴ πυρκαϊᾶς as connected with the Areopagus' supervision of public buildings. Intentional arson—for an accident was, most probably, not punishable—was regarded as an offence against the person and life of another; arson, as we know it, to gain some pecuniary advantage, could not happen then. It is only in this way that we can explain the fact that the γραφὴ πυρκαϊᾶς is included in the νόμος φονικός. Plato, too, Laws, 9, 862, mentions murder πυρὸς προσβολῇ.

[2] Penalty for φόνος ἑκούσιος: Dem. 21, 43; Antiph., de caede Her., 10; Philippi 109 sqq.; for τραῦμα ἐκ προνοίας, Lys. 3, 38; Dem. 40, 32; Philippi 113/4: for φάρμακα: Philippi 120.

[3] Dem. 23, 71: τὸ δικαστήριον τὸ ἐπὶ Παλλαδίῳ. The legend of the origin of the court quoted from Cleidemos and Phanodemos in Suid. ἐπὶ Παλλαδίῳ. See Harp. Poll. 8, 118; Paus. 1, 28, 8/9; Philippi, 13 sqq.

[4] Arist. 57, 3: τῶν δ' ἀκουσίων (sc. φόνων) καὶ βουλεύσεως κἂν οἰκέτην ἀποκτείνῃ τις ἢ μέτοικον ἢ ξένον οἱ ἐ[πὶ] Πα[λλ]αδίῳ. Cf. Harp. ἐπὶ Παλλαδίῳ and βουλεύσεως, for which Isaios makes the court the Palladion, Deinarchos the Areopagus. Forchhammer brings arguments to shew that Deinarchos' statements are of little weight, and Philippi, 43 ff., agrees with him. What information we have about βούλευσις makes in favour of the Palladion, as Philippi shews, 29 sqq. His view is opposed by Lipsius, in Bursian's Jahresber., 1878, pp. 289/90, and in Meier [2] 384 sqq., and by Heikel, die sogen. βούλευσις in Mordproc., Helsingfors, 1886. Forchhammer, de Areopago, 30 ff., defines βούλευσις as the inception or origination of a plot to murder; W. Passow,

were: for unintentional manslaughter, exile without confiscation of property for a limited period until the murderer had propitiated the relatives of the murdered man, or, in case they would not relent, exile for a certain time, the length of which we do not know; for inciting another, the same punishment as if the offender had himself committed the crime.[1]

The third Athenian court for cases of bloodshed also sat outside the walls, on the east side of the town, near the Delphinion, the sanctuary of Apollo Delphinios.[2] This court tried those who pleaded that the homicide which they had committed was by law exempt from punishment.[3]

τὸ δικαστή-
ριον τὸ ἐπὶ
Δελφινίῳ.

---

de crimine βουλεύσεως, Goett., 1886, will have it to be a murder committed by a man "insidias machinatus quaslibet clandestinas consilio magis quam vi aperta" (p. 17), while αὐτόχειρ in his view is a man who kills another "manifesta vi" (p. 12), or "cruenta caede" (p. 14). The erroneousness of this, as Thalheim has already noticed, *Berl. phil. Wochenschr.*, 1887, p. 784, is evident from Plato, *Laws*, 9, 865B: ἐὰν δὲ αὐτόχειρ μὲν, ἄκων δὲ ἀποκτείνῃ τις ἕτερος ἕτερον, εἴτε τῷ ἑαυτοῦ σώματι ψιλῷ εἴτε ὀργάνῳ ἢ βέλει ἢ πώματος ἢ σίτου δόσει ἢ πυρὸς ἢ χειμῶνος προσβολῇ ἢ στερήσει πνεύματος, αὐτὸς τῷ ἑαυτοῦ σώματι ἢ δι' ἑτέρων σωμάτων, πάντως ἔστω μὲν ὡς αὐτόχειρ, δίκας δὲ τινέτω τὰς τοιάσδε. A new explanation by Kohm, in *Progr. von Olmütz*, 1890, is refuted by Thalheim, *Progr. von Schneidemühl*, 1892, p. 3 ff. Passow, 37 sqq., thinks that there never was such a thing as γραφὴ βουλεύσεως. So Heikel, *ibid*. But now that we have the express statement of Aristotle himself, there can be no further doubt about it; see also Plato, *Laws*, 9, 872. The Palladion is proved by Arist. to have been the court also for the trial of the murderer of a foreigner, a fact previously doubted by Philippi, 52 ff.; Welsing, however, took the right view, *de inquilinor. et peregrinor. ap. Athen. iudiciis*, 48 sqq., Münster, 1887. That the murder of a foreigner was punished differently to that of a citizen was inferred by Lipsius, in *Bursian's Jahresber.*, 1878, p. 290, from Dem. 23, 89. Cf. the same writer in Meier [2] 379. Lex. Seguer. 194, 11 says: ἐὰν μέτοικόν τις ἀποκτείνῃ, φυγῆς μόνον κατεδικάζετο· ἐὰν μέντοι ἀστόν, θάνατος ἡ ζημία.

[1] Punishments for φόνος ἀκούσιος: C.I.A., I. 61; Dem. 23, 45. 72; see Philippi 114 sqq.; for βούλευσις: Andoc., *de Myst.*, 94; without πρόνοια to murder: Antiph., *de Chor.*, 7; with πρόνοια: Antiph., *Accus. Venen.*, 27; Philippi 118 sqq. As to the punishment for the murder of a foreigner, we know that the murder of a metic was punished with banishment: Lex. Seguer. 194, 11.

[2] Dem. 23, 74 sqq.: τὸ δικαστήριον τὸ ἐπὶ Δελφινίῳ. Harp. ἐπὶ Δελφινίῳ. The legend of the origin of the court in Paus. 1, 28, 10; Poll. 8, 119. See Philippi 15/6.

[3] Arist. 57, 3: ἐὰν δ' ἀποκτεῖναι μέν τις ὁμολογῇ, φῇ δὲ κατὰ τοὺς νόμους, ο[ἷον]μοιχὸν λαβὼν ἢ ἐν πολέμῳ ἀγνοήσας ἢ ἐν ἄθλῳ ἀγωνιζόμενος, τού[τῳ] ἐπὶ Δελφινίῳ δικάζουσιν. Cf. Harp. ἐπὶ Δελφινίῳ. Leist, *graeco-italische Rechtsgeschichte*, 850 ff., assigned the two last cases to the Palladion; this is now shewn by Arist. to be an error.

The following cases were exempt according to the laws of Draco: unintentional killing of another competitor in an athletic contest, or of a comrade in time of war; slaying an adulterer detected with one's wife, mother, sister, daughter, or free concubine; and homicide in self-defence.[1] If the prosecutor recognised the homicide as unpunishable, the court probably had simply to confirm this. But it would usually happen that the prosecutor brought a charge of premeditated murder, while the Basileus, accepting the defence of the accused that the case was one of justifiable homicide only, brought the case before the court at the Delphinion.[2] As this defence might be rejected by the court, and the murder be pronounced premeditated and punishable, the court at the Delphinion must have had the power of passing sentence of death.[3]

The fourth court, "in Phreatto," sat in the Piræus on the seashore, but was probably very seldom needed. It tried any man who was banished for an unintentional murder and was accused of an intentional murder or intentional wounding—whether before or during his exile is doubtful. As the exile was not allowed to enter the country, he conducted his defence from a ship before judges sitting on the shore. If he was found guilty, he incurred the penalty for the crime in question; if he was acquitted, he returned into exile until his reconciliation with the relatives for the unpremeditated murder had been effected.[4] (τὸ δικαστήριον τὸ ἐν Φρεαττοῖ.)

The fifth court, that at the Prytaneion, composed of the four φυλοβασιλεῖς under the presidency of the βασιλεύς, had only a ceremonial importance. If a murder was (τὸ δικαστήριον τὸ ἐπὶ Πρυτανείῳ.)

---

[1] That Draco enumerated the several cases in his laws is evident from Dem. 20, 158. Among the cases specified by Draco, Philippi 55 sqq. reckons those given in Dem. 23, 54 sqq. The correctness of their inclusion is partly confirmed by the psephism of B.C. 409/8 (C.I.A., I. 61), and by the formula frequent in the Orators: ἐάν τις ἀμυνόμενος ἄρχοντα χειρῶν ἀδίκων κτείνῃ, of which there are also traces in C.I.A., I. 61, line 33. Later the number of cases of δίκαιος φόνος was increased still further; see Philippi 57 sqq.

[2] Philippi 59 sqq.

[3] Philippi 123 ff.

[4] Dem. 23, 77 sqq.: τὸ δικαστήριον τὸ ἐν Φρεαττοῖ, from which Harp. ἐν Φρεαττοῖ is taken. Arist. 57, 3 says: ἐὰν δὲ φεύγων φυγήν, ὧν αἴδεσίς ἐστιν, αἰ[τίαν ἔχῃ ἀπο]κτεῖναι ἢ τρῶσαί τινα, τούτῳ δ' ἐν Φρεάτου δικάζουσιν. [ὁ δὲ ἀπολο]γεῖται προσορμισάμενος ἐν πλοίῳ. Cf. Poll. 8, 120; Hellad. in Phot., Biblioth., 535a, 28; Lex. Seguer. 311, 17 sqq. The legend of the origin of the court in Paus. 1, 28, 11. See Philippi 18/9.

committed, and the murderer could not be discovered, then this court pronounced sentence upon him, and condemned the tools that had been employed in the murder; it also tried and convicted inanimate objects that had fallen and caused the death of a human being. These were then thrown by the Phylobasileis beyond the frontier.[1]

In early times, none but the relatives of the murdered man were entitled to vengeance; similarly, in historic times, the right to prosecute for murder was restricted to certain persons. Such a prosecution could only be instituted by the man himself, if wounded, or if death followed, by his relatives; and the law directed that notice of the charge was to be given to the murderer, and the accusation brought before the Basileus by the sons, brothers and sisters, or nephews and nieces, of the murdered man, and that they were to be assisted in the prosecution of the murderer by his cousins and their sons, his relatives by marriage, sons-in-law, father-in-law, and Phrateres.[2] For slaves the master, for metics the προστάτης, had to prosecute.[3]

Right to prosecute a murderer.

---

[1] Dem. 23, 76: τὸ δικαστήριον τὸ ἐπὶ Πρυτανείῳ.—τοῦτο δ' ἐστίν, ἐὰν λίθος ἢ ξύλον ἢ σίδηρος ἤ τι τοιοῦτον ἐμπεσὸν πατάξῃ καὶ τὸν μὲν βαλόντα ἀγνοῇ τις, αὐτὸ δ' εἰδῇ καὶ ἔχῃ τὸ τὸν φόνον εἰργασμένον, τούτοις ἐνταῦθα λαγχάνεται. From this are derived Harp. ἐπὶ Πρυτανείῳ, Poll. 8, 120: δικάζει περὶ τῶν ἀποκτεινάντων, κἂν ὦσιν ἀφανεῖς, καὶ περὶ τῶν ἀψύχων τῶν ἐμπεσόντων καὶ ἀποκτεινάντων. The addition προειστήκεσαν δὲ τούτου τοῦ δικαστηρίου φυλοβασιλεῖς, οὓς ἔδει τὸ ἐμπεσὸν ἄψυχον ὑπερορίσαι (see also Paus. 6, 11, 6) is set right by Arist. 57, 4: ὅταν δὲ [μ]ὴ ε[ἰδ]ῇ τὸν ποιήσαντα, τῷ δράσαντι λαγχάνει, δικάζει δ' ὁ βασιλεὺς καὶ οἱ φυλοβασιλεῖς καὶ τὰς τῶν ἀψύχων καὶ τῶν ἄλλων ζῴων. For the connexion of these usages with the ceremonies of the Bouphonia see Paus. 1, 28, 10; 24, 4. For the Bouphonia see Mommsen, *Heort.*, 449 sqq.; Philippi 16 sqq. [Sandys on Arist. 57, 4, and Gleue, *de Homicid. in Areop. Ath. Iud.*, Göttingen, 1894.]

[2] For the obligation of the relatives to prosecute the murderer see the law in Dem. 43, 57, which is confirmed by C.I.A., I. 61. Cf. for the meaning of the expressions there employed the explanations of Philippi 68 sqq. Lipsius, in *Bursian's Jahresber.*, 1878, p. 291, doubts the correctness of the explanation of ἐντὸς ἀνεψιότητος καὶ ἀνεψιῶν in Philippi, p. 70 sqq., "exclusive of the cousins." He bases his objections on a single passage in Dem. 43, 51, where, however, ἐντὸς has yet to be shewn to be an Athenian legal term. This law has been declared spurious by Seeliger, in *N. Rh. Mus.*, 31, 1876, p. 176 ff., and Grasshoff agrees with him, *symb. ad doctrin. iur. att. de hereditatib.*, Berlin, 1877, p. 8. When a murdered citizen had no relatives, or when, if he had, they would not do their duty, it is natural to enquire whether one who was not a relative might represent him and prosecute in a δίκη φονική: but the authorities at present accessible to us do not enable us to decide this point. See Philippi 100 sqq.

[3] For the prosecution for the murder of slaves or metics see Philippi 98 ff.

Trials for Homicide.

In murder cases, certain formalities had to be observed in giving in the information, in recording the pleadings, and at the trial. After the interment of the murdered man, at which, as a sign that he had lost his life by violence, a spear was carried before the body and then fixed upon the grave, the man whose duty it was to prosecute filed his information before the Basileus, and, probably under his authority, forbade the murderer to enter the market-place or the temples, and summoned him before the proper court.[1] In the trial itself there were two stages—the preliminary investigation and the actual proceedings in court. The preliminary investigation was conducted by the Basileus in a particularly solemn manner in three προδικασίαι in three successive months; in the fourth month the case was brought before the proper court.[2] This preliminary inquiry was held to enable the Basileus to decide, from the depositions of the prosecutor, the defendant, and witnesses, before which court the case was to be brought on.[3]

Procedure.

---

[1] For the ἐπενεγκεῖν δόρυ ἐπὶ τῆς ἐκφορᾶς see Harp. s.v., Poll. 8, 65; Lex. Seguer. 237, 30. The filing of the information took place after the interment, Antiph., de Chor., 37/8. I agree with Philippi, 69/70, that our authorities know of only one notification to the defendant—by the prosecutor after he had entered the accusation. So Hauvette-Besnault, de archonte rege, 101 sqq. See Antiph., ibid., 35: πείσαντες δὲ τούτους ἀπογράφεσθαι καὶ προαγορεύειν ἐμοὶ εἴργεσθαι τῶν νομίμων, i.e., according to Poll. 8, 66, ἱερῶν καὶ ἀγορᾶς. Cf. Arist. 57, 4: ὁ δὲ τὴν αἰτίαν ἔχων τὸν μὲν ἄλλον χρόνον εἴργεται τῶν ἱερῶν καὶ οὐδ' εἰς τὴν ἀγορὰν δ[έδοται ἐ]μβαλεῖν αὐτῷ. τότε δ' εἰς τὸ ἱερὸν εἰσελθὼν ἀπολογεῖται. Antiph., de Caede Herod., 10; Dem. 20, 158. That the notification was connected with the summons into court may be gathered from such an expression as (Dem.) 59, 9: προεῖπεν αὐτῷ ἐπὶ Παλλαδίῳ φόνου. Arist. 57, 2 says: καὶ ὁ προαγορεύων εἴργεσθαι τῶν νομίμων οὗτός (sc. ὁ βασιλεύς) ἐστιν (see Poll. 8, 90; Lex. Seguer. 310, 6 sqq.): we must understand this to mean that the notification was made on his authority.

[2] Antiph., de Chor., 42. As the same Basileus had to conduct the preliminary investigation and the actual trial, murder cases cannot have been entered during the last three months of the year.

[3] I do not think Philippi's view (p. 85 sqq.) probable, that the Basileus referred the case to a definite court even before the preliminary investigation, and that this investigation was conducted in the presence of the judges. Cf. Schömann, griech. Alterth., 1, 496. Hauvette-Besnault, 107 sqq., opposes this view. The reason which Philippi gives—that oaths before the Areopagus (Lys. 10, 11; Dem. 23, 67) and at the Palladion ([Dem.] 47, 70) are mentioned, and that the taking of oaths belonged to the preliminary investigation—will not bear examination, as the latter hypothesis is not proved to be true as regards accusations for murder. The

The sittings of all the courts of homicide were held in the open air, in order that the prosecutor and the judges might not be under the same roof as a man polluted by bloodshed.¹ In the court on the Areopagus, about which we are somewhat better informed than about the others, and whose procedure must have been similar to theirs, the defendant and prosecutor stood on unhewn stones, the one called λίθος ὕβρεως, the stone of offence, the other λίθος ἀναιδείας, the stone of implacableness.² The proceedings began with the oath taken by the parties appealing to the Σεμναί, as they stood by the pieces of a sacrificed boar, ram and bull.³ In this oath the prosecutor declared that he was related to the murdered man and therefore entitled to prosecute, and that the murder was committed by the defendant; while the defendant avowed his innocence. Both invoked a curse upon themselves and their children if they swore falsely.⁴ Each side might make two speeches; in these they had to confine themselves to the case.⁵ If it is a fact that the proceedings lasted three days, the first day was probably taken up with the first speech of the prosecutor, the evidence of the witnesses and their oath, and the first speech of the defendant, the second day with the second speech of both

oaths mentioned in Dem. 23, 67 sqq. were taken at the actual trial, to judge from the context.

¹ Antiph., de Caed. Herod., 11. Arist. 57, 4 says: εἰσάγει δ' ὁ βασιλεὺς καὶ δικάζο[υσ]ι . . . καὶ ὑπαίθριοι.

² Paus. 1, 28, 5: τοὺς δὲ ἀργοὺς λίθους ἐφ' ὧν ἑστᾶσιν ὅσοι δίκας ὑπέχουσι καὶ οἱ διώκοντες τὸν μὲν ὕβρεως, τὸν δὲ ἀναιδείας αὐτῶν ὀνομάζουσιν. The correct explanation of the names of the stones was given by Forchhammer, de lapidib. in Areop. quib. insistebant reus et accusator, p. 7 sqq., Kiel Ind. Lect., 1843/4. See also Istr. ap. Suid., Phot. Θεός —ἐτιμᾶτο δὲ καὶ 'Αθήνησιν ἡ 'Αναίδεια καὶ ἱερὸν ἦν αὐτῆς, ὡς Ἴστρος ἐν ιδ'.

³ Poll. 8, 117, in his account of the trial before the Areopagus: ἐγίνετο δὲ διωμοσία καὶ μετὰ τὴν διωμοσίαν κρίσις. Oath by the Σεμναί: Dein. in Dem. 47 87. For the sacrifice see Dem. 23, 68.

⁴ For the oaths of the parties see (Dem.) 47, 72; Lys. 10, 11; Antiph., de Chor., 16; de caede Herod., 11; Dem. 23, 67. The same oath also at the Palladion: (Dem.) 59, 9/10. For the meaning of these oaths see Philippi 89 sqq. The Schol. to Dem. 23, 68, Bullet. de' corr. Hell. 1, 137, says on the διωμοσία: ὅταν οἱ φονικὴν δικαζόμενοι δίκην ὤμνυον πρὸ τῆς δίκης ἑκάτεροι τἀληθῆ λέξειν, ἐξώλειαν ἑαυτοῖς ἐπαρώμενοι, εἰ ἐξαπατήσαιεν. Æschin., de F. L., 87, mentions an oath taken by the prosecutor, after getting a conviction: of this we know nothing further. See Philippi 93, 33.

⁵ Poll. 8, 117; Lys. 3, 46; Lyc., Leocr., 12. The same regulations were observed too in the Palladion; see de Chor. (before the Palladion: Philippi 32 sqq.) 9, 14.

parties, and the third day with the voting.[1] Even after the first speech of the parties, the defendant might escape sentence by voluntary exile.[2] If the votes were equal, the defendant was acquitted.[3] If acquitted, he offered a thank-offering in the sanctuary of the Σεμναί.[4]

The wilful murderer who had escaped punishment by flight, and the unintentional murderer who was exiled by the court, were both under the protection of the laws. If they avoided Attica, the public games, and the Amphictyonic festivals, to assassinate them was a punishable offence; any one who did so was condemned like an ordinary murderer. But if they were caught within Attica, they might be killed with impunity, or taken for execution to the Thesmothetai or informed against.[5] *Position of the murderer.*

A murderer whose crime was only punished by exile and one who had committed a murder that was exempt from punishment, were permitted to return, under certain formalities, to civil and religious membership of the State. For this, religious purification and atonement were required. Whoever had committed a murder that was exempt from punishment needed only religious purification, but that was necessary because every one who had shed human blood was considered unclean.[6] *Atonement.*
If a man who had committed an unpremeditated murder wished to return from exile before his legal term of banishment was expired, he had first to seek reconciliation with the relatives of the slain. To make this valid, however, the unanimous consent of the father, the brothers, and the sons of the murdered man was necessary. If there were no such relatives, the Ephetai had to select ten members from the man's Phratry, who could, if they chose,

---

[1] Separate proceedings on separate days were first suggested by Schömann, *Antiquit.*, 292. Whether indeed Poll. 8, 117 can be taken as authority for this is very doubtful: καθ' ἕκαστον δὲ μῆνα τριῶν ἡμερῶν ἐδίκαζον ἐφεξῆς, τετάρτῃ φθίνοντος, τρίτῃ, δευτέρᾳ. For the witnesses and their oath see Antiph., *de Caede Herod.*, 12.

[2] Dem. 23, 69. Poll. 8, 117 excepts parricides.

[3] Antiph., *de Caede Herod.*, 51.

[4] Paus. 1, 28, 6.

[5] The laws as to the intentional murderer are given in Dem. 23, 38. 29 ff., 51 ff.; according to C.I.A., I. 61, they also applied to the unintentional murderer. See Philippi 129 sqq.

[6] Philippi 62/3. In this the exegetai assisted; see Suid. ἐξηγηταί, Art. 2: ἐξηγηταὶ τρεῖς γίνονται πυθόχρηστοι, οἷς μέλει καθαίρειν τοὺς ἄγει τινὶ ἐνισχηθέντας.

consent to a reconciliation.¹ The reconciliation of the murderer with the relatives of his victim was followed by a religious purification.² In the case of premeditated murder, however, where the murderer had gone into exile before the court had pronounced sentence, reconciliation could not be granted by the relatives, but the murdered man himself might grant it before his death.³

Civil cases for the most part fell within the jurisdiction of

Arbitrators. public arbitrators or διαιτηταί.⁴ These officials, who, there can be no doubt, existed even in the fifth century, were a body composed of those Athenians who, upon attaining the age of 60, were removed from the list of those liable to military service. They held office one year, after which they were relieved by the next body of men who had completed their time of service. Whoever avoided this duty of serving as a Diaitetes was punished with Atimia unless he were excused as holding some other office or being abroad at the time.⁵ The Diaitetai formed

---

¹ The αἴδεσις for a φόνος ἀκούσιος is dealt with in C.I.A., I. 61, and in the law in Dem. 43, 57, which fills up the gaps in the inscription. Philippi 137/8 conjectures that, in the inscription, before the 10 phrateres of the murdered, the nephews, cousins and cousins' children were also mentioned, an assumption, however, which is not confirmed, at least by the law in Dem. It is probable that the relatives were permitted to excuse the murderer from exile altogether; see Philippi 142/3. After the expiration of the legal term of exile the relatives were no doubt obliged to grant the αἴδεσις; see Philippi 115.

² Dem. 23, 72.

³ The first regulation is educed by Philippi 143 sqq. from Dem. 21, 43; the second from Dem. 37, 58 sqq.

⁴ For the Diaitetai cf. Hudtwalcker, *üb. d. öffentl. u. Privat-Schiedsrichter —Diaiteten—in Athen u. d. Proc. vor denselben*, 1812; M. H. E. Meier, *die Privatschiedsrichter u. d. öffentl. Diaiteten Athens*, 1846; Westermann, *über die öffentl. Schiedsrichter in Ath.* in *Ber. d. sächs. Ges. d. W.*, 1, 236 sqq.; Hubert, *de arbitris att. et privatis et publicis*, Leipzig, 1885; Lipsius in Meier², 1009 sqq.

⁵ Meier 28/9 assumes that they were only introduced under Eucleides: for the contrary view see Schömann, *Verfassungsgesch. Ath.*, 44 sqq.; Hubert 20 sqq.; Lipsius 1009 sqq. Arist. 53, 4: διαιτηταί δ' εἰσὶν οἷς ἂν ἐξηκοστὸν ἔτος ᾖ. τοῦτο δὲ δῆλον ἐκ τῶν ἀρχόντων καὶ τῶν ἐπωνύμων. Then follows a description of the arrangement of the muster-roll of those liable to service—p. 315³—and then Arist. 53, 5 continues: τὸν δὲ τελευταῖον τῶν ἐπωνύμων λαβόντες οἱ τετταράκοντα διανέμουσιν αὐτοῖς τὰς διαίτας καὶ ἐπικληροῦσιν, ἃς ἕκαστος διαιτήσει. καὶ ἀναγκαῖον ἃς ἂν ἕκαστος λάχῃ διαίτας ἐκδιαιτᾶν. ὁ γὰρ νόμος, ἄν τις μὴ γένηται διαιτητὴς τῆς ἡλικίας αὐτῷ καθηκούσης, ἄτιμον εἶναι κελεύει, πλὴν ἐὰν τύχῃ ἀρχὴν ἄρχων τ[ιν]ὰ ἐν ἐκείνῳ τῷ ἐνιαυτῷ ἢ ἀποδημῶν. οὗτοι δ' ἀτελεῖς εἰσι μόνοι. And this is all that is told us about the age, number and appointment of the Diaitetai. See Suid. διαιτητάς; Lex. Seguer. 186, 1; 235, 23; Poll. 8, 126;

a judicial corporation, apparently divided into 10 sections corresponding to the 10 tribes.[1] The members of these separate sections had not necessarily to be taken from the tribe for which they officiated.[2] Each section sat in some court or temple appointed for it.[3] The procedure was as follows. The Deme-judges in civil suits for sums exceeding 10 drachmas, and the other officials in such civil cases as were brought before them (a few special classes of actions alone excepted) appointed by lot for the parties a Diaitetes, taken no doubt generally from the section for the tribe to which the defendant belonged. The Diaitetes was at once president and jury. Trial before him was speedier, cheaper (for plantiff and defendant paid only one drachma each, and as much again for each motion for adjournment) and less hazardous, since the Diaitetes was only permitted to inflict a fine. If at the conclusion of the case the parties could not come to terms, the verdict of the Diaitetes was given at an appointed time.[4]

Hesych. διαιτηταί; Ulpian on Dem., *Mid.*, 542. The list of the Diaitetai of the year 325/4 with the heading: Διαιτηταί οἱ ἐπὶ 'Αντικλ(έους ἄρχοντος) ἀνέθεσαν στεφανωθέντε(ς ὑπὸ τοῦ δή)μου contains the names of 103 persons, 13 from the Erechtheis tribe, 14 from the Aigeis, 3 from the Pandionis, 12 from the Leontis, 9 from the Acamantis, 11 from the Oineis, 16 from the Kecropis, 9 from the Hippothontis, 9 from the Aiantis, 7 from the Antiochis; see C.I.A., II. 943. Other fragmentary Diaitetai-lists are C.I.A., II. 941, 942. But 944 can hardly be such a list.

[1] The Diaitetai, as a body, pass resolutions: C.I.A., II. 1172, dedicate votive offerings: 1182. For the sections for the separate tribes see (Dem.) 47, 12: οἱ γὰρ τὴν Οἰνηῗδα καὶ τὴν 'Ερεχθηῗδα διαιτῶντες ἐνταῦθα (*i.e.* ἐν τῇ ἡλιαίᾳ) κάθηνται. Bergk, in *Zeitschr. für Alterthumsw.*, 7, 1849, 273 sqq., infers from Dem. 21, 83 sqq. a body of Diaitetai constituted under the presidency of Prytanes.

[2] This follows from the fact that in the law-suit between Demosthenes of Paiania (Pandionis) and Meidias of Anagyrus (Dem. 21, 68 Erechtheis) Straton of Phaleron (Dem. 21, 83 Aiantis) was Diaitetes.

[3] For the places of trial see Poll. 8, 126: διῆτων δ' ἐν ἱεροῖς. ἐν τῇ ἡλιαίᾳ: (Dem.) 47, 12; ἐν τῇ ποικίλῃ στοᾷ: Dem. 45, 17; ἐπὶ Δελφινίῳ: Is. 12, 9; Dem. 40, 11. Arist. 55, 5 says of the stone of swearing at the βασίλειος στοά (Poll. 8, 86): ἐφ' οὗ καὶ οἱ διαιτηταὶ ὀμόσαντες ἀποφαίνονται τὰς διαίτας.

[4] Lex. Cantabr. 673 under μὴ οὖσα δίκη: Δημήτριος ὁ Φαληρεὺς ἐνίους λέγει τῶν κρινομένων κακοτεχνεῖν τοῖς διώκουσιν ἀντιλαγχάνοντας τὴν μὴ οὖσαν. ἔδει γὰρ τοὺς ὑπὲρ δέκα δραχμὰς ἀμφισβητοῦντας διαιτητὰς εἰς δίκην ἑκάστην (Müller's reading for the διαιτητεῖς δέκα ἔτη of the MSS.) λαμβάνειν· διὸ καὶ ἔκειτο νόμος μὴ εἰσάγεσθαι δίκην, εἰ μὴ πρότερον ἐξετασθείη παρ' αὐτοῖς τὸ πρᾶγμα. See too Poll. 8, 126. Arist. 53, 1. 2 describes the procedure that was usual in the suits tried by the Deme-judges: τὰ δ' ὑπὲρ τοῦτο τὸ τίμημα (10 drachmas) τοῖς διαιτηταῖς παραδιδόασιν. (53, 5 he says: τὸ δὲ τελευταῖον τῶν ἐπωνύμων λαβόντες οἱ τεττα-

There were two legal remedies against the verdict. If the sentence had been pronounced in default and if the defaulter maintained that the verdict in default had been given although he was innocent, he might bring a motion to quash the verdict, which was probably decided by another Diaitetes. If it were not a judgment in default, he might appeal to a Heliastic court. In the latter case the documents prepared by the president were transferred to the Heliastic court.[1]

Against any proceedings of any individual Diaitetes an Eisangelia could be brought before the whole body; the defendant was free however to appeal from them to a Heliastic court. The penalty, if he was condemned, was Atimia.[2] It does not appear

ῥάκοντα διανέμουσιν αὐτοῖς τὰς διαίτας καὶ ἐπικληροῦσιν, ἃς ἕκαστος διαιτήσει· καὶ ἀναγκαῖον ἄς ἂν ἕκαστος λάχῃ διαίτας ἐκδιαιτᾶν.) οἱ δὲ παραλαβόντες, ἐὰν μὴ δύνωνται διαλῦσαι, γιγνώσκουσι, κἂν μὲν ἀμφοτέροις ἀρέσκῃ τὰ γνωσθέντα [καὶ] ἐμμένωσιν, ἔχει τέλος ἡ δίκη. See also Poll. 8, 100; Phot. τετταράκοντα; Lex. Seguer. 306, 15 sqq. For the procedure in other private suits, exclusive probably of δίκαι ἐμπορικαί, see Hubert, 37 sqq. Cf. Dem. 21, 84 sqq. Ἡ κυρία is the appointed day for the Diaitetes to give judgment; the general word for that is ἀποφαίνειν, to acquit is ἀποδιαιτᾶν, to condemn καταδιαιτᾶν. See also Hubert 42 sqq. Plaintiff and defendant each paid into court a παράστασις of one drachma: Poll. 8, 39. 127, and the same amount at each ὑπωμοσία: Harp. παράστασις.

[1] For the quashing of a sentence see Lex. Cantabr. 673 in the preceding note; Poll. 8, 60; Lex. Seguer. 278, 29; Hubert 48 sqq. Cf. however Thalheim in *Progr. v. Schneidemühl*, 1892, p. 5. sqq. Arist. 53, 2, describes the procedure in an appeal: ἂν δ' ὁ ἕτερος ἐφῇ τῶν ἀντιδίκων εἰς τὸ δικαστήριον, ἐμβαλόντες τὰς μαρτυρίας καὶ τὰς προκλήσεις καὶ τοὺς νόμους εἰς ἐχίνους, χωρὶς μὲν τὰς τοῦ διώκοντος, χωρὶς δὲ τὰς τοῦ φεύγοντος, καὶ τούτους κατασημηνάμενοι καὶ τὴν [γνώ]σιν τοῦ διαιτητοῦ γεγραμμένην ἐν γραμματείῳ προσαρτήσαντες, παραδιδόασι τοῖς δ' τοῖς τὴν φυλὴν τοῦ φεύγοντος δικάζουσι (these are οἱ τὴν φυλὴν δικάζοντες in Arist. 58, 2, i.e. the four Deme-judges of the particular tribe; see Arist. 53). οἱ δὲ παραλαβόντες εἰσάγουσιν εἰς τὸ δικαστήριον, [τὰ μὲν ἐ]ντὸς χιλίων εἰς ἕνα καὶ διακοσίους, τὰ δ' ὑπὲρ χιλίας εἰς ἕνα καὶ τετρακοσίους. οὐκ ἔξεσ[τι δ' οὔ]τε νόμοις οὔτε προκλήσεσι οὔτε μαρτυρίαις ἀλλ' ἢ ταῖς παρὰ τοῦ διαιτητοῦ χρῆσθαι ταῖς εἰς τοὺς ἐχίνους ἐμβεβλημέναις. See also Harp., διαιτηταί = Suid., διαιτηταῖς; Poll. 8, 126/7; Hubert 46 sqq.

[2] Arist. 53, 6: ἔστιν δὲ καὶ εἰσαγγέλλειν εἰς τοὺς διαιτητάς, ἐάν τις ἀδικηθῇ ὑπὸ τοῦ διαιτητοῦ, κἂν τινος καταγνῶσιν, ἀτιμοῦσθαι κελεύουσιν οἱ νόμοι· ἔφεσις δ' ἐστὶ καὶ τούτοις. Harp., εἰσαγγελία makes the Eisangelia come πρὸς τοὺς δικαστάς. Bergk, *ib.*, wished to read in Harp. διαιτητὰς instead of πρὸς τοὺς δικαστάς, supposing the Eisangelia to be brought before the whole body of Diaitetai. This is confirmed by Arist. For an instance of such a proceeding he refers to Dem. 21, 83 ff. Fränkel, *d. att. Geschworenger.*, p. 72, 4, and Hubert 51 ff. agree with him; R. Schoell, *de synegor. att.*, p. 15 sqq. refers the passage in Demosthenes to the submission by the Diaitetai of an account of their office for scrutiny.

probable that the Diaitetai were bound at the close of their year of office to give account for their proceedings; adequate security against possible irregularities was found in the Eisangelia just mentioned.[1]

From these public Diaitetai we must distinguish the Diaitetai who arbitrated when an action was compromised. These Diaitetai were appointed by the parties themselves by mutual agreement; and there was almost always more than one, generally three. They based their decisions on considerations of equity, and the parties bound themselves by a written contract, often even by giving bail, to accept their arbitration. Against this neither a motion for quashing the sentence nor an appeal was permitted.[2] *Private Arbitrators.*

The third and largest body of judges at Athens was the Ἡλιαία.[3] The number of members varied at different times. When the power of the First Athenian Confederacy was at its height, there were 6,000, chosen doubtless once a year from those who had made application for the office.[4] In the fourth century, when the allies no longer brought lawsuits to Athens for trial, there ceased to be any occasion for 6,000 jurors. Besides, the political energies of the Athenians, it would seem, were now *Ἡλιαία.*

---

[1] Meier 15 sqq., Schoell p. 15 sqq. assume that a εὔθυνα took place; Fränkel, p. 72, 4, takes the opposite view.

[2] Meier, p. 3 ff.; Hubert 8 sqq.; Dem. 33, 14/5; Isocr. 18, 11: ὡς οὐκ εἰσαγώγιμος ἦν ἡ δίκη διαίτης γεγενημένης.

[3] The etymology of the word is uncertain; I would refer the reader to Wachsmuth 2, 1, 361 sqq. for a discussion of the point.

[4] Arist. 24, 3 says expressly of the time when the fortunes of the First Athenian League were in the ascendant: δικασταὶ μὲν γὰρ ἦσαν ἑξακισχίλιοι. This disposes of Fränkel's arguments *d. alt. Geschworenger.*, p. 1 sqq. The lines in Arist., *Wasps*, 661 ff: ἀπὸ τούτου νῦν κατάθες μισθὸν τοῖσι δικασταῖς ἐνιαυτοῦ· Ἐξ χιλιάσιν, κοὔπω πλείους ἐν τῇ χώρᾳ κατένασθεν, Γίγνεται ἡμῖν ἑκατὸν δήπου καὶ πεντήκοντα τάλαντα mean "there have never been more than 6,000 Dicasts, and sometimes less," so that the calculation is even more unfavourable for earlier times. The numerous lawsuits brought to Athens by the allies no doubt necessitated a great number of Dicasts, and they were enabled to devote themselves to the work under the polity which Arist. describes, since in it most of the citizens took a share in the administration, and were paid for their services. That the Dicasts in the fifth century were selected by lot from those who applied to serve appears from Arist. 27, 4: ἀφ' ὧν (in consequence of the introduction of the payment of Dicasts by Pericles) αἰτιῶνταί τινες χείρω (τὰ δικαστήρια) γενέσθαι, κληρουμένων (as there were chosen by lot, and therefore applied to serve) ἐπιμελῶς ἀεὶ μᾶλλον τῶν τυχόντων ἢ τῶν ἐπιεικῶν ἀνθρώπων.

not so vigorous that such a number of men should offer themselves every year as jurymen that 6,000 Dicasts could be selected from them. Accordingly in the fourth century all who applied were apparently entered on the jury-list, if they possessed the necessary qualifications, *i.e.*, if they were over 30 years of age, were not indebted to the State, and were not under Atimia. Any one who did not fulfil these conditions, yet surreptitiously obtained a place on the jury-list was brought to trial and punished.[1]

All Athenians who had applied to serve as Heliasts for any year took the Heliastic oath on the Ardettos at the beginning of the year.[2] It ran as follows: "I will judge according to the laws and resolutions of the Athenian people and of the Council of the Five Hundred, and in those cases which are not determined by the laws, according to the best of my judgment, without favour or animosity. I will decide on the actual case before me. I will hear both sides impartially. I swear this by Zeus, by Apollo, and by Demeter: may much good befall me, if I keep my oath, but if I prove false to it, may destruction fall upon me and my family."[3]

Heliastic Oath.

---

[1] Arist. 63, 3: δικάζειν δ' ἔξεστιν τοῖς ὑπὲρ λ' ἔτη γεγονόσιν, ὅσοι αὐτῶν μὴ ὀφείλουσιν τῷ δημοσίῳ ἢ ἄτιμοί εἰσιν· ἐὰν δέ τις δικάζῃ, οἷς μὴ ἔξεστιν, ἐνδείκνυται κ[αὶ εἰς] τὸ δικαστήριον εἰσάγετ[αι], ἐὰν δ' ἁλῷ, προστιμ[ῶσιν αὐτ]ῷ οἱ δικασταί, ὅτι ἂν δοκῇ ἄξιος εἶναι παθε[ῖν] ἢ ἀποτεῖσαι. ἐὰν δὲ ἀργύριον τιμηθῇ, δεῖ αὐτὸν δεδέσ[θαι], ἕως ἂν ἐκτείσῃ τό τε πρότερον ὄφλημ[α, ἐ]φ' ᾧ ἐνεδείχθη, καὶ ὅτι ἂν αὐτῷ προστιμήσῃ τ[ὸ δικ]αστήριον. Cf. Poll. 8, 122: ἐδίκαζον δ' οἱ ὑπὲρ τριάκοντα ἔτη ἐκ τῶν ἐπιτίμων καὶ μὴ ὀφειλόντων τῷ δημοσίῳ.

[2] Harp. Ἀρδηττος—τόπος Ἀθήνησιν ὑπὲρ τὸ στάδιον τὸ Παναθηναϊκόν, πρὸς τῷ δήμῳ τῷ ὑπένερθεν Ἀγρυλέων. ἐν τούτῳ, φασί, δημοσίᾳ πάντες ὤμνυον Ἀθηναῖοι τὸν ὅρκον τὸν ἡλιαστικόν. ὠνομάσθη δὲ ἀπὸ Ἀρδήττου ἥρωος ἀρχαίου, ὃς Ἀθηναίους πρῶτος ἐξώρκισεν. Θεόφραστος δ' ἐν τοῖς περὶ νόμων δηλοῖ, ὡς κατελέλυτο τὸ ἔθος τοῦτο. Cf. Lex. Seguer. 443, 24; Suid. ἡλιαστής; Poll. 8, 122, with the remarks of Lipsius in Meier [2] 161, 29. That the Heliasts took the oath once only and not before each meeting of the court follows from Isocr. 18, 34. The oath is called ὁ ὅρκος ὁ ἡλιαστικός: Hyper., *Euxenipp.*, xlix.; ὁ τῶν ἡλιαστῶν ὅρκος: Dem. 24, 148; ὁ δικαστικὸς ὅρκος: Lex. Seguer. 207, 5; ὁ τῶν δικαστῶν ὅρκος: Æsch. *in Ctes.* 6. That the Heliastic oath was taken every year is proved by Isocr. 15, 21.

[3] For the value of the Heliastic oath in Dem. 24, 149 ff. see Westermann *comment. de iurisiur. iudicum Ath. formula*, Leipz., 1858, 1859, pars 1. 2. 3. Cf. Lipsius in Meier [2] 153, 17. I do not consider that its defence by Hofmann is successful *de iuris iurandi ap. Athen. formulis*, 8 ff., Darmstadt, 1886. The genuine oath, according to Fränkel's careful reconstruction from passages referring to it (Herm. 13, 452 sqq.), ran somewhat as follows: ψηφιοῦμαι κατὰ τοὺς νόμους καὶ τὰ ψηφίσματα τοῦ δήμου τοῦ Ἀθηναίων καὶ τῆς βουλῆς τῶν πεντακοσίων, περὶ δ' ὧν ἂν νόμοι μὴ ὦσι, γνώμῃ τῇ δικαιοτάτῃ καὶ οὔτε χάριτος ἕνεκ' οὔτ'

The Heliaia was a political body presided over by the Thesmothetai and having its special place for meeting.[1] As representing the community, it formed the supreme court of justice, and sat for that purpose either as a body or in larger or smaller sections. Our authorities mention courts of 200, 400, 500, 1,000, 1,500, 2,000 and 2,500 members, to which numbers however we have always to add one extra Dicast.[2] Special courts were constituted in military cases from the comrades

The Great Court and the Small Courts.

ἔχθρας (restored from Æschin. *in Ctes.* 6; Dem. 19, 179; 89, 40; 57, 63). καὶ ψηφιοῦμαι περὶ αὐτῶν, ὧν ἂν ἡ δίωξις ᾖ. (from Æsch. *in Tim.* 154, 170; Dem. 45, 50). καὶ ἀκροάσομαι τῶν τε κατηγορούντων καὶ τῶν ἀπολογουμένων ὁμοίως ἀμφοῖν (from Dem. 18. 2. 6; Isocr. 15, 21; Luc., *de Calum.*, 8). ὄμνυμι ταῦτα νὴ τὸν Δία νὴ τὸν Ἀπόλλω, νὴ τὴν Δήμητρα, καὶ εἴη μέν μοι εὐορκοῦντι πολλὰ καὶ ἀγαθά, ἐπιορκοῦντι δ᾽ ἐξώλεια αὐτῷ τε καὶ γένει (from Poll. 8, 122; Andoc., *de Myst.*, 31; cf. C.I.A., II. 578). The passage given in Andoc., *de Myst.*, 91, was perhaps only a temporary addition inserted in the oath for a little while immediately after the amnesty.

[1] The Heliaia was a political body; for οἱ δικασταὶ swear with the Boule to the treaty with Chalkis in 445; see C.I.A., IV. 27a. The body of Heliasts is in this document called ἡ ἡλιαία ἡ τῶν θεσμοθετῶν. V. Wilamowitz-Moellendorf, in *Phil. Unters.*, Heft 1, p. 90 ff., takes this as the official quarters of the Thesmothetai, "the sunny hall," close to the θεσμοθέσιον, perhaps immediately connected with it. He is opposed by Wachsmuth 2, 1, 359 sqq. The same expression has been restored by Taylor in Antiph., *de Chor.*, 21 for εἰς τὴν ἡλιακὴν τὴν τῶν θεσμοθετῶν, ἡλιαία here meaning the place. In the same way the ἡλιαία in (Dem.) 47, 12 is the place where the whole of the Heliasts meet, called in Andoc., *de Myst.*, 28, τὸ τῶν θεσμοθετῶν δικαστήριον. Cf. Paus. 1, 28, 8. In Dem. 23, 97 ἡ ἡλιαία means the body of jurors. Their place of meeting was by the market; see Curtius, *att. Stud.*, 2, 42; Wachsmuth 2, 1, 359. Courts composed of two or three sections of the Heliasts also sat there; cf. Harp. ἡλιαία; Lex. Seguer. 189, 20; 262, 10; Phot. Et. M. *s.v.*

[2] In the fragment of Demades περὶ δωδεκαετίας, no. 52, in *Herm.* 13, 494: ἕκαστον τῶν ἀδικημάτων ἰδίας ἔχει τὰς οἰκονομίας· ἃ μὲν γάρ ἐστι δεόμενα τῆς Ἀρείου πάγου βουλῆς, ἃ δὲ τῶν ἐλαττόνων δικαστηρίων, ἃ δὲ τῆς ἡλιαίας, τὰ ἐλάττω δικαστήρια are the sections, contrasted with the ἡλιαία, where the court was regularly held when several sections combined; see Harp. ἡλιαία. A court of all the Heliasts initiated into the Mysteries, we are told, tried the Diadicasia mentioned by Andoc., *de Myst.*, 28; 200 judges: Arist. 53, 3. Poll. 8, 48; 400: Arist. 53, 3. Poll. 8, 48; 500: Is. 5, 20. (Dem.) 50, 10; 1,000: Poll. 8, 53. Dem. 24, 9; 1,500: Dein. *in Dem.* 107; 2,000: Lys. 13, 35; 2,500: Dein. *in Dem.* 52. See Fränkel, pp. 103/4 ff.; Meier [2] 167 sqq. More exact information with the extra judge added to make the number unequal is given in Arist. 53, 3. (the source of Poll. 8, 46) and Dem. 24, 9, on which the Schol. adds: διὰ τοῦτο δὲ ὁ εἷς προσετέθη ἀεὶ τοῖς δικασταῖς, ἵνα μὴ ἴσων γενομένων τῶν ψήφων ἐξ ἴσης ἀπέλθωσιν οἱ δικαζόμενοι, ἀλλ᾽ ἐκεῖνος δόξῃ νικᾶν, ᾧ ὁ εἷς προστεθῇ. See Schömann, *op. ac.*, 1, 215. However, according to C.I.A., II. 778, 499 jurors acted at one trial.

of the defendant, in Mystery-cases by the initiated, and perhaps in mercantile cases by expert Heliasts.[1]

It is highly probable that even in the fifth century the 6,000 Dicasts were divided into sections, each containing 500 members.

Divisional Courts. The number of these sections may have been 12, or—as 10 is the number we find in the fourth century—10 with 1,000 reserves. Whether, if there were 10 sections, they comprised only members of the same tribe, or whether, as in the fourth century, they were composed of men drawn from all the tribes, must be left undecided.[2] It is probable that in the fifth century each section was assigned by sortition or otherwise to some particular president, and that he always sat in a particular court. These arrangements probably lasted for the year.[3]

With the remodelling of the constitution under the Archon

---

[1] For the γραφαὶ δειλίας, λιποταξίου, ἀστρατείας, see Lys. 14, 5; for Mystery-cases, Poll. 8, 123; Andoc., de Myst., 28; for commercial suits, Dem. 35, 43: καὶ ἔγωγε καὶ αὐτὸς συγχωρῶ σοφώτατον εἶναι τοῦτον, ἐὰν ὑμᾶς πείσῃ τοὺς περὶ τῶν συμβολαίων τῶν ἐμπορικῶν δικάζοντας.

[2] As a single δικαστήριον in the fourth century still consisted of 500 members (Dem. 24, 9; Harp. ἡλιαία; Poll. 8, 123), although in all probability this was then only a theoretical number, we must suppose 500 to have been the number in the 5th century: to be retained afterwards as a fictitious number, it must have once had a real meaning. In the trial of Pericles there were 1,500 judges: Plut., Per., 32. The view that there were 10 Dicasteria of 500 each, and 1,000 substitutes, was first advanced by Matthiae, de iudiciis Atheniensium, in Miscell. phil., 1, p. 251, and adopted by Schömann, op. ac., 1, 200 ff. Schoell, in Ber. d. bayr. Ak., 1887, pp. 7/8, supposes that the several δικαστήρια consisted of members of the same tribe. He does so on the strength of the following words in an inscription of the fifth century: (ἱ)εροποιοῦ(ς δ)ὲ οἵτινες ἱεροποιήσουσ(ι τὴν θυσίαν ἄνδρας δέκα δια)κλη(ρῶσαι) ἐκ τῶν δ(ικα)στῶν ἕνα ἐκ τῆς φυλῆς ἐκ τοῦ (πίνακος),('Εφ. ἀρχ., 1883, pp. 167/8, lines 10 ff.). This, however, is not an absolutely inevitable conclusion, as such a selection by lot is also conceivable if we imagine all the tribes to be represented in each section. Fränkel 95 infers from Arist., Wasps, 233 sqq., that each section contained members from all the tribes, as the Dicasts mentioned in that passage seem to belong to the same section.

[3] This is a probable inference of Bamberg's (Herm., 13, 508/9) from Aristoph., Wasps, 303 sqq.: ἄγε νυν, ὦ πάτερ, ἢν μὴ Τὸ δικαστήριον ἄρχων Καθίσῃ νῦν, πόθεν ὠνη-Σόμεθ' ἄριστον. The jurymen know beforehand whom they have to try; see Wasps, 156/7. 240. 286 ff. Philocleon is at the κιγκλὶς of his δικαστήριον while it is still dark. He has not to be first drawn by lot, therefore; see Wasps, 124, 103/4. The author of De Rep. Ath., 3, 7, regards the size of the courts as a security against bribery; this seems to make against the idea that they were drawn by lot immediately before the case began. That the several Hegemones had their own courts follows from Aristoph., Wasps, 1107 ff.; Antiph. ap. Harp., Παράβυστον.

Eucleides, there seems also to have been a reorganization of the judicature. From this date all probably who applied were enrolled as jurors, if they fulfilled the conditions already mentioned. Each of the ten sections of Dicasts (of which we have certain evidence in the fourth century) was composed of members of all the tribes, and contained the tenth part of those who had applied. Five hundred was retained as the normal strength of a section; but, as there can hardly have been 5,000 Heliasts in all at this time, we must assume 500 to have been a theoretical total, only realized by allowing Heliasts to belong to several sections at once. The new arrangement presumably was that each section was composed of members drawn by lot at the beginning of the year to serve in it, with a number of substitutes added, who were ordinary members of another section.[1] To guard against the possibility of the courts being bribed (as was first done, it appears, by Anytos, towards the end of the Peloponnesian war), the sections were now not allotted to the several courts sitting on any particular day, until just before the hearing of the cases began. Nor is it probable that this was productive of any serious inconvenience—by Heliasts being drawn for several sections at once; for the days for the courts to sit and the cases to be tried on each day were determined by the Thesmothetai. Thus for each day they could set down cases for hearing, for which the legal number of Dicasts could easily be raised simultaneously. And here it should be remarked that most cases required considerably less than 500 jurors.[2]

New organization under Eucleides.

---

[1] Arist. 63, 4: νενέμηνται γὰρ κατὰ φυλὰς δέκα μέρη οἱ δικασταί, παραπλ[ησ]ίως ἴσοι ἐν ἑκάστῳ τῷ γράμ[μα]τι, sc. from A to K as appears from the preceding words. This division, as Aristoph., *Eccl.*, 680 ff., shews, was already in use in the year that the *Ecclesiazusai* was brought out. The normal figure for the sectional δικαστήρια was still 500 in Demosthenes' day: Dem. 24, 9. That individual Heliasts were members of several sections is inferred by Fränkel, 96 sqq., from Arist., *Plut.*, 1166/7: οὐκ ἔτος ἅπαντες οἱ δικάζοντες θαμά Σπεύδουσιν ἐν πολλοῖς γεγράφθαι γράμμασιν, where, as Fränkel shews, there evidently can be no question of any merely fraudulent practice, however common.

[2] Bribery first practised by Anytos, Arist. 27, 5; Diod. 13, 64. The new method of drawing the jurors and the courts by lot is parodied in Arist., *Eccles.*, 676 ff.; see Schömann, *op. ac.*, 1, 215 sqq. Praxagora wishes to draw for the various sections from the whole body of Athenians: κᾆτα στήσασα παρ' Ἁρμοδίῳ (sc. τὰ κληρωτήρια) κληρώσω πάντας, ἕως ἂν Εἰδὼς ὁ λαχὼν ἀπίῃ χαίρων ἐν ὁποίῳ γράμματι δειπνεῖ. The judges are chosen by lot from those that have made application at the beginning of the year. Then Praxagora wishes to

Aristotle's account of the arrangements in his own day shews that the method of drawing Heliasts for the several courts was **Arrangements in Aristotle's day.** subsequently made much more complicated—probably with the object of preventing bribery as far as possible. The division of the jurors into 10 sections was retained, but apparently no special regard was paid to this division at the drawing.[1]

There were at that time, it appears, 10 courts, with differently coloured lintels.[2] As to the names of courts, we hear of **Courts.** δικαστήριον τρίγωνον, παράβυστον, μέσον, μεῖζον, καινόν, τὸ πρὸς τοῖς τειχίοις, βατραχιοῦν, φοινικιοῦν, τὸ Μητίχου, τὸ Κάλλιον. But cases were tried also in the Odeion and in the στοᾷ ποικίλῃ.[3]

make proclamation by the herald what places the various sections are to go to for their meals: καὶ κηρύξει τοὺς ἐκ τοῦ βῆτ' ἐπὶ τὴν στοιὰν ἀκολουθεῖν Τὴν βασίλειον δειπνήσοντας· τὸ δὲ θῆτ' εἰς τὴν παρὰ ταύτην, Τοὺς δ' ἐκ τοῦ κάππ' ἐς τὴν στοιὰν χωρεῖν τὴν ἀλφιτόπωλιν. That the courts were assigned to the sections by sortition follows from Blepyros' objection: ὅτῳ δὲ τὸ γράμμα Μὴ 'ξελκυσθῇ, καθ' ὃ δειπνήσει, τούτους ἀπελῶσιν ἅπαντες, which will not happen, Praxagora answers, in the New Ideal State. A bronze medal in the cabinet of coins in Berlin Royal Museum, bearing on one side four owls with the superscription, θεσμοθετῶν, and on the other an 'Ε, is most likely a balloting counter for section E; see Fränkel, in *Sallets Zeits. f. Numism.*, 3, 883 ff. A second specimen with the letter A was noticed in the Παρνασσός, Febr., 1883. The Thesmothetai fix the court-days; Arist. 59, 1: οἱ δὲ θεσμοθέται πρῶτον μὲν τοῦ προγράψαι τὰ δικαστήριά εἰσι κύριοι, τίσιν ἡμέραις δεῖ δικάζειν, ἔ[π]ε[ιτα] τοῦ δοῦναι ταῖς ἀρχαῖς· καθότι γὰρ ἂν οὗτοι δῶσιν, κατὰ τοῦτο χρῶνται. From this Poll. 8; 87 is derived. On the mode of constituting the courts see Fränkel 98 sqq. The smallest court, according to Dem. 21, 223, contained 200 members. A court of this size decided cases involving sums of not more than 1,000 drachmas, according to Arist. 53, 3=Poll. 8, 48. Fränkel justly remarks that the serious criminal and political cases, which our authorities record, were rare and exceptional.

[1] That the sections were retained even then is shewn by Arist. 63, 4: νενέμηνται γὰρ κατὰ φυλὰς δέκα μέρη οἱ δικασταί, παραπλ[ησ]ίως ἴσοι ἐν ἑκάστῳ τῷ γράμματι. The account of the drawing that follows shews that at it no regard was paid to the sections.

[2] I obtain the number of the courts from a comparison of ἕτερα κιβώτι[α δέκα, εἰς ἃ ἐ]μβάλλεται τῶν λαχόντων δικαστῶν τὰ πινάκια in Arist. 63, 2, with col. 31, 29 ff., as to which something will be said further on. In favour of the number 10 we have also the testimony—decidedly dubious, it is true—of the *Schol.* on Arist., *Plut.*, 277. For the different colour of the courts see Arist., col. 32, 8 sqq.: [τοῖς γὰρ δικαστηρ]ίοις χρῶ[μ]α ἐπιγέγραπτ[αι ἑκάστῳ] ἐπὶ τῷ σφη[κ]ίσκῳ τῆς εἰσόδου. So in the quotation from Aristot. in the *Schol.* to Aristoph., *Plut.*, 278. For the meaning of σφηκίσκος see Wachsmuth 2, 1, 382, 2. I have followed Boeckh, *kl. Schr.*, 7, 478 sqq., in the text.

[3] That most of the courts of justice were situated near the market is an

The Dicasteries.

Every morning those Heliasts who were prepared to administer justice on that day assembled in the market-place, before the place where the drawing took place, provided with their juror's tokens of boxwood, on which were inscribed their own name, their father's name, that of their Deme, and the letter of their section.[1] The place where the drawing of the juries took place was called κληρωτήριον, or, as each tribe had its own division, perhaps also κληρωτήρια; it was, perhaps, the same as the great court called Ἡλιαία. It had ten entrances, one for each tribe, leading into the compartments of the several tribes. In each compartment there were 2 κληρωτήρια, 10 κιβώτια, with the letters Α to Κ on them, 10 others with the letters Λ to Υ, and 2

Mode of making up the courts.

inference from Isocr. 7, 54; Lys. 19. 55. But there was also one πρὸς τοῖς τειχίοις: Arist., *Wasps*, 1109; and others in the street of the Hermoglypheis: Plut., *de gen. Socr.*, c. 10. Perhaps several of the following names denote the same place: τρίγωνον: Poll. 8, 121; Paus. 1, 28, 8; *Schol.* on Arist., *Wasps*, 120; Harp., *s.v.*; παράβυστον: Poll.; Paus.; *Schol.* Arist.; Harp. Phot., *s.v.*; Lex. Seguer. 292, 24; C.I.A., II. 822; μέσον: Poll.; *Schol.* Arist.; μεῖζον: Poll.; καινόν: Arist., *Wasps*, 120; δικαστήριον πρὸς τοῖς τειχίοις: Arist., *Wasps*, 1109; βατραχιοῦν: Paus.; φοινικιοῦν: Paus.; τὸ Μητίχου: Paus. 8, 1, 21; Lex. Seguer. 309, 17; τὸ Κάλλιον: Poll.; Phot., *s.v.* Trial in the Odeion: Arist., *Wasps*, 1109; in the στοὰ ποικίλη: C.I.A., II. 778. For the various courts of justice compare Meier[2] 172 sqq.

[1] The drawing took place in front of the Dicasteries, most of which abutted on the market-place: Isocr. 7, 54 ἐπεὶ νῦν γε τίς οὐκ ἂν ἐπὶ τοῖς γιγνομένοις τῶν εὖ φρονούντων ἀλγήσειεν, ὅταν ἴδῃ πολλοὺς τῶν πολιτῶν αὐτοὺς μὲν περὶ τῶν ἀναγκαίων, εἴθ' ἕξουσιν εἴτε μή, πρὸ τῶν δικαστηρίων κληρουμένους; the market is referred to as the place where the drawing took place by Eubulos, in the *Olbia* in Athen., 14, 640B, where we read: ἐν τῷ γὰρ αὐτῷ πάνθ' ὁμοῦ πωλήσεται Ἐν ταῖς Ἀθήναις, and then, besides other articles for sale, κληρωτήρια are mentioned. Cf. Wachsmuth 2, 1, 382. All the Dicasts assembled in order to be drawn (Dem.) 25, 27: ἀλλ' ὑμεῖς αὐτοὶ πάντων ἄρτι κληρουμένων Ἀθηναίων (sc. those who had taken the jurors' oath) καὶ πάντων εὖ οἶδ' ὅτι βουλομένων εἰς τοῦτο λαχεῖν τὸ δικαστήριον, μόνοι δικάζεθ' ἡμῖν. διὰ τί; ὅτι ἐλάχετε, εἶτ' ἀπεκληρώθητε. ταῦτα δὲ οἱ νόμοι λέγουσιν. For the tokens of the Heliasts cf. Arist. 63, 4: ἔχει δὲ ἕκαστος ⟨ὁ⟩ δικαστὴς πινάκιον πύξινον, ἐπιγεγραμμένον τὸ ὄνομα τὸ ἑαυτοῦ πατρόθεν καὶ τοῦ δήμου καὶ γράμ[μα] ἓν τῶν στοιχείων μέχρι τοῦ κ. See also Hesych. χαλκοῦν πινάκιον; *Schol.* Arist., *Plut.*, 277. As the official tokens were made of boxwood, we must suppose that the bronze tokens of this kind which have been found were ornamental ones, which enthusiastic Heliasts had made for them, to carry with them to their graves. They have been discussed by C. Curtius, in *N. Rh. Mus.*, 3, 283 sqq.; Klein, in *Jahrb. d. Vereins v. Alterthumsfreunden im Rheinl.*, 58, p. 57 sqq., 1876; Girard, in *Bull.*, 2, 1878, p. 521 sqq.; Rayet in *Annuaire de l'association pour l'encouragement des études Grecques*, 12, p. 201 sqq. They are now collected in C.I.A., II. 875–940; *Bull.*, 7, 32 sqq.; Ἐφ. ἀρχ., 1888, 105 sqq., 1887, 53/4.

ὑδρίαι.¹ The nine Archons, with the secretary to the Thesmothetai, had to draw the juries, each drawing for one tribe in one of the compartments of the hall.

Before the drawing began a letter from Λ onwards was drawn for by the Thesmothetai (whose duty it was to arrange all matters relating to the judicature) to be given to each of the courts that were that day to be used. These courts were already fixed upon, as it was known what magistrates were to be sitting on that day. In this way if, for instance, trials had to be held in five courts, the letters Λ to Ο, representing the five courts that were to be constituted, had to be drawn for. The letter, drawn for each court, was fixed up by a servant of the Thesmothetai, probably over the entrance to the court.² Next the Thesmothetai appor-

---

[1] The κληρωτήριον is the name given to the place by C.I.A., II. 441, and by Aristophanes ap. Poll., 10, 61. The plural occurs in Lex. Seguer. 47, 18: κληρωτήρια· ἔνθα κληροῦνται οἱ δικασταί. The plural is either because each tribe had its own κληρωτήριον—Arist., col. 31, 17: ὁ ἄρχων τὴν φυλὴν καλεῖ [εἰς τὸ κ]ληρωτήριον—or, according to the well-known Attic idiom (Harp. δεῖγμα—ἔστι δὲ τὸ ἔθος 'Αττικὸν τὸ σημαίνειν ἀπὸ τῶν ἐν τῷ τόπῳ τοὺς τόπους αὐτούς. Instances in Wachsmuth 2, 1, 463, 1) because there were 20 κληρωτήρια in it. Arist. 63, 2 says: εἴσοδοι δέ εἰσιν εἰς [τὰ] δικαστ[ή]ρια δέκα, μία τῇ φυλῇ ἑκάστῃ, καὶ κλη[ρωτήρια] εἴκοσι, δ[ύο] τῇ φυλῇ ἑκάστῃ, καὶ κιβώτια ἑκατόν, δέκα τῇ φυλῇ ἑκάστῃ, καὶ ἕτερα κιβώτι[α δέκα, εἰς ἃ ἐ]μβάλλεται τῶν λαχόντων δικαστῶν τὰ πινάκια, καὶ ὑδρίαι δύο. This description refers to the hall where the drawing took place, as appears from the account of the drawing in col. 31. The awkward {τὰ} δικαστ[ή]ρια in Arist. may perhaps be taken to mean the 'Ηλιαία, i.e., the place (see p. 393¹) where several sectional δικαστήρια regularly assembled, and where, perhaps, all of them met under certain circumstances; otherwise δικαστήρια must be changed into κληρωτήρια. The preceding [κ]ληρ[οῦσιν] is sufficient to prepare the way for this mention of κληρωτήρια; and the alteration of κληρωτήρια into δικαστήρια in the MS. may be explained by supposing that the copyist ignorantly objected to the first κληρωτήρια on account of the following καὶ κληρωτήρια εἴκοσι, and so substituted δικαστήρια for it from the clause before. For the letters on the different κιβώτια see below.

[2] Arist. 63, 1: τὰ δὲ δικαστήρια [κ]ληρ[οῦσιν] οἱ θ' ἄρχοντες κατὰ φυλάς, ὁ δὲ γραμματεὺς τῶν θεσμο[θετῶν τῆς] δεκάτης φυλῆς. In C.I.A., 567b, it is said of Phyleus, the priest of Asclepios, appointed by lot, who is supposed to have been a Thesmothetes in the year in which the document was drawn up: ἐπιμελεῖται δὲ καὶ τῆς κληρώσεως τῶν δικαστηρίων. The drawing of letters, from Λ onwards, to be attached to the courts that were to be used on the particular day, is described by Arist. 63, 5 in these words: ἐπειδὰν δὲ ὁ θεσμοθέτης ἐπικληρώσῃ τὰ γρ[άμ]ματα, ἃ δεῖ προσπαρατίθεσθαι τοῖς δικαστηρίοις, ἐπέθηκε φέρων ὁ ὑπηρέτης ἐφ' ἕκαστ[ον τὸ δικ]αστήριον τὸ γράμμα τὸ λαχόν. That the letters from Λ onwards are here meant follows from Arist. 63, 2, where we find that the βάλανοι had these letters, and according to col. 32, 3 ff. the δικαστήριον had the same letter as the βάλανος.

tioned among the ten compartments of the allotment-hall a number of bâtons and acorns. The bâtons were marked with the colours, and the acorns with the letters, of the various courts; and as many bâtons of each colour and acorns of each letter were taken as there were jurors required for the corresponding court. Thus, for example, if the courts τὸ βατραχιοῦν and τὸ φοινικιοῦν were to sit, and the former had been allotted the letter Λ and the latter M, and the first was to have 200, the latter 400 jurymen, then 200 green bâtons, and 400 red, 200 acorns marked Λ and 400 marked M had to be apportioned. Probably the bâtons and acorns were divided among the compartments in proportion to the number of jurors coming from the several tribes. The bâtons were deposited at the entrance to the ten compartments, and the acorns in one of the two hydriai placed in each compartment.[1] Then the drawing began. The jurors from the various tribes were drawn for in different compartments. The sortition was done by the nine Archons, the tenth tribe being drawn for by the Secretary to the Thesmothetai. According to Aristotle's account (which however is by no means complete), the sortition proceeded in some such way as this. Inside each compartment there were 10 κιβώτια, each marked with one of the first ten letters of the alphabet. Every Heliast, who was prepared to serve on the particular day, deposited his juror's token in the κιβώτιον, which had the same letter as was upon the token.[2] Their tokens having been thus grouped in the several boxes, an attendant gave them a good shaking, and then the presiding official drew from each box one token. The ten Heliasts, whose tokens were drawn, had to assist in the rest of the sortition and were called ἐμπῆκται. For what followed each κληρωτήριον required 10 κανονίδες. Each of these, like the boxes, was marked with one of the first ten letters. The ἐμπήκτης fastened the tokens that were drawn out from his κιβώτιον in the κανονίς that bore the same letter as the κιβώτιον. We must

[1] Arist. 63, 2: καὶ βακτηρίαι παρατίθενται κατὰ τὴν ε[ἴσοδον] ἑκάστην, ὅσοιπερ οἱ δικασταί, καὶ βάλανοι εἰς τὴν ὑδρίαν ἐμβάλλονται ἴσαι ταῖς βακτηρίαις, γέγραπται δ' ἐν ταῖς βαλάνοις τῶν στοιχείων ἀπὸ τοῦ ἑνδεκάτου, τοῦ λ, ὅσαπερ ἂν μέλλῃ [τ]ὰ δικαστήρια πληρωθήσεσθαι. The ὑδρία here is one of the two mentioned just before as standing in each compartment of the allotment-hall.

[2] Arist. col. 31, 2 ff.:—[κ]αθ' ἑκάστην τὴ[ν φυ]λήν. ἐπ[ὶ] γέ[γραπται δ']ἐπ' αὐτῶν τὰ σ[τοι]χεῖα μέχρι το[ῦ κ. ἐπ]ειδὰν δ' ἐμβάλωσιν οἱ δικαστ[αὶ] τ[ὰ πινά]κια εἰς τὸ κιβώτι[ον], ἐφ' οὗ ἂν ᾖ ἐπι[γεγρα]μμένον τὸ γρά μ[μα] τὸ αὐτό, ὅπ[ε]ρ ἐπ[ὶ τῷ] πινακίῳ ἐστίν. These are the 10 κιβώτια which Arist. 63, 2 first informed us of.

suppose these κανονίδες to have been contrivances in which the tokens were set, as they were drawn, or (if they were perforated) on which they were strung; so that they could only be removed again from the κανονίς in the reverse order.[1] After twice as many tokens had been drawn (an equal number from each κιβώτιον) as the tribe had to supply jurors for the day, the presiding official placed one white and one black die for every five of the tokens drawn, in the second κληρωτήριον, and then called the Heliasts of his tribe (who had until then been waiting at the entrance) into the allotment-hall.[2] Then the Archon drew the dice for his κληρωτήριον, whilst the ἐμπῆκται for each die drawn took the five uppermost tokens from their κανονίς, most probably taking their turn in the order of the sections they had charge of from A to K. If the die was white, they put the tokens in the second unused ὑδρία, retaining them and afterwards restoring them to their owners if the die was black. When the drawing was finished, the Archon took the tokens one by one from the ὑδρία calling out the names written on them. The ἐμπῆκται eo ipso were included in the jury-list for the day.[3] The juryman, whose name was

[1] Arist col. 31, 7 sqq.: ἀ[πὸ] τῶν στοιχεί[ων δια]σείσαντος τοῦ ὑ[πη]ρέτου ἕλκει ὁ [θεσμο]θέτης ἐξ ἑκάσ[τ]ου τοῦ κιβωτίο[υ πιν]άκιον ἕν. οὗτο[ς] δὲ καλεῖ[τ]αι ἐν[πήκτ]ης καὶ ἐνπήγνυσι τὰ πι[νά]κια [τὰ ἐκ το]ῦ κιβωτίου εἰς τὴν κανονίδα, [ἐφ' ἧς τὸ α]ὐτὸ γράμμα ἔπεστιν, ὅπερ ἐπὶ τοῦ [κιβωτίου. κληροῦται δ'] οὗτος, ἵνα μὴ ἀεὶ ὁ αὐτὸς ἐνπ[ηγνύων] κακουργῇ. εἰσὶ δὲ κανονίδες [δέκα ἐ]ν ἑκάστῳ τῶν κληρωτη[ρίων], i.e. in the 10 compartments of the hall. Hesych. is hardly accurate: ἐμπήκτης· ὁ τὰ δικαστικὰ γραμματίδια (for the γράμματα διὰ of the MS.) παρὰ τοῦ θεσμοθέτου (θεσμοφόρου MS.) λαμβάνων ὑπηρέτης καὶ πήσσων εἰς τὴν κανονίδα (MS. κανευνίδα). The meaning of κανονίς is not clear: according to Suid. it is ἐργαλεῖον καλλιγραφικόν· ἐν ἐπιγράμμασι (Anth. Pal. 6, 62) "καὶ κανονίδ' ὑπάτην." In that place it means some apparatus used in writing.

[2] Arist. col. 31, 17 sqq.: [ἐπειδὰν δ'] ἐνβάλῃ τοὺς κύβους ὁ ἄρχων, τὴν φυλὴν καλεῖ [εἰς τὸ κ]ληρωτήριον. εἰσὶ δὲ κύβοι [ξύλινοι, μέ]λανες καὶ λευκοί. ὅσους δ' ἂν δέ[ῃ λαχεῖν] δικαστάς, τοσοῦτοι ἐ[μ]βάλλον[ται λε]υκοί, ⟨οἷον?⟩ κατὰ πέντε πινάκια εἷς, οἱ δ[ὲ μέ]λανες τὸν αὐτὸν τρόπον. Just as the white beans in the election of magistrates showed the persons elected (Lex. Cantabr. 671 κυαμεύονται), so the white dice doubtless showed the jurymen who were to sit for the day. That twice as many tokens were drawn from the 10 κιβώτια as there were dicasts required, follows from the number of white and black dice being equal.

[3] Arist. col. 31, 23 sqq.: ἐπειδὰν δ' ἐ[ξέλῃ] (so I read with most of the editors, though Blass supplies ἐξαιρῇ) τοὺς κύβους, καλεῖ τοὺς εἰληχότας ὁ [ἄρχων]. ὑπάρχει δὲ καὶ ὁ ἐνπήκτης εἷς [ὦ]ν [αὐτῶ]ν. The text is a conjectural expansion of these words. The calling out of names began according to Arist. after the drawings were finished. ὁ ἐνπήκτης is used collectively for the ten ἐμπῆκται. The ὑδρία mentioned in the text is the second of the two men-

called, walked up to the ὑδρία containing the acorns, drew one and showed the presiding officer the letter inscribed upon it. The latter then placed that juryman's token in that one of the ten other κιβώτια which bore the same letter as the acorn. The whole of these κιβώτια were not used except when all ten courts sat on the same day; only so many boxes (beginning with the letter Λ) were placed beside the Archon as there were courts sitting that day.[1] The dicasts thus selected received from an attendant bâtons of the colour of the courts where they were to sit—each dicast sitting in the court which for this day had the same letter as the acorn he had drawn. Armed with acorn and bâton the Dicast proceeded to his court, while the κιβώτιον was also sent there with the tokens of the Dicasts drawn for that Court, so as to check the names.[2] On entering the Court the Dicasts, probably upon the

tioned in Arist. 63, 2; in the first were the βάλανοι. Arist. 63, 2 gives two κληρωτήρια for each tribe, which I should explain by supposing that in the one were the πινάκια on or in the 10 κανονίδες of the κληρωτήριον, in the other the κύβοι. (Dem.) 25, 27 distinguishes between λαγχάνειν and ἀποκληροῦν at the drawing of the jurors. Λαγχάνειν is the drawing of the πινάκια from the κιβώτια before described, ἀποκληροῦν is the process now in question.

[1] Arist. col. 31, 25 sqq.: ὁ δὲ κληθεὶς καὶ [εἴλη]χ[ὼς] ἔλ[κ]ει [βάλανο]ν ἐκ τῆς ὑδρίας καὶ [π]ρο[δεί]ξας αὐτὴ[ν] . . . ὧν τὸ γράμμα, δ[εί]κνυσιν πρ[οσελθὼν] τῷ ἄρχοντι τῷ ἐφεστηκότι. ὁ δὲ ἄ[ρχων ἐπειδ]ὰν ἴδῃ, ἐνβάλλει τὸ πινάκιον α[ὐ]το[ῦ εἰς τὸ κ]ιβώτιον, ὅπου ἂν ᾖ ἐπιγεγραμ[μέν]ον τὸ αὐτὸ στοιχεῖον ὅπερ ἐν τῇ βαλ[άνῳ, ἵ]ν' εἰς οἷον ἂν λάχῃ εἰσίῃ καὶ μὴ εἰς [οἷο]ν ἂν βούληται, μηδὲ ᾗ συναγαγεῖν [εἰς] δικαστήριον οὓς ἂν βούληταί τις. πα[ράκει]ται δὲ τῷ ἄρχοντι κιβώτια, ὅσ' ἂν ἀεὶ [μ]έλλῃ τὰ δικαστήρι[α] πληρωθήσεσθαι, [ἔχο]ντα στοιχεῖον ἕκαστον ὅπερ ἂν [ᾖ] τοῦ δικαστηρίου ἑκάσ[του].—The κιβώτια here are evidently the same as those of which it is said in Arist. 63, 2: καὶ ἕτερα κιβώτι[α δέκα, οἷς] ἐμβάλλεται τῶν λαχόντων δικαστῶν τὰ πινάκια. Ten κιβώτια of this kind with the letters Λ to Τ were ready in case all the ten courts sat simultaneously. This was not ordinarily the case. Πληροῦν τὰ δικαστήρια is a very expressive term for the process described in the text. The phrase is used of the Thesmotheta in a number of grants of citizenship: ὅταν πρῶτον πληρῶσιν δικαστήριον εἰς ἕνα καὶ πεντακοσίους δικαστάς. C.I.A., II. 395, 396, 402, 455, etc. Cf. Lys. 26, 6; Is. 6, 37; Dem. 21, 209; 24, 58. 92. In C.I.A., II. 809a, 205, the verb παραπληροῦν is used. Cf. Forster's collection of passages in *N. Rh. Museum*, 30, 284 ff., 1875.

[2] Arist. col. 32, 3 sqq.: ὁ δὲ ὑπηρ[έτης δίδωσιν αὐτῷ βα]κτηρίαν [ὁ]μόχρων τῷ [δ]ικα[στηρίῳ ἐφ' οὗ τὸ αὐτὸ γρ]άμμα [δ]περ ἐν τῇ βαλάνῳ, ἵ[να ἀναγκ]αῖον ᾖ αὐτῷ [ε]ἰσελθεῖν εἰς τ[ὸ] ἑαυ[τοῦ δικασ]τήριον. ἐὰν γὰρ [ε]ἰς ἕτερον εἰ[σίῃ, ἐξελέγχεται ὑπὸ τοῦ] χρώμα[τ]ος [τ]ῆς βακτηρίας. [τοῖς γὰρ δικαστηρ]ίοις χρῶ[μ]α ἐπιγέγραπτ[αι ἑκάστῳ] ἐπὶ τῷ σφη[κ]ίσκῳ τῆς εἰσόδου. [ὁ δὲ λαβὼ]ν τὴν βακτηρί[α]ν βαδίζει εἰς [τὸ] δικα[στήριον] τὸ ὁμόχρων μὲν [τ]ῇ βακτ[ηρί]ᾳ ἔ[χον δὲ τὸ αὐ]τὸ γράμμα ὅ[περ ἐν [τ]ῇ βαλ[άνῳ]. Cf. Arist. in the *Schol. Arist., Plut.*, 278. Lex. Seguer. 220, 17 sqq. Schol. Arist., *Wasps*, 1110. Suid. βακτηρία καὶ σύμβολον. That the κιβώτια with the πινάκια drawn were sent to the courts for the purpose of

production of their acorn, received the σύμβολον, a counter on returning which they were paid their fees at the close of the day's sitting.[1]

The arrangement of all the courts must have been pretty much the same. In the first place there probably stood in all of them a statue of the hero Lycos in the shape of a wolf.[2] The place where the court was held was fenced round with railings and closed by a trellised gate.[3] The public were allowed up to the railings provided that there was no Mystery-

Arrangements in court.

checking the names is a natural suggestion and is perhaps confirmed by Arist. col, 82, 19 sqq.: οἱ δὲ ὑπη[ρέται] οἱ δημοσίᾳ . . . . [τ]ῆς φυλῆς ἐκάστης π[αραδι]δόασιν τὰ κ[ι]βώτια ἐν ἐπὶ τὸ δικα[στήρ]ιον ἔκαστον, ἐ[ν οἷς] ἐστιν τὰ . . . a . . . [τῆς] φυλῆς τὰ ὄντ[α] ἐν ἑκάστῳ τ[ῶν δι]κα[στηρί]ων.

[1] Arist. col. 32, 13 sqq.: ἐπε[ιδὰν δ᾽ εἰσέλ]θῃ παραλαμβάνει σύνβολον δη[μοσίᾳ π]αρὰ τοῦ ε[ἰληχό]τος ταύτην τὴν ἀ[ρχήν]. Cf. Arist. in the Schol., Arist. Plut., 278. The Dicast on entering the court probably gave up his βάλανος and received the σύμβολον, as the σύμβολον and the βακτηρία were the insignia of a Dicast. Cf. Dem. 18, 210: καὶ παραλαμβάνειν γε ἅμα τῇ βακτηρίᾳ καὶ τῷ συμβόλῳ τὸ φρόνημα τὸ τῆς πόλεως νομίζειν ἕκαστον ὑμῶν δεῖ, ὅταν τὰ δημόσια εἰσίητε κρινοῦντες, εἴπερ ἄξια ἐκείνων πράττειν οἴεσθε χρῆναι. Βακτηρία and σύμβολον also appear at the voting—Arist. col. 36, 35 sqq.—but the βάλανος is not mentioned again. See Suid. βακτηρία καὶ σύμβολον—τὸ μέντοι σύμβολον μετὰ τὴν κρίσιν ἀποδιδόντες ἐκομίζοντο τριώβολον· ὅπερ καὶ δικαστικὸν γέγονεν. Examples of such σύμβολα in Benndorf in Zeitschr. f. österr. Gymnasialw., 1875, p. 601. In the Schol. Arist., Birds, 1540, we find: 'Αριστοφάνης ὁ γραμματικὸς τούτους (sc. τοὺς κωλακρέτας) ταμίας εἶναί φησι τοῦ δικαστικοῦ μισθοῦ. See also Lex. Cantabr. 672, 15; Lex. Seguer. 275, 22. But the κωλακρέται have not so far been found in inscriptions of the fourth century. C.I.A., II. 809a, 213 sqq., says: τὸν δὲ μισθὸν διδόναι τοῖς δικαστηρίοις τοὺς ταμί(α)ς τῶν τῆς θεοῦ κατὰ τὸν (νό)μον. Arist. col. 37, 5 sqq., says: ἐπειδὰν δὲ αὐτοῖς ᾖ δεδικασμένα τὰ ἐκ τῶν νόμων, ἀπολαμβάνουσιν τὸν μισθὸν ἐν τῷ μέρει οὗ ἔλαχον ἕκαστοι. These are the δέκα μέρη mentioned in Arist. 63, 4: so that the sections must have been paid separately.

[2] That this, according to Athenian ideas, was indispensable in a Dicasterion follows from such passages as Arist., Wasps, 389 sqq., 818 sqq., and is also attested by Eratosthenes ap. Harp: Λύκος ἐστὶν ἥρως πρὸς τοῖς ἐν Ἀθήναις δικαστηρίοις, τοῦ θηρίου μορφὴν ἔχων, πρὸς ὃν οἱ δωροδοκοῦντες κατὰ δέκα γιγνόμενοι ἀνεστρέφοντο, ὅθεν εἴρηται Λύκου δέκας. The meaning of Λύκου δέκας is uncertain. See Wachsmuth 2, 1, 376, 2. Lex. Cantabr. 672, 26: Λύκος ἥρως· ἱδρυμένος οὗτος ἦν ἐν τοῖς δικαστηρίοις, ᾧ καὶ αὐτῷ τὸ δικαστικὸν ἔνεμον, ὡς Ἰσαῖος ἐν Τεμενικῷ. I hold with Hudtwalcker, Diæt., p. 14, that τὸ ἐπὶ Λύκῳ δικαστήριον in Poll. 8, 121 is due to a misunderstanding of this statue of Lycos in front of all the courts. Schömann, op. ac., 1, 225 takes another view.

[3] For the δρύφακτος see Arist., Wasps, 830, with the explanation of the Schol.: δρύφακτος τὸ παρατεινόμενον ξύλον τοῖς δικασταῖς. κιγχλίς=door: Arist., Wasps, 775; Harp. κιγχλίς—αἱ τῶν δικαστηρίων θύραι κιγχλίδες ἐκαλοῦντο· 'Αριστοφάνης Δαιταλεῦσιν "ὁ ἡλιαστὴς εἷρπε πρὸς τὴν κιγχλίδα." Cf. Poll. 8, 17, 124; Suid. κιγχλίδες; Phot. κιγχλίδες.

case proceeding. At Mystery-cases a rope was drawn round the court at a distance of 50 feet and public slaves were stationed to keep off the people.[1] The Dicasts sat within these railings on wooden benches, the president probably on the βῆμα.[2] In all probability this was also used as a tribune for both parties; if they were not speaking, they sat[3] on either side of a stone table, placed most likely in front of the βῆμα. On this table the votes were counted.[4] In the fourth century each of the two parties had his own βῆμα, on which he sat. This was different from the tribune for speaking also called βῆμα, which perhaps was placed on the platform, where was also the βῆμα of the president.[5]

Courts sat on every day of the year except festivals and unlucky

[1] The public at the bar of the court: Æsch., de F.L., 5, in Ctes. 55; Dem. 18, 196; Is. 5, 20; Dem. 30, 32. On the secrecy in Mystery-cases see Poll. 8, 123/4. 141.

[2] The Dicasts on wooden benches: Arist., Wasps, 90. Poll. 4, 121; 8, 133. In the fifth century there was only one βῆμα in the court in all likelihood, as the parody on the Dicasterion in Arist., Eccl., 676 sqq., shews. Blepyros asks: τὸ δὲ βῆμα τί σοι χρήσιμον ἔσται; Praxagora answers: τοὺς κρατῆρας καταθήσω Καὶ τὰς ὑδρίας, καὶ ῥαψῳδεῖν ἔσται τοῖς παιδαρίοισιν Τοὺς ἀνδρείους ἐν τῷ πολέμῳ, κεἴ τις δειλὸς γεγένηται, "Ἵνα μὴ δειπνῶσ' αἰσχυνόμενοι. The κρατῆρες and ὑδρίαι most probably answer to the κάδοι for the voting pebbles. Wachsmuth 2, 1, 871, 4, on the words of Philocleon in Arist., Wasps, 349: οὕτω κιττῷ διὰ τῶν σανίδων μετὰ χοιρίνης περιελθεῖν refers the σανίδες to the βῆμα.

[3] Andoc., de Myst., 101.

[4] That the two parties sat on either side of a stone table apparently follows (Wachsmuth 2, 1, 371/2) from Arist., Ach., 683 sqq.: τονθορύζοντες δὲ γήρᾳ τῷ λίθῳ προσέσταμεν, Οὐχ ὁρῶντες οὐδὲν εἰ μὴ τῆς δίκης τὴν ἠλύγην. Ὁ δὲ νεανίας ἑαυτῷ σπουδάσας ξυνηγορεῖν Ἐς τάχος παίει ξυνάπτων στρογγύλοις τοῖς ῥήμασι. But they did not speak from there. That Aristoph. is referring to a trial in court is evident from 694: ταῦτα πῶς εἰκότα, γέροντ' ἀπολέσαι πολιὸν ἄνδρα περὶ κλεψύδραν. Beyond a doubt it is the same stone of which Philocleon says in Arist., Wasps, 332: ἢ δῆτα λίθον με ποίησον, ἐφ' οὗ τὰς χοιρίνας ἀριθμοῦσιν. When Praxagora, in the parody on the Dicasterion in Arist., Eccl., 676 sqq., says she will place on the βῆμα mixing-bowls and ὑδρίαι, and that the boys are to sing from there of the deeds of brave men, it sounds like a parody on the speeches there delivered by both parties. That the parties ascended a βῆμα when they spoke is plain from the suit against the dog Labes in the Wasps, 891 sqq. Cf. especially 905. 944. 963. 977. 979 sqq.

[5] Dem. 48, 31: καὶ οὑτοσὶ Ὀλυμπιόδωρος ἠγωνίζετο πρῶτος (sc. ἐν τῷ δικαστηρίῳ) καὶ ἔλεγεν, ὅτι ἐβούλετο καὶ μαρτυρίας παρείχετο ἃς ἐδόκει τούτῳ· κἀγώ, ὦ ἄνδρες δικασταί, σιωπῇ ἐκαθήμην ἐπὶ τοῦ ἑτέρου βήματος. Æschin. in Ctes. 207: φάσκων τοὺς μὲν ὀλιγαρχικοὺς ὑπ' αὐτῆς τῆς ἀληθείας διηριθμημένους ἥκειν πρὸς τὸ τοῦ κατηγόρου βῆμα, τοὺς δὲ δημοτικοὺς πρὸς τὸ τοῦ φεύγοντος. It is clear from Æschin. de F. L., 59, in Ctes. 165, that these βήματα of the parties were not the same as the speaker's tribune. See Lipsius in Meier² 182, no. 91; Wachsmuth 2, 1, 372.

days and, in the age of Demosthenes, days when Ecclesiai were
Court-days. held: in time of war, when the city of Athens itself was threatened, there was often a suspension of legal business.[1]

The suits which came before the Athenian jurors may be variously classified according to the principle of division adopted.[2] **Classes of** The ground of action, the ἔγκλημα, was either an **legal Actions.** offence against an individual, or against the State. In the first case the action was a private action, ἀγὼν ἴδιος, δίκη ἰδία, or simply δίκη; in the second case it was a public action, ἀγὼν **Private** δημόσιος, δίκη δημοσία, or γραφή. The characteristic **Actions.** features of private suits were that, in the first place, they could only be brought by the man who was directly interested in the establishment of the contention, or in obtaining satisfaction for the wrong, or by his κύριος, or, if he were a metic, by his προστάτης; secondly, if the action was successful, the object in dispute or the compensation went, with few exceptions, exclusively to the plaintiff; thirdly, court-fees called Prytaneia were paid; and, lastly, the plaintiff was not punished, if he withdrew the action.

Public suits were divided (though Attic law had no special names for the two classes) into those where the offence affected the **Public** individual directly and the State indirectly, that is, **Actions.** what we should regard as criminal cases; and those where the offence affected the State directly and the individual indirectly, or, as we should say, offences against the State. The distinctive features of all public suits were that they could be instituted not only by a plaintiff who had suffered direct injury, but, with few exceptions, by every citizen who possessed the franchise; that the penalty or compensation was paid to the State, in all but

---

[1] No court on feast-days: (Xen.), *de Rep. Ath.*, 3, 8; Lys. 26, 6; nor on ἀποφράδες ἡμέραι: Luc., *Pseudol.*, 13; Suid. *s.v.* Arist., *Wasps*, 661 sqq., in a context where the temptation would be to exaggerate if anything, gives 300 court days. Before Eucleides courts sat and the Ecclesia met on the same day, as is shewn by Arist., *Wasps*, 594/5; see von Bamberg in *Herm.*, 13,506 sqq., against Fränkel, p. 11, who thinks that this could only happen with an ἐκκλησία σύγκλητος. In the time of Demosthenes an ἐκκλησία and a sitting of a δικαστήριον could not fall on the same day, as is shown by Dem. 24, 80. Iustitium in time of war: Dem. 45, 4; Isocr. 21, 7; Lys. 17, 3; Is. 5, 7. Cf. Meier[2] 185 sqq.

[2] In this classification I have followed Meier [2] 191 sqq. I take this opportunity of referring the reader once for all to that work for details.

a few cases entirely, and even in the exceptions a part was paid—penalties affecting the person, honour, or life of the delinquent being regarded as paid to the State: that no πρυτανεῖα were paid, and that the prosecutor, if he withdrew from the prosecution or failed to obtain the fifth part of the votes cast, had to pay a fine of 1,000 drachmas, and forfeited the right of ever bringing a similar action again.

According to a second principle of division suits were divided into δίκαι κατά τινος and πρός τινα. The first were directed against the person of the defendant—to have him punished for an infraction of the laws; in the others there was either no question of any personal infraction or none at least of any for which he could be prosecuted.[1]

Actions κατά τινος and πρός τινα.

Lastly, suits were either ἀγῶνες ἀτίμητοι or τιμητοί. The ἀγῶνες ἀτίμητοι were those suits in which the penalty was previously fixed by law, or, occasionally in certain public suits, by special psephism, or, in private suits, by a previous agreement between the parties as to the forfeit for a breach of contract. The ἀγῶνες τιμητοί, on the other hand, were suits in which the amount of compensation was not fixed beforehand, but had to be determined by the jury. If they condemned the defendant, they voted again as to the penalty after hearing what punishment the prosecutor proposed and what the defendant.[2]

Actions with the penalty determined and undetermined.

A special kind of action must here be mentioned, the διαδικασία. This was an action to decide rival claims or disputes in regard to property, or to the obligation to discharge a public Leiturgy.[3]

διαδικασία.

Before giving a short description of the usual procedure in a lawsuit, it will be well to give some account of one or two special kinds of action. Under one head may first be mentioned ἀπαγωγή, ἐφήγησις and ἔνδειξις. It seems to have been a peculiarity of all three that they could only be

ἀπαγωγή, ἐφήγησις, ἔνδειξις.

---

[1] Heffter has shown, *d. athenäische Gerichtsverf.*, p. 124 ff., that the division into δίκαι κατά τινος and πρός τινα extended to all suits, and not to private suits only.

[2] These suits are correctly defined by Harp. ἀτίμητος ἀγὼν καὶ τιμητός. ὁ μὲν τιμητός, ἐφ' ᾧ τίμημα ὡρισμένον ἐκ τῶν νόμων οὐ κεῖται, ἀλλὰ τοὺς δικαστὰς ἔδει τιμᾶσθαι, ὅτι χρὴ παθεῖν ἢ ἀποτίσαι· ὁ δὲ ἀτίμητος τοὐναντίον, ᾧ πρόσεστιν ἐκ τῶν νόμων ὡρισμένον τίμημα, ὡς μηδὲν δεῖν τοὺς δικαστὰς διατιμῆσαι.

[3] Meier[2] 471 ff.; Heffter 272 sqq.

employed when the offence was patent and undeniable. They were limited to certain particular crimes; there was no summons; and as soon as the president of the court that would try the case had accepted the accusation, the defendant was obliged to go to prison until the trial, unless he could produce as sureties three citizens belonging to the same assessment-class as himself. The three actions may be thus distinguished:—in the ἀπαγωγή the accused was taken by the prosecutor before the official who had jurisdiction in the case; in the ἐφήγησις the accuser took the official to the place where the defendant had committed the offence or where he lived, to arrest him; in the ἔνδειξις it has been very reasonably conjectured that the prosecutor lodged an information with the official, leaving him to secure the criminal.[1]

The peculiarity of the φάσις seems to have been that, although it was an action against one who had injured the State, yet half of the fine, if a conviction followed, was given to the prosecutor. *Phaseis* were brought against those who had injured the fiscal interests of the State, especially those who had contravened the laws relating to trade, the customs, and mining, and also against guardians who had either omitted altogether to invest their ward's fortune or had made a bad investment.[2]

φάσις.

The ἀπογραφή was an action for the confiscation of anything in private hands, which was claimed as State-property.[3]

ἀπογραφή.

The εἰσαγγελία and the προβολή have been discussed already.[4]

The regular mode of procedure (which was pretty much the same in public and private suits) began with the summons (πρόσκλησις) of the defendant by the plaintiff, who was commonly accompanied by two witnesses (κλητῆρες). The witnesses had to prove the summons in the court, before which the case was brought, in order that judgment might be given in default, if the accused failed to appear on the day named in the summons.[5]

Ordinary Process.

Summons.

[1] For details see Meier[2] 270 ff., 776 ff.
[2] Meier[2] 294 sqq.
[3] Meier[2] 302 sqq.
[4] P. 304 ff. and 308 f. For two special kinds of εἰσαγγελία cf. Meier[2] 332 ff.
[5] Meier[2] 769 sqq.

The action was entered by handing in a statement of the accusation in writing to the magistrate who presided at trials of that particular class. **Lodgment of the suit.**

If the suit was accepted by the competent magistrate, then the court-fees had to be paid. These were called πρυτανεῖα in civil actions and were paid by both parties, but the loser had to return to the other what he had paid. The fees were 3 drachmas, if the amount in dispute was from 100 to 1,000 drachmas, and 30 drachmas, if it exceeded 1,000 drachmas. In public actions only the prosecutor had to pay—whether in all cases is doubtful—and the fee was a small fixed sum, called παράστασις, probably one drachma; πρυτανεῖα were paid only when the prosecutor had a claim to part of the penalty which the defendant would have to pay if condemned. Lastly, in suits concerning inheritances, where the plaintiff tried to recover an inheritance which had already been taken possession of by another party, and in suits to recover property seized by the State, the plaintiff had to deposit the παρακαταβολή, as it was termed, which in the first case amounted to one-tenth, in the second to one-fifth of the property in dispute. This was not returned if the case were lost.[1] **Court-fees.**

After lodgment of the suit, the competent court fixed a day for the preliminary investigation (ἀνάκρισις), and during the interval the articles of the charge were published, sometimes in extenso, sometimes abridged.[2] At this preliminary investigation an oath was taken by both plaintiff and defendant. The plaintiff swore to the truth of his accusation, the defendant to that of his defence (which had at the same time to be sent in in writing).[3] **Preliminary investigation.**

If the accused admitted that the institution of the action was formally and technically correct, the process was called εὐθυδικία; he was free however to enter special pleas or objections —διαμαρτυρίαι and παραγραφαί. In the διαμαρτυρία witnesses for and against the legality of the suit were produced, and its admissibility was discussed. In the παραγραφή the objection was not supported by witnesses; recourse was had **Demurrers and Special Pleas.**

---

[1] See Boeckh, 1, 461 sqq. (Bk. 3, ch. 9), Meier² 809 sqq. Παράστασις for all public suits is assumed by Boeckh, 466 (Bk. 3, ch. 9). From Arist. 59, 3, this seems doubtful. See also Lipsius in Meier² 73/4, 813/4.

[2] Meier² 790 ff.; Wachsmuth 2, 1, 297, 2; 387 ff.

[3] Meier² 823 sqq. Philippi, *d. Areop. u. d. Eph.*, 87 sqq., supposes that the plaintiff alone took the oath.

to other means of proof. The accused was now the plaintiff and so had the right of speaking first. Both forms of objection had to be decided before the original suit could be proceeded with. If the decision were in the defendant's favour, the main suit was either quashed as inadmissible or, at any rate, could not be prosecuted in the way proposed or before the same court.[1]

The ἀντιγραφή or cross-action was different. The defendant would bring this against the plaintiff, and it might relate either to the subject of the original accusation or to any other subject. The verdict in the ἀντιγραφή did not affect the issue of the original suit.[2]

ἀντιγραφή.

In the preliminary examination laws, documents, depositions of witnesses or slaves, and affidavits could be produced as evidence.

Evidence. The laws bearing on the case were produced in copies; the documents, if they were public papers, in copies; if private, the original was if possible produced. If the original was in the possession of the other party, he was challenged to produce it, that a copy of it might be taken; if it was in the hands of a third person, he was required to give a copy of it certified by witnesses, and in case this was refused, a δίκη εἰς ἐμφανῶν κατάστασιν could be instituted. The depositions of witnesses were either made before the presiding official himself and taken down in court, or if the witnesses were prevented through illness or other cause from appearing personally they might be sent in in writing. In such a case, their authenticity had to be certified by witnesses. Depositions by slaves were not accepted as evidence, unless made under torture. This examination by torture probably took place, in most cases, out of court in the presence of both parties, and the evidence thus extracted was certified by witnesses present at the torture, and then added to the other documents in the case. The party interested in extracting a deposition from slaves used either to offer his own slaves for examination by torture or to challenge his opponent to produce his. It was not obligatory however for the party challenged to accept such a πρόκλησις εἰς βάσανον, but a refusal would create a presumption against his case. The oaths which the parties offered to take themselves, or were challenged to take by their opponents, were taken before the presiding magistrate and reduced to writing. If such a challenge were refused, this fact was likewise put down in

---

[1] Meier [2] 883 ff.   [2] Meier [2] 857 sqq.

writing. At the close of the preliminary investigation, the documents in civil cases were first sent on to a public Diaitetes to try amicable mediation. In all public cases, and in private suits when an appeal had been made from the decision of the Diaitetes, the presiding official sealed up the documents relating to the case in a vessel called ἐχῖνος and took charge of them until the case came into court.[1]

Not infrequently the trial was postponed for some time; but in certain cases the suit had to be decided within a month; such suits were consequently called δίκαι ἔμμηνοι.[2] The date of the trial might be postponed either by mutual agreement or in consequence of a motion for delay made by one party. This would be made on the day of the trial by the attorneys or friends of the absent party, who had to shew cause under oath for his absence. Hence this motion was called ὑπωμοσία. The other party to the suit could object to the adjournment of the case by an ἀνθυπωμοσία, in which he impugned the validity of the reasons advanced to explain the absence of his opponent. If the motion for delay was refused by the court, and it was the accused who did not make his appearance, judgment went by default; if the prosecutor failed to appear, the defendant was acquitted.[3]

Date of trial.

At the trial the same official presided as had conducted the preliminary inquiry. To keep order, he had some Skythai at his disposal. The proceedings were interrupted, if διοση- μίαι occurred. They began with a solemn sacrifice, after which the bars of the court were closed.[4] Then followed the reading by the clerk of the accusation, and of the defendant's reply. After that the plaintiff first addressed the court, and the defendant followed. The law required every man to conduct his own case; but it seldom happened that the Dicasts refused to give

The Trial.

---

[1] Meier² 865 ff. That the Diaitetai necessarily first heard private causes is proved by Lex. Cantabr. 673, μὴ οὖσα δίκη. Cf. Arist. 53 [where see Wyse in *Sandys*, p. 190]=Poll. 8, 126; Lipsius in Meier² 1009 sqq.

[2] For the δίκαι ἔμμηνοι cf. Arist. 52, 2. 3; Poll. 8, 63. 101; Harp. *s.v.*; Lex. Seguer. 237, 33; Meier² 907. The δίκαι ἐμπορικαί had at one time not been ἔμμηνοι: (Dem.) 7, 12; cf. Xen., de Vect. 3, 3.

[3] Meier 906 sqq.

[4] For διοσημίαι see Poll. 8, 124. Skythai at the trial: Poll. 8, 131. That there was a sacrifice at the outset of the proceedings appears from Arist., *Wasps*, 860 ff., which is evidently copied from the real courts. Closing of the bars after the sacrifice: *Wasps*, 891/2; cf. 775. For the trial itself cf. Meier² 917 ff.

either party permission for the appearance, after their own speeches, of one or more advocates (συνήγοροι). In many cases the first speeches were followed by a second speech and a second reply. The duration of the speeches was in some cases fixed by law and checked by a water-clock (κλεψύδρα): in other cases no limit was fixed. The defence of the accused was not unfrequently supported by the entreaties of his friends and relations.[1]

After the speeches were over, the votes of the jury were taken; most likely this always was by ballot.[2] The mode of voting in the fifth century differed from that in the fourth. In the fifth century they voted with muscle shells, at first with real shells, later probably with artificial ones of bronze. Each juror received a shell, which he cast into one of two vessels placed one behind the other and probably covered over. By depositing his shell in the front vessel, the juror declared himself in favour of acquittal; by depositing it in the second, he voted for condemnation. If the penalty was not determined by law, a second vote was taken, after hearing the penalties proposed by both parties. Wax-tablets were used for this: by a long line on them the Dicast pronounced in favour of the plaintiff's proposal, by a short line for that of the defendant.[3]

The voting.

---

[1] Arist., *Wasps*, 894 sqq. Dem. 19, 213 shows that λόγοι ὕστεροι were not allowed in all suits.

[2] Our evidence of secret voting begins at a time subsequent to Eucleides: Lys. 12, 91; Dem. 19, 239; Lyc. 146. But from the antithesis in Lys. 13, 37: δύο δὲ τράπεζαι ἐν τῷ πρόσθεν τῶν τριάκοντα ἐκείσθην· τὴν δὲ ψῆφον οὐκ εἰς καδίσκους ἀλλὰ φανερὰν ἐπὶ τὰς τραπέζας ταύτας ἔδει τίθεσθαι, τὴν μὲν καθαιροῦσαν ἐπὶ τὴν ὑστέραν ... it seems that τὸ τὴν ψῆφον εἰς καδίσκους τίθεσθαι was not φανερόν. Szanto in *Wiener Stud.*, 3, 24 sqq., concludes from Dem. 43, 10 (cp. Is. 11, 21. 23) that the voting in private suits was generally open. But his authorities do not necessarily prove this; for it always may be supposed that the καδίσκοι were covered.

[3] In Poll. 8, 16 χοιρίναι are mentioned among the σκεύη δικαστικά, and the passage continues: πάλαι γὰρ ἀντὶ ψήφων χοιρίναις ἐχρῶντο, αἴπερ ἦσαν κόγχαι θαλάττιοι· αὖθις δὲ καὶ χαλκᾶς ἐποιήσαντο κατὰ μίμησιν. καὶ σπόνδυλοι δὲ ἐκαλοῦντο αἱ ψῆφοι αἱ δικαστικαί, χαλκοῦ πεποιημέναι. Cf. Arist., *Wasps*, 332/3: ἦ δῆτα λίθον με ποίησον, ἐφ᾽ οὗ τὰς χοιρίνας ἀριθμοῦσιν. 849: οὕτω κιττῷ διὰ τῶν σανίδων μετὰ χοιρίνης περιελθεῖν. In Aristoph., *Equit.*, 1332, Demos after his reformation is οὐ χοιρινῶν ὄζων. For the two καδίσκοι cf. Phrynichos in his *Muses* ap. Harp. καδίσκος: ἰδοῦ, δέχου τὴν ψῆφον, ὁ καδίσκος δέ σοι 'Ο μὲν ἀπολύων οὗτος, ὁ δ᾽ ἀπολλὺς ὁδί. In the suit against Labes in the *Wasps*, Bdelycleon 987/8 says to Philocleon: τηνδὶ λαβὼν τὴν ψῆφον ἐπὶ τὸν ὕστερον Μύσας παράξον κἀπόλυσον, ὦ πάτερ. But Philocleon wishes to condemn, and consequently he asks 991: ὅδ᾽ ἔσθ᾽ ὁ πρότερος; cf. Xen., *Hell.*, 1. 7, 9. Lipsius in Meier

In the fourth century, οἱ λαχόντες ἐπὶ τὰς ψήφους, after the speeches were over, handed to each juror openly before the eyes of both parties, two ballots, one perforated and one not perforated. These ballots were discs of bronze with an axis in the centre, protruding on both sides of the disc, and either perforated or whole.[1] Then the herald called upon the parties to declare whether they intended to bring a δίκη ψευδομαρτυριῶν against any witness, and after that he called on the jury to vote, saying: "The perforated ballot for the first speaker," *i.e.* for the plaintiff, "the unperforated for the second," *i.e.* for the defendant.[2] In all probability two vessels stood on the speaker's platform, the one of copper, the other of wood; the copper vessel, called ὁ κύριος ἀμφορεύς,

940/1 supposes that secrecy was ensured even in the fifth century by handing to the juror, besides the real ψῆφος, another counter like it, which was deposited in the other vessel. This is rightly disputed by Wachsmuth 2, 1, 871. He assumes that the position of the voting-urns in the fifth century was different from that in the fourth. According to Dem. 19, 311 the urns stood in front on the βῆμα; according to Arist., *Wasps*, 849: οὕτω κιττῷ διὰ τῶν σανίδων μετὰ χοιρίνης περιελθεῖν (if Wachsmuth, 869, 4 is right in referring the line to the moment of voting) behind the βῆμα. Bdelycleon too (990), in speaking of leading his father to the urn, uses the verb περιάγω. Poll. 8, 16 mentions among the σκεύη δικαστικά, πινάκιον τιμητικὸν μάλθῃ, ᾗ καταλήλιπτο τὸ πινάκιον, ἐγκεντρίς, ᾗ εἶλκον τὴν γραμμήν· μακρὰ δὲ ἐκαλεῖτο, ἣν καταδικάζοντες εἷλκον. Cf. Phot. μακρὰν τίμησιν· τοῖς δικάζουσι πινάκιον ἐδίδοτο, ἐν ᾧ ἔγραφον μακρὰν γραμμήν, ὅτε τινὰ καταλαμβάνοιεν ἐν τῷ τιμήματι, βραχεῖαν δέ, ὅτ᾽ ἀπολύοιεν καὶ μὴ καταδικάζοιεν. See also Phot. and Suid. μακρὰ γραμμή. That this arrangement belongs to the fifth century, is clear from Aristoph., *Wasps*, 106, 166/7.

[1] Arist., col. 35, 27 sqq. (the restorations here are confirmed by the quotation from Aristotle in Harp. τετρυπημένη): [ψῆφοι δέ εἰσι χαλκ]αῖ αὐλίσκον [ἔχουσαι ἐν τῷ μέσῳ, αἱ μὲν ἡ]μίσειαι τετρυ[πημέναι, αἱ δὲ ἡμίσειαι πλήρεις· οἱ] δὲ λαχόντες [ἐπὶ τὰς ψήφους, ἐπειδὰν εἰρημέ]νοι ὦσιν [οἱ λόγοι, παραδιδόασιν ἑκάστῳ τ]ῶν δικαστ[ῶν δύο ψήφους τετρυπημένη]ν καὶ πλήρη, [φανερὰς ὁρᾶν τοῖς ἀντιδίκοις, ἵν]α μήτε πλή[ρεις μήτε τετρυπημένας] ἀ[μφο]τέρας λαμβάνωσιν. Cf. Phot. τετρυπημένη; Lex. Seguer. 307, 18; C.I.A., II. 778. On one side the ballot had the inscription, ψῆφος δημοσία, on the other a letter. The specimens we possess have Γ or Κ, and belong, therefore, most likely to a time when the sections of Heliasts sat in different courts. On the ψῆφοι that have been preserved cf. Vischer, *Kl. Schr.*, 2, 288 ff.; Wachsmuth in *Arch. Anz.*, 1861, 223/4.

[2] Arist., col. 36, 10 sqq.: ἐπειδὰν δὲ διαψηφίζε[σθαι] μέλ[λ]ωσιν [οἱ δικασ]τα[ί], ὁ κῆρυξ ἀγορ[εύ]ει πρῶτον, ἂν ἐ[πι]σκή[πτων]ται οἱ ἀντίδικοι ταῖς μαρτυρίαις· [δε]ῖ γὰρ [πρότερον] ἐπισκήψασθαι [αὔ]τα[ῖς ἢ ἀπ]αντα[ς] διαψη[φίσασ]θαι. ἔπειτα πά[λι]ν [ἀνακη]ρύττε[ι] "ἡ τε[τρυπη]μένη τοῦ προτέρου [λέγο]ν[το]ς, ἡ [δὲ] πλή[ρης το]ῦ ὕστερον λέγο[ν]τος." For the δίκη ψευδομαρτυριῶν, sometimes called specially ἐπίσκηψις, see Meier[2] 490 sqq. Ἡ τετρυπημένη ψῆφος condemns. Cf. Æschin, *in Tim.* 79.

was intended for the ballots with which the Dicasts meant to vote, while the wooden vessel, ὁ ἄκυρος ἀμφορεύς, received the second ballot given to each juror. The juryman, taking the axis of the ballot with which he intended to vote between two fingers, so that no one could see whether it was perforated or not, approached the κύριος ἀμφορεὺς and dropped the ballot (κυρία ψῆφος) into the copper vessel through a slit just wide enough to admit it. He then dropped the other disc (ἄκυρος ψῆφος) into the wooden vessel, which was open at top. In this way the secrecy of the ballot was tolerably certain.[1] When all had voted—probably giving up their bâtons at the same time—the κύριος ἀμφορεὺς was set on a table and the ballots sorted out by οἱ ἐπὶ τὰς ψήφους εἰληχότες. The president then counted the votes—the perforated ballots for the plaintiff, those not perforated for the defendant. He then had the result given out by the herald. The party that received most votes was victorious, a tie counting in favour of the defendant.[2]

[1] Arist., col. 86, 3 sqq.: εἰσ[ὶ δ'] ἀμφ[ο]ρεῖς [δύο κεί]μενοι ἐν τῷ δικαστηρίῳ, ὁ μὲν χ[α]λκοῦς, [ὁ δὲ ξύ]λινος, διαιρετοι, [δ]πως [μ]ὴ [τινε]ς ὑπο[β]άλλων[ται ψήφ]ους, εἰς οὓς ψηφίζονται οἱ δικαστα[ί], ὁ μὲν [χαλκοῦ]ς κύριος, ὁ δὲ ξύλινος ἀκυρ[ος]. ἔχ[ει δ' ὁ] χαλ[κοῦς ἐ]πίθημα διερρη[η]μένο[ν], ὥστ' αὐ[τ]ὴν [μόνη]ν χωρεῖν τὴν ψῆφον, ἴν[α μ]ὴ δύο [ὁ] αὐτὸς [ἐμβάλ]ῃ. Schol. Arist., Equit., 1150: ὕστερον δὲ ἀμφορεῖς δύο ἵσταντο ἐν τοῖς δικαστηρίοις, ὁ μὲν χαλκοῦς, ὁ δὲ ξύλινος καὶ ὁ μὲν κύριος ἦν, ὁ δ' ἄκυρος. ἔχει δὲ ὁ μὲν χαλκοῦς, ὥς φησιν Ἀριστοτέλης, διερρινημένον ἐπίθημα εἰς τὸ αὐτὴν μόνην τὴν ψῆφον καθίεσθαι. See also Poll. 8, 123. The ἀμφορεῖς stood upon the same platform as that on which the speaker's tribune and, perhaps, the βῆμα of the presiding magistrate stood. Dem. 19, 311: νῦν τοίνυν ὑμᾶς οὐκ εἰς Πελοπόννησον δεῖ πρεσβείαν πέμπειν οὐδ' ὁδὸν μακρὰν βαδίσαι οὐδ' ἐφόδια ἀναλίσκειν, ἀλλ' ἄχρι τοῦ βήματος ἐνταυθοῖ προσελθόντα ἕκαστον ὑμῶν τὴν ὁσίαν καὶ τὴν δικαίαν ψῆφον ὑπὲρ τῆς πατρίδος θέσθαι κατ' ἀνδρὸς κ.τ.λ. It is quite immaterial whether ἐνταυθοῖ be taken as referring to the speaker's tribune (where of course the speaker would be standing), or whether with Wachsmuth 2, 1, 370, 1, we suppose it merely put in contrast to long journeys on embassies far away from the city of Athens. On the voting see Arist., col. 36, 16 sqq.: [ὁ δὲ δι]καστ[ὴς] λα[βὼν] . . . ἐ[κ] τοῦ λυχνείου τὰς ψήφους, πιέ[ζει] τὸ [μέσον] τῆς ψῆφου, καὶ οὐ δεικνύων [τ]οῖς ἀ[γωνιζο]μένοις οὔτε τὸ τε[τρυ]πημένον [οὔτε τὸ] πλῆρες ἐνβάλλει τὴν μὲν κυ[ρία]ν εἰς [τὸν χαλκ]οῦν ἀμ[φορέ]α, τὴν [δὲ ἄκυρον] εἰς [τὸν ξύλ]ινον.

[2] Before the close of the voting the herald asked whether all the Dicasts had voted: Arist., Wasps, 751 ff., where Philocleon says: κείνων ἔραμαι, κεῖθι γενοίμαν, Ἵν' ὁ κῆρυξ φησι, τίς ἀψήφισ-Τος; ἀνιστάσθω. Κἀπισταίην ἐπὶ τοῖς κημοῖς Ψηφιζομένων ὁ τελευταῖος. It seems likely that the bâtons were given up at the voting, because, when a second vote was necessary, the jurymen first received them back again. See the next note. For the counting of the ballots see Arist., col. 36, 22 sqq.: οἱ δὲ [τεταγ]μένοι λαβ[ό]ντες [δύ' ὑ]πηρέτ[ας τὸν ἀ]μφορέα τὸν κύριον [ἐπαφ]ιᾶσιν [ἐπ'] ἄβα[κα τρυ]πήματα ἔχοντα [ὅ]σ[αιπέρ εἰσι[ν] αἱ [ψ]ῆ[φοι] . . . ΑΥΤΑΙ . . . ΗΧ. Ρ . . . τοῦ ἀ[ρ]ιθμῆ[σαι . . .]

If the suit was an ἀγὼν τιμητός, the Dicasts voted again, after again hearing the parties, as to the amount of the penalty or compensation. At this second ballot they had to declare themselves in favour either of the proposal of the plaintiff or of that of the defendant. The voting was taken in the same way as before.[1] In suits where several parties laid claim to some object in dispute, the voting was somewhat differently conducted. Καδίσκοι were put up equal in number to the claimants. The Dicasts, it would seem, received each one ballot, which they deposited in the καδίσκος of that party in whose favour they pronounced.[2] It appears that besides the method of voting just described the old method was also used in the fourth century, but probably only for Eisangeliai. The Dicast received only one voting stone, which he had to deposit, either in the urn for condemnation or in that for acquittal.[3] If

καὶ τὰ [διάκ]ενα [αὐτ]ῶν [καὶ] τὰ πλήρη δηλ[οῖ τοῖς ἀν]τιδ[ί]κοις· οἱ δ[ὲ ἐπὶ] τὰ[ς] ψήφους [εἰ]λη[χότες] δια[ριθμοῦσιν α]ὐτὰς [ἐπ]ὶ τοῦ ἄβακος, [χωρὶς] μὲ[ν τὰ]ς πλήρεις, χω[ρὶ]ς δὲ τὰς τε[τρυπ]ημένας. καὶ ἀνα[γο]ρεύει ὁ κῆ[ρυξ] τὸν [ἀριθ]μὸν τῶν ψήφων, τοῦ μὲν διώ[κον]τος τὰς τετρυπημένας, τοῦ δὲ φ[εύγοντος τ]ὰς πλήρεις· ὁποτέρῳ δ' [ἂν πλείων γ]ένη[ται, οὗ]τος νικᾷ, ἂν δὲ [ἴσα]ι, ὁ [φεύγων]. See Aristot. ap. Lex. Cantabr. 670: ἴσαι αἱ ψῆφοι αὐτῶν. Cf. Antiph., de Cæde Herod., 51: εἴπερ γε καὶ τῶν ψήφων ὁ ἀριθμὸς ἐξ ἴσου γιγνόμενος τὸν φεύγοντα μᾶλλον ὠφελεῖ ἢ τὸν διώκοντα. Æschin. in Ctes. 252: καὶ ἴσαι αἱ ψῆφοι αὐτῷ ἐγένοντο· εἰ δὲ μία μόνον μετέπεσεν, ὑπερώριστ' ἂν ἢ ἀπέθανεν. The president counts the ballots: Is. 5, 18.

[1] Arist., col. 36, 85 sqq.: ἔ[π]ειτα πάλιν τιμῶσιν, ἂν δέῃ τιμῆσαι, τὸν αὐτὸν τρόπον ψηφιζόμενοι, τὸ μὲν σύμβολον ἀποδιδόντες, βακτηρίαν δὲ πάλιν παραλαμβάνοντες. ἡ δὲ τίμησίς ἐστιν πρὸς ἡμίχουν ὕδατος ἑκατέρῳ. Apparently the jurymen gave up their σύμβολα when they received back the βακτηρίαι for the second vote, so that their numbers might be checked. They received them again on returning the βακτηρίαι at the voting. This passage in Aristotle is an indirect proof that at this second ballot the jury had to choose between the proposal of the plaintiff and the counter-proposal of the defendant; see Meier [2] 216 sqq. For a possible προστίμημα by the jury, see Meier [2] 218 sqq.

[2] Dem. 48, 10: καὶ τοῦτον τὸν τρόπον ἐπιβουλευσάντων καὶ συναγωνιζομένων ἀλλήλοις ἐφ' ἡμᾶς, καδίσκων τεττάρων τεθέντων κατὰ τὸν νόμον, εἰκότως, οἶμαι, οἱ δικασταὶ ἐξηπατήθησαν καὶ ἐστασίασαν ἀλλήλοις καὶ παρακρουσθέντες ὑπὸ τῆς παρασκευῆς ἐψηφίζοντο ὅτι ἔτυχεν ἕκαστος. καὶ αἱ ψῆφοι ὀλίγαις πάνυ ἐγένοντο πλείους, ἢ τρίσιν ἢ τέτταρσιν, ἐν τῷ Θεοπόμπου καδίσκῳ ἢ ἐν τῷ τῆς γυναικός. Cf. Is. 11, 21. Secrecy was possible here too, if the καδίσκοι were covered and were approached by the Dicasts one after another.

[3] This theory rests upon a passage in the speech of Lycurgus on the Eisangelia against Leocrates, § 149: ὑμῶν δ' ἕκαστον χρὴ νομίζειν τὸν Λεωκράτους ἀποψηφιζόμενον θάνατον τῆς πατρίδος καὶ ἀνδραποδισμὸν καταψηφίζεσθαι, καὶ δυοῖν καδίσκοιν κειμένοιν τὸν μὲν προδοσίας, τὸν δὲ σωτηρίας εἶναι, καὶ τὰς ψήφους φέρεσθαι τὰς μὲν ὑπὲρ ἀναστάσεως τῆς πατρίδος, τὰς δὲ ὑπὲρ ἀσφαλείας καὶ τῆς ἐν τῇ

the prosecutor did not obtain a fifth part of the votes cast, he had, in a large number of private suits, to pay the defendant the ἐπωβελία, *i.e.* an obol for each drachma of the property in dispute; in public suits he was fined 1,000 drachmas, and lost the right of bringing similar actions in future.[1]

Punishments. The punishment voted by the court might be either pecuniary or personal; pecuniary punishments were employed in both private and public suits, personal in public suits only. Personal punishment might mean sentence of death, selling into slavery (allowable only in the case of foreigners), banishment or Atimia; these were not unfrequently accompanied by confiscation. Imprisonment was never decreed except as an additional punishment.

In public cases the sentence was carried out by the State itself, through its servants. A sentence of death was executed under **Execution of the Sentence.** the superintendence of the ἕνδεκα, in ancient times by hurling the criminal into the Βάραθρον, but later by giving him a draught of hemlock (κώνειον), and also probably in the case of common crimes by cudgelling him to death (τυμπανίζειν). A sentence of Atimia was enforced by the severe penalties annexed to any contravention of the restrictions imposed by the Atimia. Fines were collected by the Practores; confiscated property was sold by the Poletai.

In private suits the execution of the sentence was left to the plaintiff himself, except when the State was to share the fine imposed, or when imprisonment had been decreed, and also in the δίκαι ἐμπορικαὶ, where the condemned party was imprisoned until the fine was paid, unless he could find bail. The plaintiff had the right of distraint or seizure of property, if the defendant failed to satisfy him within the time fixed by the law or by the court; and if the defendant interrupted the distraint, he could bring a δίκη ἐξούλης, which made the defendant a State-debtor for the same amount as he owed the plaintiff.[2]

πόλει εὐδαιμονίας. The two κάδισκοι here must mean one for condemnation and one for acquittal; see Lipsius in Meier [3] 941. 949. But I cannot see a second proof of this in Is. 5, 17/8. I take ἐξαιρεθεισῶν τῶν ψήφων to refer to taking the ballots out from the κύριος ἀμφορεὺς and separating the perforated discs from the others. For it is only after this has been done that the ἀριθμεῖν can begin. And then this counting is a συναριθμεῖν, not a διαριθμεῖν, so that Szanto's suspicions, *ib.*, 29, are groundless.

[1] Meier [3] 947 ff.; Boeckh., *St. d. Ath.*, 1, 479 ff.
[2] Meier [3] 956 ff.

There was no appeal (ἔφεσις) from the verdict of a Heliastic court. A plea for cassation could, however, be brought (τὴν ἔρημον sc. δίκην ἀντιλαχεῖν), if the condemned party proved that judgment had been given against him by default, through no fault of his. Lastly, the sentence was annulled if the condemned man procured the conviction of the witnesses of his adversary in a δίκη ψευδομαρτυριῶν for false evidence. The process under such circumstances was begun afresh as δίκη ἀντίδικος.[1]

Restitutio in integrum.

The plan of entrusting the administration of justice to the common people proved a failure in the form in which it was tried in the Athenian Heliaia.[2] The Heliasts, led away by their irresponsibility, too often disregarded the laws, and acted on the mere impulse of the moment.[3] More than this, bribery and interested motives not unfrequently determined the decisions of the courts.[4] Further, the Heliasts' ignorance of the laws demoralised the speakers, who, not unfrequently, trading on this ignorance, misinterpreted and misrepresented the laws to suit their case.[5] The system of allowing the people to administer justice produced a crop of sycophants at Athens, who made their living by false accusations, and by levying blackmail, which their victims were afraid to refuse

General Criticism of the Athenian Judicature.

---

[1] Meier [2] 971 sqq.

[2] Cf. Fränkel 106 sqq.; Beloch, *d. att. Polit. seit Perikles*, 8 sqq.

[3] On the irresponsibility of the Heliasts see Arist., *Wasps*, 587. 548 sqq. Its effect on the feelings of the Dicasts: (Xen.), *de Rep. Ath.*, 1, 18; *Wasps*, 552 sqq.; see also Dem. 19, 1; 21, 4. Judgment dependent on the impression made by the speeches: Xen., *Mem.*, 4, 8, 5. Condemnation after the first speech without hearing the other party: Dem. 45, 6; Isocr. 15, 22. In general Isocr. 18, 10: καὶ ὅτι τύχῃ μᾶλλον ἢ τῷ δικαίῳ κρίνεται τὰ παρ' ὑμῖν. See also (Xen.), *de Rep. Ath.*, 1, 13.

[4] The great number of Dicasts in courts rendered bribery difficult: (Xen.) *de Rep. Ath.*, 3, 7. Nevertheless it was managed, according to Arist., 27, 5, also Harp. δεκάζων, and Diod. 13, 64, first by Anytus. Cf. Eratosth. *ap.* Harp. δεκάζων, where, however, the proverb Λύκου δεκάς, used by the old comedy, is unintelligible with the explanation of Eratosth. Attempts at explanation by Wachsmuth 2, 1, 376, 2. A case of bribery is attested by Lys. 29, 12. The Athenians had the reputation of being corrupt: Diogen. 3, 12: 'Ἀττικὸς ὑπέχει τὴν χεῖρα ἀποθνῄσκων· ἐπὶ τῶν φιλαργύρων. φιλοκερδεῖς γὰρ οἱ 'Ἀθηναῖοι. Corruption of the Athenian judges is denied by Oncken, *Ath. u. Hell.*, 1, 274 sqq. Another motive for an unjust verdict in Lys. 27, 1: ἐνθυμεῖσθαι δὲ χρή, ὅτι πολλάκις ἠκούσατε τούτων λεγόντων, ὁπότε βούλοιντό τινα ἀδίκως ἀπολέσαι, ὅτι, εἰ μὴ καταψηφιεῖσθε ὧν αὐτοὶ κελεύουσιν, ἐπιλείψει ὑμᾶς ἡ μισθοφορά. Cf. Arist., *Equit.*, 1356 sqq.

[5] Cf. Buermann in *N. Rhein. Mus.*, vol. 32. 383/4. See Dem. 20, 166; Æschin. *in Tim.* 178.

owing to the vagaries of the Dicasteries.[1] The result of this state of things was a general uncertainty in the administration of justice, which made it impossible even for the most upright citizen to live in peace at Athens, if this did not suit the caprice of some malicious neighbour.

6. THE ATHENIAN LEAGUE.

A. *The First Confederacy.*

After the battle of Mycale the Greeks of the Islands—among them the Samians, Chians, and Lesbians—were received into the Pan-Hellenic Confederacy that had been formed against the Persians. The Ætolian and Ionic cities of Asia Minor, however, were refused admittance, and in consequence threw themselves on the protection of Athens. Leotychidas subsequently returned home with the Peloponnesian fleet, while the Athenians and their allies from Ionia and the Hellespont laid siege to Sestos and at last, late in the winter, succeeded in reducing it. In the following spring a fleet was fitted out by the Peloponnesians, the Athenians, and the other allies, under the command of Pausanias. Sailing to Cyprus, he subjugated the greater part of that island, and thus closed the sea to the Persians. Such of the Greek islanders as had not yet joined the League now came in. The Greek fleet next sailed to Byzantion and took it, thus securing the only other approach to Greece. While at Byzantion, Pausanias, by his overbearing, violent behaviour, drove the Greeks of the Hellespont and Ionia, who were already allies of Athens, and the island Greeks, who were members of the Pan-Hellenic alliance, to seek the protection of the Athenians. Their request was granted, and before the Archon Timosthenes' year of office was over (478/7 B.C.), Aristeides had assessed the tribute to be paid by each city, and thus established the First Athenian League. It is extremely probable that even before this a number of Greek cities in Thrace had joined the alliance, but it was not till two years later that every vestige of the Persian dominion over that district was removed by Kimon's capture of Eion. And by the battle of the Eurymedon the Greeks of the Carian, Lycian and Pamphylian coasts were also gained for the confederacy.[2]

Foundation and extension of the League.

---

[1] Xen., *Mem.*, 2, 9, 1. Lys. 7, 39. Dem. 25, 41; 58, 65.

[2] Kirchhoff's view in *Herm.* 11, 1 ff. of the gradual extension of the Athenian League is opposed, and I think justly, by Beloch in *N. Rh. Mus.*

The original objects of the League thus formed by the Athenians were the emancipation of the allies from Persian rule and the repulse of any Persian invader.[1] To effect this an armed force was necessary to the allies, and as of course at the formation of the League all the members did not possess a navy, we must suppose that, from the very first, the duties of members differed, States which possessed a regular navy furnishing a contingent of ships, while those which did not had to pay a war-contribution to the treasury of the League. This treasury was kept at Delos and was administered by Athenian officials, the Hellenotamiai. It was at Delos, too, in the sanctuary of Apollo that the periodical meetings of the Federal Council were held. That body determined the policy of the League and at the same time acted as the Federal Court of Justice.[2]

Original objects of the Confederacy.

Even before the League was completed by the accession of the Carian, Lycian and Pamphylian cities, circumstances had arisen within it which naturally led to a change in its character. The allies soon grew weary of the war, the continuance of which interfered seriously with their pursuit of their ordinary avocations. Most of them accordingly agreed with the Athenians that instead of fur-

The Confederacy converted into an Athenian Empire.

43, 104 ff. Cf. Nöthe, d. del. Bund, 1 sqq., Magdeburg, 1839. The island-Greeks received into the Pan-Hellenic Alliance after the battle of Mycale: Hdt. 9, 106. Notwithstanding Diod. 11, 37 the Ionic and Hellespontine cities, which revolted from Persia (Hdt. 9, 104) seem not to have been admitted into this general confederacy, but to have been allies of the Athenians: Thuc. 1, 89; Leo in Verh. d. Philologenvers. in Wiesbaden, 60 sqq. Capture of Sestos: Thuc. 1, 89; Hdt. 1, 121. In 478 B.C. reduction of Cyprus and Byzantion: Thuc. 1, 94. 128. The Hegemony of the Greeks of the islands and the coast of Asia Minor transferred to the Athenians: Thuc. 1, 95; Plut., Arist., 23; Leo 65. Constitution of the League by Aristeides in 478/7 B.C.: Arist. 23, 5; Thuc. 1, 96. The terms of the Peace of Nikias show that at this time cities in Thrace already belonged to the confederacy: Thuc. 5, 18; Beloch 110. Eion, it seems, reduced in 476 B.C.: Thuc. 1, 98; Hdt. 7, 107; Diod. 11. 60; Plut., Kim., 7; Schol., Æschin., 1, 131, p. 48, 11 Diod. ἐπὶ ἄρχοντος Ἀθήνησιν Φαίδωνος. The Carian and Lycian cities: Diod. 11, 60.

[1] Thuc. 3, 10; 1, 96; Arist. 23, 5: διὸ καὶ τοὺς φόρους οὗτος (Ἀριστείδης) ἦν ὁ τάξας ταῖς πόλεσιν τοὺς πρώτους ἔτει τρίτῳ μετὰ τὴν ἐν Σαλαμῖνι ναυμαχίαν ἐπὶ Τιμοσθένους ἄρχοντος, καὶ τοὺς ὅρκους ὤμοσεν τοῖς Ἴωσιν, ὥστε τὸν αὐτὸν ἐχθρὸν εἶναι καὶ φίλον, ἐφ' οἷς καὶ τοὺς μύδρους ἐν τῷ πελάγει καθεῖσαν.

[2] Thuc. 1, 96, 97; Köhler, Urk. u. Unters. z. Gesch. d. del.-att. Bundes, 88 ff;. Nöthe 7/8; [Abbott, Hist. of Greece, ii. 293 ff.].

nishing a contingent of ships as the constitution of the League required, they should pay annually a sum of money, in return for which the Athenians were to supply the requisite contingent themselves. The greater States alone continued to furnish their own contingents. But even they were not infrequently reluctant to furnish them, or declined altogether to do so; while those States which had agreed to pay sums of money often refused to pay. In either case the Athenians took vigorous measures against the recalcitrant members. Those States which had already commuted their contingent into money payments were incapable of resistance; those which still possessed military forces were subjugated, frequently not without serious resistance. Their position in the League was thus lost, and they became subjects of Athens on conditions determined in each case by a special treaty.[1] Thus Naxos was subdued by the Athenians and deprived of its autonomy just before the battle of the Eurymedon. Not long after, Thasos met with the same fate, as indeed did all the other States that tried to desert; for by neglecting their duty as members of the League they were virtually deserting their allies.[2] By about 454 B.C. all the allied States (except Samos, Lesbos, and Chios, which had separate treaties with Athens) had ceased, either of their own accord or under compulsion, to furnish contingents of their own, and had become tributary. It was only the natural and indeed the inevitable result of these new conditions that the Athenians (who, in consideration of these tributary payments, had themselves undertaken the military duties of their subjects) came to regard the chest of the League, into which this tribute-money was paid, as an Athenian treasury, and removed it about 454 B.C. to Athens.[3] A squadron of 20 guardships and a body of

[1] Thuc. 1, 99; 6, 76; Köhler 93 sqq.; Kirchhoff 23 sqq.; Nöthe 9 ff.; [Abbott p. 295 ff.].

[2] Thuc. 1, 93. 100. 101. For the other allies see Thuc. 1, 98: πρώτη τε αὕτη (Νάξος) πόλις ξυμμαχὶς παρὰ τὸ καθεστηκὸς ἐδουλώθη, ἔπειτα δὲ καὶ τῶν ἄλλων ὡς ἑκάστῃ ξυνέβη.

[3] Arist. makes Aristeides the author of this change in the relations between the allies and Athens. In 24, 2 he describes its character: πεισθέντες δὲ ταῦτα καὶ λαβόντες τὴν ἀρχὴν τοῖς [τε] συμμάχοις δεσποτικωτέρως ἐχρῶντο πλὴν Χίων καὶ Λεσβίων καὶ Σαμίων · τούτους δὲ φύλακας εἶχον τῆς ἀρχῆς, ἐῶντες τάς τε πολιτείας παρ' αὐτοῖς καὶ ἄρχειν, ὧν ἔτυχον ἄρχοντες. In 405/4 B.C. the Athenians resolved in regard to the Samians: τοῖς δὲ νόμοις χρῆσθαι τοῖς σφετέροις αὐτῶν αὐτονόμους ὄντας καὶ τἄλλα ποιεῖν κατὰ τοὺς ὅρκους καὶ τὰς συνθήκας καθάπερ ξύνκειται Ἀθηναίοις καὶ Σαμίοις: 'Αρχ. δελτ., 1889, p. 26, ll. 15 ff. The transfer of the Federal Treasury from Delos to Athens about 454 B.C. follows

2,000 men for garrison duty were sent out annually to maintain obedience among the allies.[1] The few confederate States which remained independent were still entitled, nominally at least, to a voice in the direction of federal affairs.[2] The number of States that were still independent in 454 B.C. was in course of time more and more diminished. First the cities of Eubœa revolted in 446, and after their reduction became tributary, with the exception of Hestiaia, whose inhabitants were expelled, and its territory taken possession of by Athenian Cleruchs.[3] In 440 B.C. Samos revolted, but after a hard struggle she submitted in 439, and was deprived of her army and navy.[4] Mytilene revolted in 428 B.C., but was retaken in the following year, and deprived of its fleet, while the whole of Lesbos, the territory of Methymna alone excepted, was divided into 3,000 Cleruch Lots.[5] The last members of the

from the preamble of C.I.A., I. 260; cf. Sauppe in *Nachr. d. Götl. Ges. d. W.*, 1865, p. 5; Köhler 102 sqq.; Busolt, in *N. Rh. Mus.*, 37, 312 ff.; Nöthe 12; [Abbott, pp. 357 sqq.]. According to Theophr. *ap.* Arist. 25 it was the Samians who proposed the transference.

[1] According to Arist. 24, 3 when the fortunes of the League were in the zenith, there were regularly νῆες δὲ φρουρίδες εἴκοσι, ἄλλαι δὲ νῆες αἱ τοὺς φρουροὺς ἄγουσαι τοὺς ἀπὸ τοῦ κυάμου δισχιλίους ἄνδρας.

[2] Köhler 101 supposes that the Federal Council had been definitely abolished before the chest was conveyed to Athens. The narrative in the speech of the Mytilenæans (Thuc. 3, 10. 11) supports the view that the independent allies were entitled to vote upon Federal affairs. Cf. καὶ εἰ μὲν αὐτόνομοι ἔτι ἦμεν ἅπαντες, βεβαιότεροι ἂν ἡμῖν ἦσαν μηδὲν νεωτεριεῖν · ὑποχειρίους δὲ ἔχοντες τοὺς πλείους, ἡμῖν δὲ ἀπὸ τοῦ ἴσου ὁμιλοῦντες κ.τ.λ. And again: ἅμα μὲν γὰρ μαρτυρίῳ ἐχρῶντο μὴ ἂν τούς γε ἰσοψήφους ἄκοντας, εἰ μή τι ἠδίκουν, οἷς ἐπῆσαν, ξυστρατεύειν. We cannot say positively, however, whether a regular Federal Council was still in existence, as Wachsmuth 1, 545, 1 imagines. Thuc. 3, 36 says of the Mytilenæans, οὐκ ἀρχόμενοι ὥσπερ οἱ ἄλλοι. It is impossible to say what τὸ κοινὸν τῆς —— may refer to in C.I.A., IV. 38a, a psephism dealing with conditions of tribute.

[3] Thuc. 1, 114; Diod. 12, 7; Plut., *Per.*, 22, 23. 1,000 Athenian Cleruchs were sent to Hestiaia according to Diod. 12, 22; 2,000 according to Theop., *fr.* 164 in Müller's *fr. hist. gr.*, 1, 305. The treaty with Chalkis is preserved, C.I.A., IV. 27a.

[4] Thuc. 1, 115. 116. 117; Diod. 12, 27. 28; Plut., *Per.*, 24-28. H. Droysen, in *Herm.*, 13, 566/7, doubts whether Samos became tributary. He supposes that part of the island was seized for Athenian Cleruchs. From C.I.A., I. 38 and Thuc. 7, 57 it appears that we must regard her as tributary, but the name of Samos has not been found in the Tribute-Lists yet: Köhler, *Urk. u. Unters.*, etc., p. 142, 1. Beloch, in *N. Rh. Mus.*, 39, 36 ff., believes that the customs in Samos were collected wholly or in part for the Federal chest. With this he connects τὰ ἐχ Σάμου (χρήματα) in C.I.A., I. 188.

[5] Thuc. 3, 50.

League left independent, Methymna and the island of Chios, had to submit to Athenian encroachments on their independence.[1] They remained faithful to Athens, however, till 412 B.C., when the League was broken up.[2]

The members of the Athenian Confederacy were styled officially οἱ σύμμαχοι or αἱ πόλεις; they were also commonly known as ὑπήκοοι.[3] They were divided into two classes—autonomous and non-autonomous allies.[4] The autonomous allies had to furnish the Athenians with a specified contingent of ships of war ready manned, but they were independent so far as their internal administration was concerned.[5] The non-autonomous allies had to pay an annual tribute, and were subject to restrictions as to the character of their constitution and internal administration.[6]

Members of the League—how designated and classified.

The total amount of tribute which the tributary States had to furnish was at first 460 talents. Diminished for a time in some particulars, it was again raised to the same amount by the assessment of B.C. 439/8. It was not till the assessment of 425/4 that the tribute was raised to 1,200 talents, though even then only 800 to 900 talents a year were paid in reality.[7]

Tribute.

The tributary allies were subsequently divided into Tribute-

---

[1] Thuc. 7, 57: Μηθυμναῖοι μὲν ναυσὶ καὶ οὐ φόρῳ ὑπήκοοι. Χῖοι οὐχ ὑποτελεῖς ὄντες φόρου, ναῦς δὲ παρέχοντες αὐτόνομοι ξυνέσποντο. Cf. 6, 85. Prayers for the welfare of the Chians were offered at the public sacrifices in Athens: Arist., Av., 878 ff., and Schol. on l. 880. In 425 B.C. the Chians pulled down their new walls on the order of the Athenians: Thuc. 4, 51.

[2] Thuc. 8, 14. 22.

[3] For the official title, see C.I.A., I. 31. 37. 40; I. 9 has ἡ Ἀθηναίων ξυμμαχία. For their usual name, see Thuc. 7. 57; 6, 22. 43. 69. Cf. A. Fränkel, de condicione, iure, iurisdict. sociorum Atheniensium. Leipzig, 1878, p. 9ff.; Christensen, de iure et condicione sociorum Atheniens. In Opusc. philol. ad Madvigium a discipulis missa, p. 1 ff., 1876.

[4] Thuc. 7, 57 distinguishes αὐτόνομοι and ὑποτελεῖς φόρου. This is not exact. Cf. 1, 19; 3, 10; 6, 85.

[5] Thuc. 6, 85 says: Χίους μὲν καὶ Μηθυμναίους νεῶν παροχῇ (or παροκωχῇ as Stahl reads) αὐτονόμους; 7, 57: Χῖοι ναῦς παρέχοντες αὐτόνομοι. Μηθυμναῖοι ναυσὶν ὑπήκοοι. Among the autonomous allies we find aristocracies or oligarchies, as at Samos (Thuc. 1, 115) and Mytilene (Thuc. 3, 27. 47) before their subjugation. On the limits of Federal autonomy, cf. Busolt, d. zweite ath. Bund in Suppl. vol. 7 of Jahrb. f. cl. Phil., p. 645 ff.

[6] Thuc. dwells only on their tributary position: 6, 85; 7, 57. But he makes the Mytilenæans say 3, 10: οἱ ξύμμαχοι ἐδουλώθησαν πλὴν ἡμῶν καὶ Χίων.

[7] See p. 357.[1]

Districts, which, it appears, were also used as divisions for administrative purposes.[1] These divisions form the basis of classification in the tribute-lists which have been preserved to us from 446 B.C. onwards; after 443 B.C. they are strictly observed, and the cities arranged under definite heads. Five districts are given ὁ Ἰωνικὸς φόρος, ὁ Ἑλλησπόντιος φόρος, ὁ ἐπὶ Θρᾴκης φόρος, ὁ Καρικὸς φόρος, and ὁ νησιωτικὸς φόρος. After some time the district of Ionia was united with that of Caria, at first under the former name, but afterwards under the latter. The date of this union was probably 437 B.C.[2] According to Aristophanes the number of tributary cities was 1,000, but this figure far exceeds what appears in the tribute-lists.[3] The difference is partly explained by the fact of several cities in the lists being representatives of Synteleiai, that is, of groups of cities, most of which perhaps stood in a kind of dependent relation to their representative; and Aristophanes most likely counts these dependent cities as separate States. Synteleiai paid their tribute in one sum, but they were liable to dissolution at every assessment, in which case the members were assessed separately.[4]

Tribute districts.

[1] That the Tribute-Districts were also divisions for purposes of administration seems to follow from the Quota-List C.I.A., I. 37 [Hicks, *Gk. Hist. Inscr.*, 47], and from a passage in the psephism for the foundation of Brea, C.I.A., I. 31 [Hicks 29] : κατὰ τὰς ξυγγραφάς, α(ἱ ἐπὶ—)του γραμματεύοντος ἐγένον(το περὶ τῶν πόλε)ων τῶν ἐπὶ Θρᾴκης. Köhler 125/6 denies that the Districts were used as administrative divisions; so Nöthe 6.

[2] *Vid.* the lists in C.I.A., I. 234 sqq., IV. 2, 239 sqq., p. 72. 3, 272d sqq., p. 175. The titles were Ἰωνικὸς φόρος, Ἑλλησπόντιος φόρος, ἐπὶ or once ἀπὸ Θρᾴκης φόρος, Καρικὸς φόρος, Νησιωτικὸς φόρος. Cf. Köhler, p. 124. Löscheke, *de aliquot tit. att.*, p. 11 sqq., explains the conjunction of the Ionian and Carian districts by supposing that, in consequence of the revolt of Samos, the more inland towns of Caria deserted too, and were not reconquered; see also Busolt in *Phil.* 41, 684 ff.

[3] Arist., *Wasps*, 707, gives 1,000 tributary cities, a round number, including cities only nominally dependent and those which paid in Synteleiai. Cf. Köhler, p. 110 sqq. A list of about 200 cities in the League is given from the inscriptions by Kirchhoff in C.I.A., I. p. 226 ff.; Curtius, *griech. Gesch.*,[5] Index and Supplement, p. 113 ff.; Busolt in *Phil.* 41, 653.

[4] Antiphon discussed these Synteleiai in his speech on the tribute of Samothrace (Harp. συντελεῖς), and in the course of it gave a definition of ἀπόταξις (Harp. *s. v.*), the technical expression for the dissolution of such a Synteleia. Instances of Synteleiai expressly described as such are Λύκιοι καὶ συν(τελεῖς): C.I.A., I. 234; Σερμυλιῆς κα(ὶ) συν(τελεῖς): I. 235. *Vid.* Köhler, p. 122/3; Busolt, *ib.*, 656 ff. The several cities of the Carian Chersonese appear with their separate assessments in C.I.A., IV. 3, 272d, p. 155, under the heading: αἴδε τῶν πόλεων Χερρονή(σου) συντελεῖς οὖσαι ἀπέδοσαν (τὸμ φόρον?).

The allies were usually assessed every four years, this period running, at least after 454 B.C., from one Great Panathenaia to another. This festival was celebrated in the third year of every Olympiad. Shortly before the outbreak of the Peloponnesian war, probably in 437 B.C., the beginning of this tribute-period was changed from the third to the fourth year of the Olympiad.[1] It was the duty of the Boule, as an administrative body, to draft the assessment; but their rating had to be confirmed by the Ecclesia.[2] The preliminary work was done by τάκται, an elective body, eight in number at the assessment in the year 425/4, two for each of the four Tribute-Districts then existing.[3] In the first instance the allied cities assessed themselves before these τάκται just as men who were liable to the εἰσφορὰ assessed themselves. Those cities, whose own rating was approved by the τάκται and by the Council, and confirmed by the

Assessment.

---

[1] (Xen.) de Rep. Ath., 3, 5: τὸ δὲ μέγιστον εἴρηται πλὴν αἱ τάξεις τοῦ φόρου· τοῦτο δὲ γίγνεται ὡς τὰ πολλὰ δι' ἔτους πέμπτου. The Quota-Lists shew that assessments were made in 450 and 446 B.C., and this is evidence that the assessment was quadriennial even before the Peloponnesian war. Even after the beginning of the Tribute-Period was changed, the assessment was made at the time of the Panathenaia (the Lesser Feast, of course, after the change); see C.I.A., I. 40: ὃν (sc. φόρον) τοῖς προτέροις Παν(αθηναίοις) ἐτατάχατο φέρειν. Cf. Köhler, p. 127. 184.

[2] C.I.A., I. 87: (κατὰ τάδε ἔτα)ξεν τὸμ φό(ρον τῇ)σι πόλεσιν ἡ (β)ουλ(ὴ) ᾗ (Πλ)ειστίας π(ρῶτος ἐγραμμ)ά(τευε—ἐ)πὶ Στρατοκλ(έους ἄ)ρχοντος, ἐπὶ (τῶ)ν (ἐσ)αγωγ(έω)ν, οἷς Κα(—ἐγραμμάτευε). That the Ecclesia had the final voice in the matter is proved by the first decree for Methone, C.I.A., I. 40: δι(α)χειροτονῆσαι τὸν δῆμον αὐτίκ(α πρὸς Μ)εθωναίους εἴτε φόρον δοκεῖ τάττειν τὸν δῆμο(ν αὐτίκ)α μάλα—. Heydemann has written against this, de senatu Atheniensium in Diss. phil. Argentorat. sel., 4, 177, but I cannot agree with him. Köhler, p. 66 ff., holds that the same formalities were observed in making the assessment as in passing a law: but Köhler himself admits in effect that this statement needs qualification, by expressing a doubt as to whether all the figures were examined by the court, and I cannot regard his view as correct. He is followed, however, by Schoell in Ber. d. bayr. Akad., 1886, p. 127 ff., though Schoell does not share his doubts. Guirand, De la condition des alliés pendant la première confédération Athénienne, p. 44, Paris, 1883, conceives that the tribute was assessed by a psephism; and it is true that the assessment was sanctioned by a psephism, for Crateros' ψηφισμάτων συναγωγὴ contained Tribute-Lists: see fr. 2, 12 in Müller, fr. hist. gr., 2, 618. 622. Fränkel, p. 43 ff., is substantially correct. In the second Athenian League, too, the estimate of the συντάξεις was made by a psephism: (Dem.) 58, 37/8.

[3] C.I.A., I. 87: χειρο(τον—ἐπὶ τὰ)ς πόλεις δύο (μὲν ἐπὶ τὰς ἐπὶ Θράκης), δύο δὲ ἐ(πὶ 'Ιωνίαν, δύο δ)ὲ ἐπὶ ν(ήσους, δύο δὲ ἐπὶ 'Ελλήσπ)οντο(ν). There can be no doubt that the τάκται mentioned in C.I.A., I. 266 are here meant.

Ecclesia, appear in the Tribute-Lists without any separate heading. These form the bulk of the allies. Cities that carried their own assessment in the Ecclesia as against the assessment of the τάκται are called πόλεις αὐταὶ φόρον ταξάμεναι.[1] On the other hand, cities that were unsuccessful in their appeal to the Ecclesia against the rating of the τάκται, formed the class known as πόλεις, ἃς ἔταξαν οἱ τάκται.[2] Just as it was allowable to move an amendment in the Ecclesia to any proposal of the Council, so it was open to any private citizen, when the Assessment was before the Ecclesia, to move an increase or a reduction for this or that allied city. If such a motion was accepted by the Ecclesia, the cities thus assessed were placed under the heading πόλεις, ἃς οἱ ἰδιῶται ἔταξαν or ἐνέγραψαν φόρον φέρειν.[3] As any member of the Ecclesia might appeal to a Heliastic court against its resolutions by a γραφὴ παρανόμων, we may presume, by analogy, that any private person might appeal to a Heliastic court against any assessment fixed by the Ecclesia. And no doubt the sense of justice was sufficiently alive at Athens to lead the people to accord a similar privilege to the allies. Cities whose assessment had ultimately been made in this way came under the heading of πόλεις, ἃς ἡ βουλὴ καὶ οἱ πεντακόσιοι οἱ ἡλιασταὶ ἔταξαν.[4] The proceedings

---

[1] This heading is found C.I.A., I. 243. 244. 256. Köhler, p. 187, understands it to mean the cities that had carried their appeals in the law-court. But these form another class: C.I.A., I. 266. A passage in the oath of the Chalkidians seems to point to the cities assessing themselves: καὶ τὸν φόρον ὑποτελῶ 'Αθηναίοισιν ὃν ἂν πείθω 'Αθηναίους, C.I.A., IV. 27a. This formula is restored by Foucart, Revue arch., 38, p. 261, in C.I.A., II. 92. Cf. Thuc. 1, 101: Θάσιοι—χρήματά τε ὅσα ἔδει ἀποδοῦναι αὐτίκα ταξάμενοι. Where the same cities appear under the same headings in different years, the old heading had been retained because there was no need to change the assessment. The Καλλιπολῖται, Σαρταῖοι, 'Αμόργιοι, who in 437 and 436 are πόλεις αὐταὶ φόρον ταξάμεναι (C.I.A., I. 243. 244) are assessed by the τάκται in another list, C.I.A., I. 266. Busolt, 658 ff., believes that this self-assessment was a special privilege possessed by certain States.

[2] C.I.A., I. 266: (πόλεις ἃς ἔτ)αξαν οἱ τάκται.

[3] C.I.A., I. 257: (πό)λει(ς ἃς) οἱ (ἰδι)ῶ(ται ἔ)τ(α)χ(σαν). Usually this heading runs: πόλεις ἃς οἱ ἰδιῶται ἐνέγραψαν φόρον φέρειν: C.I.A., I. 243. 244. 256. Köhler, p. 187, supposes that such motions by private persons were made in the Boule. According to Busolt, 669 ff. (cf. 659 ff.), the ἰδιῶται were the phil-Athenians in any allied city who procured its separation from some other city and its entrance on the list as paying a separate tribute.

[4] The formula of this heading has not been completely preserved; see C.I.A., I. 266: (πόλεις ἃς ἡ) βουλὴ καὶ οἱ πεντακόσιο(ι . . . ἔτ)αξαν. Köhler, p. 82, fills up the lacuna after πεντακόσιοι with ἡλιασταί. In any case, it is

before the Heliasts were conducted as at an ordinary trial, the pleadings being recorded and the suit introduced by the εἰσαγωγεῖς. The allies conducted their own cases, but they were free to engage the assistance of Athenian συνήγοροι.[1]

Besides the ordinary φόρος, the Athenians occasionally imposed an additional tax on some of the allies. This was called ἐπιφορά.

ἐπιφορά. It is impossible now to ascertain the reasons which led them to make these impositions: but it appears that the principle underlying this ἐπιφορά (which we first hear of in 440 B.C.) was that in extraordinary emergencies the Athenians had a right to tax the confederates beyond the ordinary imposts.[2] Occasionally a city was exempt from tribute for a longer or shorter period, and in this case had simply to pay to the treasury of Athena the customary ἀπαρχή, $\frac{1}{60}$ of the tribute.[3]

The allies regularly paid in the tribute to the Hellenotamiai before the Council at Athens; the time was during the great Dionysia in the month of Elaphebolion.[4] The Hellenotamiai kept an account of the payments, and entered the names of the persons who paid the tribute for the various cities.[5] Cities which omitted to pay or made only part payment

---

clear that the πεντακόσιοι are a court of law. Cf. C.I.A., I. 37: (τ)ὸ δικαστήριον, ὅταν περὶ τῶν τάξ(εων) ᾖ). In the time of the second Athenian Confederacy, too, a γραφὴ παρανόμων was allowed against συντάξεις fixed by a psephism: (Dem.) 58, 37/8.

[1] That the εἰσαγωγεῖς played no unimportant part at the assessment may be inferred from C.I.A., I. 37 lines 47 ff., where the assessment of the year 425 B.C. is dated by them as well as by the Archon: (ἐ)πὶ Στρατοκλ(έους ἄ)ρχοντος, ἐπὶ τ(ῶ)ν (ἐσ)αγωγ(έω)ν, οἷς Κα(. . . ἐγραμμάτευε). They are mentioned again in lines 7 ff., but in what connexion does not appear. We see from the fragment of Antiphon's speech on the tribute of the Samothracians in Suid. Σαμοθρᾴκη that the allies conducted their own cases. Yet συνήγοροι are mentioned in Antiphon's speech on the tribute of the Lindians; see Harp. συνήγοροι.

[2] Mention of the ἐπιφορά: C.I.A., I. 240-4. 249, 252. 256.

[3] C.I.A., I. 257: αἴδε τῶ(ν) πόλεων αὐτὴν τὴν ἀπαρχὴν ἀπήγαγον. Methone is exempted, 428/7 B.C.: C.I.A., I. 40. Besides this we hear of an ἄτακτος πόλις Κυστίριοι: C.I.A., I. 243 and in B.C. 438 Φαρβήλιοι ἀτακ(τοι) and Μιλτώριοι ἀτακτο(ι): I. 242, both of these cities appearing in 437 and 436 B.C. among those that made their own assessment: I. 243. According to Busolt, 665/6, these ἄτακτοι πόλεις were previously συντελεῖς, and continued to pay their old tribute until they assessed themselves.

[4] Arist., Ach., 502 sqq.; Schol. to 504: εἰς δὲ τὰ Διονύσια ἐτέτακτο Ἀθήναζε κομίζειν τὰς πόλεις τοὺς φόρους, ὡς Εὔπολίς φησιν ἐν Πόλεσιν. According to (Xen.) de Rep. Ath. 3, 2 it is one of the duties of the Council φόρον δέξασθαι.

[5] So much may be inferred for certain from C.I.A., I. 38 fr. c. d.

had ἐκλογεῖς sent out to them to collect the money. These ἐκλογεῖς were chosen from the first class of the census, and were probably appointed for the first time in B.C. 446; of course none were chosen, unless there was tribute-money still owing. They were protected in the execution of their duty by a squadron of ships under the command of one or more Strategoi.[1] If any city then insisted that it had paid its tribute, an inquiry was held at Athens and the case decided in a court of law.[2]

In order to raise more money from the allies the Athenians introduced the εἰκοστή, a duty of 5 per cent. *ad valorem* on all imports and exports of the allied cities. This took the place of the old tribute, and according to Thucydides the change was made in 413/2 B.C. It is clear, however that this duty was not levied on all members of the League, for we find some of them paying tribute even after 413/2 B.C.[3]

εἰκοστή.

Originally the non-autonomous allies were not liable to military

---

[1] Election of the ἐκλογεῖς, C.I.A., I. 38 *fr. f. g.*: ὅπως ἂν αἱρε(θῶσι οἱ ἄνδρες οἱ) τὸν φόρον ἐγλέξοντες and towards the end: (φ)όρου ἐγ(λογῆς ἢ)ρ(έθησαν οἵδε.) Cf. Harp. ἐκλογεῖς οἱ ἐκλέγοντες καὶ εἰσπράττοντες τὰ ὀφειλόμενα τῷ δημοσίῳ. Ἀντιφῶν ἐν τῷ περὶ τοῦ Σαμοθρακῶν φόρου· ᾑρέθησαν γὰρ ἐκλογεῖς παρ' ἡμῖν, οἷς πλεῖστα ἐδόκει χρήματα εἶναι. Λυσίας ἐν τῷ πρὸς Ἀρέσανδρον· νῦν δὲ πρὸς τοὺς ἐκλογέας τοῦ φόρου ἅπαντα ἀπογραφόμεθα. Suid. *s.v.*, Lex. Seguer. 245, 33. Köhler 132/3 supposes that ἐκλογεῖς were first appointed B.C. 446, because, from that date onwards, there are but few and doubtful traces of arrears in the tribute-lists. Hence some new method of collecting the tribute must have been introduced at that time. The ships which convoyed the ἐκλογεῖς were called νῆες ἀργυρολόγοι, Thuc. 3, 19; 4, 50. 75. There were no officials called ἀργυρολόγοι: *Beitr.*, p. 67, 26.

[2] This follows from C.I.A., IV. 38a.

[3] Introduction of the εἰκοστή in B.C. 413/2: Thuc. 7, 28; as to the motive for the change he says πλείω νομίζοντες ἂν σφίσι χρήματα οὕτω προσιέναι, and so Beloch in *N. Rh. Mus.*, 39, 43 ff.; according to Köhler, however, in *Mitth.*, 7, 316, it was because of the irregularity with which the tribute was paid. Another proof of the existence of the εἰκοστή in the fifth century may be found in the fact that, when the Athenians were endeavouring to found a new confederacy at the beginning of the fourth century, they introduced an εἰκοστή at Clazomenai and Thasos, probably in 390/89 B.C. An Athenian psephism of 387/6 B.C. speaks of (ὑπ)οτε(λοῦν)τας Κλαζομενίους τὴν ἐπὶ (Θ)ρασυβούλου εἰκοστήν: *Mitth. d. dtsch. arch. Inst. in Ath.*, 7, 174. An εἰκοστή in Thasos: *ibid.*, 314. Even after B.C. 413/2 tribute was paid: Xen., *Hell.*, 1, 3, 9; C.I.A., I. 258; IV. 51. Müller-Strübing, *Thukyd. Forsch.*, 30 ff., following Grote, maintains that the new system of taxation was never extended to the whole League: but this does not prove that it was not introduced in a number of allied States; *Beitr.*, 285 sqq. The εἰκοστή is mentioned in Lex. Seguer. 185, 21.

service, nor indeed had they any other duty to the League beyond the obligation to pay tribute.[1] But when the League was converted into an Athenian Empire, and its administration conducted with greater strictness, a change took place in this respect, and more was exacted from the dependent States. At any rate during the Peloponnesian war, the allies were regularly drafted for military service.[2]

Personal obligation of the Allies to serve in time of war.

The allied cities had each to contribute a ram and a couple of sheep for the sacrifices at the Panathenaia. This was not required as tribute; it was a symbol of their relation to Athens, and the Cleruchs had to make a like contribution.[3] Similarly, the allies took part in the sacrificial festivities, and had to present to the Eleusinian goddesses the same tribute of grain as did the Athenians: on every 100 medimnoi of barley a ἑκτεύς, on every 100 medimnoi of wheat a ἡμιεκτέον.[4]

Tithes to the gods.

The form of government usually established in the cities of the

---

[1] That the tributary cities were not originally liable to military service appears from Thuc. 1, 99, where we read that they preferred to pay tribute rather than furnish ships, ἵνα μὴ ἀπ' οἴκου ὦσι. Cf. Plut., Per., 12: ἐδίδασκεν οὖν ὁ Περικλῆς τὸν δῆμον, ὅτι χρημάτων μὲν οὐκ ὀφείλουσι τοῖς συμμάχοις λόγον προπολεμοῦντες αὐτῶν καὶ τοὺς βαρβάρους ἀνείργοντες, οὐχ ἵππον, οὐ ναῦν, οὐχ ὁπλίτην, ἀλλὰ χρήματα μόνον τελούντων κ.τ.λ., a passage taken, as Sauppe argues, *Quellen d. Plut. im Leben d. Perikles*, 26 ff., 1867, from the speech actually delivered by Pericles, and preserved by Ion of Chios in his Ἐπιδημίαι.

[2] Many instances of this are to be found in Thuc., as 4, 23. 42. 58. 51; 5, 2; 6, 43; 7, 17. 20. 57; C.I.A., I. 432. Thuc. 2, 9 says of the Athenian allies: τούτων ναυτικὸν παρείχοντο Χῖοι, Λέσβιοι, Κερκυραῖοι, οἱ δ' ἄλλοι πεζὸν καὶ χρήματα. In the oath to be taken by the Chalkidians there occur the words: καὶ τῷ δήμῳ τῷ Ἀθηναίων βοηθήσω καὶ ἀμυνῶ, ἐάν τις ἀδικῇ τὸν δῆμον τὸν Ἀθηναίων, C.I.A., IV. 27α; cf. C.I.A., I. 40. And in the treaty with Selymbria we read: (ἂν ἐπαγ)γέλλ(ωσ)ι Ἀθην(αῖοι— κ)ατάλογον κατ—, referring to the right of conscription; C.I.A., IV. 61α. According to Busolt *N. Rh. Mus.*, 37, 637 ff., allies who revolted were made liable to conscription after their reduction; cf. v. Wilamowitz-Möllendorf, in *phil. Unters.*, 1, 71 ff.; his views have been challenged, however, on several points by Busolt, *ibid.*; Guirand 39 ff.; Gülde, *d. Kriegsverf. d. ersten att. Bundes*, Progr. v. Neuhaldensleben, 1888.

[3] C.I.A., I. 87: βο(ῦν καὶ—) λ(—ἀπάγειν ἐς Παναθ)ήναια τὰ μέ(γαλα) ἁπάσας. Cf. the treaty with the Erythraians: C.I.A., I. 9. For the Cleruchs cf. I. 31.

[4] See the psephism of 440 B.C. in Dittenberger, *Syll.*, 13: ἀπάρχεσθαι δὲ καὶ τοὺς χσυμμάχους κατὰ ταὐτὰ (sc. τοῖς Ἀθηναίοις, whose contribution was fixed before at what is stated in the text). τὰς δὲ πόλεις (ἐγ)λ(ο)γέας ἐλέσθαι τοῦ καρποῦ, καθότι ἂν δοκῇ αὐτῇσι ἄριστα ὁ καρπὸ(ς) ἐγλεγήσεσθαι. ἐπειδὰν δὲ ἐγλεχθῇ, ἀποπεμφσάντων Ἀθήναζε. τοὺς δὲ ἀγαγόντας παραδιδόναι τοῖς ἱεροποιοῖς τοῖς Ἐλευσινόθεν Ἐλευσινάδε.

League was some species of democracy.[1] As to the extent of their independence in matters of internal administration, no general statement is possible. We have seen the direction in which the constitution of the League developed, and have traced the progress of that development; and we can feel how natural it consequently was that, as time went on, separate treaties with single States superseded the federal treaty perhaps originally concluded. The result was that Athens did not retain precisely the same rights over the allies as she originally possessed; in some cases she gained more powers, in others she lost some of those formerly conceded to her.[2] In Erythrai, for instance, the Athenians regulated the constitution down to the smallest details. A psephism of the time of Kimon contains rules as to the number of Bouleutai there, the mode of appointing them, their Dokimasia and their age, the time to elapse between two βουλεῖαι, and the oath they were to take, the very words of which are prescribed. Not only did Athenian ἐπίσκοποι revise the Erythraian constitution in harmony with this psephism, but the Athenian φρούραρχος continued to exercise an immediate control over the administration; every year, assisted by the retir-

Form of Government in the allied cities.

---

[1] That a democratic constitution was the rule in the confederate cities follows from Thuc. 8, 48. 64. 65. The Lesbians, Chians, and Samians were in a privileged position, for Arist. 24, 2 to say: τούτους δὲ φύλακας εἶχον τῆς ἀρχῆς ἐῶντες τάς τε πολιτείας παρ' αὐτοῖς καὶ ἄρχειν ὧν ἔτυχον ἄρχοντες. It is quite incredible that oligarchical States, which revolted from Athens and were again subdued, should have had their oligarchies left intact. Hence we should not reject Diodorus' statement (12, 28) that a democracy was established in Samos after its subjugation in 439 B.C. (cf. Thuc. 1, 115). We may explain Thuc. 8, 21 by supposing that the democrats, who formed the government, proceeded against those of oligarchic sentiments. Similarly, there can be no doubt that a democracy was established in Chalkis 446 B.C., and the expulsion of the Hippobotai confirms this idea: Plut., *Per.*, 23; cf. Thuc. 6, 76. I mention this fact because it has been overlooked by Fränkel, *de condic. iure iurisdict. soc. Ath.*, p. 23 ff. It is evidently an exceptional privilege when Athens guarantees to the Selymbrians, 409 B.C. (εἶναι δὲ καταστῆσαι Σηλυμβ)ριανοὺς τὴμ πολι(τείαν—τρόπῳ) ὅτῳ ἂν ἐπίστωντ(αι): C.I.A., IV. 61a. Cf. Guirand 22 ff.

[2] This has very rightly been insisted on by H. Droysen in *Herm.*, 18, 567. We should regard as separate treaties of this type the psephisms touching Erythrai: C.I.A., I. 9, 10. 11; Colophon: I. 13; Miletus: I. 22a; whilst the psephism touching Chalkis, C.I.A., IV. 27a, seems to have merely defined with greater precision some conditions in the treaty of peace proper. We can still discern differences of detail in these treaties, notwithstanding their fragmentary character. Even the oath for the Council at Erythrai varies from that for the Council at Colophon.

ing Boule, he appointed the new Bouleutai by sortition, and they formed the supreme executive power in the State. The psephism also contained detailed regulations relative to the administration of justice, determining in each case the appropriate court and penalty. The magistrates were expressly bound to obey the resolutions of the Athenian people.[1] We need have no hesitation in supposing that similar conditions also obtained in the other cities of the League. At Miletus, for instance, where even the tribes of Cleisthenes were introduced, the constitution was remodelled by five Athenians chosen for the office.[2] And when the members of the second Athenian Confederacy, besides having liberty and autonomy secured to them, are guaranteed the right to live under any constitution they choose, with no garrison to keep, no officials to admit, no tribute to pay, these express assurances justify the conclusion that in the first Confederacy the very reverse must have been the case.[3] A mass of evidence makes it practically certain that the Athenians maintained garrisons in many of the confederate towns, and their commanders would inevitably have as commanding a control over the administration of the place as the Phrourach had at Erythrai.[4] The ἐπίσκοποι were Athenian officers chosen by sortition to go and supervise the internal administration of the various cities of the League.[5]

[1] C.I.A., I. 9. 10. 11.
[2] C.I.A., IV. 22a. The tribes of Cleisthenes at Miletus: Lebas, *Asie Min.*, 238. 240. 242. See vol. 2, 141.
[3] C.I.A., II. 17, lines 19 ff.: ἐξεῖναι αὐ(τ)ῷ(ι ἐλευθέρ)ῳ ὄντι καὶ αὐτονόμῳ, πολιτ(ευομέν)ῳ πολιτείαν ἣν ἂν βούληται, μήτε (φρουρ)ὰν εἰσδεχομένῳ μήτε ἄρχοντα ὑπο(δεχ)ομένῳ μήτε φόρον φέροντι.
[4] Before the time of the Thirty Tyrants, Isocr. 7, 65 speaks of the Athenians as τὰς τῶν ἄλλων ἀκροπόλεις φρουροῦντας. Φρουρὰ in Erythrai: C.I.A., I. 9. 10; Miletus: IV. 22a; Kyzicos: Eupol. *ap. Schol.* Arist., *Pax*, 1176; Samos: Thuc. 1, 115; the cities of Thrace: Thuc. 4, 7. 108; 5, 89. The φύλακες mentioned by Theophr. *ap.* Harp. ἐπίσκοποι, are evidently the same as the φρούραρχοι. (Xen.), *de Rep. Ath.*, 1, 19, mentions τὰς ἀρχὰς τὰς ἐς τὴν ὑπερορίαν. According to Arist. 24, 8 there were ἀρχαὶ ὑπερόριοι εἰς ἑπτακοσίους, but this number is open to question. In a psephism subsequent to the Sicilian expedition, security is guaranteed at Athens and in Athenian territory to Leonidas of Halicarnassus; he is to be protected by those ἐν τῇσι ἄλλησι πόλεσι οἵτινες Ἀθηναίων ἄρχουσι ἐν τῇ ὑπερορίᾳ, ὅτι ἂν ἕκαστοι δυνατοὶ ὦσι, ὡς ἂμ μὴ ἀδικῶνται: *Bull.* 12, 180=C.I.A., IV. 8, 27c., p. 164. An Athenian psephism of 408 B.C. mentions τὸν ἄρχοντα τὸν ἐν Σκιάθῳ, ὃς ἂν ᾖ ἑκάστοτε: *Bull.* 13, 153=C.I.A., IV. 8, 62b, p. 166. Zenob. 6, 32 thus explains the proverb φρουρεῖν ἢ πλουτεῖν: 'Ἀθηναῖοι γὰρ φρουραῖς διαλαβόντες τοὺς νησιώτας, μισθοὺς ἔταξαν μεγάλους τοῖς φυλάττουσιν ὑπ' αὐτῶν χορηγεῖσθαι τῶν νησιωτῶν.
[5] Harp. ἐπίσκοπος· Ἀντιφῶν ἐν τῷ περὶ τοῦ Λινδίων φόρου καὶ ἐν τῷ κατὰ

But the independence of the allies was curtailed most seriously by their deprivation of the right of trying any important lawsuit. It was of course only natural that Athens should pronounce on all offences against federal institutions or against herself as head of the League.[1] But, besides this, all penal processes against the citizens of an allied city were finally decided at Athens. The power of sentencing members of a Federal city to death, to banishment, or to Atimia, was expressly reserved to the Athenian Heliaia.[2] And even in private suits the

Jurisdiction.

Λαισποδίου. ἐοίκασι ἐκπέμπεσθαί τινες ὑπὸ 'Ἀθηναίων εἰς τὰς ὑπηκόους πόλεις ἐπισκεπτόμενοι τὰ παρ' ἑκάστοις; Suid. ἐπίσκοπος; Lex. Seguer. 254. 15; cf. Arist., *Birds*, 1021 sqq. Appointed by lot: *Birds* 1022. On the ἐπίσκοποι see also A. Fränkel, *ib.*, p. 17 ff. They are mentioned in C.I.A., I. 9, 10. Whether they administered justice to the allies is uncertain. The title has been conjecturally restored in C.I.A., IV. 96, but perhaps ἐπιμελητὰς should be read instead, as in C.I.A., I. 38, IV. 22a. In Arist., *Birds*, 1032, 1053, the ἐπίσκοπος always takes κάδω with him. Remuneration by the city in which they administered: 1025. In Lex. Seguer. 273, 33 ff., we find κρυπτοί mentioned as Federal officers, but nothing is known of them.

[1] Cf. Stahl, *de sociorum Atheniensium iudiciis*, Münster, 1881; Guirand 30 ff. The Athenian courts tried cases of treason, and of hostility on the part of allies against Athens: Arist., *Wasps*, 288 sqq.; *Peace* 639 sqq.; and also offences against Federal institutions: C.I.A., I. 38, ἐὰν δέ τις κακοτεχνῇ(ι, ὅπως μὴ κύριον ἔστα)ι τὸ ψήφισμα τὸ τοῦ φόρου (ἢ ὅπως μὴ ἀπαχθήσετ)αι ὁ φόρος 'Ἀθήναζε, γρά(φεσθαι ἐξεῖναι ἕκασ)τον τῶν ἐκ ταύτης τῆς πό(λεως π)ρὸς τοὺς ἐπιμελητάς· ο(ἱ δὲ ἐπιμεληταὶ ἐσαγό)ντων ἔμμηνα ἐς τὸ δ(ικαστήριον, ἐπειδὰν οἱ κ)λητῆρες ἥκωσι; cf. IV. 38a. Such suits are referred to in a passage in the oath of the Athenians to the Chalkidians (see Köhler in *Mitth. d. dtsch. arch. Inst. in Ath.*, 1, 192=C.I.A., IV. 27a): οὐδὲ ἰδιώτην οὐδένα ἀτιμώσω οὐδὲ φυγῇ ζημιώσω οὐδὲ ξυλλήψομαι οὐδὲ ἀποκτενῶ οὐδὲ χρήματα ἀφαιρήσομαι ἀκρίτου οὐδενὸς ἄνευ τοῦ δήμου τοῦ 'Ἀθηναίων. Stahl p. 18 ff. refers this to suits between Chalkidians and Athenians. The meaning of ἄνευ τοῦ δήμου τοῦ 'Ἀθηναίων here is not clear. Köhler 191/2 translates it "except by order of the Ecclesia." But it is impossible to see what this could mean in an oath taken by the Dicasts, and the words quoted are in the oath of the Dicasts (Dittenberger. *Syll.*, 10, 5). It can hardly mean: "I will not condemn any man without giving him an opportunity to defend himself, unless the Ecclesia so decrees." The δημόσιοι κλητῆρες were employed for the summonses in these cases; cf. C.I.A., I. 37–38. Aristophanes, in the *Birds*, 1422 ff., introduces a κλητὴρ νησιωτικὸς assisting at a summons, but we cannot say whether he is one of these δημόσιοι κλητῆρες.

[2] Antiph., *de caede Herod.*, 47: ὃ οὐδὲ πόλει ἔξεστιν ἄνευ 'Ἀθηναίων οὐδένα θανάτῳ ζημιῶσαι, where ὃ οὐδὲ πόλει ἔξεστιν applies to *all* the cities of the League, as has been shewn by A. Fränkel, p. 83 ff. Cf. (Xen.), *de Rep. Ath.*, 1, 16, where we are told that in consequence of the citizens of the allied cities being tried at Athens: καὶ τοὺς μὲν τοῦ δήμου σῴζουσι, τοὺς δ' ἐναντίους ἀπολλύουσιν ἐν τοῖς δικαστηρίοις· εἰ δ' οἴκοι εἶχον ἕκαστοι τὰς δίκας, ἅτ' ἀχθόμενοι τοῖς 'Ἀθηναίοις, τούτους ἂν σφῶν ἀπώλλυσαν, οἵτινες φίλοι μάλιστ' ἦσαν 'Ἀθηναίων

competence of the courts in the allied States was limited to cases involving not more than a certain sum of money, probably 100 drachmas, and to certain punishments : where a greater sum was at stake or a heavier punishment necessary, the case had to be carried to Athens.[1]

It is however impossible to make any general statement as to how far the Athenians exercised the power of judicature in the domestic affairs of the Federal cities. The extent of their powers differed in various cities according to the regulations in the treaties between those cities and Athens.[2]

τῷ δήμῳ. Cf. Isocr. 12, 66. That the Athenian Heliaia was the supreme court of appeal is shown by the treaty with Chalkis, C.I.A., IV. 27a (Hicks 28): τὰς (δ)ὲ εὐθύνας Χαλκιδεῦ(σ)ι κατὰ σφῶν αὐτῶν εἶναι ἐν Χαλκίδι καθάπερ ᾽Αθήνησιν ᾽Αθηναίοις πλὴν φυγῆς καὶ θανάτου καὶ ἀτιμίας. περὶ δὲ τούτων ἔφεσιν εἶναι ᾽Αθήναζε ἐς τὴν ἡλιαίαν τὴν τῶν θεσμοθετῶν κατὰ τὸ ψήφισμα τοῦ δήμου. Cf. Stahl pp. 17/8. The treaty of alliance with Erythrai, C.I.A., I. 9. decrees death and exile for certain crimes, which were evidently to come for trial before an Erythraian court, though the confirmation of the sentence must have been reserved to the Athenians. This follows from the words in the oath of the Bouleutai: οὐδὲ τῶν μενόντων ἐξελῶ (ἄ)νευ τῆς γν(ώμης) τῆς ᾽Αθηναίων καὶ τοῦ δήμου.

[1] In the treaty with Miletus, concluded about 450 B.C., C.I.A., IV. 22a, its juridical powers are determined with great precision of definition ; cf. e.g., τὰς δὲ δίκας εἶναι Μιλησίοις κα—(fr. c. 8) (τὰ δ)ὲ πρυτανεῖα τιθέντων πρὸς— (10) (αἱ δ)ὲ δίκαι ᾽Αθήνησι ὄντων ἐν τ(ῷ)—(11) τὰς δὲ ὑπὲρ ἑκατὸ(ν δραχμὰς)—(25) μείζονο(ς ἅ)ξ(ι)ος ᾗ ζημίας ᾽Αθη(να—) (fr. d. e. 10) (ἐπιβ)αλόντε(ς '(οπόσης ἂν δόκῃ ἄξ(ιος εἶναι) (fr. d. e. 11). We may conclude from these fragments that the jurisdiction of the courts of Miletus was limited to suits where the claim did not exceed a certain sum of money, 100 drachmas, or the penalty a certain limit. Lipsius in Meier[2] 1004 holds that in cases involving 100 drachmas an appeal might be made to Athens. (Xen.), de Rep. Ath., 1, 16, mentions as one consequence of the allies bringing their suits to Athens, πρῶτον μὲν ἀπὸ τῶν πρυτανείων τὸν μισθὸν δι᾽ ἐνιαυτοῦ λαμβάνειν. Boeckh supposes (1, 466 sqq.) that πρυτανεῖα were only paid in private actions, and therefore (1, 531) takes these words to relate to them. A. Fränkel p. 34 ff. tries to refute this view. To me it seems that the regulations in the treaty with Miletus must refer to private actions only; Stahl, however (24 ff.), maintains this to be impossible. That private suits of the allies were decided at Athens is proved by Isocr. 4, 113: ἀλλὰ πρὸς τοῖς ἄλλοις καὶ περὶ τῶν δικῶν καὶ τῶν γραφῶν τῶν ποτε παρ᾽ ἡμῖν γενομένων λέγειν τολμῶσιν (sc. the oligarchs when they governed the cities under Spartan protection), αὐτοὶ πλείους ἐν τρισὶ μησὶν ἀκρίτους ἀποκτείναντες, ὧν ἡ πόλις ἐπὶ τῆς ἀρχῆς ἁπάσης ἔκρινεν. So Isocr. 12, 63 says that the censurers of the Athenian people καὶ τάς τε δίκας καὶ τὰς κρίσεις τὰς ἐνθάδε γιγνομένας τοῖς συμμάχοις καὶ τὴν τῶν φόρων εἰσπραξιν διαβαλεῖν.

[2] Such separate treaties as to the right of judicature must be meant by Arist. ap. Lex. Seguer. 436, 1 (probably from the mutilated conclusion of the ᾽Αθ. πολ.): ᾽Αθηναῖοι ἀπὸ συμβόλων ἐδίκαζον τοῖς ὑπηκόοις· οὕτως ᾽Αριστοτέλης.

Administration of the First League.

It appears that suits of the allies were not prepared for trial by officials differing according to the character of the case, although this was the custom in all suits of Athenian citizens. All suits of allies (except perhaps murder cases) were brought into court by the same board of magistrates, the ἐπιμεληταί; and they presided in cases of offences against Federal institutions, private suits, and ἀπαγωγαί for murder.[1] *Presidents at lawsuits of Confederates.*

So Hesych. ἀπὸ συμβόλων., Poll. 8, 62. In inscrr. these treaties are called ξυμβολαί until the beginning of the 4th century: C.I.A., IV. 96, I.G.A. 322, Ἀρχ. δελτ., 1889, p. 26, l. 18. Arist. by ἀπὸ συμβόλων δικάζειν cannot mean the σύμβολα customary in the 4th century, which regulated the administration of justice in disputes between different States; C.I.A., II. 108. Whether σύμβολα, II. 86, is a treaty about the administration of justice is doubtful. The singular σύμβολον is found later *Bull.* 8, p. 24, l. 13, p. 25, l. 28, 37. In C.I.A., II. 308, σύμβολον is probably a treaty for an arbitration between two States. Cf. (Dem.) 7, 9-13; (Andoc.) *in Alcib.* 18; Harp. σύμβολα. It is true that Arist., *Pol.*, 3, 1, p. 59, 7 ff.; 3, 9, p. 72, 18 ff. Bekker uses σύμβολα in this sense: but, if he meant σύμβολα of this kind in the passage cited above, we should have had ἀπὸ συμβόλων δικάζεσθαι and not δικάζειν. I cannot adopt Köhler's opinion (*Mitth. d. dtsch. arch. Inst.*, 1, 194) that these rights of the Athenians were not extended further before the last decades of the Athenian Empire. By the treaty with Chalkis, the Chalkidians were empowered to inflict any punishment except death, banishment and Atimia. But we do not know how it was with the decisions of private suits, though there can be no doubt that the treaty of peace contained regulations regarding them; cf. Fränkel 46 ff. Fränkel too, p. 46, believes that, whenever an ally rebelled and was again subjugated, Athens was in the habit of arrogating to herself a share in the rights of judicature. The regulations upon this point were different, it would appear, in the case of Miletus (C.I.A., IV. 22a) from what they were for Chalkis.

[1] The ἐπιμεληταί presided at trials for offences against Federal institutions: C.I.A., I. 38; in private suits to judge from C.I.A., IV. 22a fr. c, line 19: Ἀθήναζε τοῖς ἐπιμελετ(ῆσι); and in ἀπαγωγαί for murder. For as the ἐπιμεληταί can be proved to have presided at suits of the allies, we must take Antiph., *de caede Herod.*, 17, as referring to them: τῶν δὲ ἄλλων ξένων ὅστις πώποτ᾽ ἠθέλησε καταστῆσαι ἐγγυητάς, οὐδεὶς πώποτ᾽ ἐδέθη. καίτοι οἱ ἐπιμεληταί τῶν κακούργων τῷ αὐτῷ χρῶνται νόμῳ τούτῳ. Here τῶν κακούργων depends on νόμῳ, the whole forming an abridged expression for the phrase preserved in C.I.A., II. 476: οἱ ἐπὶ τῶν κακούργων κείμενοι νόμοι; cf. § 9. By all the rules of language it is no more and no less possible to connect τῶν κακούργων with the words that follow it than it is to connect it with ἐπιμεληταί (cf. Lipsius in Meier[2] 1005, no. 668). The speaker says: "My imprisonment is illegal, as I offered three sureties for my appearance. No other foreigner has ever been imprisoned, if he offered bail. And, in point of fact, the ἐπιμεληταί do use this very law about κακοῦργοι, *i.e.* they are bound by the same law as οἱ ἕνδεκα. So that this law, observed in the case of all other foreigners, has been disregarded in my case and mine alone." This gives a clear and intelligible sense. But οἱ ἐπιμεληταί τῶν κακούργων would be as unprece-

The preliminary inquiry, however, was probably held in the federal cities, as a rule, by Athenian officers appointed for the purpose.[1]

In the δίκαι συμβόλαιαι, that is, suits originating in commercial agreements, a distinct procedure seems to have been employed *Trial of δίκαι* within the Athenian League.[2] In a treaty between *συμβόλαιαι.* Athens and Phaselis, of some date between 394 and 387 B.C., it is ruled that any lawsuit, arising from an agreement, concluded at Athens, between merchants of Athens and Phaselis, should be tried before the πολέμαρχος, but that suits arising from agreements not concluded at Athens should be tried in accordance with the provisions of the former treaty with Phaselis. If any Athenian official agreed to try suits of this character, in defiance of this article of the treaty, his judgment was to be void.[3] As

---

dented an expression for οἱ ἕνδεκα as if in a military suit, *e.g.*, the defendant were to call the Strategoi, who would preside at such a suit, οἱ ἐπιμεληταί τοῦ πολέμου. Finally, καίτοι οἱ ἐπιμεληταί τῶν κακούργων τῷ αὐτῷ χρῶνται νόμῳ τούτῳ, if applied to the ἕνδεκα, would be an entirely superfluous remark; they would, of course, be guided by the law about οἱ κακοῦργοι. The only other hypothesis possible is that τῶν κακούργων is a gloss. The speaker—a Mytilenaian (§ 77)—might have been summoned before one of the Homicide courts (§ 8 sqq.). Whether in that case the ἐπιμεληταί would have been the presiding officers, cannot be proved from this speech. On other allusions in it cf. Blass, *d. att. Beredsamkeit*, 1, 162 ff.

[1] The Athenian ἄρχοντες, mentioned by Antiph., *de caede Herod.*, 47, seem to have conducted the preliminary inquiry. The treaty with Miletus C.I.A., IV. 22a fr. c, has, line 18: (π)ρὸς τοὺς ἄρχοντας τοὺς Ἀθ(ηναίων), line 19: Ἀθήναζε τοῖς ἐπιμελετ(ῇσι). Perhaps the ἄρχοντες, again mentioned line 24 (')οι ἄρχοντες οἱ Ἀθηνα(ίων), held the preliminary inquiry in this case. Ἄρχοντες among the allies are also mentioned in Arist., *Birds*, 1050, where we cannot suppose that only the ἐπίσκοποι are meant.

[2] Cf. Stahl, p. 6 ff.

[3] C.I.A., II. 11 (Hicks 73): (τοῖ)ς Φασηλίταις τὸ ψ(ήφ)ι(σμα ἀν)αγράψαι, ὅ τι ἂμ μὲ(ν) Ἀθ(ήνησι συμβό)λαιον γένηται (πρὸς Φ)ασηλι(τ)ῶν τινα, Ἀθή(νησι τὰς δ)ίκας γίγνεσθαι π(αρὰ τῷ πολ)εμάρχῳ καθάπερ Χ(ίοις καὶ) ἄλλοθι μηδὲ ἀμοῦ τῶ(ν δὲ ἄλλων) ἀπὸ ξυμβόλων κατ(ὰ τὰς Χίων) ξυμβολὰς πρὸς Φα(σηλίτας) τὰς δίκας ε(ἶνα)ι, τὰς (δὲ . . .) ἀφελεῖν· ἐὰν δὲ τ(ῶν ἀλλαχοῦ ἀρ)χ(ω)ν δ(ἐ)ξ(η)ται δ(ίκην κατὰ) Φασηλιτῶν τ(ι)νος, (τοῦτον μὴ τίν)ειν καταδίκας, (ἀλλ' ἡ μὲν δίκη) [or as Dittenberger, *Syll.*, 57, perhaps more correctly, reads: (τοῦτο δ' ὀφε)ίλειν καταδικασ(θῆ, ἡ μὲν δίκ)η] ἄ(κυρ)ος ἔστω, ἐ(ὰν δὲ ἐκβῆν)α(ι) δ(οκ)ῇ τὰ ἐψη(φισμένα, ὀφ)ει(λ)έ(τ)ω (μ)υρ(ί)ας δ(ραχμὰς) ἱερ(ὰς) τῇ Ἀθηναίᾳ. Here κατ(ὰ τὰς Χίων) ξυμβολὰς is a restoration made by Sauppe, and now adopted by Köhler, though formerly, *Herm.* 7, 159, he read κατ(ὰ τὰς πρὶν) ξυμβολάς. I agree with A. Fränkel, pp. 61/2 in doubting Sauppe's restoration: Köhler's original suggestion seems more probable. With Sauppe's reading, κατὰ τὰς Χίων ξυμβολὰς πρὸς Φασηλίτας must be taken together, "according to the treaty of the

this treaty between Athens and Phaselis refers to the earlier treaty between them only in regard to suits arising from commercial agreements not concluded at Athens, it is probable that the article as to the treatment of suits arising from agreements that were concluded there, was not contained in the older treaty. From this we may infer that, under the old treaty, the place where the agreement was concluded did not determine where the case was to be tried. It would appear from this that a Phaselite could not in the fifth century be proceeded against at Athens for breach of an agreement not concluded there; in other words, he could only be sued at Phaselis. And, if this notion be correct, the character of other principles, which we can trace in Athenian treaties drawn up in the fourth century to settle similar disputed questions of jurisdiction, justifies the inference that among the principles accepted by the Athenians and their allies this had taken its place even in the fifth century: *that in all mercantile suits the case should be heard at the town where the defendant resided.* And this supposition seems to be confirmed by at least one important piece of evidence.[1]

Chians with Phaselis." But it is not likely that the Athenians would refer to a treaty, the protocol of which was not in their possession, without quoting the particular clauses intended. If, on the other hand, we take πρὸς Φασηλίτας with the following τὰς δίκας, we must make κατὰ τὰς Χίων ξυμβολὰς mean " according to the treaty concluded by the Athenians with Chios," which is hardly possible. Stahl, p. 11, reads, κατ' (αὐτὰς τὰς) ξυμβολάς.

[1] In the present edition I have abandoned the position I formerly held in regard to the treatment of mercantile suits between Athenians and the allies. I now agree with Lipsius in Meier[2] 996, no. 647. But it seems to me that to take ἀπὸ ξυμβόλων in C.I.A., II. 11 with τὰς δίκας in spite of the interval which separates them, and so make it refer to a treaty to determine questions of jurisdiction between Athens and the allies, is a very dubious construction on account of the κατ(ὰ τὰς πρὶν or Χίων) ξυμβολὰς πρὸς Φα(σηλίτας). The words ὅτι ἂμ μὲν 'Αθήνησι συμβόλαιον γένηται πρὸς Φασηλιτῶν τινα are answered by τὰ ἄλλα sc. συμβόλαια, and τὰ ἄλλα ἀπὸ ξυμβόλων (if we take ξύμβολα to mean private commercial agreements) will be merely a synonym for this. If this be so, the words in C.I.A., IV. 61a: ὅτι δ' ἂν ἀμφισβη(τῶσι, δίκα)ς εἶναι ἀπὸ ξυμβόλων, will mean, " disputes arising out of the commercial agreements previously mentioned are to count as δίκαι ἀπὸ ξυμβόλων," *i.e.* " are to be decided in accordance with the regulations obtaining within the Athenian confederacy, in regard to all suits arising from commercial agreements." We cannot demonstrate from contemporary authors that σύμβολα meant a private contract. As to the legal principles observed by the Athenians in the fourth century in deciding mercantile suits between citizens of different cities, cf. (Dem.) 7, 9. It is best to ignore

Such commercial treaties might be concluded by one private company with another, by the State with private persons, or by private persons with the State. The most important subjects dealt with in them were loans, deposits, rights of citizenship, sales and purchases, and rents.[1] As has been said, the Athenians, in regulating the administration of justice among their allies, allowed suits, arising out of these treaties, to be tried at the place where the defendant lived. Obviously this was a departure from the ordinary custom, and there can be no doubt that Athens, in making this concession, was actuated by a desire to extend her commerce, the growth of which must have been considerably promoted by the confidence this system gave the allies as to the security of pecuniary transactions with Athenian citizens.

Final result. The political rights of which the Athenians deprived their allies were considerable enough to cause the situation of the latter to be regarded as one of subjection.[2]

---

[1] Antiph., *de caede Her.*, 78; Fränkel 49 ff. has shown that there is some *lacuna*. But evidence of the observance of the principles mentioned in the text may be found in Thuc. 1, 77: καὶ ἐλασσούμενοι γὰρ ἐν ταῖς ξυμβολαίαις πρὸς τοὺς ξυμμάχους δίκαις καὶ παρ' ἡμῖν αὐτοῖς ἐν τοῖς ὁμοίοις νόμοις ποιήσαντες τὰς κρίσεις φιλοδικεῖν δοκοῦμεν,—words of the Athenian ambassadors intended to show the moderation of Athens towards her allies. I suppose ἐλασσούμενοι to be antithetical to ἐν τοῖς ὁμοίοις νόμοις ποιήσαντες τας κρίσεις, and the words παρ' ἡμῖν αὐτοῖς in the second clause stand in opposition to the allies in the first clause. I translate: "For although we are, on the one hand, unfairly treated (*i.e.* by the law courts of the allies) in lawsuits arising out of commercial treaties with the allies, and on the other hand in our own courts we decide the cases by laws equally fair (to us and to our allies); in spite of all this, we are supposed to be litigious" [cf. Jowett's translation]. Fränkel, p. 56 ff. gives another explanation. Köhler in his *Urk. u. Untersuch.*, etc., p. 97, 3, takes an entirely different view of the passage. See also Stahl, p. 28 ff. and Herbst on Thuc., p. 80 ff. [Goodwin, *Amer. Journ. of Phil.*, 1, 4 ff; Welsing p. 40².]

[1] Who the contracting parties in such agreements were is shown by C.I.A., IV. 61a: (ὅσα δ' ἀ)λλα ξυμβόλαια προτοῦ ἦν (so I read with Dittenberger, *Herm.*, 16, 188, and Stahl, p. 9) τοῖς ἰ(διώταις πρ)ὸς τοὺς ἰδιώτα(ς) ἢ ἰδιώτῃ πρὸς τὸ κ(οινὸν ἢ τῷ κοι)νῷ πρὸς ἰδιώτη(ν) ἢ ἐάν τι ἀ(λ)λο γίγ(νηται, δια)λύειμ π(ρ)ὸς ἀλλήλους· ὅτι δ' ἂν ἀμφισβη(τῶσι δίκα)ς εἶναι ἀπὸ ξυμβόλων. On obligations arising from agreements, and the legal processes by which they were enforced, see Meier² 675 ff. That these δίκαι ἀπὸ συμβόλων are not to be identified with the δίκαι ἐμπορικαί, which could be instituted by ἔμποροι and ναύκληροι only, is proved by the words quoted above from the commercial treaty with Selymbria. Fränkel, p. 59 ff., is therefore wrong.

[2] Thuc. 1, 98; 3, 10; 6, 76.

B. The Second League.

Soon after the victory off Cnidos, when Conon had rebuilt the walls of Athens with the help of Persian gold, and prepared the way for a new Athenian fleet, the Athenians began to **Development** renew their former connexions with the various cities **of the League.** on the coasts and islands of the Ægean Sea. Here too Conon had prepared the ground for them, for, wherever he went with the Persian fleet, he favoured the establishment of democracies, which naturally were well inclined towards Athens.[1] The first state to come into closer alliance with Athens was Chios, after the expulsion of its Lacedæmonian garrison in 394 B.C. Mytilene, which had also liberated itself after the battle of Cnidos, soon followed suit, and both towns sent contingents to the Athenian fleet in 390.[2] The Athenians liberated Byzantion in 390, and set up a democratic government there; whereupon the Byzantines permitted Athens to establish a depôt for exacting tolls on the Bosporos; this however was soon abolished. Calchedon also made a friendly alliance with Athens. Samothrace, Thasos, Tenedos, Cos and Carpathos soon came over to Athens; but in Rhodes, although it had deserted the Spartan alliance as early as 395 B.C., it was only after a long struggle between the partisans of Sparta and Athens that the latter finally prevailed.[3] Lastly in 387 B C., shortly before the peace of Antalkidas, Clazomenai joined the alliance. Thus the Athenians had in a few years laid the foundation of a new League, in arranging which they re-established the institutions of their earlier League. The allied States were probably autonomous, but the Athenians seem to have had the right of establishing garrisons in them; and the εἰκοστή of the later period of the Peloponnesian war was revived. The Athenian law courts apparently had jurisdiction over various offences committed in the allied States. The treaties, which had been concluded during the first League, regulating the decision of lawsuits arising out of commercial contracts, were now renewed with various States; among them being, as we know, Chios and Phaselis.[4]

[1] Cf. Xen., *Hell.*, 4, 8, 12; Diod. 14, 85.
[2] For Chios and Mytilene cf. Diod. 14, 84. 94.
[3] Cf. Xen. 4, 8, 27, 28. 31; 5, 1, 6/7; Dem. 20, 60. 61. For Cos, Rhodes and Carpathos cf. the decree of Athens in the *Bull.*, 12, 155/6; for Rhodes Diodor. 14, 79 and Busolt's paper in the 7th Suppl. vol. of the *Jahrb. f. cl. Phil.*, p. 671 ff.
[4] A decree of the Athenian demos of 387 B.C. (*Mitth. d. dtsch. arch. Inst.* in

Even the King's Peace of 387 B.C. did not sever these connexions completely. On the contrary, Chios petitioned Athens for a formal treaty of alliance, apprehensive that the oligarchs might make some violent attempt now that the coast of Asia Minor was in Persian possession. The Athenians granted their request, and a defensive alliance was concluded between them, Athens giving assurances that she would respect the freedom and autonomy of Chios as guaranteed by the King's Peace.[1] Similar alliances were in all probability made with Mytilene and Byzantium.[2] The first steps towards the formation of a more extensive League were taken by Athens in the summer of 378 B.C.[3] Ambassadors

---

Ath., 7, 174/5) mentions the Clazomenians as (ὑπ)οτε(λοῦν)τας Κλαζομενίους τὴν ἐπὶ (Θ)ρασυβούλου εἰκοστήν. And since the decree directs: (περὶ δὲ ἀρχ)οντος καὶ φρουρᾶς διαχειρο(τονῆσαι τὸν δῆμον αὐτί)κα μ(ά)λα, εἴτε χρὴ καθιστάναι ε(ἰς Κλαζομενὰς εἴτε αὐ)τοκράτορα εἶναι περὶ τούτων (τὸν δῆμον τὸν Κλαζομε)νίων ἐάν τε βούληται ὑποδέχε(σθαι—), Athens must as a rule have had the power of putting garrisons in the allied cities. An εἰκοστή in this period is attested in the case of Thasos too: *Mitth.*, 7, 313 ff. In a fragmentary decree of the Ecclesia dating from this period autonomy is guaranteed to the Eteocarpathoi. Any violation of it is to be punished by fine: δίκην δὲ εἶνα(ι πρὸς θεσμο)θέτας ἐν 'A(θηναίοις): *Bull.* 12, 155/6. On the foundation of this new league see Swoboda in the *Mitth.*, 7, 188 ff. Beloch, *d. att. Politik seit Perikles*, 344 ff. For the judicial procedure in συμβόλαια cf. C.I.A., II. 11, the treaty with Phaselis, where reference is made to a similar arrangement with Chios.

[1] See *Mitth. d. dtsch. arch. Inst. in Ath.*, 2, 188 ff. The passage concerning the treaty reads thus: συμμάχους δὲ ποιεῖσ(θα)ι Χίους ἐπ' ἐλευ(θε)ρίᾳ καὶ αὐτονομί(α)ι μὴ παραβαίνοντας τῶν ἐν ταῖς στήλαις γεγραμμένων περὶ τῆς εἰρήνης μηδέν, μηδ' ἐάν τις ἀλ(λ)ος παραβαίνῃ πειθομένους κατὰ τὸ δυ(να)τόν· στῆσαι δὲ στήλην ἐν ἀκροπόλει (πρό)σθεν τοῦ ἀγάλματος, ἐς δὲ ταύτην ἀνα(γρ)άφειν, ἐάν τις ἴῃ ἐπ' 'Αθηναίους, βοηθε(ῖν) Χίους παντὶ σθέ(νε)ι κατὰ τὸ δυνατόν, (καὶ) ἐάν τις ἴῃ (ἐπὶ Χί)ους, βοηθεῖν 'Αθηναίου(ς π)αντὶ σθέ(νει κατὰ τ)ὸ δυνατόν. C.I.A., II. 13 888/7 B.C. is a fragment of a decree of honour for a Chian.

[2] Although Busolt, p. 677 ff., doubts the accuracy of the testimony of Isocr. 14, 28 for the period after 387 B.C.: καὶ Χῖοι μὲν καὶ Μυτιληναῖοι καὶ Βυζάντιοι συμπαρέμειναν, it has been confirmed by inscriptions so far as the Chians are concerned, and this makes it much more credible for the case of Mytilene and Byzantium too. In the fragments of the treaty between Athens and Mytilene, at the foundation of the second Athenian League, an earlier treaty is referred to; cf. C.I.A., II. 18.

[3] Busolt p. 679 ff. says that the Athenians took the first steps towards founding the League immediately after the liberation of Thebes; Schaefer, *Dem. u. s. Zeit.*, 1¹, 16 ff., relying on Xen. 5, 4, 34 and Plut., *Pelop.*, 15, says that nothing was done till after the acquittal of Sphodrias in summer 378 B.C. I think the latter view the more probable, though Diod. 15, 28 certainly puts Sphodrias's attempt after the foundation of the League.

were sent to the cities unfriendly to Sparta, inviting them to unite with Athens in a League for securing against Spartan aggression the freedom and autonomy guaranteed by the King's Peace.[1] The League thus formed was simply an extension of the alliance already existing between Athens and Chios. The first States to join the League were Chios, Mytilene, Methymna, Rhodes and Byzantium, and they were soon followed by Thebes.[2] Early in 377 B.C., to remove the distrust of Athens still prevalent in Greece, an authoritative declaration was put forth, by decree of the Athenian Demos, of the principles on which the constitution of the League should be based, and by which its administration should be governed. During the next few years after this the successful operations of Chabrias and Timotheus induced many other States to join the League, each concluding a special treaty with Athens.[3] In 374 B.C., when the Lacedæmonians recognised the naval *hegemony* of Athens, in the peace then concluded at Sparta, the League already numbered about 60 members, and by 357 B.C. they had increased to about 75.[4]

Nevertheless the permanence of the League was by no means

---

[1] Diod. 15, 28; C.I.A., II. 17, 1. 9 sq.: ὅπως ἂν Λα(κε)δ(αιμόν)ιοι ἐῶσι τοὺς Ἕλληνας ἐλευθέ(ρ)ους (καὶ) αὐτονόμους ἡσυχίαν ἄγειν τ(ὴν χώραν) ἔχοντας ἐμ βεβαίῳ τὴ(ν ἑαυτῶν)—. (Οἱ ἐς τοὺς συμμά)χους πρεσβεύσαντες are mentioned in C.I.A., II. 18 also.

[2] Diod. 15, 28. Chios heads the list of allies: C.I.A., II. 17, l. 79; cf. also l. 23 sq. Chios, Mytilene, Methymna, Rhodes and Byzantium were already members of the League when C.I.A., II. 17 was written, for their names are inscribed by the same hand as the decree above them. Fragment of the treaty with Mytilene: C.I.A., II.18; with Byzantium: II. 19. An Athenian decree permitting the people of Methymna, who were already in alliance with Athens, to enter the League is in *Bull.* 12, 188/9. For Thebes cf. Diod. 15, 29; C.I.A., II. 17. 23 sq.; Fabricius in the *N. Rh. Mus.*, 46, 595 ff.

[3] C.I.A., II. 17 contains this declaration. See Schaefer, *Dem. u. s. Zeit.*, 1¹, 29 ff. The same inscription gives the list of the allies. This list and the dates of the admittance of the various cities have been discussed by Schaefer, *commentat. de soc. Ath. Chabriae et Timothei aetate in tab. pub. inscriptis*, and by Busolt, *op. cit.*, p. 787 ff. See also Fabricius, *op. cit.*, 597 ff. The treaties made by Athens with the various States have been preserved in a more or less fragmentary condition; that with Mytilene: C.I.A., II. 18; with Byzantium: II. 19; with Chalkis: II. 17b; with Kerkyra : II., 49b, complete *Bull.*, 13, 354 ff.

[4] For the number of the allied States see Busolt, p. 763 ff. He makes the statement of Æsch., *de Fals. Leg.*, 70—(cf. Diod. 15, 30)—refer to 357 B.C., Schaefer, *Dem. u. s. Zeit.* 1¹, 52, makes it refer to 373 B.C. For the peace of 374 B.C. and the recognition of Athenian maritime supremacy by Sparta cf. Diod. 15, 38; Busolt, *ib.*, 771 ff.

secure. After the peace of 371 B.C. Thebes deserted, and in 370/69 she was followed by the cities of Eubœa, which were not recovered till 357.[1] As a result of the naval expedition of Epaminondas in the spring of 364 or 363 Byzantium definitely abandoned the League, and in other allied towns too movements hostile to Athens apparently occurred, which it required energetic measures to suppress.[2] But the rudest shock to the stability of the League was inflicted by the outbreak of what was called the Social War in 357 B.C. Chios, Rhodes, Cos and Byzantium, through the intrigues of the Carian dynast Maussollos, were induced to form a League hostile to Athens. The establishment of Athenian Cleruchs in Samos and Potidæa, and the interference of Chares in the party warfare at Kerkyra may have been the immediate occasions of this step; but it was to a great extent the result of oligarchic intrigues. The peace of 355 B.C. recognised the seceding States as independent of the Athenian League; and other allied towns which had remained neutral during the war now practically severed themselves from the alliance, Athens being too exhausted to prevent them.[3] After this the League dragged on a nominal existence till the battle of Chaironeia, when it was finally dissolved.[4]

The original object of the Second Athenian Confederacy[5] was to lend assistance to any member that required it for the main-

[1] For Eubœa cf. Xen. 6, 5, 23; 7, 5, 4. For the recovery of the island see Busolt, *ib.*, p. 816 ff.; Schaefer, *Dem. u. seine Zeit*, 1¹, 142 ff.

[2] Cf. Diod. 15, 79, where it is said of Epaminondas in reference to Rhodes, Chios and Byzantium: ἰδίας τὰς πόλεις τοῖς Θηβαίοις ἐποίησεν. Isocr. 5, 53 shows that the expedition went as far as Byzantium. Byzantium was never recovered: Busolt 810/1. Köhler, *Mitth. d. dtsch. arch. Inst. in Ath.*, 2, 142 ff., sees another result of Epaminondas's expedition in the hostile proceedings of the Kean towns against Athens described in an Athenian decree which he publishes. On this decree see also Hartel, *Stud. üb. att. Staatsrecht u. Urkundenw.*, p. 88 ff.

[3] Cause of the Social War: Dem. 15, 3. For the Athenian Cleruchies at Samos and Potidæa see Schaefer, *Dem. u. seine Zeit*, 1¹, 87/8. 90. Busolt, p. 804 f. maintains that they were justifiable. Chares and the civil dissensions at Kerkyra: Diod. 15, 95; Æn., *Takt.*, 11, 7. Busolt, 821 ff., refutes the statement that the second Athenian empire was a mere arbitrary domination. For the peace of 355 B.C. and its sequel see Busolt, p. 858 ff.

[4] Paus. 1, 25, 3 says of Philip: Ἀθηναίοις δὲ λόγῳ συνθέμενος ἔργῳ σφᾶς μάλιστα ἐκάκωσε, νήσους τε ἀφελόμενος καὶ τῆς ἐς τὰ ναυτικὰ παύσας ἀρχῆς.

[5] The terms of the alliance have been discussed by Boeckh, *Pub. Ec.*, 1, 646 ff.; Rehdantz, *vitæ Iphicr. Chabr. Timoth.*, p. 54 ff.; Schaefer, *Dem. u. s. Zeit*, 1¹, 25 ff.; Busolt, pp. 684-737.

tenance of its freedom and autonomy against Spartan aggression.[1] In course of time this professed object became unmeaning, as all danger from Sparta disappeared, and the League continued to exist simply because Athens would not permit its dissolution. Since the terms of alliance recognised the King's Peace of 387 B.C., only those Hellenes or barbarians on the mainland or coast could be admitted, who were not subjects of the Persian king. All the States of the League were to be autonomous, and to live under any form of government they pleased, and they were not to be required to admit any Athenian garrisons or officials.[2]

Objects of the League.

There were two parties to the League, the Athenians and the allies; the interests of the latter were represented by the Federal Council. Accordingly the official title of the League was οἱ Ἀθηναῖοι καὶ οἱ σύμμαχοι.[3] Athens was the Hegemon of the League, and as such exercised supreme control over military matters and represented the League in foreign affairs.[4] The Federal Council, οἱ σύνεδροι τῶν συμμάχων, was an assembly of representatives of the allied States; each State, irrespective of its size, had one vote in the Council. The Council sat at Athens, where its members appear to have permanently resided.[5] As regards the rights and duties of the allies, we must

Constitution of the League.

---

[1] C.I.A., II. 17, l. 9 ff.: ὅπως ἂν Λα(κε)δ(αιμό)νιοι ἐῶσι τοὺς Ἕλληνας ἐλευθέ(ρ)ους (καὶ) αὐτονόμους ἡσυχίαν ἄγειν τ(ὴν χώραν) ἔχοντας ἐμ βεβαίῳ τὴ(ν ἑαυτῶν). l. 46 sqq. ἐὰν δέ τις (ἴῃ) ἐπὶ πολέμῳ ἐπὶ τ(οὺ)ς ποιησαμένους τὴν συμμαχίαν ἢ κατὰ γ(ῆ)ν ἢ κατὰ θάλατταν, βοηθεῖν Ἀθηναίους καὶ τοὺς συμμάχους τούτοις καὶ κατὰ γῆν καὶ κατὰ θάλατταν παντὶ σθένει κατὰ τὸ δυνατόν.

[2] C.I.A., II. 17, l. 15 sq.: ἐάν τις βούλ(ηται τῶν Ἑλ)λήνων ἢ τῶν βαρβάρων τῶν ἐν (ἠπείρῳ ἐν)οικούντων ἢ τῶν νησιωτῶν, ὅσ(οι μὴ βασι)λέως εἰσίν, Ἀθηναίων σύμμαχ(ος εἶναι κ)αὶ τῶν συμμάχων, ἐξεῖναι αὐ(τ)ῷ(ι ἐλευθέρ)ῳ ὄντι καὶ αὐτονόμῳ, πολιτ(ευομέν)ῳ πολιτείαν ἣν ἂν βούληται, μήτε (φρουρ)ὰν εἰσδεχομένῳ μήτε ἄρχοντα ὑπο(δεχ)ομένῳ μήτε φόρον φέροντι. Cf. II. 17b.

[3] For the official title of the League cf. C.I.A., II. 17. 19. See also *Bull.* 12, 138/9, where, at the admission of the Methymnaians, the Strategoi and Hipparchoi appear as representatives of Athens, while the σύνεδροι τῶν συμμάχων represent the allies.

[4] Diod. 15, 28; Xen., *de Vect.*, 5, 6. In 357/6 in the Social War Athens had φρουροί in Andros (C.I.A., II. 62), though in general the allies were not required to receive a φρουρά; cf. C.I.A., II. 17, l. 22. Athenian ἄρχοντες in the Hellespont 355/4 B.C.: II. 69.

[5] Inscriptions style the Council οἱ σύνεδροι τῶν συμμάχων; cf. C.I.A., II. 17, l. 43/4; *Bull.* 12, 139; cf. also Æsch. *in Ctes.* 74. In C.I.A., II. 51. 57b we have simply οἱ σύμμαχοι. Diod. 15, 28: ἐτάχθη δ' ἀπὸ τῆς κοινῆς γνώμης τὸ μὲν συνέδριον ἐν ταῖς Ἀθήναις συνεδρεύειν, πόλιν δ' ἐπ' ἴσης καὶ μεγάλην καὶ μικρὰν μιᾶς ψήφου

suppose that there never were any articles of Federation proper in which these were precisely defined, but that Athens made separate treaties with the various States, all of them to much the same effect.

The Federal Council represented the common interests of the allies, as distinct from those of Athens, Athens herself not being represented in the Council.[1] The Federal Council was a purely deliberative assembly. When we remember how the voting was taken, that each State had one vote and one only, whatever was its power and importance, we can hardly imagine that Athens was in any way bound by the decisions of the Council, where a majority of votes might sometimes be nothing more than the voice of a large number of small towns. Community of interests made a conflict of opinion between the Federal Council and the Athenian Ecclesia a very rare occurrence; still, whenever such an event did occur, the will of the dominant city prevailed. This is shown by the proceedings in connexion with the peace of Philocrates in 346 B.C., when the Federal representatives had to swear to observe the

---

κυρίαν εἶναι. That the Federal Council remained permanently at Athens is not proved by Isocr. 14, 21, but seems probable from the fact that Æsch., *de Fals. Leg.*, 86, cites τοὺς συνέδρους τῶν συμμάχων as witnesses to an event that happened in the Federal Council 3 years previously; Busolt, p. 698; cf. Lenz, *d. Synedrion d. Bundesgen. im 2 Ath. Bund*, pp. 6/7. Königsberg. A σύνεδρος τῶν Τενεδίων is mentioned in 'Εφ. ἀρχ. 1886, p. 187=*Herm.* 24, 134/5. C.I.A., II. 52c shows that single States might have more than one σύνεδρος at Athens; see Höck in the *Jahrb. f. cl. Phil.*, 1878, p. 478 ff. In that case of course they still had only one vote between them.

[1] We may infer from C.I.A., II. 17 that there were no Articles of Federation, defining the constitution of the League. Had there been, the provisions concerning the League in this decree would have been superfluous: and further, the names of the new States admitted would have been recorded not in this decree, but in the Act of Federation. The treaties of alliance were in general made by each State separately with Athens; cf. C.I.A., II. 49, 109. 17b. 49b.=*Bull.* 13, 354 ff., 12, 139. The conclusion of no. 49, so far as it is legible, will not justify us in arguing from it, as Lenz 16 ff. does, that the Federal Council had any voice as to the reception of new members. In the passage in question the allies are required to be parties to the oath of allegiance, but so also are the Knights, though we cannot suppose that the Knights had any special rights in the matter. See also *Bull.* 12, 139. 57b is no exception, for that inscription is simply a treaty between Athens and her allies on the one part and the Peloponnesian States there mentioned on the other. See also Lenz p. 17 ff. The treaty by which Kerkyra joined the League is headed: συμμαχία Κορκυραίων καὶ 'Αθηναίων (εἰ)ς τὸν (ἀεὶ) χρόνον: *Bull.* 13, 354.

conditions of the peace, though it was made against their expressed opinion.[1]

The usual course of procedure in Federal affairs was that a *dogma* was drawn up by the Federal Council, and sent up to the Athenian Boule for discussion. If it met with the approval of the Boule, it was adopted by that body in their probouleuma, with an intimation that it had primarily proceeded from the Federal Council. If the Boule did not approve of it, an amendment or counter-proposal of the Boule was sent, with the original *dogma*, for the consideration of the Ecclesia. In either case, the final decision rested with the Ecclesia.[2] The Athenian Boule sometimes requested the Federal Council to send their *dogma* direct to the Ecclesia; but this was probably a departure from the ordinary rule. Here again, of course, the Ecclesia determined what course should be taken.[3]

Procedure in the management of the affairs of the League.

[1] The δόγμα τῶν συμμάχων concerning peace with Philip 346 B.C. in Æsch., *Fals. Leg.*, 60 sq., *in Ctes.* 69. 70, was rejected by the Athenian Ecclesia on the 19th of Elaphebolion, and a few days afterwards the Ecclesia decreed that the allies should be required to swear to keep the peace concluded in opposition to their δόγμα; cf. Æsch. *in Ctes.* 73/4. Höck, *op. cit.*, 475 ff., arguing against Busolt, p. 691. 701/2, supposes that the allies had consented to the Athenian decree in the interval (see also Lenz, p. 60), but this is a mere conjecture which cannot be proved, and seems to me highly improbable. I see no sufficient reason for supposing that the limitation of the Federal Council to merely deliberative functions, as Busolt, p. 691 (see also Hartel, *Demosth. Stud.*, 2, 46/7. 82) correctly describes it, was true of the period after the Social War merely.

[2] Cf. C.I.A., II. 57b: (ἐπειδὴ δ)ὲ οἱ σύμμαχοι δόγμα εἰσήνεγκαν εἰς (τὴν βουλὴν δ)έχεσθαι τὴν συμμαχίαν, καθὰ ἐπαγγέλ(λονται οἱ Ἀρ)κάδες καὶ Ἀχαιοὶ καὶ Ἠλεῖοι καὶ Φλε(ιάσιοι, καὶ ἡ βου)λὴ προυβούλευσεν κατὰ ταὐτὰ δεδό(χθαι) κ. τ. λ. See Köhler, *Mitth. d. dtsch. arch. Inst. in Ath.*, 1, 198. That this was the usual procedure is the view adopted by Lenz also, p. 33. The history of the peace of Philocrates shows that the Ecclesia had the ultimate voice when the Federal Council and the Boule made different proposals.

[3] The evidence for this procedure is supplied by C.I.A., II. 51, discussed by Köhler in the *Mitth. d. dtsch. arch. Inst. in Ath.*, 1, 13 ff.; see also Höck, in the *Jahrb. f. cl. Phil.*, 1883, 515 ff. I agree with Hartel, *demosth. Stud.*, 2, 48 ff. (see also Busolt, p. 690), in opposition to Köhler, that the inscription shows no distinction between the letter of Dionysios and the oral messages of the envoys. The expressions περὶ τῶν γραμμάτων ὧν ἔπεμψεν Διονύσιος and περὶ ὧν λέγουσι, i.e. οἱ πρέσβεις οἱ παρὰ Διονυσίου ἥκοντες, are, in my opinion, too, mere synonyms. The subject-matter of Dionysios's message is referred to in l. 33 sq., where it says of him and his sons: βοη(θοῦσιν τῇ βασ)ιλέως εἰ(ρή)νῃ ἣν ἐ(π)οιήσα(ντο Ἀθηναῖοι) καὶ Λακεδαιμόνιο(ι) κ(α)ὶ (οἱ ἄλλοι Ἕλληνες), which in one point, at any rate, agrees with the contents of the γράμματα l. 5 sqq.

The occasions on which it was customary to obtain a *dogma* of the Federal Council were mainly those when foreign affairs were **Competence** to come under discussion.[1] Thus, the Federal Council **of the Federal Council** gave its opinion on questions of war, peace, and alliance; it sometimes sent representatives on embassies along with Athenian ambassadors; its members sometimes ratified treaties of peace or alliance by oath.[2] Further, a *dogma* of the Federal Council was apparently customary when it was proposed to occupy an allied town with an Athenian garrison,[3] or when the employment of the revenues of the League upon some object was to be sanctioned.[4] Lastly, the Federal Council acted as

The Boule proposed in return for this the grant of Athenian citizenship to Dionysios and his sons. The inferences which have been drawn from the formulæ of this inscription are none of them certain. Lenz, p. 84, does not convince me. That C.I.A., II. 52 is in close connexion with 51 cannot be demonstrated.

[1] Lex. Seguer. 302, 14: σύνεδροι οἱ ἀπὸ τῶν συμμάχων μετὰ τῶν Ἀθηναίων βουλευόμενοι περὶ τῶν πραγμάτων.

[2] C.I.A., II. 51. 57b. Höck, *op. cit.*, p. 477 (see *id.* in the Husum Progr., 1881, p. 8 ff., and also Lenz, p. 24 ff.) goes much too far when he infers from the oaths taken by the Athenians and Kerkyraians, at the admittance of the latter into the naval alliance in 375/4 B.C., C.I.A., II. 49b, that the Athenians could not commence war or make peace in cases where the League was interested without the consent of a majority of the Federal Council. Cf. the passage in the treaty between Athens and Kerkyra: πό(λ)ε(μ)ον δὲ καὶ εἰρήνην μὴ ἐξεῖναι Κ(ορκυρ)αίοις ποιήσασθαι (ἄ)νευ Ἀ(θηναίων) καὶ (τοῦ π)λήθους τῶν συμμάχων· ποιεῖν δὲ κα(ὶ) τἆλλα κατὰ τὰ δόγματα τῶν συμμάχων, and the corresponding oath of the Kerkyraians (l. 31 sqq.): περ(ὶ) πολέμ(ο)υ κ(αὶ εἰρ)ή(νης πράξω καθότ)ι κα Ἀ(θ)ηναῖο(ι)ς κ(α)ὶ (τῷ) π(λήθει τῶν συμμάχ)ων (δο)κῇ κ(αὶ τἄ)λλ(α) ποι(ήσω κατὰ τὰ δόγματα) τὰ Ἀθηνα(ί)ων κα(ὶ τῷ)ν (συμμάχων) and the passage in the oath of the Athenians (l. 20 sq.): καὶ περὶ πολέμου καὶ εἰρήνης πράξω καθότι ἂν τῷ πλήθει τῶν συμμάχων δοκῇ καὶ τἆλλα ποιήσω κατὰ (τὰ δ)όγματα τῶν συμμάχων. These passages all assume that the Athenians and the allies always agreed in their opinions. Who had the preponderant voice in matters on which they did not agree is shown by the conclusion of the peace of Philocrates. Federal Council swearing to observe treaties: *Mitth. d. dtsch. arch. Inst. in Ath.*, 2, p. 144, 1. 57/8; *Bull.* 12, 139. In 371 B.C. the entire Federal Council was at the peace congress at Sparta, and swore to observe the peace: Xen. 6, 3, 19. The σύνεδροι swore to the peace of Philocrates: Æsch. *in Ctes.* 74; *Fals. Leg.*, 85; previously only Aglaocreon of Tenedos, whom the Athenians elected for the purpose from among the σύνεδροι, went with the Athenian ambassadors to Philip: Æsch., *Fals. Leg.*, 20.

[3] C.I.A., II. 17b; see Höck, p. 479. An Athenian ἄρχων at Arkesine in Amorgos: *Bull.* 12, 225; in Andros: Æsch. *in Tim.* 107.

[4] C.I.A., II. 62 records an employment of the συντάξεις κ(ατὰ τὰ) δό(γματ)α τ(ῶ)ν συμμάχων; in II. 108. 117 decrees on the subject are made by simple

the court of justice for trying certain classes of offences against the fundamental principles of the League.[1]

For the first few years after the foundation of the League probably no contributions of money were exacted from the allies. This is indicated by the fact that the allies were pledged to mutual assistance, and by the statement in the Athenian declaration of the principles of the League that none of the allies should be required to pay tribute.[2] But soon the same change which had taken place in the character of the first League began to transform the second. The smaller States commuted their liability to military service for the payment of an annual sum of money; the citizens of the larger States continued to serve in person.[3] To avoid the hated name of tribute, which might have awakened memories of the First Confederacy, these payments were styled συντάξεις, or contributions.[4] The quotas were fixed by decree of the Athenian Ecclesia, and this might be

Federal taxes.

---

resolution of the Ecclesia. Lenz, p. 24, holds that the Athenians could not make use of the συντάξεις except when the Federal Council had passed a resolution to that effect.

[1] Any Athenian who became owner of property within the territory of the allies was brought before the cognisance of the σύνεδροι τῶν συμμάχων, who confiscated his property: C.I.A., II. 17, l. 41 sq., and again l. 51 sqq.: ἐὰν δέ τις εἴπῃ ἢ ἐπιψηφίσῃ ἢ ἄρχων ἢ ἰ(δ)ιώτης παρὰ τόδε τὸ ψήφισμα, ὡς λύειν τι δει τῶν ἐν τῷδε τῷ ψηφίσματι εἰρημέν(ων, ὑ)παρχέτω μ(ὲν) αὐτῷ ἀτίμῳ εἶναι καὶ τὰ (χρ)ήμα(τα αὐτ)οῦ δημόσια ἔστω καὶ τῆς θ(εοῦ τ)ὸ ἐπιδ(ἐκα)τον καὶ κρινέσθω ἐν Ἀθην(αίο)ις καὶ τοῖς συμμάχοις ὡς διαλύων τὴ(ν) συμμαχία(ν, ζ)ημιούντων δὲ αὐτὸν θανάτῳ ἢ φυγῇ, οὔ(περ) Ἀθηναῖοι καὶ οἱ σύμμαχοι κρατοῦσι(ν). Lenz, p. 9 ff., makes the judicial functions of the Federal Council more extensive, and on p. 15 ff. he infers from l. 41 ff. that it had even a power of general supervision.

[2] C.I.A., II. 17, l. 46 sq., 23.

[3] Busolt's contention, p. 703 ff., that all the allies paid contributions, is rightly rejected by Hahn in the *Jahrb. f. cl. Phil.*, 1876, p. 455 ff. Xen. 6, 2, 1 shows that Thebes paid no συντάξεις. See also Schaefer, *Dem. u. s. Zeit*, 1¹, 27. In the words of the Kerkyraians in Xen. 6, 2, 9: ἐξ οὐδεμιᾶς γὰρ πόλεως πλὴν γε Ἀθηνῶν οὔτε ναῦς οὔτε χρήματα πλείονα ἂν γενέσθαι, χρήματα refers to the money spent on their own fleet; see Hahn, p. 458. Lenz's arguments to the contrary, p. 22, do not appear sound. Cf. Isocr. 7, 2, a piece of evidence not invalidated by Busolt's criticisms, p. 711 ff.: ὥσπερ τῆς πόλεως—ἔτι δὲ συμμάχους ἐχούσης πολλοὺς μὲν τοὺς ἑτοίμως ἡμῖν, ἤν τι δέῃ, βοηθήσοντας, πολὺ δὲ πλείους τοὺς τὰς συντάξεις ὑποτελοῦντας καὶ τὸ προστατόμενον ποιοῦντας.

[4] Cf. Harp. σύνταξις—ἔλεγον δὲ καὶ τοὺς φόρους συντάξεις, ἐπειδὴ χαλεπῶς ἔφερον οἱ Ἕλληνες τὸ τῶν φόρων ὄνομα, Καλλιστράτου οὕτω καλέσαντος, ὥς φησι Θεόπομπος ἐν ί Φιλιππικῶν.

attacked by a γραφὴ παρανόμων.[1] The συντάξεις were usually paid by the allies at Athens. If they fell into arrears, payment was exacted by force.[2]

The συντάξεις were paid into the federal treasury, out of which all war expenses were defrayed. Besides this, the Strategoi were often instructed to exact contributions for purposes of war direct from the allies.[3] The amount of the annual revenue from συντάξεις during the most flourishing period of the League cannot be stated with precision.[4]

The autonomy of the allies, though recognised by Athens as a leading principle of the League when it was first founded, seems to have been subjected to some limitations, as regards the administration of justice, where States had seceded and been recovered by conquest, or had been compelled to join the League against their will. At any rate, the treaty which Athens made with the towns of Keos, when that island, after seceding in 364/3, in consequence of Epaminondas' naval expedition, had been again subdued, allowed an appeal to Athens from judgments given by the Kean courts of justice.[5] Again, in

Supreme Court of Justice.

---

[1] (Dem.) 58, 37/8.

[2] Συντάξεις as a rule brought by the allies to Athens: Plut., *Phok.*, 7. For exaction of arrears see *Mitth.*, 2, 142, l. 13: οἱ ᾑρημένοι ὑπὸ δήμου εἰσπράτ(τ)ειν τὰ ὀφειλόμενα χρήματα τῶν νησιωτῶν. C.I.A., II. 62.

[3] The existence of a Federal chest is shown by C.I.A., II. 17, l. 45/6; II. 65. Fines were also paid into it. The συντάξεις=war funds: (Dem.) 49, 49: ἐκ γὰρ τῶν κοινῶν συντάξεων ἡ μισθοφορία ἦν τῷ στρατεύματι. Particular συντάξεις would be assigned to the Strategoi; *e.g.* to Chares, Charidemos, and Phokion, (χρ)ήματα τῶν συντάξεων τῶν ἐλ Λέσβῳ: C.I.A., II. 108; Cf. Isocr. 15, 113; (Dem.) 49, 49.

[4] Busolt's computation, p. 723 ff., is purely conjectural. See also Hahn 461 ff. According to Dem. 18, 234 the συντάξεις in 355 B.C. amounted to 45 tal.; before 346 B.C., according to Æsch., *Fals. Leg.*, 71, 60 tal.

[5] Cf. the Athenian decree of 363/2 B.C. published by Köhler in the *Mitth.* 2, p. 142 ff. (=Dittenberger 79), and Köhler's remarks *ibid.* Line 44 sq. says, with reference to a particular class of people who are to be banished from Iulis and their property confiscated: ἐὰν δέ (τινες τῶν) ἀπογραφέντων ἀμφισβητῶσι μὴ εἶναι τούτων τῷ(ν ἀνδρῶ)ν, ἐξεῖναι αὐτοῖς ἐγγυητὰς καταστήσασι πρὸς (τ)οὺ(ς) σ(τρ)ατηγοὺς τοὺς Ἰουλιητῶν τριάκοντα ἡμερῶν δίκα(ς ὑποσχεῖ)ν (κα)τὰ τ(οὺ)ς ὅρκους καὶ τὰς συνθήκας ἐν Κέῳ καὶ (ἐν τῇ ἐκκ)λήτῳ πόλει Ἀθήνησι. Similarly the passage in the oath of the Kean towns, l. 74 sq.: τὰς δὲ δίκας καὶ (τὰς γραφὰς) . . . πάσας ἐκκλήτους . . . (ἑκ)ατὸν δραχμὰς (a restoration of the passage is given in Dittenberger) must be regarded as referring to appeals to Athens. The maximum limit of 100 dr. seems to occur again in an inscription, probably from Arkesine in Amorgos, *Bull.* 12, 230 ff., l. 40: ἐξεῖναι αὐτοῦ δι(κάσασθαι ἐπ') ἀστικοῦ δικαστηρίου μέχρι ἑκατ(ὸν δραχμῶν).

the case of Naxos, when the island was obliged to surrender in consequence of the Athenian victory off Naxos 376 B.C.,[1] a treaty was concluded, making Athens the ἔκκλητος πόλις for the ἐφέσιμοι δίκαι of the Naxians.[2]

C. The Athenian Cleruchies.

The planting of Cleruchies contributed very materially to the growth of Athenian supremacy over the first League; when the second League was founded the Athenians explicitly pledged themselves not to plant any Cleruchies.[3] No part of the Athenian policy was so odious to the

History of the Athenian Cleruchies.

Szanto has restored and discussed this inscription in *Mitth.* 16, 33 ff. Again, in the decree of the Kean town Coresos, after directions as to the legal proceedings to be instituted at Coresos in case of violation of the laws concerning the export of red earth, the decree continues: (εἶν)αι (δὲ) καὶ ἔφεσιν 'Αθήναζε καὶ τῷ φήναντι καὶ τῷ ἐνδεί(ξαντι). Cf. C.I.A., II. 546, l. 20. Sonne, *de arbitris externis, quos Graeci adhibuerunt ad lites et intestinas et peregrinas componendas*, 101 ff., Goett., 1888, refuses to admit that an appeal lay to Athens, and understands by ἔκκλητος πόλις the State to which jurisdiction was entrusted for a shorter or longer period by one or more towns.

[1] Schaefer, *Dem. u. s. Zeit*, 1¹, 38, cf. his *de soc. Ath.*, 10 ff., is right in dating the accession of Naxos to the Athenian League immediately after the battle of Naxos. Busolt, p. 757 f., holds that Naxos never joined the League, but this is controverted with good reason by Hahn, pp. 465/6. We cannot imagine that after his victory Chabrias would have omitted to resume the blockade and reduce Naxos to capitulation. The statement of Diod. 15, 35 : Χαβρίας μὲν οὖν ἐπιφανῆ ναυμαχίαν νικήσας κατέπλευσε μετὰ πολλῶν λαφύρων εἰς τὸν Πειραιᾶ does not prove that he did not, before his return to Athens, induce various States to join the League, as Dem. 20, 77 says that he did.

[2] The fragments of the treaty are published by Kumanudes in the 'Αθήν., 7, p. 95 ; he dates the inscription in the first quarter of the fourth century. In l. 6 ff. we read : ὁπόσα δ' ἂ(ν)—(τοῦ) 'Απόλλωνος κατὰ τοὺς νόμους—(τὸ)ν διαιτητικὸν νόμον, ἐὰν μὲν ο(ἱ)—(δικασ)τήριον τὸ ἐν Νάξῳ, τὰ δὲ προσαγο(—)ται τὰ ἐκ τοῦ νόμου· τοὺς δὲ θεσμοθέτας—(κα)τὰ τὸν νόμον· ἐὰν δὲ μὴ συμφέρωνται (—) τὸ δικαστήριον τὸ 'Αθήνησι· τὰ δὲ προ— (ἐ)ὰν ἡσσηθῇ· μισθὸν δὲ τοῖς δικασταῖ(ς παρέχειν τὸν δῆμον τὸν 'Αθηναίω)ν, ἐν δὲ τῇ ἐκκλήτῳ παρέχειν Ναξίο(υς)—(λ)αμβάνοντας τά τε πρυτανεῖα καὶ τὰ—(ἐ)νάγειν δὲ τὰς ἐφεσίμους δίκας κ(αὶ)—(ἐσ)τιν τοὺς θεσμοθέτας εἰς τὸν χρ—. No certain restoration is possible. I believe the fragments justify us in conjecturing with fair probability the arrangements described in the text. Sonne 73, 46 gives a restoration consistent with his theory; another by Szanto is in the *Mitth. d. dtsch. Arch.*, etc. 16, 42/3.

[3] C.I.A., II. 17, l. 35 sq.: (d)πὸ Ναυσινίκου ἄρχο(ντ)ος μὴ ἐξεῖναι μήτε ἰδίᾳ μήτε δημοσ(ί)ᾳ 'Αθηναίων μηθενὶ ἐγκτήσασθαι ἐν τ(α)ῖς τῶν συμμάχων χώραις μήτε οἰκίαν μήτε χωρίον μήτε πριαμένῳ μήτε ὑποθε(μ)ένῳ μήτε ἄλλῳ τρόπῳ μηθενί. The Athenians, it is true, planted Cleruchies during the second League, in spite of this, in Samos: Schaefer, *Dem. u. s. Zeit.*, 1¹, 87/8, in Potidaia: Schaefer 1¹, 90, in Sestos: Schaefer 1¹, 400; 2¹, 28 ff.

members of the first League as this system of Cleruchies. As a natural consequence, on the disastrous termination of the Peloponnesian war, the Athenians were forced to abandon those they had established in the fifth century.[1] Even Lemnos, Imbros and Skyros were then lost, but we soon find these three islands again in the possession of the Athenians; they were recognised as Athenian property by the King's Peace of 387 B.C., and in later times they still appear, though with some temporary interruptions, as Athenian possessions.[2] Even the Romans in 197 B.C. gave Athens Imbros and Skyros, which she had held up to 200 B.C., and added Paros; in 166 B.C. these possessions were increased by the grant of Lemnos and Delos (also former possessions of Athens), and of her ancient frontier town Haliartos.[3]

The lands on which the Athenian Cleruchs of the fifth century were planted were acquired by Athens, either by right of conquest, or by pacific agreements with the States to which they originally belonged. In the first case the earlier population was completely removed and a compact territory was formed, inhabited exclusively by Cleruchs; or, if the former owners were only deprived of a portion of their lands, the Cleruchies lay, scattered here and there, in the midst of the territory retained by the older inhabitants. In the second case, where the Athenians acquired the territory pacifically in return for some equivalent concession,—generally a reduction of tribute,

Different Types of Cleruchies.

---

[1] Cf. Xen., *Mem.*, 2, 8, 1. In my opinion the provisions in the decree of the Ecclesia 378/7 B.C., C.I.A., II. 17, l. 25 sq.: τοῖς δὲ ποιησαμέν(οι)ς συμμαχίαν πρὸς 'Αθηναίους καὶ τοὺς συ(μμ)άχους ἀφεῖναι τὸν δῆμον τὰ ἐγκτήματα ὅ(π)όσ' ἂν τυγχάνῃ ὄν(τα ἢ ἴδι)α (ἢ δ)ημοσία 'Αθ(η)ναίων ἐν τῇ χ(ώρᾳ τῶν ποιου)μένων τὴν συμμαχίαν κ(αὶ περὶ τούτων π)ίστιν δοῦναι ('Αθηναίους) (cf. Diod. 15, 29), refer, not as Schaefer supposes (*Dem. u. s. Zeit.*, 1¹, 30), to estates still occupied by Athenians, but to claims to property, dating from the period of the first League.

[2] Among the terms of peace in the Skytale of the Ephors in Plut., *Lys.*, 14, was: καὶ ἐκβάντες ἐκ πασῶν τῶν πόλεων τὰν αὑτῶν γᾶν ἔχοντες. Andoc., *de Pace*, 12, shows that even Lemnos, Imbros and Skyros were relinquished. Before the peace of 387 the Athenians had again occupied these islands, though the possession was disputed (cf. Xen. 4, 8, 15), and was not formally guaranteed till the peace was made. Cf. Xen. 5, 1, 31.

[3] Cf. Liv. 33, 30 (adicit Antias Valerius) Atheniensibus insulas datas Parum (so Cod. Mogunt. for the Vulg. Lemnum), Imbrum, Delum (?), Scyrum. For their acquisitions after the defeat of Perseus cf. Polyb. 30, 18 (21). For the history of the Athenian Cleruchies see Köhler in the *Mitth.* 1, 257 ff., 5, 278/9; Wachsmuth, *d. St. Ath.*, 1, 637 ff.

—the Cleruchies were scattered allotments within the territory of the other State.[1]

The Athenians had two reasons for sending out their Cleruchies. First, they served to secure the supremacy of Athens in the League, and may be regarded, according to the manner in which they were founded, either as Athenian military outposts, or as permanent garrisons.[2] The second object in view was to secure the means of livelihood for needy Athenians by granting them allotments of land.[3] The Cleruchs were accordingly taken from the lower Solonian census classes.[4] The size of the allotments of land varied in the different Cleruchies according to the quality of the land to be allotted; but the income each Cleruch was to be granted was fixed normally at a certain amount, which may be estimated from the annual revenues of the Cleruchs of Lesbos at 200 drachmas *per annum*. Now an annual revenue of 200 drachmas corresponds to the minimum census of the Zeugitai. Hence Thetes, sent out as Cleruchs, were thereby promoted into the class of Zeugitai.[5] In this way the State obtained an accession of military strength; for the hoplite forces, in which the Thetes did not serve, were considerably increased by the transformation of so many Thetes into Zeugitai. In about 50 years of the fifth century Athens can be proved to have sent out more than 10,000 Cleruchs, and to have thus increased her hoplite forces by that number of men.[6]

Purpose of the Cleruchy System.

---

[1] For the various kinds of Cleruchies distinguished in the text see Kirchhoff in the *Abh. d. Berl. Ak.*, 1878, p. 1 ff., where there is also a list of the Cleruchies planted in the fifth century.

[2] The military object, Plut., *Per.*, 11: φόβον δὲ καὶ φρουρὰν τοῦ μὴ νεωτερίζειν τι παρακατοικίζων τοῖς συμμάχοις. Cf. Isocr. 4, 107. In 441 B.C. the Samian hostages were left in the custody of the Cleruchs in Lemnos: Thuc. 1 115; Kirchhoff, *op. cit.*, 32.

[3] Plut., *Per.*, 11: καὶ ταῦτ' ἔπραττεν ἀποκουφίζων μὲν ἀργοῦ καὶ διὰ σχολὴν πολυπράγμονος ὄχλου τὴν πόλιν, ἐπανορθούμενος δὲ τὰς ἀπορίας τοῦ δήμου. Hence the Cleruchy system was very popular at Athens; cf. Aristoph., *Nubes*, 202 sq.

[4] Cf. the clause in the decree concerning the foundation of Brea: ἐς δὲ (Β)ρέαν ἐχ θητῶν καὶ ζευγιτῶν ἰέναι τοὺς ἀποίκους, C.I.A., I. 31.

[5] Incomes of Cleruchs in Lesbos: Thuc. 3, 50. For the Zeugite census see p. 130[2].

[6] As late as 427 B.C. the Thetes did not serve as hoplites; cf. Aristoph., ap. Harp. θῆτες. The numbers recorded for the Athenian Cleruchs of about 460 B.C. to 410 B.C. are as follows:—1,000 to the Thracian Chersonnesus (Plut., *Per.*, 11, 19; Diod. 11, 88), 250 to Andros (*Per.* 11), 500 to Naxos (*Per.* 11), 1,000 to Euboea (Diod. 11, 88), 1,000 or 2,000 to Hestiaia

When a Cleruchy was to be established,[1] the Cleruchs were either appointed by lot, out of the total number of applicants, or if there were no limit to the amount of land to be allotted, all applicants were accepted.[2] The Cleruchs thus appointed were then conveyed to their new residence. The Brea decree orders ten γεωνόμοι to be appointed to measure out the land to the Cleruchs, while the ἀποικιστής of the Cleruchy has full powers to superintend their establishment. Besides his allotment of land, each Cleruch apparently received a sum of money to enable him to stock his estate. The State probably reserved part of the lands as State domains; but we cannot say for certain whether it retained any rights of ownership over the allotments of the Cleruchs, nor whether the Cleruchs had to make annual payments to the State for the use of the lands: neither alternative, however, seems probable.[3]

Method of Establishing Cleruchies.

The Cleruchs took part publicly in the principal religious festivals of Athens, *e.g.*, the Panathenaia and the Dionysia. In the Cleruchies themselves they kept up not only the Athenian cults which they brought with them, but also the religious observances which they found in their new home.[4]

Cults observed by the Cleruchies.

(Diod. 12, 22; Theop. *ap.* Strab. 445), 1,000 to Brea (*Per.* 11), 1,000 to Potidaia (Diod. 12, 46), 2,700 to Lesbos (Thuc. 3, 50), 500 to Melos (Thuc. 5, 116). Total, 8,950 or 9,950 Cleruchs, to which must be added others sent within the same period to Lemnos, Imbros, Amphipolis, Ægina, whose exact numbers are not recorded.

[1] See Foucart, *Mémoire sur les colonies Athéniennes au cinquième et au quatrième siècle*, in the *Mémoires présentés par divers savants à l'Académie des inscriptions*, etc., 1880, p. 328 ff.; Oskar, *Kius d. att. Kleruchie*, in the *Progr. of the Friedrichs-Gymn. in Cassel*, 1888. The latter supplies no new information.

[2] Cleruchs appointed by lot: Thuc. 3, 50; Plut., *Per.*, 34. But C.I.A., I. 31, states: ὅσοι δ' ἂν γράψωντα(ι ἐποικήσειν τῶ)ν στρατιωτῶν, ἐπειδὰν ἥκωσ(ι Ἀθήναζε τριά)κοντα ἡμερῶν ἐμ Βρέᾳ εἶναι ἐ(ποικήσοντας). A list of Cleruchs is given in C.I.A., II. 960.

[3] Cf. C.I.A., I. 31; Thuc. 3, 50. I infer that the Cleruchs received money grants to stock their farms from the words of the Brea decree: (Α)ἰσχίνην δὲ ἀκολουθοῦντα ἀπο(διδόναι τὰ χρή)ματα. Cf. the *argument* to Dem. 8. For the ἀποικιστής of the Cleruchy see also Boeckh, *Seeurk.* XIV., l. 170 ff., p. 457 =C.I.A., II. 809a, 144 sq.; Thuc. 5, 11. State-lands in the Cleruchies: Æl., *Var. Hist.*, 6, 1; Hdt. 8, 11; Köhler in the *Mitth.*, 9, 121. The question whether the State continued to be the owner of the Cleroi, and whether the Cleruchs made any payment for the lands to the State, has been discussed by Foucart, *ib.*, p. 341 ff.

[4] See Foucart, *ib.*, 381 ff. C.I.A., I. 31 says of the Cleruchs at Brea: βοῦν

The footing, on which the Cleruchs stood towards Athens, was defined by a decree of the Athenian Ecclesia drawn up in the sixth century. The wording of that decree shows that it was made at a time subsequent to the creation of the oldest Athenian Cleruchy, that in Salamis. Its provisions determined the legal status of the Cleruchs in Salamis, and formed the precedent on which all subsequent Cleruchies were modelled. It is fairly certain that Cleruchs were bound to reside permanently in their Cleruchy, and were subject to the financial and military obligations of ordinary Athenian citizens.[1]

Relations of the Cleruchs to Athens.

Those Cleruchies, which covered a compact and continuous territory, from which the former inhabitants had been entirely expelled, differed, even in matters of internal administration, from those which lay scattered here and there in the territory of an allied State;[2] but all Cleruchs alike remained Athenian

---

δὲ καὶ (πρόβατα δύο ἀπά)γειν ἐς Παναθήναια τὰ μεγάλ(α καὶ ἐς Διονύσι)α φαλλόν. Cf. C.I.G. 2270. A certain portion of the allotment land was consecrated to the gods; cf. C.I.A., I. 81: (τὰ δὲ τεμ)ένη τὰ ἐξῃρημένα ἐᾶν καθά(περ ἐστι καὶ ἄλ)λα μὴ τεμενίζειν; cf. Thuc. 3, 50. Temenos of Athene at Ægina: C.I.A., I. 528. ὅρος τεμένους 'Αθηναίας: C.I.A., IV. 3, 528a; in Samos: Curtius, *Lübeck Progr.*, 1877, p. 9; C.I.G. 2246; τέμενος ἐπωνύμων 'Αθήνηθ(ε)ν at Samos: I.G.A. 8; τέμενος 'Ίωνος 'Αθήνηθεν at Samos: *Bull.* 8, 160; τέμενος of Athene in the Lelantian plain: Ælian, *Var. Hist.*, 6, 1. Cult of Apollo Patroos, of Nemesis and of Zeus Hypsistos at Imbros: Conze, *Reise auf d. Ins. d. Thrak. Meeres*, pp. 87. 88. 90. Examples of indigenous cults adopted by the Athenian Cleruchs are the worship of Hera at Samos: Curtius, *op. cit.*, p. 10 ff., and of the θεοὶ μεγάλοι: *Monatsber. d. Berl. Ak.*, 1855, p. 632.

[1] This decree has been repeatedly published with conjectural restorations, by Köhler in the *Mitth.* 9 (1884), 117 ff., by Kirchhoff in C.I.A., IV. (1887) 1a, p. 57, by Foucart in the *Bull.* 12 (1888), 1 ff., by Gomperz in the *Mitth.* 13 (1888), 137 ff.; a small additional fragment was published by Lolling in the 'Αρχ. δελτ., 1888, pp. 17/8 and *arch. epigr. Mitth. aus Oesterr.-Ungarn.*, 1888, p. 61 ff., and, since then, Lipsius has edited the whole inscription in *Leipz. Stud.*, 1890, 221 ff. No certain restoration is possible unless more fragments are discovered. Some approach to certainty may however be claimed for the restoration of the first lines, which I quote from Lipsius: (τὸν ἐ Σα)λαμ(ῖνα λαχόντα) οἰκέν ἐ(ν) Σαλαμῖνι (ἀεὶ π)λὲν (σὺν 'Αθηναίοι)σι τε(λ)ὲν καὶ στρατ(εύεσ)θαι—. For the rest I must refer to the restorations mentioned above. For Salamis as an Athenian Cleruchy see Meinhold, *de rebus Salaminiis*, p. 15 ff., Goett. The provisions concerning the Salaminian Cleruchs are quoted as the model in decrees for subsequent Cleruchies: C.I.A., II. 14b, 7. In the fourth century the Cleruchs seem no longer to be burdened with financial contributions to Athens: Dem. 14,16.

[2] The various terms, ἄποικοι, ἔποικοι and κληροῦχοι, are interchangeable, and do not represent any differences of status. See the evidence collected

citizens although they were designated by the name of the place where they were settled. They still were members of the Phyle and Deme to which they belonged before they were sent out. Being Athenian citizens, they paid no tribute; but they naturally had to meet the financial requirements of the Cleruchy from their own resources.[1]

As regards the internal government of the Cleruchies, those which occupied continuous territories, from which the former **Internal government of the Cleruchies.** inhabitants were entirely removed, formed miniature copies of Athens, with but trifling variations. As at Athens, so in the Cleruchy, the sovereign power was represented by a Council and a popular Assembly. At Samos in 346/5 B.C. the meetings of the Council and of the Ecclesia were presided over by 9 πρόεδροι, the Phylai holding the Prytaneia in rotation; but these πρόεδροι, contrary to Athenian practice, were nominated by lot from all the tribes, including the φυλὴ πρυτανεύουσα. At Imbros, about the end of the fourth century, we find the presidency of the Ecclesia and the Council in the hands of an

---

by Kirchhoff, *op. cit.*; cf. also C.I.A., I. 31, 339. 340, IV. 96, II. 14; Foucart, *op. cit.*, 841, 1.

[1] For the denominations of the Cleruchs cf. Thuc. 7, 57. Οἱ Ἀθηναῖοι οἱ οἰκοῦντες ἐν Ἑστιαίᾳ: C.I.A., I. 29, l. 11. 21; οἱ ἐν Σαλαμῖνι κατοικοῦντες Ἀθηναῖοι: II. 465; ὁ δῆμος ὁ Σαλαμινίων: 469. 470. 594. 595; οἱ κατοικοῦντες ἐν Λήμνῳ: 489; ὁ δῆμος ὁ ἐν Λήμνῳ: II. 1343; οἱ οἰκοῦντες ἐμ Μυρίνει: II. 593; ὁ δῆμος ὁ Ἀθηναίων ὁ ἐν Μυρίνει: *Bull.* 9, 54, 58/9. 68; ὁ δῆμος ὁ ἐν Ἡφαιστίᾳ: II. 284; Ἀθηναίων ὁ δῆμος ὁ ἐν Ἴμβρῳ: II. 1353; ὁ δῆμος ὁ ἐν Ἴμβρῳ: II. 1342; ὁ δῆμος ὁ ἐν Σάμῳ: II. 1347; ὁ δῆμος ὁ Ἀθηναίων τῶν ἐν Δήλῳ: C.I.G. 2270; ὁ δῆμος ὁ Ἀθηναίων τῶν ἐν Δήλῳ κατοικούντων: *Bull.* 13, 245. 421; Ἐφ. ἀρχ., 1891, p. 140; Ἀθηναίων οἱ κατοικοῦντες ἐν Δήλῳ: 13, 415; see Foucart, *op. cit.*, 363 ff. In a list of men fallen in war, dating from the time of the Peloponnesian war, some members of the Erechtheis, Aigeis, Hippothontis and Aiantis tribes appear under the heading, Λημνίων ἐγ Μυρίν(ης); cf. C.I.A., I. 443 and 444. Decrees of the Cleruchs show that they were members of Demes also. Cf. the inscription of the Samian Cleruchs, C.I.A., II. 592 sq. Ἐπώνφης Ἀθηναῖος Παυδιονίδος φυλῆς Κυθέρριος from Melos: *Bull.* 1, p. 44=I.G.A. 9; Conze, *Reise*, p. 85, 109; cf. Æsch. *in Tim.* 78. The Lemnians and Imbrians Athenian citizens: Dem. 4, 34; cf. Xen., *Mem.*, 2, 8, 1. Boeckh's view, *Publ. Econ.*, 1, 565 ff., that the Cleruchs were subject to tribute is refuted by Kirchhoff, *op. cit.* Beloch, in *N. Rh. Mus.*, 39, 45 ff., supposes that the Lemnians and Imbrians mentioned in the tribute lists were Athenian Cleruchs, because, according to Hdt. 6, 140; Thuc. 4, 109; Diod. 10, 19; Nep., *Milt.*, 2, there were no non-Athenian communities on the island. He supposes that Cleruchs of a later date paid no tribute. For the general subject see Foucart, p. 348 ff. For a property tax on the Cleruchs at Potidaia cf. (Aristot.), *Œc.*, 2, 5.

ἐπιστάτης and two πρόεδροι. At Hephaistia in Lemnos, at Salamis, and at Delos, the procedure at meetings of the Council and of the Ecclesia was the same, or nearly the same, as at Athens.[1] Again, the magistrates of Athens reappear, with the same names, in the Cleruchies, though our fragmentary records only supply us with a few casual instances in the various Cleruchies. For example, we find an ἄρχων ἐπώνυμος at Skyros, Imbros, Samos, and Salamis; a πολέμαρχος, with two πάρεδροι, at Imbros; θεσμοθέται at Samos; πράκτορες at Imbros; a γραμματεὺς τοῦ δήμου at Hephaistia in Lemnos, at Imbros, Skyros, and Salamis; 10 ταμίαι τῆς θεοῦ, that is, of Hera, at Samos; a ταμίας at Skyros, Imbros, and Salamis; and ἀγορανόμοι at Delos. Instances of a scrutiny of the accounts of retiring officials are found at Imbros, Salamis, and Delos.[2] As might have been expected from the military character of the Cleruchies, the Athenians in the fourth century sent out to them military officers, Strategoi and Hipparchs, to exercise supreme authority there. We find instances of such Athenian officers in the fourth century at Skyros, Lemnos, Imbros, and Samos; a Hipparch at Lemnos; Strategoi for Hephaistia and Myrina; a Strategos for Skyros; a Strategos and a Hipparch for Salamis. In the second century, when Lemnos, through Roman complaisance, had again become an Athenian possession, there was once more a Strategos and a Hipparch for Lemnos, and also Strategoi for the several towns of the island.[3] In the Lemnian towns there was

[1] See Foucart 372 ff. For Samos see C. Curtius, *Inschr. u. Stud. z. Gesch. v. Samos*, Lübeck Progr., 1877, p. 10; for Imbros, *Bull.*, 7, 154/5; for Hephaistia in Lemnos, *Bull.*, 9, 50; for Salamis C.I.A., II. 469. 470. 594; for Delos C.I.G. 2270, 2271; *Bull.* 10, 35. 37; Schoeffer, *de Deli ins. rebus*, 198/9. πρόεδροι: *Bull.* 13, 245, 410. 415. 421.

[2] Ἄρχων ἐπώνυμος at Skyros: *Bull.*, 3, 63; at Imbros: 7, 154/5; at Samos: Curtius, *ib.*, 10; at Salamis: C.I.A., II. 469. 594. In the fourth century an ἄρχων sent out from Athens to Salamis: Arist. 62, 2. The ἄρχων ἐπώνυμος at Delos is the Athenian Archon. See Nenz, *quaest. Deliacae*, 14, Halle, 1885;· Schaefer 199 ff. Πολέμαρχος and two πάρεδροι at Imbros: *Bull.*, 7, 154/5. Θεσμοθέται at Samos: *Mitth.*, 7, 368. Πράκτορες at Imbros: *Monatsber. d. Berl. Ak.*, 1855, p. 629, 1865, 121 ff. Γραμματεὺς τοῦ δήμου at Hephaistia: C.I.A., II. 592; at Imbros: Conze, *Reise*, p. 88; at Skyros: *Bull.*, 3, 63; at Salamis: C.I.A., II. 469. 470. 594. 595. 10 ταμίαι τῆς θεοῦ at Samos: Curtius 10. A Ταμίας in Skyros: *Bull.*, 3, 63, at Imbros: *Monatsber.*, 1865, p. 123, at Salamis: C.I.A., II. 469. 470. 594. Ἀγορανόμοι at Delos: *Bull.*, 10, 33. C.I.A., II. 985, three in number: *Bull.* 13, 410. Εὔθυνα at Imbros: *Bull.*, 7, 154/5; at Salamis: C.I.A., II. 594; at Delos: *Bull.*, 13, 415.

[3] Arist. 62, 2: λαμβάνουσι δὲ καὶ ὅσαι ἀποστέλλονται ἀρχαὶ εἰς Σάμον ἢ Σκῦρον ἢ Λῆμνον ἢ Ἴμβρον εἰς σίτησιν ἀργύριον. The ἄρχων εἰς Σαλαμῖνα has been men-

also, in the fourth century, an ἐπιμελητής; and an official with this title occurs again as the supreme Athenian officer for Delos, Paros, and Haliartos.[1]

It may be inferred, from what we know to have been the case at Hestiaia, that the Cleruchies were also subject to some restric-
Administration of Justice in the Cleruchies. tions in regard to the administration of justice. In the case of Hestiaia, a Cleruchy established after a complete expulsion of the former inhabitants, Athenian psephisms not only laid down with great minuteness rules for the trial of all suits between Athenians and Cleruchs, but even imposed limitations on the freedom of the Cleruchs to decide lawsuits with one another. Imperfect though they are, the fragments still preserved of these decrees are sufficient to show that one specific class of lawsuits, in which both the parties were Cleruchs, were decided by the Nautodicai at Athens as δίκαι ἔμμηνοι, while other cases were tried before Dicasts appointed by lot from among the Cleruchs, and accountable to them for their conduct.[2] As regards their political rights, the Cleruchies were

---

tioned before. Hipparch at Lemnos: Hypereid., *pro Lycophr.*, XIV. 2 sq.; Dem. 2, 27; Arist. 61, 6; C.I.A., II. 14. 387/6 B.C., where we should perhaps read (Ἱππαρχ)οῦντος ἐν Λήμνῳ. In 329 B.C. ἐγ Μυρίνης στρατηγὸς and ἐξ Ἡφαιστίας στρατηγός: Ἐφ. ἀρχ., 1883, 128/4, l. 63/4. ἐ Σκύρου στρατηγός: *ib.*, l. 62. A Strategos in Salamis in 318 B.C.: Paus. 1, 35, 2; cf. C.I.A., II. 469. 595. A Hipparch at Salamis: *Mitth.*, 7, 40 ff. A Strategos and Hipparch for Lemnos in the second century: C.I.A., II. 593; cf. Ἐφ. ἀρχ., 1884, p. 194; *Bull.*, 4, 543. Contemporaneously with the στρατηγὸς ἐπὶ Λήμνον we have evidence of στρατηγοί also at Myrina: C.I.A., II. 598. In a decree of Hephaistia, after mention of the στρατηγὸς ἐπὶ Λήμνον, we read στρατηγοῦντος κατὰ πόλιν τ. δ.: *Bull.*, 4, 543.

[1] In the fourth century an ἐπιμελητής at Hephaistia: *Bull.*, 9, 50, at Myrina: *Bull.*, 9, 54. In the second century at Delos: C.I.G. 2286. 2287. 2293. 2298. 2806, and frequently elsewhere; see also Nenz, *op. cit.*, 14/5. Schoeffer 200 ff.; at Paros: *Mitth.*, 1, 258=Dittenberger, *Syll.*, 288; at Haliartos: Lebas 661. Köhler, in the *Mitth.*, 1, 267, 3, regards the ἐπιμεληταί as officials of the Cleruch communities. This seems to be corroborated by C.I.A., II. 469. 470. 594; on the other hand, C.I.A., II. 595: (ἐ)πειδὴ καὶ ὁ στρατηγὸς κα(ὶ οἱ) ἐπιμεληταὶ συναποφ(αί)νονται, ἔστω εἰς φυλακὴν seems rather to suggest Athenian ἐπιμεληταί. See also Meinhold 29.

[2] Cf. C.I.A., I. 28. 29. I. 29, l. 2–10 seems to have contained provisions for the cases which came before the Athenian tribunals, l. 11 sq., for those which were decided by the local juries. Whether we may adopt the restoration (τ)ὰ δὲ ὑπὲρ δι(ακοσίας δραχμάς) in line 28, and assume that 200 drachmas was the maximum amount within the competence of the latter, must be left undecided. For the Cleruchy at Hestiaia see Kirchhoff, *op. cit.*, 4. Euthyphro intended to prosecute his father for homicide before

in a similar position to the Attic Demes; they had a communal organisation, but were not completely independent.

As has been before observed, those Cleruchs who lived isolated from one another, within the territory of an allied State, were in a different position. That they possessed a communal constitution is as improbable a conjecture as that they were in any political community with the States in whose territory they were settled. Jurisdiction over Cleruchs of this description was exercised in minor matters probably by the Athenian ἐπίσκοποι, in more important cases by the Athenian courts.[1] From the scanty materials at our disposal it is impossible to give a more detailed account of their condition.

the βασιλεύς at Athens: Plat., *Euthyphr.*, 2 and 4. Both father and son are to all appearances Cleruchs in Naxos: Plat., *Euthyphr.*, 4.

[1] The provisions of C.I.A., IV. 96 probably applied to the Athenian Cleruchs and the Mytilenaians: (δί)κας διδόν(τε or τα)ς πρὸς Ἀθην(αίων τοὺς ἐπισκόπους κα)τὰ τὰς ξυ(μβο)λάς, αἳ ἦσαν πρὸ τούτου τοῦ χρόνου. The trial for the murder of Herodes was held at Athens. The ἄρχοντες mentioned in Antiph., *de caede Herodis*, 47, are probably the ἐπίσκοποι—a notion supported by the entire context of Aristoph., *Birds*, 1050.

APPENDIX TO PAGE 210.

In the Demosthenic oration against Boiotos, the facts of the case were, I should conceive, as follows:—Mantias had, during the lifetime of his wife, contracted an intimacy with an Athenian woman, Plango, the daughter of Pamphilos. Th. Thalheim, in the *Schneidemühl Programm*, 1889, p. 7 ff., holds that Mantias must have been originally married to Plango, because she was of too good a family for us to suppose that she lived in concubinage with Mantias. Subsequently, according to Thalheim, he divorced Plango, and married the mother of the speaker, but after her death he returned to Plango. But Pamphilos died in debt (Dem. 40, 22), and hence it is possible that Plango may have been willing to become Mantias' mistress. This was while he was married to the speaker's mother (39, 26; 40, 8/9). The speaker deals very cautiously with the relations between Mantias and Plango before the death of his mother, because he wishes to persuade his audience that Plango's two sons were not Mantias' children at all; indeed he declares that Plango was intimate with other men at the same time. That, he says, was why Mantias did not wish to acknowledge them (39, 2; 40, 9), and why, as he declares, Mantias did not keep the δεκάτη for Boiotos (39, 22; 40, 28, 59). After his wife's death, which occurred while her son was yet a child, Mantias set up a separate establishment for Plango, his legitimate son being brought up in another house on the interest of his mother's dowry (40, 9. 27. 50/1). He now concluded a lawful marriage with Plango. Had this not been the case, the speaker would have met Boiotos's claim to Plango's dowry, not by shewing that she could have brought none, but by proving that she was never married to his father at all (40, 22–26). The legitimation of her two sons, which Mantias still struggled to avoid, was effected by chicanery. In collusion with their mother, the youths brought an action to compel Mantias to acknowledge them as his legitimate sons, as Plango was now his legal wife. Plango assured her husband that she was prepared to swear, if

Appendix.

put on her oath, that her sons were not Mantias' children. Mantias fell into the trap; Plango swore just the opposite to what she had promised, and since, as Arist., *Rhet.*, 2, 23, says with reference to this very case, περὶ τῶν τέκνων αἱ γυναῖκες πανταχοῦ διορίζουσι τἀληθές, Mantias was obliged to acknowledge the sons of Plango, now his ἐγγυητὴ γύνη, and to have them enrolled in his Phratry (39, 2 sqq.; 40, 8 sqq.).

With regard to the sixth oration of Isaios, I would make the following observations. The relation of Alke to Euctemon while he was married to Philoctemon's mother was concubinage (18–21). When he attempted to introduce Alke's eldest son into his Phratry (21), declaring him to be a freedman's child (20), he must have pretended that the child was the son of an Athenian woman who had been his former wife; in fact the counter-claimants to Philoctemon's estate actually contended that Alke's sons were really the children of an Athenian woman, Callippe, Euctemon's lawful wife (11, 13 sqq.). Philoctemon, the son of Euctemon, raised objections to the introduction of the son into the Phratry. Euctemon threatened to contract a fresh marriage, and so Philoctemon finally agreed to his brother's introduction into the Phratry, with certain reservations as to his rights of succession to property (22-24). Euctemon therefore must have introduced the son of Alke, pretending—and Philoctemon tacitly admitting—that the child was Euctemon's legitimate son. There is therefore no need to suppose that there was any "lawful concubinage" in this instance either. Nor do Euctemon's proceedings when Philoctemon prevented the introduction of Alke's son into the Phratry afford any proof of it. § 22 says of Euctemon: ἐγγυᾶται γυναῖκα Δημοκράτους τοῦ Ἀφιδναίου ἀδελφήν, ὡς ἐκ ταύτης παῖδας ἀποφανῶν καὶ εἰσποιήσων εἰς τὸν οἶκον, εἰ μὴ συγχωροίη τοῦτον εἰσαχθῆναι (22). The union, into which Euctemon entered by this ἐγγύησις with Democrates' sister, was a lawful marriage, as the repeated use of γαμεῖν §§ 24/5 demonstrates clearly. (See Zimmermann 18.) But Buermann 571 shews from §§ 21 and 39–41 that it is a mistake to suppose that Euctemon had previously divorced his wife. It follows that Euctemon proposed to commit bigamy (see Hruza, *Beitr. z. Gesch. d. griech. u. röm. Familienrechtes*, 27 ff.), for the ἐγγύησις proved that he contemplated a lawful marriage. But his object was simply to break down Philoctemon's opposition. In all probability it never came to an actual γάμος: had that been so, a divorce from his first wife would have probably followed. Philoctemon gave up his opposi-

Appendix.

tion before the γάμος was consummated; and that explains the expression in § 24: ἀπηλλάγη τῆς γυναικὸς (sc. Democrates' sister) ὁ Εὐκτήμων καὶ ἐπεδείξατο ὅτι οὐ παίδων ἕνεκα ἐγάμει. Here ἐγάμει is the imperfect of an incompleted action, and, instead of ἀπηλλάγη, the technical expression, if the γάμος had taken place, would have been ἀπέπεμψε τὴν γυναῖκα.

INDEX.

The index and table of contents supplement each other. The index does not mention subjects which can readily be found in the table of contents.

A.

Αχνιάδαι Phratry, 210.
Acropolis, 275.
ἄδεια, 288, 336, 356.
ἀδιάτακτοι, 176.[4]
Adoption, 196.
ἀδύνατοι, 347.
Æschines, 374.
'Αγιάδαι, 5, 42.
Aglauros, 310.
ἀγὼν ἴδιος and δημόσιος, 404; ἀτίμητος and τιμητός, 405.
ἀγωνοθέτης, 360.
ἀγορά of the Phylai, 202.
of the Demes, 207.
ἀγορανόμιον, 259.[1]
ἀγορανόμος at Kainepolis, Gytheion, 29.
at Delos, 451.
Agra hill, 99.
Agyrrhios, 245, 345.
Αἰγεῖδαι, 19.
Αἰγικορεῖς, 103.
αἶτας, 65.
ἀκοντιστής, 314.
Alcman, 30.[1]
Alcmeonidai, 145.
Alkibiades, 187.
Amazons, 100.
ἀμπαιδες, 60.
ἀμφορεὺς κύριος, ἄκυρος, 411-2.
ἀναγραφεύς, 271.
ἀνάκρισις, 407.
ἀνδρεῖα, 65.
'Ανθεστήρια, 254.
ἀνθυπωμοσία, 409.

ἀντίδοσις, 252.
Antigonos, 161.
ἀντιγραφή, 408.
ἀντιγραφεύς in Roman period, 166.
ἀπαγωγή, 257, 281.
ἀπαρχή, 244, 335, 424.
'Απατούρια, 192.
ἀπελεύθερος, 175.[4]
ἀπέλλα, 9, 10, 29.
ἀφέτης, 314.
Aphidna, 99.[2]
Aphrodite, 100, 258,[3] 287/8.
ἀπογραφή, 257.
ἀποικιστής, 448.
Apollodoros, 245, 388.
Apollo, 99-100, 107, 150, 219.
ἀπόφασις, 285.
ἀποφορά, 173.[2]
ἀποστολεῖς, 327.
ἀπόστολος, 325, 327.
ἀποθέται, 62.
'Αραί, 380.
Aratos, 161.
ἀρχαγέται, 43.
ἀρχαιρεσίαι, 197.
ἀρχηγέται, 201.
Archestratos, 155.
ἄρχων τῶν σκευοφόρων, 74, 76.
at Athens, 111, 120, 136.
ἄρχοντες, 131, 136.
ἐπὶ τὴν δημοσίαν τράπεζαν, 165.
τοῦ γένους, 211.
of the Μεσόγειοι, Τετραπόλεις, 212.
in Skyros, Imbros, Samos, Salamis, 451.
'Αργαδεῖς, 103.
ἀργυρολόγοι, 425.[1]

Index.

ἀργυροταμίαι, 165.
Ares at Sparta, 77.
Aristogeiton, 254.
Artemis at Sparta, 76 ; Athens, 254.
Asclepios, 252.
Asteropos, 20.
Asylum, 172, 379/80.
ἀτέλεια, 182, 199-200.
'Αθῆναι, 101.
Athena at Sparta, 8, 9, 59, 76.
  at Athens, 99, 150, 384.
ἀτιμία, 199, 388, 390.
ἄξονες, 140.

B.

Babyka, 9.
βαγοί, 43.
βαφά, 67.
βάραθρον, 414.
βασιλεύς, 109, 120, 125, 136.
βασίλιννα, 253.
βασίλισσα, 253.
βῆμα, 408.
  ὁ περὶ τό, 166.
Bendis, 361.
βωμονίκης, 28,[3] 64.
βοῦα, 63.
βουάγορ, 63.
βουαγός, 68.
βουκόλιον, 112, 113.
βουλή at Kainepolis Gytheion, 29.
  at Samos, Imbros, Lemnos, Salamis, Delos, 450.
βουλεία, 265.
Βρασίδειοι, 34.[3]
Βραυρών, 99.[2]

C (and χ).

Caiadas, 80.
Carians, 97, 100.
Cassandros, 159.
Cheilon, 20.
χορηγός, 202-3, 252, 359/60.
χοροδιδάσκαλος, 359.
Chrysa, 100.
Chthonian deities at Ath., 99.
Cleomenes, 145.
Cleon, 344.
Cleophon, 245.
Cnakion, 9.

Corn distributions, 346.
Crowns of honour, 200.

D.

Damasias, 141.
οἱ περὶ δαμοσίαν, 75.
Decarchies, 86.
Dechas, 80.
Decrees of Ecclesia, their form, 297 sq.
δεκάτη, 191.[2]
δήμαρχος, 204-5.
Demetrios Poliorketes, 160-1.
  of Phaleron, 159-61, 248, 359.
Demiurgoi, 135.[1]
δημόσιος, 238, 240.
Demosthenes, 247, 339, 373.
δημόται, 204.
Δημοτιωνίδαι, 194, 210.
Diacria, 143.
διαδικασία at Sparta, 46,
  at Ath., 193-4, 375.
διαιτηταί, 388.
διαμαρτυρία, 407.
διαμαστίγωσις, 64.
διαψήφισις, 208.
δίκαι ἀγαμίου κακογαμίου ὀψιγαμίου
  at Sparta, 39.[1]
ἀλογίου, 228.
ἀποστασίου 175.
εἰς ἐμφανῶν κατάστασιν, 408.
ἔμμηνοι, 238, 409, 452.
ἐμπορικαί, 378, 414.
ἐφέσιμοι, 445.
ἐξούλης, 414.
κατά τινος and πρός τινα, 405.
φονικαί, 155.[1]
συμβόλαιαι, 432.
ἀπὸ συμβόλων, 255.
ψευδομαρτυριῶν, 411.
δικασταὶ οἱ κατὰ δήμους, 144, 157.
δικαστήρια, 396.
Dionysia, 252.
Dionysos, 258.[3]
διοσημία, 292, 409.
Dodecapolis, 99.
δοκιμασία, 255.
δραχμή, 329.
Δυαλεῖς Phratry, 210.
Δυμᾶνες, 40.
Δύμη, 41.

Index.

E.

εἰκοστή, 425, 435.
εἰσαγγελία, 255, 281, 890.
εἰσαγωγεῖς, 424.
εἰσιτήρια, 266.
εἰσφορὰς εἰσφέρειν μετὰ Ἀθηναίων, 181, 182.
ἐκκλησία at Sparta, 50.[1]
  κυρία, 285 sq.
  σύγκλητος, 286/7.
ἔκκλητοι at Sparta, 50.[1]
ἐκλογεῖς, 425.
Ἐλασίδαι, 210.[2]
ἐλεῶναι, 165.
Ἐλευσίνιοι τριττύς, 209.
Eleusis, 98.
ἔμφρουρος, 72.
ἐμπήκτης, 399/400.
ἔνδειξις, 255, 257.
ἐγγύησις, 189.
ἐγκεκτημένοι, 204.
ἔγκλημα, 404.
ἔγκτησις, 135, 182, 183.
ἐγκτητικόν, 204.
ἐννόμιον, 207.
ἐνωμοτάρχης, 70, 71, 75.
ἐνωμοτία, 67, 69, 70.
Enyalios, 254.
ἔπαικλα, 67.
Ἐπακριεῖς, 99,[1] 212.
Ἐπακριεῖς τριττύς, 209.
Ἐπεύνακτοι, 18, 35.[2]
Epheboi at Sparta, 25, 57.
ἔφεσις, 415.
Ephialtes, 155.
ἔφοροι in Laconian towns, 29.
ἐπιβάται, 326.
ἐπιβολή, 205, 355.
ἐπιδικασία, 189.
ἐπιγραφεῖς, 180, 365.
Ἐπιλύκειον, 112, 254.
ἐπιμεληταί, at Kainepolis, 29.
  at Athens, 165, 168.
  τῆς φυλῆς, 202.
  of religious associations, 213.
  τῆς πομπῆς τῷ Διονύσῳ, 252.
  τῶν μυστηρίων, 254.
  of the Symmories, 371.
  federal officials, 431.
ἐπιφορά, 424.
ἐπίσκοποι, 428.
ἐπιστάται τοῦ νεώ, ἀγάλματος, 263.[3]
ἐπιστάτης, 166.
  τῶν πρυτάνεων, 272 sq.
  τῶν προέδρων, 274 sq.
Epitadeus, 14.
ἐπιτάφια, 254.
ἐπιτιμηταί, 206.
ἐπιτιμία, 199.
ἐπιτριηράρχημα, 375.
ἐπωβελία, 414.
ἐπώνυμοι, 166, 251,[2] 315.
ἐρανισταί, 212.
τὴν ἔρημον ἀντιλαχεῖν, 390. 415.
ἐργαζομένων, τὸ κοινόν, 214.
Eubulos, 245.
εὐεργέτης, 181.
Eumolpidai, 254.
Eupatridai, 135.[1]
Euryleon, 7, 19.[1]
Eurypontidai, 42.
Eurystheus, 42.[3]
εὐθυδικία, 407.
εὔθυνα, 255.
εὔθυνοι in the Demes, 207.
  of the State, 224–5.
ἐξηγητὴς τῶν Λυκουργείων, 23.[3]
ἐξελεύθερος, 175.[4]

F.

Flamininus, T. Quinctius, 25.

G.

Γαμηλία, 189.
Γῆ at Athens, 99.
Γελέοντες, 103, 150.[2]
γένη, τὰ καλούμενα, 107,[2] 148, 195.[3]
Georgoi, 135.[1]
γεωνόμοι, 448.
γερωχία, 47.
γεροντία, 47.
γνώμονες, 283.
γραμματεῖον ληξιαρχικόν, 198, 205.
  φρατερικόν, 196, 210.
γραμματεύς in general, 229.
  τῆς βουλῆς καὶ τοῦ δήμου, 270 sq.
  κατὰ πρυτανείαν, τῆς βουλῆς, 268 sq.
  in the Cleruchies, 451.
  of the Epheboi, 314.
  ἐπὶ τοὺς νόμους, 270[1].
  of religious societies, 213.
  in Rom. per., 166, 168.

Index.

γραφή, meaning of, 404.
ἀδικίου, 226.
ἀπροστασίου, 177, 239.
ἀργίας, 284.
ἀσεβείας, 155, 283.
ἀστρατείας, 318.
δειλίας, 318.
δώρων, 227.[1]
κλοπῆς δημοσίων χρημάτων, 226-7.
λιποταξίου, 318, 375.
παρανόμων, 184, 255, 302, 423, 444.
πυρκαϊᾶς, 155.
ὕβρεως, 171.
ὑποβολῆς, 196.
ξενίας, 196, 239, 378.
γυμνασίαρχος, 202, 253.
γυναικονόμοι, 160.
Gytheion, 77.

H.

Habron, 248.[2]
αἱματία, 67.
ἄμιπποι, 324.
Harmodios, 254.
ἁρμοσταί, 36, 75, 86.
ἕδραι, 275.
ἡγεμών of the Symmory, 368, 371.
ἡγεμονία δικαστηρίου, 215, 376,
Ἑκτήμοροι, 117 and Addenda.
Ἑλλανοδίκαι, 75.
ἕνδεκα, 181, 186.
Hephaisteia, 181, 360.
Hephaistos, 99.
Heptachalcon, 100.
Heracles, 42,[3] 97, 100.
ἑστίασις, 361.
ἑστιάτωρ, 202.
ἱέρεια τῆς Ἥβης καὶ τῆς Ἀλκμήνης, 206.
ἱερεὺς τῶν Ἡρακλειδῶν, 206.
of the Phratry gods, 210.
ἱεροποιοὶ εἰς τὸ τῆς Ἥβης ἱερόν, 206.
of religious associations, 213.
ἱππαγρέται, 72.
ἵππαρχος, 120-1.
in the Cleruchies, 451.
ἱππαρμοσταί, 74-5.
ἱππεῖς, 115, 120, 122, 130, 132.
Hippias, 144.
ὁμόταφοι, 214.
Ὁπλῆτες, 103.
ὁπλομάχος, 314.

ὁρισταί, 206.
Ὑλλεῖς, 40.
ὑπήκοοι, 420.
ὑπερβατήρια, 76.
ὑπηρέται, 230,[2] 314.
ὑπογραμματεῖς, 166, 229,[2] 271.
ὑπωμοσία, 299, 409.

I.

Ὑλαι, 63.
ὕλαρχος, 63.
Ion, 96, 101, 103.
Isagoras, 145.

K.

καδίσκοι, 413.
Kaiadas, 80.
κανονίς, 399.
καταβολαί, 356.
κατάλογος, 316 [1 and 2].
καταλογεῖς, 321.
καταπελταφέτης, 314.
κατάστασις, 322.
κελευστής, 327.
Κεραμεῖς τριττύς, 209.
κήρυκες, 166, 168, 229, 271.[4]
Κήρυκες clan, 254.
Kinadon, 22, 32.
κλάρια, 45.[2]
κλεψύδρα, 410.
κλῆροι, 81.[3]
κληρωτήριον, 397.
κλητῆρες, 406.
Knakion, 9.
κοινὸν τῶν Ἐλευθερολακώνων, 29.
κωλακρέται, 113, 131, 136.
κώνειον, 414.
κοπρολόγοι, 258.[2]
κοσμητής, 311, 314.
κούρειον, 193.
κουρεῶτις, 192.
κρεωδαίτης, 75.
Κροτανοί, 41.
κυβερνήτης, 327.
Κυδαθηναιεῖς τριττύς, 209.
Κυνόουρα, 41.
Κυνόσαργες, 187.
κύρβεις, 140.
κύριος, 189, 404.
Κυθηροδίκης, 86.

Index.

L.

Lachares, 161.
Λακεδαιμόνιοι, 38.
Λακιάδαι τριττύς, 209.
Lampadephoria, 253.
λαφυροπῶλαι, 75.
Leipsydrion, 145.
Leleges, 97, 100.
Λήναια, 258.
λῃτουργίαι, 358.
ληξίαρχοι, 289.
Λίμναι, 41.
λίθος ὕβρεως, ἀναιδείας, 386.
λοχαγοί at Sparta, 69, 70, 71, 75.
λόχος, 68, 69, 70, 71.
λογισταί, 207, 223, 225.
Lycos, 402.
Lycurgus, the Athenian, 142, 248, 358.
Lycurgos, Spartan king, 24.
Lysander, 22.

M.

Machanidas, 24.
Marathon, 97.
Medon, 111.
Megacles, 118, 143.
μεῖον, 193.
Melite, 97, 100.
μελλίρανες, 63.
μεράρχαι, 206.
Μεσόα, 41.
Μεσόγειοι, 99,[1] 212.
Messenians, 81–2.
Μετοίκια, 102.
μητρῷον, 297.
μισθός, 156.
μνᾶ, 329.
μοῖρα ἡ ἀρχαία, 14.[1]
μόρα, 70, 74.
Μυρρινούσιοι τριττύς, 209.
Mysteries, 253.

N.

Nabis, 24.
Names at Athens, 198.
Nauarchia, 47.
ναυβάται, 326.
ναυκραρία, 133.
ναύκραρος, 133.
ναυπηγοί, 327.

ναῦται, 326.
νεωροί, 261.[3]
Nicanor, 159.
Nobles, Spartan, 12.
νομοφύλακες at Athens, 155, 160.
νομοθεσία, 255.

O (and Ω).

ὠβαί, 9, 25, 41–2.
ὀβελίσκοι, 78.
ὀβολός, 329.
ὀργεῶνες, 149, 212.
ὀστρακισμός, 288.
οὐλαμοί, 74.

P (Π, Φ, Ψ).

Παιανιεῖς τριττύς, 209.
παῖδες, 63.
παιδοτρίβης, 314.
Πάμφυλοι, 40.
Pan, 361.
Παναθήναια, 101, 181, 324, 360, 422, 448.
πανοπλία, 319, 317.
παραγραφή, 407.
παρακαταβολή, 407.
Πάραλιοι, 143.
Paralos, 348.
παράστασις, 407.
πάρεδροι, 225, 228, 252, 254, 255.
Parthenon, 334.
Pasiphaa, 59.
Pausanias, 22.
Πεδιακοί, 142.
Πειραιεῖς τριττύς, 209.
Peisistratos, 144.
πέλανορ, 78.
πελάται, 117.
πεντακοσιομέδιμνοι, 115, 120, 122, 130, 131, 132.
πεντηκόνταρχοι, 327.
πεντηκοντήρ, 70, 71, 75.
πεντηκοστύς, 70, 71.
πεντήρεις, 325.
Pericles, 154.
περίπολοι, 312.
περίστια, 291.
περιστίαρχοι, 291.
Περρίδαι, 98.[5]
Phalanthos, 18.[3]
Phaleron, 97.
φάσις, 261, 281.

φελλεῖς, 95.
φιάλαι ἐξελευθερικαί, 176.
φιδίτια, 66.
Φιλαΐδαι, 98.[5]
Philopœmen, 25.
Phœnicians, 97.
φόρος, 420.
   βασιλικός at Sparta, 87.[8]
φρατρίαρχος, 210.
φρουρὰν φαίνειν, 56.[2]
φρούραρχος, 427.
φυλαί at Sparta, 9, 25.
φυλή = military division, 319.
φυλοβασιλεῖς, 109, 388.
πίνακες ἐκκλησιαστικοί, 199, 289.
Πιτάνη, 41.
πλυνεῖς, 214.
πόλεις, 420, 422, 428.
πολεμαρχεῖον, 112.
πολέμαρχοι at Sparta, 69-71, 75.
πολέμαρχος, 110 sq., 120, 153, 182.
   at Imbros, 451.
πωληταί, 131, 136.
πολῖται ποιητοί, 184.
Polydoros, 17.
Polysperchon, 159.
Poseidon, 100.
πράκτορες in Imbros, 452.
πρᾶσιν αἰτεῖν, 172.[2]
πρεσβυγενεῖς, 47.
προβολή, 255.
προβούλευμα, 293 ff.
πρόβουλοι, 85.
προχειροτονία, 298.
Procles, 42.[3]
προδικασία, 385.
πρόδικος, 43.[2]
προεδρία, 199.
πρόεδροι, 166.
   in the Cleruchies, 450.
προεισφορά, 370.
πρόγραμμα, 273, 275, 287.
πρόκλησις εἰς βάσανον, 408.
Προμήθεια, 181, 360.
πρῳράτης, 327.
πρῳρεύς, 327.
προσκαταβλήματα, 356.
πρόσκλησις, 406.
πρόσοδος, 182.
προστάτης, 404.
πρωτίρανες, 63.

πρόξενος, 181-2.
πρυτανεία, 271.
πρυτανεῖα, 407.
πρυτανεῖον, 112, 251, 347.
πρυτάνεις, 120-2, 166.
ψηφίσματα, ὁ ἐπὶ τά, 271.
   ἐπ' ἀνδρί, 307 ff.
   τὰ κατὰ ψ. ἀναλισκόμενα, 339-40.
Psephisms, their form, 297 sq.
ψήφους, οἱ λαχόντες ἐπί, 412.
πύρφορος, 76.
Πύθιοι, 45.

Q.

Quadriremes, 325.
Quinqueremes, 325.

R.

Rhetra of Lycurgus, 7-8.

S.

Sanctuary, right of, 172, 379.
Sciritai, 35.[3]
Scythians, 173.
σημεῖον of the Ecclesia, 291.
Σεμναί, 386-7.
σίτησις, 199-200.
σιτώνης, 165.
σιτωνικὸν ταμιεῖον, 165.
Skias at Sparta, 28, 51.
   at Athens, 273.
Skiritai, 35.[3]
Skirophorion, 266.
σωφρονισταί, 206, 311.
σφαιρεῖς, 28,[3] 63.
Speusinii, 173.
σπονδαὶ αἱ παλαιαί, 85.
Statues, 347.
στοὰ βασίλειος, 140, 258, 282.
στρατηγεῖον, 280.
στρατηγοί, 120, 153.
στρατηγὸς ἐπὶ τὰ ὅπλα, 163.
   in the Cleruchies, 451.
στρατεία, 317.
στρατεύεσθαι τὰς στρατείας μετὰ 'Αθηναίων, 182.
συλλογεῖς τοῦ δήμου, 289.
σύμβολον, 402.
σύμβουλοι, 47.[1]
σύμμαχοι, 420.

συμμορίαι μετοικικαί, 180.
συμφορεῖς, 75.
σύνδικοι 168, 207.
σύνεδροι at Gytheion, 29.
τῶν *συμμάχων*, 439.
συνήγοροι, 195, 207, 225, 301, 410, 424.
συνήγορος τοῦ ταμιείου, 165.
Συνοίκια, 102.
συντάξεις, 444.
συντέλεια, 372.
σύσκηνοι, 65.
συσσίτια, 67, 68.[1]
σύσσιτοι, 214.

T (and Θ).

τάκται, 422.
τάλαντα τὰ δέκα, 340.
τάλαντον, 329.
ταμίαι at Kainepolis and Gytheion, 29.
at Sparta, 75.
at Athens, 120, 131, 136, 165, 166, 180, 202, 213, 250, 271.
in the Cleruchies, 451.
ταφροποιοί, 264.
τάξις, 319.
Tegea, 82.
τειχοποιοί, 264.
τέλη, 54.[3]
Τετράκωμοι, 99.[1]
Τετράπολις, 99,[1] 212.
τετρακόσιοι οἱ, 158.
τετρήρεις, 325.
θαλαμῖται, 326.
Θαργήλια, 252.
Theopompos, 16, 17.
Theoriai, 252, 343.
θεωρικόν, 333, 342-3.
θεωροί, 85.
Theras, 6.

Θερρικιάδαι Phratry, 210.
Θερρικωνίδαι Phratry, 210.
Theseus, 101.
θεσμοθέται, 112, 120.
at Samos, 451.
θεσμοθετεῖον, 112, 255.
θῆτες, 130.
θίασοι, 148-9, 194-5, 211.
θιασῶται, 212.
θόλος, 272,[3] 273.[2]
θρανῖται, 326.
Θριάσιοι τριττύς, 209.
Thyreatis, 82.
Timomachos, 7.
Τιτακίδαι, 98.[5]
τόξαρχοι, 320.
τοξότης, 314.
τραπεζίτης, 247.
τριακάς at Sparta, 67, 68.[1]
τριάκοντα οἱ, 158, 225.
τριηράρχημα, 375.
τριήρεις, 325.
Τριηροποιοί, 264.
Τρίκωμοι, 99.[1]
τριττύαρχοι, 210.
τριττύες, 133.
τρόφιμοι, 39.[2]
τυμπανίζειν, 414.
Tyrants, 83.

X (Ξ)–Z.

ξεναγοί, 89, 90.[1]
Xuthos, 96.
Year at Ath., 220-1.
Ζακυάδαι, 210.[2]
ζευγῖται, 119, 120, 122, 130, 132.
Zeus at Sparta, 8, 45, 76.
at Athens, 99, 107, 150, 219, 252, 258,[3] 324.
ζυγῖται, 326.

School Edition. Strongly bound in cloth extra, 10s. 6d.
Presentation Edition, 4to. 21s.

A DICTIONARY
OF
CLASSICAL ANTIQUITIES
MYTHOLOGY, RELIGION, LITERATURE AND ART

FROM THE GERMAN OF

Dr. OSKAR SEYFFERT

REVISED AND EDITED, WITH ADDITIONS, BY

HENRY NETTLESHIP, M.A. | J. E. SANDYS, Litt.D.
Fellow of Corpus Christi College and Corpus Professor of Latin Literature in the University of Oxford. | *Fellow and Tutor of St. John's College, and Public Orator in the University of Cambridge.*

WITH MORE THAN 450 ILLUSTRATIONS

London: SWAN SONNENSCHEIN & CO.
New York: MACMILLAN & CO.
1895.

SOME EXTRACTS FROM PRESS OPINIONS.

"It is hardly necessary to add anything to the chorus of general approval with which this English edition of Dr. Seyffert's *Lexikon der klassischen Alterthumskunde* has been widely received. Professor Nettleship's notes on Latin literature and the important articles by Dr. Sandys are alone enough to give an independent value to this edition."—Professor A. S. Wilkins, in *The Classical Review.*

"At once more concise and more comprehensive than the well-known *Dictionary of Antiquities*, which has so long held the field in this country. For that very reason it will be more adapted to the requirements of certain classes of students; while its scholarly execution, and its copious illustrations render it, within its limits, a formidable rival."—*Times.*

"The standard of the work is excellent, the additions of Professor Nettleship and Dr. Sandys are judicious and valuable, and the illustrations are almost uniformly first-rate. On the whole, we have a most useful book for school and college use."—*Academy*.

" There was room for such a Dictionary as that which is given us in this handsome volume. Partly perhaps from the clear and generous typography, but mainly from the vivid and animated writing, this Dictionary bears the palm for interest; it may be read like a magazine filled with very brief articles. It covers a field not covered by any other single volume, and it will not merely be an ornament to any library, but will bring light, and therefore add value, to the other volumes which compose our libraries." —Dr. MARCUS DODS, in *The British Weekly.*

"We are inclined to believe that the book, though of course mainly intended for guidance and reference, could be read through without any feeling of weariness, so attractive is its matter, so interesting the method of treatment. Its value would be hard to exaggerate for the use of sixth and fifth form boys. We unhesitatingly express our opinion that it is a most valuable work, important for both reference and comment, and one that is sure to give fresh interest to the study of the great writers in Greek and Latin literature. It would make a noble classical prize."—*Education*.

"This is a handsome book, well illustrated, and printed in a type that it is a pleasure to read. In these respects it has an advantage over Dr. Smith's well-known series of Dictionaries, as also in the fact that it puts together, in one volume, a variety of information for which one has to consult five volumes of the older work. It is likely to be a very useful book, and to fulfil a function of its own."—*Pall Mall Gazette.*

"It is delightfully written, and admirably arranged: and the comprehensiveness of its scope may be judged from its full title, which is an accurate description of its contents. The illustrations are so well executed, so carefully selected, and so lavish in point of number, that they draw the indolent reader on from page to page, and compel him to study the learned but never dull letterpress. Playing with the pages of this handsome book is as pleasant as walking through the galleries of the British Museum by the side of a learned guide. We have tested several scores of the articles, and in no case have we found that the author and his editors have failed to incorporate the results of most recent research, or to notice the chief heads of dispute of any point of controversy. More than this, no classical dictionary can or should attempt, and to do this well is a feat as useful as it is difficult. We may thank and congratulate Professor Nettleship and Dr. Sandys for their labours, and upon their success. They have produced a book of reference valuable to scholars of all sorts, from the schoolboy beginning to get a grip upon his work, to the commentator writing in Bodley, or the British Museum, and absolutely indispensable in any respectable library."—*St. James' Gazette.*

"A vast deal of information has been compressed into a small space by dint of careful selection, and by the omission of all references. The statements are clear and well-arranged, and are illustrated by an abundant supply of woodcuts. It is well suited to the older schoolboy and the younger college student; but even wider will be its use for that large and growing class of readers, who, though they know no Greek and little Latin, yet have a lively interest in ancient art and letters, and often turn to a really sound and suitable book of reference on these topics."—*Manchester Guardian*.

"Dr. Seyffert is one of the leading lights of present day classical learning in Germany, and to his own researches, based upon the most valuable works in his own country, are added the observations of Dr. Nettleship, the representative of Latin scholarship at Oxford and of Dr. Sandys, one of our leading Grecians at Cambridge. The result is a magnificent volume of over 700 pages; it is printed in large and clear type that need strain no eyes; it is beautifully and copiously illustrated, and it may be appealed to with confidence on almost any subject connected with classical antiquities on which information is desired."—*Glasgow Herald*.

"Among existing works this handsome volume naturally challenges comparison chiefly with Dr. Smith's well-known Dictionary of Antiquities. Dr. Seyffert's work differs from Dr. Smith's, chiefly by reason of its wider range, and its more popular character. The information is everywhere brought up to the present standard of knowledge. As a popular manual of classical antiquities, it may be commended almost without reservation." —*Literary World*.

"The volume is one that every classical scholar will desire to have beside him as he reads. It far more than satisfies the requirements of a book of reference for educational purposes."—*Scotsman*.

"Some of the articles, *e.g.*, that on Philosophy, and that on Vases, are marvels of expression and precise statement. Indeed, for school and general use the book has not been equalled. It is, of course, impossible in the compass of some 700 pages, to treat at all exhaustively such wide subjects as ancient literature and art, but the main points have been skilfully detected and emphasized."—*Cambridge Review*.

"The translation is carefully done, and reads well. Those who know how difficult it is to make a translation of a learned German work look like English, will be able to judge what careful revision this implies on the part of the Editors. Their names may fairly be accepted as a guarantee for the general excellence of the work, which is one of great value, not only to students and even professed scholars, but to that large class which, without knowing very much about the classical languages and literature, is thoroughly interested in their mythology, and especially in their art. The book, too, should find a place in every school library, and even perhaps on the private shelves of every master of the sixth form. It fills a place not precisely occupied by any work accessible to the English public."—*Speaker*.

"The subject of mythology is treated with great tact; there is no temptation here to young students to waste time over the details of idle fairy tales and endless genealogies, but what is of vital interest in the most beautiful of important myths is given in an interesting shape, and the freedom of this part of the book from anything in the least degree gross or indelicate is highly praiseworthy, and an additional recommendation for its use in schools."—*Educational Review.*

"The book looks well; it is printed well; it is liberally illustrated. It even goes so far as to mark quantities where any doubt could be. Its authorities are good, its Editors capable, and its style far more English than some works which are not translated from a German original. We can heartily congratulate the coalition of Oxford and Cambridge training on the result of its labours, and we can entirely recommend the book to that ever-growing class of learners who aspire to a London degree, for it will tell them all and more than all they need, and combines in one the hitherto separate provinces of the *Dictionary of Antiquities*, and the *Classical Dictionary.*"—*University Correspondent.*

"This is a work well fitted to do for schools and the lower classes in colleges what Smith's *Dictionary of Antiquities* does for more advanced students. The original is already in wide use in Germany, although it appeared only in 1882. Its particular merit is that, besides supplying articles on the subjects usually treated in a Dictionary of Antiquities, it contains also information on matters of mythology and literature, for which one generally goes to a Classical Dictionary. Thus the student finds all these topics treated in one easily handled volume of 700 pages, excellently printed in large clear type on fine paper. The English editors have not rested content with a mere translation into real English free from every trace of Germanisms. They have corrected (with the help of Dr. Seyffert) and enlarged the original as well."—*Nation* (New York).

"Certainly a very handsome and useful volume. We get here, in the compass of some seven hundred pages, printed in a very pleasant and readable type, the important items of classical literature, art, and archæology. The book is distinctly useful as far as it goes, supplies a want, and has a definite function of its own. It puts together in one convenient volume information which illustrates the ordinary course of classical study."—*The Spectator.*

www.ingramcontent.com/pod-product-compliance
Lightning Source LLC
Chambersburg PA
CBHW020858020526
44116CB00029B/353